WASHINGTON

Washington in 1798. Crayon drawing by Charles de Saint-Mémin.
Courtesy of Harry MacNeill Bland.

WASHINGTON

An abridgment in one volume

BY RICHARD HARWELL

of

the seven-volume

GEORGE WASHINGTON

BY DOUGLAS SOUTHALL FREEMAN

CHARLES SCRIBNER'S SONS · *New York*

This condensation of Douglas Southall
Freeman's *George Washington* is dedicated
to Mary Wells Ashworth in gratitude for
her interest and encouragement and with
the conviction that Dr. Freeman would
like this volume so dedicated.

R. B. H.

Table of Contents

List of Illustrations

List of Maps

Introduction

At the close of many months of working with Douglas Southall Freeman's *George Washington* the abridger of it faces a paradox in setting out to write an introduction, however brief, to the shorter *Washington*. Why should he add words to this volume when he has been trying so long and so hard, sometimes almost desperately, to retain the essence of Dr. Freeman's work and, at the same time, to subtract as many words as possible from the story of a life so full of meaning to Americans that it should be told as completely as possible? The answer is twofold: First, it is incumbent on one who has worked so closely with a book to give his view of its meaning and relevance; second, it is only fair that the reader know how and to what extent this one-volume biography of Washington differs from Freeman's monumental and definitive seven-volume biography of him.

Washington's life can stand almost any number of books about it. It can also withstand—in Stephen Vincent Benét's phrase—the "picklock biographer," the peephole historian, the myth-maker, and the muckraker. It has withstood many bad books. Freeman's is certainly one of the few that it has deserved. *George Washington* is the true and complete story—fully researched, felicitously written, and unembellished by foolish myth or by false and pretentious piety. It is a remarkable tribute to Washington that the twentieth-century scholarship of Freeman leads to the same conclusions about him as did the work of his first great biographer, Chief Justice John Marshall.

Freeman did not live to complete his work on Washington, and his associates, Mary Wells Ashworth and John Alexander Carroll, who wrote its seventh volume, did not presume to include there the kind of summary of the first President's character which Freeman had written into his narrative at appropriate intervals. At the end of Volume V (in the chronology of the biography, just after the close of the Revolution) Freeman wrote:

> . . . if at the end of the Revolutionary War he had to be characterized in a single sentence, it would be substantially this: He was a patriot of conscious integrity and unassailable conduct who had given himself completely to the revolutionary cause and desired for himself the satisfaction of having done his utmost and of having won the approval of those whose esteem he put above every other reward.
> . . . In accepting the integrity, the dedication and the ambitions of Washington as realities, one does not face an insoluble problem when one asks how

this life, at the end of the Revolution, had reached the goal of service, satisfaction and reward. George Washington was neither an American Parsifal nor a biological "sport." What he was, he made himself by will, by effort, by ambition and by perseverance. For the long and dangerous journeys of his incredible life, he had the needful strength and direction because he walked that "straight line." [1]

Doubtless Freeman used the simple reference to the "straight line" here because it was his general custom to use in writing of each period in Washington's life only the letters, comments, and other materials relating directly to that period. Quite possibly he used the phrase at this point with the intention of establishing a tie to a full quotation of the letter to Fairfax when he came, in his final volume, to summarize and to characterize the whole of Washington's life.

Chief Justice Marshall had written, almost a century and a half before:

In [Washington], that innate and unassuming modesty which adulation would have offended, which the voluntary plaudits of millions could not betray into indiscretion, and which never obtruded upon others his claims to superior consideration, was happily blended with a high and correct sense of personal dignity, and with a just consciousness of the respect which is due to station. Without exertion, he could maintain the happy medium between that arrogance which wounds, and that facility which allows the office to be degraded in the person who fills it.

It is impossible to contemplate the great events which have occurred in the United States under the auspices of Washington, without ascribing them, in some measure, to him. If we ask the causes of the prosperous issue of a war, against the successful termination of which there were so many probabilities? of the good which was produced, and the ill which was avoided during an administration fated to contend with the strongest prejudices that a combination of circumstances and of passions could produce? of the constant favour of the great mass of his fellow citizens, and of the confidence which, to the last moment of his life, they reposed in him? the answer, so far as these causes may be found in his character, will furnish a lesson well meriting the attention of those who are candidates for political fame.

Endowed by nature with a sound judgment, and an accurate and discriminating mind, he feared not that laborious attention which made him perfectly master of those subjects, in all their relations, on which he was to decide: and this essential quality was guided by an unvarying sense of moral right, which would tolerate the employment only of those means that would bear the most rigid examination; by a fairness of intention which neither sought nor required disguise; and by a purity of virtue which not only was untainted, but unsuspected.

[1] Mrs. Ashworth, in her charming Preface to Volume VII of *George Washington,* elucidates the final phrase quoted here:

These words of Washington's also offer the best explanation for his success in the Presidency and for the whole of his adult life. They are from a letter to his friend Bryan Fairfax, written early in 1799: "The favorable sentiments which others, you say, have been pleased to express respecting me, cannot but be pleasing to a mind [sic] who always walked on a straight line, and endeavored as far as human frailties, and perhaps strong passions, would enable him, to discharge the relative duties to his Maker and fellow-men, without seeking any indirect or left handed attempts to acquire popularity."

Thus do the estimates of Washington by his most recent great biographer and by his first great biographer coincide. So, too, have the estimates of the dispassionate historians in all the generations since his death been unanimous in his praise. So it was in his own time, with all but a few—the few who, from their own corruptibility or overweening political partisanship turned praise into its perverted counterpart, invective. Abigail Adams, the wife of Washington's successor as President, gave the judgment of his contemporaries after her meeting with Washington in 1775. She wrote John Adams her first impression of the General who had come to direct operations before Boston in the initial months of the Revolution. "You had prepared me," she noted, "to entertain a favorable opinion of General Washington, but I thought the half was not told me. Dignity with ease and complacency, the gentleman and soldier, look agreeably blended in him. Modesty marks every line and feature of his face." And Mrs. Adams had what might equally well serve as the last word—except there will never be a "last word" about Washington—when she recorded shortly after his death: "Simple truth is his best, his greatest eulogy. She alone can render his fame immortal."

The perfection of Washington's character was marred by only two flaws, his ambition—which was as much a virtue as it was a fault—and his rather incomprehensible lack of strong affection for his mother. His conduct likewise bears two stains—his avoidance of his responsibilities at Fort Cumberland during the time of his over-zealous efforts to assure his supremacy in command over Capt. John Dagworthy and his peremptory treatment of Edmund Randolph during the second term as President. The first is easily excused on the ground of youthful ambition; if not excused, the second can be rationalized as a product of extreme and extenuating circumstances. This having been said, all else must be praise.

As a military man Washington did not burst upon the world as a genius nor did he ever achieve distinction deserving of the appellation, but he heeded his own advice written to his youthful captains on the frontier in 1757: ". . . devote some part of your leisure hours to the study of your profession, a knowledge in which cannot be obtained without application; nor any merit or applause to be achieved without a certain knowledge thereof. Discipline is the soul of an army." So was self-discipline the soul of Washington's success. In military matters, as in all things, he constantly improved himself. (It can be appropriately added that in self-discipline lay also much of the reason for the success of Douglas Freeman. It can be written of him, as he wrote of Washington: "He never could have finished all his duties—to say nothing of keeping his books and conducting his correspondence—had he not risen early and ordered his hours.")

Washington had a pragmatic view of history. "We ought not to look back," he said, "unless it is to derive useful lesson from past errors and for the purpose of profiting by dear bought experience." Certain it is that Americans have much to learn about their present and for their future by looking back on him and on his "dear bought experience." There are lessons in the history of every day of the Revolution; there is wisdom in every line of Washington's Farewell Address; there is example in almost his every act. There is advice for the present in the Count d'Estaing's letter to Washington after rash moves on the part of Gen. John Sullivan had threatened a rupture of the Americans' relations with their French allies:

> If during the coming centuries, we of America and France are to live in amity and confidence, we must banish recriminations and prevent complaints. I trust the two nations will not be forced to depart from moderation in their conduct but that they will reflect in all their public affairs that firmness and consideration for public interests necessary to unity between two great nations.

And in the words Washington spoke to a minority group—in that case the Jewish Congregation at Newport—on his visit to Rhode Island in 1791:

> It is now no more that toleration is spoken of, as if it was by the indulgence of one class of people, that another enjoyed the exercise of their inherent natural rights. For happily the government of the United States, which gives to bigotry no sanction, to persecution no assistance requires only that they who live under its protection should demean themselves as good citizens, in giving it on all occasions their effectual support.

What "straight line" Washington would mark for America in a time of a foreign war longer than the Revolution, of unprecedented social unrest, and of a degree of personal danger to public figures never known to him is speculation. Would his admonishment against American involvement in European affairs in a period when a youthful America had much to fear from older and stronger powers be repeated in a world grown small and an America grown large; would it be extended into argument against involvement in Asia? "The great rule of conduct for us, in regard to foreign nations," he wrote, "is, in extending our commercial relations, to have with them as little political connexion as possible. So far as we have already formed engagements, let them be fulfilled with perfect good faith. . . . Here, let us stop." Would he say, in the face of demands from the socially and economically disadvantaged, what he wrote "Light Horse Harry" Lee in 1786 concerning the malcontents led by Daniel Shays? He told Lee that grievances should be corrected, but that if the uprising in western Massachusetts represented no valid complaint the force of the government should be employed against it: "Let the reins of government . . . be braced and held with a steady hand, and every violation of the constitution be reprehended: if defective let it be amended, but not suffered to be trampled upon whilst it has an existence." Can public men any longer say what Washington said on his arrival at New York for his inauguration as President in April of 1789? He declared, when he met the officer in charge of a guard that had been arranged for him: "As to the present arrangement, I shall proceed as is directed, but after this is over, I hope you will give yourself no further trouble, as the affection of my fellow-citizens is all the guard I want."

* * *

When Mrs. Ashworth and Dr. Carroll undertook Volume VII of *George Washington*, Wallace Meyer, their editor and long Dr. Freeman's editor at Scribner's counselled them: "Keep your sights on biography, holding hands with history." The emphasis in this *Washington* is necessarily heavily on biography; to emphasize the story of Washington, the background descriptive of his time has been reduced as much as possible. Certainly the history of Washington's time and those who worked with, or against, him is of importance. But if Freeman's seven volumes were to be reduced to one, his text would manifestly (as he would say) require some major excisions, and a great many small ones. The text was compressed everywhere. Second and third examples of what Washington did, reiterative and corroborative quotations were dropped. Many details had to be omitted, especially those which, as Freeman noted of Washington's tour of the Northeastern States, were "delightful to experience but dull to read about now." Some details "dull to read about now"—and especially in their reduction to a bare-bones narrative—were retained because of their importance in the interlocking story of Washington's life. All of the appendices, all of the footnotes were eliminated. Even style was altered in minor ways when doing so would save a few words. The total of changes is large; it had to be to reduce the original 3582 pages of narrative text to the present 754. I hope the abandonment of details has not distorted the record. I hope Dr. Freeman, who wrote carefully and did not waste words, would forgive me for creating from his words sentences he would never himself have written. At least the words are his—very few mine—even if they have sometimes been reordered. I have tried to retain Freeman's interpretation as well as his words. In general his sections which evaluate Washington have been reduced less drastically than others. I hope most of all that I have done no disservice to the reader. This is a volume for the reader who had rather read one volume than seven. For the student who wants all the facts: The facts and all their substantiation are there in the seven-volume *George Washington*.

* * *

Gratitude to those who have helped in the course of this work is due many. First, of course, it is due the original work of Dr. Freeman and of Mrs. Ashworth and Dr. Carroll and to the editorial work of Mr. Meyer. I am particularly indebted to Mrs. Ashworth for advice and encouragement and to Mrs. Inez Goddin Freeman and the other members of Dr. Freeman's family for their willingness that I should undertake this condensation. I am little less indebted to Mr. Charles Scribner, Jr., to Mr. Wayne Andrews, to Mr. Thomas J. Davis, III, and to Miss Elsie Koeltl at Charles Scribner's Sons. They have been patient with my delays. To my sister Mrs. Marion B. Harwell of Greensboro, Georgia, thanks are due for a fast and massive job of typing. For other favors and help in the preparation of this volume I thank Mr. Stafford Kay of Madison, Wisconsin; Mr. Arthur Monke and Mrs. Lena E. Browne of Brunswick, Maine; Dr. James S. Coles of New York City, formerly President of Bowdoin College; Mr. Philip N. Racine of Atlanta; Mr. Roger E. Michener of Stirling, New Jersey; Dr. Wilbur Jacobs of the University of California, Santa Barbara; and the Henry E. Huntington Library and its staff, particularly its Director, Dr. James Thorpe, its Senior Associates, Drs. Allan Nevins, A. L. Rowse, and

Ray Billington, its Librarian, Robert O. Dougan, and staff members Carey S. Bliss and Mary Isabel Fry.

In writing this introductory note I have tried to avoid repeating what I said in my introduction to *Lee,* a similar one-volume version of Freeman's *R. E. Lee.* I cannot forbear however, recalling once more how Dr. Freeman liked to speak of the pleasure of his years of work on *R. E. Lee* and *George Washington* as time spent in "the company of great gentlemen." So has it been with me, but the great gentlemen have been three: LEE, WASHINGTON, and FREEMAN.

RICHARD HARWELL

Bowdoin College
24 June 1968

WASHINGTON

CHAPTER / 1

It was amazing how the settlers between the Potomac and the Rappa-hannock Rivers in Virginia progressed. They had not come in any consider-able number to that long peninsula until 1640 and after. A few were gentle-men of good descent; most were small farmers, artisans, clerks, tradesmen or adventurous younger sons of the middle classes who believed they would have a better chance in the new world than in the old. Many paid with their lives for their enterprise, but in spite of everything, the families in-creased fast and with no loss of vigor. The second generation began to buy luxuries from England and enjoyed larger leisure. Men of the third genera-tion considered themselves aristocrats. Within seventy-five years a new and prosperous landed society had been organized.

In every part of the development of the Northern Neck men named Washington had a modest share. The first was John Washington who came early in 1657 as mate and voyage partner, aged about twenty-five, in the ketch *Sea Horse of London*. The son of an English clergyman who had been ousted from his parish by the Puritans in 1643, John had received decent schooling and, on making the voyage to Virginia, saw possibilities of self-advancement on the Northern Neck. Circumstance favored him. When the time came for the ketch to start home with a cargo of tobacco she ran aground and a winter storm sank her. Her tobacco was ruined, but there was a chance she could be raised, and John helped in getting her above water. During the time he was sharing in this task he made new friends, among them Nathaniel Pope, a well-to-do Marylander who had a marriage-able daughter Anne. For this or other persuasive reasons, John prevailed on Edward Prescott, the master of the *Sea Horse,* to allow him to remain in Virginia. Anne Pope and her father both approved him. The father, in fact, was so hearty in his blessing of the union that when his daughter married John he gave her seven hundred acres of land and lent him £80 or more, with which to get a start.

In the autumn of 1659 a son was born to Anne and John Washing-ton. The next spring Nathaniel Pope died and in his will cancelled the debt due him by John. John promptly began to acquire more land by importing servants whose "headrights" he could claim, by purchase, by original patent, and by taking up grants of deserted land. By 1668 he owned considerably more than five thousand acres. He sought and gained an ascending order of profitable offices and court appointments. His family increased with his honors and his acres, and in 1668, Anne, who had borne him five children, died. She was lamented, no doubt, but not so poignantly that John refused to seek a second wife, Anne Gerrard, who previously had married Walter Brodhurst and, after his death had been the wife of Henry Brett.

John's eldest son and principal heir, Lawrence Washington, was born in September 1659 on the farm his grandfather had given Anne Pope on her union with John Washington. Apparently the boy was schooled in England. Soon after his father's death in 1677, Lawrence was back in Virginia and was taking up some of the public duties his parent had discharged. He was Justice of the Peace before he reached his majority; at twenty-five he was a Burgess; thereafter came service as Sheriff. He did not marry until he was approximately twenty-seven, but then he found in Mildred Warner a wife of character and established position. Mildred's father was Augustine Warner of Gloucester, Speaker of the House of Burgesses and a member of the Council. Economically Lawrence Washington began at a higher level than his father; socially he went further, but it was for a few years only. In his thirty-eighth year, 1698, Lawrence died.

At the time of his death, Lawrence Washington had three children, John, Augustine and Mildred. John was then almost seven years of age; Augustine was three; Mildred was an infant. Provision for them was not lavish but was adequate. Like his father, Lawrence had stipulated that his personal property be divided equally into four parts for his wife and the three children. During their minority, or until their marriage before they became of age, John, Augustine and Mildred were to remain under the care and tuition of their mother, who was to have the profits of their estates in order to pay for their support and schooling.

Mildred Washington probably remained a widow longer than was customary, but in the spring of 1700 she married George Gale. He took his wife, her children, and some of their possessions and migrated to England. Mildred was pregnant at the time and, following her arrival at White Haven, Cumberland, was stricken with a serious malady. A few days after her child was born, she made her will, January 26, 1701, and bequeathed £1000 to Gale. The balance of her estate she divided among him and her children. Care of the three young Washingtons was entrusted to the husband. Upon her demise, George Gale duly filed bond for the proper custody of the children and sent the boys to Appleby School, Westmoreland. There they might have remained, to be reared as young Englishmen, had not questions been raised across the Atlantic. Some of the Washingtons disputed Mildred's will. They insisted that Lawrence had left to his children estates in which Gale had no legal interest. John Washington, Lawrence's cousin and executor, put the question to counsel. The opinion of the lawyer was that Mildred could not bequeath the property, the income, or the custody of the children to her husband. As a result, within slightly less than twenty-four months, they were in the custody of the court and under the care of John Washington, the executor to whose diligence may be due the fact that they grew up as Virginians and not as residents of White Haven.

Augustine came of age in 1715. Gus, as he was called, was blond, of fine proportions and great physical strength and stood six feet in his stockings. His kindly nature matched his towering strength. Together, they made it easy for him to select a wife from among the daughters of the planters of Westmoreland. The girl who filled his eye returned his affection, and he was married, in 1715 or 1716, to Jane Butler. With Jane's lands and other property to supplement his own holdings, Augustine began his married life as proprietor of more than 1740 acres. Like his father and his grandfather, he soon became a Justice of the Peace and took his seat on the bench of the county court; in the energetic spirit of the immigrant John, he began forthwith to trade in land.

Augustine was in the first heat of this acquisition of new land when the reappointment of Robert Carter as agent of the proprietary was followed by the Treaty of Albany. Not only "King" Carter himself, but also George Turberville, Mann Page, who was Carter's son-in-law, Charles Carter, Robert Carter, Jr., George Eskridge and others of like station and speculative temper, took out patents for large acreage. Washington did not venture as far westward as these rich planters did, nor could he hope to equal the size of the tracts they acquired, but he caught so much of the speculative spirit that he extended himself to the limit of his means and perhaps beyond his resources.

First in interest to Jane and Augustine was the purchase in 1717 of land to add to the farm John the immigrant had acquired. Five years later, Augustine was prepared to build a new residence on the enlarged tract. The structure, finally occupied in 1726 or 1727 and later known as Wakefield, must have been a simple abode. Augustine Washington had too many uses for his money to build extravagantly. Next, a bargain seemed to be offered Augustine in the 2500 acres of land that represented Grandfather John Washington's share of the land patented at the "freshes" of the Potomac opposite the Indian village of Piscataway. John had bequeathed this to Lawrence; Lawrence had left his holding to his daughter Mildred. Mildred and her husband were willing to sell this "Little Hunting Creek Tract" for £180 sterling. On May 17, 1726, the agreement was signed. By this purchase Augustine advanced his landed interests to a point within twenty-four miles, as the river ran, of the Great Falls of the Potomac, then the dividing line between the old and the new settlements.

The improvement of the Pope's Creek property and the purchase of the Little Hunting Creek tract were by no means the end of Gus Washington's enterprises. He bought more land to cultivate or to resell in the region of Potomac shore known as Chotank. More particularly, he began to share in the development of ore-bearing lands and iron furnaces. These were the backward children of Colonial industry and they never had thriven; but they had the attention of several companies of adventurous Marylanders and Virginians, who would not permit themselves to be discouraged. The solid results had been achieved in Maryland. There, as early as 1718, at what later became the Principio Iron Works, John Farmer had produced and sent to England three and a half tons of the metal. England was then at odds with Sweden, whence came the greater part of the island's best iron. To replace this, Colonial furnaces were encouraged. The Principio partners did their utmost to supply the needed iron and to reap a coveted profit, but they did not have in Farmer a man of requisite vigor and ability. To spur or to succeed him, they sent to Maryland an experienced ironmaster, John England.

Either England's wide prospecting or Augustine Washington's own search brought to light what appeared to be rich iron deposits on land patented in part by Washington along Accokeek Creek, about eight miles northeast of Fredericksburg. England was eager to use this ore. By January 1725 he reached an informal agreement for its use with Augustine who was to receive a share in the Principio works as his compensation. This preliminary bargain seemed to England to be so advantageous to Principio that he was anxious the partners across the Atlantic sign at once to bind Augustine Washington. In urging on them promptness and legal care, England suggested that they send the Virginian a small present of wine as evidence of their approval. Augustine, for his part, quickly acquired on Accokeek 349 acres that were desired for the enlargement of the mining enterprise.

The furnace was a profitable venture, but Augustine was equivocal and irresolute in his relations with his associates in England. This was perhaps the prime reason why he determined in the summer of 1729 to go to England and deal directly with his partners. If, in dull days aboard ship, he took occasion to review his career, he had reason to be gratified. At thirty-five, he had a wife and three children, Lawrence, Augustine and Jane. He was not rich, but he was prospering and was discharging the duties and holding the offices that usually fell to a gentleman of the county. In spite of vexations and occasional reverses, Augustine Washington was established and, it would appear, was financially stronger every year.

Augustine's strange attitude toward a new bargain kept him a long time in England. When he returned to Pope's Creek May 26, 1730, he had the shock of his life: his wife had died the preceding November 24.

One thing that could not be deferred by the father of three young children was the finding of a new mother for them. Augustine looked about, visited and, on March 6, 1731, married a healthy orphan of moderate height, rounded figure, and pleasant voice, Mary Ball, aged twenty-three. Augustine took her to his home on Pope's Creek, where it was not for many months that Mary's thoughts of children were confined to those of her husband's first marriage. By June 1731 she knew that she was pregnant and that, if all went well, she would be delivered in midwinter. At 10 A.M. on February 22, 1732, Mary Ball Washington was delivered of her first-born child, George Washington.

As George grew to consciousness and learned to walk, there was a new sister, Betty, born June 20, 1733. Before she was a year and a half old, another baby arrived, a brother christened Samuel. In his friendly little neighborhood of Washingtons, Monroes, Marshalls and like-minded folk of the Northern Neck George experienced the first sorrow of his life: On January 17, 1735, shortly before he was three years old, they told him that his half-sister Jane was dead.

Another event of 1735 led George in a new direction. Augustine purchased from his sister Mildred 2500 acres more on Little Hunting Creek. As this property, then called Epsewasson, included land that had never been under the plow, Augustine caught anew the spirit that was carrying settlement up the Potomac and concluded that it would be to his advantage to establish his family on his up-river farm. On the new site, he probably owned a dwelling that may have been built by his father. It was not large but neither was his household. Lawrence and Augustine (familiarly "Austin") were at school in England, and the family to be sheltered at Epsewasson consisted of five only—the parents, George, Betty and Samuel —until it was increased to six by the birth of Mary Washington's fourth baby and third son, John Augustine, on January 24, 1736.

Augustine Washington was faced with a serious business dilemma when in 1735 the death of John England raised a question concerning the future of the iron furnace at Accokeek. It was profitable to a reasonable degree but it was not making the partners rich. There was no assurance that the deposits of ore were large enough to support indefinite operation. Could it be continued; should it be suspended? Where could an experienced and diligent ironmaster be hired? How was the quality of the product to be maintained? For an answer to these questions, Augustine concluded to consult his partners. In 1736 or early in 1737 he went again to Britain. When he returned in the summer, he had signed a beneficial contract under which more of the work of the furnace fell to him. On occasion he had to set an example of manual labor. Strong as he was, he could not direct a plantation, look after his other farms and at the same time supervise an iron furnace thirty miles from Epsewasson. If he was to have a continuing personal part in the management of the furnace he had to be closer to Accokeek.

It probably was while Augustine was reasoning towards this conclusion that George made two new acquaintances. One was of a sort no longer to be classed as a surprise. On May 2, 1738, he had his first look at another brother, Charles. This boy was the fifth child of Mary Ball and the ninth of Augustine by his two marriages. Of the nine, only two had died—an unusual record in a Colony of hot summers and hosts of flies. George's other new acquaintance of 1738 was his elder half-brother Lawrence who, at twenty, returned to Virginia. As a result of his long and careful schooling in England, the young gentleman had grace, bearing and manners that captivated George. The lad quickly made a hero of Lawrence and began to emulate him. Augustine, for his part, entrusted to his eldest son a part of the management of Epsewasson in order both to train the young man in agriculture and to lighten his own load.

There appeared in the *Virginia Gazette* of April 21, 1738, an advertisement that seemed to offer Augustine a means of continuing as a planter and a manufacturer, too. William Strother of King George County had died in the winter of 1732–33 and had left land which his wife was authorized to sell for her benefit. As she took a second husband who had an establishment of his own, she offered for sale the Strother place of about 260 acres on the left bank of the Rappahannock about two miles below the falls. This property attracted Augustine. It was within easy riding distance of Accokeek. Moreover, its location across the river from Fredericksburg held out the possibility of sending the boys to school there. Investigation deepened

Augustine's interest and led him to acquire the land. In addition, he leased at £4 per annum three hundred acres that adjoined the place he had bought. By December 1 he moved to the new home, which then or thereafter was styled Ferry Farm. In the advertisement the residence was pronounced a "very handsome dwelling house," but it probably did not deserve the extravagant adjective. With a nearer approach to accuracy it could have been described as a livable residence of eight rooms. The site was high and fine, but there was an unhappy difference from Epsewasson in the width of the water. Compared with the Potomac, the Rappahannock was a mere creek. Pleasant or unpleasant in this particular, Ferry Farm was now George's home, the third of his seven years, and it was located opposite something the boy had never seen before, a town.

George had his seventh birthday soon after the family established itself at Ferry Farm; that was the age at which boys were taught to read and then to write and to cipher. George was in the first stages of this bewildering but rewarding process when he had a new sister; he was progressing in his reading when the Colony, his father, and particularly his brother Lawrence were stirred by news of war with Spain. On January 11, 1740, the *Virginia Gazette* reported that Admiral Edward Vernon had carried his British warships to Cartagena on the Gulf of Darien, opposite the Isthmus of Panama, "taken a view of it," returned to Jamaica, prepared an expedition, and gone back to the South American coast to deliver an attack on Cartagena. Three weeks later, the paper announced that Vernon had proceeded with seven men-of-war to Porto Bello in the hope of burning the Spanish ships there. Actually, these accounts reversed the sequence of events. Vernon, then in home waters, received orders July 19, 1739, to open hostilities against Spain, and on the twenty-third he started for the West Indies. By October 19, when war was declared formally, he was at Port Royal, Jamaica, and ready for action. He descended swiftly on the coast of Panama and boldly assailed the defences of Porto Bello. Finding them feeble, he pressed his attack and within forty-eight hours after his arrival off the town, forced its full surrender. This easy success fired the imagination and fed the pride of Britain.

After the first confused reports were set right, Virginians' next news was that three thousand troops for the land expedition to accompany Vernon were to be Colonials. All the company officers, except one lieutenant for each company, were to be nominated by the Governors of the Colonies that supplied the men. Virginia's quota was to be four hundred men. Immediately every wealthy planter's son who had military ambitions wondered how he could get one of these commissions from Gov. William Gooch or through former Gov. Alexander Spotswood. Spotswood had proposed that an American contingent be raised and was entrusted with the task of recruiting men but death at Annapolis on June 7, 1740, spared him the pain of saying "No" to some applicants and denied him the pleasure of smiling "Yes" to others.

Among those who sought Gooch's signature on the King's commission none was more determined than George's older half-brother. Lawrence had diligent rivals. To procure a captaincy, Richard Bushrod of Westmoreland raised a company at his own expense. So far as the records show, Lawrence did no recruiting, but he must have procured the strongest endorsements from influential Colonials, because when the Governor announced to the Council June 17, 1740, the four leaders he had chosen for the Virginia companies, Lawrence was the first named. Beside him and Bushrod, the fortunate young Captains were Charles Walker and James Mercer. There was much satisfaction at Ferry Farm over Lawrence's advancement, but, as often happens in war, long delay occurred between the promise of a command and embarkation for foreign service. Although shipping was supposed to be available by August 20, 1740, it probably was not until October that Lawrence said farewell and sailed with his companions in arms.

After Lawrence went away life at Ferry Farm dropped back to its unexciting norm. Only rumor born of rumor mocked the minds of those whose sons had gone. The infant Mildred died October 23, 1740; George continued at school; Augustine probably had more than the usual troubles with the iron furnace. Other such enterprises were closing down or were operating amid continued discouragements. As for Lawrence, he wrote often but the receipt of his letters was uncertain. Summer was approaching, probably, when the family heard that Lawrence had reached Jamaica and then had sailed to Cartagena. While vague snatches of bad news were arriving thereafter, the Washingtons suffered a fire that involved formidable loss; but that soon was made to appear small in comparison with the good news received in another letter from Lawrence: He was safe after a disaster that had shamed British arms.

Lawrence Washington had been denied a part in the operations ashore. For the period of fighting, he had been among those held on the vessels and had been given no more exciting task than acting as Captain of the Marines on the flagship. His view of the disaster was typically that of the young officer who wished to think that his side had inflicted heavy losses to pay for those it had sustained; but he could not make out a case. He had to admit: ". . . the enemy killed of ours some 600 and some wounded and the climate killed us in greater number. Vast changes we have in each Regiment; some are so weak as to be reduced to two thirds of their men; a great quantity of officers amongst the rest are dead. . . . War is horrid in fact but much more so in imagination. We there have learned to live on ordinary diet; to watch much and disregard the noise or shot of cannon." Finally, word reached Ferry Farm that the American Regiment had been broken up and that Lawrence had sent the Council of Virginia a memorial in which he had set forth a claim to the vacant office of Adjutant General of the Colony. Later he brought back to the Old Dominion some of the survivors of the expedition. It was not a triumphant return, nor did he receive until later the post of Adjutant of Virginia.

When the veteran of Cartagena came back to Ferry Farm, his full brother was there to welcome him. In June 1742 Austin had returned from Appleby, the English school where his father and Lawrence also had been instructed. George soon came to love Austin, but he found his interest and his admiration more than ever fixed on Lawrence—on the brother who had seen the forts of Cartagena, had heard the cannons roar, and had watched the battle. In study for George, and in business activity for Augustine,

Lawrence and Austin the winter of 1742–43 passed. With the coming of spring and the approach of Easter, George was permitted to go down into the Chotank district of the Potomac to visit some of his cousins. He was in the full enjoyment of the sports of the farm, when a messenger rode up with instructions for him to return home at once: his father was dangerously sick. George set out as soon as practicable. He had seen little of his father and later was to remember only that his sire had been tall, fair of complexion, well proportioned and fond of children; but, of course, it was a deep grief for George when he reached home. The stricken man had made his will and now faced death in content of soul. It was on April 12, 1743, that he died.

The body of Augustine Washington was carried to the family grave-yard on Bridges Creek and buried there. His will was probated by Lawrence May 6, 1743. It divided an estate that included seven or more tracts, of a total acreage in excess of ten thousand. Slaves numbered at least forty-nine. Lawrence, as the eldest son, received much the largest share of his father's estate. Everything on Little Hunting Creek was to be his, as was land on Mattox Creek. He was to have, also, Augustine's interest in the iron furnace, subject to the purchase from the profits of three young slaves for Austin and the payment of £400 to Betty. Half of the debts due Augustine were to go to Lawrence on his assumption of a proper share of Augustine's obligations. To Austin went all the lands in Westmoreland not otherwise bequeathed, together with twenty-five head of cattle, four Negroes and a moiety of the debts due his father, less 50 per cent of the liabilities of the testator.

George received the Ferry Farm, half the Deep Run tract, ten slaves and three lots Augustine had acquired in Fredericksburg. In addition, he was to have his fifth of residual personal property that the father wished to be divided among his wife and her four sons. Samuel, John Augustine and Charles received farms and Negroes besides shares of the personalty. Almost in the language of his own father's will, Augustine wrote that the estates of all these children of his second marriage were to remain in their mother's care during the minority of each of them. Protection of their interest was to be assured in the event their mother remarried.

The widow was to have certain slaves in lieu of dower right in the Negroes as a whole. Besides her fifth of the undivided personalty and her tenancy of her sons' property during their minority, Mary Washington was given current crops on three plantations and the right of working the Bridges Creek quarter for five years, during which time she could establish a quarter on Deep Run.

A businesslike document the will was. If Augustine had not attained to the goal of the rich planters, who sought to have every male heir main-tain the baronial style of the family on a great estate, he had assured a living to all his sons who would make discreet use of what he had left them. So far as eleven-year-old George was concerned, the farm he would receive when he became twenty-one was of moderate size, in a district not particu-larly fertile. His other property was not valuable. The boy was too young at the time to realize it, but his inheritance was just large enough to raise a question: Would he be lulled into contentment as a planter of a second class, or would he be spurred by what he had to seek more?

Circumstance shaped in a natural manner the first approach to an answer. Lawrence was now seated permanently on Little Hunting Creek and was courting Anne Fairfax, daughter of Col. William Fairfax, cousin and agent of Thomas, Lord Fairfax, proprietor of an almost boundless tract in northern Virginia. William Fairfax was fifty-two at the time, and, besides acting for His Lordship in the issuance of land grants and the settlement of quit rents, he held office as Justice, as Burgess and as Collector of Customs for the South Potomac. After a residence comparatively brief on the Potomac he had become the most influential man in that part of the Northern Neck. On a point of land on the southern shore of the river Colonel Fairfax had acquired a pleasant tract and had built a handsome house which justified the name Belvoir.

On July 19, 1743, a little more than two months after Augustine's death, Anne Fairfax became the wife of Lawrence Washington. It was both for Lawrence and for George a fortunate day. To Lawrence it meant alliance with the most powerful interests of the Northern Neck and marriage to a girl who already had valuable lands and before many years was to hold patents for a total of four thousand acres. George, in his turn, found new and desirable associations. Increasingly, after Lawrence's marriage, George visited on Hunting Creek and at Belvoir, where he came under the fine influence of Colonel Fairfax.

George's brother Lawrence, about fourteen years his senior, stood almost *in loco parentis* and had developed the character his friendly face displayed. To Fairfax and to all his seniors, Lawrence was carefully courteous and deferential. Among men of his own age and station, he showed energy, ambition and the urbanity of good schooling. His greatest gifts were social, but they did not make him soft. In business, his judgment was average, or better. If he lacked the mathematical mind George was beginning to develop, he was genuinely intellectual. His letters were well reasoned and well written. Lawrence possessed political sense and he had religion without bigotry or pious protestation. Arms were his avocation. He preferred horses to books, apparently, but he had culture and probably gave the impression of wider learning than he had mastered. For the enlargement of George's mind and the polishing of his manners, Lawrence was almost an ideal elder brother.

At Ferry Farm life had not been stinted or meagre, but neither was it opulent or gracious; on Little Hunting Creek social relations were more polished and discourse was often of larger subjects. The house itself was perceptibly different from the little dwelling in which George had lived on the Potomac in 1735–38. Lawrence either tore down that structure, or else fire had saved him the trouble. A new residence was rising over the cellar and foundations of the original house. The structure was of wood and not of fine interior finish, but it was comfortable and soon well furnished. In this new house George found delight not only because it was new, but also because its master was his beloved Lawrence. There was still another stimulus: In honor of the Admiral of the Cartagena expedition, Lawrence styled his home Mount Vernon and, in so doing, unconsciously made the very name a challenge to the imagination of his younger brother. Lawrence talked, too, of war and of the honors and glories of a soldier's life—not a distant theme to a boy who lived within two days' ride of the trail the Indians sometimes followed in their raids.

Conversation at Mount Vernon was of lands as well as of armies. Lawrence had the confidence of his father-in-law, and of course knew of the patents issued from Colonel Fairfax's office to speculators who were looking eagerly to the west. Everyone hoped, through the years, that Lord Fairfax would win in the long controversy over the boundaries of his domain. Hope there was also, that the Five Nations could be induced to make the Allegheny range and not the Blue Ridge the eastern line they would not cross. If these two uncertainties were resolved favorably, the Shenandoah Valley would be open to settlers, and by their knowledge of conditions there and farther westward, William Fairfax and Lawrence Washington might enrich themselves. If the Indians could be induced to make a larger bargain, the great valley of the Ohio might be tapped.

When George went from Ferry Farm or from Lawrence's home to his brother Austin's plantation on Pope's Creek, he found the chief interests of that household to be farming and horses and the life of the river. Austin, like Lawrence, had found himself a bride of birth and station. This new mistress of the older Washington home on the Potomac was Anne Aylett, a daughter of Col. William Aylett of Westmoreland. In the household of Anne and her husband, George doubtless spent many pleasant weeks, though his mother probably kept him at Ferry Farm during the months of his schooling. He was developing fast, both physically and in knowledge of "ciphering" which soon became his absorbing interest.

West of the fall line, near which George had his home, the settlements fringed towards the frontier of the Blue Ridge and the Valley of the Shenandoah. Democracy was real there where life was raw, but in the Tidewater, the flat country east of the fall line, there were no less than eight strata of society. The uppermost and the lowliest, the great proprietors and the Negro slaves were supposed to be of immutable station. The others were small farmers, merchants, sailors, frontier folk, servants and convicts. Each of these constituted a distinct class at a given time, but individuals and families often shifted materially in station during a single generation. Titles hedged the ranks of the notables. Members of the Council of State were termed both "Colonel" and "Esquire." Large planters who did not bear arms almost always were given the courtesy title of "Gentlemen." So were church wardens, vestrymen, sheriffs and trustees of towns. The full honors of a man of station were those of vestryman, Justice and Burgess. Such an individual normally looked to England and especially to London and sought to live by the social standards of the mother country. Men of this level of society were fortunate and were not unmindful of it.

The wealth of such men assured Virginians the reputation of living nobly. One of their own historians wrote of "the families" as if all of them flourished opulently on great plantations. In reality, owners of expansive estates dominated completely the political life of the Colony in 1750 and gave its society a certain glamour, but these men were a minority. The majority of the white population was composed of farmers whose holdings of land were small in comparison with those of the great planters. Racially, in background and in native intelligence no line could be drawn between the owners of the larger and the lesser properties.

Economically the gradation was downward from great estates to self-dependent farms and then to small holdings. Almost 40 per cent of the 5066 known farms in the older Tidewater counties of the Colony, outside the Northern Neck, contained 200 acres or less in 1704. Farms of 100 acres or less represented 13 per cent of the total. The mean of all farms at that time was about 250 acres. Those agricultural properties with an acreage between 1000 and 5000 numbered only 448. Again with the exception of the Northern Neck, Tidewater plantations of more than 5000 acres are believed to have numbered eighteen. Later acquisitions swelled the holdings of the rich planters who speculated in western lands, but these additions did not affect greatly the size of farms east of the fall line. Where change occurred there between 1704 and 1750, it involved a substantial reduction in the mean.

The houses of Virginia exhibited the emergence of the wealthy and the lag of the poor in a Colony now almost 150 years old. Habitations, like their residents, were, so to say, in their second or third generation. The settlers' first homes had been succeeded by stouter buildings. Some of these—notably William Byrd's Westover and Thomas Lee's first home in Westmoreland—had been burned. Newer and still finer structures were rising. Most of the "great houses" erected after 1710 were of brick without portico and contained large but not numerous rooms. The favored design was a rectangular building, two storeys high, with a central hall from front to rear. On either side were two rooms. The same arrangement usually was made on the second floor. One chamber was that of the master and mistress. Another usually was described as "the boys'." A third was "the girls'." In the fourth guests or parents might be accommodated. If a dwelling of this size and type was outgrown, wings were added, but not to the satisfaction of the aesthetically minded. Opposite the angles of some of the more imposing residences, four smaller brick houses were constructed. If four were too many or too expensive, there might be two outbuildings at the same angle to the front or rear of the main structure. Often these corner buildings served to set off the "great house." Behind it were wooden sheds, barns and workshops so numerous that a stranger might think, from a distance, he was approaching a village. Such places always were few.

In almost every item of lighting, furniture and equipment, George's own home at Ferry Farm was typical of the second order of Virginia houses: it was far below the level of luxury that prevailed on the greatest estates, but it was adequate. The hall, which had a bedroom in rear of it, was painted and was not adorned with pictures. A mirror hung on one wall. Most of the eleven leather-bottomed chairs probably were arranged around the larger of two tables. The arm chair doubtless was that in which Augustine Washington had rested near a fireplace supplied with screen and fire-irons. This hall served, also, as dining room. Its china, modest in value, was ample in quantity. The linen was in keeping with the china. Glasses were few, because of breakage. There was no plate, but the silver spoons numbered twenty-six. The room intended for a parlor had been made to serve as a chamber in which were three beds. Four other bedrooms contained a total of eight beds, two of which were old. The dairy was well equipped and was used, also, for washing clothes. Ironing was done in the kitchen. Numerous old tubs were kept in the storehouse. There, too, were the reserve pots and pans and cloth for making garments for the Negroes. To George's eyes, doubtless, none of these things was comparable in interest to a tripod and certain boxes that Augustine Washington himself had put carefully away in their appointed place. These were the surveying instruments which, with the rifle and the axe, were the symbol of the extending frontier.

The food of Ferry Farm, as of every plantation, was supplied almost entirely from its own acres. To some visitors the consumption of bread and meat seemed incredible. A large family, servants included, disposed daily of fifty pounds of fine flour and a like weight of "seconds" at the master's house alone. On a plantation with approximately 250 slaves, the consumption of food and drink in a year was estimated by one owner at 27,000 pounds of pork, 20 beeves, 4 hogsheads of rum, 150 gallons of brandy, 550 bushels of wheat and an unreckoned quantity of corn, which was the principal food of the field-hands.

In dress, as in almost all else, London was the model for the wealthy. The wives and daughters of the great planters were forever sending to England orders that must have been in complexity and particularity the despair of the merchants. Men's dress was elaborate on high occasions. Fortunately, for persons not of exalted social station, dress did not have to be formal except on the King's birthday and then only in Williamsburg where every Englishman—of office or of station—was supposed then to put on "handsome, full-dress silk clothes" and call on the Governor. At other times the individual could dress much as he pleased. Fashions did not change rapidly. A male might "wear the same coat three years." Men shaved almost universally and much esteemed their collections of razors. The dress sword was the main appurtenance of the gentleman's attire when, for example, he called at the Governor's Palace. A Virginian of station was content to have one such sword or to borrow one; a landed lord as careful in such matters as was King Carter might own several swords and might protest he had "never a belt that's fit to wear." Jewelry was frequently but not generally used. Women often wore rings but they seldom had necklaces. Men had gold shirt studs, carried seals or snuff boxes, or wore wedding or mourning rings.

The pride of the Colony was its capital, Williamsburg, the seat of the Governor and the meeting place of the General Assembly, Council, and General Court. Rivaling any of these was the College of William and Mary, chartered by the Crown in 1693. The town took on the dignity of a city by royal letters patent of July 28, 1722. By 1759, Williamsburg consisted of about two hundred houses, ten or twelve of which were rated as permanent residences of gentlemen's families. The principal, though often dusty, street was proclaimed one of the most spacious in America; the appearance of the town was handsome; its population was about one thousand.

Most of the other important towns of the Colony were close to Williamsburg. Across the narrow Peninsula between the York and the James was Yorktown. Its rise had been due to the depth of the York at that point and to the proximity of Chesapeake Bay. Many vessels made it their destination. Merchants built large stores there. No town in all Virginia had a fairer site or an appearance more picturesque. Above the masts and yards of the ships in the sparkling river, houses were perched along the hill-mounting road as if they merely were resting in their climb. On the flat and cheerful cliff were the homes of the merchants, the Court House and the better ordinaries.

Farther down the Peninsula, almost at its tip was Hampton. This was next to Jamestown in age among the Virginia outposts and, after the abandonment of Jamestown, it was to be the oldest English settlement of continuous existence in America. Across Hampton Roads, and a few miles up the tolerant and hospitable river that bore the name of Queen Elizabeth, the town of Norfolk was thriving in the 1750's. It enjoyed a brisk trade with the West Indies from which it imported more of throat-searing rum than was good for the Colony.

Williamsburg, Yorktown, and Norfolk were within a circle of twenty-five miles from Hampton. The Colony's next town of rising dignity was Richmond, more than fifty miles up the James from Williamsburg and at the falls of the river. It was laid out in 1737. Five years later, it was incorporated as a town and in 1751 was chosen as the site for the Court House of Henrico County. The population of Richmond at the middle of the century probably did not exceed 250 or perhaps 300.

The magnitude of the domain inhabited by the Virginians was their pride, the basis of much of their hope and speculation. The Tidewater was well settled, the Piedmont was being occupied, the realm beyond the mountains lured and excited. In 1744–45, precisely when George was beginning to understand something of the life around him, two events widened the frontier of Virginia. After the signing of the Treaty of Albany in 1722, there had been doubt whether the Five Nations had relinquished title as far westward as the crest of the Blue Ridge or the higher saddle of the Alleghenies. The preamble of the Virginia ratification of the preliminary treaty had mentioned only the "great ridge of mountains." The "greater" ridge was that west of the Shenandoah, but the term "ridge" was used primarily for what previously had been called the "Blew Mountains," east of the rich Valley of the Shenandoah. The Colonials interpreted the treaty to cover everything as far westward as the crest of the Allegheny Mountains; the Indians were not willing to allow this extended claim otherwise than for solid gifts.

Patient maneuvering finally brought together at Lancaster, Pennsylvania, the representatives of the Five Nations and the emissaries of Virginia and of Maryland. From June 22 until July 4, 1744, the negotiations continued. Final agreement, stoutly compensated by gifts from the white men, gave the Colonials the land they sought and more. The Shenandoah Valley was not to be entered by Indians. Settlers could open in peace its fat lands and those beyond it.

Announcement of this treaty was news to whet the appetite of every land-hungry Virginian, but the extent to which princely patents could be issued through the King's office in Williamsburg depended, in part, on the outcome of the contest over the boundaries between Virginia and her sister Colonies. The argument with North Carolina could wait because most of the disputed lands were far from navigable streams. With Maryland, the issue was narrow. A doubt of a singular nature existed concerning the line between Virginia and Pennsylvania. West of the boundary of Maryland, the contention of the authorities of the Old Dominion was that "Virginia resumes its ancient breadth and has no other limits . . . than what its first royal charter assigned it, and that is to the South Sea, including the island of California." Part of this domain manifestly was taken from Virginia by the charter given William Penn in 1681, but subsequently there was dispute whether the western boundary of Pennsylvania, which was to be five degrees west of the Delaware River, conformed to the windings of that stream or was a straight line drawn directly north and south at a distance of five degrees from some fixed point on the Delaware. This rendered doubtful a district small in area but valuable for its streams, even though the wealth of its minerals was not then realized.

Controversy over the boundary of Lord Fairfax's proprietary, the Northern Neck, was on a vast scale. If his contention were denied by the Privy Council, then almost the whole of the new country acquired from the Five Nations would be royal domain; but if Fairfax prevailed, all the finest land close to the Potomac and as far west as the South Branch of that river would be his, to patent or to withhold, to sell to all comers or to parcel to his family and among his friends. The case was a close one. The Governor and Council maintained that the Northern Neck extended from the forks of the Rappahannock, above Fredericksburg, to the junction of the Shenandoah and the Potomac. With this western limit, the estimated area between the Rappahannock and the Potomac was 1,470,000 acres. By assuming the northern fork of the Rappahannock to be the base of the western line, acceptance of the same northern limit, where the Shenandoah entered the Potomac, would make the proprietary consist of 2,053,000 acres, as nearly as the Governor could compute. If Fairfax's contention were upheld in full, his boundary would run from the headwaters of the Rapidan, the southern fork of the Rappahannock, all the way to the "head springs" of the Potomac, far in the mountains west of the Alleghenies. The proprietary then would include approximately 5,282,000 acres, or as much land as that on which quit rents were paid the Crown in the remainder of the Colony.

An order in Council for the determination of the boundaries had been issued in November 1733; the report of Fairfax's surveyors and that of boundary commissioners named by the Colony had been completed in August 1737. Thereafter, year on year, the peer had attended the meetings of the Commissioners for Trade and Plantations and had sought to get favorable action on his plea for the widest boundaries of the Northern Neck.

MAP / 1

THE THIRTEEN COLONIES

THE THIRTEEN COLONIES
NEW HAMPSHIRE · MASSACHUSETTS · CONNECTICUT
RHODE ISLAND · NEW YORK · NEW JERSEY · PENNSYLVANIA
DELAWARE · MARYLAND · VIRGINIA · NORTH CAROLINA
SOUTH CAROLINA · GEORGIA

MILES

Drawn under the supervision of RANDOLPH G. ADAMS

Finally, in the winter of 1744–45, he received permission to appear before the Privy Council and offer a compromise: If his contention regarding boundaries was allowed and quit rents for lands within those limits were paid him in the future, he would confirm all royal patents issued in the disputed area, would waive all accumulated quit rents on his own account there, and would pay to the Crown all arrearages he collected of rents due under the King's patents. In the early summer of 1745 word reached Belvoir that on April 11 the Privy Council had taken final action in the case of Fairfax *vs* Virginia. The Proprietor's compromise was accepted; his title was recognized in toto.

George was then thirteen and, though he was precocious in all that related to business, he still was too young to understand the full meaning of Fairfax's victory and of the vast speculative movement that began as soon as the Colonials knew where the Proprietor would set his stakes. Around young George whenever he was at Mount Vernon, the talk was of patents, of surveys, of trails, of settlements and of the profits that might be made by organizing land enterprises beyond the farthest bounds of Fairfax's grant. Much of this was dream, much was speculation, though a few bold men already had penetrated from Virginia to the Mississippi and had descended it. There was admiration for the explorers, but there was envy of the speculators where their plans were known. Rivalry was stirred among different patentees; ugliness showed itself; but Fairfax's following, which included the Washingtons, had both content and ambition. Under the decision of the Privy Council, lands taken out by them within the western reaches of the proprietary would have secure title. Beyond those lands was the unclaimed Valley of the Ohio—with the promise of a fortune for young men of enterprise and courage.

George appeared to have in 1746 small prospect of any part in exploring the domain the decision of the Privy Council awarded Fairfax. In fact, Lawrence did not believe it was to George's best interest to become in time another of the young speculators who were looking to the Shenandoah Valley and beyond. Aboard Vernon's flagship in the Cartagena expedition Lawrence had seen something of the better side of life at sea, and he could think of no finer career for his tall young brother. George was not averse to this, but he was dependent on his mother's will, whim and judgment. As his guardian, she could approve or she could veto. Short of running off, there was no way of starting a sailor's life otherwise than with the acquiescence of a lady who seemed to have little of the Balls' ancestral interest in shipping and the sea.

Mary Ball Washington was positive. A thousand trifles were her daily care to the neglect of larger interests, but mistress of much or of little, mistress she was resolved to be, and in nothing more certainly than in deciding what should be done by her first-born, her pride and her weakness. Lawrence might counsel and plan, but she would decide. This must have been plain to her elder stepson. He realized that any dealings with her and any effort by him to persuade her to permit George to go to sea had to be conducted with high caution and superlative diplomacy.

So, on September 8, 1746, George went across the ferry from the farm to Fredericksburg and there met Col. William Fairfax, who was preparing, with William Beverley and Lunsford Lomax, to mark the newly established boundaries of the proprietary. Colonel Fairfax had come directly from Belvoir. He brought news of Mount Vernon and, more particularly, he put into George's hands two letters from Lawrence. One was addressed to George himself; the other was to Lawrence's stepmother. Fairfax explained that Lawrence wished George to ponder the letter meant for him but not to mention to his mother that he had received it; the letter to Mrs. Washington doubtless was deferential and probably did no more than mention the benefits that might come to George from service on the deck of a good ship. George understood the diplomacy of this approach. He promised Fairfax to follow the advice of Lawrence, who, he said, was his best friend.

Either from George or from an acquaintance in Fredericksburg, Colonel Fairfax learned that a Doctor Spencer was visiting often at Ferry Farm and exercising some influence over Mrs. Washington, then not older than thirty-seven and consequently not beyond thought of remarriage. The Doctor was urged to influence the widow to look favorably on the plan for George to go to sea. Mrs. Washington was half-converted, but within a few days was back to her original state of mind. As a friend of the family, Robert Jackson, wrote Lawrence about a week after the delivery of Lawrence's letter, "she offers several trifling objections such as fond and unthinking mothers naturally suggest and I find that one word against [George's] going has more weight than ten for it."

There, for the time, the matter rested, though it continued to be discussed in family letters and eventually in one from some of the kinsfolk to Joseph Ball, Mary's half-brother in England. Mary had plans of her own that involved Joseph. She had to look forward to 1753 when George would be of age and would come into possession of Ferry Farm. Not far down the Rappahannock was the property that Mary's father had divided between her and Joseph. If the brother would permit her to cut timber and collect stone from his part of the property, she could assure herself a home there when she should leave Ferry Farm. Joseph was the wealthy member of the Ball family. Mary thought he should give her the timber and the stone for foundations and chimneys and that he could afford, indeed, to make a handsome present to his niece, Mary's daughter Betty. To solicit these gifts Mary wrote her brother on December 13, 1746.

If George was not to go to sea until his mother had made up her mind, he had abundant, nearer activities. He seemed to pass in a single year from boyhood to young manhood. Strong of frame and of muscle, he still was studying mathematics and he was learning to write a swift, clear hand that made copying less tedious than for most boys. Among young Virginians of his class there was circulating an abbreviated version of Francis Hawkins's *Youth's Behaviour*. George read this and transcribed the rules with boyish lack of discrimination. He did not attempt to discard those intended for urban English or Continental life rather than for the Colonies; as the text was, so was it copied. At the end he transcribed: "Labour to keep alive in your Breast that Little Spark of Cetial fire Called Conscience." He did so well with his copying that he scarcely deserved a black mark for writing

"Cetial" instead of "Celestial." He was to apply the maxim though he marred the word.

Of religion, there was at Ferry Farm an acceptance of belief in God and a compliance with the ritual of the church, but no special zeal or active faith. Such religious instruction as George received was of a sort to turn his mind towards conduct rather than towards creed. He was beginning to reason that there were certain principles of honesty and fairplay by which a man ought to live. In his small world he tried to practice those principles, but already he was looking beyond Ferry Farm and the Rappahannock. Everywhere the talk was of surveys and of the designs Lawrence and some of his friends were formulating for a company to develop the Ohio country that was accessible under the new Treaty of Lancaster. Whatever career the sea might hold later, the land was full of interest and of promise. George was developing an ambition to share in the profits his seniors were predicting.

The means of advancement were at hand—the surveyor's instruments that had belonged to George's father. George quickly learned the elements of surveying and began to run lines at Ferry Farm or on the plantations of his kinsmen. The work entranced him. By August of 1747 he had attained to the required standard of accuracy on simple assignments. Soon he was proficient on surveys that were not unduly complicated. One batch of surveys at the beginning of October brought the boy £2 3s. It was welcome coin to a boy who already had money-making as one of his ambitions. Surveying not only was excellent training, but it also had interest and yielded a profit.

Young Washington was in the first excitement of this engrossing work and of his first acquisition of earned money when his mother received a somewhat strange reply to the letter she had written her brother Joseph concerning the use of timber from his woods. Joseph wrote (in part) on May 19, 1747:

> I think you are in the Right to leave the House where you are, and to go upon your own Land; but as for Timber, I have scarce enough for my own Plantations; so can spare you none of that; but as for stone, you may take what you please to build you a House. . . .
>
> I understand you are advised, and have some thought of sending your son George to sea. I think he had better be put aprentice to a tinker; for a common sailor before the mast has by no means the common liberty of the Subject; for they will press him from a ship where he has 50 shillings a month and make him like a Negro, or rather, like a dog. And as for any considerable preferment in the Navy, it is not to be expected, there are always too many grasping for it here, who have interest and he has none. And if he should get to be master of a Virginia ship (which will be very difficult to do) a planter that has three or four hundred acres of land and three or four slaves, if he be industrious, may live more comfortably, and leave his family in better Bread, than such a master of a ship can . . . . beforehand, let him begin to chinch, that is buy goods for tobacco and sell. . . .

The arguments against a mariner's life for George probably were decisive with Joseph's half-sister. Nothing more was said in advocacy of such a career at a time when to Mrs. Washington's refusal were added George's profitable employment and a further event that might open many opportunities: Lord Fairfax—the Proprietor himself!—had arrived in Virginia and had established himself at Belvoir. It probably was in February 1748 that George journeyed to Mount Vernon and soon afterward went down to the next plantation to pay his respect to the great landlord. Lord Fairfax was fifty-four in 1748 and was not conspicuous either for good looks or for ugliness. Doubtless in the eyes of the youthful visitor, who was of the age and temperament to admire dress, the strangest characteristic of the owner of the Northern Neck was a disdain of fine apparel. Fairfax would buy of the best and the newest and never wear what he purchased. Year by year his unused wardrobe increased, while he went about in the plainest garments. Another peculiarity was Fairfax's dislike of the company of women. Even among men, as his Virginia kinspeople were to find, he occasionally was silent and sullen; in the presence of ladies he almost always was reserved and embarrassed. If these were peculiarities discernible to young Washington, there was about Fairfax nothing that barbed antagonisms. His intellect was far from brilliant, but he was sufficiently wise to employ competent counsel when he needed to supplement his own. If some accounted him dull, none accused him of being vicious. He never was to have—and never undertook to have—an influence on George comparable to that exerted by Colonel Fairfax or by Lawrence.

Among the Fairfaxes were young women who had grace and good manners and wore fine clothes as if born to them. The resplendent young man of the circle was Colonel Fairfax's oldest son, George William, born in the Bahamas but well-schooled and well-polished in England. He was twenty-three in 1748, seven years older than George, and already a Justice of the County and a newly elected Burgess. With these acquisitions would be coupled a great fortune in land. What finer model could there be, or one more certain to arouse emulation in the heart of George Washington?

Chance offered George in the spring of 1748 an opportunity of being in the company of this young gentleman in circumstances that would permit George to be useful at the same time that he was having a fascinating experience. A surveying party was about to start for the remote South Branch of the Potomac. James Genn, the commissioned County Surveyor of Prince William, was to be in charge; the Proprietor was to be represented by George William Fairfax. Chairmen and other helpers were to be recruited on the frontier. If George cared to do so, he could go with the party. Somewhat surprisingly, permission was given by George's mother.

March 11, 1748, was fixed as the date for leaving Mount Vernon and Belvoir. An important date it was in George's life, because it marked his farthest journey from home and brought his first personal contact with the frontier. George was not unequipped for the enterprise; although he had just observed his sixteenth birthday, he was physically his father's son and, in strength, almost a man. He was systematic, he had achieved his ambition of learning to write swiftly and clearly, and he could perform readily enough the simple mathematical problems of surveying. His mind found interest chiefly in matters of business, concerning which he was mature beyond his age, though he had little imagination except for planning how he could advance himself. On nearly all aspects of farm life, he had the information and the attitude of the plantation owner. For good land he was developing a critical and appraising eye. He rode admirably. He made on adults an excellent impression of vitality, courtesy and integrity at the same time that he won the good will of the young. Along with these excellencies he had the softness of the young gentleman who would ride horseback by the hour but always would come back to a comfortable house and a good bed. Although he was far from rich, he was accustomed to an ease quite different from the life of the frontier. Instead of wearing a hunting shirt and telling time "by sun," he carried a watch and enjoyed some of the clothes of fashion.

Thus apparelled, George and "Mr. Fairfax" set out. Soon, instead of riding past plantations that were taking on something of the appearance of established estates, they turned northwest, at the Occoquan, and traveled through a country which, in part, was one stage only in development from the primal wilderness. Farms were few and trails were dim. Twenty miles the young men had to journey in woodland and new ground, by way of the recently established second Court House of Prince William County; and forty miles they had covered for the day when, at last, they drew rein at the ordinary of George Neville, located about two-thirds of the way to Ashby's Bent on the trail from Fredericksburg.

The next morning, March 12, up rode Genn, who lived on the road to Falmouth. He had been one of the men responsible for the survey in 1746 of the boundaries of the proprietary and had been employed, also, on other work for Lord Fairfax. A more experienced surveyor for drawing lines in the frontier scarcely could have been George's good fortune to find in Virginia. Under Genn's guidance, the two young gentlemen passed northwestward, at times almost northward, until they reached the crest of the Blue Ridge at Ashby's Bent. Ahead of George then, almost directly under the mountain, was the beautiful Shenandoah, the valley of which was a vast plain that spread almost to the horizon on the south. Beyond the plain, to the west and northwest, were lofty, enclosing mountains. For the splendor of this scene, George did not have imaginative eyes. With his companions he rode down from the mountain top by the road to Ashby's Ferry. There, at the house of Captain John Ashby, the travelers spent the night. In a little blank book George had brought with him he wrote down briefly the details of the day's journey and concluded: "Nothing remarkable happen'd."

George perceived quickly why the country was exciting gamblers and attracting settlers. About four miles south of Ashby's Ferry, beyond the western bank of the Shenandoah was the tract of some thousands of acres that Lord Fairfax had established as a "quarter" the previous year. This land, which became known as Greenway Court, George William Fairfax and George Washington set out to examine on March 13. After he got back to Captain Ashby's he wrote in his journal with the enthusiasm of a planter and land speculator: "We went through most beautiful groves of sugar trees and spent the best part of the day in admiring the trees and the richness of the land."

The first surveying of the expedition was not to be at Greenway

Court but about twenty miles northward, down the Shenandoah, on tracts known as Cates Marsh and Long Marsh. For men working there the vicinity of Frederick Town, subsequently Winchester, was better suited as head-quarters than was Ashby's Ferry. On March 14 Genn, Fairfax and George proceeded along the river bank where early settlers had cleared some of the finest land and had planted it in grain, hemp and tobacco. George saw and admired. George observed a survey of lands that George William Fairfax had patented in the two "marshes" where the party was working. It was a commonplace survey and it may have made no impression on Washington; but like many a similar incident that was to come under his eye, it was typical of what the enterprising young men of the Colony were doing: they were moving ahead of actual settlement and were buying up some of the best of the lands. When George could, he would too. That was so natural a way of making money that he probably never became conscious of reaching any formal decision to share in land speculation.

Next ahead of the party was the task of reaching by the easiest practicable route the upper waters of the South Branch of the Potomac, where a large and almost inaccessible tract was to be divided into small parcels. Had the ride been directly from Frederick Town to the designated part of South Branch, the distance would not have been more than forty miles; but that would have involved a battle with roadless mountains, through muddy bottoms and across unbridged, swollen streams. A round-about way was selected. The start for the South Branch of the Potomac was delayed by rain the morning of the seventeenth, but George and his com-panions, by the day's end, reached the residence of Andrew Campbell, about twenty-five miles from town.

As the trails ran, the ride the next day to the Potomac was thirty-five miles and was disappointing besides. On the Potomac northwest of the mouth of the Shenandoah the water was six feet above normal and rising. As Genn planned to cross the river and proceed on the Maryland side, he was balked. The surveyors had to go back to Frederick Town and wait, or stay impatiently where they were, or find some occupation of their time till the flooded Potomac fell. Their decision was to visit the Warm Springs about twenty-five miles upstream. It was large labor to small end. George had to write again that "nothing remarkable happen'd."

March 21 found the surveyors across to the Maryland shore and plodding westward. In continuous rain they pushed their mounts forward over what George pronounced the "worst road ever trod by man or beast." The riders escaped accident and came at last to the well-stocked trading post and the sizeable residence—half home, half fort—of Thomas Cresap, a renowned frontiersman.

All day March 22 the rain fell; the next morning it still mocked the young gentlemen from Fairfax. After noon, the downfall ended and the skies cleared; but the Potomac still was too high and the road too wet for Genn to think of riding farther towards the point where he intended to recross to the Virginia side. There was the prospect of continued boredom when thirty Indians appeared from nowhere. They were a war party, they told their friend Cresap, but they were somewhat chagrined to own that their expedition had been unprofitable. One scalp was all they had to show for their hardships and their journey.

George never before had seen so many savages together nor encountered a war party that had a contingent of young braves. He watched them with charmed eyes. Presently, from the store of liquor the surveyors carried with them, a friendly offering was tendered the Redmen. It raised their spirits and stirred them to preparations for a dance. Some of them borrowed one of Cresap's pots and half filled it with water. Then they stretched a deer skin over it to make a drum. Another savage brought out a dry gourd to which was attached a part of a horse's tail. In this gourd were shot enough to yield a rattle. Other natives, all the while, were clearing a piece of ground and fetching wood. Damp as was the day, they soon had a roaring fire around which they seated themselves in a circle. One of their leaders then launched into a speech unintelligible in every grunt but manifestly done in the best manner of sylvan eloquence.

As to all speeches, there was an end at last. No sooner had the speaker emitted his liberating grunt than a lithe savage jumped into the circle as if he still were dazed with sleep. Whether that was part of the ceremony or a pantomime of the somnolent effect of the speech, George could not determine, but the comedy of it was entrancing. Other Indians joined the first performer; the drummer and the man with the rattle began their accompaniment of the dance. George watched closely and later wrote carefully in his journal a brief account of the whole occurrence. It would be something to tell the household at Mount Vernon and friends in Chotank, and, of course, if it was to be described at all, it must be recorded accurately. That already was part of George's code.

The current of the river west of the mouth of the South Branch did not seem to be swift enough on the twenty-fifth to endanger a horse that undertook to swim to the Virginia shore. The men, it appeared, could get across in a canoe. The party left Cresap's and rode upstream to a point opposite Patterson Creek. There the crossing was made without incident. On the south bank, the caravan proceeded up Patterson Creek. Nightfall found the party at the farm of Abram Johnston, fifteen miles up the creek. The twenty-sixth brought the surveyors to the settlement of Solomon Hedges. On the twenty-seventh the men left the creek, turned east and reached the long-sought middle stretches of the South Branch of the Potomac at the cabins of Henry van Meter, an Indian trader. At van Meter's, the surveyors were about thirty miles from the district where they were to undertake some surveys for James Rutledge. On March 29, eighteen days after the start from Belvoir, the first tract of Rutledge's was surveyed, and, on March 31, George himself ran the lines of one of the surveys.

Interesting experiences crowded the next week. George found the wild turkeys of the region a difficult target for his rifle; he had the excitement of a fire in the straw where he and his companions were asleep; the tent was blown down twice. On April 3, some German settlers came to visit the camp, and on the next day the surveyors were followed through the woods by a great company of men, women and children. Young Washington observed these Germans with amazement. Their lack of acquaintance with

English seemed to him positively perverse. Said he: "I really think they seemed to be as ignorant a set of people as the Indians. They would never speak English but, when spoken to, they speak all Dutch."

Fairfax left the party temporarily on April 4, perhaps to arrange for new supplies. His absence deprived George of most of the fun of the expedition; Genn and his assistants were not companionable, nor was the weather of a sort to comfort young Washington. On the sixth the party started back to van Meter's, only to be caught in so violent a rain that refuge had to be taken. The rain continued until about 1 P.M. on the seventh. A little later, George heard the good news that Fairfax had returned and was at Peter Casey's, two miles away. Off went Washington to see his friend. That night they spent at Casey's—"the first night I had slept in a house," George proudly wrote in his journal, "since I came to the Branch." He doubtless felt he was getting to be a pioneer.

Although the young gentlemen would do their own cooking where they must, they at least wanted something to cook and did not relish what they had the next day, empty stomachs. The man who was to bring supplies did not appear. While an all-day quest for food was being made, George and Fairfax remained at the camp, under the canvas, and none too happy; novelty and excitement were giving place to hunger and discomfort. They decided they had had enough of the wilderness, or else their designated time was up. In any event, they ate some of the food that reached the camp between 4 and 5 P.M. and then said good-bye and headed for the lower Potomac.

They lost no time on the road. When that journey ended April 13, their expedition to the Valley could not be described as an adventure of frontier hardship unflinchingly borne, but it could be written down as compassing the most useful thirty-three consecutive days that George ever had spent. All the milder, less arduous experiences of the frontier had been crowded one upon another. Some days had been wet and tedious and some nights long and smoky, but George had learned that he could run a line in the wilderness. He had camped out, though neither with skill nor to his satisfaction; he had cooked his food over the flames, and he had slept by a fire in the open; he had been among Indians, and he had observed as much of their ways as he could in two days. He had seen with his own eyes the fine western lands. He had felt the frontier.

The story of George's half-amusing, half-instructive experiences beyond the mountains was one, of course, that all his kinsmen wished to hear. After telling it at Mount Vernon to Lawrence and Nancy, the young gentleman who had been to the frontier had to repeat his narrative at Ferry Farm, probably at Pope's Creek and, in June, among the pleasant families of Chotank. After some enjoyable days there, George paid a visit to the Turner plantation, on the north bank of the Rappahannock, opposite Port Royal. Another journey of the summer carried him on his first visit to Yorktown, where he did some shopping for his mother. There was more ready cash in the family that summer because the active executors of Augustine Washington's estate—Lawrence Washington and Nathaniel Chapman—had sold on George's account about 165 acres of the Ferry Farm to Anthony Strother.

In August George rode to the falls of the Potomac with Lawrence, whose continuing interest in western lands was evidenced by his purchase during 1748 of more than thirteen hundred acres in the Shenandoah Valley. Promising a profit was a plan in which Lawrence, Austin and others were engaged, to move the Colonial capital from Williamsburg to a more convenient, healthier site in the region where the Washingtons and their friends were large landowners. The plan was an old one but it had a new argument behind it that year: Williamsburg was suffering from an epidemic of dysentery so serious that a postponement of the meeting of the House of Burgesses was advocated.

This proposal to change the seat of government interested George as a young man of business but it did not excite him. He was making occasional surveys and he was reading the *Spectator* and a little of English history, but, above all, he was enjoying life. Besides billiards, George had learned whist and loo by the autumn of 1748, and he did not object to playing for stakes that were worth winning. George was enjoying other social pleasures, too. His clothes and his appearance became increasingly his concern. Another new acquirement was dancing. In the acquisition of social graces, George's model and mentor continued to be Lawrence, who was acquainted with the best usages as well as with the best families of the Colony.

Sickness now was interfering with Lawrence's service to the public. From the time Fairfax had separate representation in 1744, George's older half-brother had been a Burgess and a member of the important committee on propositions and grievances. Seniority and influence were rising when, in December 1748, he had to ask leave of absence because of ill-health. He returned to Mount Vernon, where George remained with him for part of the cold season.

If this was a time of solicitude on account of Lawrence, it was a time of pleasurable excitement, also, because of a shining event at Belvoir. George William Fairfax had wooed and won Sarah Cary, daughter of Col. Wilson Cary of Ceelys, an excellent estate on James River about three miles from Hampton. The marriage had been solemnized December 17; the proud young Fairfax had brought his bride immediately to his father's house and had introduced neighbors who, of course, were eager to see her. As George observed her that winter of 1748–49, Sally was an altogether charming and somewhat tantalizing person. She was eighteen, not two years older than George, and she had much grace. Belvoir, indeed the whole sweep of that part of the Potomac, was the brighter for her presence. Having met her, it was difficult for George to go back to Ferry Farm, even for a brief period, or to find full pleasure in visits elsewhere.

The spring of 1749 found Lawrence plagued with so stubborn a cough that he talked of leaving Virginia. He took up his duties when the House of Burgesses was convened, but in May he had again to be excused from attendance. The distress created by this illness was deepened by loss of one after another of Nancy's children by Lawrence. Three times the mother had seen the body of her only child carried to the grave. There was the unhappy prospect that if Lawrence yielded to his malady, which looked more and more like consumption, he would have no heir of the body. Augustine had provided that in this event, the land and mill left to Lawrence should pass to George unless Austin desired the Hunting Creek property. Should Austin wish to own Hunting Creek, if Lawrence died without issue, then, Augustine had stipulated that his second son must transfer the Mattox-Pope Creek estate to George.

Lawrence's illness and loss of his children were the saddest but not the only concerns of the family in 1749. Mary Washington had abandoned her plan for building a house on her lower farm. Mrs. Washington simply "stayed on" at Ferry Farm as if the property were her own and was not to pass to George when he became twenty-one. Besides there was a threat that a ferry might be authorized across the Rappahannock at her lower tract—in George's indignant words, "right through the very heart and best of the land."

George explained this to Lawrence in May 1749, at a time when the younger brother was busy as a surveyor and was planning still larger things in that profession. The long-desired town at Belhaven, on the Potomac, was about to become a reality. The General Assembly had authorized the establishment of the town on sixty acres of land that belonged to Philip and John Alexander and to Hugh West. The place was to be "called by the name of Alexandria," in honor of the owners of the greater part of the tract. The trustees, all three of the Fairfaxes among them, were resolved to establish the town at once. On May 27 the *Maryland Gazette* announced that lots would be sold to the highest bidders July 13. To have all the parcels laid off by that time, the regular surveyor, John West, Jr., used young Mr. Washington as an assistant. George worked fast. By approximately July 17, he had finished his part of the survey and had drawn a plan of the town.

Lawrence was in bad condition physically. His cough defied local doctors and home treatment. In growing concern, he determined to consult physicians in London and while there to advance a business enterprise that was exciting him and some of his neighbors. With toasts for a pleasant voyage and prayers for a sure and swift recovery, he was bidden farewell shortly before the vendue at Alexandria.

This was the grief of the summer of 1749. The gratification was the success of George in his application for the surveyorship of Culpeper. On the last day of July, he completed the long ride to the temporary quarters of the Court and received his commission from the President and Masters of the College of William and Mary. George proceeded immediately to exercise his new authority. He surveyed four hundred acres in Culpeper for Richard Barnes of Richmond County on July 22 and received promptly his fee of £2 3s. Soon, too, George was copying for customers deeds already recorded. Of other work in the proprietary, there was little during the summer. The principal reason was controversy regarding the title of Jost Hite to certain lands he had acquired in the Shenandoah Valley and then had resold in part. Because of Hite's threat, Lord Fairfax closed the land books of Frederick County to most applicants in 1749. This action denied George any surveying of new tracts in Frederick, where business otherwise would have been brisk. He scarcely could have undertaken to ride over the mountains, even had the land office been open, because of an attack of malaria, which, said he, "I have had to extremity."

With the return of Lawrence, a short time prior to November 7, interest shifted. As a student of the art of making money, George now had a new lesson. Although Lawrence had not improved in health and had not even learned the nature of his malady, he displayed the energy of renewed interest in a project that had been shaping itself ever since the completion of the Treaty of Lancaster. Thomas Lee, Lawrence Washington, and some of their speculating friends planned a bold project for an "Ohio Company." With the help of the Duke of Bedford and of John Hanbury, a wealthy London merchant, the company received a grant of 200,000 acres from King George on February 23, 1749. If the terms attached to that grant were executed, an additional 300,000 acres were to be allotted.

Lawrence and his associates were convinced they could attract settlers and secure the frontier against the possibility of occupation by French who might come down from Canada. Lawrence reasoned that a fort and an Indian trading post in the western country could be supplied from the upper Potomac far more readily and regularly than would be possible for the French from the St. Lawrence River and the Lakes. Thus a larger part of the fur trade might be captured. The Indians, getting the goods they wanted, might be more firmly the friends of England. Nor could Lawrence overlook the fact that if the upper Potomac became the base for this new trade, land owners in that region might profit handsomely. The immediate task was to establish the trading post. All advice to the stockholders of the company from frontiersmen indicated that the junction of the Allegheny and Monongahela Rivers would be the ideal site for the post. Until it could be established, a warehouse was to be maintained on Wills Creek, forty-five miles northwest of Frederick Town.

The prospect had appeared bright early in 1749, but it had been clouded somewhat by the time of Lawrence's return from England. "Those very Indians that had encouraged [the company] at first," wrote Thomas Lee in disgust, "had been persuaded that our design was to ruin, not to trade with them." In addition, on the day that the Governor and Council had confirmed the grant to the Ohio Company, they had allotted 800,000 acres to a somewhat similar enterprise, that of the Loyal Company. The lines of the two companies were far enough apart to avoid direct conflict, but rivalry was stirred. Neither company was willing to trust the other or to withhold a blow that could be delivered secretly.

These matters were vexing to Lawrence and exciting to George. As a qualified County Surveyor, he could work anywhere he was engaged, and he accepted gladly an invitation from Fairfax to meet the Proprietor in Frederick at the November term of Court. The ground Fairfax now wished surveyed was to be similar, in general, to that George had seen in 1748, but there was a most material difference: On this new expedition Washington was to be responsible for surveys, not merely a volunteer assistant.

Work began November 2, 1749. For a few evenings, George was close enough to Frederick Town to go to the ordinary and sleep in a bed. The other nights he spent by a fire on straw or bearskin. The dwellers in the

Valley he disliked as acutely as on his previous visit. "A parcel of barbarians . . . an uncouth set of people," he termed them. He said of his life among them, "There's nothing would make it pass off tolerably but a good reward." He confided with pride: "A doubloon is my constant gain every day that the weather will permit my going out, and sometimes six pistoles." This was fine compensation for a young man not yet eighteen but it could not be earned for long. His last surveys for the season were made November 11.

When George came back to Mount Vernon, he continued to hear discussion of business ventures and speculative enterprises. Contact with Lawrence and the Fairfaxes was itself a business education for the younger Washington. Although the health of Lawrence was no better, he discharged patiently his duties as one of the trustees of Alexandria, engaged in additional land transactions, and sought to hasten the dispatch of goods to the frontier for the Ohio Company. Its affairs were not developing as rapidly or as favorably as the Virginia promoters had hoped. The suspicions on the part of the Redmen were unrelieved. In addition to the threat presented vaguely by the French, moving from Lake Erie southward, there was nearer rivalry by Pennsylvanians who showed every intention of competing for the fur trade and asserted title to part of the territory given the Ohio Company.

George went to Fredericksburg in January 1749–50 and spent some time at Ferry Farm. Conditions there had not changed greatly. Death had taken none of the family, though Catherine Washington Lewis, wife of Fielding Lewis, was near the end of her brief years. George's mother continued busy with many small things and was charged with three young sons as well as with Betty, who was now sixteen and, naturally, would soon be marrying.

He went back to the Potomac early in the year. George now had to be regarded as a serious young man of business. Pleasure had its place; making a fortune came first. Pistoles and doubloons were to be sought in strict accordance with the code of honorable conduct that George was developing steadily, but within the limits that character and honesty imposed, gold was to be pursued and caught. Settlers were increasing rapidly on the lower stretches of the Shenandoah; there was work enough there for George, highly profitable work that would reconcile him to sojourning among the "barbarians." He rode over the mountains to the Valley, made on March 30, 1750, his first survey of the spring and continued to use his compass and Jacob's staff, with scant interruption, until April 28. Before George had gone to the Valley, he had bought himself a handsome set of pole-chair harness at £10 15s. On his return, he had money for the enjoyment of his equipage, and he likewise had the consciousness that when he came upon a particularly good piece of unpatented land, he could afford to pay the quit rents on it.

Much had happened on the well-settled part of the Northern Neck while George was in the Valley. Catherine Washington Lewis had died February 19 and had left a son, John, about three years of age. Her husband, Fielding Lewis, turned at once to George's sister Betty. The siege was brief; on May 7 Betty was married to him. That event was pleasant, if somewhat precipitate; but at Mount Vernon and at Belvoir, there were troubles. Sally Fairfax Carlyle, Nancy's sister and the wife of the rich merchant and shipmaster, John Carlyle, was pregnant and had symptoms that suggested cancer of the breast. Col. William Fairfax had gone to England. Most of these clouds were swept from the sky in the spring and summer of 1750. Betty's venture in matrimony was manifestly a happy one; Sally Carlyle improved in health; George made some remunerative surveys in Culpeper and had a round of visits that extended from Yorktown to Pope's Creek.

The continuing distress of the Washington-Fairfax circle was Lawrence's physical condition. Warm weather brought him no relief. Another change of climate seemed desirable. As the springs of Berkeley, which George had visited in 1748, were gaining in reputation, it was thought that a visit there might invigorate Lawrence. George gladly agreed to go as companion and, if need be, as nurse. By July 25 the brothers were en route to the primitive resort. With a great bend of the Potomac lying to the north, the approaches to the baths were interesting, but the immediate surroundings were commonplace or worse. While the benefit to Lawrence was transitory if perceptible at all, the sight of much good land in the region of the Shenandoah revived his speculative impulse. Either on the basis of patents already issued to him, or else in the knowledge that his father-in-law would approve grants for any unoccupied land he desired, Lawrence had George survey three tracts.

George's departure from the Shenandoah Valley was not earlier than the afternoon of August 26, but he lost no time in getting home and in picking up a few honest pounds. Work alternated with play. Late in September or early in October there was an excursion to Yorktown. From October 11 to October 24, he ran the lines of approximately sixteen tracts. Then, on October 25, George had a new and delightful experience. He had saved much the greater part of his earnings as a surveyor while cherishing ambition to buy good land when he found a tract that appealed to him in price and quality. The time now came. On October 17 he had the satisfaction of asking transfer of patent for a tract of 453 acres which he bought of Capt. John Rutherford—the first spread of friendly Shenandoah land to become his. This was not all: on the twenty-fifth he submitted to record a deed from Lord Fairfax for 550 acres of land in Frederick.

Back George went to his work. Now that he was buying land, cold and adverse weather were less of a deterrent to surveying. Not until November 26 did Washington make his last survey west of the mountains for that season. This done, George rode back over the Blue Ridge, but he was not quite through with his investments for the year. On Bullskin Creek were 456 acres of James McCracken's that would make a most desirable purchase. As soon as George was at Mount Vernon and could arrange the details, he paid McCracken £45, took a deed, and promised to tender the balance of £77 within a few months. George duly met this second payment to Mc-

Cracken and could list the farm as his unencumbered own. Surveying was profitable! Besides a handsome income, it had yielded him 1459 acres of good land, part of which he soon leased to a tenant.

George found the household at Mount Vernon busy with a different balance-sheet. While he had been absent in the Valley, his sister-in-law Nancy had given birth to her fourth child, another girl. The new baby was named Sarah, in honor of her grandmother Fairfax. If Lawrence was disappointed that the child was a girl, no record survives. Nancy was young and strong enough to bear him other children, but the condition of the health of Lawrence raised more acutely than ever the question whether he would live to look into the face of a boy who would bear his name and inherit his property. George must be, in a sense, son as well as younger brother.

Lawrence's work that winter of 1750–51 was not a sort to improve his physical condition. In November Thomas Lee, president of the Ohio Company, came to the end of his career; the direction of much of the business of the company devolved on Lawrence Washington. Harassment over the affairs of the Ohio Company and a further decline in health forced Lawrence to return to the Warm Springs early in 1751. George preceded or escorted him. While Lawrence "took the cure" and told German settlers about the riches of the Ohio country, George undertook the usual round of surveys in Frederick. By March 26 Lawrence was ready to leave.

Travel was more and more difficult for Lawrence. Although he remained courageous, it did not appear wise to subject him to another winter in Virginia. A few months in a balmy climate might stay his malady and perhaps restore his health. Barbados Island had a reputation as a haven for persons with diseases of the lungs. Lawrence could not take Nancy there with him; she could not leave her baby. If Lawrence was to make the journey and to have companionship, which was almost essential, the arrangement made for the visits to the springs must be repeated; George must accompany his half-brother.

In a measure the voyage would be a fascinating experience for a young man who once had thought he would be a sailor. Financially, long absence from Virginia would involve the loss of the autumn season of surveying and the sacrifice of the chance of finding some new bargains in frontier lands. No hint of any balancing of loss against gain or of cost against duty appears in anything George is known to have said then or afterward. Family obligation came first; Lawrence needed his company. That was enough. Everything else could wait.

Their vessel left the Potomac September 28, 1751, and by October 4 had gone far to the southeast of the Virginia capes and was standing eastward in the latitude of the Bermudas. At the end of the voyage, beating inshore and entering shallow Carlisle Bay was slow work but was completed November 3. Lawrence and George went ashore to a tavern in Bridgetown, the principal settlement on the island. Arrangements were made for an examination of Lawrence the next day by Dr. William Hilary, a physician of much experience in treating diseases of the lungs.

George must have waited in affectionate anxiety as Dr. Hilary talked with Lawrence on the fourth, and he must have felt relief when he heard the physician's conclusion: Lawrence's disease was not so deeply seated that it could not be cured. This encouragement led the two young men to start in quest of lodgings, which the doctor urged them to take outside the town. As there were no inns or taverns in the rural parts of the island, inquiry had to be made at private homes. No suitable quarters were found that evening; but if this was a disappointment to Lawrence, the ride was exciting to his younger brother. George was almost overwhelmed by the beauty of the tropical landscape. Letter writing on the sixth and much hospitality on the seventh were followed the next day by conclusion of a bargain for board and lodging at the house of Captain Crofton, commander of Fort James. The price was outrageously high—£15 a month exclusive of liquors and washing—but to George the site was almost ideal. It was close to the water and not more than a mile from the town. "The prospect," George wrote, "is extensive by land and pleasant by sea, as we command the prospect of Carlisle Bay and all the shipping in such manner that none can go in or out without being open to our view."

The delights of the view were equalled by the cordiality of the residents of the island. Except for the Governor, Henry Grenville, who kept himself aloof from nearly all society on the island, each of the dignitaries seemed anxious to entertain the Virginians. One of George's visits was to Fort James, which he viewed as critically as if he had been a military engineer. "It's pretty strongly fortified," he wrote in his diary, "and mounts about 36 guns within the fortifications, but [has] two fascine batteries mg. 51."

On the morning of November 17 the younger Washington felt a curious rigor and then had a high fever. Before evening he was seized with a violent headache and with pains in his back and loins. The next day the debilitating symptoms were the same. By the twentieth, red spots were discernible on the young man's forehead and among the roots of his hair. In a few hours, these spots became thickly set papules. George had the smallpox. He was busy with his painful battle against the disease until about the twenty-eighth. Then the "suppurative fever" diminished and disappeared. Soon the scabs began to fall off. Underneath were reddish brown spots. George knew that these would leave "pits" which he would carry with him through life, but he had won the fight that almost every man of his generation expected to have to wage. On December 12 Washington was dismissed by his physician.

George and Lawrence attended a succession of dinners every day, except one, between the thirteenth and the twentieth. In private, discussion concerned their own plans. Lawrence was discouraged. He gave no indication of sudden or swift decline, but he had not gained in health and he greatly missed Nancy and their little girl. The sameness of the climate depressed him. No diversion was offered other than dancing, which was supposed to bring on yellow fever. Although not quite prepared to call his visit a failure, he was close to a decision that if he did not improve soon, he would go to the Bermudas. If that did not help, he would return home and try once more the dry air of Frederick County. All this would involve more months away from Mount Vernon. During that time, George could be of small assistance to his brother; he might as well return to Virginia. This was agreed. On December 21 George said farewell to Lawrence and the friends he had made on the island.

After landing at Yorktown, January 28, 1752, George hired a horse and rode over to Williamsburg to call on the Governor and present letters entrusted to him. Governor Dinwiddie had gone to Green Spring, but he was expected back later in the day. When the Governor returned he received George cordially, invited him to stay and dine, and inquired concerning the health of Lawrence. It was George's first chat with a man he was to know much better. From Williamsburg, George returned to Yorktown. There he found Col. John Lewis, who had come to town, along with the gentry of that region, to witness a great main of cocks. The two left together in Lewis's chariot and rode to that gentleman's home. Thence George went to Hobbs Hole and on to Layton's Ferry. It probably was on February 5 or 6 that he reached Mount Vernon and reported to Nancy on Lawrence's condition and plans and on his own experiences.

Besides giving him some acquaintance with the economy of the island, George's visit to Barbados had shown him something of the markets offered Virginia in the British West Indies. More personally, he had demonstrated on the island what he probably had no reason to doubt—that he could go into new society and, when he accepted an invitation, could so conduct himself that he received new invitations from guests he met. That was not the sole gain from the voyage. The worst feature of the stay on the island proved to be the best: That pain, that burning fever, that ugly eruption of smallpox had left George immune. He could go now to frontier, camp, or barrack without fear. The ancient foe could not strike him down.

The six months that followed George's return from Barbados were crowded with incident. After rest and visits to kinspeople, he went to Frederick County in March and undertook new surveys that occupied his time until nearly the first of May. In gross receipts, the work was as profitable as ever, but it was subject, at least in theory, to a deduction not previously made. Under the charter of 1693, which gave the College of William and Mary exclusive authority in Virginia to commission county surveyors, the institution received one-sixth of the fees those officers collected. Lord Fairfax and his surveyors apparently had ignored the law. Governor Dinwiddie tactfully admonished Lord Fairfax to have the suveyors procure commissions and pay the College the stipulated one-sixth of their receipts. The first of these two requirements did not trouble George, but compliance with the College's share of his fees would reduce his gross income by 16⅔ per cent. In spite of this, George's thrift and diligence yielded money enough in 1752 for him to increase his holdings on Bullskin Creek. Both he and Lawrence regarded that part of Frederick County as particularly desirable.

On his return from Frederick, George was stricken with pleurisy. This embarrassed him and irritated him because, at that particular season he was engaged in what he considered a most important negotiation. George was in love. From early youth he had been confident in all his work and all his pleasure, so long as men were involved; with girls, he must have been self-conscious. Occasionally he wrote vague, sighing poetry to them, or about them. More direct associations had not been lacking, though they had not been taken too seriously. He had sighed over a "Low Land Beauty" when he still was too young to marry, and he had found attraction in an unidentified "Sally" when he was a little older. The girl with whom he was most frequently thrown at Belvoir and at Mount Vernon was Mary Cary, younger sister of the tantalizing Sally Cary, whom George William Fairfax had married. He might have fallen in love with Mary had he not been in a tangle of affection for other girls.

Now, in the spring of 1752, he turned seriously in another direction. At Naylor's Hole in Richmond Country lived William Fauntleroy. Fauntleroy was of the established, dominant class, though not of the wealthiest or most eminent. By his first wife, Elizabeth, he had a daughter of the same name. Familiarly "Betsy," this girl was in her sixteenth year when she dazzled the eyes of George. As befitted a young gentleman who had examined critically the fortifications of Barbados, he undertook the siege of Betsy's heart by formal approaches. Repulsed in his first attack, he had to wait until he had recovered from the pleurisy to make a second. Diplomacy and persistence alike were unrewarded. Betsy's answer again was in the negative, so strongly negative that George abandoned the siege.

If George felt grief over his rejection by Betsy, he now had a deeper, absorbing concern over his elder half-brother. As previously planned, Lawrence went to Bermuda. His letters from that island indicated that he had moved too early in the year. The chill of the spring had renewed the worst of his symptoms. After a time he showed some improvement but, as he wrote, he was "like a criminal condemned, though not without hopes of reprieve." Lawrence's next letter was grimmer in tone: "The unhappy state of health which I labor under makes me uncertain as to my return. If I grow worse I shall hurry home to my grave; if better, I shall be induced to stay here longer to complete a cure." Sometime prior to June 16 Lawrence landed from Bermuda—with his death sentence written on his face. He knew his end was at hand and proceeded hurriedly to put his affairs in such order as was possible. "In consideration of love and affection," he transferred to George his share in the reversion under his father's will of the three lots in Fredericksburg, and he had his mother and his younger half-brothers witness the paper. On June 20 he hastily completed and signed his will; and on July 26, 1752, he breathed his painful last. George had the sombre duty of arranging for the funeral and for the construction of a burial vault. His, too, was much of the early work in the execution of Lawrence's will.

The master of Mount Vernon bequeathed his wife a life interest in that property and in his lands on Bullskin Creek, together with half his slaves; and he provided that all his estate, exclusive of specific bequests, should descend to his infant daughter, Sarah. Were Sarah to die without issue, part of her estate was to go to her mother, if alive, and part of her lands were to be divided equally among Lawrence's brother and half-brother. George was to share equally in the real estate that was to go to Lawrence's brothers in the event of Sarah's childless death. Further, if Sarah died without issue, George was to have Mount Vernon and all of Lawrence's other real estate in Fairfax County when Nancy's life ended. Executors named by Lawrence were Col. William Fairfax, George Fairfax, Nathaniel Chapman, John Carlyle and Austin and George Washington.

The settlement of Lawrence's affairs was slow and complicated. It was December 23 when the inventory was completed and was copied by the young surveyor. A sale of personal effects was held that month, when George, one of numerous purchasers, bought live-stock to the value of £33. Final balancing of his accounts with the estate of his brother was to be delayed thereafter for more than three years.

Lawrence's death involved the transfer of his varied duties as a trustee of Alexandria, as a stockholder in the Ohio Company and as Adjutant of the Colony. This last office either had been vacated before Lawrence's death or else had been held with the understanding that Lawrence would resign when a successor was chosen. To seek to succeed his brother was, for George, a natural ambition. Even before Lawrence's death it had been understood that the adjutancy would be divided among three men, to each of whom would be assigned a district. George knew that if Col. William Fitzhugh would accept it, that gentleman could have direction of the district in which the Northern Neck was to be included, but, as his second wife had large property in Maryland, Fitzhugh had moved his residence to that Colony.

George had been anxious to know if this change of abode meant that Fitzhugh would forego the office of Adjutant of the Northern Neck. A short time before Lawrence's return, George had ridden to Williamsburg, had seen the Governor, and then had gone to Maryland to consult Fitzhugh. Apparently Fitzhugh would accept the office if he could discharge the greater part of his duties from the Maryland shore and, when circumstance admitted, would erect a house in Virginia and reside there "sometimes." Fitzhugh gave George a letter in which he told the Governor of the terms he would have to impose if he took the office. George went back to Ferry Farm, wrote the Governor of his visit and enclosed Fitzhugh's letter.

George had pending, in a short time, application of a different sort. On September 1, 1752, a new lodge of Masons held its first meeting in Fredericksburg and soon attracted members. Under Daniel Campbell as Master, a class of five was initiated on November 4. George, one of this group, paid his initiation fee of £2 3s. as an Entered Apprentice.

Two days afterward, the situation created by the death of Adjutant Lawrence Washington was reviewed by the Council of Virginia. Governor and Council agreed that one man could not discharge the duties of the office. Virginia consequently was divided, not into three districts, but into four—each of which was to have an Adjutant. For the frontier, Thomas Bentley was chosen; the "Middle Neck" between the Rappahannock and the York was assigned to George Muse; the Northern Neck was made the district of William Fitzhugh. To George was allotted the southern district, the most remote and least interesting. It extended from Princess Anne County to the western fringe of settlement and covered the entire region between James River and the North Carolina boundary. It was a distinction for George to be named Adjutant before he was twenty-one, and to be allowed pay of £100 per annum. On February 1, 1753, he presented his commission to the Court of Spotsylvania and took the various oaths; but, meantime, he sought and procured the influence of the powerful William Nelson for the vacancy that might occur if Fitzhugh found himself unable to serve.

When George took the oaths as Adjutant, he became officially Major Washington. He might have regarded the title as a present for his twenty-first birthday. How well he had advanced during the ten years that had passed after his father's death! The younger son of a second marriage, he had received as his inheritance ten slaves, the small Ferry Farm, three Fredericksburg lots and half of the Deep Run tract. He now had a remunerative profession as County Surveyor and from his own earnings he had bought ample clothing and good equipage. In the rich Shenandoah Valley he held two thousand acres of excellent land. If he counted his moiety of the Deep Run tract and what remained of Ferry Farm, he already was the owner of 4291 acres of unencumbered land and thus was in the class of the larger proprietors. With the advantage of immunity to smallpox, he could travel freely. He was strong and was able, without complaint or great discomfort, to sleep out of doors, in his clothing and on the ground. The softness of 1748 was gone, but without the loss of his love of good apparel and comfortable living. Fixed in his methodical habits, he kept his accounts carefully. If his English grammar and composition still were poor, he was progressing in these, too. Socially, he was capable of entering the best of Colonial society. He could dance, and he had proficiency in cards and billiards. While not particularly accurate as a marksman, he squared accounts by the superlative excellence of his horsemanship. Now, with the thoroughness that marked his every performance, he was to learn the duties of District Adjutant of Virginia.

George had to instruct himself in order that he might train the county officers. Study must in consequence have occupied much of his spare time during the spring and summer of 1753. Available books on tactics were hard, complicated reading for a man who did not have opportunity of drilling and exercising soldiers. As far as surviving records show, he did not visit in 1753 any of the counties under his care. George's interest shifted as his duties changed. His few letters of later boyhood contained not one line on public affairs and not a single reference to the duty a Virginian owed King and Crown. Now, as Major Washington, Adjutant of the Southern District, he began to learn more about the political aspect of dealings on the frontier, and, in particular, about the advance of the French.

The Treaty of Aix-la-Chapelle, October 18, 1748, had ended the war of the Austrian Succession; but, so far as England and France were involved, the settlement merely provided for restitution of the territory each had taken from the other. Like wrestlers well matched, the two ancestral adversaries broke off their struggle in order to get a new hold when an opening was offered. No boundary was drawn on the watershed of the Ohio, which both countries claimed. The French thought the English planned to separate Louisiana from Canada and to conquer the two Colonies separately; the British suspected that the French intended to cut them off from the back country and to pin them to the Atlantic coast. In the foreground was the prospect of winning or losing the fur trade.

In full appreciation of what the loss of the fur trade would mean, the French had become aggressive. During the first days of the Ohio Company the protection of the frontier had been little more than an argument to facilitate large grants to Virginia land speculators; now it was a reality. In 1749, the Marquis de la Galissonière, French Governor of Canada, had sent the Chevalier Céloron de Bienville to the Ohio Valley to reassert the claim of France to that region. Céloron had visited numerous Indian tribes and had penetrated to Logstown. There he had warned the Indians against the English. When the word of Céloron's expedition reached the English Colonies, it convinced both Pennsylvanians and Virginians that they should strengthen their ties with the Six Nations and that they should confirm the treaty which had been made at Lancaster in 1744 but never had been ratified acceptably. Forts must be built to resist the French if they should return.

It was shortly after this that Governor Dinwiddie had arrived in Virginia and had become interested, financially and politically, in the Ohio Company and in the settlements it proposed to establish in the region claimed by the French. Soon he commissioned Joshua Fry, Lunsford Lomax and James Patton to deliver a present to the Six Nations at Logstown on May 15, 1752, procure the desired ratification of the Treaty of Lancaster, and renew friendly relations and gain new concessions. Fry and his companions had to spend many days in coaxing the Indians into a new agreement. Finally, on June 13, 1752, they won full confirmation of the treaty. Permission was given the English to build two strong trading posts on the Ohio and establish settlements south of that river.

This success of English Colonial diplomacy was offset that same month when Charles Langlade, a French trader, mustered 250 Ottawas and Ojibwas and badly defeated the Indian Chief, Old Britain, oddly styled the Demoiselle, a known friend of England. After that, nothing was heard of French activity in the disputed region until the winter of 1752–53. Word then reached Dinwiddie that the Miami Indians had gone over to the "other side" and that fifteen or sixteen French had come to Logstown and were establishing themselves there. Dinwiddie was alarmed. "We would fain hope," he declared, "these people are only French traders, and they have no other view but trade. I hope there is no great army of French among the lakes."

His hope was vain. A force of 1500 French troops landed in the spring of 1753 on the southern shore of Lake Erie and built forts and some stretches of road. These soldiers of King Louis spread their dominion swiftly and without resistance, only to find disease a worse foe than the Indians or the negligent English colonists. By autumn most of the survivors were sent back to Montreal. The number of those who remained at Forts Presque Isle and Le Boeuf was not known to the Virginians, but this much was plain: These men from Canada were in territory claimed by England, and if they pushed southward, they would reach the Ohio and close to English traders and settlers the rich lands that speculators had been eyeing ever since the Treaty of Lancaster had been signed.

The young Adjutant of the Southern District read in the *Virginia*

Gazette of some of these events, and doubtless he learned from Colonel Fairfax that the situation on the Ohio had been described in dispatches to the home government. Perhaps, too, it was Fairfax who told him that the Governor had resolved to send a warning to the French commander to leave the country of the British King. George reflected, saw an opportunity, determined to seize it—and set out for Williamsburg: He would volunteer to carry the message to the Ohio.

CHAPTER / 2

When George Washington reached Williamsburg at the end of October 1753 he found the taverns crowded with Burgesses. The General Assembly had been called to meet November 1, in circumstances that aroused more than the usual curiosity of Colonials eager for news. On October 21 a sloop of war had brought special dispatches to the Governor, who promptly had sent letters under the King's seal to the executives of the other Colonies. The proclamation for an early session of the Virginia lawmakers had then been issued.

George soon learned part of the reason for this activity. At the Palace, he was ushered into the presence of the Governor. Dinwiddie was aroused and probably impressed by the importance of the steps he was about to take. On June 16 he had written the home government concerning the need of building forts to prevent the French from occupying the Ohio country. Dispatches of August 28 had brought him instructions that accorded with his judgment. Encouraging promises of military equipment had been made. As a first step, Dinwiddie had been instructed to warn the French of their encroachment and formally call on them to leave British territory.

Governor and Council accepted promptly George's offer to carry the message. Orders were drafted. Without delay he was to proceed to Logstown and there call on friendly Indian Sachems for a guard to attend him as far as he thought proper en route to the French commanding officer. When he reached the French station, Washington was to present a letter, which Dinwiddie handed him, and demand a reply, for which he was to wait not more than a week. This answer having been given, Major Washington was to request a French escort on his way back to the Virginia settlements. In addition, George was to procure all the information he could of the numerical strength, armament, defences, communications and plans of the intruders.

Besides his written instructions, George received detailed verbal orders: He was to proceed first to Wills Creek and there deliver to Christopher Gist, an experienced frontiersman, a written request from the Governor and Council that Gist act as Washington's guide on the mission. The Virginia messenger, moreover, was to inquire of the French why they had made prisoners of British subjects trading with the Indians and why they had driven trader John Frazier from the house where he had lived for twelve years. Finally, speed was enjoined.

This mission was assigned young Washington when sparkling

autumn weather was turning to the rains and the bleakness of November. George knew how unpleasant that month could be; but he was being honored by the assignment, and he had such an opportunity as no young Virginian had enjoyed in his generation of winning reputation. Off he went to Fredericksburg, and as he rode he planned: Besides Gist as guide, he would need men to look after the horses and baggage and to pitch a tent. Unless Gist knew the Indian tongues, it would be necessary to procure an interpreter. Further, someone must make the journey who could translate French and converse in it. George believed he could procure such a man. To the vicinity of Fredericksburg in 1752 had come a young Hollander, Jacob van Braam. Though his English was meagre, he was said to have a knowledge of French.

On reaching Fredericksburg, November 1, George found van Braam, who agreed to accompany him; and the two set out for Alexandria. From Alexandria the road of the emissary and the interpreter was for Wills Creek, which they reached November 14. Near at hand, on the Maryland shore, was the cabin of Gist. When George delivered the letter which asked Gist to accompany the Major, the frontiersman consented. While Gist made ready, George hired four men as "servitors." One of these, an Indian trader Barnaby Currin, was to prove himself capable of bearing some of the responsibility of the wilderness. Of the others, John MacQuire also had traded with the Indians, and Henry Steward had some knowledge of the frontier. When the party set out on November 15 it consisted of seven men with their horses and baggage. Everything had been included that Washington had thought necessary—even an "Indian dress" for the Major.

Washington was to find Gist capable of handling both compass and canoe, a man altogether conscientious in the performance of duty. More than any other man, Gist was to be George's teacher in the art of dealing with the uncertain savages. George scarcely could have had a better instructor: he had now to demonstrate how apt a pupil he would be.

The opening days of George's apprenticeship as a frontiersman were novel and interesting enough, but not exacting. He and the others climbed upward, descended to the narrow valleys, mounted again to the tops of the passes, and crossed the stony streams. The journey was as rapid as the difficult country permitted. Northward the men moved through the mountains and, as they advanced, encountered their first snow. George and his companions crossed the Youghiogheny November 19. On the twenty-second the Englishmen reached the Monongahela at the mouth of Turtle Creek, close to Frazier's settlement.

The trader had much news to relate. Friendly natives recently had visited him and had left wampum and a message for the Governor of Virginia to the effect that three nations of French Indians had taken up the hatchet against the English. Frazier passed the wampum to George along with the warning. Another item of information was that French troops had been advancing towards the Ohio from Lake Erie when mounted messengers had arrived with news that the "General" of the French, Pierre Paul, Sieur de Marin, had died. After that, the greater part of the French had been withdrawn northward to winter quarters. In this intelligence, the good and the bad were mingled. George knew that Dinwiddie and the royal government depended, in large measure, on friendly Indians of the Six Nations for the defence of the Virginia frontier. As for the French withdrawal, it might have large meaning for the future and might give England an advantage.

On November 23 George reached the strategic objective of the rival English and French, the wind-swept, uninhabited point of land where the Allegheny received the waters of the powerful Monongahela. There, or nearby, Governor Dinwiddie planned to erect the fort that was to keep the French from the Ohio and the Monongahela. George studied the ground carefully in order to ascertain, if he could, how the nearer stretches of the rivers could be commanded by English guns. He reached conclusions which he jotted down in notes for the rough journal he was keeping. Later he elaborated his views to this effect: "The land in the forks . . . I think extremely well situated for a fort, as it has the absolute command of both rivers. The land at the point is twenty or twenty-five feet above the common surface of the water; and a considerable bottom of flat, well-timbered land all around it, very convenient for building."

About the time George finished the examination of this site, Currin and Steward arrived with the canoe and the baggage. They unloaded safely on the farther side of the Allegheny and then ferried over the other members of the party. Camp was made on the shore. The night was uneventful but it opened an interesting and eventful day. Nearby lived the Indian Chief Shingiss, a Delaware whom it seemed wise to invite to the council George had been instructed to hold with the powerful Indian, Half King, at Logstown. Policy and politeness dictated a personal call on Shingiss and on a lesser Chief, Lowmolach. Shingiss and Lowmolach both were, when acquainted with George's purpose, entirely agreeable: They would go at once with the white men to Logstown.

On the first march George ever had made with Indians, between sunset and dusk they came to a rich bottom where were the huts and the long house known as Logstown, scene of Indian conferences and the home of Half King. This was the beginning of the serious part of the mission. Now, under his instructions, George was to find Half King and the other Sachems and ask them to supply guards for the journey to the French post. George's call on Shingiss had been of small importance compared with this visit. To deal with Half King, the most influential leader of the district, George needed an interpreter, because Gist had never learned the Indian tongues of that region. What Gist lacked, the well-known trader John Davison possessed, and attended by this experienced master of the Indian speech, George sought the Indian.

Half King was away at his cabin on Little Beaver Creek, but George learned that Monakatoocha, a Chief second only to Half King, was in the village and went to call ceremoniously on him. Through Davison, he explained that he was a messenger to the French commander and was directed by the Governor of Virginia so to inform the Sachems. Then, George presented the Chief a string of wampum and a twist of tobacco. This done, he asked Monakatoocha to send for Half King. When the Chief promised to

MAP / 2

THE FORKS OF THE OHIO, 1754–1759

FORKS OF THE OHIO
1754-1759

Lake Ontario

Fort Niagara
La Belle Famille
Little Niagara

SENECA

Lake Erie

Chautauqua Lake

Conewango Creek

Presque Isle

Le Boeuf

French Creek

Allegheny River

DELAWARES

Venango
Fort Machault

West Branch

DELAWARES

SHAWNEE

Kuskuski

Murthering Town

Connoquenessing Creek

Beaver Creek

Sawcunk

Kittanning

Penn Creek

River
Fort Augusta

Penn Creek
Massacre

Ohio River

Logstown

Allegheny River

Kiskiminetas River

Little Juniata

Juniata

River

MOUNTAINS

Susquehanna

Braddock's Defeat

Fort Duquesne (Fort Pitt)

Turtle Cr.

Loyalhanna Creek

Conemaugh River

Raystown Branch

Carlisle

Harris Ferry

Catfish Camp
(Washington)

Monongahela River

FORBES

Loyal Hannon
(Ligonier)

ROAD

Aughwick
Fort Shirley

Shippensburg

York

Redstone Old Fort
Fort Burd

Gist's

CHESTNUT RIDGE

LAUREL RIDGE

ALLEGHENY

WILLS MOUNTAIN

Fort
Littleton

TUSSEY MOUNTAIN

SIDELING MOUNTAIN

Fort Loudon

Fort Necessity

GREAT MEADOWS

Fort Cumberland

BRADDOCK'S ROAD

Wills Creek

Raystown
(Bedford)

SOUTH MOUNTAIN

Oldtown
(Cresaps)

Potomac River

Potomac River

Winchester

Baltimore

MILES
10 5 0   25   50

Drawn under the supervision of ALFRED P. JAMES

dispatch a runner the next morning, George thanked him and invited him and the other great men of the tribe to visit the English tent. It was a satisfactory though not a brilliant interview.

The next day, November 25, was one of sensation. Into the town came a small group of French deserters. George talked at length with them and with the man who had them in charge, a British fur trader named Brown. The French deserters said that they were part of a force of a hundred who had been sent up the Mississippi to meet at Logstown a similar detachment from the garrisons on the south side of Lake Erie. All this seemed to confirm what had been suspected at Williamsburg. George doubtless guessed that the French had intended to advance to the forks and build a fort there. Eagerly, therefore, he continued his first examination of deserters, a distasteful but indispensable military duty.

Word came at 3 P.M. that Half King had arrived from Little Beaver Creek. Etiquette required that the English visitor should make the first call. George accordingly went over to the Sachem's cabin and met Half King. This cherished friend of the English was an intelligent man, vain, brave, as candid as an Indian ever was, and possessed of an unusual knowledge of white men and their methods of fighting. When his passion was stirred, Half King would assert that the reason he hated the French was that they had killed, boiled and eaten his father. More immediately he had a bitter grudge because of treatment he recently had received at the hands of the Sieur de Marin.

George found Half King more than willing to talk—anxious to give all the information he could and to set forth his grievances with the full fury of outraged pride. All routes were quickly described. The better of them was impassable because of the swamps made by the overflow of streams. It would be necessary to proceed via Venango. Five or six good days' journeys would be required. This explained, Half King launched into an account of his visit to the French fort. He had been received by de Marin with much sternness and had been asked very brusquely what he wanted. Half King had prepared in advance a speech for the occasion, and as he told George of the episode he insisted on repeating the substance of what he had announced to the French commandant.

If Half King told the truth about his speech, it was a bold call on the French to leave the watershed of the Ohio. The Indian manifestly thought it a good speech, and he went on to tell George that he had followed it by returning to the French commander a string of wampum, symbolic of one the French had given the Indians when they had made a previous, amicable visit. Then the Chief gamely and with burning eyes repeated the defiant reply of de Marin, a reply deliberately phrased to humiliate the Redman. With few preliminaries, the Frenchman had demanded: "Where is my wampum that you took away, with the marks of towns in it? This wampum I do not know which you have discharged me off the land with. But you need not put yourself to the trouble of speaking, for I will not hear you."

This had infuriated Half King; but, as repeated by him, it must have confused and alarmed and, at the same time, pleased George. George had new evidence of the French determination to occupy the Ohio, though he could afford to be happy that de Marin had outraged Half King's pride. Half King explained what he had seen of French defences in the country between Logstown and Lake Erie. There were two forts, said the Chief. One was on the lake; the other was fifteen miles inland on French Creek and near a small body of water. A wide wagon road connected the two places. The forts were alike, though the one on Lake Erie was the larger. At length Half King left the tent with the understanding that he would assemble his great men to hear Washington's request for an escort.

Next morning George greeted the assembled leaders and, with Davison as interpreter, undertook to explain his mission. What Washington asked in the way of an escort might involve Half King's followers in a quarrel with French Indians or with the French themselves at a time when the English allies of the friendly tribes were far off. This danger probably had been increased by the clash between Half King and de Marin. If the Indians furnished a large escort and went boldly northward, they might be marching straight into a wintry war.

Half King was altogether for compliance with the Englishmen's request. He was determined, in fact, to go back to the French fort and repeat to the new commandant what he had told de Marin. He urged the other Sachems to approve doing this, and after some discussion, they apparently acquiesced.

Half King's promise had been that the guard would be ready to start on November 29, but early that morning he and Monakatoocha came to George's tent with a plea for one more day. November 30 brought evidence that the friendly Chief might not always be able to control the other Sachems; four men only appeared with equipment for the trail. Half King explained that after he had visited Washington the previous evening he and the other Sachems had held a council at the Long House. Their conclusion had been against sending any large escort because, if they did so, the French might become suspicious and might treat them rudely. It would be better to send only the three "great men" with a single hunter. The young emissary might have been tempted to ask the Indians why they expected any other than a rude reception if they were, in effect, to notify the French of a rupture of friendly relations, but debate would delay a departure for which he had been waiting with far more impatience than he had shown. Off he went with his companions and his Indian friends on the trail.

Gist led the party toward the junction of French Creek and the Allegheny River. December 4 brought George to Venango. He knew the village was in French hands, but his heart must have beat faster when he saw the fleur-de-lis flying over the trading post from which Frazier had been driven.

George, with van Braam and Gist, went to the building. At the entrance the trio were met by three French officers whose leader introduced himself as Capt. Philippe Thomas Joincare. Politely, he invited the visitors to enter. Captain Joincare was the son of a Seneca squaw by a French officer, and he had been so reared that he could deal equally well with his mother's and with his father's people. From the time of his father's death in 1740, Joincare had been the man to whom the French Indians of the region had looked for guidance. He operated the trading post and the portage at Niagara and made large profits from both. In the service of France, along with his rank as Captain, he had the title of Chief Interpreter for the Six Nations. Having accompanied Céloron on the expedition of 1749, he knew the Ohio country and the characteristics of the savages who dwelt on its upper watershed. He was one of the ablest and most resourceful of the French spokesmen in Canada.

The reception these men gave Washington was flawless. In answer to Washington's inquiry concerning the French commander, to whom a communication was to be delivered, Joincare replied that he himself was in charge on the Ohio, but that there was a general officer at Fort Le Boeuf, close to Lake Erie. Joincare's advice was that George carry his letter thither. Meantime, would Monsieur Washington and the other gentlemen sup with him and his comrades that evening? George was not pleased at having to go forty or fifty miles farther up the creek but he accepted the invitation to eat with the distinguished Captain. Washington left the Indians behind deliberately. Joincare set out for his guests the best he had and offered and drank wine in abundance. Most politely he promised a French escort for the messenger on the ride to Fort Le Boeuf. As he and the others talked to George, who kept sober and listened intently, their tongues and their Gallic pride were loosed. They had perceived that a contest for the Ohio was brewing. It was their design to take possession of the river, they said, and, by God, they would prevent the settlement of English on it or any of its tributaries.

Rain reasserted its power on December 5. The Indians had by that time become engaged in council with their allies the Delawares, who lived in and near Venango. Before long Joincare heard that a council had been held and that Half King was in it. He ordered one of his men to go to the natives' camp and invite the Chiefs to visit him forthwith. When they arrived, Joincare did not display a touch of the biting sternness that de Marin had exhibited towards Half King. He acted as if these Indians were the closest of allies and the warmest of friends. How could they be so near, he inquired, and not come to see him? He made them a few presents and plied them with brandy until the savages were too drunk to realize what they were doing. Not a word could Half King say of the warning he had sworn he would give the French to leave the land. When George in disgust went back through the rain to his tent, he realized what previously he perhaps had sensed dimly—that he was engaged in a diplomatic battle with the French for the support of the Indians. He had come to deliver a message; he found himself called upon, with Gist's understanding aid, to save an alliance.

This challenging turn of events was even plainer the next day. Early in the morning Half King was at the entrance to George's tent, completely sober, probably ashamed of himself, and once again entirely resolute. It was his purpose to make his speech to the commander of the French and repeat his order that they quit the Indians' country. Earnestly the Chief urged that they delay their departure long enough for him to serve this notice on Joincare.

George's observation the previous day made him anxious not to expose the Chief again to the Captain's wiles and wine. Besides, the mission must be completed as soon as possible. George tried to persuade Half King to withhold his warning until they reached Fort Le Boeuf. Half King would not yield: Joincare, he said, was to light a council fire at Venango; that was to be the place where all business of this sort was transacted; Joincare had sole management of Indian affairs. George unwillingly consented: There was no escape. He had to remain, listen, and take whatever risks might develop from Half King's defiance of the French. He did not misjudge his orator. The council assembled about ten o'clock, but the preliminaries must have been interminable. Finally Half King began his speech. It was in substance the one he had delivered to the Sieur de Marin, but it produced no such effect on Joincare as it had on the French commander at the fort. When Half King reached his climax and returned the speech belt, Joincare refused to accept it. Displaying no anger, he insisted that the belt should be presented at Le Boeuf.

It had been a disquieting day of a sort George had not been called on to endure previously. The next, December 7, scarcely gave promise of being any better. Commissary La Force came to the Englishmen's quarters with three soldiers and reported himself ready to escort Monsieur Washington to the fort. George and his white companions were prepared to start but the Indians were not there. Washington, in desperation, sent Gist to bring them to the trail. It was nearly eleven o'clock when the guide came back. He had the three Chiefs and the young hunter with him, but prevailing upon them to forego the allurements of Venango had taxed his powers of persuasion.

After sunset on December 11, the end of the fourth day on the trail, the party reached the point on the creek opposite Fort Le Boeuf, and George sent van Braam across to notify the commandant of his arrival. Several French officers came over in a canoe and invited the emissaries to the fort. Major Washington was agreeable, and soon was received, as Gist put it, "with a great deal of complaisance." Nothing official was undertaken that evening.

As early as he thought polite the next morning George presented himself, with Gist and van Braam, at Headquarters. The second in command received him and ushered him into the presence of the senior officer of the post, the Sieur Legardeur de St. Pierre de Repentigny, Knight of St. Louis. He had been sent to the post after the death of de Marin and had been there only a week when the English mission arrived. Through van Braam, Washington begged leave to show his passport and commission and then tendered the letter from Governor Dinwiddie. St. Pierre declined to receive it at that time. Would Monsieur Washington retain the papers until the arrival from the next fort of Monsieur Repentigny, who had been sent for and was expected shortly?

The delay gave George time to examine the fort casually. He found it a stout frontier structure of four houses built as corner bastions with the space between them stockaded. Before he was able to study the armament, he was informed that the officer from Presque Isle had arrived. George again went to Headquarters, and after an introduction to Captain Repentigny, delivered the papers. St. Pierre took them and went into another room so that the Captain, without distraction, could turn the documents into French. When the translation of this was approved, Washington asked for an early answer; the commandant said he would call a council to consider the question. George retired to await a decision and, meantime, to get such information as he could of the fort and the minor matters covered by his instructions.

Had the young Virginian undertaken that night to analyze the information he and his men had acquired at Fort Le Boeuf, he would have found two items important. First, there did not appear to be the least doubt in the mind of the commandant that the French had a valid title to the Ohio and could hold that river and its tributaries. Second, the intruders were preparing to extend their occupation the next spring. On this point, George's companions reported along the creek at Fort Le Boeuf fifty birch canoes and 170 of pine. Many others were being blocked out. These preparations convinced Washington that the French were making ready on a large scale for an early descent on the Ohio. Virginia must act quickly and in strength. Not one day must be lost in getting to Williamsburg the news of what the French were undertaking.

Equally apparent was the French aim to detach the Indians from their British alliance. The tactics employed to entice Half King at Venango were being repeated at Le Boeuf. The Chief was as anxious as ever to return the treaty belt, but, he said, the commandant would not give him an audience. St. Pierre was seeking to delay the Indians in the hope that George would leave without them. If that happened, the French knew precisely how to wean the natives from the English and win them with rum, presents and promises.

Perhaps it was a game in which all the odds were against George, but it was not a contest the young man would forfeit. His aim must be to procure an early answer, depart with the Indians and, after that, get to Williamsburg as soon as possible. In this spirit he flatly declined St. Pierre's next proposal—that Washington proceed to Quebec and present to the Governor of Canada the communication from His Excellency of Virginia. His orders were to deliver the letter to the commander on the frontier the French had occupied. He had no authority to go farther or to place the paper in the hands of anyone else. From this stand he did not permit himself to be shaken. George would do his utmost to spur Half King to press for the council St. Pierre was trying to avoid. Immediately after Half King made his speech and returned the treaty belt, young Washington intended to start down the creek.

Washington got the horses off without difficulty, and then he urged Half King again to seek an interview with the commandant. Half King got St. Pierre to receive him late on December 14, but this was done privately and with only one or two other officers—virtual defeat in itself, because the Chief had wished the return of the treaty belt to be formal and public. St. Pierre had not been willing to accept it, even though de Marin previously had demanded it. St. Pierre had protested that he had great friendship for the Indians over whom Half King held sway. The French wished to trade with the tribes, the commandant had assured him, and, as proof of this, would send goods immediately to Logstown.

That evening George received the formal written answer to Governor Dinwiddie's letter. Along with the paper was assurance that two canoes would be at Washington's disposal the next morning. St. Pierre was as good as his word. Early on December 15, there was much activity on the part of the French in seeing that the emissary be made comfortable for his voyage down the creek, but at the same time every blandishment was offered the Indians to keep them from leaving with the Englishmen. In this critical affair, on which the continued support of the Six Nations might depend, the young Virginian instinctively relied on moral force. He went to Half King and, with all the strength of argument at his command, tried to prevail on the Chief to depart with him. For the first time in George's dealings with Half King, the Indian palpably evaded: The commandant, he said, would not let him go until the next day. George walked forthwith to St. Pierre and squarely faced the old soldier: Would the commandant complete his business with Half King and permit the natives to leave? Ill treatment was being accorded an emissary, because to delay the Indians was to hamper his own departure.

The Indians were waiting because the French had promised they would receive the next morning a present of guns and the supplies they most loved. For the sake of a few rifles, the savages were delaying a return journey on which English control of the Ohio might depend. George quickly made up his mind that he also would remain. Then, if the French redeemed their promise, the savages would get the presents and still go with the Virginians; if the French delayed the gifts, then George could accuse them before the Indians of breaking promises.

The next morning St. Pierre and his lieutenants saw that Washington had the advantage. Without further chicanery the presents were given the Sachems with appropriate ceremony and fine words. Then the French played their last card: Liquor was offered the Redmen. George knew that if the savages took any of it, they soon would get drunk and neither would nor could attempt that day the difficult work of steering their canoe down the creek; so, once again, George appealed to the Indians. The party must start, and at once! Half King and this three companions looked at the jugs, and then, to Washington's immense relief, they went about the final preparations for departure. Soon both canoes were ready. George gave the word. They were off, all hands. George had won.

George and his party reached Venango December 22. He made ready to start for Logstown the next day and sent for Half King in order to learn whether the Indians were going overland with the Englishmen or intended to continue by water. Half King explained that he would use the canoe for the rest of the journey. George no longer had to depend on Half King and could not wait indefinitely at Venango to protect the Chief against the cunning of Joincare, but he took pains to warn the Indians against Joincare. Half King was reassuring in answer: Washington need not be concerned; the Chief knew the French too well to be deceived by them. He had not yet satisfied himself concerning George's abilities but he had a measure of affection for the tall Major and a certain belief in the future of the young white emissary. Half King already had given him an Indian name, Caunotaucarius, Towntaker. What this new brother of the Six Nations needed, the tribes would endeavor to supply.

George thanked the Chief and bade him farewell. The next day the white men set out from Venango for Murthering Town. Five miles only were covered before early twilight and the weariness of the animals forced Washington to call a halt. By the morning of December 26, three of the men were so badly frost-bitten that they could do nothing. George stood inflexibly to his resolution to get the answer of the French to Williamsburg without the loss of a day that could be saved. He proposed to Gist that they strike out on foot. The veteran frontiersman did all he could to dissuade the Virginian, but the Major was insistent. Although the two men followed the easiest trail that led towards Murthering Town, the pace was exhausting, the cold, in George's own words, "scarcely supportable," and the small streams so tightly frozen that it was difficult to get even drinking water. The guide was correct: this was not the life for a gentleman. At Murthering Town they found among the natives one who spoke English and professed to know Gist. It seemed good fortune that this fellow had been encountered, because George now was determined to leave the trail and make for the nearest crossing of the Allegheny. The Indian might be able to show them the shortest route. On inquiry, he said he could, and would do so gladly.

With this guide Washington and Gist set out. As the Indian carried George's pack easily, in addition to his own rifle, they made good speed for eight or ten miles. Then the Major had to admit that his feet were getting very sore and that he was weary. It would be well, he said, if they camped. On this, the Indian offered to carry George's gun as well as his pack, but George did not wish to part with his rifle or to give the strange Indian two. Refusal displeased the savage. He became churlish and insisted that the party press on because, he said, there were Ottawas in the woods. If the white men stopped and went to sleep, these Indians would attack and scalp them.

Gist had become suspicious by this time and had noticed that the man was proceeding too far to the northeast to reach the nearest crossing of the Allegheny. George had not received either a glance or a whisper from Gist to show that the frontiersman distrusted the Indian, but he himself was growing dubious. Soon, in the belief that the Indian was leading them astray, Washington told him that when they reached the next water, they would stop. If the native guide made any reply over his shoulder, George did not remember it afterward. He noticed only the back of the savage, less than fifteen paces ahead, and the wideness of a meadow spotted here and there with trees. The three had gone a little way into this meadow when George saw the Indian wheel, lift his rifle and fire straight at them.

"Are you shot?" George cried to Gist.

"No," answered Gist, who had not seen the Indian fire.

As they looked, the man ran ahead a little way, got behind a big oak and started to reload his rifle. Almost instantly the two white men were upon him. Gist would have killed him without a word, but Washington restrained his companion. Silently and alertly, then, with the Indian in front of them, the travelers went on downgrade to a little run. There George called a halt and directed the savage to make a fire, while George either stood by the guns or saw that Gist was within instant reach of the weapons.

Presently Gist whispered: "As you will not have him killed, we must get him away and then we must travel all night."

George agreed. Gist went about arranging things as if they were to camp there, and at length turned to the Indian. "I suppose," said he, "you were lost and fired your gun."

The bewildered savage answered only that he knew the way to his cabin and that it was nearby.

"Well," Gist answered indulgently, "do you go home, and as we are much tired, we will follow your track in the morning; and here is a cake of bread for you, and you must give us meat in the morning."

The native had thought he was going to be killed, and when he saw that he had a chance to get away alive, he was happy to depart without word, loot or scalps. Gist followed him some distance and listened to be sure the Indian continued to put many yards between him and the campfire. Not long after nine o'clock, Gist came back and told George they must move to another site. Weary as Washington was, he picked up his pack and tramped about a mile. Then Gist stopped again and lighted a fire so they could see to set their compass. This done, they fixed their course and started for the Allegheny. Although George had thought early in the day that he could not go any farther, new strength came with danger. In the knowledge that his trail could be followed rapidly in the snow, he was able to travel all night and all the next day.

On the twenty-ninth the two reached the shore of the Allegheny about two miles from Shannopin's Town. One glance at the stream was enough to dishearten: Instead of the solid sheet across which he had expected to walk, George saw only about fifty yards of ice adjoining each of the banks. In midstream was angry, open water, down which broken ice was driving. A raft offered the only means of traversing that turbulent and forbidding stream, a raft that had to be built of standing timber, for felling which the pack included only one hatchet! An all-day job the two men had, but just after sundown the raft was complete. George and Gist shoved it to open water and got the rough platform into the stream. Before they could push halfway across they were in an ice jam that threatened to overwhelm the raft. It flashed over George, on the downstream side, that he might be able to stop the raft and let the ice run past. Quickly and with all his strength, he pushed his pole downward in about ten feet of water. Then he swung to it. On the instant, the force of the current threw the raft against the pole with so much violence that the top of the pole was dashed forward —with George hanging to it. He fell into the water and might have lost his life had not one of his long arms reached a log of the raft. He gripped it, pulled himself up, and, in freezing garments gave such help as he could to Gist in handling the raft. It was to no purpose. The two men could not push to either shore. At last, finding a little island in the river, they left the raft and got on the bit of ground. George was sheeted in ice; Gist had his fingers frost-bitten. The island was of all resting-places the bleakest and the coldest; but the two men were still alive and had their packs, their guns, their hatchet . . . and the dispatch to Dinwiddie.

Daylight brought an entrancing sight: from the shore of the little island to the bank, the river was frozen over stoutly enough to bear the weight of men with packs. George and Gist crossed without any trouble and, after a tramp of ten miles, entered the hospitable door of Frazier's trading post.

The remaining days of the mission were tedious but not dangerous. At Gist's new settlement, which he reached January 2, 1754, Washington bought a horse and saddle, so that Frazier's might be sent back to him. Then George started for Wills Creek. It was speed, speed, speed to arouse Virginia for the prompt occupation of the country the French were preparing to seize. George was at Belvoir on January 11, but he did not feel he could linger when he had news for the Governor. He hurried to Williamsburg and, on January 16, 1754, placed the letter from St. Pierre in the hand of the official who anxiously had been awaiting his return.

The firm but noncommital answer and George's description of conditions on the frontier so impressed Dinwiddie that he asked Washington to write a report that could be laid before Council the next day. This required George to throw together hastily the entries he had made almost daily in his journal. The product was a narrative of seven thousand words, loosely constructed and in some passages obscure; but it had interest and it contained much information at once accurate and apropos.

When George moved about Williamsburg he found himself and his mission the objects of much curiosity. He was applauded by the friends of the Governor and accused secretly by the enemies of His Honor and by rival speculators of magnifying the danger in order to get help for the Ohio Company. Washington's immediate desire was to know what would be done to anticipate the advance of the French to the Ohio. Dinwiddie believed that success hung on speed. Unless the English hastened their march, the French would get to the Ohio first and would so strongly secure themselves that the might of England would be taxed to drive them away. As surely as with Washington on the way home, it was speed, all speed. Soon after George's return, the Governor changed the date for the meeting of the prorogued Assembly from April 18 to February 14.

In advance of the session of the lawmakers, Dinwiddie felt he should provide an adequate guard for the protection of the men whom he already had dispatched to build a fort at the junction of the Monongahela and the Allegheny. Accordingly, on January 21, five days after his return, Major Washington, as Adjutant of the Northern Neck District, was authorized to enlist one hundred of the militia of Augusta and Frederick Counties; the Indian trader, Capt. William Trent, was directed to raise a like force among men of his own calling, whose property and livelihood were most threatened. The quota did not seem high. Of the three hundred English traders who went out yearly into the Indian country, a third should be expected to volunteer. By the time these two hundred men had reached the Ohio, four hundred to be requested of the General Assembly could be enlisted. If other Colonies then would send contingents, these combined forces, "with the conjunction of our friendly Indians," Dinwiddie explained, "I hope will make a good impression on the Ohio and be able to defeat the designs of the French."

George examined the instructions given him. He found that fifty of his men were to be supplied from the militia of Frederick by Lord Fairfax, County Lieutenant. James Patton, County Lieutenant of Augusta, was to furnish a similar number. By February 20 these two detachments were to be in Alexandria, where George was to train and discipline them. Many of the militiamen were expected to volunteer for service; but if volunteers did not suffice, the required total was to be reached through a draft by lot.

To speed the muster, George procured the Governor's permission to send Jacob van Braam to assist the County Lieutenant of Augusta. George hurried to Frederick to act with Fairfax. He quickly uncovered that the militia, as the Governor phrased it, were in "very bad order." George waited impatiently but helplessly until about February 11 and then, disillusioned, started back to Williamsburg with a letter in which Fairfax confessed that the draft was a failure. Like reports came from Augusta, though it had suffered during the previous summer from an Indian raid.

About the time George brought to Williamsburg the news from Frederick, the General Assembly met. On the opening day Dinwiddie delivered a message in which he summarized Major Washington's report of the mission to Fort Le Boeuf. His Honor gave warning that 1500 French, with their Indian allies, were preparing to advance early in the spring, rendezvous at Logstown, and "build many more fortresses" on the Ohio. With a fervent description of the horrors of a frontier war, the Governor called on the Burgesses to vote a "proper supply."

With this information in hand, the Burgesses began to review the Governor's appeal for funds. There was no enthusiasm for an expedition to the Ohio. Some officials insisted that the report was "a fiction and a scheme to promote the interest of a private company"—the Ohio Company, of course. Debate was precipitated; dissent was vigorous. "With great application," Dinwiddie subsequently reported, "many arguments and everything I possibly could suggest, the [Burgesses] at last voted £10,000 for protecting our frontiers."

As soon as the £10,000 had been voted, Dinwiddie undertook to raise six companies of fifty men each and to dispatch these new soldiers to the contested river. To command the volunteers, officers had now to be commissioned by the Governor—a fact that immensely interested George; if new military service was to be offered and new honors won, Washington must have a share in them! Ambitious as George had become, he told himself in all candor that he did not have the age or the experience to justify him in aspiring immediately to the general command of the expedition to the Ohio; but he believed that if he could get a commission as Lieutenant Colonel under a qualified senior, he would not fail.

George went about the task of recruiting for the new force. His headquarters were in Alexandria, where he had close relations with John

Carlyle. That gentleman, on January 26, had been appointed Commissary of Supply for the expedition to the Ohio. George had a good opinion of Carlyle and, after experience with him, concluded that the Commissary was altogether capable and most painstaking. At the time there was nothing in Carlyle's record to indicate that he was a man too ready to accept promise as performance.

There was no enthusiasm for enlisting. After approximately a week of hard persuasion, George enlisted about twenty-five individuals, most of whom he described as "loose, idle persons," devoid of shoes and almost every garment. Haplessly, there were no uniforms and no credit for buying any. A few recruits who were enlisted elsewhere drifted into Alexandria, but the upbuilding of the force to the stipulated strength of three hundred was slow, dangerously slow in the light of news that came from Trent on the Ohio. Trent repeated in a letter to Washington what friendly Indians had told him of great threats made by the French and urged that Washington hasten to him.

Dinwiddie, sifting all he knew, soon chose Joshua Fry as the man best qualified to command the expedition. Fry, a former professor of mathematics at William and Mary, an engineer and cartographer who had gone in 1745 to the new County of Albemarle in the Piedmont, had done no fighting but he knew men, won their respect easily, and displayed always a justice and serenity of spirit in dealing with them. George Muse was named Captain and soon was promoted Major. Of the appointment of a third officer, Capt. Adam Stephen, George probably heard also. The other commissions, as he ascertained gradually, went in most instances to ambitious young men who wished to learn something of the frontier.

Of his place in the organization, George had received some assurance before he knew who were and were not to be his companions-in-arms. By March 20 a messenger brought him a letter of instructions from the Governor and a note in which Richard Corbin said briefly: "I enclose your commission. God prosper you with it." The commission was at the rank of Lieutenant Colonel, the second in command of the expedition. Dinwiddie expressed surprise that the French were expected to move so early in the season to the Ohio. This, said he, "makes it necessary for you to march what soldiers you have immediately to the Ohio, and escort some wagons, with the necessary provisions." Colonel Fry was to follow with the other troops as soon as possible. There was an opportunity! The Lieutenant Colonel was to command the vanguard on an advance to the river and meet whatever adventure awaited the Virginians there.

The speed of preparation increased at Alexandria. As George tried to make soldiers of his homeless and destitute volunteers, Carlyle sought to procure supplies and equipment. George decided to start with supplies sufficient only for the march to Winchester and get additional wagons and provisions there for the long journey to the Ohio. When his troops at Alexandria increased to 120, he organized them into two companies, one temporarily under van Braam and the other under Peter Hog, who had the Governor's commission as Captain. With these two officers, five subalterns, two sergeants and six corporals, all probably inexperienced, George continued to give his men such drill and inculcate such discipline as they would take; but they still were raw recruits when, at the beginning of April their Lieutenant Colonel issued marching orders. On the morning of April 2 George led his little column out of Alexandria and westward in the direction of the "Blew Mountains." This was the first time he ever had commanded troops on the road. A long and a strange road it was to prove, the road of a career he coveted but had not planned.

When Washington reached Winchester he found there the company raised in that area by Captain Stephen. He looked next for the transportation to carry to Wills Creek and on to the Ohio the supplies his men and horses must have if the expedition was to succeed. Virtually nothing had been done to assemble the needed vehicles. Dinwiddie had called Carlyle's attention to the impressment law and had said that it must be invoked if wagons could not be hired at reasonable rates, but no official in Frederick had acted. Forty wagons George impressed, fifty, sixty—and received at his camp not one in seven of them. He waited for the arrival of others that had been requisitioned, and when they did not arrive, he impressed still more. When a week of fruitless impressment and argument had passed, George felt he no longer could wait, because all indications had been that the French would start early for the Ohio. About April 18, Washington and 159 men started westward across the mountain.

Towards western country George rode over North Mountain and then northward down the right bank of the Cacapon. He had crossed this river when he met a man who rode rapidly towards him with an express. This horseman brought from Trent a number of letters that Washington read eagerly. They were an appeal for reenforcement at the forks of the Ohio with all possible speed: Eight hundred French troops were approaching, Trent wrote; he was expecting attack at any hour.

More trouble awaited George at Wills Creek. When he inquired for the pack animals to be used for a swift, light march westward, he found that Trent had failed to redeem the promise to collect the horses. Not one was there. Lack of transport might doom the expedition. Amid George's first grim reflections on this paralysis came the blackest news of all: Ensign Edward Ward who had been in immediate command at the mouth of the Monongahela rode up to Wills Creek on the twenty-second and reported that the fort had been captured. The French had won control of the forks of the Ohio. George had lost the race almost before it had begun.

Ensign Ward had a humiliating story to tell—the forks of the Ohio lost, a French force estimated at more than one thousand men there to defy the 159 under Washington, the Indians clamoring for reenforcements, of whom only a few weak companies were within marching distance. Short of the defection of the Six Nations and the destruction of the little force at Wills Creek, the situation was about as bad as it could be, but it did not appall the young commander. He felt, instead, what he termed a "glowing zeal." George's mind and military inexperience would not yield to odds or circumstance. The Indians needed help and asked it in a spirit of loyalty that made George doubly anxious to extend it. Besides, to withhold aid would be to lose the savages' support. Even with the insignificant force he had, George felt that he must advance as far as he could and must hold a position from which the column, when reenforced, would proceed to the forks, recover the fort and drive the French away.

When the young Virginian had reached this conclusion, his knowledge of the country shaped his action. The best station at which to hold his detachment until reenforcements arrived in sufficient number to justify an offensive was, he thought, a place he had not visited, the junction of Red Stone Creek with the Monongahela, thirty-seven miles above the forks. From that point it would be possible to send the artillery and the heavy supplies by water to the mouth of the river. In order to reach Red Stone Creek with the heavy guns and the wagons it would be necessary to widen the trail into a road, but this could be done with the men George had.

Progress was hideously slow. Everywhere the trail had to be widened and repaired. Effort availed scarcely at all. Never was the column able to advance more than four miles a day. When conditions were at their worst, night found the wagons no farther than two miles from their starting point. One English trader after another would arrive at camp from the west with his skins and his goods and explain that he was fleeing from the French and tell of the strength of the force that had come down from Lake Erie. Some merely repeated rumor; but one of them, Robert Callender, reached Washington's detachment with information of a nearer potential enemy: At Gist's new settlement, Callender had encountered a party of five French under Commissary La Force. The number was trifling; their proximity was suspicious. Ostensibly, they were searching for deserters; but actually, in Callender's opinion, they were reconnoitring and studying the country.

That news was enough to give a faster beat to any young officer's heart, especially when Callender brought word that Half King was marching with fifty men to join the English detachment. George determined to send out twenty-five men under Captain Stephen on May 11 to reconnoitre and to meet Half King.

There followed a week of discouraging reports, brightened by dispatches from Williamsburg. An express brought letters in which George was informed that Colonel Fry had reached Winchester with more than 100 men and soon would march to join the advanced contingent. Other troops were coming, too. North Carolina was to send 350 men; Maryland was to supply 200; although Pennsylvania would furnish no soldiers, she would contribute £10,000; from New England, Gov. William Shirley was to march 600 troops to harass the French in Canada. George had not yet learned how readily hopes and half-promises might be accepted as assurances and guarantees. He took all the reports at face value and rejoiced, in particular, over the prospect of a demonstration against Canada.

Ensign Ward, whom Washington had sent on to Williamsburg, came back to camp on the seventeenth with a letter from Dinwiddie. The Governor told of the arrival in Virginia of an Independent Company from South Carolina and of the expectation that the two similar companies from New York would reach Virginia waters within about ten days. He wrote that Council approved of George's caution in planning to halt at Red Stone Creek until reenforcements arrived. Somewhat deliberately in this same letter, George and the other Virginia officers were admonished not to let "some punctillios about command" interfere with the expedition.

Ward probably supplemented this with news that a committee controlling pay of the officers and men had limited to £1 6s. the allowance for enlisting each soldier, and Council had not raised the scale of compensation of officers or added to the ration previously allowed, which merely was that of the private soldier. This had been a sore subject with the officers. Now they soon would be serving with Captains, lieutenants and ensigns of Independent Companies who would be receiving higher pay. This prospect combined with hard work, wet weather and poor fare to produce near-mutiny among the Virginia officers. Under the chairmanship of Stephen, they drafted a formal protest to the Governor, and, reviewing their hardships, concluded with at least a threat of resignation en masse. This document they signed and brought to George for transmission. George felt the sting of poor pay as sharply as they did, but resignation was a different matter. Although he would not fail to stand his ground against discrimination, he wished to do this in a manner that would not jeopardize his continuance as Lieutenant Colonel.

Reflection suggested a means of achieving both ends. On May 18 George wrote the Governor a letter that was at once boyish, wrathful and shrewd. He confessed his sympathy with the protest and went on to explain that the officers would have resigned their commissions had they not felt themselves obligated by the nearness of danger to remain on duty. Then he deliberately began a new paragraph to distinguish their intentions from his own: "Giving up my commission is quite contrary to my intention. Nay, I ask it as a greater favor, than any amongst the many I have received from your Honor, to confirm it to me. But let me serve voluntarily; then I will, with the greatest pleasure in life, devote my services to the expedition without any other reward than the satisfaction of serving my country; but to be slaving dangerously for the shadow of pay, through woods, rocks, mountains—I would rather prefer the great toil of a day laborer, and dig for a maintenance, provided I were reduced to the necessity, than serve upon such ignoble terms. . . . Be the consequence what it will, I am determined not to leave the Regiment, but to be amongst the last men that quit the Ohio, even if I serve as a private volunteer, which I greatly prefer to the establishment we are now upon."

Ward brought, also, a message from Dinwiddie to Half King, whom the Governor was anxious to have with him at the conference soon to be held in Winchester. George did not forward the message itself. He reasoned that Half King and the other Chiefs, possessing full measure of curiosity, would proceed more quickly if informed that a speech from the Governor was at the headquarters of the English. Speed seemed imperative, in spite of high water, because two friendly Indians who came to camp now reported that Frenchmen on reconnaissance had been within six or seven miles of the English. George continued to hope he would be able to bag some French. To do this he would need the assistance of Half King, and he consequently took much pains with the "speech" of invitation to the Chiefs.

On the twenty-third Stephen had a strange report to make. The

Captain and his men had reached the Monongahela not far from Red Stone Creek, and there they had met Indian traders whom the French had permitted to return towards the English settlements. All that these men could tell Stephen was that some French soldiers under a young officer styled Jumonville had been reconnoitring along the Monongahela, but had gone back the previous day to the fort at the forks of the Ohio, Fort DuQuesne as it now was styled.

The next day some small information of a reliable character began to arrive from the country ahead. The Indian previously sent to Half King returned with a companion who had a message from the Sachem. This was a clear warning and a definite encouragement. The French in undetermined number were advancing to fight; Half King was coming to counsel. Later in the day, after the column had reached the Great Meadows between Laurel Hill and Chestnut Ridge, an Indian trader reported that he had seen two Frenchmen the previous day. He was certain that a strong hostile detachment was on the march. This information appealed to George as accurate and as calling for immediate defensive preparation. He sought out favorable ground in the Meadows and at length found two gulleys that were close together and, to his inexperienced eye, adequate as natural trenches. These he promptly manned and then he placed his wagons between them.

The morning of May 27 brought the most explicit information George had received of the movements of the French. Gist rode into camp and described how the previous noon La Force and fifty soldiers had come to his new settlement, which he had left in the charge of two Indians. The French were in hostile mood; Gist hurried off to warn Washington. En route, about five miles from camp, Gist found the tracks of numerous white men whom he took to be those who had been at his place on the twenty-sixth. The canoes of this advance party, Gist had learned, were at Red Stone Creek. If the Frenchmen were far from their landing place, and close to his camp, George thought he had an excellent chance of cutting them off.

Night was bringing the blackest of darkness when, about 9 P.M., an Indian runner subsequently known as Silverheels came to the camp with stirring news from Half King. The Chief sent word that he was about six miles away and that he had seen footprints of two Frenchmen who had crossed the trail. Half King believed these men belonged to the party who had passed Gist's. All of them, the Chief thought, were nearby.

George resolved immediately to join Half King and attack the French. Although he had scarcely more than eighty men, he called up forty of them and, within an hour, started for the bivouac of the friendly natives. Day was breaking when the guide stopped at the crude shelter of Half King. The inevitable council was brief. Half King and the others agreed to make common cause and join the English in attacking the enemy. Quickly the Virginians and the natives went to the spot where the footprints of the Frenchmen had been seen. Then Half King told two of his Indians to follow the trail and ascertain where the French were encamped.

At length the two Indian scouts returned: They had found their quarry! About half a mile from the trail, in a bower well concealed among rocks, was a body of French troops. The situation was ideal. By proceeding carefully, George's men could surround the French and attack on all sides.

Between 7 and 8 A.M. deployment was completed. The Virginians and Indians crept nearer until they were within a little more than a hundred yards of the unsuspecting French. George waited until he was sure everything was in order. Then he stepped forward and gave his command. Almost on the instant his tall figure was under the eyes of Frenchmen. As fast as they could, these soldiers ran back to their bower to get their rifles. A moment later, shots rang out. Men began to fall. George heard the whistle of passing bullets as they cut the air and somehow felt exhilarated. Stephen closed in with his platoon and captured an officer. Some of the French gave ground, made off, and then, at a shout from their commander, came running back with uplifted hands. These men had seen the Indians in their rear and, knowing what their fate would be at the hands of the savages, preferred to surrender to the British. Behind them came half a dozen Indians who fell upon the wounded, brained and scalped them.

By this time firing had ceased. All the twenty-one unwounded French survivors had thrown down their weapons. On the ground were ten dead and one wounded man who had escaped the hatchet of the Indians. One French soldier, Mouceau by name, had been seen to make off. An Englishman was dead. The wounded on Washington's side numbered only two or three. From first shot to last surrender, not quite fifteen minutes had elapsed. The surprise had been complete; George's first skirmish had achieved the ideal of the soldier, the destruction of the adversary as a fighting force. The commander of the French part, Joseph Coulon, Sieur de Jumonville, had been killed by Half King, or at least the Chief so boasted. Jumonville's second in command, Druillon, and two cadets were among the captured; but the most valuable of the prisoners was La Force, whom Washington described as "a bold, enterprising man and a person of great subtlety and cunning."

Washington started the prisoners and his men back to the camp in the Meadows. On the way, the captured French officers began to protest that they had come as an embassy to serve notice on the English to leave the domain of the French King. They insisted they should be treated as attendants of an ambassador, not as prisoners of war, and should be returned with an escort to Fort DuQuesne, precisely as the French had treated Washington the previous winter.

Washington's officers argued, if the French were an embassy, why were they so numerous and why so careful to hide themselves? Why did they not come boldly out and declare their presence and their mission? There was evidence that the French had been two miles closer to the camp than when they were discovered and that they had moved back and had sent off runners to report to Claude Pierre Pécaudy, Sieur de Contrecœur, the strength and position of Washington's party. Behind this reasoning was conviction that the French seizure of the fort at the forks had been an act of war. In the minds of Washington and the other Englishmen, the French already were the enemy. Half King was wholly of this view. The French, he said, never intended to come otherwise than in hostility: if the English were fools enough to let them go, he never would assist in taking another Frenchman.

George announced no decision after this discussion of the twenty-eighth. The next morning the French formally asked him in what manner he regarded them. They were prisoners, said George; they were to march under guard to Winchester, where Dinwiddie was assumed to be. In a letter written later that day George cautioned His Honor against listening to the "smooth stories" of the Frenchmen concerning their alleged embassy. ". . . In strict justice," he said, "they ought to be hanged as spies of the worst sort. . . ."

Not for an instant did Lieutenant Colonel Washington permit the protests of the French prisoners to divert him from two other matters of much concern—his answer to the Governor on the sore question of pay, and his preparations to meet the attack he expected in retaliation for the defeat of Jumonville's party.

The Governor's reply to the protest George had forwarded was a sharp letter written from Winchester May 25 in which Dinwiddie took up the complaints of Captain Stephen and the other officers. Where the Governor thought the complaint justified, he promised such correction as he could make; where he believed the officers wrong, he said so, and reminded them that other applicants for commission "were desirous to serve on those conditions." The Governor gave the commander a verbal spanking, professed his understanding of George's difficulties and assured the young man that merit would not "pass unnoticed." The letter disturbed George. It touched his pride and his pocket, concerning both of which he was sensitive, and it raised, vaguely, the question of his continuance in command. On the day after the fight with Jumonville, he sat down and wrote Dinwiddie an answer that displayed his youth and his ambition. He argued the issues in detail, and not unskillfully, and promised to do what he could "to reconcile matters"; but he could not forbear stating how he figured he was receiving almost ten shillings less per day than an officer of like rank on the regular establishment would receive, to say nothing of the fact that he had no prospect of half-pay on retirement. As he did not consider his circumstances permitted, he would not insist on serving without pay and would continue to accept the *per diem* of 12 s. 6d. Not until he made this completely, indeed tediously, plain, did he even announce to the Governor the victory he had won.

The effect of that success on his state of mind was what might have been expected in the case of an inexperienced but intelligent soldier: It increased his self-confidence and created an unwarranted contempt for the enemy at the same time that it admonished him to prepare against an attack by a force numerically much superior to his own. He began on May 30 to strengthen the ground where he had found the "natural entrenchments" between which he had placed his wagons. The French did not approach, but the fort was not finished in reasonably defensible form until June 3 and then was by no means as strong as its young engineer believed. The English escort brought in, on June 2, eighty or more Indians, but that total included women and children.

Badly as George needed more men, the arrival of the squaws and the children along with the warriors gave new seriousness to a condition that had troubled him for several days: Food had become scarce; flour, in particular, was almost exhausted. Every issue lowered the supply until, on June 6, the sergeant came to the bottom of the last sack.

In the wretched crisis this shortage of food presented him, George had new responsibility placed on his shoulders. Gist, on the very day of the exhaustion of the flour, brought news that Fry was dead. The Colonel had sustained a fall from his horse, several days prior to May 29, and had succumbed on May 31. As a result, George now had the chief command of the expedition, the post to which he had not dared aspire a few months previously.

As if to exemplify his extension of command, George received on June 9 the first reenforcements, aside from Indians, that had joined him after he had left Wills Creek. These were the remaining three companies of the Virginia Regiment under Capts. Robert Stobo and Andrew Lewis and Lieut. George Mercer, who had been advanced slowly by their temporary commander, Maj. George Muse. In the charge of Stobo, Lewis and Mercer were approximately 181 soldiers, few of whom had ever fired a rifle at any other target than game. These men brought scant supplies, but with the convoy there arrived nine small guns and the swivels on which to place them so that they could be fired horizontally in any direction. These were the first swivel guns George had received and they were to be the principal armament of the little stockade.

More interesting than anything else Major Muse brought with him was an emissary and interpreter, Andrew Montour, who spoke good French and English, as well as several Indian tongues. Along with Montour and the English reenforcements, or on their heels, George received three letters from Dinwiddie. In one written after receipt of the news of the death of Fry, the Governor informed George that he was to take Fry's place with the rank of Colonel. Muse was to be Lieutenant Colonel; the senior Captain, Stephen, was to be made Major. The executive went on to say that Col. James Innes, "an old, experienced officer," was expected daily and "is appointed Commander-in-Chief of all the forces, which I am very sensible will be very agreeable to you and the other officers."

Dinwiddie already had written George that the Independent Companies were on their way to the fort, and now renewed his admonition that controversy with the commanders of these troops be shunned. The coming of the Independent Companies most certainly would raise the vexatious issue of rank and command. George was a Virginia Colonel; the officer in charge of the nearest Independent Company was James Mackay, a Captain by royal commission. Was rank so to be disregarded that the Captain would command the Colonel, or—what was more probable—would the Captain be exempt from the orders of a man three grades his senior? George asked himself the question in manifest disturbance of spirit. "Your Honor may depend I shall myself and will endeavor to make all my officers show Captain Mackay all the respect due to his rank and merit; but [I] should have been particularly obliged if your Honor had declared whether he was under my command or independent of it; however, I shall be studious to avoid all disputes that may tend to the public prejudice, but as far as I am able, I will inculcate harmony and unanimity."

Righteous resolution and correspondence alike were interrupted that June 10 by reports of the approach of a party of French. George at once sent out Indian scouts and made ready to receive the enemy, but no French appeared and no fire was opened. The next day, Washington pushed out another detachment to find the foe. Two of these scouts returned on the twelfth with news that they had seen a small number of French in the woods.

On about June 14, Captain Mackay arrived with the Independent Company from South Carolina. George was at a loss how to act or what to do concerning the use of the company, but he was determined to receive Mackay as a gentleman and a comrade. When, therefore, he saw Mackay ride up, he greeted him in friendly manner and gave him no orders. Mackay picked his own campsite; George did not go to the company or inspect it. The first test came when Washington, as commander, sent the Captain the parole and countersign. Mackay replied that he did not think he should receive these from the Colonial Colonel. Mackay insisted that his command was a separate force and maintained that the Governor could not issue a commission that would command him. Another complication arose over the duty the Independent Company was to perform. The Colonials were working on the road to Red Stone. Would Mackay have his troops share in this labor? No—that was to say, not unless Colonel Washington was prepared to allow the men the regular pay of one shilling sterling per day for such special service. George, it will be remembered, was allotted eight pence daily for his own soldiers; he could not give more to those of the Independent Company.

At first, George did not know what to do when he came to this impasse. He wished that Mackay were somewhere else. As the Virginia Colonel could not detach the Independent Company, he concluded that he would himself leave: He would take his own men and their part of the remaining provisions, and would start for Red Stone Creek; Mackay could remain at the Meadows with the Independent Company. George assembled his troops on the morning of June 16 and prepared to start for Red Stone Creek. By persistence and in spite of many obstacles, he reached Gist's new settlement and from that point sent back all except two of his wagons and teams to haul provisions.

The Colonel now had to return to a diplomatic role. George had heard that the Delawares and the Shawnees had taken up the hatchet against the English. Doubtless on the advice of Half King, the commander had sent messengers and wampum to those tribes and had invited them to a council at Gist's. Washington felt better equipped now for negotiations with the savages because he had as his counsellors not only Montour and Half King but also the trader, Indian diplomatist and interpreter, George Croghan.

The Delawares and several Shawnee emissaries came promptly, but before Washington could employ Croghan's arts on these Indians, there arrived from Logstown eight Mingoes who seemed curiously in a hurry. They asked to see Washington without delay and told him they had a commission that required an immediate council. Surprised by this haste, the Colonel brought some of his advisers together and let the Mingoes explain themselves. They went on with so many expostulations in discussing the French that George and his companions became suspicious: These Mingoes might be spies! Because of this possibility, George proceeded to act with appropriate caution and told the Mingoes that he could not receive their speech until Half King could be present. Delaware spokesmen similarly were asked to wait until that friend of the English could sit with the white men.

After Half King reached the camp, the English and about forty Indians opened a council. It lasted three days and, in the slow preparation and translation of long speeches, must have been exceedingly tedious. The substance of the speeches George made the Indians was that he and his men had come to fight by the side of the Six Nations and the Delawares, who were invited to send their women and children to safety in the English settlements. All other Indians of the Ohio were put on notice to choose between French and English and take the consequences.

The council, terminating June 21, was held under the eyes of the eight Mingoes, whose behavior confirmed the suspicion that they were spying on the force and were spreading false information concerning the strength of the French. To verify or disprove the statements of the Mingoes regarding the dispositions of the enemy, Washington sent out friendly natives as counter-spies. "I left off working any further on the road," George explained later, "and told [the Mingoes] that as we intended to continue it through the woods as far as the fort, felling trees, etc., that we were waiting here for the reenforcements which were coming to us. . . . But as soon as they were gone, I set about making out and clearing a road to Red Stone."

In spite of this deception of the enemy and the encouragement of friends, George discovered promptly that the council had been a failure. The Delawares could not be induced to go to the camp in the Meadows with their families. The Shawnees silently vanished. These were not the only disappointments. When the council was over, Half King and all his people started back to camp. As a consequence of this defection, George had to use his own inexperienced men as scouts to prevent surprise by the French.

This failure shook the faith of Washington in Montour and Croghan, who never were able to bring into camp more than thirty Indians, and not more than half of the thirty serviceable. Deeper than this reason for the Indians' reluctance to fight was the meagreness of the presents George could offer. More Indian goods were coming but they had not arrived when most needed. Still another reason why the Indians had begun to hold back was their belief, not openly voiced, as yet, that the forces of the English were inferior to those of the French. The zeal of the Indians was dampened, further, by the shortage of provisions. All the flour and bacon of the advanced party had been consumed by June 23; nothing was left but a few steers, the milch cows and their calves. Until more provisions arrived, the English and their Indian guests would have to subsist on a little parched corn and on unsalted fresh meat.

George did not hesitate in the face of that contingency. He steeled himself to carry through what he had undertaken. He reasoned that the French either would come up the Monongahela and thence up Red Stone Creek or would follow the trail from Fort DuQuesne to Gist's settlement. It appeared that the best attainable result was to be had by dispatching Captain Lewis with a few officers and sixty men to clear a road to the mouth of Red Stone Creek. The remaining troops must stay at Gist's. Mackay and the Independent Company, presumably, still were at Great Meadows.

That night or the next morning, June 28, there arrived a message from Monakatoocha, a most startling message: The Chief had been at Fort DuQuesne two days previously, had witnessed the arrival of reenforcements there, and had heard the French say they were going to march forward and attack the English with eight hundred white troops and four hundred Indians. In Washington's judgment, the fact that this report came from so experienced and trustworthy a man as Monakatoocha gave it credibility. An early attack by a greatly superior force was altogether probable, almost certain. He immediately sought the counsel of the few officers with him. Common judgment was that the scattered parts of the little force, Mackay's Independent Company, Lewis's detachment and Washington's own contingent, should be united as soon as possible at Gist's.

Captain Mackay understood the plight of his Colonial comrade and, as became a good soldier, hurried forward with his troops. Lewis, too, pressed his detachment and, by the forenoon of the twenty-ninth, was at Gist's. In spite of this successful reunion of the scattered forces, the Indian allies became more and more alarmed. Some of them had scouted around Fort DuQuesne; some had heard exaggerated stories of the overwhelming strength of the French. All the natives soon gave warning that they would leave the English unless Colonel Washington returned to the fort in the Great Meadows.

The fort at Great Meadows would be more accessible to supplies. In addition, it should not be difficult there to get an early report of a French advance, whereas, at Gist's, there always was the possibility that the French would slip eastward from Red Stone and lie in wait across the English line of supply. In favor of the strategy that would avoid this possibility there was, finally, the insistence of Indians on a withdrawal. Loss of the Indian scouts might be fatal in that difficult country. These considerations led George and his brother officers to decide unanimously that the column should retreat forthwith to Great Meadows. It was not an easy task. Besides the mountainous character of the country and the badness of the road, George had once more to contend with the lack of transport that had cramped and cursed the expedition from the day it reached Winchester. Only two teams, a few horses and the officers' mounts remained with the troops. These animals and the men themselves were all the resources George had for moving the nine swivels, the ammunition and the baggage. The soldiers must draw the swivels; the ammunition and as many as possible of the other articles must be carried in the wagons and on the pack horses.

The retreat commenced—an ordeal that men endured only because the alternative was death in the woods from the bullet or war hatchet of an Indian. There was nothing to eat except parched corn and lean beef slaughtered, cooked and swallowed in the same hour. Every grade was a despair, every furlong a torture. The worst was the attitude of the men of Mackay's Independent Company. They refused to help in getting the ammunition ready for transportation and, once the march began, would not lend a hand in dragging the swivels or removing obstacles from the road. These, said the regulars, were not the duties of soldiers, and could not be required of them.

It was the first of July when the exhausted men pulled the swivels into their feeble fort in the Great Meadows. The fort must be strengthened so that it would be safe until an enlarged force was able to take the offensive against the French. Tired as were the men, those who had the mettle and the muscle must clear a longer field of fire, fell trees, work on the stockade or dig trenches outside. The position did not now appear to be the "charming field for an encounter" that Washington had thought it when he first had sheltered his wagons behind "natural entrenchments." It was possible, George quickly perceived, to carry his crude trench beyond a small branch, so that his men could be sure of getting water. Moreover, as part of the ground around the fort was so marshy that a direct assault by infantry probably could be made from one direction only, the south, it might be possible, also, to complete the little stockade in the middle of the entrenchments and to secure there the powder and provisions. This was the measure of advantage. For the rest, the fort was in a damp "bottom"; woods came within easy musket range of it; high ground surrounded it. Time did not permit the selection of a stronger, more defensible site. The best had to be made of a weak position. George gave it the name of Fort Necessity. Its effective total of fighting men was 284.

About daybreak on July 3, a single shot rang out. The troops were ordered to get under arms. Sleepy soldiers scarcely had made ready for action when a steady rain began to fall. For five hours, the unsheltered men had rain, rain, rain. In preparation for the enemy's arrival, George could do almost nothing except to urge the men to keep their powder dry. Mud was deep inside the fort; water was rising in the trenches. About eleven o'clock, an alert sentinel caught a glimpse of armed men and sounded a new alarm by firing his musket. It was a challenge the French accepted. George saw them emerge from cover and move forward in three columns. The shout of the white men and the wild yell of the Indians told the garrison to expect the utmost in soldierly skill and the worst in savage cruelty. George met valor with vigor. He moved his troops into the open and formed them to repel a charge. When the French halted and opened fire at approximately six hundred yards, there was no wavering by the English and, fortunately, no loss. George did not let the men return the fire at that distance.

Now the French began to advance as if they intended to press their attack home. At the word of command, the English slipped back immediately into their trenches, which were deeper than ever in water. From the low parapet of these defences, the Virginians and the regulars prepared for a volley that would repulse the onslaught, but the charging soldiers dropped to the ground, scattered and almost disappeared. "They then," wrote Washington, "from every little rising, tree, stump, stone and bush kept up a constant, galling fire upon us. . . ." He saw, too, that it was not directed against his men only. The French deliberately shot every horse, every cow and even the dogs in the camp, until, while the engagement still was young, the English realized they had lost already their transport and their meat.

The Virginians and Carolinians felt sure they killed many a Frenchman and kept the others from pressing closer, but they themselves now were losing steadily and were having more and more difficulty in keeping their weapons and their cartridges dry enough to use. The unequal fight continued into the late afternoon and rose in the fury of fire until the rain filled the trenches, got into the men's cartridge-boxes, wet their firelocks and reached even the powder that had been placed carefully in what was thought to be the driest spot inside the stockade. The fire fell off.

About eight o'clock, there came a cry from the French, *"Voulez-vous parler?"* No. There was a wait and then another shouted question from beyond the trenches: Would the commander send out an officer to receive a proposal, an officer who could speak French? The messenger would be permitted to return unhurt.

Washington, heavy-hearted, but convinced of his duty, called two French-speaking officers, van Braam and William La Peyroney, and sent them out between the lines to ascertain what the French proposed. They soon brought back assurance that the French were willing to permit the English to return to Virginia without becoming prisoners of war. Probably because of the vagueness of these terms, Washington rejected them and instructed his representatives to return for further parley. La Peyroney either had been wounded earlier in the day and collapsed about this time, or else he received a shot that dropped him now. Van Braam was left as the one French-speaking officer to carry on the negotiations. The Dutchman left the entrenchments and returned, after a time, with a folded sheet. On the first page were the badly penned opening paragraphs of a *Capitulation*, in French, accorded by Coulon de Villiers, commanding the troops of His Most Christian Majesty, to the English troops *dans le fort De Necessité*. As best van Braam might, he undertook to translate the difficult handwriting. In the Dutchman's own poor English the document set forth that it never had been the intention of the French to disturb the peace and *bonne harmonie* that subsisted between the two princes, "but only to avenge . . ."

There van Braam came to a word over which he probably hesitated as at least one other translator did subsequently. It may have looked as if it were *l'assailir*, which did not make sense. Van Braam finally translated it as "death," or "loss" or "killing"—there later was some doubt which word he used. The text then went on *"qui a été fait sur un de nos officiers,"* which of course was easy. Washington and others believed the language meant that the French said they sought to avenge the death of one of their officers, who, of course, was Jumonville.

At the moment, less thought was given to this than to the specific terms. First, the English commander could retire with his entire garrison to his own country. No insult would be offered by the French, who would do all they could to restrain their Indians. Second, the English could carry with them all their belongings except their artillery and "munitions of war," which the French "reserved" to themselves. Third, the defenders of the fort would receive the honors of war and could march out of the entrenchments with drum beating and with one small cannon. Fourth, as soon as the terms were signed, the English were to strike their colors. Fifth, at daybreak, a detachment of French would see the English marched off and the French left in possession of the fort. Sixth, as the English had no horses or cattle with which to remove their effects, they could put these *en cache* until they could send draft animals for them; and to this end they could leave a guard, on condition that they should not work on any establishment in that vicinity or on that side of the mountains for one year. Finally, as the English held prisoners taken at the—again that word van Braam translated "loss" or "death" or "killing" of Jumonville—they must liberate and deliver these men, under escort, at Fort DuQuesne. As surety for this and for the general agreement two Captains were to be left as hostages until the arrival of the French and Canadian prisoners. The victors offered to provide a guard for these hostages, who promised return of the French prisoners in two and a half months at latest.

The main provisions were honorable. George balked at one stipulation only: the English ought not to be compelled to surrender their "munitions of war," because that phrase would include ammunition. If the troops started back without powder and ball, every man of them might be killed and scalped by the Indians. Van Braam must return to the French and insist on the elimination of that phrase.

Back once more went the Captain. He soon returned: The French had been reasonable. From the capitulation the words *et munitions de guerre* had been stricken by a penstroke. There remained the question of hostages. Who of the Captains should be delivered to the French? Van Braam and Stobo, young, unmarried and unattached, were the most available hostages. The French commander was so informed. George signed the capitulation in a hand that showed neither excitement nor exhaustion. Mackay, too, attached his name because he would not recognize the authority of a Colonial to act for his troops. It was then about midnight of July 3.

Destruction of belongings took some hours. It was close to ten o'clock on July 4 when the survivors marched out of the fort. They stepped to beat of drum; their colors were flying; they carried their arms; they received the honors of war; but they could not keep the Indians from plundering what they left behind or anything they did not guard vigilantly while they carried it with them.

When the survivors of Fort Necessity were counted at the bivouac the next morning they numbered 293 officers and men. By the time it reached Wills Creek on July 8 or 9, the Virginia Regiment had been reduced by death, wounds, detachment, lameness and desertion to 165 rank and file. Total killed finally were counted at thirty and the wounded at seventy for the entire force, which, at the beginning of the expedition, had consisted of about four hundred of all ranks.

George and most of his officers soon recovered from the physical strains of the battle and the retreat, but the surviving private soldiers of the Virginia Regiment less quickly responded to rest and full rations. This exhaustion could lead to demoralization, but, in retrospect, there had been little in the conduct of the men that should shame them or their Colonel. Cowardice there doubtless had been, but the only notorious display of lack of mettle had been by an officer. Lieutenant Colonel Muse had shown himself unable to endure the dangers of combat. Speedy resignation was acceptable.

This was individual humiliation. General distress was created in the command when some officer with a reading knowledge of French scrutinized the text of the capitulation. The word that van Braam had translated "loss" or "death" or "killing" proved to be in one place *l'assassin* and in the other *l'assassinat*. For the first time it was plain to the English officers that they unwittingly had made an acknowledgment that they had assassinated Jumonville. George, Mackay and Stephen were willing to swear that van Braam had not once used the word "assassination" in translating the paper; but there the word was. In their wrath, they suspected the worst and denounced van Braam as treacherous.

Their indignation would have burnt even more deeply had they realized with what satisfaction the French regarded the entire operation against Fort Necessity. De Villiers, one of six brothers of Jumonville, was furiously anxious to avenge his brother's death and was in command. The fight, according to de Villiers, had cost him two killed and seventeen wounded. When de Villiers' comment appeared in print, it was not lacking in self-praise or in derogation of his adversaries: "We made them consent to sign that they had assassinated my brother in his camp; we had hostages for the security of the French who were in their power; we made them abandon the King's country; we obliged them to leave their cannon, nine pieces; we destroyed their horses and cattle and made them sign that the favors granted were evidence that we wanted to use them as friends."

Dinwiddie was balanced in his criticism and was relieved, in a sense, that the disaster had not been worse. When the Governor learned of the defeat, he soon persuaded himself that he explicitly had ordered George not to attack until "the whole forces were joined in a body." Although he blamed George to this extent, Dinwiddie adhered to his belief that larger responsibility rested on the other Colonies and, among Virginians, first on those who, having contracted to deliver flour promptly, had failed to do so. Croghan was as much condemned at Alexandria and in Williamsburg as he had been at Fort Necessity. Criticism was not limited to the Colonies in general, to Washington, to Croghan and to other traders who did not meet their contracts for provisions or transport. Gradually, after George came back to the settlements, he learned how and why the Governor had been disappointed, most of all, in the failure of the North Carolina contingent and of the two New York Independent Companies to reach Great Meadows.

Col. James Innes had been told by Governor Dinwiddie as early as March 23 that the position of Commander-in-Chief of the expedition to the Ohio had been intended for him. Delay had attended the organization of the North Carolina troops whom Innes was to bring to Virginia, but the Colonel himself had proceeded to Winchester. He had arrived in the Valley town on June 30 and had begun to exercise command under orders and commission of Dinwiddie. As Innes held also an old commission as Captain in the regular establishment, he seemed well chosen. He could give orders to the young Captains of Independent Companies and thereby could escape the disputes over rank that George had encountered. Because their Colony had no magazine, Innes's men had no arms except those that private individuals chose to bring along with them. Two of his five North Carolina companies had disembarked at Alexandria late in June, but they found no weapons there. The other reenforcements on which Dinwiddie had relied for months were the two Independent Companies from New York. These troops had received in March orders to move to Virginia, but they had not reached Norfolk until June 16 and then proved to be poor human material, feebly equipped.

When blame for the capitulation at Fort Necessity was apportioned, Dinwiddie and Washington and all their friends could point to the number of idle troops: of the eight companies, approximately 550 men, who had been expected to support the Virginia Regiment, only Mackay's company had joined Washington. The delay of the regulars and of the North Carolinians, the Governor told some of his correspondents, had been "monstrous." Dinwiddie did not once suggest that, as conditions were, the more men Washington had, the sooner they would have gone hungry. The Governor never seemed to appreciate the part that feeble transportation played in the defeat of the expedition. He continued rightly to blame the contractors; he did not realize, or at least did not admit, that he had been culpably overoptimistic in his assumption of the speed with which vehicles could be assembled and men and supplies moved to the Ohio over the rough, mountainous road George slowly had reopened.

Detailed judgment of the misadventure had not been formulated fully by the time George and Mackay hurried to Winchester, where they reported to Colonel Innes, their Commander-in-Chief. They left Winchester on July 11 to ride to Williamsburg to report to the Governor. It was July 17, a fortnight after the bloody day at Fort Necessity, that the two officers reached Williamsburg.

The Governor received George, heard the details of what had happened, and began to make his preparations for the next phase of the struggle. His new orders to Colonel Innes were for the building at Wills Creek of a log fort to receive six months' provisions. ". . . I think it's not prudent to march out to the Ohio," the Governor wrote, "till you have a sufficient force to attack the enemy, and that you be properly provided with everything for that purpose." This policy was accepted as sound and fixed.

George found that his expedition was the theme of every man's talk in Williamsburg. He was himself conspicuous, not to say famous. The victory in the skirmish with Jumonville had been much applauded. Public men shared his humiliation at having signed a document that admitted the "assassination" of the young French officer, but this word was attributed more violently than ever to treachery on the part of van Braam. No blame was attached to Washington for the capitulation itself.

Otherwise than by Dinwiddie, official commendation of George and the other officers could not be expected immediately in Virginia because the General Assembly was not in session; but the Governor and Council did have authority to make a grant to the men from money voted at the previous session. When, therefore, Washington started back to his command, he had in his baggage three hundred pistoles for distribution among the men of his Regiment and of the South Carolina Independent Company "as a reward for their bravery in the recent engagement with the French."

George found the survivors of the expedition in worse condition than they had been at any time. The Independent Companies remained at Wills Creek; his own men had come—or soon came—to Alexandria. They were demoralized, half naked, without hats or blankets, and were in resentful temper because they had not been paid. Some had created disorder at Winchester; others had deserted and carried their arms with them. Miserable as was their plight, George could do little to relieve it, except to appeal to the Governor to remit funds with which to pay them. George learned, also, that the North Carolina troops were close to dissolution because the fund for their support was almost exhausted. The Independent Companies, especially Mackay's, remained under discipline and in fair condition, but they were numerically weak.

George knew that, lamentable though it was, the men who had been engaged at Fort Necessity were incapable of another effort that year. Clarke's and Innes's troops were not equipped or seasoned for the attempt. Even if they were, they lacked adequate transport, without which advance was self-murder. Colonel Washington, for these reasons, was stunned when he opened, a few days later, a dispatch from Dinwiddie dated August 3. Another attempt was to be made forthwith to drive the French from the Ohio. It seemed incredible that such a thing could be considered by a Governor who a fortnight previously had been content to talk of building a fort at Wills Creek and of victualling it for six months' supply of troops who were not to start westward until they were equipped and concentrated.

George's orders were that he was to proceed as soon as possible to Wills Creek with the troops he had. The Council, Dinwiddie explained, had decided that, as the French probably would be stronger in the spring of 1755, it would be wise to recross the Alleghenies at the earliest possible moment and either to capture Fort DuQuesne or to construct defences at some point selected by a council of war. Washington was to join Innes for this purpose.

George stood aghast at Dinwiddie's plan. It seemed the counsel of madness. At the moment he did not trust himself to address the Governor. He reflected and, as soon as he could muster his arguments and discharge his temper, he wrote William Fairfax a long critique of Dinwiddie's plan. George tore the plan to bits and, in doing so, gave himself an excellent drill in military analysis. If he realized, when he finished it, how much he had learned since the previous November concerning the management of troops and preparation for war, he did not drop a boastful word. The subject was too grim for self-praise. Study of a theoretical military problem was not enjoyable when he might be required to attempt an impossible solution.

The next day he wrote Innes that he was withholding the letter "to Williamsburg," until he heard from the North Carolinian, so that he might "write nothing inconsistent with what" his immediate superior proposed. Then George recorded explicitly: "If you think it advisable to order me in the shattered condition we are in to march up to you, I will, if no more than ten men follows me (which I believe will be the full amount). . . ."

Events of the next few days made this prediction almost a probability. Desertion continued. Every night or so, some of the ragged men of the Virginia Regiment would slip away. Strength of the Regiment dropped steadily towards a minimum of 150. Among the North Carolina soldiers conditions were even worse. One company mutinied in Augusta County; a like spirit was said to prevail among the others. With alarming speed, companies disbanded for lack of money with which to provide pay or purchase subsistence. By the end of August barely twoscore or, at most, fifty North Carolinians remained as an organized force in Virginia.

Soon George heard at Alexandria that Dinwiddie had declared the plans for an offensive "entirely defeated" by the "obstinacy of our Assembly" in its failure to provide financial support to contest the French, the disbanding of the North Carolinians and the reduction in the strength of the Virginia Regiment. The Governor argued stubbornly that if the Burgesses had provided the money, he could have raised six hundred troops and thereby could have offset the loss of the Carolinians. Plans for an offensive in the autumn of 1754 were suspended. New alarm seized frontier families who expected Indian attacks.

About September 15 marching orders reached Washington, but they opened with the statement by the Governor: "I fear we are not numbers sufficient to attack the fort taken from us by the French." George was to proceed to Wills Creek with such men as he could muster after detaching forty or fifty, who were to go to Augusta County as a guard against incursions of small bodies of Indians and perhaps of French. At Wills Creek George and the remnant of the Regiment would receive further orders. In all these dealings there was one consolation only: The General Assembly, before prorogation, had voted thanks to George and Mackay and to their respective officers, except Muse and van Braam, "for their late gallant and brave behaviour in the defence of their country."

As it eventuated, circumstances and sickness probably relieved George of the unnecessary march to Wills Creek that autumn. The loss of health he attributed to the hardships he had endured; the hampering circumstances were the preparations for the departure of Captain Lewis's men for Augusta, and, doubtless, Washington's inability to get others equipped for a winter on the upper Potomac.

Avoidance of that dull service was not escape from all annoyance. On the contrary, there were new irritations, regrets and further humiliation. Gov. Horatio Sharpe of Maryland made criticisms of the affair at Fort Necessity in a manner that showed misunderstanding of what had happened. The principal regret was over news of the death of Half King. Half King had been the most loyal of the supporters of England in the realm of the Six Nations. It was distressing to learn that he had arrived at Paxton,

Pennsylvania, on October 1 in ill health. Three days later he died. George's new humiliations were over the prospect that if he went back to Wills Creek, he no longer would be commander of the forces. Instead, he would be subordinate to Innes and in unpleasant relationship to the Captains of the Independent Companies. Either he would have to remain entirely separate from those officers or recognize their authority as superior to his.

George had an accumulation of discontent and humiliation weighing on his mind when he started for Williamsburg about October 17, the date to which the House of Burgesses had been prorogued by the Governor. On October 21 he was in Williamsburg. He found the Governor busy in the entertainment of distinguished men and in the planning of a larger war with greater means. The Governor of North Carolina, Arthur Dobbs, had arrived in Williamsburg after a dismal voyage from Spithead. He had brought from the home government £10,000 in specie for Dinwiddie's use in securing the defence of the Colony, and he had delivered also a crown credit for a like sum and notice that two thousand stands of arms were to be sent to Virginia. Important dispatches had been in Dobbs's hands for Governor Sharpe, whom Dinwiddie in His Majesty's name was to summon to Williamsburg for conference with the Governors of Virginia and North Carolina. Obediently, Sharpe had been able to reach the Virginia town on the nineteenth and had been closeted with Dinwiddie and Dobbs.

Washington learned at least something of what was contemplated. Together, the three executives were working on a plan similar to the one Dinwiddie had formulated in August and had abandoned when money ran out and the North Carolina troops scattered. The information of the Governors was that the French force on the Ohio was so reduced that a new opportunity was offered the English. If practicable, Sharpe, who had received a Lieutenant Colonel's commission from the King, was to raise seven hundred men who, with the Independent Companies, were to proceed forthwith to the Ohio and capture Fort DuQuesne before the French could reenforce it.

Amazement over this rash scheme was effaced almost immediately by news for which Washington was altogether unprepared. The Virginia Regiment was to be broken into Independent Companies! George would cease to be a Colonel and would become a Captain, and that not even on the King's commission, unless and until His Majesty approved Dinwiddie's recommendation that the Colonials be on the regular establishment. His pride rebelled against such a thing. Sharpe tried to prevail on George to serve with the troops he was to raise. When George declined, Sharpe asked that Washington at least promise to consider any proposition he might be able to make after he returned to Maryland. George could not refuse this but he did not believe Sharpe could tender a position he could accept. "I think," he said later, "the disparity between the present offer of a company and my former rank too great to expect any real satisfaction or enjoyment in a corps where I once did, or thought I had a right, to command. . . ."

In that spirit, proud and indignant but not openly wrathful, Washington tendered his resignation as Colonel of the Virginia Regiment. Dinwiddie accepted it. George turned decisively to other matters and completed his shopping in Williamsburg by purchasing new fittings and horse furnishings of the sort a planter of station required. Then on November 2, he started home.

George had no rendezvous except with his own lands, to which he had given little attention during the year that had elapsed since he had undertaken to carry Dinwiddie's message to Fort Le Boeuf. On November 15, 1753, he had been at Wills Creek and had been engaging Gist as a guide for his first great adventure in the wilderness. November 15, 1754, he was sitting at a desk in Colonel Fairfax's Belvoir. Within twelve months had come, first, the journey almost to Lake Erie and the struggle in the snow as George hurried back to warn Dinwiddie that the French were preparing to descend to the Ohio. They had done so quickly enough and had driven off Ward before Washington could reach the Monongahela. The responsibilities and excitement of acting as leader of the advanced column, the anxieties and disappointments of command, promotion to the rank of Colonel after the death of Fry, the difficulties with Mackay, the doubtful conferences with the Indians, the affair with Jumonville, the attempt to cut a road to Red Stone Creek, the shameless delay of contractors, the hunger of the soldiers, the disappearance of the red warriors, the blood and the mud of July 3, the humiliation of retreat and of that word "assassination," the journey to Williamsburg, the thanks of the House of Burgesses, and then the blow, almost the insult, of dropping from the first post of field command to the rank of Captain subordinate to every half-pay officer who might come from England—all this had been hard. George had given his every energy to his duty and had endured more of hardship than any Virginian of his day had been called on to suffer in the public service. It had been shabbily rewarded, he thought. He himself had been repudiated and humiliated. Now the whole of it was behind him. In front of him, there on the desk, was the single sheet on which he was to accept or decline the offer Governor Sharpe had extended on November 4 through William Fitzhugh in accordance with the promise made at Williamsburg.

Sharpe had done his best: If George would reconsider his resignation, Colonel Innes would be no obstacle to his service, because the North Carolinian was merely to exercise post command at Wills Creek. When Sharpe himself was not afield, Fitzhugh would see to it that George would not be required to take orders from those who had been his juniors when he was on the frontier. A letter from Sharpe to Dinwiddie, written to give assurance of this, was enclosed with the Marylander's invitation and could be forwarded to Williamsburg if George accepted the offer. Fitzhugh added his personal advice "by no means to quit."

No! He would not accept it. Sharpe and Fitzhugh deserved, of course, the best and most polite answer he could pen, because they had been considerate and generous; but the decision stood—no. Col. George Washington would not submit to loss of rank which Sharpe did not have authority to change. George so wrote Fitzhugh, gravely and politely, and explained that as he could not use it, he was returning Sharpe's letter to Dinwiddie. Of the Maryland Governor, George wrote: ". . . assure him, sir, as you truly may, of my reluctance to quit the service and of the pleasure I should have received in attending his fortunes. Also inform him that it was to obey the call of honor, and the advice of my friends, I declined it, and not to gratify any desire I have to leave the military line."

Then he added, in regret and in confession, in memory of stirring days and perhaps in vague thought of the future: "My inclinations are strongly bent to arms."

CHAPTER / 3

George Washington's resignation as Colonel of the Virginia Regiment in November 1754 did not destroy his ambition for a military career. He quit the service because he felt that Governor Dinwiddie had humiliated him personally and had deprived him of public honors by dividing the troops into Independent Companies. Instead of his former position as Colonel, George would have had that of Colonial Captain only, outranked, as he wrathfully put it, by "every Captain, bearing the King's commission, every half-pay officer, or other, appearing with such a commission." He would not endure that, but he still wanted to learn more of "the military art," and he began to ask himself and his influential friends if there might not be some way by which he could serve in the campaign of 1755 as a volunteer. Especially was he disposed to this when he heard that the next march on Fort DuQuesne was to be under the direction of an experienced British general and not under Colonel Innes or Governor Sharpe, neither of whom he esteemed as a soldier.

Whatever the prospect of new military service as a volunteer, George had his own fortune to advance. For a man not yet twenty-three he was well-to-do, but he had no home of his own. He wanted an establishment, he could afford one, and he had now a prospect of leasing the property he most desired, Mount Vernon. Colonel and Mrs. George Lee (she was the widow of Lawrence Washington) agreed December 17 that George might have the use of the estate and of the eighteen resident slaves at a fixed annual rental of 15,000 pounds of tobacco per annum, or the equivalent in current money of Virginia at the rate of 12s. 6d. per hundredweight of tobacco. As George had little experience in housekeeping and had kind and sympathetic neighbors, it is likely that he consulted often the family at Belvoir and, in particular, the charming Sally Cary Fairfax. His feelings for her may not have been conscious, but he certainly admired her as much as it was proper to regard the wife of a close friend.

George's share in the settlement of Lawrence's affairs, his interests in Belvoir, and his numerous activities on his own plantation did not occupy all his thought. He had too deep a devotion to arms, even after his unhappy experience over his commission, to ignore events subsequent to his resignation. Much of interest had occurred during the autumn and winter; still more was in prospect. Both Governor Dinwiddie and Governor Sharpe, now acting Commander-in-Chief, were resolved to press the campaign against the French in 1755 and recover the territory and prestige lost the previous year.

Plans for the operations of the spring and summer had five essential aspects: First, the Colonies must have the leadership of officers and troops "from home"; second, the Colonies themselves must supply soldiers of their own and provisions for them and for the forces from England; third, Colonials and Redcoats should seek the assistance of all the Indians who could be won to their side; fourth, to prevent hunger and loss of time when the season for active fighting began, a large store of provisions must be accumulated in advance and transported as far towards the Ohio as practicable; fifth, for the proper storage and custody of these rations, a fort was to be constructed at Wills Creek.

Indian alliances, Colonial recruits, the begrudging supply of stinted funds by suspicious assemblies, the tedious upbuilding of provisions at Wills Creek—all these preparations looked to the arrival of disciplined regulars from England. Well-trained troops led by professional soldiers would be the core of the column that would advance irresistibly to the Ohio and drive away or destroy the French. This was the conviction of Dinwiddie. He had warned the Lords of Trade: ". . . without two Regiments of men from Britain, we shall not be able effectually to defeat the unjust invasion of the French." By December 12, 1754, he had received confirmation of his hopes that the troops would be sent—that transports had been taken in October and that Capt. Augustine Keppel would convoy them with a fifty-gun ship. Shortly after hearing this good news, Dinwiddie learned also that two additional regiments were to be raised in New England and were to be led by Governor Shirley of Massachusetts and Sir William Pepperell, the first native American ever to be made a baronet.

As this information was printed in the *Virginia Gazette,* George soon saw it at Mount Vernon. He felt a new stirring of his military ambition, and he admitted that he would like to share in the campaign; but he took no step to recover his commission or volunteer for service. Almost every subsequent issue of the newspaper whetted his appetite for honors. He had just returned from a visit to Col. John Baylor's plantation and probably to Ferry Farm when word came that a distinguished British officer had reached Williamsburg from England—Sir John St. Clair, baronet of Scotland and former Major of the Twenty-second Foot, who had been assigned as Deputy Quartermaster General of forces in America with local rank as Lieutenant Colonel. George probably learned in February that St. Clair most heartily had damned the road from Winchester to Wills Creek as the worst he ever had traveled. At that outpost, now styled Fort Cumberland, St. Clair had reviewed the Independent Companies and had discharged more than forty of the men as unfit for service. The Deputy Quartermaster General manifestly was a positive officer who knew his own mind.

While the Colonials were beginning to discover what manner of person St. Clair was, they received information that the two promised regiments were en route and that they were commanded by Col. Sir Peter Halkett and Col. Thomas Dunbar. During the last week in February, George ascertained that on the night of February 19/20, Commodore Keppel's flagship, the *Centurion,* had dropped anchor off Hampton along with the *Syren* and the *Norwich,* on which last vessel was Maj. Gen. Edward

Braddock, His Majesty's Commander-in-Chief of the forces in North America.

The *Virginia Gazette* announced also that the General was accompanied by "Captain Orme, Aide-de-Camp and Mr. Shirley, secretary." George read and envied. These young men were doing exactly what he wanted to do: they were in close daily relationship with an experienced soldier of long service from whom they could learn much of the "military arts" that fascinated George. Soon the young Virginian identified "Mr. Shirley" as William Shirley, son of the Governor of Massachusetts. A little later George found that Braddock was to have another aide-de-camp, Roger Morris, who bore the surname and might be a kinsman of the Governor of Pennsylvania. If they could serve with Braddock as members of his "military family," why should not a Virginian also? George did not solicit appointment directly, but he took pains to write a letter of congratulations to Braddock on the General's arrival in America and thereby he let His Excellency know there was such a person as George Washington.

Braddock remained in Williamsburg, hard at work. Newspapers and returning travelers told of vigorous recruiting to fill out the expected British Regiments, and of the organization of Virginia companies of rangers, carpenters and light horse to be commanded by officers of Braddock's selection. In addition George, of course, heard gossip of Braddock, Keppel and St. Clair, because three such notables could not come to the quiet Virginia capital and not create chatter. Never had there been such planning, such talk of ships and soldiers, such contracts—for two hundred hired wagons, among other things, and 2500 horses. In comparison with George's expedition of 1754, the scale of everything was trebled or quadrupled; promises made by the Colonials were in proportion.

To the young master of Mount Vernon, the resigned Virginia Colonel, all this was at once far off and familiar. He knew what the preparations involved and forecast, but he was out of the service . . . until March 14, 1755, when this letter was delivered to him:

Sir: The General having been informed that you expressed some desire to make the campaign, but that you declined it upon the disagreeableness that you thought might arise from the regulation of command, has ordered me to acquaint you that he will be very glad of your company in his family by which all inconveniences of that kind will be obviated.

I shall think myself very happy to form an acquaintance with a person so universally esteemed and shall use every opportunity of assuring you how much I am

Sir

Your most obedient servant

ROBERT ORME *aid de camp*

Williamsburg, Mch. 2, 1755

The opportunity of joining Braddock's staff came, unfortunately, at a time when George's military ambitions clashed with his personal economy. The lease and partial equipment of Mount Vernon had involved considerable expense; he had no manager of his property; if he followed his impulse and went again to the Ohio he might lose heavily at the very time he otherwise might profit. The impulse persisted; so did the doubt. Balancing gain and sacrifice, he at length decided to postpone a final answer until he met Braddock and talked with the General.

George did not have long to wait. The last of the transports from Ireland arrived at Hampton with the rear companies and stores of Braddock's command. The men were ordered to proceed on the same vessels to Alexandria, whither Braddock himself took ship with Keppel and Dinwiddie. On March 28 these celebrities disembarked at the proud new town.

Braddock decided quickly that the tall young Virginian was worth attaching to his family. He offered George a Captain's commission by brevet and had it explained carefully this was the highest position he had authority to fill. In turn, George described his perplexity over entering the service in any capacity and asked whether, if he did join the staff, he could devote to his own affairs the time that would elapse before Braddock was ready to establish headquarters at Wills Creek. When Braddock readily agreed to this, George thanked him and said he would give an early answer to the offer.

An interview with the General was not all. George must have made several visits to the quarters of the younger officers or often have met them socially, because he soon was on friendly, bantering terms with Orme and Shirley. When George left the company of these young officers, it always was with the feeling that if he joined Braddock he would be associated with pleasant men not much older than himself. Deliberately he debated whether he should accept the invitation to be one of them. Pride and previous utterance led him to exclude even the possibility of accepting a Captain's commission by brevet. The essential question was whether he could afford to serve as a volunteer aide. He decided about April 1 that he would do this, if he could perform the duty the General expected of him without too great or too prolonged neglect of his private affairs. The bargain struck, George took pains to let his friends know he was to serve as a volunteer and without pay.

Secrecy was not a virtue of military planning at so great a distance from the French. Without being inquisitive, George soon ascertained that Braddock's plan had been drafted in Britain, chiefly by the Duke of Cumberland, and was covered by instructions and by letters. These provided for attack at three points that formed a concave arc from the Ohio at Fort DuQuesne to Lake Champlain. First, Braddock was to march from Wills Creek to the junction of the Allegheny and Monongahela. If, as expected, he made short work of Fort DuQuesne, he was to look to Fort Niagara, near the western end of Lake Ontario and on Niagara River, about two hundred miles north and slightly east of the first objective. In addition, a plan was formulted for an attack on Nova Scotia. It was a plan to appeal to a young soldier because, if its daring was rewarded, it would crush the enemy and terminate in speedy triumph the war with France. Washington had yet to discover how readily even experienced soldiers may be tempted to let their imagination outmarch their armies and their ambition disdain the limitations of their resources. The Virginian had lost his small battles with mud and mountains and haggling farmers who would risk a war to save a wagon. Would these commanders from home show him where he had erred and how he might have won?

Washington heard, also, of the Governors' other deliberations with Braddock—how they regretfully had told the General the Colonies would not provide a common fund for the support of the campaign, and how they had pledged their Colonies to provide a fund for presents to friendly savages and to make arrangements for garrisoning Fort DuQuesne when Braddock had captured it and had moved on towards Fort Niagara.

In the remembrance of the hunger of his men the previous year, George felt that transportation was the problem of all problems for a successful advance. In his opinion, the mountains would be crossed with minimum difficulty by a large train of pack horses. Braddock was a believer in wheeled transport rather than in pack animals; but he increasingly was disturbed by the difficulty and expense of procuring wagons. In some manner he had misunderstood what was told him about the distance over the mountains to Fort DuQuesne. He thought he had to traverse fifteen miles of rough country. When he learned that he had ahead of him between sixty and seventy miles of mountain and hill he became peevishly sensitive to everything that delayed an early start on the long and toilsome road.

Non-fulfillment of Colonials' promises to supply wagons shaped Braddock's next move. He had been induced to send part of the troops through Maryland because he had the assurance that the farmers of that Colony would not rent their wagons for use outside its bounds but would supply vehicles on the Maryland side of the Potomac. Now that he was ready to have the artillery follow the infantry toward the frontier, he found that the wagons promised by Sharpe were not available for the guns. Angrily the General sent an express to St. Clair, who had gone to Winchester and was expecting, when he had repaired the road, to proceed to Wills Creek. After a few days, Braddock impatiently decided to ride to Frederick, Maryland, and see for himself what could be done there to get wagons.

George remained behind to finish his business, and, on May 1, started out to join Braddock in Frederick. A long, roundabout ride it was, and one that fatigued even George, but it carried him to the Maryland village—a place of abundance—just in time to catch Braddock before that officer was departing in disgust and wrath over conditions that in some respects duplicated and in others exceeded those George had to endure the previous year.

The General had arrived at Frederick on the twenty-first; St. Clair had reached the settlement the same day. They found few cattle accumulated for the troops and no wagons ready for the journey to Wills Creek. Braddock, complaining of the cost of everything, was forced at heavy expense to send into the country around Frederick to purchase beeves; and he was compelled to threaten dire things unless the Justices of the Peace procured wagons for the movement of stores and ammunition to Fort Cumberland. At length twenty-five wagons were delivered, but twenty-five only, and some of them not fit for the road. Braddock almost went mad. The expedition was at an end, he swore; he could not go on. He must have not less than 150 wagons and must have them speedily!

The visitor who toned down Braddock was a soft-spoken man of forty-nine, regarded as one of the ablest as well as suavest of Philadelphia leaders. He was Benjamin Franklin, who had come to Frederick in an effort to assuage the wrath of Braddock and St. Clair against Pennsylvania and he believed he had removed some of their prejudices. Now, in desperation, the General appealed to Franklin: would he undertake to contract in Pennsylvania for 150 wagons and 1500 horses to be delivered by May 10 at Fort Cumberland? Franklin agreed to make the effort, whereupon Braddock advanced £800 from the army chest for the initial expenses.

Braddock, reaching Winchester May 3, lingered unwillingly there because he had been led to believe, from what Dinwiddie had told him at Williamsburg, that Indian Chiefs would meet him in the Valley town and would join in a council designed to strengthen alliances against the French. The General found no Indians at the rendezvous and heard that none had been there. As excessively hot weather was added to disappointment, Braddock probably was boiling inwardly and outwardly, but, of course, he was unwilling to stir until he was convinced that no Indians were on the road to attend the council.

Braddock left Winchester for Wills Creek May 7 in the conviction that longer waiting for the Indians would be time wasted. With his staff and the Virginia Troop of Light Horse, he reached Cresap's on the eighth. All hands rested on the ninth; but on the tenth they were astir. Dunbar's Regiment started early; later Braddock climbed into his chariot and gave the nod. Off rolled the vehicle. George, Orme, and the others attended at a slow trot; the Virginia Troop acted as guard and escort. The ride was pleasant through the greenery of early May and without dust. Not far from Wills Creek, George and his companions passed the Forty-eighth Regiment on the road. The men gazed at the fat gentleman in the carraige; the drums beat the "Grenadiers' March"; the Colonials marveled: A new style of war had come to the wilderness.

Fort Cumberland now was a formidable-looking structure, but crudely put together. To George, the setting was familiar, but there were differences from his earlier experiences at the outpost. Never had George seen so many soldiers at the Fort, or so many supplies. That was the principal difference. The next was the contrast between a professional commander and staff and the extemporized, inexperienced organization George had known under Fry and later under Innes. A third difference was symbolized by twelve words written in the orderly book of Headquarters that day, May 10, 1755: "Mr. Washington is appointed aid de camp to His Excellency General Braddock." That meant new honor, new authority, new opportunity.

George's duties as aide to General Braddock scarcely accorded at the outset with the distinction the young Virginian attached to the post. His principal regular assignment was to see that the orderly book was written up carefully. Further, in common with all other officers, George was supposed to wait on the General at the morning levee, held daily between ten and eleven o'clock. Then and always, Washington received the fullest consideration of Braddock, who soon formed an attachment for him and gave him patronage any of the Southern Governors would have coveted: in the hands of his new assistant the General placed several blank commissions for ensigns, and authorized him to fill them out in the name of young men he approved. This pleasing evidence of Braddock's goodwill was appreciated, but the selection of a few ensigns for these commissions, and the discharge of his trivial routine duties occupied only a small part of George's time.

George doubtless saw before many days what some of his comrades-in-arms already had observed—that something besides horses and wagons was lacking. Beneath the show of strict conformity to military standards, and of blunt, open dealing on the part of the General, there was much slowness, inefficiency, stupidity, lack of resourcefulness and some laziness. As one officer subsequently wrote, Braddock "was a man of sense and good natured too, though warm and a little uncouth in his manner—and peevish—withal very indolent and seemed glad for anybody to take business off his hands." Young Washington, in the still-sensitive memory of the difficulties of transportation in 1754, wondered whether it would be possible for Braddock to get the artillery over the mountains. If that could be done, George believed the military task beyond the ridges could be discharged with ease and honor. A second concern was that of assistance from the Indians. Besides the certainty of delay and the uncertainty of Indian allegiance, a third difficulty developed during the first days at Wills Creek. As a result of high temperature and poor packing, much salt meat spoiled. Braddock at once set up a public market but offerings were far below the requirements of the camp.

Although Braddock advanced some gold for the encouragement of his feeble trade, funds for these purposes were running low because of the high prices demanded for everything. He had now to replenish his stock of money, and on May 15 he gave George instructions to proceed to Hampton and to get £4000 from the Paymaster of the expedition, John Hunter. George got back to Wills Creek with the money on May 30, the fifteenth day after his departure. He had made excellent time and found himself at the journey's end in "tolerable health," as he put it, though he was somewhat worn.

Much had happened during his absence. All the troops intended for the expedition had arrived or soon would. The artillery had experienced much trouble in reaching Fort Cumberland because of the usual shortage of wagons and teams. Had not Lt. Col. Thomas Gage impressed vehicles and horses as he went forward, he might never have reached Wills Creek. The last contingent known to be on the road, Dobbs's North Carolina Company, tramped into quarters the day of George's return. There then were in the camp the two British Regiments of seven hundred men each, three Independent Companies, and one North Carolina, one Maryland and nine Virginia companies, together with sixty regulars of the artillery train and thirty seamen accustomed to the use of block and tackle in moving heavy guns. The Maryland Company had made a favorable impression on St. Clair, in spite of the fact that recruits from the Colony for the regulars had included some convicts and a number of servants who had scurried to the colors in the hope of terminating their indenture. The Virginia troops had been well drilled by Ensign Allen of the regulars, but, in the judgment of Orme, "their languid, spiritless and unsoldierlike appearance, considered with the lowness and ignorance of most of their officers, gave little hope of their future good behavior."

George found, further, that the Governor of Virginia now had lost standing with the General and shared in Braddock's eyes the undependability of the soldiers of the Old Dominion. One of Dinwiddie's contractors had failed to deliver cattle he had promised; Michael Cresap had repeated his father's performance of 1754 and had not sent to Wills Creek an adequate supply of flour; Thomas Cresap had attempted to sell pickled meat so bad that it was condemned and buried. In wrath and desperation, Braddock had been compelled to return wagons all the way to Winchester for provisions and had been forced to dispatch 300 pack horses to the Conococheague for flour. Only the 150 vehicles promised by Franklin and about 500 of the desired 1500 pack animals had been delivered in specific and punctual performance of contracts. Little had been accomplished with the Indians. The soldiers had found some of the Indian girls not unattractive and altogether obliging, with the result that patrols had to be organized to scour the woods where assignations were being held. Stern and still sterner penalties had been imposed on soldiers who gave or sold liquor to the Indians. Most of the savages were offended by the severity of the camp regulations; the troops, in turn, were demoralized by the presence of native women. Drunkenness, theft and gambling were increasing.

Braddock had fixed his order of march and had designated Major Chapman to move with five hundred men to the Little Meadows, in order to improve the trail, construct a small fort and establish an advanced store of provisions. This was the only action Braddock took toward the establishment of an advance base. In every other respect he proposed to move his men, artillery and wagons directly to the Ohio from Fort Cumberland, which thus became his general base. This projected march from Wills Creek to Fort DuQuesne was in six stages. The distance to be covered was about 110 miles, the greater part of it through rough, heavily wooded country. The column had to be self-sustaining because the country itself would supply nothing.

The march of Chapman's advanced force was under way when George rode into camp. British officers were appalled by the difficulties presented on this first stretch of a long, long road. Such warnings as George and the frontiersmen had felt themselves free to give Braddock had failed to prepare the General for the realities of the road. Concern and irritation increased in the camp—concern because a bloody flux had shown itself widely among the soldiers and irritation because Braddock had lost all patience and no longer could argue anything without wrath. Consideration and every quality of moderation were thrown away. Convinced more than ever of slothfulness, rascality and lack of truth among the Colonials, the General would concede no virtue to any of them otherwise than to admit that Franklin had kept the contract to deliver 150 wagons. Braddock often renewed his arraignment of the Virginians and Marylanders before George, who would defend them against sweeping allegations. George's resentment would have been even greater had he seen the dispatches the General was sending the home government: The Virginians were "very indifferent men"; there was "want of honesty and inclination to forward the service"; the promises of the people of Virginia and Maryland were "not to be depended on"—and so, endlessly.

On June 10 Lt. Col. Ralph Burton reported to Braddock that he had taken two days to move the train of artillery and wagons five miles and reminded the General that the road over which they had passed at so slow a pace was better than they could expect farther on. The horses available simply could not haul the loads they had. It was found that the wagons brought from England had too much weight of their own and carried shafts too wide for the light American horse. The return of these wagons to Fort Cumberland for exchange left the expedition with small net gain in vehicles. The "King's wagons" had been fitted and used to carry powder. The Colonial wagons had to be protected against the weather when it was decided to use them for the explosive. Two days were devoted to preparing the vehicles and shifting the powder.

Then the column started again. George watched, counselled, and in the memory of his own difficulty in crossing the mountains, became convinced that success demanded a further reduction of transport. More particularly there had to be an increase in the number of pack animals at the front, even though it was manifest that the inferior creatures supplied for the expedition would carry only half the load that could be borne by strong horses.

Washington was unhappily accurate in his forecast. The first "division" marched about five miles on the thirteenth and went into camp, but the second "division" did not cover that distance until the fourteenth. Men and horses were so worn that Braddock had to order a day's rest. George shared the day of idleness, but he did not get refreshment. Instead he developed fever and sharp pains in his head, symptoms that might mean typhoid fever or the bloody flux, or, as he hoped, merely a brief indisposition. He found he could not remain in his saddle. Much as he disliked it, he had to get permission to ride in one of the wagons while the column passed through the dense woods known as the "Shades of Death," beyond which were the Little Meadows.

There George found Sir John St. Clair. He was ashamed to have spent eight days in covering twenty miles, but he blamed his slow advance on the size of his train and on the fact that the road was "either rocky or full of bogs." St. Clair was convinced that Braddock could not get to Fort DuQuesne until more wagons and supplies were at hand and a road from Shippensburg was opened. The probability of meeting increased opposition, as a result of slow approach, became a serious consideration in the General's planning.

Braddock did not wait for counsel. He sought it. George received a summons to the commander's tent. The Virginian still was sick; but he had a clear head for the question the General put to him: What should be done

next? George argued that if Braddock would push on with a chosen detachment, supported by artillery, Fort DuQuesne could be taken from its few
defenders before French reenforcements arrived. While a lightly equipped
English column was moving rapidly forward, the wagons could follow
slowly and in safety because the advanced force would be between the trains
and the enemy.

The next day, June 17, sicker than before, George probably heard
that Braddock was talking of the plan he had suggested. St. Clair knew of it;
so did Halkett and Dunbar. Apparently, none of these had any intimation
that the design was not the General's but the young aide's. George was
exceedingly proud and too discreet to boast that the army now was to
proceed as he, an uncommissioned Colonial, had recommended.

As preparations were made to organize the advanced detachment,
George had to steel himself to proceed with it. His pain was ceaseless; at
intervals he may have been delirious. When the troops actually took the
road, George felt what he subsequently described as "the most infinite delight"; a fortunate company was about to sweep on to the Ohio and to plant
the flag of England on the parapet of Fort DuQuesne. Pain and fever did
not yield to patriotic impulse. Braddock knew of the aide's illness and
unhappiness and considerately notified the Virginian that when he was
strong enough to go forward a wagon would be at his command. Later that
same day, George received written orders not to go on! Although he had to
obey, he appealed to the General for one concession: Would Braddock
promise that he would be brought to the front before the fort was reached?
The commander gave word of honor but coupled with the promise the
surgeon's warning that if George persisted in going forward immediately he
would be risking his life. Grimly and reluctantly George had to yield and
had to stay at Little Meadows while the drums beat and his comrades rode
away.

To the wretchedness of George's pain and fever there now was added
the feeling of separation from the scene of action, and of loneliness besides.
Definite relief of mind consequently was afforded on the twenty-second by
the arrival of Dunbar and his command, though as it proved, the Colonel
was bristling with resentments. Dunbar felt that he had been deceived by
the General. He felt keenly the handicap put on him by the organization of
the advanced column. As soon as Braddock had set out with Halkett for
Fort DuQuesne, Dunbar discovered that the General had taken the best
wagon horses and many spare animals and had left him only a sufficient
number to move two-thirds of the wagons at a given time with full teams of
four. The distance between the fast-moving men at the front and Dunbar's
heavily burdened force was certain to be increased hourly.

Dunbar had a bitterness to keep fresh and he scarcely could have
shown affectionate concern for a sick member of his commander's "family,"
but with Dunbar was Dr. Murdock, a surgeon whom George could trust.
Braddock had sent back positive command that George should be given
Doctor James's Powders, a patent medicine. The prescribed treatment was
administered. To the restless young patient Doctor James's Powders seemed,
in George's own words, "the most excellent medicine in the world, for it

gave me immediate ease. . . ." Almost from that date the fever diminished.

As George's fever fell, his interest in the movement of the troops ahead rose higher than ever. His desire to rejoin them became more intense every time an express or a returning drover brought news from the front. Indian and French scouts were harassing Braddock's column. Other Indians had penetrated close to Fort Cumberland and into Frederick County, Virginia, and had scalped and slain white families. A nearer concern to George was the humiliating slowness of the advance of Braddock's men. By the twenty-sixth George was sufficiently improved to proceed in a covered wagon to the Great Crossing of the Youghiogheny but there he had to remain because the physician did not think he had regained sufficient strength to cover the twenty-five miles that now separated him from the advanced force. Not until July 1/2 could the first of Dunbar's wagons be dragged despairingly to a camp between the Great Crossing of the Youghiogheny and the site of George's battle of the previous July. Probably on July 1, a messenger arrived with orders from Braddock to forward beeves and one hundred pack horses loaded with flour.

Doubtless by the bearer of this order, the officers at Dunbar's camp were given news of Braddock's advance. Progress had been slow, as George had apprehended. The men had felt that their numbers were too small for the work they had to do. Poor food caused grumbling. Still more complaint was made because the men had nothing to drink but water. Struggle with road and river had carried Braddock and his men by nightfall of June 30 no farther than one mile beyond Stewart's crossing of the Youghiogheny north of Gist's.

George did not attempt to go with Adam Stephen and the guard of a hundred men for the train of pack-horses that carried the flour from Dunbar's camp to Braddock's force. He still was far too weak for the long rides on horseback, but the next time wagons started for the front, George climbed feebly into one of them. On the eighth Washington had his reward for the pain of his journey. He reached the army about two miles from the east bank of the Monongahela and not more than twelve miles from Fort DuQuesne. George found, as always, a hearty welcome at Headquarters that were busy with important decisions after a march that had been arduous but not costly in life. He had arrived in time: One more day's march, that of the ninth and then . . . Fort DuQuesne and "the land in the Fork," which he had said, when first he had seen it, "I think extremely well situated for a fort". . . . He had come back to share in taking it . . . and in holding it!

It is not in the heart of man, aroused at two o'clock in the morning, to have cheer or conscious, pulsing courage; but when the British camp began to stir at that hour on July 9 there was confidence as well as expectancy in the minds of those who knew the plan for marching on Fort DuQuesne. Even soldiers of cautious mind felt that if the troops, artillery and wagons could get across the Monongahela unresisted, the remainder of the campaign would be easy.

George's responsibility was neither for strategy nor for tactics but for being mounted and afield on the day of all days in his twenty-three years.

His fever and his pain were gone; but they had left him so weakened that he did not know whether he could endure the jolt of a fast-moving horse. He determined to try it, and, to lessen his ordeal, he procured cushions and tied them into his saddle.

Starting his mixed column was such slow work that watches pointed to eight o'clock when Braddock reached the first crossing. Passage of the river was easy. When it had been completed, Braddock formed his line of march and set off down a road that had been cut roughly parallel to the stream. The General, George and others had proceeded a mile only when a messenger brought fine news: Colonel Gage presented his compliments to His Excellency and begged to report that he had completed the second crossing without encountering opposition and had taken position as ordered, on the right bank where his guns commanded the lower ford. En route to the first shallow, Gage had flushed thirty Indians, who had made off. At the second crossing the men of the advance guard had noticed that the water was muddy, as if there had been recent passing, and they had seen many footprints on the river bank. If these particulars were reported to Braddock, no importance was attached to them.

The march along the left bank continued without incident until, at length, the head of the column halted at a point slightly downstream from the mouth of Turtle Creek, which flowed into the Monongahela from the opposite side. As George and his companions looked, they saw on the other bank a sandy bluff about twelve feet high through which St. Clair's men busily were cutting an incline at the point chosen for the passage of the troops. The advanced parties were across the river at the place where a vigilant enemy might have repelled them. Braddock proceeded, in spite of this clear advantage, to do what his English and German seniors had said an officer should do in a like situation: he ordered all the vehicles drawn up properly on the bank and posted pickets on the high ground behind him. Then he and his officers had opportunity of examining the country ahead of them as far as it was visible from their position.

Inspection was as deliberate as the prospect was beautiful. Completion of the passageway through the bluff occupied St. Clair's men until almost 2 P.M. When the incline at last was ready, Braddock sent Captain Morris to order Gage and St. Clair to start down the ridge with their detachments and open a road as they advanced. After the last of the advanced parties had cleared the other side of the ford, Braddock gave the word for his column to cross. It was easily and flawlessly done—in George's eyes the most thrilling sight of his entire life.

As the men came up the incline from the river the line of march was complete. In front were the guides and a few of Stewart's Company of Virginia Light Horse. Behind them was the engineer who was blazing the trees that had to be felled to provide a roadway. His task was not difficult. The woods were so open that a vehicle could be driven almost anywhere among the trees. Besides, orders were to prepare a twelve-foot road—no wider. All that was needed now, in the judgment of the responsible officers was room enough for the guns and wagons. The men could look after themselves. Gage's covering party followed in files four deep. On the flanks were the grenadier companies, spread in parties of twenty men, each under a sergeant. Next were the carpenters and pioneers, and then the two six-pounders with the ammunition wagon and a guard. Together, these men were the advanced force. Closing on them now was Lieutenant Colonel Burton with the vanguard, most of the wagons and part of the guns. The rearguard, with the remainder of the cannon, was under Colonel Halkett. If the proper intervals were being observed, everything was in the best style of the regular establishment.

Half-past two o'clock and close to 1500 men confidently in motion; then, suddenly, the sound of firing from the front! George was stiff in the saddle at the first crash. So was every officer.

Harry Gordon, the engineer, had ridden ahead of the advanced guard to find the guides and had been looking for them when they hurried back and reported the enemy close at hand. The engineer had seen about three hundred men, French and Indians, approaching on the run. At their head was an officer who wore a piece of decorative armor at his neck. He, too, was looking vigilantly ahead but had not yet discovered the British. When the French commander caught a glimpse of the grenadiers, he motioned with his arms. His men then divided to encircle the head and flanks of the British column. An Indian warwhoop swelled through the woods and froze the blood of the soldiers who never before had heard that sound. After their first startled fright, the grenadiers delivered a volley and then loaded and fired again. Some of their bullets brought down the conspicuous French officers and a number of Indians, but the Redmen and their white comrades did not intend to form line of battle and exchange volleys with the British in the woods. Before most of the English soldiers saw a single rifleman, the French and Indians disappeared, quickly and mysteriously. The hair-raising whoops continued. Down both flanks the fire spread. Soon it began to strike the British from the high ground on the right of the halted column. All except one of the English flanking parties ran in; one company of grenadiers and one of carpenters were in danger of being cut off. The whole of the advanced force fell back fifty or sixty yards.

The Captains and lieutenants were able to restore a confused line, but it was for a few minutes only. Bulking above the heads of the crouching troops, the mounted leaders were ideal targets for the invisible marksmen. Down the officers tumbled from their steeds, dead or wounded. Most of those who escaped with their lives lost their horses. Colonel Gage kept his saddle, but he found few subordinates to help him rally men who had no idea how to fight an enemy they could not see. Now Sir John St. Clair rode up to ascertain what was happening—and got the information in the form of a bullet through his body.

In rear of what had been the right flank the fire was heavier every minute. With front and both flanks thus enveloped, the British were within a half-moon of yelling adversaries. Suddenly the rumor spread that the French and Indians were attacking the baggage train. Stunned men under triple fire from an unseen foe did not stop to ask whether the rumor had probability. They concluded instantly that if the enemy was closing on their rear, they soon would be surrounded, scalped, massacred. With one impulse,

Gage's men ran eastward, carried St. Clair's workers along, abandoned the two six-pounders—and stumbled into the uncertain files of Burton's vanguard which had been advancing to their support up the twelve-foot road. The situation was completely beyond the control of the few officers who remained on horseback.

Now Braddock rode up, attended by George. The General had waited only a few minutes at the point where he had halted the column. Then he had started for the front. At first he was half paralyzed by the indescribable confusion and the unfamiliar ground. Braddock could not decide, on the instant, what to do or how to do it. While he hesitated, St. Clair made his way through the press of men and called to the General for God's sake to take the northern hill in order to keep the army from being surrounded. Before the Quartermaster could say more, he lost consciousness because of his wound.

Capt. Thomas Waggener, a veteran of Fort Necessity, had kept his men together and now undertook to lead them up the hill to the trunk of a great fallen tree that he thought he could use as a parapet. He succeeded in getting there with the loss of three men only, but to his amazement he found himself subjected to the fire of British who mistook his company for French. Some of the regular officers concluded that he and his soldiers were attempting to run away, and they discouraged those who were willing to reenforce him. In getting back under fire, the Captain lost all except thirty of his men.

Braddock at last realized that the hill must be wrested from the savages and that the two six-pounders must be recaptured. He sent George off to find officers and tell them to organize one party of 150 to charge up the hill and another party of like size to recover the cannon. George managed to stay in his saddle despite his weakness. During the action, he had two horses shot under him, but he found another and skillfully made his way through the woods. His tall figure was a mark for hidden riflemen. One of them sent a bullet through his hat; another bullet, a third, and still another slit his uniform with hot lead.

Braddock again and again undertook to rally the men, to form a line and lead them against the hidden enemy and the high ground north of the road. Nothing could be done. The survivors would not budge. At last, in desperation, he decided to withdraw to the right and east in order to cover his wagons. The General did not proceed far with this. Already five bullets had struck the horses he had ridden; now it was his turn. A missile crashed through his right arm and penetrated his lungs. After he was placed on the ground he remained conscious, but of course, could not direct the withdrawal to the wagons.

The situation was desperate but not altogether hopeless. Two hundred men were held together by uninjured commanders and by officers returning from the surgeons with bandaged wounds. These troops, keeping their heads, still were able to hold the enemy at a distance, though they were deaf to every order to mount the eminence or to rush out and put the six-pounders into action.

Those officers who had received the order to withdraw to the wagons undertook to do so and carry their commands with them. They were powerless. The men in the road stayed where they were and continued their blind fire. Orders no longer meant anything. Hopelessly the men continued to ram home their charges and to level their pieces aimlessly. Ammunition was almost exhausted; few officers remained on their feet; the cannon were deserted; the rain of bullets from hidden marksmen did not cease or even diminish. That same paralyzing, fiendish whoop of the savages rang through woods carpeted with dead and dying men. Frightened soldiers plunged past comrades of stouter heart and gave themselves to mad panic. Many of the troops threw away arms, even parts of their clothing, to speed their flight down to the river. Soon the straggling men were choking the passageway that led to the crossing.

When all hope of rallying the soldiers on the right bank was gone, George's first duty was to get the wounded General safely across the river. Washington found a little cart that had not lost its team and into this put Braddock, who still was master of himself. In the company of the best of the troops, Washington then descended to the bank and, under fire, conveyed the hard-breathing commander over the ford. Had George looked back while he was crossing, he would have seen some battle-maddened Indians plunge into the water and kill exhausted fugitives there. Otherwise, there was no immediate pursuit. Most of the savages remained on the battlefield to plunder the wagons, rob the dead, and scalp the wounded and the slain. If the savages had not stopped to pillage, they might have confronted the survivors from the right bank at the upper ford. Had the French and their allies done that, then all the British who had escaped from the battleground might have been starved or slaughtered.

With Burton and Orme, George now shared the task of trying to restore order among the survivors. High ground was chosen, about a quarter of a mile from the river and some two hundred yards from the road—a position strong enough to be held till Colonel Dunbar came up. Burton made an appeal to the soldiers and prevailed upon the least shaken of them to serve as outposts. Braddock observed this, approved it, and directed George to ride farther back along the line of the morning advance and rally the men who had fled in that direction.

Obediently, George turned his horse's head. Beyond the upper ford, he found Lieutenant Colonel Gage. How the commander of the advance party got that far to the rear, George did not ascertain. Gage had with him eighty men, whom he apparently had rallied and now had under some discipline. George, about sundown, recrossed the upper ford to return to Braddock. On the way back to the hill the officers had agreed to make their stronghold, George met a grim cavalcade—Braddock and such of the troops as had held to their duty after the first panic was overcome. The other soldiers had slipped away from the eminence and were trying to put more distance between them and the enemy.

Nothing remained except to retreat as quickly as possible without further loss. Colonel Dunbar was supposed to be at no great distance; he could cover the retreat and could forward provisions and liquor to the hungry and exhausted men. For sending orders to Dunbar, Braddock looked once more to young Washington. Having been on horseback for more than twelve mad hours of incredible strain, George had to set out again. He did, though he had to muster all his moral courage to undertake it.

It seemed impossible for any human being to keep his saddle after twenty-four hours and more of riding, fighting, and witnessing the horrors of the battlefield. George gripped his saddle with exhausted knees and held fast to his bridle-rein. The resolution that had carried him through the snow-covered wilderness and over the floating ice of the Allegheny did not fail him now. Late in the morning of July 10, George's horse staggered into the area of Dunbar's wagons, near "Rock Fort" seven miles northwest of Great Meadows, the Virginian so fatigued and overwrought that he scarcely was able to discharge his mission.

Rumor of bad news had spread through the camp after nine o'clock that day. The whisper was that Braddock's force had been wiped out. About noon, Colonel Dunbar lost his head and ordered the drummers to beat "To arms." Instead of bringing the men to their places, this spread panic among cowardly soldiers and teamsters. Some of them broke for the rear as if the enemy were about to open fire. The impulse to retreat gripped even officers. Fortunately, Dunbar recovered sufficient self-command to resolve to hold his position at least for the next night. The wagons for which George brought orders were hitched, loaded with supplies, and sent forward.

George did not go with the convoy; his powerful will could not drive his exhausted body any longer. He had to remain at Dunbar's to rest, but, when he awakened on the morning of the eleventh, he found new anxiety in the confusion of the camp and in the virtual disappearance of all discipline. Demoralization was so general that Dunbar probably deserved credit for being able to comply with a further order from Braddock to send to him additional wagons and two companies of infantry.

In the evening, Braddock and the main body of wounded and un-hurt survivors arrived at Dunbar's Camp. The General had been trans-ferred from the cart to a hand-litter and, when soldiers refused to carry him, he had been forced about 3 P.M. on the tenth to mount a horse. How he endured the agony of his wound on the long ride none could understand; but he retained consciousness and undertook to give orders. He directed that available teams be assigned for the wounded, the two six-pounder cannon that had been left with Dunbar, and such indispensable provisions as could be conveyed by the remaining animals. Everything else was to be destroyed. Then the crippled army was to be removed farther from the victorious enemy.

Braddock had not been talkative at any time after he left the Mo-nongahela, but his orders and his few remarks indicated that he had suffered no loss of memory through shock and that he knew what was happening around him. "Who would have thought it?" he asked, in ref-erence to the defeat. Now, after he had traversed approximately one mile of the road between Rock Fort and Great Meadows, he received an inquiry from Dunbar concerning some doubtful question. This seemed to make Braddock realize that he should not attempt to direct the retreat. He called

Dunbar to him and in a few words turned over the command to the Colonel. About two miles west of Great Meadows, Braddock called a halt. To Orme, Braddock gave new instructions: he must acquaint Keppel promptly with what had happened, and must tell him that "nothing could equal the gallantry and good conduct of the officers nor the bad behavior of the men." In that pride of his corps and with that shame of his troops, the General died about 9 P.M. on July 13.

George was charged with the burial of the defeated General. George had by no means recovered from his own strain but he had strength enough to perform the last services for a man who had admired him and had given him coveted opportunity. On the morning of the fourteenth, he selected a place in the road near the head of the column and there had a squad dig a short, deep trench. He chose that spot because the French Indians might hear of the death of Braddock and seek to find the grave in order that they might disinter and maltreat the body. When the ground was ready, George had the General's corpse brought forward with such honors of war as the condition of the troops permitted. Then, when the column began to move eastward again, he had all the wagons pass over the grave and all the footmen tramp the earth down, so that no mark of the burial should remain. The device was successful. French and Indians learned that Braddock had expired but they did not find his grave.

On the brief remainder of the march to Fort Cumberland, George's particular care was for the comfort of his fellow staff-officers, Morris and Orme, and of their traveling-companion, Colonel Burton. All three were on horse-litters, and by the morning of the sixteenth, they were safe at the fort. The wounded who reached Wills Creek numbered twenty-three officers and 364 men. The final list of casualties was to show sixty-three officers and 914 men killed or wounded, a total of 977 in a force of 1459. Virginians had sustained losses that almost destroyed the three participating companies.

These Virginia casualties became the more serious in the face of what George heard of plans. He knew by mid-July that Dunbar intended to leave Fort Cumberland and proceed to Philadelphia. This meant, as George wrote Dinwiddie, "there will be no men left here unless it is the poor remains of the Virginia troops who survive and will be too small to guard our frontiers." More than that Washington did not say concerning Dunbar's decision, which was based on the belief that the situation was hopeless.

On the death of Braddock, George's appointment as a volunteer aide had come to an end. He still was willing to work to redeem the disaster, but he felt that as the army had been "drove in thus far"—to Wills Creek—he was at liberty to go home when his strength permitted. By the twenty-second, he was able to undertake the journey. On July 26 he had the joy of drawing rein on his own lawn.

All the way back to Fort Cumberland and to Mount Vernon George heard the complaints of soldiers who felt they had been led into the wilderness to be slaughtered. Officers who survived the battle had praise for their corps and contempt for the alleged cowardice of the ranks. Criticism from other sources now became audible. George began to discover what Colonial Governors and public men thought of the campaign, and for months afterward he read comment on a defeat so overwhelming that it stunned the strongest. There was no disposition to take one inclusive view in England and another in America. Different men emphasized different mistakes of strategy and tactics, but geography did not shape the critique except in two particulars. One of these concerned blame of the Colonials for failing to furnish a sufficient number of horses and wagons; the other had to do with the superior attitude most of the British officers assumed in dealing with the Colonials.

The most general complaint was of Braddock's overconfidence in an unfamiliar country where warfare was different in almost every way from that for which he had been trained. Nearly everyone agreed that Braddock should have heeded the warnings of the Colonial officers. They told him, as plainly as they dared, that stand-up fighting and line fire would not avail in a heavily wooded country, where the men scattered and hid themselves while firing from shelter. Instead of changing his tactics, "General Braddock," as Adam Stephen said in accurate epitome, "unhappily placed his confidence and the whole dependence on the Regiments."

Doubtless to his last hour, Braddock believed that the failure to provide promptly the wagons, horses, flour and meat needed for the expedition denied him an early start that would have assured easy capture of Fort DuQuesne. Governor Dinwiddie was of the same mind, though he blamed Braddock, not the Colonies, for the delay. That the teams and the supplies were not placed at the disposal of Braddock when he expected them, none could deny; but so far as the Colonial governments were responsible, the reason was inexperience, not rascality. Had the Governors been informed accurately of what they could do, through contractors above the average in honesty, Braddock would have known what was practicable and what was not. It does not follow that he would have been sufficiently wise to use his wagons to establish a series of advance bases to one of which he might have withdrawn, after a disaster, without having to abandon the entire country west of the Allegheny Mountains. In war, good transportation never was a satisfactory substitute for good sense.

This, too, must be remembered: Vexatious as was the delayed arrival of the wagons, the nature of the country was such that, regardless of supplies, advance was not possible until the roads had been dried by the sun of May. Braddock at Fort Cumberland consequently did not have to chafe in idleness crying for more vehicles much more than a fortnight longer than he would have had to wait, in the best of conditions, for General Mud to retreat. Moreover, if the French figures of their own strength are correct Braddock stood on the defensive with something over 1400 men, speaking one language, to receive the attack of not more than 900 French, Canadians and Indians, a majority of whom could not communicate with one another. Delay did not give Braddock inferiority of force on the day of battle.

On the day of battle, what Braddock lacked primarily, in approaching the field, was not more wagons but more Indians. It is easy to exaggerate this failure of Braddock. Had he been diplomatic instead of blunt, skillful instead of inept, he scarcely could have been expected to overcome the advantage the French had gained before he reached America. Everything indicated that the defeat of Washington at Fort Necessity in 1754 led the Shawnees and the Mingoes to conclude that the French would win the war. Even those tribes of the Six Nations that had long and friendly ties with England found it prudent to remain neutral if not openly to espouse the cause of Britain's adversary. Braddock's country thus had lost temporarily the support of the Indians before he so much as had a chance to woo them. He needed allies in order to win a victory; he could not hope to regain the allies until he had won the victory. It was an impossible situation.

Braddock was entirely ignorant of the type of combat that prevailed in America. What was worse, he was not a man to learn. He lacked all originality of mind and exemplified the system that produced and schooled him, a system traditional, methodical and inflexible. A man of his training was not apt to fail to do everything the regulations and the accepted tactics prescribed. It was still less likely he would do anything more. Braddock believed that the tactics in which he had been drilled for forty years were close to perfection; but he did not even apply well the tactics in which he and his troops were trained. He was inexcusably careless in not making certain that Gage had reconnoitred thoroughly before proceeding towards Fort DuQuesne from the lower ford. The result contains a warning to every soldier: Great dangers often are rendered small by vigilance; lesser dangers always are enlarged by negligence.

On either side of Braddock's advanced parties, at the time Gage met the enemy, there chanced to be ravines sufficiently deep to serve as natural trenches for the French and Indians. These ravines were close enough to afford the enemy a perfect field of fire against the head and flanks of the British column. Braddock's guides and engineers had not discovered them or else, finding them empty, had disregarded them. Once the French and their savage allies had occupied the gulleys without being observed, the question was whether the British would charge and clear the ground. If they did not, the only other question was that of the slaughter the British would endure before they broke and ran.

Washington's responsibility at the time of the debacle was limited by his position. As a volunteer aide-de-camp he had no troops under his command. According to the letter of military usage, he discharged his duty when he delivered the General's orders and set an example of courage and diligence in action. There remains the moral question whether he did all he should have done in making his experience available to Braddock. Obviously, the three matters that related most directly to the lessons George had learned in 1754 were, first, the employment of pack horses instead of wagons; second, the necessity of fighting the French Indians in their own way, and, third, the wisdom or unwisdom of making the final advance with a part only of the small army, in light order. George was correct in urging pack animals, though shortage of transport was not decisive. He did all that a volunteer aide-de-camp could do in warning his seniors concerning the tactics of their forest foe. In advising Braddock to divide the army and to hasten forward with a small, light column, George was incorrect in some of his reasoning; but Braddock's acceptance of George's plan did not give him inferiority of force on the day of battle, nor, probably, would rejection by Braddock of the advice of Washington, and the consequent employment of the entire army, have changed the outcome.

George's military conscience was clear.

CHAPTER / 4

At the time, George Washington was not of mind nor of mood to consider Braddock's strategy. The nearer realities of fatigue and humiliation absorbed the young Virginian. Old resentments rose again; George's military experience seemed to be a succession of unregarded sacrifices. He would not have it so another time! Never would he engage on the same terms. Command must be his, and under conditions he would himself impose.

Both Dunbar and Sharpe considered a westward advance impractical, and Colonel Dunbar had the troops leave Fort Cumberland and proceed to Philadelphia. Dinwiddie protested: Dunbar had no authority whatsoever for carrying them to Philadelphia—to go into "winter quarters" in the middle of August! As Dinwiddie saw it, the British had opened an easy road of French advance from the Ohio to the Virginia frontier. The worst seemed to be in prospect when Indians appeared in Maryland and on the northwestern frontier of Virginia and began to murder isolated families.

It was manifest from the hour the General Assembly met on August 5 that what was left of the Virginia Regiment must be augmented, equipped and assigned the task of dealing with the savages and with any French who might descend on the frontier. This prospect aroused George's interest and led him to consider a journey to Williamsburg, but he was discouraged by continued physical weakness and conviction that he could not get a new command on terms he would care to accept. He abandoned the idea of visiting the capital and began to devote such energies as he possessed to his private affairs and the musters he was expected to hold as District Adjutant.

As August slipped by and the exposure of the frontier became apparent, George underwent a slight change of mind. On August 13 he received a letter from his friend and cousin, Warner Lewis, who had been in Williamsburg the previous week: The General Assembly had voted £40,000 for the defence of the Colony; there was talk of raising as many as four thousand men to repel the French and Indians. "Everyone of my acquaintance," Lewis wrote, "profess[es] a fondness for your having the command of the men now to be raised."

Within a week George had more positive information: He learned that Dinwiddie was willing to name him commander of the forces to be raised. He felt that he should go to Williamsburg and hear what the Governor might propose. Before George reached Williamsburg, Dinwiddie issued commissions to Captains of most of the sixteen companies that were to be formed into a regiment. This must have been a disappointment to George. When he had written Lewis of the conditions under which he might accept command he had put first "having the officers in some measure appointed with *my* advice, and with my concurrence."

Dinwiddie offered George command of the enlarged Regiment and met the other conditions he had imposed—that he have a military chest and two needed assistants, one an aide-de-camp and the other a secretary. If Commissary Charles Dick resigned, as he had indicated he would, Colonel Washington would be free to name his successor. Finally, there was a new distinction: George would not only be in charge of the Regiment but also "commander of all the forces that now are or may be employed in the country's service." Everything was offered except that which George considered most essential, a voice in the selection of his subordinate officers.

Would Colonel Washington accept? With all thanks to the Governor for the compliment paid him, he would *not*. Dinwiddie was not prepared for George's refusal, but the Scotch Governor was not to be downed. At length, he offered a compromise: As he had named the Captains, George might select the field officers. This meant much, not only as the vindication of a principle but also because it assured George the continuing service of Adam Stephen and Andrew Lewis, whom he had tested. Probably, also, at some stage of the negotiations and without the Governor's knowledge, members of the committee charged with the expenditure of funds made a financial proposal that appealed to Washington: he could have pay of 30s. a day, £100 yearly for his table, an allowance for batmen and a commission of 2 per cent on all funds he handled. When all the considerations were weighed, George concluded that if he stood to lose reputation by assuming a difficult command, he might lose still more in public esteem by persistent refusal.

Once he said "Yes," August 31, 1755, all his energies were given to his new duties. He issued recruiting orders promptly to the officers in Williamsburg and left September 3 with a small amount of public funds to resume active duty.

The new Commander-in-Chief found trouble at the first town he reached after he left Williamsburg. When he arrived in Fredericksburg September 5, he learned that as volunteers had not been forthcoming, some vagrants had been drafted. The recruits had protested so violently that it had been necessary to lock them in jail to prevent desertion. This had incensed friends of the prisoners, who had broken into the building, released the mutineers, and defied the militia officers. A more ominous beginning to the campaign for new troops George scarcely could have experienced. It convinced him that drafted men would be worthless as soldiers unless they were under strong officers who would have the weapon of positive and punitive law. Major Lewis, who had the firmness and vigor to control the men, was directed to come to Fredericksburg and assume command there.

George had another disillusioning experience in Fredericksburg. He had been told by Dinwiddie that it would be well to retain Dick, who had threatened to cancel an agreement he had made to deliver provisions and supplies at Wills Creek. George saw Dick and on September 6 talked fully with him. He was not satisfied that Dick's heart was in the enterprise. Thus, the old difficulty of provisioning the army, the old problem of getting food to the frontier, was rising once more. It seemed to be one of the essential things that somehow never were well done.

From Fredericksburg George rode to Alexandria where he found a situation scarcely better. At the regular muster of the militia an effort had been made to get recruits for the Regiment. Not a man stepped forward. The new officers who had accepted commissions to raise troops began to express apprehension of failure as soon as they had the coveted papers in their hands. No men, no discipline, no clothing, no organization, no money—within a week after Washington had taken command, more and more of the story of the spring of 1754 was repeating itself.

George hurried on to Winchester and to Wills Creek and Fort Cumberland. This badly placed defence was not yet complete and still was exposed to easy rifle-fire from woods that had been left standing across the creek. The garrison consisted of the survivors of the Virginia Regiment, together with the Maryland Company of Capt. John Dagworthy, who had been with Braddock's army. Many had deserted, but 198 rank and file remained. Stephen was nominally in command but he did not have the men under firm discipline. With his usual amiability in his treatment of officers, Washington set his subordinates to their duties. After that, orders were issued in steady flow—to deal with drunkenness, swearing and obscene language, to terminate traffic in liquor, to complete the work on the fort and, in general, to improve discipline.

As soon as he had put affairs in order at Fort Cumberland, Washington started up the Shenandoah Valley, past Winchester, and over the Allegheny Mountains. By September 25, he reached Fort Dinwiddie. Its condition was bad enough to dishearten. Troops who had erected the stockade had answered so many alarms that they had not had time to build the bastions. Ammunition was low. There was no salt for fresh meat and no prospect of pickling any beef for winter unless salt, tools and implements were sent.

Far worse were conditions to the west. On the Greenbrier River the approach of Indian raiders in August had caused settlers to hurry to a feeble little fort. About sixty persons had been huddling there when the Indians descended on them. The defenders in four days lost thirteen and perhaps more before the savages made off. The Indians, in addition, took perhaps a dozen lives, carried off two girls, burned eleven houses and slaughtered or drove with them horses and cattle estimated to number five hundred.

This hurried tour of inspection dramatized the impossibility of George's task in defending a long frontier with a handful of men. Recruiting had to be expedited. Lives depended on it. So did the security of the Colony, and, in part, the recovery of the Ohio. The experience of his first month in command convinced him that he had a multitude of perplexities some of which must be discussed with the Governor and with the Burgesses' committee on expenditures. Washington stopped at Alexandria only long enough to issue some essential orders, and then took the road to the capital.

George had proceeded as far as the plantation of his friend Col. John Baylor on October 7 when an express pushed up the lane with a dispatch from Stephen. This bore date of Winchester, October 4, and began: "Matters are in the most deplorable situation at Fort Cumberland." There followed some information about items of less importance at the fort and then: "Unless relief is sent to the back inhabitants immediately none will stay on this side Monocasy or Winchester." George read on: "I have reason to believe Captain Dagworthy will look upon himself as commanding officer after you have joined the troops."

That sentence may or may not have stuck in Washington's mind at the moment. The rest of the letter shaped instant duty: he must report the situation to the Governor; he must tell His Honor he could not proceed to Williamsburg; and he must go back full speed to Fredericksburg and thence to the frontier.

Within less than three hours after he wrote the Governor, George rode into Fredericksburg where he met Stephen, who, like himself, had started for Williamsburg. The Lieutenant Colonel had an even worse situation to report than described in his letter. Washington listened, put the new information in focus, left Fredericksburg late on the eighth and proceeded to Winchester. When he arrived there he found a madhouse. Except at Fort Necessity and on the dreadful day of Braddock's defeat, he never had encountered so much confusion and panic. Facing it, he kept his head and went instantly to work.

On the eleventh George wrote the Governor of the situation and of his inability under existing statutes to compel the obedience of the militia. Less than six weeks after his appointment to command, he was so discouraged that he talked of quitting. He told Dinwiddie: "I must with great regret decline the honor that has been so generously intended me; and for this only reason I do it—the foreknowledge I have of failing in every point that might justly be expected from a person invested with full power to exert his authority."

About 8 P.M. that evening a fear-stricken express staggered into Winchester with a report that Indians had reached a plantation about twelve miles from the town and that the settlers in that neighborhood were fleeing. George strengthened the guard and sent two scouts to ascertain how numerous the Indians were and in what direction they were moving. On the morning of October 12 another express dashed into Winchester, "ten times more terrified," as George judged him, than the man who had arrived the previous evening.

The next day brought a change for the better. Although George received information that the militia on the South Branch intended to leave their post, reports from scouts were that the Indians were leaving the stream. Major Lewis, with the recruits from Fredericksburg, was within one day's march of Winchester. Capt. Thomas Waggener arrived on the morning of the thirteenth with thirty men after a rapid advance from Alexandria. George now sent out expresses on all the roads to assure fleeing farmers that danger was past and posted public notice that the Indians were believed to have returned home and that the frontiers soon would be well guarded. Preparations were made, also, for Washington himself to proceed to Fort Cumberland to strengthen its garrison.

Wills Creek was reached on October 25. Fort Cumberland was intact, though Indians had come almost within gunshot. Families of nearby settlements had been victims of cruelty that made survivors blanch. On one farm, the unburied bodies of a scalped woman, a small boy and a young man lay near a burned house. A party of soldiers found three persons who had been brained with stakes, scalped and thrown into a fire that had half consumed the victims. Adequate security, in Washington's opinion, depended on four things—recruiting the Regiment to full strength, strengthening the militia law, a successful effort to procure the services of friendly Indians, and erection of a few small, temporary forts to serve as cover for rangers and their provisions.

In settling such of these matters as had to be arranged north of the Potomac, Washington moved fast because he had encountered a stubborn man who had raised a contentious issue, John Dagworthy, Captain of the Maryland Company at Fort Cumberland. In 1746 Dagworthy had received a royal commission as Captain and had undertaken to raise a company to share in the Canadian expedition. He worked hard and had 103 officers and men in his company, one of five raised in New Jersey, but those troops saw no active service. After they were discharged, Dagworthy and another captain went to England, with the endorsement of the Council of New Jersey, to see if they could continue as officers of the regular establishment. They did not succeed in this ambition, but Dagworthy effected an arrangement whereby he received a sum of money in lieu of half pay or further service. He was not, apparently, required to return the document by which he had been commissioned in 1746. Sometime after his return to America, Dagworthy removed to Maryland. He was residing there when, in August 1754, Governor Sharpe undertook to raise a company for the defence of the frontier. Command of this small force was given Dagworthy. It participated in Braddock's campaign, during the course of which Dagworthy asserted that his royal commission of 1746–48 still obtained and therefore gave him seniority over Colonial officers. Braddock had to sustain this contention and, indeed, to admit that Dagworthy, by date of commission, outranked all except two Captains of the regiments from England. With the defeat of Braddock and the scattering of the forces, Dagworthy's contention temporarily was forgotten, but about October 1, 1755, he returned to Fort Cumberland, where some thirty survivors of his Maryland Company were included in the garrison. Command of the fort had been vested by Dinwiddie and then by Braddock in Colonel Innes, who, on leaving the post, had assigned the command to Stephen as senior officer present. Dagworthy insisted that he outranked Stephen and had authority to direct affairs at the fort. He did not push his argument to the point where he actually gave orders to the Virginia Regiment, but he contrived to take over the fort itself from Stephen and he demanded and received all the honors due the commander.

There was no disposition on the part of George or of Dinwiddie to discredit Dagworthy, but neither would admit the validity of Dagworthy's assertion of the right of command. There was a question in their minds whether his royal commission had not lapsed when he was given a flat sum on expiration of service instead of being put on half pay. However that might be, Dagworthy, as the Virginians saw it, would have been entitled to command if, but only if, he had been sent to Fort Cumberland by the King's order to serve where regular and Colonial troops were stationed together. He had not come to the fort under orders "from home" but by direction of the Governor of Maryland. Dagworthy, in George's eyes, was the Captain of thirty Maryland soldiers—that and no more. So firmly was Washington convinced of this, and so fully determined to maintain his seniority, that he resolved he would surrender his commission before he would accept Dagworthy's pretensions to command. At the same time, George remembered that Braddock had recognized Dagworthy's commission and reasoned that he might have to accept the Captain's orders so long as he was at Fort Cumberland. In the circumstances, it was desirable to leave the fort before this issue came to a test.

Another reason for finishing speedily all official business on Wills Creek was a letter from Dinwiddie concerning better regulation of the Virginia troops. The Governor wrote that he realized the defects of the existing military statutes and had called the General Assembly to meet on October 27 and correct them. He hoped George would be in attendance to explain the need of stronger laws. Washington could not possibly get to Williamsburg by the date the session opened, but he determined to go there as fast as he might.

As the revised bill stood when George arrived from the frontier, it provided the death penalty for mutiny, desertion, the refusal of an officer to obey his superior, and and any act of violence by such an officer against the person of a senior. Lesser punishment might be meted out at the discretion of a court martial. If such a court decreed death, two-thirds of the members had to concur. Execution could not be carried out until the Governor had reviewed and approved the sentence. Provision was made for the apprehension of deserters and the reward of persons who captured the culprits and returned them to their command. Some defects of this act may have been apparent to George when he first read its terms. Others were to be brought to light by test, but, despite imperfections, the act was so much stronger than the law it replaced that Washington was encouraged.

Encouragement there was, also, in dealing with the pretensions of Dagworthy. George explained more fully to the Governor this revival of the issue of the seniority of royal commissions. Dinwiddie was irritated. He could not see the slightest basis for Dagworthy's argument. The Governor felt he must renew to his home government his request that the officers of the Virginia Regiment be given King's commissions. Meantime, he would write General Shirley and ask that the acting British commander issue brevet commissions to Washington, Stephen and Lewis at the rank they held in Virginia service. This would give them a status Dagworthy could not challenge. Until Shirley passed on this request there could be no settlement of the dispute unless the Maryland officer receded from his position.

It was the middle of November when George set out for Winchester via Fredericksburg. At the Rappahannock town, George received reports from Stephen and others of quiet on the frontiers. The greatest need was a large supply of salt for pickling beef. George reasoned that he would do better to get the salt than to proceed in person to the Valley. If all went well, he told himself, he could remain near home, encouraging recruiting, until Dinwiddie received an answer from Shirley. By waiting on the lower Potomac George, moreover, could avoid a clash of authority with Dagworthy.

On December 5, George wrote the Governor for the first time since he had left Williamsburg. He explained that he had come to Alexandria to get salt and to procure recruits and supplies, and then blurted: "I have impatiently expected to hear the result of your Honor's letter to General Shirley and wish that the delays may not prove ominous. In that case, I shall not know how to act, for I can never submit to the command of Captain Dagworthy, since you have honored me with the command of the Virginia Regiment &c." George went on to discuss some vexations in supplying the troops and next, as if conscious his absence from Wills Creek might be criticized, he wrote: "As I cannot now conceive that any great danger can be apprehended at Fort Cumberland this winter, I am sensible that my constant attendance there cannot be so serviceable as riding from place to place, making the proper dispositions and seeing that all our necessaries are forwarded up with dispatch. I therefore think it advisable to inform your Honor of it, hoping that it will correspond with your own opinion."

No news came from Shirley. Such information concerning Dagworthy as reached George from Fort Cumberland was an added blow to the pride of the Virginia Colonel. Stephen still had not formally surrendered command of the fort or of the troops to Dagworthy, but he had not resisted with vigor the exercise of authority by the Captain. George's friends elsewhere were indignant that the commander of thirty Marylanders should presume to tell five hundred Virginians what they should and should not do.

Washington, about a week before Christmas, journeyed from Alexandria to Winchester. There, on the twenty-seventh, he received a letter Dinwiddie had written almost a fortnight previously. It was a paper to deepen depression. The Governor stated that the express had returned from New York, but that General Shirley had not reached the city when the messenger left. An answer from Shirley concerning Dagworthy's status might be expected soon by another hand.

Stephen came to Winchester shortly after New Year's Day, 1756, and brought word that Dagworthy held to the position previously taken. Washington heard from Stephen of other developments at Fort Cumberland—of a renewed petition by Virginia officers to be put on the regular establishment and of a discussion among them of the honors to which their own commanders were or were not entitled if Dagworthy actually had the authority for which he contended. On these matters George did not pass anticipatory judgment, and, as he felt he had done everything he could on the frontier for the time being, he started back to Alexandria during the second week of January. When George left the Shenandoah Valley his resolution was fixed: he would not accept Dagworthy as his superior officer. If he did not receive a favorable answer from Shirley, he would go to Boston in order to ask for a ruling on Dagworthy's status and to lay before the General a petition his officers had drawn up for inclusion in the regular establishment. In event this appeal was vain, George would resign.

George gradually learned what Shirley had done in answer to Dinwiddie's letter. The New England Governor and acting Commander-in-Chief wrote Dinwiddie December 4 that he had instructed Governor Sharpe to settle the dispute between Washington and Dagworthy. Sharpe promised compliance and wrote Dagworthy to confine himself to the command of the fort and not interfere with any troops in the barracks or assume any authority over the Virginians who might be posted there. Before Dinwiddie received information to this effect, Dagworthy had boasted at the fort that Sharpe had told him to keep the command. The Captain took care to obey the remainder of Sharpe's orders, but he said nothing about his orders to leave the Virginia troops to their own officers. Dinwiddie and Washington concluded, therefore, that Sharpe had not carried out the instructions of Shirley but, on the contrary, had written Dagworthy to retain the command previously exercised. When, therefore, Dinwiddie gave his approval to a personal appeal by Washington to Shirley, the Colonel did not permit the weather of midwinter to deter him. He would go to Boston to establish his seniority as readily as he had ridden to Fort Le Boeuf to deliver the message of the Governor.

Washington remembered the fine impression that Shirley had made on him at Alexandria, but he left nothing to chance. He would make his best approach. George planned to appear in a style that befitted the "Colonel of the Virginia Regiment and the Commander-in-Chief of all the forces that now are, and shall be raised &c &c." He arranged for Capt. George Mercer, his aide, to accompany him and act as paymaster. Capt. Robert Stewart, also, was to ride with his chief. George's body servant was to be in attendance. A second servant, Thomas Bishop, would be useful. He perfected his arrangements and, during the first days of February 1756, set out from Alexandria.

George and his companions reached Boston February 27. Governor Shirley received George with the courtesy and kindness that had impressed the young man at Alexandria. George delivered formally his officers' petition to be accepted on the regular establishment. Along with this he doubtless stated his opinion of Dagworthy's asserted right to command at Fort Cumberland. Shirley was surprised that the issue had arisen, because Sharpe had promised him months before to end the dispute. Now the General listened and questioned Washington concerning recruitment, prospects and support of the war by the southern Colonies. After a time Shirley said that he would consider the question of Dagworthy's status and would give George his decision later.

Apparently the Governor concluded that he could do nothing about the award of brevet commissions and the inclusion of the Virginia troops in the regular establishment, but on March 5, he called Washington to his office and gave him a paper that read:

Boston, 5 March, 1756

Governor Dinwiddie, at the instance of Colonel Washington, having referred to me concerning the right of command between him and Captain Dagworthy, and desiring that I should determine it, I do therefore give it as my opinion, that Captain Dagworthy, who now acts under a commission from the Governor of Maryland, and where there are no troops joined, can only take rank as a provincial Captain and of course is under the command of all field officers, and, in case it should happen, that Colonel Washington and Captain Dagworthy should join at Fort Cumberland, it is my order that Colonel Washington shall take the command.

W. SHIRLEY.

In a letter to Sharpe the General directed that Dagworthy either be removed from Fort Cumberland or else be informed that if he remained he had "put himself under the command of Colonel Washington." Shirley told Sharpe that Roger Morris had informed him Braddock had named Colonel Innes to command at Fort Cumberland and had so announced officially. "If that be so," Shirley wrote, "the matter must remain on the same foot [Braddock] put it upon."

It seemed a clear-cut victory for George, but there was one unhappy disclosure: On February 23, Shirley had appointed Sharpe to head all the troops to be raised in Pennsylvania, Maryland, Virginia and South Carolina. At the very minute Shirley was giving George seniority over Dagworthy, an express was spurring towards Maryland, with a commission under which the man whom George believed to be responsible for Dagworthy's stand would have control of him—and of the next expedition against Fort DuQuesne. The vindicated senior of Captain Dagworthy and the new subordinate of Governor Sharpe wasted no time in Boston after he received Shirley's decision. Once across the Potomac again, George scarcely paused before setting off for Williamsburg to report to Dinwiddie.

By the date George started from Mount Vernon to the capital, March 25, it was known generally that Sharpe had received command of all the forces to be raised in the south for another march to the Ohio. Sharpe had himself notified both the Governor of Virginia and Stephen, who still had in his care the Virginia troops at Fort Cumberland. Dinwiddie had been prompt to extend congratulations, but Stephen was chagrined. He wrote that Captain Dagworthy boasted of influence with the new commander and strutted more than ever. Actually, Sharpe undertook to execute Shirley's instruction that the Captain accept Washington's orders or leave the fort; but the Governor of Maryland believed George had created the tangle by staying away from Fort Cumberland after Dagworthy had been instructed to confine himself to command of the fort and not to interfere with the Virginia troops. Before many weeks were past, George was to confess: "I know that the unhappy difference about the command . . . has kept me from Fort Cumberland. . . ." At the moment, however, he was in no mood to admit that he had evaded a test of authority with Dagworthy. On the contrary, he felt aggrieved anew that his rival's friend and patron, Sharpe, had been put over him. It was futile to continue! When he reached Williamsburg he would resign.

When Washington arrived in Williamsburg March 30 the General Assembly was in session. The Burgesses realized that the recruiting of volunteers had not filled the Virginia Regiment and would not. A draft was unavoidable. Sentiment was strong for the construction of a long chain of small forts to protect the frontier, a policy which Washington believed the Colony could not execute without a far larger number of men than there was any reason to believe Virginia would call to service. Few hours were given Washington at the capital. There was not time, in fact, to explain to the Governor why he once again had resolved to resign. When the Colonel had been in Williamsburg only a day or two, an express brought bloody news: French and Indians had broken into the frontier settlements. Details were few; danger was acute. George started back to his command.

On the long, familiar road, George had time for reflection. Immediately ahead there might be excitement and tragedy. Then, sooner or later, there would be another offensive. With that in prospect, Washington's ambition triumphed over his pique and disappointment. Resignation seemed no longer to be demanded by his pride. If there was to be a march to Fort DuQuesne, he must share it—and, at the least, must be second in command. George did what more than once he had found effective—he asked directly for the position he wanted. He wrote a formal request to Shirley to commission him as second officer in the new enterprise.

George reached Winchester April 6 and found the people in "a general consternation." Indians had overrun most of the back settlements and murdered an unreckoned number of persons with the cruelty of hell's own tortures. Nearly all the frontier families had abandoned their homes and fled to Winchester or to the nearest of the few garrisoned stockades. George was almost helpless. In Winchester he could not muster more than forty armed men. Gunpowder was low. The greater part of supplies and provisions of the Regiment were at Fort Cumberland. From that base, Winchester virtually was cut off. Washington had endured and survived the raids of the previous autumn, but his experience then did not equip him to stop panic or deafen him to the horrible stories of murder and pillage.

Relief of a sort came suddenly. On the seventh, into George's quarters strode Richard Pearis, Indian trader and interpreter: He and some companions had run into a small party of Indians with whom they had exchanged fire for about half an hour. One of Pearis's men had been killed and two wounded, but the Virginians had hit several of the enemy and had slain the leader, a Frenchman. Pearis produced the scalp and a bag taken from the dead man. This bag contained instructions from the commander at Fort DuQuesne and identified the slain officer as the Sieur Douville. The instructions, signed by Dumas—a well-known officer who had distinguished himself in the battle of the Monongahela—bade Douville conform to the usages of honor and humanity and restrain the savages. At the same time, he was to undertake to burn the magazines at Conococheague, far inside the settlements. The very boldness of this design made the outcome of the first skirmish all the more pleasing to Washington. He forwarded Douville's scalp to Dinwiddie, with the recommendation that the men who took it be rewarded as Indians would have been for the same feat. The Colonel proceeded to send out scouting parties, but the killing of Douville appeared to have discouraged the raiders. Although frightened settlers continued to flee, no additional murders were reported for several days.

George took advantage of this breathing spell to plan for the future: At the earliest possible date he would undertake a sharp offensive. To succeed in this, he must have the aid of courageous Redmen immediately. "Indians are the only match for Indians," Washington said, "and without these we shall ever fight upon unequal terms." Looking beyond the instant crisis Washington reasoned that troops of the type of his own Virginia Regiment had to be the backbone of any permanent force. As he did not think it possible to procure volunteers, he reasoned that the new draft should be of able-bodied marksmen for a term of eighteen to twenty months. By the end of that period, George somewhat grimly observed, two campaigns would have brought "matters nearly to a crisis one way or other." The General Assembly was expected to vote £20,000 and authorize an increase of his command, by means of the draft, to two thousand men. All these troops George wished to incorporate into a single regiment, under his own direction, rather than to see them organized into two regiments, with someone else as colonel of the second.

On April 18 Colonel Innes arrived from Williamsburg, which he had visited after some months in North Carolina. Innes was not unwelcome *per se* at Winchester, but he was the bearer of a letter from Dinwiddie that infuriated Washington. The Governor enclosed a commission to hold courts martial, and then went brusquely on: "I hope the affairs of the Regiment are not in so bad a condition as represented here. The Assembly were greatly inflamed, being told that the greatest immoralities and drunkenness have been much countenanced, and proper discipline neglected; I am willing to think better of our officers and therefore suspend my judgment till I hear from you."

Washington wrote the Governor a vigorous denial. Then he made his indirect confession that pride and a desire to avoid possible humiliation at the hands of Dagworthy might have been responsible in part, for what now was alleged: "I . . . know that the unhappy difference about the command, which has kept me from Fort Cumberland, has consequently prevented me from *enforcing* the orders, which I never fail to *send*."

George was in this state of mind—sensitive, humiliated and half convinced of error—when, on April 19, a sergeant of the Virginia Regiment brought a most alarming report from Lieut. William Stark at Edwards's Fort. Stark reported a losing engagement in which two officers and fifteen men had been left, some of them dead, in the hands of the enemy. Stark's letter indicated that many French were participating and that they had surrounded, and were preparing to storm, the feeble defences.

Edwards's Fort was on Cacapon River in Hampshire County, distant not more than twenty miles from Winchester. The first attack might be preliminary; the town itself might be the real objective of a powerful raid. Washington called into council Colonel Innes and those officers of the Virginia Regiment in Winchester. What did the council recommend? Judgment was unanimous. The militia of Frederick and adjoining counties must be raised immediately; when a strong force was available, it should take the offensive.

Washington accepted these recommendations. Capt. William Peachey was hurried off to notify the Governor and ask for a muster of the militia. Lord Fairfax was urged to call on the militia of Frederick and the adjacent counties to move to Winchester as rapidly as possible. Washington did all that was recommended, but he felt that reliance of any sort on the militia was worse than doubtful.

Bad news followed bad. From several outposts George received expresses that informed him of isolation, threatened attack and shortage of provisions. The story was one of gloom, danger and murder. Indians and French were believed to be prowling almost every road; attack on Winchester appeared imminent. Every day, every hour—almost every minute as it seemed to George—brought new alarms, but no report of reenforcements. One express after another was dispatched with appeals for help from other counties. George sent a second officer to Williamsburg to explain the situation and ask for arms and ammunition.

He had learned from Williamsburg that the General Assembly probably would pass a bill for the erection of a new and longer chain of forts. His most recent information was, also, that the total armed force to be authorized by the lawmakers was to consist of only 1500 men. On the twenty-fourth George wrote a letter in which he put these two probabilities together and discussed the defensive policy of Virginia with as much of calm logic as if he had been, on an untroubled day, at the Governor's Palace or in the council chamber of the capitol. He did not muster all his arguments at the moment and had to return to the subject three days later; but in the two papers he disclosed ability to rid his eyes of the motes of the day and fix them in undeviating scrutiny on a single issue. His argument was not in vain. The bill for erecting the forts had been passed before his letters reached Williamsburg, but the measure was forthwith amended to authorize what he particularly recommended, a strong fort at Winchester.

George had to write the Governor April 27: "Desolation and murder still increase, and no prospects of relief. The Blue Ridge is now our frontier, no men being left in this County except a few that keep close with a number of women and children in forts, which they have erected for the purpose. There are now no militia in this County; when there were, they could not be brought to action."

The prospect now changed. Dinwiddie had not been idle. After Lord Fairfax's appeals for help had been sent out, the Governor had ordered the Lieutenants of Frederick and the nine counties east of the Blue Ridge and nearest the lower Shenandoah Valley to muster their militia, draft one-half of them, and have them rendezvous at Winchester. Almost to Washington's surprise, they "actually came."

By cruel chance, it now seemed that the invaders had begun to leave precisely when the militia commenced to reenforce the small Virginia Regiment. Information was scant and not convincing, but by the end of April it indicated that the raid was over and that the Indians had started back to Fort DuQuesne. Indeed, the Colonel had the embarrassing prospect of more militiamen than he could shelter or use or willingly would feed and pay at the expense of the Colony. In tones almost ludicrously different from those of his recent calls for help, George now wrote the Governor "humbly to offer it to Your Honor's superior judgment if it would not be advisable to stop all the militia that are ordered from the ten Counties, save about five or six hundred from the adjacent ones?"

There was no stopping the flow of militia once they began to descend on the Valley. Three days brought Washington about 670 militiamen. He had to elaborate his plans for employing them. Otherwise the "quarrelsome fellows" would war among themselves. It was difficult to find employment for all. After the garrisons were drafted and artisans enlisted, the others either should be dismissed or sent to defend the exposed southern part of the western frontier. To make a wise choice, George called the field officers into council on the fourteenth. They were unanimously against attempting to use the militia at a great distance and of one mind in advising the discharge of all not "absolutely necessary to resist a second invasion upon this quarter." Washington accepted this decision.

When he came to compute the number of militiamen required at the ten places he had chosen as their posts, he found he would need at least 482 of the 877 men, or thereabout, around Winchester and in the town. At sunset on May 16 part of the militia were ready to march to their stations on the basis of a fair drawing of names; the others were going home; from among the whole number, seventy had been employed as carpenters to work in Winchester at six pence per day in addition to their regular pay. The situation thus appeared to be better.

That very night brought mockery, suddenly and incredibly. An express rode into town with letters from Ashby's, Cocke's and Pearsall's forts, all to the same effect: A considerable body of Indians was said to be astir in the region of Patterson Creek and the South Branch. Incautiously, the express let the contents of his dispatches be known to some of the militia. Men under orders to go to the South Branch or to Patterson Creek pictured themselves as scalped already. They deserted en masse. So ruinous were the desertions, fired by reports of the return of the savages, that Colonel Washington had to revise his assignments for guarding the forts and reduce the number of places to be defended. He sent messengers off, also, to the militia officers who were marching men homeward. These leaders were told to reverse their steps and bring back their soldiers to take the place of those who had disappeared, but they could not. The militia had vanished as a fighting force.

Fortunately, the rumors that had produced the final panic of the militia were as untrue as the runaways. No additional murders were committed; no hostile Indians were seen. Washington sent forward militiamen who had not deserted and stationed them where they would encourage and assist the planters in reestablishing themselves.

The decision for the maintenance of a defensive in Virginia had been made by the Burgesses. To secure the frontiers a chain of forts must be constructed and extended southward almost to North Carolina. Over the size, number and location of these forts, conference and argument appeared endless. George's view was that it was impossible with scanty forces to maintain additional forts on the upper stretches of Patterson Creek or the South Branch of the Potomac because of the distance from Winchester and the difficulties of supply. Fort Cumberland, on the other hand, was so isolated that its garrison neither could serve usefully in the defence of Virginia nor receive and forward promptly information of the enemy's movements towards the region of the Shenandoah. It might be wise to keep a small number of men on Wills Creek. Chief reliance must be on a fort at Winchester, strong enough to serve as a magazine and as a refuge for the settlers during Indian raids. Roads converged at Winchester; it was the starting point for an advance on Fort DuQuesne. That French stronghold was the supreme objective. Nothing was safe and nothing stable till the enemy was driven from the Ohio.

To connect Fort Cumberland and the new defences at Winchester, George thought another large work might advantageously be erected, but the line between the Valley town and Wills Creek, Washington kept insisting, was the most advanced that could be held in 1756. Based on this line the companies of the Regiment not employed in the main forts could be placed "equidistant," in Washington's own words, "or at proper passes along our frontiers." George had been careful not to protest too vigorously against the extension of the chain of forts as far southward as the General Assembly desired, but he had been no less careful to point out that 1500 men could not cover the whole of the Virginia frontier.

The weeks after the departure of the savages brought Washington some mild satisfaction and, as always, a measure of new distress, personal and official. On May 12 the King proclaimed more liberal regulations on the subject of rank. Recognition of a sort was given Colonial general and field officers. They remained the juniors of all officers of like insignia and royal commission, but in North America they were to take rank as the "eldest Captains." There was gratification, besides, in the assurances friends were giving George that charges now being raised of immorality and drunkenness in the Regiment were not leveled against him. Another development made Washington feel "much affected" because his whole future as a soldier might be involved. In a communication received from Dinwiddie during the last week of April, George read: "Letters from Britain leave us still in uncertainty as to peace or war. Two Generals are appointed for America— Lord Loudoun and General Abercrombie—and it's thought they will bring over two Battalions, but whether for this place or New York remains uncertain; but it's further said His Majesty intends to send blank commissions for the Americans. If so, I doubt not you will be taken care of."

On April 16 Shirley had learned through private letters that Lord Loudoun had been appointed Commander-in-Chief of His Majesty's forces in North America and that Gen. Daniel Webb was coming over at once to assume direction of military affairs until Loudoun arrived. Shirley had felt that as his notification was unofficial, he should go ahead with his preparations for the campaign of 1756. In that spirit he wrote Sharpe on May 16 that he would name Washington second in command of the Ohio expedition "if there is nothing in the King's orders, which I am in continual expectation of, that interferes with it."

Washington did not wait for these developments. As soon as it was apparent that Loudoun was to be the man to decide on operations and the subordinates who were to participate in them, he wrote Dinwiddie and asked the Governor to recommend him to the new Commander-in-Chief. "His Honor" almost was grieved that Washington had thought this necessary. "You need not have wrote me," he said, "to recommend you to the Earl of Loudoun." The Governor explained: "I wrote fully to General Abercrombie, who is second in command, and my particular friend, in your favor, which I think much better than writing to his Lordship, as I know the influence he has with him." In the letter to Abercromby, the Governor praised Washington as a "very deserving Gentleman," for whom, had Braddock lived, he doubtless would "have provided . . . handsomely in the regulars." Dinwiddie went on to say of Washington: "If his Lordship will be so kind as to promote him in the British establishment, I think he will answer my recommendation."

Washington left Winchester June 4 and rode to Williamsburg to settle his accounts and discuss plans for the new forts. Arriving on the sixth, he found the Governor ailing. Unless his health improved during the summer, said Dinwiddie, who was sixty-three, he would ask permission to go home. There was another and a sure indication that the old Scot was failing: He readily referred troublesome decisions to the young commander. When Washington rode away from the capital on June 10 he had more authority and responsibility than ever had been assigned him officially. As respected fundamental strategy, Dinwiddie had been compelled to reiterate, and Washington to agree, that Virginia must remain on the defensive in 1756 unless regulars and artillery could be made available by Loudoun. At the same time, regardless of the delays and supineness of adjoining Colonies, Virginia must do her part for her own people and, if possible, make her advanced settlements secure. Washington's Regiment therefore was to be recruited to full strength by a draft; the chain of forts was to be completed along the whole of the frontier.

On his arrival at Winchester, Washington intended to remain for a few days and then proceed to Fort Cumberland, but it was July 1, or later, when once again he established temporary headquarters on Wills Creek. The Indians had made no new raids of any magnitude, though the prospect of their return at any time could not be disregarded. When Washington had heard the little there was to tell, he held a council on plans for the forts, and he put into effect the first of a series of orders for stiffer discipline. Then, shortly after July 13, he returned to Winchester, and, amid recurring alarms, proceeded to work on the three heavy tasks that were his lot—recruitment, discipline and fort building.

A draft was the positive phase of recruitment but it was not all that Washington had hoped it would be. Too much was expected of ignorant men. Low pay, fatiguing service and severe hardships were discouragements that vigilance could not overcome. As late as August 1, the total of Regiment, rangers and scouts was not more than 926 of an authorized 1500 and a needed 2000. Discipline remained a grim business for the Virginia commander. Building forts was hampered by lack of faith. Both Dinwiddie and Washington did what they could to execute the will of the General Assembly, but the Governor did not believe George had sufficient men to construct the forts, and the Colonel did not think they were worth building as the lawmakers planned them.

One of Washington's substantial conclusions during the summer was that Fort Cumberland should not remain in the care and charge of Virginia, which was to centre her frontier defences on Winchester. Maryland was to build a new fort far to the east of Wills Creek; therefore, George could see no reason for maintaining troops and keeping stores on that remote stream. When Governor Sharpe was on the frontier during July, George explained this to the Maryland commander, who made no objection. Dinwiddie would not have it so. Cumberland, he said, was a "King's fort" which could not be abandoned without the consent of the home government or of the new Commander-in-Chief for North America.

By orders "from home," proclamation was made in Williamsburg on August 7 of the official declaration of war by Britain against France on May 17, 1756. This was repeated in Winchester on August 15 by the young soldier whose skirmish with a French youth in May 1754 had been the "first shot" of a war that was to shape the lines of empire on the richest of continents. With the leading citizens of the town, Washington marched three companies of the Virginia Regiment to the fort, where the declaration was read aloud. Toasts were drunk, the cannon thrice discharged, and three rounds of musketry fired.

Harder service it now promised to be. A few days before Washington announced the proclamation of war disaster had befallen the King's arms in northern New York. After a winter of suffering and hunger, the survivors of three regiments and of detachments of the Royal Artillery had been trapped in three feeble forts at Oswego, subjected to serious casualties, and compelled to surrender. This was an unhappy introduction to the new Commander-in-Chief, Lord Loudoun, who had landed in New York on July 23.

In spite of pains taken to settle the estate of Lawrence Washington, the obscure provisions of his will had prevented this. What was worse, a controversy had arisen between Col. George Lee and the Washington brothers over the property to be divided between them and Lawrence's widow, who had married Lee. At length, the parties to the dispute arranged to meet about the middle of September in an effort to reach a final adjustment. George asked to go to Alexandria if conditions on the frontier permitted. The Governor consenting, Washington arrived at Mount Vernon about September 15—and rode squarely into disappointment. Several of the men whose presence was necessary for the conference regarding the estate had been summoned to Williamsburg as Burgesses to attend a session the Governor had advanced in date because of the disaster at Oswego.

In spite of postponement that would necessitate another journey, a week at home, where John Augustine ("Jack") Washington and his bride, Hannah Bushrod, now were residing, would have been delightfully acceptable had not George found himself involved in a matter that seemed to concern his character as a man and his reputation as an officer. For some months the *Virginia Gazette* had been publishing at irregular intervals a series of numbered articles, signed "L. & V.," and printed under the heading "The Virginia Centinel." "The Virginia Centinel. No. X" occupied nearly the whole of the front page of the *Virginia Gazette* of September 3, 1756. Bombast and pseudo-scholarship ran through it. Nowhere did the anonymous author give a hint of his identity unless it was in a line that suggested as author some militia officer who had been to Winchester the previous spring and had not been treated acceptably there. The profession of the soldier was declared noble, but "no profession in the world can secure from contempt and indignation a character made up of vice and debauchery." The "Centinel" left no doubt that he was speaking of the Virginia Regiment, even if he did not call it by name: ". . . when nothing brave is so much as attempted, but very rarely, or by accident, or for necessary self defence; when men whose profession it is to endure hardships and dangers cautiously shun them, and suffer their country to be ravaged in their very neighborhood; then, certainly, censure cannot be silent; nor can the public receive much advantage from a Regiment of such dastardly debauchees."

In his usual sensitiveness, Washington took every word of this to himself, but with one difference: Previously, he would have ridden to Williamsburg and returned his commission or he would have written that he would not continue to serve when he was subjected to such censure. This time, instead of resolving he would resign, he asked himself whether he should. Nor did he become so absorbed in the controversy or so depressed by it that he neglected other things. He wrote Austin a letter in which he answered the charges of "The Virginia Centinel." This he forwarded to his half-brother and, with it, money to pay for its insertion in the *Virginia Gazette* if Austin considered publication desirable.

Still in uncertainty of mind concerning his probable action, Washington received at Winchester bad news from the southern part of the Virginia frontier. That region had been subjected to Indian raids at intervals since June 25, when a force of French and Indians under de Belestre had appeared at the palisade Ephraim Vause had erected near the Roanoke River. Its defenders were a handful of ill-disciplined rangers under newly commissioned Capt. John Smith, who negligently permitted men to leave the place until the French commander realized those who remained were too few to defend it. De Belestre closed in, and, when two of the garrison had been killed and five wounded, he offered the survivors terms, which they accepted. Now, late in September, came word of new raids in Augusta.

The situation was one that Washington felt he must examine in person; so he rode up the Shenandoah Valley to Vause's Fort. The country was ideal for ambuscade, with neither settlers nor patrols to give warning of the presence of savages; but George's good fortune attended him. He found Peter Hog at his post, but scarcely more than that could be said of the

MAP / 3

WASHINGTON'S TOUR OF
THE FRONTIER, 1756

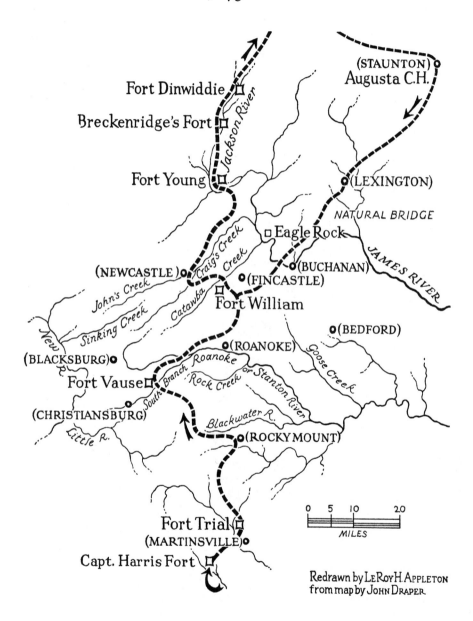

WASHINGTON'S TOUR
OF THE
FRONTIER, 1756

(STAUNTON)
Augusta C.H.

Fort Dinwiddie

Breckenridge's Fort

Jackson River

Fort Young

(LEXINGTON)

NATURAL BRIDGE

Eagle Rock

JAMES RIVER

Craig's Creek

(NEWCASTLE)

(BUCHANAN)

(FINCASTLE)

John's Creek

Catawba Creek

Fort William

Sinking Creek

(BEDFORD)

(ROANOKE)

New R.

(BLACKSBURG)

Goose Creek

Roanoke

Fort Vause

South Branch

Rock Creek or Stanton River

(CHRISTIANSBURG)

Little R.

Blackwater R.

(ROCKY MOUNT)

Fort Trial

(MARTINSVILLE)

Capt. Harris Fort

0   5   10   20

MILES

Redrawn by Le Roy H. Appleton
from map by John Draper

Captain. His company had dwindled to eighteen men, too few to do much work on the fort which was to be erected near the one Vause had built. Hog himself had degenerated as a commander during a long period of detached duty. His discipline was lax in some things and in others non-existent. The waste of manpower and feebleness of discipline shocked Washington.

The pass at Vause's farm was of great importance, George saw, and if it were defended properly it would protect all of Bedford and the greater part of Augusta. His disgust with misuse of the position led him to explode later with: "They have built three forts here, and *one* of them, if no more, erected in my opinion in a very out-of-the-way place. This they call Fort Trial." Washington continued southward, because he now resolved to make his inspection of the Virginia defences complete by going on to the forts in Halifax, next the North Carolina line. He found nothing to change his impression of the worthlessness of the militia and the inadequacy of the chain of feeble forts. Discontent, half-despair accumulated on the long, lonely road from Winchester to the North Carolina line. Militia were undependable; employment of them was wasteful; the Regiment was not strong enough, even when recruited fully, to do the work expected of it; there was censure and insinuation even in times of hardship and trial. At the southern end of the projected long line of forts, all these things had grown into an acute irritant.

With emotions confused and complicated, he wrote Dinwiddie:

I scorn to make unjust remarks on the behavior of the militia as much as I despise and condemn the persons who detract from mine and the character of the regiment . . . I only want to make the country sensible how ardently I have studied to promote her cause, and wish very sincerely my successor may fill my place more to their satisfaction in every respect than I have been able to do. I mentioned in my last to your Honor that I did not think a less number than 2,000 men would be sufficient to defend our extensive and much exposed frontier from the ravages of the enemy. I have not one reason yet to alter my opinion, but many to strengthen and confirm it. And I flatter myself the country will, when they know my determinations, be convinced that I have no sinister views, no vain motives of commanding a number of men, that urge me to recommend this number to your Honor, but that it proceeds from the knowledge I have acquired of the country, people, &c. to be defended.

In this state of mind Washington reversed his direction on October 10. He felt he had seen what there was to see, and all of it discouraging. On October 22 he rode into Winchester and found new distress there. Indians had resumed their raids on the South Branch and elsewhere; farmers' appeals for help were reaching Winchester daily; the whole situation was so alarming, that Washington had to confess himself deeply anxious. Fortunately, the alarm was of brief duration.

The Virginia officers at Fort Cumberland did not see the article of the "Centinel" until October 5, while Washington was on his tour of inspection. They met the next day and sent Lieutenant Colonel Stephen a furious letter. The angry young Virginians served notice: "We are resolved to obey as officers no longer than the twentieth day of November next, unless we have as public satisfaction as the injury received." That was serious. In several past crises the extreme utterance of others had led George to draw back. This time he perceived that what he had been tempted to do himself was dangerous when done by others. Cost what it might, he must keep the officers from leaving the service when their resignation would mean disintegration of the Regiment and further exposure of the Colony to attack. As soon as a few essential duties were performed, George hurried to Fort Cumberland and undertook to convince the officers that they had allowed too little time for the Governor, the Council or the Burgesses to give them "satisfaction." He asked them to defer action until he could investigate and report. They assented, but they insisted they must have the thanks of the General Assembly and an avowal of disbelief in the charges of the "Centinel." The alternative was set forth with deliberate sarcasm—that the Governor or the lawmakers must appoint in their place "a set of gentlemen who will more fully answer their and his expectation and perform that for their country which it seems their Governor, if not they, little hope for from a company of dastardly debauchees."

Washington agreed that their appeal should be presented. To seek vindication and to transact an accumulation of business, he prepared to start for Williamsburg. On this mission, the Colonel had reached Alexandria when he received an extraordinary letter from Dinnwiddie. The Governor had been confined to his room and not been improved in body or in temper. He had taken offence at a reference Washington half casually had made to the arrival in Winchester of eleven Catawba Indians whose number might have been increased by the use of responsible guides. Dinwiddie for months had been humiliated by the failure of his efforts to procure substantial help from the southern Indians and doubtless had been shamed anew by the arrival of Andrew Lewis with a ludicrous reenforcement of seven Cherokee warriors and three squaws. Hit where he was sore, the Governor struck angrily at Washington.

Temper colored the whole of Dinwiddie's letter. Most startling was a succession of brief, concluding sentences in which he said that the proposals concerning the future of Fort Cumberland had been reviewed by himself and the Council:

In consequence thereof, I hereby order you immediately to march 100 men to Fort Cumberland from the forces you have at Winchester, which Captain Mercer says is 160 men. You are to remain at Fort Cumberland and make the place as strong as you can, in case of an attack. You are to send out parties from the fort to observe the motions of the enemy if they should march over the Allegheny Mountains. Any stores at the fort not absolutely necessary for its defense you are to send . . . to Winchester. You are to order one of your subaltern officers (in whom you confide) to command at Winchester and to oversee the finishing of the fort building at that place. These orders I expect you will give due obedience to, and I am with respect, sir, your most humble servant. . . .

This was sharp, stern discipline for the young Colonel who was on his way to Williamsburg to tell the Governor that the officers at Fort Cumberland demanded they be replaced unless the attack on them by "The Virginia Centinel" was disavowed! Washington was astonished and stunned. To dispatch one hundred additional men to Fort Cumberland would leave Winchester undefended, the stores unprotected, and Fort Loudoun (as the defence at Winchester was now called) not only uncompleted but also exposed to the elements and to thieves who would carry off the building materials accumulated there. Of all the occasions on which Washington might have thought himself justified in throwing up his commission, this certainly was the most provoking and warrantable; but the effect on him of Dinwiddie's criticisms was exactly the reverse. The risk to the "country" and to the work he had taken in hand cooled and calmed him.

He obviously had to be in the Valley and not at Williamsburg. Accordingly he made his arrangements to return to Winchester and then replied to Dinwiddie's letter point by point. He apologized for what Dinwiddie had considered his "unmannerly" reference to the Indians' guides. "[I] am sorry," he wrote, "to find that this and my best endeavors of late meet with unfavorable constructions." He went on: "What it proceeds from, I know not. If my open and disinterested way of writing and speaking has the *air* of pertness and freedom, I shall redress my error by acting reservedly, and shall take care to obey my orders without offering at more." After a review of the other matters of which the Governor had complained, he returned to the proposal for the abandonment of Fort Loudoun, told Dinwiddie what this involved, and then wrote a final sentence that was apt to make the Governor reconsider: "So, to comply with my order (which I shall do literally if I can) not a man will be left [at Winchester] to secure the works or defend the King's stores, which are almost wholly removed to that place."

Three days later, November 27, Washington left Alexandria for Winchester and, on arrival, called immediately for a return of the troops in the Valley town. If Washington abandoned Winchester completely, he learned, he could not furnish the whole of the reenforcement ordered to Fort Cumberland. Wagons and flour for the transfer of the troops and their equipment to the Maryland post were not available immediately. Without disobedience of orders, time sufficed for an appeal to the Governor. George wrote deferentially and set forth the loss that would attend the evacuation of Winchester.

Dinwiddie and the Council had a change of heart when they learned reenforcement of Fort Cumberland would necessitate abandonment of the unfinished fort at Winchester. Washington received instructions December 15 to evacuate all the smaller forts except Waggener's on the South Branch and to divide available men between the garrisons of Winchester and of Wills Creek, so that Fort Cumberland might be strengthened and Fort Loudoun still be held. This meant that Indian raiders could penetrate easily the abandoned area between the two main forts, but the danger to settlers during the winter season would not be great. It was less bad to take that risk than abandon Fort Loudoun and its supplies to plunderers. Washington had won a partial victory. Fort Loudoun had been saved.

In his letter ordering the abandonment of the stockades, the Governor had quoted a paragraph from a communication in which Lord Loudoun had said of the proposed evacuation of the small forts: "If [Colonel Washington] leaves any of the great quantity of stores behind, it will be very unfortunate; and he ought to consider that it must lie at his own door." That was alarming. George felt that Loudoun had somehow been prejudiced against him. He could perceive that the General wrote in misconception of the facts, if not in ignorance of them; but misconception and ignorance are sources of prejudice, not cures of it. The recourse that occurred to George was to wait in person on the new Commander-in-Chief and present the reasons for what he had proposed. Washington pressed for information of the General's arrival. Then, on December 20 or 21, Washington took all his wardrobe, his camp equipment, his horses and the puppy he had bought that month and set out for Fort Cumberland.

The weeks of waiting for the visit of Lord Loudoun to Virginia could not be for Washington a time of idleness even at Fort Cumberland in winter. After the Christmas holdiays, George had to find clothing for the half-naked troops, who had been expecting it since October, and had to submit to controversy with the Governor over the appointment of a Commissary. More serious was a mutiny on the South Branch. This was put down promptly and sternly. These unpleasant matters faced and endured, Washington turned to the preparation of a report to Loudoun on the condition of the Virginia forces and the situation on the frontier. He wrote this paper with much care because he intended to use it as an introduction to the new Commander-in-Chief, who had been compelled to defer plans for visiting Virginia and whom Washington wished to impress as a vigilant commander.

Washington began a covering letter to Loudoun's senior aide, with the assertion that a British offensive, if practicable, was necessary: "Our all in a manner depends upon it. The French grow more and more formidable by their alliances, while our friendly Indians are deserting our interest. Our treasury is exhausting, and our country depopulating. . . ." He assured Loudoun that three thousand men could cut communications between Fort DuQuesne and the Lakes and, with artillery, could destroy the fort. The difficulties that weakened the Virginia Regiment and hampered its operations were the burden of the report.

Washington held to his purpose to find the earliest possible opportunity of "testifying" to the qualities of the man who could advance him quickly. When he learned Loudoun had called a conference of Governors to meet in Philadelphia, he sought and received Dinwiddie's permission to attend. Washington reached the place of conference about February 21, 1757—only to find that the new Commander-in-Chief had not made his appearance. Pending that gratifying event, Washington had to make the most of such dull diversions as idle days in Philadelphia could offer in midwinter. At last on March 14, the guns of the Association Battery and of ships in the harbor announced Loudoun's arrival. As the waiting Governors had become impatient, they sat down eagerly to confer with him and hear the little Loudoun had to say about his military plans. There were some ceremonials, but, in the main, there was solid discussion, which soon turned to the means by which the people could be aroused to support the war with vigor.

Washington found Lord Loudoun, a bachelor of fifty-two, stout and below middle height but strongly muscled and apparently fit for the field. The General had the marks of high station and good living and he displayed an interest in administration. From Loudoun's senior aide, Washington soon learned the General had been much pleased with Washington's report on the situation in Virginia. Loudoun doubtless was equally pleased when he met the young Virginian who succeeded in nothing more certainly than in winning the good-will of his seniors. George was not invited to all meetings of the conference, but he was called in March 20 when a choice was to be made concerning the forts to be held in western Virginia and the garrisons to be employed there.

The council of Governors sat with Lord Loudoun through March 23. Loudoun told the council virtually nothing concerning his plan of operations in the north, but he and the Governors agreed that no offensive could be undertaken in Pennsylvania or to the south during 1757. A defensive must be maintained there and particularly in South Carolina, where a French attack from Santo Domingo or from the Alabama fort in the Creek country was apprehended. Washington knew nothing of the situation in South Carolina and expressed no opinion of it. From his point of view, the single gratifying decision of the council was a minor one—that Maryland was to assume responsibility for Fort Cumberland.

Washington already regarded himself as a fatalist. He was disposed now to take a gloomy view of the future, in so far as his own military future was concerned; and when he reached Alexandria early in April he had added another to the long list of disappointments that had been his in pursuit of military fame. His initial command had been hampered by Mackay and then by defeat at Fort Necessity; Braddock had been good enough to promise advancement but had been killed; after George had been named Commander-in-Chief of Virginia troops under his second commission, first Dagworthy and then Sharpe had stood in his way; when Dagworthy had been eliminated and Sharpe had been won over to ask for him as second in command, Shirley had promised to give him that post—and then Shirley had been superseded; now Loudoun was favorable, but there was to be no offensive against the Ohio in 1757.

At Alexandria he found a letter in which Captain Mercer, commanding at Winchester, said that ninety-five Catawba Indians had arrived in the town. This presented possibilities of a sort that revived Washington. Perhaps these warriors could be used in an expedition towards Fort DuQuesne. In the transfer of Fort Cumberland to the custody of Maryland, someone must see that all Virginia property, except provisions, was removed to Winchester. Weakening of the Regiment in order to strengthen South Carolina must be resisted. Evacuation of Fort Cumberland would release some troops for garrisoning the stockades between that post and Winchester. These men must be posted wisely. Finally, the Governor had directed George to come to Williamsburg during the session of the General Assembly beginning

April 14 and report on arrearages of pay. If immediate tasks were to be discharged, Washington must be off to the Valley.

Busy days followed. The Governor was as anxious to get a contingent for South Carolina on its way as George was to hold it. Transfer of Fort Cumberland involved delays as well as formalities. Much had to be done in anticipation of the coming of a larger force of Cherokees and Catawbas. Meantime, the French Indians were appearing again, almost under the stockade of Fort Cumberland, and waylaying small parties of men on the road. Officers at that fort were renewing their appeal for King's commissions. George visited Wills Creek briefly and then started at his usual speed for Williamsburg. He was in Fredericksburg April 24 and by the twenty-seventh was in the capital.

Washington was receiving thirty shillings per diem pay and 2 per cent commission on all funds he handled for the troops. Dinwiddie regarded this as too high a rate compensation, but George now earnestly asked the Governor not to lower either pay or commission. It was not altogether a vain plea. The General Assembly heard Washington's statement of the arrearages due the Regiment and gave him good-will and admiration; but members did not change the plan to entrust financial administration to the Governor nor did any of them prevail upon the Governor, if even they tried, to continue the commission of 2 per cent. Dinwiddie kept George's salary at thirty shillings, agreed to provide for the men who attended his horses and allowed him a flat £200 per annum for his table and expenses.

The remonstrance of the officers was unavailing; relief and recognition must come from the Crown, not from Burgesses who were conscious of the Colony's financial distress. They were well-inclined, if powerless, and as always, they were sociable. George accepted entertainment and gave it. Conferences came at last to an end. Washington completed all his business by May 17 but left the General Assembly still in dispute over the size of the forces to be employed for the operations to be undertaken that year and in 1758. Return was by Fredericksburg, to Alexandria and then to Winchester, which he reached May 24.

In Winchester and nearby Washington found a larger number of Indians than ever he had seen together previously. He could not escape the presence or the importunity of Cherokees, Catawbas, Nottaways and Tuscaroras. Negotiation, treaties, presents and promises had brought Washington more savages than he could employ advantageously while Virginia remained on the defensive. "They are," said Washington, "the most insolent, most avaricious and most dissatisfied wretches I have ever had to deal with."

The nuisance was immediate; the benefit *in futuro;* the danger that the Indians would march off in dudgeon could not be blinked. Responsibility of conciliating them was not long to be Washington's. The home government had named Edmund Atkin Superintendent of Indian Affairs in the Southern Colonies in recognition of a long report on the southern natives, written by Atkin. Atkin did nothing in haste and preferably did nothing at all. He had come to Williamsburg on April 9, but he resisted all prodding to go to Winchester. If the management of the Indians was the affair of

Atkin, then George wanted to be relieved of the Indians and wished the new official to be present to look after them. Washington sent an express with a request that the Governor speed the agent, but it was not until June 2 that Atkin arrived and, after some diplomatic delays and pretended indifference, began a council with the savages. This was long and complicated. Atkin professed to act in superior knowledge of the Indians, but he did not impress Washington. It would be far better, the Colonel thought, if Virginia had a single agent of her own—Christopher Gist, for example—who would transact all business with the Indians.

Circumstance for some weeks saved Washington from the tedium of administrative routine. A delicate negotiation was that of determining the military relationship Washington was to bear to Col. John Stanwix of the Sixtieth Infantry, whom Loudoun had named to command five companies of regulars assigned to support Colonials in the defence of the western frontiers of Virginia, Maryland and Pennsylvania. Washington took pains to inquire of the Governor: "If I should meet with anything from [Stanwix] at any time that may clash with your instructions to me, how I am to conduct myself in the affair[?]" The reply was: "You are to follow such orders [as] Colonel Stanwix may send you from time to time, without any regard to any orders you may have received from me."

This answer referred specifically to a situation that developed in mid-June. When Washington returned to Winchester from Williamsburg he found that several raids to the west had been undertaken by the Virginians and their Indian allies. One such thrust had been made by the natives who had brought in four scalps and two prisoners. Major Lewis later led toward the Ohio a scalping party of considerable size, but, as he had not been able to prevail on the savages to take more than eight days' provisions with them, he soon was back with no scalps on any warrior's belt. Two parties remained out, one with whom Capt. Robert Spotswood had started in the direction of Fort DuQuesne, and another under Lieut. James Baker, who had taken fifteen Indians and five white men toward Logstown.

An express on June 12 brought news that Baker had returned on the ninth with five French scalps and one French prisoner. That left only Spotswood and his party afield. Washington was beginning to feel concern for them when, during the night of June 15/16, an express rode into town with this dispatch:

Fort Cumberland June 14, 1757

Sir,

Six Cherokee Indians who just now came from Fort DuQuesne, say that six days ago they saw a large body of troops march from that garrison with a number of wagons and a train of artillery, and by their route, must intend an attack on this garrison.

I am, sir, your most humble servant,
JNO. DAGWORTHY.

The Indians said they had heard a great gun fired near the battle-field of Monongahela. The French, according to the Cherokees, had "numbers of wheeled carriages and men innumerable and had marched two days before they quit the Monongahela waters." Washington credited the news—called for a council of all the commissioned officers then in Winchester. Unanimously the council voted to recall the garrisons to Winchester and hold them there, working on the fort, till more was known about the French advance.

The orders issued by Washington during the next few hours showed that he was acquiring experience. Washington sent Dagworthy an account of the steps that had been taken. "I have no doubt that a very considerable force will be with you in a very short time," he added. For three days thereafter, if George had further word from Fort Cumberland, it merely repeated rumor and echoed suspense.

On the twenty-first Washington received a somewhat embarrassed letter from Dagworthy. Other Indians had arrived from the vicinity of Fort DuQuesne and asserted that previous reports of a French advance with artillery and wagons were untrue. A large scouting party had left the Ohio and was moving in the direction of Fort Cumberland, but the tale about vehicles and heavy guns was the imagining of badly scared young warriors who had hurried eastward after a glimpse of the enemy.

These more experienced natives of the second party Dagworthy sent to Winchester in order that the Virginians might question them. Washington did so and concluded that they had not actually been close to Fort DuQuesne but that they had been on the trail of a considerable force of French and Indians who were moving towards the English settlements. These enemies had no artillery and they were following a route they recently had been employing for all their raids, whether against Virginia, Maryland or Pennsylvania. Dagworthy's first alarm might have been due to the mistakes of an interpreter; but there still was sufficient doubt about the whole expedition to justify the retention for a time of the militia who were arriving.

By June 24 suspense was diminished. Thereafter, Washington observed hopefully the indications that the French and Indians from Fort DuQuesne, on reaching the English settlements, had divided into separate scalping parties which did comparatively little damage. At the end of the first week in July there still were signs of hostile savages; but by mid-July Washington could report, "we are pretty peaceable."

The last echo of Captain Dagworthy's false alarm was not pleasant to the ears of Virginians. If the men at Winchester and on the South Branch could mock the Marylanders for creating foes through tales told by friends, Dagworthy's men soon could say that Washington's advisers would make enemies by misusing friends. In blundering confidence that he knew how to punish as well as reward the savages, Atkin locked up ten of them for some infraction and thereby created a turmoil so serious that Washington had to act quickly to placate the offended natives before they set out in wrath for their own country.

While doing what he could to counteract the mistakes of Atkin, the Colonel had the doleful duty of relieving of command one of his earliest officers. Captain Hog had failed to maintain discipline and to build economically a properly situated fort at Vause's. There was no alternative to getting rid of him. After Hog was sent home, the supervision of the southern end of the western defences was placed in the competent hands of Lewis. Some shifts were made, also, in the disposition of the detached companies, but the greatest change was the absence of Stephen in South Carolina. Frontier garrison duty had not carried him, as it had Hog, in a descent to incompetence; but where Stephen was, trouble was. His acceptance of Dagworthy's seniority never had been explained, though Stephen's letters often contained sharp criticisms of the Marylander. It was against Stephen, however unjustly, that some of the charges of drunkenness and immorality at Fort Cumberland had been directed. He had been loyal to Washington, but Washington found, after resuming command of all his troops, that Stephen so often had given orders contrary to those he had received that, said Washington, "it will be with great difficulty, if it is even possible, to extricate the officers and myself from the dilemma and trouble they have occasioned."

These occurrences were incidental to the main task, rebuilding the Virginia Regiment in conformity to the new legislation of the General Assembly. The bill that finally met with the Burgesses' approval authorized a total force of 1272, organized into twelve companies. Two of those to be recruited, in addition to two already in existence, could be dispatched to South Carolina if the commanding officer of His Majesty's forces in North America thought necessary. One company was to garrison the fort in the Cherokee country; the remaining seven were to be employed for the general defence of the Colony. Furthermore, three companies of rangers, each of one hundred men, were to be enlisted for the protection of the southwestern counties.

A regimental roster continuously below authorized strength represented the principal failure of an exasperating year on the defensive. Washington did not blame himself for this weakness, nor did his superiors charge him with it. Washington had distress, also, over Captain Spotswood and his scouts, soldiers who by now had been given up as lost after their failure to return from their raid towards Logstown. Another distress was over the continuing slow progress of work on Fort Loudoun. Overtopping all the unhappiness of the service was the feeling of Washington that he had been treated unfairly by the Governor, that he and his officers had been maligned, and that they had been denied the right they believed they had earned of inclusion in the regular establishment.

Such were the events of the early summer of 1757; such the balance of satisfaction and disappointment, of compensation and distress—the Regiment still below strength, Spotswood dead, Stephen agreeably dispatched to South Carolina, Fort Loudoun taking shape slowly, Dagworthy somewhat discredited, Dinwiddie still quick to argue, but sick, anxious, and soon to pass off the stage. Washington himself was depressed and perhaps bored, but he was not disheartened. Pride, anticipation and experience were echoed in a letter of instruction he wrote the Captains who were about to take their companies to the more remote forts. ". . . devote some part of your leisure hours to the study of your profession, a knowledge in which cannot be attained without application; nor any merit or applause to be achieved without a certain knowledge thereof. Discipline is the soul of an army."

Before one perplexity vanished another mocked. About August 1 George developed a mild dysentery, which he ignored to the extent that he did not reduce his activities in the least. Among compelling personal duties was that of going to Alexandria for another attempt at a settlement of Lawrence's estate. He set out on August 4 and, on arrival, found few questions to be discussed. The books were in order. When all the adjustments with Lee had been made there was no credit to Washington to offset the debts of £125 12s. 9d. contracted in 1753–55 and represented by purchases from the estate. This sum he duly paid. A fine crop of tobacco was growing on the land and was especially encouraging because Washington had decided that he would undertake to raise the best leaf in considerable quantities. From his salary and allowances he had saved money with which he soon was to buy five hundred additional acres on Dogue Run for £350, and he had invested £300 in additional slaves from November 1756 through May 1757. Thus would he have more "hands" for more work. Nothing specific could be undertaken immediately for the repair and furnishing of Mount Vernon, but much had to be pondered and planned, doubtless with the assistance of Jack Washington and his young wife. All business was completed as far as it could be by the beginning of the last week in August, when Washington went back to Winchester.

Washington had not made more than his initial approach to the perplexities usual to his life at that place when a messenger brought sad news: On September 3 death had taken Colonel Fairfax, the man who had done more than any other to counsel and advance young George Washington. Fairfax had transferred to George the moral assistance he first had given to Lawrence. He could not have been kinder to the son-in-law than to the dead man's younger brother. From Fairfax George had learned more of the arts of society than from any other person except Lawrence. It was, therefore, as much a personal duty as it was a neighborly obligation to ride over the mountain to Colonel Fairfax's formal funeral later in the month, even though the continuance of the bloody flux made the journey difficult and painful.

When the last tribute had been paid to Fairfax, Washington hurried back to the Valley. Those days between the news of the Colonel's death and the time of the obsequies had been among the unhappiest of Washington's whole period of command. About September 14 he received a letter written by William Peachey, one of the captains of the Regiment who had been discharged when the number of officers had been reduced. Peachey described with great particularity how Charles Carter had quoted William Claiborne as saying Richard Corbin had quoted Peachey as affirming in the spring of 1756, when sent to Williamsburg for aid, "that the whole business at that time was to execute a scheme of [Washington's] to cause the Assembly to levy largely both in money and men, and that there was not an Indian in that neighborhood, that the frontiers or even Winchester and the adjacent county did not appear to be in any more danger at that time than any other. . . ." Peachey reported that this "piece of deceit or imposition of yours (as they term it) has lessened the Governor's and some of the leading men's esteem for you."

In Washington's eyes few things could be so calamitous to him as to lose the good opinion of the outstanding men of the Colony. He was conscious that he had lost favor with Dinwiddie, and he was inclined to believe that Corbin had spoken as Claiborne and Carter had reported. For this reason he wanted to know, first of all, whether the Governor had heard the accusation and knew its source. On the seventeenth George copied in a letter to Dinwiddie what Peachey had written and then asked: "I should take it infinitely kind if your Honor would please to inform me whether a report of this nature was ever made to you, and, in that case, who was the author of it?" With characteristic candor he admitted that he might have made military mistakes through lack of experience. "I think it would be more generous," he said, "to charge me with my faults, and let me stand or fall according to the evidence, than to stigmatize me behind my back."

Now returned from Fairfax's funeral, Washington wrestled over the meaning of Governor Dinwiddie's reply to this letter. The Governor said: "I would gladly hope there is no truth in it. I never heard of it before, nor did I ever conceive you'd have sent down any alarms without proper foundation. However, I shall show it to Col. Corbin when he comes to town, but I'd advise you not to credit every idle story you hear, for if I was to notice reports of different kinds, I should be constantly perplexed. My conduct to you from the beginning was always friendly, but you know I had good reason to suspect you of ingratitude, which I am convinced your own conscience and reflection must allow I had reason to be angry, but this I endeavor to forget; but I can't think Col. Corbin guilty of what is reported. However as I've his Majesty's leave to go for England, [I] propose leaving this November, and I wish my successor may show you as much friendship as I've done."

This letter caused Washington as much pain as it relieved. George answered almost despairingly: "I do not know that I ever gave your Honor cause to suspect me of ingratitude, a crime I detest and would most carefully avoid. If an open, disinterested behavior carries offence, I may have offended, because I have always laid it down as a maxim to represent facts freely and impartially, but no more to others than I have to you, sir. If instances of my ungrateful behavior had been particularized, I would have answered to them. But I have long been convinced that my actions and their motives have been maliciously aggravated."

There the matter had unhappily to rest, but if Dinwiddie soon was to leave, Washington felt it was desirable to go to Williamsburg and to settle accounts. The Colonel asked permission to do this, but the Governor snappishly met his request with a refusal. Rebuffed, George had to await a more favorable time, when the Governor's humor was better or his successor had come. How soon that might be, George could not guess. He certainly did not anticipate the reality—that he had written the last words he ever was to address to "His Honor." It was to be regretted that the last months of Dinwiddie's relations with Washington were clouded with misunderstanding, after almost four years of pleasant association. Part of the final ill-feeling perhaps had its origin in Dinwiddie's illness that shook his judgment and his temper. Had he recovered, he might have been reconciled.

At the same time, a certain complaint and contention ran through Washington's letters of the summer of 1757 and for the same reason that Dinwiddie was bad-tempered: he was sick. The dysentery persisted relentlessly and reduced his strength day by day. About November 1 this bloody flux became more violent. Soon George was so weak that he scarcely could walk. On the seventh he was in such violent pain that the physicians had to give him warning: If he did not suspend all activity and seek a "change of air," they could not be responsible for him; and even if he went away, he could not hope for early recovery. That decided him. Without attempting to write either Dinwiddie or Colonel Stanwix, he turned over the command to Captain Stewart, instructed that officer to notify his superiors of his illness and started for Alexandria.

On arrival in Alexandria, Colonel Washington went to the home of John Carlyle and there he remained long enough to consult Dr. Charles Green. For a time, the patient grew worse; then, after he went to Mount Vernon, he gained slightly in his battle with his malady. At Christmas, he was strong enough to transact some personal business, and subsequent to New Year's Day he talked of going to Williamsburg, though at least one friendly neighbor discouraged the effort.

Neither pride nor physic, neither resilience nor resolution sufficed to break the grip of Washington's affliction. The bloody flux ceased, only to return again. Some indications of "decay," as the Colonials termed consumption, were apparent. With the coming of March, Washington grew desperate. Temporarily he would put himself under a strict regimen; when he had done his utmost, he would go to Williamsburg and consult the best physicians there. ". . . My constitution is certainly greatly impaired," he told Colonel Stanwix. It might be necessary for him not only to resign but also, as he put it, to "retire from all public business."

Painfully he set out March 5, 1758, and, in contrast to his usual galloping speed, rode slowly southward. He reached Williamsburg and consulted Dr. John Amson. This physician's long experience apparently convinced him that George's fears were unfounded and that cure was near. Assurance to this effect had immediate result. Washington almost overnight cast off thought of death and proceeded to a new reconnaissance. He rode from Williamsburg to the White House, home of Martha Dandridge Custis, widow of Daniel Parke Custis.

CHAPTER / 5

In a society so small and so intimate as that of the great planters of eastern Virginia, Colonel Washington probably had known the young widow Custis during her married life, and he could not have been ignorant of some of the good fortune and of the bad that had fallen to the Custises and to the Parkes during the century and more of their residence in Virginia.

In 1749 Daniel Parke Custis fell in love with Martha Dandridge, aged eighteen, daughter of John and Frances Jones Dandridge of New Kent. Martha Dandridge was one of the fairest and most amiable girls of her society but by no means one of the wealthiest. Daniel Custis in due time married Martha, took her to the White House plantation on the Pamunkey River and there led with her a happy and opulent life. After the death of his father in 1749 Daniel Parke Custis, the heir of Parkes and Custises, held no less than 17,438 acres on modest quit rents, and he undertook to raise superior tobacco and to bundle and prize it with care. He operated fisheries; he drained his marshes and leased swamp land for the run of horses; he rented farms to tenants and he shared crops. Custis never became a Burgess but he had another of the usual honors of a great planter, that of being a warden of his parish, with which Parkes and Custises and Dandridges had all been connected. Good looks he set off with fine clothes from a Williamsburg tailor and with furnishings from London, where Martha bought freely of the market's best ribbons and laces and silks and stomachers. Besides fine horses, Custis kept a chair and a chariot and visited often in Williamsburg.

Children were born to Martha. The first and the second babies, Daniel Parke and Frances, died in childhood. A second son, John Parke, was born late in 1754; the fourth child, a dark-haired girl, was born in 1756 and named Martha. Other daughters and sons might be added, because the young mother was healthy, but when June 1757 ended and the rich month of July opened, Custis fell ill and developed symptoms that defied home medication. Dr. James Carter of Williamsburg was summoned and was at Custis's bedside on the fifth. Effort and vigil were vain. Custis died on July 8 at the age of forty-five years and nine months.

Custis died without a will and thereby put upon Martha full responsibility of administering the estate and serving as guardian for her children. She undertook the task with little experience but with abundant common sense. On affairs of law she promptly consulted attorneys she knew to be competent and trustworthy. In many matters she followed the forms her husband had used, and she painstakingly drafted and revised her letters to merchants and other correspondents until they were explicit and adequate. She was careful, too, in taking receipts even for small sums paid out on account of the estate, though she soon found she could entrust this detail to her husband's manager, Joseph Valentine.

Although George secretly regarded himself as in love with Sally Cary Fairfax, he knew that nothing more than the happiest of friendships could or would exist between him and his neighbor's wife. It became a young man of station to look elsewhere for a bride. The Colonel looked towards the White House and Mrs. Custis. The young widow was among the wealthiest and most desirable in Virginia when the tall young Col. George Washington bowed low to her on March 16, 1758. Washington did not stay then more than a day or a day and a half at the White House, but as he looked at the lovely Martha and across the broad, rich fields of level land, he resolved to come again. He did so the next week, and when he went back to Williamsburg after that second visit he had either the promise of Martha to marry him or her assurance that she would consider the proposal he made her. Then he finished his business at the capital, rode to Fredericksburg and to Alexandria, paused briefly, and rushed on to Winchester. There he spent his earliest spare hour in ordering from London "by the first ship bound to any part of Virginia . . . as much of the best superfine blue cotton velvet as will make a coat, waistcoat and breeches for a tall man, with a fine silk button to suit it . . . six pairs of the very neatest shoes . . . [and] six pair gloves. . . ." In New Kent, perhaps about the same time, a certain lady was ordering from the same capital of fashion "one genteel suite of cloathes for myself to be grave but not to be extravagant and not to be mourning."

By the time of the Colonel's reopening of his Headquarters in Winchester, much had changed during the five months of his absence. Most conspicuous was the presence of the largest body of southern Indians that ever had come to support the English in their war against the French. Some four hundred savages were in the town or were roving the country west of the English settlements; an additional 140 were on the way from their villages. In spite of the cost, these contingents were encouraged to remain, but Washington was almost as uneasy when he had Indian warriors as when he lacked them.

About the time Washington had been taken sick, Lord Loudoun's expedition against Louisburg had failed so completely that no attempt could be made even to land troops. The French under the Marquis de Montcalm had attacked and destroyed Fort William Henry at the lower end of Lake George. Almost the entire garrison had been captured. It was a disaster as humiliating as any British arms had sustained in a war that had included already the defeat of Braddock and the loss of Oswego.

What was to be done in 1758? William Pitt had been recalled to office June 29, 1757, as a Secretary of State and had been given supreme control of the war and of foreign affairs. When Pitt found no plan set forth in Loudoun's dispatches, the Secretary concluded to relieve the commander in America. Pitt left Major General Abercromby as titular head of the forces in America. Nominally in the care of Abercromby but actually under Pitt himself were to be three expeditions, one against Louisburg as a preliminary to an advance on Quebec, the second against Fort Ticonderoga, and the third against Fort DuQuesne. To command the new attack on Louisburg, Pitt named Jeffrey Amherst. The thrust for Ticonderoga was to be Abercromby's charge. For the operation against Fort DuQuesne, Pitt's choice fell on Col. John Forbes, of the Seventeenth Foot, who was made Brigadier General.

To Colonel Stanwix came a step upward to the rank of Brigadier, with orders to share in the campaign on the Lakes. This transfer of Stanwix and the recall of Loudoun meant to Washington that he had to repeat the process of winning the good opinion of officers who replaced those whose esteem he had acquired.

He proceeded once again to have himself recommended to the new General—and to have it done promptly. Forbes assumed command about March 21. In a letter of congratulation that Washington wrote Stanwix April 10, less than a week after his return to Winchester, he said:

. . . I must . . . beg that you will add one more kindness to the many I have experienced, and that is, to mention me in favorable terms to General Forbes (if you are acquainted with that gentleman) and not as a person who would depend upon him for further recommendation to military preferment, for I have long conquered all such expectancies (and serve this campaign merely for the purpose of affording my best endeavors to bring matters to a conclusion) but as a person who would gladly be distinguished in some measure from the *common run* of provincial officers, as I understand there will be a motley herd of us.

Had Washington known more at the time of Forbes, he would have realized that he could learn much from him. Forbes's special distinction had been as a quartermaster, a service in which there had been much backwardness and lack of skill throughout the operations in Virginia. Washington could not have found in America a better instructor in the art of army administration, nor could he have been associated with a man of greater patience, cheer and cordiality in relations with officers and men. Forbes was cautious in not wishing to advance until his troops were equipped and supplied, but he was tireless in effort to prepare them. While he had never been proclaimed brilliant, he was able, courageous and thorough.

Now Washington was to have a regiment of infantry, as previously, but he was to serve "in the line" under any colonel or brigadier of the regular establishment who might be designated. Nor was he to be Virginia's sole colonel, at the head of her only regiment. The General Assembly had passed a bill to raise the armed forces of the Colony to two thousand men, exclusive of the previously created ranger companies. The additional one thousand volunteers were to be allowed a bounty of £10 each, and were to be enlisted for service to December 1, 1758, and no longer. John Blair, President of the Council and acting Governor, accepted an offer William Byrd III of Westover made to recruit and to lead the new troops.

These three developments—the presence of Indians, the change of command, and the recruiting and equipment of the larger force—set Washington's task for the two months that followed his return to the Valley.

Recruiting proved less difficult than in the past. Although Forbes did not believe he would receive more than half the two thousand troops Virginia had authorized, Washington's Regiment numbered 950 or more by May 28, and Byrd, with 900, was so close to authorized strength that the official formation of his Regiment was set for May 29. Even St. Clair, who had found no words too contemptuous for describing the Virginia troops of 1755, had to admit that their successors were "a fine body of men."

Indians raised new problems daily. Raids of hostile scalping parties took heavy toll in West Augusta. The need of Indians with whom to fight Indians was as manifest as ever; diplomacy, firmness and understanding of them were imperatives. Such hope as the English had of overcoming the adverse odds in the struggle for the frontier might depend on winning over some of the Indians who were said to be dissatisfied with their French allies.

Throughout this time of recruiting, adjustment to new commanders, and effort to satisfy the insatiable Indians, preparations were being made hourly to move the Virginia regiments across the Potomac and, in due time, to Pennsylvania for the advance on Fort DuQuesne. At the outset the questions that most concerned Washington, St. Clair and others had to do with wagons, tents, cartridge boxes, powder horns, blankets, hatchets and varied items of equipment relatively unimportant in themselves but essential to such an orderly advance as Forbes proposed to make. Before St. Clair could put Washington's troops under marching orders, he determined to procure such equipment as he could from the Colony and accordingly directed Washington to go to Williamsburg to ask for arms and tentage and to "settle the affairs of the two Virginia Regiments." For a manifest personal reason, Washington was glad to go to the vicinity of the White House, but he hurried his trip as he was anxious to get back to the frontier in time to share in an offensive he so long had been urging.

St. Clair took Washington to Conococheague with him on June 13 for a conference with Governor Sharpe and Col. Henry Bouquet. Although Washington had often exchanged letters with Bouquet, this was the first time he had met the man who was to be Forbes's most trusted lieutenant and Washington's immediate superior. Swiss-born and thirty-nine years of age, Bouquet was portly and undistinguished in appearance but of attractive and friendly manners. Next to his definite ability and rounded training as a soldier, Bouquet's greatest quality was his freedom from the binding tradition of the British and German armies. In Charleston, South Carolina, he had amazed the holders of Colonial commission by his considerate treatment of them and their troops. With like understanding, after he returned to Pennsylvania, he had begun to study new, more flexible tactics for forest fighting by British regulars. He was as careful as he was skillful, and on matters he did not understand, such as dealings with the Indians, he sought the best counsel he could get. By temperament as by training, Bouquet probably was second only to Forbes among all the soldiers in America from whom Washington could learn.

At the conference where Washington became acquainted with this remarkable man, Bouquet did not give the Virginia troops their marching orders, but, instead, left the duty to St. Clair. With orders from St. Clair Washington returned to Winchester and, on June 24, left that place for Fort Cumberland with five companies of the First Virginia and a company of artificers of the Second—close to six hundred men, and probably more than George had ever before commanded on the road in a single body.

It was not a fast or flawlessly managed march. Not until the afternoon of July 2 did the Virginian, his tired men and his twenty-eight wagons reach Fort Cumberland. By that time the last of Forbes's artillery and supply ships had reached Philadelphia; his cannon had been put in the road to catch up with his infantry; and he himself was on his way to Carlisle, where he was to arrive on the fourth. The heads of his three columns then were at that post, Raystown and Fort Cumberland. His force was to number close to seven thousand, of whom about 1400 were Scottish Highlanders. Operations were to be different from Braddock's in this fundamental: Braddock had established an advance base at Cumberland and had undertaken to proceed straight from that point to Fort DuQuesne. Forbes intended to establish successive depots as he advanced. Braddock had attempted a long jump; Forbes was to make a number of hops. Washington had seen the one method result in failure; he now was to share in a test of the other.

In all respects save one, the first few weeks at Fort Cumberland did not differ greatly from those that Washington had spent on Wills Creek under other Commanders-in-Chief. There were the usual alarms and murders by Indians; after the arrival of Col. William Byrd with eight companies of his Regiment on July 6, much effort had to be devoted to equipping troops for service they were expected to perform directly under Bouquet. The first contingents of two hundred under Maj. Andrew Lewis marched away promptly and arrived July 10 at Raystown, where they won praise from Bouquet both for the "extraordinary dispatch" of their advance and for the utility of their dress. Washington had taken pains to have the men procure hunting shirts and leggings, and he had satisfaction in the prompt decision of Bouquet and then of Forbes to make that garb "our pattern in this expedition." Lewis's contingent was followed by other companies until, by July 12, 535 Virginians, six companies, were at the Pennsylvania post under the command of Adam Stephen, who believed the entire Regiment would soon be assembled there. Discipline and the prospect of a final thrust at the enemy on the Ohio had made the Regiment more efficient than ever it had been.

What made this tour of duty different was that George was now a candidate for office. He wished to be a member of the House of Burgesses, from which he so often had received orders, and he had taken care to give early notice of his candidacy. Before he had left Winchester he had declared himself for one of the two seats of Frederick County, then represented by Hugh West and Thomas Swearingen. Col. Thomas Bryan Martin, young nephew of Lord Fairfax, had served as a Burgess of Hampshire County in 1756-58, but he too decided now to stand in Frederick County, where the peer had given him the 8840 acres styled Greenway Court. Martin had decided to conduct his canvass primarily against West, and, by so doing, he made Washington, in a sense, the challenger of Swearingen. Although Washington had good assurances of support, he suffered because of this circumstance: The writs of election did not reach Winchester until July 4; as twenty days had to elapse before the election could be held, the poll could not be conducted until July 24. Washington, therefore, might be absent at Fort Cumberland during the time the other aspirants were afield.

Friends did all they could to offset this disadvantage. George William Fairfax and John Carlyle agreed to visit the Valley and to assist in lining up their tenants. James Wood, the most influential man in the County, was wholeheartedly for Washington, though he preferred West to Martin. Gabriel Jones, one of the Burgesses from Augusta, was so determined to have Washington chosen that he neglected his own solicitation of votes to assist the Colonel. Washington's officers in Frederick were as active in his behalf as military proprieties admitted, perhaps more active than they should have been. Lieut. Charles Smith, in command of Fort Loudoun, assumed responsibility with innkeepers and merchants for the beverages that were to be served voters on the day of election.

At first Washington's success appeared certain, but after he left for Fort Cumberland some of his adherents thought the tide turned to the incumbents. Fairfax feared the Colonel would be "very hard pushed." John Kirkpatrick had to report that some of the voters "entertain a notion of the inconvenience you lie under of attending the Assembly and of defending them at the same time." He thought it desirable and Jones considered it imperative that Washington return temporarily to Frederick and solicit votes. Washington naturally wanted to go and to do his utmost to achieve what he had undertaken; but he could not get the full approval of his conscience. Marching orders might reach him; an emergency might develop; the service might suffer, and censure might fall on him if he were absent on personal business.

Washington could do nothing except to await the result. Late in the night of June 25, or on the morning of the twenty-sixth, he had it. He had been elected. What was more, he had led the poll. It stood: Washington, 309; Martin, 239; West, 199; Swearingen, 45. Now he was to be a lawmaker and was to see how those who authorized the drafts and levied the taxes looked on the officers who spent the revenue in the bloody business of war.

In letters to thank the friends who managed his canvass, Washington spoke gloomily of the military outlook: "Our expedition seems overcast with too many ills to give you any satisfaction in a transient relation of them. God knows what's intended; for nothing seems ripe for execution; backwardness, and I would (if I dared) say more, appears in all things." This pessimism was born of slow preparations for the advance to the Ohio and of the fact that the support of Indians seemed almost as uncertain as ever. Apparently Washington did not know that Forbes was seeking, and with good prospects of success, to detach the hostile Indians from their French allies. In addition Washington was profoundly concerned over the selection of the best approach to the French stronghold on the Ohio. In June and during the first days of July, it had been reported widely that Forbes intended to follow the road used in 1755, but now Washington feared that the General had been misled into choosing a line of advance where a serviceable road did not exist.

Advanced Redcoats were at Raystown. The question was whether the General should attempt to proceed from that point directly northwest for eighty miles or should pursue Braddock's route across the Alleghenies and over Laurel Hill and Chestnut Ridge. If the advance were by a new road from Raystown, then the greater part of the troops at Fort Cumberland would have to be moved to the Pennsylvania base. This would involve the abandonment of the line of supply from Alexandria to Fort Cumberland for all purposes other than the victualling of the few men who might be left on Wills Creek. Trade might follow the road the army smoothed. The rival interests of Pennsylvania and Virginia thus were at stake.

Washington did not admit and probably did not feel he had any selfish or personal interest in the continued use of a line of supply, via Fort Cumberland, that would make the Potomac the watergate to the Ohio. From the military point of view, he was so convinced of the superiority of Braddock's road that he was to attribute advocacy of a different policy to "Pennsylvanian artifice." His argument was positive: From the time a road to the Ohio first was discussed, the Indians had said that the trail from Wills Creek was much the best. On the basis of their experience, the road had been built: it must be "firmer and better" than a new one could be. In the next place, circumstance demanded that a blow be struck on the Ohio in 1758 because the central and southern Colonies were making their maximal effort during the year and could not do as much again in 1759. The Indians would not remain friendly in event the English continued inactive. Of all the reasons for using Braddock's road, the one that Washington most emphasized was that of saving time. The season, he maintained, was too far advanced to permit of the construction of a new road that year.

Neither Forbes nor Bouquet was committed irrevocably, though they tentatively had decided on the route from Raystown. This line of advance had been recommended to them by responsible men in Philadelphia. The commanders had no reason to suppose they had been misled by self-interest. The matter seemed so completely one of wise choice that Forbes and Bouquet were puzzled by the vehemence of the Virginian's insistence on the use of Braddock's road. Washington, in the judgment of his superiors, minimized the obstacles which had balked Braddock many times in 1755.

Because of the stand taken by Washington, Byrd and other men from south of the Potomac, Bouquet reviewed the choice of the Raystown approach and collected such additional information as he could concerning the relative advantages of the two routes. In summarizing the reports for Forbes, he took pains to say of the most conspicuous dissenter: "Colonel Washington is filled with a sincere zeal for the success of the expedition and will march wherever you determine with the same activity. He is sure that, with all the information he can gather, the route we have chosen is the most impracticable for horses; that the mountains are bad and that Braddock's Road is the only one to take." At the end of July Bouquet arranged a conference with the Colonel in the hope, as he phrased it, "that we might all centre in one and the same opinion." Washington went to the meeting resolved to urge speed and to get leave "to advance on with the Virginians to the crossing [of the Youghiogheny] at least, opening the road and constructing posts as we go." All this and more he told Bouquet July 30—and all without convincing his superior.

Washington was profoundly disappointed. He went back to Fort Cumberland and wrote out his arguments in full for Bouquet, who had asked for such a paper in order that it might be placed before the General. Then Washington did a dangerous thing. He believed that Bouquet was the special advocate of the Raystown route, and that Forbes probably was being deceived regarding it. As it happened, Francis Halkett, a comrade of Braddock's army, was Brigade Major of the British forces in Pennsylvania and often was acting secretary to the commander. Washington reasoned that if he explained the situation to Halkett, that officer might pass the information to the General. Without going over the head of Bouquet, it might be possible to appeal to Forbes in a matter concerning which Washington was convinced he was correct. The Virginian accordingly addressed a letter to Halkett the day he completed the long argument he intended to send Bouquet.

Three days later, and before his letter could reach Halkett, word came to Washington from Bouquet that the choice of the General was for the route directly from Raystown. Virginia's spokesman replied with dignity and with just a touch of stiffness that he would obey orders, but that he was of the same opinion still. This was by no means the end of it. Washington did more than adhere to his opinion. He continued to argue for advance along the old road, and he kept predicting calamity from the attempt to cut a new one during the brief remaining period of open weather. Within a few days he was on the black books of the commanding General. Forbes came accidentally upon Washington's letter to Halkett, read it and felt that it explained the source of the Virginians' opposition to the Raystown route. On the strength of this disclosure, Forbes began to build up a distrust of the author of the communication.

Even this neither changed Washington's opinion nor silenced him. Both he and Colonel Byrd had written Virginia's new Governor, Francis Fauquier, that they did not expect large results from the advance in Pennsylvania. Fauquier replied that it might be too late to prevent the attempt to build the Raystown road but that he hoped Washington and Byrd would explain to their commanding officers that Virginia's enlistment of troops and her supply of money had been based on the belief that a decisive effort would be made in 1758 to take Fort DuQuesne. Those officers needed no urging. The trial of their judgment was under way.

Bouquet's men cut the road to the top of the Allegheny Mountains, got the first division of the artillery over the crest and started work on the crossing of Laurel Hill. Beyond that barrier was the settlement of Loyal Hannon, which Bouquet intended to make his advanced base. General Forbes directed that Washington proceed westward from Fort Cumberland by the old road. These instructions were a triumph for the Virginian. He immediately wrote Bouquet a letter in which he told of the orders from

Forbes, described the good prospect ahead and concluded with an expression of hope that Bouquet's advance from Raystown would be successful. At the same time, Washington did not believe the army should move west in two columns. He wanted everything concentrated on Braddock's road for an immediate start and continued his criticism of the new route and the delay in getting the troops on the march.

There were many troubles and some hopes at Forbes's Headquarters, which had been moved on August 12 from Carlisle to Shippensburg. The General was struggling with the bloody flux and was better one day and worse the next. Forbes was having difficulty with Sir John St. Clair. St. Clair on his own account got into an altercation with Adam Stephen and called the Virginians "mutineers." Forbes was conscious that delay on his part was provoking comment. It was due primarily, he insisted, to the "horrible roguery and rascality" of the farmers who did not supply promised vehicles and teams. As the passing of September reduced steadily the time during which the army could hope to advance on Fort DuQuesne, every new difficulty was a test of the nerves of the commanders. A rain appeared to be a calamity, a day of warm sunshine an occasion of rejoicing.

Such was the situation when Washington had the long-desired opportunity of a personal conference with Forbes at Raystown. There, on September 16, he received one clear order from his commander: He was to return to Fort Cumberland and move thence as promptly as possible to Raystown with his own and Byrd's troops. This put an end to Washington's hope of an advance on Braddock's road—but it meant participation, which Washington had been craving. He and Byrd and their officers were to rejoin the advanced contingents and mingle with the largest armed force Washington ever had seen. Soon after they reached Raystown, Stephen informed the Virginia Colonels he had been told by everyone that the road from Loyal Hannon to Fort DuQuesne was impracticable. One of the Virginians passed this information to Forbes, who took advantage of the occasion to speak his mind to Washington and to Byrd. The General felt they actually would be glad, rather than sorry, that the new route could not be used, because they had so predicted. Forbes's was a stern rebuke and it was not without warrant.

Washington had news on September 20 or 21 of a strange and costly misadventure. Maj. James Grant of the Seventy-seventh Regiment had gone over the Allegheny Mountains and Laurel Hill and, with his troops, had joined Colonel Bouquet at Loyal Hannon. Bouquet had abundant force to beat off any surprise attack, but he was harassed by small bands of Indians who lurked around his camp, picked up stragglers and fired almost daily at men sent to care for the horses in nearby woods. About the time of Grant's arrival, Bouquet had decided to send out a number of detachments to scour the country and, if possible, waylay the French Indians and recover the prisoners that had been carried off. Grant disapproved this. If Bouquet would give him five hundred men, Grant stated, he would make a secret march to Fort DuQuesne, ascertain conditions there and, if circumstance favored him, make a night attack on the Indians supposed to be camped around the fort. Bouquet demurred. Grant pressed tenaciously, and at length Bouquet yielded, but he cautiously increased to about 750 the number of troops, exclusive of Indians, whom Grant was to take. Only when all the decisions had been made by Bouquet did he call in the officers who knew more about woodland warfare—James Burd, who commanded the Pennsylvanians, and Andrew Lewis, in charge of the advanced companies of Washington's Regiment. Lewis's experience warned him against the dispatch of so small a force as 750 white men, with a few native scouts, to reconnoitre close to the French fort and at so considerable a distance from his own base. These objections being overruled, Lewis was ready to obey orders but he was insistent that it be remembered he had not approved the plan.

Off, then, the column moved September 9—300 Highlanders of the Seventy-seventh, 100 men of the new Royal American Regiment, about 175 of the First Virginia, 100 Pennsylvanians, 100 Marylanders, and a mixed Indian contingent of Nottaways, Tuscaroras and Catawbas. No opposition was encountered anywhere along the line of march. At 3 P.M. on the twelfth Grant was on what appeared to him to be advantageous ground, at a distance, according to his guides, of ten or twelve miles from Fort DuQuesne. There he halted, made preparations for the final stage of his advance and at length shaped his plan to conform approximately to his orders from Bouquet, which were to this effect: He was to reconnoitre the route from Loyal Hannon to Fort DuQuesne and procure information concerning the garrison, the condition of the French defences and the number of Indians at hand. If he succeeded in reaching the vicinity of the fort without being detected, he would be free to occupy the adjacent hill and open fire on the Indians camped outside the parapet. In the event he discovered the savages huddled around their fires after dark, he was authorized to have a detachment put on white shirts over their jackets and proceed to attack the Indians shortly after midnight. For the successful execution of this strange plan, Grant had to preserve the maximum possible secrecy during the final stage of his advance and regulate his march in such a manner that he would approach the fort after dark but with adequate information concerning the ground.

By 11 P.M. of September 13 Grant reached the hill a few hundred yards from the fort and there he assembled 750 men or more almost within rifle-range of the French. So far as he knew, he still enjoyed all the advantage of surprise. How best to utilize that advantage, when he manifestly could not capture the fort by regular approaches, was the question Grant had to answer. Few Indian fires were around the fort; this might indicate merely that the fires had burned out; or it might be a warning that the natives had learned of the approach of the English and had withdrawn into the fort.

Grant sent for Lewis and explained that the absence of Indian fires prevented the execution of the original plan. It still would be possible, he said, to remain a day in front of the fort without being discovered. The utmost should be made of that opportunity, and at once. Lewis must take two hundred provincials and two hundred Highlanders and "attack anything that was found about the fort." In spite of the midnight blackness,

Grant felt absolute confidence that these orders could be obeyed. The troops had on the prescribed white shirts and could distinguish one another a short distance apart; they did not have far to move; four hundred seemed a sufficient number to deal with all adversaries who might be found outside the fort.

After the attacking force started down the hill Grant disposed the other troops. Minutes passed. No sound of rifles came from the vicinity of the fort; no fires flared. Grant did not know what had happened to muffle or engulf his attack. After a time of nervous waiting, Lewis came out of the darkness. It was impossible to proceed, he said; the road was bad, logs blocked it, the men were bewildered. They might fire into their own divided ranks and might not find their way back. Grant hurried down from the hill to see conditions for himself. "I found the troops," he said later, "in the greatest confusion I ever saw men in, which in truth was not surprising for the Major had brought them back from the plain when he returned himself, and every man took a road of their own." It was too late, Grant said in his official report, to attempt to re-form Lewis's command or move forward the men who had been left on the hill. All he could do was to move forward a detachment of fifty men towards the place where on arrival during the night he had seen two or three fires burning.

This was attempted, but no Indian camps were found. The detachment had to content itself with setting afire one of the storehouses, where the flames soon were extinguished. About the time this party was mounting the hill again, in foggy dawn, Grant sent Lewis back with 250 men to the point, two miles from the front, where Capt. Thomas Bullett had been left with the baggage.

Now, with about 550 men at his command, Grant shifted some of his Highlanders to the left and put Pennsylvanians on his right. Soon, when he learned that the position of the detachment on the left had been discovered by Indians, Grant directed his drums to beat the reveille. He noted later: "I must own I thought we had nothing to fear," but disillusionment was immediate. Out from the fort poured the French garrison, with their Indian allies in front. Small parties, working together, scattered among the trees, fired, loaded again and then dashed forward to new shelter. The Highlanders' officers, imprudently exposed, were shot down at once. Startled soldiers became bewildered and broke.

As soon as the swelling sound of the fire made it clear that Grant was attacked and being compelled to give ground, Lewis yielded to the pleas of his officers and men that he go to the rescue. He pushed forward but could not establish contact with Grant, whose men now were scattered and in hopeless confusion.

A few minutes more and the situation was beyond repair. Panic gripped the men who had received the first attack. Even Lewis's veterans of forest warfare did not linger behind their trees for many shots at the enemy. Soon the survivors were flocking back to the baggage and to the guard under Captain Bullett. That officer did not wait for refugees and pursuing French and Indians to engulf him. Although he could count only his fifty rifles, he attacked as furiously as if he had a regiment. The fast and determined fire of this contingent made the enemy hesitate long enough for the surviving Highlanders and Colonials to escape. Bullett's Virginians continued to load and fire, but they were too few to turn a bad retreat into a drawn battle. Then Bullett's men, too, stubbornly and reluctantly withdrew. The enemy did not pursue far. Losses were severe for the force engaged. A subsequent list covered twenty-two officers and 278 men killed. The Virginians slain in Washington's Regiment numbered sixty-two.

Disgust was general. Forbes was sure "no man [could] justify" the affair, which he attributed primarily to Grant's acceptance of the story that the French forces at Fort DuQuesne were small. At Headquarters, there was no disposition to shield Grant or deny the Colonials full credit for what they had done to prevent a worse defeat, but there was not at Raystown a touch of the despair that prevailed at Fort Cumberland after the surrender of Fort Necessity or after the disaster to Braddock. The loss was not considered serious enough to weaken materially a force that believed itself definitely superior. In Forbes's mind, the only foe that could stop the British advance was continued bad weather. Washington was convinced that the operation was poorly planned and was out of sympathy with the direction of the whole enterprise. He echoed his old complaint: ". . . I see no probability of opening the road this campaign: How then can we expect a favorable issue to the expedition?" He was not reconciled or even mollified when General Forbes publicly complimented him on the behavior of the Virginians in Grant's fight.

Forbes daily was issuing prudent directions of instructional value to a young officer who never had operated with so large a body of men as Forbes had under his command. There were lessons, also, in such matters as Forbes's arrangements for putting the army in condition to move on an hour's notice. Equally informative was the General's careful explanation of the manner in which soldiers were to get themselves and their arms in order after exposure to a heavy rain. As one of these well-fashioned orders followed another, Washington did not disdain them; he read them carefully and compared them with his own experience. Disappointed though he was, he was not disgruntled. He still differed from his chief, but he did not sulk.

While Forbes, resolute, though now too sick to ride a horse, battled with nearly all the usual perplexities of the field and with some that were exceptional, the French became active. "Having a mind," in Forbes's words, "to repay Major Grant's visit," the enemy sent a column against Loyal Hannon. Its approach was discovered on the morning of the twelfth by the firing of twelve guns southwest of the camp. The French boldly approached and opened a hot fire, but they did not make a direct assault. After about two hours they withdrew with many stolen horses—only to return that night. Discouraged then, they disappeared. Forbes was disappointed that the French were not pursued, but he wrote cheerfully, "I fancy they will not visit soon again."

It was now his turn, his last chance of 1758. In the knowledge that he had left only a brief period in which to strike at Fort DuQuesne, Forbes strained every man, horse and wheel in an effort to get close enough to deliver a swift and sudden blow. All troops were to be held in readiness for advance at the beat of the drum.

The road over Laurel Hill made Bouquet and Forbes wonder if, after all, they possibly could win the race with winter. As in the struggle with the Allegheny Mountains, the odds changed almost daily. Forbes had been told that October and November were the best months for a campaign because it then was possible to see a little way through the woods and thereby avoid surprises. Instead, he found the season forbidding, but every day that the weather permitted, Forbes pushed his men forward and at length, on October 23, he advanced Washington to Loyal Hannon.

A brave, unusual achievement now lighted the darkness of the rainy autumn and strengthened the heart of Forbes. He had been mindful of the dangers he would face on the way to Fort DuQuesne if the Indians were his enemy and he had been unwilling to acquiesce in the conclusion of some of the Colonial leaders that the Indians of the Ohio country were now bound permanently to France. Forbes believed the Indians could be brought to see that Britain would win the war and that it was to their interest to be on the winning side. He had undertaken to induce the government of Pennsylvania to negotiate for peace with France's savage allies. Partly because of Forbes's persistence, Gov. William Denny and the Council of Pennsylvania had asked Fredrich Post to make a journey to the Ohio and invite the Indians to renew their old treaties with England. Post was a Polish lay missionary of the Moravian sect Unitas Fratrum and for sixteen years had been laboring among Indians in whose language he had acquired proficiency. He left Philadelphia July 15 and went to Fort DuQuesne. In spite of French machinations and the treachery of one of his companions, Post displayed so much courage, honesty and simple address that the Indians agreed to make peace if all the Colonial Governors would join in it. With this assurance and the promise of some of the Indians to attend a conference at Easton, Pennsylvania, Post succeeded in getting to Fort Augusta September 22.

While Post had been persuading the savages to end their war with England, Sir William Johnson and others had been inviting the Chiefs of many tribes to the meeting at Easton. Forbes had followed eagerly each step in this adventure of diplomacy and had countenanced military delays he otherwise would have rebuked, because he was afraid a premature blow against Fort DuQuesne might involve the death of some of the Indians who, by patience, might be prevailed upon to make peace and desert the French. At last, about October 27, Forbes heard that a treaty had been signed under which some of the Indians would make common cause with England, but, as he reported to Pitt, "[they] require time, a thing at present so precious to me that I have none to spare." Then he stated his stark alternatives: "[I] must in a day or two choose either to risk everything and march to the enemy's fort, retreat across the Allegheny if the provincials leave me, or maintain myself where I am to the spring."

These alternatives were not hypothetical. Apart from the paralyzing halt that might be caused by weather, there was danger the little Army might be wrecked by discharge. The Second Virginia would cease to exist, under the terms of its enlistment, on December 1. Provision had been made for the muster-out of the First Virginia Regiment on May 1, 1759. It was much the same with the Pennsylvania, Maryland and North Carolina troops. No pay beyond December 1 had been provided for them. They might start home with the Virginians and leave the General no troops but the survivors of his 1500 Highlanders. Forbes consequently had to work more vigorously than ever to put the troops in condition to go forward at full speed if November brought a sufficient number of clear days to dry the road.

Skies remained dark. Uncertainty prevailed both as to the weather and the strength of the enemy. None of the Indians would undertake reconnaissance as far as Fort DuQuesne at that bleak and treacherous season. Daily there was grim subtraction; every day left one less of life for the force, one less of hope of victory. The outlook was more discouraging than ever when, on November 12, the outposts sent word that the enemy again was approaching Loyal Hannon. Forbes immediately sent Washington with five hundred of the Virginia troops to pursue the French, who were assumed to be making another raid on the cattle and horses of the British. Behind Washington, George Mercer was to proceed with another five hundred men and try to surround the enemy. Washington proceeded briskly and came upon a party of French and Indians around a fire. In an exchange of musketry, one of the alien soldiers was killed. By closing in quickly on the others, the Virginians captured a white prisoner and two Indians.

Washington held these prisoners near the fire and awaited developments. Presently, through the growing darkness, a considerable force was observed. Almost at the same instant, both sides delivered a volley. Men fell; the wounded cried out. From the approaching troops there likewise came shouts. Officers yelled their orders—and yelled in English. The men were Mercer's. Virginians were firing into the ranks of their friends. Each side had mistaken the other for French. As soon as the grim mistake was realized, the men lowered their guns and turned to the care of their wounded. The toll was heavier than in any action Washington had witnessed after Braddock's defeat: one lieutenant dead; thirteen other soldiers killed; twenty-six wounded. The enemy, disappearing in the darkness, might say mockingly that he did not need to attack the English: they would kill one another.

Washington's humiliation was not without balm. The white prisoner taken by the Virginia Regiment proved to be a British subject, one Johnson, who had thrown his fortunes with the French and had served in the garrison at Fort DuQuesne. If he could be made to tell the truth, he could give Forbes the information most desired, that of the strength of the enemy at Fort DuQuesne. Faced with the promise of life and gold as the alternative to torture and death, Johnson talked freely. The French at Fort DuQuesne were weak. The contingent that had made the raid on Loyal Hannon had quit the forks of the Allegheny and Monongahela; the Ohio Indians had gone home. Similar information was given by the two captured Indians Forbes believed his opportunity, his last opportunity, had come: he would gamble on the truth of this new intelligence; his advanced units must cut a road quickly over the last barrier of Chesnut Ridge; then with an unencumbered, fast-moving force he would march for Fort DuQuesne. To assure fullest mobility, Forbes divided his attacking force into three brigades. One of these was to be commanded by Colonel Bouquet and another by Lt. Col. Archibald Montgomery of the Seventy-seventh. The third, the only one entrusted to a Colonial officer, was assigned to Washington. His command was to be his own Regiment, two companies of artificers and the Maryland, North Carolina and Delaware contingents.

Forbes now sent out three forces. One of Pennsylvanians under Col. John Armstrong was to proceed ahead of the others and build redoubts one or two days' marches apart. Washington was to follow and cut a road; Montgomery was then to proceed, as a reenforcement of the troops ahead and as a vanguard of the main body of infantry and artillery.

November 18—twelve days and twelve only before the army would begin to break up! The weather held fair. There was a chance, if still a gambler's chance, that the fort could be reached and taken.

On the twenty-first, the army was close to Fort DuQuesne, exactly how close none could say with certainty, but near enough to invite surprise attack. Vigilance already had been carried far beyond the care the average prudent commander would display; overnight it was made an absolute imperative for every man. With Bouquet's troops in advance, the columns made good progress on the twenty-second and camped on the farther side of Turtle Creek. The men lay on their arms that night in complete silence.

Before Forbes began the march on the twenty-third the weapons of all soldiers were examined again. Warning was given that any man who fired his piece without an officer's order would receive two hundred lashes on the spot. Then the troops started through the woods and marched briskly in the cold weather. When distances were computed after they bivouacked, one estimate put the column fifteen miles from Fort DuQuesne; another scout reckoned the distance twelve miles. The men once more were told what they were to do in the event of sudden attack. Flour for six days and meat for four were issued; all the felling axes were ground. Most careful were the efforts to determine what the enemy was doing and whether he knew the English were close enough to lunge. Patrols were sent to search the woods nearby. Reconnaissance to Fort DuQuesne itself was entrusted to Indians who went out separately.

The anxious twenty-fourth of November was spent in camp—the beginning of the last week during which the army could be held together. If Forbes had only seven days, he was resolved to make the most of them.

Night came early, a bleak night of foreboding and of expectancy. The next day might bring, perhaps must bring, the battle to which Washington had been looking forward since that July day almost three and a half years previously, when he had been compelled to turn his back on the Monongahela and the ghastly field of Braddock's debacle . . . and now . . . Now a Redman was going to Headquarters—one of the scouts who had been sent out on the twenty-third. No great news was his. He had not been to the junction of the rivers, but he had been on ground whence he could look directly toward DuQuesne, and billowing there he had seen a great column of smoke.

Smoke! Had the French learned of the approach of the English, and, despairing of successful defence, burned and abandoned their stronghold? It was a mystery of minutes only: another scout arrived. He had been to Fort DuQuesne—or rather where Fort DuQuesne had been. It was gone. So were the French. They had abandoned the site!

No battle, then, was ahead—perhaps no flags, no surrendered arms, no booty—but the prize would be England's! As soon as the light horse could saddle and get off, they must ride to the junction and, if the fire still burned, they must put it out. The infantry would follow the next morning.

A long, long morning it must have been and a still longer afternoon. Twelve miles of unbroken woodland and all its little streams had to be crossed by men whose eager ambition ran far ahead of them. Darkness had fallen when, at six o'clock, the army reached its goal. There, at the junction, stood the wreck of the ramparts of the stout square fort. Two hundred yards away, on the bank of the Allegheny, was the shell of another burned fort, the deserted outworks of which had never been finished. In the gathering darkness, this seemed a poor reward for so much of sickness and shivering, of muddy marches and long nights' misery—an ugly, disappointing scene to men who doubtless had pictured a frowning fort, its bastions crowded with stubborn French. No fort, no food, no booty the British found, but almost beneath them was the Ohio, the mighty stream that watered a valley of fabulous richness as it swept to the Mississippi.

Indians in considerable number were on an island in the river, ready to make their peace with the victor. The British learned that the French had placed the cannon of the forts on boats and had carried them down the river. Then the garrison, reported to consist of about five hundred, had set fire to everything that would burn. The troops had departed, some by water, and some on foot down the bank of the Ohio. They were going, the Indians believed, to the Illinois country.

Forbes had made a great conquest at small cost in life. Neither ambition nor illness blinded him to the possibilities of the land where, once again, the standard of Britain had been set. He would be compelled, he said, to keep a small force of Colonials at the fort during the winter, after which he hoped Pennsylvania would give him support "to fix this noble, fine country, to all perpetuity, under the dominion of Great Britain." Ceremonies attended so great an advance—a service of thanksgiving November 26 with a sermon, a day of celebration on the twenty-seventh, and then a solemn march to Braddock's field, where the skulls of more than 450 men were buried. Their bones long before had been scattered by wolves.

If Washington had a part in these events it probably was perfunctory because he was looking now to Williamsburg and to the White House on the Pamunkey. Reluctantly he obeyed the order of Forbes to assign some of the ragged men of the First Virginia Regiment to the garrison of Fort DuQuesne. Justice and gratitude prompted Washington to urge that arrangements be made for provisioning and clothing these men more heavily during the bleak months they must remain on the icy Ohio. The entire Regiment, in fact, was worn and must be refitted; help to them best could be rendered where his heart was calling him. So, when Forbes suggested that Washington might be able by personal representation to get early assistance from Virginia for the troops of the Colony, it was not necessary for the General to use persuasion. Washington was off. On arrival at Winchester during the night of December 8, he was sick and exhausted, but, after brief efforts at recuperation, he made his way to Belvoir and before the year's end was in Williamsburg.

It had now been five years and two months since Washington had started for the Ohio to warn the French to leave that region. He had required fifty-two days only to reach in December 1753 the "land in the Fork," which he had thought "extremely well situated for a fort"; after that visit, nearly the whole of his energies for four years and a half had been devoted to getting there again. Now, he was looking to the future, matrimony, the management of a much-enlarged estate, and service as a Burgess. He took pride in what he had done as a soldier, but he considered his years of military duty a closed chapter of his life.

Had Washington sat down to analyze the scope of his training, he would have found that the stern master, Experience, sometimes to the scourging of a sensitive skin, had taught him many fundamentals of command but had given him few of the higher qualifications. What he had learned on the frontier, what every officer had to learn in that school of experience, were the A B C's of leadership, commonplace but irreplaceable.

Washington had been able to assume responsibility. He could not have acted as he did on a score of occasions if he had not seen clearly that a soldierly trust carries with it the obligation to make decisions and take the consequences. Washington had found that he often must deal with subordinates who were not men of his own choice or even of any special aptitude for arms. He had to take the human material given him and ascertain its worth in order that he might use every officer at that individual's best. He learned in time how to gain the affectionate confidence and enthusiastic good will of most of these subordinate officers, though he did not succeed in winning a similar measure of personal esteem from many officers of his own rank in the regular establishment or in the service of other Colonies. Most of these men regarded him as competent, but they considered him ambitious and not particularly likeable or conspicuously able.

Washington quickly realized the value of absolute justice in dealing with his officers and learned equally well the ensnaring danger of any sort of favoritism. Justice was instinctive with him. He learned a different code for the men in the ranks, the traditional code of punishment as the basis of discipline. He found that drunkenness and desertion had ceaselessly to be combated with every weapon a commanding officer could fashion. Tippling-houses had to be under sternest regulation and, if possible, suppressed. As for desertion, it was the nightmare of command. Washington tried all the expedients. Nothing availed. Washington learned that as desertion steadily sapped his Regiment, he could not hope to raise it to full strength by the voluntary enlistment of free men. He was convinced of the futility of relying upon the militia. The only substantial resources of manpower were indentured servants, vagrants and such unmarried men as county officers would be willing to draft. Washington's lesson in recruiting was largely negative: He knew where he could *not* get men; he did *not* know where he could.

Washington acquired, among others, this fundamental of military administration: Transport and supply called for early planning and constant, detailed attention; but if these qualities were displayed energetically, it was possible to provide food for troops in spite of the small number of wagons and the badness of roads. One of the most protective of all the lessons he learned was that of timing with reasonable accuracy the preparation and delivery of supplies and provisions. Another basic lesson in military administration was that shortages in clothing, equipment and tools and deficiencies of medical care were inevitable and that the most had to be made of what was procurable. It was repeatedly impressed upon him that the backwardness of American industry, the limitations on exports and the resulting scarcity of money made the sternest economy a *sine qua non* of military defence.

Such were the principal lessons Colonel Washington learned by the time Forbes reached the site of the burned and abandoned Fort DuQuesne. All were elementary lessons, but they were essentials of warfare that might unhappily be renewed in America. War could be waged with ill-trained and sometimes reluctant and sullen soldiers who would be poorly supplied with transport, weapons, equipment and provisions by a feeble government that lacked solid financial resources. The only commanding officer who would have any prospect of success with such an army, under such a government, would be one who had learned how to make much of little, one who had, above all other qualities, resolute patience.

Washington had acquired that patience and some of the other essentials, but his training was deficient in seven disciplines of importance among the many an officer should master. He had not acquired the art of dealing with the private soldier in a manner to arouse the individual's sense of responsibility for a cause. He had been a definite failure in recruiting. He had shown that he could lead a regiment; he had not demonstrated that he could raise one quickly. He had learned scarcely anything about the utilization of militia and apparently never made allowance for their ignorance and their lack of weapons the law unreasonably expected them to provide. Their reluctance to serve, their readiness to desert and the cowardice that many of them exhibited in the presence of the enemy created early in Washington's mind a disgust that soon became a prejudice. He had to call on them frequently, but he never did so with any confidence. Nor did he press his proposals for their training under sterner law and through longer service.

Washington's next deficiency in training was his limited acquaintance with officers from other Colonies. He had much to learn concerning the manner in which ambitious, self-important officers of the different Colonies could work together. Akin to this was his failure to adopt precisely the right attitude towards his superior officers. The more Washington dealt with the senior officers of the regular establishment, the less, in general, was his

MAP / 4

THE REGION OF THE ADVENTURES
OF YOUNG GEORGE WASHINGTON, 1732-1759

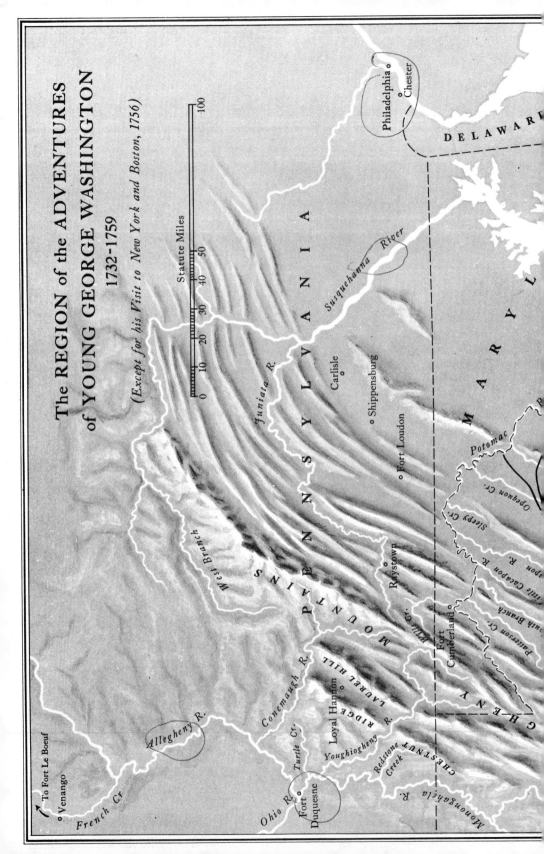

The REGION of the ADVENTURES of YOUNG GEORGE WASHINGTON
1732-1759
(Except for his Visit to New York and Boston, 1756)

Statute Miles

0 10 20 30 40 50 100

DELAWARE

Philadelphia
Chester

Susquehanna River

P E N N S Y L V A N I A

Carlisle
Shippensburg
Fort Loudon

Juniata R.

M A R Y L A N D

Potomac

Opequon Cr.

Sleepy Cr.

Little Cacapon R.

Cacapon R.

South Branch

Patterson Cr.

West Branch

Raystown

Fort Cumberland

A L L E G H E N Y

M O U N T A I N S

Conemaugh R.

Loyal Hanton

LAUREL HILL

CHESTNUT RIDGE

Youghiogheny R.

Will Cr.

Redstone Creek

Monongahela R.

Allegheny R.

Ohio R.
Fort Duquesne

Turtle Cr.

French Cr.

Venango

To Fort Le Boeuf

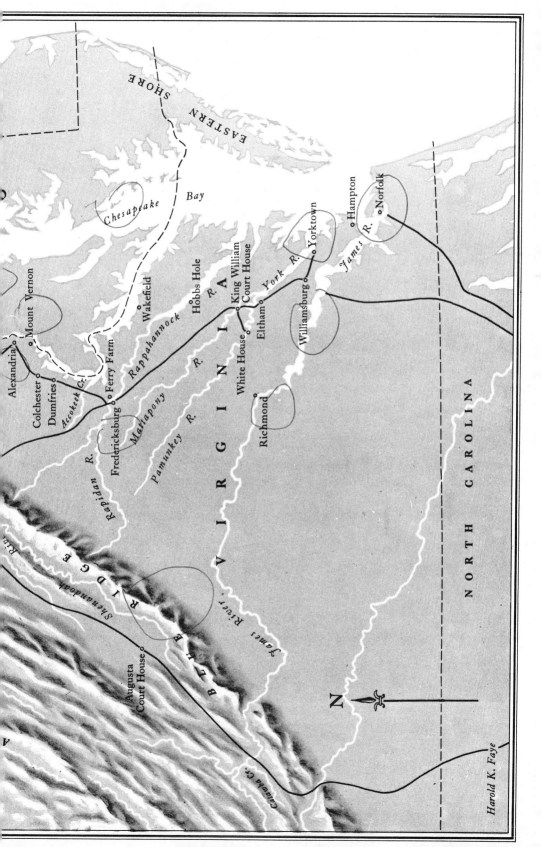

FAMILY LIFE

1. Lawrence Washington. Painting attributed to John Wollaston.
Courtesy of the Mount Vernon Ladies' Association.

2. Martha Dandridge Custis. Painting by John Wollaston. *Courtesy of Washington and Lee University.*

3.   Martha Washington. Painting by Charles Willson Peale. *Courtesy of
the Yale University Art Gallery, Mabel Brady Garvan Collection.*

4. John Parke Custis. *By the Kind Permission of E. L. R. Smith of Baltimore, Maryland, Owner of the Original.*

5. The Washington Family. Painting by Edward Savage. *Courtesy of the Philadelphia Museum of Art.*

6. Washington in 1777–1778. Painting by Charles Willson Peale.
Courtesy of the Mount Vernon Ladies' Association.

7. George William Fairfax.

8. Washington in 1787. Painting by Charles Willson Peale. *Courtesy of the Pennsylvania Academy of the Fine Arts.*

9. Washington in 1796. The "Lansdowne" Portrait by Gilbert Stuart. *Courtesy of the Pennsylvania Academy of the Fine Arts.*

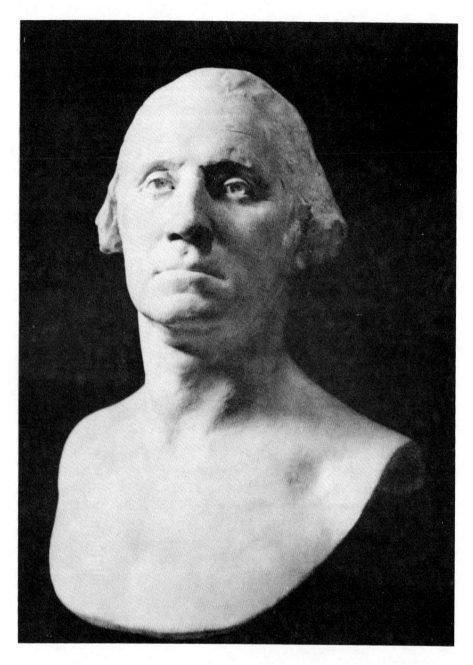

10. Washington in 1785. Clay Bust for the Statue by Jean Antoine
Houdon. *Courtesy of the Mount Vernon Ladies' Association.*

respect for their accomplishments. Forbes and Bouquet were the best soldiers with whom he had served. He could have learned much from them concerning matters of military administration. Instead, he opposed so persistently the choice of the Raystown route that he probably became prejudiced against them and certainly, for a time, created suspicion in the mind of Forbes. There scarcely could be denial that Washington went beyond the bounds of what the military etiquette of the times allowed a subordinate.

Washington's other deficiencies as a young commander were circumstantial. He had been given little opportunity of handling any large body of men on the road until the last weeks of the campaign under Forbes. Even then, he never directed the advance of more than one thousand. That number he apparently commanded with ease, and he employed a road-building contingent with success. No fair-minded man could have said he gave evidence of having reached the limit of his ability to command. Washington seems never to have had any misgiving of his ability to keep his head while engaged with the enemy. His baptism of fire had convinced him, apparently, that he could meet the challenge of conflict. It was by chance and by reason of modest rank that Washington had been given no opportunity of employing in a strategic plan of his own design the tactics he had learned thoroughly. Even so, he had not been lacking in strategical study, nor had he been deficient in strategical sense, that refined, acute military judgment indispensable to the soldier. The Virginia commander, though displaying no genius in strategy, appeared to have sound conceptions and just appreciation of the value of the wisely timed offensive.

None of Washington's contemporaries made the effort, at the end of 1758, to weigh his military virtues against his shortcomings. The only man who might have been interested in doing this was Forbes, and he was close to death. Washington's own officers did not look on him with the eyes of cold valuation as a soldier but with something of the ardor of young men for a successful leader of their own age. They prepared and, on the last day of the year, signed a paper which, in spite of exuberant rhetoric, was solid proof of the progress he had made in one great essential of leadership, that of arousing the enthusiasm of his subordinates. The twenty-seven company officers who subscribed to this address spoke gratefully of the happiness they had enjoyed with their Colonel, the honor they had won under him, and the affection they felt for him: "Your steady adherence to impartial justice, your quick discernment and invariable regard to merit, wisely intended to inculcate those genuine sentiments of true honor and passion for glory, from which the great military achievements have been derived, first heightened our natural emulation and our desire to excel. How much we improved by those regulations and your own example, with what cheerfulness we have encountered the several toils, especially while under your particular direction, we submit to yourself, and flatter ourselves that we have in a great measure answered your expectations." Assurance was added: "In you we place the most implicit confidence. Your presence only will cause a steady firmness and vigor to actuate in every breast, despising the greatest dangers and thinking light of toils and hardships, while led on by the man we know and love."

Did Washington deserve these words? At the end of 1758, as he approached his twenty-seventh birthday, what manner of man was he?

The company officers had seen their Colonel in many tests. A few of the ranking Captains had stood resolutely beside him in the flooded trench of feeble Fort Necessity. One or two of his subordinates had been where they could have observed the suppressed pain and perplexity in his honest eyes as he rode through the confused ranks near the bank of the Monongahela. His finely proportioned figure and his flawless horsemanship were the model of his juniors; his physical endurance had become a tradition in his Regiment. He was mature beyond his years, with all the vigor of growth from the good earth of character. To officers who discharged their duties with courage, intelligence and spirit, he always was amiable and attractive and sometimes he was affectionate.

Slow to praise excellencies, he was equally slow to forget them. If he seldom applauded, he always remembered. He did not cross the gulf that regulations had fixed between officers and men; and he did not feign admiration of the ignorant, common man who was more apt, he thought, to be a coward than a hero. In his dealings with troops, Washington's reliance was not on human nature but on military discipline. The possibility of promotion for the diligent and refreshment for the faithful was not disregarded; no substitute was offered for the performance of duty as duty. Daily practice exemplified what orders had proclaimed: "Discipline is the soul of an army."

Behind the flap of his own tent, the young commander sought the self-discipline he inculcated. This was not easy for a man of complicated emotional character. His ambition burned so steadily that it gave to all his efforts a concentration and a seriousness never relieved by the relaxing balm of humor. Even after he was convinced that high rank in his beloved profession of arms never would be his, he retained all the driving energy and all the instinctive planning required to press towards the goal of wealth, distinction and honor; but he could not laugh at his own relentless pursuit of pounds and epaulettes, and he could not smile at his own defeats. Instead, his consciousness of steadfast, wholehearted adherence to duty made him unhappily sensitive to criticism. He battled with this thinness of skin and, after five years in the field, reached the state of mind in which he could grip his temper and repress his sensitiveness if his resentment of criticism was likely to injure the defence of the Colony in a day of danger. He had achieved that much; he had not conquered a pride that had on occasion the color of self-righteousness.

His principal weaknesses were superficial or circumstantial. Facility of speech never would be his. It would not be possible for him to move a multitude; but if Washington could not stir emotion he could accomplish something that might be less impermanent: he could win support by sound judgment and disinterested zeal. He had no rock of refuge in religion. Instead of adhering to a creedal religion he held steadfastly, almost ostentatiously, to the principles of conduct he regarded as the code of gentlemen.

The foundations of that code were not love and mercy, faith and sacrifice, but honesty and duty, truth and justice, justice exact and inclusive, justice that never for an instant overlooked his own interests. Justice demanded that he do his utmost and that, in return, he receive what he had earned, whether it was the public esteem he cherished or the last penny due him by "the country" for the food of every batman the letter of military regulations allowed him.

What he demanded for himself, he allowed with equal exactness to all his fellow men. Anything that any person deserved at his hands, that person must receive on balanced scales, whether in monetary payment, reward, courtesy, candor or truth-telling. Justice never could walk with Compromise. Nor did adherence to justice require that young Washington be a partisan of individuals. If injustice to any individual came under Washington's eye in his own command, he would correct it as a matter of course, but there he drew the line. He would do his part to relieve human misery and he might be the champion of public causes. Rarely did he become the advocate of any man, lest support of one be injustice to another.

Justice was not "the be all and the end all" of Washington's code of conduct, but it was as basic in that code as the development of patience was in his training. The officer who tapped on the tent-pole to make a report to his Colonel probably would not feel that he was in the presence of a great man, but he knew that Washington would hear him with sure patience and dignified amiability, would reason logically and methodically, would concentrate on whatever duty the report imposed, would display sound judgment and cold, calm courage in the execution, would demand discipline and—always and inflexibly—would measure out exact justice.

Such was the soldier and the man. Some of his deeper characteristics were not known to the officers who addressed him at the end of 1758; but they wished to pay tribute to him as best they might, and they had now an occasion besides that of the conclusion of the campaign for expressing their affection for him: He had decided to resign—finally and without thought of reconsideration. His officers hoped against hope that he would remain with them, but if he would not, then those young Virginians wished to record that "as you have hitherto been the actuating soul of the whole corps, we shall at all times pay the most invariable regard to your will and pleasure. . . ."

This was honor of the sort he loved, but there were other ambitions now. A new Fort Pitt was rising on the ruins of DuQuesne; the Virginia frontier would be secure. Washington felt he had done his part for the King's domain. Let the northern Colonies take Quebec. For himself now, there was Mount Vernon and a seat in the House of Burgesses and Martha and the rich plantations of the Custises and the Parkes on slow-flowing, pleasant rivers!

CHAPTER / 6

No regret was in the heart of Col. George Washington as he resigned his commission at the end of 1758 and turned his horse from Williamsburg towards the plantation on the Pamunkey River where Martha Dandridge Custis was waiting for him. Lack of recognition by the British government "at home" had destroyed his military ambition but it had not lessened his conviction that he had done his part, and more, in defending both "the country," as he termed Virginia, and the other American domain of Great Britain. In the memory of service he was willing to put neglect behind him. Besides, there was no bleakness on the road that led to the estate of the woman of twenty-seven who was to be his bride. Fires would be burning and wedding garments would be ready at the White House. Beyond spread the tobacco plantations and the prospect of opulent years.

Every expectation was realized. The marriage ceremony was performed January 6, 1759, after which a happy honeymoon was spent at the well-furnished Custis home on the bank of the Pamunkey. George now found easy and cheerful companionship in a young woman, who, though not brilliant, had her full share of good nature. She had ample common sense, also, except where her two children were involved. The son, John Parke Custis, called "Jackie" by the family, was now four and a healthy, normal boy. His sister "Patsy"—christened Martha Parke Custis—was less vigorous at two, but was an attractive child.

The bridegroom, as a good man of business, made his first inquiries concerning the details of the new duties he was to assume as fiduciary, and then he had to go to Williamsburg where he began February 22—his twenty-seventh birthday—his service in the House of Burgesses.

The control and management of the House, as usual, were in the hands of a small number of powerful seniors. In the chair sat John Robinson, Treasurer and Speaker and Washington's consistent friend during the struggle for the Ohio. With him in the House worked Richard Bland, Edmund Pendleton, the Carters (Landon and three Charleses), and Peyton and John Randolph. These men did not always agree among themselves but whatever a majority of them advocated, the House customarily approved. The leading Burgesses usually worked together in complete understanding, and they carefully apportioned among themselves the chairmanships of the important committees. Not antagonistic to these men but developing steadily in thought and in knowledge of the law were several young members whom Washington probably met for the first time. One of the ablest of these was the Burgess for the College of William and Mary, George Wythe, personal adviser of the resident Governor, Francis Fauquier, whose title was officially that of Lieutenant Governor. Several other young Burgesses scarcely were inferior to Wythe in ability and diligence. From the counties still other youthful Virginians were looking towards Williamsburg and were hoping soon to be sitting among the members.

If Washington surveyed with polite curiosity those leading Burgesses whom he did not know already, they were interested in him as the most conspicuous of the younger soldiers of America. One of the lawmakers, his old friend and companion-in-arms, George Mercer, said of Washington in a letter written in 1760:

. . . He may be described as being straight as an Indian, measuring 6 feet 2 inches in his stockings, and weighing 175 lbs when he took his seat in the House of Burgesses in 1759. His frame is padded with well developed muscles, indicating great strength. His bones and joints are large as are his hands and feet. He is wide shouldered but has not a deep or round chest; is neat waisted, but is broad across the hips, and has rather long legs and arms. His head is well shaped, though not large, but is gracefully poised on a superb neck. A large and straight rather than a prominent nose; blue-grey penetrating eyes which are widely separated and over-hung by a heavy brow. His face is long rather than broad, with high round cheek bones, and terminates in a good firm chin. He has a clear tho rather colorless pale skin which burns with the sun. A pleasing and benevolent tho a commanding countenance, dark brown hair which he wears in a cue. His mouth is large and generally firmly closed, but which from time to time discloses some defective teeth. His features are regular and placid with all the muscles of his face under perfect control, tho flexible and expressive of deep feeling when moved by emotions. In conversation he looks you full in the face, is deliberate, deferential and engaging. His demeanor at all times composed and dignified. His movements and gestures are graceful, his walk majestic, and he is a splendid horseman.

The young soldier, thus described, had been in the House only four days, among old friends and new, when on February 26 an admirer rose and offered this resolution: ". . . that the thanks of the House be given to George Washington, Esq; a member of this House, late Colonel of the First Virginia Regiment, for his faithful Services to his Majesty, and this Colony, and for his brave and steady behavior, from the first Encroachments and hostilities of the French and their Indians, to his Resignation, after the happy Reduction of Fort DuQuesne." The resolution was passed immediately with a roar of "Ayes"; Mr. Speaker leaned forward in his chair to voice the thanks of the House; instinctively Washington arose, listened, blushed and sat down again, amid more applause.

The new member from Frederick found much that was instructive in the reports of committees and discussion of the subject for which, primarily, the General Assembly had been convened. As Fauquier explained in his address to the two houses on the opening day, General Amherst had written to ask that, for a final offensive on the Great Lakes against the French, Virginia supply him in 1759 with as many troops as the Colony had paid during the campaign of 1758.

The House responded that if the Colony fell short of Amherst's expectations in 1759, it would be because of "poverty alone, which has often obstructed many a noble and honest intention." This was polite notice that troops would not be supplied for an expedition on the Lakes, but it was not final. When the Committee of the Whole began to deliberate on a bill to raise the strength of the Regiment to one thousand men and continue it in service until December 1, 1759, the advocates of a strong war policy proposed that an additional five hundred be raised to guard the frontiers and that the Regiment be placed at the disposal of Amherst for such use as the military situation required.

In the intervals of the discussion, Washington had his first experience with embarrassing local bills and measures that affected counties in which he had special interest—a plea of Augusta for better protection of the frontiers, petitions for the extension of the bounds of Winchester, various appeals for changes in the tobacco-inspection laws and a measure to remove the Court House of Spotsylvania from Fredericksburg. Definitely in the line of business was an appeal from the merchants of Winchester, influential constituents of Washington's, for protection against Pennsylvania pedlars in skins and furs. The parliamentary course of these bills was not of a sort to call for great display of the art of government, but, taken together, the enactment of the measures was, for a beginner, an informative lesson in the processes of legislation.

Committee hearings and participation in the work of the House did not occupy all of Washington's time. The evenings were free for social affairs, and there always was delight in quiet conversation with Martha. The end of March approached while the Washingtons enjoyed the company of the children, planning for the future and the life of the town. No action had been taken on the bill concerning the supply of the Regiment, but there were indications that even the most prolix orators were exhausting their arguments. Washington was anxious to prepare his farms for spring planting but was not willing to leave the House until the bill to continue his old Regiment had been brought to a vote. He resolved his dilemma in his usual direct fashion: he would remain in Williamsburg for the passage of the measure and then apply for leave of absence for the remainder of the session. On April 2 the bill was passed. The next business of the House was the grant of a leave to Mr. Washington.

As soon after that as Martha, the children, the servants and luggage were ready, the journey to Mount Vernon began. The plantation to which Washington brought his new wife that April was close to the centre of an interesting neighborhood framed by the Potomac River. The Mount Vernon estate would have been merely a large Virginia plantation had not the Potomac given it a setting of dignity, charm and everchanging color. Eight and a half miles upstream was Alexandria. Southwest at a distance of near a mile and a half was the mouth of Dogue Run. On the south side of this was Belvoir, dear to Washington through a hundred associations. Another mile and a half of the river led to George Mason's recently completed Gunston Hall.

Washington had other neighbors back of Belvoir; downstream was Westmoreland County, Washington's birthplace and the home of the Lees. The largest interest was up the river at Alexandria, but the social boundary

MAP / 5

WASHINGTON'S "BURGESS ROUTE" TO WILLIAMSBURG

WASHINGTON'S "BURGESS ROUTE" *TO* WILLIAMSBURG

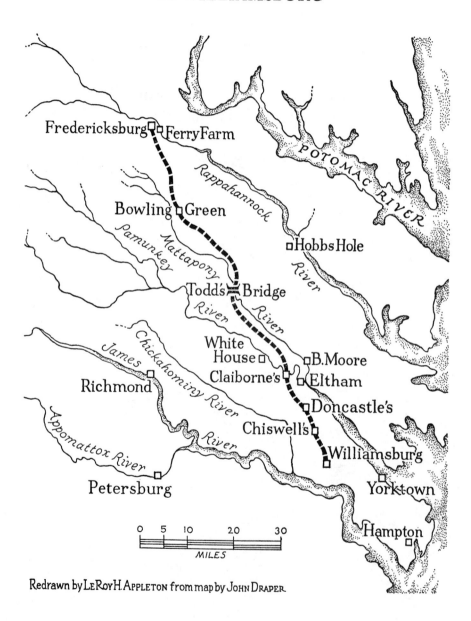

Fredericksburg Ferry Farm

POTOMAC RIVER

Rappahannock

Bowling Green

Hobbs Hole

Pamunkey

Mattapony

River

Todd's Bridge

River

River

White House

James

Chickahominy River

B. Moore

Claiborne's

Eltham

Richmond

Doncastle's

Appomattox River

River

Chiswell's

Williamsburg

Petersburg

Yorktown

```
0    5   10      20        30
|————|———|————————|—————————|
         MILES
```

Hampton

Redrawn by LeRoy H. Appleton from map by John Draper

now was not that town. In effect, it was the little stream above Alexandria known as Four Mile Creek, not far from the falls of the Potomac. A fixed agricultural economy prevailed below the falls. West of them conditions were beginning to change. Ownership might be vested in rich Virginians; development might depend on those Pennsylvania Germans who ten years previously had disgusted young Washington.

The Colonel and his lady belonged, distinctly, to the society that lived below the falls. While Washington never forgot that more money could be made by patenting and holding land beyond the mountains than in almost any other way, he had at hand a task that would absorb for a long time all his energy and, as he soon discovered, the greater part of the capital he would get from Martha. The unhappy fact—not to be evaded, blinked, minimized or quickly ended—was this: Mount Vernon had been misman-aged during the later years of his service in the army. In the Colonel's absence, Jack Washington had made an effort to take care of the estate, but the younger brother had not been there all the time, or successful when there. Almost everything needed for good management was worn out or lacking altogether. Washington saw immediately that he had much to do; he was not equally quick to perceive that he lacked part of the experience he needed in order to do it well.

Washington went to Williamsburg late in April to qualify for the administration of the Custis estate. He appeared with Martha's attorney, John Mercer, before the General Court and asked that he be named to administer the two-thirds interest vested in Jackie and Patsy, along with the third he already controlled as husband of Martha. He did not request the Court to name him instead of Speaker Robinson as guardian of the chil-dren. The Court entered the appropriate order. Simultaneously, Mercer and Washington recommended to the Court a division of the property of the estate. As finally apportioned, the estate was handsome. The real estate consisted of 17,438 acres. Without inclusion of this, the sum credited to each of the three heirs was £1617 sterling and £7618, currency of the country, in slaves, livestock, notes and bonds and accounts receivable—an aggregate in personality of almost £20,000 sterling. No less than £8958 of these assets in the currency of the country were represented by slaves. Washington was resolved that his accounts of the estate should be accurate to a penny; at the same time he insisted on getting all that was due him as husband of the former Mrs. Custis.

On returning to Mount Vernon he had forthwith to organize the household in order to assure comfortable management and conform to his custom of doing everything with system. "I have quit a military life," he said, "and shortly shall be fixed at this place with an agreeable partner, and then shall be able to conduct my own business with more punctuality than heretofore as it will pass under my own immediate instruction, a thing impracticable while I discharged my duty in the public service of the coun-try." He ordered the best books on agriculture and farm management and, as the tobacco crop of 1759 promised a handsome return, became almost enthusiastic over the future of the staple on his own lands.

Along with hope and the happiness of new love, despite the wretched condition of the estate, the summer brought a cargo of good news about the war. Except for what might be happening in the unknown region of Detroit, the enemy now had been driven back to the Great Lakes and the St. Lawrence and was being held, in the main, to the line of the river, northeast of Lake Ontario. The only strong positions still in French hands were Montreal, Quebec, and the 150 miles of country between them in the region south of Quebec. Now Washington saw the long-awaited successes he had craved for his country. This point of view he expressed in a letter to a British merchant: "The scale of Fortune in America is turned greatly in our favor, and success is become the boon companion of our fortunate Generals." Three days before Washington wrote this, Quebec had surrendered after a siege that had cost the lives of General Wolfe and the Marquis de Montcalm. Many of the details, when read by Washington, must have stirred his soldierly pride, because they covered some of the most magnificent achievements in the history of the British Army, but they found no place in any of his letters. Quebec, its graves and its glory, were far off; Washington's prime interest now was in restoring the buildings, the livestock and the implements of Mount Vernon.

On October 22 he took the road to Williamsburg: The personal property in the Custis residence there was to be sold at public sale on October 25; the House of Burgesses was to meet November 1. In Williamsburg, as business did not press, he was able to enjoy such festivities as the town offered before the Burgesses assembled in a session not particularly interesting. After the General Assembly adjourned, Washington lingered long enough to see that the tobacco on the Custis plantations was inspected and delivered at the ship's side and then returned to Mount Vernon in contentment of spirit. The tobacco crop along York River had been large; the market seemed favorable. When Washington rode into the stableyard at home two resolutions were firm in his mind—to increase his production of tobacco, which he was resolved to raise to the highest quality and cure, and to acquire more land on which to employ idle servants in growing that staple.

After the Christmas holiday of 1759, the first he had spent with his wife and her children, Washington expanded these plans and, meantime, directed the winter activities at Mount Vernon. Hogs had to be killed and the meat cured; timber was sawed; a house was moved; fencing was repaired; such grubbing was undertaken as the ground permitted; hundreds of bottles of good cider were filled; before the end of February it was possible to begin some of the plowing for oats and clover; March brought more plowing for clover and some for lucerne, along with several experiments in sowing grass seed and considerable activity in grafting cherry and nut trees.

The crop of 1759 had been grown on two plantations by Washington's own slaves and on nine tracts by tenants. The Colonel had not been able to prepare for it and scarcely regarded it as a test of his management. It would be different now. "The greater pains imaginable," Washington wrote subsequently, "[were] used in the management of this tobacco"; but before it was primed, there were reminders that other considerations than those under the grower's control might affect the return. The *Deliverance,* which was carrying some Washington and Custis tobacco to the British Isles, was lost on the coast of France. At least one merchantman with tobacco belonging to the same owners was taken by a French man-of-war. Rains threatened to ruin the crop of 1760. Reports on the sale of the leaf of 1759 were worse than depressing. Nor was it encouraging to an ambitious young proprietor to note the figures at which the invoices sent to England for clothing and supplies had been filled. Washington was shocked at the charges on his account. Truth was, larger orders at higher prices were eating up an expanded income and a part of the money Martha had brought him. If Washington observed that fact in the summer of 1760, he did nothing to correct it.

Through a growing season that seemed in retrospect to be one of "incessant rains," Washington spent most of his time at Mount Vernon with his wife and stepchildren. When September opened, it was manifest that the tobacco crop, which had been spotting badly, would be short but would be better than had been expected. It consequently was with some eagerness that Washington looked forward to October, when he would go to Williamsburg for the session of the General Assembly and could visit the plantations on the York and see what had been produced. As Martha wished to make the journey with him, the Colonel decided to travel in style, with chariot and six—the first time he ever had set out for the capital with the equipage that was the unchallengeable emblem of a planter of the highest affluence.

The session was opened on October 6 in a balance of cheer and of gloom. Intelligence confirmed the complete surrender at Montreal September 8 of the last organized French force in Canada. Every Virginian rejoiced with Governor Fauquier when he proclaimed: ". . . the war is gloriously brought to a happy end. . . ." The unhappy news was that all hopes of avoiding war with the Cherokees had been blasted. The Burgesses responded by voting to raise the Regiment to its full strength of one thousand men and continue its pay and subsistence until April 1, 1761, with the proviso that the men should not be employed outside the Colony. Costs were to be paid from the £52,000 that represented Virginia's part of funds voted the Colonies by Parliament. In making these arrangements the Burgesses probably availed themselves of Washington's experience, but he was not conspicuous in debate nor were there many calls on the committees to which he belonged.

When the House adjourned October 20, Burgess Washington became immediately the diligent proprietor and trustee, eager to know what the weight and quality of the tobacco crop would be. The showing was not good. Some tobacco on low grounds had been drowned, and some on the uplands had "fired." Much of the leaf was poor; the total was below the average in weight and bulk as well as in quality, but the aggregate of Washington's various crops was 147,357 pounds in spite of the bad year. It looked as if he was achieving his ambition to grow superlative tobacco in volume sufficient to crowd the hold of a proud merchantman.

The first ships to leave Virginia in the autumn of 1760 with tobacco grown that year doubtless passed westbound vessels that carried announcements of the death of George II. He had succumbed October 25—the only King to whom Washington ever had sworn allegiance. News of the demise of the monarch reached the Colonies at the end of December, but it was February 4, 1761, when Governor Fauquier received instructions to proclaim the new King, George III. Whatever else the year 1761 held, it probably would involve a dissolution of the House of Burgesses, a journey to Frederick, visits to influential citizens and a polling of freeholders. It was not a pleasant prospect for a man who desired most of all to remain at home and attend to his own affairs; but if it had to be done, Washington would do it. Membership in the House of Burgesses was at once the duty and the avocation of a gentleman. He could not discharge the duty if he shunned the contest.

Pending a call from friends in the Valley or dissolution of the House, Washington busied himself with farm affairs. The Colonel had at length to pull himself away and to go to Williamsburg, where the General Assembly had convened. Washington went tardily because he had been detained in Fairfax by a development that changed his status. On March 14 Anne Fairfax Lee, the widow of Lawrence Washington, had died. Anne had no issue within the terms of Lawrence's will, and the estate consequently passed to George.

When Fauquier delivered his final address, April 10, he made the expected announcement of a dissolution and sent the Burgesses home to seek reelection or to participate in the choice of their successors. Washington felt that he should go to Frederick to counteract the electioneering of Adam Stephen. He had not been in Frederick when the election of 1758 had been held; it would be neither proper nor prudent to have the voters of the county regard him as indifferent. Doubtless he would have been reelected decisively in any event, but he could not have been given a much stronger vote of confidence than the poll of May 18 showed: Washington, 505; George Mercer, 399; Stephen, 294; scattering, 3. Washington and Mercer had been elected.

It was victory at a price. A severe cold Washington caught while visiting among his constituents persisted and stirred up old maladies. Fever produced a lassitude that Washington in some humility of spirit attributed to indolence. Most of the conferences of a hard, tedious summer were with physicians. He wrote late in July: "I have found so little benefit from any advice yet received that I am more than half of the mind to take a trip to England for the recovery of that invaluable blessing, Health." Another suggestion was that he consult Philadelphia physicians. The final decision was to try the waters of the Berkeley Baths. George had no faith whatever in "the air," which he believed unwholesome, but he was willing to test the effect of the mineral water, and he accordingly set out August 22 with Martha and the children. The Colonel was so weak that the easiest part of the journey was an ordeal; adverse weather made the later stages torture. After the crude resort finally was reached, August 25, the water, the weather, his state of mind or the vigor of his body—one or more than one of these—soon brought improvement. When he reached Mount Vernon about

September 18, he was in a mood to pick up business matters that had been neglected.

While his own financial war seemed now to face defeat and now to promise victory, Washington never ceased buying and planning for the future, even though he had thought at one time that he would lose the fight for his own life. Now that stimulating autumn weather had come to Virginia, he felt able to make the journey to Williamsburg for the first meeting of the new General Assembly. After arrival in the capital November 2, he was able, also, to transact some private business and write with cheer not only of the prospect of peace with the Cherokees but also of a settlement of the larger struggle between Britain and France.

Able to give his crops the attention he could not bestow during his illness, Washington visited the plantations in New Kent and on the York. He found they had enjoyed a more favorable season than in 1760; the yield was larger. The merchants' returns in 1762 should demonstrate whether Washington was winning or losing—whether his special care for the quality of his leaf was a profitable expenditure.

The General Assembly met January 14, 1762, without the senior Burgess from Frederick. Washington knew that the session was to be devoted to one question, the continuance or disbandment of the Virginia Regiment. He probably anticipated the decision of the lawmakers and did not feel that members from the more remote counties were so badly needed that they should be called upon to make the long journey in midwinter. The Burgesses were not convinced of the need of retaining an armed force in the service of the Colony, but they were unwilling to disband it until they had positive assurance that the war with the Cherokees had been ended. That view shaped the law. The statute "for preventing mutiny and desertion," one that had been strengthened after many exhortations by Washington, was revived for the period that ended May 1, but no further provision was made for the pay of the troops. Officers fared better. Each of those in service at the time was allowed a full year's compensation beyond that due him on the date the Regiment was disbanded.

Washington now had the normal operations of his plantations in full swing and was busying himself with an interesting routine. By February 9 the master of Mount Vernon began plowing for oats. Sowing and harrowing followed. About March 24 the tobacco beds were burned over and then seeded. While the plows were turning the earth where corn rows soon were to stretch, Washington had grim news from Westmoreland: His brother Austin had succumbed to an illness that had pursued him for years. His end had come at Wakefield, where he had lived amply. Washington journeyed as quickly as he could to the home of the dead brother who never quite had succeeded to Lawrence's place in the affection of George but always had counselled him wisely and with patience. George could do nothing now to show his appreciation except to stand by his brother's grave.

In a short time, Washington had again to travel to Williamsburg for a reason that was becoming monotonous—another session of the General Assembly. Fauquier had arrived in Virginia during June 1758 and in three years and nine months had held eleven sessions. This time, at a meeting begun on March 30, the Governor reported that he had disbanded the Virginia Regiment as soon as he had received formal news of peace with the Cherokees. Later he had notice that the King desired a regiment to "be kept in the pay of the Colony." In addition, His Majesty demanded that a quota be raised to aid in filling the regiments under Amherst. This was not all. The day before the General Assembly met, the Governor had received notice that Spain had joined France in the war on Britain. If, therefore, peace had been made with the Cherokees, a new adversary had to be accepted in their stead. The General Assembly voted to raise one thousand men for a new Regiment and to recruit Virginia's quota for Amherst's forces. For the discipline and control of its soldiery the Assembly passed a new mutiny and desertion act.

In the spring of 1762 there was interesting work and the prospect of comforting profit from good management of the land to which he returned when the brief session ended. All went well except for the essential—good weather. A drought began at the very time plants most needed moisture. Washington had to replant tobacco and corn, also. There was prospect, of course, that if the tobacco crop was small, prices would be high—but even that hope was eclipsed by reports that the Mount Vernon product had not been sold at a good figure in London.

While buyers withheld shillings and Nature begrudged rain on the banks of the Potomac, Washington busied himself with some of the many improvements he had projected. In spite of debt and doubt concerning the tobacco crop, he continued steadily to restore and improve the plantation. He bought more slaves; title was acquired to acres which raised his total to 8505. Business always was interesting to the master of Mount Vernon, especially if there was profit in it; but the bargain in land had to be a promising one that absorbed him as completely as did provision for new equipage, for good wine, for the furnishings and beautification of the house, and for the pleasure of Martha and the children. His desire to select and enjoy the best was sharpened as he increasingly became a family man. For these reasons, the year 1762 was one of much purchasing and planning.

He had ordered a new still in 1761 and intended to put it into service in the autumn of 1762 if it arrived by that time. Use of it could eliminate numerous bills for spirits used on the plantation. Among the milder beverages, the one he most used and most frequently served was Madeira, which he imported directly from the Islands. Drink in itself made no strong appeal to him: he liked three or four glasses of Madeira at dinner, but these were merely a part of the grace of living.

The entire household must have been made conscious of abundance when on July 20 the *Unity* discharged the goods Washington had ordered in the fall of 1761. From salt to saddles, from spirits of lavender to diversified leather portmanteaux, from "one dozen augurs, sorted" to "three pecks almonds in the shell," from the plainest fabrics for the slaves' garments to egrets for the headdress of Martha, the goods were brought forth and were appraised and admired or criticized and pronounced too expensive.

This cargo arrived in the year when Jackie became eight and Patsy six. Their mother had put into the orders from England many articles for them, but, of course, life for Jackie and Patsy was not to consist altogether of opening trunks over which Aladdin himself might have rubbed his lamp. Colonel and Mrs. Washington had resolved that the children must begin the acquisition of serious knowledge and that Patsy, in addition, must learn the graceful arts of a young lady of fashion. They had a tutor now in the person of Walter Magowan. A challenging list of Latin grammars, dictionaries and texts had been ordered. Soon the invoices were to include Greek books with stern titles in Latin. Furthermore, Miss Custis now had a spinet that had been ordered for her with superlative care.

Already, in other matters, there were indications that the gentleman who had preserved on the frontier both the discipline of his Regiment and his own amiability might not be equally successful with his wife's children at Mount Vernon. The reason would not be special perversity on the part of the children but the indulgent extremity of their mother's love for them. The oddest aspect of this was Martha's own recognition of a weakness she could not overcome.

The sowing of wheat was begun August 16 and was continued to September 8. Soon the tobacco was cut, and the annual argument over the probable size and price of the new crop was renewed. Washington set out November 10 for Williamsburg, where the General Assembly had met on the second—for the third time that year. En route, he found the crops on the York relatively better than those on the Potomac and he permitted himself to hope, as he phrased it, that "the tobacco, what there is of it, will prove exceedingly good this year. . . ."

The legislative session was interesting to him in his role of planter. Governor Fauquier explained that he had called the Assembly together to enter upon the usual business of the country and provide for the future safety and well-being thereof. Of particular importance, said the Governor, were carefully matured action to relieve the shortage of bullion and measures of similar wisdom to regulate trade with the Cherokees. Military operations on American soil had ended, though the war against the French and Spanish continued at sea. The Burgesses enacted a new election law, amended militia legislation, put on the books a measure for the relief of insolvents, provided for the inspection of pork, beef, flour, tar, pitch and turpentine, and fashioned a modified plan to encourage wine-making and silk-culture in Virginia.

This diversified legislation kept the General Assembly in session until December 23, but it did not detain the senior Burgess from Frederick until so close to Christmas. He reached home December 1 in time to see the corn crop measured and shared with the overseers. Of meat he set down the total for the use of "the family" at 6632 pounds. This weight of meat, virtually three tons, was typical of the magnitude of many of the operations at Mount Vernon. Everything was expanding; some things were prospering. The Washington and Custis tobacco crop from the several plantations was almost 60,000 pounds.

That seemed a reassuring figure but, now that he was completing his fourth year's work after his retirement from the army, a number of circumstances should have kept the Colonel from financial complacency. He had done the essential things at Mount Vernon. In 1759, neglect was visible under every shed and in every field. Even now repair seemed endless; but the place was decently equipped in almost every requirement—teams, livestock, implements, buildings, Negroes. All this made the estate more valuable but it had cost many hundred pounds and it had not demonstrated what Washington had taken for granted—that first-class tobacco could be grown at Mount Vernon in quantity and at a sufficient profit to pay off the debt and keep up the plantation.

These were the concerns of a man who intended to remain a planter, grow richer if he could, and enjoy the luxury of a life he had earned for himself. In larger preparation for the uncertainties of the future, political and personal, he had learned more of law-making, had gained in good will to men, and, facing the vagaries of season and of human nature, was becoming more patient and more willing to bear what he could not cast off. By the thorough performance of commonplace, daily duties he was building slowly the stronger structure of the spirit that men call character.

During four years of struggle to make Mount Vernon a profitable tobacco plantation, Washington had been drawn closer to the church and October 25, 1762, had been elected a vestryman of Truro Parish. His first important official duty was to attend a vestry meeting at Falls Church and consider the need of a new structure there. Beyond this election, Washington had no new public distinction. He did not shine as a Burgess, though his character and his military reputation gave him influence. More and more he was becoming a planter who had his holidays and enjoyed them but had, between them, to discharge duties that were as humdrum as they were numerous.

Good bargains seemed better and bad crops appeared not quite so intolerable when set against the joyful news of the Treaty of Paris, signed February 10, 1763. The struggle then ended between France and England had cost the lives of 853,000 soldiers and of unreckoned hundreds of thousands of civilians. England was supreme in North America and had gained enormously in India. The Earl of Granville did not exaggerate when he aroused himself from the languor of his last illness to affirm this "the most glorious war, the most honorable peace, this nation ever saw." Very different were the comments of the Virginia former Colonel. "We are much rejoiced at the prospect of peace which," he wrote, " 'tis hoped will be of long continuance and introductory of mutual benefits to the merchant and planter, as the trade to this Colony will flow in a more easy and regular channel than it has done for a considerable time past." That was all: peace meant easier, profitable trade.

Climbing debt and dragging repayment did not keep Washington from ordering another pipe of a "rich, oily" Madeira, nor was he deterred from new expenditure by a controversy over exchange that now threatened the amity of Virginians. British merchants trading in the Dominion had filed in February a protest against the volume of paper money issued by the Colony. The injustice of the act for the relief of insolvent debtors likewise had been challenged in the memorial, which the Lords Commissioners for Trade and Plantations had hastened to transmit to Fauquier. The Gover-

MAP / 6

THE PROCLAMATION LINE OF 1763

PROCLAMATION LINE OF 1763
INDIAN CESSIONS
AND THE LAND COMPANIES

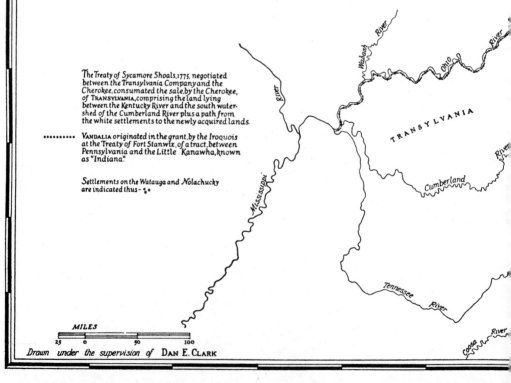

— — — The Proclamation of 1763 forbade the purchase or settlement of Indian lands westerly of a line running through the heads of the rivers which fell into the Atlantic from the west or northwest.

—x—x— Tryon's Line, 1767, (by agreement with the Cherokee) directed that no white settlement should be made westerly of a line running from a point where Reedy River was intersected by the then North Carolina-South Carolina boundary, to Tryon's Mountain and thence to Fort Chiswell.

—+—+—+— The Treaty of Fort Stanwix, 1768, (with the Iroquois) extinguished Iroquois claims to the lands southeasterly of a line running from Fort Stanwix to Fort Pitt, and thence along the southern bank of the Ohio to the mouth of the Tennessee (Cherokee) River.

—o—o— The Treaty of Hard Labor, 1768, (with the Cherokee) confirmed Tryon's Line

—x—x— of 1767 and extended it from Fort Chiswell to the mouth of the Kanawha River.

—•—•— The Treaty of Lochaber, 1770, (with the Cherokee) moved the northern part of the line established at the Treaty of Hard Labor westerly to run from six miles east of Long Island of Holston directly to the mouth of the Kanawha River. Lochaber was the name of the plantation of Alexander Cameron, Assistant Commissioner of Indian Affairs for the Southern Provinces.

—••—••— Donelson's Line When Col. Donelson acting for Virginia, and Chief Attakullakulla and Alex. Cameron, acting for the Cherokee, came to run the Lochaber Line, some agreement was entered into by which it was turned westward and made to run with the Kentucky (Louisa) River.

The Treaty of Sycamore Shoals, 1775, negotiated between the Transylvania Company and the Cherokee, consumated the sale, by the Cherokee, of TRANSYLVANIA, comprising the land lying between the Kentucky River and the south watershed of the Cumberland River plus a path from the white settlements to the newly acquired lands.

··········· VANDALIA originated in the grant, by the Iroquois at the Treaty of Fort Stanwix, of a tract, between Pennsylvania and the Little Kanawha, known as "Indiana."

Settlements on the Watauga and Nolachucky are indicated thus- ⟂₀

MILES

25   0   50   100

Drawn under the supervision of DAN E. CLARK

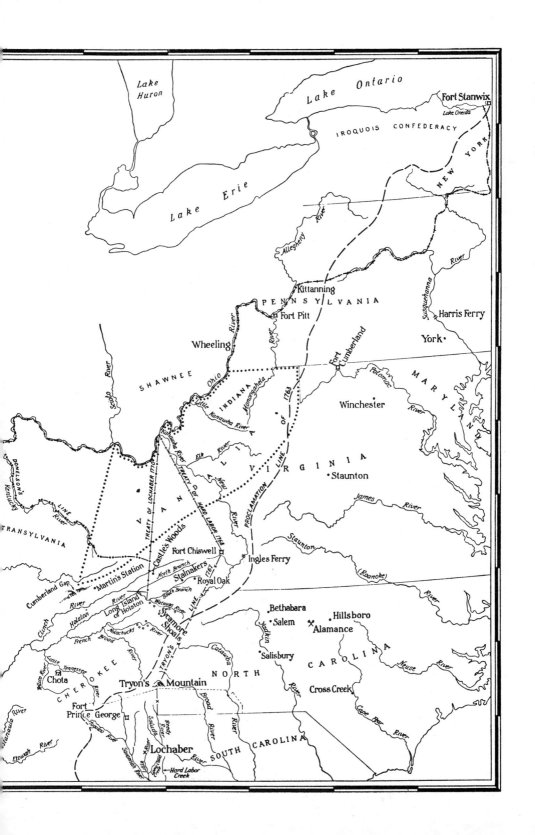

nor, in turn, had laid the paper before the Council on April 28 and had said he thought it imperative that the Assembly be convened. A call then had been sent out for May 19.

When the Burgesses filed into the council chamber, they found the friendly and diplomatic Governor in a mood of unwonted stiffness. Fauquier did not undertake to suggest how the merchants were to be satisfied, but he urged the lawmakers to provide adequately for the redemption of the paper currency on maturity and called on them to repeal the amended act for the relief of insolvents. The Burgesses were ready for the Governor. Emission of treasury notes had been necessary, the Burgesses maintained, because there had been no other means of meeting the King's requisitions. The notes had been made legal tender, except for quit rents, in the conviction that this was essential justice to all. Provision for judicial determination of disputed rates of exchange was proper; sufficient funds had been provided for the redemption of the notes; "no person trading to this Colony could receive any injury"; British merchants would gain as much as they would lose in the fluctuations of exchange. The general tone was one of professed surprise that the House was censured for what it had considered "acts of duty to our Sovereign." To this view, the Burgesses adhered. No appeal, no persuasion, could shake them. The insolvency act of the previous November was repealed. More than this the Burgesses refused to do.

In this discussion, Washington had no place of prominence. He probably was not present when the Governor called the Burgesses to the council chamber May 31, scolded them mildly for their failure to act, and then prorogued them. The absence of the senior member from Frederick was not due to unconcern over sterling debts but to a desire to increase his fortune and discharge some of his own debts otherwise than from the uncertain returns of an unpredictable crop. Washington was convinced that land speculation held as good a promise of profit as ever. He still was looking westward; but, along with some of the planters and merchants, he now turned to an undeveloped area not far away, the Great Dismal Swamp.

There was general belief that if the swamp were drained, tens of thousands of acres of ideal farming land would be the reward. William and Thomas Nelson and a few of their friends had decided to seek the patent of the unoccupied and waste land of the swamp and to draw off the water from the best of it. These men readily interested Washington, who agreed to visit the Great Dismal and see for himself what it would offer of fine timber while it was being drained and of rich flatlands when it was cleared. The ground seemed, in his own phrase, "excessive rich." The prospect was one of undisguised speculation; but if the swamp could be drained successfully, the reclaimed land might yield fabulous crops, close to the market of Norfolk and the open sea. Washington decided he would make the venture along with the Nelsons, Robert Tucker, Robert Burwell and the others who had shown special interest in it.

Washington returned north to resume his everyday life as a planter, but he did not abandon his reawakened interest in speculative land enterprises. Almost immediately he became a sharer in a new Mississippi Company that had bold, ambitious designs: Fifty subscribers, and no more than that number, were to contribute funds with which to send to England an agent to solicit the grant directly on the Mississippi River of a domain large enough to allow each member of the company fifty thousand acres. The terms, like the aims that shaped them, were the ideal of speculation, such an arrangement as the land-hungry dream about.

Later in June Washington went to Frederick County and while there had news of the sort grimly associated in his mind with that region. After the surrender of Montreal, many of the French Indians, particularly those around Detroit, had refused to accept the rule of the conquering English. During the spring of 1763, these Indians captured English outposts north of the Potomac and the Ohio. No massacres had been reported from any part of Virginia, but terror once again had gripped the frontier. Washington knew what to expect. When he returned home at the end of June he wrote: ". . . it is melancholy to behold, the terror that has seized them and the fatal consequences that must follow in the loss of their harvest and crops, the whole back country being in forts or flying."

Happily for the Colonies, some of the Highlanders who had fought in Forbes's campaign of 1758 had been left in Pennsylvania under Colonel Bouquet. That veteran struck west from Carlisle on July 18 with approximately 460 regulars. Detaching a handful to garrison Raystown, which now had become Bedford, and another score and a half to guard Fort Ligonier, formerly Loyal Hannon, he hurried along the route he had followed five years previously. On the afternoon of August 5 the Indians attacked in force on Bushy Run. Their tricks were those that had led to the massacre of Braddock's men; but Bouquet was not Braddock, nor were his troops untrained in the warfare of the woodlands. Bouquet matched the Indians' worst until nightfall, and, when they renewed the battle August 6, he lured them forward by a pretended retreat, then delivered a fierce bayonet charge and finally routed them. Relief of Fort Pitt followed immediately. West of that outpost, the savages still were violent, but the retired Colonel of Mount Vernon knew that the defeat administered by Bouquet would dull their zeal for war.

Closer at hand Washington had a multitude of vexatious duties that would have alarmed a timid planter or have harassed a man less reconciled to detail than he was. By October 1 Washington had harvested his summer crops, sown his winter wheat and cut his tobacco. He was pessimistic about his "money crop." The yield on the York appeared to be good, "but," Washington had to write his London dealer, "my crops on the Potomac are vastly deficient; in short, a wet spring, a dry summer and early frosts have quite demolished me." When the hogsheads had been filled on all the plantations, the total was better than the Colonel had thought it could be. On the other hand, quality was so lacking in the leaf that bulk and weight were more than cancelled. Washington realized this and did not purchase luxuries as recklessly as in the past. His largest single item in the orders that fall was for chariot harness for six horses.

Land was different; he could not resist that. By the end of summer he had carried his total holdings to 9381 acres, and almost before the tobacco crop was housed he went to Stafford Court House to attend a meeting of the men who sought the vast grant on the Mississippi. Later in October Washington started again for the Great Dismal Swamp—to get still more land. Washington "went the rounds" of the swamp, as he said, and visited its southern border in North Carolina where he saw some excellent land he subsequently determined to purchase. He concluded that profitable drainage of the swamp was possible and, with the other speculators, returned to Williamsburg in an effort to procure action on a petition filed the previous May for the grant of lands in the swamp. It developed that the petition itself had disappeared and that the Council had done nothing about it. Thereupon a new paper was circulated in the names of the original applicants, their kinsmen, friends and tenants, to a total of 148 persons. On presentation of this paper, the Council was quick to make amends for delay and neglect. It resolved November 1, "that each of the petitioners have leave to take out a patent for 1000 acres of the said land upon condition of giving legal notice to the proprietors of the contiguous high lands and that they will not interfere with any entries antecedent to this day. . . ." Seven years were allowed for the return of the surveys.

The Governor's irresistible inclination to consult the Assembly prompted His Honor to summon the lawmakers on January 21, 1764. The reason was the familiar one—a call for Virginia troops to join in a new campaign against the Indians. The Redmen still were halting the advance of English settlement and were threatening to bring the torch and the scalping knife to the frontier again. Thomas Gage, who had served in Braddock's campaign, was now Major General and American Commander-in-Chief and urged that Virginia supply five hundred men for a western offensive to relieve Detroit and annihilate the resisting Indians or force them to make peace.

Fauquier asked the lawmakers whether it was not better "to march into the enemies country than by waiting at home to revenge yourselves when they think proper to enter yours and commit all kinds of outrages and murders." He had been employing the militia, Fauquier said, and had found it expensive. The force had been reduced to five hundred men and would have been diminished still further had not the call for the Assembly been sent. The Assembly preferred using the militia to raising troops by extravagant bounties, and it promptly named a commission, with Washington as chairman, to examine the accounts of the militia and certify them for payment. After the close of the short session, Washington remained in Williamsburg long enough to arrange for the shipment of fifty-two hogsheads of tobacco.

Washington was not stinting the luxuries he, Martha and their guests enjoyed. He, indeed, was becoming a bit reckless, not to say extravagant. He was not deterred from the purchase of luxuries or of Negroes by the size of the debt he owed Robert Cary & Co., his factors in London; he scarcely was restrained by the fact that money was scarcer than ever, that many planters were in difficulty, and that several bills of exchange given him in repayment of loans proved worthless at the time. His eyes were opened to reality, if not to frugality, by a letter he received shortly before May 1 from Cary & Co. The merchants informed him that Jackie Custis's balance had shrunk to

£1407 and that Washington was in their debt for no less than £1811. They would be pleased to have him reduce that obligation and, meantime, to pay interest on it. As a matter of right, Cary should be told to charge interest. The merchant might be reminded that poor crops and bad debtors explained the magnitude of the debt. Buying need not be stopped. Cary & Co. could wait for their money from a customer who was sending them fifty-two hogsheads of tobacco, with more to follow.

While some of that tobacco still was at sea, America received unwelcome word of new taxes that might be levied by Parliament. In the war with France from 1754 to 1763, Britain had increased her national debt to £130,000,000. Her interest charge alone was £4,500,000; new and continuing expense must be assumed for the protection of the American frontier. George Grenville, Chancellor of the Exchequer, had raised the question of Colonial contribution to the cost of defending the English settlements. He asserted and the Commons promptly agreed that "it may be proper to charge certain stamp duties in the said Colonies and plantations." No action to this end was taken at the time, but Parliament seemed ready to act whenever the Ministry brought in the bills.

Reports of this reached Virginia and Maryland about the middle of May and met with instant challenge. Direct taxation of the Colonials by act of Parliament never had been attempted. Such general levies as had been imposed in any Colony had been by laws of its own Assembly, chosen by the people who were to pay the taxes. This had been so unvarying a practice that only constitutional lawyers of inquisitive mind had taken the pains to analyze taxation in terms of inherent political right. Colonials had now to unlock the forgotten armory of their rights to get weapons for their defence against parliamentary taxation. Practice had to be vindicated by principle. The Colonials rediscovered their inheritance in protecting their interests. Had not their forefathers possessed all the rights of British subjects, including the right of taxation through representatives of their own choice, when they came to America? What had they done that deprived them of any guarantee they possessed under the English constitution? The first rumors of direct taxation of Americans by Parliament prompted every Colonial who knew anything of history to think of Runnymede and of the long struggle of Parliament itself to establish taxation as the right of the taxpayer. Even before the precise form of contemplated British action was known, Washington's fellow-Burgess, Richard Henry Lee, put the question that shaped endless protests: "Can it be supposed," he asked a correspondent in London, "that those brave adventurous Britons, who originally conquered and settled these countries . . . meant thereby to deprive themselves of that free government of which they were members, and to which they had an unquestionable right?"

Washington, like most Virginians, was concerned and instinctively disposed to resist, but, as usual, was not inclined to anticipate events. That applied to taxation and, more immediately, and more personally, to his debts. Summer brought from Cary & Co. a letter which its recipient somewhat indignantly regarded as a dun. Washington undertook to answer it with a statement that "mischances rather than misconduct" had been responsible for his financial ills. He was chagrined but not chastened. Orders from England must be reduced. Luxuries for the time being were banned. He would defer other purchases in order to reduce his debt.

That was one measure of relief. His other and more acceptable recourse was an increase of income. Substantial increase in farm income at Mount Vernon might be through the substitution of some other large crop for tobacco. Culture of the troublesome and exacting tobacco-plant would continue until a profitable staple could be grown in its stead. Perhaps it would be wise on the lower Custis farms to make no change; but at Mount Vernon the coveted leaf could not be matured and marketed in a quality to make it yield anything more than cost, if even cost, on the London market. The fact was: Mount Vernon tobacco was second rate. Washington must try something else—wheat, hemp, flax, anything that was profitable. In Alexandria, the firm of Carlyle & Adam was seeking more vigorously each year to encourage the growing of wheat. The market was only a few miles up river, and the financial settlement at 3s. 6d. per bushel would be with friends. Washington was sufficiently encouraged to increase the acreage he normally devoted to wheat. This wheat was in the ground and some at least of the tobacco of 1764 was ready for shipment when, about October 28 or 29, Washington completed another journey to Williamsburg for a session of the General Assembly.

The Burgesses wished to consider, in particular, the subject that had alarmed the Colony in the spring. According to a letter from a committee of the Massachusetts Assembly, passage of a direct tax on the Colonies might be as close as the next session of Parliament. Virginia lawmakers must decide what they would do about it. On November 14 the Burgesses reached their main conclusion. It was the traditional one—to address the throne and protest to the Lords and the Commons. So delicate a task naturally was assigned those members of the House best skilled in letters and in the lore of the British constitution. Peyton Randolph was appointed chairman. With him were associated Richard Henry Lee, Landon Carter, George Wythe, Edmund Pendleton, Benjamin Harrison, Archibald Cary, and John Fleming. The session dragged interminably on while the House debated uninteresting bills, and the special committee weighed words and sanded phrases in perfecting the address to the King and the appeals to the Houses of Parliament.

Relief broke tedium December 10 when the Governor forwarded a letter from Bouquet reporting that he had pressed on from Pittsburgh into the Ohio country and had forced the Indians there to make peace. Col. John Bradstreet had made a treaty in August at Detroit with savages who from the outset showed little intention of respecting it; but the Burgesses were so confident peace would be enforced that they advised the Governor to disband the militia still guarding the frontier.

At last, on December 13, the address to the King and the memorial to the Lords and the remonstrance to the Commons were ready for consideration. The core of the address was a plea that the King would protect the people of Virginia "in the enjoyment of their ancient and inestimable right of being governed by such laws respecting their internal polity and taxation as are derived from their own consent, with the approbation of their sovereign or his substitute." In the memorial to the Lords, the central argument was that the settlers of Virginia had all the rights and privileges of British subjects and that the descendants of the first comers had done nothing to deprive them of this inheritance. The arguments in the remonstrance to Commons were the same with the added protest that if taxation were justified, it would be unwise because it would be intolerable to a people already burdened by the costs of the war with the French. Virginians would be "reduced to extreme poverty, would be compelled to manufacture those articles" they formally had imported from Britain. Together the three documents included about two thousand words, and they meant much more than their authors realized. The Virginians were not asking a favor: they were asserting a right. They had explored their inheritance and had faith in the weapons they found there. Right, rediscovered, was reenforced. What pride and self-interest prompted, the constitution vindicated. In that spirit the session and the year came to a close. It might not be easy to get the address of Virginia before the King, but the papers could be printed and circulated.

Whatever burden of taxation 1765 might or might not bring Virginia, the year called for no less than seven things at Mount Vernon: Invoices from England must include nothing beyond the articles indispensable in the operation of the farms; no more slaves should be bought; no additional lands should be acquired. These were the economies. Income must be increased by the planting of more wheat, an effort to produce and market hemp profitably, large use of the mill, and greater hauls of the river's fish.

This was not an impossible plan for reducing the debt to Cary & Co. Good crops and sound management of a property well-stocked, would in time clear the account. The servants were now nearly sufficient in number—eleven in the house, seven on the home plantation, eleven working at trades, nine at Muddy Hole, ten at Dogue Run and seven at the mill—a total of fifty-five. For directing this labor more carefully and undertaking larger farm activities the owner employed his remote cousin, Lund Washington. Lund could discharge many of the irksome duties that had crowded the Colonel's days. The winter months passed quietly, and the hands were preparing to sow oats, hemp and lucerne when Washington once again set out for Williamsburg. The House met on May 1, 1765, and prepared to debate the subject for which the session primarily had been arranged. This was the revision of the tobacco law, a measure so clumsily amended that it was in great confusion. Indications were for a dull meeting; attendance was below average. Four vacancies were reported—one each in Chesterfield, Amelia, Lunenburg and Louisa. Writs for new elections were requested of the Governor; the session got under way and rumbled slowly along.

Days of routine followed so drearily that many members procured leave to go home for the remainder of the session or left without permission. Then, about May 20, sensations began to develop. Louisa County reported that she had complied with the writ of election and had chosen Patrick Henry of Hanover. Although it was unusual to name a man from another county when he owned no property in the county that chose him, there was nothing in the election law to prohibit it. The oath was administered.

On the twenty-third Washington, the new member from Louisa and the others who had ears for it heard some of the seniors of the House explain the details of the plan, even to the rate of interest Virginia was to pay, for a loan of £250,000 in London and the form of the tax she was to impose until 1795 in order to meet the debt. Debate was not prolonged. Those Burgesses sufficiently versed in matters of finance to understand the resolutions had been lined up in advance; those who did not comprehend could not oppose. The Committee of the Whole reported the resolutions that same day.

On May 24 the measure came up for action by the House. The fledgling Burgess from Louisa arose to challenge the measure. Henry had no schooling in public finance, but he sensed that one aim of the proposal was to permit rich debtors to mortgage their lands to pay for luxuries and he skillfully brought down the complicated "resolves" to language the least-tutored member from the newest frontier county could understand. Vehemently he exposed what he declared to be the favoritism of the plan and the abuses to which it certainly would lead. The leaders had the vote, if not the answer, and proceeded to pass the resolves; but they were doubtful of their handiwork as they sent the resolutions to the Council for concurrence. Either because the unwisdom of the resolutions led a majority to say "No," or because the patrons took alarm at Henry's attack, there came back no message from the council chamber that concurrence had been voted. On the contrary, Council rejected the measure.

On the twenty-sixth only a few minor measures remained. Most of the members had started home. Of a total of 116 Burgesses, only thirty-nine besides the Speaker were in their seats when George Johnston of Fairfax moved that the House go into Committee of the Whole to consider the "steps necessary to be taken in consequence of the resolutions of the House of Commons of Great Britain relative to the charging certain Stamp duties in the Colonies and Plantations in America."

The motion itself announced what had not been published officially—that Commons had set in operation the parliamentary procedure for passing the Stamp Act. A copy of the bill had "crept into the House," as Governor Fauquier later expressed it, and had convinced members that the new tax was to be stiff and inclusive. Some of the details probably were known at the time Johnston made his motion, which Henry seconded. The motion was put and carried; the Speaker left the chair and sat as committee chairman; the thin House looked to Johnston; he deferred to Henry. From his place, the junior Burgess of Louisa County rose, took out a paper and submitted a series of resolutions:

Resolved—

That the first Adventurers and settlers of this his Majesty's Colony and Dominion brought with them and transmitted to their Posterity and all other his Majesty's Subjects since inhabiting in this his Majesty's said Colony, all the Privileges, Franchises and Immunities that have at any Time been held, enjoyed, and possessed by the People of Great Britain.

That by two royal Charters, granted by King James the first the Colonists aforesaid are declared entitled to all the Privileges, Liberties and Immunities of Denizens and natural-born Subjects, to all Intents and Purposes as if they had been abiding and born within the Realm of England.

Resolved—

That the Taxation of the People by themselves or by Persons chosen by themselves to represent them, who can only know what Taxes the People are able to bear, and the easiest Mode of raising them, and are equally affected by such Taxes themselves, is the distinguishing Characteristic of British Freedom and without which the ancient Constitution cannot subsist.

Resolved—

That his Majesty's liege People of this most ancient Colony have uninterruptedly enjoyed the Right of being thus governed by their own Assembly in the article of their Taxes and internal Police, and that the same hath never been forfeited or in any other way given up, but hath been constantly recognized by the Kings and People of Great Britain.

Resolved—

Therefore, That the General Assembly of this Colony have the only and sole exclusive Right and Power to lay Taxes and Impositions upon the Inhabitants of this Colony and that every Attempt to vest such Power in any Person or Persons whatsoever, other than the General Assembly aforesaid, has a manifest Tendency to destroy British as well as American Freedom.

A majority of the Burgesses favored a protest of some sort against a Stamp Act, but some of the older leaders frowned and shook their heads as they listened to Henry's paper. One after another of them assailed the resolutions. Their argument must have been that in so far as the resolutions were proper, they duplicated the address, memorial, and remonstrance of 1764 and that conciliation, not denunciation, should be the weapon of the Colonies. When the utmost had been made of this general objection, a motion was put and passed to consider Henry's resolution *seriatim*.

Where reference was made to "the Privileges, Franchises and Immunities" the "first Adventurers and settlers" brought with them from Great Britain, the word "liberties" was inserted ahead of the other nouns. Henry probably had no objection to this strengthening of the first resolution, and he certainly could not fail to thank the Burgess who suggested how the language of the second resolution could be improved without any change of meaning. The same thing happened to the third resolution. On each of the first four resolutions the old leaders demanded a division—and in each case lost narrowly. None of the resolutions commanded a larger majority than twenty to seventeen. The firmest of all the declarations, the fifth, now was up for approval or rejection. To some, the mild conclusion may have seemed anti-climactic; but the fifth resolution was the one to which all the others led. That was why Henry had put "therefore" after that particular "resolved" and not after any of the others. There was no power outside the General Assembly that had any right to tax Virginians. Were that power usurped, it would be tyranny. So Henry reasoned.

The debate had angered him. Abuse by his adversaries was a goad. Henry took the floor thoroughly aroused. His words took on the nobility of his theme. Listeners were carried to new heights of thought. Young Thomas Jefferson, standing at the door, was swept back to Troy by the rhythmic eloquence of Henry. "He appeared to me," said Jefferson long afterwards, "to speak as Homer wrote." The air became wine. A tax was lost in a principle. Williamsburg became Runnymede. The walls of the chamber melted into the deep background of the Englishman's struggle to shape his own destiny. Henry's imagery took bolder and bolder form. With a voice that impaled his hearers, he shouted: "Tarquin and Caesar each had his Brutus, Charles the First his Cromwell, and George the Third—"

"Treason," ruled the outraged Speaker.

Henry lifted his shoulders still higher as he paused for an instant only—"and George the Third may profit by their example! If *this* be treason make the most of it!"

Skillful as this was, the Speaker did not intend to permit the utterance or the apparent acquiescence of the House to go unrebuked. Robinson again ruled Henry's words treasonable. Henry had made his point; he had no intention of having prejudice aroused against his resolutions because of a ruling that the author of them had uttered treasonable words. He apologized to the Speaker and the House and avowed his loyalty to the King. Division was demanded. The count showed the declaration to have been carried by twenty to nineteen.

The Committee of the Whole rose; Peyton Randolph reported to the House that certain resolutions had been adopted and that he was ready to deliver them. As the hour was late, the House voted to receive the report the next day. May 30, when the seniors undertook to defeat Henry's resolutions, his lines held. All five were adopted with some slight amendments.

In the belief that the declaration of the Colony was now firmly a matter of record, Henry started back to Hanover. The following morning his absence was noted in a House perceptibly thinner than it had been even during the debate on the Stamp Act. Randolph and other leaders proceeded to move that the resolutions be expunged, but, as the five parts of the paper had been adopted one by one, the chair ruled, that the expunging vote be put separately on each resolution. Weakened though Henry's supporters were by his absence, they held together and beat down the motion to efface from the record the first, the second, the third and the fourth resolutions. The fifth, the resolution carrying the climactic "therefore," they lost. It was stricken from the Journal.

Governor Fauquier, on June 1, summoned the Burgesses to the council chamber, signed the completed bills and joint resolutions and then, without a word of thanks or reproach, dissolved the House. The King must appeal to his people in new elections. Appeal he might, but Henry had not penned his resolutions in vain. Virginia's resolves gave the signal for a general outcry over the continent.

It is unlikely that Washington attended the final days of the General Assembly. He probably left Williamsburg early, for there were serious matters to consider at Mount Vernon. A new uncertainty was creeping into the life that defeat of the French had given promise of stability. Washington found the family well, but conditions on the farms were bad. Drought had settled on the Hunting Creek estate. Besides drought, there was rust on the wheat crop which Washington was hoping would offset the decline in returns from the Potomac tobacco.

The hard summer was not without its satisfactions and its honors. Writs of election went out in June for the new House. In Fairfax, there was to be a vacancy. George Johnston decided that he would not be a candidate for the seat he had held since 1758. Washington accordingly declined in Frederick County and declared himself a candidate in Fairfax. The result of a light vote on July 16 was: Washington, 201; John West, 148; John Posey, 131. Washington and West were elected. Washington was entirely satisfied. It was, he confessed, "an easy and a creditable poll."

Attendance on the new Assembly seemed immediately in prospect. Washington was preparing to start for the capital when word came on July 28 that the session had been prorogued. "I am convinced . . ." said Washington, "that the Governor had no inclination to meet an Assembly at this juncture." That was the belief in every part of Virginia. The lawmakers of Massachusetts had sent on June 8, 1765, a call for a meeting in New York October 7 of representatives of all the Colonies: Governor Fauquier did not want the Houses of Burgesses to approve participation in this enterprise which he regarded as seditious.

Opposition to the Stamp Act was shifting from argument to resistance. The stamps had been printed in England and were being sent to each of the Colonies for allotment. For Virginia, the designated "Distributor" was Col. George Mercer. Mercer's known acceptance of the office had cost him already his place in the affection of many of his own people. On the Northern Neck he had been burned in effigy. Thousands of the Colonials were resolved they would not use the tax-paper in any circumstance. Some members of county courts were saying that they would not serve a day after legal processes had to be stamped. Whispers were passed that if an attempt were made to execute the law, men would come from the upcountry to Williamsburg and would seize and destroy the stamps. Washington heard and pondered. He was not excited and had not made common cause with those who advocated an extreme course.

Whether or not the new ministers of a coalition headed by Lord Rockingham ended the calamity of the Stamp Act, the year in Virginia was certain to be a disastrous one on the plantations. While the drought did not prove as ruinous as Washington had expected, the yield of his enlarged acreage of wheat was not more than 1112 bushels. The experiments with flax and hemp bore out Washington's earlier fears of partial failure that season. Quality was low and the market was undeveloped, though the prospect was not altogether disheartening. The difficult crop year was ending when Washington read the details of the meeting in New York during October of the "Stamp Act Congress." Twenty-seven from nine Colonies had conferred for about a fortnight and had formulated a "Declaration of Rights and Grievances" to which most Virginians would have subscribed.

Then Washington heard that a startling new scene in the drama of the Stamp Act had been staged in Williamsburg. Mercer had crossed the Atlantic with a full stock of stamps and had arrived in Hampton Roads at a time when the Colony's anger over the tax measure was rising to new resentment with the approach of November 1, the date on which a stamp would be required to validate almost any act of business or law. Little besides the Stamp Act was discussed in Williamsburg as October was closing and attorneys, merchants and planters gathered for the usual settlement of accounts at the meeting of the General Court, scheduled for the same fateful November 1.

On October 30, when the throng was close to its crest, Colonel Mercer arrived in Williamsburg and went forthwith to private lodgings, but he brought none of the detested stamps with him from the vessel. Word of his presence reached the Governor who decided immediately to go to Mrs. Campbell's Virginia Coffee House to be at hand in event of disorder. About mid-afternoon, someone shouted "One and all!" Others took it up and began to move towards the building where Mercer was supposed to be. "This concourse of people," the Governor said afterwards, "I should call a mob, did I not know that it was chiefly if not altogether composed of gentlemen of property. . . ." The crowd came upon Colonel Mercer at the Capitol. He had shown abundant courage during the French and Indian War and he did not cringe now. The question was shot straight at him: he saw how the people felt about the stamps; was he going to distribute them or would he stand with his own people and resign the office? Mercer kept his head. The issue meant a great deal to him, he said. He could not attempt to answer the question immediately. Friday, the day the stamps had to be used, he would make his answer—in front of the Capitol—at ten o'clock in the morning.

With that he started towards the coffee house. There on the porch, seated together, were the Governor and most of the members of Council. Mercer, of course, went straight to the Governor, whom he had not seen since his arrival. The crowd did not like this. Cries were rising from the street: "Friday is too late," "The law goes into effect then," "Promise to give your answer tomorrow." After various messages and appeals, Mercer reluctantly agreed to give his answer at five o'clock Thursday afternoon.

By the next afternoon at five o'clock the crowd was larger than ever and was collected in the Capitol, where Mercer had promised to appear. In a few minutes he arrived, faced the throng and read a letter which said in part:

> I do acknowledge that some little time before[,] I heard of and saw some resolves which were said to be made by the House of Burgesses of Virginia, but as the authority of them was disputed, they never appearing but in private hands, and so often and differently reported to me, I determined to know the real sentiments of my countrymen from themselves and I am compelled to say that those sentiments were so suddenly and unexpectedly communicated to me that I was altogether unable to give an immediate answer upon so important a point. . . .
> I should be glad to act now in such a manner as would justify me to my friends and countrymen here and the authority which appointed me but the time you have all allotted me is so very short that I have not yet been able to discover that happy medium and therefore must entreat you to be referred to my future conduct with this assurance in the meantime that I will not directly or indirectly

by my deputies or myself proceed further with the Act until I receive further orders from England and not then without the assent of the General Assembly of this Colony and that no man can more ardently or sincerely wish the prosperity of than myself. . . . Your sincere friend and humble servant. . . .

That was enough! Those who had seemed willing to kill him on Wednesday now made a hero of him and carried him out of the Capitol in triumph.

The General Court met the next day, but not a litigant appeared and not a lawyer, except the Attorney General. Fauquier subsequently reported: ". . . I called for Colonel Mercer and asked him in open court whether he could supply the Court with proper stamps that the business might be carried on, according to law. He replied he could not, and gave the substance of the answer he had given the evening before. I then asked the Clerk whether he could carry on the business without them. He said he could not, without subjecting himself to such penalties as he would not expose himself to. . . . Then the Court was unanimous that we might adjourn to the next court in course, which was accordingly done."

There was more—an effort by Mercer to tender his resignation to the Governor who refused it, and the transfer of all the stamped papers to a war vessel—but that tableau in the General Court was the ominous climax. "The first and most obvious consequences of all this," Fauquier reported, "must be the shutting up all the ports and stopping all proceedings in the courts of justice." A few days later the optimistic Governor was wondering whether the Colonials would stand fast: ". . . I am very credibly informed that some of the busy men in opposing the reception of the stamps are already alarmed at the consequences of the imprudent steps they have taken."

"Credibly informed," the Governor said he was—not concerning the man who read of this at Mount Vernon, nor Henry, nor that young student Jefferson whose heart had beat high as he listened to Henry cry, "Caesar had his Brutus. . . ."

The temper displayed towards Mercer and his stamps was warning that 1766 might prove a year of grim and stubborn contest in Virginia. Plans had to be based on the possibility that no ships would be cleared, no debts collected and no legal business of any sort transacted because no stamps would be purchased or used. To prevent the rusting of all the wheels of trade the Stamp Act must be repealed. England must realize that the measure was as unenforceable as it was unjust. Should this effort prove vain, then Mount Vernon and every like plantation must produce the articles necessary for self-support.

Washington did not undertake to grow any tobacco in 1766 on the Potomac, though he did not forbid his tenants doing so. He determined, instead, to increase his wheat and, at least experimentally, continue with flax and hemp. In addition, as Capt. David Kennedy offered to rent the Bullskin plantation for £28 per annum, that gentleman should have it. A schooner was finished and rigged and could be used during the spring for fishing and, later, for bringing plank from the Occoquan sawmill. The outlook was not hopeless. Unfavorable conditions would correct themselves if Parliament would abandon direct taxes in frank realization that the Colonies would not yield, could not be made to do so and would be quick and violent in dealing with any attempt to comply with the law.

Hot blood on the Rappahannock did not wait. A merchant and shipowner of Hobbs Hole, Archibald Ritchie, declared at the court in Richmond County during February that he intended to clear his vessels on "stamped paper" and that he could get stamps. The countryside was enraged. Everywhere along the Rappahannock the comment was the same: If merchants yielded, the Stamp Act could be enforced in part at least, and the right of exclusive Colonial self-taxation would be destroyed. On February 27, 1766, a number of prominent planters met at Leedstown to decide what they should do about Ritchie's defiance. They proceeded to formulate the principles on which they would act and to draw up articles of association.

Then the "Associators" decided to make Ritchie sign a declaration that was duly drafted and approved. The next day, no less than four hundred men assembled at Hobbs Hole—"Sons of Liberty" they called themselves in proud acceptation of the name Col. Isaac Barre had applied during the debate in the House of Commons on the stamp bill. A committee went to Ritchie's house to demand that he sign the paper. Ritchie protested: Would not the gentlemen name a committee to "reason with him on the subject?" No! His case had been passed upon. It was for him to say whether he would go willingly to the street where the other Sons of Liberty were waiting for him. Ritchie could not hesitate otherwise than at the risk of worse things to come. He went out, listened as the declaration was read to him, signed and swore to this paper:

Sensible now of the high insult I offered this County by my declaration at Richmond Court lately of my determination to make use of stamped paper for clearing out vessels; and having been convinced such proceedings will establish a precedent by which the hateful Stamp Act might be introduced into this Colony to the utter destruction of the Public Liberty, I do most submissively in the presence of the public sign the Paper meaning to show my remorse for having formed so execrable a Declaration and I do hereby solemnly promise and swear on the Holy Evangelist that no vessel of mine shall clear on stamped paper; that I never will on any Pretence make use of Stamped Paper unless that use be authorized by the General Assembly of this Colony.

ARCHIBALD RITCHIE.

At Norfolk, Virginia, the Sons of Liberty resolved to use "all lawful ways and means" that Providence had put in their hands for preserving the right "of being taxed by none but representatives of their own choosing, and of being tried only by a jury of their own peers"; in London, the agents of the Colonies and some of the merchants were pleading before Committees of Commons for the repeal of the Stamp Act. Benjamin Franklin underwent examination at great length, by friends and by adversaries, before Commons in Committee of the Whole, and he won great praise by his answers. The prime distinction he drew in his argument was between a tax on commerce, imposed and accepted in the interest of the empire, and a direct internal tax on the American Colonies, levied without their consent.

Mercer was still another witness before the Committee. He thought the burden of the stamp tax would fall most heavily on the poor because the great part of the taxes were "very trifling" in amount and would mean little to persons of wealth. Mercer made the distinction on which Franklin had laid much emphasis: "The grand objection was to any *internal* tax, and this is the only institution to which the Legislature has been opposed."

Other witnesses were equally firm in saying that attempted enforcement of the Stamp Act would be calamitous and that nothing less than complete repeal would satisfy the Colonials or save the merchants. Perhaps the most vehement cry of all was in a petition of the London merchants, who described the markets that had been created in the Colonies for British goods and the benefits that had been Britain's from commodities the Colonies had shipped in part payment for the products sent them. ". . . this commerce," the merchants told the Commons, "so beneficial to the State and so necessary for the support of multitudes, now lies under such difficulties and discouragements that nothing less than utter ruin is apprehended without the immediate interposition of Parliament."

Virginians did not hear promptly of any of this, but they learned that the Rockingham ministry still held office and that friends of the Colonies were urging the repeal of the Stamp Act. Commerce remained at a standstill. Conversation was changed, too. When men of station were not talking of repeal of the act, their speech was of how to carry on the business of plantations in spite of it. Ladies of fashion had pride no longer in what they were importing from England but in what they were doing without. Refusal to send orders to Britain now was as sure a distinction as the high cost of an invoice of fine dress previously had been. The enforced self-dependence of the frontier had become the voluntary law of life in the Tidewater.

In the midst of this period of protest and uncertainty Washington made a journey in April to the Dismal Swamp with his brother-in-law, Fielding Lewis. They found the Negroes making sufficient progress to renew faith in the undertaking. So hopeful were the visitors that they decided to purchase on their own account approximately 1100 acres of Marmaduke Norfleet's land for £1200 Virginia currency. It was a dangerously large obligation to be assumed at a time of perplexity by a man already in debt to his London merchant for a considerable sum; but Washington believed in the future of the swamp. When he believed in anything he would stake his money on his judgment.

The early days of May brought developments that seemed to justify faith in the future. As if she were proud to be the messenger, the ship *Lady Baltimore* arrived in York River May 2 with news for which the entire Colony had been hoping: the Stamp Act had been repealed! After a resounding debate in which Pitt was the strategist against the measure, Commons had voted to erase the offending tax from the statute books. On the first division, the Lords voted fifty-nine to fifty-four for the execution of the

Stamp Act, but in the end they accepted the repeal bill. Royal assent was given March 18. Merchants had been so confident this would be the action of Parliament that some of them already had started cargoes to America. Commercial England's gratification was as nothing compared with the jubilation of America. Resistance had justified itself, one element proclaimed; faith in King and Parliament, said others, had been vindicated.

So completely were Washington's fellow-planters convinced of the sympathy of Parliament with the Colonies' interpretation of constitutional principles that scarce attention was paid in Virginia to a "Declaratory Act" that had been responsible, in part, for the willingness of the Lords to reverse their vote against repeal. The measure, passed almost simultaneously with the repeal bill, referred to the assertion by the Colonies of the exclusive right of taxing themselves. In plain words the Colonies were told they did not possess that right without qualification. The act set forth that Crown and Parliament "had, hath and of right ought to have the full power and authority to make laws and statutes of sufficient force and validity to bind the Colonies and people of America, subjects of the Crown of Great Britain, in all cases whatsoever." Further, Colonial proceedings of every sort that challenged or disputed the powers of King and Parliament were "utterly null and void to all intents and purposes whatsoever."

This declaration was warning to the Colonies that the repeal of the Stamp Act was not to be regarded as an admission that the law itself was unconstitutional or that the provisions of it were arbitrary and tyrannical. Parliament, in fact, did more than assert full authority to do again what it voluntarily had undone: it served notice that it could and, if need be, would declare Colonial laws of no effect—a power that previously had been exclusively the prerogative of the Crown. This was minimized, if not ignored by the leaders of the General Assembly who felt that it mattered little, as they saw it, that powers had been declared that never would be exercised by Parliament.

It was tragic for the leaders of the General Assembly that the news of the repeal should be followed on May 11 by the death of Speaker Robinson, who for many years had seemed to exemplify good will. Death was not his worst fate. Robinson was buried with honor and lament; Robert Carter Nicholas was named in his place as Treasurer. Then in a short time the new official reported that Robinson was delinquent in some vast, undetermined sum, which enemies styled defalcation and apologists declared to be loans made to protect the estates of friends.

Governor Fauquier formally proclaimed the repeal of the Stamp Act on June 6 and thereby gave justices and lawyers, merchants and planters the signal to go back to work. Washington wrote his merchants: "The repeal of the Stamp Act, to whatsoever causes owing, ought much to be rejoiced at, for had the Parliament of Great Britain resolved upon enforcing it, the consequences I conceive would have been more direful than is generally apprehended both to the Mother Country and her Colonies. All therefore who were instrumental in procuring the repeal are entitled to the thanks of every British subject and have mine cordially."

It was gratifying to get rid of so provocative an issue; doubly so because conditions at Mount Vernon called for the undiverted attention of the owner. The transfer from tobacco to wheat was not easy. A controversy was brewing with Carlyle & Adam over the proper weight of wheat per bushel. That firm, moreover, was far from prompt in paying. Information was discouragingly meagre concerning the growing and shipment of flax and hemp and the collection of the bounty offered by Parliament. Goods from England were high in price and, sometimes, poor in quality or shipped without regard to specifications. Unpleasantness found its place in letters and ledger-entries; the happiness of domestic life left no record except in the heart. Private life was better, not worse.

In this atmosphere the new Burgess from Fairfax received the usual summons to Williamsburg: Fauquier had set a date for a session of the General Assembly in March, then May, then July, and once again in September, only to postpone it finally to November. Washington went in style this time, with coach-and-six and with Martha and the children. He found himself immediately on the scene of a vigorous contest for the office of speaker, vacated by the death of Robinson. The potentates were divided over a choice between Peyton Randolph and Richard Bland. The majority were for Randolph, who proceeded at once to take the chair and organize the House. First action was a unanimous vote for the appointment of a committee to examine the state of the Treasury and, in particular, to scrutinize all receipts and check all issues of Virginia paper money after 1754. Bland was named chairman, with ten associates from among the ablest members of the House.

The committee had to go back in Robinson's accounts to April, 1755, from which date it followed all the issues of Treasury notes, all the collections and all the major disbursements—a long and troublesome task. The committee concluded that the balance due by Robinson was £100,761, and his administrators asked three years in which to settle. The Assembly was loath to prolong the period during which the Colony might be crippled by the defalcation. After discussion in Committee of the Whole, the decision was, first, to request the Governor to institute suits against Robinson's estate, and, second, to instruct the Attorney General, after obtaining judgment against Robinson's securities, not to issue executions in a larger sum than was necessary to make good the difference between what Robinson owed and what his estate would yield. Measures thought to compass all that could be done at the moment to recover the £100,000 of which the people had been defrauded were enacted. The legislation was prompt and uncompromising, but the humiliation persisted: through Robinson, the integrity of the ruling class had been assailed.

Washington bore his part of responsibility for the decisions in the Robinson case, and he took advantage of his proximity to the Dismal Swamp to visit the new enterprise for a week. He continued to believe that money devoted to the work would prove an investment of high value. It was pleasant to look forward to the development of new, rich farms because some of those on the Potomac still seemed to rebel against anything that was planted after the plow had passed over. Washington now owned 9581 acres of land on which he was paying quit rents of 2s. 6d. per hundred acres—a total that did not include any of the plantations acquired through Martha. Custis farms that year had grown tobacco to fill seventeen hogsheads for Washington and fifty-one for Jackie Custis—a short crop. From the Potomac, Washington received none of the staple other than "rent tobacco" which eight tenants had raised. The wheat crop of 1766 had been good, but neither yield nor weight had been exceptional. Nor were relations with the purchasers, Carlyle & Adam, marked by any closer approach to the spirit of full friendliness that Washington desired.

If Washington had sought or needed consolation, he would have found it in the delights of home life and the knowledge that Mount Vernon was better equipped every year. If money could be made on the thin land of the area adjacent to Hunting Creek, Washington now had the slaves and the implements to make it. He was becoming more and more rooted into the life of the Potomac. Seven years of almost constant residence on the river had increased his love of his land and waterfront and his interest in the advancement of the simple institutions of Fairfax County and Alexandria. On the death of George Johnston, one of the trustees of the town, Washington was named in his place. Another continuing, perhaps increasing, interest was in the affairs of Truro Parish. Now that he was a vestryman, he had duties which he discharged with diligence. Dr. Charles Green having died in 1765, the Rev. Lee Massey became minister and proceeded to appeal for the erection of a new church. Washington was one of five named to "view and examine" the structure at intervals. The master of Mount Vernon was designated also to handle the parish collection and, with George William Fairfax, to sell the parish tobacco for the payment of the minister and the erection of the new place of prayer. In signing these accounts, Washington soon was authorized to write "Warden" after his name.

Plans for 1767 at Mount Vernon were explicit. No tobacco was to be grown by Washington on any of his Potomac farms, though eight or ten of the "renters" would continue to pay in leaf. The main crop was to be wheat. Under the contract with Carlyle & Adam, all that grain grown by Washington would be delivered to that firm; but as the mill on Dogue Run was now operating smoothly on a moderate scale, it could grind the wheat of other planters from whom Washington might buy flour as well as take toll. More corn would be planted. Experiments with hemp and flax would be continued for another year. The schooner could be used in fishing and, when not needed for other purposes, might be chartered by planters or shipmasters. Weaving would be the farm industry Washington would develop most vigorously, because the shortage of specie had increased the demand for homespun. The carpenters would erect a barn on the Neck Plantation. There would be vigorous prosecution of the bold venture of draining Dismal Swamp; and if fine western land could be found at a low figure, it must be purchased, even though Cary & Co. had to wait a little longer for the balance due them. These plans were followed in 1767 with few disappointments.

In February Washington went to Williamsburg on business of the Custis estate, and in mid-March he had to attend another session of the House of Burgesses. It did not prove exciting. Perhaps the report that created most talk was another on the state of Treasurer Robinson's accounts, which showed a payment to the Colony of only £553 by his administrators. His outstanding delinquency, recomputed, was set down as slightly over £102,000. The familiar, almost unendurable shortage of money that made the sale of Robinson's property slow and expensive was the subject of attempts at relief legislation. The day the Council said "No" to these proposals, April 11, the Governor prorogued the Assembly.

Washington again found occasion for a visit to Dismal Swamp, and he arranged for advertising a lease of the Custis plantation near Williamsburg. Then he went home and, among other things, renewed a controversy with Carlyle & Adam. The issue was that of weight per bushel. Contention was sharpened because the merchants had written Washington bluntly that they "had rather be £1000 in any other gentleman's debt than the trifling sum of £100" in debt to him.

Washington's code of noblesse oblige would not permit him to turn away debt-distraught friends, perplexed farmers of humble station who valued his judgment above the advice of lawyers and the more so because it cost them nothing, old soldiers who seemed to think their Colonel must remain their counsellor, or aging planters of wealth who wanted a prudent executor of their will or a careful guardian of their sons. All these were beginning now to call on Washington. To hear them took hours; to solve their problems or relieve their distress sometimes called for days. It was costly but it was not shunned. Instead, Washington's service for his neighbors daily increased his sense of obligation to them and, at the same time, gave him longer patience and new understanding of men. Contact with human woe subtly slackened his acquisitive impulse and tightened his self-discipline. He had to be more diligent and orderly than ever in looking after his own business, because he had to give so much of his time to the affairs of others. All this service was training, though he probably did not so regard it and certainly did not ask himself for what purpose this training would be used.

While the wheat crop still was being stored in the driest barns on the plantations, Washington went with Martha and the children to the Berkeley Springs. Along with the cripples and the feeble, Washington met at the Springs an old comrade of the French and Indian War—Col. John Armstrong, senior officer of the Pennsylvania contingent in Forbes's campaign of 1758. Washington did not have much of the Pennsylvanian's company at the resort, but he learned that Armstrong was residing at Carlisle and had some connection with a public land office in Pennsylvania.

By the middle of the second week in September Washington was back at Mount Vernon with his appetite for western lands whetted by developments in controversies over the boundary lines of Pennsylvania. To ascertain the Maryland-Pennsylvania boundary, Charles Mason and Jeremiah Dixon had started work in 1764. Their survey had been suspended in November 1766 but now was being extended. Washington received information that valuable lands, previously unpatented, were to be declared within Pennsylvania and might be procured under grants of that Colony. He began a campaign to get 1500 or 2000 or even more acres of the best of this land. Capt. William Crawford, another old comrade of Forbes's march to the Ohio, resided on the Youghiogheny, in the very country towards which Washington was looking. Two letters went promptly to the Captain to enlist his services. Crawford must find out how patents could be had; Colonel Armstrong would help him; if Crawford succeeded, Washington would compensate him and, in the spring of 1768, would visit him on the Youghiogheny to explain the whole matter and another of even greater importance, which he proceeded to sketch.

This was the patenting of a very large tract west of the Pennsylvania boundary and west, also, of the "Proclamation Line" set over the royal seal, October 2, 1763. That frontier separated the eastern settlements of all Colonies from the lands left to the Indians for their hunting and occupancy. Washington confided to Crawford: ". . . I can never look upon that proclamation in any other light (but this I say between ourselves) than as a temporary expedient to quiet the minds of the Indians and must fall of course in a few years especially when those Indians are consenting to our occupying their lands. Any person therefore who neglects the present opportunity of hunting out good lands and in some measure marking and distinguishing them for their own (in order to keep others from settling them) will never regain it. . . ." A loose partnership was to be formed: Crawford must locate the lands in the closed area and must mark them; Washington would pay all the costs of surveys and patents and would engage to procure the lands as soon as possible. A letter was dispatched to Colonel Armstrong: would he please advise concerning the procedure for patenting lands in Pennsylvania? Armstrong would do all he could to assist; Crawford was entirely at Washington's command.

CHAPTER / 7

The close of 1767 would have been peaceful and the beginning of 1768 cheerful but for action of the British Parliament. There was insistent exercise of the right of taxation asserted in the Declaratory Act. Import duties were fixed on paints and their ingredients, glass, many kinds of paper, and all tea. Proceeds were to pay for a central customs system and then for the compensation of Governors and other officials of the Crown. These Townshend Acts, so styled after the name of the Chancellor of the Exchequer, were passed between June 15 and July 2, 1767. When known in America, they were denounced as violations of the fundamental rights of Englishmen in America. Everywhere, public men renewed the argument that it was tyrannical to have taxes levied without the consent of the people who were to pay them.

The future of all the Colonial legislative bodies might be forecast by the punishment imposed on the New York Assembly under the first of the Townshend Acts. Because the greater part of the British troops in America had been billeted on New York, the Assembly had declined to vote salt, vinegar and cider or beer, on the ground that these were not allowed His Majesty's troops in European barracks, though the Assembly did not withhold the grant it previously had made under the Quartering Act of 1765. When Gen. Thomas Gage reported this to the home government, Charles Townshend had Parliament pass a stern act: The New York Assembly was suspended from the exercise of its functions until it complied with all the requirements the British commander set for billeting his troops.

Alarm over this "Suspending Act" spread throughout the Colonies. Previously assemblies had been convened, prorogued and dissolved by the Governor, as the representative of the Crown. Now it appeared that Parliament had usurped royal authority at the behest of an irritated politician. Parliamentary control of Colonial lawmakers, taxation without representation, a royal rein on Governors and judges because they had to look to the King for their pay, the denial to the assemblies of control over customs—these provisions of the Townshend Acts, taken together, were regarded as a threat to the most essential rights of America. If these rights were lost, what remained?

For Colonel Washington 1768 began with hope for benefits from the shift from tobacco growing to wheat. The change meant vast saving in labor, for no Virginia crop is quite so demanding of time and toil as tobacco. New tasks now could be undertaken—the development of farm-fisheries, improvement of the mill, expansion of weaving, construction of a new barn and enlargement of the residence at Mount Vernon. Washington had more time for hunting and could look forward to visiting in summer Martha's kinsfolk and his own. He entered zestfully into fox hunting, shooting and card-playing. March called for more farm activities, and the Colonel had to contend with his first illness in several years.

A session of Assembly opened the last day of March and was prorogued April 16, without attendance by the junior Burgess from Fairfax. It was a session of some distinction. To the general grief of the Colony, Governor Fauquier had lost on March 3 a long struggle with illness. Burial in the Williamsburg church was with every honor the people could give him. His temporary successor, under existing practice, could be none other than the President of the Council. John Blair, who held that office, was eighty-one years of age, but was alert, acceptable and able, though reluctant to assume the duties of Governor. On assuming the post, "Mr. President" had believed that Fauquier's call for a session of Assembly at the end of March should stand, because the reason for it remained. Encroachment by white settlers on Indian lands had aroused the Redmen to threats of reprisal that were alarming the frontier. The Assembly resolved politely to urge Indians and frontiersmen to avoid hostilities. Its most serious deliberations were on the Townshend Acts. Freeholders of half a dozen counties had sent protests against these measures and in support of the appeal the Massachusetts General Court had made February 11 for united action of the Colonies against measures that deprived them of their rights. Virginia Burgesses drafted another address to the King, a memorial to the House of Lords, and a remonstrance to the House of Commons.

These papers were more argumentatively explicit and somewhat less rhetorical than those adopted prior to the passage of the Stamp Act. The Virginians maintained more vigorously than ever that the fundamental principle of British government was, "No power on earth has a right to impose taxes upon the people or to take the smallest portion of their property without their consent, given by their representatives in Parliament." As the Colonies were not and could not be represented in Commons, the right of self-taxation must rest exclusively in the Colonial legislative bodies. The "Suspending Act" aimed at the New York Assembly presented the Virginians with possibilities they had not canvassed in any of their previous declarations, but in their appeal to Parliament they merely branded the statute as even "more alarming" than the other measures. The Burgesses were not divided as in 1764; they were unanimous in approving all three papers. The Council concurred, and agreed that its representative in England would join the regular agent of the Colony in supporting address, memorial and remonstrance. Finally, and again with unanimity, Speaker Randolph was given two instructions: First, he was to reply to the "circular Letter" of the Massachusetts House "that we could not but applaud them for their attention to American liberty and that the steps we had taken thereon would convince them of our opinion of the fatal tendency of the acts of Parliament complained of and of our fixed resolution to concur with the other Colonies in their application for redress." Second, he was "to write to the respective Speakers of the Assemblies and Representatives on this continent to make known to them our proceedings on this subject and to intimate how necessary we think it is that the Colonies should unite in a firm but decent opposition to every measure which may affect the rights and liberties of the British Colonies in America." Common danger created common cause.

Colonel Washington's absence denied him the right of voting "Aye" on the adoption of these papers. Had he been present he would not have hesitated for an instant. Once the issue became that of the rights of Virginians, it no longer was in the realm of debate with him. Thereafter his course of duty was plain.

That spring, the children's tutor, Walter Magowan, decided to proceed to England to seek admission to holy orders. Mrs. Washington might provide instruction for Patsy at Mount Vernon or in the neighborhood, but the stepfather had to find a teacher for Jackie. Washington had heard of the well-attended school for boys that Jonathan Boucher, rector of St. Mary's, Caroline County, was conducting on the minister's glebe, twelve miles from the church. The Colonel wrote forthwith to Boucher. Boucher's replies contained first a doubt, because the school might be moved to Maryland, and then an eagerness to have "Master Custis." About July 1, Jackie was escorted by Washington to Caroline County along with his body servant, two horses and luggage but without sundry Latin texts he soon was to need.

On June 13 Washington and Martha rode to Belvoir, where Colonel and Mrs. Fairfax were entertaining. On their return home Patsy suddenly became ill and had what unmistakably was a fit. Dr. William Rumney was summoned and was able to relieve the twelve-year-old girl. She recovered to such an extent that the physician felt justified in leaving the next morning, but the child's illness was alarming. Fits might recur. The solicitous mother could do nothing more than the doctor suggested, except to give Patsy the pleasure of pretty possessions.

Tobacco once again had a bad season. Four years in five Washington had received less money, net, for the leaf he had sent to England than he could have commanded for it at Dumfries. This year he sold 53,000 lbs. at 22s. 6d. per hundredweight, Virginia currency, to Hector Ross of Colchester. The crops of 1768 from the York were twenty hogsheads of Washington's and thirty-six of Jackie's. These probably would go to England. The debt to Cary & Co. had not yet been discharged, but Washington's credits were accumulating. A fine wheat crop yielded more than 4900 bushels. Washington ordered a new chariot, the specifications of which he drew with much care. Circumstances seemed, also, to justify expenditure for handsome clothing and more luxuries. During the spring and summer Washington attended two meetings of the company that sought acreage on the Mississippi, and in October he set out again for the Dismal Swamp where he spent three days.

From the Great Dismal, Washington went back to Williamsburg to make an inspection of the Custis farms and attend the autumn session of the General Court. As soon as he reached the capital, Washington learned that a proclamation had been issued October 27 for the dissolution of the General Assembly. This was the act of the new Governor, Norborne Berkeley,

Baron de Botetourt, who had arrived ceremoniously the day before he signed the paper. Lest the Virginians assume that his proclamation indicated a suspension of the General Assembly, the Governor announced in the document that he intended "shortly to issue writs for the election of Burgesses to serve in the new Assembly at such time as by the advice of his Majesty's Council shall be judged most fit and convenient." The attitude of the new Governor was conciliatory. He said nothing of instructions to curb the resentful Colonials; no word came that dissolution was punishment for the papers of protest adopted in April. To most of the Burgesses the proclamation meant only that if they wanted to retain their seats they had to undergo the expense and annoyance of an election in the late autumn.

Washington had no thought of declining the contest. He felt the responsibility and enjoyed the distinction. Besides, he just now had attained to the full honors of a gentleman of the county and he did not wish to forgo any of them. In addition to holding the office of Burgess and that of Warden of Truro Parish, he was appointed in September a Justice of the County Court of Fairfax and a member of the Court of Oyer and Terminer of the County.

At Mount Vernon he found everything in order. There was ample leisure for fox-hunting. Dinners followed hunts; the pheasant as well as the fox was sought. In anticipation of success in the election December 1, Washington arranged a ball to which his adherents were invited. The poll justified both the plan and the expense, which reached the stout sum of £25 12s. Washington and John West were re-elected—Washington by a somewhat smaller lead than in the previous poll. Capt. John Posey again was the third man in the field and the loser. When the vote had been counted and proclaimed, well-wishers danced till the night was gone.

After that came Christmas and, in the New Year, 1769, new plans and commitments. At home, the slaves worked on opening an avenue to the house; from Pennsylvania Crawford wrote of the land he had procured in his own name for Washington, though the Captain had to admit the prospect of getting large tracts on the Kanawha did not appear bright. In the green upcountry, Washington had bought 2682 acres in Loudoun and Fauquier Counties from the estate of George Carter, and in March he went to survey it and divide it into small tracts.

On his return to Mount Vernon he did not find the usual cheer. Patsy had suffered more fits and apparently had to face recurring affliction. Washington grieved with Martha and with the girl, but he did not let sorrow in his own household blind him to opportunity in other homes. Having no son of his own, he was interested in the promising boys of his neighbors, and as his means increased so did his beneficence. The old acquisitiveness remained: it was dignified by a new philanthropy. He found it inconvenient at the moment to comply with the request his friend William Ramsay of Alexandria made for a loan, but he had heard Ramsay speak in praise of New Jersey College as if it were the wish of the father to have young William Ramsay attend that school. Washington accordingly wrote that he would make £25 a year available for the education of the youth. In what was the most generous sentence that ever had come from his pen,

Washington wrote: "No other return is expected or wished for this offer than that you will accept it with the same freedom and good will with which it is made, and that you may not even consider it in the light of an obligation, or mention it as such; for be assured that from me it will never be known."

These were the channels in which life was moving—now over shoals, now over rocks and now through pleasant pastures when, early in April, Washington received from Dr. David Ross of Bladensburg, Maryland, papers in which proposals were made for "associations" of merchants and citizens who would agree not to import or buy non-essential British goods so long as Parliament undertook to impose direct taxes or suppress Colonial assemblies. Washington read the papers and then forwarded them to George Mason. Vigorously Washington wrote: "At a time when our lordly Masters in Great Britain will be satisfied with nothing less than the deprication [sic] of American freedom, it seems highly necessary that something should be done to avert the stroke and maintain the liberty which we had derived from our ancestors; but the manner of doing it to answer the purpose effectually is the point in question." He dropped a line and continued as if what he was about to say was almost too obvious to labor: "That no man should scruple, or hesitate a moment to use a-ms in defence of so valuable a blessing, on which all the good and evil of life depends, is clearly my opinion; yet A-ms, I would beg leave to add, should be the last resource, the denier [dernier] resort."

Washington continued his letter after he had spoken grimly of an appeal to arms as the last resort of the Colonials. The northern Colonies, Washington went on, were using associations of merchants to put pressure on British trades. This method might be an effective weapon if generally employed. Clashing interests would make difficult cutting off importation of British goods. This would be particularly true in the tobacco Colonies, Washington reasoned, because trade there was diffused and conducted not by native merchants but by factors "at home." Even so the enterprise would not be hopeless if gentlemen would stop importation and purchase and would "explain matters to the people." "The more I consider a scheme of this sort," Washington wrote, "the more ardently I wish success to it. . . ." Public gain might be uncertain, because, if Parliament could tax, it could prohibit manufactures in the Colonies. Methods had to be considered. It might be well to delay action until the General Court and the Assembly met in May and agreed on a plan that could be put in operation simultaneously in all the counties.

There scarcely was a clause in any of this to show Washington realized he was entering the field of political leadership. As a Burgess since 1759 he had transacted his constituents' public business, presented their petitions, voted according to his judgment and convictions and learned much about the mind and methods of lawmaking bodies. He had not yet essayed to be a leader.

Mason already had concluded that Virginia should follow the northern Colonies in organizing firm associations for the non-importation of British goods, though he believed the tobacco Colonies had to use certain

British goods the northern Colonies could do without because New England, New York and Pennsylvania had some manufactures of their own. Now he prepared a list of the articles he thought Virginia could refuse to buy in Britain. Mason sent Washington the first text of this paper and later forwarded a few amendments. Neither Mason nor Washington had ever looked at exports and imports from the viewpoint of the plain farmer. Consequently they drafted the terms of the proposed association according to the requirements of plantation management. The view of both men was that if this association led to repeal of the Townshend Acts, a full resumption of trade across the Atlantic was to be desired, because it was beneficial both to the mother country and to America. Should Parliament be unwilling to ease the statutes, then, said Mason, Virginia should stop exports to England, particularly of tobacco, "by which the revenue would lose fifty times more than all their oppressions could raise here."

When Washington set out for Williamsburg April 30 he had with him the final text of Mason's paper. The journey, which took four days, was not given over entirely to reflection on the grievances of his Majesty's subjects in America. Washington had a new, nearer and more personal interest. The Treaty of Fort Stanwix with the Iroquois, November 5, 1768, and the Treaty of Hard Labour with the Cherokees, October 14, 1768, had wiped out the "Proclamation Line" of 1763. The Iroquois had agreed to surrender their claims to territory on a line from Fort Stanwix near Lake Oneida, New York, to Fort Pitt and thence along the eastern bank of the Ohio to the mouth of the Cherokee (Tennessee) River. By their treaty, the Cherokees yielded everything east and northeast from Fort Chiswell to the mouth of the Great Kanawha. The two pacts threw open country to which Washington long had been looking. By prompt action with Captain Crawford he could hope to patent some thousands of acres. Another prospect was having the Colony execute the formal pledge of Governor Dinwiddie and the Council in 1754 to allot two hundred thousand acres of land to those who would volunteer to go to the Ohio "to erect and support" the fort to be built at "The Forks." Now, Dinwiddie's promise could come into effect. Two hundred thousand acres, divided "in a proportion due to . . . respective merit"! That was a promise no government should be allowed to forget: By any arithmetic it meant some thousands of acres to be added to the holdings of George Washington.

At Williamsburg he found most of the old leaders returned in the December election. Edmund Pendleton, Richard Bland, Peyton Randolph, Archibald Cary and Charles Carter all were there. Patrick Henry now represented Hanover. An unusual number of new members appeared. Among these was a tall, thin young man of twenty-six who represented Albemarle —Thomas Jefferson. During the term of the Assembly's sessions Washington found time and opportunity to acquaint the Governor with the terms of the proclamation of February 1754. While he did this in a cursory manner, he had no intention of leaving so large and valuable a grant where it might or might not be remembered by Lord Botetourt. The Colonel was sowing the seed now; he would come again, to till and then to harvest.

As legislation was neither large in volume nor important in scope,

Burgesses talked much of what might be accomplished by such an association as Mason had modeled after those in the northern Colonies and had
sketched in the paper entrusted to Washington. There was discussion of
threats in Parliament to have persons accused of treason in the Colonies sent
to England for trial. A statute of Henry VIII, authorizing this, had been
unearthed and brandished over the heads of the Colonials. This alarmed
Vriginians. They had begun to lose faith in appeals to Parliament and felt
that a blow at England's trade was a better defence than was argument.

A motion was made on May 16 to refer to the Committee of the
Whole the early British acts on treason trials that had been cited as justification for sending offending Colonials to England. Debate on these statutes
and on the operation of the tax laws disclosed no difference of opinion.
Inclusive resolutions were presented for reaffirmation of the principle that
the sole right of taxing the inhabitants of Virginia was and always had been
vested in the House of Burgesses. A second resolution asserted the right of
petition to the throne. Next came solemn affirmation of the right of trial in
Virginia of any person charged with any crime there. Unanimously, the
House approved its own action in Committee of the Whole, resolved to
continue its discussion of the state of the Colony, and directed that the
Speaker send copies of the paper to the presiding officers of all the American
Colonies, with a request that the other Assemblies concur.

The House proceeded to routine business the next day. At length
about noon, the Sergeant-at-Arms called out: "Mr. Speaker, a message from
the Governor!"

Nathaniel Walthoe, Clerk of the General Assembly, strode down the
aisle and halted. "Mr. Speaker," he said, "the Governor commands the
immediate attendance of your House in the Council Chamber."

Down from his chair and out of the House Randolph walked. Behind
him the Burgesses streamed up the stairs to the council chamber. Governor
Botetourt waited until the last members had massed around the table and
along the walls. Then he said: "Mr. Speaker, and Gentlemen of the House
of Burgesses, I have heard of your resolves, and augur ill of their effect:
You have made it my duty to dissolve you; and you are dissolved accordingly."

Dissolved! If this was the spirit of a Governor well-disposed to Virginia, what was to be expected of a Parliament that was threatening to
invoke against Americans a two-hundred-year-old treason act? Soon word
was passed that there was to be a meeting at Raleigh Tavern. Thither most
of the Burgesses flocked and into its largest room, the Apollo. Randolph was
elected Moderator. The House reconvened unofficially and listened as members gave warning that the Colony soon might lose its liberties. Washington
was the one man who had a definite plan—in the form of Mason's project
for an association—and he consequently had to take a more prominent part
than ever before in a deliberative body. Motion was made that an Association be formed and that a committee be chosen to prepare a plan. At length
the motion was put and passed; the committee was named with Washington
one of its members; adjournment was taken until the next day to give the
committee time to draft its recommendations.

The questions to be determined by the committee were the practical ones of the articles to be excluded, the date when the Association should become operative, duration of the agreement, and methods by which all citizens could be induced to sign. On almost all these points Mason's draft was accepted. In an effort to make non-importation hurt Virginia as little as possible, while alarming Britain by the loss of exports, the committee endorsed a highly complicated scheme: No taxed article—tea, paint, pigment, paper other than the cheapest sheets—was to be imported. Of the supply in the Colony, none was to be purchased after September 1, 1769, for so long as it was taxed by Parliament. During the continuance of the tax on those particular items, none of a long list of untaxed luxuries and articles of British manufactures was to be brought to America on new invoices or was to be purchased after September 1. The Association could be dissolved only at a general meeting of the subscribers after a month's prior notice of the meeting or automatically after the taxes were terminated. Even if the Association were abandoned by consent, the pledge against the importation and purchase of taxed articles would remain in force.

The next morning the document was approved and signed by the members. By no means all the Burgesses signed. Absentees included, twenty-two members of a House of 116 failed to attach their signatures. Even in the face of this dissent the majority represented three-fourths of the House and nearly all the men apt to have influence in prevailing on the people to join the Association. Virginia would stand with her northern sisters.

At Mount Vernon when Washington drew rein on the evening of the twenty-second, the house was full of guests. Jackie was there with the Reverend Boucher, his new instructor. Magowan had come to report himself back from England, duly accepted for holy orders. Dr. Rumney was paying a social call. Mrs. John Bushrod and Mrs. Warner Washington, with their families, were on a visit. Plans were afoot for attending a race at Cameron and a barbecue in Alexandria.

After a brief season of festivities, Washington again took up a life that combined direction of his own farms, patient effort to solve some of the problems of his neighbors and steadfast planning for the increase of his estate. In the early summer of 1769 he had, also, a measure of responsibility to make it certain that planters of his county understood the Association and subscribed to it. He followed closely and shared personally in what was done to acquaint the residents of Fairfax and Prince William Counties with the Williamsburg agreement, and he hoped for hearty endorsement of it everywhere in Virginia. Reports from the capital were not encouraging. The fact was, the Association soon proved itself too rigid and too complicated.

Washington, Martha and Patsy set off July 31 in the chariot and on August 6 reached Berkeley Springs. Lord Fairfax and George William Fairfax were in residence; life was as agreeable as it could be at so crude a place; but Patsy's recurring illness did not improve. By September 9, chill, circumstance and the calls of business led the Washingtons to start home. Then the Colonel had to go to Alexandria for the election of a new House of Burgesses. Nobody challenged the incumbents; Washington and West were declared the county's choice.

Lord Botetourt called the General Assembly to open on November 7. For the sake of Martha's company and her own pleasure, Washington wished to take his wife and Patsy with him. Jackie prevailed on his mother to let him go, too. For so many travelers, the new chariot would be needed. It had never been shown in Williamsburg, and it should be. Its carved exterior and its green leather furnishings were not altogether unworthy of appearing on the same street with Governor Botetourt's coach. It was the last day of October when the chariot left Mount Vernon and November 6 when Washington reached Williamsburg. Martha and Patsy were to stop with Mrs. Washington's sister, Mrs. Burwell Bassett, at Eltham. Later the family would come to Williamsburg and join in the festivities there. In Williamsburg, also, there would be opportunity to have Patsy examined by the Colony's leading physicians. Jackie was to spend a few days at each place and then go back to school.

The day after Washington reached town he attended the opening of the General Assembly, took the oaths and, with his fellow-members, listened to a speech which showed why the Governor, Lord Botetourt, so readily enlarged good will already acquired. Although the membership was substantially that of the General Assembly he had sent home in May, His Excellency had not a word to say regarding the circumstances of the dissolution. Instead, the Governor told of the King's approval of a farther extension of the boundary in the Cherokee country if Virginia would bear the expense of negotiating it. Botetourt hastened to repeat assurance from Lord Hillsborough "that his Majesty's present administration have at no time entertained a design to propose to Parliament to lay any further taxes upon America for the purpose of raising a revenue, and that it is their intention to propose in the next session of Parliament to take off the duties upon glass, paper and colors, upon consideration of such duties having been laid contrary to the true principles of commerce."

Botetourt scarcely could have phrased it more skillfully, nor have announced more deftly what was in reality a proposal for a compromise —that the tax on tea only was to be left but that the repeal was to be ostensibly in the interest of commerce and must not be regarded as an admission that Parliament had no right to levy internal taxes on America. Most of the Burgesses accepted the Governor's statement as the proclamation of a truce, but they did not overlook the fact that the tax on tea was to remain.

The most important general measure in which Washington had personal interest was an address to the King, accompanied by a memorial to the Governor, on the extension of the western boundary in the Cherokee country. Determination of this line might affect the claim that veterans of the expedition of 1754 had to bounty land. Washington's eager examination of the chances of getting this land had uncovered three obstacles. The first was the multiplicity of large western grants and "orders" for land. At least one of these must be taken seriously—an enterprise to be associated with the names of Samuel Wharton and Thomas Walpole and to be known as the "Walpole Grant." This might lead to the establishment of a large new colony, with its own government and with authority to make or to deny land grants. Second was the occupation of so much land around Fort Pitt by previous patentees that it was doubtful whether the one hundred thousand acres promised in that region to the veterans would be anything more than barren mountainside. Third was the question: Did not the volunteers of 1755 have a right to share this bounty?

Washington first made these difficulties clear in his own mind. Then he developed means of dealing with them. He and other interested persons had Dinwiddie's proclamation of February 18, 1754, read in the House and placed on the table "to be perused by the members"—a familiar preliminary to the introduction of a motion for the drafting of a bill. The next day the House voted an address to the Governor concerning the lands between the Allegheny Mountains and a line drawn from the western boundary of North Carolina to the confluence of the Ohio and Mississippi. In those instances where the usual terms of "seating" grants had not been met in this area, the Burgesses wished to know whether the government of the Colony had made any pledge to confirm "orders" previously approved by Council. Further, would the Governor be pleased to discourage monopolies of land in Virginia? On the third day Washington wrote the Governor, outlined the history of the claim and explained why he thought no veterans except those of 1754 had any right to share in the grant. He had completed this letter and was preparing to transmit it to the Governor, when one of his fellow-claimants, Dr. Thomas Walker, told him that the lands close to Fort Pitt had been reserved for traders. Washington mentioned this in a postscript and added that if this were the case, the former soldiers would rather have good lands laid out for them elsewhere than await a final determination in England of their rights at the forks of the Ohio in competition with those of the traders.

The Governor answered the address of the House with the assurance that no commitments had been made and that no monopolies would be approved by him. Then, on December 15, in formal petition the officers and men of the expedition of 1754 asked His Excellency that the land promised them be granted "in one or more surveys" on the Monongahela, New River, the Great Kanawha, Sandy Creek and adjacent streams.

The response of Governor and Council on the question of allotting the land was one of hearty acquiescence: Virginia would keep her word. If one very large area of rich land could be located, all the grants might be within it, but if exploration showed that the men could do better for themselves by searching out individual stretches of good land, they would be free to do so. Then Council decided that claimants could make as many as twenty surveys but no more. In these twenty areas must be contained all the two hundred thousand acres the veterans were to receive. On lesser details, Council's action conformed to the petitioners' wishes: Washington was free to urge the College of William and Mary to appoint some properly qualified person to survey the land and authorized to say this would be agreeable to Council. He was directed to advertise that all claims should be attested by October 10, 1770. As he knew his old soldiers individually, they were to present their claims to him. He was to certify them to Council for final determination. Five years were to be allowed for surveying. No person could qualify "who entered the service after the Battle of the Meadows in 1754."

So much legislation had Washington and his fellow-members to consider that it was December 21 when they were able to adjourn. Washington left Williamsburg that day, slept that night at Eltham, and on the twenty-second set out with his family for home. On the twenty-eighth, the Colonel and Martha and Patsy were back at Mount Vernon, where Jackie and Mr. Boucher joined in the festivities of the Year's End.

It had been the best year of the eleven spent at Mount Vernon after Washington's return from the French and Indian War. The collection of debts had been almost impossible; the burden of counselling the luckless had been heavy; a few loans had been made to embarrassed friends when it would have been more prudent to say "No." In nearly every other aspect of Washington's business affairs there had been success. More of the tenants were paying in cash; tobacco rents were still in excess of 8000 pounds, but this simply reflected increase in the number of farms leased to tenants. On Custis plantations a crop that had suffered from early drought had the prospect of a favorable market. Farm industries were thriving in a small way. Besides his weaving room and his smithy, Washington in 1769 developed his fisheries; a small consignment was available for shipment in the autumn to Antigua.

The main development of 1769 was in milling. Washington delivered to Carlyle & Adam 6241 bushels of wheat—almost six times as much as in 1765 when he first had undertaken large scale production. He had concluded in June that if there was a profit for Carlyle & Adam in selling his wheat to a miller, and a profit for the miller in dealing with the baker or merchant, he could make money by grinding his own wheat into flour. On December 30 he made an agreement with John Ball to build a mill in which he was feeling already an ambitious interest.

It would be a busy year, 1770! Washington's largest stake was in the lands promised the volunteers of 1754. In apportionment of the acres, he might get 10,000 or even 15,000. There was another speculative opportunity under a royal proclamation of 1763. This authorized the Governors of the Colonies to grant "without fee or reward, to such reduced officers as have served in America during the late war, and to such private soldiers as have been, or shall be disbanded in America; and are actually residing there, and shall personally apply for the same, the following quantities of lands, subject at the expiration of ten years, to the same quitrents as other lands are subject to in the province within which they are granted, as also subject to the same conditions of cultivation and improvement, viz. To every person having the rank of a field officer, five thousand acres; to every Captain three thousand acres; to every subaltern or staff officer, two thousand acres; to every non-commissioned officer, two hundred acres; to every private man fifty acres." There was doubt whether this was designed for soldiers of the Colonies as well as for those of the regular establishment. In either event, the initiative rested with the individual. Each veteran must make personal application. Few veterans knew what to expect or whether they actually would get anything. Former Lieut. Charles Mynn Thruston, for example, questioned Washington concerning this in a spirit of skepticism. Thruston would be entitled to two thousand acres under the proclamation but he was so discouraged that for £10 he forthwith sold his claim to Washington, who thought, for reasons of policy, that it would be well to have the transfer of the rights of Thruston made out to Lund Washington rather than to himself.

To Washington this was a gamble, nothing more nor less. "Could I purchase 12,000 or 15,000 acres upon the same terms," he said, "I would do it, considering of it as a lottery only." In telling his brother Charles of his plans to acquire additional claims under the proclamation of 1763, Washington wrote him to make inquiry about the willingness of former soldiers to sell their claims, and enjoined, "do not let it be known that I have any concern therein." The form of agreement in the bargain with Thruston was to be followed. Charles was to act for his brother as Lund had done in the first purchase of rights.

Washington thus broadened his plans for the acquisition of western lands to embrace: first, his own claims and such others as he might procure for the bounty-lands promised in 1754; second, similar personal claims and those of indifferent or necessitous veterans under the proclamation of 1763; third, such patents of desirable land as might be taken out for him in Pennsylvania by Crawford; fourth, any further patents of large, well-watered fertile tracts that Crawford might find outside districts where grants already had been made, and finally, any rival or established claims that could be bought up at a low figure to assure a good title or single, sure ownership of wide stretches. Bold plans these were, and all the bolder because they might call for large outlays of cash when, as one merchant wrote, "the scarcity of money is so great in this country that it is impossible for ablest men to comply with their engagements." Washington was willing to take the risk.

When he went to Williamsburg in May Washington had the advancement of the claims of the veterans of 1754 as one of his principal duties. He found little legislation of importance in prospect but much concern over the violence with which British troops in Boston on March 5 had fired on a crowd of about sixty rioters who had been engaged in a fight with a squad of soldiers. New England had been outraged and the other Colonies alarmed by this "Boston Massacre." Another cause of concern in Williamsburg was the failure of the Association of May 18, 1769, to scare Parliament. Lord North, on May 1, 1769, had prevailed on the British Cabinet, by a majority of one, to keep the tax on tea, and seven months later, as First Lord of the Treasury, he took over the direction of affairs. This was not encouraging. In addition, there were in Virginia known and suspected cases of importation and purchase of goods contrary to the terms of the Association. Many planters had found the terms too exacting, and some had confused the provisions of the complicated document. Others may have professed ignorance to cover design. Even the most enthusiastic had to admit that if the non-importation agreement was to be kept alive, it had to be revised.

On May 25 Washington attended a meeting of the Association, where so many divergent opinions were expressed that a committee of twenty was appointed to formulate a new association on which general agreement might be reached. Washington was named to this committee, which uncovered opposition of such stubborn temper that hours of debate did not bring a meeting of minds.

The dispute on importation was dual—whether there should be any association at all, and, if so, whether it should be stern or moderate in its terms. Edmund Pendleton and others argued at least inferentially that the Association should be abandoned. Parliament, they said, had compromised; the Colonies should be equally reasonable. Landon Carter recorded this proposal and gave the answering argument: "Fine language this, as if there could be any half way between slavery; certainly one link of the former preserved might be the hold to which the rest of the chain might at any time be joined when the forging smiths thought proper to add to it." Washington was for the sternest of non-importation agreements—"I could wish it to be ten times as strict," he said later, but he felt that a covenant which did not command support of the merchants and supply the minimum requirements of planters would fail.

Final agreement was reached June 22, 1770, on a more moderate compact than the one of the previous year. Instead of denouncing prospective violators, it promised support to those "truly worthy merchants, traders, and others, inhabitants of this Colony, who shall hereafter conform to the spirit of this association." Prohibited goods were limited, in the main, to luxuries and to expensive products. Washington signed this Association, resolved to conform fully to it, and did not deceive himself concerning the terms. It was, he said, "the best that the friends to the cause could obtain here, and though too much relaxed from the spirit with which a measure of this sort ought to be conducted, yet will be attended with better effects (I expect) than the last, inasmuch as it will become more general and adopted by the trade."

In the House of Burgesses that sat while the Association was being revised, Washington was able to do no more in furtherance of the claim of the veterans of 1754 than to arrange for a meeting of beneficiaries in Fredericksburg. At this meeting, August 2, Washington met comrades whom he had not seen after he had left Wills Creek in 1754. He was less military now, of course, but not less businesslike. Agreement was reached on the percentage of the whole that would go to men of each rank. All participants were called upon to make a pro rata payment for surveys and other expenses. Washington was prevailed upon to assume the handling of this thorny business. He had a pleasant round of visits with Martha and Patsy in the Fredericksburg district. The only disappointment was that the girl gained nothing from the treatment of Dr. Hugh Mercer, whose professional reputation perhaps led the Colonel and Mrs. Washington to hope for more than any physician could accomplish.

When Washington brought Patsy and her mother back to Mount Vernon August 9, he had made one firm resolution on the whole question of western claims: he would go to the Ohio and Great Kanawha and make his own choice of vacant lands as soon as the dispatch of his business and the fall of the leaves favored the journey. Much had to be done in advance.

First was the duty of having the planters and merchants in Fairfax sign the new Association, printed copies of which were available with the names of the original signers attached. Washington circulated these papers among his neighbors and doubtless entrusted to other hands copies for Alexandria and Dumfries. Nearly everyone signed; until the total reached 420. This done, the Colonel was ready to accept duty on the Fairfax Associators' Committee whenever it was formed. Next was the building of the mill, a troublesome task that involved a controversy over encroachments on his land and a dispute over riparian rights. There were half-a-score of lesser, time-consuming matters to settle—invoices to be made out subject to the repeal of the British tax, a troublesome arbitration to be undertaken for friends, preparations for the shipment of a cargo of herring to the West Indies, a discussion of the possible navigation of the upper Potomac, and a review of a long, earnest correspondence with Boucher regarding Jackie's immediate future.

The reverend instructor had concluded that a tour of Europe, with himself as mentor, would be a proper part of the education of Jackie who, the minister admitted, was proving himself, at seventeen, "constitutionally too warm, indolent and voluptuous." Washington recoiled. Boucher had said that the travel would cost £1500 or £1600 a year; Washington explained that the sum exceeded the boy's annual income, that he did not wish to expose himself to censure for reckless use of Jackie's property and, in general, that while young Custis had "what is called a good estate, it is not a profitable one." It was the first time Washington ever had made any such confession regarding the proudly held Custis plantations. He did not say that Jackie could not go; he left the question in abeyance with the probabilities somewhat against his approval of the "grand tour."

By the time Washington had most of these matters behind him, autumn had come and the range of vision in western forests would be far enough to show where the axe might widen meadows or open new fields. Crawford had reported continued uncertainty about lines and boundaries, though he had selected for Washington, Lund, and two of George's brothers what he considered patentable tracts. Washington had lacked information concerning the Walpole Grant and had written the Governor to inquire whether it was true, as rumored, that the grant had been made for a separate colony. Botetourt had replied, through the Clerk of the Council, and had enclosed some extract from correspondence that showed where the proposed new colony was to be established. Before leaving for the Ohio Washington concluded that he should make formal reply of such a nature that Botetourt, if willing, could dispatch it to England, as in effect a petition to the Crown to protect the rights of the volunteers of 1754. The Walpole Grant, he told the Governor, would devour four-fifths of the territory Virginia had voted to purchase from the Cherokees and to survey at a combined cost of £2500. He argued for full recognition of the grant of the two hundred thousand acres. The day Washington finished this letter, October 5, he set out with his friend and wartime Surgeon, Dr. James Craik, three servants and a packhorse. After an absence of nine weeks and one day Washington returned home on December 1. The journey and voyage had been expensive, in large part tedious and not altogether satisfying. Again and again Washington had used the words "exceeding fine" to describe particular tracts, but he had seen much poor land along with the good and a great deal that was neither better nor worse than the average new ground of eastern Virginia. There nowhere appeared such rolling, rich dark earth, mile on mile, as had been desired for division among the veterans of 1754. In fact, Washington had not grown as enthusiastic over any land he had seen on the lower Ohio and Kanawha as he had over acreage Crawford had procured for him near the Youghiogheny. Next that, the finest land Washington had seen in a single large tract was that which George Croghan was offering between Raccoon Creek and the Monongahela. Washington resolved to buy fifteen thousand acres of this at £50 per thousand if Crawford could find that much of quality in a single tract to which Croghan could give title.

The patenting of the Kanawha lands for the veterans of 1754 must be pressed. Perhaps as many as ten of the allotted twenty surveys would have to be used to provide even a third of the two hundred thousand acres wanted. Land-hunters from Virginia and elsewhere already had reached the Little Kanawha; in another summer they would get at least as far as the Great Kanawha. Then, Washington reasoned, "a few settlements in the midst of some of the large bottoms would render it impracticable to get any large quantity." Behind these difficulties was doubt concerning the new boundary line in the Cherokee country and the boundaries that would be set for the Walpole Grant if it should be perfected. During Washington's absence something had occurred that made all the obstacles harder to surmount: Lord Botetourt had died October 15. It would be necessary for Washington to start again under a new Governor.

A further exchange had to be completed with Boucher on Jackie's behavior. The boy was growing up: he required the most friendly aid and counsel, Washington thought, especially as Boucher was now operating his school at Annapolis, where temptation would be greater than in Caroline County. "I would beg leave to request," Washington wrote the teacher, "that he may not be suffered to sleep from under your own roof, unless it be at such places as you are sure he can have no bad examples set him; nor allow him to be rambling about of nights in company with those who do not care how debauched and vicious his conduct may be." Boucher was back promptly in a long letter with the somewhat disconcerting central theme: "I must confess to you I never did in my life know a youth so exceedingly indolent or so surprisingly voluptuous: one would suppose Nature had intended him for some Asiatic Prince."

But for that unhappy affirmation and Patsy's continued fits, Christmas, 1770, would have been one of the best that had been spent at Mount Vernon. Nearly everything was going well on the farms. The fisheries had done well. The weaving had developed now to include woolen plaid, striped wool, wool and cotton, broadcloth, dimity, thread and cotton, jump stripe, calico, barricum, striped silk and cotton, and other fabrics. Even of hemp, though it was not flourishing, enough had been grown to bring a bounty of almost £5. Far more interesting to Washington was the fact that the new mercantile flour mill was nearing completion. The contract for the delivery of wheat to Carlyle & Adam had expired; a miller, William Roberts, had been employed at £80 per year. Washington now had ground enough to grow wheat for half-a-dozen such mills—9263 acres—and he hoped to add many other thousands. He soon would be a planter of the very front rank.

The general shortage of specie was one of several reasons why some of the veterans who had claims under the proclamation of 1754 had been slow to pay their part of the cost of the surveys of the western lands. Other claimants were discouraged by the news that powerful interests in England most certainly would get the region they sought on the Ohio. "Our affairs, never in a very promising way," Washington later wrote, "began to grow very alarming"; but that did not keep him from setting out March 2, 1771, for Winchester to participate in the meeting of those who, like himself, were willing to gamble for the stake of those two hundred thousand pledged acres.

Attendance was not large, but it included Col. Adam Stephen, Capt. Peter Hog, Doctor Craik, and several others. Washington reported on his visit to the Great Kanawha. His associates promised to meet another assessment, which amounted in the case of field officers to more than £11 each, and they cheerfully gave Washington full authority over Crawford as surveyor. He continued resolute in all that related to veterans' lands, but, as he wrote one claimant, he realized that, "We have many difficulties and some uncertainties to struggle through, before our rights to these lands will be fully recognized."

Back from Winchester March 13, he was eager to have news of the mill. The work was not complete. To speed it, Washington rode almost daily to the creek and on April 5 had the satisfaction of seeing the sluice opened. Soon it was operating on a scale that made the delivery of 497 barrels more an occasion of rejoicing than strain on mill and workers. The spring was as interesting on the river as at the mill. Washington had an immense catch at the spring "run." In addition to herring kept for use on the plantation, 679,000 were sold to Carlyle & Adam. Shad caught and salted by Washington's men numbered 7760.

The Colonel started for Williamsburg April 27 with Martha and Patsy. As usual, Martha's plan was to stay at Eltham and, if special attraction offered, to go to Williamsburg for a few days. When the Bassett home at Eltham was reached, Washington halted with the others to enjoy the hospitality that always was superlative there and then went on to the capital on May 3 to meet the merchants and transact with them his business and that of the estate. Apparently he did not attempt to do anything about the soldiers' lands under the proclamation of 1754, but he probably heard at least one thing that pleased him: The President of the Council told the members he had received a letter in which the Earl of Hillsborough promised that attention would be given the equitable claims of bona fide settlers under the grant to the Ohio Company and to "such [claims] as were passed in consequence of the instructions from his late Majesty or Lieut. Gov. Dinwiddie's proclamation at the commencement of the late war." Washington left Williamsburg May 11 and gave another ten days to the enjoyment of Eltham, visiting the Custis farms, hunting and fishing, and calling and dining.

The question of Jackie's tour of Europe remained in doubt. Washington's inclination to let the boy spend the money for the journey was challenged by his judgment. In reviewing all the arguments, he had come almost to the conclusion that Jack was too immature to profit greatly by the tour. Washington began to ponder whether Jack should not be taken from Boucher and sent to college. He himself had a poor opinion of William and Mary; Boucher was anxious that Jack should go to King's College in New York. Boucher was of the opinion that one "general fault" of young men educated in America was "that they come out into the world furnished with a kind of smattering of everything and with very few exceptions, arrant coxcombs." Jack Custis did not deserve that appellation, but the young gentleman was increasing his love of fine plumage and, as always, fond of luxuries in general.

For many Virginians the lifting of the ban on the importation of luxuries would mean little, if it came in 1771 or in 1772, because calamity had befallen them. The second and third weeks of May had been bright and almost cloudless in eastern Virginia. Then, overnight, such a flood as never had been known there swept down the valleys of the Rappahannock, the James and the Roanoke. The water rose rapidly to a height of forty feet. At some warehouses all the tobacco was swept away or was hurled ashore, mud-covered and watersoaked. On the James alone more than 2,300,000 pounds were lost or damaged. Houses rolled down the stream; frenzied animals struggled to keep afloat; dead bodies were tossed on the foaming surface. Direct loss was estimated at £2,000,000; the dead were reckoned at 150. Life on James River was shattered. Debt-ridden planters were bankrupted.

William Nelson, President of Council and acting Governor, summoned the General Assembly to meet in Williamsburg July 11. Washington had seen nothing of the flood, because it had not swept the Potomac Valley. He did not lose a shilling either on his own property or on the Custis farms. In realization of the magnitude of the "great calamity," he assumed it would mean higher prices for tobacco, and now he prepared to see what could be done for relief of the victims. He supervised his wheat harvest through June 11 and reached Williamsburg on the fifteenth. He found no disagreement in the House of Burgesses other than over the details of how the actual loss of planters' tobacco was to be determined and compensated.

No other legislation of large importance was considered; but most of the men who sat by day as Burgesses discussed by night as "Associators" the future of the non-importation agreement. The compact of 1770 had been no more successful than that of 1769. When a decision was reached to drop the Association, abandonment of the agreement was quiet, almost sheepish. In one of the Gazettes the only notice to the public was a single paragraph that at "a general meeting of the gentlemen of the Association at the Capitol [on July 15], it was agreed upon to dissolve the same; except as to tea, paper, glass and painters' colors of foreign manufacture upon which a duty is laid for the purpose of raising a revenue for America."

Washington had said that he wished the Association of 1769 to be ten times as strict as it was. He preferred a strong to a weak agreement and he labored for the most effective terms that would be supported by the mass of Virginians. Now, if the Association was at an end, obligation was, also, except for the articles directly taxed. As soon as the Association was dissolved Washington prepared an elaborate invoice of the expensive English clothing, fittings and horse-furnishings he had been waiting to purchase. He ordered eight pairs of shoes and boots for himself, and for Jack a "very handsome and fashionable suit of clothes, made of superfine broadcloth" for dress, a thinner but similar suit for summer wear, together with sundry modish waistcoats and breeches, and "a fashionable sartout [surtout] coat of best, blue beaver coating." He would adhere to the agreement if there was one; he would conform to fashion if that was not forbidden and look to his meadows and his mill and the western lands for the money with which to buy the best that London dealers would send.

A crisis in the affairs of Washington's mother soon demanded his counsel and decision. Mrs. Washington continued to live at Ferry Farm, which was in reality George's, and manage it according to her way. Ferry Farm had declined steadily. By September 1771 affairs had dropped to such an ebb that Washington was called to confer with his brother, Charles, and his brother-in-law, Fielding Lewis, on the disposition to be made of Mrs. Washington and of the property. It was decided that Mrs. Washington was to relinquish all care of the property. George was to take over the management through the overseer, was to supply her with such needed food and poultry as the place yielded, and was to pay her a fixed rent for the lower quarter and the Deep Run tract. She was to remove to Fredericksburg as soon as the proper residence could be chosen by her. In restored ownership of Ferry Farm, it doubtless was a relief to Washington to put affairs in such order as was possible and, on the fifteenth, to go back to Mount Vernon. After a few days at home and two days on the bench of the county court, he proceeded to Annapolis for the races and the plays staged in the town's annual season of gaiety.

Washington had thought that when he went to Williamsburg for the fall meeting of the merchants he also would attend a session of the General Assembly, which had been prorogued to October 24. The successor to Governor Botetourt arrived shortly before that date. He was John Murray, Earl of Dunmore, who had been Governor of New York. One of Dunmore's first acts was to dissolve the Assembly and shortly afterward to issue writs of election. Washington consequently could look forward to a visit to Williamsburg during which he could devote himself to his private affairs and to presentation of the veterans' surveys for the approval of Governor and Council.

Washington renewed his plea that Council fix the allotments and remove the limit on the number of surveys that could be made. The Councillors were ready enough to fix the allotments and did so generously. Field officers were to have 15,000 acres each, captains 9000, lieutenants 6000, cadets 2500, sergeants 600, corporals 500, privates 400. Inasmuch as many men in the ranks had not filed their claims, 30,000 acres were reserved for them and for those who bore the expense of making the surveys and of assuring their comrades' rights, but on the question of the number of surveys Council refused to yield. Its original action had provided "not more than twenty"; that number must suffice. Ten surveys had yielded less than a third of the total promised. There had to be careful exploration before the other ten surveys were undertaken, so that a minimum of poor lands would be included with the good.

In the late autumn, Washington received news of the death of Joseph Valentine, who had been in charge of all the Parke and Custis plantations on the York and its tributaries when Washington married Martha. In that position Valentine remained to the end of his days, the steward of properties left almost completely in his care. Washington could not hope to find another such man, but his choice was to fall eventually on James Hill. Before many months, Washington could be reasonably sure that every letter from Hill would catalogue so many agricultural calamities that it seemed miraculous the farms themselves had not disappeared.

Washington himself was of different temper. Now that he was closing the books of 1771 and was approaching his fortieth birthday, he was inured to such vexations as debtors who could not pay, tenants behind on their rent, unreasonable applicants for counsel or assistance, Jack's procrastination, and the idolatry of the mother for the boy. Patsy's illness was hard to bear, the more so because physicians seemed unable to do anything to relieve her. Washington again was elected to the House of Burgesses on December 1 and was host at the usual ball. The mill was working profitably; all the farm industries, the fisheries in particular, were thriving; tobacco was certain to bring a good price. He held 12,463 acres and might look forward, not unreasonably, to doubling his land holdings. In nearly all respects, Washington could say, at the beginning of 1772, that life never had been so rich or the promise of the future so bright in all that made for the opulent comfort of a restored plantation.

On January 26, 1772, snow began to fall in tons, as if the gods of wind and rain had repented the mercy they had shown the Potomac Valley during the floods of the previous May. By the twenty-ninth, snow was "up to the breast of a tall horse everywhere." The fall was, Washington wrote, "the deepest . . . I suppose the oldest man living ever remembers to have seen in this country." Not until February 21 could an open boat cross the Potomac. Even on the twenty-sixth, when Washington started to Williamsburg to attend a session of the General Assembly that had begun on February 10, Accotink Creek was so high from rains which had washed away the deep snow that he had to turn back and wait a day for the water to fall.

When Washington arrived at the capital March 2, little had been done by the House of Burgesses, and little of importance was done thereafter. The theatre was open; entertainment was extensive, though somewhat below the activity of most sessions. Personal and distinctly painful was the work of Surgeon-Dentist Baker who extracted £4 and perhaps several teeth in an effort to save what was left of Washington's feeblest physical equipment. By April 9 the dentist had done his best and the Assembly had nearly reached the end of its calendar. Washington prepared to start home.

The weeks that followed were full of activities which showed that the life of a speculating planter of station could not be spent in ease and idleness. Always something demanded attention at home or a journey from the plantation. Most particularly, Charles Willson Peale, who lived then at Annapolis, had succeeded so well in portrait-painting that to sit for him had become the fashion of the Potomac Valley. Washington of course was one of those whose countenance must be put on canvas for the delight of his household and the adornment of his walls, but it proved a new and not entirely pleasant experience. The sittings ended May 22; soon the portrait was finished. It was a success in every way except, perhaps, that the "grave mood" made the line of the mouth a little too taut. All the while, Washington continued to prod the men who could help in bringing to a conclusion the grant of the Ohio lands he wanted. He attended, also, to his part of a new transaction, shipment of 273 barrels of his flour to the West Indies. The proceeds were to be laid out in Negroes, provided the cost of "choice ones" was less than £40 sterling. Washington was planning to increase his slaves because he wanted workers for the lands he hoped to acquire.

Affairs of duty and of business punctuated one of the most delightful seasons the family at Mount Vernon ever enjoyed. There was hunting, fishing, and visiting in Maryland and in Virginia, entertainment of numerous guests and a journey to Annapolis for the races, the plays and much feasting. After that came ten days at home and then on October 21 Washington left with Martha and the young Custises for Eltham, where once more they enjoyed the hospitality of the Bassetts. In addition, Washington worked there with Crawford, who was to bring with him the field notes of the new surveys of soldiers' lands. From these Washington was to make plats of the tracts on the Ohio and on the Great Kanawha, take them to Williamsburg, lay them before the Governor and Council, and try to procure final orders for the patents.

Crawford and Washington labored from October 25 through the thirtieth over the surveys. The notes were adequate, and all the lines could be drawn, but Crawford had been able to cover 127,899 acres only. Including those surveyed the previous year, there now were thirteen tracts, one of which covered 51,302 acres, another 28,627, and another 13,532. From what Washington had seen of the country, he apprehended trouble in dividing these tracts because good land and bad would be mingled. How was justice to be assured all the officers and men? Washington decided he would make another plea for free choice in the form of a large increase in the number of permissible surveys.

Council held its ground without compromise: It had declined previously to increase the permissible number of surveys; twenty it would remain. The Council was of one mind with Washington on his basic proposition—that the private soldiers should receive their full allotment forthwith and that the officers should have their acreage in proportion to the financial support they had given the effort to establish their claims.

Those who had met the assessments were to receive all the land due them; those who had contributed nothing must await the second distribution of land. Where a man had paid half, he would get 50 per cent of his allotment.

Then the Council took up the suggestions Washington had prepared for apportioning the different tracts among the individuals according to their respective shares. He sought his own allowance of 15,000 acres as a field officer and he had bought the claim to 5000 of the 15,000 acres due George Muse, together with the claim of "Sergeant Brickner" for 600 acres—a total of 20,600 acres. For the satisfaction of these claims, Washington asked one surveyed tract of 10,990 acres, another of 4395, a third of 2448, and a fourth of 2314. The total of these, 20,147, was 453 below Washington's claim. Like the other officers he would wait to have this remainder filled out from the subsequent allotment; but if he got these four tracts, he would have no more surveying to do and could proceed as quickly as he might to occupy, "seat," clear and develop.

After these allotments to Washington were passed, those to the noncommissioned officers and the privates were made easily. Then came the question, Was the distribution equitable as respected the quality of the land? Washington answered that a conference of the officers of the First Virginia was to be held November 23 at Fredericksburg: If complaint then were made that the distribution of land was inequitable in quality, he would bring the allegations before Council, and if Council found complaint justified "he would give up all his interest under his patent and submit to such regulations as the Board may see fit to prescribe." This was enough for Council. If the officers and men themselves were satisfied with the distribution, nobody else had any right to protest.

Until the veterans' meeting, there was pleasure in Williamsburg and ample work with the new steward of the Custis plantations. On November 20 Washington carefully paid the fees for patenting the two hundred thousand acres, so there could be no future question about the entry. That afternoon he left the town and on the twenty-second stepped out of his chariot at Fielding Lewis's in Fredericksburg. The next day and the next, Washington explained the surveys to the officers, answered their questions, and reviewed the proceedings before the Council. When he had made everything plain, the officers approved the distribution he had recommended. More than that, the veterans who had known him since 1754 passed a resolution in which they asked Council to relieve him of the offer to turn back his own lands if complaint were made and Council found it justified.

It was the afternoon of the twenty-ninth when the driver pulled up the horses at Mount Vernon. Washington was anxious to be afield, but he had to report the result of the meeting in Fredericksburg. Word from Williamsburg came about December 13. Unless Council by June 1773 received and affirmed the justice of a complaint that the land had been allotted with disregard of quality, then all that Washington had included in those four grants would be his! Later in the month he received the formal patents, duly signed and sealed. Together they would increase Washington's patiently accumulated acres to a total of 32,885.

Washington devoted part of the Christmas season to preparing for publication a suitable notice of the allotments of land. To justify himself, he reported at length on the different tracts. He explained the request of Council that he advertise what had been done and told how he had promised to return his quota if inequity were alleged by veterans and proved to the satisfaction of Council.

Recovery of his costs from officers who had contributed nothing to the surveys was one of a number of difficulties that confronted Washington during a winter that was soft and beneficent in comparison with the preceding icy season. Unpleasant was the prospect that his dearest friends, the Fairfaxes of Belvoir, were going to leave Virginia for a prolonged visit and perhaps permanent residence in England. Their absence would be deprivation. Washington, of course, would collect Fairfax's accounts and do what he could to look after the absent proprietor's interests: there could be no new neighbors at Belvoir like those who were about to depart.

The superlative vexation was the attempt to establish a mill on the Youghiogheny. To improve his land and direct the building of the mill, Washington entered into a partnership with Gilbert Simpson, member of a family who had been among Washington tenants as early as 1762. Simpson, although his spouse was opposed, agreed to go to the Youghiogheny with some of Washington's slaves, tools and implements, and with his own horses and utensils, and start a joint adventure. This seemed a promising arrangement, but from the time Simpson wrote his first report to his partner he was despairing. There was no better land in that part of the world, Simpson said, but he never was in good health from the time of his arrival. "I intend to do the best I can to improve your land until the fall," the unhappy, homesick man wrote, "and then to quit the concern. . . ."

Disappointments were sharpened and business snarled that winter and spring by one of the strangest disasters that had been visited on Virginia. In January 1773 the Treasurer observed peculiarities in notes of the issues of 1769 and 1771 that had been returned for retirement. This currency was well-executed counterfeit in which even the watermark of the notepaper had been duplicated by impression. The Treasurer promptly published a warning of the circulation of the false notes and a description of them. Public apprehension convinced the Governor he must act. Council was hurriedly assembled. Soon there appeared in Williamsburg a man named John Short, who was described as a one-time participant in the counterfeiting. The criminals, he said, included a ringleader who resided in North Carolina and fifteen or sixteen men of influence in Virginia. Unless arrests were made quickly, Short warned, it soon would be exceedingly dangerous to deal with the culprits. The Governor placed warrants in the hands of Capt. John Lightfoot, a man of known resolution, and gave him full authority to call for help from the County Lieutenant and other trustworthy men of Pittsylvania, where the workshop of the counterfeiters was said to be. Back to Williamsburg on February 23 came Lightfoot. In his custody were five men who had been caught at work in a complete counterfeiting shop. Several suspects were said to have fled. Still others were reported to have been locked up in county jails. The men caught by Lightfoot were examined by Speaker Randolph in the presence of the Governor and other notables, all of whom agreed that the prisoners, with one exception, should be held. Soon afterward the accused were given a hearing before the Court of York County and remanded to the Williamsburg jail where they were joined by a suspect who showed a disposition to confess and become the King's witness. At this stage of the proceedings the General Assembly met, March 4, 1773, in answer to the Governor's summons.

Washington's departure for this session was hampered by plans he was making for Jack. That young gentleman manifestly was wasting time with the Reverend Boucher. Washington's decision to send the boy to college now had become fixed. Boucher was all for King's College in New York, because it was located in what he understood to be "the most fashionable and polite place on the continent," and he was able to bring Washington to acquiesce in this choice. The Colonel made plans for going to New York and entering Jack in college before making the journey to Williamsburg for the spring settlement of accounts; but the summons to an early session of the Assembly upset this schedule.

With Martha and Patsy, Washington reached Williamsburg the day the Assembly met. The talk was of the counterfeiting and the methods Dunmore had used in dealing with it. Every Burgess admitted that so extreme a case called for strong measures. At the same time, the Burgesses were disturbed that Dunmore had disregarded the Court of Pittsylvania County and taken men from their own vicinage for trial. Should this be permitted to pass without protest? The answer of the Burgesses was creditable to them. When they prepared the usual address to the Governor, they thanked him for endeavoring to bring the counterfeiters to justice; "*but,*" they affirmed in sharpest antithesis, "the proceedings in this case, my Lord, though rendered necessary by the particular nature of it, are nevertheless different from the usual mode, it being regular that an examining court on criminals should be held, either in the County where the fact was committed, or the arrest made." Dunmore did not like this. In replying to the address, he expressed surprise that when he was seeking to punish the guilty, his conduct "could by any means be thought to endanger the safety of the innocent." He held his ground and had the support of more than half the members of the General Court that the proceedings were legal.

Washington was preparing to leave Williamsburg when, on March 12, a motion was made that the House resolve itself into Committee of the Whole on the state of the Colony. Some of the members who followed the leadership of Patrick Henry had been conferring on the course of action Virginia should take to establish the truth or falsity of what was being reported concerning stern measures the home government was to employ against Colonies that resisted the Ministry. Rhode Island and Massachusetts, especially, were in controversy with Britain, but how they proposed to defend their rights, the Virginians did not know. Discussion in the taverns consequently had dealt with proposals for the establishment among the Colonies of committees similar to the one Virginia long had maintained in order to correspond with her agent in England.

The motion was passed, the chair was vacated, the House was in

Committee of the Whole. Recognition was given Dabney Carr, junior Burgess from Louisa. Carr read a brief preamble and then proposed that eleven Burgesses be named as a Committee of Correspondence. These eleven were "to obtain the most early and authentic intelligence of all such acts and resolutions of the British Parliament, or proceedings of administration, as may relate to or affect the British Colonies in America, and to keep up and maintain a correspondence and communication with our sister Colonies, respecting these important considerations; and the result of such their proceedings, from time to time, to lay before this House." Carr argued that it was imperative all the Colonies know what was threatened against any one of them. Accepted in Committee of the Whole, Carr's proposals were adopted unanimously by the House.

Estimates of the resolutions varied greatly. Jefferson and Carr agreed that the effect would be a call for a meeting of representatives of all the Colonies for maintenance of common rights. In New England, Samuel Adams said the "truly patriotic resolves" of Virginia would gladden "the hearts of all who are friends of liberty." Governor Dunmore was not inclined to take seriously the action of the Virginia lawmakers. "Your Lordship will observe," he wrote the Earl of Dartmouth, "there are some resolves which show a little ill humor in the House of Burgesses, but I thought them so insignificant that I took no matter of notice of them."

At intervals during the session, Washington had numerous opportunities of talking with Dunmore, a hard-headed Scot of Washington's own age, who had a kindred appetite for land. As a result, Dunmore engaged to go with Washington to the Ohio country that summer. After the Colonel found when he could undertake the journey, Dunmore was to come to Mount Vernon, whence the start was to be made. Washington was looking also to West Florida where, as he understood the facts, bounties of land were available to veterans of the French and Indian War in accordance with the proclamation of October 1763. Washington had not exercised his rights under that proclamation and now asked James Wood, who was about to go to West Florida to explore the country, to take up there for him all the land to which a field officer was entitled.

Back at Mount Vernon on March 16, Washington had two days in which to catch up with accumulated business. Then he enjoyed a few spirited fox hunts. After that he had a surprise of first magnitude: Jack had become engaged to marry. The girl was Eleanor, more familiarly "Nelly," Calvert, second daughter and one of the ten children of Mr. and Mrs. Benedict Calvert of Mount Airy, across the Potomac in Maryland. Benedict Calvert was the illegitimate son of Charles Calvert, fifth Lord Baltimore, who acknowledged paternity and gave the young man a start but never let the name of the mother be known. In 1745 Benedict became Collector of Customs at Patuxent, the next year he received appointment to the Council, and in 1748 he married a distant cousin, Elizabeth Calvert, daughter of Gov. Charles Calvert. As Benedict Calvert's connections were of this eminence, his accident of birth was not regarded as a social stigma. Washington and Jack's mother were hurt that the boy had not confided in them on a matter that might shape his entire life, but their decision was to accept the engagement—what else could be done?—and by joint consent to have the marriage postponed until Custis had gone to college. The immediate procedure was for Washington to write Calvert, approve the match and state his hope that Jack would progress further in his studies before the marriage should be solemnized. It was a task which, Washington confessed, was embarrassing to him, but one he discharged forthrightly. He closed with an invitation for the Calverts to visit Mount Vernon. Calvert replied with thanks for praise of Nelly and expressed his entire agreement that "it is, as yet, too early in life for Mr. Custis to enter upon the matrimonial state." He hoped that Jack's attendance on college would make for the future happiness of the young people and that "this separation will only delay, not break off, the intended match."

If Jack was fated to become engaged to a girl when he should have been engaged only in his studies, Washington well may have hoped that the boy had escaped, without dishonor, from premature marriage. The task immediately ahead was getting young Custis off promptly to New York with the least reluctance and the fewest tears. In proceeding to do this, Washington and Martha did not attempt to keep Jack from Nelly. They visited the Calverts, entertained them at Mount Vernon and made some of Nelly's friends a part of their own circle. When the date for departure approached, it was agreed that Jack should start two days ahead of Washington and should spend the time at the home of his fiancée, where Washington called for him May 10.

Washington found New York, where he arrived May 26, preparing for a farewell to an old acquaintance of his. Thomas Gage, now a Lieutenant General and still Commander-in-Chief of the British military forces in America. Gage had been on the continent almost continuously after 1755; now he was to leave with all the ceremonies New York could stage for him. It was pleasant to share on May 27 in the "elegant entertainment" the merchants and other citizens gave the General. Three days later Washington dined with Gage and, meantime, enjoyed numerous social affairs. At King's College no difficulty was encountered in registering Jack. The President, the Rev. Myles Cooper, proved to be full of zeal for King and church, a warm advocate of an American episcopate and a vehement enemy of dissenters. Washington started for home May 31 and reached there June 8.

Much pleased that the boy was at a good school and away from the temptation to marry on sudden impulse, Washington resumed his normal enjoyments and encountered the usual vexations, together with some he had not known previously. Troublesome boundary-disputes had developed on the Custis property on the Eastern Shore and on one of the plantations near the White House. Tobacco was selling very poorly. Gilbert Simpson had abandoned the joint settlement and mill-site on the Youghiogheny, had left Washington's slaves and property there and returned to his own farm in Loudoun County. Washington was angered by Simpson's behavior, but at the moment he was unable to do anything.

Mount Vernon was crowded with guests. Nelly Calvert and one of her girl friends were there; on the eighteenth Jack Washington, his wife and two children arrived for a visit. The next day, shortly before five o'clock, there was a stir of a sort that came often and unhappily—Patsy had been seized with one of her fits. This time the girl did not utter a word. Not a groan and scarcely a sigh escaped her lips. In less than two minutes she was dead. Martha, of course, was overwhelmed. Washington himself was shaken. Immediately, there was nothing he could do except comfort Martha as best he could, notify Jack and the kinsfolk around Williamsburg, and have the body of the seventeen-year-old girl made ready for burial.

Everything was done decorously and quietly. Condolence was as candid as kindly. Governor Dunmore understood instinctively that the proposed western journey with Washington had to be delayed. He wrote: ". . . as the poor young lady was so often afflicted with these fits, I dare say she thinks it a happy exchange." Fielding Lewis said: "Poor Patsy's death must have distressed Mrs. Washington very much, but when she considers the unhappy situation she was in and the little probability of ever getting well, she must conclude that it's better as it is, as there was little appearance of her ever being able to enjoy life with any satisfaction."

Patsy's death might end the greater part of Washington's financial distress. Thanks to prudent administration, her estate had increased to £16,000 and more. Half this went to Jack and half, through Martha, to Washington. He wrote his London factors briskly: ". . . as I would choose to discharge my debt to you I would apply her money . . . to that purpose, provided I can sell out without loss; be so good therefore as to let me know as soon as you can what steps are necessary to be pursued, in order to do this, and upon what terms it is to be done."

Washington the planter now became Washington the land broker. He was resolved that he would comply promptly with all the statutory conditions of "seating" new lands. He reasoned that settlers who went to western lands in order to advance their own fortunes would do better by him than would overseers or managers and undertook to draw settlers to his lands which, he said in an advertisement, were "among the first which have been surveyed in the part of the country they lie in"; but none came. Difficulties attending the development of this land were not a barrier to the acquisition of more—and more and more. Washington was committed to his view that the road to wealth ran on the frontier, and he set no limit to what he would patent if he could find low-lying, easily-developed tracts of first quality, no matter where—on the Scioto River, the western boundary of the proposed new Ohio Colony, or on the Mississippi in West Florida, though the prospect of this was dimming.

To find time for steadfast pursuit of wealth in the west, Washington learned how to organize and perform the work he had to do as plantation-owner, as counsellor of his neighborhood, as executor and administrator, as stepfather of the somewhat unstable Jack, as the husband of a grief-stricken wife, as a private gentleman who enjoyed his rightful share of sports—and so endlessly. He never could have finished all his duties—to say nothing of keeping his books and conducting his correspondence—had he not risen early and ordered his hours.

He turned much to a gratifying task—the enlargement and further adornment of Mount Vernon. A gardener had been employed in January;

much painting was in contemplation; 60,000 brick had been burned for new foundations and buildings; close to 15,000 shingles had been purchased. Although Patsy was missed hourly, the place was more beautiful than ever when, on October 19, Washington set out for Williamsburg to settle his business with the merchants who would assemble there at the end of the month. Martha traveled with him, as did Jack, who had come home from New York for vacation. The boy had been much shocked by Patsy's death, but he brought with him good reports from Cooper and a tutor. Washington was pleased to hear these and, now as always, he had satisfaction in the company of Martha and her son as they rode on to Eltham, which they reached on October 23.

After two days there, Washington went to Williamsburg, and renewed the veterans' agitation for land. In so far as the proclamation of 1763 was a basis of claims, he could do no more than submit the petition he had prepared in the name of the prospective beneficiaries. Those of the volunteers of 1754 who had received the tract of 51,302 acres had called a meeting at the mouth of the Great Kanawha, October 20, to make a final partition. Delinquent contributors, passed over in the first distribution, were now to receive their acreage. At the same time, Washington and a few others who had benefited in the first allotment had a new chance of increasing their holdings. No formal protests over inequitable distribution had been received, and all claims appeared to be satisfied. Left over were 18,887 acres. Washington proposed that this be divided among those who "had been at all the trouble and whole risk" of advancing their full part of the cost of exploration, surveys and patents. He urged that these men share in percentages that corresponded to the proportions of the original allotment; had not the Governor and Council provided that part of the reservation of thirty thousand should be for those who sustained extra expense in seeking to procure suitable lands for the soldiers? The Colonial officials now made the "second apportionment" as Washington recommended and added what Washington termed "the dividend" to those who had footed the bills for exploration and surveys.

So far as Washington was involved directly, one thing only remained for him to do. That was to collect what he could from those who had received their full bounty and had contributed meagrely or not at all. This task yielded scarcely enough to repay his trouble. Even so, Washington had not been rewarded poorly for pursuing the promise made in 1754, a promise which would never have been redeemed without his money, determination and persistence. On his own account, he had received 18,500 acres and at small expense he had bought up claims for an additional 5600, a total of 24,100 acres of good land on the Kanawhas and the left bank of the Ohio.

Back at length Washington went to Mount Vernon, by way of Fredericksburg, where he paid his mother £30 and took pains to note that he did so in the presence of his sister Betty. At home, December 9, he found himself at once subjected to a new plea—that Jack be not required to go back to college but be permitted to marry Nelly Calvert as soon as arrangements could be made. Determined as Washington was by nature, it was futile for him to attempt to resist the forces arrayed against him, Jack's own inclination, the desires of his mother and the acquiescence of almost all his relatives.

Thus did the prospects of Jack's marriage and increasing expenses make Washington more careful than ever about the frugal administration of the Custis trust. On his own account, though he was unrelaxing in his study of how he could acquire more land and drive off those who encroached on his new possessions, he continued to enlarge his benefactions. In his service to his neighbors he was so generous of his time he now was close to the limit of his resources, great as was his skill in ordering his days. Patsy's death was both grief and relief in 1773; Jack's unwillingness to remain at college was a distress; vexations had been numerous. The great events were the prospect of cancelling the debt to Cary & Co. and the completion of the patenting of the lands under the proclamation of 1754. A year of proud and profitable achievement ended before word came to Virginia of strange occurrences in Boston harbor on the night of December 16.

CHAPTER / 8

After repeal of all the Townshend duties except that on tea, the edge of the issue of taxation was dulled. Some Colonials gradually disregarded even their covenant not to use tea. By 1773, official silence might have produced public forgetfulness had not Lord North's ministry approved a new policy to enforce the tax on tea and relieve financial distresses of the East India Company. The Company was authorized to ship tea directly to merchants in America. On entry, the produce was subject to the tax on 3d. a pound which had been in force since 1767. It did not seem a hopeless undertaking; tea shipped and taxed in this manner would be cheaper than it ever had been in the Colonies and far less expensive than in England.

The new plan did something besides reawaken Colonials to the tax which they had denounced as a tyrannical levy imposed without their assent. Previously, the East India Company, which alone could bring tea into Great Britain, had been required to offer it at public auction to merchants who then sold it to other dealers with agents in America or directly to distributors in the Colonies. None of these men could take a middleman's profit under the new law. All organization in the trade might topple to ruin when the Company itself supplied the American dealer who dispensed the tea over the counter. To the citizen's familiar cry of taxation without representation, the merchant class now added that of monopoly without recourse. Tea was denounced as the drug of the tyrant, the scourge of the master, the bane of health. To frustrate the changes in the trade merchants used New England "Sons of Liberty," who demanded that the British government should not tax the Colonies; the champions of popular rights were glad to make common cause with the powerful mercantile class. As a result of their joint agitation, directed with skill and vehemence by Samuel Adams, a number of men carelessly disguised as Indians, clambered aboard three ships at a Boston dock on the night of December 16, 1773, and dumped into the waters of the harbor 342 chests of tea belonging to the East India Company.

Information of this affair reached Mount Vernon about New Year's Day. It did not excite Washington greatly, nor did it produce any general stir in Virginia, where the merchants were not as numerous or influential as in Massachusetts. Resentment over the tea tax was revived somewhat in the Old Dominion, but the "Boston tea party" was not approved by Washington and apparently was not regarded by him as immediately serious. He was busy that January 1774, and for many weeks afterwards, with an accumulation of troubles over tenants and leases, land claims and controversies.

Some of Washington's duties of management had to be discharged immediately, but some of them fortunately could be deferred until the celebration of the event that most interested the entire Mount Vernon household—the marriage of Mr. Custis, as he now was respectfully styled. The date was February 3; the place was Mount Airy. Washington witnessed the ceremonies and shared in the celebration. Generously, as became the stepfather of the groom, he remained for the festivities of the "second day." Then, leaving the bride, her husband and the friendly hosts, the Colonel returned to Mount Vernon, whence, in a few days, he sent to the young couple what Jack gratefully described as "many kind offers." It was Martha's hope and doubtless Washington's expectation that Jack and Nelly would spend their time at Mount Vernon until a decision concerning a permanent home was reached.

A whirl of new and continuing business at Mount Vernon was rendered the more difficult because of daily coming and going of visitors whose entertainment consumed hours. Washington did not permit himself to engage in foolish hurry and he did not pass hasty judgment on weighty affairs, but he found himself fully occupied and often annoyed. In the spring of 1774 there was gain to offset loss, irritation to match satisfaction. Even to Washington himself, the detail must have been tedious—an accident that put the treasured chariot into the river whence it had to be fished, seizure of Captain Crawford by law officers while he was visiting Mount Vernon, forced abandonment of the dream of patenting Florida lands and so through time-consuming trifles to one matter of large moment—a calamitous frost on May 4. This appeared at the moment to have destroyed about half of the wheat on the thousand acres Washington had planted in that grain. It was fortunate for Washington in this discouraging situation that he had a large store of wheat on hand and that he did well with it when he marketed it as flour.

Along with the killing frost came evil news. John Connolly, on the authorization of Governor Dunmore, had seized Fort Pitt in the name of the Colony of Virginia. That meant strained relations between Virginia and Penn's Colony and might jeopardize negotiations Washington was reopening for land on Chartier's Creek. Worse still was threat of renewed Indian warfare. Connolly was expected to proceed against the Shawnees, but the result was uncertain. More immediately, so far as Washington was involved, the upstir caught at Redstone the expedition he was sending to "seat" his Kanawha lands.

Before the extent of this financial reverse was known, Washington made ready to go to Williamsburg for a meeting of the General Assembly, most inconveniently called for May 5. Remaining at home as long as he could, he set off on the twelfth for the capital. When he arrived May 16, he found little done but much dreaded. King, ministry and Parliament had made their first response to the action of the Boston mob in throwing tea overboard. No protest, no threat, no action of violence by the Colonials had so outraged their critics in England or had alienated so many of their friends. A majority even of those who had been firmest in defence of the rights of the Americans admitted that the people of Boston should be punished. Franklin had written in dejection: "I suppose we never had since we were a people so few friends in Britain. The violent destruction of the tea seems to have united all parties here against our province. . . ." A bill was introduced to close the port of Boston after June 1 until the town paid for the destroyed tea, gave "reasonable satisfaction" to injured revenue officers, and convinced the King "that peace and obedience to the laws shall be so far restored in the said town of Boston, that the trade of Great Britain may be safely carried on there, and his Majesty's customs duly collected. . . ." The other Colonies were to be warned by that example. Lord North said: "Let us continue to proceed with firmness, justice and resolution: which, if pursued, will certainly produce that due obedience and respect to the laws of this country, and the security of the trade of its people, which I so ardently wish for." Gov. George Johnstone replied: "I now venture to predict to this House, that the effect of the present bill must be productive of a general confederacy, to resist the power of this country." He concluded that the bill "instead of quieting the disturbances of Boston . . . will promote them still further, and induce the inhabitants to cut off all communication with your ships of war, which may be productive of mutual hostilities and most probably will end in a general revolt." This warning and even the thunderous logic of Burke were in vain.

The text of the law reached Boston May 10 and both angered and appalled. A town meeting showed a determination to resist to the utmost. All the Colonies were to be asked to break off trade with Britain and Ireland till the act was repealed. Virginians did not learn of the precise terms of the act until shortly before May 19. Then the universal comment, in varying phrase, was that if one port could be closed in this manner, all could be—to the complete destruction of American rights. "The Parliament of England," wrote Landon Carter, "have declared war against the town of Boston and rather worse." He recorded the force being mustered and affirmed, "This is but a prelude to destroy the liberties of America. . . ."

In Virginia's General Assembly May 24, when petitions had been presented and referred in the usual order, the grave and religious Treasurer, Robert Carter Nicholas, took the floor and presented a paper that began: "This House, being deeply impressed with apprehension of the great dangers to be derived to British America from the hostile invasion of the city of Boston in our Sister Colony of Massachusetts Bay, whose commerce and harbor are, on the first day of June next, to be stopped by an armed force, deem it highly necessary that the said first day of June be set apart, by the members of this House, as a day of fasting, humiliation and prayer, devoutly to implore the divine interposition, for averting the heavy calamity which threatens destruction to our civil rights and the evils of civil war; to give us one heart and one mind firmly to oppose, by all just and proper means, every injury to American rights; and that the minds of his Majesty and his Parliament, may be inspired from above with wisdom, moderation and justice, to remove from the loyal people of America all cause of danger from a continued pursuit of measures pregnant with their ruin." The remainder was an order for the House to assemble June 1 and proceed, with the Speaker and the mace, to the church where prayers were to be said and a sermon delivered. Publication of the resolutions was directed in order that the public might share in the services and in the fast.

The resolutions of Nicholas were adopted on Tuesday the twenty-fourth; Wednesday week would be June 1. Burgesses expected they would be dissolved, but not until they had completed their major legislation the latter part of June. The House went on at its usual pace on the twenty-fifth. Much the same order of business was in progress between 3 and 4 P.M. on the twenty-sixth when the Clerk of the General Assembly brought the familiar message, "The Governor commands the House to attend his Excellency immediately, in the Council Chamber." In a few minutes the life of the legislature was ended in a single sentence from Dunmore: "Mr. Speaker and Gentlemen of the House of Burgesses, I have in my hand a paper published by order of your House, conceived in such terms as reflect highly upon his Majesty and the Parliament of Great Britain; which makes it necessary for me to dissolve you; and you are dissolved accordingly."

It had happened that way in May 1769. Burgesses remembered how they had gone from the Capitol to Raleigh Tavern and there had begun the discussion that led to the first Association. They flocked to the same building on the twenty-seventh and took counsel for the future. A basis of action was suggested in resolutions Richard Henry Lee had drafted. One of these called for the non-use in Virginia of the tea of the East India Company so long as the tax remained. Another denounced the Boston Port Act as "a most violent and dangerous attempt to destroy the constitutional liberty and rights of all British America." Then came a paragraph for the appointment of Deputies to meet with like representatives from other Colonies in order to consider means of stopping exports and securing the constitutional rights of America.

A paper containing substantially these ideas was adopted without haggle or hesitation. The central conclusion was this: "We are further clearly of opinion, that an attack, made on one of our sister Colonies, to compel submission to arbitrary taxes, is an attack made on all British America, and threatens ruin to the rights of all, unless the united wisdom of the whole be applied. And for this purpose it is recommended to the Committee of Correspondence, that they communicate, with their several corresponding committees, on the expediency of appointing deputies from the several Colonies of British America, to meet in general congress, at such place annually as shall be thought most convenient; there to deliberate on those general measures which the united interests of America may from time to time require." The proclamation of a common cause and the suggestion of an annual Congress were revolutionary developments.

On the twenty-eighth most of the Burgesses went home, but Washington stayed in Williamsburg to complete private business. Several other members of the dissolved House remained to attend a meeting of the Committee of Correspondence. This body took up the duty assigned it of communicating with the other Colonies on the "expediency" of an annual Congress of Delegates from all the Colonies. The Virginians approved a circular letter in which the dissolution of the House was explained. Then the committee wrote: "The propriety of appointing deputies from the several Colonies of British America to meet annually in general Congress, appears to be a measure extremely important and extensively useful, as it tends so effectually to obtain the united wisdom of the whole, in every case of general concern. We are desired to obtain your sentiments on this subject which you will be pleased to furnish us with."

That was on Saturday. The next day, Washington in grave mood went to church for both the morning sermon and the afternoon prayers. It perhaps was during churchyard conversation following the second service that Washington heard of the arrival of important dispatches from Maryland, with enclosures of serious moment from Philadelphia and Boston. Soon word spread that Peyton Randolph asked that all the Burgesses in Williamsburg assemble the next morning. Calls were dispatched, also, for those nearby. Washington of course responded and, on the morning of the thirtieth, found that twenty-four of his former colleagues had done likewise. The paper from Maryland was read to them. With it were a letter and a notice of a meeting held in Philadelphia. These, in turn, had been prompted by a communication Samuel Adams had addressed to the Philadelphia Committee of Correspondence to cover resolutions adopted in Boston.

Some of the resolutions of the Colonies above the Potomac were enough to make even the calm eyes of Washington flash. Adams reported that Boston alone could not "support the cause under so severe a trial." He went on: "As the very being of each Colony, considered as a free people, depends upon the event, a thought so dishonorable to our brethren cannot be entertained, as that this town will now be left to struggle alone." Maryland's Committee, writing May 25, was in favor of ascertaining what the people thought of a drastic plan of resistance—commercial non-intercourse, an association "on oath" to assure compliance, refusal of lawyers to enter suits for debts due in Britain and abandonment of all dealings with any Colony that declined to join with a majority of the others.

The argument quickly centred on a severance of trade with Britain. Washington could not endorse this. He favored cutting imports to absolute necessities, but he did not believe Virginians should refuse to pay their debts to Britain, and he reasoned that if planters and merchants were to pay, they had to export their goods. In this stand he was by no means alone. It was argued, also, that where so small a part of the subscribers to the existing Association were present, they should not undertake to modify the agreement. The decision was to invite the members of the former House to meet in Williamsburg and to consider what should be done. A date two months later, August 1, was set, in order that ample time might be given to arrange private business in advance of the gathering. Meantime, members would "have opportunity of collecting the sense of their respective Counties." The meeting adjourned with the understanding that the names of those present were to be signed to a letter that would be dispatched to the entire membership of the House.

Washington intended to seek re-election to the House of Burgesses and do his full part in the name of his constituents and on his own account, but he had hoped that a deft writer, such as George Mason or Bryan Fairfax, would be a candidate for the seat vacated by John West. When

Bryan declined because he was out of step with his neighbors, Washington renewed his appeal to Mason. Mason's declination left Charles Broadwater the only new candidate. The Fairfax election was held July 14 and completed in about two hours. There was a hogshead of punch for all comers, but if Washington furnished this, he was not so informed. He paid for the cakes served freely, and he left the details of the ball that evening to Capt. John Dalton, who computed Washington's share of the cost at approximately £8.

During the preliminaries of the election, and on election day itself, no resolutions on the Boston Port Act were passed. The reason probably was a desire the leading men of the county had expressed that Mason prepare for a selected committee a paper that would set forth the principles at stake. When Mason had completed a draft of resolutions and a designated committee had approved them, the final text was to be presented at a meeting over which Washington was to preside. On July 17, Mason brought to Mount Vernon his resolutions, which he doubtless discussed with Washington that evening. The next day the two rode to Alexandria and reviewed with the other committeemen the long statement Mason had fashioned. With no acrimony and little debate various amendments were made. Then the party went to the Court House, where Washington and the other members of the Committee mounted the bench. The proceedings had been opened when someone handed Washington a bulky letter. He broke the seal and found the contents to be a lengthy argument by Bryan Fairfax for petition and reconciliation, rather than for protest and reprisal. After looking over the paper, Washington passed it down the bench. One only of those who examined Fairfax's appeal was favorable to it. All the others were for ignoring it as unlikely to have the slightest support.

Mason's resolutions then were presented, explained and adopted. The observations on the rights of Americans contained little that had not been expounded previously by Mason, but they now were phrased with deliberate simplicity. Vigorous language was followed by the firm declaration "that it is our greatest wish and inclination, as well as interest, forever to continue our connection with and dependence upon the British government; but, though we are its subjects, we will use every means which Heaven hath given us to prevent our becoming its slaves."

Washington was so firmly convinced that when he returned home and explained to Fairfax why he had not read that friend's letter to the meeting in Alexandria, he powdered no phrases: ". . . Shall we, after this, whine and cry for relief when we have already tried it in vain? Or shall we supinely sit and see one province after another fall a prey to despotism? . . . [I] should much distrust my own judgment upon the occasion, if my nature did not recoil at the thought of submitting to measures which I think subversive of everything that I ought to hold dear and valuable, and did I not find, at the same time, that the voice of mankind is with me." All else failing, there remained the "one appeal" from the Sovereign that Mason had now incorporated into the Fairfax County resolutions. That was to be the same "last resource" of which Washington had set the very steel in his soul on full, if patient resistance. Neither fear nor argument could shake him. In all earlier discussion he had assumed that somehow, sometime, differences with Britain would be adjusted. Independence had not been a part of his political creed. Now his view was changing. Valuable as were the ties of trade, of defence and of inheritance, a deliberate attempt to deny Colonials their fundamental rights would justify complete separation. The Boston Port Act and the related measures of repression did more than all previous controversy to turn Washington from faith in reconciliation to a belief that a struggle for independence might be the only recourse of a people determined to preserve their liberties.

He had a direct duty to perform now. Among the resolutions adopted at the meeting in Alexandria was one that named him and Broadwater to attend the Convention the Burgesses had recommended. Washington rode into Williamsburg August 1. Others arrived hourly until the Convention had more members present than Washington had ever seen at any session of the House of Burgesses. Nearly all the old leaders were in attendance; so were the younger spokesmen of a vigorous policy, with the regretted exception of Jefferson. He had fallen sick on the way and had sent on the text of an uncorrected paper, "A Summary View of the Rights of British America, Set Forth in some Resolutions Intended for the Inspection of the Present Delegates of the People of Virginia, now in Convention." This was laid on the table and was so often read and discussed that it was published immediately. Washington was one of the first purchasers.

Daily deliberations were searching and detailed. By August 5 the Convention reached its decisions. There was agreement among the Delegates to accept Philadelphia as the place and September 5 as the time for the meeting of the General Congress. On the sixth, the participants unanimously approved their declaratory resolutions and instructions to the seven men who were to represent Virginia. The opening statement was an uninspired paper that contained few new ideas and did not express the accepted views with the ring of high determination. Instructions to the Delegates were written with stubborn repetition of familiar arguments, to which was added sharp denunciation of arbitrary orders issued not long previously by Gen. Thomas Gage in Boston. Pains were taken to make clear the reasons why Virginia did not favor the immediate prohibition of exports. Washington, himself an unimaginative man, may have been altogether content with these resolutions, which reflected his opinions almost to the letter; but there must have been some Delegates who wished that the proposal for united resistance through a General Congress had been proclaimed by Patrick Henry in the full sweep of his eloquence.

For Delegates to the Congress Peyton Randolph, Moderator of the Convention, was deferentially the first choice; next was Richard Henry Lee, whose effort had in large part been responsible for the Convention; Washington came next, then Henry, Richard Bland, Benjamin Harrison and Edmund Pendleton. In the absence of Jefferson, the length of whose disability was uncertain, and the preoccupation of Robert Carter Nicholas with his duties as Treasurer, these seven were the most distinguished members of the House.

Now Washington had to ride back to Mount Vernon and arrange his affairs in the knowledge that Henry would join him on the thirtieth and go with him to Philadelphia. The principal incidents of the days that preceded the start for the Quaker City concerned the sons of that good friend William Fairfax who gave him the news that led him to tender his services in 1753 for what proved to be his first great adventure—the journey to Fort Le Boeuf. George William Fairfax was gone, gone permanently; the contents of Belvoir were for sale; Washington had to assume some of the direction of this sad vendue. It was grim business to have men and women of every station peering and poking through the handsome chambers of that beloved house, but it was consoling to know that some of the furnishings most delightfully associated with Belvoir would adorn Mount Vernon.

The other experience was an attempted renewal by Bryan Fairfax of the argument which the committeemen had declined at Alexandria. He disavowed any desire to create a party, but he held to his views and wrote Washington a disquisition of some 2500 words on the rights of Parliament and of Colonials. Washington realized that where opinions were as far apart as his and Fairfax's it was useless to argue. His answer was modest and at the same time convinced: ". . . I am sure I have no new lights to throw upon the subject, or any other argument to offer in support of my own doctrine, than what you have seen; and could only in general add that an innate spirit of freedom first told me that the measures which administration hath for some time been, and now are most violently pursuing, are repugnant to every principle of natural justice; whilst much abler heads than my own hath fully convinced me that it is not only repugnant to natural right, but subversive of the law and constitution of Great Britain itself. . . ."

Punctually Henry arrived at Mount Vernon. With him was Pendleton. Mason came also, spent the night, and the next day discoursed no doubt on the rights of free peoples and the blindness of rulers. Henry listened and shared—"the first man upon this continent," in the opinion of Mason. The counsel of Pendleton was, as always, conservative but penetrating. Washington probably said little and that not argumentative. His mind was made up. All through the morning they reasoned and planned. Then, after dinner, the three delegates bade Mason good-bye and started for the ferry.

When Washington, Henry and Pendleton reached Philadelphia September 4, they found Delegates assembling from all the Colonies except Georgia. The next morning, Washington went to the City Tavern where they were to meet. At the tavern it was explained that the Pennsylvania Assembly had voted the Congress the use of the State House and that the carpenters of the city had offered their handsome hall for the meeting. Although Washington may have been unaware of it, politics were involved: The carpenters were adherents of the cause of the Colonies; the State House was the stronghold of a conservative element, under the leadership of Joseph Galloway. Delegates decided to view both places, but when they examined Carpenters' Hall, they liked it so much that a member asked whether they need look further. The hall was accepted; the Congress proceeded to organize; Randolph was unanimously named Speaker.

Argument began almost immediately over a motion to name a committee to draw up "regulations" for the Congress. This motion was construed to involve determination of the fundamental question, whether each Colony should have one vote or a number proportionate to the population. The decision was to allow each Colony a single and equal vote. The morning of the sixth brought rumors that Boston had been bombarded by the British garrison that occupied the town, but expresses who arrived on the eighth reported that the rumors had no better basis than the seizure of the Colony's powder at Charlestown. Congress briskly decided that two committees be named—one "to state the rights of the Colonies in general, the several instances in which these rights are violated or infringed, and the means most proper to be pursued for obtaining a restoration of them," the second "to examine and report the several statutes which affect the trade and manufactures of the Colonies."

As Washington was not appointed to either of these committees, he had no official duties from September 8 to 17 when the Congress merely adjourned from day to day or, at most, received a new Delegate and approved his credentials. This time was not wasted. Washington dined almost daily at the home of some conspicuous and hospitable Pennsylvanian, where talk ranged far. It was the largest, longest opportunity Washington ever had enjoyed of conversing with men of station from all the Colonies. He was advantaged in making the most of their educational discourse, both because he was a good listener and because he was treated with deference and courtesy. His reputation as a soldier was known; his wealth was exaggerated. Washington did not rely altogether on this method of extending his knowledge of the issues before the Congress. Philadelphia had a press quick to print pamphlets and it now had both supply and demand. In political papers, Washington invested more than seventeen shillings and he doubtless read from his purchases during the rare evenings he spent alone at his lodgings.

Most of the Delegates were impressed by the magnitude and intricacy of the task assigned them. The humble-minded were disturbed by their lack of familiarity with the problems of neighbors whose cause was now theirs. Some members who were esteemed eminent in their own Colony felt they must vindicate their reputation by eloquence and profundity. The cautious fencing and the deliberate finesse, the suspicious aloofness and the formal delivery of Ciceronian speeches, took a realistic turn with the first major event of the session, the submission to Congress on September 17 of resolutions adopted on the sixth by citizens of Suffolk County, Massachusetts. If those "Suffolk Resolves" in most respects were merely a restatement of the Colonial defence of liberties, they had an undertone of defiance and this bold endorsement of reprisal: In event any of the leaders of the popular cause were arrested, the people should "seize and keep in safe custody every servant of the present tyrannical and unconstitutional government throughout the County and Province, until the persons so apprehended be liberated from the hands of our adversaries and restored safe and uninjured to their respective friends and families."

Boston, in a word, was expressing the full argument of the Colonial cause and was serving notice sternly that reprisal would be the answer to arrest, that scuffs would be returned as blows, and, if need be, that war would be met with war. The principle in all this was one that Washington long previously had decided for himself. To his way of thinking, Massachusetts' determined stand did not justify hesitation or warrant discussion. The position was right, and, being right, must be defended. Congress' answer was equally decisive and in the same spirit, and was given that very day.

This answer delighted the members from Massachusetts at the same time that it afforded an opportunity of testing the sentiment of Congress as a whole. Thereafter more confidence was shown in preparing committee reports and in urging resolutions on the floor of the Congress, though there still was caution and a lack of planning and of leadership. Convinced and impatient Delegates were willing to go slowly if all the Colonies would move together. Unity was worth the time spent in assuring it. By the twenty-second, Delegates were agreed that the entire continent should enter into a non-importation pact, a traitor-proof "association."

In the fifth week of the Congress came a letter, October 6, from the Boston Committee of Correspondence which described the strict military rule there and asked the advice of the Congress on the course the people should follow. Congress came to the sternest resolution the Delegates had thus far adopted—"that this Congress approve of the opposition by the inhabitants of the Massachusetts-bay to the execution of the late acts of Parliament; and if the same shall be attempted to be carried into execution by force, in such case, all America ought to support them in their opposition." In another day's deliberations, October 10, the people of Boston were advised not to leave their town unless compelled to do so; but they were told that if the Colony's Council should consider removal of the population necessary, Congress would recommend that all America contribute towards making good the loss citizens would sustain. Further, the people were counselled to dispense, where practicable, with the administration of justice, if it could not be procured "in a legal and peaceable manner" under the charter and the laws of the Colony. Finally, Congress was mindful of the enemy within the gates. It resolved that all persons who accepted office or served in any way under the parliamentary act changing the government of Massachusetts "ought to be held in detestation and abhorrence by all good men, and considered as the wicked tools of that despotism which is preparing to destroy those rights which God, nature and compact have given to America."

There followed a three-day debate on the rights of the Colonies. As the debate progressed the report was made an omnium gatherum of affirmations, reiterations of action already taken and resolutions on contingencies. When the whole was adopted, October 14, even its authors would have had difficulty in saying what the document made final and what it left the Congress to elaborate. In the absence of any plan or leadership, men who had been successful lawmakers in their own Colonies found it difficult to put together an orderly plan of action, even after their differences had been reconciled. Members were aware of this and were becoming restive.

Consciousness of this feeling, exhaustion of argument, desire to get home, completion of reports over which committees had spent uncounted hours—some or all of these circumstances were responsible for a less leisured tempo of discussion after October 17. On the eighteenth, the Terms of Association were adopted for transcription and signature. The completed paper reviewed the "ruinous system of colonial administration" and the specific acts of which America had complained. "To obtain redress of these grievances, which threaten destruction of the lives, liberty and property of his Majesty's subjects in North America"—so ran the last paragraph of the preamble—"we are of opinion that a non-importation, non-consumption and non-exportation agreement, faithfully adhered to, will prove the most speedy, effectual and peaceable measure. . . ." Delegates committed themselves and the people of their Colonies to a broad agreement against the importation of British and Irish goods and of all slaves after December 1, 1774. Non-consumption of tea and other taxed goods was pledged; non-exportation was set at September 10, 1775. Local committees were recommended to see that the Association was enforced. All these matters were put together in a long document, so long, in fact, that after it was signed by the members present October 20 and delivered to the printer, it had to be issued as a pamphlet.

The Congress was in a mood of decision. October 21 it took into account repeated rumors that some of the members were to be arrested and transported to England for trial there and resolved "that the seizing, or attempting to seize, any person in America, in order to transport such person beyond the sea, for trial of offences committed within the body of a County in America, being against law, will justify and ought to meet with resistance and reprisal." The next day the Congress dismissed Galloway's plan for a Grand Council of all the Colonies and recommended that the Colonies choose Delegates to a new Congress that would assemble in Philadelphia May 10, 1775.

Was there anything more a Congress could do? Most of the Virginians did not think the remaining deliberations of particular importance and, on October 23 or 24, all of them except Washington and Lee started homeward. Bland, Harrison, Randolph and probably Pendleton left in Washington's hands a power of attorney to sign their names "to any of the proceedings of the Congress." Delegates still had to consider the final form of their address to the King and the text of an appeal to the people of Quebec. On the twenty-fifth the address was approved, and on the twenty-sixth the remaining papers on the calendar were completed and approved; fair copies of the address were signed. Lee subscribed for himself and for Henry, whereupon Washington attached his signature and those of Pendleton, Bland and Harrison. Then, at long last, the Congress was dissolved.

So lacking in plan had been the deliberations and so meandering the stream of debate that when members undertook to say what the Congress had done they might have had difficulty in stating in one-two order the resolves and recommendations. There had been so much of hesitation and confusion that many must have been disappointed. In detail, the rights of the Colonials had been asserted, and the nature of their grievances had been set forth. More important than all the Colonies had pledged in their Congress was the fact that all had pledged it. "A determined and unanimous resolution animates this continent," said John Dickinson, "firmly and faithfully to support the common cause of the utmost extremity in this great struggle for the blessing of liberty—a blessing that can alone render life worth holding. . . ."

In contributing to this, Washington had displayed no deftness of pen or skill of exhortation. In a list of Convention celebrities compiled by the observant John Adams he was not mentioned. Among the Virginia Delegates, Lee and Henry had displayed more of parliamentary leadership and had outshone him completely. Unpraised, he had not been unobserved. Members esteemed him for his military reputation and found that the soundness of his judgment compensated for the awkwardness of his public utterance. They respected him more, rather than less, for his lack of desire to parade his opinions on the floor. He impressed his colleagues as a resolute man of integrity. Washington, moreover, had widened his horizon to the north and to the south. His view was increasingly continental.

The Congress did not make any formal recommendation that the Colonies prepare for their defence. The possibility of war could not be blinked; the probability of it was believed to hang on offensive action by the British. Argument was unnecessary where agreement was almost unanimous that if hard blows were struck, harder would be returned. An oddly dressed, eccentric British half-pay officer, Charles Lee, who had been in the service of the pro-Russian faction in Poland, had talked much in Philadelphia about the organization of a battalion which it was manifest he wished to command. Washington of course met him but made no record of it. In the eyes of some members Washington himself was essentially a soldier, but of his employment as such by the Congress there had been no suggestion.

A great change was observable when Washington reached home. The people of Virginia were much more in a mood of preparation for defence. Older men and matrons busied themselves with enforcing the Association or adapting plantation life to it; young men were intent on organizing companies, finding arms and drilling. These volunteers were confident because men of their blood had just won a victory in Governor Dunmore's War. At Point Pleasant, where the Kanawha enters the Ohio, Col. Andrew Lewis and a force of Virginia militia had encountered a mass of savages on October 10. The Indians had fought stubbornly but at length had broken and quit the field. News followed soon that the Indians were asking peace and had given hostages for the delivery of the white prisoners in their villages. It was the swiftest and the most decisive campaign the Virginians had waged against the Redmen.

Washington found that committees could be set up readily enough in accordance with the resolutions of the Philadelphia Congress. In Fairfax no difficulty was encountered in dealing with a shipment of forbidden linens, to the value of £1101, reported by the consignees, Fitzgerald & Peers. The goods were sold by package to the highest bidder; the proceeds were set aside for the relief of the poor of Boston. Nothing similar to the feeling aroused by the Boston Port Act, the suppression of the Massachusetts Council and Assembly, and the occupation of Boston by British troops ever had been witnessed in Virginia.

Washington daily was busy from early morning until three-o'clock dinner. He was able, once in a while, to go fox-hunting, but that was the limit of all recreation not incidental to business. In the winter of 1774–75, one of the most troublesome affairs was the breakup of the party of indentured servants and slaves sent in March to the Kanawha lands and halted at Redstone by the outbreak of Dunmore's War. Lacking firm control, one after another of the workers disappeared, and with them the implements and supplies Washington had entrusted to the men in charge. Washington computed his loss at £300.

The larger interests held first place in his mind. On January 15, 1775, George Mason, Martin Cockburn and others returned with Washington to Mount Vernon after service at Pohick Church, and talked of plans for having their county do its part in defence of Colonial rights. This was not easy. Fairfax County possessed no ammunition beyond the normal requirements of planters. Fowling pieces were the only weapons. Besides this, there was an obstacle of law: by whose authority were the Independent Companies being organized?

Discussion of these subjects was resumed on the sixteenth at Alexandria, whither Washington rode, probably in the company of his overnight guests. Ammunition could not be purchased with money raised by formal county levy for that purpose unless the prior consent of the General Assembly was had, but powder and shot could be bought at the common cost of the inhabitants of the county. The Committee therefore voted: "It is . . . recommended that the sum of three shillings per poll . . . be paid by and for every tithable person in this County, to the Sheriff or such other collector as may be appointed, who is to render the same to this Committee, with a list of the names of such persons as shall refuse to pay the same, if any such there be." Washington and Mason agreed to advance the money required for purchase of the explosive. As for the weapons, the committee concluded these could be provided quickly in no other way than by conforming to the principle of the militia law and requiring every man to have his own firelock and to keep it in good order.

A solution of the other perplexity—that of arming without risk of arrest—already had been offered in Maryland and now was adopted, tongue in cheek. Citizens across the Potomac had decided that the Colonials would be safe if they acted on the ostensible theory that they simply were making the authorized militia more effective. So, some good draftsman, with a sense of humor—almost certainly Mason—prepared this "resolve," which might have made even the stern-visaged Washington smile: ". . . that this committee do concur in opinion with the Provincial Committee of the Province of Maryland that a well regulated militia, composed of gentlemen freeholders and other freemen, is the natural strength and only stable security of a free government, and that such militia will relieve our mother country from any expense in our protection and defence, will obviate the pretence of a necessity for taxing us on that account, and render it unnecessary to keep standing armies among us—ever dangerous to liberty; and therefore it is recommended to such of the inhabitants of this County as are from 16 to 50 years of age to form themselves into Companies."

A new Virginia Convention was called in line with the recommendation of the Philadelphia Congress of 1774 that each Colony select Delegates to a similar Congress in May 1775. Peyton Randolph "requested" the election in each county of Delegates who were asked to meet in Richmond March 20. Washington was named Fairfax's representative along with his fellow-Burgess, Charles Broadwater.

The Convention met with many auguries of peace with Britain. This was meat and drink to the Delegates who still had faith in their King and unpalatable to those who believed the monarch a tyrant. Initial division among members did not interfere with a sympathetic review of the recommendations of the Philadelphia Congress. The proceedings of the Congress were approved by unanimous vote, and the Delegates were thanked. On March 23, the fourth day of the Convention, Henry won recognition and offered a series of resolutions. They repeated substantially the Maryland and Fairfax argument regarding a "well regulated militia, composed of gentlemen and yeomen" as the "natural strength and only security of a free government." After that came words with a rumble: "Resolved, therefore"—the Convention must have become tense as the Clerk read on—"that this Colony be immediately put in a posture of defence; and that [blank] be a committee to prepare a plan for the embodying, arming and disciplining such a number of men as may be sufficient for that purpose." Henry then took the floor. He launched into a bold argument that the increase of British force in America was intended for the enslavement of the Colonies. In one way only could Americans retain their liberty. "We must fight!" he cried, as if the command were from Heaven. Henry swept furiously onward until his words were the call of bugles and the roar of guns: "Is life so dear, or peace so sweet, as to be purchased at the price of chains and slavery? Forbid it, Almighty God! I know not what course others may take; but as for me, give me liberty or give me death!"

Men sat as if they had been stunned or condemned or called to a task so much beyond their strength but so lofty and commanding that it awed them. A few were vain or reckless enough to attempt to match their eloquence against Henry's; others felt they must dispute his logic though they could not rival his delivery. They could not believe the King would permit the controversy to reach the dreadful pass where British subjects would be at one another's throat. The vote, in the end, was for putting the Colony "into a posture of defence."

Henry was named first on a committee of twelve to bring in a plan for "embodying, arming and disciplining such a number of men as may be sufficient for that purpose." Washington was assigned to the committee with most of the leading members of Henry's following. This committee could do so little for the immediate strengthening of the Colony's defence that it had its report ready by the next day. As adopted, the report was essentially an appeal for the organization of volunteers. As the weakness of Virginia's defence was certain to be the lack of arms, ammunition and equipment of every sort, the committee recommended that each county levy the equivalent of a head tax, as in Fairfax, for the purchase of ammunition. A central committee of three was created to buy military supplies for counties that did not know how to procure them. The Convention likewise selected a committee of thirteen to "prepare a plan for the encouragement of arts and manufactures in this Colony," a euphemism for employing the pitifully undeveloped resources of war. Washington was on this committee, too. A third and far more important assignment also was his. When the seven members to the new General Congress were elected, Washington was the second chosen. Randolph's name alone preceded his; Henry's followed. All the other members of the delegation to Philadelphia in 1774 were re-elected. The committee on the encouragement of arts and manufactures threw together a plan that covered a diversity of objects. The Convention approved the report and, after transacting a variety of other business, adjourned March 27.

Washington left Richmond March 28 and reached home March 31. He scarcely had rested when he heard an alarming rumor—that Governor Dunmore was going to cancel all the land patents issued under the proclamation of 1754 because William Crawford who surveyed the tracts was alleged to have failed to qualify in the manner prescribed by statute. Washington was aghast. Twenty-three thousand acres of his land were involved! They must not be lost. Washington concluded he should inquire directly of the Governor whether the story had anything more behind it than excited gossip. Promptly enough there came a terse and formal answer from his Lordship: "Sir, I have received your letter. . . . The information you have received that the patents granted for the lands under the proclamation of 1754 would be declared null and void, is founded on a report that the Surveyor who surveyed those lands did not qualify agreeable to the act of Assembly directing the duty and qualification of surveyors. If this is the case, the patents will of consequence be declared null and void."

The letter was one to ponder. If in some manner unknown to the man most heavily concerned Crawford had failed to qualify, all the cost and all the labor would go for nought. Could the whole affair be an attempt to bribe Washington and the others into acceptance of royal policy? If Washington suspected blackmail or reprisal, it did not deter him from a single act of military preparation or from the utterance of a word he would have spoken in aid of the Colonial cause.

Now came a visit to Alexandria for the muster of the Independent Company, and five days of discourse by Gen. Charles Lee, at Mount Vernon on a visit. After that, when lengthening April days brought spring to the Potomac, the greater part of Washington's time was given to the direction of plantation affairs. It was on the twenty-sixth or twenty-seventh that a hurrying express brought a startling letter from Fredericksburg, signed by Hugh Mercer and three other men interested in organizing troops for the defence of the Colony. They had heard from Williamsburg that on the night of April 20/21, the captain of a British armed schooner had landed with fifteen marines, gone to the magazine in Williamsburg and taken from it the powder stored there. Mercer and the committee in Fredericksburg reported: "The gentlemen of the Independent Company of this town think this first public insult is not to be tamely submitted to and determine with your approbation to join any other bodies of armed men who are willing to appear in support of the honor of Virginia as well as to secure the military stores yet remaining in the magazine. It is proposed to march on Saturday next for Williamsburg properly accoutred as light horsemen. Expresses are sent off to inform the commanding officers of Companies in the adjacent Counties of this our resolution, and we shall wait prepared for your instructions and their assistance."

Besides this from Fredericksburg, Washington had an express from Dumfries; volunteer officers had voted to answer a summons from Mercer but awaited Washington's instructions. Events in Williamsburg had been substantially as reported. When the townspeople discovered what had happened, wrath rose. The call was "To the Palace." They would demand the immediate return of the powder; it was theirs of right, theirs with which to defend themselves. Before the crowd could start up the street, Randolph, Treasurer Nicholas and others urged that the Common Hall of the city was the proper body to act. This seemed reasonable to men who had not yet lost their heads completely. The Common Hall met, debated, drafted a paper and proceeded in a body to the Governor's residence, where Randolph presented the address. It was a simple argument that the magazine and its contents were for the security of the Colony, which might require ammunition quickly in event of an uprising by the slaves. Would the Governor explain why he had removed the powder and would he return it?

The reference to a rebellion by the Negroes gave Lord Dunmore a peg on which to hang a cloaking excuse: Reports of a servile insurrection in a neighboring county, he said, had led him to remove the powder to a place of security, whence it could be returned in half an hour were it needed to combat the uprising. He had been led to send it off at night to avoid excitement and was surprised to hear that the people had taken up arms. In that situation he did not think it prudent to put powder in their hands. The members of the Common Hall left the Palace unsatisfied; Dunmore armed his household and the naval officers who happened to be in town. The townspeople showed a temper that seemed to threaten attack, but, after a time, they began to disperse. Dunmore was a liar, they told one another. He had no information about a revolt of the slaves; all that the Governor was doing was for one purpose only—to make the people defenceless! They must have their powder.

At the very time when peace or conflict in Virginia appeared to hang on the temper of Dunmore and the restraint of the Colonials, the news that had been half dreaded and half awaited for weeks arrived from the north: a clash had occurred in Massachusetts; much blood had been shed. In the early morning of April 19, a British infantry force had appeared ten miles northwest of Boston in the village of Lexington, where part of a volunteer company was awaiting them. The British commander called on these Colonials to disperse and, when they did not move swiftly enough to suit him, he ordered his front ranks to fire. At the volley, the company scattered, but the Americans left eight dead on the ground. Ten more were wounded. The British then marched on to Concord. At Concord, Massachusetts volunteers were gathering but fell back on the approach of the regulars. Then, while a hundred British held the bridge over the Concord River, others searched the town for military stores they had been told the Colonials had hidden there. Little was found but fires were lighted that angered the volunteers, who, after a time, returned to the bridge, where an exchange of musketry occurred. This and the menacing advance of the Colonials caused the British to leave the little stream. Presently the whole body of regulars reassembled and started back to Boston. Word of their presence had been heard throughout the countryside. Men hurried out with their rifles to reenforce the volunteers, and soon the Americans opened fire on the flank and rear of the British. A running fight began and kept up to Charlestown, within range of the British men-of-war.

The British had struck the blow the Colonials had served notice they would resist. War might follow this bloody encounter: Washington was not the man to blink the reality or to change plans based on the probability. If he must, he would stay in Virginia to combat any violent acts of Dunmore; but if the semblance of peace were preserved in his own Colony, he would continue with plans to go to Philadelphia, there to share common council for the continental cause. Washington waited anxiously for more news. The thirtieth brought information that about six hundred men had rendezvoused at Fredericksburg for a march on Williamsburg, but that they had delayed their start because of a letter of advice from Randolph. Randolph wrote: ". . . the Governor considers his honor at stake; he thinks that he acted for the best, and will not be compelled to what, we have abundant reason to believe he would cheerfully do, if left to himself." The Speaker continued: "If we, then, may be permitted to advise, it is our opinion and most earnest request that matters may be quieted for the present at least; we are firmly persuaded that perfect tranquility will be speedily restored. By pursuing this course we foresee no hazard, or even inconvenience that can ensue, whereas we are apprehensive, and this we think upon good grounds, that violence may produce effects which God only knows the effects of."

This was counsel not to be disdained by men of sanity. The committee of volunteers and other citizens appointed to consider an answer approved a strong written summary of the Colonial case and recommended: "Whilst the least hope of reconciliation remains . . . that the several Companies now rendezvoused here do return to their respective homes; but considering the just rights and liberty of America to be greatly endangered by the violent and hostile proceedings of an arbitrary ministry, and being firmly resolved to resist such attempts at the utmost hazard of our lives and fortunes, we do now pledge ourselves to each other to be in readiness, at a moment's warning, to reassemble, and by force of arms, to defend the law, the liberty and rights of this or any sister Colony, from unjust and wicked invasion." In place of the "God save the King" that ended the Governor's proclamation, the officers who read the volunteers' paper to their men shouted boldly and defiantly: "God save the liberties of America."

Washington was justified in looking now to Philadelphia instead of to Williamsburg. The hours of the last days before departure were eaten up by visitors. Among others, came Washington's long-time friend, Horatio

Gates, who had commanded an Independent Company in Braddock's expedition. Gates now was a half-pay Major, residing in Berkeley County, and was wondering, no doubt, what place, if war came, he could find in the armed forces of the Colonies whose cause he had resolved to espouse. On May 3, while Gates still was at Mount Vernon, Richard Henry Lee arrived with his brother Thomas Ludwell Lee and Charles Carter. The parlors in the evening were a rostrum for much discourse on the part of the two Lees, Carter and Gates. As host, Washington listened and, when he had observations, made them briefly. Perhaps, when the guests had gone to their rooms, and Washington was alone with Martha, there was some of the sadness of farewell, but optimism had the upper hand of grief: it was only another visit, unpleasantly long, perhaps, though in a pleasant city. When the Congress adjourned, he would come back—unless that affair at Concord and Lexington, that bloody clash of Colonials and ministerial troops, meant war. Even in that event, one campaign would decide whether Britain would recognize the rights of the Colonials or would suppress the uprising and punish the leaders. Should the darker fate be America's, then there would be a refuge on those frontier lands Washington was trying to save.

Washington rode off from Mount Vernon with his colleagues on May 4. The next day he reached Baltimore, where he was invited to review on the sixth the volunteer companies. There was significance in the invitation. For ten years and more Washington had been welcomed as a wealthy planter who had been a conspicuous Colonial soldier. Now the scale of values was tipped the other way: he was one of the few experienced military officers in the Colonies and, by chance, a man of high financial standing.

When Colonel Washington and a number of other Virginians were within six miles of Philadelphia on May 9, they met a party of horsemen later reckoned at five hundred. These were officers of the military companies, together with leading citizens, who had come out to welcome the Delegates. Guests and hosts rode four miles towards the city and there found a band and an escort of foot and riflemen. From that point onward, the column was a parade. The spirit of almost everything seemed encouragingly different from the opening of the Congress of 1774. Most of the suspicious rivalry of the previous year had been dissipated by the volleys on the Concord Road.

Where that temper prevailed, no time was lost in organization. On the tenth, the Delegates met in the Pennsylvania State House, re-elected Peyton Randolph President and, on the eleventh, ordered the doors closed for deliberations that were to remain secret until a majority voted otherwise. Procedure was smooth; papers were submitted to the Congress as if it were an established parliament. In the mass of communications, the one that meant most was from Dr. Joseph Warren, acting President of the "Provincial Congress" of Massachusetts. "We have . . . passed," he wrote, "an unanimous resolve for thirteen thousand, six hundred men, to be forthwith raised by this Colony; and proposals are made by us to the Congress of New Hampshire, and governments of Rhode Island and Connecticut Colonies for furnishing men in the same proportion." Thirteen thousand from Massachusetts alone! Warren justified the number with sound military logic: ". . . We beg leave to suggest," he wrote, "that a powerful army, on the side of America, hath been considered by [Massachusetts] as the only mean left to stem the rapid progress of a tyrannical ministry." Clearly he saw: "Without a force, superior to our enemies, we must reasonably expect to become the victims of their relentless fury: With such a force we may still have hopes of seeing an immediate end put to the inhuman ravages of mercenary troops in America. . . ." In the very hour of the conception of an American army, he had laid down the germinating ideal—superiority of force.

The first application of military policy by Congress came during the opening week of the session, in answer to an inquiry by New York: British troops were en route to the city at the mouth of the Hudson: what should American sympathizers do? The decision of Congress was that so long as the Redcoats remained in their barracks, they should be left alone, but if the British constructed fortifications, committed hostilities, or invaded private property, they must be resisted. This raised a question in answering one: If that was the policy for New York City, what of the Colony? To aid in deciding this, Washington received his initial assignment. He was named to head a group that included Samuel Adams of Massachusetts, Thomas Lynch of South Carolina, and all the New York Delegates.

Patrick Henry arrived on the seventeenth or early on the eighteenth and gave details of occurrences regarding which the Virginia Delegates already had a variety of rumors. Word of the fighting at Lexington and Concord had reached Henry and his neighbors ahead of information concerning Randolph's letter to the troops at Fredericksburg. The wrath of Henry already had been aroused by the seizure of the powder at Williamsburg; this intelligence of a British march to purloin the supplies of the Massachusetts people convinced him that the Ministry was proceeding swiftly and systematically to destroy the Colonials' means of defence. Outraged, the orator sent for the Hanover County Committee and had the commanding officer order the volunteer company to assemble at Newcastle on May 2. Henry proposed that they make reprisal in an amount large enough to purchase as much powder as Dunmore had seized. The crowd shouted its approval. Capt. Samuel Meredith, the company commander, resigned his commission so that Henry might exercise full authority. Henry thereupon had the Committee pass a resolution for the detachment of a party of seventeen to proceed to the home of Receiver-General Richard Corbin, and demand the money. If it was not forthcoming, the detachment was to seize Corbin and bring him to Henry who would be moving meantime towards Williamsburg with the remainder of the company.

Corbin chanced to be in Williamsburg, but when news reached the town that Henry had demanded payment for the powder and was marching on the capital, the Governor arranged that a bill of exchange for £330, the estimated value of the powder, be sent in Corbin's name to Henry. The leader of the expedition triumphantly receipted for the money, which he said he would turn over to the Virginia Delegates in Philadelphia, to be laid out in powder. Then, after conference and assurances that all was quiet in Williamsburg, the men of Hanover marched home again.

Washington temporarily could dismiss his concern for his own Colony and could devote his mind to his committee assignment, which had new importance because of surprising news from upper New York. On May 10 a loose organization of Colonials had overrun Fort Ticonderoga at the northern end of Lake George. If that site or Crown Point or even the southern end of Lake George could be held, the British route between Canada and the waters around New York City would be blocked. That possibility was of first importance to Washington and his committee in their study of the defence of the Colony of New York; but the daring of the plan for the seizure of Ticonderoga and the boldness of the execution startled Congress. Colonials had assumed the offensive. With such information as could be supplied by the messenger from Ticonderoga, Washington and his committee finished their report in time to submit it May 19. Randolph left on May 24 to attend the session of the Virginia General Assembly that Dunmore at length had called. In his place, John Hancock, of Massachusetts, was named unanimously to preside over the Congress. It was under Hancock's rulings, that the committee's report concerning the defence of New York was approved May 25.

No sooner had Washington discharged this duty than he received more formidable assignment—the chairmanship of a committee of six, "to consider ways and means to supply these Colonies with ammunition and military stores and to report immediately." With him were to work Philip Schuyler, Thomas Mifflin, Silas Deane, Lewis Morris and Samuel Adams. The committee proceeded to confer, but little could be done immediately except to recommend that the Colonies collect the supplies already in America and that they undertake to manufacture gunpowder where practicable.

Washington continued to vote with the majority of the Delegates for all measures that looked to a reconciliation, but he had no faith in the success of any of them. As he fashioned plans and read reports, his soldierly impulses rose. He had brought with him from Mount Vernon a uniform he had worn in the French and Indian War—and now he was wearing it daily, as if to signify to his fellow-Delegates that he believed the time had come to take the field. He scrutinized all the accounts he could get of the fighting at Concord and Lexington and found encouragement in them. Gratifying as it was to know that Americans could and would fight, the tragedy of fraternal conflict oppressed him. He wrote: "Unhappy it is, though, to reflect that a brother's sword has been sheathed in a brother's breast and that the once-happy and peaceful plains of America are either to be drenched with blood or inhabited by slaves. Sad alternative! But can a virtuous man hesitate in his choice?"

On June 2 Congress had before it this puzzling question from Massachusetts: What should the Colony do about the establishment of civil authority, which had, in effect, been suspended? To their own inquiry on this subject, leaders of the Bay Colony added counsel: "As the Army now collecting from different Colonies is for the general defence of the right of America, we would beg leave to suggest to your consideration the propriety of taking the regulation and general direction of it, that the operations may more effectually answer the purposes designated." Still again, money was demanded for everything the Congress undertook. On June 3, therefore, Congress voted to appoint a committee to estimate the funds that had to be raised. That Congress had not yet acted on the report Washington and his colleagues had filed June 1 on procuring ammunition and military stores did not excuse him from additional service; he was named to this new committee.

There was zeal; there were endless proposals for advancing the American cause; so much was urged on the floor or asked in letters from the Colonies that members doubtless became confused. When they took up proposals for active defensive preparation, they could do little so long as they were uncertain whether differences were to be reconciled or a struggle for independence had to be faced. Cruel tasks multiplied and difficulties piled up hourly. The best minds, after hardest effort, could suggest little that was genuinely useful. Confidence was changing to discouragement, but spirit shone in the resolution Congress adopted June 12 for the observance of a fast day July 20. The Congress incorporated a firm assertion of the "just rights and privileges of the Colonies"; and two days later authorized the raising in Pennsylvania, Maryland and Virginia of a total of ten companies to march to Boston.

The next decision had been shaping itself for days, perhaps for two weeks, because imagination, as always, outran action. In the paper for raising the ten companies it was specified that when these troops reached Boston they should be employed as light infantry "under the command of the chief officer in that army." A leader of ability and character must be commissioned in the name of the United Colonies and must be sent to Boston to take command of troops paid and fed by "the continent" and reenforced promptly with volunteers from every province. Such a leader must personify the unity of Americans, their character, their resolution, their devotion to the principles of liberty. Perhaps a majority of the New Englanders favored the selection of Artemas Ward, Commander-in-Chief of the Massachusetts troops in front of Boston, or some other of several general officers familiar with their own region. John Adams, increasingly the spokesman of the best judgment of Massachusetts, thought it politic to name a man from a different part of America. Elbridge Gerry and Joseph Warren favored Charles Lee. If he was unacceptable because he had not been born in America, they looked with favor on "the beloved Colonel Washington."

Washington had known for days that he was being advocated by some Delegates. One after another had told him, in effect, "You are the man." Every such expression alarmed and depressed him. His reluctance was manifest to his colleagues. He did not once "insinuate"—the verb was his—that he wished the command, and he did his utmost to restrain his friends from advocating his election, but, now, he had Edmund Pendleton draft a will for him; and in his letters to Martha, he avoided any mention of the probable time of his home-coming. As the middle of June approached he began to feel that destiny, and nothing less than destiny, was shaping his course.

Washington went to the Congress on the fourteenth and listened to discussion of the number and type of troops that should be raised. At length

John Adams rose. Adams was a convinced advocate of separation from Great Britain, but his reputation as a revolutionary did not weaken his position as the most influential representative of New England. He proceeded now to show the need of action to save the army in front of Boston. The Colonial forces, Adams argued, must have heartening evidence that the whole of British North America was behind them; this could best be done by placing the army under the direction of a man who represented the Congress and the continent. For his part, Adams went on, he did not hesitate to say that he had one person in mind, one only. At the words Hancock showed manifest pleasure, as if certain Adams was about to call his name. Washington, fearing otherwise, felt embarrassment creep over him. Adams did not prolong the suspense: The commander he had in mind, he said, was a gentleman from Virginia. On the instant Hancock's expression changed: his disappointment was beyond concealment. Adams went straight on: he referred, he said, to one whose skill and experience as an officer, whose independent fortune. . . . With that, Washington bolted for the adjoining library: Adams could be talking of no other than of him.

He went out; he stayed out; but after adjournment, he of course was told what happened. Mild dissent was immediate, though not general. Several members reasserted the familiar argument that as the whole of the army came from New England and had succeeded in confining the British in Boston, the men were entitled to a general of their own. In this view, Edmund Pendleton concurred. All who expressed this opinion were careful to state that their objection was not to Washington personally. The debate ended that day without any decision, but now that Washington's name had been proposed, those who advocated him did not hesitate in seeking to convert friends. Southerners who cherished regional pride but had deferred to New England needed to hear no other argument than that the choice of Washington would be acceptable to Massachusetts and Connecticut; men from the threatened Colonies had no answer to those of their neighbors who told them the election of Washington was expedient because it would assure full Southern support of the struggle against the British. No advocate of Washington's preferment showed any disposition at the outset to attribute superlative military qualities to him. Expediency prevailed even where the impression of Washington's martial ability did not convince some of the members that he was preeminently the man to head the Army. Within a few hours after Adams spoke, the opposition to Washington evaporated.

When the discussion was resumed on June 15, everything pointed to the selection of Washington. He stayed away and knew nothing of the deliberations until, about dinner time, the Delegates left the hall and, as they met him, greeted him as "General," and told him how, when the Committee of the Whole finished its debate and went through the formality of reporting, Congress resolved "that a General be appointed to command all the continental forces, raised, or to be raised, for the defence of American liberty." Then Thomas Johnson of Maryland rose and proposed Washington. No other name was put forward; election was unanimous; adjournment followed almost immediately.

Washington was overwhelmed, but he did not have time to think at length of the immense task he had taken upon himself. He had to attend a meeting of the committee to draft regulations for the government of the Army. Opportunity had to be found, also, for the preparation of a reply to the formal notification he was to expect the next day. In this he had the aid of Pendleton, but he doubtless specified that Pendleton make it plain he did not seek the command and did not feel qualified for it. Washington wanted it understood, also, that he did not accept the position for the pay of five hundred dollars a month that Congress had attached. Were he to take the salary, critics would say he wanted to make money rather than to serve his country. If he waived all pay and failed later, he could not be accused of having acted from mercenary motives, and, if he won, he would have the warmer praise and gratitude because he had no monetary compensation.

The next day Hancock had recovered somewhat from his disappointment over failure to receive the command, and he solemnly began: The President had the order of Congress to inform George Washington, Esq., of the unanimous vote in choosing him to be General and Commander-in-Chief of the forces raised and to be raised in defence of American liberty. The Congress hoped the gentleman would accept. Washington bowed, took out the paper and read his acceptance.

Congress agreed to name a committee to draft a commission and formal instructions for the General and then, after some discussion of Indian relations in New York, decided that it later would choose two major generals, five brigadiers and various staff officers whose pay was fixed forthwith. The next day, Washington's commission was reported by the committee—Richard Henry Lee, Edward Rutledge and John Adams. The paper ran in the name of "The Delegates of the United Colonies," each of which was specified. It proceeded to assign him the command of all the forces for the defence of American liberty and for repelling invasion; "and you are hereby vested with full power and authority to act as you shall think for the good and welfare of the service." Obedience and diligence were enjoined on Washington's subordinates; he was himself exhorted to "cause discipline and order to be observed in the army," to see that the soldiers were exercised, and to provide them "with all convenient necessities." When Congress approved this document, the members unanimously declared that "they [would] maintain and assist him, and adhere to him, the said George Washington, Esq., with their lives and fortunes in the same cause." All this was as well done as the members knew how to do it and it could not be otherwise than acceptable to Washington. If his experience as a soldier made him realize that it would be difficult for a committee of Congress to direct a military campaign, his common sense told him there was at the time no source of authority other than Congress, which had to act through committees. In the best of circumstances, with the wisest of committees, the morrow of the contingency of war would be dark, dark, dark! Washington knew that and he agonized over it. As he talked with Patrick Henry of his lack of training, the new General had tears in his eyes. "Remember, Mr. Henry," he said, "what I now tell you: from the day I enter upon the command of the American armies, I date my fall, and the ruin of my reputation."

The next action of Congress was the choice of the two major generals, who were to be Washington's senior subordinates, and of an adjutant general, who would keep the headquarters records and perform minor executive duties for the Commander-in-Chief. Washington resolved that he would use his influence to procure the election of some, at least, of those on whose military qualities he had to depend. In the initial selection he could not intervene. The Eastern Colonies expected the General who held Boston Neck to receive immediate recognition. The ballot of Congress for "first Major General" consequently was in favor of Artemas Ward. Next chosen was the Adjutant General, who was voted the rank of Brigadier. This was Major Horatio Gates, whose name almost certainly had been put forward by Washington. The second Major General elected by Congress was another man Washington recommended—Charles Lee, who had made already a favorable impression on some Congressmen by his manifest knowledge of European affairs and by his confident familiarity with military organization.

These long proceedings were on Saturday, June 17, the last day of the most fateful week in Washington's forty-three years. That evening Washington could survey the outlines of a task that would appal any man. Staff, command, army, equipment, supplies—all these had to be created from nothing! Washington was not feigning modesty when he told Congress his "abilities and military experience [might] not be equal to the extensive and important trust" the members put in his hands.

"Extensive" was about the most conservative word he could use to describe a task for the performance of which he had certain qualifications of experience and still greater equipment of character. Youthful experience had been ripened by the reflection of a maturing mind. He believed as firmly as ever that "discipline is the soul of an army" and that the first reliance of a commander had to be on well-trained troops.

As Washington undertook to begin anew on a larger scale where he had left off as temporary Brigadier, he did not have to adjust himself to changed tactics. Armies fought as they had when Washington took off his uniform at the end of 1758, but this persistence of a tactical system gave less of reassurance to the new Commander-in-Chief than might be assumed, because his scanty combat experience had been in woodland warfare. Washington's other apparent military deficiencies in 1775 included almost complete lack of training in the formulation and subsequent practical test of strategical plans of any magnitude. Fundamentally, his chief experiential weakness was in scale. He who had operated a regiment on a frontier was now, after sixteen years, to direct an army on a continent.

Some of his colleagues in Congress believed he would win the gamble because they credited the myths that had grown up concerning his early exploits, the magnitude of his acquisitions and the valor of his Virginia troops of the 1750's. This, of course, had the fragility of "the bubble reputation" but at the moment it was an advantage to Washington in assuring the support of a Congress on whom he would be dependent. It was an advantage increased by the fact that he looked the part of a soldier. Everything about him suggested the commander—height, bearing, flawless proportions, dignity of person, composure, and ability to create confidence by calmness and by unfailing, courteous dignity.

Discerning members of Congress had additional ground for believing that Washington would win the gamble with fate and with the circumstance of war, because they had observed how wisely he described in committee and in private the military pitfalls America must avoid and the hard road she must travel. In dealing with Congressmen and in winning their support, Washington's experience as a member of the Virginia House of Burgesses was of value beyond calculation. Nothing he possessed, save integrity, helped him so much, from his very first day of command, as his sure and intimate knowledge of the workings of the legislative mind. Now that he had met and conversed with some of the best men of every Colony, he was able to understand their problems and those of America. His horizon never had been provincial but it had been regional. Service in two Congresses had made it continental.

In the matter of equipment for his task, Washington had acquired, also, at least something of most forms of honest and useful experience that America had to offer in farming, manufacturing, shipping, frontier development, lay service on the bench, foreign purchasing, finance and exchange. Caution and daring were close to a balance in his mind. Deliberately, coldly bold, he was patient in waiting for an advantageous opening and wary until he found it. Along with daring, he had developed skill in adapting and improvising. He had shown ingenuity during the French and Indian War in employing feeble materials, human and man-made, to create and equip a regiment. After the war he had learned additional homely lessons in utilizing what he could get, instead of what he desired, and in making shift where he lacked a machine. Washington's large experience in the subsistence of slaves would be of use in the commissariat. He would find for his troops the best food he could; but if gaunt hunger threatened, he knew on what simple rations, and of what kind, men might keep their health.

Admirable as was this equipment, unique as it perhaps was among Americans who lived in a simple, essentially agrarian society, it did not give Washington conceit, arrogance or overconfidence. Always he kept his head. Careful in what he said before strangers, he was candid among friends and as modest in manner as he was just in judgment. In his undeviating adherence to what he called "principles," Washington had not changed from 1755 to 1775. The same was true of his conception of duty. Although he now was acquiring a nascent taste for humor, he still was too sparing with the tonic of laughter. Fear of censure continued. In most qualities of mind and spirit the Washington who put on his shoulders the heavy burden of continental defence in 1775 was different from the young officer who had ridden eastward from Fort Pitt in December 1758. Many men mature after twenty-five; Washington was almost transformed. The goodness of youth had not perished in manhood; modest characteristics had grown into positive virtues. The surest evidence of this was in his attitude toward money. He had not lost his acquisitiveness and was as stiff as ever in his dealings with overseers, tenants and tradesmen. If any man flattered himself that he could cheat Colonel Washington, let him beware! In all other transactions, Washington was increasingly disposed to think of the other party. Assured position, broadened sympathy and the financial ease that had come through his marriage to Martha—the most influential single event of the sixteen years after 1758—multiplied his benefactions.

Washington was far simpler in character, and clearer in his sense of values. In 1755 there had been the most careful weighing of advantage against disadvantage, cost against "honor." Now he did not seem to be thinking always of his own advancement or of public approval. Still deeper, Washington was distinctly more religious than in the days of the French and Indian War, and he was more frequently mindful of Providence, though he still was puzzled to distinguish Providence from destiny. His sensitiveness was as sharply painful as ever, but he was capable now of combatting every expression of it—not because he was callous but because he soon learned that he had to endure hurt lest he hurt his cause. High among his qualifications for command were spiritual attributes that some might have accounted weaknesses—patience, pity, understanding of the shortcomings of men. Washington did not realize and could not gauge at the time the extent to which his judgment had matured. The utmost that could be affirmed on this score was negative; he had not come to any blank wall of reasoning or of judgment beyond which he knew, in his heart of hearts, that he could not penetrate.

His dignity was innate; his calm was in part deliberate and in some degree the unconscious expression of his sense of rectitude. Goodwill begat amiability that shone in his countenance. The habit of command did not mar the benevolence of his visage. Although there was as yet no marked restraint in his mien, his continuing lack of facility of speech disposed him to be cautious in expressing himself outside the circle of friends who would not abuse confidence. This wariness might become reserve that would give a certain frigidity to his address. Apart from this possibility that his native kindliness might be covered with ice, his unfailing good manners were consonant with his appearance as Commander-in-Chief.

If, then, the balance of circumstance was against Washington, because the visible resources of America were not comparable to those of Britain, the balance of personal character and qualification was indisputably favorable to him. The final casting of the fateful account could not be that simple. To what extent did he possess two of the supreme qualities demanded of the man who was to head so small and feeble an army as his country would put into the field? If he and his colleagues were justified in expecting that a single campaign would end in reconciliation or accommodation, the question might not be one on which the fate of a continent hung, but if a long war lay ahead, those two special virtues must be displayed by a General dutiful to the Philadelphia Congress and in command of soldiers of such temper as could be brought into Colonial ranks. He would need many elements of strength but, most of all, patience and determination, inexhaustible and inextinguishable. Did Washington have as much patience as he now might be called upon to display? Would pride outride patience, or would he be able to endure cowardice, quarrelsome rivalries and the hideous greed of a continental struggle? Men would have credited him with steadfastness of a sort to be admired if the end of man was honest self-advancement; but there had been no special evidence of any dedication of spirit, except as Washington had adhered unflinchingly to the cause of American liberty regardless of the effect on his private estate. Did he have the high order of determination that could be combined with his patience in self-effacing leadership of a desperate cause in its most desperate hour?

Before he would be called upon to face any part of that test he wrote to acquaint Martha with his decision and to ease as much as he could the emotion he knew his letter would stir. In the same spirit he wrote Jack Custis and confessed to "very anxious feelings" on account of the boy's mother. Short of issuing a direct parental command, Washington said everything he could to induce the young Custises to reside at Mount Vernon in his absence.

CHAPTER / 9

When the Delegates came together June 19 they proceeded to put into effect some political agreements that had been reached over the weekend. A commission as Major General was voted Delegate Philip Schuyler, a New York landed proprietor and man of business who had seen service in the war of 1754–63 and had been active in the Colonial cause—in many respects the northern counterpart of Washington. The other command as Major General was awarded to Israel Putnam of Connecticut, a picturesque, little-schooled representative of the New England small farmers who were rallying to the Colonial cause.

When Washington had been assigned these principal lieutenants, he received instructions to cover his journey to Massachusetts, his assumption of command, his discretionary powers, and the steps he should take to organize, recruit and supply the Army. He was authorized to make brevet appointments of colonels and of officers below that rank until vacancies were filled by the Colony from which the troops and their commanders came. June 21 witnessed the choice of eight Brigadier Generals. Three of these were from Massachusetts, Seth Pomeroy, William Heath and John Thomas, and two from Connecticut, David Wooster and Joseph Spencer. New Hampshire was honored by the commissioning of John Sullivan; Rhode Island was credited with Nathanael Greene. An Irish resident of New York, Richard Montgomery, completed the list. Washington's sense of justice made him wait hopefully to see what qualities these men possessed. By his restrained attitude towards this delicate business of appointments and by his other dealings with Congress, he increased as a General the good opinion he had won as a Delegate. Once the members had made him their choice, they instinctively became his champion in order to justify themselves. Thus did Washington have the initial advantage, if no more than that, on the fields in front of Boston to which he had now to proceed. Two able young Philadelphians, Thomas Mifflin and Joseph Reed, agreed to go with him temporarily as members of his staff. Charles Lee and Schuyler were making ready to depart on the twenty-third with their Commander-in-Chief. Soon Washington completed his meetings with Congress or its committees on the compelling questions that had to be settled before his departure. Neither he nor the New England leaders felt he could wait in Philadelphia to deal directly with small issues when his presence with the troops in Massachusetts was required.

It was an interesting cavalcade. Washington's immediate attendants, Mifflin and Reed, were attractive young men of charming manners. Reed, thirty-four, was of distinguished courtesy and accustomed to dealing with men in high station. Because he had seen something of the world and was a skillful writer as well as a man of high intelligence, Washington was gratified to have him as military secretary and as a conspicuous member of the Headquarters "family." This was true, also, of Mifflin, who was ranked as aide-de-camp. Mifflin had wealth, position and much felicity in speechmaking. Lee and Schuyler had training to complement his own as a soldier and as a purveyor to the needs of fighting men in the field. The escort of some of the foremost young men of the Quaker City, the detachment of the Philadelphia Light Horse under Captain Markoe, seemed altogether appropriate.

A committee of the New York Provincial Congress met them at Newark during the forenoon of the twenty-fifth and announced among other things, that Gov. William Tryon, an uncompromising Loyalist, was returning to New York and had sent word that he would disembark that day. The King's Governor and the Congress' General to land in the divided town the same day—the oddness of it had humor and presented manifest danger. It was not a pleasing prospect but certainly not one over which Washington would hesitate. Washington and his cavalcade made their way to the ferry. For his first appearance in New York as American Commander-in-Chief, Washington put on a new purple sash with his blue uniform, and laid aside his travel hat for one that bore a fine plume. Philadelphia's generous reception and grateful farewell were small affairs when set against this welcome that awaited him and Lee and Schuyler.

It was about four o'clock Sunday afternoon that Washington stepped ashore, shook hands with the officials and acknowledged the huzzas. He proceeded from the landing and, after more introductions, accepted Col. Leonard Lispenard's invitation to dinner. Something besides savory viands awaited him. Excited members of the Provincial Congress told him that an express had arrived with a number of papers, among which was a letter to the President of the Continental Congress from the corresponding body in Massachusetts. It doubtless contained news of the battle of Bunker Hill, of which Washington had heard a sketchy account before leaving Philadelphia. Washington hesitated to break the seal of a communication addressed to the presiding officer of the body to which he was responsible, but the paper might contain facts that would be of value on the journey ahead of him. Reluctantly he took the letter from the express. The battle of the seventeenth was described in some detail. The number of Americans killed and missing was supposed to be about sixty or seventy, and the former President of the Provincial Congress, Dr. Joseph Warren, was among the victims. One report put casualties among the ministerial troops at one thousand, "but," said the Massachusetts legislators honestly, "this account exceeds every other estimation." Washington knew that casualty lists usually are to be corrected by adding to one's own losses and subtracting from those of the enemy; but even if the final figures were half as favorable as the first estimates, Americans could stand up against British regulars. An ominous note followed the report of the battle: "As soon as an estimate can be made of public and private stocks of gunpowder in this Colony, it shall be transmitted without delay, which we are well assured will be small, and by no means adequate to the exigence of our case." Powder shortage! It had been known, deplored and discussed in Philadelphia, but it had not been relieved and now was a threat to the defence of an army which had earned by its valor the right to protect itself and the Colonial cause.

Washington's sense of duty prompted him to spur on towards Boston, but at the moment he had to consider the instructions he was to give Schuyler, for that officer was to remain as commander in New York. Washington requested Schuyler to report to Congress and to him as frequently as developments required. Orders could not be explicit or restrictive: "Your own good sense must govern in all matters not particularly pointed out," Washington said, "as I do not wish to circumscribe you within narrow limits." In his first orders Washington thus abdicated the right of a Commander-in-Chief to have every decision of importance made at his Headquarters. Distance itself vested discretion. Schuyler could operate independently when, in his judgment, such a course was expedient. Washington would advise and perhaps could supervise; he could not direct or administer, and he neither would try nor would pretend to do so.

The next morning Washington was told that William Morris and Isaac Low wished, on behalf of the Provincial Congress, to present him an address. The General was anxious to start for Boston, but he could not decline this civility. Meantime, he directed his companions to have everything ready for departure as soon as the ceremonies were concluded. At the designated hour the members of the Congress waited on him with an address diplomatically fashioned to attest their devotion to the continental cause without giving unendurable offence to those who feared military rule in America and still hoped for reconciliation with England. Washington had his answer ready. His reply included a note of clear simplicity that reassured: "When we assumed the soldier we did not lay aside the citizen." The words, widely circulated, came to represent Washington in the eyes of many Americans.

Washington's whole impulse was to put on to Boston. Boston was "the front," Boston the place where, if anywhere, success might produce an honorable settlement, without the acute agony and ruinous cost of a long struggle. Even if that contest was unavoidable, the camps around Boston must be the training school of victory. The sooner the start, the earlier the ending.

The ride to Springfield June 30 put Washington in touch for the first time with men who were sharing as Massachusetts legislators in the contest with the British in Boston. Dr. Benjamin Church and Moses Gill presented themselves as a committee named by the Provincial Congress of Massachusetts to receive the Generals "with every mark of respect due to their exalted characters and stations." These hosts explained that the Massachusetts Congress had directed that gentlemen of the larger towns on the road to Cambridge serve as an escort to the new Commander-in-Chief and his second. That prospect was equivalent to lengthening the highway to the besieged city, but there was no avoiding what manifestly was meant to be honor and courtesy.

With Church and Gill and a number of the leading men of Springfield, Washington rode July 1 to Brookfield, where his escort was changed, and thence to Worcester, where the same thing happened. From Worcester the next stage was to Marlborough. July 2 he covered early the distance to Watertown. The Provincial Congress was holding its sessions there and the week previously had named a committee to prepare for the reception of the General. At the head of the committee was the President of the body, James Warren. The entire Congress gave him a grateful welcome and presented him an address that was cordial in spirit and honest in warning the General he would not find "such regularity and discipline" in the Army as he might expect.

Then Washington was able to start on the last stretch of his journey, the three miles to Cambridge. There he was conducted to the residence of Pres. Samuel Langdon of Harvard where, he was advised, the Massachusetts Provincial Congress had given orders that he and General Lee were to have all the rooms, except one allotted Langdon. Washington met the officers who already had assembled or who called as soon as they heard of his arrival. Conspicuous among them was Artemas Ward, in general command. Another was Israel Putnam. As Putnam had been the choice of Congress for one of the commissions as Major General, Washington thought it appropriate to hand him the formal paper that attested his rank. Some incident of the meeting brought Washington a first, unpleasant surprise: It was manifest that the seniority prescribed by Congress for the New England Generals did not accord with the opinion the leaders had formed of the relative merits of those commanders. Soon he learned that Seth Pomeroy, for whom he had a brigadier's commission, had left the Army because of disappointment. Another new Brigadier, Joseph Spencer, was said to be angry because Putnam, whom he had outranked in the service of Connecticut, had been given a higher continental commission. This was not the last or the most embarrassing case. Dr. John Thomas was regarded as one of the best officers of Massachusetts, but in ignorance of existing seniority Congress had made him a Brigadier and had listed him as junior to William Heath and Pomeroy, both of whom he had outranked in Massachusetts service. Washington was immediately on the alert. Quarrels must not divide the leadership of the Army on which the vindication of the Colonial cause depended.

Washington rode out in the company of Putnam, Lee and other officers in the afternoon for a view of the fortifications. In a short time the horsemen covered the three-quarters of a mile to Prospect Hill. Washington had almost immediately in front of him at a little more than a quarter of a mile an excellent gun position his guides called Cobble Hill. Across a wide millpond was Bunker Hill where he could see British sentinels. Below their post and under Breed's Hill were the ruins of Charlestown, which had been set afire and almost consumed in the fighting of June 17. The entire Charlestown Peninsula was British ground, isolated and easily defended, except perhaps against night raids by men in boats. Southeastward he could see a considerable part of Boston, distant about two miles. Beyond Boston, in the fine harbor, were the ships of the British fleet. The waters in which the vessels were riding could be swept by the naval guns. Two miles and a

MAP / 7

BOSTON, 1775–1776

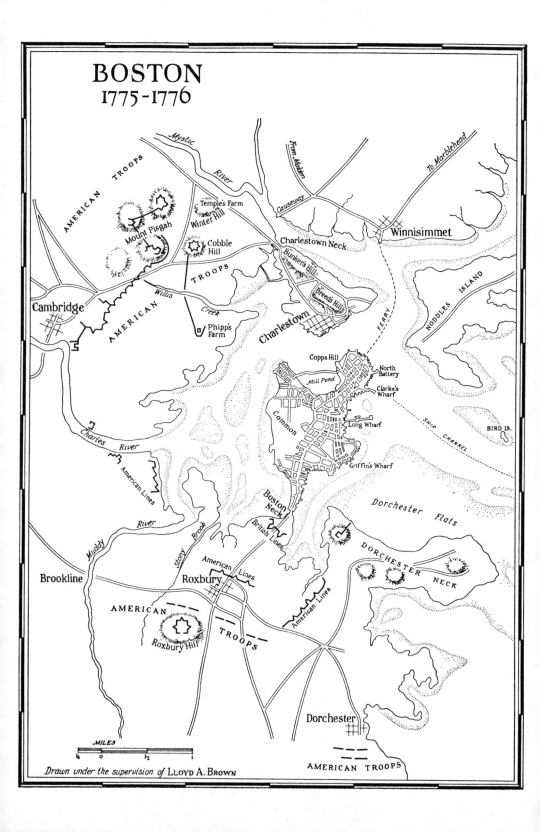

BOSTON
1775-1776

Mystic

River

From Malden

To Marblehead

AMERICAN TROOPS

Temples Farm

Winter Hill

Causeway

Mount Pisgah

Cobble Hill

Charlestown Neck

Winnisimmet

Bunker's Hill

AMERICAN TROOPS

Willis

Breed's Hill

FERRY

NODDLES ISLAND

Cambridge

Creek

Phipp's Farm

AMERICAN

Charlestown

Copps Hill

North Battery

Charles River

Mill Pond

Clarke's Wharf

SHIP CHANNEL

BIRD IS.

Common

Long Wharf

American Lines

Muddy River

Stony Brook

Boston Neck

British Lines

Griffin's Wharf

Dorchester Flats

Brookline

Roxbury

American Lines

DORCHESTER NECK

AMERICAN TROOPS

Roxbury Hill

American Lines

Dorchester

MILES

¼ 0 ½ 1

Drawn under the supervision of LLOYD A. BROWN

AMERICAN TROOPS

half from the eastern rim of Boston, Castle Island had its armament and its garrison. Thus land and harbor were commanded by the King's long arm, his cannon. Washington saw at a glance that the redoubts prepared by the Americans were feeble and in several instances badly placed, but he could observe, also, that some of the positions were strong naturally. With vigor and good engineering, he could hope to confine the British to Boston and the hills above Charlestown. By choosing advantageous ground for batteries he might discourage landings from the fleet. Together, these possibilities shaped his first mission: He must bottle up the British while he trained his Army.

Transfer of command by Ward on July 3 was more or less formal, but did not impress itself on witnesses as ceremonious. Morning General Orders, the first issued by Washington, included a call for a "return" of the troops to ascertain immediately the number of men under his direct command and the strength of the different regiments. Along with their returns, the colonels were to file a statement of the ammunition in the hands of their men. To Washington's annoyance he found that the returns could not be supplied that day, but he had a satisfying report on powder: The store was 308 barrels, or roughly sixteen tons. For the moment, as the shortage of powder would not be serious, Washington could devote his energies primarily to strengthening the fortifications. Not a day must be lost in making the defences as nearly impregnable as they could be in the hands of inexperienced troops.

Washington rode over the ground, examined the works, and had his first glance at the Colonial troops around Roxbury, two Connecticut and nine Massachusetts Regiments. The discipline of none of these was good, by professional standards. Arms were poor and of every age and type; many men were almost naked because they had lost their clothing at Bunker Hill and had not received that which the Provincial Congress had voted them. Many officers did not know their duties or how to do them. Washington was tolerant and was resolved to be patient because he knew the human material out of which the Army and its command had to be created.

Washington took up his administrative duties vigorously and with his usual regard for detail. Warren and Joseph Hawley, leading members of the Massachusetts Provincial Congress, believed they had found a way of righting the wrong they thought Congress had done General Thomas when the Philadelphia lawmakers had put Pomeroy and Heath ahead of Thomas in continental service. The inactive Pomeroy was a hundred miles away. If the Commander-in-Chief found it consistent with his instructions to withhold Pomeroy's commission until he could hear from Congress, they would try to prevail on Heath to acquiesce in the restoration of Thomas's seniority. Washington had no objection to this and realized that it would be desirable to give seniority to Thomas if that officer was as good as Massachusetts leaders said he was.

This affair out of his way, Washington could devote himself to fundamental needs of the Army that were plainer every day, secure fortification, accurate intelligence, the discipline of understanding minds and the strength of good organization. Cover and training both might soon be im-

perative, because Gen. Thomas Gage's men gave every indication of a purpose to attack somewhere on the American defences. Washington had first to
build up his Army defensively but he saw at the same time an opportunity
of using his extended works as a cordon to intercept the supply of the
British in Boston from the surrounding country. If the summer's campaign
would end the war, then he had no greater duty than that of confining the
British, hungry and helpless, in Boston.

Discipline, order and sound organization could not wait on the raising of parapets to the required height. Washington set out to train the
troops to make their numbers count to the fullest. During the first days that
fortification and discipline were being improved, Washington was calling
for returns of the strength of the Army. He was told that from 18,000 to
20,000 men were on the lines, but nobody could speak with certainty. He
fretted over the delay in compiling figures he thought every regimental
commander would have had at hand. As delivered on July 9, the returns
were alarming. Washington found only about 16,600 enlisted men and
NCOs, of whom the rank and file, present for duty, fit, numbered 13,743
foot. The artillery were listed as 585.

Effective strength was so much below estimates that it raised immediately a question larger than any that Washington ever had been called upon
to answer: Should these half-trained and poorly disciplined Colonials attempt to continue the siege and to invite attack, or for safety's sake should
they retire beyond the range of the British heavy guns? Washington determined immediately to refer it to a council of war and, regardless of his
Generals' advice on the question of siege or withdrawal, to proceed at once,
by every legitimate means, to get more men into the Army. The answer of
the council was that the Army must continue the siege, and must offer the
sternest resistance it could in event the British made a sally.

If the Army was to stand in front of Boston, it must stand on the
A-B-Cs of war: it must be thoroughly disiplined, well organized, ceaselessly
vigilant and numerically stronger. To this basic policy, after the council of
war, Washington returned even more positively than ever. He stressed it in
his initial dispatch to the President of Congress. The one cheerful passage in
a realistic report was that "there are materials for a good army, a great
number of men able bodied, active, zealous in the cause and of unquestionable courage." At Headquarters there were other encouraging conditions.
Gates assumed his duties as Adjutant General, greatly to the relief of Washington. When the Massachusetts Provincial Congress learned that the President's house at Harvard was not altogether adequate as Headquarters, it
directed the Committee of Safety to place at Washington's disposal and at
Lee's any other dwelling that suited them. As a result, the two Generals
transferred Headquarters to the house of John Vassall, who had gone to
Boston when the Colonials occupied Cambridge.

Another encouragement was a new turn in the case of General
Spencer. After that Connecticut commander had taken offence at the appointment of Putnam over him, he had left his quarters on July 6 without
leave from the new Commander-in-Chief, and he either inspired or else said
nothing to prevent a written protest on July 5 by forty-nine of his officers.

The effect was to bring Spencer into general disfavor. In the end, he had the good sense to swallow his pride and return on July 18, at the rank assigned him by the Continental Congress. This relieved Washington of a delicate situation which he had not created and could not himself correct. Wooster's discontent persisted; Pomeroy might perhaps be disregarded; if Thomas could be reconciled to the rank given him or could be made the senior Brigadier, then jealousies of this nature might cease for the time to threaten the cause of the Colonies. Washington deferred action temporarily, but Congress promptly voted to make Thomas senior Brigadier, vice Pomeroy. To remove all ground of future difference, the Delegates stipulated that Thomas's commission bear the same date as Pomeroy's. If this displeased Heath, he made no formal protest and by his silence let the controversy end. Washington could mark off his list of difficulties the "great dissatisfaction" with the appointments of general officers. Not till this was past did he admit the full seriousness of the danger he thought the controversy carried. Then he confided to Philip Schuyler that because of the incompetence and clashes among the officers, "confusion and disorder reigned in every department, which in a little time must have ended either in the separation of the army or fatal contests with one another."

Washington proceeded to battle with mounting duties and, in particular, to execute a plan for dividing the Army into three "Grand Divisions" of two brigades each. Ward was named to command the right, with the brigades of Thomas and Spencer. The central Grand Division, lacking as yet an organized second brigade, was to be Putnam's. Its existing brigade, in which Putnam had been ranking officer, was entrusted to its senior colonel. On the left were the brigades of Sullivan and Greene, with Lee in general command. A Judge Advocate General was named to organize the work of the military courts; similarly, a Commissary General was appointed in the person of Joseph Trumbull. Many articles required for the camps would be crude, and some were unprocurable in a region deprived of imports; but Washington found he could count on everything the New England Colonies could supply.

Abatement of jealousies over rank, first steps in organization and discipline, the progress of fortification, the support of the New England Colonies—all these were facilitated by hearty acceptance of Washington as a man of character and a leader of judgment and resolution. In the Bay Colony as in Pennsylvania, he was credited with so great a fortune that his willingness to risk it in the Colonial cause bred confidence in him. Henry Knox told his wife: "General Washington fills his place with vast ease and dignity, and dispenses happiness around him." Abigail Adams assured her husband: "You had prepared me to entertain a favorable opinion of General Washington, but I thought the half was not told me. Dignity with ease and complacency, the gentleman and soldier, look agreeably blended in him. Modesty marks every line and feature of his face."

Washington was fortunate, more than fortunate, in his adversary. Bunker Hill had shaken both the strength and the confidence of the British. Although some of the officers around Charlestown expressed special confidence in Gen. William Howe, they had respect for American marksmanship and resentment of the Colonials' vigilance. The British delayed the attack Washington expected. On July 8 some of General Thomas's men surprised the guard at an advanced post on the Roxbury line and destroyed the dwelling and barn there. On the twenty-fifth three men-of-war and six transports sailed out of Boston and disappeared on a raid on the smaller islands of Long Island Sound.

Indications multiplied that the enemy might be preparing to break the siege. On the night of the twenty-ninth, two patrols were sent out to capture a prisoner and ascertain what was happening at Charlestown. The patrols crept forward and were about to join forces when they ran into the British relief guard and had an exchange of fire. Two British prisoners were taken without loss. This brush led to scattered fire along the line and two small actions. On the thirtieth, the British demonstrated on Boston Neck and west of Bunker Hill. Late in the night of July 30/31, a British party advanced towards Roxbury but failed to gain surprise because a deserter had slipped ahead and given warning. An American force of three hundred landed that same night on the island where the British were repairing the Light House. The object was to stop the work and capture the carpenters and a guard of thirty-two marines under a subaltern. American success was complete.

These activities might forecast major attack. The American commander knew that a fleet of transports had brought reenforcements to Boston, and he had learned that these consisted of four regiments, "a miserable relief," as one British officer put it. Washington's estimate of the total strength of the British was 10,000 to 12,000, admirably equipped in every particular, with good artillery. The effectiveness of this force was increased vastly by its ability to concentrate at almost any point in superior numbers.

Washington never let himself forget that British advantage. He increasingly suspected that the British would begin heavy bombardment of the American lines in the hope of driving the troops from them. He scarcely could hope to answer this fire because he did not have the powder for such an exchange, even though nothing had occurred during July to reduce materially the stock of 308 barrels he had been told was in store. In any event, cartridges must be issued the men. As the continental stock amounted to 35,000 only, appeal was made forthwith to the Massachusetts authorities to furnish the remainder from their store. Elbridge Gerry replied that the supply of the Bay Colony amounted to no more than thirty-six barrels of powder. Thirty-six barrels? Impossible. What did the troops of the other Colonies have? Their total was about fifty-four barrels. Thirty-six and fifty-four—ninety barrels or 9900 pounds. Was that all? Absolutely! When the return had been made after Washington's arrival, the men who gave the General the figure of 308 barrels had included all the powder that had been collected—what had been fired as well as what remained. If the British attacked, the Army had barely powder enough to issue each man nine cartridges. One brisk action might render the Army defenceless: it must not be!

The next day brought reports that eighty thousand flints and eight tons of lead were in transit to the Army and that "fifteen hogsheads of powder" had been received in New York and would be reported to the Commander-in-Chief; but "reports" were one thing and deliveries quite another. Washington had to be miserly with every grain of explosive the Army possessed, and he had to call for every pound left in New England, without being at liberty to tell the people how overwhelming was the need. Unless there was the tightest secrecy, the British would hear of the Colonials' plight. Faced with that prospect the Army must stop wasting cartridges. Every man's ammunition was to be examined at evening roll call. Those soldiers who were short of their allotment were to be confined. The Governors must be acquainted with the essentials. The next step was to report the stark danger to the President of the Continental Congress. This was done as briefly as might be, with the stern conclusion: "I need not enlarge on our melancholy situation. It is sufficient to say that the existence of the Army and salvation of the country depends upon something being done for our relief both speedy and effectual and that our situation be kept a profound secret."

How could desperate danger be abated? Within approximately a week after the discovery of the critical shortage, Washington received an answer of unexpected nature: From Philadelphia under date of August 1, Richard Henry Lee wrote that Congress had adjourned for approximately a month. "The capital object of powder," Lee said, "we have attended to as far as we could by sending you the other day six tons, and tomorrow we shall propose sending you six or eight tons more, which, with the supplies you may get from Connecticut, and such further ones from here, as future expected importations may furnish, will I hope enable you to do all that this powerful article can in good hands accomplish."

Arrival of this supply before an attack by the British would give the Continentals a fighting chance. The odds against the Army no longer would be hopeless. Eagerly Washington traced the progress of the wagons with the powder and learned that if all went well, they would draw up in his camp on the sixteenth. The promised supply would not give the Army more than 184 barrels, or a bare thirty cartridges per man; but that would be a condition at least three times better than the one that had existed. It would raise the spirits of the men, too. Besides, the arrival of the powder would be heartening proof that Congress had been mindful of the Army and energetic in seeking supplies.

Congress was not the only contributor to the magazines. The powder it collected in Philadelphia was supplemented by lead that Schuyler, on order, forwarded from Ticonderoga. Gov. Nicholas Cooke, of Rhode Island, likewise purchased for the army seven thousand pounds of powder, seventy hundredweight of lead and five hundred stand of arms. Soon two additional tons of powder were sent from Philadelphia. Gradually the situation was being changed to the extent that instead of dreading an attack, Washington was to lament the fact that his supply still did not suffice for him to take full advantage of his positions.

Washington still hoped against hope that the war would be concluded in 1775 and that peace would be restored. What he could not understand was why the British withheld the blow that might decide the campaign. Was Gage preparing by regular approaches to force the Americans from their lines; or were the British counting winter as an ally before whose blasts the Army would scatter? Could there be truth to the rumor that the King's men would use their seapower and transfer the war to New York, where the waters of the Hudson and the northern lakes might give them contact with their comrades in Canada?

For such light as could be shed on these questions, Washington undertook to develop a rough-and-ready intelligence system that had been established before his arrival. Chelsea, north of the approaches to Boston harbor, was an ideal place from which to observe movements of British shipping. After Washington's coming, Col. Loammi Baldwin was made responsible there and at Malden for daily intelligence reports. Besides the results of Baldwin's observation, much of fact and more of rumor was supplied at Chelsea, in Cambridge and at Roxbury by Boston residents who were passed through the lines in spite of orders to the contrary. Almost a full history of what happened in the city could be pieced together, in time, from questioning those General Gage authorized to leave the town in order to reduce the consumption of food there. Of the deserters, another traditional and unreliable source of intelligence, a few knew much; others knew or would tell nothing.

Washington steadfastly refused to detach any large part of his Army to serve as garrison or combat raids, even though he told himself that he would "be accused of inattention to the public service and perhaps with want of spirit to prosecute it." He continued securing his positions and improving his organization and discipline. It was not enough to be safe against attack; he must place his guns where he could answer the enemy's bombardment as soon as he had the powder with which to do so.

On the northwestern flank of the American lines was an eminence known as Plowed Hill. This elevation did not obstruct in the least the American fire from Prospect Hill or that of the British from Bunker Hill, but there were rumors that the British intended to seize it in order to command the low ground between that eminence and Bunker Hill. It was ground worth fighting for. Washington resolved to seize and fortify it. Colonial troops moved out to Plowed Hill on the night of August 26 and threw up so much earth that when daylight came they had cover against enemy fire. The British cannon slumbered until 9 A.M. but when they did wake up, they barked all day, though with little hurt to the Americans. For making the fortifications proof against this fire, Charles Lee was given credit. Washington was pleased and at the same time was distressed because he could not expend the powder required to answer the British effectively.

Organization must progress along with fortification while Washington waited either for the enemy to attack or for the coming of powder with which to seize the initiative. The commissioning of Thomas as senior Brigadier on the Boston front and the return of General Spencer had put an end, apparently, to what one officer described as "uneasiness in camp." Further down the scale of rank, men had been granted Continental commissions without inquiry into their fitness. Washington had to deal vigorously with the inevitable result of this bad system and, in particular, with the inertia of ignorance. One remedy, he thought, was in naming officers from other Colonies, now that the Army was continental. A second means of improving the quality of officers was for Congress to keep open a number of commissions as rewards of merit. Still another was that of setting an example of what an officer should be. On occasion, too, as when Col. William Woodford of Virginia wrote for his advice on the duties of an officer, Washington could put on paper some of the essentials of his code of command: "Be strict in your discipline; that is, to require nothing unreasonable of your officers and men, but see that whatever is required be punctually complied with. Reward and punish every man according to his merit, without partiality or prejudice; hear his complaints; if well founded, redress them; if otherwise, discourage them in order to prevent frivolous ones. Discourage vice in every shape, and impress upon the mind of every man, from the first to the lowest, the importance of the cause, and what it is they are contending for." In applying this to his immediate subordinates, Washington undertook to see that their rights were not disregarded, that their seniority was established and respected, and that they were treated as individuals and gentlemen. The rotating officer of the day, the officer of the guard and the adjutant of the day, no matter who they might be, had standing invitation to dine at Headquarters: Washington was resolved, having done what he could in ridding the officers' corps of cowards, rascals and incompetents, to acquaint himself thoroughly with the others and develop their good qualities.

Washington could not always find men equipped to fulfill the ideal he set before Colonel Woodford, but he selected them with care from the class he thought most conscious of obligation and best qualified to meet his special needs. He made Thomas Mifflin Quartermaster General with rank of Colonel; he approved the best brigade majors he could procure, and after a bit of finessing in avoiding political appointments, he named Edmund Randolph and George Baylor as aides. Both were Virginians and both of the upper stratum of the Colony's society.

While improving the organization of his officers during the time he was awaiting Gage's attack, Washington continued his efforts to make the troops comfortable and healthy and to better their discipline. This second task was rendered more difficult by the arrival in camp of rifle companies recruited in accordance with a resolution Congress adopted June 14. The idealized argument for companies of this type had been compressed by Richard Henry Lee into a few clauses when he wrote of these men's "amazing hardihood, their method of living so long in the woods without carrying provisions with them, the exceeding quickness with which they can march to distant parts and above all, the dexterity to which they have arrived in the use of the rifle gun." Lee added almost with awe: "There is not one of these men who wish a distance less than 200 yards or a larger object than an orange—Every shot is fatal." Washington wanted some of them; he probably did not desire too large a contingent. When they began to arrive late in July, everyone marvelled at the speed with which the men had enlisted, settled their affairs at home and covered on foot the hundreds of miles to Boston. The very first comers showed a marksmanship that taught the British to keep their heads below the nearer parapets, but the anticipated deficiency soon was apparent: These riflemen had no such word as "discipline" in their vocabulary. They saw one duty and one only; that was to kill the British. Whenever they saw a "Lobster," as the Americans now styled the Redcoat, they would take a shot at him even if he was within the very farthest range of their rifles. The result was much wastage of powder and no increase in British casualties.

There were many matters in which the members of his staff could be of service to the General. This was increasingly true of Reed, whom James Warren described as "a man of sense, politeness and abilities for business." Gates was similarly useful and soundly versed in military affairs. The Adjutant General was operating as smoothly as could be expected with men still inexperienced in military usages. The Army was improving. If it was not yet good, it was less bad by far than it was at the beginning of July. The General doubtless would have been reluctant to have his men attempt, as yet, to stand up against the British in the open field; but, assuming that powder and ball sufficed in quantity, he would not be afraid to meet a British attack—if only the British would come out and assault American positions.

That continuing uncertainty was worse than all the remaining woes and perplexities of the Army put together. Suppose Gage still refused to attack as autumn brought warning of the long months when sentries might freeze at their posts and the tents of the camp be deep in snow. Winter quarters would be required, and they would have to be built with much labor and cost. Besides, virtually all the enlistments had been to December 7 or to the end of 1775; what would happen then?

Whatever had to be done, Washington would do. If winter quarters had to be provided, all the buildings of Harvard College that could must be closed in; those officers who were erecting board-covered retreats must allow them to be occupied by as many persons as could be accommodated. The Commissary General must formulate plans for feeding the men.

Washington cast aside his theory that his strategical task simply was to confine the British to Boston. He reflected on the possibilities, deliberated with Massachusetts lawmakers and Congressional Delegates on vacation, and decided to undertake three things: First, now that he had stopped all deliveries to Boston by land, he would arm some coastal vessels and try to cut off the supplies that were reaching the British by sea. Second, he would attempt to give help to Schuyler, if the New York commander was able to formulate a plan for the early invasion of Canada. Third, he would himself deliver with his Army a direct attack of some sort on Boston.

The effort at sea had to be made with armed schooners by some of the numerous mariners in the regiments from the coastal towns. Nicholson Broughton was appointed Captain in the Army and was directed to proceed with the armed schooner *Hannah* to capture, if he could, any craft laden with men, arms, ammunition or provisions inward or outward bound from Boston.

Plans for a diversion in Canada were now considered. They had probably originated in reports that the British had few troops in the region wrested from France and that the native population was still hostile to the Redcoats. Washington learned that there was a route by which he could cooperate with Schuyler in attacking in Canada. The previous spring Col. Jonathan Brewer had offered to follow this trail and, if five hundred men were assigned him, make a demonstration against Quebec. His proposal was to move troops up the Kennebec River to a carrying place opposite a stretch of Dead River, then west on that stream to its headwaters near Lake Megantic and thence northward again down the Claudière to the St. Lawrence almost directly opposite Quebec. The advance up the Kennebec and down the Chaudière would force the British commander in Canada, Gen. Sir Guy Carleton, "either to break up and follow this party to Quebec," by which Carleton would leave Schuyler's approach on Montreal unopposed, or else to "suffer that important place, [Quebec] to fall into our hands, an event which would have a decisive effect and influence on the public interests." Washington regarded the detachment of a small column to Canada as a risk worth taking. The essentials were, first, to be certain Schuyler was going to advance in the general direction of Montreal; second, to procure the necessary batteaux for the ascent of the rivers; and, third, to find an able man to lead the expedition.

Washington lost no time in ascertaining whether General Schuyler intended to move north. He outlined the plan in an urgent letter of August 20, which he sent express to his New York comrade, and in it he admitted that much of success depended on the response of the Canadians themselves. Schuyler was prompt to reply. He expressed his agreement with Washington's proposals and gave assurance that Gen. Richard Montgomery was making ready to leave Ticonderoga for Canada. He would join his Brigadier at Crown Point, Schuyler said, but he would not have in the two columns more than 1700 men. These would be too few to employ against Quebec after necessary detachments had been left at the places he would undertake to seize. Then he said: "Should the detachment of your body penetrate into Canada, and we meet with success, Quebec must inevitably fall into our hands. Should we meet with a repulse, which can only happen from foul play in the Canadians, I shall have an opportunity to inform your party of it, that they may carry into execution any orders you may give, in case such an unfortunate event should arise."

Washington felt a measure of confidence about the enterprise, first, because he was reassured concerning the attitude of the Canadians and the Indians, second, because everyone said the route of the Kennebec-Claudière was practicable, and, third, because he believed the limitations of transport and supply could be overcome by the man he now selected to lead the expedition. This was Benedict Arnold. For his exploit in seizing Ticonderoga with Ethan Allen May 10, 1775, Arnold had received much applause and had proceeded to the head of Lake Champlain where he had destroyed Fort St. John. Then had followed an ugly succession of quarrels over command of a pitifully equipped little force to which four Colonies and the Continental Congress were contributing meagerly. Arnold had wished to attack Canada without delay, but his violence and the stubbornness of his rivals had paralyzed effort. At length, when he was told to recognize the seniority of his most persistent rival, Col. Benjamin Hinman, he resigned his Massachusetts command, dismissed his men and, before many weeks, appeared at Watertown for the settlement of his accounts. He had boldness, energy and ambition of a sort that would not permit him to be unoccupied in wartime and soon presented himself to Washington. Washington quickly saw that Arnold was furnished with much of the stuff that must be in a man called to head a swiftly moving expedition that was to fight water and wind and winter. Besides, as a trader, Arnold had been to Quebec and probably knew more about the town and the approaches to it than did any officer of Washington's immediate command. Arnold could get there! He must start his march before the summer slipped away.

Washington's discussions with Arnold and others led him to conclude that the force should consist of the equivalent of a battalion, and that three companies of riflemen should be provided—roughly 1100 men altogether. Washington apportioned the footmen among the regiments, pro rata, with the understanding that volunteers would be accepted at a parade on September 6. The riflemen were chosen by lot and as units—William Hendricks' Cumberland County Pennsylvanians, Matthew Smith's riflemen from Lancaster County in the same Colony, and Daniel Morgan's Virginians. For service with these riflemen, many volunteers were forthcoming; preparations were hurried to begin the march by September 13; a resounding address to the people of Canada was completed in Washington's name and translated into French. Washington told Arnold: "Upon your conduct and courage and that of the officers and soldiers detached on this expedition, not only the success of the present enterprise, and your own honor, but the safety and welfare of the whole continent may depend." Arnold rolled the drums as soon as the different parts of his force could take the road to Newburyport.

On September 11—the very day Arnold's men were put under marching orders—Washington met with the eight members of his council of war. He wished to know whether his Generals believed an offensive for a dual attack up the "Neck" from Roxbury and by boats from other parts of the front should be taken in hand. Lee believed an attack should be delivered. His fellow-commanders voiced concern. Boston Neck was too narrow, the officers maintained, and the approaches by water too much exposed to give the Colonials a decent chance of success. Other argument was political and hung on the hope—indeed, on the expectation—that the ministry of Lord North would fall and friends of America come into power. No word had been received of the King's action on the appeal of the Continental Congress; but news probably had arrived of the "Humble Address, Remonstrance and Petition" which the Lord Mayor, Aldermen and Livery of London had adopted on June 24 and were seeking to present to the Monarch. This paper called on the King to dismiss his present ministers and advisers, dissolve Parliament, and put his future confidence in servants whose attachment to the constitution, when joined to the King's own wisdom and integrity, "may enable your Majesty to settle this alarming dispute upon the sure, honorable and lasting foundations of general liberty." Colonials who read this would conclude, not unnaturally, that even if the King ignored

MAP / 8

THE INVASION OF CANADA, 1775–1776

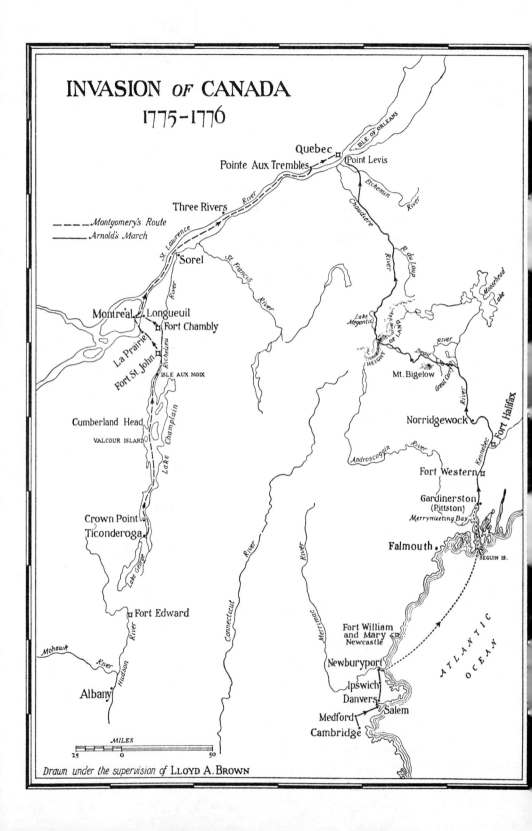

INVASION of CANADA
1775–1776

Isle of Orleans

Quebec

Pointe Aux Trembles

Point Levis

Etchemin River

St. Lawrence River

Three Rivers

Chaudiere River

R. du Loup

- - - - Montgomery's Route
——— Arnold's March

Sorel

St. Francis River

Lake Megantic

Moosehead Lake

Montreal · Longueuil

Fort Chambly

HEIGHT OF LAND

River

La Prairie

Fort St. John

Richelieu River

ISLE AUX NOIX

Dead River

Mt. Bigelow

Great Carr...

River

Cumberland Head

Lake Champlain

VALCOUR ISLAND

Norridgewock

Fort Halifax

Androscoggin River

Kennebec River

Fort Western ⌑

Crown Point

Ticonderoga

Gardinerston
(Pittston)

Lake George

Merrymeeting Bay

River

Falmouth ·

SEGUIN IS.

Fort Edward

Connecticut River

Merrimac River

ATLANTIC OCEAN

Mohawk River

Hudson River

Fort William
and Mary
Newcastle

Newburyport

Ipswich
Danvers

Albany

Medford
Cambridge

Salem

MILES

25   0   50

Drawn under the supervision of LLOYD A. BROWN

the appeal of the Continental Congress, he certainly must consent to receive and answer the address of the most powerful single body of his subjects. In the light of this, an attack on Boston well might be delayed, but "unanimously" was not precisely the word for rejection of the plan. Lee doubted; Washington at heart dissented. "I cannot say," he told Congress, "that I have wholly laid it aside."

For a fortnight and longer, after Arnold's volunteers marched away, there was spiteful dispute by the artillery, but nothing that indicated preparation by the British for an immediate attack. The British made ten shots or more for every one from an American cannon, because Washington demanded unrelaxed care to prevent the wastage of powder. Each grain was guarded as if it were a coin in the last treasure of America. Some additional powder arrived at the camp, but almost as much went out of the store as ammunition for the men. The feeling grew in Washington's mind that if powder could be had, the enemy could be driven from Boston; but, meantime, angry artillerists had to endure the annoyance of British fire and shivering sentinels had to be clothed. The work of constructing barracks was pressed, though not at a speed to equal the evidences that the need would be early and inclusive. Weather, rather than slow-handed workmen, was responsible for most of the delay in building winter quarters. The soldiers themselves were not laggard.

Washington, as everyone else, was unprepared for what developed at the end of September when Brig. Gen. Nathanael Greene called at Headquarters and asked to see the Commander-in-Chief privately. He entered with another man, Godfrey Wainwood, a baker of Newport, Rhode Island, and handed Washington a letter that Wainwood had brought from Henry Ward, Secretary of that Colony. Ward's letter and Wainwood's statement had to do with a woman who had come to Wainwood's house in Newport early in August and, on the basis of previous acquaintance in Boston, had asked him to arrange for her to see Capt. James Wallace of H.M.S. *Rose,* or the Royal Collector, Charles Dudley, or George Rome, a known Tory, who was a rich merchant and shipowner. The manner of the woman led the baker to wonder if she might not have some secret communication to make to a Loyalist. Wainwood at length got from her an admission that she had received in Cambridge a letter she was to deliver to one or another of the men she had named in order that it might be forwarded to Boston. Finally, the woman acceded to Wainwood's suggestion that she entrust to him the letter, which he said he would deliver at first opportunity. She disappeared and presumably went back to Cambridge. Wainwood related the circumstances to a Newport schoolmaster named Maxwell, a stout supporter of the Colonial cause. Without hesitation, Maxwell broke the seal and opened the communication. It was to no purpose that he scrutinized the sheet, because the letter was written in strange characters and was completely unintelligible. Maxwell gave the paper back to Wainwood, who put it away again and troubled himself no more about it until, days later, the woman wrote him in much trepidation.

Wainwood was a man of native shrewdness and concluded that the person who had employed the mysterious cipher had been in communication with the addressee in Boston and had learned that the letter had not been received. He went to Maxwell, told him what had occurred and agreed that the two of them would proceed to Providence and report the circumstances to Ward.

So, there they were, Greene and Wainwood, with the letter the woman had sent the baker and with the cryptogram she had left with him earlier. Who was the woman? Wainwood gave her name and confided that she was a female of easy virtue with whom he had consorted in Boston before the war. Washington gave orders that search be made for her. That evening she was brought to Headquarters but was obdurate. The next day she was worn to the point where she could resist no longer: the man who had given her the letter to carry to Newport was Dr. Benjamin Church.

Dr. Church? The Director General of the Hospitals, a leader in the Massachusetts Congress and a member of the Boston delegation, along with Samuel Adams and John Hancock in the new House of Representatives? Could it be possible that a man so distinguished for public service, one of those sent to Springfield to escort Washington and Lee to Watertown, could be engaged in a correspondence that certainly was clandestine and suspicious and probably was traitorous?

In a few hours the Doctor appeared under guard and submitted to questioning. Yes, the letter was his and was intended for his brother, Fleming Church, who was in Boston. When deciphered, the Doctor said, the document would be found to contain nothing criminal. He accompanied this with protestations of loyalty to the Colonies, but he did not offer to put his letter in plain English. Nor did he explain why he had said nothing of the correspondence to any person but the woman who, it eventuated, Church had been keeping as his mistress.

Church must be put under surveillance; the letter must be deciphered. The key was found easily. By October 3 Washington received the deciphered document. The letter evidently was to a person with whom Church previously had conducted a correspondence. The Doctor recorded his own movements, told of a visit to Philadelphia, described the strength and equipment of the Colonial forces, mentioned a plan for commissioning privateers, and stated that an army would be raised in the Middle Colonies to take possession of Canada. The letter concluded with elaborate instructions concerning the dispatch of an answer. The last sentence was, "Make use of every precaution or I perish." In Washington's eyes, Church was in traitorous communication with the enemy. His sense of justice did not protest for an instant against the verdict of his military judgment.

Procedure was another matter and one concerning which Washington was not certain. He felt the need of advice and convened a council. Grimly he informed the general officers of the discovery of Church's activities and laid before them the text of the letter. The other Generals, like Washington, were stunned and unable at the moment, to reach any other decision than that they should summon Church and judge for themselves. Church was brought before the Generals October 4 and was confronted again with the deciphered text of the letter: did he acknowledge it? Church did not hesitate. He had written the letter; it was deciphered properly; he had penned it deliberately in the hope he might deter ministerial forces from attacking at a time when the Army's supply of ammunition was low.

The argument was unconvincing. Dr. Church was taken from the room still declaiming about his loyalty to the American cause, and Washington asked the members of his council for their judgment. Unanimously they were of opinion that Church had carried on a criminal correspondence. What, then, should be done with him; what did the Army regulations prescribe? The offence was one so little contemplated that none of the officers was quite certain of the punishment. A search of the regulations adopted by Congress in June disclosed an odd provision: Under Article XXVIII, a person communicating with the enemy was to suffer such punishment as a general court-martial should mete out; but under Article LI, it was disputable whether a military court was authorized in such a case to impose any penalty heavier than that of cashiering, a fine of two months' pay, or thirty-nine lashes. Apparently the Delegates in Philadelphia had not considered carefully the limitations set to the authority of courts-martial. This penalty was absurdly unfitted to the crime. There was nothing the council could do except have Washington call the attention of Congress to the inadequacy. Pending further instructions from the Delegates in Philadelphia, Church must be confined closely and denied all visitors except those who had the General's permission.

Washington remained determined to have the man punished. He saw to it that Church was kept in confinement to await the judgment of Congress and also of the Massachusetts Assembly, which could act independently on the treason of one of its members. Church was sent for custody to a Connecticut jail "without the use of pen, ink or paper, to be conversed with in the presence of a magistrate only, and in the English language."

Word reached the Americans, in the midst of the excitement over Dr. Church, that General Gage had been ordered home and that Maj. Gen. William Howe had been named to act in Gage's absence as head of the armed forces in that part of America. The change was one to justify the conclusion that Gage had been recalled because he had been too cautious, too discreet in using his forces or, perhaps the vainglorious might say, too much afraid of the Colonials to take the offensive against them. Beyond this, there was no ground for rejoicing over the transfer of command. On the contrary, Washington might well have reasoned that he was exchanging an adversary he knew for one with whom he was unacquainted, except as Howe had shown fighting spirit at Bunker Hill.

At the beginning of the third week in October, with the camps buzzing over Church's arrest and the recall of "Blundering Tom," as the men styled Gage, it was too early to expect important news from Arnold; but barracks had to be built and ceaseless vigilance displayed, and the possible break-up of the Army had to be faced. The enlistments of the Connecticut and Rhode Island troops would terminate December 1; none of the men from other New England Colonies had covenanted to remain in service beyond the end of 1775; the riflemen, in the main, would be subject to martial law until July 1. If the majority of the foot soldiers reenlisted, the ranks might be filled by vigorous recruiting; but if most of the men marched off, how were they to be replaced?

Congress wished to know what number of men would suffice for a winter campaign? Could soldiers' pay be reduced? Of what should the ration consist? Were further regulations necessary for the Army? To these questions Washington added several of his own and, in particular, one concerning the term of future enlistments. The General was notified from Philadelphia that a committee of Congress would come immediately to Headquarters to confer with him. To the meetings Washington was directed to invite representatives from the legislatures of the New England Colonies and the Governors of those Colonies that had such officials. This arrangement was acceptable to Washington in both its parts and not the less so because of the members chosen for the committee of Congress: Benjamin Franklin, Thomas Lynch, and Washington's friend Benjamin Harrison of Virginia.

When the committeemen reached Cambridge, October 15, Washington had ready for them the advice of his council of war on the questions of organization, pay, rations and the like; but in the absence of the President of the Congress of New Hampshire the committee waited before beginning discussion of subjects that seemed to grow in intricacy and in number. The time was not lost. Among the instructions given by Congress to the committee's members was one that they declare the sense of the Congress respecting an attack on the troops at Boston: If before the last of December Washington should think it practicable it will be advisable to make attack upon the first favorable occasion and before the arrival of British reenforcements; if the troops did not suffice, Washington should be authorized to call in as many minutemen as he thought proper. Washington felt that he should resubmit the question to his senior officers. He called them together October 18 and told them that he had "an intimation from the Congress that an attack upon Boston, if practicable, was much desired." Not one of the eight believed it feasible.

The committee met with Washington that same day and before it took up matters of administration requested the officers of the Connecticut regiments to ascertain how many of their men were willing to remain in service until the other troops finished their enlistment at the end of December—a necessary first step in determining what strength would be at Washington's disposal during the last month of the year. The conference accepted the council's figure of 20,372 as the minimum strength of the new Army, and proceeded to deliberate on what should be done if reenlistments did not reach that total. The decision was to encourage in every way general continuance in service, to look to individual officers to fill their own ranks and, if all else failed, to summon the militia.

Optimistic early reports indicated that most of the officers would be willing to remain with the Army through 1776 and many beyond that date; but detailed reports soon led Washington to doubt whether more than one-half, or at maximum, two-thirds of the company officers would promise to stand by the colors to December 31, 1776. Whether the Connecticut private soldiers would agree to remain until the expiration of the enlistment of the Massachusetts and New Hampshire troops on the last day of December was a subject of sharp division of opinion. Many officers thought the greater number of the troops would stay to the year's end if, meantime, the men could go home on furlough, see their families, and get winter clothing. Unhappy knowledge that even the warmest coats would not protect the men from cold was a special consideration with the committee in urging the utmost speed in ascertaining the sentiment of the soldiers. If the men were doubtful about committing themselves while autumn weather lingered, they almost certainly would insist on leaving, if they could, when December had frozen the fields and sent paralyzing chill into unfinished barracks.

Actual polling of the rank and file of the Connecticut regiments was disheartening. "After breakfast," one Lieutenant of the Eighth wrote, "we called out the company and made a trial to see who would stay in the service till the 1st of January, but not a man would engage." If this was typical, the Army would be dangerously weak in December, after the Connecticut men went home. During that month, moreover, a new force must be created. The least difficult situation that Washington could anticipate, in short, was that of having thirty-one days in which to muster out one army and replace it with another while in the presence of the enemy.

Would it be possible to reduce that danger by attacking the British? Twice a council of war had decided against an offensive by the Americans. The approach of winter suggested something that had not previously been mentioned in Washington's reports to Congress: Suppose the harbor of Boston were frozen so tightly that the British warships could not maneuver; suppose sufficient powder and long-range cannon were collected at suitable positions; could the city be bombarded so heavily that the British would be forced to surrender? If this was possible, would it be humane? Should the people of Boston have death that America might have liberty? These were questions for common counsel. On the last day of the conference, October 24, Washington reviewed what had been said about attacking Boston. The matter, the committee said, was of "too much importance to be determined by them"; they would refer it to Congress on their return to Philadelphia.

What the bombardment of a town of wooden houses might involve, commander and Congressmen learned in sickening detail while they were discussing future operations. Washington received from an intelligent Boston refugee a report that a considerable squadron, including two transports that could provide quarters for a total of six hundred men, was to have sailed from that port October 4—a warning that was passed on, as soon as possible, to most of the coastal towns. The squadron was delayed, but on the thirteenth it was standing out to sea. Nothing more was heard of it until the twenty-fourth, when the three members of Congress were catching up the last loose ends of their instructions. On October 16 four British vessels had appeared off Falmouth under the command of Capt. Henry Mowat. After much bluster, warning, futile negotiation and demand for cannon and hostages, Mowat's ships opened fire on the eighteenth. The town was set afire and the greater part of the prosperous place destroyed

—139 dwellings and 287 other structures. Captain Mowat was alleged to have orders to burn all the seacoast towns between Boston and Halifax. The lesson of Falmouth could be applied in Boston. With proper artillery, Boston could be destroyed if that was the only way of driving the enemy out—a different plan, most certainly, from Washington's expectation in July that his prime duty would be to confine the enemy to Boston.

Hopeful impatience mounted for news of Arnold. About October 4, Washington had received a letter written by Arnold September 25 announcing that he had reached the Kennebec River promptly, September 20, but that he had found some of the batteaux so poorly constructed he had felt it necessary to build others. While this delayed his general advance, he had sent forward two reconnaissance parties and was following with two other "divisions." Col. Roger Enos was to bring up the rear. After that report, Washington received none from Arnold for days. The General comforted himself with recollection of one explicit order he had given Arnold: If anything went amiss, Arnold was to notify him by express. For a time, Washington was equally apprehensive of delay in Schuyler's expedition against Montreal, because the New York commander continued to report obstacles that were vexatious and dangerous. Gen. Richard Montgomery was pushing toward St. John's and Fort Chambly but, said Schuyler, he himself was beset by many difficulties. During the first week of November, Schuyler reported that Montgomery had captured Chambly with its garrison of eighty men, 124 barrels of gunpowder and 125 stand of British arms on October 20. Within three or four days, Washington received a dispatch that Arnold had written October 13 at the second portage from the Kennebec to Dead River. Arnold expressed the hope that the worst of his difficulties were behind and that he would reach the Chaudière River within eight or ten days. Washington was immensely relieved. He wrote of Arnold on November 8: "I think he is in Quebec. If I hear nothing more of him in five days, I shall be sure of it." Five days of silence followed, but on the sixth day good tidings from Schuyler arrived: St. John's on the Richelieu River had fallen to the Americans. So fine an achievement presaged the isolation and almost certain fall of Montreal. Montgomery had done his part well. If Arnold matched him, Quebec as well as Montreal would be wrested from Britain.

Five days more and then, on the nineteenth, more news, incredible news: There arrived from Arnold another dispatch, dated at Chaudière Pool, not at Quebec, and forwarded by Colonel Enos. The heading and opening words of Colonel Enos's own explanatory letter were enough to make the eyes bulge and the blood run to the face:

> Brunswick, near Kennebeck, November 9, 1775
> Sir: I am on my return from Colonel Arnold's detachment. . . .

Enos went on to relate how, as he had advanced, Arnold had sent back for provisions with which to feed the men in front. Enos had forwarded what he could and then had decided that he should turn back with his three companies because, if he went on, the provisions of all would give out before supplies could be had from the French settlements on the Chaudière. Retreat seemed desertion of Arnold. Arnold's letter appeared to make the withdrawal all the more infamous. Arnold had been much impeded by heavy rains. Provisions were short; Colonel Enos and Col. Christopher Greene had been directed to bring forward no more men than they could supply with fifteen days' rations. Although the route was far worse than Arnold had been told to expect, he would press on and would get provisions. Indications pointed to a welcome by the French in Canada; reports were that few troops, if any, were stationed at Quebec.

Surely a man who wrote in that spirit should have the support of the last musket even if the rearguard had to march and fight on an empty stomach. So Washington reasoned from Arnold's letter and from that of Enos. Washington assumed that when Arnold's advance became known, General Carleton could be expected to bring together at Quebec the British forces that had survived the fall of Chambly and of St. John's and the expected occupation of Montreal by Montgomery. The task of Arnold now would be much more difficult than it would have been if, with Enos's men in support, he had reached the vicinity of Quebec a fortnight earlier. In spite of this ill fortune Washington did not despair of the success of the resolute man who had ascended the Kennebec.

Anxiety over Arnold's plight was deepened by hourly concern over reenlistments and barrack-construction. Another and serious problem was procurement of powder and artillery for operations against Boston. Washington decided to extend his earthworks beyond Plowed Hill more than halfway to Bunker Hill from the dominating ground of Winter Hill. As far as the Commander-in-Chief could foresee, he would not have to pay too high a price for Cobble Hill, an excellent position three-quarters of a mile south of Plowed Hill and slightly less than that southwest of Bunker Hill. The three positions were a triangle with the apex to the east, a circumstance that some day might make it possible to direct a converging fire on Bunker Hill. If Cobble Hill was to be taken, it had to be at once, because the ground was freezing fast and deep. Whether the British would be content to let the Americans hold this ground must be ascertained by the new move. Howe might conclude that a stop had to be put to the gradual shortening of the range. It seemed much like trying to tighten a noose around the neck of the enemy, but the experience at Plowed Hill was duplicated incredibly. Under Washington's own eye, high parapets were thrown up on the night of November 22/23 and were undisturbed by the British for days.

Thus many things seemed to be shaping to a climax, when Colonel Enos returned to Cambridge with his three companies. Washington put him under arrest and ordered a court of inquiry under the presidency of Charles Lee to sit on November 28. During the evening of the day on which the order for the court was issued, the twenty-seventh, an express from General Montgomery brought tidings of the unopposed occupation of Montreal on the morning of the thirteenth. General Carleton got away with his troops and his powder, but when Montgomery wrote, at Montreal, he was hopeful he could capture the explosive. Almost as important was a paragraph that began: "By intercepted letters, I find Colonel Arnold is certainly arrived in the neighborhood of Quebec; that the King's friends are exceedingly alarmed, and expect to be besieged, which, with the blessing of God, they shall be, if the severe season holds off, and I can prevail on the troops to accompany me."

There was fine news from the sea, also. Washington received during the second week of October word of the departure from England, August 11, of "two north country built brigs of no force," laden with arms, powder and other stores for Quebec. These vessels were proceeding without convoy. Washington must undertake to send out armed craft and capture the immensely valuable prizes. Many delays had been encountered, but two vessels had left port October 21, and the armed schooner *Lee,* Capt. John Manley, had sailed from Plymouth November 4. Manley had the initiative and the good fortune to recapture a schooner, laden with wood, that a British prize crew was carrying into Boston. Now, November 27, Washington received intelligence that the diligent Captain had brought to Cape Anne an infinitely richer prize, the large brig *Nancy,* believed to be one of the vessels of which word had been sent from England. Almost before the handshaking over the good news was ended, Washington ordered four companies to Cape Anne, gave authority for the impressment of teams to haul away the stores and directed the minutemen of the adjoining country to assist in removing the cargo to a place of safety. As the men went about this task, every lift from the hold of the *Nancy* seemed to bring a military treasure into daylight. When he saw her papers, Gates exclaimed that he could not have made out a better invoice if he had tried. Although she carried no powder, she yielded two thousand stand of small arms, many flints, tons of musket shot and a fine brass mortar with a maw of thirteen inches and a weight in excess of 2700 pounds.

When this giant was brought to Cambridge, General Putnam was to christen it with a bottle of rum and Colonel Mifflin was to name it "Congress"; but before that festive celebration, many things happened. First among them was the assembly of the court of inquiry in Enos's case. Contrary to Washington's expectation, by no means all the testimony was adverse. There was doubt, in fact, whether Enos had not helped Arnold by sending forward all the supplies he could spare, instead of marching ahead to add more mouths to those already exhausting Arnold's provisions. The court was somewhat reluctant to recommend action in the light of the evidence, but it concluded that a formal trial was necessary "for the satisfaction of the world," as it said, and for Colonel Enos's "own honor." Washington accordingly ordered a court-martial with John Sullivan as President.

Washington thus far had endured without flinching all the venality, all the incompetence and all the ignorance of war with which he had been confronted, but he had to face the prospect that if the long-desired British attack was delivered, it might be at the most unwelcome time conceivable, the freezing days when the Connecticut troops would be marching home. In writing Joseph Reed of this and of some skirmishing around Lechmere Point, he explained that "a scoundrel from Marblehead, a man of property," had gone to Howe, told of the reluctance of Continentals to reenlist and assured the British commander that the ministerial forces easily might make themselves master of the American lines. Washington undertook to counter. He began a bomb battery at Lechmere Point on the night of November 29/30. He could not tell whether this activity would serve its immediate purpose in deterring the British, but he confided to Reed that the Army expected an attack. What more perfect time for it could there be? In his months in command Washington had watched with growing repugnance the cunning of the place-hunters and sensed the acuteness of a danger the slothful disregarded. He had had to struggle with himself to keep his patience and his faith. To Reed he broke out:

Such a dearth of public spirit, and want of virtue, such stock-jobbing and fertility in all the low arts to obtain advantages of one kind or another in this great change of the military arrangement, I never saw before, and pray God I may never be witness to again. What will be the ultimate end of these maneuvers is beyond my scan. I tremble at the prospect. We have been till this time enlisting about three thousand, five hundred men. To engage these I have been obliged to allow furloughs as far as fifty men a Regiment, and the officers, I am persuaded, indulge as many more. The Connecticut troops will not be prevailed upon to stay longer than their term (saving those who have enlisted for the next campaign and mostly on furlough), and such a dirty, mercenary spirit pervades the whole that I should not be at all surprised at any disaster that may happen. In short, after the last of this month our lines will be so weakened that the minutemen and militia must be called in for their defence. . . .

He rushed angrily on:

. . . these [men], being under no kind of government themselves, will destroy the little subordination I have been laboring to establish, and run me into one evil whilst I am endeavoring to avoid another; but the lesser evil must be chosen. Could I have foreseen what I have, and am likely to experience, no consideration upon earth should have induced me to accept this command. A Regiment or any subordinate department would be accompanied with ten times the satisfaction, and perhaps the honor.

Washington's information on November 29 was that at least 1500 men were absent on furlough as a reward for reenlistment and that the force with which he had been defending his lines thus was reduced by almost 12 per cent. The report was, also, that the Connecticut troops absolutely could not be induced to continue in service beyond the first of the month. Something had to be done; the situation was critical; delay was dangerous. He summoned a council for the next morning. At the council, the grim-faced seniors could give no encouragement: the Connecticut troops stood fast in their resolution; pleas and argument alike were vain; patriotism no longer stirred them. They must be replaced at Continental expense with minutemen from other Colonies until January 15, 1776, by which date the new Army would be organized or the American cause hopeless.

Again on December 1 the Connecticut companies were addressed by their officers and asked to keep their faces towards the enemy until other soldiers took their places. The report was the same: Unless they were given extra pay, most of the men were resolved to go home, regardless of what happened. When some actually started, that was more than Washington would endure. He sent after the men; apprehended most of them, brought them back and sternly warned them not to leave until they received their formal, written discharges. At the same time, he put all the troops on the alert and undertook to make the camps as secure as possible. The certain loss of the Connecticut regiments within ten days put an attack on the British so far beyond reach that Washington scarcely need spend thought on it. He had in candor to tell himself there was no reason for expecting the troops from the other Colonies to do any better, when their enlistments ended, than the Connecticut soldiers had done. He could not believe that voluntary enlistment would bring the Army to the accepted maximum—20,372.

After the departing Connecticut troops were brought back, they did their duty for several days without complaint. No mutiny swept the camps; the sentinels gave no indication of any preparation for an assault; December 3 passed without alarm, a movement of troops to Charlestown on the fourth amounted to nothing. The fifth was quiet. Routine was restored in the Army. The court-martial acquitted Colonel Enos "with honor," a verdict that Washington accompanied, on publication, with an order for immediate release from arrest and with no other comment.

Washington received on December 4 a dispatch from Schuyler, dated November 22, that contained letters of Montgomery and of Arnold. Montgomery reported that American artillery fire had kept Carleton and his men from moving on their ships down the St. Lawrence, and past the mouth of the Richelieu to Quebec. Arnold wrote at St. Mary's. He told of his purpose to cross the St. Lawrence in a few days and to attack the city, though he feared it might have been reenforced. If it was too strong for him, he would march to join Montgomery at Montreal. The natives seemed friendly and willing to supply provisions. This was encouraging and led Washington to hope that Montgomery's early juncture with Arnold not only would assure the capture of Quebec but also would complete the conquest of Canada.

Some of the Connecticut troops refused on the tenth to perform any military duty and at least passively demanded that they be allowed to start home at once. Washington again had to refuse, but this time he had an encouraging reason: militia from other New England Colonies were beginning to arrive in noticeable numbers. If they continued to move into the camps, the Connecticut regiments might leave, but not until then. The safety of the lines had to prevail over the letter of old enlistment resolutions. On the eleventh it looked as if a new necessity was developing. Fretful activity was observed around Bunker Hill; large numbers of men moved from their encampments and crossed to Boston by the ferry. Washington concluded that the British either were reconcentrating in the city for an attack at some undisclosed point or were transferring the men to less exposed winter quarters. The more formidable of these alternatives was enough to make Washington ask once again whether Howe might be withholding his attack until the day some secret agent would hurry to British Headquarters and say, in effect, "The rebels are at their weakest now!"

Keep the Connecticut regiments, then—will they, nil they—till a corresponding number of militia filed into the tents and barracks. That, in substance, was the order. Mercifully, the worst of the danger appeared to be over almost before the Connecticut men had time to get angry. The British made no further movement at Bunker Hill or from Boston; militia companies reported with a briskness that surprised the General. The militia came the more readily because they were outraged by the news that the Connecticut troops were going to leave regardless of what happened to Boston. Within a few days it was to be manifest, also, that the leaders of Connecticut and many of the humble folk were humiliated and outraged by the virtual defection of so many of their troops in an hour of peril.

If the uncertainty created by the departure and arrival of these desperately needed troops had not absorbed Washington's thought on December 11, he might have indulged a different and sentimental resentment. It would have been this: After much exchange of correspondence, long preparation and the muster of a considerable entourage, Martha had started for Cambridge from Virginia and she arrived that day. Her vehicle poured out Virginians as if they had been apples from a barrel—herself, Mrs. Horatio Gates, Jack Custis, his wife and George Lewis. There were, of course, affectionate greetings for Martha and for her fellow-travelers and there was as much of comfort at Headquarters as could be provided by fumbling males; but a man of other temperament might have complained that of all days on which a chivalrous foe and a considerate Army should have left a Commander-in-Chief alone, it would have been when he wished to receive a wife whom he had not seen for seven months.

Behind all other burdens of command was gnawing concern over Arnold's Canadian expedition and over the course of the reenlistment, a double dread—to darken a Christmas that Nature did her best to brighten. Christmas Eve brought heavy snow, but Christmas Day itself was full of sunshine. Some of the officers came, of course, to call on the General and his lady during the day. In the unfinished barracks and in the crowded houses of the towns the soldiers made such mirth as they might. A few who had money and the courage with which to face untrodden snow went out into the country and bought themselves such fruit and fowl as the farmers had. The enemy, too, kept the peace of the Prince of Peace.

It was altogether a quiet day, but on the roads to Cambridge, two expresses were fighting their way through the snow. One of them came from Fort George with a dispatch from young Henry Knox, whom Washington in November had sent to New York and thence to Ticonderoga to get additional cannon and ammunition. Knox, writing December 17, reported excellent progress on his own account, but he said that Colonel Arnold was obliged to go to Point-aux-Trembles, about six miles from Quebec and that Montgomery had gone to join him and added: "I have very little doubt that General Montgomery has Quebec now in his possession." That had been Washington's hope, but his confidence could not be fixed until he learned that Montgomery was with Arnold.

What of opportunity at Boston? The Massachusetts committee for the supply of wood was hinting to the townships of the "great danger the country is exposed to from a dispersion of the Army, which must take place if it is not supplied with wood"; Washington's concern was whether reenlistment would yield a sufficient force to hold the line at the Year's End, when those men from the other New England Colonies who would not reenlist for 1776 would leave the Army and go home. By the last returns prior to December 15, not more than 5917, including Connecticut volunteers, had agreed to sign for another year. On December 18, total reenlistments were computed at 7140. The task seemed an impossible one. As the Year's End came within a bare hundred hours or so, Washington received from the second express who had been on the road at Christmas the answer of Congress to the question the committee of Franklin, Lynch and Harrison had submitted to Philadelphia. The reply was, "Resolved, that if General Washington and his council of war should be of opinion that a successful attack may be made on the troops in Boston, he do it in any manner he may think expedient, notwithstanding the town and property in it may thereby be destroyed." Here was the authorization: would there be an opening and the men to make the most of it? If Howe was pretending to be cautious in order to deceive the Americans, would there be men to repulse him, or could he sweep aside a thin and shivering line? Amid desperate attempts to prevail on men to stay and fight for their country, the final day of the year came. Present, fit for duty, were 11,752 rank and file. Enlistments of every sort for the new establishment were 9650. Nathanael Greene heard the figures and spoke for his chief and for all his patriotic brother-officers when he wrote: "Nothing but confusion and disorder reign. . . . We never have been so weak as we shall be tomorrow. . . ."

The New Year, 1776, began with so few troops in the redoubts and the barracks that the lines at some points were bare of defenders; but the British did not stir, and Washington issued a long appeal for "order regularity and discipline," as if he were sure of "the new army, which," he said, "in every point of view is entirely continental." All offenses of the old establishment were pardoned; the guardhouse doors were opened for all imprisoned American soldiers; the British union flag was raised as if to honor the birthday of the Army. This was done with an air of confidence, almost of bravado. Washington was far less sure of the morrow than he appeared to be. He told Reed "How it will end, God in his great goodness will direct. I am thankful for his protection to this time. We are told that we shall soon get the army completed, but I have been told so many things which have never come to pass that I distrust everything."

Two days after Washington had hoisted the union flag "in honor of the United Colonies" the camps received the long-delayed text of the King's speech to Parliament on October 26. George III then had announced his intention of putting "a speedy end" to what he described as a "rebellious war . . . manifestly carried on for the purpose of establishing an independent empire." The monarch went on to say that he would give "authority to certain persons upon the spot to grant general or particular pardons and indemnities . . . as they shall think fit, and to receive the submission of any Province or Colony which shall be disposed to return to its allegiance." This evoked nothing but ridicule from Chelsea to Dorchester Neck, but when Boston Tories saw the union flag lifted on the first day of the New Year they assumed that the Americans had put up the flag as a symbol of submission. News of this feeling in the occupied city amused even Washington.

Relief came with laughter. By the evening of January 4 sufficient militia had arrived for the Brigadiers to reoccupy thinly those parts of the line that had been undefended for three days. In another four days the number of men present for duty, fit, was to rise to 10,209, but that was less than half the authorized strength of the Army, and even that figure now might face subtraction because of new developments to which Lee insistently called attention.

Lee had gone to Rhode Island to advise Governor Cooke concerning the defence of the Colony. Upon his return shortly before the beginning of January, Lee was alarmed by reports which indicated that the British in Boston were fitting out a fleet. The objective of this force might be New York and its aim might be not only to seize the most valuable point strategically on the coast but also to rally and recruit Tories, who had made that city their stronghold. New York must be occupied and the Tories curbed— that became Lee's temporary creed.

Washington as long previously as October had considered the possibility of a British descent on New York and had asked whether he should detach troops, should await instructions, or should rely on the men of that and nearby Colonies to defend the city. No decision by Congress had been communicated to him. Now that a British movement from Boston was in the making, Washington shared Lee's view that immediate action should be taken and urged that New Jersey troops be thrown into the city. More than this he did not think he should urge, because of his lack of familiarity with conditions in New York. Distance and circumstances had made his position as Commander-in-Chief more nominal than directional. He held the inclusive title; he was not sure he should exercise all the powers his title seemed to confer. Lee made a detailed proposal for the occupation of New York City and the nearby country. The plan appealed to Washington; but he remained in some doubt concerning his authority, and, as John Adams happened to be near at hand, Washington consulted the Congressman. His long experience as a legislator had taught the General that the time to avoid criticism was in advance of action and that the way to do this was to consult and convince those who might be critical later. Washington told Adams that if the plan was to be executed, it should be undertaken at once and by Lee. Adams's reply was unequivocal: Washington should seize New York; it was entirely within his authority to do so. Specifically, said the Massachusetts leader, "your commission constitutes you commander of all the forces . . . and you are vested with full power and authority to act as you shall think for the good and welfare of the service."

Lee's instructions were drafted forthwith. He was to raise volunteers in Connecticut, proceed to New York, get assistance from New Jersey, and put New York City "into the best posture of defence which the season and circumstances will admit of."

The day after he gave Lee his papers Washington received the first detailed returns of the new Army. He had estimated from incomplete weekly figures that the total would be 10,500, or about 45 per cent of the authorized strength. Now he was appalled to find that actual enlistments were 8212, and that the number of men present for duty, fit, was 5582 only. In the light of these unhappy facts he was so discouraged that he doubted whether the Army ever could be completed by voluntary enlistment. He said so without advocating immediately an alternative policy, though he believed a draft or a bounty for long-term enlistment would be necessary. He had once again to look to the militia. The time of those called to the lines in December would expire January 15. Although Washington's anxiety prompted him to ask the Massachusetts Legislature to keep these men with the Army until February, his experience admonished him of the old, ugly, fact that a great part of the militia would not extend their service even for two weeks.

Weakened in this way, Washington felt that he should call a council to consider how he could get the men with whom to carry out the plan to which he always returned from every wrestle with adverse circumstance, the plan of attacking Boston or of inducing Howe to come out and fight. Washington asked John Adams and James Warren to attend along with his general officers, and on January 16 he laid before them "a state of the Regiments in the Continental army, the consequent weakness of his lines, and, in his judgment, the indispensable necessity of making a bold attempt to conquer the ministerial troops in Boston, before they can be reenforced in the spring, if the means can be provided, and a favorable opportunity offered, and then [he] desired the opinion of the council thereon." This time, all the doubters were convinced: the attack should be made as soon as practicable; to facilitate it, Washington should call for thirteen militia regiments to serve from February 1 to the end of March; these regiments should have the same number of officers and men as were authorized for the Continental regiments. Massachusetts must be asked for seven, Connecticut for four, and New Hampshire for two.

The call went out accordingly. What the result of this new application might be, Washington could not foresee; but in the acuteness of his anxiety he opened his heart to his friend Reed: "Could I have foreseen the difficulties which have come upon us; could I have known that such a backwardness would have been discovered in the old soldiers to the service, all the Generals upon earth should not have convinced me of the propriety of delaying an attack upon Boston till this time. When it can now be attempted, I will not undertake to say; but this much I will answer for, that no opportunity can present itself earlier than my wishes."

Opportunity! The word seemed to be mocked by papers that lay in Washington's Headquarters as he wrote. He discovered now that, if such a thing was possible, he was even worse off for arms than for soldiers. His long anxiety over the outcome of the advance of Montgomery and Arnold to Quebec was more and more acute. Schuyler had written January 5 that Arnold and Montgomery had formed a junction, "but," the New Yorker said, "their force is so small and the weather has been so severe that I fear they have not been able to possess themselves of Quebec." Unhappy and in ill-health, Schuyler had added: "I tremble lest Canada should be lost." Receipt of this letter deepened Washington's dread and when, on January 17, he broke the seal of a dispatch written by Schuyler from Albany on the thirteenth, the opening words were so many blows in the face: "I wish I had no occasion to send my dear General this melancholy account. My amiable friend, the gallant Montgomery, is no more; the brave Arnold is wounded; and we have met with a severe check in an unsuccessful attempt on Quebec." The situation, Schuyler wrote Washington, called for "an immediate reenforcement that is nowhere to be had but from you."

This news stunned. The invasion of Canada had been ordered by Congress but the cooperation of Arnold through an advance on Quebec had been Washington's own design, his first adventure in strategy on a scale of any magnitude. It had failed, with heavy loss and with dark potential consequences: If Canada were lost to the Americans, that country would be a secure base for the confident planning of an offensive down the lakes and down the Hudson simultaneously with an attack on New York City by the British fleet and perhaps by Howe's army. Were this joint operation to succeed, then the Colonies would be divided and might be subdued. As Washington saw it, the question was not one of detaching troops from his command to reenforce Arnold; it was, instead, how could additional soldiers be found elsewhere for the relief of a gallant man and the capture of the enemy's northern base?

He summoned an immediate council, to which Adams accepted an invitation, and when he had the Generals and the Delegate together in a private room, Washington inquired "whether it proper, in the present circumstances of the lines, to detach a reenforcement from hence to the succor of the troops in Canada?" The senior officers were convinced that this was "improper," but there was unanimous assent to a proposal Washington made that the New England Colonies be requested to supply men to aid Arnold. As Canada went, the balance might turn; the winter of 1775-76 would be decisive there because, when spring came, the enemy most certainly would send large reenforcements to the St. Lawrence. Washington had more confidence than ever in Arnold, and he hoped that officer, recovering promptly, would add, as he wrote him, "the only link wanting in the great chain of continental union."

Scarcely had this exhortation been written than Washington found affairs in Canada involved anew and differently with those of New York. During the last week in January he learned that Lee had been halted at Stamford, Connecticut, by an attack of gout and had been confronted there by a strange and disconcerting letter from the Committee of Safety in New York City. The committee told of reports it had received that Lee was about to enter the city with a considerable body of troops, and it informed him that it had little powder and no defensive works. Because of this situation, members felt that hostilities in New York City should not be provoked before March 1, if then. Lee was requested to halt his troops on the western confines of Connecticut "till we shall have been honored by you with such an explanation on this important subject as you may conceive your duty may permit you to enter into with us. . . ." Lee's letter to Washington enclosed this document and his reply, the substance of which was that his object was to keep the British from taking post in the city or from effecting lodgment on Long Island. ". . . I give you my word," Lee had written the committee, "that no active service is proposed as you seem to apprehend." He specified: "If the ships of war are quiet, I shall be quiet; but I declare solemnly that if they make a pretext of my presence to fire on the town the first house set in flames by their guns shall be the funeral pile of some of their best friends—but I believe, sir, the inhabitants may rest in security on this subject." Further, Lee wrote his chief, he had concluded he would receive instructions from Congress, to which he had written on the subject. The response of Congress was to send a committee of three members—Harrison, Lynch and Andrew Allen—to decide what should be done for the defence of New York.

Before Lee had recovered sufficiently to proceed on his way, his direction of defence at New York for any length of time was put in doubt. At Headquarters it was surmised by some, that Schuyler did not wish to exercise general command in Canada, but Washington thought he might be prevailed upon to accept the responsibility. If the New Yorker did not, then Charles Lee would be the logical man to head the operation. When Washington received a request from Congress that he designate one of his Generals for the Canadian command, he suggested that Lee be left temporarily in New York and that Schuyler be entrusted with the Canadian command.

Soon papers that came to Cambridge told of plans for the dispatch of Lee, rather than of Schuyler, to Canada. Lee was willing, and he was insistent only in asking for the essentials of war most difficult to get in America—trained subordinates, cannon and ammunition. He wished to have either Greene or Sullivan assigned him, but the qualities that made him desire the services of one or the other of them were the very excellencies that led Washington to want both men to remain with the Army in front of Boston. Lee did not insist. He was in good spirits; because his proposal to occupy New York brought him much praise. This aroused no jealousy in Washington's heart. He wanted Canada, he would part with his most experienced lieutenant were that necessary to get it; he regretted that he could spare no troops to help in the northern province, but he was convinced he could not afford to detach even a battalion.

This unyielding insistence by Washington on concentration of force accorded with his answer to previous appeals for detachments: If Howe did not attack, he would, and to do so he required every man. He needed, too, more powder than ever, and he had relatively less, both because of wastage and because he now had more heavy guns. Knox had arrived at Framingham with fifty-two cannon, nine large mortars and five cohorns, which he had hauled over the snow from Fort Ticonderoga. Washington might hope

to drive the British from the wharves of Boston if ever he had in store sufficient powder for a long bombardment.

Artillery was Knox's assignment and was well handled; transaction
of much of the other public business was more difficult now because of
changes in Washington's staff. Edmund Randolph had been compelled to
start back to Virginia in November to look after the estate of his uncle,
Peyton Randolph, who had died suddenly in October. To Washington's
distress, Joseph Reed had set out for Philadelphia to look after certain
cases pending in his law practice. Reed had proved himself so nearly indispensable that Washington had written Richard Henry Lee to endeavor to
prevail upon opposing counsel to agree to postpone trials in order that
Reed might return promptly to Cambridge. For the discharge of the less
important duties of aide, Washington procured the services of Robert Hanson Harrison. Stephen Moylan gave such help as he could, but he had his
own regular work to do as Mustermaster General.

February 13 Washington went to Lechmere Point. He found the ice
there solid all the way across the channel to Boston. Would it be practicable to attack across the ice and to rely primarily on the fire of small arms?
If this bold move was to be undertaken at all, it should be attempted at
once, because the ice might break up and British reenforcements might sail
into Boston. So, on February 16 Washington submitted his plan to his
Generals.

Every man of them was against it. Washington was set back by this
counsel. He had reckoned the cost of the long assault over the ice and had
agreed that success would depend on the good behavior of the troops, but
he had been willing to take the risk because this seemed the one feasible
operation for an army that lacked powder for a sustained bombardment.
When his Generals were decidedly of opinion that he was wrong, he could
not persist in asserting himself right. He did not change his mind but, he
admitted subsequently, "the irksomeness of my situation . . . might have
inclined me to put more to hazard than was consistent with prudence."
Washington had to turn again to the almost hopeless task of building up a
reserve of powder and the enterprise the council had recommended, that of
occupying some of the hills of Dorchester Neck in the hope the enemy
would attempt to drive the Americans from the high ground. In spite of
ice, everything seemed to be proceeding well. The secret reports from Boston were to the effect that the British were putting heavy guns and a
quantity of bedding aboard ship. Townsfolk believed Howe was preparing
to move to New York or Virginia.

Washington reasoned that Howe might be fashioning a ruse, might
actually be about to leave Boston or might be making ready in anticipation
of orders to evacuate the city. Speculation on Howe's designs was not permitted to slow the preparations for the seizure of high ground on Dorchester Neck. As Washington developed his plans for this operation, he gained
faith in it.

Time seemed now to run swiftly towards a decision. At all the batteries within easy range of Boston, solid shot and shell were brought for-

ward, and the precious kegs of powder were placed where no moisture could reach them. Nurses were sought; bandages were prepared. Every effort was made to get full information of the enemy and stop passage from the American lines to Boston, but this precaution did not suffice. On February 27 Washington learned of the desertion of a rifleman who of course would disclose to the enemy as much as he knew.

As the extra day of the Leap Year gave place to a cold first of March it was known in the camps, by the soldiers' own strangely accurate intelligence system, that the Dorchester Heights were to be occupied. By the second engineers had placed a thirteen-inch mortar and a ten-inch at Lechmere Point and a thirteen-inch companion at Lamb's Dam in Roxbury. The Massachusetts Legislature was sending up militia Washington had asked from the Dorchester area. The bombardment would be started that night:

Cambridge, March 2, 1776

[General Ward, Roxbury]
Sir: After weighing all circumstances of tide, &c, and considering the hazard of having the posts on Dorchester Neck taken by the enemy, and the evil consequences which would result from it, the gentlemen here are of opinion that we should go on there Monday night [March 4]. I give you this early notice of it, that you may delay no time in preparing for it, as everything here will be got in readiness to cooperate. In haste I am sir, etc.

GEORGE WASHINGTON.

For the operation Washington had approximately 14,000 foot soldiers, of whom about 9000 were Continental troops and 5000 militia. Militia of Roxbury and Dorchester could man part of the lines in event the regular defenders had to be moved. Artillerists under Knox were counted at 635. The supply of powder probably amounted to 174 barrels, exclusive of what had been issued for small arms.

On the night of March 2 Abigail Adams, at Braintree, was writing for all New England women when she shaped these words to her husband: "I have been kept in a continual state of anxiety and expectation ever since you left. It has been said, 'tomorrow' and 'tomorrow' for this month, but when the dreadful tomorrow will be, I know not." At that instant, across field and water came the sharp sound of an explosion. It was a cannon shot—that was certain. The house shook; the young wife of John Adams went to the door and listened. Another explosion, another, and another! Word spread mysteriously that this was it; all the remaining militia were to repair to the lines by midnight of Monday. Abigail came back to her writing: "No sleep for me tonight."

Except as the bombardment indicated that the Americans had seized the initiative, it was a trifle—only eleven shells and thirteen solid shot. The British reply was prompt and lively but was not of a sort to make a quaking militia fearful of instant death. The enemy's fire inflicted no damage, but two of the Americans' large-bore mortars at Lechmere Point and one at Roxbury split. Washington's chief concern was that the enemy had intelligence of the impending attack and might seize Dorchester

Heights before the Americans could. Occupation of the high ground must not be delayed. General Thomas was to be in immediate charge; General Ward was to have supervision of everything on his part of the front and now was assured he would get reenforcement of infantry and riflemen.

After a day of diligent preparation, the artillery opened on the night of March 3/4 at 9 P.M. from Cobble Hill, Lechmere Point and Lamb's Dam. Bombardment did no damage except to the Americans' pride; on the third shot the brass "Congress" split as shamelessly as the iron mortars had. The British fire was less bad than on the previous night, but it ceased when that of the Americans ended early March 4.

Washington now had come to the day on which occupation of Dorchester Heights was to begin. The auguries were contradictory. "Long Faces," as the militia were called, continued to put in their appearance, but word came about ten o'clock that British troops were embarking in boats opposite Lechmere Point. Immediately the alarm was sounded, and the American regiments in that district were put under arms and hurried to their posts. Two hours of uncertainty passed. Then Washington heard that the British had given up whatever design they had.

From that time until nightfall everything outwardly was quiet. Around Roxbury teams were assembled, fascines loaded and the men were made ready to march. The entrenching tools were put into carts and barrels filled with stone and sand were lifted into the stoutest vehicles. These barrels were to be rolled down the hills in order to bowl over the Redcoats who delivered the assault. The surgeons met with the Medical Director and received their assignments, hospitals were cleared for the arrival of the wounded, and so with many other details as the clock ticked the crowded minutes. At dusk the bombardment began. The three thousand troops that Thomas had chosen started from Roxbury for the hills on Dorchester Peninsula. American fire now was almost ten times as fast as it had been either of the two previous nights. British artillerists answered as if they knew that this time something serious impended.

The moon was full; the night was mild. About three hundred teams started with their fascines, chandeliers and barrels and as early as 8 P.M. were climbing the nearer hills. The infantry moved in silently; the riflemen spread themselves out along the waterfront. Men who previously had surveyed the ground saw that the dumping was at the proper places. Next was the sad business of cutting down orchards to provide abatis. Washington scarcely could have asked better performance.

Dawn came at last on March 5. Near Cambridge two regiments were mustered for an early march to Roxbury. The alert was ordered all the way around the crude arc of the American lines as far as Chelsea. On Dorchester Heights the men were surprised and proud to observe how much had been accomplished under the curtain of a single night. Six fortifications had been laid out on the higher hills and on the tableland—cover for the flank and rear against fire from the British on Boston Neck. In the first hours of day there was no sign of any assembly of British troops, no activity in the fleet to suggest that men were to be taken aboard. Washington was not deceived. He knew that flood tide would be about noon and that nothing except artillery fire could be expected until the water was high enough to permit the landing of a force on Dorchester Peninsula. Everything indicated that the "Lobsters" would come in with the tide.

The British began cannonade of the new works, then suspended it; they could not elevate their guns to reach the high parapets. With the halt of the enemy's cannon there were signs of commotion in the town. Late in the forenoon troops could be seen embarking, with their artillery, on small boats that carried them to transports. A few of these vessels thereupon dropped down to anchorages off the Castle. By the time this was done the hours of best opportunity had been lost. The tide was past the flood. Washington's troops meanwhile were wheeling a larger number of field pieces into their works, and they continued to pile up earth; but they could do no more than that—except to swear that when the Redcoats came they would "give it to them." During the late afternoon the weather became colder and the wind shifted. By evening a furious storm roared in from the south with a cruelly cold wind and lashing rain. Before darkness settled it was plain that in that full gale man's implements of wrath were feeble and futile. Washington let no powder be wet in attempted bombardment. When he awoke the next morning the storm was still roaring, but the rain slackened and, by eight o'clock, ceased. The wind remained high and was holding the transports to their anchorage. If there was to be an attack, it could not come by water until the wind dropped. Howe might sally on Boston Neck. Any such attempt must be met with vigilance and prompt fire. Four thousand men were to be held in readiness to cross the river to Boston should the Redcoats stream down the Neck. Work on the fortifications was renewed; at high water the American positions on the Peninsula were to be manned. Conditions were better hourly. Defences on the high ground of Dorchester soon would be so strong that if the British assaulted their troops would be mowed down. If they did not, Nook's Hill could be occupied by Washington's men. This done, American cannon would be so close to the town that the wharves of Boston would be untenable.

On the seventh Washington felt the situation sufficiently stabilized to justify dismissal of those militiamen who lived in the area and had brought with them three days' provisions only. They had done their duty so well that Washington praised and thanked them in both General Orders and the detailed report he wrote that day to Congress. That was not all that a dispatch to the President of Congress should cover. Washington proceeded to review the need of a third major general. The senior in line of promotion was Brigadier General Thomas, who had acquitted himself admirably in Dorchester Neck. Washington of course esteemed Thomas, but, because he knew jealous eyes in Philadelphia might criticize his words, he wrote with restraint: "General Thomas is the first Brigadier, stands fair in point of reputation and is esteemed a brave and good officer." Then he went on to recommend Col. William Thompson, for advancement to the rank of Brigadier: ". . . as far as I have had an opportunity of judging . . . a good officer and a man of courage. What I have said of these two gentlemen, I conceive to be my duty, at the same time acknowledging whatever promotions are made will be satisfactory to me."

During those early hours of March 7 work was going briskly on. The fortifications were stronger every hour. One thing only of possible importance had occurred: The British most certainly and unmistakably were moving cannon in Boston. Could it be that they were preparing to abandon the city? There were other vague indications, also, that the Redcoats might be preparing to leave.

Now it was March 8 and just such a day as the seventh, busy but unexciting—until, about 2 P.M., a flag of truce was seen at the British advanced post on Boston Neck. Col. Ebenezer Learned, commanding on that part of the front, went out to meet a man in British uniform and three civilians. The British officer introduced himself as Maj. Henry Bassett of the Tenth Regiment. His companions were Thomas and Jonathan Amory and Peter Johonnot, who produced a letter from the Selectmen of Boston. The flag went back, and the communication was forwarded in haste to Washington.

He took it, glanced at the inscription, broke the seal and began to read:

Boston, 8 March, 1776

As his Excellency General Howe is determined to leave the town with the troops under his command, a number of the respectable inhabitants, being very anxious for its preservation and safety, have applied to General Robertson for this purpose, who at their request have communicated the same to his Excellency Genl. Howe, who has assured them that he has no intention of destroying the town, unless the troops under his command are molested during their embarkation or at their departure, by the armed forces without, which declaration he gave Genl. Robertson leave to communicate to the inhabitants; If such an opposition should take place, we have the greatest reason to expect the town will be exposed to entire destruction. As our fears are quieted with regard to Genl. Howe's intentions, we beg we may have some assurances that so dreadful a calamity may not be brought on by any measures without. As a testimony of the truth of the above, we have signed our names to this paper, carried out by Messrs. Thomas and Jonathan Amory and Peter Johonnot, who have at the earnest entreaties of the inhabitants, through the Lt. Governor, solicited a flag of truce for this purpose.

JOHN SCOLLAY, TIMOTHY NEWELL, THOMAS MARSHALL, SAMUEL AUSTIN

If there was exultation, it was momentary, because Washington had to decide what answer he would make to a paper which appeared "under covert, unauthorized and addressed to nobody." The largest instant question was whether Howe himself stood behind a proposal to abandon the city if he were permitted to sail away unmolested and "with the honors of war." Those general officers unoccupied and near at hand were asked to come to Headquarters and were shown the Selectmen's letter. Washington found his Generals distrusted any proposal for a bargain. Caution was the first law of conduct where treachery was possible. Washington should acknowledge the letter, point out that it covered no written pledge by Howe, and reserve all the rights of war. A letter for the signature of Colonel Learned was drafted to that effect.

On the morning of the ninth the Americans laid out on Nook's Hill, in plain view of the British, the work they proposed to construct that night. They paid for their imprudence! No sooner did they start work after darkness fell than shells fell also, and precisely where the Americans were to put their fascines and raise their parapets. The undertaking was abandoned for the night. The fire of the British was the heaviest against any of the new American positions and might indicate that Howe had resolved to stay in Boston. Washington did not so interpret it. All the shot came from the narrow, near arc of British gun positions, a fact which indicated that cannon from the other redoubts had been put aboard ship. Besides, there was as much bustle as ever in the town and on the wharves. Washington concluded that the British were not ready to leave and that they repelled him because they knew he could force them to abandon the Massachusetts capital as soon as he secured artillery positions on Nook's Hill.

Events of March 10 seemed to vindicate Washington's judgment. A great stir was visible at the landing-places of Boston. Soon one ship after another raised sail and dropped down the harbor. This was a signal for Washington's troops to move out from Roxbury and man their positions on Dorchester Heights, but no indications of a landing were observed. Nor was there any perceptible change on March 11. Boston yielded the same picture of preparations for general departure of army and fleet. While expectancy remained and some anxiety lingered in Washington's mind, he was now more confident of the outcome and talked with Boston refugees concerning the occupation of the town as if he were certain of the complete departure of the British.

The waiting was exasperating. If and when Howe sailed, where would he head? Was Halifax or New York the destination of the fleet? The American General held to the belief that the objective was the mouth of the Hudson and brought his general officers together on the thirteenth to ask their judgment on the number of troops he should send to New York and the time when it would be safe to start the movement. The advice of his council was that he could begin the transfer immediately but that he ought not to dispatch any men besides the rifle companies and one brigade until the British actually had left Boston. Plans were made accordingly.

To reduce risk of having the mouth of the Hudson virtually undefended when the British arrived, Washington appealed to Governor Trumbull to send two thousand men to New York. From Jersey one thousand were to be sought. It was better to prevent a lodgment at New York than to have the task of ousting an adversary already entrenched there.

March 15 was the eighth day after the receipt of the Selectmen's announcement of the impending departure of Howe—and the British still held Boston. The wind was favorable for the departure of the British but they loitered still. Then before the fifteenth ended, the wind shifted so adversely that the King's men could not leave if they would. Washington felt that he had nothing further to gain by delaying longer the fortification of Nook's Hill. Once the British saw his battery planted there, they must leave Boston or take the risks of a short-range bombardment. Up the hill, then, the men were ordered to go on the night of March 16/17. British artillery challenged the workers as it had on the ninth, but no American had been hurt when, at daylight, the workers could see the fruits of their labor and, at a distance, the effect on their adversary. The wind was from the quarter favorable for departure; the wharves were thronged with men in uniform. Troops could be seen to enter boats and start in great numbers for the vessels that were riding comfortably at anchor below the Castle. Word came that troops in large number were marching away from Bunker Hill.

Had all the British left the town? For many minutes there was doubt. Then, from in front of the outposts on Boston Neck, sentinels heard the shouts of American boys. The British were all gone, the lads cried; Selectmen were on their way to Roxbury. Soon, down the Neck came Austin, Scollay, Marshall and others, who were hurried to General Ward's quarters. When their tale was told, Ward gave his orders: Colonel Learned was to select five hundred men who had experienced smallpox and with this force and two companies of artillery was to enter Boston.

Washington showed no elation over an event he long had anticipated. He ordered Sullivan to occupy Charlestown while Putnam collected men who could enter Boston without fear of smallpox. It was done with enthusiasm and alacrity. Ward's force of five hundred proceeded to the British outpost and then to the advanced line, where Colonel Learned ceremoniously unbarred and opened the gates on the main road. Nowhere did they encounter British soldiers, but there was abundant work for "Old Put" in locating and salvaging the public property, cannon, small arms and weapons the British left behind.

Washington did not indulge himself in a triumphant entry. He had too much to do and had to ask himself once again a question to which he gave the same convinced answer: Howe's objective certainly was southward, Washington thought, and most probably was New York. The troops that had been delayed in their departure for the mouth of the Hudson could now be dispatched. Such was the end of the most encouraging day Washington had spent after he had assumed command at Cambridge eight and a half months previously. He had forced the Redcoats to evacuate Boston almost without loss of American life. There was one regret, one doubt only: The British fleet had not actually gone to sea. Vessels that had sailed from Boston prior to the seventeenth were in Nantasket Road; the transports that had left Boston on St. Patrick's Day were riding between the Castle and the Light House.

They were close, dangerously close, and they still were there the next morning, March 18. As Washington could do nothing against the fleet, he took time to visit Boston and view for himself the damage that had been wrought. Several of the churches had been stripped of their pews and turned into riding schools; numerous old wooden buildings had been torn down for firewood; the stores around the wharves had been looted of groceries which had been dumped in the filthy streets. Strangely, none of the possessions of John Hancock had been disturbed. "The town," Washington wrote, "although it has suffered greatly, is not in so bad a state as I expected to find it." Washington was much impressed by the fortifications. Boston, he subsequently wrote, was "amazingly strong . . . almost impregnable, every avenue fortified." On Boston Neck, where the defences were much stronger and better built than elsewhere, the works were complete and of a sort to evoke the admiring praise of the captors. The heavy cannon had been spiked but so carelessly that some were quickly cleared again. Miscellaneous ordnance stores, almost the whole of the British medical supplies, a stock of three thousand blankets and much equipment were found on the wharves.

Washington was so suspicious because of the enemy's continued presence in Nantasket Road that he ordered immediately the construction of a strong work on Fort Hill, a dominant position. As the parapet rose fast, while the enemy remained close at hand, Washington's state of mind was one of disappointment and misgiving. On the night of March 19/20 the British demolished the defences at the Castle and blew up buildings that could not readily be burned. The enemy made some efforts, also, to block the channels. If, as seems logical, these were the acts of a commander who was abandoning Boston, why did he not proceed to Halifax, as his men had told Boston people he intended to do; and if Howe was going, instead, to New York or Long Island, as Washington still believed, what deterred him from gaining the advantage of early arrival? Washington started Heath and a brigade of foot for New York on the twentieth; but more men than this he did not think he ought to detach until he could ascertain what the British intended. If *ever* they started for New York—Washington saw clearly his duty. New York, he told Governor Cooke, who feared for the safety of Rhode Island, "secures the free and only communication between the Northern and Southern Colonies, which will be entirely cut off by their possessing it, and give them the command of Hudson's River and an easy pass into Canada. . . ." This made it "absolutely and indispensably necessary for the whole of this army, which is but inconsiderable . . . to be marched from hence for defence with all possible expedition." Barring direct invasion, no part of the Army could be detached to Rhode Island, and no more troops would be left in Boston than were required to give the town protection against surprise attack.

The British should go to New York if their strategy was intelligent: why did they linger, and why, in particular, when the wind was favorable? Six additional American Regiments were made ready for the road. Days dragged anxiously on. On the twenty-seventh, a day when the waters of Massachusetts Bay were running high, and a fair wind with the promise of spring in its breath was blowing steadily, Washington had much to do. All business had been transacted, dinner had been eaten, the end of the day was at hand, the twenty-fifth day after the opening gun on Dorchester Heights—when a messenger drew rein at Headquarters. He brought news, *the* news: That morning at eleven, the flagship *Fowey* had hoisted signal; at 3 P.M., the fleet had made sail from Nantasket. Now the whole of it, except for three or four vessels, was standing out to sea.

"General Howe has a grand maneuvre in view or has made an inglorious retreat"—that was Washington's comment, and it was accompanied almost in the same breath by orders for the dispatch of additional troops to New York. Washington continued to believe the strategic importance of New York so great that he was not justified in delaying the march to that city of all his Army except regiments needed to garrison Boston. On arrival in New York, the whole force was to be under the command of General Putnam till Washington moved Headquarters there. Washington transacted business as fast as he could get it before him. To regular matters were added the vexatious details of moving nine or ten thousand men; and on this were superimposed the ceremonials of congratulation and farewell.

The Massachusetts Assembly presented Washington an address on March 28 which praised his achievements as if the man who had wrought the deliverance of Boston was assured a place among the immortals. A few days later he received from the Selectmen of Boston a brief, laudatory address, which pleased him almost as much as the paper from the General Court. Harvard, in its turn, voted him the honorary degree of Doctor of Laws, but delays in preparing the diploma prevented its delivery.

Had Washington in the last days of March reviewed his conduct of this first campaign, he would have told himself, as an honest-minded man, that he had somewhat underestimated the effective strength of Howe and overestimated the mobility of the Boston forces at sea and on land. A positive mistake, perhaps the most serious Washington made, was the dispatch of Arnold's small, ill-equipped and poorly provisioned force over a wilderness route concerning which information was inadequate and inaccurate. He appears to have exaggerated what one thousand men could do in that savage country. Daring sometimes could defy men, but it could not disregard nature. The other mistake, that of not seizing Dorchester Heights earlier, was it really a mistake? If Howe or Gage had taken a chance of securing the high ground of the peninsula, Washington might have been forced to buy it in blood or to deliver his assault under great disadvantage up narrow Boston Neck. When the British failed to occupy the elevations that overlooked the town, then Washington doubtless reasoned that he could not afford to do so prior to March, because that would have inspired a British attack which he might not be able to beat off with the powder he had. His apparent lack of aggressiveness was lack of powder.

Washington's mistakes had been few and explicable; his shortcomings—the negative as set against the positive—had been more numerous. He had not shown any large skill or any sense of direct responsibility for the enlistment of men. He had devoted too much of his own time to "paper work." A third shortcoming, primarily attributable to distance, was his virtual failure to exercise the full functions of Commander-in-Chief. Washington had a realistic and probably a correct sense of the fundamental strategy of New England and of New York, but he had not demonstrated he could supervise all the plays on the continental chessboard.

Washington had demonstrated that he knew how to make an army out of a congeries of jealous contingents, and he had learned while he had been teaching. He had studied gunnery in the track of the missiles and now he had sufficient acquaintance with that arm to know what he could not expect artillery to do. This self-instruction was acquired while his youthful chief of artillery, Henry Knox, was getting mastery of the cannon. General and Colonel must have gained knowledge together by conversation and test. It was different with Washington's adherence to the great fundamental of concentration of force, and different, too, with that categorical imperative of American defence—sea power. Much was taught Washington and, through him, his country, by his observation of what a few American ships in the hands of courageous men had done in cutting off supplies from Boston, but, basically, he seemed to have from the beginning of the campaign a correct understanding of the larger principles of naval warfare and of American defence. These doctrines, the quintessence of common sense, had been absorbed as matters of course by a man who was the personification of that quality. Moreover, Washington was learning more and more about men. He had shown that he could discharge the business of an army with justice, diligence and excellent judgment. His absolute integrity had been demonstrated again and again; his singleminded devotion to his task had been exemplified in his refusal to leave the camps for any personal reason during the whole of the siege; the dignity and dispatch with which he transacted business, and his courteous good humor in dealing with all comers created an aura.

Washington had fulfilled the highest expectations of his admirers and had exceeded by far anything that would have been anticipated by those who realized how vastly out of scale with his experience as a Colonel were his responsibilities as Commander-in-Chief. He had not gained this esteem by genius, in the sense of specialized ability incomparably greater than that of the average man. He had won this place by the balance of his parts. In nothing transcendent, he was credited with possessing in ample measure every quality of character that administration of the Army demanded. Already he had become a moral rallying-post, the embodiment of the purpose, patience and determination necessary for triumph of the revolutionary cause.

Nowhere was there a hint by Washington that he had surprised himself by his accomplishments in front of Boston. He wrote and acted as if he had been schooled and prepared for the victory that had been won, and he was proud of his achievements and of the applause they had drawn. A few days after the British mastheads disappeared over the horizon, he wrote John Augustine:

I believe I may with great truth affirm that no man perhaps since the first institution of armies ever commanded one under more difficult circumstances, than I have done. To enumerate the particulars would fill a volume. . . . I am happy, however, to find and to hear from different quarters that my reputation stands fair, that my conduct hitherto has given universal satisfaction. The addresses which I have received, and which I suppose will be published, from the General Court of the Colony—the same as our General Assembly—and from the selectmen of Boston upon the evacuation of the town and my approaching departure from the Colony, exhibits a pleasing testimony of their approbation of my conduct and of their personal regard, which I have found in various other instances, and which, in retirement, will afford many comfortable reflections.

In this spirit, on April 4, he left Boston for New York, a prouder man by far, and more self-confident, than when he had arrived nine months previously to undertake his first campaign. He had won; he believed he could do it again.

CHAPTER / 10

Washington's route to New York was by Providence and the towns near Long Island Sound in order that he might expedite the march of his troops; Martha and her entourage proceeded via Hartford. She had made a good, if not a dazzling impression on Massachusetts society. Washington received warm welcome by Governor Cooke and some of the gentlemen of Providence on the sixth. By the afternoon of April 13 he was in New York.

In the city Tories were diminishing in number but still were strong and not lacking in confidence, because they had the protection of British men-of-war that could set the town afire at any hour. The "Sons of Liberty" were not cowed by the cannon of the ships and not disposed to let the Loyalists plot mischief. Feeling, already tense, was rising daily. Some defensive works had been completed by militia who had just been discharged; other fortification was in progress. Putnam was in command with Heath under him; troops were fewer than Washington had expected to find and were rashly dispersed.

The situation was disorganized and confused because it lacked the experienced direction of Charles Lee who had designated sites but had left execution in its first stage when he had received command of a newly created Southern Department. Lee had thought it "more prudent" that he be dispatched to Canada, because of his knowledge of French, but he wrote of the southern command, "I shall obey with alacrity and hope with success." Washington had said: "As a Virginian, I must rejoice at the change; but, as an American, I think you would have done more essential service to the common cause in Canada." Privately Washington had begun to doubt the stability, perhaps the dependability, of his senior lieutenant. "He is," Washington had written his brother Jack, "the first officer in military knowledge and experience we have in the whole Army. He is zealously attached to the cause, honest and well-meaning but rather fickle and violent I fear in his temper."

Before Washington could master the details of the fortifications Lee had left unfinished, the Commander-in-Chief was compelled to deal with a dismal situation in Canada. Congress had decided on February 15 to name three commissioners to proceed to Canada and had determined to send to the St. Lawrence an officer of high rank and recognized ability. As Schuyler was physically unfit to take the field, Congress had chosen John Thomas for this mission and had made him a Major General. Thomas had left Roxbury March 22 and on the twenty-eighth had reached Albany. There he had caught the echo of much doubt and misery voiced by officers and men in Canada. When fragmentary reports could be pieced together during April, they showed many discouragements. Gen. David Wooster had transferred his headquarters to the camp of the small American force that was keeping up the pretence of a siege of Quebec; Arnold had gone to Montreal, which was still in the hands of Continental troops. Before Arnold had left Quebec, he had been hampered by the sullenness of discontented men and the presence of no less than five feet of snow. He had four hundred sick and wounded, though he himself had almost recovered. After Wooster reached the lines across from Quebec, he had an even gloomier tale to tell. The American forces on that front numbered between two and three thousand, of whom not more than half were fit for duty. Many were determined to leave April 15, when their enlistment expired. New troops were arriving slowly and were of small use because of the prevalence of smallpox. Col. Moses Hazen had sent Schuyler a discouraging report. "We have brought on ourselves by mismanagement," Hazen wrote bluntly, "what Governor Carleton himself never could effect."

Before the worst of this was known, Congress had reaffirmed its resolution to add Canada to the United Colonies and to retrieve the defeat Montgomery had sustained. Washington had been directed to detach four battalions to Canada. In addition, the able Commissioners of Congress—Franklin, Samuel Chase and Charles Carroll—had been given instructions, vested with discretionary power to raise companies, and started on their way.

It now was time for Washington to do his part to win Canada to the Colonial cause. Washington alone could supply trained men in sufficient strength to shift the balance again. Desire to destroy the enemy's strongholds in Canada disposed him to relax his insistence on concentration of force and comply vigorously with orders he would in any event have obeyed. He was inclined, also, to give more credit than formerly to the reports that Howe's fleet was bound for Halifax, whence it would be easy to detach men and transport up the St. Lawrence to Quebec. Washington felt confident that New York was too much a prize strategically for a competent British commander to ignore. In the same way, he regarded Canada as a base so convenient and valuable for the British that the Americans were justified in risks and sacrifices to wrest the northern province from the enemy.

The strategy of the struggle was changing. It was becoming a contest for the control of the Hudson: If Howe could seize and occupy the mouth of the river, he might be able to sever the eastern Colonies from the others. If Washington could close the St. Lawrence between Quebec and Montreal, he could prevent the use of that river for operations against the Hudson. It was a dramatic race—Washington to Quebec, Howe to New York.

Four battalions were made ready to proceed up the Hudson under the command of William Thompson. By the time Washington received word on April 27 of the arrival of these troops in Albany, he had new orders from Philadelphia: He was to send six additional regiments to Canada and if he thought this force insufficient to assure the capture of Quebec, he was to indicate whether still more men could be spared from New York. Washington immediately designated the regiments to go and named John Sullivan to the command. On the question of still larger assistance for the Canadian expedition he said: ". . . I should wish indeed that the army in Canada should be more powerfully reenforced; at the same time I am conscious that the trusting this important post (which is now become the Grand Magazine of America) to the handful of men remaining here is running too great a risk: The securing this post and Hudsons River is to us also of so great importance that I cannot at present advise the sending any more troops from hence." Then he went on to explain that his officers thought a garrison of ten thousand necessary for New York.

In restless, divided New York the soldiers were subjected to temptations different from those they had faced in small New England villages and in camps from which women were excluded. The neighborhood known satirically as "the holy ground" was shocking to some of the men of Puritan descent. Wild tales were told of what was done by denizens of dark places. Many of the soldiers went to the dives with the result that venereal disease was prevalent in some commands. There were, too, numerous cases of desertion and some instances of drunkenness, combined with so much disorder that the offenders had to be brought before general court-martial. A considerable part of the Commander-in-Chief's orders on disciplinary matters dealt with camp sanitation and with the protection of the houses, trees and gardens of citizens. Washington requested the Committee of Safety to put an end to trading with the enemy and, when that did not suffice, he served notice that traffickers would be punished.

The defences of New York were strengthened. Along with his scheme of fortification, Lee had given Congress his analysis of the tactical possibilities of coping with an adversary who commanded the waters around New York City. Lee's theory was that the town scarcely could be made a tenable fortress, but that it could be "made a most advantageous field of battle, so advantageous, indeed, that if our people behave with common spirit, and the commanders are men of discretion, it might cost the enemy many thousands of men to get possession of it."

Long Island Sound could be dominated by the Americans; Long Island itself could be defended by four to five thousand men with redoubts at its western end. Cross fire from these fortifications and those of New York would make it almost certain that East River could be closed to the British. North River was so wide and deep that the enemy could navigate it but might have less power to do mischief than had been assumed. The ground offered some protection from naval ordnance; batteries could keep men-of-war at a distance. Barriers and redoubts must be erected; King's Bridge must be so fortified that communication would be "free and open" with Connecticut, to which New York would have to look for reenforcements. New Jersey could not be relied upon in an hour of sudden danger because the North River made easy contact precarious.

Lee had been able to interpret only a part of his program into terms of parapets and ditches before he had been sent south. Washington had to complete what Lee had begun. That was the easier part of the task. More

MAP / 9

NEW YORK, 1776

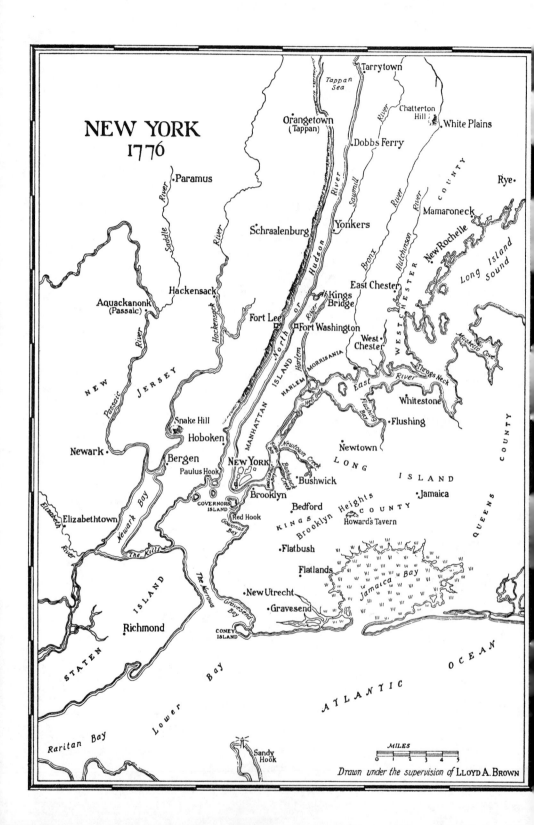

NEW YORK
1776

Tarrytown

Tappan Sea

Orangetown
(Tappan)

Chatterton
Hill
•White Plains

Dobbs Ferry

•Paramus

Saddle River

River

WESTCHESTER COUNTY

Rye •

Mamaroneck

Schraalenburg

Yonkers

Sawmill River

Bronx River

Hutchinson River

New Rochelle

Long Island Sound

Hackensack

Hackensack River

North or Hudson River

East Chester

West Chester

WESTCHESTER COUNTY

Mosketto Cove

Aquackanonk
(Passaic)

Fort Lee

Kings
Bridge

☐Fort Washington

Harlem River

MORRISANIA

NEW JERSEY

Passaic River

MANHATTAN ISLAND

HARLEM

Hell Gate

East River

Throgs Neck

Whitestone

Snake Hill

Hoboken

Newtown Creek

Flushing Bay

•Flushing

LONG

Newark •

Bergen

Paulus Hook

NEW YORK

Wallabout Bay

Bushwick

•Bushwick

Newtown

ISLAND

QUEENS COUNTY

GOVERNORS
ISLAND

Brooklyn

Bedford

Brooklyn Heights

•Jamaica

Elizabethtown

Elizabeth River

Newark Bay

The Kills

Red Hook

Gowanus Bay

KINGS COUNTY

Howard's Tavern

•Flatbush

STATEN ISLAND

The Narrows

•New Utrecht

Flatlands

Jamaica Bay

Richmond

Gravesend Bay

•Gravesend

CONEY
ISLAND

Lower Bay

Gravesend Bay

ATLANTIC OCEAN

Raritan Bay

Sandy
Hook

MILES
0 1 2 3 4 5

Drawn under the supervision of LLOYD A. BROWN

troops had to be made available for service whenever the lookouts signalled that the King's canvas was visible on the horizon. Washington had barely 8300 men fit for duty as of April 23. He appealed to the New York Committee of Safety to provide 2000 to 2500 militia for an emergency and, while setting no figure, he made a like request of New Jersey. Connecticut, too, was enjoined to have men ready for the instant succor of their comrades in New York.

Bickering and argument between Whig and Tory became more violent. If the Loyalist looked down the harbor towards the masts of the *Asia* and prayed for the arrival of a delivering fleet, the Americans talked increasingly of proclaiming independence and of jailing spies and traitors. The anniversary of Concord and Lexington was past. Uncertainty had prevailed for a year: there soon must be a decision. Washington sensed or saw it all from his Headquarters at Abraham Mortier's, where Martha had joined him April 17.

Of honor, there was as much as he who loved the approval of his fellowmen could ask. John Adams informed him that Congress had voted thanks and a gold medal for Washington's accomplishments at Boston. As author of this motion and chairman of the committee on the design of a medal, Adams wished Washington's "sentiments concerning a proper" device. Formal notification, approved by Congress on April 2 and duly signed by Hancock, overtook Washington on the seventeenth. It contained a eulogistic review of the campaign. Then followed official thanks which Washington was to communicate to the Army. The General's reply was, in part, an assurance "that it will ever be my highest ambition to approve myself a faithful servant of the public; and that to be in any degree instrumental in procuring to my American brethren a restitution of their just rights and privileges will constitute my chief happiness." Then, in justice to his men, Washington said: "They were indeed at first 'a band of undisciplined husbandmen' but it is (under God) to their bravery and attention to their duty that I am indebted for that success which procured for me the only reward I wish to receive, the affection and esteem of my countrymen." Always the approval and applause of his fellow-men had been the supreme goal, next that of acquiring a fortune. It had been to deserve this approval that he had shaped his life and disciplined his spirit. Now, in larger measure than ever, he had honor and something already approaching veneration.

Now, he had to contend with an acute shortage of small arms, with the slow progress of recruiting, the termination July 1 of the enlistment of the riflemen, and the possibility that neglect of the refortification of Boston might invite a return of the British. Artemas Ward had presented his resignation as Major General on the grounds of ill-health, but Congress had failed to name a successor. Ward remained, though he still asked to be relieved. Washington had no high opinion of Ward and said nothing to indicate regret at the news that he had decided to leave the Army.

The possibility of an attack on Boston seemed at times to be remote and, in other circumstances, to be not unlikely; but as of May 5, Washington had to admit: "The designs of the enemy are too much behind the curtain for me to form any accurate opinion of their plan of operations for the summer's campaign." He still thought that no place was of more importance to the British than the mouth of the Hudson. He and Congress soon had information that the enemy might be strong enough to reenforce their troops in Canada, send Howe to New York and, perhaps, strike simultaneously at some other point. By the second week in May, American leaders came to believe there was truth to reports that the King had hired German troops from continental princes. Regiments were known to have been dispatched from Ireland, also. A stronger Britain would confront an America weakened by dispersion of force, losses of many sorts and the ravages of smallpox.

The worst nightmare was disaster in Canada. Thomas had arrived in front of Quebec May 1 and had taken general command; Thompson, promoted to Brigadier, was known to have reached Fort George. Sullivan and his command were supposed to be proceeding north from Albany; Schuyler was doing his utmost to forward supplies. The Commissioners to Canada reported from Montreal that a supply of coin was necessary and that the lack of it was responsible, along with "other arbitrary proceedings," for many of the difficulties the troops were encountering. By May 15 papers that passed through Washington's hands led him to conclude: "nothing less than the most wise and vigorous exertions of Congress and the Army there can promise success."

It did not so befall. Two days after writing this letter, Washington received from Schuyler a report that covered a tale of calamity. Smallpox, paper money, poor transport and divided leadership had weakened the Americans hopelessly in the face of a strengthened adversary. A British squadron of five vessels had reached Quebec May 6. There followed an affair thus summarized in the American Commissioners' letter to Schuyler, the paper Washington read: "The enemy made a sally . . . in a body supposed not to be less than a thousand. Our forces were so dispersed that not more than two hundred could be collected at headquarters. In this situation, a retreat was inevitable, and made in the utmost precipitation and confusion, with the loss of our cannon on the batteries, provisions, five hundred stands of small arms and a batteau load of powder. . . ."

Washington had hoped that the besiegers of Quebec could remain in front of the city until the reenforcement of ten regiments from his own Army arrived, but he did not interpret the bad news to mean that the major effort of the British was certain to be directed south from that stronghold. On the contrary, his office was preparing to draft orders for a continuing general alert in New York. He had, in short, to face the possibility that the vital line of the Hudson might be assailed from the north and from the south; he felt that the response to this should not be vain regret but active resolution. He encouraged and exhorted Schuyler and undertook to rally Sullivan.

Washington received on the eighteenth from an escaped prisoner of war, George Merchant, a number of papers, among which were copies of the treaties England had made for the employment of approximately seventeen thousand German troops. This action was enough to quicken demand for a final break with the mother country, and, so far as Washington's military problem was concerned, it meant also that the enemy with more troops, could strike heavier blows in more places—and speedily. Merchant brought with him a letter that indicated fifteen British regiments were at sea or soon would be bound for America.

Washington concluded that Adjutant General Gates should go at once to Philadelphia. He did not feel that he himself should leave New York when there was a prospect the British fleet might descend on that city at any time. He turned over to Gates the copies of the German treaties and, in a communication to Hancock let it be understood that Gates had the largest latitude to make suggestions. On the evening of the day Washington wrote this letter, there arrived from Hancock an invitation for Washington to visit Philadelphia for his health and for consultation with Congress. Along with this came highly interesting Army news: Horatio Gates had been promoted Major General, and Thomas Mifflin had been made a Brigadier. With this much Washington was heartily in accord. The disturbing note was in a request from Hancock that both Gates and Mifflin be assigned to duty in Massachusetts, where Washington did not believe there was material danger of a British landing. It was too much to lose Gates as Adjutant General and, in addition, to have him shelved on Beacon Hill.

Washington drew up careful instructions for Putnam to press the fortification of New York and set out for Philadelphia, where he found a great diversity of business to be transacted in an atmosphere of excitement over possible independence and depression over Canada. When the Commissioners prepared their report, four days after Washington dismounted in Philadelphia, they listed circumstances to humiliate the continent: "General Wooster is, in our opinion unfit, totally unfit, to command your Army. . . . Your army is badly paid; and so exhausted is your credit that even a cart cannot be procured without ready money or force. . . . Your army in Canada do not exceed 4000; above 400 are sick with different disorders. . . . We cannot find words to describe our miserable situation. . . ." Washington told himself that America must expect a "bloody summer" for which she was not prepared; but he could not believe the situation in Canada beyond redemption by courage and effort. The force in Canada must be augmented, but not at the expense of the Army that was to defend New York against almost certain attack. That was the major premise of his recommendations to Congress.

On May 24 and 25 Washington appeared before Congress to answer inquiries of members. When this proved an awkward arrangement, he, Gates and Mifflin held frequent conferences with a committee named for that purpose. The broad conclusion was to contest "every foot of ground" occupied by the Americans in Canada and to do the utmost to hold a position below the mouth of the Richelieu River. Entry of the British into the upper country of the United Colonies was to be prevented by American operations on the St. Lawrence; efforts were to be made to prevail on Indians to attack Niagara and Detroit; New York and the mouth of the Hudson were of course to be defended. A two-to-one superiority of force was desired and was to be had, substantially, by enlisting until December 1 approximately twenty thousand militia, who were to be apportioned among the Colonies from New Jersey northward. Indians not exceeding two thousand were to be hired in Canada. In addition, the Middle Colonies of Delaware, Pennsylvania and Maryland were to provide until December a total of ten thousand militia who were to constitute a "Flying Camp," under "such continental general officers as the Commander-in-Chief shall direct." All this was agreed upon readily. Washington believed short-term enlistment responsible for much of the woe of the Army in Canada and urged the grant of a bounty to men already in the Army who would enlist for a term of years or for the "continuance of the war." He found Congress not yet willing to vote the bounty or provide for enlargement of the Continental Line on the basis of two or three years' service. Reliance still was on the militia for emergencies. Washington acquiesced.

While this discussion of "survive or perish" called for Washington's full participation, the other subject of talk at every table—whether and when the Colonies should declare their independence—was one with which he scarcely had patience. He wrote his brother: ". . . things have come to that pass now as to convince us that we have nothing more to expect from the justice of Great Britain." Washington found this the view of virtually all those members of Congress with whom he had been on closest terms during the months he had belonged to the Virginia delegation. Having gone so far, they felt they now might as well go all the way. Most of New England was impatient over delay. As the end of May approached, Virginia and North Carolina were believed to be ready for action. It was understood that the Middle Colonies and some of those in the south would be the last to assent, but there was a disposition to wait for a few weeks in the belief that unanimity might be achieved. Soon, it seemed, an answer was to be made to the warning of Charles Lee: "If you do not declare immediately for positive independence, we are all ruined."

Washington's immediate task was to counsel regarding the means by which the evil day in Canada could be redeemed, and his, too, was the duty of advising on the choice of men to take the place of Gates as Adjutant General and of Mifflin as Quartermaster General. Now it was possible to offer Joseph Reed the post of Adjutant General and invoke the aid of members of Congress in prevailing on him to accept. Reed's lack of precise knowledge of the Adjutant's functions and duties did not weigh decisively, in Washington's mind, when set against the quick perception and social skill of the Philadelphian. Divided New York called for the finesse Reed could display. Washington had been showing great deference for the feelings of New York, but he wanted to have at his command the diplomatic address and diversified knowledge of men and of law that Reed possessed. With some difficulty, he prevailed.

For Mifflin's successor as Quartermaster General, Washington turned to another member of his military "family," his recently appointed aide Stephen Moylan, who previously had been Mustermaster General. He had energy and a ready tongue and gave promise of as good an administration as could be expected where almost everything a Quartermaster sought was crude and costly or unprocurable.

Throughout these consultations with Congress, Washington felt heightened concern for the safety of New York, but no weary express knocked at Washington's door with the anticipated news from North River. Business in Philadelphia was concluded in comparative calm. On June 3 Hancock expressed to Washington the thanks of Congress for "unremitted attention" to his trust and especially for assistance in making plans for the defence of the Colonies. The General was free, Hancock wrote, to return to Headquarters when he saw fit. Washington waited only to get copies of the various resolves of Congress that concerned his duties, and then, leaving Martha in the Quaker City, he was off on the fourth for New York, where he arrived June 6.

Good news and bad awaited him. It was good because all was quiet and because visible progress had been made on the defences: it was bad in that letters from Canada gave alarming if vague details of a new defeat at The Cedars, about thirty miles up the St. Lawrence from Montreal. Washington feared the next intelligence would be of the loss of Montreal. From other sources, he heard that General Thomas had smallpox and, on the eighth, he had the shocking announcement that the vigorous New Englander was dead. Washington reiterated to Schuyler what he had said to more than one correspondent: "The most vigorous exertions will be necessary to retrieve our circumstances there, and I hope you will strain every nerve for that purpose. Unless it can be done now, Canada will be lost forever, the fatal consequences of which everyone must feel." Thomas's death would have meant normally that Brigadier General Wooster would have assumed temporary command; but on the day Washington learned of it, notice was received from Hancock that Wooster had been relieved of command. Charles Carroll and Samuel Chase, two of the Canadian Commissioners of Congress, had reached New York and now reported to Washington. Their particular object of wrath was Wooster, who soon would be on his way to New York. "I wish to know what I am to do with him," Washington asked Congress, "when he comes."

Supplies for Canada had to be hurried up the Hudson; the fortification of New York was continued, that of Powles Hook on the Jersey side of North River was pressed, and the task of guarding the New York highlands was entrusted to Col. James Clinton. Discipline was enforced with even more vigor than previously. These and kindred tasks were discharged in an atmosphere of expectancy. Hour by hour, suspense was heightened.

As early as June 10 Governor Tryon was credited with saying that a frigate from Halifax had brought news of the embarkation of Howe's army for New York. In the camps it was predicted that the enemy would attack within ten days. Washington felt that this information originated with Loyalists who were reporting all American activities to the *Asia* or to the ships off Sandy Hook and were supplying them with fresh provisions. When he had gone to Philadelphia he had been hopeful that the New York authorities would arrest the men most apt to aid the King. Now a vigorous policy was pursued by the New York patriots; a general search for disaffected persons was begun.

During the first stages of this hunt for Tories, Washington had no concern over the prospective vote on independence. He doubtless was informed promptly that Congress had decided June 10 to postpone further discussion of the issue for three weeks in the hope that the Delegates of the most hesitant Colonies would receive authority to vote for separation from England.

Even if nothing of consequence was to come from Philadelphia before July, news might be expected at any time from Canada, news so grim that Washington almost dreaded its arrival. When the first additional budget reached him in the form of two dispatches from Sullivan he felt distinct relief. Sullivan described enthusiastically what he pronounced a "strange turn" in the American cause. "The Canadians," he said, "are flocking by hundreds to take a part with us." He had ordered General Thompson to proceed to Three Rivers and, if that officer did not find the enemy greatly superior in numbers, attack. This was what Washington had been advocating—the American front as far as possible in the direction of Quebec. He approved Sullivan's plan with heartiness and, at the same time, with cautious understanding of both the ambitious officer and the difficulties that had to be overcome. Sullivan manifestly was "aiming at the command in Canada." Washington accordingly decided to transmit Sullivan's letter to Hancock and, after presenting as fair a sketch as he could of the character of the New Hampshire General, to say nothing to influence the decision of Congress whether Sullivan should be placed at the head of the little army in Canada.

Embarrassment was escaped by prompt action in Philadelphia. The very day Washington's letter to the President was written, Congress decided to vest in Horatio Gates the Canadian command and direct Washington to expedite the departure of the new Major General. Whether Gates would be acceptable to Sullivan, it was impossible for Washington to say. Nor was it certain that Gates would go there in the most cooperative state of mind. In confidential letters to New England friends, he was becoming critical of Washington.

Washington probably knew nothing of this correspondence, but he doubtless felt that he had good fortune in avoiding a disagreeable encounter with General Wooster, who arrived in New York June 17. No high officer of the Army was held in such low opinion by most of those whose opinion was of value. When Wooster arrived the Commander-in-Chief had received no answer to his inquiry concerning what he should do with the Connecticut officer, but he heard that Wooster desired to go home for a visit; so, in renewing his question about the employment of the veteran, Washington told Congress of the General's wish. Patience paid its practitioner. Wooster announced that he wished to proceed to Philadelphia and to talk with Congressmen before going home. Gladly and promptly Washington assented.

Thus stood matters when on June 21, David Matthews, Mayor of New York, was "charged with dangerous designs and treasonable conspiracies against the rights and liberties of the United Colonies of America" by a committee of the Provincial Congress; Washington was authorized and requested to apprehend and secure the Mayor and all his papers. Matthews had been listed a few weeks previously by the Provincial Congress of New York as one of those whom the people were "naturally led to consider . . . as their enemies" because of failure to aid the American cause, but no action had been taken against him. On June 17, a man named Isaac Ketcham, who was in jail for complicity in an attempt at counterfeiting, informed the Provincial Congress that he believed two fellow prisoners, Continental soldiers, Thomas Hickey and Michael Lynch, belonged to some "corps" that was receiving money from the British fleet. These culprits and persons who came to see them in prison talked of cutting down King's Bridge and of going over to the enemy when the British fleet came. The Provincial Congress listened in alarm to Ketcham and, after a meeting between Washington and one of its spokesmen that day, named a committee to confer with the General.

As a result of this, John Jay and Gouverneur Morris, of the special secret committee, examined William Leary who had come to town from Orange County on the seventeenth in search of a runaway servant of Erskine's Bigwood Ironworks. Leary found the absconder but lost him at the Powles Hook Ferry to a Sergeant who enlisted the man in Captain Roosevelt's Company. While waiting at the ferry, Leary chanced upon one James Mason, who previously had been in the employ of the operator of the ironworks but had been discharged. After some cautious fencing, Mason confided that he and several companions had sworn to quit New York and go on board a British man-of-war. Until they could be carried out safely to the ship, they were receiving wages and provisions, he said, from a man who represented the Mayor of the city or the Governor of the Colony. Leary then went with Mason to visit Mason's friends and later made an attempt to lure them to one of the American camps, but they became suspicious and scattered. Leary's testimony to the committee was that enlistment for service aboard a British ship was in progress and that the Mayor or the Governor was alleged to be paying the costs. Leary believed the money came from Mayor Matthews but was not certain.

It was on the basis of the testimony of Mason and Leary that the committee asked Washington to take Matthews into custody. Matthews surrendered at his residence without resistance, but no written evidence was found there. Gilbert Forbes, a gunsmith incriminated by Leary's statements, was also apprehended and taken before the committee but he was unwilling to say anything. The next morning, a young minister, Robert Livingston, visited him and sympathetically exhorted him to tell the truth as he probably had only a few days of life. This stirred Forbes either to clear his conscience or to try to save his neck. He offered to go before the committee and confess everything. The net thereupon was carefully and widely spread. Even suspects who belonged to Washington's Headquarters Guard had no warning of danger until they were confronted with the bayonets of the Provost Marshal's men.

Matthews was examined on June 23 before Philip Livingston, Jay and Morris. Washington believed that Matthews was guilty and that the conspiracy originated with Governor Tryon, but he concerned himself first with the allegation that soldiers of his own Guard, even, had been charged with crimes that ranged from threats of desertion to treasonable communication with the enemy. The men who had been plotting together apparently had considered little that was definite, but they had talked vaguely of destroying King's Bridge to cut off reenforcements and of seizing a battery when the fleet attacked. Conspiracy must be dealt with immediately. Drummer William Greene of the General's Guard, though among those most criminally involved, was willing to confess and throw himself on the mercy of the court. The most obdurate suspect was Hickey, one of two Continental soldiers jailed for an alleged attempt to pass counterfeit. After his arrest for trafficking in bad money, he and his companion, Lynch, were said by one witness to have sworn they never would fight any more for America. Hickey and Lynch had boasted, moreover, that almost seven hundred men had promised to stand by the King, and the two culprits confided to other inmates of the jail that the American Army had become damnably corrupted, that the fleet was soon to arrive, and that a band was to turn against the Americans then. Eight of the General's Guard, Hickey had said, were participants in the plan.

In these circumstances, it seemed best to make an example of Hickey. He was arraigned before a court-martial on the twenty-sixth. Greene and other witnesses adhered to their previous statements; Hickey produced no witnesses and only a pathetically feeble defence. The verdict was immediate and unanimous, death by hanging, a sentence which Washington confirmed the next day and put in execution a little before noon June 28. As far as the records show, no other was punished, though Mayor Matthews was in jail. Washington believed some of the Tories capable of almost any crime to defeat the American cause, but, with characteristic restraint, he said of Hickey's execution, "I am hopeful this example will produce many salutary consequences and deter others from entering into like traitorous practices." That was written at a time when events more serious, by far, than a scotched conspiracy, called for Washington's attention.

On the day Matthews had been arrested, June 22, an express from General Schuyler had reached Washington with news that contradicted all the high hopes in the letters from Sullivan. Thompson had proceeded to Three Rivers, had attacked the British, and had sustained a reverse on June 8. He and a considerable number of his officers and men surrendered. The remainder of the original force of approximately two thousand counted themselves lucky in getting back to Sorel, which it now was manifest the Americans could not hold. By the evening of the twenty-third Washington had dispatches which indicated that the only question in dispute among the officers immediately responsible for operations in Canada was the depth of their withdrawal. Some of those who should have best judgment on the issue thought the Army should not attempt to hold a position north of Crown Point, 150 miles south of Sorel. Arnold, meantime, on the night of June 15 had evacuated Montreal with his force of three hundred and had proceeded to Ile aux Noix. As reunited at that point, the American forces numbered approximately seven thousand men, about half of whom were sick and unfit for duty.

Washington was profoundly alarmed by this reverse; Canada was lost; Sullivan would be fortunate if he could escape and, with Schuyler's help, fortify and hold the passes of the New York lakes. Gates must proceed north at once and take command of the troops under the discouraged but still ambitious Sullivan. No detailed orders could be given the new Major General. Gates could hope to accomplish little unless there was early attainment of the goal set in Congress' resolution of June 25 that "the number of men destined for the Northern Department be augmented to 4000." To provide reenforcement Congress at length had heeded Washington's plea for a bounty and offered ten dollars to every sergeant, corporal and private soldier who would enlist for three years.

Gates had to do what he could in reorganizing the broken forces that had survived the campaign. Washington, for his part, had to face the high probability that soon the British would be hammering at both ends of the waterline and portages that linked the St. Lawrence with Sandy Hook. If Gen. John Burgoyne already had begun the ascent of the Richelieu, it could not be long before Howe would be pointing the bows of his ships up the Hudson. While giving all possible assistance to Gates's expedition, Washington had to struggle with the supreme vexation of command, that of trying to achieve quickly and securely what ignorant men with rude implements and feeble equipment were apt to do slowly, awkwardly, and in slovenly style. Fortunately, brigade and regimental organization now was familiar with its duties and was able to take some of the detail off the hands of the commanding General.

So much had to be done! The establishment of a Troop of Light Horse had to be approved and encouraged; fortification had to be pressed; obstructions were placed in North River to discourage a naval commander who might feel confident he could pass the batteries; arrangement had to be made for the prompt summons of the militia from other Colonies when the fleet hove in sight; greater vigilance in the patrol of nearby waters was ordered to prevent communication between ship and shore; additional arms were sought from captured stores in Boston; snarls in the negotiations of Schuyler with the Indians had to be untangled.

Information that appeared to be indisputable was laid before the busy General on June 28 that Howe had left Halifax for New York on June 9 with 130 sail. It was reported that his flagship already was at Sandy Hook. Washington at once called on the authorities of Massachusetts and Connecticut to "lose not a moment's time in sending forward the militia of your province as the enemy will undoubtedly attack us in our weak state as soon as a sufficient force arrives to enable them to attempt it with the least probability of success. . . ." About nine o'clock the next morning, as officers looked through The Narrows to the high ground on Staten Island, they saw flags were up—the agreed signal that the British fleet was in sight. By the time Washington sat down to write a dispatch to the President of Congress forty-five ships had come in; when an express arrived from the lower bay about 2 P.M., he reported that almost one hundred rigged vessels had arrived and had anchored in the Hook. Washington called a council to review plans for defence; and he wrote briefly and grimly to Hancock without any attempt at literary finish or rhetorical flourish: "I am hopeful before [the British] are prepared to attack that I shall get some reenforcements, but be that as it may, I shall attempt to make the best disposition I can for our troops, in order to give them a proper reception, and to prevent the ruin and destruction they are meditating against us." There was no blinking the desperate task ahead of him and no disposition to ignore the possibility that the enemy's men-of-war might slip past the batteries on the shores of the North River and pass upstream to a junction with Burgoyne.

Preparation at New York was hampered by the shortage of senior officers. Now that Thomas had died and Gates had followed Lee away from Headquarters that were the Colonies' one military training school, Washington had a single Major General at New York, "Old Put." Washington also was encumbered by a mass of paper work he could not pass on readily to the inexperienced men who had joined his small staff. The American force at Washington's command was being increased slowly, and some days scarcely at all, by the militia for whom Washington continued to call urgently. The term of the rifle companies was expiring; few of these men were willing to reenlist. Then, as the militia of Massachusetts seemed loath to assemble and start a march for the relief of New York, Washington had to arrange for the transfer of three of the five regiments of Continental troops he had left in the Bay Colony. The exposed situation in Jersey made him all the more anxious to see Congress organize the Flying Camp that had been authorized. He had to get Martha started homeward, because New York under threat of attack was no place for her, and he had as much vexation and anxiety as he would permit himself concerning developments in northern New York.

Sullivan had reached Crown Point with all his troops except six hundred whom he had left to assist the armed vessels on Lake Champlain. He was somewhat apologetic; but he was in better spirits and felt as strongly as ever ambition to command. Within a few days he learned that Gates had been sent north to take charge of operations, and he blazed with resentment. He asked Schuyler to permit him to leave the department, with the intimation that he would resign. Schuyler, smoothing him down, gave permission for him to go to see Washington; but Schuyler himself was engaged in controversy with Gates over their respective authority. Schuyler maintained that Gates had no control of the northern troops except in Canada; Gates contended that he had command of the little army wherever it was. Both men displayed candor and good temper, but neither yielded anything to the other. Washington read with regret of their clash and referred it to Congress with a request for prompt decision. With a veritable palisade of British masts down the harbor, Washington felt he could best leave such a dispute to the gentlemen in Philadelphia.

The movements of the British fleet indicated that Howe was about to attack one part or another of the district around New York. On July 1 many vessels raised sail, came closer to The Narrows and anchored off Gravesend, Long Island. Washington sent five hundred men to strengthen the force stationed there under Nathanael Greene. The next day some of the British men-of-war were within eight hundred yards of Long Island; before nightfall approximately fifty-five had maneuvered close to Staten Island and anchored. A heavy British landing on Staten Island, July 3, deepened concern; but when the enemy began throwing up works there, July 5, Washington concluded that his adversaries had no more serious immediate design than to make themselves masters of the island, a stronghold of Tory feeling. Other information suggested that the British might be planning an advance in Jersey simultaneously with an attack on New York by another column, which would have the support of the fleet. This operation, it was thought, the British would not undertake prior to the arrival of Gen. William Howe's brother, Richard, Admiral Viscount Howe, newly appointed to the command of the North American Station. Prediction was that he soon would reach Sandy Hook with 150 sail and more troops.

Washington a year before had held at Cambridge his first council of war. Incredibly, in the twelve months that had elapsed, he had fought no battle. Not once had lines been drawn where Americans and British exchanged volleys. Washington had demonstrated that he could organize, train, discipline and administer an army. By complete devotion to duty, justice to his men, moderation of judgment and unchallengeable integrity he had become the symbol of what the best of the Americans wished their cause to represent. But the stubborn fact remained: he had fame without fight. Now it would be different. It had to be; Howe, not he, had the initiative. Washington and the Army had to meet the test of battle—and meet it now with the assurance that if they failed, nobody would plead for mercy on devoted, if errant subjects of the King. The Delegates in Philadelphia had renounced that allegiance. On the evening of the fourth, the rumor spread that the Congress in Philadelphia had declared the Colonies independent. It was not until July 9 that official notice was at hand for Washington to include the intelligence in General Orders:

The Hon. The Continental Congress, impelled by the dictates of duty, policy and necessity, having been pleased to dissolve the Connection which subsisted between this Country, and Great Britain, and to declare the United Colonies of North America, free and independent States. . . .

There was a report on the tenth that British regulars in large number were drawn up at the Staten Island ferry. Before Washington could be certain whether this forecast an incursion of the Jersey shore, he had alarming proof that Howe was preparing for the long-dreaded move to open the Hudson to the British. On the afternoon of July 12, the forty-gun *Phoenix* and the *Rose*, twenty guns, with the accompanying schooner *Tryal* and two tenders, were seen to move towards North River. The alarm was sounded; within twenty-five minutes the vessels were close enough to the town for the American batteries on both shores to open. In comparison with the days of stinted artillery fire at Boston, there was a veritable avalanche of round shots and even a few shells; but few of these projectiles hulled the British oak. In a short time the two men-of-war, the schooner and the tenders were up the river, almost intact, and ere long were casting anchor in the Tappan Sea. The vessels, in the judgment of the American commander, were to be employed to stop the shipment of supplies between New York and Albany by land as well as by water or the crews were to put arms ashore for the Tories of the region. Washington was prompt to urge vigilant defence of the highland passes, and he was relieved to hear from the Commissary General that interruption of the flow of supplies would not hamper operations in northern New York. Sufficient food was stored there, Washington was told, to provide for ten thousand men over a period of four months.

One serious aspect of this affair of the *Phoenix* and the *Rose* was the misbehavior of many American soldiers, who, at the sounding of the alarm, should have hurried to their posts. They did almost everything except that. Not more than half the artillerists even went to the guns. Hundreds of the troops appeared to forget their duty in watching the race of the ships up the stream. "Such unsoldierly conduct," Washington said the next day in General Orders, "must grieve every good officer, and give the enemy a mean opinion of the Army, as nothing shows the brave and good soldier more than in case of alarms, coolly and calmly repairing to his post and there waiting his orders, whereas a weak curiosity at such a time makes a man look mean and contemptible."

While the ill-disciplined American troops were running up the east bank of the Hudson something potentially more serious was happening in the lower harbor: a tall ship flying St. George's flag at her fore topmast head was making her way to anchorage. Experienced seafaring men identified her as the *Eagle* and knew from the position of her flag that she had a vice admiral aboard. Vice Admiral Lord Howe had arrived; behind him would come transports and escorts that were supposed to number 150 sail, with a reenforcement of fifteen thousand men.

This was a prospect of adverse odds for the American commander of Continentals and militia who did not reach a higher aggregate than that of the hostile reenforcement. To strengthen the small American force, New England was to be stripped of Continentals who were to be brought to the mouth of the Hudson or were to be sent to Gates as soon as they were free of smallpox. Indians were to be enlisted; artillerymen were to be recruited; troops already in service were to receive the bounty of ten dollars, if they, like the recruits, enlisted for three years; further militia drafts were to be expected.

Suddenly there was an entirely new development. On the afternoon of July 12 a messenger brought word that a British naval officer had come up the harbor with a flag of truce and a letter which he desired to deliver to Washington. Some intimation was given that the paper might not be addressed acceptably, for which reason Washington immediately called into council the Generals close at hand. They agreed with him that he should give safe conduct to any officer who brought an official message to him as American commander but that he should not receive any communication that did not recognize his position as head of an organized force. Reed met the British officer and found the letter was addressed: "George Washington, Esq."

"You are sensible, sir," Reed said, "of the rank of General Washington in our Army."

"Yes, sir, we are," replied Lieutenant Brown of the *Eagle*, "I am sure Lord Howe will lament exceedingly this affair, as the letter is quite of a civil nature and not a military one. He laments exceedingly that he was not here a little sooner."

That ended it, except as the Americans wondered whether the final remark of the British officer meant that Lord Howe regretted he had not reached New York before the Declaration of Independence.

Washington decided he should submit his action for the approval of Congress, and he wrote at once for further instruction. Evidently, Lord Howe wished to negotiate and, while endeavoring to do so, might not strike a blow. This judgment was confirmed on July 16 by the tender, again declined, of a letter to "George Washington, Esq., &ca, &ca." On the seventeenth there came a third flag with an inquiry whether His Excellency, General Washington, would receive the Adjutant General of General Howe. Immediate assurance of the American commander's willingness to do this was given, with the result that an appointment for noon on the twentieth was made.

Washington dressed for the occasion with much care. The visitor proved to be Lieut. Col. James Patterson, a suave and experienced officer. Colonel Patterson proceeded to explain that Lord Howe and his brother the General had large powers as the King's commissioners to settle the unhappy differences with America. Patterson wished his visit to be considered as the first advances to that end. Washington was prepared for this approach, which he met with the statement that he had no authority to treat on that subject. He added in plain words that he thought the Howe brothers were empowered only to grant written pardons. These papers, said the General, were not desired by Americans who felt they had committed no fault but were defending their indisputable rights. This discouraged Colonel Patterson who then brought the conversation to the exchange of specific prisoners.

Definite encouragement was found in news received a few hours after Patterson's departure to the effect that Charles Lee and the South Carolinians had beaten off Sir Henry Clinton's attack on Charleston. Along the front for which Washington was responsible, everything indicated a desperate contest of doubtful issue as soon as ships brought the final contingent of Howe's army. In Washington's own Army, hot weather and bad water were causing much sickness; desertion was on the increase. Provincial jealousies showed themselves ominously.

In northern New York and in Canada, Washington had "more trouble and concern," than in front of Howe. Among the difficulties was that of placating Sullivan. Before Sullivan arrived July 21, Washington learned that the Generals of the Northern Department had decided on a withdrawal to Ticonderoga. This had seemed to some of the field officers so dangerous a move that twenty-one of them had joined in a formal protest. Washington himself had never been on the northern lakes but some of the Generals and senior colonels in New York were familiar with that country. Their description and the argument advanced in the protest almost convinced Washington that a mistake had been made in the abandonment of Crown Point in favor of Ticonderoga. Washington stated this to Gates. A sense of danger made Washington less careful than otherwise he would have been in addressing even so close a comrade as Gates, and Gates and Schuyler, forgetting their own rivalries, made common cause in denouncing what they took to be the judgment of a council of war in New York on their strategy. Before he could restore understanding, Washington had to withdraw somewhat from his criticism of the decision to quit Crown Point.

The number of British sail off Staten Island was rising ominously. Almost daily the lookout reported ships in the offing. August 1 brought approximately forty vessels, which Washington took to be the transports of part of the expected Hessian force. Regularly he would receive from the lookout on Long Island a report of arriving and departing vessels and of boats that passed from ship to shore, but the American commander could not learn anything specific about the men those dark hulls hid. He could go to sleep at night knowing that every ship of the British fleet was in its place, but he had to admonish himself that the next morning he might find all of them riding near the shore of Long Island, in line off the Grand Battery, or preparing to ascend East or North River to land troops in his rear.

Washington had finished a letter to Congress on August 7 when he was informed that two men who had deserted from the fleet had told an almost incredible tale: Their ship was among those that had arrived August 1, but they did not belong to Hessian reenforcement. They were part of the army of Sir Henry Clinton; they had been sent to South Carolina and, having been repulsed there, had joined General Howe in order to share in the capture of New York and the occupation of New Jersey. Clinton! He had been left out of all calculations regarding New York after he had gone south. Now he was back. Washington had to admit that this had not been anticipated.

Washington had not asked and Congress on its own initiative had done nothing for an increase in the number of Continental regiments in the Army directly under his command. Besides, it was now too late to recruit on a large scale for a campaign that might develop within a week. If help was forthcoming at all, it must be from the Flying Camp being set up in New Jersey and from the militia. These two sources were in reality one, because the ten thousand men proposed as a Flying Camp were to be militia from the Middle Colonies; and all of the additional fifteen thousand Congress had asked of Massachusetts, Connecticut, New York, New Jersey and Pennsylvania were of the same category. Both forces were to be employed to December 1 unless sooner discharged. The principal difference among these contingents would lie in the possibility that some of the more populous and patriotic States would forward their quotas with less than the normal delay. Washington resolved that he would do his utmost to speed the militia of the nearest Colonies, but there could be no certainty regarding the number of militiamen who would be available, the time they would arrive or the spirit in which they would fight. While Washington sought reenforcement wherever it could be mustered, he had at his disposal no more than ten thousand effectives in a total of 17,225, with whom he had to oppose an army of thirty thousand experienced veterans on a front of approximately fifteen miles.

These perplexities were presented when Washington's staff scarcely was able to cope with day-by-day problems. Transfer of Gates to the Canadian command had been so recent that the new Adjutant General, Reed, could not be expected in an acute crisis to discharge all the duties of that office. Besides this untrained administrative officer, Washington had two new aides and an assistant secretary, Alexander Contee Hanson, who was unfamiliar with the office. As Moylan had left Headquarters to undertake his new labors as Quartermaster General, the Commander-in-Chief was dismally burdened. Occasionally he would seek to have others transact business that came to his desk, but he was loath to call for more assistance in his office. It was July 25 when he brought himself to explain his circumstances and ask of Congress "an increase of my Aid de Camps"—a request the Delegates answered in the singular. Besides more secretaries, Washington needed additional senior officers, needed them desperately, and had written Congress on the subject. He had one Major General only, Israel Putnam, though three were the minimum to discharge essential duty. Three Brigadiers were desired in New York, also, and an equal number, or more, were required elsewhere. Congress was quick to respond with the promotion of Heath, Spencer, Sullivan and Greene to the rank of Major General, and of six colonels to brigade command.

Ninety-six ships or more came into the lower harbor on August 12 and 13. Approximately twenty others dropped anchor on the fourteenth. These, surely, must be bringing the Hessians and must be the last of the tremendous fleet. If they were, then the onslaught would come in a few days. On the fourteenth, there was much stir of small boats and indications both of landing and embarking troops, but Washington's last reports of the day were that the newly arrived Hessians were being put ashore on Staten Island. A heavy rain that day disrupted movement, broke a long drought and ushered in a brief, blusterous period of sickness and uncertainty. "The badness of the weather," Washington told his men, "has undoubtedly prevented an attack," and he admonished them to keep their canteens filled and have two days' dressed rations on hand.

There was some good news along with the bad. Militiamen arrived in such numbers that by the nineteenth they had raised Washington's total strength to twenty-three thousand. Another gratifying item was an attack August 16 of fire-rafts on the *Phoenix* and the *Rose*. This failed after threatening for a time to set the larger ship aflame; but the daring move so alarmed the British commander that he abandoned his station and rejoined the fleet. For the moment the Hudson again was open to the Americans, but they had woes enough. The long, dry weather had polluted the water supply; the chill days of rain were attended by much sickness. In some regiments all the field officers were incapacitated. Foremost among the victims was the man in command of what might be the battleground—Nathanael Greene on Long Island. His had been the duty of watching the enemy's movements and of guarding an estimated one hundred thousand pastured cattle and an even larger number of sheep. This livestock could not be removed to the mainland though it would supply food for months to an adversary whose landing could not be prevented. Greene had developed more in Washington's fourteen months of command than had almost any other officer. He was the man who probably could get the utmost in whole-hearted defence from the troops allotted him; and now he had to report himself confined to bed with a raging fever. Greene's early discharge of military duty was impossible; someone had to be assigned in his stead—and who?

Washington's choice fell on Sullivan. That officer had little or no acquaintance with the island, but in Washington's opinion he was the best available man for a most difficult assignment. He appreciated the importance of Long Island and believed that it had to be held if New York City was to remain in American hands. To Long Island, Sullivan went on August 20, under orders that made plain the assignment was temporary. Gen. Lord Stirling was to command Sullivan's Division during the service of that officer at Greene's post.

The day after Sullivan was named, several ships of the British fleet, crowded with soldiers, dropped down from the anchorage to The Narrows. Whether these vessels were bound on some special mission or were making the first move in an operation all the warships were to share, Washington could not ascertain before darkness. The next morning more of the four hundred transports and thirty-seven men-of-war off Staten Island had gone to The Narrows. Then came ominous intelligence: British troops were disembarking on the shore of Gravesend Bay, Long Island; Sir Henry Clinton's Grenadiers and the Light Infantry formed the van; the force already ashore numbered about eight thousand. Detachments had pushed on to Flatbush, a village about three miles from the outer American positions. Six battalions were promptly hurried across East River. The men went off in fine fighting mood, though some of them were without prescribed provisions.

Morning reports on the 23rd were, in effect, "No change." The enemy had extended his front but had delivered no attack during the night. Washington thought this increased the probability that Long Island was to be the sole immediate objective of the British, but he did not feel he should leave Manhattan Island until flood tide passed without indication of attack there. Then, as he could discern no preparations aboard the British fleet for a new landing, he had five more battalions made ready and crossed to Long Island. Either his observations there or pleas of Putnam convinced him it would be well to send that General to the island to supervise the defence. Putnam went accordingly—and to his immense satisfaction. Washington observed, studied the ground and the disposition of the forces and then returned to New York. There late in the day, he received from Sullivan a dispatch that told of an affair in which the British had been worsted. Washington doubted whether the attack of the Redcoats was on the scale the Major General thought, but as the repulsed advance might be the first move of a larger effort, Washington decided to send four more regiments and post them where they could be used by Sullivan or ferried back to New York.

On the morning of the twenty-fourth it still seemed to the anxious

Commander-in-Chief that his powerful adversary would not be content to strike one blow only. Washington was deepened, too, in his conviction that with his inferior forces he could do no more than hold his works and the approaches to them. Offensive operations were precluded unless Governor Trumbull of Connecticut could organize a force of perhaps one thousand men to cross the sound and harass the British who otherwise would be free to ravage nearly the whole of Long Island. Washington asked the Governor to do this, though with little faith in the accomplishment of it. Then, once again, Washington went to Long Island, rode along the front and saw enough to draw from him a firm and reproachful letter to Putnam. The soldiers, Washington wrote, were wasting their shots; riflemen should be placed in a wood near a strategically important fortification at Red Hook; traps and ambuscades must be prepared; a line must be drawn and held.

Nine Connecticut militia regiments, approximately three thousand men, reported on the twenty-sixth. Otherwise, there was no great change in the situation. If new intelligence reports contained anything positive it was to the effect that British attacks at two points were not in preparation. "We are led to think," Washington now wrote Congress, "[the British] mean to land the main force of their army on Long Island, and to make their grand push there." More American troops were rowed across to strengthen Putnam. The essential of American strategy was holding Brooklyn Heights, which commanded East River and New York. To secure Brooklyn, a line of parapets and a string of forts had been constructed near the western tip of Long Island from the salt marshes overlooking Wallabout Bay to those of Gowanus Creek, which were believed to be impassable. About a mile and a half from this man-made line was the nearest point of the natural defences of Brooklyn—a long row of hills almost parallel to the fortifications.

Putnam decided to guard in person the main defensive line of Brooklyn and to deputize Sullivan to the management of the battle on the "outwork" of the hills. Sullivan followed traditional seniority: he put Stirling in command of the right. Direct command of the centre and supervision of the left were under himself. His left element was Col. Samuel Miles's Pennsylvania Regiment of Stirling's Brigade, which had its exposed flank in the air. Miles was under orders to patrol in the direction of the road that led around the eastern end of the ridge to Jamaica; but as he had no mounted troops, he did not attempt to place vedettes far in advance or to maintain them anywhere outside his lines at night.

Washington observed and doubtless approved the principal dispositions. Everything he saw and heard of the enemy indicated that the blow was about to fall. Additional troops had been brought ashore by the British; the hostile camps, where visible, were astir. If an attack of magnitude was in the making, it had to be upgrade through the woods, Washington reasoned, and it could be hampered by the parties that had been posted along the routes over the hills. On the assumption that his soldiers behaved well, Washington could hope his main strategical objective would be achieved to the extent that by holding the approaches to his position at Brooklyn, he could withdraw safely and in good order to that line after taking stiff toll of the enemy.

About 1 A.M. the alarm was sounded at the front; General Putnam was notified; he aroused Stirling and sent that officer and Gen. Samuel H. Parsons to the right front. Sullivan went out in general command. Counting four hundred already in front on three roads—Gowanus, Flatbush and Bedford—there now were approximately 3500 American troops on the high wooded ground along slightly less than three miles. On the right, this reenforcement seemed adequate. Eight o'clock of a clear, cool and pleasant day found the opposing forces briskly skirmishing. It probably was about this time that Washington reached the scene from New York. He had directed the movement to the island of reenforcements, and he had watched with anxiety the effort of five British war vessels to enter East River so that they might bombard the rear of American positions in Brooklyn and sever communications with New York. Mercifully, the wind had shifted against the British and favored the Americans.

On the island, the American commander faced the first pitched battle he ever had directed. At the moment, there was little that he could do. Stirling seemed to be holding his own on the right. On the centre and left, though the Hessians persisted in their fire, they gave no indication that they intended to advance within the next hour or so. Every experienced soldier reasoned the British would not be demonstrating so widely unless they planned a heavy blow. Even so, orderly withdrawal to the fortified line of Brooklyn should be entirely possible.

At nine o'clock the sound of a cannon shot was audible, followed immediately by another—signal guns, undoubtedly: British troops in large number were on the Bedford Road, in rear of Sullivan's men who were facing the Hessians around Flatbush. In an amazingly short time the Redcoats were pushing forward. Soon the British would cut off Stirling's line of retreat to the fortifications. Unseen and unopposed, the enemy had gone around the eastern end of the hills and then had turned to the left and south. A surprise had been executed as complete as that which had overwhelmed Braddock. The British quickly covered their left and pressed furiously onward. At the signal, the Hessians pushed up the wooded ridge. The troops in front of Stirling abandoned their teasing tactics and opened in earnest. Everywhere the command seemed to be the same—to force the American volley and then close with the bayonet before the Continentals could reload.

Outwitted and outnumbered, the troops saw no alternative to destruction except immediate retreat. By early afternoon, most of the Continentals who had escaped the bayonets of the British had reached the Brooklyn defences, where Washington himself shared the work of rallying them. "Remember what you are contending for," he cried to some of them but he did not have at hand the leaders the men knew best. Stirling was missing. Sullivan had failed to fight his way out. Several promising officers were known to have been killed. Casualties obviously ran into the hundreds and might rise higher because the British were drawing nearer, as if they were preparing to assault the American line. Some officers, at least, became conscious of the weakness of the defences in front of Brooklyn. Troops were put to work to complete several fortifications, particularly those that were de-

MAP / 10

THE LONG ISLAND APPROACHES TO THE BROOKLYN DEFENSES

LONG ISLAND APPROACHES
TO THE
BROOKLYN DEFENSES

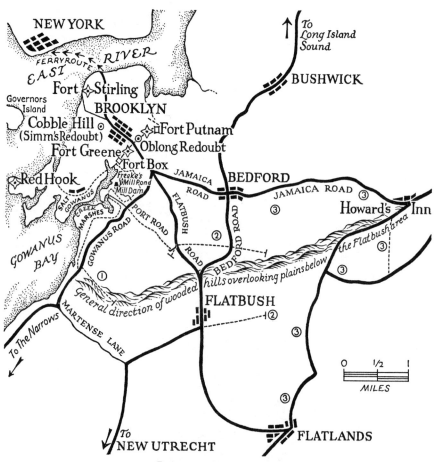

Redrawn by LeRoy H. Appleton from map by John Draper.

① Stirling's advanced position on the morning of August 27, 1776
② The front and left flank of Sullivan
③ The direction of the principal British movement

signed to cover the approaches on the Jamaica Road; but in the haste and excitement of the afternoon hard tasks were slighted and dangerous duty was dodged. The one immediate relief was the discovery that the British men-of-war had been able to do no more than send a few shots in the direction of the fort at Red Hook and then, in the face of an ebbtide, anchor out of range. The royal regiments in front of Brooklyn might or might not be held off; there was no danger the defences would be bombarded from the rear that evening.

After the action the British drew back, out of cannon range, and halted as if they had other plans afoot than those of an assault. It was a respite; it must not be an informal truce. American officers still had sufficient fight left to order riflemen into a wood near the British front. From that cover the marksmen opened a steady fire after 4 P.M. This irritated the British and cramped their movement without provoking either a farther withdrawal or an attempt to clear the Americans from among the trees. Were the British and Hessians being rested for a night attack? Such trained and experienced regulars were able to execute that difficult maneuver, even over unfamiliar ground, but now Washington began to suspect that, instead of attacking forthwith, Howe might prefer to undertake regular approaches.

Darkness fell and dragging minutes crept to a midnight that threatened never to come. There was no attack. Silence continued. Washington had some sleep but by four o'clock on the twenty-eighth he was astir. The British were still in the position they held the previous evening. Washington did what he could to see that the men found their regiments, got food, put their arms in order and, if wounded, had the attention of a surgeon. Out in East River, the wind still favored the Continentals; communication between Long Island and New York could be maintained.

Anxiously the morning passed without a British movement. Afternoon brought a measure of temporary security at the price of hours of wretched discomfort. A cold rain fell on ground already watersoaked. The temperature dropped; chill and moisture pervaded everything; it was impossible for many of the soldiers to keep even their firearms dry.

On the morning of the twenty-ninth Washington saw through the downpour the carefully drawn outline of a British redoubt, for which the enemy had broken ground during the night. The earthwork was arrogantly close—not more than six hundred yards from the American left—and on a site well chosen. Washington immediately accepted the rising mudbank as confirmation that the British were to undertake the capture of the American lines by regular approaches over a stretch of land favorable to that type of operation.

If Brooklyn was to be besieged, it was imperative that the wounded be sent to New York and that fresh troops take the place of those who were weary, wet and disheartened. Washington thought it probable that the British might attack New York while part of Howe's army held him in Brooklyn and did not strip New York of its last guards. Instead, he called additional reenforcements from the Flying Camp of Gen. Hugh Mercer at Amboy. The number who could be supplied from that quarter was small and the troops themselves were newly mustered militia, but any help would be an encouragement.

The day wore on wearily, in unrelenting rain and deepened gloom. Arms could not be put in order; much ammunition was spoiled by dampness; honest-minded commanders had to ask themselves whether their wet and weary men could stay in the flooded trenches if the British delivered a strong attack. An alarming report came of the presence of British ships at Flushing Bay. There was fear that the British might be moving part of their troops to Flushing, perhaps to cross to the mainland and assail King's Bridge. Added to these circumstances was the regretful assurance informed Brooklyn citizens gave that even if the obstructions in the main channel stopped the British men-of-war, armed ships of light draft could pass between Long Island and Governor's Island. No obstruction had been placed on that stretch because the water had been regarded as so shallow that no vessel could nagivate there. This and almost every other strategical aspect of the operation were a reminder Washington scarcely needed—that he continued to keep his small Army dangerously divided in the face of an adversary who controlled the waterways and therefore could concentrate in force wherever desired, whenever wind and tide permitted.

These adversities combined so manifestly to threaten the destruction of the dispersed American Army that Washington felt he should consult his council of war. That afternoon, at Philip Livingston's country house, he asked the seven Generals then in the Brooklyn defences whether, in the words of the minutes, "under all circumstances, it would not be eligible to leave Long Island and its dependencies, and remove the Army to New York." The decision of the council was unanimous for evacuation and was affirmed in a brief paper to which all subscribed. Washington himself reduced the decision to its simplest terms when he said the decisive facts were the regular approaches of Howe over favorable ground and the prospect of being cut off by the fleet.

Preparation had to be started at once for the transfer of ten or twelve thousand men across East River in the darkness. In a short time the activity of officers, whispered exchanges, the arrival and dispatch of messengers made it plain to the troops that something was afoot. As the men speculated, many concluded they were to be called on to attack the British, but as quickly as possible after nightfall, men and moveables were sent to the ferry landing whence they were rowed to New York. The hours seemed agonizingly long for those who had to wait, and not long enough for officers charged with getting all the troops and equipment to New York. Effort tipped the scale. Before dawn all the men except a few sentinels had been put aboard. The heavy guns only had to be left behind, because they sank hub-deep in mud from which they could not be pulled by all the men who could put hand to rope.

The battle had been lost; the campaign must not be!

On August 30 and 31 the small garrison of Governor's Island was transported to New York under the very eyes of British naval officers still balked by that persistent northeast wind, a strong if temporary American ally. Washington ruefully was reckoning the number of good leaders he had lost on Long Island. Stirling, cut off, had surrendered in person to Gen. Leopold von Heister; Sullivan had been caught on the twenty-seventh about a hundred yards from the post of one of the Hessian commanders. Now, on the thirtieth, Sullivan came over to New York on parole, sent by Lord Howe to give notice that the British Admiral wanted to see some members of Congress in order that he might explain to them the nature of the peace mission with which he and his brother, the General, were entrusted. Washington was of opinion that in a matter important in form, even if deceptive and fragile in substance, he should not deny Sullivan the privilege that officer sought of going to Philadelphia and repeating to the Delegates what Howe had told him. Off Sullivan rode—to put the match to a controversy hot and furious.

The success of the British operation, as Washington saw it, was due to lack of vigilance on the part of Sullivan's men, who guarded the Flatbush and Bedford Roads but failed to prevent surprise along the Jamaica Road. Washington was justified in this judgment, to the extent at least that the field officers on the left had neither the force nor the experienced direction required to thwart a flank march soundly conceived and executed with brilliant precision. In plain words, the Redcoats had outclassed the Continentals. The American Commander-in-Chief had appeared to be a tyro, a bungler as well as a beginner, in comparison with the English General. Washington himself did not attempt to review the details and set down in full the reason for the defeat. The decision to evacuate Long Island was sound and militarily economical. A very different story might have been written had Washington attempted to escape the night after the battle or even August 28/29. He had been the more willing to take the risk of remaining until he could leave without heavy loss because he was inclined to think that Howe was going to undertake regular approaches. In this, Washington was correct. Despite urging by some of his subordinates, the British commander had refused to press his attack on the evening of the day he turned the American left.

The defeat led immediately to a crisis that absorbed Washington's thought so completely he had no time for retrospect or for self-reproach: Before he could complete the reorganization of the Army necessitated by the death or capture of officers, he found, as he said, that "the check our detachment sustained . . . dispirited too great a proportion of our troops and filled their minds with apprehension and despair." Militia began to melt away. Almost by regiments they left their camps and started home—discouraged and unpaid, disillusioned and embittered. Other temporary soldiers were coming from Massachusetts and Connecticut to take the place of those going home; but these unwilling recruits had no small arms, tents or even camp-kettles, and, in most instances, no stomach for a fight. Washington knew there would be some conscientious individuals among the Long Faces, but he did not believe these new militia, *en masse*, would be any better than the old.

The situation threatened the dissolution of the Army—in the face of a powerful, confident adversary free to maneuver almost at will because of British sea power. It was Washington's good fortune and perhaps the salvation of America that the British, with the *élan* of victory, were under the command of a man whose innate caution was deepened by the desire of his brother, the Admiral, and by his own ambition to pursue negotiations for peace before employing to the utmost bayonets and cannons. General Howe's slowness was a boon; it could not be an escape. Sooner or later the British would strike somewhere on the front of sixteen to eighteen miles defended by half-demoralized men whom Washington reckoned at less than twenty thousand effectives. The militia continued to slip away in such numbers that General Mercer did not believe Washington could muster among them more than five thousand dependable soldiers.

Certain defensive arrangements could be made. The enemy could be confronted with the most vigilant of the officers; reenforcements from Virginia and Maryland, as well as the incoming militia, could be hurried forward; the sick could be removed from exposed New York; surplus supplies could be hauled beyond the snatch of the British lion; seasoned troops could be taken from the forts and could be replaced by men of the Flying Camp; all the roads that flanked American positions could be blocked; North River could be obstructed more stoutly and could be subjected to a heavier cross fire from batteries; the garrisons of the highland defences of the Hudson might be strengthened; available troops might be posted where they could be moved quickly to meet any force landed from British transports. Other expedients might suggest themselves after the form of the attack on New York was disclosed; but would they, could they suffice? Nathanael Greene, well enough by September 5, was of opinion that no effort should be made to save the town. It should be burned and evacuated, he said; two-thirds of the property there belonged to Tories anyway. Heath argued that the city should be held, if possible. Rufus Putnam, acting Chief Engineer, considered fortification a waste of energy where so many landing places existed. Washington said, "Till of late I had no doubt in my mind of defending this place, nor should I have yet, if the men would do their duty, but this I despair of." It was for Congress, he thought, to say whether the town should be destroyed or left alone. As he phrased it in its least painful form, the question was, "If we should be obliged to abandon the town, ought it to stand as winter quarters for the enemy?" The answer he gave himself was plain: he would apply the torch to the entire city if permitted to do so.

Congress had a different view, of which he was informed by September 6: "Resolved, That General Washington be acquainted, that the Congress would have especial care taken, in case he should find it necessary to quit New York, that no damage be done to the said city by his troops, on their leaving it: The Congress having no doubt of being able to recover the same, though the enemy should, for a time, obtain possession of it." Washington read this in the belief that it might represent one of the capital errors of Congress, but he determined to make the best defence he could. Manhattan Island was thirteen miles in length. The town of New York occupied slightly less than the lower three miles. North of the town was the district called Bloomingdale. Beyond that, the land rose gradually in a rocky formation, known as Harlem Heights that ran southeast-northwest to a declivity about eight miles from the lower end of the island. Beyond this stretch the ground rose higher on the western side of the island and formed a cliff with an elevation of two hundred feet and a little more. King's Bridge, which spanned Harlem River, was one of the important military positions. Whoever held firmly that crossing and its approaches could open or shut the gate upstate and into New England.

To cover King's Bridge the Americans had constructed Fort Independence at the southern end of the Fordham Heights. On the cliff south of King's Bridge the Continentals were erecting a large earthwork which they called Fort Washington. The whole of the adjoining high ground had recently been dubbed Mount Washington. Almost directly opposite these works was Fort Constitution, soon to be renamed Fort Lee, on the Jersey side of North River. Its fire and that of Fort Washington crossed where obstructions had been placed in the river to keep the British from using the Hudson. Below Mount Washington on Manhattan no large work had been erected except in New York City itself, but a high ridge could be used for defence against an adversary who commanded the plains of Harlem. In the city a redoubt had been erected on Bayard's Hill, and trenches had been dug wherever a landing seemed likely or a field of fire was offered. Most of these works appeared later to a British observer to have been "calculated more to amuse than for use." The key positions were King's Bridge and Fort Washington. During the difficult days of early September Washington suspected that the enemy intended to land near King's Bridge, hem him into the area south of Harlem and sever his communications. Proper disposition to meet such a move called for a council, which Washington brought together September 7. Over the vigorous opposition of Greene, a majority of the council recommended that an effort be made, as Congress desired, to hold New York.

The British by September 7 were feeling their way up East River with a contentious frigate and were completing a battery on Long Island opposite Horne's Hook. On the eighth this battery opened but quickly drew the fire of American gunners who were confident of their skill after having had the better of exchanges with the British frigate. Then, on the tenth, the British occupied Montresor's Island. From that post they could land either on the plains of Harlem, south of King's Bridge, or on the Morrisania estate, whence they could flank the position at King's Bridge by a march of six or seven miles. A bad situation was getting worse. Signs multiplied that the enemy's attack was to be both north and south of King's Bridge.

The apparent imminence of this two-pronged thrust at the vitals of the Army led Greene to circulate on September 11 a petition to Washington for review of the decision to defend New York. Washington himself believed it futile and perhaps fatal to attempt to hold the town, and he responded immediately with a call for a new council September 12. This time all except three of the participants were for the evacuation of the area south of Harlem River, with the exception of Fort Washington, as soon as supplies could be withdrawn. Washington reported this decision to Congress. He warned the President of Congress that the council regarded the situation as "extremely perilous."

September 13 brought more evidence that the onslaught might be close at hand. A forty-gun ship started up East River and opened on the batteries, which responded angrily. British guns on Governor's Island went into action. Washington rode over to one of the forts to see whether the movement of the enemy had begun, but he found no indication of an immediate landing. On the fourteenth came assurance from Congress that its resolution against the burning of New York was not to be construed to mean that Washington "should remain in that city a moment longer than he shall think it proper for the public service that the troops be continued there." About sunset word reached Washington that six ships or more were proceeding to a station in East River, that British troops were being assembled on the islands in Hell Gate, and that widespread movement was observed by scouts and lookouts. Anxiously, Washington hurried to Harlem in the belief that the blow would fall there or across the mouth of Harlem River at Morrisania. On arrival he saw what others had reported but no additional preparation. Fire had not been opened; no landing had been attempted. Washington rode back to new Headquarters opened at the home of Roger Morris, near King's Bridge and on Harlem Heights, whence he thought he could proceed more quickly to a threatened position than from his old office.

The next morning was quiet until about eleven o'clock, when a sound of heavy firing rolled up to King's Bridge. It did not come from the plains of Harlem or from Morrisania but from a point farther down East River than Washington had expected. The apprehensive General started for the scene of the bombardment. While six transports had remained off Bushwick Point, five warships had left that temporary station at earliest dawn and had anchored broadside the New York shore from Kip's Bay southward at a distance of about eleven hundred yards. Up North River at that very hour a trio of ships were making their way to Bloomingdale. If those men-of-war in North River were intended to cover a landing there simultaneous with one on East River, then the hour of decision had come.

About ten o'clock Americans who had a clear view of Newtown Cove on Long Island, saw British flatboats move out of the mouth of the creek and take shelter astern the transports. Men from other boats climbed up the sides of the ships, which manifestly were to convey the troops to some landing place—but what place? Eighty British guns began to roar shortly before 11 A.M. American supports did not venture within less than half a mile of the shore; the men who were expected to meet the first landing were pinned to their lines. Paralyzing fire continued for more than an hour. About 1 P.M. the bombardment ceased and different sounds became audible, shouted commands, the grinding of bows on the river bank, the dull percussion of heavy feet on boat bottoms, and then—British and Hessians splashing ashore and forming on both sides of Kip's Bay, at one point within forty yards of the Continentals' breastworks.

It was not long after this landing that Washington rode up at furious pace with his aides—only to find that the militiamen had abandoned their trenches without firing a shot and were retreating in mad confusion. Generals Parsons and Fellows were doing everything they could to rally the men but their commands were unheeded. Washington and the young officers with him rode among the scattered troops and tried to form them. It was in vain—Washington's wrath rose. "Take the wall," he shouted, "take the cornfield," and he pointed to the positions. Some men filed out from the road to do as he said; Parsons tried to get them into a line, but the panic-stricken outnumbered those who kept their heads. Fellows' Brigade broke and scattered. In Watts's orchard, on the right of the assailed front, a few men disputed the advance of Hessians—only to see the Germans shoot down and bayonet Americans who came forward with uplifted hands to surrender. Nearer the landing place at Kip's Bay Washington continued his efforts to rally the half-frenzied men, but just when it looked as if he might get some hundreds of them to stand, a body of sixty or seventy British soldiers started towards them. The Americans broke, ran away, and left Washington and his aides to face the attacking party without a single musket. Washington had to give ground himself and, intensely humiliated, had to send orders for Harlem Heights to be secured. Over on the Bloomingdale Road, about that time, the cry was raised that British light horse were attacking the rear. That completed the panic of some and speeded the retreat of the others. The British pursued as far as Murray's Hill, while the advance was pushed towards Harlem Heights and was extended by the left flank across to North River.

This fixed the fate of New York. Establishment of the British line across the island put an end to the orderly evacuation of supplies by land, precisely as all water transit had been stopped early that morning by the dispatch of three British warships to Bloomingdale. The defeat was as grievous in loss of property as it was shameful in the cowardice it uncovered. There never had been a more outrageous affair and seldom so complete a British victory for so small an expenditure of blood and bullets. The action at Kip's Bay was no more than a skirmish in itself, but it was of high importance in that it precipitated the evacuation of New York and deepened the anxiety of Washington over the morale of his soldiers and the competence of some of his commanders.

During the early morning of September 16 the General sent out reconnoitering parties and then he sat down to report to Congress on the humiliating events of the preceding day. He had not completed the drafting of his letter many minutes when word reached him that the enemy was astir. If there was even a possibility of an engagement that day, Washington wanted to be on the scene before action opened in order that he might guard against surprise and make proper disposition of his regiments. He soon set out and on his arrival at the advance posts heard firing to the south, occasioned by a clash between Lt. Col. Thomas Knowlton's Rangers and a British advance party. The exchange was not in a volume to indicate anything more than a skirmish. Washington listened and prepared to receive attack, but he had no further report of a general advance by the main body of the British. Some time passed. Then a number of Knowlton's men began to climb back up the hill to their own positions, where they gave encouraging news of a stiff encounter still in progress with a body of Redcoats who were concealed in a wood. Joseph Reed assured his chief that Knowlton's men had done admirably and deserved support. Would the General approve an advance in some strength to encourage the men? As Washington pondered the British came in sight and sounded their bugles—not with a command to halt or deploy but with the call of hunters who have killed the fox and are ending their chase.

Whether or not this taunt angered him, Washington presently gave orders for a small demonstration directly in the enemy's front. Knowlton simultaneously was to take his men and three rifle companies of Gen. George Weedon's Third Virginia Regiment to get in rear of these contemptuous British. Washington saw the men start from the left of the line and made ready from Gen. John Nixon's Brigade the force that was to demonstrate in front of the British. In the early afternoon Nixon's men were sent down into the wide declivity that separated the northern part of Harlem Heights from Vandewater's Heights, the next high ground to the south. The British, regarding this as a challenge, came down from Vandewater's Heights and took position behind a fence and among bushes. Fire was opened at once but at too great a range to be effective.

Soon there came to Washington's ears the sound of an exchange of musketry from the left front, but manifestly this fusillade was not from the rear of the British who had advanced to the fence. Something had gone awry: Instead of getting behind the enemy to cut off his retreat, Knowlton's men had attacked the enemy's right flank. Washington heard shortly that Maj. Andrew Leitch had been brought out with three bullets through his body. After him came Colonel Knowlton, mortally wounded. Washington concluded that the flanking column, now fighting under captains, needed further support and dispatched parts of two Maryland regiments and some New Englanders. Within a few minutes the enemy's advance party was gone, ingloriously gone. American troops had not previously seen the enemy "on the run" and could not resist the temptation to pursue; but Washington reasoned that the British would send up reenforcements and did not think his shaken Army should risk a general engagement. He ordered the men to cease their pursuit and return to their lines.

The Americans had forced British troops to flee before them in the open field. That never had happened before. The British had retreated from Lexington and from Concord, but they had intended to return to Boston anyway. They had quit that city the next March, but they had not been worsted in a stand-up battle. The victory won by Lee in South Carolina had been an affair of naval guns. Long Island and Kip's Bay were subjects too sore for mention. This time it was different: The Americans had proved that the British army was *not* invincible. Redcoats had backs! It was a great discovery. Washington was pleased but cautious. "The affair," he said to Congress, ". . . seems to have greatly inspired the whole of our troops."

CHAPTER / 11

Washington promptly extended his new lines across the upper end of Harlem Heights from North River to Harlem River, and he soon felt that if the men would fight, the defences would make any success costly to the British whom he expected to advance at an early date. A great fire that destroyed about a fourth of New York City on September 20–21 seemed to Washington to be an instance in which, as he later wrote Lund, "Providence, or some good honest fellow, has done more for us than we were disposed to do for ourselves," but he had to admit regretfully that "enough of [the city] remains to answer" the purposes of the British. The conflagration was followed on the twenty-third by the easy British occupation of Powles Hook. Thereafter, one or two suspicious movements convinced Washington the British would attack during the remaining weeks of open weather.

Vigilance and discipline and leadership and almost everything else that went into the making of an army were threatened with ruin. The militia continued to disappear in such numbers that Washington despaired of getting from them a service that justified their pay. These militia were being replaced, and they represented slight numerical net loss; but they escaped with so little punishment for their contempt of discipline that many Continental troops followed their evil example. Washington had to issue successive General Orders against straggling, plundering, cowardice, malingering and desertion. He tried to be fair to the temporary soldiers, but his experience with their undependability had led him to believe that the Army must be reorganized on a basis of long enlistment under sterner articles of war. This was now absolute necessity and it called for attractive bounties of money and of land. Congress had been talking of long-term service and it acceded to most of Washington's requests. The Delegates passed a series of resolutions for the enlistment of eighty-eight battalions, by quotas among the several States, "to serve during the present war." Battalions already in service were to be counted in the total if they were recruited for the duration of hostilities. Every private and NCO who enlisted for that service was to receive twenty dollars and one hundred acres of land. Officers were to be commissioned by Congress, but "the appointment of all officers, and filling up vacancies (except general officers) [was to] be left to the governments of the several States." Arms and other necessities were to be supplied by the States; clothing was to be charged against the pay of the soldier. New articles of war were adopted for the maintenance of better discipline and the firm establishment of justice to the individual soldier.

This, in Washington's opinion, was good as far as it went, but it did not go far enough. The bounty was too small to attract recruits in competition with higher British offers; nothing was done to encourage good officers to remain in the service or assure the appointment of leaders of station and intelligence. Elbridge Gerry, Roger Sherman and Francis Lewis, who were named by Congress to visit Washington's camp, arrived there about September 25 and held numerous conferences in which Washington and his Generals disclosed frankly what they had not thought proper to put into official correspondence with Congress—that the corps of officers was unworthy of the country, lacking in competence, and in large measure responsible for poor discipline. Privately, Washington affirmed that even his Continental troops "never had officers, except in a few instances, worth the bread they eat"; officially he was "sensible that the very existence, that the well doing of every army depends upon good officers." When the three Congressmen went back to Philadelphia a mildly phrased committee report was seconded by the most desperate letter Washington had addressed to the President of Congress. He pleaded for the utmost speed in procuring action by the States on the names of new officers; he insisted on the clothing bounty for soldiers; and he argued almost vehemently for a scale of pay that would make it possible for officers to support their character as gentlemen. His conclusion was startling: ". . . such a cloud of perplexing circumstances appears before me without one flattering hope that I am thoroughly convinced unless the most vigorous and decisive exertions are immediately adopted to remedy these evils, that the certain and absolute loss of our liberties will be the inevitable consequences. . . ." One unhappy stroke, he added, would "throw a powerful weight into the scale against us."

This language from a trusted leader was decisive with Congress. Members voted a clothing bounty. Officers' pay was increased. The States were urged to complete their levies of new troops by November 10 and to officer them with "men of honor and known abilities." As far as they went, these moves gratified Washington, but a measure simultaneously adopted by Congress alarmed him. This was a call on the States that had Continental regiments in New York or in Pennsylvania to send committees to the Army "to appoint all the officers of the Regiment to be raised by their States under the new establishment." This was to be done in order that the officers of the new regiments might "proceed immediately to enlist such men as are now in the service, and incline to reenlist during the war." Washington saw what Congress apparently had overlooked: Until the committees arrived and chose the officers, there could be no recruiting for the new regiments.

In the memory of his sleepless nights of December 1775, he could not be otherwise than apprehensive as December 1776 approached with the same problem of organization, but as he looked to the future he had faith in the potentialities of the American soldier. He devoted himself vigorously to the execution of the plan for long enlistment. He wrote those Governors whom he knew well and exhorted them to see that qualified officers were chosen for the new battalions. In addressing Patrick Henry, the General tactfully asked for care in the selection of officers to head the Virginia troops: "The true criterion . . . is . . . a just pretention to the character of a gentleman, a proper sense of honor, and some reputation to lose." Washington did not want this vital requirement to wait on words. In a knowledge that the state commissioners were instructed by Congress to "advise with the general officers," Washington instructed some of his principal subordinates to prepare lists of the competent officers in their commands.

There he had for the time to leave it. Discipline and morale were no better; the commanding General's barge was hit in North River and three men were killed by a careless mistake; several members of Washingon's staff were restive; Reed was pessimistic and soon was to ask that he be replaced. The most disquieting failure in staff work was that of Quartermaster General Stephen Moylan. In spite of his devotion to the American cause, Moylan could not handle acceptably the business of procuring teams, tents, and other equipment of the Army. He confessed his failure and accepted advice that he resign. This made way for the reappointment of Thomas Mifflin at the continuing rank of Brigadier; but with the best of fortune, Mifflin could not hope soon to find and buy the clothing and blankets on which the life of the Army in large measure depended during the winter. As a result of the increase in duties without improvement in his staff, Washington was overloaded. He divested himself, as far as he could, of responsibility for naval affairs and he reduced or eliminated his detailed reports to Governors and Legislatures; but he took in hand much of the correspondence regarding a general exchange of prisoners and at times, it would seem, he deliberately turned to letter writing as if he wished to keep his mind from bootless reflection on problems he could not solve.

Overwork, strain and the endless vexations of command brought Washington lower in spirits than he had been at any time during the war. At the end of a long review of his desperate situation, he told Congress: ". . . the difficulties which have forever surrounded me since I have been in the service, and kept my mind constantly upon the stretch; the wounds which my feelings as an officer have received by a thousand things which have happened, contrary to my expectations and wishes; the effect of my own conduct, and present appearance of things, so little pleasing to myself, as to render it a matter of no great surprise (to me) if I should stand capitally censured by Congress; added to a consciousness of my inability to govern an army composed of such discordant parts, and under such a variety of intricate and perplexing circumstances; induces not only a belief, but a thorough conviction in my mind that it will be impossible unless there is a thorough change in our military systems for me to conduct matters in such a manner as to give satisfaction to the public which is all the recompence I aim at, or ever wished for."

An enemy who had remained quiescent during critical days now was bestirring himself where it had been assumed he would. A British force embarking at the scene of the panic of September 15 could leave the transports at Throg's Point and, marching less than nine miles to the northwest, not only would reach King's Bridge, but also turn that position, force the evacuation of Harlem Heights, and isolate Fort Washington, the main American land defence against the free passage of the lower Hudson. Nature thus dictated strategy that was not the less effective because it was elementary and obvious. Howe adopted it in the knowledge that it might save him from having to storm the works on Harlem Heights and would put him where he could cut the shortest line of Washington's land communications between New York and the lower Connecticut towns. On October 9 a squadron of three ships with their tenders passed the obstructions in North River, defied the land batteries and ran up as far, Washington guessed, as Tarrytown, where they could stop river shipment of supplies to Washington from Albany. On the morning of the twelfth, flatboats and small vessels brought ashore at Throg's Point a strong force that had been embarked the previous night at Kip's Bay and conveyed successfully through Hell Gate in a thick fog. The landing was unopposed, but the news was transmitted quickly to Headquarters. Washington believed he held defensible ground between the Neck and King's Bridge. It was a district of stone fences that would confine artillery and large bodies of infantry to the main roads. Washington's reconnaissance was encouraging; he found the men apparently in good spirits; Greene, commanding at Fort Constitution, offered, without so much as a hint from Headquarters, to bring three brigades to help his chief.

The next day, Washington gave instructions for vigilance and for stronger guards on the lines of probable advance from Throg's Neck. Then, as the enemy remained immobile, Washington made another reconnaissance on the fourteenth and reassigned part of his forces in order to put the best troops under the most experienced commanders and place militia where they would do least harm. Washington designated Israel Putnam and Spencer to supervise strengthening of the fortifications and assigned Heath to command south of King's Bridge, where an attack seemed least probable.

The most conspicuous aspect of reorganization was the return of Charles Lee to command. Lee had come to Philadelphia after his victory in Charleston harbor and had received a triumphant welcome. Ill as was his temper, his knowledge was needed where Washington did not have to count five in order to list his general officers of intelligence, promptness, decision and courage. Greene met most of the qualifications, but he was across the Hudson at Fort Constitution. Sullivan might be disciplined to full efficacy. He was on active duty again, an exchanged prisoner of war, and was assigned a division. Stirling likewise had been exchanged and was in command of a brigade. Brigadier Thompson, captured at Three Rivers, had been brought to New Jersey but had not yet been liberated. The new Major General of Massachusetts Militia, Benjamin Lincoln, who had just arrived, was showing unusual promise but still was to be tested. Eagerly, Washington received Lee and placed under him the troops above King's Bridge.

Washington concluded that it was possible to hold Fort Washington and not only protect the navigation of the Hudson but also establish near the fort "an easier and better communication" between the northern and southern States. Now he had to review that conclusion: The British repeatedly had run their warships past Fort Washington and over or through the obstructions in North River. This meant that they could send a squadron up the Hudson and land troops in rear of the American Army. Simultaneously, the enemy could move westward from Throg's Point and turn the flank of Washington's unhappy regiments. The danger was that the jaws of the trap would be closed suddenly. American forces might be compelled to fight when and where the enemy pleased or might be cut off and starved into surrender.

Washington read to his council of war on the sixteenth reports of Tory stirrings upstate and of deserters' predictions of early attack. He asked whether the Army could hold its position and prevent a severance of communication. The answer of the Generals, with the exception of George Clinton, was that the Army could not keep communications open and that new positions had to be occupied. This involved the removal northward of troops in the works on Harlem Heights, because the Army could not afford to remain divided by Harlem River. Must Fort Washington be evacuated also? That earthwork was slightly more than two miles south of King's Bridge and was considered strong. If Fort Washington were garrisoned by courageous troops with a competent leader, it would occupy the attention of a considerable British force and would make General Howe cautious in movements of men and supplies. Council advised Washington to hold the fort as long as possible.

The test of the first of the council's conclusions appeared to be near. Four miles north of Throg's Neck on the coast of Long Island Sound was a better landing-place, Pell's Point, east of Hutchinson's River and within easy striking distance of the road from Connecticut to King's Bridge. On the eighteenth British troops were ferried to Pell's Point and disembarked there; those on Throg's Neck then were moved to a junction with the men who had been landed at Pell's Point. Washington had placed in that quarter about 750 well-schooled troops under Col. John Glover, acting Brigadier. That officer fell back gradually. At the end of the day the British were well secured on a front of about two miles and a half.

On October 19 and 20, as the British remained where they were, it was reasonable to assume that they planned to proceed up the shore of Connecticut or that they purposed to continue north in an effort to turn Washington's left. If the British strategy was to confine the American Army between the sound and North River, then Howe's advance probably would be to White Plains. At White Plains the Redcoats would have three advantages: they would command the upper road to Connecticut; they would have the Croton River to cover their rear; and from White Plains they could proceed with fair ease five miles west and reach the Hudson at Tarrytown. Washington went to White Plains on the twenty-first to examine the ground and resolved to anticipate a British movement to that position and take measures to withdraw provisions and other stores from exposed towns in southern Connecticut.

Several skirmishes occurred, but no action of importance was staged. Washington moved Headquarters to Valentine's Hill. While at Valentine's, Washington heard that Benedict Arnold had met the British fleet on Lake Champlain and had lost practically all the little vessels built with much toil; but from the reports received then and later Washington saw that in stubborn, stand-up fight, Arnold's defeat was a victory of courage over the impulse to run away. It had been Washington's hope that if October and November passed without a British advance down the New York lakes, nothing need be feared from that quarter until the spring of 1777; now he could give little time to reflection on dangers upstate because he needed every minute to concentrate his troops for the attacks he expected. It was October 23 when he opened Headquarters at White Plains in a position which was of some strength but was by no means as formidable as well-drawn lines would be in the higher hills north of the village. He took the less secure position because he wished to hold White Plains until the supplies there could be removed.

While the Quartermaster's men were doing their best to transport these stores, Washington began to show some confusion of thought on strategy. Sound though his maneuvers had appeared to be, he now questioned their adequacy. Would it not be better to set up two armies, one to be stationed east of Hudson and the other to operate in New Jersey, where it could maneuver freely to combat any advance from New York in the direction of Philadelphia? Washington directed the subject to the consideration of Congress; but he had to defer more detailed personal review of it because he learned that the enemy was in movement towards White Plains. Then he virtually severed land communication with Fort Washington and called his troops from their posts on the Bronx. Lee, as the most experienced of Washington's lieutenants, was entrusted with the rear of the column that came up Bronx River to the position at White Plains.

During the forenoon of the twenty-seventh the Americans heard the sound of heavy cannonade from the direction of Fort Washington. When a messenger reached Headquarters, the Commander-in-Chief learned that two frigates had come up North River and anchored at contemptuously short range to halt movement between Fort Washington and Fort Lee. A British land force simultaneously had presented itself in front of the southern outworks of Fort Washington and begun demonstrations. The whole undertaking was a quick failure. One of the frigates was mauled remorselessly; the British infantry did not attempt assault.

By dawn of the twenty-eighth, Washington had decided he must fortify and hold Chatterton's Hill if he was to retain even briefly his position at White Plains. Colonel Reed was directed to take a force to the eminence, dispose the men and have them entrench. Spencer and Maj. Gen. James Wadsworth were sent out with five or six hundred mixed militia and Continentals to delay the British and collect such information as they could. While the Army waited, Reed went about his task of securing the hill. Spencer's and Wadsworth's troops presently came back to the lines with reports that the British were moving up the East Chester Road. Soon the enemy could be seen. In a short time, the British artillery opened with vigor on widespread targets. The American troops broke and were rallied with difficulty. The enemy increased his bombardment. Troops began to move from the British left and form for a crossing of Bronx River. Ere long, smoke was rising from an eminence almost directly south of Chatterton's Hill: The enemy had climbed the ridges and was firing across. The crackle of small arms was almost continuous. Then came silence on the extreme right and a humiliating message to Washington: Hessians and British had stormed Chatterton's Hill; the militia had run away again. The hill was lost, and so was the day. The right of the American lines at White Plains no longer was tenable.

Capture of Chatterton's Hill did not expose immediately the whole of the Continental lines to British fire. The ground so abounded in natural defences that the American right could be drawn in and the remainder of the front held. Howe himself contributed to this by failing to press the advance. Washington shifted some of his troops to better positions on high ground October 28 and 29 and, all the while, removed as many supplies from White Plains as the wagons could carry. Howe kept his men under cover but by October 31 it was apparent that he was working on four or five batteries that could sweep most of the American positions. Washington accordingly withdrew that night to North Castle, a more rugged country where assault by the Redcoats would be expensive.

So far as rock and grade gave his Army protection, Washington felt he would be secure in the hills north of White Plains as soon as he could add to nature's bulwarks. Open field combat was impossible at the time. Washington scarcely knew where to look for new soldiers or how to keep the veterans. He appealed to the militia to remain with the Army beyond the expiration of their term of service, but he might as well have asked them to scale high heaven. In the attempted enforcement of discipline, he threatened, he exhorted, he admonished. General Orders of November 3 read in part: "The General is sorry to find that there are some soldiers so lost to all sense of honor and honesty as to leave the Army when there is the greatest necessity for their services: He calls upon the officers of every rank to exert themselves in putting a stop to it, and absolutely forbids any officer, under the rank of a Brigadier General, discharging any officer or soldier or giving any permission to leave the camp on any pretence whatsoever."

Such was the plight of the Army when, on the morning of November 5, Washington received news that the British had abandoned their camps and started in the direction of King's Bridge. Headquarters buzzed with interpretation. Washington thought the move might be a feint and did not believe Howe could be preparing to go into winter quarters. It was more likely, he reasoned, that the British intended to besiege Fort Washington, attempt the subjugation of New Jersey and perhaps send an expedition to one or another of the southern States.

A council on the sixth agreed that if the British retreat were towards New York, Howe might be planning to invade New Jersey and that additional American troops should be moved thither. It was suggested that the regiments for this service be those of States below the Hudson and that men from the eastern States be returned to that region if circumstances permitted. Three thousand soldiers, the council decided, would be an appropriate guard for the New York highlands. This advice looked to the creation of two armies in accordance with the suggestion previously submitted to Congress by Washington, and it reflected the weary confusion of mind to which he was coming in his consideration of strategical plans. Too weak to take the offensive with one army, he was in a fair way of destroying even its defensive power by dividing it in circumstances that would increase his dependence on militia. At the moment, all the General could do to make this dangerous proposal an experimental reality was to apportion troops and make preliminary arrangements for the march and for the crossing of the Hudson.

The British withdrawal from White Plains gave the American commander almost a week in which to struggle with plundering, half-mutiny, widespread desertion and some obstacles of a sort that had not been put in his way when he had striven to replace the Army at the end of 1775. To have called his situation desperate would have been to brighten the picture. The danger of a complete dissolution of the Army was so imminent that while Washington did what he could to relieve the misery of his men, he could not afford to admit the justice of some of the soldiers' complaints. Scores of tents had been lost in the evacuation of New York. Compelled to sleep on the ground, many of the recruits fell sick and went to hospitals which were worse than the camps. Some of the troops had no cooking utensils; others had to man the works all night when they were weary and shivering for lack of clothing. They could not be expected to respond with huzzas to the plea that they reenlist for the duration of the war. To Washington, the attitude of the men could not have seemed unreasonable, but he believed that if vigorous, persuasive officers were authorized to recruit on the terms Congress had allowed, some of the veterans could be induced to continue in service. The obstacle to this was a new one: no officer of a regiment due to leave at the end of the year knew whether he was to remain an officer and whether he had any right to recruit. Under the resolves Congress recklessly had adopted, nothing could be done in this direction until the state commissioners selected the men who were to command the regiments from their States. As of November 6, not a single officer of a state regiment had been chosen in this manner and invested with authority to recruit.

The addition of these man-made perplexities to the leadership of a dispirited and feeble army in the presence of a superior foe imposed on Washington the heaviest load under which he could hope to stagger on. It did not seem possible for patience to endure another frustration or for faith to bear up if disaster came. When, in bafflement and approaching despair, Washington brought his general officers together in council November 6, he asked their advice on recruitment: Could anything be done to preserve the Army? The answer of the council was the old one, perhaps the only one that could be made: As there inevitably would be a gap of some months between the time the Army of 1776 disbanded and the Army of 1777 was ready for the field, each of the nearby States must be called upon to supply a considerable force of militia to serve until March 1, 1777. To this weak and worn expedient was the Commander-in-Chief reduced, he who remembered militiamen's negligence on Long Island, their panic at Kip's Bay, their flight from Chatterton's Hill and their mass desertion when weariness or homesickness overtook them.

After the council Washington addressed his appeal to some of the

States for these new drafts of militia. He particularly exhorted Gov. William Livingston of New Jersey to put militia in readiness to take the place of men whose term of service was soon to expire. Washington's tone in this was calm if urgent, but when he reported to Congress, which had authorized him to call for militia, he scarcely could conceal his desperation: "The propriety of this application [to the States] I trust will appear when it is known that not a single officer is yet commissioned to recruit, and when it is considered how essential it is to keep up some show of force and shadow of an Army."

"Shadow of an Army"—was that all he was to have in the day when Howe manifestly intended to assail Fort Washington and, if successful there, might move against Philadelphia? Washington had to prepare as best he could for these eventualities, but he was wearier than he knew. His judgment increasingly was clouded; his decisions were made more slowly and with hesitation. In his exhausted state of mind, Washington thought the contemplated transfer of American forces across the Hudson was immediately strategic and perhaps imperative. He would divide the artillery, leave Heath to guard the New York Highlands, name Lee to direct operations north of King's Bridge, and cross the Hudson with the troops from the States west and south of the river. These men would be few in number, but they could be reenforced, Washington believed, by two brigades of "five-months" troops from the Flying Camp and by Jersey militia. He estimated that from these two sources he could get at least five thousand troops. With these and his Continentals, he hoped he could hold the British until the development of their offensive made possible the reconcentration of all his troops except, perhaps, those left to garrison the passes of the highlands, the bastion that must be held if it was possible for a small army to do so.

In this expectation, Washington left the camp above White Plains November 10 and by the evening of the thirteenth reached Greene's Headquarters at Fort Lee. Nearly all the troops from south or west of the Hudson then were across that river under the immediate command of Stirling—and were in number less than three full regiments would have been. Greene commanded 3500 men. With the inclusion of all the militia except those in Fort Washington, the Army east of the Hudson consisted of 13,123 fit, rank and file, on November 3. Approximately seven thousand of these had been left with Lee; Heath had about four thousand. Washington had reduced his own force to two thousand Virginians and Marylanders. He received information from Greene that was a stunning blow: The Flying Camp did not include anything like as many men as Washington had assumed were there; practically no Jersey militia had rallied to Greene. Instead of the five thousand recruits he had expected Washington had virtually no immediate accession of strength beyond the troops Greene had in Fort Lee.

In the face of this dispersion of force, the military situation was more and more bewildering. On November 11, while Washington had been reconnoitering the highlands, nearly two hundred sail had left New York, in the wake, as it were, of twenty-two that had stood out to sea on the ninth. Whither were these vessels bound? Washington was puzzled, too, by the failure of Howe to cross into Jersey. It was to be assumed that the British commander would undertake to reduce Fort Washington, but did Howe have some other plan, of which the Americans had as yet no information? There might be one more thrust. After that the Redcoats might go into winter quarters, but the direction of the probable offensive was put in deeper doubt now by reports Lee sent November 13 of a British march down North River from Dobbs Ferry in the direction of King's Bridge.

As Washington, in hesitant mood, read all this and listened to the varying interpretations of the situation by the men about him, he felt that the prudent course for the time being was to leave Heath and Lee where they were and dispose the troops with him on the various roads leading into New Jersey, unless Congress had become anxious for the security of Philadelphia and wished him nearer that city. Never had he been so confused regarding his adversary; never had he been so hesitant—and seldom had he been called upon to decide quickly so close a question as that which had been presented for a week and more by Fort Washington: Should it be held or should it be evacuated? Could its garrison beat off attack that seemed certain, or would the place be taken and the officers and men be made prisoners unless they could get to Fort Lee?

Washington knew little about conditions at Fort Lee. He had lost direct communication with the place about October 22 and had left its defence to Greene. On November 5, the frigate *Pearl* and two victual ships had gone up North River, had passed the forts and the obstructions and had anchored off Spuyten Duyvil in defiance of the "rebels" and the cannon on the heights. Washington had been shaken when he had heard of this exploit. He wrote Greene: "If we cannot prevent vessels passing up, and the enemy are possessed of the surrounding country what valuable purpose can it answer to attempt to hold a post from which the expected benefit cannot be had . . . ?" The letter to Greene proceeded to urge that all stores and provisions at the forts or in the adjacent districts be removed or destroyed, except for those immediately needed, because experience had shown that the enemy had "drawn great relief" from supplies found in the area of operations.

Greene, in answer, advanced arguments for retaining Fort Washington: It occupied the attention of a considerable British force; it compelled the enemy to keep troops at King's Bridge to prevent American sorties; it could hold out, according to Col. Robert Magaw, to the end of the year. Greene renewed his assurance that if the situation grew serious, he could remove the garrison of Fort Washington to Fort Lee and then could unite his command with the troops Washington brought over.

Now, November 14, at Fort Lee, on hearing Greene's verbal report, Washington met with a disappointment: Greene had begun the reenforcement of the garrison at Fort Washington and had not removed surplus supplies and equipment from the works on either side of the Hudson. He still had strong conviction that the defences east of the river could be held and had exercised the discretion he thought Washington had given him regarding Fort Washington. Washington had to ask himself whether he should let Greene's orders stand, increase the garrison and defend the place to the utmost, or attempt, even at the last hour, to follow his own judgment and evacuate the garrison and such artillery and supplies as he could. The weary General could not bring himself to a choice. There was "warfare" in his mind, he confessed later, and hesitation. He did not change Greene's orders, but, leaving the management of affairs to that officer, he went on to Hackensack to study the dispositions that should be made to resist the expected advance of Howe. Greene, as confident as ever, sent across to Fort Washington reenforcements who increased the defenders of the works to nearly seventeen hundred men.

At Hackensack, November 15, Washington received a brief dispatch from Greene, who enclosed one sent him by Colonel Magaw at Fort Washington. Magaw reported the receipt of a flag of truce from King's Bridge, with the British Adjutant General in the party. The American officer wrote: "The Adjutant General would hardly give two hours for an alternative between surrendering at discretion, or every man being put to the sword." Magaw concluded: "We are determined to defend the post or die," and he appended a copy of his flat rejection of the demand for surrender.

Back then to Fort Lee the Commander-in-Chief rode to determine whether to make an effort to bring the garrison across the river or to let Magaw fight it out with the British. Shortly before dawn of the sixteenth Washington started across North River with Putnam, Greene and Mercer in order to decide, finally and positively, what should be done. Almost at the instant the Generals took their places in the boat the sound of firing became audible from a part of the ridge where some skirmishing had occurred November 11. When Washington and his companions climbed to the crest, they learned that the enemy had passed easily the first line across the King's Bridge Road on the southern side of Mount Washington. The second and stronger line was being assailed. Washington was told, also, that British columns had been moving on other approaches, as if they were reconnoitering. Colonel Magaw had made his dispositions, which appeared to be proper.

Down the heights and back across the river Washington and his party went—to listen, wonder, and—presently—despair. The sound of the firing soon indicated that the British were closing from the south and were within the range of small arms. Stiff resistance was being offered on the northern face of the earthworks. Fighting of indeterminable scope was in progress to the east. Gradually the firing converged; ere long Washington had to conclude that the troops were being driven into the fort itself. If it was possible, the garrison ought to be withdrawn to the Jersey shore; but evacuation could not be undertaken till night. Someone must contrive to get into Fort Washington with a message to Magaw that if he held out till darkness, the Commander-in-Chief would see that the men were brought safely to New Jersey. A young officer was found who was willing to cross the river; the message was dispatched. A little later the tortured Commander-in-Chief sent another volunteer to see if affairs were as desperate as they appeared. At length the officer who had taken the first message to Magaw succeeded in getting back to Fort Lee with intelligence to depress the stoutest heart:

Colonel Magaw sent his thanks to the General but had to report that he had gone so far with negotiations for surrender that he could not in honor break them off.

Later, the second man who had crossed the river returned to report. He, too, had the worst to tell. The only terms the British would allow were those of immediate and absolute surrender as prisoners of war. While Washington listened to that calamitous news he knew he had to deduct from the rolls of his small Army the men who might at that very hour be marching to some foul prison. They numbered, he thought, about two thousand—many of whom, as he sadly wrote Congress, "have been trained with more than common attention." Actually, the total was 2818 officers and men. These were lost, altogether lost!

The details of what had happened to Magaw's men and the actual terms of surrender were not yet known on the Jersey side of North River, but criticism did not wait on fact. Those who were wise after the event or were secretly jealous of Greene made him their scapegoat and indirectly assailed Washington.

Washington realized that the disaster of the sixteenth was not to be the end of adversity. Tired as he was, he saw that when Fort Washington was lost, Fort Lee was worthless and, if held, might be another trap. As soon as it was threatened, it must be evacuated. This would sharpen criticism and would deepen public disappointment. Better that than a second Fort Washington. When he went again to Hackensack to resume preparations for withdrawal southward he was appalled to find there scarcely any of the New Jersey militia on whose support he had relied. Although the state was apt to be invaded and property plundered, it appeared as if Jerseymen either were cowed by British victories or at heart not sympathetic with the American cause.

It scarcely seemed possible that so tremendous a change had come within the ten days since Washington left White Plains, but this now was the frightful prospect: By the end of November Washington would not have more than two thousand fit soldiers of the Continental establishment with whom to oppose Howe in the region west of the Hudson. "Oppose" was his own verb: he knew it was a mockery, but he scarcely could afford to say so to any of those about him, not even to Reed, whom he loved and trusted. The one person to whom the agonized commander could unburden himself was his always prudent confidant, his brother John Augustine. So, at Hackensack on the nineteenth, Washington finished a letter started at White Plains, November 6.

Indignantly he wrote: ". . . all the year since, I have been pressing [Congress] to delay no time in engaging men upon such terms as would assure success, telling them that the longer it was delayed the more difficult it would grow; but the measure was not set about till it was too late to be effected, and then in such a manner as to bid adieu to every hope of getting an Army from which any services are to be expected; the different States without regard to the merits or qualifications of an officer, quarreling about the appointments, and nominating such as are not fit to be shoe blacks from the local attachments of this or that member of Assembly." He could not stop even when he had put some of his junior officers lower than shoe blacks: "I am wearied almost to death with the retrograde motions of things, and I solemnly protest that a pecuniary record of £20,000 a year would not induce me to undergo what I do; and, after all, perhaps, to lose my character, as it is impossible under such a variety of distressing circumstances to conduct matters agreeably to public expectation, or even of those who employ me, as they will not make proper allowances for the difficulties their own errors have occasioned."

In this furious disappointment, Washington resumed his efforts to dispose his troops for combat or retreat. He felt himself most disadvantageously placed for either, because what remained of his small Army still was divided in four fragments—his own feeble force at Hackensack and Fort Lee, Stirling's eight small regiments, about one thousand men, at Rahway and New Brunswick, Lee at White Plains, and Heath at Peekskill. The last of these forces must be left on guard in the highlands. To keep Howe and Burgoyne from forming a junction and isolating New England remained an imperative of strategy. Washington's columns, Lee's and Stirling's must be reunited if Howe made the expected move and attempted to take Philadelphia.

Washington had the multiple phases of this problem before him November 20 when an express brought him a dispatch from Greene: A heavy British force had crossed North River that morning below Dobbs Ferry and appeared to be marching rapidly to Fort Lee. Washington in a few minutes was galloping towards the fort. He confirmed reports that the British were in greatly superior numbers and ordered the place evacuated immediately, even though this meant that pots had to be left boiling and tents standing. There was only one avenue of quick escape—across the Hackensack, which had a single bridge. Once across that stream the country was flat and offered no natural strongholds. It was necessary for Washington to order a withdrawal beyond the Passaic and leave a fine country to be ravaged by the Hessians. On the twenty-first he made the necessary moves and proceeded with his short files to Aquackanock Bridge on the Passaic. He wanted now to reunite his scattered forces. This, he reasoned, would involve a farther withdrawal, probably to New Brunswick, in order to be in touch with Stirling, who had made ready to join him on receipt of the news that Howe's vanguard, under Cornwallis, had passed North River. As soon as the full strength of the British offensive in New Jersey was manifest the essentials of the plan adopted in advance by Washington were to become operative: In accordance with instructions given Lee before the Army moved from White Plains, that officer was to leave Heath to guard the highlands. With militia included, Heath now had about four thousand men. Lee's numbers had risen to more than 7700 and included some of the most experienced and best disciplined troops of the Army. These were Washington's principal source of strength and were to be moved forthwith to Jersey, though Lee had been asserting, ever since the fall of Fort Washington, that sound strategy dictated retention of the area around White Plains. From the Passaic River, Washington wrote his senior lieutenant about the evacuation of Fort Lee and proceeded to answer Lee's arguments against a shift from

White Plains. Washington told Lee: "Unless, therefore, some new event should occur, or some more cogent reason present itself, I would have you move over by the easiest and best passage."

Lee's coming was in reality a matter of life and death in the sternest, most realistic addition and subtraction. If he brought five thousand and Stirling could count one thousand bayonets, these could be added to the fragments of Continental regiments, Greene's men from Fort Lee, the militia and the survivors of the Flying Camp, all of whom had now been assembled under Washington to an unstable aggregate of 4400. On paper, then, the arrival of Lee and Stirling would give the reconcentrated Army a temporary strength of 10,400, but that figure, if attained at all, would be illusory. Within less than ten days the Army would be reduced by slightly over two thousand on the expiration of the service of the Maryland and New Jersey regiments of the Flying Camp. Eight hundred and fifty more would be free to go home January 1. That would leave slightly over 7500, of whom 5000 represented brigades, with Lee. Continuance of resistance, in any serious sense, thus depended on that officer's prompt compliance with the instructions sent him. Those instructions were positive but, of course, were phrased considerately.

The weather, which had been unusually fine, now grew bad. The British seemed willing to wait on the elements. At Newark, where Washington established temporary Headquarters, there was much work and planning for the commander. Washington decided Thomas Mifflin should visit Philadelphia and explain to Congress the weakness of the Army and the necessity of immediate help. Joseph Reed was dispatched on a similar mission to Governor Livingston of New Jersey. Congress was besought to forward money for the payment of the soldiers of the Flying Camp.

In the Quaker City crisis was shaking the revolutionary leaders out of their addiction to defer that which was pressing and to consider promptly that which might be postponed. Congress, city authorities and Council of Safety were almost frantic as they heard one report after another of British plans for marching on Philadelphia. A committee was named by Congress to visit Washington, and another was chosen to devise means of reenforcing him and of obstructing the advance of the enemy. The Commander-in-Chief was authorized to recall the New Jersey and Pennsylvania regiments then in the Northern Department.

From all of this and from recruits the bounty would attract, there might rise in 1777 a new and more stable Army if, meantime, the frail remnant of the Army of 1776 could survive. For the next few weeks, everything would depend upon the activity of Howe, the contingencies of war and the prompt arrival of Lee with his veteran brigades. Rain or hesitation or both appeared to be holding back the royal army; Lee's coming was taken for granted; the adverse developments at the beginning of the last week of November were a spread of desertion and the report of a Tory uprising in Monmouth County, New Jersey. As nothing worse was apparent, a few of the courageous and philosophical men in the Army began to reknit their ravelled hope.

Then, November 24, Washington opened a letter addressed by Lee to

Reed, who still was absent in consultation with Governor Livingston. It was an astonishing document: Lee was not bringing his troops. Instead he was ordering the detachment to Washington of two thousand of Heath's men. Washington read with dismay. He had not meant to give Lee discretion; politeness had not been intended to modify orders; the one thing about which he had been most explicit before leaving White Plains had been that Heath should remain to guard the highlands; now Lee was taking two thousand of Heath's men and was leaving at White Plains the very troops Washington most needed, and needed without an hour's delay! There might be several interpretations of Lee's action. Anyone who regarded him as an ambitious adventurer might scrutinize that letter to Reed and might consider some of the language suspicious, arrogant even. Had a critic, moreover, read the correspondence book at White Plains he would have seen other communications that would have puzzled him. The day before Lee wrote Reed, he had scratched off to his friend Benjamin Rush a letter in which he had boasted "I foresaw, predicted, all that has happened" at Fort Washington. Lee had concluded: "I could say many things—let me talk vainly—had I the powers I could do you much good, might I but dictate one week; but I am sure you will never give any man the necessary power. . . ." There was much almost as vainglorious as that—for example, a paper addressed to Gov. James Bowdoin of Massachusetts concerning separate armies on either side of the Hudson, with the assurance that if the enemy attempted to enter New England or force the passes of the highlands, "I should never entertain a thought of being succoured from the Western Army"—and more in like strain, along with no little that was sound, soldierly and sensible.

Washington had not seen these letters, of course, nor had he observed anything to change his opinion that Lee was fickle; but now he took the view that Lee merely had misunderstood or misinterpreted orders and wrote immediately to leave no doubt of his wishes. He proceeded then to give such instructions about the march as seemed to be necessary. In a letter received late November 26, Lee stated that he had received Washington's "orders" and would "try to put 'em in execution," but, he said "[I] question much whether I shall be able to carry with me any considerable number of men, not so much from a want of zeal in the men as from their wretched condition with respect to shoes, stockings &c, which the present bad weather renders more intolerable." Then Lee went blandly on: "I sent Heath orders to transport two thousand men across the river, apprize the General and wait for further orders, but that great man (as I might have expected) entrenched himself within the letter of his instructions and refused to part with a single file, though I undertook to replace 'em with a part of my own."

This was disconcerting in that it showed Lee apparently unfamiliar with Washington's plan to keep Heath in the highlands, regardless of other moves. Further, Lee spoke of "two days' delay"—as if two days might not mean the difference between surviving and perishing. Heath, in his turn, reported the first phase of a correspondence with Lee, whose demand for the dispatch of the two thousand men he refused as contrary to his direct orders from the Commander-in-Chief. Washington's secretary gave assurance to Heath: "In respect to the troops intended to come to this quarter, his Excellency never meant that they should be from your Division."

On the twenty-seventh there still was no news that Lee was marching to help his commander, and all the reports were that more of the British were across the Passaic. There were indications that a force to support Cornwallis might land at Amboy. Washington could not give battle and must retreat at least as far as New Brunswick. The move began November 28. As the American rearguard left Newark, the British entered the opposite side but they did not attempt pursuit. At noon, November 29, Washington reached New Brunswick and halted the Army, which, in spite of all its freezing and splashing in the mud, doubtless was interested to hear of abundant liquor there. If the survivors of Washington's luckless campaign found rum and fought among themselves and disturbed the uncertain sleep of an anxious town, who could blame them unduly?

Washington did not have precise figures before him on November 30; but he had a calendar and he had a tabulation prepared for Congress while he was at Newark. This was the paper which had shown that of the 5410 troops, more than two thousand had the right December 1 to start home. "If those go whose service expires this day," Washington had to write the President of Congress, "our force will be reduced to a mere handfull"—when a division of the enemy was at Elizabeth Town and the King's quartermasters were busy in the choice of shelter five miles farther south. Never had the situation been so desperate, not even on the corresponding date of 1775 when the Connecticut militia were about to march off, or on December 31, the last day of the "old Army." It seemed futile to appeal to the common man; only the exceptional individual was patriotic. If liberty was to be won in America, it must be by the patience, the courage, the intelligence, the character of a few leaders. These men must stand together.

An express from General Lee arrived with a letter addressed to Colonel Reed. In Reed's absence, the express insisted on putting the letter in the hands of the Commander-in-Chief. If it was official, it was to be opened as a matter of course by Washington. A twist of the sheet, the crackling of the sealing-wax, and then:

Camp, Nov'r the 24th, 1776

My Dr. Reed:
    I received your most obliging, flattering letter—lament with you that fatal indecision of mind which in war is a much greater disqualification than stupidity or even want of personal courage. Accident may put a decisive blunderer in the right, but eternal defeat and miscarriage must attend the man of the best parts if cursed with indecision.
    The General . . .

There followed an explanation of Lee's reasons for not wishing to march to Jersey; then came a summary of what he hoped to do to "Ranger" Rogers and nearby British. Next a few words about the prospect of recognition by France, and—

I only wait myself for this business I mention of Rogers & Co. being over—shall then fly to you—for to confess a truth I really think my Chief will do better with me than without me.

Washington was more hurt than outraged by the accidental discovery that his Adjutant General and his senior division commander apparently had been exchanging letters critical of him. For months he had been on his guard against the "fickleness" of Lee. Now that Lee's state of mind had been disclosed bluntly, Washington would be more careful than ever in dealing with that soldier. Officially, there could be no change of attitude. Lee's professional knowledge must be utilized for the country's sake. It was Reed whose secret correspondence mortified—Reed who had shared the most intimate conversation, Reed who knew all that went on at Headquarters. Why had not Reed told him what had been passed on to Lee? As it was, the circumstances of opening the letter had to be explained to Reed; that was the obligation of a gentleman. Washington sat down on that most miserable of his wretched days and wrote this:

[New] Brunswick, November 30, 1776

Dear Sir:
  The enclosed was put into my hands by an express from the White Plains. Having no idea of its being a private letter, much less suspecting the tendency of the correspondence, I opened it, as I have done all other letters to you, from the same place and Peekskill, upon the business of your office, as I conceived and found them to be.
  This, as it is the truth, must be my excuse for seeing the contents of a letter, which neither inclination or intention would have prompted me to.
  I thank you for the trouble and fatigue you have undergone in your journey to Burlington, and sincerely wish that your labors may be crowned with the desired success. My best respects to Mrs. Reed. I am, Dear Sir, etc.
  PS. The petition referred to I keep.

This letter was to be all, unless Reed himself opened the subject.
  Of his larger problem Washington wrote, "I will not despair"; but before another sun had set he needed to summon all the resolution that lay behind his words. On the morning of December 1 scouts reported the enemy at Bonum, about ten miles from New Brunswick. Rumor had it that reenforcements from Staten Island had joined Earl Charles Cornwallis, a possibility that Washington could not disregard when he put an estimate of six to seven thousand on the force of his adversary. The American Army, on the other hand, continued to dwindle. With scarcely 3400 effectives, Washington had to undertake a new retreat. Orders were issued for every man and every vehicle to cross the Raritan at once. It was done in the early afternoon and without loss, but the margin was so narrow that the whole of the bridge could not be destroyed.
  Now that odds were so heavy and the future so black, Washington felt that he should not halt until he reached the Delaware and put himself where he could move readily to the Pennsylvania side of that river. He continued to send out earnest calls for reenforcements as he proceeded on

his way, via Princeton. At the college town he hoped Lee would meet him, but neither Lee nor any dispatch from that officer was waiting. Stirling, with about twelve hundred men, was left at Princeton to act as a check-rein on a galloping chase by Howe; the remainder of the little Army passed on to Trenton December 3.

There Washington received a dispatch from Lee, but the content was as depressing as silence had been. Lee's letter was four days old, and it was in the mood of a man anxious to do as he pleased in quest of fame. Now Lee justified his delay on the ground that when he entered Jersey he would bring "Four thousand firm and willing troops. . . ." If the advance had been begun earlier, said the tardy General, "I should have only led an inferior number of unwilling." Lee concluded: "I could wish you would bind me as little as possible, not from any opinion, I do assure you, of my own parts, but from a persuasion that detached Generals cannot have too great latitude, unless they are very incompetent indeed."

Washington had to adjust himself to the fact that no help could be expected from Lee for several days. Meantime, Howe might advance before militia arrived in number large enough to give hope of a successful defence. When the report of a powerful British onmarch was verified, Washington did not delude himself: He could not make a stand otherwise than by risking a hopeless fight with his back to the river. The ghost of the American Army must be transported across the Delaware and, if possible, must be revived. December 7, by nightfall, the troops were in Pennsylvania, opposite Trenton. No public property, other than a few boards, had been left on the Jersey side of the river. On the eighth the enemy had a part of his column at Maidenhead and at Princeton and he pushed his van to Trenton. Report was that Howe's train included boats in which to ferry Redcoats to the Philadelphia Road. If this were true, then the Americans must be spread, thinly, along the Pennsylvania shore and the crossings fortified. Orders for the collection and removal of boats from the left to the right bank of the Delaware were being executed, but these instructions must be enlarged to cover the entire navigable stretch of seventy miles above Philadelphia. This only was certain: If Howe had any boats, they had not been brought forward, nor had any considerable number thus far been found by his men on the Jersey shore. What could be done? Washington must concentrate his troops and procure militia reenforcement in order to prevent, if possible, the British capture of Philadelphia before the American Army of 1777 could be recruited and brought into the field. He was not sure this could be done; he did not believe Philadelphia could be saved unless the troops under Lee joined the other Continentals when Howe started his march on the city. Even with Lee's aid, whatever was done to keep Philadelphia from falling into the hands of the enemy must be done quickly, because Washington could expect no more than three weeks' further service from some of the best of his troops. The time of nearly all the Continental regiments, except those of Virginia and of Maryland, would expire with December. The history of 1775 was being paralleled in a manner that sickened and appalled.

Washington did not deceive himself. His resolution was inflexible; his hope was waning fast. He remained of the opinion that the enemy would attempt soon to cross the Delaware and move on Philadelphia. Nothing, he thought, except lack of boats held the British back. All calculations, all argument, came back to the same ugly fact: If any basis of hope remained, it lay in Lee. With his troops, some of them battle-tested, to augment Washington's Continentals and the Philadelphia militia there was a chance that Howe might be halted, or so discouraged that he would go into winter quarters north of the Delaware. Without Lee, those strong British and Hessian battalions almost certainly would destroy with ease the wraith of the Army that lingered after the losses of 1776.

Lee began his crossing of the Hudson on December 2 and proceeded to Morristown, which some of his troops did not reach until the tenth. The previous night Washington received a letter written by Lee on the eighth. On the evening of the tenth another of the same date arrived. In one of these communications, Lee reported his own troops as 2700 and "our Army," militia included, as 4000. Then Lee said: "If I was not taught to think that your Army was considerably reenforced, I should immediately join you; but as I am assured you are very strong, I should imagine we can make a better impression by hanging on [the enemy's] rear, for which purpose a good post at Chatham seems the best calculated." He proceeded to explain briefly the advantage of that position.

Washington read this in full appreciation of the advantage of having a force in the rear of Howe's army, a strategical possibility of which Cornwallis was already unhappily conscious. Washington was not disposed to dwell on the fact that Lee now spoke of four thousand men, though in a previous letter he had mentioned "an army of 5000 good troops in spirits." The main issue dominated. Lee must be brought to the main Army, but how, how, how? Additional orders would be ineffectual; a personal appeal was the only recourse. Humiliating as it was to beseech a subordinate to do what was properly to be commanded of him, Washington felt that the cause and the crisis required that meek diplomacy. He gave directions to Stephen Moylan to proceed at once to Morristown and to push forward Lee's troops and Gates's as well. As Lee of course could balk Moylan, the Commander-in-Chief wrote his senior lieutenant: "I cannot but request and entreat you and this, too, by the advice of all the general officers with me, to march and join me with all your whole force, with all possible expedition." Washington wrote briefly of route and of the disposition of British forces, who seemed to be making ready for an attempt to cross the Delaware above Trenton. "Do come on," he coaxed, "your arrival may be happy, and if it can be effected without delay, may be the means of preserving a city, whose loss must prove of the most fatal consequences to the cause of America."

In reporting to Congress, Washington already had said he did not know how to account for the slowness of Lee's march; now he summarized Lee's letters and said only, "as I have not at present, nor do I see much probability of further reenforcements, I have wrote to him in the most pressing terms to join me with all expedition." From Washington's point of view, that was self-protective because it put on record the fact that Lee was insubordinate.

The crisis tightened. On December 13 Washington doubtless heard that Congress had left Philadelphia for Baltimore, where it was to reassemble not later than the twentieth. Intelligence reports indicated that the enemy might be making dispositions for an attempted crossing. Events seemed to show, also, that the British were so confident of their strength they could afford some dispersion of force in a desirable minor operation. The fleet that had left New York December 1 had discharged near Newport, Rhode Island, on the eighth a force of sufficient magnitude to evoke from state authorities loud and instant calls for assistance. Washington ordered Joseph Spencer and Benedict Arnold to proceed there, but he could spare neither Greene nor Gates, whom the Rhode Islanders were anxious to procure.

From Lee, on the thirteenth, there came another strange letter, under date of December 11. It began with the statement, "We have three thousand men here at present; but they are so ill-shod that we have been obliged to halt these two days for want of shoes." With no elaboration of this reason for delay, Lee's letter proceeded: "Seven Regiments of Gates's corps are on their march, but where they actually are, is not certain." Then, for some reason, the letter was shifted to the third person: "General Lee has sent two officers this day; one to inform him where the Delaware can be crossed above Trenton; the other to examine the road toward Burlington, as General Lee thinks he can, without great risk, cross the great Brunswick post road, and by a forced night's march, make his way to the ferry below Burlington. Boats should be sent from Philadelphia to receive him. But this scheme he only proposes, if the head of the enemy's column actually pass the river. The militia in this part of the province seems sanguine. If they could be sure of an Army remaining amongst 'em"—and here Lee shifted back to the first person, "I believe they would raise a very considerable number."

Washington did not lose patience in answering: "I am much surprised," he wrote, "that you should be in any doubt respecting the route you should take." With a brief explanation, once more, of the crossing arranged for Lee, the commanding General proceeded: "I have so frequently mentioned our situation and the necessity of your aid that it is painful to me to add a word upon the subject. Let me once more request and entreat you"—he did not withhold the humiliating verb—"to march immediately for Pittstown, which lies on the route that has been pointed out, and is about eleven miles from Tinnicum Ferry, that is more on the flank of the enemy than where you are. Advise me of the time you will arrive there, that a letter may be sent you, about your future destination and such other movements as may be necessary." Washington had said substantially the same thing previously and with no observable result. This time he was going to hold out a prospect that he believed no soldier could disregard. Stirling was to follow Moylan to Lee and was to dispatch other officers to Gates and to Heath. The object of this was to ascertain the condition of the various forces, learn when the columns could be expected at Pittstown, and see what proposals Lee, Gates and Heath could make for an attack on the British in concert with Washington's forces.

"Use every possible means without regard to expense," said Washington, "to come with certainty, at the enemy's strength, situation and movements; without this we wander in a wilderness of uncertainties and difficulty, and no plan can be formed upon a rational plan." Stirling well may have gasped at his orders: A General who had declared himself almost certain to fail in the effort to keep the British from Philadelphia without the help of Lee now was hinting that the Army would turn from defensive to offensive. Washington sketched only in the vaguest way the possibility of recrossing the Delaware, but the spirit of the offensive was rising. It might be desperation; it might be military madness; but there would be no more hesitation of the sort that cost Fort Washington and more than 2800 men.

That day, the fourteenth, a heavy freeze began. If it continued, the muddy roads would be hard, but the Delaware might be covered with ice. If the covering soon were thick enough to support men and cannon, then Cornwallis might cross and attack before the American plan of action could be matured. Again, if the river did not freeze heavily enough to present danger of a British advance on too long a front to guard it, the ice might present an obstacle to the Continentals' returning to the north bank. Washington faced these possibilities and refused to permit them to discourage him. Like every other man, he might have better days and worse, might find sunlit hours short and black night long, but he now had conquered the confusion of mind that had paralyzed him early in November. Said Thomas Paine: "Voltaire has remarked that King William never appeared to full advantage but in difficulties and in action. The same remark may be made on General Washington, for the character fits him." Paine had seen Washington at Fort Lee and in the ghastly retreat across Jersey and testified as an eye-witness. Washington's planning justified this praise. On the day he once more "entreated" Lee to advance—the day when Stirling was riding fast over treacherous roads toward Morristown—Washington wrote Gates of the Army's weakness, of the depth of the retreat, of the great strength the British showed, and of the lack of help from the militia. Washington could not or would not believe that Lee would fail him, and he told Gates: "I expect General Lee will be here this evening or tomorrow, who will be followed by General Heath and his Division. If we can draw our forces together, I trust, under the smiles of providence, we may yet effect an important stroke, or at least prevent General Howe from executing his plans."

As soon as Lee arrived, Washington would explore with him the possibilities of an offensive. Noon of the fifteenth and no message from the outposts that the van of the veteran Division was close to the upper crossings of the Delaware, safely beyond the extended right flank of the British. At one o'clock a spattered horseman drew rein at Headquarters—an express from General Sullivan. So often had expresses brought bad news and so seldom had they been the bearers of good tidings that Washington had trained himself to expect anything, but he had now something new, something bewildering; Sullivan reported that on the thirteenth, about ten o'clock in the morning, at a temporary lodging some three miles from the American lines, General Lee had been captured by a British patrol.

Washington, in his first announcement to Congress, felt it proper to write: "I will not comment upon the melancholy intelligence, only adding that I sincerely regret General Lee's unhappy fate, and feel much for the loss of my country in his captivity." Comment by others ranged from dismay to puzzlement and suspicion. The facts were not known in their fullness for days and, when known, scarcely explained Lee's conduct. He had ridden to before he had finished breakfasting and bickering. Most of his guards had must have retired at a late hour and slept long, because it was ten o'clock before he had finished breakfasting and bickering. Most of his guards had slipped off to a nearby building and were trying to warm themselves in the sun when a party of British—four officers and thirty mounted men—dashed up the lane, surrounded the tavern and demanded that Lee come out to them. After a few minutes and with scarcely a show of defence, Lee yielded. The British quickly put him on a horse, hatless and not fully clothed, and dashed off with him to New Brunswick. The party had been organized by Lieut. Col. William Harcourt who had volunteered to reconnoiter the position and strength of Lee's forces, when he learned that Cornwallis had no acceptable intelligence of the American column. Accidental capture of an American light dragoon with a dispatch for Lee had given the clue that prompted Harcourt to sweep down on the inn. Harcourt and his men rode seventy miles on their circuit without loss or accident and they had high welcome when they brought in their prisoner. It was doubtful whether the British or the Americans put the higher valuation on him and his importance to the Continental cause. Congress was anxious to relieve the hardships of Lee's imprisonment and voted him one hundred half-joes. Robert Morris was to supply these to Washington, who was requested to forward them through British channels. Others found consolation in the fact that Gates was at hand and could be used by Washington for tasks that would have been assigned Lee. Fear of what the less informed public would make of the affair was voiced by one of Washington's aides, Samuel Webb. ". . . We shall find hard work," he wrote, "to convince many officers and soldiers that [Lee] is not a traitor."

Heath and Gates had recent letters from Lee that would have created suspicions of other and puzzling sorts if the papers had been made public. Lee's letter to Gates was written the morning he was captured and had been snatched up by Gates's messenger as the British troops came thundering up the lane that led to White's Tavern. Had this document fallen into hostile hands it would have been juicy meat to British teeth and exceedingly hard for Lee to swallow. Said Lee: "The ingenious [sic] maneuver of Fort Washington has unhinged the goodly fabric we have been building—there never was so damned a stroke—*entre nous,* a certain great man is damnably deficient—He has thrown me into a situation where I have my choice of difficulties—if I stay in this Province I risk myself and army and if I do not stay the Province is lost forever."

Whether or not Washington had sensed any of this, he did not waste words on the situation. His reply to Sullivan's announcement of the capture of Lee contained two sentences of regret and then—"the event has happened. And I refer you to the several letters which I had wrote him, and to one which now goes to Lord Stirling, who I presume is with you, and who was fully possessed of my ideas when he left me, for the measures you and he may judge necessary to adopt." There was no more than that, because every hour added problems and multiplied perplexities. Washington continued to face those maddening questions on which life or death of the Revolution depended: when would Sullivan and Gates arrive; how could the crossing of the Delaware by the British be prevented; was it really possible to forge a counterbolt, or was the situation hopeless?

Judgment and resolution warred hourly over the answer. Every day after the fifteenth there was hope that Sullivan and perhaps Gates also would arrive. But as every bleak dawn brought tragically nearer the end of the enlistment of most Continental troops, Washington lost one prospect after another of reenforcement. Prudence dictated the return of Heath's six hundred to the highlands; Clinton, too, would be needed there, along with his militia; reports of the reenlistment of New England troops in the regiments marching to Washington's aid proved false. If rumor hopefully had it that Howe was going into winter quarters, Washington told himself that his adversary would stay there so short a time and would emerge with so much strength that the new American Army must be organized quickly. He had to admit in a confidential letter, "If every nerve is not strained to recruit the New Army with all possible expedition, I think the game is pretty near up. . . ."; but the deep determination of his spirit, his innate refusal to accept defeat, dictated this sentence in the same letter: ". . . under a full persuasion of the justice of our cause, I cannot entertain an idea that it will finally sink, though it may remain for some time under a cloud."

The Army must be increased to 110 battalions, the artillery enlarged, a corps of engineers established—half-a-score changes must be made at once if the new Army was to be recruited or be efficient when created. Deferential as Washington always had been in his attitude towards the men who spoke for America, he felt now that the choice was between country and Congress. On the twentieth, in resolute mood, he wrote the Delegates of his need, announced that he would enlist additional artillery and stated in plain terms that "if any good officers offer to raise men up on continental pay and establishment in this quarter, I shall encourage them to do so, and regiment them when they have done it."

As Washington finished his letter word came that Sullivan had arrived with Lee's troops and that Gates had reached camp. From plans for the Army that must somehow be brought into being within twelve dark days, Washington turned again to the troops who had to be put across the Philadelphia Road as a bar to Howe or to be thrown against the British. The 5000 troops whom Lee had said he would bring turned out to be about 2000; Gates's regiments had no more than 600; Washington computed his own force at between 2400 and 2500, plus the militia who had joined since he crossed North River. Formal returns were to show total effectives to be 7659, far too few and too dispirited, apparently, for the duty to be performed! Fairweather friends of American freedom were going over to the British and accepting the pardons Howe was dispensing. Howe was gaining strength from arms-bearing American Tories. Eleventh-hour attempts to offset some of the adverse odds were being made in the fever of fear. Old clothing was being sent shivering soldiers; blankets were being collected; a start was being made towards the establishment of depots of supplies in the less exposed towns of Pennsylvania. Almost frantically, everything that could be undertaken for the Army was being done except as respected the supply of soldiers.

Washington did not withhold a single detail of this tragedy from Congress, which had named Robert Morris head of a committee to conduct affairs in a Philadelphia that had taken on the look of a plundered town. Washington wrote Morris in plainest words:

. . . unless the militia repair to the city of Philadelphia for defence of it, I see no earthly prospect of saving it after the last of this instant; as that fatal vote of Congress respecting the appointment of new officers has put the recruiting business upon such a footing, and introduced so much confusion into the old Regiments, that I see no chance of raising men out of them; by the first of next month then, we shall be left with five Regiments of Virginia, one of Maryland, General Hand's and the remains of Miles'; reduced so much by sickness, fatigue &ca. as in the whole not to exceed, but short of 1200 men. Upon these and the militia is all our dependence, for you may as well attempt to stop the winds from blowing, or the sun in its diurnal, as the Regiments from going when their term is expired.

Then Washington reiterated, "I am satisfied the enemy wait for two events only to begin their operations upon Philadelphia," thick ice on the Delaware and the dissolution "of the poor remains of our debilitated Army."

The gods of weather appeared to be neutral. A heavy snow on the night of December 19/20 had been followed by a partial thaw on the twenty-first, with the result that the ice on the Delaware Christmas morning was not heavy enough to support troops or prevent the passage of well-handled boats. The ominous condition was a shift of wind toward the northeast. If that meant colder weather and more ice . . .

The wind was rising rapidly and men hovering around the camp fire were talking of their departure for home within another week and commiserating the 1500 who had to remain. But Washington had on his table that Christmas Day an order that his troops were to start for McKonkey's Ferry, "as soon as it begins to grow dark . . . and embark on board the boats . . ." Even if he had an Army for only a week more, Washington was going to attack.

He had to attack. If boats became available, or the river was frozen deeply over, Howe had it in his power to strike directly south from Trenton or on the road to Philadelphia, or else to cross in rear of Washington's Army and make it impossible for the Continentals to interpose their front between their adversary and Philadelphia. Washington's chief reliance had to be on prompt intelligence of British movements and wise use of the boats he had and the enemy lacked. Washington would have the initiative until the ice on the river permitted a British crossing or his Army disintegrated at the year's end. He must use that initiative.

Trenton, Washington believed, was occupied by two to three thousand Hessian troops, who had six field cannon. Hessian contingents of varying size were encamped to the east and southeast of the town, as far downstream as Black Horse. The main British forces were north of Trenton—at

Princeton, New Brunswick and Amboy. Christmas afternoon, the Continental regiments, to a total of about 2400 men were to parade behind the Pennsylvania hills at McKonkey's Ferry, approximately nine miles upstream from Trenton. General Ewing was to assemble opposite Trenton a force of New Jersey and Pennsylvania militia, who aggregated six to eight hundred. Farther downstream John Cadwalader, acting Brigadier, was to bring together Continentals, Pennsylvania troops and Philadelphia "Associators"—about eighteen hundred men—who held the line of the Delaware between Bordentown and Dunk's Ferry. Cadwalader's point of assembly was to be Bristol.

The main force of Continentals was to cross at McKonkey's Ferry, make a surprise attack at Trenton and, if successful there, push on to Princeton. The calculation was that the passage of the river could be completed by midnight and that the blow could be delivered at Trenton by 5 A.M. on the twenty-sixth. Brig. Gen. James Ewing, opposite the town, was to time his passage of the stream so that he could land before day and cut off the enemy's easiest line of retreat down the left bank of the Delaware. Detailed orders were given the general officers who were to cross with Washington. Discouragements developed, but Washington did not permit them to deter him. After darkness fell the troops began to move towards the ferry.

Every ounce of courage was needed as night went on. Blocks of ice began to float down the river, which was high and flowing fast. New ice began to form; the wind rose and made the handling of the boats difficult. At midnight, when Washington had hoped his men and guns would be on the Jersey shore, the task was hours from completion. Not until 3 A.M. was the last artillery-piece safely on Jersey soil. Another hour was required to put all the regiments at their stations around the landing place. Four o'clock, nine miles of road to cover, sunrise about 7:23, and light by 7:10 —in these circumstances Washington reasoned that the advantage of surprise would certainly be lost. He did not hesitate. His judgment told him that the loss of surprise scarcely could be worse than the harassment and casualties involved in a retreat across the river in the presence of the enemy. The advance must be made; the Hessians must be assailed the moment the town was reached.

The Army pressed on. At Birmingham John Sullivan took about half the troops and cannon down the lower road which followed the general course of the Delaware. Nathanael Greene, with a like force, took the upper or Pennington Road. Washington soon joined Greene. As closely as the General could estimate it, the two columns had nearly the same distance to march—between four and five miles—to Trenton. He had all the officers set their watches by his and gave orders that when either column struck the Hessian outposts, it was, without waiting to hear from the other, to push into Trenton before the enemy had time to form line of battle.

A light snow had covered the ground when the Army left camp; now, snow began to descend again. With it was mingled sleet or rain that froze and glazed the road. A more difficult time for a march over an unfamiliar route could not have been devised by the devil himself; it was a night when the indifferent soldier would cover his head with his blanket and the mercenary would hug the fire.

Day began to dawn when the column of Greene was still two miles from Trenton. Soon Washington noticed that Greene's advance had halted and went forward to ascertain the reason. He saw ahead a small company of men in a field. Before Washington could identify them, word was passed that they were Americans. What were they doing there? Capt. Richard Anderson of the Fifth Virginia explained that Gen. Adam Stephen had sent him to reconnoiter. He had carried out his orders and had just been to the Trenton outpost where his men had encountered and shot down a sentinel who apparently had not seen them in the storm until the moment they caught sight of the Hessian.

Stephen was at hand when the Captain reported. Washington turned on the Brigadier in wrath he did not attempt to conceal: How had Stephen dared send a patrol across the river, the day before the expedition started, when he had not asked or received authority to do so? "You, sir," Washington cried, "may have ruined all my plans by having put them on their guard!"

This colloquy did not consume many moments, but the Pennington Road now was so heavily covered with sleet and frozen rain that advance became a slow, treacherous slide and stagger. It was half an hour after daylight when Greene's van was at a point the guides reckoned as one mile from the town. As the enemy's advanced guard was believed to be about half-a-mile from Trenton, Washington had now to halt and prepare himself and his men for the execution of his plan.

Nothing had been heard of General Ewing, but Sullivan's column was moving on steadily and without opposition. The General himself pushed on in Greene's van, through the unrelenting storm, with the men at a "long trot" and about eight o'clock he left the woods about half-a-mile from the village. Ahead was a cooper's shop which the Germans were using as an advanced picket post. In a few moments, the Americans were challenged; there were shouts and commands; almost a score of Hessians emerged from the building. The Continentals opened fire at once, though the range was overlong; the officer in charge of the post waited until Washington's men were closer. Then the Germans delivered a volley which went wild in the roaring storm. Without making any pretence of further resistance at their advanced post, the pickets fell back. Three minutes after the first shot, there came from the south the welcome sound of musketry. Sullivan evidently was as far advanced as Greene and, like him, was rushing the outpost. Even if there was not to be a complete surprise of the enemy, resolution, storm and circumstance were giving Washington the closest approach to it. Push forward, then, with all possible speed and fullest strength; lose not a minute in hurrying the cannon to the head of King and Queen Streets. The Hessian pickets could offer slight opposition, but "for their numbers," Washington said later, "they behaved very well, keeping up a constant retreating fire from behind houses." This fire did not delay the advance. Washington could see the Germans forming in the town and beyond, but he could not ascertain what they were attempting to do. A few

MAP / 11

THE NEW JERSEY AND PHILADELPHIA CAMPAIGNS, 1776–1778

NEW JERSEY AND PHILADELPHIA CAMPAIGNS 1776 - 1778

Drawn under the supervision of LLOYD A. BROWN

MILES

5   0   10   20   30

minutes more and Washington was on high ground whence he could view almost the whole of Trenton. He stopped the long trot of the infantry and bade them give more room to the artillerists to bring pieces into position. Every movement seemed clumsy and exasperatingly slow; but in reality, the well-drilled artillerists lost few seconds. Their great moment had come. Soon the "b-o-o-m" of the opening gun shook the heavy air. The second shot followed on the instant.

Visibility was so low at times that Washington probably could see nothing of what was happening where Sullivan was attacking. Nearer, Hugh Mercer's men of Greene's command were closing in. Some were breaking into houses the enemy held, some slipping through alleys and walkways and directing their fire against Germans along the street and beyond it, in the direction of Assunpink creek. For a few minutes it looked as if the enemy might make a bold charge, but this was broken up by American artillery. Then large numbers of the Hessians gathered on the open ground east of the town and formed their line as if they were going to file off to the American left. That was the direction of the road to Princeton, the only avenue of retreat available to the Hessians if Sullivan or Ewing by this time had occupied the bridge across the Assunpink. Washington sent Col. Edward Hand's veterans and the Philadelphia German Battalion to take position directly across the line of Hessian retreat towards Princeton. As soon as the Continentals' bayonets barred the way, Washington thought he saw the Germans halt and then begin to shift again as if they knew it was futile to attempt a retreat up the Princeton Road. Stirling's impatient troops were allowed to go forward, the leading company, the Third Virginia, under Capt. William Washington and Lieut. James Monroe. When these Virginians took the German guns Washington could close the trap on the Germans. Their front was blocked; at their back were the cold, deep waters of the creek. Washington saw the trap shut. Then, presently, up the street spurred a young soldier who drew rein and cried rapturously that German regiments in the field had surrendered.

How numerous they were, Washington did not know; but firing from the vicinity of the bridge led him to believe that Sullivan's column still was fighting. Washington started to see for himself what was happening. About half-way to the bridge he came upon some Germans who were assisting badly wounded Col. Johann Rall, senior officer in the town. At that moment a young American came up the street. He was James Wilkinson, who represented Sullivan and carried the best of news: Another Hessian regiment, the last in the town, had grounded arms. Washington's face shone with satisfaction. "Major Wilkinson," he said, "this is a glorious day for our country."

It was victory! In the most desperate hour of the Army, less than a week from its virtual disbandment, the Continentals had won their greatest success. Ewing had not been able to cross at Trenton ferry because of the ice; at that hour, nothing had been heard from Cadwalader. The troops who had operated under Washington, and they alone, had defeated a force that consisted, prisoners said, of three German regiments. In the whole engagement not one American life had been lost. How the Hessians had permitted themselves to be surprised, nobody was able as yet to explain.

Washington had now to decide whether he could follow up this lucky success. The prisoners must be placed where they could not be rescued. It would be politic to treat them with consideration and, perhaps, to wean them from the British. In the absence of the Continentals' flanking forces, all the Hessians east and southeast of Trenton could be brought together to challenge any move Washington might make. The number of these Germans he believed to exceed that of his own force. Besides, there had been no contradiction of reports that a strong British battalion was stationed at Princeton. To undertake a new advance involved so many hazards that Washington thought he should consult his general officers. The conclusion was that of Washington himself: The American regiments must not take the chance of losing much by seeking more.

When encamped at Newtown, Bucks County, and listed by rank, the German prisoners ran to a total the Americans never before had captured —918. German dead were estimated as "about twenty-five or thirty."

Resolution to exploit advantages shaped Washington's congratulatory orders:

The General with the utmost sincerity and affection, thanks the officers and soldiers for their gallant and spirited behavior at Trenton yesterday. It is with inexpressible pleasure that he can declare that he did not see a single instance of bad behavior in either officers or privates; and that if any fault could be found, it proceeded from a too great eagerness to push forward upon the enemy. Much! very much indeed, is it to be lamented that when men are brought to play the part of soldiers thus well, that any of them, for the sake of a little temporary ease, should think of abandoning the cause of liberty and their country at so important a crisis. As a reward to the officers and soldiers for their spirited behavior in such inclement weather, the General will (in behalf of the Continent) have all the field pieces, the arms and accoutrements, horses and everything else which was taken yesterday, valued and a proportionate distribution of the amount made among the officers (if they choose to partake) and the men who crossed the river. The Commissary is strictly ordered to provide rum for the troops that it may be served out as occasion shall require.

These, surely, were terms on which soldiers would contract to deliver the second blow that Congress and the country expected of them. At the moment, too, prospect of reenforcement seemed brighter: a regiment of light horse soon would arrive from Virginia; Arnold probably would push forward from the Hudson some New England militiamen; perhaps a few would be raised in New Jersey. The revival of hope in Philadelphia was instant. "This affair," wrote John Nicholson, "has given such amazing spirit to our people that you might do any thing or go any where with them."

With militia assembled on the Delaware, near Bristol, Colonel Cadwalader was displaying on his own account bold and intelligent leadership. On Washington's table December 27 were two letters Cadwalader had written him. One gave details of the failure on Christmas Day—how it had been impossible to land artillery in Jersey after dark because of the ice. Washington already knew the essential facts, but the letter had ideas that displayed firm spirit: Cadwalader proposed that he ferry the Delaware downstream and effect junction with troops General Putnam was expected to land in Jersey in order to reenforce the militia left at Black Horse by Col. Samuel Griffin. Combined, said Cadwalader, these men "would make a formidable body—this would cause a diversion that would favor any attempt you may design in future and would expose their baggage and stores if they attempt to cross." Cadwalader's other communication was equally bold: He was going to cross on the twenty-seventh, he said, and if Washington would send part of the main Army to Crosswicks, "we might perfectly surround the troops at Bordentown, so as to prevent one man escaping."

Here was a challenge. Washington had to match Cadwalader's offer, but as soon as the General began to consider ways and means of doing this, difficulties eclipsed hopes. The Continentals had to be rested before they could be trusted in action again. Bad management and worse weather had so nearly emptied the Commissary that the men could not be given the contented vigor of strong meat until December 29 or 30—within two days, or even one, of the time when the greater number of the soldiers who finished their term of service would start home. If that happened, Washington would be almost as badly crippled as before victory at Trenton.

Washington did not permit the prospect to deter him. The puzzle might perplex; it would not baffle! In that unyielding state of mind he wrote Cadwalader: "If we could happily beat up the rest of the [enemy's] quarters bordering on and near the river, it would be attended with the most valuable consequence." He had called a council, Washington explained, and recommended that Cadwalader and Putnam defer movement till they heard from him again. On the twenty-eighth another dispatch from Cadwalader presented breath-taking opportunity: Although cooperation with troops from Philadelphia had not seemed probable on Christmas, General Mifflin was moving five hundred men from that city towards Burlington and would send more. Cadwalader himself had acted with the greatest boldness: At the head of about fifteen hundred men, he had crossed the Delaware into New Jersey December 27 in the expectation of finding the main Army still there; but even after he learned of its return to Pennsylvania he had decided to stay on the left bank. More than that, he had occupied Burlington.

Washington ascertained that the Commissary wagons would bring up sufficient provisions December 29 and 30 to supply the Army until it was reestablished in Jersey. Somehow, the Army must get across. Orders were issued for the troops to move into Jersey on the thirtieth. The crossing proved altogether as difficult as Washington had anticipated. Snow was six inches deep; everywhere the cold was cruel. Except for darkness, shivering soldiers underwent all the suffering they had endured Christmas night. So slowly was the battle with ice won by each boat's crew that it was manifest some troops would not get to the left bank until the thirty-first. Washington himself went to the Jersey shore on the thirtieth and proceeded to Trenton. Nowhere on the road was there any opposition. Information was meagre. Reports of the enemy were vague, conflicting or blank. Washington could learn nothing more definite than that Howe probably was effecting a new concentration and fortifying Princeton. Washington sent a detachment of Philadelphia Light Horse to reconnoiter in the direction of the college town and posted his troops at Trenton, south of Assunpink creek, where he felt they would be secure from surprise while he considered the possibilities of maneuver.

Then Washington played his last card in the gamble of American independence. Before he had left the Pennsylvania side of the river he had resolved to offer a special bounty of ten dollars, besides continuance of pay, to each man who would agree to remain with the Army six weeks after the expiration of service on December 31. As an economical manager he felt this a "most extravagant price," but the bounty had to match Pennsylvania's offer of that sum to militiamen who would bear arms in a brief, winter campaign. If the New England regiments disbanded on the thirty-first, the Virginians remaining with Washington would not be sufficiently numerous to set the pace for the militia. To keep men of any state after their time had expired, Washington had learned that one appeal only was effective, the dollar.

So—sound the drums and put a New England regiment in line; the Commander-in-Chief wanted to address it. He described the success of the twenty-sixth and explained why the veterans were needed. They could do more for their country during the next few weeks than ever they could again. He announced the bounty and, as one Sergeant wrote years afterward, "in the most affectionate manner [he] entreated us to stay." Regimental officers took charge and called on those who would accept the bounty and would remain six weeks to step forward. The drums rolled; Washington ran his eye along the line. Not a man moved, not one.

Was that the humiliating, disgraceful answer? Would it be given by all the regiments in silent and sullen refusal? It must not be so! Washington wheeled his horse again and rode back to the centre of the immobile line. He would renew his plea; he must get the men's consent—he must, must, must! When he had finished and the drums had rolled a second time, either his earnestness or their own reflection made the soldiers look questioningly at one another. A few stepped boldly out; others followed, and more and more; soon only those who were too feeble to fight or too nearly naked to face the wind remained in the original line.

It was much the same in the next regiment to which the offer of the bounty was made that day. After that, some of the men of a third regiment volunteered for longer service; then, part of a fourth did. All the Continental troops along the Delaware acted and their decision seemed to increase the *élan* aroused by the success at Trenton the day after Christmas. The response was by no means as emphatic as needs required, but it took the worst of the gloom from the approaching first of January.

In offering the bounty that gave him the Continentals he must have if he was to keep an army through the winter, Washington had violated one of the fundamentals of his official conduct: he had made an irrevocable pledge of public credit with no authority whatsoever. In a matter of heavy expense and perhaps of costly precedent, he acted boldly and without even consulting Morris's committee of three in Philadelphia to whom Congress had delegated large authority. It was a case of pay or perish. His own private credit and that of every responsible and discerning American had to be pledged, if need be, to get money with which to push success.

Never in Washington's life had boldness been vindicated more dramatically: That last evening of 1776 an express from Philadelphia brought him a series of resolves adopted by Congress on December 27. The Delegates had been commanded by necessity and had been compelled to approve what, in any other circumstances, they would have shouted down. The Commander-in-Chief was authorized to establish whatever system of promotion he and his council thought likely to produce the widest satisfaction. Another measure empowered Washington to do the very thing he had done—"to use every endeavor, by giving bounties and otherwise, to prevail upon the troops whose time of enlistment shall expire at the end of this month to stay with the Army so long after that period as its situation shall render their stay necessary." A third resolve was in this language:

That General Washington shall be, and he is hereby, vested with full, ample, and complete powers to raise and collect together, in the most speedy and effectual manner, from any or all of these United States, sixteen battalions of infantry, in addition to those already voted by Congress; to appoint officers for the said battalions; to raise, officer, and equip three thousand light horse; three regiments of artillery, and a corps of engineers, and to establish their pay; to apply to any of the states for such aid of the militia as he shall judge necessary; to form such magazines of provisions, and in such places, as he shall think proper; to displace and appoint all officers under the rank of brigadier general, and to fill up all vacancies in every other department in the American armies; to take, wherever he may be, whatever he may want for the use of the army, if the inhabitants will not sell it, allowing reasonable price for the same; to arrest and confine persons who refuse to take the continental currency, or are otherwise disaffected to the American cause; and return to the states of which they are citizens, their names, and the nature of their offences, together with the witnesses to prove them:

That the foregoing powers be vested in General Washington, for and during the term of six months from the date hereof, unless sooner determined by Congress.

Washington reacted with none of the pride he would have felt as a younger man. Responsibility outweighed everything except the cause that created it. He wrote: "Instead of thinking myself freed from all *civil* obligations by this mark of [the Delegates'] confidence, I shall constantly bear in mind that as the sword was the last resort for the preservation of our liberties, so it ought to be the first to be laid aside when those liberties are firmly established."

CHAPTER / 12

Washington estimated that 2200 or 2300 men had made the second crossing to Jersey with him, and he calculated now that the bounty had been accepted by half of those whose time expired on the thirty-first. As nearly as he could compute, those who remained were between 1500 and 1600. He could not expect the immediate arrival of any reenforcements other than perhaps a few more from Pennsylvania, which already had responded largely.

The British in Jersey numbered between five and six thousand men, chiefly at New Brunswick and Princeton. Report was that General Howe had landed at Amboy an additional one thousand soldiers who were moving forward. Was Howe making ready to advance, or was he going into winter quarters? Washington put first the defensive concentration of his regiments, in belief that the Redcoats were almost certain to attack. He could not repel assault with the force he had at Trenton, but if he retreated he would discourage Jersey militia. The position at Trenton was by no means ideal, but it included a road that led to Princeton as well as the one that followed the course of the river. If the enemy decided to move on Philadelphia was it more likely that the adversary would move via Princeton and Trenton or via Crosswicks and, say, Burlington? Washington chose to gamble on the route by Trenton. This had to do with a defensive. If an opportunity were presented of attacking the enemy, Washington would try to strike one or more of the enemy's posts in Jersey.

Without hesitation, therefore, Washington on the thirty-first ordered Cadwalader to move to Trenton and sent similar instructions to Mifflin. Washington knew that many hours would elapse before these troops could take position by the side of the Continentals. Meantime it was prudent to post a reliable body of veterans on the line of the enemy's most probable advance, the road from Princeton. Fermoy's brigade, Hand's regiment, the German Battalion, Scott's Virginia Regiment and a detachment with two cannon of Forrest's battery were stationed on Five Mile Run, about halfway between Trenton and Princeton.

New Year's Day Cadwalader's men began to arrive, though some of them did not reach the encampment until the second. Before that time, Washington received word that the British were on the march from Princeton to Trenton. To retard the advance of the British and ascertain their strength, Washington directed the troops on Five Mile Run to hold back the enemy as long as possible. Reports from the front indicated that delaying action, though brisk, was not costly. For a reason he did not explain,

Gen. M. A. de Roche Fermoy had left his troops and come back to Trenton, but this helped rather than hurt because it put the detachment under Colonel Hand. That veteran employed time and cover with much skill. His fire and a brief pursuit of an incautious advance guard of Redcoats were so effective that the British thought the Americans intended to make a stand. The enemy formed line of battle, brought up artillery and poured fire into the woods, with little injury to Hand's troops. His men checked the British for two hours and then withdrew in good order towards Trenton.

North of the town a ravine offered a defensive line, where the Americans next undertook to face the British. Both sides employed artillery as well as musketry in this clash, which Washington urged the Americans to prolong, because he did not wish to leave the British daylight hours for a general assault. Obediently, the Continentals held out for a short time, and when they had to give ground, they did so stubbornly.

He scarcely could have asked for a better delaying action than now was ending. Zeal, discipline and intelligent leadership had been shown. When, in the late afternoon, a vigorous cannonade began, Henry Knox's artillerists handled their guns, some thirty or forty in number, with skill and steadfastness. A "feeble and unsupported effort" by British troops to storm the bridge to Trenton was beaten off easily.

At nightfall the firing ceased, but to some of Washington's officers and men his position seemed desperate. In Washington's eyes the controlling realities of the situation were that the British were in greatly superior force and that they planned to surround and destroy his Army. He did not believe he should risk a battle where he stood, but if he was not to fight on the bank of the Delaware, what was he to do? The alternative to battle was a retreat, but that could not be completed in a single night directly across the river and would destroy hopes raised by defeat of the Hessians. If battle might be ruinous and retreat full of hazards, was there an alternative? The Army might move by its right flank, cross Assunpink creek beyond the British left and then march to Princeton and New Brunswick, where the enemy was believed to have large supplies. Instead of a defensive if, by using roads more or less familiar to numerous officers and men, the Army could reach a crossing called the Quaker Bridge unobserved and unopposed, it then could proceed almost due north to Princeton about six miles from the bridge.

The chief obstacle to an advance on Princeton was the condition of the roads, which thaw had transformed into deep mud. When details had been resolved and Washington had sent orders for a start at midnight in complete silence, he had a pleasant surprise: In the course of a few hours the weather had changed and the roads were beginning to freeze. Midnight found arrangements complete, and the Army ready to move. Five hundred remained to guard the Assunpink bridge at Trenton, feed the fires temporarily, and use pick and shovel as if they were constructing earthworks; all the other troops stole quietly off to the right and soon were moving eastward. By 2 A.M. of January 3, 1777, the mud was gone, and the ground was hard frozen.

As the regiments plodded on in the darkness, it was a cruel ordeal even for those who had crossed the Delaware in the first advance to Trenton. If there was any mercy under the black canopy of the heavens, it was the absence of sleet or snow. When, at last, there was a cast of gray in the east, the troops were approaching a stream known as Stony Brook which at that point forms a bow to the south as if to protect the town of Princeton. In another hour Washington began to pass his column over the stream. Ahead was an extension of Quaker Road that followed roughly the course of Stony Brook until it joined the Post Road from Princeton to Trenton. The main Post Road ran from the creek to Princeton. Another, nameless, led from the vicinity of the meeting house to the town. This route could be used advantageously in the execution of the simple plan Washington had formulated. The greater part of the American force was to pass from the Quaker Road into the back road and advance into Princeton. The defences of the town were designed to resist attack up the Post Road and could be turned almost completely from the back road. While the main body of Washington's troops was undertaking this, approximately 350 men were to proceed under General Mercer along the creek to the Post Road. At that point, close on Mercer's left, would be Worth's Mill and the Post Road bridge over Stony Brook. Mercer was to destroy this crossing and thereby make it impossible for any British from Trenton to reach Princeton quickly by the main highway.

All the preliminaries accorded with the plan. Everything was moving smoothly when Washington received unexpected news: The British had been found on the Post Road, down which their troops had been marching in considerable number on the way to Trenton. These Redcoats turned and started back at a rapid pace towards Princeton. Mercer's men began to run from the road along the creek. They climbed a little hill in the direction of Princeton and then descended on the opposite slope as if they were making their way towards the back road. As these men were passing through an orchard a small British force fired on them, whereupon the Americans changed front and dislodged the British who had delivered the first fire from the shelter of a fence. Mercer formed his line along this fence and was preparing to contest the advance of the British, who left the Post Road in considerable numbers and turned on him. Close to the enemy, Capt. John Fleming of the First Virginia shouted, "Gentlemen, dress before you make ready." The British heard him, and answered, "Damn you, we will dress you," and opened fire. The Virginians stood the blast and delivered so effective a volley "that the enemy screamed as if many devils had got hold of them."

Washington probably saw just enough of this clash to make him realize that Mercer must have support. Cadwalader's militia were soon coming over a low hill—only to find Mercer's men falling back from the orchard and being pursued. The British advance reached a fence not more than a hundred yards from the Americans; the whole scene appeared to be a prologue to ruin. Then, from the hill over which Cadwalader's column had been moving, two American field pieces began to bark as if they had been awaiting a rescue signal. Their fire forced the British behind the fence to run back to the main body. The British answered with their brace of field cannon and brought into play, also, the pair Mercer had been forced to abandon; but these did not silence the guns on the hill. Exposed to this fire, the British hesitated to attack. While they waited, Washington and his companions did their utmost to rally survivors of the fight in the orchard and halt the retreat of the Pennsylvania militia.

Now there was encouragement. Col. Daniel Hitchcock's Brigade was coming up. Its veterans could be trusted to deliver hard blows. Washington ordered Hitchcock to the right and placed Hand's riflemen beyond the right of Hitchcock. Then Washington rode among the militia, whom Cadwalader was striving to put into line. "Parade with us, my brave fellows," Washington cried, "there is but a handful of the enemy, and we will have them directly!" He did not appeal in vain. In a surprisingly short time they were ready. Washington placed himself at their head and ordered a general advance. Forward the men moved. Even when British bullets began to whine, the line did not break. Steadily the Americans approached the unflinching Redcoats. At thirty yards Washington drew rein, shouted "Halt," and gave the command to fire. The volley was delivered and answered in an instant; smoke enveloped everything; when it cleared, Washington still was on his horse, unscathed.

The British realized now that they must quit the field. As the red line broke and fell back, officers undertook to rally it and check the advance of the Americans. It could not be done. A few minutes later the enemy was in flight. Washington had for the first time an opportunity of chasing an adversary across an open field, and he could not, would not, restrain himself.

When he returned, he found that his Generals had become alarmed by his absence. His reappearance was occasion for a double rejoicing, first because he was safe and, second, because his men had occupied Princeton with ease. After the troops in front of Washington had been defeated, the King's men on the hill had hurried to Princeton and joined a regiment left there as a garrison. Together, these soldiers had moved out to the edge of a ravine south of the town, but they offered no more than perfunctory resistance there. Then some of them fled to the college building. When the Americans brought up artillery, those who had taken shelter in the college surrendered. The remainder disappeared in the direction of New Brunswick.

Within two hours, Washington received word that a British column was advancing up the Post Road and was close to the bridge at Worth's Mill. Experienced men had been at work on the demolition of that crossing, and well-placed artillery were covering them; but if the British were the troops who had occupied Trenton no time should be lost in eluding so strong a force. Washington's Army was too weary to give battle even if the General had been willing to do so. He had no intention of hazarding a general engagement and hoped he might seize some other British post that was not held by a garrison too large to be challenged. New Brunswick would be the great prize; but perhaps the most that Washington could hope to do with his weary men would be to seize Somerset Court House where 1300 hostile troops were supposed to be stationed. The long roll was beaten;

the men fell in; the captured guns were left behind; the column got under way and cleared the town before the van of the British reached Princeton. From Princeton, Washington's route was to Kingston, where the right fork of the road led to New Brunswick and the left to Somerset Court House. At the crossroads the final decision had to be made on the cherished plan of capturing New Brunswick. It was negative. Washington was regretful but convinced. He set it down, however, that "six or eight hundred fresh troops upon a forced march" could have taken Brunswick, its stores and military chest, and could have "put an end to the war."

From Kingston the Army staggered on to Somerset Court House, with no other hindrance than the presence across the Millstone River of a body of horse that finally disappeared. Some of the American troops reached the Court House at dusk but the belongings of the British encountered at Princeton had left there under a small escort a bare hour previously. Not one command in Washington's Army had strength left to organize pursuit. The next day, the fourth, the troops moved to Pluckamin. To the men the village was a paradise, because there, in the language of young Capt. John Clinton's diary, "we got plenty of beef, pork, &c., which we had been starving for a day or two, not having time to draw and dress victuals." On January 5 and 6 the march was to Morristown where Washington hoped to get shelter and rest for his men.

It scarcely was possible to exaggerate the effect of the operations at Trenton and Princeton on the self-confidence of the Army, the spirit of New Jersey, the policy of Congress and the faith of all the States in the attainment of independence. A dying cause was revivified; timid men who had been afraid to participate in what the British termed "rebellion" now came cheerfully to camp. Metaphorically, the situation might have been described with accuracy in an entry Capt. Thomas Rodney had made in his diary: ". . . the sun rose as we passed over Stony Brook."

Now that he was at Morristown, Washington could hope that, after he had refreshed his men, he could renew his effort to drive the British out of Jersey, but soon he faced discouragements of a familiar sort. By January 7 he had to write the President of Congress:

The severity of the season has made our troops, especially the militia, extremely impatient, and has reduced the number very considerably. Every day more or less leave us. Their complaints and the great fatigues they have undergone induced me to come to this place, as the best calculated of any in this quarter to accommodate and refresh them. The situation is by no means favorable to our views, and as soon as the purposes are answered for which we came, I think to remove, though I confess I do not know how we shall procure covering for our men elsewhere.

An Army that had thrown the winning card in the last hours of a months-long adverse gamble could not be blamed if, by the fire in winter quarters, it spoke boastfully of the manner in which it had worsted a wily opponent at Trenton and Princeton. Nor was it unnatural that British who had driven the Americans on Long Island and herded hundreds of prisoners at Fort Washington should make the utmost of the fact that before the third of January ended, Princeton again was in the keeping of the King's men.

Later in January soldiers had a new subject of debate: How far should the United States go in reprisal if it were true, as reported, that General Lee would be tried as a British deserter. In the narrower circle of the better informed, the argument was whether Congress was right in twice deciding it would not comply with Lee's repeated application for the appointment of a committee to confer with him on an undisclosed question of importance. Washington conducted the correspondence on reprisal and confessed he could see no valid reason for denying Lee a conference with members of Congress; but to these and other developments he could give no more of his hurrying minutes than duty and courtesy exacted. Most of the dangers that had threatened his Army continued. Some of them grew worse.

Incredibly, too, an Army that had thought it had endured all the woes of a military existence and all the plagues of politics found itself beset by new miseries and challenged by unfamiliar perplexities. Early in the new year Washington had the task of holding a sufficient number of militia to give the semblance of an army to a force of Continentals that once again was vanishing. Of the one thousand to twelve hundred who had agreed to stay in return for the bounty of ten dollars offered on December 30–31, 1776, only about eight hundred remained on January 19. Although the return of the main Army showed a paper strength of 17,812, Washington's actual numbers were so few he confessed to Jack Custis his doubts concerning the future: "How we shall be able to rub along till the new Army is raised, I know not."

Washington was in a position that both humiliated and crippled him. His troops were too few to attack or even to accept battle in open country. The Commander-in-Chief reasoned that the best practicable services by his shadow regiments were to destroy or remove the grain, provender and livestock near the hostile camps and harass constantly the parties sent farther afield to get supplies that could not readily be brought to New Brunswick by ship. Attacks on the British foraging parties had to be made persistently by courageous soldiers under skillful, cool-headed leaders, but these affairs must never be pushed so far that an inferior American force would be compelled to fight. The perseverance of American advance parties compelled the British to employ more and more men in foraging parties. Thereby the ill-fed horses were worn down progressively.

Washington could not believe the British were ignorant of his numerical weakness and undertook to reduce the adverse odds by prevailing on General Heath to make so heavy a demonstration around King's Bridge that Howe would send reenforcements to New York and give the troops at Morristown opportunity of striking the Redcoats left at New Brunswick. Washington's hope rose the day he heard at Headquarters the sound of firing from the direction of King's Bridge; but Heath did no more than move close to Fort Independence, demand its surrender, waste some gunpowder and march away to the accompaniment of mocking British laughter. This failure deepened the apprehension that Howe was gaining, not losing strength, and, when his preparations were complete, probably would advance overland towards Philadelphia.

Until the Army of 1777 was at his command, Washington would continue to harass the British in Jersey, but he put first in all his planning and correspondence the completion of recruiting for his Army and, in particular, for sixteen new regiments authorized by Congress. Lack of money hampered everything. Recruiting an army in the presence of the enemy never was easy, and now it might be harder than ever. About the date of the departure of some of the New England troops who had accepted the bounty at Trenton the time of a large part of the Pennsylvania militia expired. The cavalry of Morris County, New Jersey, were decamping before January was half spent. Two infantry regiments from that state could not be held beyond February. Whether officers had fresh enthusiasm or the disillusionment of experience, they encountered still other obstacles of many sorts—rival enlistment for state forces, state and local bounties for men who would enter the old regiments, unanticipated shortage of arms, paucity of funds, discontent of men who were not to receive the bounty, fear of sickness that would take men to the notoriously bad Army hospitals, and suspicion that some venal officers were putting on the rolls the names of fictitious recruits, pocketing the bounty and then pretending that these non-existent volunteers had deserted.

After surveying these maddening difficulties Washington had to reconcile himself once again to seeking from nearby States militia who would take the place, numerically, of the departing troops and would remain until the recruits for the Army of 1777 arrived. "My situation with respect to numbers," said Washington on January 20, "is more distressing than it has ever been yet. . . ." and it was rendered still worse by an extensive renewal of desertion. Unless the people gave notice of the presence of deserters in their neighborhood, "we shall be obliged," Washington warned Congress, "to detach one half of the Army to bring back the other."

Part of this loss might be reduced by saving the lives of some of the sick and wounded sent to hospitals and thereby condemned, all too frequently, to death in those wretched charnel houses. The main contribution that Congress could make to the welfare of the Army in the winter of 1776–77 was the promise of a better system. In recognition of many protests against the hardships the patients had been called upon to endure needlessly, the Delegates on January 9 voted to dismiss Dr. John Morgan, Director General of the Hospitals, and Dr. Samuel Stringer, Director of the Northern Department. At Washington's request, Dr. William Shippen, Jr., and Dr. John Cochran drew up a plan of reorganization which the General forwarded to Congress with the reminder that, while the expense of establishing and operating the proposed hospitals would be "very great," ultimately the new arrangement would "not only be a saving to the public, but the only possible method of keeping an Army afoot."

Another device that Washington selected as a means of strengthening his shadowy forces was to publish January 25 a proclamation in which he called on those who had accepted the Howe brothers' offer of "protection" to surrender it and to take the oath of allegiance to the United States.

Otherwise, within thirty days, they must go into the British lines or be "deemed adherents to the King of Great Britain and treated as common enemies of the American States." Issuance of this proclamation was one of the rare instances in which Washington made use of emergency powers granted him by Congress in December 1776, and it did not fail to raise an immediate question of authority, which two of the New Jersey Delegates, Abraham Clark and Jonathan Sergeant, presented to Congress. This was a fine bone over which to growl. A committee was named at once to examine the proclamation and give its opinion whether the contention of the Jerseymen had meat and marrow. On February 27 it presented a report that probably was drafted by John Adams: ". . . General Washington's proclamation . . . does not interfere with the laws or civil government of any State; but considering the situation of the Army was prudent and necessary."

One gain was the strengthening of the staff at Headquarters. Tench Tilghman of Pennsylvania, a former Captain of the Flying Camp, had joined the staff as an unpaid volunteer in August 1776 and had performed usefully many difficult tasks. John Fitzgerald, a Major of the Third Virginia, had become Aide-de-Camp in October. George Baylor, Samuel Webb and William Grayson had left Washington's "family" at the beginning of 1777 to accept regimental command—a trio of transfers that hampered the work of the office, particularly at a time when the post of Adjutant General was unoccupied, Joseph Reed having resigned. George Johnston joined the staff as aide about January 20, John Walker took a like position in February, and Capt. Alexander Hamilton, already distinguished as an officer of New York Artillery, and Richard K. Meade did so in March. The vacancy in the Adjutant General's office was continued for almost five months, in part because Washington hoped Congress might prevail on Horatio Gates to resume the duties. Washington wanted Gates's skilled service at Headquarters, but he felt that the choice should be left to Gates. His own wishes and convenience should not be put above those of the former head of the Northern Department, who might, said Washington, regard the place as in some sense a "degredation." There the matter stood until circumstance called for Gates's employment elsewhere. The only other man considered for immediate assignment as Adjutant General was Maj. Appolos Morris, but he was suspected of hesitating in allegiance to America. When Morris was eliminated, Congress was favorable to Col. William Raymond Lee. That officer generously stood aside for Col. Timothy Pickering, who was prevailed upon to accept.

There sometimes had been a surplus of militia officers and the applicants for rank as junior officers exceeded vacancies and new positions; but it was difficult to find competent field officers, establish a seniority system, advance able men, and get rid of those who lacked courage or enterprise. Because qualified colonels were few, Congress had difficulty in finding ten whom conscientious Delegates could promote to brigadier in partial fulfillment of Washington's request that the total number of officers of that rank be raised to thirty. Congress elected five additional Major Generals as well as the ten Brigadiers. Lord Stirling, Thomas Mifflin, Arthur St. Clair and

Benjamin Lincoln were made Major Generals; Enoch Poor, John Glover, John Paterson, Anthony Wayne, James M. Varnum, John P. DeHaas, George Weedon, Peter Muhlenberg, John Cadwalader and William Woodford, all of them Colonels, were promoted to brigade command; but these choices disappointed more officers than they gratified. Instead of getting relief, Washington had to spend hours smoothing down Brigadiers Benedict Arnold and Andrew Lewis, who thought they should have been promoted. In the end, Cadwalader declined, John Armstrong and Andrew Lewis resigned. Washington had repeatedly to point out the needs of the troops before he could prevail on Congress to name three additional Brigadiers —Edward Hand, Charles Scott and Ebenezer Learned—to fill vacancies, and even then he felt a continuing lack of generals of that rank. The one solace of this vexatious upstir was the application of Artemas Ward for relief from command in Massachusetts. This permitted Washington to oblige Heath, who wished service in his own state, and made possible a change of command in the highlands.

Accumulation of woes shook even the strong nervous system of Washington, made him irritable, and contributed to an illness that sent him to bed at the end of the first week in March. His staff kept from him all business that did not call for his personal decision, but, as Hamilton wrote, the General was "much pestered with things that [could] not be avoided." By the fifteenth, when Washington was able again to carry his full burden, Jersey "three-months' men," the militia of Cecil County, Maryland, and the Virginia volunteers began to stir in their quarters. On April 1 their time would expire. The flow of incoming new soldiers had ceased temporarily. Nathanael Greene, who had continued to develop the art of dealing with men, must go to Philadelphia, whither Congress now had returned from Baltimore, and must report on the condition of the Army.

During the time that Greene was in Philadelphia, Washington had bad news. Shortly before Heath left his post on the Hudson, General Wooster withdrew his Connecticut militia from New Rochelle and did not succeed in getting them to return. This provoked from Washington a rebuke and an order to Wooster to advance towards King's Bridge and do what he could to confine the British to Manhattan Island. Further intelligence from the Hudson led Washington to suspect in mid-March that the British might be planning to move their Canadian forces by sea to join Howe in an overwhelming attack on Philadelphia. It then seemed best to the American commander to concentrate at Peekskill the New England part of the sixteen new regiments. Troops could be moved easily from Peekskill in any direction. While Washington still was exerting himself to get fighting men to that station, he learned on March 25 that a British force had gone ashore there two days previously. Gen. Alexander McDougall was at Peekskill, but his infantry were so few that he could do no more than burn some of his stores and evacuate the village. This might be the first in a series of British expeditions to seize the forts and passes of the Hudson. Several days passed without any report from McDougall. So long as uncertainty prevailed, Washington continued to plead for help from Governor Trumbull, and he directed most insistently that Heath forward to Peekskill or to

Ticonderoga the troops recruited in Massachusetts for the Continental Army.

It was in the course of this effort to strengthen the northern forces that Washington received his second budget of bad news during the time Greene was in Philadelphia: Recruitment was progressing so slowly that it might be termed a failure, not to say a scandal. As Washington cited figures in explaining why more troops had not reached Peekskill, he grew almost sarcastic:

. . . sorry I am to observe, the militia have got tired, and . . . the Colonels of the Continental Regiments have been greatly deceived themselves, have greatly deceived me, or the most unheard of desertions or most scandalous peculations have prevailed, among the officers who have been employed in recruiting; for Regiments, reported two or three months ago to be half completed are, upon the Colonels being called upon in positive terms for a just state of them, found to contain less than 100 men; and this is not the case of a single Regiment only, but of many.

There were black clouds in the spring sky when Greene returned, but some bright spots could be seen. The brig *Sally* had arrived in the Delaware with 6800 muskets, 1500 gunlocks and other ordnance stores. An express brought word on the twenty-ninth that the French ship *Mercury* had anchored safely March 17 at Portsmouth, New Hampshire, with nearly twelve thousand firelocks, one thousand barrels of powder, forty-eight bales of woolens and many scarce articles.

Other wants were not relieved by anything that Greene had been able to accomplish in Philadelphia, though many of the Army's problems had been explained to Delegates who were disposed to assist as best they could under their awkward system of administration by committee. Greene brought back much news of appointments, reproofs and suspension. Gates was to proceed to Ticonderoga and to take command there in place of Schuyler; Congress on receipt of charges against the senior naval officer, Commodore Esek Hopkins, had suspended him from command; the position of commandant of the forts in the New York highlands had been created and George Clinton had been named to it.

Washington digested Greene's report and turned again to his task of confining Howe, clinging to restive militia, trying to expedite recruiting, and arousing officers from their lassitude. In particular, Washington sought to improve his system of intelligence so that he could discover quickly and accurately the direction of the enemy's advance. The test was certain to come, he thought, long before the Army was large enough to meet it victoriously. That raid on Peekskill might mean that Howe was planning to ascend the Hudson. Now, on the last day of March, an American captain of a "tobacco ship" who had escaped from New York reported at Headquarters. About three thousand troops, he stated, had embarked there and apparently were ready to sail. "It was generally said," Washington wrote after the examination of the captain, "they had in contemplation an expedition to Chesapeake Bay, and to make a descent on the Eastern Shore." Further, "there were some who conjectured, they mean to go up the North River and to take the highland fortifications if possible."

The first days of April brought no confirmation of the report by the captain but the news, whether correct or erroneous, heightened the pitch of the argument at Morristown over the perennial question, where would the British strike? Washington's opinion was that Howe's army was about to move up the Hudson or to Philadelphia, with the probability in favor of the Quaker City. Congress was so nearly convinced the enemy was to descend on Philadelphia that it adopted measures to safeguard the approaches and remove the more valuable stores. Defence of the city had to be fitted into Washington's broader strategical plan, which, as in the past, was to avoid a general engagement and, at the same time, prevent the severance of the New England States from those to the south. General Carleton was expected to make the utmost of controlling Lake Champlain. He or General Burgoyne would be able to invest, or at least approach, Ticonderoga without effective challenge. Washington considered it essential to hold Ticonderoga and the highland passes at any price short of removing his own Army from in front of Howe. All the while, too, he had to keep an eye on Rhode Island and on the British fleet.

"In short," Washington wrote one of his Brigadiers April 3, "the campaign is opening, and we have no men for the field." It was incredible, but substantially true: By the middle of April the weakness of the Army was more ominous than it had been in late winter. Even in that plight Washington refused to fall back on the policy of short-term enlistments. He had to fight, he confessed, to "keep the life and soul of this Army together," but he retained the confidence of most of his men and he did not weaken in determination. Three times in March he had been compelled to give warning that the debacle might not be far distant unless the Army was recruited heavily and at once with dependable troops. April 12 he set down the statement, "I wish I could see any prospect of an Army, fit to make proper opposition, formed anywhere," and nearly two weeks later he told Schuyler that the Army already had "a much longer indulgence" at the hands of the enemy than Americans "had any right to expect."

Many men were disaffected and the incidence of desertion was alarming. Washington believed the cure for military disorder was prompt pay, good provisions and the general improvement of discipline. ". . . Nothing," he said, "can be more hurtful to the service than the neglect of discipline, for . . . discipline, more than numbers, gives one army the superiority over another." Sound discipline of this sort was not inculcated easily. The long tedium of the spring had inevitably its demoralizing effect on some of the officers. In spite of everything, Washington tried to hold each officer to the highest standard the individual could attain, but so long as men with commissions did not fall below the minimal requirements of their rank, he did not expect of the dullest and least lettered what he demanded of the ablest and best schooled. He counselled those he found within his reach and in need of admonition or assistance; but in this hard labor of training soldiers, he needed more help than he had.

Snow disappeared from the hills around Morristown; spring came to the fields of New Jersey; roads mysteriously seemed to find bottoms that had been lost in mud. Once only, in the whole of April, however, did the British attempt to do more than protect their foraging parties and then in only a small affair at an outpost at Bound Brook, seven miles upstream from New Brunswick on the Raritan. The Redcoats wasted little time after they found their quarry gone and Bound Brook almost without stores. As soon as the British satisfied themselves they could get no booty, they left the village and returned as they had come. The episode led Washington to reduce the number of posts, in order that the forces might be less exposed to surprise and more readily assembled in event the enemy made the expected major thrust.

The General had very soon to justify in the eyes of Connecticut the application of this policy of maintaining the minimum of posts. At 3 A.M. of April 28 Washington was awakened to receive a dispatch in which General McDougall forwarded reports that a British force had landed on the coast of Connecticut and started inland towards Danbury. That town had become an extensive base, because it was supposed to be safe from raiders and was convenient to Peekskill, where stores were exposed to attack from the Hudson. The morning of the thirtieth Washington received a further report from McDougall: the British had reached Danbury unopposed and burned the stores and some private buildings; on their withdrawal, April 28, they had been assailed by a small body whom General Wooster had scraped together. Another column was organized by Gen. Gold S. Silliman, who yielded command to Benedict Arnold when that officer arrived. Wooster assailed the British rear; Arnold threw his force across the road by which the King's men were retiring, and, when pushed aside, continued to harass flank and rear. Wooster was mortally wounded, approximately twenty Americans were killed. British casualties were estimated at figures as high as "500 or 600" and in reality ran to the substantial total of about 154 killed and wounded.

Materially, one loss was more serious than all the others combined. Tents to the number of almost seventeen hundred had been sent to Danbury for safe-keeping and were destroyed there. These were irreplaceable otherwise than by importation. Another result of the raid was increasing reluctance on the part of Connecticut authorities to send their militia to Peekskill, lest another raid be made on their state, though the raid had shown that Connecticut and the country immediately east of the Hudson were strategically one defensive area.

Washington somehow endured the confinement of his work. Thanks to his habit of early rising, he usually dispatched his routine business by dinner time, when, if conditions permitted, the senior officers and brigade majors of the day were his guests. As a hostess, Martha now presided. She had come to Morristown in mid-March and was to remain until nearly the end of May. It was a relief to him to ride with interesting women; and it was a physical stimulation, when the afternoon was free, to catch ball with some of his juniors. Riding and sports were part of the life for which he yearned.

After Washington had sent General Putnam to the vicinity of New

York, in the command vacated by Heath, the Commander-in-Chief had to spend time on letters designed to coax Putnam into an attack on King's Bridge or, at the least, into a demonstration against that post. Ticonderoga demanded attention. Washington did his utmost to get the New England States to complete the recruiting of the additional regiments and to hurry them to Ticonderoga, where Gates was given the service of the alert Arthur St. Clair. Schuyler had won vindication at the hands of Congress, had worked usefully for some weeks in Philadelphia, and soon was to have again the command of a redefined Northern Department, in which Gates was to serve under him or else resume duty as Adjutant General. In May, as in every month after Gates had left Headquarters, Washington could have used the experience and reasoning power of that officer, because perplexities continued to multiply. It was impossible for Washington to know all that was happening in his Army. He found it particularly difficult to get trustworthy estimates or prompt action from Commissary General Joseph Trumbull, who remained in New England, and from recruiting officers, scattered everywhere.

A case of large possibilities of injustice concerned Arnold and his dissatisfaction over the outcome of his political campaign to recover his "rights" to promotion. A resolve of Congress made him a Major General but it did not restore him to the seniority he had when he was among the Brigadiers. Arnold came to Headquarters on May 12 with the statement that he wished to go to Philadelphia for a settlement of his accounts and an examination of charges made against his integrity. In explaining this Arnold probably asked for a letter to the President of Congress in order to assure a hearing. Washington wrote such a paper, in which he concluded: "These considerations are not without their weight, though I pretend not to judge what motives may have influenced the conduct of Congress upon this occasion. It is needless to say anything of this gentleman's military character. It is universally known that he has always distinguished himself as a judicious, brave officer of great activity, enterprise and perseverance."

Through the early months of 1777 the policy of Congress had been to discourage foreign officers from coming to America, but not to discredit Silas Deane, agent in Paris, or to offend the Comte d'Argoud of Martinique, an enthusiastic supporter of the American cause and the sponsor of numerous applicants for commission. The feeling had been confirmed that most foreign officers arriving in 1775–76 were adventurers who had been given rank beyond their merit. There was agreement, also, that officers who did not understand English should not be commissioned; but exceptions were frequent. The broad exception in this policy concerned engineers and artillerists.

On May 8, a French officer of approximately Washington's own age arrived at Headquarters and introduced himself in English as Col. Thomas Conway of the Army of His Most Christian Majesty. Conway explained his name and his knowledge of English by saying that he was Irish-born, though educated in France. He spoke of some of the French officers who had come with him to America aboard a ship that brought a much-desired cargo of cannon, but he may not have told of a controversy with an engineer who had tried to dismiss him before their ship left France. Washington formed a good first opinion of Conway and sent him to Philadelphia with a letter more commendatory than the General usually wrote of a stranger. Congress received the Frenchman enthusiastically, accepted at face value all that Deane wrote of him in a letter of introduction and elected him a Brigadier General. Hearing of this, American colonels of long service might have pondered alternatives: They themselves must be exceedingly poor officers or else Conway must be superlative.

Behind Conway came the man who had wished to get rid of him in advance, Philippe Charles Tronson du Coudray. This gentleman, the most extravagant acquisition of Deane, had no less than eighteen other officers and ten sergeants in attendance on him. He had stopped May 14 in Boston where he had expressed much contempt for the British who let themselves be driven from so strong a position. Du Coudray put the highest valuation on his professional standing, his connections and his writings on military subjects. He did not tell Washington precisely what he expected to do, but he dropped hints to other officers that led to the belief he had a contract with Deane under which he was to be vested with the chief command of the artillery.

Washington prepared a letter to the President of Congress in a determination to have the dangers of such an appointment plain. "General Knox," wrote Washington, ". . . has deservedly acquired the character of one of the most valuable officers in the service, and . . . combatting the almost innumerable difficulties in the department he fills, has placed the artillery upon a footing that does him the greatest honor." Were he superseded, Knox "would not think himself at liberty to continue in the service." In that event, Washington gave warning, the artillery would be convulsed and unhinged. Would it not be possible to satisfy du Coudray by appointing him to some other position? Du Coudray hurried to Philadelphia and presented to amazed members of Congress articles of agreement between him and Deane. These carried a variety of financial guarantees for du Coudray, prefaced by the statement that he was to have the title of General of Artillery and Ordnance with the rank of Major General. His was to be "the direction of whatever relates to the Artillery and Corps of Engineers, under the order and control only of the Congress of the United Colonies, their Committee of War, or the Commander-in-Chief for the time being." The agent had no authority to make such a contract. Were it accepted, it would give du Coudray and his French artillerymen seniority over all American officers of like rank who had been recommissioned January 1, 1777.

These vexations were among the worst Washington had to endure in the endless task of finding intelligent officers, training those who gave promise and putting incompetents where they could do least harm if they could not be dismissed. Lesser troubles with American officers were presented, solved, compromised or deferred; the Frenchmen remained a continuing enigma when Washington should have been free to devote a mind otherwise untroubled to what might prove the decisive test of the year.

Howe manifestly was to move soon; but there was as much doubt as ever in Washington's mind regarding the objective of the enemy, except that it probably was one that required the use of both the transports and the fleet. All the probabilities and the few known facts led Washington to decide that he should move closer to New Brunswick and into a strong position, whence he could follow quickly any British advance, whether towards the eastern States or toward Philadelphia. He selected as the most advantageous position a well-protected valley at Middle Brook, on the left bank of the Raritan, seven miles northwest of New Brunswick, and moved Headquarters to the new encampment on the evening of May 28. The greater part of the Army followed May 31.

Washington took advantage of warm weather and field encampment to discipline the men, drill the officers in military etiquette and watch the enemy. Prior to June 7 nothing of importance was reported concerning Howe's plans. It was known that troops had left Rhode Island, but their destination had not been established. Troops from New York had joined Howe. On the seventh word was received that "many vessels" at New York were being fitted out for horses. Three uneventful days followed. Then, on June 10, Col. David Forman reported he had seen much activity in shipping off Sandy Hook, Amboy and Prince's Bay. In the belief the next express might bring news that would set every wheel turning, Washington ordered all baggage loaded, except the tents. June 12 brought intelligence of the arrival of additional regiments from Europe, the ferrying of British troops from Staten Island to Amboy and the gathering of British shipping in Prince's Bay.

What, then, was afoot? Was Howe about to proceed by land, by sea, or by both a voyage and a march along the coastal plain? Washington, weighing reports and probabilities, believed that the British were reenforcing New Brunswick heavily and that they were aiming at the destruction of the American main Army or were preparing an expedition to capture Philadelphia. The Hudson seemed the less probable objective. The advice of the council was that all troops in excess of one thousand be called from Peekskill. Morristown was to be held lightly; Sullivan should move from Princeton to Millstone River, where his flank could not be turned by the enemy though he would be free to maneuver.

Two days later American Headquarters learned that Howe had started his movement: the British advance was at Somerset Court House. As far as the Continentals could ascertain, the enemy was occupying New Brunswick still. Washington was ready. Mifflin had been directed to collect boats on the upper Delaware; Congress had ordered Arnold to proceed to Trenton and take command there; Washington dispatched a call for the New Jersey militia and expected news that the enemy was headed for the Delaware or for a general attack along the upper Raritan.

Howe did neither. He merely stayed where he was. The American General waited in vain with tents struck, wagons loaded and horses harnessed and hitched to the vehicles. So little happened that Washington found the hour in which to write a letter that restored full, friendly relations with Joseph Reed, to whom he vainly had offered command of the cavalry. With Charles Lee no longer talking freely and writing carelessly from American Headquarters, reconciliation was easy. It would have been gratifying if at that very hour, Reed had been present to add his suggestions for ascertaining what the British were to do next and how they could be checkmated. American outposts were commanded to keep on the alert; Sullivan was told to get beyond the right flank of the Redcoats by moving to Flemington. Were he to remain on the left of the British he might be separated from the main Army. To their surprise, both Washington and Sullivan received a steady flow of militia.

The British continued work on redoubts but made no move. Early June 19 Washington had a report that puzzled him: The British were withdrawing to New Brunswick. They had started during the night and as they had so short a march, they could not be overtaken or injured. Why had they gone back without making a single attack? From the fact that the King's men had been working the previous day on their redoubts, Washington concluded that the decision to end the watch on the Raritan was reached suddenly. He assumed that the British had found it difficult to assault the advantageous ground the Americans had strengthened at Middle Brook, and he reasoned that Howe perhaps had been discouraged by the extent to which militia had flocked to the American camp.

Had Howe let down his guard? Washington did not yield to the temptation to strike. He followed the retreat but did not attack. At the end of the twenty-second the Redcoats were concentrated in Amboy. Washington moved up at six o'clock the next morning to take a look at the British defences. The enemy's position appeared unassailable by such a force as Washington could throw against it. Howe's flanks rested on waterways; strong redoubts ran across the neck on which Amboy stood. Army Headquarters consequently were opened about five miles north of New Brunswick at Quibble Town.

In the face of reports that many of the British troops had been sent to Staten Island, Washington was notified June 26 that the British had sallied from Amboy in greater strength than ever and were advancing several columns as if they intended to do one or more of three things—to cut off Stirling at Metuchen Meeting House, bring the main Army to battle, or occupy the high ground in the vicinity of Middle Brook. The march of the British was said to be rapid, as if they hoped to overwhelm Stirling or get to elevated positions before Washington could. This was not a fisherman's cast at which Washington would snap. His forces at Quibble Town he put on the march for Middle Brook, and he doubtless directed Stirling to disengage himself from troops who already were assailing the position at Metuchen. The British columns pursued as far as Westfield and halted there, and on the twenty-eighth returned to Amboy. On July 1 the jubilant word brought to Middle Brook was that the enemy the previous day had evacuated Amboy completely and reestablished themselves on Staten Island.

It was true. The operation that began November 20 when Cornwallis crossed the Hudson and moved against Fort Lee had now ended in withdrawal from New Jersey of all large bodies of British. A cause that had been close to complete ruin seven months previously was not yet assured of victory; but it had recovered to a vigor justifying John Hancock's statement that the British evacuation of Jersey "will be the most explicit declaration to the whole world that the conquest of America is not only a very distant but an unattainable object."

Washington himself was not elated; he knew the deficiencies of his Army and the immensity of the advantage Howe still enjoyed. "Our situation," Washington told Gov. John Rutledge of South Carolina, "is truly delicate and perplexing and makes us sensibly feel now, as we have often done before, the great advantage they derive from their Navy." Always, too, Washington had to ask himself whether the scanty American forces were balanced strategically between New Jersey and the Hudson, or whether the danger of having Carleton and Burgoyne sever New England from the rest of the country was greater than the risk that Howe, if confronted with too few, might subdue the middle States.

Before Washington could measure the improvement in his military situation or even give himself rest from strain, his Army was involved anew in troubles as baffling as those he had to face in the winter of 1776–77. On July 3 he withdrew his troops to his former station at Morristown, whence he could move swiftly to the Hudson or Philadelphia as Howe's next maneuver might require. Washington had no convincing intelligence reports on British preparations but the probabilities seemed decisively on the side of an advance by Howe to form a junction with Burgoyne when the latter assailed Ticonderoga. A more immediate danger was that of a surprise attack by Howe on the highland defences. Putnam was invoked to watch vigilantly for the coming of the enemy and keep his forces concentrated. Gen. George Clinton was asked to cooperate and call out the New York militia. Sullivan's Division was moved to Pompton, sixteen miles northeast of Morristown and about twenty miles west of the Hudson. From that point, if necessary, Sullivan could hasten to the support of Putnam in balking an attack on the forts of the highlands, "the thing of all others," Washington wrote Schuyler, "most fatal to our interests," because "the possession of the Highlands [by the British] would effectually bar all mutual assistance of our two Armies."

The Commander-in-Chief could not devote himself exclusively to study of the defence of the Hudson. He had to give it his prime thought, but he had to deliberate also on other conditions that were exasperating in themselves and full of danger to the Army. One of these was the violent resentment Greene, Knox and Sullivan were showing because of the pretensions the Frenchman, du Coudray, was making. Another cause of uneasiness was a murmur that Washington was devoting too much to the defence of the Hudson and disregarding the danger of an attack on Philadelphia. Quartermaster General Mifflin had been among the first to voice such complaint and was becoming progressively alienated on this account from Washington.

A more acute concern was the plight of the Commissary. Washington had felt that Carpenter Wharton, Deputy Commissary General at Headquarters, was incompetent and that Joseph Trumbull, head of the department, should come to Morristown and remain there. Trumbull was in Connecticut and was not in accord with Washington's view that the balancing of his books was less important than personal supervision of the feeding of the main Army. Congress was cognizant of Wharton's derelictions and the smell of scandal. Trumbull first was urged, then commanded, to come to Philadelphia and set right the muddled affairs of his subordinates. He arrived April 22, reassured Congress regarding provisions immediately available and dismissed Wharton; but he did not silence other complaints. A crisis came at the end of May when Washington told Trumbull that he must visit Morristown and procure sufficient supplies or see the Army disperse for lack of food. These circumstances and the loss at Danbury prompted prolonged debate in Congress, during the course of which some of Trumbull's assistants quit and some became demoralized. On June 10 Congress adopted new regulations for the commissariat and on June 18 fixed the pay and named the men to direct a complicated organization. Trumbull looked with some favor on the plan of the new service, though he had felt that its success and his labor for it depended on the compensation allowed him, the nature of the regulations and the character of the man in charge of the department. The organization provided no longer for one inclusive category of commissaries, but for two classes, one to have charge of purchase and the other to control issue. Trumbull resigned his old post and agreed with reluctance to act temporarily as Commissary General of Purchases.

At the moment the question was whether the troops could be provisioned to the end of the month, or even to the close of the next week. Trumbull sent one of his deputies to Washington July 9 with a letter in which he said that the bearer, Maj. Robert Hoops, had found it impossible to act because of the "difficulties arising from the strictness of Congress' new regulations." Trumbull wrote earnestly: "I really fear the Army will suffer if not be disbanded soon if some effectual measures for my relief are not taken." He proposed that Congress be requested to send a committee to Morristown as soon as possible in order that members might see the danger and recommend corrective measures. Washington forwarded this to Congress with the warning that unless something was "done in aid of Mr. Trumbull immediately, this Army must be disbanded." Washington went on to say that the Army might be obliged to move within a few hours and might have more to dread from the disorder of the Commissary than from the acts of the enemy.

This, then, was the situation: a ragged citizen Army too small for the task assigned it and under dissatisfied officers, might be compelled to scatter in order to keep from starvation at a time when every regiment should be ready to move swiftly if it was to continue maneuver against a powerful professional force able to strike anywhere on deep water. Washington's greatest need was for a prolongation of quiet in order that provisions might be collected and distributed. Instead, the express who arrived on the morning of July 10 brought a dispatch from Schuyler, dated July 7, to this effect: a report had been forwarded that St. Clair had evacuated Ticonderoga; it was feared the greater part of the garrison had been captured.

The movement Washington previously had dreaded—a British advance on Philadelphia—now appeared the lesser of evils. If Howe's army were embarked, prompt notice of its departure for the Delaware would give Washington time to reach Philadelphia ahead of the foe; and if Howe started overland toward Pennsylvania, the Americans could outstrip him. Every consideration of strategy seemed to indicate that instead of doing either of these things, Howe would proceed up the Hudson to a junction with the northern army as soon as he confirmed the report that Burgoyne had reached Ticonderoga. On like grounds of military logic, Washington believed that Burgoyne would not proceed farther southward until he knew Howe's drums had sounded the advance up the river. The three essential and immediate tasks were to move the main Army closer to the highlands of the Hudson, assure utmost vigilance at posts the enemy would pass or assail in moving to cooperate with Burgoyne and prevail on the eastern States to send their militia to strengthen Schuyler. Temporary troops assembled to resist the advance of the enemy from the New York lakes should be placed under some aggressive man. Orders must be prepared for Continental brigades to start northward. Their unannounced objective was Pompton Plains, eighteen miles from Morristown. Thence Washington intended to proceed through Smith's Clove to the vicinity of West Point and await word of what was happening up the Hudson.

Neither the news nor the march was pleasant. En route to Pompton, during the evening of July 11, Washington received verification of the evacuation of Ticonderoga. Although details were lacking, he had to accept the event, which he put "among the most unfortunate that could have befallen us." The disaster might be worse than reported, because Washington did not yet know what had happened to St. Clair's garrison after it had abandoned Ticonderoga on the sixth. Washington advanced most of his small Army to a point eleven miles in the Clove, Orange County, New York, and there he halted July 22 until he could clarify reports he had received of the presence of British ships up the sound, in North River, off Sandy Hook, and at sea on voyages to unascertained anchorage. On the twenty-fourth, Washington felt sure the British fleet had left Sandy Hook. Philadelphia seemed its most probable destination, but he had to admit that the descent of the King's ships might be on New England. Once more he paid tribute to sea power when he said simply: "The amazing advantage the enemy derive from their ships and the command of the water keeps us in a state of constant perplexity and the most anxious conjecture."

The imperative task was placing the Continental brigades where they would have the shortest distance to cover when the plan of the enemy was disclosed. The light horse should proceed towards Philadelphia; the best disposition of the main Army probably would be at the crossings of the Delaware, on either side of Trenton, whence the march to Philadelphia or North River would not put too heavy a strain on the men. Washington moved southward the larger part of his Army. On July 27 he received word that seventy sail of the British fleet had been sighted off Egg Harbor. He felt it more probable than ever that the destination of Howe was Philadelphia, but he was not quite convinced. "Howe's in a manner abandoning General Burgoyne," Washington said, "is so unaccountable a matter that till I am fully assured it is so, I cannot help casting my eyes continually behind me."

The British fleet appeared off the capes of Delaware Bay on the thirtieth, and presumably was making ready to enter. It was an easy matter to start a movement that had been anticipated. Orders were prepared and circulated; instructions were sent Sullivan to march for Philadelphia by the shortest route; Washington hoped his leading division would reach the city August 1. He hurried on in advance with his staff towards Philadelphia. His first task, after his arrival, was to ride through the environs of the city in order to ascertain where the troops could best be placed. He was at Chester on this mission the night of August 1 when up from Cape May rode an express: The fleet had sailed off on the thirty-first. Two hundred and twenty-eight sail had been counted off the capes—manifestly the entire fleet. If its objective had not been Philadelphia, why had it entered those waters; and if Howe had designed to attack the city, what had deterred him? Was the voyage to the Delaware a feint to draw the Continental Army to that region? Had the British slipped away to land in New England or ascend North River while the American column toiled through New Jersey again?

Military common sense directed that Washington start his troops back to the middle ground of the Delaware Valley and that Sullivan and two brigades that had been summoned from Putnam's Army proceed to Peekskill. Orders were issued accordingly. Joint action by Burgoyne and Howe appeared to Washington to be "so probable and of such importance" that he would, he said, "with difficulty give into a contrary belief" until the evidence demanded it. Pending that, he would halt the Army at a convenient place and wait.

Washington remained in Philadelphia until August 5 and found time to attend at least one dinner. It was interesting because of the presence of a young Frenchman, not yet twenty, to whom Congress had voted the rank of Major General, though with the implied understanding the commission was honorary and without compensation. As Washington had been taxed to find some accommodation between ambitious foreigners of excessive rank and American officers jealous of their high position in the Army, the Commander-in-Chief could have been pardoned some misgiving when the young man was introduced as Major General the Marquis de Lafayette. Lafayette appeared to be modest, tactful, admiring and not at all inclined to tell the Americans how to manage their affairs. He made a deliberate effort to win the good will of Washington, and Washington invited him to visit the camp and took the young soldier with a party that made examination of the water defences of Philadelphia.

Washington had to treat half-a-score, more or less, of administrative ills. Some of these problems of August 1777 had been a torture from the time he had assumed command; others represented friction or weakness that had developed while the Army was on the march. The new organization of the Commissary was ill. As many complaints of neglect and mismanagement had been made, Congress adopted the greater part of the suggestions made somewhat tardily by the committee that had been to Headquarters. Meantime, Trumbull was relieved and William Buchanan named Commissary General of Purchases. Clothing was another subject of inquiry by the committee of Congress. In humiliating contrast to their adversaries, the men of the American Army had been in tatters at the opening of spring. Clothier

General James Mease gave the fullest effort to the discharge of his duties, but the continuing demand was beyond the resources of the country. The committee included in its report recommendations for ascertaining what clothing the Army would need during the winter. This was to be imported or provided by each state for its own men at Continental cost. Needless to say, this arrangement disregarded the tightening of the British blockade, the frequent inability of the Board of Treasury to provide even the depreciated Continental currency and the general carelessness that seemed to be spreading from the office of the Quartermaster General.

Almost as vexatious to Washington was a problem represented by two words that had made some Americans flush with anger whenever they were uttered—"foreign officers." Violent rivalries developed between du Coudray and additional French engineers employed by Deane. Three of these had arrived in Philadelphia during the last week of June and had let it be known that they would not take orders from du Coudray. Congress commissioned the senior, Louis le Beque Duportail, a Colonel and gave his two subordinates, Bailleul la Radiere and Obry Gouvion, the rank of Lieutenant Colonel and Major respectively. Two weeks later Congress settled some of the rivalries by voting that Duportail should "take rank and command of all engineers previously appointed." Washington was alarmed by the preference shown Duportail and even more by the knowledge that Greene, Sullivan and Knox had been angered and humiliated that du Coudray would have seniority over them. Knox, in particular, was outraged by what he considered an inexcusable slight. Greene, Sullivan and Knox addressed individual, but conditional, resignations to the President of Congress. Washington was quickly directed by Hancock to let the three Generals know that Congress regarded their letters as "an attempt to influence its decision"; if the officers were "unwilling to serve their country under the authority of Congress, they shall be at liberty to resign their commissions and retire." To all Washington's burdens and perplexities now was added this vehement rebuke of three of his best officers, because they protested against the apparent grant of seniority to a French soldier who had not marched a mile in America or faced even one bullet in the battle for independence! Washington acknowledged Hancock's letter, stated that he had transmitted the resolves of Congress to Greene, Knox and Sullivan —and for the moment, said no more. Congress finally decided to give du Coudray staff, instead of line appointment, at the promised rank of Major General, and to make him Inspector General of Ordnance and Military Manufactories—a compromise that proved acceptable to Greene, Sullivan and the officer most directly concerned, Knox.

Washington had good opinion of one or two of the younger Frenchmen who had come to America, and he welcomed to Headquarters the young Lafayette who had come to learn, not to teach; but it soon was apparent that Lafayette wished to share and not merely observe the Army's hardships, marches and battles. Washington had to inquire of Benjamin Harrison whether he correctly had understood Congressmen to say that Lafayette's commission was nominal only and did not cover, even prospectively, the direction of troops at the rank voted him. The young Frenchman, said Harrison, "could not have obtained the commission on any other terms."

Washington at the moment could give little time to foreigners because maddening doubt with respect to Howe's objective once again absorbed his hours and shaped his action. In the absence of all news of the fleet, Washington guessed that the British commander was bound for Charleston, South Carolina. Perhaps the British intended to block the harbors in that region, garrison the important coastal towns and then come north again. As it was impossible to move overland and confront Howe at so great a distance, Washington and his council decided on August 21 that the Continental troops should break camp in Bucks County and march against Burgoyne. This involved exposure of Philadelphia to possible attack, for which reason Washington thought he should ask Congress' approval of his proposed move. Colonel Hamilton was hurried off to Philadelphia with a statement of Washington's plans and with an inquiry concerning the control of operations in event Washington entered the Northern Department which, said the Commander-in-Chief, "has been all along considered as separate and in some measure distinct." The Delegates endorsed the plan and affirmed that "General Washington was to act as circumstances may require."

Within a few hours the prospect of a long northward advance was forgotten. A messenger arrived from John Page, member of the Council of Virginia, who announced that a British fleet had appeared off the entrance to Chesapeake Bay August 14 and that it seemed to be standing in. Washington scarcely could credit the reports. Had Howe intended to sail into Chesapeake Bay, he certainly would have arrived there before now. The next day indisputable reports, reaching camp at sunset, showed Howe far up the Chesapeake. The British General evidently was putting into operation a variant of a plan that had been credited to him during the winter and early spring. Instead of attempting to capture Philadelphia overland from the north or by the Delaware, the British were to land at the northern end of Chesapeake Bay and proceed northward about fifty-five miles, as the roads ran, to the city that probably had been their objective all the while. American marching orders were reversed; regiments must turn about and concentrate at Chester. General Putnam must convince the New England States that Howe could do them no harm and that they should put every musket in line to destroy Burgoyne.

Washington felt relief both because the mystery at last was resolved and because the British debarkation would be far enough from Philadelphia for him to interpose his Army between the Redcoats and their goal. The prospect was brightened, too, by fine news from the north. A strong detachment of British and German troops had proceeded from Burgoyne's main army towards the village of Bennington, in the New Hampshire Grants, presumably to seize provisions and horses. The enemy had been met on the sixteenth by an American force of two thousand, most of them militia, under John Stark. In confused fighting, the raiders had lost thirty-two officers and staff and about seven hundred prisoners. British and Hessian dead were reckoned at two hundred; American casualties were put at seventy or eighty.

While the soldiers were in the confident mood this news stimulated, some of Washington's officers urged him to march his brigades through Philadelphia en route to Chesapeake Bay. They maintained that the appearance of so many armed men might impress Tory sympathizers and those who had been awed by reports of British superiority. Washington agreed and, as his troops still lacked uniforms, directed that clothes be washed, arms burnished and every soldier's hat dressed with a "green sprig, emblem of hope." On August 24, the march of the Continentals through the Quaker City was a gallant and, at the same time, pathetic two-hour display of what the troops were and were not. John Adams wrote later in the day: "The Army . . . I find to be extremely well armed, pretty well clothed, and tolerably disciplined . . . Much remains yet to be done. Our soldiers have not yet quite the air of soldiers. They don't step exactly in time. They don't hold up their heads quite erect, nor turn out their toes exactly as they ought. They don't all of them cock their hats; and such as do, don't all wear them the same way."

Washington probably was satisfied with the showing his men made. He believed in discipline as firmly as in the justice of his cause, but he knew that the real test went beyond the manner in which the soldiers turned out their toes and cocked their hats. Now, as he marched south, he had more evidences of unsuccessful leadership than of unselfish spirit. Sullivan had attempted to deliver a surprise attack on Staten Island August 22 but had failed. In withdrawing, the Americans had lost perhaps 150 men and had a score wounded.

Leadership had become involved almost simultaneously in rivalry between Gates and Schuyler. After Schuyler had been restored to full command of the Northern Department, Gates had proceeded to defend himself and assailed his critics with angry demands. When Congress found the time and temper for considering the proper employment of a man who manifestly had lost his head, it voted that he repair to Headquarters "and follow the directions of General Washington." The Commander-in-Chief decided, at length, that the best employment of a senior officer unwilling to resume his old duties of Adjutant General would be to assign him Lincoln's Division during the absence of that officer. Then came the evacuation of Ticonderoga which was blamed in part on Schuyler. Delegates who questioned Schuyler's ability made common cause with those who felt he should be replaced because he did not have the good will of the New England militia. Gates's friends proclaimed anew his military excellencies. The result of a long debate was a decision by Congress on August 1 to call Schuyler to Headquarters and direct Washington to name "such general officer as he shall think proper" in Schuyler's place—a task from which the embarrassed friend of both men asked at once to be excused. Congress appreciated Washington's feelings and itself chose Gates as head of the Northern Department. Washington forthwith issued the orders and wished his comrade success; but the circumstances of this appointment were among the reasons why he asked

Congress on August 21 to define his responsibility for operations in the department that included the upper Hudson and the adjacent lakes. The day after the march through Philadelphia, Washington was assured "that Congress never intended by any commission heretofore granted by them, or by the establishment of any Department whatever to supersede or circumscribe the power of General Washington as Commander-in-Chief of all the continental land forces within the United States."

At the beginning of the last week in August reports were that Howe soon would disembark at Head of Elk. Washington continued mindful of the imperative need of strengthening the water defences of Philadelphia and did all he could to draw militia to him; but he hurried on to Wilmington, put his entire force on the alert, reconnoitered with considerable risk and small success on the twenty-sixth, and then moved up his Army so that he could resist any effort Howe might make to clear the road to Philadelphia. Strategy demanded that he advance his most mobile forces, keep them close to the British and harass the foe without exhausting his own men. The main Army should remain perhaps as far as eight or ten miles from the enemy, but the American light horse and some of the small parties of foot could drive off cattle and remove supplies and provisions from the reach of the enemy.

The British covered their front skillfully, kept inquisitive cavalry at a distance and contrived to mystify Washington almost as completely as when the Royal Army had been at sea. Nothing of importance occurred until, on September 5, the British appeared to be ready to start their offensive. The fleet began to drop down the Chesapeake and on the eighth was so far south that Washington was convinced the ships of war were to be used against Philadelphia, via the Delaware. An assault by water was to be simultaneous with an advance by land. The British forces took the road towards Christiana, on the creek of the same name which flows into the Brandywine close to Wilmington. The American commander suspected that Howe would attempt to turn the flank of the Continentals and to get between them and Philadelphia. To prevent this, Washington put the Brandywine Creek between his men and Howe's and took position near one of the principal crossings of that stream, Chad's Ford. If Howe was advancing in full strength, Washington would attempt no more than a continuance of skirmishing and harassment; but he would have satisfaction, of a sort, when he knew precisely where the British were and what they were trying to do.

Unless the enemy were held on the Brandywine, he scarcely could be stopped until he reached the Schuylkill. Once on that stream, he might maneuver without great difficulty into Philadelphia. As a defensive barrier the Brandywine had no particular value other than that it was of sufficient depth to require troops to use the fords. The position taken by the Americans at Chad's Ford appeared to be about as good as any for an Army that wished to be free to maneuver and avoid or accept the enemy's attack as the contingencies of the hour might dictate.

Early September 11 word reached Washington that the enemy was advancing to Chad's Ford. If Howe offered battle there and tried to cross the creek under fire, Washington scarcely could hope to engage his adversary in circumstances more advantageous, except for a thick fog for several hours after dawn. About eight o'clock British troops filed into position on the high ground in rear of the ford and challenged Gen. William Maxwell of Lincoln's Division with musketry and, a little later, with artillery. Maxwell found that a fresh brigade came up in rear of the enemy so he gave the order to withdraw. This was followed by the skillful, partly concealed advance of more British troops to the sheltered ground on the left bank of the Brandywine opposite Chad's Ford. Howe's guns soon were roaring across the stream; Washington answered them in kind. Howe appeared to be disinclined to attack. Washington saw no opening.

As minutes passed without the slightest effort by the enemy to cross the Brandywine, Washington and his officers began to suspect that Howe was trying to amuse them at Chad's Ford while he made his crossing elsewhere. Washington consequently could not have been surprised when reports began to reach Headquarters of a British column marching from Howe's left upstream, parallel to the Brandywine. Col. Moses Hazen, who was guarding Jones's Ford, sent word by Maj. Lewis Morris, Aide-de-Camp to Sullivan, that these British were proceeding to the forks of the creek. Washington directed Stirling and Stephen to move their Divisions to a site that commanded the road over which the British were most apt to advance from the upper fords of the Brandywine. Confirmation of Hazen's report and the wisdom of this shift was forthcoming almost immediately in a dispatch from Lt. Col. James Ross of the Eighth Pennsylvania, who with seventy men had been patrolling the Great Valley Road on the right bank of the creek. Ross wrote at 11 A.M. and said that "from every account five thousand with sixteen or eighteen field pieces, marched along this road just now."

If Howe had started five thousand men upstream, comparatively few troops could have been left at the position first occupied that morning by the British. Washington's opportunity of striking with superior force might be at hand: The Continentals at Chad's Ford and the one directly above it, where Sullivan had his station, must cross the Brandywine and attack and destroy the men left there. The troops were prepared, almost, to plunge into the water when Sullivan forwarded this dispatch:

> Since I sent you the message by Major Morris I saw some of the Militia who came in this morning from a tavern called Martins on the forks of the Brandywine. The one who told me, said he had come from thence to Welches Tavern and heard nothing of the Enemy above the forks of the Brandywine and is Confident that [sic] are not in that Quarters. So that Colonel Hazen's Information must be wrong. I have sent to that Quarter to know whether there is any foundation for the Report and shall be glad to give your Ex'y the earliest information.

Was Hazen mistaken? Was Ross or were the militiamen correct? The individual who gave Sullivan the information in this new dispatch proved to be Major Spear, a militia officer sent out the previous day to reconnoiter. Washington concluded that where there was an unresolved conflict of intelligence reports, it would be rash to assume the offensive.

Early in the afternoon a farmer rode up to Headquarters. He blurted out, in much excitement, that the Army must move immediately; otherwise it would be surrounded; the enemy was coming down the eastern side of the creek and was near at hand. Washington could not believe it. The farmer insisted he was relating facts of his own observation and spoke with so much positiveness that the General decided to see for himself whether the man possibly could be correct. Washington probably had started for the right when messages from Col. Theodorick Bland and Sullivan confirmed the farmer's report.

The enemy in the rear—the same maneuver against the man who had been outflanked on Long Island a year previously! Ross and Hazen had been correct. A great opportunity had been lost by not attacking the force that Howe had left to hold Chad's Ford. Sullivan must march at once to meet the column advancing on his rear. Stephen's and Stirling's divisions must proceed at a trot to Birmingham Meeting House. Sullivan, as senior Major General "of the right" wing, should direct the fighting. Washington himself should remain at Chad's Ford, where he could keep his hand on all the troops.

About 4:30 straining ears at Chad's Ford heard cannon-fire. Soon the stammer of uneven volleys was audible, and then the spiteful bark of rifles. It was difficult for Washington to restrain himself and stay at Headquarters while a battle of uncertain issue was raging within two miles; but he noticed that the artillery fire from across Chad's Ford was quickening, as if an infantry attack were in preparation. Soon Washington's concern got the better of his consideration for Sullivan's natural wish to fight an independent battle. The commander of the right wing should have help. Greene still was in reserve. He must move at once to the right. Washington would go with him. Lincoln's Division must remain at Chad's Ford and repulse any attempt of the enemy to cross there.

Off went Washington with his staff and a guide. Behind the General, Greene's men half ran, half walked towards the sound of the firing. Washington had to ascertain what was happening as a result of a confused struggle around a plowed hill southwest of the Birmingham Meeting House. Stirling and Stephen had reached that elevation and had found the enemy approaching in greater strength than reports had indicated. They had occupied strong ground and almost had completed their dispositions when Sullivan, who had not been on that part of the field before, found his advance guard an eighth of a mile from an oncoming British column. Sullivan was to the left and almost half-a-mile in front of Stephen and Stirling. He ordered their divisions to extend to the right to give him space to form. The change was made disadvantageously. While Sullivan's men were being shifted they were attacked and thrown into some confusion.

At the moment of Washington's arrival, the left was beginning to break, and the whole of the line was sagging under pressure by the British. A rout of the Army's staunchest veterans appeared imminent. So long as mounted officers shouted and threatened close to the front, they were able to hold part of the line together. When they rode back from a position then within about two hundred yards of the foe, many of the men ran off, but good handling of the brigade in the last hour of daylight forced the weary British to abandon pursuit.

At Chad's Ford the enemy had thrown himself vigorously after the departure of Washington. The troops of Gen. Anthony Wayne and of Maxwell put up the best defence they could, but they had to retreat and lost their artillery. The militia on their left, unassailed, made an easy withdrawal. So tangled were the troops along the road to Chester, that Washington did not get them in order until nearly midnight. Fears that casualties included many prisoners were relieved somewhat the next day by the emergence of men who had lost their way or had spent the night in the woods for fear of running into an enemy patrol if they went out to the road. Hundreds, however, did not come back. American wounded had been left on the field where Howe was so little able to provide care that he invited Washington to send surgeons to attend them. These bleeding men, together with the dead and the uninjured prisoners, were estimated at twelve or thirteen hundred.

Washington had lost the field, the lives of hundreds of men, and a considerable part of his artillery. The reasons were plain. There was on the part of the Americans a most discreditable ignorance of the ground. Little or no reconnaissance was undertaken. Neither Washington nor any of his staff or division commanders or colonels of cavalry appears to have known the location of the fords. The Commander-in-Chief has to be charged with being less careful than usual in his dispositions. He was tired or temporarily overconfident or else the instance was one, familiar if not frequent, in which an able man for some unascertainable reason fails to grasp the realities of a problem he normally would master without prolonged effort.

The other reason for the defeat on the Brandywine was an aspect of the poor reconnaissance and lack of knowledge of the ground. "A contrariety of intelligence, in a critical and important point," Washington wrote about a fortnight later, "contributed greatly, if it did not entirely bring on the misfortunes of that day." His reference was more specific in one of his letters to Sullivan: ". . . I ascribed the misfortune which happened to us on the 11th of September principally to the information of Major Spear, transmitted to me by you. . . ." but Washington did not permit himself to finish the sentence without making it plain that he did not blame Sullivan for "conveying that intelligence." In fact, the importance of what Spear had to tell the commanders was misinterpreted by them because of their unfamiliarity with the region. If the American commanders had examined the ground or had questioned informed residents of the area around the East Branch, they could have learned that the absence of British on the road they knew of was no guarantee the enemy was not moving to the right on another road and in the manner both Colonel Hazen and Colonel Ross reported.

Opinion might and did vary concerning the responsibility of Sullivan for the defeat and for the misinterpretation of intelligence that contributed to the loss of the day, but the heaviest judgment that could be imposed on Sullivan would not exculpate his Commander-in-Chief. Washington conducted the Brandywine operation as if he had been in a daze. The General who always had stressed the necessity of procuring fullest intelligence and of analyzing it correctly had failed to do either or to employ his light horse adequately when the price of error might be the loss of Philadelphia.

Explain the Battle of the Brandywine as one might, it was a defeat that called for an immediate deep withdrawal. From Chester, Washington moved the greater part of his Army to the Schuylkill and over it to Germantown, where he had the stragglers collected and the lost detachments sent back to their regiments. All the troops were given rest and such food as the feeble and disorganized Commissary could provide. In shaping his strategy anew, Washington's deep caution reasserted itself. Speedy reenforcement of the Army was essential if even the semblance of resistance to an advance on Philadelphia was to be maintained. Trained men could come in number from one source only, Putnam's command. In full appreciation of the risks involved in reducing the force on North River and the highlands of New York, Washington decided first that he must draw to him fifteen hundred men whom Congress had ordered Putnam to send to New Jersey. Then the Commander-in-Chief concluded that another one thousand men could be spared by "Old Put" without excessive risk.

Washington's plan was to harass the British with regiments still south of the Schuylkill and then, when the other Continentals had recovered from the shock of battle, leave the militia on guard at the fords towards which the British were heading. With the veteran organization, he would recross the Schuylkill and watch the enemy. This maneuver was exacting but it was attended by no widespread demoralization of the troops or of American supporters in Philadelphia. The rally was firmer and faster than Washington had thought it would be. Almost everywhere the result of the Battle of the Brandywine was accepted without flinching and in the spirit of "better next time."

Congress' sole openly voiced resentment, as respected the battle, was against Sullivan, who was blamed by some for the loss of the field. Washington already had been directed to hold a court of inquiry on Sullivan's handling of the expedition against Staten Island and now was informed that Congress had recalled that officer from command until the inquiry should be completed. At Sullivan's instance Washington attested that in all he had seen at Brandywine the accused General had behaved well. Washington asked and Congress reluctantly consented to let the Major General continue temporarily in service because Washington had so few officers of that rank.

On September 15 Washington called his still-weary soldiers to pass southward over the Schuylkill once again in an effort to prevent the entry of the British into Philadelphia or, at least, make them pay heavily for the town. On the sixteenth reports indicated that swift maneuver might give the Americans an opportunity that seldom had been theirs—the opportunity of delivering a sudden blow against the enemy while his column was in motion. Washington saw his opening near Warren Tavern, on the road from Lancaster to Philadelphia, and prepared to strike. His prospect was of the fairest when, of a sudden, he encountered something he never before had faced on like scale. The wind rose to a gale from the northeast and brought a rain that did not relent for a second. Washington's Continentals had learned to defy the worst northeasters that swept in from the North Atlantic, but this time they were caught with forty rounds of ammunition in their cartridge boxes. The better containers turned the rain; the others proved worthless against a long-continued, searching deluge. Before the day ended, Washington was told that tens of thousands of rounds had been ruined and that many regiments could not fire a shot. It was the first time in his experience as Commander-in-Chief that "the whole safety of the Army," as Washington later wrote the Board of War, depended in action on the "goodness" of a simple and familiar accouterment. There was no immediate hope of drying any of this ammunition, because the rain continued all night and most of the next day. Washington's men had no shelter and little food; no less than one thousand of them were barefooted. Opposite the dripping, woebegone American columns the British, moreover, maneuvered as if they intended to envelop both flanks and gained such definite superiority of position that on the nineteenth, though the day was lovely and the wind from the northwest, Washington again decided to recross the Schuylkill by way of Parker's Ford. He left on the British side of the stream the Brigade of Smallwood and the Division of Wayne, who then were separated but were to make common cause in harassing the enemy's flank and rear and especially in trying to cut off the British baggage.

On the evening of September 20 Wayne encamped his small Division near Paoli, about twelve miles from Philadelphia. During the night three British regiments made a skillful approach, attacked furiously and, in a short time, scattered the division. Wayne lost at least 150 killed, captured or wounded.

The disaster to Wayne cost the Army experienced troops and accelerated the disappearance of militia who, as always, quickly yielded to fear. Washington felt that he must be wary of every move of the British. In the eyes of Nathanael Greene, the Commander-in-Chief seemed to be drifting back into the hesitation of mind that had plagued him before the fall of Fort Washington. A newcomer, Gen. Johann Kalb—the Baron de Kalb he styled himself—wrote:

Washington is the most amiable, kind-hearted and upright of men; but as a General he is too slow, too indolent and far too weak; besides, he has a tinge of vanity in his composition, and overestimates himself. In my opinion, whatever success he may have will be owing to good luck and to the blunders of his adversaries, rather than to his abilities. I may even say that he does not know how to improve upon the grossest blunders of the enemy. He has not yet overcome his old prejudice against the French.

The concern of Kalb and Greene doubtless was shared by other ranking officers not quite so self-confident, but actually at this time Washington was almost as hopeful as he was cautious and apparently of doubtful mind. He believed that time would bring him reenforcements with which to meet the British, even if the enemy occupied Philadelphia. He successfully resisted an effort of Congress to take troops from him and use them in the construction of defences on Delaware River. He sought to hasten the 2500 men called from Putnam and to draw to him other contingents. Until reenforcements assembled Washington could do no more than keep vigilant, render difficult the British passage of the nearby watercourses and repair, as far as time permitted, the manifest weaknesses of his command.

The worst and most pressing of these was in the light horse. Washington had hoped that Joseph Reed would accept the command of the mounted arm, for which he had shown aptitude; but after Reed had declined in June, Washington deferred action. He gradually became convinced that if the cavalry were brought together and employed as a unit they might prove a powerful instrument. This decision had been due, in considerable measure, to the persistence of Count Casimir de Pulaski, a Polish officer who had come to Headquarters with letters from the American Commissioners in France. When Pulaski described how he had used cavalry in a Polish uprising, the American commander had concluded that the leadership of the American troopers might make that officer "extremely useful." A letter to that effect had been written Congress in August. Pulaski most unwisely had imperiously sought rank subordinate only to that of Washington and of Lafayette. This had created a prejudice against him, but September 15 Congress created the post of "Commander of the Horse," with rank of Brigadier, and elected Pulaski to it. If Pulaski succeeded in winning the support of the cavalry colonels, the light horse might strike many a stout blow to aid the infantry when—or did Washington have to say "if"—the footmen could find shoes for bad roads and clothing for wintry bivouacs.

That dark contingency was deepened almost immediately. The danger to Philadelphia had compelled the removal to magazines in less exposed towns all stores not immediately required in the city. Ten days after the Battle of the Brandywine the Americans concluded not only that Howe had heard of this transfer but also that he knew the particular value of supplies deposited in Reading. A march begun on the twenty-first seemed to be directed straight at that new base. Washington shifted his right in the same direction, whereupon the British reversed their march, slipped back down the river and on September 26, unopposed, moved into Philadelphia with the easy air of proprietorship. The American commander had been outmaneuvered so easily that the sole immediate question became that of where he should place and how he should employ his troops now that he had lost the largest American city in a manner more humiliating, if possible, than that of his forced abandonment of New York.

As he waited about six miles north of Parker's Ford on the Schuylkill for reenforcements, Washington and his senior officers had an astonishing experience: they found that British capture of the city meant little compared with what they had feared in the autumn of 1776 the fall of Philadelphia would involve. Now that the calamity had fallen, it was manifest that the course of the campaign had lessened the importance of Philadelphia. The British found there virtually no public property of value. The city was a shell. To some it might be a symbol, but it no longer contained the living organism of independence. Washington's soldiers had come to regard the fall of Philadelphia as inevitable and they did not permit it to dampen a spirit that was rising again now that tired men were rested. A weightier reason was the joyous certainty that the darkest cloud of the war was losing its blackness. The strategical danger that Washington had dreaded most was being dissipated. On September 19, at Freeman's Farm, north of Albany, Gates had worsted his opponent so thoroughly that the Commander-in-Chief felt the Americans could "count on the total ruin of Burgoyne." Unless there was an incredible reversal of fortune, the Hudson no longer would have to be shielded, hourly and vigilantly, as the jugular of America, the severance of which meant death.

Washington's Army was reenforced at the same time it was reanimated. McDougall's Brigade arrived about September 27. Other troops were close at hand in numbers estimated to raise the total strength of the Army to eight thousand Continentals and three thousand militia. "I am in hopes," Washington wrote Heath, "it will not be long before we are in a situation to repair the consequences of our late ill success. . . ." He moved forward to within about twelve miles of the British to await either an advantageous opening or additional men.

Opportunity outmarched militia. At the beginning of October Washington received two intercepted letters which mentioned the detachment of a British force to proceed against Billingsport to aid there in the attempt of the British navy to open the Delaware River. Other intelligence reports showed that the main army of Howe was encamped at and near Germantown, a handsome, sprawling village five miles northwest of Philadelphia. When Washington communicated this information to his general officers, they were unanimous in advising attack at Germantown. The Commander-in-Chief now marched into Worcester Township and made camp.

This advance put the Army fifteen miles from Germantown—as close as Washington dared advance in daylight because he hoped to surprise the enemy by attacking at dawn over roads that seemed to form an ideal stage for surprise. The road from Reading and the Shippack Road ran parallel to each other until about four miles from the centre of Germantown. Then they met at Chestnut Hill and ran southward together as the "Main Street." The course of the two roads would facilitate a deployment at Chestnut Hill or south of it. Moreover, northeast of the Shippack Road was the Lime Kiln Road which came into Germantown from the east. West and southwest of the Main Street and connected easily with it was the Manatawny Road. Washington could advance on three or even on four roads and assail simultaneously the front and flanks of the British.

Into a detailed battle order Washington put what appeared to be the essentials of coordinated attack. Once only before in his three years and more of command of the Army had Washington drafted and executed a General Order for offensive action by the whole of his infantry. That had been for the advance on Trenton December 25–26, 1776. This new order was more elaborate. Reading it, critics in the Army who sometimes accused Washington of overcaution must have been silenced for the moment: Trained reenforcements had not begun to arrive until September 27. One week later the "American Fabius" was to take the offensive.

The Army started its march on the evening of October 3. Probably to avert further criticism of Sullivan, the Commander-in-Chief decided to re-

main on the right with that officer and entrust management of the left wing
to Greene. The longer road was Greene's by as much as four miles, because
a part of his route was circuitous. The night wore dismally on, but by 3 A.M.
on the fourth Washington, riding near the head of Sullivan's column, was
inside the area covered by the British patrols. No alarm was audible; the
troops continued quietly on their way towards the known picket posts of the
enemy. Washington had given instructions that the pickets should be seized
or bayonetted before they could make an outcry. The weather during the
night had not been unpromising, but as morning approached the advance
of the Army ran into fog, which limited vision, distorted the appearance of
landmarks and confused every sound.

A bad setting did not balk a good beginning. Unchallenged, Sullivan's
men tramped down the main road; Conway's Brigade shifted towards the
right across the fields. About dawn, Washington heard the rattle of a few
muskets, contrary to orders. Evidently the British pickets had been reached,
but they had not been surprised altogether. After that, in less time than
should have been required for these men to fall back on the first line, the
roll of a British volley reached Washington's ears. The pickets, Sullivan
explained later, "were suddenly reenforced by all their Light Infantry,"
who seemed to be drawn up in an orchard, unprotected by trenches or
redoubts. Gen. Thomas Conway had to halt his flank march and form his
brigade in line: soon Washington learned that the enemy was advancing.

Was this the first act of familiar tragedy all over again—a repulse
and then a rout? The answer was reassuring for the moment: The British
musketry was no nearer; the American line must be standing firm. Perhaps
that fog drowned the sound of Greene's advance. Nothing had come from
him, neither a messenger nor the roll of a single volley: he might be succeeding so well that he did not have to use small arms, but it was possible
that Greene had lost his way or had met some overpowering obstacle. Why
did Gen. John Armstrong and his Pennsylvania militia on the extreme right
withhold their fire? It looked as if Sullivan's Division might have to fight
the battle alone. Sullivan ordered Wayne to form on his left where Greene's
troops were to have taken position, started two regiments in the direction of
Armstrong's advance and dispatched Moylan's light horse to aid the infantry. By these dispositions, Sullivan sought to secure his flanks as well as
possible, though he might be compelled to pull both of them back.

About the time this was done the snatches of information that came
to Washington indicated that the attack of the British light infantry had
been beaten off. The initiative had passed to Sullivan, whose men began to
push forward again across fields planted in buckwheat. Troops found this
slow work and doubly dangerous, because they might encounter the enemy
behind any fence or hedge and in the enclosure of any residence. Fog, now
thick with mingled smoke, made the Americans' pursuit a grope, but it
blinded the British and at some points cut visibility to thirty yards. The fog
was more protection to the troops on Main Street than they or their officers
realized. When the Continentals drove the enemy from one fence line, they
did not hesitate to run to the next and then to the next. Soon the troops
were far in front of the Commander-in-Chief and were firing furiously.

Verbal confirmation came from Sullivan of what the firing already told: the enemy was giving way, Sullivan said; Wayne should push on. Washington agreed. What was more, he ordered Gens. Maxwell and Francis Nash, leaders of the reserve brigades, to put their troops on the flanks of the advancing line.

As Maxwell's Brigade moved up to support Sullivan it ran into considerable musketry from the windows of a large stone residence, which natives called the Chew House. From second-story windows, which had stout and heavy shutters, Redcoats delivered a sharp fire. An American battery was brought up, but the cannon were placed at an angle to the structure and struck only glancing blows. When the reserve was instructed to keep out of range of the Chew House and otherwise to disregard it, half an hour had been lost, but Sullivan apparently had not been hampered by the delay. His men were pressing gallantly on through blinding, choking smoke and fog. Wayne's troops were equally aggressive in their resolution to get revenge for the slaughter at Paoli. It was in vain that officers tried to protect the British wounded or the occasional Redcoat who was captured unhurt. All these were bayonetted. Washington pressed so far to the front that Sullivan had to ask him to retire—a request he heeded for a few minutes but then forgot as his soldiers kept their pace.

All this time there had been intense concern over the lack of any news from Greene, but anxiety was relieved. Adam Stephen's men appeared on the left of Wayne; from the countryside beyond came the bark of cannon and the rattle of small arms. Greene apparently was in position and driving the British. Victory appeared closer: Defeat of Howe when disaster was about to overwhelm Burgoyne might mean the end of the war! Washington was about to give the order for a general advance towards Philadelphia, when something happened. On the left, there was confused firing. Shouts were heard and were answered from a greater distance. On Sullivan's front a loud volley shook the ground but provoked an uneven answer. Out of the fog men came back on the run, some frantic with fear, some able to gasp a few words—that the enemy was in the rear, that the flank had been turned, that friends had been mistaken for foes, that orders to retreat had been shouted. Presently the artillery galloped past and took the road to the rear. Officers swinging their swords and swearing or pleading, tried to stop what in the course of a few minutes became a mad panic. It was as if they were shouting to the fog to dissipate itself. By ten o'clock, incredibly, the action was over. Two hours and forty minutes had sufficed to see a victory won, as the Americans believed, and then thrown away. Washington could do no less than order the retreat continued till pursuit was shaken off. With intervals of rest for the men who remained together, the backward march dragged for twenty miles and more, until the Army was at Pennypacker's Mill.

What had caused the panic? That was the question every one asked and none could answer to the satisfaction of his comrades. In the fog some of Wayne's men and some of Stephen's mistook a dim and distant line for the enemy and exchanged fire several times; the retreat had continued for some distance before the identity of Stephen's right flank was understood by

Wayne's soldiers. Also, about that time the British cut off the Ninth Virginia and thereby disordered the left wing. The main cause of the retreat probably was that on the right the British advanced fresh troops with much vigor when Sullivan's men were extended, half exhausted and almost without ammunition. Washington, Sullivan and most of the others believed that the halt at the Chew House, the exchange of fire on the left, and confusion created by the fog had given the beaten British troops time to rally.

Much was made of Greene's failure to attack at the time General Orders directed. In most respects the reason was misfortune, not misconduct. Greene's march was longer than had been reckoned; his troops had been formed at too great a distance from the enemy; certain of the troops had marching orders so complicated that even their guide lost his way. In spite of this, some of Greene's men had pushed gallantly on but had encountered unexpected resistance. Greene's retreat on the left had about the same justification—whether it be deemed full or partial—that Sullivan's had on the American right. Apparently the most serious failure on the left was Stephen's. He was alleged to have given the order to retreat, though he maintained he shouted to his men that they were running away from victory. The principal charge against Stephen was that, if not actually drunk, he had been drinking so heavily for so long that he was not able to discharge his duty with sound judgment.

Had the British been surprised? Did the speedy appearance of the light infantry indicate that they were under arms when the attack began? Washington was of opinion that surprise was achieved "so far as reaching their guards before they had notice of our coming." General Howe insisted, on the other hand, that the only surprise was that of an attack by Washington so soon after the defeat in the Battle of the Brandywine. Patrols had learned at 3 A.M. of the approach of the American columns and had notified the British commander without letting the Continentals know their advance had been discovered. All the British regiments had then been put under arms promptly, but some of the senior officers had remained skeptical and thought the alarm had been created by a mere "flying party."

Strangely, the details of the attempted simultaneous convergence of Washington's columns received little analysis by the Americans. Washington scarcely could have demanded more of his officers than that they conduct their illshod troops in darkness over comparatively unfamiliar roads to distant positions, deploy and form them and have them ready to attack together at dawn. The American commander patiently studied the routes and timed the march of the separate columns by the condition of the various roads as well as by the distance to be covered; but he did not succeed in drafting orders that put every movement in simple, understandable language. The marvel is not that the left elements were late because the guide lost his way, but that they reached their objective at all.

The results—were they in keeping with the effort, or were they, too, a frustration? Perhaps the answer was given unwittingly by a Germantown diarist who wrote October 5: "Great numbers came out of town today to satisfy their curiosity as to the battle yesterday, and everyone spoke as they affected." That was it: each man's sympathy shaped his judgment. Washington's faith in the fundamental rightness of his cause led him once again to assume the enemy's losses must be larger than his own, though, actually, his gross casualties, including prisoners, were close to eleven hundred and those of the British about half that. The American commander shared, also, belief that the advance halted and panic began when Howe was about to retreat across the Schuylkill and perhaps even to Chester—a belief for which there is not a shadow of justification in Howe's report to his government.

Heavy as were losses, mistaken as was the Commander-in-Chief regarding nearness of victory at the onset of panic, the undertone of army comment on the battle was even more optimistic than after the contest on the Brandywine. The struggle in the fog around Germantown yielded no ground to the Americans and imposed on the British no damage serious enough to hamper their efforts to open their line of supply up the Delaware River, but in spirit, losers were gainers. Thomas Paine reported to Franklin that the troops appeared "to be sensible of a disappointment, not a defeat." Washington was distinctly of that mind. The most he conceded to adversity was: "Upon the whole, it may be said the day was rather unfortunate than injurious."

MAP / 12

THE HUDSON HIGHLANDS, 1776–1783

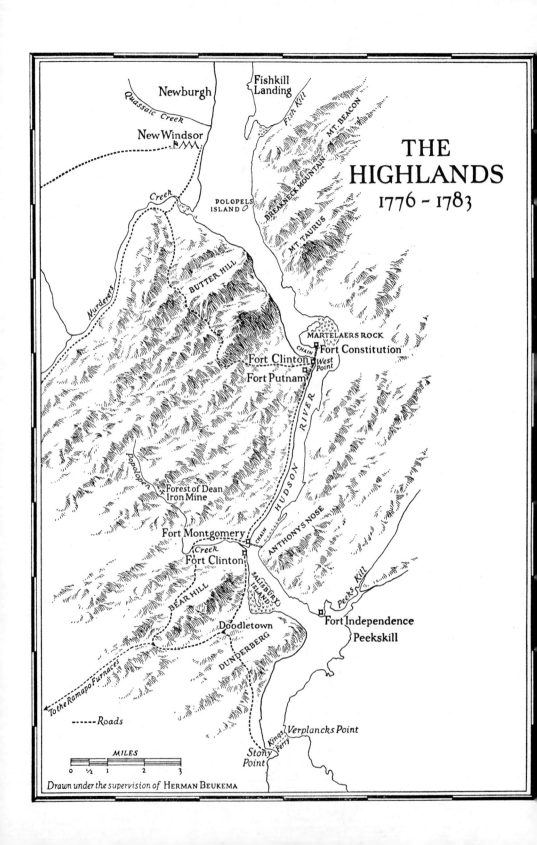

Newburgh

Quassaic Creek

Fishkill Landing

FISH KILL

New Windsor

MT. BEACON

BREAKNECK MOUNTAIN

Creek

POLOPELS ISLAND

MT TAURUS

Murderers

BUTTER HILL

THE HIGHLANDS
1776 – 1783

MARTELAERS ROCK

CHAIN

Fort Constitution

Fort Clinton

West Point

Fort Putnam

HUDSON RIVER

Popolopen

Forest of Dean Iron Mine

Fort Montgomery

CHAIN

ANTHONYS NOSE

Creek

Fort Clinton

SALISBURY ISLAND

Peeks Kill

BEAR HILL

Fort Independence

Doodletown

Peekskill

DUNDERBERG

To the Ramapo Furnaces

----- Roads

Verplancks Point

Kings Ferry

Stony Point

MILES

0   ½   1   2   3

Drawn under the supervision of HERMAN BEUKEMA

CHAPTER / 13

American troops were learning their bloody business and tactically were by no means as inferior to the British as they had been a year previously. Many officers were increasing both in understanding and in appreciation of their seniors. Washington rose, rather than waned, in esteem, as a result of the Battle of Germantown. His plan was not criticized; his boldness in attacking so soon after the defeat on the Brandywine was applauded. He and his Army received the thanks of Congress. Hope for the future was buttressed by the spirit of the Army. American soldiers had shown, Washington reminded them, that "the enemy are not proof against a vigorous attack, and may be put to flight when boldly pushed."

During the night of October 12/13, Washington had news that on the sixth a British force had stormed successfully the two guardian defences of the Hudson, Fort Montgomery and Fort Clinton, on the west bank of the river, approximately four miles northwest of Peekskill and about forty-eight from New York harbor. Washington had said often that the loss of the passes of the highlands would be well nigh fatal to the American cause in New York and the eastern States. It was for this reason, among others, that he had regretted the necessity of calling on Putnam after the Battle of the Brandywine for 2500 troops. Washington had directed that the garrisons of all non-essential outposts under Putnam's command at Peekskill be recalled. He had hoped that Connecticut militia would replace the withdrawn Continentals and, in the gamble of probability, thought it likely that if Sir Henry Clinton's British troops made any move from the vicinity of New York, they would attempt an overland march to join Howe. Washington now was proved in error. He took pains to make clear the circumstances in which he had felt compelled to recall troops from Putnam and did not blame that officer for the reverse. Neither did he attempt to minimize the possible consequences for which both Congress and he were held by some to be responsible.

Then came a strange revival of good fortune. By their capture of Forts Montgomery and Clinton the British had unlocked the southern gate to the region in which Clinton and Burgoyne were to meet; the very next day Horatio Gates slammed the northern gate. For a second time on Freeman's Farm Burgoyne offered battle, October 1, and advanced a column which the Americans repulsed and pursued in a savage action that continued till late evening. Burgoyne could not hope to penetrate farther southward. General Gates hoped that even retreat would not be possible. Incomplete news of this action reached Washington late on the fourteenth and changed instantly the outlook on the Hudson. It was confirmed on the eighteenth when an express laid before him this dispatch from George Clinton:

> Albany, October 15, 1777
>
> Last night at 8 o'clock the capitulation, whereby General Burgoyne and the whole army surrendered themselves prisoners of war, was signed, and this morning they are to march out towards the river above Fisher's Creek with the honors of war (and there ground their arms). They are from thence to be marched to Massachusetts Bay. We congratulate you on this happy event and remain, yours &ca.

Great possibilities seemed to lie ahead—the Hudson no longer a possible boundary line between free and subjugated States; troops to reenforce the thin divisions that confronted Howe, restoration of faith in victory and the rally of militia to the cause. Hopes built up at Germantown were raised higher. Washington was gratified personally as well as officially, because he had done all in his power to assist first Schuyler and St. Clair at Ticonderoga and then Gates, but he and many other persons were now to be much irritated. Gates was guilty of incomprehensible tardiness in forwarding a detailed report. When the triumph was confirmed, it was so "important and glorious," in Washington's words, that he stifled the anger he felt because of the failure of Gates to send the dispatch through Headquarters. There was no undertone of jealousy in anything Washington said of the victory. Perhaps the closest approach was in the observation that Gates was said to have had fourteen thousand militia with him. Washington remarked of the New England States that mistakenly were supposed to have sent so many men to the Northern Department:

> Had the same spirit pervaded the people of this and the neighboring States, we might before this have had General Howe nearly in the situation of General Burgoyne, with this difference, that the former would never have been out of reach of his ships, whilst the latter increased his danger every step he took having but one retreat in case of a disaster, and that blocked up by a respectable force.

Never for an hour, while operating close to deep water, could Washington forget seapower.

As if in acknowledgment of the change in its prospect the Royal Army vacated Germantown on the night of October 18/19 and drew back to Philadelphia. Washington moved his camp to White Marsh, but he could do no more than "hover" around the Quaker City. Below that city an effort was being made by the British to clear the way for the supply ships, without which Howe could not hope to hold the town. Washington was responsible for manning the forts and selecting the officers to command them, but the defence on the water was in the hands of officers responsible to the Navy Board and working in cooperation with Commodore John Hazelwood, who had full power over the Pennsylvania Navy. In so clumsy an engine of war, loss of motion was unavoidable; friction was all too likely. Two days before the Battle of Brandywine, the British had occupied Billingsport on the Jersey shore of the Delaware but they made no effort to seize Red Bank, five miles above Billingsport. On the Pennsylvania shore, the British were hoping to place batteries on Province Island, a marshy part of the mainland cut off by small creeks. The Americans worked steadily on the defences at Red Bank, styled Fort Mercer. The other principal American fortification consisted of four blockhouses and a battery of ten eighteen-pounders. These works were known as Fort Mifflin and were located on the treacherous ground of Port Island, nineteen hundred yards from Fort Mercer. The defenders had fashioned heavy timber obstructions which had been sunk across the channel. If the enemy tried to remove these chevaux-de-frise they could be swept by artillery in the forts. Above these barriers were light craft, most of which were galleys that could be maneuvered rapidly and with precision.

With patient enterprise, the British succeeded in planting their siege guns on Province Island and began, October 10, a steady bombardment of Fort Mifflin. By the twenty-first, it was manifest that a general assault on the river defences was impending. The destruction of Fort Mifflin was undertaken October 22 by British land batteries and by six men-of-war that came through an opening where two of the chevaux-de-frise had been pulled up. Fort Mercer and American craft gave hearty help to the guns of Fort Mifflin. At length, badly punished, the British vessels started back down the river, but a sixty-four-gun ship, the *Augusta,* and the frigate *Merlin* ran aground. The same day a force of about twelve hundred Hessians attempted to storm Fort Mercer. The effort was defeated completely at a cost to the assailants of about four hundred casualties. The final stroke of this successful phase of the defence came on the twenty-third, when an explosion wrecked the *Augusta* and fire destroyed the *Merlin.*

This repulse, in Washington's judgment, was nothing more than a respite, but it afforded time to strengthen Fort Mercer and it gave him a few more hours each day in which to meet, as far as he could, increasing needs of an enlarged Army. The Commissary still was demoralized by loss of men and by the regulations Congress had shaped unwisely. Quartermaster General Mifflin had neglected his duties for months and was now in such ill health that he had to quit his office. Where the issue of shoes was concerned, the men in the ranks doubtless would have insisted that no change could be for the worse. The need of blankets was equally desperate. During November Washington was to write: "There are now in this Army by a late return 4000 men wanting blankets, near 2000 of which have never had one, although some of them have been twelve months in service."

Washington faced all his familiar difficulties and some he had not experienced previously. Over certain periods, he lost more men by desertion than he gained by enlistment. Now that the forests around the camps were flying the red and yellow warnings of autumn, the Army began to dissolve. Besides losing the militia, Washington soon would have to say farewell to some and perhaps all the troops of the first nine Virginia regiments because their time was expiring. In their place, if for a short period only, Washington must get Pennsylvania militia, but how he did not know.

There was one other area from which men might be drawn, trained men at that: the line of the Hudson no longer would need as many troops as were with Gates and Putnam. Many could be sent to Pennsylvania, but in this, as in much besides, the gulf between *could* and *would* was wide.

Washington did not have the uniform support of able lieutenants who understood his perplexities and intelligently endeavored to relieve them. Though he had some senior officers like Greene, Lincoln and Knox, who were developing steadily, several lacked essential qualities of leadership. The Army had been for weeks without sufficient generals and now Francis Nash, a promising North Carolina Brigadier, died of wounds. In addition, five general officers of experience faced charges—Prudhomme de Borre for mismanagement or worse at Brandywine, Sullivan for the affair on Staten Island and for the action of September 11, Wayne for the attack on his troops near Paoli, Stephen for misconduct and excessive drinking, and Maxwell for substantially the same charges. De Borre resigned; Sullivan was acquitted unanimously and given by Congress a vote that was an apology in all but explicit words; Wayne was said by the court to deserve "highest honor." Maxwell was given something of a Scotch verdict, but Adam Stephen was not that fortunate. He was convicted of "unofficerlike behavior" and of "drunkenness" and was recommended for dismissal. Washington approved the sentence. While the Commander-in-Chief did not say so, he undoubtedly was glad to be rid of Stephen, but the need of additional officers remained. Congress named Alexander McDougall of New York a Major General and gave like rank to Robert Howe, a North Carolina Brigadier, whom Washington did not know. Among the effects of this shortage of senior officers was a lack of discipline among ambitious, place-hunting colonels. Other regimental commanders were discouraged by the low purchasing power of their pay and promotion over them of foreigners and staff officers regarded as pets of powerful generals. The main Army was outraged, in particular, by the compliance of Congress with the request of Gates that Lt. Col. James Wilkinson be given brevet as Brigadier for bringing the news of Burgoyne's surrender. There was, as always, the canker of controversy over seniority.

Applications of foreigners for high rank in the American service continued. The Commissioners in France were embarrassed by what Silas Deane styled the "rage" among Frenchmen for this adventure. The agents in Paris were told firmly that the decision of Congress to refuse commissions to foreigners who did not understand the English language must not be construed to mean that all those who had knowledge of that tongue would be employed. Meantime, Congress begrudgingly advanced money to French officers who either were extravagant or were without funds of their own. In the embarrassing case of du Coudray accident served where diplomacy had failed. On September 15 this ambitious officer had insisted on remaining astride his horse when he was going aboard the Schuylkill ferry. The animal had taken fright and plunged into the river. Du Coudray was drowned—a "dispensation," said John Adams, "that will save us much altercation." Thanks to the example set by Lafayette, Duportail and a few others, Washington was undergoing a change of mind concerning qualified foreign officers, but at this time most of them added to burdens which soon led Greene to say: "I think I never saw the Army so near dissolving since I have belonged to it." Apparent disintegration had been a continuing process, the worst of which had not been realized yet; but this time it had not brought Washington as low in spirit as he had been in 1776 when he had written his brother: "If every nerve is not strained to recruit the New Army with all possible expedition, I think the game is pretty near up. . . ." Now, when he sketched for the same brother's eye the perplexities he faced, Washington said: "I am doing all I can in my present situation to save them; God only knows which will succeed."

A shocking incident on October 15 would have justified Washington in saying of the moral fibre of Americans substantially what he had written of their war for independence: God alone knew whether it would outwear adversity. A devout woman of culture, Mrs. Elizabeth Graeme Ferguson, came to Headquarters that day and asked to see the General. Washington knew her not only by her own reputation for literary attainments but also as the daughter of a distinguished Philadelphian, Dr. Thomas Graeme, who had died five years previously, and had full faith in her. Mrs. Ferguson handed Washington a bulky package of fourteen folio pages. It proved to be a letter to Washington from a man he admired, the Rev. Jacob Duché, a Philadelphia clergyman whose eloquence had stirred the heart of every Delegate to Congress in 1774. It was a blow in the face to read long, fervent paragraphs in which the minister urged that Washington call on Congress to rescind the Declaration of Independence and open negotiations for peace. Duché was confident that such a move would meet with favor in America. "If it should not," the former Chaplain of Congress said, without abashment, "you have an infallible recourse still left; negotiate for your country at the head of your Army."

Washington reflected immediately that if he had been given an inkling of the contents of the letter he would have returned the paper unopened. As he could not do that now, he would transmit it to Congress lest it be found among his records in event they were stolen or he was killed or made prisoner. Congress shared his amazement and decided to make the paper public. Delegates, attachés and Pennsylvanians talked of the incident with a zest little below that of discussion of Burgoyne's surrender. As Duché saw them, "cause" and "commander" were almost synonyms. He believed this was the opinion of "the whole world" and he set in contrast to the rise of Washington the decline of Congress. Said Duché:

Take an impartial view of the present Congress, and what can you expect from them? . . . These are not the men you engaged to serve; these are not the men that America has chosen to represent her. Most of them were chosen by a little, low faction, and the few gentlemen that are among them now are well known to lie on the balance, and looking up to your hand alone to turn the beam. 'Tis you, sir, and you only that support the present Congress; of this you must be fully sensible.

Had Washington been disposed to discuss the composition of Congress he would have insisted that Duché erred in generalizing, but he would have been compelled to admit that Congress no longer represented America's best. Nearly all the members of that body who had voted unanimously in June 1775 to put their Virginia colleague at the head of the Army had died, terminated their service or taken long leave. Seven only remained—John Adams, Samuel Adams and John Hancock of the Massachusetts delegation, Eliphalet Dyer of Connecticut, James Duane of New York, Samuel Chase of Maryland, and Richard Henry Lee of Virginia. Of these, Chase was saying his farewells and the three senior members from Massachusetts were preparing to leave York, where Congress now held its sessions. Before December arrived, Dyer and Duane were to be the only Delegates in a shrunken body of twenty-one or twenty-two who had seen Washington in uniform when Congress had filled the seats during the late spring of 1775 and a majority still had hoped for reunion with England. Newcomers were acquainted, of course, with Washington's high reputation; most of them had never seen him in committee or council of war and did not know the quality of his judgment.

Duché wrote that Washington alone supported Congress, but the question in reality was, would Congress continue to support Washington? His good name was at the mercy of strangers, some of whom were divided by sectional jealousies and were dazzled by Gates's easy success in the Northern Department. Inexperienced Delegates did not realize that Washington had to do much more than maneuver an army. When these men compared Gates's decisive victory near Saratoga with Washington's defeats on the Brandywine and at Germantown, they naturally would reason that Gates was the better General. He had captured an entire army. While he was achieving that, what had been Washington's next accomplishment? The loss of Philadelphia—so members of Congress might be disposed to answer. In doing so, they failed to perceive the vast difference between Gates's task and Washington's.

Gates made the utmost of the praise he received. One immediate effect was an abrupt change of attitude towards Washington. Most of the careful deference to "Your Excellency" disappeared from his communications, which became less and less frequent. When young Colonel Wilkinson at last reached Headquarters with the dispatches, which were addressed to the President of Congress, not to Washington, the aide observed the surprise over Gates's disregard of "channels of command" and wrote back to his chief in partisan spirit: "The dissensions, the jealousies, calumnies and detractions which pervade a certain quarter must be reserved for some other opportunity. I am often asked the cause of your not writing to General Washington, so that this omission has been noticed publicly." Gates continued to communicate directly with Congress and later forwarded to the President the news of the British evacuation of Ticonderoga, though by that time he had received, along with Washington's congratulations on the defeat of Burgoyne, a mild reprimand for failing to send official notice to Headquarters.

Washington did not build a grudge on this disregard of his position as Commander-in-Chief; but he could not fail to observe how promptly some officers now became his critics and Gates's avowed supporters. In the foreground, rather because of arrogance than of eminence, was Thomas Conway, the Irish-French officer who had made a somewhat favorable impression on Washington. Conway had been in Sullivan's Division and at Brandywine had won in the mind of Sullivan a respect that amounted almost to awe. Two weeks after Brandywine Conway addressed to President Hancock a letter that began: "It is with infinite concern that I find myself slighted and forgot when you have offered rank to officers who cost you a great deal of money and have never rendered you the least service. Baron de Kalb to whom you have offered the rank of Major General after having given him large sums of money is my inferior in France." Then in a tone half boastful, half scolding, Conway set down seven reasons why he thought he should be made a Major General and ended with more of a bark than a bow: "Your very speedy and categorical answer will very much oblige him who is with respect. . . ."

This letter greatly offended Congress but it by no means included all that Conway had to say. He visited widely and discussed personalities without restraint. "No man," said he of the Commander-in-Chief, "was more a gentleman than General Washington, or appeared to more advantage at his table, or in the usual intercourse of life; but as to his talents for the command of an Army they were miserable indeed." Washington ignored such of this as may have come to his ears. Although he was scarcely less sensitive than he had been, he did not have the time to notice every man who disliked or disparaged him. Nor, in this instance, was he inclined to put a high estimation on Conway's abilities or judgment.

Conway found after Saratoga that what he had been saying in dispraise of Washington fitted perfectly into the arguments advanced by those who were trying to exalt Gates. Some members of Congress previously incensed by Conway's arrogance now were willing to listen, accept his estimate of himself and ask whether, after all, it might not be in the country's interest to use his much applauded military knowledge by giving him the rank he sought. One report reached Washington that this had been done, or soon would be voted, and it both aroused his fears and outraged his sense of justice. The Army was suffering already from a downpour of resignations; men considered their duties so difficult and were themselves so tired that obligation to country no longer had first place in their minds. Besides, their pay in depreciated currency left them little or nothing for their families. All twenty-three of the American Brigadiers were Conway's seniors in date of commission. If now a boastful self seeker, a foreigner at that, and the most recently created Brigadier were promoted over these men, they would have a grievance that would seem to justify what some were anxious to do anyway. The best method of preventing this seemed to be for Washington himself to protest to Congress against the elevation of Conway.

Washington addressed his appeal to Richard Henry Lee, the only member of the Virginia Delegation of 1777 with whom he had served. He told Lee the appointment of Conway would be "as unfortunate a measure as ever was adopted" and "I may add (and I think with truth) that it will give a fatal blow to the existence of the Army." Forthrightly he explained:

"General Conway's merit . . . as an officer, and his importance in this Army, exists more in his imagination than in reality: For it is a maxim with him to leave no service of his untold, nor to want anything that is to be had by importunity."

Lee's reply was reassuring and at the same time alarming. Conway had not been elected Major General and would not be "whilst it is likely to produce the evil consequences you suggest." The Virginia Delegate then proceeded somewhat coldly to discuss the reorganization of the Board of War and the identity of three individuals who were to take the place of Congressmen and constitute the membership. Washington doubtless needed all his self-control as he read what some members of Congress favored: they wanted to put on the board Joseph Reed, Timothy Pickering, who was Washington's Adjutant General, and Robert H. Harrison, the indispensable Headquarters secretary, and they talked of electing Conway Pickering's successor as Adjutant General. Did Congress wish to make life intolerable for him?

During the evening of November 8 a messenger brought Washington a letter written by Lord Stirling at Reading on the third, principally a report on numerous small affairs. At the end was this sentence: "The enclosed was communicated by Col. Wilkinson to Major McWilliams"—Stirling's aide—"such wicked duplicity of conduct I shall always think it my duty to detect." The enclosure itself consisted merely of this: "In a letter from Genl. Conway to Genl. Gates he says—'Heaven has been determined to save your country; or a weak General and bad Counsellors would have ruined it.'" Conway in correspondence with Gates—that, and not the Frenchman's sarcastic reference to Washington, struck home. Had Conway and Gates made common cause against their senior officer? Washington's amiability led him to conclude that Wilkinson had communicated the message at the instance of Gates and as a means of warning him. Nothing could be done about the matter, but the next day he let Conway know that his contemptuous criticism had been reported.

Washington knew members of his military family would see this note, and he talked with them confidentially about Conway's apparent effort to stir up strife, but little time or thought could be given the incident because every officer was busy with preparations to meet the enemy's anticipated final attacks on the river defences of Philadelphia. Washington did his absolute to reenforce Fort Mifflin and Red Bank, eliminate bickering, employ and then preserve the armed craft, and try every tactical device that ingenuity could suggest and common sense approve; but the task was almost hopeless. The end of a gallantly stubborn defence was the evacuation of the ruins of Fort Mifflin on the night of November 15/16 and of Fort Mercer on the night of November 20/21 before Cornwallis could deliver an intended assault. The river now would be open to the British.

What next? The Army was not strong enough to attack. "Our situation, . . ." Washington told Greene,

is distressing from a variety of irremediable causes, but more especially from the impracticability of answering the expectations of the world without running hazards which no military principles can justify, and which, in case of failure, might prove the ruin of our cause; patience and a steady perseverance in such measures as appear warranted by sound reason and policy must support us under the censure of the one, and dictate a proper line of conduct for the attainment of the other; that is the great object in view.

More specifically, he would put his Army in winter quarters close to Philadelphia and would try to keep his barefoot men from starving or freezing. The more vigilant part of the light horse and such infantry as could move swiftly with decent shoes and satisfied stomachs, he would employ to guard against surprise, discourage raids by Howe's forces and prevent the movement of supplies into Philadelphia. If Washington saw an opening, he would try to make the most of it; in general, he would remain on the defensive.

The struggle for the forts on the lower Delaware and the reconcentration that followed their loss so occupied Washington during November that he had little time to study a bright event of that dark month—the completion by Congress of the Articles of Confederation and the dispatch on the seventeenth of the text to the States for ratification. In Washington's eyes the close cooperation of the States had been and still was the first essential of success in the attainment of independence, but not one line had he, the soldier, written of the compact Congress had been discussing at intervals since July 12, 1776. The perfection of those articles, as far as it was attainable at all, was the work of the civil arm of government. He who held the sword must not use its point as a pen.

Conway made immediate reply to Washington's blunt note of November 9 which had enclosed the text of the Frenchman's observations in his letter to Gates. He asserted:

. . . I am willing that my original letter to General Gates should be handed to you. This, I trust, will convince you of my way of thinking. I know, sir, that several unfavorable hints have been reported by some of your aide de camps as the author of some discourse which I never uttered. These advices never gave me the least uneasiness because I was conscious I never said anything but what I could mention to yourself.

In its entirety this letter could be regarded either as candid or as cunning. At Headquarters, Washington's opinion probably was echoed some weeks later by John Laurens, a most intelligent aide, who said of the Frenchman, "the perplexity of his style, the evident insincerity of his compliments, betray his real sentiments and expose his guilt." Washington did not think Conway's explanation called for a reply and probably felt some satisfaction when he learned that, in a letter of November 14 to the President of Congress, the French officer had submitted his resignation. This was followed by a request to Washington from Conway for a leave of absence in which to collect his scattered effects. The request was granted through Colonel Harrison the evening it was received. Washington himself signed a letter in which he explained that acceptance of the resignation of Conway was the prerogative of Congress.

When the Frenchman's resignation was presented to Congress there was no motion to accept it, but, instead, an order to refer it to the Board of War, on which, at this stage of the reorganization, the most powerful member was Thomas Mifflin. He had consented on November 18 to serve and was entering on the discharge of his duties. Pickering had agreed to become a member, though as yet he could not leave Headquarters in the absence of anyone who was qualified to be the Adjutant General. As Colonel Harrison had declined, Congress filled out the membership of five by electing Gates, Joseph Trumbull, and Richard Peters, who had been Secretary of the "old" Board. Delegates voted that Gates should be President, should retain his military rank, and should "officiate at the Board, or in the field, as occasion may require."

Washington probably was aware by this time that Mifflin, though cautious and adroit, was regarded as head of the movement to make the largest use of the abilities of Gates. That was the best face to put on the activities of Mifflin, who had been among the most useful and active of Washington's supporters until, in the summer of 1777, he had been alienated by the refusal of the Commander-in-Chief to disregard the possibility of a British attack based on New York. Mifflin had wanted all the American forces employed to save Philadelphia. Increasingly his name was being associated with those of men who sometimes spoke mysteriously of their unwillingness to pay homage to "the image."

So far as Conway and his resignation were entangled in these matters, the Board did not report to Congress on his resignation, but some leaders in York began to support a proposal for which Conway took credit, that Congress name an Inspector General who would instruct troops, apprehend deserters and see that public property had careful custody. When the Board of War asked the opinion of the Commander-in-Chief on what such an inspector might do, Congress did not wait on Washington's views, expression of which was delayed until December 14 by field duties. On the thirteenth the Delegates adopted a long resolve on the establishment of a system of inspection. Conway forthwith was elected Inspector General and was made a Major General.

Washington might well have regarded the resolve as a carefully planned affront. Had such an incident occurred while he had been in the French and Indian War, he would have resigned wrathfully and at once. Now it was different. When liberty was at stake, pride and personalities dwindled in perspective. He would see to it that official dealings with Conway were in every way correct, though personally he would not pretend to like a man he distrusted. Moreover, if Congress wished to decide questions that previously had come to his desk, he would tell correspondents to communicate directly with that body. Was there dissatisfaction with him as Commander-in-Chief? Did Congress think Gates a superior General? Washington would make no defence of what had been the best he could do; if another were preferred, let the gentleman have the sash, the epaulettes, and the daily, devouring duties!

Doubts and resentments in Congress created for Washington an opportunity of showing members depressing realities it had not been prudent to set down even in a letter read behind closed doors. A committee of Delegates was named to consider means for conducting a winter campaign. Congress voted to scrutinize the "causes of the evacuation of Fort Mercer" and followed that with orders for like investigation of the loss of Fort Montgomery and Fort Clinton. The failure of the Rhode Island expedition also was to be investigated. This, in turn, was fortified with bristling assurance that whenever an operation failed or a post fell to the enemy, Congress would seek to establish the reason by inquiry conducted "in such manner as [it] shall deem best adapted for the investigation of truth in the respective cases."

When the committee came to White Marsh, Washington told the members how nearly naked and how ill-shod his troops were. When the committee inquired if a large body of militia could not be called out to give him added strength for an attack on Philadelphia, he asked his Generals for their views, with full assurance of what their answers would be. The commanders pointed out that the season was too far advanced to summon militia from distant States and that, even if the men reached the camp, it was doubtful "whether they could be furnished with provisions and forage, and brought to act in concert with the regular Army." Committeemen questioned and consulted and informed Congress that, in their opinion, a winter offensive was "ineligible." The Army should take up winter quarters where it would "be most likely to overawe the enemy," protect the country and find provisions and shelter. In like understanding of unhappy realities and long disregarded needs, the committee endorsed Washington's proposals for improving the corps of officers and for assuring the continued service of leaders qualified to "introduce that order and discipline amongst the troops so essential to the military character."

Congress was not content to accept the committee's findings without the papers on which the report was based. By resolves of December 19 the Delegates called for these documents. The facts might not satisfy the element critical of Washington but they were a final answer to those who looked at the actual condition of the Continental Army vis-à-vis Howe's. Congress did not have to rely on Washington's interpretation only. The testimony of all the senior officers was the same: strategical mistakes and tactical blunders had been made but none of these meant as much as the fundamental inferiority of the Army in almost every thing fighting men required. At bottom, the issue was not that of supplanting Washington but that of supplying him where he and his officers decided they would post the Army.

Warm argument and sharp division arose over the selection of winter quarters, because the extent of the area open to British depredation might depend on the distance of the American camp from Philadelphia. If Washington's divisions were close to the city, they would be exposed to surprise, an excessive price to pay for reducing by a few square miles the district exposed to British pillaging. Conversely, if the Army were remote, it would not be able to deal with parties that might improve British rations by stripping bare a prosperous countryside. A related subject of discussion was whether the forces should or could requisition quarters in nearby towns and villages, which already were overcrowded with refugees from Philadelphia. The Council and Assembly of Pennsylvania sent Congress a vigorous remonstrance in which they pointed out the danger of exposing lower Jersey and that part of Pennsylvania east of the Schuylkill. The Pennsylvanians maintained, also, that many families had fled from Philadelphia and had so crowded nearby towns that soldiers could not be quartered there. Before this paper reached Congress or came to Washington's hand the choice of a campsite had been made—a wooded region on the south side of the Schuylkill, eighteen miles northwest of the occupied city, at a place called the Valley Forge.

The area into which the Army was to move a week before Christmas 1777 formed a crude right-angle triangle that covered the Fatland Ford, about four and a half miles north and slightly east of the scene of the "Paoli Massacre." A few redoubts and a line of entrenchments would consolidate the hills and high ground into a strong defensive position. Thick woods would offer fuel and logs for the construction of quarters. Streams would supply water in abundance. A few scattered dwellings and farm buildings were the sole man-made facilities of which the Army could avail itself. Most of the precinct was windy and forbidding hillside. On that bleak and comfortless soil the troops must camp in their tattered tents until axemen went into the woods, felled trees and brought in logs that must be raised and roofed and made into cabins which the soldiers were to fit with hearths and chimneys.

The shortage of provisions continued and rapidly became worse. Some brigades had a small amount of salt pork issued them December 21 from a Commissary in the last stages of collapse. Then provisions gave out entirely. Many soldiers got nothing and, in their mounting misery, made loud complaint. A sombre chant was repeated endlessly in the tents of one regiment after another till the long hillsides rang with the wail, "No meat, no meat." Although officers were able promptly to put an end to this defiance of discipline, they warned Headquarters they might have more trouble unless the men were fed.

By strained effort enough food was brought up overnight to permit an issue, but early on December 22 Washington was aroused by news that a British force had left Philadelphia and was moving towards Derby on what appeared to be a foraging expedition. When he ordered the Army made ready to march against this column he received a report the like of which never had come to him in the two and a half years of his command: the troops could not stir from their camps. Washington was compelled to send this alarming dispatch to Congress: ". . . unless some great and capital change suddenly takes place . . . this Army must inevitably be reduced to one or other of these three things. Starve, dissolve or disperse, in order to obtain subsistence in the best manner they can. . . ." As he put this on paper his wrath mounted against those who had sought to prevent the occupation of quarters in Pennsylvania towns nearby: "I can assure those gentlemen that it is a much easier and less distressing thing to draw remonstrances in a comfortable room by a good fireside than to occupy a cold, bleak hill and sleep under frost or snow without clothes or blankets. . . ."

Previously, at every twist of the revolutionary struggle, some essential of successful war had not been available; at Valley Forge everything was lacking. The Army might freeze before it starved; and if it found shelter and food, the shortage of clothing and footgear would keep it from taking the field. The fault was not with the place but with equipment and supplies.

Little had been accomplished either by Congress or by most of the States to collect garments. Congress and the Commander-in-Chief had been compelled to say in plain words that the Clothier General could not meet the requirements of shivering thousands. This had been followed by a pessimistic committee report to Congress on what might be expected from importation. New inquiry into the competence of the Clothier General's management, a summons of that harassed individual to Headquarters, the assurance that officers would join him in trying to find new supplies, the dispatch of representatives to Boston—these were four only of numerous desperate moves of December. So low was the stock of clothing near the end of the year that after some of the veterans of the nine original Virginia regiments offered to continue in service if the bounty was doubled and the promised clothing was allowed them, Congress had to tender money instead of garments. From "Head Quarters, Valley Forge" on the last day of a dreadful year, Washington compassed the misery of thousands in a single exclamation: "Our sick naked, our well naked, our unfortunate men in captivity naked!"

Thus, at the beginning of 1778, the Army was witnessing one of the strangest of races, a contest between the axes of the men building huts and the harsh wear-and-tear on the remaining garments of those who still had sufficient clothing to permit outdoor duty. The huts had to be finished speedily, or nakedness would be fatal to the Army. Sickness increased with exposure. Although hospital huts were built early and in what was believed to be sufficient number, they soon were overcrowded with miserable men who died fast or, if they survived, received little attention. In spite of all exertion, it was the middle of January when the last of the troops were under roof. Even then they did not always have straw to take the chill from the earthen floor of their huts. Thousands had no bed covering. The shortage of blankets had become so critical that when Virginia troops reached the end of their term of enlistment, Washington had to order taken from these men the blankets, belonging to the Army, that would have made their bivouacs endurable on the long road home.

Part of the blame rested on the shoulders of Quartermaster General Mifflin, who had not maintained his office at Headquarters from the time the Army had entered Pennsylvania. Washington had himself tried to give a measure of supervision to the department but had not been able to devote to the task time to get the best performance from Mifflin's deputies. Washington should have called on Congress to replace Mifflin or insist that the Quartermaster General discharge the duties of office. Instead, his amiability had led him to hope against hope for some betterment until, in this respect, he was unjust to his troops.

Food, of course, was the absolute essential—and food, more than even clothing or blankets or straw, was lacking at Valley Forge. Commissary General Trumbull was an able and diligent man, but he had been sick for months and in New England, with the result that his department, like that of the Quartermaster General, did not have the daily supervision of an experienced and competent head. The Commissary was in a condition so tangled that Washington did not attempt to assess blame for the scarcity of provisions, now approaching famine. "Fire cakes" frequently were all the half-naked men had to eat in their overcrowded, smoky huts. Early in the New Year most of the regiments had to be told the Commissary could issue no provisions because it had none, none whatsoever. After this second period of fasting had become almost intolerable, some flour and a few cattle reached camp. Meagerly after that, a half-allowance of meat or of bread was issued daily, until about the beginning of the second week in February, when winter fired all its siege guns. The bombardment by the gray skies was so overwhelming that no teams could reach camp. All reserve provisions were exhausted—to the last thin cow and the bottom slab of pork in the one remaining barrel. A week and more passed before any flesh was available for the men in the ranks. As Washington, intensely anxious, walked through the camp during that dreadful week he heard an ominous chant—"no pay, no clothes, no provisions, no rum."

Washington expected the disintegration of his forces or open mutiny and desertion *en masse*—alternatives so ruinous that they frightened even those members of Congress who had appeared skeptical concerning the breakdown of the Commissary. The most stubborn-minded Delegates were shaken from their persistent confidence in the dual system of purchase and supply they had set up in 1777. Fundamental changes were projected. If possible, Congress must have again the services of Trumbull, from the date of whose departure, Washington said, the Army had lived precariously. Time would not wait on deliberation.

These were desperate hours. Washington continued to watch and to warn. "A prospect now opens," he said February 17, "of absolute want such as will make it impossible to keep the Army much longer from dissolution unless the most vigorous and effectual measures are pursued to prevent it." He had been inclined to suspect that mutiny was near; thereafter it looked as if the alternative would prevail—that the Army simply would fall apart as the men left their huts and scattered in quest of food. They would have to walk because, even if they were disposed to steal the horses, the animals that had survived the lack of forage were too few and too feeble to carry them far.

The men exceeded the faith of their officers in them. They neither mutinied nor marched away. Desertion actually diminished when the shortage of provisions was most depressing. The troops had confidence in Washington and they deserved everything that John Laurens implied when he spoke of "those dear, ragged Continentals whose patience will be the

MAP / 13

CAPE ANN TO BALTIMORE:
PRINCIPAL TOWNS AND HIGHWAYS, 1775-1778

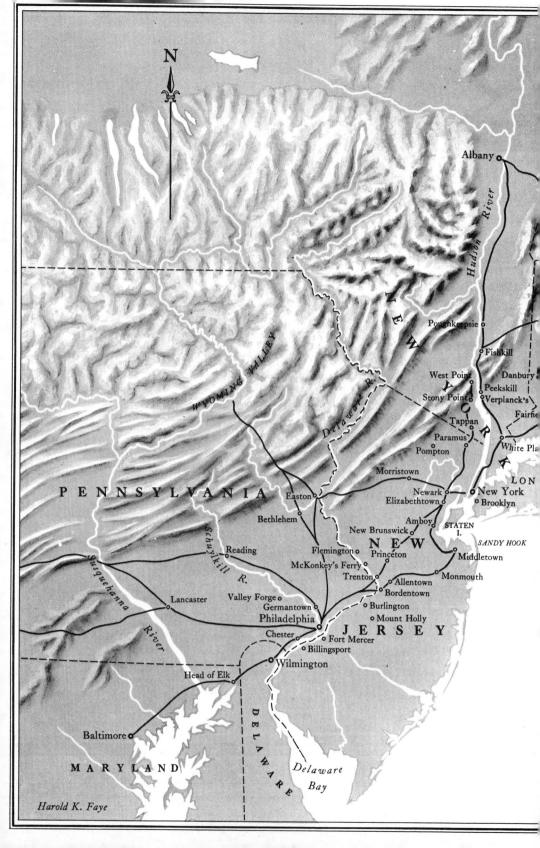

CAPE ANN to BALTIMORE

Principal Towns and some of the Highways

1759-1778

Statute Miles

0   10   20   30   40   50   100

MILITARY LIFE

11. Washington's Election as Commander in Chief of the Continental Forces. From the Journal of the Continental Congress for June 15, 1776. *Library of Congress.*

12. Benjamin Lincoln. Painting by Charles Willson Peale. *Independence National Historical Park Collection.*

13. Anthony Wayne. Painting by Peter F. Rothermel, Based on the Study by John Trumbull. *Courtesy of the Historical Society of Pennsylvania.*

14. Charles Lee. Caricature by Benjamin Rushbrooke.

15. Joseph Reed. Painting
by Charles Willson
Peale. *Independence
National Historical
Park Collection.*

16. John Sullivan. *Inde-
pendence National
Historical Park Col-
lection.*

17. Benedict Arnold. Engrav-
ings by B. Reading from
the Drawing by du Sime-
tière.

18. Friedrich, Baron von
Steuben. Painting by
Charles Willson Peale.
*Independence National
Historical Park Collec-
tion.*

19. Jean Baptiste, Comte de Rochambeau. *Courtesy of Musée Bonnat, Bayonne, France.*

20. Marie Joseph, Marquis de Lafayette. Painting by Charles Willson Peale. *Independence National Historical Park Collection.*

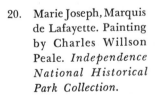

21. Horatio Gates. Painting by Charles Willson Peale. *Independence National Historical Park Collection.*

22. Thomas Mifflin. Detail from the Painting by John Singleton Copley. *Courtesy of the Historical Society of Pennsylvania.*

23. Joseph Trumbull. Painting by John Trumbull.
Courtesy of the Connecticut Historical Society.

24. Henry Knox. Painting by
Edward Savage. *Property
of the American Scenic
and Historic Preservation
Society, New York City.*

25. Nathanael Greene. Painting by Charles Willson Peale. *Independence National Historical Park Collection.*

26. Washington at Yorktown with Lafayette and Tench Tilghman. Painting by Charles Willson Peale. *State House of Annapolis, Maryland.*

admiration of future ages. . . ." Nathanael Greene was privileged to pay tribute and to relate the climax of the story as it concerned part of his command:

Such patience and moderation as they manifested under their sufferings does the highest honor to the magnanimity of the American soldiers. The seventh day [without rations] they came before their superior officers and told their sufferings in as respectful terms as if they had been humble petitioners for special favors; they added that it would be impossible to continue in camp any longer without support.

Through the worst of the ordeal, even in the dreadful third week of February, Washington retained outwardly his unshaken composure as the days of late winter dragged by and concern over provisions was aggravated by a hundred problems. His was the task of planning for the victorious long life of an Army that might die of starvation the very next week. He had, fortunately, the companionship of Martha who lighted the long evenings and directed the Spartan entertainment at Headquarters. Simple as were the diversions in officers' quarters, they were in heartrending contrast to the life of the soldiers. As his duties multiplied, Washington used increasingly a staff he now was free to augment as he saw fit. Col. Alexander Scammell, the new Adjutant General, proved competent, but he had to confess that his duties were intolerably heavy.

Washington, while laboring to prevent the starvation of his men, was busy with the hard, anxious administration of the Army and with plans for making it better able to face its foe. Reforms were advanced through a committee of Congress that had been named at his instance to discuss with him and recommend to other Delegates such changes in organization as its judgment and the counsel of officers suggested. Most of these committeemen came to camp and remained there during part of the period of hardship—a most fortunate circumstance because it gave them an understanding of what Washington had to endure. The four supreme needs, as Washington saw them, were strengthening of the officers' corps, assurance of recruits for the infantry, improvement of the cavalry and better organization of the Quartermaster's, the Commissary and other weak departments.

The plea for a reorganization of the Quartermaster's Department included the assertion that the principal post should be filled by a man of military training. Reports and parliamentary maneuvering of the usual sort delayed action but ended in the conclusion that Philip Schuyler would not be acceptable as Quartermaster General and that Mifflin was unwilling to resume the duties. Mifflin, in fact, had left his post on the Board of War and had quit York, where Congress was now meeting, in a huff because, he affirmed, he was falsely accused of seeking to displace Washington. The ablest man available for the post appeared to be Nathanael Greene, who was most reluctant to accept but at length was prevailed upon to do so. No similar man was procurable immediately for Commissary General. Trumbull's letters showed him to be unhappy and in ill health. His Deputy of Purchases, Jeremiah Wadsworth of Massachusetts, was the man who seemed most likely to succeed, but election was delayed.

The draft of militia for twelve months, as recommended by the General and approved by the committee, involved politics and public sensibilities that frightened every time-server in Congress, but it was endorsed in its essentials. Because two months of the year had passed when the Delegates voted, they decided that needs for 1778 would be met if the draft were effective for nine months from the time the recruits reached the prescribed rendezvous. The design for the organization of larger cavalry regiments was not questioned but was postponed temporarily, along with other details of the "Establishment of the American Army."

Partial reorganization was effected, and the miseries of Valley Forge were endured while Washington was having an extraordinary adventure in command. General Conway had returned to camp late in December from York, where he had spoken, to quote Lafayette, "as a man sent by heaven for the liberty and happiness of America." The Marquis observed, half humorously, "he told so to them and they are fools enough to believe it." At York and everywhere else that politicians gathered, they still were talking of the difference between Washington's apparent failure and Gates's manifest success. Washington's early resignation was predicted; Gates, Conway, Mifflin or Lee, on release, were put forward as his successor. Lafayette was shocked to observe the dissension in Congress and hear—as he wrote Washington—that "stupid men who without knowing a single word about war, undertake to judge you, to make ridiculous comparisons. . . ."

Washington explained his difficulties to Lafayette and, while the committeemen of Congress were in camp, he disclosed to them the conditions that were paralyzing the Army. John Harvie, a Virginia member of the committee, waited until he was alone with Washington and then said earnestly, "My dear General, if you had given some explanation, all these rumors would have been silenced a long time ago." Washington's answer was a question: "How could I exculpate myself without doing harm to the public cause?" He did not ask this in vain of Harvie or of other discerning members of Congress. They understood. Henry Laurens, now President of the Congress, wrote his son, the General's aide: "In [Washington's ruin] would be involved the ruin of our cause. On the other hand his magnanimity, his patience will save his country and confound his enemies."

Washington's patience was a virtue that had limits which already had been passed with Conway. The Commander-in-Chief had concluded that ambitious pretensions and incredible self-esteem made the Irish-born Frenchman an "incendiary" who would not hesitate to stir up dangerous contention and to set comrades against one another. The rank and the office of the new Inspector General were to be regarded; Washington would work as best he could with those men Congress assigned him. Personal relations were another matter. Conway was a personal enemy and must be faced.

This was the situation when Conway called at Headquarters to pay his respects. He was received with flawless, cold courtesy—the "ceremonious civility" which Washington had once described as tantamount to incivility. Conway came again and had precisely the same treatment, such a reception, he protested later, "as I never met with before from any General during the course of thirty years in a very respectable Army." As if to avoid unnecessary personal contact, Washington next sent Col. John Fitzgerald to inquire what methods Conway proposed to employ in the new office of Inspector General. The Frenchman replied, December 29, with an explanation of his plan to prepare models, together with printed rules and regulations and, meantime, to begin the verbal instruction of officers and NCOs from each regiment. This was followed by the statement that the rank of major general was "absolutely requisite" for the discharge of the duties. Conway went on: ". . . if my appointment is productive of any inconvenience or anyways disagreeable to your excellency, as I neither applied nor solicited for this plan, I am very ready to return to France where I have pressing business, and this I will do with the more satisfaction that I expect even there to be useful to the cause."

The offer in those final clauses might be accepted as arrogantly defiant or as patriotically subordinate. Washington was not concerned over alternative interpretations, but he was resolved to write the Frenchman a letter that would represent the issue as one of justice to American brigade commanders, whom the Inspector General now outranked. In words as formal as those of his reception of the ambitious Inspector General, Washington disposed of the essential matters of business and proceeded to assure Conway, "Your appointment of Inspector-General to the Army, I believe, has not given the least uneasiness to any officer in it." Washington continued:

By consulting your own feelings upon the appointment of Baron de Kalb you may judge what must be the sensations of those Brigadiers who by your promotion are superseded. I am told they are determined to remonstrate against it; for my own part, I have nothing to do in the appointment of general officers and shall always afford every countenance and due respect to those appointed by Congress, taking it for granted that, prior to any resolve of that nature, they take a dispassionate view of the merits of the officer to be promoted, and considered every consequence that can result from such a procedure; nor have I any other wish on that head but that good attentive officers may be chosen, and no extraordinary promotion take place but where the merit of the officer is so generally acknowledged as to obviate every reasonable cause of dissatisfaction thereat.

At this point the exchange might have ended with tacit assumption by Conway that he possessed the special merit to justify advancement; but he apparently was as confident of his finesse in debate as of his skill in war and replied at once with a long letter, polite to the point of sarcasm. Four things in this angered Washington—manifest insincerity of the manner in which Conway linked his name with that of Frederick the Great, the insinuation that Conway had not been received properly at Headquarters, the assumption that nobody in the Army had thought previously of creating a system of inspection, and finally the statement that Conway could "expect no support" in the discharge of his official duties because of the Commander-in-Chief's dislike for him personally.

Washington's decision was instant and sharp: If, improbably, Congress so desired, it could make its choice between him and the Frenchman. As a soldier and a gentleman, his concern was to denounce the intimation that he would fail to support Conway—or anyone else—in the performance of duties assigned by Congress. On January 2 Washington transmitted to the Delegates in York his correspondence with Conway and in plainest words told Congress how he felt:

If General Conway means, by cool receptions . . . that I did not receive him in the language of a warm and cordial friend, I readily confess the charge. I did not, nor shall I ever, till I am capable of the arts of dissimulation. These I despise, and my feelings will not permit me to make professions of friendship to a man I deem my enemy, and whose system of conduct forbids it. At the same time, Truth authorizes me to say that he was received and treated with proper respect to his official character, and that he has had no cause to justify the assertion that he could not expect any support for fulfilling the duties of his appointment.

Before this was read in Congress, Washington received an excited communication of December 8 from Horatio Gates who had heard of Washington's first letter to Conway, with the quotation Stirling had sent. Gates was much disturbed: Conway's letters to him had been "stealingly copied," he said, "but which of them, when, and by whom, is to me as yet an unfathomable secret." Gates's letter contained no denial of the accuracy of the quotation. Moreover, he twice mentioned "letters" from Conway as if they might have been sufficiently numerous to make it difficult to determine from which the extract might have been taken. Gates wrote, also, of the possibility that the letter containing the offensive words might have been shown Washington by a member of Congress: did this mean that correspondence of Conway and Gates, critical of Washington, was being circulated among Delegates?

Washington faced the same sort of challenge he had read in Conway's persiflage, a challenge of his integrity, because there was, he thought, an intimation in Gates's letter that he had received in some discreditable manner an extract from a paper "stealingly copied." Previously, Washington would have written directly to Gates about this; but now that the commander of the Northern Department had laid the indirect accusation before Congress by sending a copy of his letter to its President, Washington decided to send through the same tribunal a letter in which his statement of the facts would be his sufficient denial. In doing this, Washington could see no impropriety in saying that Gates's own aide, James Wilkinson, had talked of Conway's letter while on the way to York with Gates's victory dispatch.

As it happened, perhaps fortuitously, both Conway and Wilkinson now became objects of attack. The Brigadiers had determined to protest the promotion of Conway to Major General; the colonels were preparing to direct a similar paper against Wilkinson who overnight was given the brevet of a Brigadier for bringing a paper from Saratoga to York, though many colonels who had shared in all Washington's campaigns had been denied advancement. Nine of the Brigadiers joined in the "memorial" to Congress regarding the promotion of Conway and forwarded their paper to Washington with the request that it be transmitted to the Delegates at York as soon as convenient. Greene added a personal protest, deferential and at the same time firm in its warning that if regular promotion were denied "a sense of injury [would] mean a lessening of military service." Congress received the memorial and the communication of Greene and defiantly laid them on the table. Members doubtless affirmed they would not permit soldiers to dictate to them; but as a matter of practical politics, they did not disdain the protest. Nor could they overlook the fact that most of the senior American officers disliked, if they did not actually distrust, Conway. Manifestly, Washington did not have to fight alone against forces that sought to displace him.

With his reply of January 4 to Gates's letter Washington left the issue. Gates might answer, if he saw fit, and, meantime, might settle accounts with Wilkinson. The colonels' protest against the promotion of that gentleman to Brigadier had not yet been received by Congress, but the rumble of their dissatisfaction already had been audible. "A plan is laid by sundry members of Congress, which I believe will be carried out, to remove him by the way of appointing him Secretary to the Board of War or by sending him to Georgia." Appointment by the Board of War was made without waiting to ascertain whether it would please Wilkinson or placate the colonels over whom he had stepped.

Conway did not wait on Congress or on Gates or on anyone else. He informed Sullivan: "I depend upon my military promotion in rank for to increase my fortune and that of my family. I freely own to you it was partly with a view of obtaining sooner the rank of Brigadier in the French army that I have joined this." In that unabashed pursuit of fortune, he again wrote Washington and asked if the Commander-in-Chief intended to order an inquisition because an officer wrote such a letter of criticism as any subaltern in Europe might indite without having the least notice taken of it by his superiors. Washington had decided to answer no more of Conway's communications and did not waste time in analyzing this letter. From reports brought Washington, Conway wished a place in an expedition the Board of War was hoping to organize for an irruption into Canada. Washington did not believe this enterprise feasible but was reserved in passing judgment on the project because titular command was to be vested in his trusted young friend Lafayette.

Before the Canadian adventure took form, Conway had or thought he had, on January 19, the most powerful possible reenforcement. Gates arrived in York and brought with him the original of Conway's letter, alleged to include the reference to a "weak General" and "bad counsellors." Gates showed this paper to Conway and other friends and satisfied them it did not contain the sentence Stirling had quoted. Conway was anxious, he said, to have it printed, but he was discouraged by Henry Laurens to whom he spoke of the text, though he did not offer to let the President see it. Laurens read a copy confided to other hands and wrote that some of the contents were "ten times worse in every way" than the alleged original. In a short time it became generally known that the letter was primarily a display of Conway's military wisdom in a critique of the Battle of the Brandywine, for the loss of which the Frenchman assigned no less than thirteen reasons.

Not until January 22 did Gates receive Washington's reply of the fourth. The next day Gates wrote a long answer that said of Conway: "The reasons which, in his judgment, deprived us of the success we could reasonably expect, were methodically explained by him; but neither the 'weakness' of any of our Generals, nor 'bad counsellors' were mentioned." The communication closed with some words of regret that Washington had predicted—in a letter "which came to me unsealed through the channel of Congress"—that Conway would be proved an "incendiary." Nowhere, among all Gates's assurances of the "harmless" character of Conway's critique, was there a single quotation from that paper or the hint of an offer to let Washington have a copy of it.

Gates's letter was followed by one in which Conway made similar assertions and averred that only the arguments of Laurens and others had deterred him from publishing what he had written Gates, but he, too, failed to send a copy to prove what he affirmed. Washington had no intention of resuming personal relations with Conway and ignored the letter. The case with Gates was different. Conway was imposing on Gates, perhaps, but Gates must not be permitted to impose on Congress and the Army. It was of small importance to know what was in the critical letter, but it was a matter of duty to expose the duplicity that attended the circulation and then the suppression of it.

On February 9 an answer to Gates's defence of January 23 was completed, an answer that wisely was hung on a few brief questions, especially: If the letter of Conway was so "harmless," why was it not made public? Washington did not permit his letter to indicate that he merely differed with Conway on a question of strategy or tactics concerning which there could be two opinions. The issue was one of sincerity or its equivalent, military *bona fides*. He was determined to make that clear:

Notwithstanding the hopeful presages, you are pleased to figure to yourself of General Conway's firm and constant friendship to America, I cannot persuade myself to retract the prediction concerning him; which you so emphatically wish had not been inserted in my Last. A better acquaintance with him, than I have reason to think you have had, from what you say, and a concurrence of circumstances oblige me to give him but little credit for the qualifications of his heart; of which, at least, I beg leave to assume the privilege of being a tolerable judge. Were it necessary, more instances than one might be adduced, from his behaviour and conversation, to manifest, that he is capable of all the malignity of detraction, and all the meanness of intrigue, to gratify the absurd resentment of disappointed vanity, or to answer the purposes of personal aggrandizement, and promote the interests of faction.

Before this was dispatched and probably before it was written, Henry Laurens informed his son at Headquarters that he thought Gates desired a reconciliation with Washington. The younger Laurens showed part of this letter to Washington, who remarked, in effect, that Gates was merely the instrument of dangerous men. Greene was not precisely of that mind. He thought Mifflin was at the head of the opposition to Washington and suspected that Gates was party to it. Whoever the men might be that supported Conway in his cabal against Washington, they were, Greene thought, in great discredit and were "prodigiously frightened."

Washington scarcely cared whether they were aggressive or disheartened. He would scotch Conway; for the rest, he wished all friends of America to work amicably together. In this state of mind he received on February 23 Gates's acknowledgment of his letter of the ninth, which apparently had not reached York until the eighteenth. Gates said:

> . . . [I] earnestly hope no more of that time, so precious to the public, may be lost upon the subject of General Conway's letter. . . . In regard to the parts of your Excellency's letter addressed particularly to me, I solemnly declare that I am of no faction; and if any of my letters taken aggregately or by paragraphs convey any meaning, which in any construction is offensive to your Excellency, that was by no means the intention of the writer. After this, I cannot believe your Excellency will either suffer your suspicions or the prejudices of others to induce you to spend another moment upon this subject.

Washington replied the next day:

> I am as averse to controversy, as any Man and had I not been forced into it, you never would have had occasion to impute to me, even the shadow of a disposition towards it. Your repeatedly and Solemnly disclaiming any offensive views, in those matters that have been the subject of our past correspondence, makes me willing to close with the desire, you express, of burying them hereafter in silence, and, as far as future events will permit, oblivion. My temper leads me to peace and harmony with all Men; and it is peculiarly my wish, to avoid any personal feuds with those, who are embarked in the same great National interest with myself, as every difference of this kind must in its consequences be very injurious.

Washington prudently made reservation in the words "as far as future events will permit." He had reason for doing this because of a letter from Patrick Henry, who enclosed an anonymous missive that repeated most of the complaints against Washington. Not once was the name of Washington used, but the innuendo was that of his incompetence in command. The author took good pains to say that if his handwriting gave a hint of his identity, the name must not be mentioned. "Even the letter," one anxious sentence ran, "must be thrown in the fire." To Washington's astonishment, the autograph unquestionably was that of Dr. Benjamin Rush, who, Washington wrote Henry, "has been elaborate and studied in his professions of regard for me, and long since the letter to you." Nothing was to be gained by raising an issue over this, but it was enough to keep Washington on the alert.

Whether or not rivalry and backbiting were renewed, Washington thus far had profited by what now had come to be known as "Conway's cabal." If any ambitious officer or politician had been under the impression

that amiability and politeness covered a compliant nature readily dominated by more positive minds, they discovered in the exchange with Gates
that the head of the Army could be a vigorous, unflinching adversary—a
man best left alone or treated with the deference he showed to others. He
might not be invincible in controversy but, with the resources he commanded, personally and through his friends, he was not to be assailed by
any who took their task lightly.

All the supporters of Washington felt sure that Conway arrogantly
had conspired against him—and probably had hoped for larger pay and
greater influence under a new head of the Army; but few could believe the
Frenchman had either the finesse or the knowledge of America required to
lead so complicated an enterprise as that of getting rid of a leader whose
popularity still was greater than that of any other soldier or any Delegate.

Who, then, was prompting Conway or using him as a mouthpiece?
Gates and Mifflin were the two men most widely suspected, and they were
thought by some to have given indisputable proof of their purpose to sup-
plant Washington. Their ambitious wish was taken for granted: their
hostile acts could not be specified to the satisfaction of all of Washington's
supporters. Alexander McDougall wrote Greene, for example, "I have
heard much of the machinations of a certain junta to intrigue our Chief
out of command, but I want such proof of it as will bear the public eye."
In the case of Mifflin, even those most convinced of the Pennsylvanian's
leadership in the cabal were well nigh baffled in their attempts to draw a
moral indictment of a man who fast was acquiring the arts of political
equivocation.

Gates was in a category different from that of Conway and Mifflin.
The victor of Saratoga was believed to be anxious to succeed Washington
and was proved to have corresponded with Conway. Gates's disregard of
the channels of command was deliberate and must have been designed to
establish independent relations with Congress. In the same way, his early
acts as President of the Board of War were not those of an official disposed
to cooperate with the Commander-in-Chief. Washington believed Gates to
be hostile, but from the time Gates was caught in the inconsistencies of refusal to make Conway's letter public, Washington apparently felt that
Gates would not again associate with the Frenchman or make another
effort at an early date to win first place in army command. Even so, Washington kept up his guard.

It would have been miraculous if every influential officer at Valley
Forge had remained uncritical of Washington throughout the hardships
and hunger, the crowding and the shivering of the weeks-long torture in
the wintry camp. Complainants may have been numerous; active sharers in
the move to displace Washington were few. When the immediate exchange
of correspondence and gossip had ended, he wrote:

That there was a scheme of this sort on foot, last fall, admits of no doubt; but it
originated in another quarter . . . with three men who wanted to aggrandize
themselves; but, finding no support, on the contrary that their conduct and views,
when seen into, were likely to undergo severe reprehension, they slunk back,

disavowed the measure, and professed themselves my warmest admirers. Thus stands the matter at present. Whether any members of Congress were privy to this scheme and inclined to aid and abet it, I shall not take upon me to say, but am well informed that no whisper of the kind was ever heard in Congress.

Although Washington did not name the individuals who told him of the attitude of Congress, those who gave him assurance included, among others, President Laurens and Charles Carroll of Maryland. At strongest, the hostile, the disaffected and the unacquainted in Congress and in the Army showed themselves so feeble when challenged that this question rises: Should Washington have given attention to the cabal? Washington made no effort to answer the question while the maneuvers against him were in progress, and later he had more important concerns. His observations, at one time or another, show that he had mixed motives for giving serious attention to the affair: he confessed to Henry Laurens that knowledge that a "malignant faction" had been operating to his hurt "could not but give me some pain on a personal account. . . ." That was one consideration. The second and "chief concern," he told the same friend, arose "from an apprehension of the dangerous consequences which intestine dissensions may produce to the common cause." As he explained to Lafayette, the cabal involved the "fatal tendency of disunion." For that reason he was convinced that it should be resisted to the utmost. Washington took the action he did, in the third place, because he regarded Conway as a treacherous personal foe. The Frenchman's malignancy and, later, Gates's evasion violated Washington's sense of honor, aroused his wrath and made him resolve that he would not permit a self-seeking faction to drive him from his post of duty, service and honor. His enemies sneeringly styled him "demigod," but he was in nothing more completely human than in dealing with the Conway cabal.

Resolute as Washington proved to be in facing the cabal and trying to hold the Army together in the winter of 1777–78, he could not say until after the end of April that he had defeated Conway finally and irrevocably. While the Frenchman was at Albany preparing for the Canadian irruption, he had been deep in discontent, particularly after the coming of Kalb. By the beginning of April Conway was outraged that another man now had the place he had desired as Inspector General. Once again he professed his willingness to resign, and injudiciously did so, in tones promptly described as "taunting." Congress accepted the resignation and refused to reconsider when Conway expostulated that he had not meant his letter to be more than a private communication to President Laurens. Conway's strange influence was at an end.

Washington could not write that word "end" at the bottom of the story of Valley Forge on March 15 or on April 1. Even when the mud dried in the roads and green appeared in the fields, he had no assurance his troops would get sufficient meat every day. There was emergence, not deliverance, from the miseries of Valley Forge. If at last, by good fortune, Washington did not have to fear that his men would be half-starved before a week was out, he always had an accumulated burden of business, the most galling part of which was put on his shoulders by men who wished to leave the Army.

No particular regret was recorded when Joseph Spencer resigned the Rhode Island command and his commission as Major General, but as neither Putnam nor Heath was acceptable in his stead, Washington had to send Sullivan and with no guarantee that Congress would elect an additional officer of divisional rank. At the time the command in Rhode Island was being discussed, it was apparent that a change would be necessary in New York also. On March 16, McDougall was named to relieve Putnam whose standing as a commander was alleged to have been destroyed by indolence, ignorance and patent incompetence. Among field and company officers the "rash of resignation" had become a disease that menaced and might prove mortal. It was especially severe in the cavalry and in the Virginia regiments but was so nearly pandemic that Washington estimated the number of resignations at more than two hundred within eight months.

The Count Pulaski and the Marquis de Lafayette became problems. Pulaski spoke no English, did not understand Americans and soon found himself in so much difficulty that he resigned the general command of the cavalry and successfully solicited permission to organize an independent corps, in which he was authorized by Congress to enlist deserters if Washington approved. Washington had no intention of allowing this. The Commander-in-Chief consequently was surprised and provoked to learn, a little later, that Pulaski had been recruiting among prisoners of war. It was in part because of Pulaski's mishandling that Washington saw little prospect of having the cavalry take the field in the spring, though there was reason to hope for good performance by young Harry Lee who was promoted to Major and entrusted with recruiting and directing independently two companies of light dragoons. Lafayette was a problem of a different sort. He was able, diligent, appreciative and almost embarrassingly affectionate. At the same time he was ambitious and so insistent on the avoidance of any impairment of what he considered a high reputation that after the failure of the irruption into Canada, he had to be nursed and coddled by Congress and by Washington.

When all the whims and frailties and derelictions of malcontents were added to the doubts of the campaign, Washington still found hope for America in the performance of two men that spring, one a newcomer and the other an old lieutenant with a changed assignment. On February 23 an attractive German soldier had come to Valley Forge with letters from President Laurens, who introduced him as "Baron Steuben" and explained that Congress had voted its thanks for the gentleman's tender of service as a volunteer and had directed him to report to Washington. Washington's questions elicited the admission that Friedrich von Steuben, who said he had been a Lieutenant General in the service of Frederick the Great, was interested in the training of troops and would be glad to receive the rank and pay of a Major General, though he did not desire the command of a division.

The apparent candor, the asserted rank and the delightful personality of Steuben prompted Washington to approve a temporary arrangement which soon created confidence in the character, equipment and zeal of the Prussian. Within little more than a fortnight, Washington detached one hundred men as a supplementary Headquarters Guard and assigned them to Steuben for training. By the end of another week Washington was writing of Steuben as a "gentleman of high military rank, profound knowledge and great experience in his profession," who was to be "at the head" of a "department of inspection." Washington announced that Steuben "[had] obligingly undertaken to exercise the office of Inspector General" and, until the pleasure of Congress was known, was to be obeyed and respected in that position. Congress soon approved and made him a Major General.

While Steuben was introducing uniform and expeditious maneuver, Washington saw that better equipment and transportation would be made available to the Army through the skillful, industrious and military approach of Greene to his new duties as Quartermaster General. Hampered as Greene was by the resignation of Mifflin's deputy, he proceeded to employ to advantage the business experience of able new assistants and devote his energies to what he knew to be a task of great complexity.

Training under Steuben and the improvement of the quartermaster service by Greene soon could be left to the men in charge. Sound methods were solving a few of the difficulties that had baffled Washington's previous attempts. An arrangement by which hides were bartered for shoes worked out surprisingly well and, by the end of April, supplied footgear for most of those in painful need. Nakedness was not yet covered. The Clothier General was regarded by some officers as arbitrary and inefficient and was increasingly unpopular. As for provisions, Washington was able on March 1 to thank the Army for the patience it had shown during the days of shortage, which Commissary officers appeared to have overcome. Congress now was nervously concerned over the failure of the Commissary and no longer was disposed to defend the system disastrously adopted in 1777. Wadsworth was prevailed upon to become head of the purchasing division under amended regulations. Soon the word from optimistic officers was, "we fare much better than heretofore," though it was undeniable that life in the camp still was meager, uncertain and dirty.

A little later in the spring, evidence of jealousy of the Army on the part of a certain element in Congress led Washington to protest:

. . . without arrogance or the smallest deviation from truth it may be said that no history, now extant, can furnish an instance of an Army's suffering such uncommon hardships as ours have done, and bearing them with the same patience and fortitude. To see men without clothes to cover their nakedness, without blankets to lay on, without shoes, by which their marches might be traced by the blood from their feet, and almost as often without provisions as with; marching through frost and snow, and at Christmas taking up their winter quarters within a day's march of the enemy, without a house or hut to cover them till they could be built, and submitting to it without a murmur, is a mark of patience and obedience which in my opinion can scarce be paralleled.

Perhaps it was not unnatural that some Delegates felt the jealousy of which Washington sought to make them ashamed by recounting the misery his men had endured. A Congress of few members, and most of them undistinguished, was laboring long hours and expending too much of its time on financial accounts it tried to discharge with a currency that continued to depreciate.

Long bargaining over a special exchange of Charles Lee and Gen. Richard Prescott was successfully terminated. During the last stages of this negotiation, Washington had instructed Elias Boudinot, the Commissary-General of Prisoners, not to permit trifles to stand in the way because, said Washington, he never had needed Lee more. When final arrangements were made for the parole of Lee within the American lines as a preliminary of his full exchange, the Commander-in-Chief fashioned for his senior lieutenant such a reception as would have been accorded the victor in a campaign that had liberated Philadelphia or New York. An escort of horse under a member of Washington's staff awaited the paroled General at the British picket on April 5. The Commander-in-Chief and most of his senior officers went out to meet Lee at the lines and escorted him to Headquarters. Mrs. Washington was hostess to Lee and to those who came to do him honor.

He proved to be the same self-confident individualist. If any change had occurred it was of the sort that disposes a prisoner or invalid to be autocratic and to covet more power than usual because he has been exercising less. Even before Lee's parole ended in complete freedom of action, he forwarded Washington a new "Plan for the Formation of the American Army in the least Expensive Manner Possible . . ." with the statement, not altogether jocular: "I have taken it into my head that I understand it better than almost any man living." Reluctant to be matched with the inconspicuous Prescott, he had proposed that he be exchanged for Burgoyne. Said Lee to President Laurens: ". . . to speak plainly and perhaps vainly I am really convinced as things are circumstanced, I am of more consequence to you than General Burgoyne is to the other party." Although it may have bruised the conceit of Lee, he was traded for Prescott, not for the loser at Saratoga, and back on duty, he soon was trying to prevail on Congress to give him the rank of Lieutenant General.

Whether Lee would justify by his counsel and leadership his conception of his importance or would repeat the part he had played in the dark drama of the late autumn of 1776, Washington required all the sound counsel the Army could get, because, as April advanced, the American cause had to face the possibility of a double, perhaps triple, British offensive. One prong of the coming attack was to be political. Lord North had introduced two "reconciliation bills," one to set forth the intentions of Parliament concerning the exercise of the right to tax the Colonies and the other to appoint commissioners to "treat, consult, and agree upon the means of quieting the disorders subsisting in certain of the Colonies, Plantations and Provinces of North America." Washington wrote Laurens:

The enemy are determined to try us by force, and by fraud; and while they are exerting their utmost powers in the first instance, I do not doubt but that they will employ men in the second, versed in the arts of dissimulation, of temporizing, negotiating genius's.

It appears to me that nothing short of independence can possibly do. The injuries we have received from Britain can never be forgotten, and a peace upon other terms would be the source of perpetual feuds and animosities. Besides, should Britain from her love of tyranny and lawless domination attempt again to bend our necks to the yoke of slavery, and there is no doubt but that she would, for her pride and ambition are unconquerable, no nation would credit our professions, nor grant us aid. At any rate, their favors would be obtained upon the most advantageous and dishonorable terms.

All the Delegates were of this mind and promptly adopted resolutions designed to convince the people that the British proposals were nothing more than a snare for unwary feet. When Governor Tryon sent copies to Washington of North's bills, the American commander acknowledged the documents and said they would have a "free currency" among his soldiers. As a return compliment Washington forwarded prints of a resolve of April 23 in which Congress recommended that the States offer pardon to those citizens who had joined or aided the British forces in America. Tryon was asked to distribute this paper.

The British offer of peace thus was blunted before it was delivered. Would there be one other offensive, or two, a campaign by General Howe from Philadelphia and one by Sir Henry Clinton, based on New York City? Washington was not sure. In anticipation of active combat involving all the American forces, Washington recalled absent general officers and studied closely the confusing movement of ships to and from Philadelphia and New York; but he could ascertain nothing tangible. Reports of heavy reenforcement of Howe's army in Philadelphia seemed to be unfounded. Washington considered the possibility of an attack on New York and sought on this the counsel of McDougall. On the subject McDougall was to study, Congress had opinions of its own. Its members had been thought negligent in not providing for the better defence of the Hudson, but at length they ordered the demolition of what remained of Forts Independence and Ticonderoga and directed Gates to resume command of the Northern Department. As a result, McDougall could come back to the main Army, where he would be most welcome; Gates would be free to make his own plans which he might or might not communicate in advance to Washington. Nothing was done by Congress to reduce the authority of the Commander-in-Chief; nothing was said of any restriction of Gates's command within his department, but Congress quietly made it plain that Washington remained in fact what he was in title. Washington was "authorized and directed" on April 18 forthwith to convene a council of war and, with its advice, "to form such a plan for the general operations of the campaign as he shall deem consistent with the general welfare of these States." To this instruction, a few amendatory lines were added that may have seemed perfunctory—"that Major Generals Gates and Mifflin, members of the Board of War, have leave to attend the said council." The purpose was unmistakable: As Major Generals, these critics of the Commander-in-Chief were subject to his summons and under his orders. Congress gave them leave from the Board that they might answer the call of their superior officer.

Washington had intended to take counsel with Gates, and now he wrote not only Gates and Mifflin but also Gen. John Armstrong and invited all of them to the council. The letter to Mifflin was stiff but unexceptional. Gates could not leave York as soon as he had hoped, for which reason the council had to be deferred; but the delay was not of consequence, for by April 23 it was reported that Gen. Sir William Howe had been recalled to England and that Gen. Sir Henry Clinton was to succeed him in command. While Washington suspected Howe might try to strike a parting blow, he doubtless reasoned also that some weeks might elapse before the new commander would have a plan ready to put into execution. Washington and his senior officers meantime could consider alternatives he already had formulated—offensive against Philadelphia, attack on New York, or continued defensive. If Gates or Mifflin or anyone else could demonstrate the superiority of one plan over the others, Washington wished it done. The larger relation of Gates to the plans of the Commander-in-Chief, and of Washington to administration on the upper Hudson, was clarified by Congress on April 21 when instructions to the head of the Northern Department were adopted. Gates was not to stop supplies sent to the main Army from New England; when called on to do so, he must dispatch Continental troops to reenforce Washington, while privileged to ask for help from the divisions in the middle States. Gates was to conform, also, as far as practicable, to the plan adopted at the council of war Washington was to assemble.

In anticipation of that council, the general officers at camp were expressing a diversity of opinion. Most of them favored an offensive but all of them took into account the difficulties that compelled the Commander-in-Chief to list as the third possibility: "remaining quiet in a secure, fortified camp, disciplining and arranging the Army, till the enemy begin their operations, and then to govern ourselves accordingly."

Almost everything in the Army had suffered direly from neglect, or despair or incompetent direction during that frightful winter at Valley Forge. ". . . at no period of the war," Washington had to write Congress, "have I felt more painful sensations on account of delay than at present. . . ." Richard Henry Lee was to be more outspoken in a letter he soon was to write Thomas Jefferson: "For God's sake, for the love of our country, my dear friend, let more vigorous measures be quickly adopted for reenforcing the Army. The last draft will fall greatly short of the requisite number."

It was now the end of April; 1778 thus far had been a nightmare of cabal and intrigue in command, and of pallor, hunger, tatters and foul odors at Valley Forge. For what torture of spirit must Washington now steel his soul? That very morning of April 30, he had written Henry Laurens an appeal for a half-pay bill and almost despairingly, had said:

I do not to this hour know whether (putting half-pay out of the question) the old or new establishment of the Regiments is to take place; how to dispose of the officers in consequence; whether the instituting of the several other corps, as agreed to by the committee, and referred by them to Congress, is adopted or not; in a word, I have no ground to form a single arrangement upon; nor do I know whether the augmentation of the Cavalry is to take place, or was rejected, in order that I may govern myself thereby. . . . In short, our present situation (now the first of May) is beyond description irksome and dangerous. . . .

There had been other letters to answer and as the day wore on there came two more by express, one from McDougall and the other from Simeon Deane, a stranger. Washington opened and read: Deane had left Brest on March 8, aboard *La Sensible,* and after a swift voyage had reached Falmouth April 13. He had hurried on to York in order to deliver to Congress five packets. One of them contained the text of a treaty, signed February 6, at Versailles, by which France recognized the independence of the United States.

CHAPTER / 14

"I believe no event was ever received with more heartfelt joy"—that was the observation of Washington in the first letter he wrote Congress after receiving the news that France had recognized the independence of the United States. Soon everyone at Valley Forge heard of an agreement that opened a new and more hopeful period of the Revolution. On May 5 the Commander-in-Chief was free to inform the Army officially:

It having pleased the Almighty ruler of the Universe propitiously to defend the Cause of the United American-States and finally by raising us up a powerful Friend among the Princes of the Earth to establish our liberty and Independence up[on] lasting foundations, it becomes us to set apart a day for gratefully acknowledging the divine Goodness and celebrating the important Event which we owe to his benign Interposition.

The next morning hasty arrangements were carried out jubilantly by men whose pride covered their nakedness. At nine o'clock the bridgades assembled and listened to the reading of the treaty and a discourse by their chaplains. An hour later the regiments were inspected and commanded to load their arms. Next, the brigades marched into the field and formed. As a compliment to the French officers, Lafayette was given command of the right of the first line and Kalb was put in charge of the second. When all the troops were ready a triumphant salute of thirteen guns was delivered. A running fire of musketry followed from right to left on the first line and then from left to right on the second. A shout went up, "Long live the King of France!" A second salute and *feu de joie* were a prelude to the huzza, "And long live the friendly European powers." A final tribute, with the same accompaniment, was, "To the American States." The men marched from the field and received each a gill of rum. Washington saw it all and, when the ceremonies were at an end, entertained the commissioned personnel of the Army at a cold collation—"profusion of fat meat, strong wine and other liquors."

What would be the effect of "those fatal documents which seemed," as one British observant wrote, "to stamp a seal upon the separation of America from England"? The alliance was a boon for which Washington scarcely had permitted himself to hope; but he held to the conviction that America's first reliance had to be on herself, and he saw a danger in complacency. If this could be avoided, the alliance meant that France's aid would supply, in some measure, what General Kalb had described as the "one obstacle . . . which exceeds all others, the absence of a navy." France might not be able to end speedily the domination of American waters by the British, but she could reduce it. Arms, clothing, monetary aid and needed foreign goods likewise might be forthcoming from the ally. Beyond this, it seemed that self-help was the surest way of making French help effective.

An "immediate good consequence" of the treaty, Washington thought, would be that the States would "shake off their languor and be stimulated to complete their battalions," but when he returned to the tasks of organization he found the old story repeating itself. Congress approved a plan for the "establishment" of the Army, but it accepted an unpalatable compromise of seven years' half pay for retired and disabled officers. A shortage of arms was reduced by a shipment from New England; but inoculation, exposure and the diseases of crowding and undernourishment incapacitated close to four thousand of the troops at Valley Forge at a time when the flow of recruits was slow. Washington felt it necessary by the middle of May to call for the five thousand militia Congress had authorized.

Even in the continuing military squalor and misery of Valley Forge improvement in the Army was discernible. It was the task of Washington to see that this gain was not cancelled by the officers who usually made trouble for him. In spite of repeated notice that he was leaving America, Thomas Conway lingered in hope of being restored to command. Thomas Mifflin reappeared as a division commander—and speedily left camp to answer formal inquiry by Congress into his accounts as Quartermaster General; restraint had to be set on the zeal of Baron Steuben, whom some of the line officers suspected of ambition to take over the direction of their troops; it was not until May 9 that Gates finally quit Valley Forge to resume command of the Northern Department.

Conway, Mifflin, Steuben, Gates—to the diversified perplexities these four represented those of Lee were added. He returned to camp shortly before May 21 and received temporary command of Lincoln's Division. Washington took pains to stipulate: ". . . in case of action or any general move of the Army, the three eldest Major Generals present fit for duty are to command the two wings and second line according to their seniority." When misunderstandings developed Washington reaffirmed the orders, but he could not quite satisfy Lee, who continued to angle for promotion to Lieutenant General.

To the difficult question of administration two others now were added. The first was, what should and what could he do to aid in assuring a firm rejection by America of proposals the British ministry were certain to make in accordance with Lord North's "reconciliation acts"? On May 30 an invitation from Sir Henry Clinton for a personal interview was promptly declined on the ground that military proposals should be in writing and diplomatic matters should be addressed to Congress. A little later three British commissioners undertook to procure from Washington a passport for their Secretary, Dr. Adam Ferguson, to visit York. Washington replied that he would not issue this without instructions from Congress and during the whole of the abortive negotiations refused to do more for the commissioners than to transmit dispatches. He was relieved to hear that the main condition of the commissioners was the demand he believed Americans would not accept, that of a return to British allegiance.

The other question was the perennial, what will the British attempt and how can they be frustrated? Washington estimated he would have about twenty thousand men for the campaign, plus three to four thousand militia from the middle and southern States and an unascertained force in the north. The British in Philadelphia, according to his intelligence reports, numbered ten thousand. An additional four thousand were in New York, and probably two thousand in Rhode Island. When these totals were presented May 8 to the council that Congress had directed Washington to hold, the unanimous advice was to keep the Army at Valley Forge, strengthen it, increase the cavalry, and await developments. This accorded entirely with the judgment of Washington.

Before the American commander could do more than make his first approach to a new concentration and a protracted defensive, he received from spies the startling news that the British seemed to be preparing to evacuate Philadelphia and return to New York. Why, Washington could not guess; but if there was a prospect the enemy might move north forage must be accumulated on the roads through Jersey; troops marching south under McDougall must remain around Fishkill till the plans of the British were disclosed; and strong detachments should be moved close to Philadelphia.

For this assignment Washington selected Lafayette and gave the Marquis a select force of about 2200 men. Lafayette left camp May 18 and proceeded to Barren Hill, eleven miles from Philadelphia and about twelve from Valley Forge. Probably the next that Washington heard of Lafayette was the sound of alarm guns on the twentieth, fire that led him to order the troops at Valley Forge assembled and served with ammunition. Later he learned that Lafayette had been attacked by greatly superior force and had escaped narrowly an effort to entrap and destroy the American troops. It developed that Lafayette had chosen his initial position with care, had taken pains to acquaint himself with the adjacent ground and fords, and had kept his head. The trouble was that the "Marquis," as Washington wrote later, "by depending on the militia to patrol the roads on his left, had very near been caught in a snare; in fact he was in it, but by his *own dexterity* or the enemy's *want of it,* he disengaged himself in a very soldierlike manner. . . ." After the disappointed British went back to Philadelphia, Lafayette occupied Barren Hill a second time, and returned on May 23 to Valley Forge, where he was commended and congratulated. The Commander-in-Chief did not attempt again to set up a detached observation force within a day's march of the enemy.

Daily spies' reports indicated more and more strongly that the British were about to quit Philadelphia. The sailing of one hundred ships from the Delaware gave color to the prediction that the best of the enemy's troops were to strike out across Jersey for New York. Everything was made ready at Valley Forge, on the assumption that the British retreat would be overland to New York. Orders were drafted for the departure of Lee's Division for North River as soon as evacuation of Philadelphia was confirmed; Congress approved Washington's plans for the control of the city after the British left; Jersey militia were urged to operate in very small parties and to dog the march of the adversary. The first week of June ended with the enemy still in the Quaker City; the second week brought no change. On June 17 an impatient council of war acquiesced in Washington's judgment that the Army remain at Valley Forge until the aim of the British was clear. Then the expected news arrived: About sunrise June 18 Clinton's army had completed the evacuation of Philadelphia and assembled in New Jersey.

Washington took it for granted that the British were returning to New York; but would they proceed down the left bank of the Delaware and embark or would they move northward through New Jersey? Washington thought the enemy was preparing for the long march to the Raritan or the North River, and he gambled on this probability by starting a column of six brigades "towards Jersey" as soon as he heard of the enemy's departure from Philadelphia. He ordered Charles Lee and Anthony Wayne to carry these brigades north to Coryell's Ferry. Lafayette and Kalb were to follow with their Divisions on the nineteenth.

An easy march that day was the reward of careful preparation, but heavy rain on June 20 so delayed the troops that Washington halted for the night at Buckingham, ten miles from Coryell's Ferry. By noon of June 21, Washington was at Coryell's Ferry. On the twenty-second the advance of the enemy was at Mount Holly, about eighteen miles from Cooper's Ferry on the Delaware, opposite Philadelphia. Part of Clinton's men were at Moorestown, halfway between the ferry and Mount Holly. British shipping, except for two vessels, had dropped down the river below Reedy Island. Nearly all doubt of the enemy's prime intention was removed, but when Washington wrote Gates he displayed his usual caution: "these appearances," he said, "seem to decide that [the British] intend to traverse the Jerseys, though they do not appear to be in any hurry."

If the enemy was to operate in New Jersey, Washington now had to ask himself: Why were the British proceeding so slowly? Which of the northern routes would they pursue? How and where should they be opposed? At the moment the American commander could not surmise the reasons for so leisured a British change of base. As for line of march, Clinton could go north to Bordentown, pass around to Trenton and proceed via New Brunswick; or he could withdraw from Mount Holly on roads that ran more nearly with the meridian. After that the enemy would have a choice of points of embarkation on the lower Raritan, in Raritan Bay and at Sandy Hook.

If the British could be caught in motion on any of these roads, they would present an ideal target. Should Clinton's divisions be destroyed, now that Burgoyne's had been captured, then King George would have no troops left in the United States. Independence would be achieved. Glorious as that prospect appeared, Washington did not permit himself to think in terms of so overwhelming a single victory with an Army as feeble as the one just emerging from Valley Forge. Daring was balanced by caution:

Why stake on a single throw that which assuredly could be won by slow and careful play?

Washington was waiting for the British line of march to be disclosed. "We intend, as soon as things are in a train," he told Arnold, "to move towards them and to avail ourselves of any favorable circumstances that may offer." He wished the Jersey militia to continue the destruction of bridges and culverts; Arnold, whom he had put in command at Philadelphia, was urged to employ Pennsylvanians under the leadership of John Cadwalader in rear of the moving column to vex it; at every stage of the enemy's movement the local troops were to be exhorted to dog the Redcoats. Every leader of every detachment, regardless of size, was to do his utmost in collecting and forwarding intelligence promptly. Washington expanded in a letter to the President of Congress on June 22 what he had told Arnold: "We have been a good deal impeded in our march by rainy weather. As soon as we have cleaned the arms and can get matters in train, we propose moving to Princeton, in order to avail ourselves of any favorable occasions that may present themselves of attacking or annoying the enemy."

This shift was made by the Continental Army without incident. Before darkness on the twenty-third Washington opened Headquarters near the Baptist Meeting House at Hopewell, about twelve miles northwest of Princeton, and there he analyzed intelligence reports that were arriving in considerable number. Beyond all doubt, the enemy had reached Black Horse and probably was moving to advance on both the Crosswicks Road and the Bordentown Road. Now commenced in earnest a guessing game the like of which Washington had not seen since he had worn out his men chasing Howe's fleet. The task of the American commander was simply stated but difficult to execute: He must use his outposts, which he urged anew to vigilance and accuracy of report, in such a manner that he would have a force on almost every road the British might use, and, at the same time, must not so scatter his troops that he would be unable to concentrate quickly when his adversary's plan was disclosed.

For a day or two Washington suspected Clinton might be attempting to lure him to battle. Then it looked as if the King's men might be seeking to establish themselves on the high ground around Morristown. In the uncertainty that existed Washington decided to give his men another day's rest and hold a council of war. He found his Generals divided in judgment. Lee, who dominated the discussion, was of opinion that America would be justified in building a "bridge of gold" to expedite the march of the British across Jersey. The French alliance would assure independence; no battle should be fought at the time. Greene was strongly of opposite view but hesitated to speak out because he was performing staff duty; Wayne was for attacking; Duportail and Steuben both thought that if Washington could strike the enemy in motion he would have an opportunity which neither of them could describe adequately in English; Stirling and Knox agreed substantially with Lee; the young Marquis was vigorously in favor of detaching a strong force to assail the British baggage train or a part of their moving column.

The decision was to avoid a general engagement and to send fifteen hundred men to act as occasion might serve on the enemy's left flank and rear. All the members of the council signed this except Wayne, but few were satisfied that a correct solution had been found. Lafayette said with much feeling, "I would that a council of war would never have been called," and he, Wayne and Greene separately wrote Washington of their dissent. Greene's letter was to this effect:

> . . . I am not for hazarding a general action unnecessarily, but I am clearly of opinion for making a serious impression with the light troops and for having the Army in supporting distance. . . . People expect something from us and our strength demands it. I am by no means for rash measures but we must preserve our reputations and I think we can make a very serious impression without any great risk and if it should amount to a general action I think the chance is greatly in our favor. However, I think we can make a partial attack without suffering them to bring us to a general action.

Washington pondered this, but he complied with the council's recommendations and set up a force under Charles Scott "to fall in with the enemy's left flank and rear and give them all the annoyance" possible. The only addition made to the proposals of the council was to send Daniel Morgan and his small command to harass the enemy's right. These arrangements soon were found inadequate. Steuben reported June 24 that the enemy undoubtedly had taken the direct road from Allentown to Monmouth Court House; all other intelligence indicated that the annoyance of the British by small parties was make-believe warfare. Washington must move closer to the enemy and strengthen the force intended to worry the British. The first essential was met in part on June 25 by advancing the Army to Kingston. There Washington's main body of troops would be twelve miles from Cranbury, which Clinton would pass on his march.

This change of position was easy; the enlargement of the advance force immediately created more of those problems of pride and seniority that had burdened Washington for three years. The reenforcement of the column nearest the enemy should consist of one thousand men under Wayne, who believed in the offensive, but the senior of the forces operating on the flank and rear of the British would be Maxwell, who was not esteemed one of the best of the Brigadiers. It would be desirable, Washington reasoned, to put all these troops under Lafayette, a whole-hearted advocate of a vigorous policy. The difficulty in the way of doing this was the presence and the seniority of Lee. A man who favored a "bridge of gold" for the escape of the enemy was not a suitable officer to inflict the fullest possible punishment on the British.

Washington undertook to meet this in direct manner by personal appeal to Lee, who proved compliant. The proposed task, said Lee, more properly could be discharged by a "young, volunteering General" than by the second in command of the entire Army. Pleased and relieved by this, Washington proceeded to draft Lafayette's orders, but almost before the enthusiastic Frenchman could start Lee withdrew his consent and argued that if the detachment was to be large his "ceding it would have an odd appearance." Washington had to work out a new arrangement. The best he could advise was an awkward compromise whereby Lafayette was to have the honor of making the first move and of executing it fully if, when Lee came forward, the Marquis was engaged. After that, and earlier if Lafayette was not committed to action, Lee would have the usual authority of senior Major General.

While Washington negotiated this strange bargain on the twenty-fifth, he continued to receive intelligence which confirmed that the British were moving toward Monmouth Court House, an advance that threatened soon to put the enemy beyond reach. Washington concluded that he should shorten the gap between his Army and the Redcoats at the same time that he drew closer to his advance force. With the heavy baggage left behind, he moved his Army on the night of June 25/26 from Kingston to Cranbury, the nearest safe vantage ground in rear of the British columns.

At Cranbury he found new perplexities: the shift of his troops, the movements of the enemy and the exhaustion of men and horses in paralyzing heat had produced a temporary collapse of intelligence; the columns had outrun the Commissary wagons; Washington's own orders, certain officers' ignorance of the country and the general zeal to harass the enemy had scattered the Continentals and the militia so widely that with the possible exception of Lafayette's, none of these small forces could strike a blow or give weight to the attack any other troops delivered. The situation was almost out of hand. Unless Washington could act quickly and decisively, the supreme opportunity of assailing the enemy in motion would be gone.

Lafayette must move to Englishtown. He could be provisioned more readily there. Besides, if Lee decided to attack, Englishtown would be on the flank of the route the British were most apt to follow when they left Monmouth Court House. On the basis of this reasoning Washington directed Lafayette to move as soon as possible. Lafayette could not withhold the observation: "I do not believe General Lee intends to make any attack tomorrow, for then I would have been directed to fall immediately upon them without making eleven miles entirely out of the way. I am here as near as I will be at Englishtown."

It was now or never for an offensive against an enemy in motion. The American commander proceeded accordingly: He closed his column. Lee was directed to proceed to Englishtown and take command of the enlarged advance force of five thousand men, even though this meant that Lafayette temporarily might have no troops under him. The main Army must move up in support of Lee to Penelopen, three miles from Englishtown. Later in the day dispatches from the front indicated that the enemy still was at Monmouth Court House and might be on the point of moving ten or twelve miles northeast, to the heights of Middletown. Lee was told to confer with his subordinate general officers, secure his camp and make ready to attack the rear of the enemy the moment the British left Monmouth Court House. A strange answer came back: From his knowledge of the senior officers in the opposing Army, said Lee, he thought it highly probable they would turn about and strike, and if he had not been acquainted with them personally, he would have expected this of them as officers.

About five o'clock on the morning of June 28, a dispatch informed Washington the enemy were in motion. As this was dated 4:30 A.M., Washington had the speediest possible notice of a movement he had anticipated. With good fortune, he could hope for prompt pursuit. Troops left behind when Lee had marched off must be put in motion at once. Col. Richard K. Meade, the officer then on duty, must go to Lee, tell him to have his men leave their packs in camp, take the road, follow the enemy, and "bring on" an attack.

Washington soon afterward permitted first John Laurens and then James McHenry, a new member of his staff, to reconnoiter in the direction of Monmouth Court House, while he started the column towards that village. Washington could assume his troops well apportioned. Lee had about 5000 men and 12 cannon; Gen. Philemon Dickinson's estimated 1000 Jersey militia were close to the advanced column; Morgan was on the eastern flank of the enemy with 600 marksmen; the supporting force under Washington himself numbered about 7800. The left wing was led by Stirling, as usual; Greene was put in command of the right.

While Washington pushed his column forward he heard that Lee had shown irritation over conflicting intelligence reports but was continuing towards the rear of the enemy—a state of affairs that seemed to make it worthwhile to send new assurance that the main Army was in support. To bring that support into action at the proper time would call for the utmost energy, because men already were falling out from heat exhaustion. This was disturbing, but the reports from the vicinity of Monmouth Court House were encouraging: The enemy was moving off at "a quick pace"; Lee was about to attack the rearguard, and he had hopes of cutting it off.

About noon the sound of a cannon shot came from the vicinity of Monmouth Court House, then another and another and another to a total of four or five. No answering artillery fire was audible. The close and scorching air brought not a single echo of a small-arms volley. Washington sent Colonel Meade forward again to ascertain what was afoot, and when Maj. John Clark offered to convey to Lee any message the Commander-in-Chief wished to forward, the General bade the Major tell Lee to "annoy the enemy as much as in his power, but at the same time proceed with caution and take care the enemy don't draw him into a scrape."

No further sound of conflict rolled back. Nothing important happened until Alexander Hamilton drew rein and reported. Lee was about to engage, said the Colonel; would it not be well to turn Greene's troops to the southward, where they could cover the right flank of the Army in event the British defeated and pursued Lee? While Washington considered this, Knox returned from the direction of Monmouth Court House as hot in mood as in body. There was confusion among Lee's troops, said the Chief of Artillery; precautions should be taken against a possible reverse.

Be it so! When Greene's leading regiment came to Tennent's Church, let all the troops of the right wing file off to the south. They then would be on a road that followed for some distance the general direction of the main route from Englishtown. A couple of miles west of Monmouth the two converged at a point where, if need be, the Army could form line quickly. The left wing, meantime, need not deviate.

A stranger in civilian clothes now joined the group of officers. In a moment or two the General heard that the countryman had come from the vicinity of Monmouth Court House and had said Lee's troops were falling back. The tale could not be true. Washington rode on, but he had gone no farther than fifty yards when he had to pull in his horse once more. A few men were approaching from the east and soon were around him. One of them declared that the whole force in front was retreating. Again Washington could not believe the rumor. He had heard no firing except the cannon shot about noon; Lee had sent no word of any withdrawal; had the advance force encountered trouble, so experienced a soldier would have sent warning to a fellow-commander operating over unfamiliar ground.

Washington touched his horse and pushed anxiously on to a wooded ridge below which, to the east, a rebellious brook had spread the net of a long morass. In a few minutes he stopped, aghast: the yellow road in front of him, merciless furnace, was crowded with armed men. They were moving towards him in retreat, staggering, exhausted. The General was appalled. This was Long Island, Kips Bay, Germantown reenacted by veterans; it was defeat; it soon would be madness and chaos, because Washington had no plan or place to rally the men before the enemy was upon them.

Here was Israel Shreve, Colonel of the Second New Jersey. What, asked the General, was the meaning of the retreat? Shreve answered that he did not know; he was retiring by order. Washington turned away to seek better information and, in a few minutes saw Lee and some of his staff ahead of a withdrawing detachment. The Commander-in-Chief anxiously rode to meet him. In much astonishment, Washington asked sharply, What is the meaning of all this? Lee answered, in embarrassment, that contradictory intelligence had caused confusion, that he did not choose to meet the British when he was in that condition, that Gen. Charles Scott had abandoned a favorable position, and that the situation was no worse than that which arose when orders were not being executed properly. Besides, the attack had been made contrary to his opinion. Washington retorted hotly that whatever Lee's opinions, he expected his orders to be obeyed. If Lee had not believed in the operation, he should not have undertaken it. Washington hurried off and left Lee to expostulate that he was ready as a soldier to obey orders but was averse to general engagements and had opposed them in council.

Washington had thought for one thing only—to save those fainting and disheartened men who had retreated to strange ground, in that torturing heat, without firing a musket. At the front, where blind confusion prevailed, he met Robert Harrison. The enemy was pressing hard, the Colonel cried, and was within fifteen minutes' march! This was the first notice Washington had received that the Redcoats were so close, and for a minute or two it stunned him. How would it be possible to defend a position as

near the British as the ridge where he stood? Must he order a general retreat? While he was hesitating, Tench Tilghman spoke up: Lt. Col. David
Rhea of the Fourth New Jersey had passed a few minutes previously and
had remarked that he knew the district where they then were. It was militarily good ground. If the General wanted him, Rhea would be glad to
help.

Washington fairly leaped at the words. Send instantly for Rhea.
Washington looked about him for some shelter where he could rally the
troops of Lee. Fortune favored. Nearby, on the eastward gradient, was a
hedgerow. With terse commands Washington ordered all he met in the
field to post themselves behind this barrier. Henry Beekman Livingston on
his own initiative brought up his men and put them there—the first movement in a rally of the fugitives. Livingston was laboring firmly at this and
Washington was collecting other regiments when Tilghman returned with
Rhea, the most useful guide, surely, that ever came to Washington on a
field of battle. The ground where they stood, Rhea told the General, was
part of a long elevation. In front was a protective swamp. On the left, the
Army would find an eminence of some strength; woods in the rear would
cover any supports posted there.

The spirits of Washington rose at the words. Within a few moments
he was master of himself and of the situation. Hamilton wrote later: "His
coolness and firmness were admirable. He instantly took measures for
checking the enemy's advance, and giving time for the Army, which was
very near, to form and make a proper disposition." Wayne helped tremen-
dously in this by placing his unshaken brigade where it would be able to
hold off the approaching enemy, while Washington reassured Ramsey's and
Stewart's Regiments, ordered Varnum to form behind the hedge, and sent
an urgent call for artillery. Greene and Stirling must be left to find the
best positions they could on either wing.

Full effort achieved heart-stirring results. When, presently, smoke
and sound told of the arrival of the royal artillery on the east side of the
swamp, Col. Eleazer Oswald had four guns ready for a defiant answer.
Washington felt sure they would discourage an immediate British attack
and hurried off to see how Stirling fared on the left. There the
Commander-in-Chief came again upon Lee who apparently did not understand who was directing the action. Washington still was ignorant of what
had happened at the front, but his wrath had not cooled and he said
tersely that one or the other of them should take charge where they were.
If Lee would stay there, he would go back and form the centre. Lee was
agreeable. Washington galloped back to the ridge in anticipation of heavier assaults than Oswald's guns and Wayne's muskets could repulse for
long. The line behind the hedgerow must be strengthened. Not a second
could be lost.

The odds shifted again momentarily, because Stewart's and Ramsey's men were beginning to waver and had to be relieved. Elsewhere the
rally was taking form. Stirling was trying to get ten cannon in a good position, with Maxwell's Brigade in support of the wing; Steuben was available
to collect fugitives; Greene's men were filing in on the right; the men be-

hind the hedgerow were more numerous. Washington could reason that he soon would have a better chance of redeeming a desperate hour, but, of course, he had to expect attack here, there, anywhere the enemy might find him weak, and he might have to face a general assault, something his Army never yet had withstood. The outcome would be desperately close: it must not be fatal.

Now the British cavalry swept thunderously forward within forty paces of some of the Continentals—only to turn away in the face of the American fire. A few minutes more and Stirling's guns were biting British advancing against the American left, above the head of the morass. On the opposite flank another force had found lodgment, but it was met by such vigorous challenge that the Redcoats had to hug the ground to protect themselves. Washington saw all this and waited with what appeared to be complete self-command. In a short time the British still were using artillery with some vigor but infantry fire had ceased. It was now past five o'clock. The sun, still high, was abating its fury. Thirst, not heat, was the worst torture of the troops. Minutes passed without further attack or demonstration. Did this mean that the enemy had enough? Washington could not be sure, but, a little later, Wayne moved carefully out and succeeded, as he believed, in driving the last of the British back across the swamp. A counter-stroke, Washington thought, now might be delivered. He sent word to Steuben to bring up reenforcements for pursuit of the enemy, and he attempted to throw out Gen. William Woodford on the right and Gen. Enoch Poor on the left, with that officer's regiments and the North Carolina Brigade.

Gallantly, if not gladly, these troops went forward—only to halt because, in Henry Dearborn's words, the men were "beat out with heat and fatigue." The flanking columns remained at the point of farthest advance; the fire died away; Washington's men had unchallenged control of the field where they had been rallied. "We remained looking at each other," said John Laurens later, "with the defile between us, till dark. . . ." The next morning, the troops awakened to find the enemy gone. Only the debris of the field, the badly wounded and the unburied dead, 217 of them, were left on the ridge and on the edges of the morass. Evidence of this severe British loss and fear that the enemy were beyond pursuit gave thoughtful American officers a feeling of mingled pride and humiliation. Washington desired, of course, to press the enemy, but on June 29 heat and the weariness of the men forbade, and on the thirtieth—another exceedingly hot day—intelligence made it clear that the British could not be overtaken.

The last day of June was not destined to be merely hot and quiet. Without any hint of what was coming, Washington received from Lee a letter that began with this flourish:

From the knowledge I have of your Excellency's character, I must conclude that nothing but misinformation of some very stupid, or misrepresentation of some very wicked person, could have occasioned your making use of such very singular expressions as you did on my coming up to the ground where you had taken post:

they implied that I was guilty either of disobedience of orders, of want of conduct, or want of courage.

Lee wished to know "on which of these three articles you ground your charge, that I may prepare for my justification, which I have the confidence I can do, to the Army, to the Congress, to America, and to the world in general." With this he warmed to his subject. No one absent from the scene could be the "least judges of the merits or demerits" of Lee's maneuvers to which—he asserted it without blush—"the success of the day was entirely owing." Lee had, he affirmed, the right "to demand some reparation for the injury committed," and unless he could obtain it, he would retire, "when this campaign is closed, (which I believe will close the war) from a service, at the head of which is placed a man capable of offering such injuries. . . ."

The assertion that success was due entirely to Lee's "maneuvers" was discounted that same day by a letter in which Wayne and Scott described events of the forenoon of June 28. The two Brigadiers declared, in effect, that the advance of Lee's column had caught the enemy in motion, and that, after the British rearguard turned to attack the van, American troops thrown forward in support had repulsed the Redcoats. Wayne and Scott then had taken what they described as a position ideally formed for defense, but they found the troops on their right melting away, and when Wayne sent to Lee to have these withdrawing regiments halted and returned to their post, Lee sent back "no answer than that he would see General Wayne himself." This, said Wayne and Scott, "he never did." The two brigades had been left without support and had been compelled to pull back. Wayne and Scott concluded with these words: "We also beg leave to mention that no plan of attack was ever communicated to us, or notice of a retreat, until it had taken place in our rear, as we supposed by General Lee's order."

Washington did not intend to argue that point or any other now, but he could not ignore Lee's reference to "singular expressions," to "injuries" and to "justification." This answer was dispatched:

SIR: I received your letter (dated through mistake the 1st of July) expressed as I conceive, in terms highly improper. I am not conscious of having made use of any very singular expression at the time of my meeting you, as you intimate. What I recollect to have said was dictated by duty and warranted by the occasion. As soon as circumstances will permit, you shall have an opportunity, either of justifying yourself to the Army, to Congress, to America and to the world in general; or of convincing them that you were guilty of a breach of orders and of misbehavior before the enemy on the 28th. instant in not attacking them as you had been directed and in making an unnecessary, disorderly and shameful retreat. I am, etc.

Colonel Fitzgerald carried this in person to Lee and brought back a reply as amazing as the first letter. Lee begged pardon for the error of dating—and made another of like sort in heading his new communication June 28 instead of June 30. He then indulged himself in this: "I trust the temporary power of office, and the tinsel dignity attending it, will not be able, by all the mists they can raise to offiscate [offuscate] the bright rays of truth." Meantime, Lee concluded, "Your Excellency can have no objection to my retiring from the Army."

In a later letter of the same day, Lee said that reflection had convinced him a court of inquiry "should be immediately ordered. . . ." With this request, which was not unusual, a prudent officer would have ended the exchange; Lee would not have it so. He defiantly offered this antithesis: ". . . but I could wish it might be a court martial." With that he leveled a new threat: "for if the affair is drawn into length, it may be difficult to collect the necessary evidences, and perhaps might bring on a paper war betwixt the adherents to both parties, which may occasion some disagreeable feuds on the continent; for all are not my friends, nor all your admirers." Lee then proceeded to his final challenge: "I must entreat you, therefore, from your love of justice, that you will immediately exhibit your charge; and that on the first halt, I may be brought to a trial, and am, sir, your most obedient, humble servant."

Lee asked a court-martial. He should have it! There followed consultations, some drafting of papers, and then a brief word to one of the staff: please ask Adjutant General Scammell to come to Headquarters and bring his sword and sash with him. Scammell arrived promptly. Washington gave him this document to deliver officially and in person to General Lee:

> Head Quarters, English Town,
> June 30, 1778
>
> SIR: Your letter by Colo. Fitzgerald and also one of this date have been duly received. I have sent Colo. Scammell, the Adjutant General to put you in arrest, who will deliver you a copy of the charges on which you will be tryed. I am, etc.

Announcement of the trial was made in the next day's orders: "A general court martial whereof Lord Stirling is appointed President will sit in [New] Brunswick tomorrow (the hour and place to be announced by the President) for the trial of Major General Lee." It soon was known everywhere that the paper handed Lee by Scammell had ordered trial:

First: For disobedience of orders, in not attacking the enemy on the 28th of June, agreeable to repeated instructions.

Secondly: For misbehavior before the enemy on the same day, by making an unnecessary, disorderly and shameful retreat.

Thirdly: For disrespect to the Commander-in-Chief, in two letters dated the 1st of July and the 28th of June.

Never had the main Army experienced such a sensation; never had there been such heated discussion of personalities, not even in the Conway cabal. Young staff officers, Laurens and Hamilton in particular, were vehemently critical of Lee because they knew what his orders had been; Wayne and Scott stood squarely to their charge that Lee, in effect, had not exercised command when he met the British. Every aspect of the accused officer's conduct was reported. Fair-minded men doubtless recognized the difficulties he faced because of his unfamiliarity with the ground, the cease-less calls of his subordinates for instructions and, to quote Lee's own words, "a crowd of visitants and spectators, acting in no capacity" who "galloped in so furiously" that they might have alarmed the troops; but why he had ordered his large force to retreat before a numerically inferior foe with scarcely an exchange of fire the court would have to ascertain.

By the time that tribunal began to take testimony on July 4 the Army's talk was of the closing campaign rather than of the opening trial. Morgan had attempted to follow the retreating British, but he had been able to do little. The enemy marched almost without challenge to Nave-sink and thence to Sandy Hook, New York and Long Island. Washington gained only in deserters, who continued to slip from the British camps. Weather continued almost unendurably hot, but it did not interfere mate-rially with the observance of the second anniversary of the Declaration of Independence. The ceremonial was in a sense a celebration of Monmouth and was similar to the exercises that had proclaimed the French alliance. To many of Washington's supporters, the day in retrospect became still more joyful on receipt of news from Philadelphia of a duel Cadwalader had fought in answer to a challenge Conway had sent him because of an alleged slur. Cadwalader had shot the Frenchman in the face, not fatally, as some feared and others hoped.

The Army remained a week at New Brunswick and then marched through Newark towards position at Paramus. All reports were that the British, too, were "reposing," in Washington's own word, at the stations to which they had returned, a circumstance that led him to believe the first stage of the campaign of 1778 was at an end. As reviewed by Washington's admirers, the operations were declared a credit to him and to the troops. Congratulations from Henry Laurens were in the strain of the address by the Massachusetts Legislature after the liberation of Boston, and with this tribute came unanimous thanks of Congress to Washington and the Army.

As surely as Monmouth was a defeat for Lee, it was a victory for Wash-ington. Never had he appeared to such advantage as a combat leader. When all accounts were balanced—the dead counted, prisoners cared for and deserters marched off—Clinton's ranks were thinner by twelve hun-dred and more, losses perhaps five times those of the Americans. The battle was the best the Army yet had fought, the nearest approach it had made to victory in the field when the whole British force was at hand. Actions at Trenton and Princeton had been with detachments: This time all of Clin-ton's troops had been near enough to have participated if their commander had wished to have a full engagement.

Clinton manifestly did not want a fight in Jersey. It was not certain where or when he subsequently would seek battle. After the British had embarked, presumably for New York, Washington thought it might be wise to place part of his Army on the east side of the Hudson to strengthen the defence of the highlands, but he delayed transfer until he could ascertain the views of Gates, whose whole attitude during the march of the British through the encumbering sands of Jersey had been one of cheerful co-operation.

Change of base brought diversion and relief. Washington's troops continued the recovery they had begun at New Brunswick. Their reward was long sleep and rations usually full; Washington had larger compensation than even the thanks of Congress. He learned that the Delegates of nine States had signed the Articles of Confederation and that the "perpetual union" might become a reality when the other States assented. To no man could this mean more than to the patient General who had groaned over many a line he had written in an effort to persuade the States to support the common cause; but federation was *in futuro*.

Nearer, running through the camps, was rumor of tremendous import: New York had heard that a strong French fleet was off the coast! In a letter of General Arnold's, received on July 11 from Philadelphia, Washington read that the sailing of French men-of-war from Toulon for a voyage to Chesapeake Bay had been set down as undisputed fact. On the night of July 13 confirmation was on Washington's table in a dispatch from Congress, with a terse description of the fleet and unqualified announcement that the vessels had appeared off Chincoteague, Virginia, under the command of Vice Admiral Count d'Estaing.

Arrangements for signals and pilots were made; plans were sketched for passing the Army to the left bank of the Hudson, whence it could demonstrate against Manhattan Island at the time of d'Estaing's arrival. John Laurens, who spoke good French and had the distinction of being the able son of the President of Congress, was directed to proceed to the Jersey coast and deliver a letter of welcome to the Admiral. In this first message to his new colleague Washington had to begin the confession of the hundred humiliating inadequacies of his Army: he could not even inform d'Estaing of the strength or composition of the enemy's fleet in nearby New York.

Washington proceeded on the fourteenth with part of the Army to Haverstraw, on the west side of the Hudson, opposite King's Ferry. That evening he received a letter of June 13 from d'Estaing and a duplicate of one, dated June 8, that had not reached American Headquarters. In display of cordial spirit and desire to share immediately in decisive action, these communications were a model for any ally. D'Estaing was off Sandy Hook and was encouraging the pilots to find a channel through which he could carry his deep draught vessels to attack Lord Howe's fleet that was riding at ease "within the Hook." The French Admiral was eager to know Washington's plans. "I have orders to second them," he wrote, and added: "I dare assure you that I will do it to the utmost of my power. To act in concert with a great man is the first of blessings. . . ."

That general sentence would have been all the more gratifying to Washington if he had known the entire story of d'Estaing's landfall. The tedium of eighty-seven days at sea and a shortage of water and provisions made d'Estaing anxious to get his casks refilled and his sick ashore. When he found no conveniences available and no duty to perform at the mouth of the Delaware, he left after a single day of waiting and proceeded north. On reaching the vicinity of Sandy Hook June 11, d'Estaing was confronted with a change of heart in the pilot who had come aboard off the Delaware and had promised to take the fleet inside the Hook, where, the man said, sweet water might be obtained easily. D'Estaing, puzzled and almost desperate, soon concluded that a reconnaissance had to be made on shore, and he undertook it in person. He reached land with much difficulty, only to find himself in what appeared to be a hostile community where his host, a Quaker, proved to be more English than American in sympathy. He contrived to make his way into the estuary known as Shrewsbury River where he was told he might reach fresh water by digging. This adventure cost the life of a marine officer and four sailors. Several rowboats sank. At this stage of d'Estaing's unhappy experiences, on July 16, Laurens came out to the flagship, though he ran great risk of being drowned, and dispelled most of the Admiral's misgiving; but the best pilots thereafter procured for d'Estaing could not point out a sure and safe channel, nor could Washington comply with d'Estaing's request for a plan of action until he knew whether the French ships could assail effectively the British vessels. Delay in opening the attack on New York seemed certain, though it gave the enemy time for preparation and might involve the arrival of reenforcements for the British fleet. Meanwhile, d'Estaing was lowering his supply of water and getting reports of a steady rise in the number of men with scurvy.

Was there an alternative to swinging impatiently at anchor in the treacherous waters off Sandy Hook while pilots continued to seek a channel that might not exist? The question might be answered for Washington in a letter that brought him on July 17 a proposal by Congress that the operations of d'Estaing be directed against Rhode Island, where the destruction of a small squadron might open the way to defeat of the British garrison under Maj. Gen. Sir Robert Pigot. Washington gave this immediate study and found in it strategical excellencies that prompted him to make the basic preparation: John Sullivan, then commanding opposite Rhode Island, was authorized to call out sufficient militia to raise the total American force in that region to five thousand men. Washington decided, also, that whether the next objective was New York for the entire Army or Rhode Island for part of the troops, he now would be more advantageously placed east of the Hudson, and he executed the transfer July 15 through 18. As soon as this movement was completed, Washington dispatched Hamilton to d'Estaing to show him the proposal for an attack on Rhode Island and explain the new position of the Continental Army. The next night, July 19, Laurens returned from the French fleet and reported the Admiral so nearly in despair of finding a channel that he was considering the very course Washington had sent Hamilton to suggest. Washington consequently felt that he could assume the departure of the French fleet for Rhode Island as almost certain and that he should begin movement of troops in that direction. Gens. James Varnum and John Glover were ordered to start their brigades on the twenty-second. Some of these troops had not been twelve hours on the road when Washington learned from Hamilton that d'Estaing had abandoned hope of accomplishing anything at Sandy Hook and had decided to proceed to Newport.

Washington thus far had not seen the French Admiral, but correspondence had been altogether correct and friendly. Now d'Estaing was leaving the area of Washington's direct command and was going to the district where the retirement of Joseph Spencer had led to the appointment of Sullivan as American commander. The New Hampshire General had courage and a sense of organization, but he was excessively ambitious and disposed to be overconfident until some adversity threw him into a desperate mood. His record as a military diplomatist was negative, though he had fraternized with some of the French officers in American service. If Washington had doubts concerning Sullivan's part in the critical experiment in cooperation, he wrote nothing on the subject, but he quickly assured himself that the men who headed the reenforcements should be as suave in diplomacy as they were skilled in war. Lafayette was given divisional command of the two Continental brigades, Varnum's and Glover's. Not long previously, the sensitive feelings of Greene had been hurt because he had thought Washington critical of him. As an emollient, as well as a deserved distinction and a service to the French, Washington directed Sullivan to reorganize all the Continentals and militia into two divisions, with Greene in command of one and Lafayette responsible for the other. This was an arrangement not beneath the dignity of Greene, because Washington, in advance of the appointment, told Sullivan to disregard the authorized limit of five thousand for the expedition in Rhode Island and collect as many militia as the New England States would supply. If these temporary troops were forthcoming in adequate number, Greene and Lafayette each would have a division that counted as many men as either had commanded in earlier operations. With these two officers to assist Sullivan and d'Estaing a hopeful prospect took on shining color.

Washington was firm in belief that a glorious victory would be achieved when the French fleet reached Newport. At last the balance of power was shifting! "The fairest hopes that ever were conceived," and the "moral certainty of success," as he said later, now were America's. In that spirit he rode to White Plains on the afternoon of July 20 with the intention of establishing Headquarters at the familiar village on the upper road to Connecticut. A personal letter to Thomas Nelson included this observation:

It is not a little pleasing, nor less wonderful to contemplate, that after two years' maneuvering and undergoing the strangest vicissitudes that perhaps ever attended any one contest since the creation, both Armies are brought back to the very point they set out from, and that that which was the offending party in the beginning is now reduced to the use of spade and pick axe for defence. The hand of Providence has been so conspicuous in all this that he must be worse than an infidel that lacks faith, and more than wicked that has not gratitude to acknowledge his obligations. . . .

Had the General pursued this idea he might have been disposed to admit that if the providence of Almighty God was manifest in the confident return of a more experienced American Army to White Plains, the handiwork of the devil was to be seen there in the hearts of dissatisfied and quarrelsome officers. Rank and seniority were in dispute; contention among the Virginia Brigadiers was undiminished; Alexander McDougall and Johann Kalb were engaged in a polite exchange over the dates of their respective commissions; Steuben was angling for line command. Washington valued Steuben's service but he faced so many vexations in dealing with officers from other countries that he included even Steuben when he wrote a friend in Congress, "I do most earnestly wish that we had not a single foreigner among us, except the Marquis de Lafayette, who acts upon very different principles from those which govern the rest."

A score of other vexatious puzzles had to be solved—if that were possible—while Washington waited for a decision in Rhode Island. He seconded as best he could the efforts of the Board of War to procure clothing; he had to disapprove an operation against Detroit at a time when he might be required to send more troops to Sullivan; and he contended for weeks with varied disabilities among his senior officers. Putnam procured leave to go to Philadelphia where he had the satisfaction of getting Congress to approve the findings of the court-martial that acquitted him of culpability for the loss of Fort Clinton and Fort Montgomery. Arnold still reported himself physically unable to take the field, in spite of Washington's wish to employ him in the main Army. It seemed desirable to leave the invalid in Philadelphia, where he was making both friends and enemies by a tolerant attitude towards Loyalists.

Lee's case took a turn still different. At the time of the arrest of that officer, Hamilton had doubted whether the court would condemn the leader of the advanced force at Monmouth. "A certain preconceived and preposterous opinion of his being a very great man," said the aide, "will operate in his favor"; but the violence of Lee's reckless utterances had destroyed this illusion. "By all that's sacred," he wrote Robert Morris on July 3, "General Washington had scarcely any more to do in (the Battle of Monmouth) than to strip the dead." He credited himself "with great presence of mind and not less address," and he insisted that "although my orders were perpetually counteracted," he maneuvered the British "from their advantageous ground into as disadvantageous a one." When Lee found there was no general support of these assertions, he began to complain, "No attack, it seems, can be made on General Washington but it must recoil on the assailant." The hearing had been inclusive, though the court had been compelled to move with the Army. Lee conducted his defence with little skill and did nothing in cross-examination to shake the testimony of those who maintained, in effect, that he scarcely knew what was happening at the front. He called few witnesses and his principal aim seemed to be to establish the courage and coolness of his behavior on the field, rather than to demonstrate the wisdom of his dispositions and the skill of his maneuvers. His summing-up exhibited far more regard for phrase than for fact. The court concluded the hearing on August 9, and, on the third day of deliberation, found Lee guilty as charged. His sentence was suspension "from any command in the armies of the United States of North America, for the term of twelve months." Some observers thought the sentence so severe that they feared Lee's partisans and chronic malcontents would make an issue of it, but the event was to show no wavering in general support of Washington. Washington had resolved to say nothing of

Lee or the case before final action was taken by Congress and made no comment in forwarding the proceedings to Congress on August 16.

Even had he felt it proper to discuss the outcome of the trial, he would have been too busy. His long wait for news from Rhode Island was ending in a confusion of reports and of events worse, if possible, than the silence and the fog of the sea. Washington had received word on August 4 that d'Estaing had anchored safely off Rhode Island July 29 and that the promise of high achievement still held. Then the Commander-in-Chief heard little for days, either because Sullivan was preoccupied or because he ambitiously had resolved to conduct the campaign in his own way. Almost the only intelligence of importance developing in New York was that on August 7 Lord Howe's men-of-war had sailed from Sandy Hook—a voyage that Washington considered to have no other purpose than that of a demonstration against Sullivan and d'Estaing, unless, the British Admiral expected reenforcement while at sea. This news was followed, on the eighth, by a dispatch in which Sullivan announced that the British at Rhode Island had destroyed the whole of their naval vessels, four frigates and a tender, a little squadron that Washington had hoped d'Estaing could compel the enemy to surrender intact.

By August 13, Washington had an extraordinary dispatch of the tenth from Sullivan. Few details were given in Sullivan's letter, as he proceeded immediately to this disconcerting review: The French had on the eighth passed up the Middle Channel, and silenced two batteries. Early on the morning of the ninth, hearing that the British had evacuated the northern end of Rhode Island, Sullivan had begun landing troops in order "to prevent their reoccupying the works." This was an advance in the schedule of the operations about which d'Estaing was unaware, and he had not put his troops ashore on the opposite side of the island. Sullivan consequently threw his line across to the Middle Channel, facing south, and sent a request to the Admiral to disembark the French contingent.

Before this message reached d'Estaing or Sullivan even had completed his transfer of force to the island, some of the lookouts, nearer the open sea, had a sight that made every man gasp and wonder: the morning fog suddenly lifted; to the south were ten white dots on the gray ocean, the sails of large ships. Minute by minute the number increased until about thirty could be counted. At one o'clock steady eyes and good telescopes made out the colors. They were British. By 1:30, no less than thirty-five vessels were in sight. Lord Howe's fleet had arrived at the worst conceivable time—when the French warships were high up the Middle Channel and Sullivan's troops landed where they might be cut off and destroyed.

After Sullivan's report explained that a "small and unfavorable" wind compelled the French to keep their position for the remaining hours of the ninth, the paper before Washington's eyes ran to a climax:

> . . . this morning [the Admiral] got underway with a fine breeze, passed the batteries at Newport and those which are below, with all his ships of the line and went in chase of the English fleet. At 11 o'clock I had the pleasure of seeing them fly before him. The Count has left three frigates in the East Passage. It is out of

my power to inform you when we shall make the attack on the enemy as it is uncertain when the French fleet will return, and I think it necessary to wait their arrival as their troops are on board.

Washington knew that Sullivan's force soon would reach a total of approximately nine thousand, and he continued of opinion that Howe's appearance at Newport was no more than a demonstration, but anxiety was deepened by a violent storm from the northwest on August 12–13. D'Estaing had promised he would return, a guarantee Washington accepted. Until it could be fulfilled, Sullivan must make the best of the situation. Reports that reached White Plains during the next few days did not strengthen Washington's optimism. Nothing had been heard of d'Estaing, and the American commander felt uneasiness that a fleet short of water should be compelled to remain so long at sea, but he renewed his hopes of success when he found that Sullivan was recovering confidence.

Had the commander at White Plains been informed of happenings around Newport prior to the departure of the French fleet, he would have been alarmed no less for the outcome of the experiment in cooperation than for the safety of d'Estaing's ships. Sullivan's ambition to win a shining triumph combined with his inexperience as a military diplomat had produced discord from the first. Where Washington or Greene would deferentially have suggested cooperation, Sullivan had written in plain, direct words: "I wish . . . your Excellency would make a show of landing your troops. . . ." And again, "you will move your ships. . . ." Sullivan thus aroused a measure of resentment in d'Estaing's heart. D'Estaing was disappointed in the more serious matter of American preparations. "Creator of what was called an army by the General," the French commander wrote later of Sullivan, "we found that the troops were still at home." When Lafayette approached, "he announced that he had soldiers; he appeared with nothing but militia," though he soon won d'Estaing's admiration for the rapid disciplinary improvement of his force. The French were dissatisfied also with the arrangements for supplying water and provisions. When Sullivan had changed his plan, d'Estaing had been surprised but had resolved to do his full part. Later the arrival of the British without any previous warning from American Headquarters made the French marvel, half in disgust, at the incompetence of Continental espionage.

By August 21 Washington heard that some of Lord Howe's ships had returned to Sandy Hook on the seventeenth. Rumors were circulating, also, of a naval battle and of the approach of a British squadron under Vice Admiral John Byron. Reports told of a large concentration of transports at the southwestern end of Long Island Sound. On the twenty-fourth Washington received an alarming letter that Sullvian had written August 21. The commander on Rhode Island spoke of the "situation of *Languedoc* and another ship of the line" which evidently had been dismasted in the recent violent storm at sea. One other man-of-war was missing. With his damaged fleet, d'Estaing had returned to the vicinity of Newport but had almost determined to go to Boston for the repair of the crippled vessels. This would leave the American troops stranded where they might be overwhelmed by Pigot's force with a little help from any British squadron that might arrive. A later dispatch from Sullivan came before daylight on August 25 with a diversity of papers that had passed between French and Americans. As Washington put the facts together from these exchanges he acquired this better understanding of what had happened in Rhode Island: After the departure of d'Estaing's fleet, Sullivan had made his dispositions for attack, and under the cover of a protective fog he had established his batteries. During the progress of this work, Sullivan heard not a word from the French, with the result that by the sixteenth he became alarmed that he might not have the promised support of d'Estaing. When Sullivan at length received dispatches, the French fleet was again off Newport but d'Estaing proposed a change of base on the ground that Boston had better facilities for repairing ships. In giving notice of his proposed move, the Admiral requested that three frigates and a corvette which had remained when the ships of the line had put to sea should rejoin the fleet at Boston. Sullivan was outraged. The general officers joined in a protest that summarized the arguments for the retention of Newport as the French base. Departure, said the officers, was "highly injurious to the alliance formed between the two nations," but d'Estaing with all the war-vessels sailed away on the night of August 21/22.

Had the affair ended here, it would have been militarily disappointing but it would not have threatened danger to the alliance. D'Estaing probably could have reported nothing worse to his government than that the Americans were not sufficiently adept in war to conduct offensive operations, and the Americans could have said that they had done their utmost but had encountered delay, British good luck and an adverse act of God in the storm that scattered the French fleet. But the temperament of Sullivan and the plight of his forces prevented this easy and amicable termination of an unpleasant episode. His ambition balked and his utter defeat not improbable, Sullivan lost his head. Through General Orders of August 24 he made references to the French in these words: "The General cannot help lamenting the sudden and unexpected departure of the French fleet, as he finds it has a tendency to discourage some who placed great dependence on the assistance of it. . . . He yet hopes the event will prove America is able to procure with her own arms that her allies refused to assist her in obtaining."

This inexcusable slur prompted Sullivan's advisers, Lafayette in particular, most earnestly to urge a retraction that might reduce the ill will Sullivan's language was certain to create. The General did not change his mind but he undertook in General Orders of August 26 to erase his mistake. Whether he concealed his anger by his words might be doubted, but he probably went as far as his embittered feelings permitted.

Lafayette, according to Greene, "did everything to prevail upon the Admiral to cooperate with us that man could do," but the Marquis's "great thirst for glory and national attachment," the same witness had to confess, "often [ran] him into errors." Naturally, too, when d'Estaing was accused in officers' conversation of "deserting" the Americans, Lafayette's French blood rose and he defended d'Estaing with so much vigor that he provoked heated answers. "I am," he protested to the Commander-in-Chief, "more upon a warlike footing in the American lines than when I came near the British lines at Newport."

News of these unhappy developments came, item by item, to Washington. He concluded that further offensive attempts at Newport were impossible and that the sole strategical question was the manner in which Rhode Island could be evacuated without undue loss. What could be done for the exposed troops on Rhode Island depended both on what they could do for themselves and on the naval force that might be employed against them. When Sullivan at length reported a successful withdrawal to the northern end of Rhode Island, Washington called a council of war on his next maneuver but he did not find himself content with the advice of his Generals to stay where he was. Especially was he made uneasy by a report on September 2 of the arrival at Sandy Hook of six seventy-fours under Rear Admiral Hyde Parker. Fortunately, fear for the safety of Sullivan was relieved September 4 by a dispatch in which the General announced the uncontested withdrawal of his force on the night of August 30/31.

By September 4, d'Estaing had been for a week at Nantasket, though Sullivan and some even of his own officers had doubted whether he could complete the voyage with his crippled ships. Once there, he received a hurried visit from Lafayette, who wanted to know his plans and, particularly, whether he could not return to Newport; but the chance of this was past, and—what was more important—the passions aroused by the Admiral's departure and Sullivan's offensive order were less fiery. As soon as Washington had ascertained the heat of the feeling on both sides, he had decided that all attempts at conciliation should be deferred until tempers had cooled.

The first foreign officer whom Washington undertook to bring back to normal friendly relations was, of course, Lafayette. Washington did not run great risk that Lafayette would put salt into the wounds of expectation. D'Estaing, from the first, showed less resentment than he felt towards Sullivan. In replying to a letter Sullivan wrote after the fleet left Newport, the Admiral declined further argument. He went on: "If during the coming centuries, we of America and France are to live in amity and confidence, we must banish recriminations and prevent complaints. I trust the two nations will not be forced to depart from moderation in their conduct but that they will reflect in all their public affairs that firmness and consideration for public interests necessary to unity between two great nations." Washington, Hancock, Gates, Greene and other leaders did all they could to assuage the feelings of d'Estaing and allay the wrath of those who thought the Admiral had run from a fight. Congress did its utmost, too, in preventing a fracture of the strained alliance.

From careful observation of incidents reported to him at White Plains, Washington sensed that amity was not restored as completely as Sullivan thought and he continued to labor for fullest cooperation and quick repair of the damaged French men-of-war. He was prompted by mysterious British ship movements to start Gates's Division on September 10 for Danbury, Connecticut, in event reenforcements were needed on the coast of Massachusetts; but Washington could do nothing to prevent such outrages as developed from this British raid, which involved the burning of Bedford and Fair Haven in southeastern Massachusetts and the forced requisition of sheep and cattle on Martha's Vineyard.

This was followed by a succession of land maneuvers on the part of Sir Henry Clinton's New York forces. One or two transfers of men appeared to threaten serious consequences; other marches seemed designed to tease the Americans and keep them uneasy. Washington shifted some of his troops to deal with anything that might be involved in the landing on September 24 of strong British reenforcements at Powles Hook, but force without vigilance was vain. On the night of September 27/28, Col. George Baylor and the troopers of his small regiment were surprised at Old Tappan and were destroyed as a fighting force. A simultaneous demonstration at Dobbs Ferry necessitated a general alert, dictated the opening of Field Headquarters at Fishkill, and gave Washington an uncomfortable two weeks before the Redcoats withdrew. Washington had to face an organized protest by no less than 213 officers who felt that Congress was denying them a decent life and was stingy to the men who had led regiments that had been disbanded or consolidated. Attempted adjustment of disputed seniority in the artillery led to violent protests by two of the best-known artillerists of the Army, Lieut. Col. Eleazer Oswald, who resigned, and Col. John Lamb of New York, who fumed but stuck to his guns.

Other soreness and heartburning was connected either with the old bickering over rank and seniority or with the peculiarities of ambitious men. Mifflin had tendered his resignation; Charles Scott, a useful Brigadier, was talking of retirement. Lafayette created a sensation and made himself ridiculous by sending a challenge to the Earl of Carlisle, head of the British Peace Commissioners who still lingered vainly in America. The Marquis accompanied his theatrical gesture with a request for a furlough in order that he might return to France and survey the opportunities of service there and in Canada. Congress poured on the unction of formal thanks and yielded to his persistent application for the reward and compensation of his aides. Kalb was irritatingly maladroit in asking promotion for French officers; Thaddeus Kosciuszko was anxious to serve with Gates, was jealous of Duportail's control and was retained with difficulty in his assignment at West Point. Count Pulaski several times showed himself defiantly undisciplined, but because he was stationed in or near Philadelphia, his behavior exasperated the Delegates more than it troubled Washington.

Everything locked together in one bewildering puzzle of personnel, equipment, supplies, finance and resources in the early autumn of 1778. British ship-movements were as baffling as ever. Gates interpreted rumors to forecast an attack on Boston, an offensive that seemed improbable to Washington. Various observers thought the enemy was preparing to attempt the subjugation of South Carolina. President Laurens shared this view and doubtless sponsored in Congress the election of Benjamin Lincoln to succeed Robert Howe in command of the Southern Department. Virginia and North Carolina were called upon to supply militia reenforcements. Washington's own estimate of Clinton's plans shifted with events, but when intelligence was received in mid-October of contemplated or actual embarkation of as many as five or six thousand troops in New York, he concluded that some of these regiments were bound for the West Indies and some for South Carolina. At the same time, he conceded something to the fears of New England and increased Gates's force by three brigades, and then on October 23 he ordered McDougall eastward. Gates was authorized, at discretion, to proceed to Hartford but not to go farther until it was certain the British were bound for Massachusetts. A week passed without news. Then Washington learned of a resolution of the Delegates in Philadelphia that directed him "to order Major General Gates forthwith to repair to Boston." This made no real difference, but the action of Congress aroused the jealousy of Sullivan, offended the pride of Heath, and stirred antagonism between the more belligerent of Gates's supporters and Washington's. In this temporary, half-concealed renewal of strife, the recuperated Conway had a hand—perhaps his last disservice to America—by again presenting Gates as the persecuted savior of the country. The victor of Saratoga was left idle and isolated when the "scare" of an invasion of New England died away quickly.

Washington awaited disclosure of British plans and returned to sharpening dull tools by working the treadle of the old grindstone of disciplinary routine. Other duties of the autumn tried both his heart and his judgment. Because of the shortage of flour in New England, the "convention Troops" of Burgoyne's army were sent to Charlottesville, Virginia; numerous proposals for action against hostile Indians were canvassed and rejected or deferred; preparation was begun for a large raid into Canada but laid aside as impracticable in winter. Scarcely had this scheme been abandoned when Washington received on November 4 the text of a detailed plan for a joint French and American invasion of Canada in 1779. This had been considered by Congress, which had voted to send a copy of the plan to Benjamin Franklin and another to Washington with instructions to communicate it to Lafayette. It was not wise, Washington reasoned, to disclose to a citizen of any other country the considerations that might be decisive in passing judgment on the undertaking. Although Lafayette spoke of the project as if it had originated with him, Washington thought it might have emanated from the court of France and he examined it most carefully. His conclusion was that France and America jointly would not have sufficient strength for the conquest of Canada in 1779.

The nearer puzzle of British strategy continued to irritate and baffle the American commander. He had to confess: "I am every day more and more at a loss." Knox complained: "we cannot draw a conclusion of what will be done by what [the British] ought to do, for they often act directly against their own interest." Washington had thought Clinton and Howe might have been waiting on the result of the Peace Commissioners' efforts but when the failure of that venture was manifest, the armed forces of King George still nodded by their campfires or looked vacantly from portholes. In disgust Washington wrote of his adversaries: "They are indecisive and foolish."

Still another puzzle now was added to the mystery: D'Estaing left

Nantasket Road with his entire fleet on November 4 and gave Washington not even a hint of his plans or objective. When Washington learned the French fleet had left Boston, he could do no better than guess that it might call at Newport and assuredly would proceed to the shifted scene of international war, the West Indies. British seapower again might be uncontested in the waters of New York and New England, but it now was November. A British General who had done little since July was not apt to send out his columns to shiver in the wind. With no special misgiving, Washington put the American infantry in winter quarters at Danbury, Connecticut; West Point, New York; and Middlebrook, New Jersey, with the relative size of each station determined by the availability of supply and the strength of nearby garrisons. To find forage, the cavalry had to be dispersed all the way from Durham, Connecticut, to Winchester, Virginia.

Washington decided to establish his own Headquarters at Middlebrook, and on November 28 left for his new station with the intention of examining en route the progress of work at West Point. He stopped at Elizabeth, New Jersey,. in order to see Stirling and while there received an alarming report on December 4 that fifty-two British vessels were sailing up the Hudson. This started him toward Paramus, but news that the enemy had turned downstream again permitted him to resume the march to Middlebrook, where he arrived December 11. Headquarters were opened four miles from the village.

Conditions were incredibly different from those that had existed when the half-frozen Army had halted at Valley Forge. Provisioning now was easier, because the troops were divided. There was even greater difference in clothing, shoes and blankets. "Hutting" progressed steadily but so slowly that many men remained in tents for long weeks.

The news most frequently discussed while the huts were being raised at Middlebrook was that of final action in the case of Charles Lee. After one or two false starts, the Delegates on October 23 began intermittent discussion of the court-martial findings in circumstances that showed Lee high in the estimation of some members of Congress and still confident of acquittal. He figured in two sensations during the first week of December. One of these was a challenge to a duel with Steuben, who was satisfied when given assurance that Lee had not meant to reflect on him during the court-martial. The other was an article Lee printed in the *Pennsylvania Packet* under the heading "General Lee's Vindiction to the Public." Indirectly the paper was an exposé of the defeats Washington had sustained, but it failed to influence Congress. The Delegates voted December 5, six States to two, that the sentence of the court be executed.

Men still were discussing the case when Washington received a summons to Philadelphia for consideration of plans for the campaign of 1779. He quickly turned over command to Stirling and left Middlebrook December 21. In Philadelphia, Martha gave warm welcome, but an unpleasant number of changes had occurred: Henry Laurens had resigned as President of Congress, and John Jay had succeeded him; the Board of War was undergoing another reorganization; John Laurens had challenged and shot Lee seriously but not fatally in a duel provoked by the article in the

Packet, which the young aide had felt that Washington could not resent in terms of "the code"; Mifflin was under accusation of negligence or worse because one of his deputies was alleged to have used public wagons for the transportation of private property in what appeared to be formal trade.

The reception accorded Washington had about it no echo of any unpleasantness. Everything was done with deference and with the fullest honor on the floor of Congress, at the committee table, and in the city. Almost every night he was guest at an elaborate dinner, where he met friends of long acquaintance and officers who had come to Philadelphia on business or on leave. He was the more heavily committed to this pretense of gaiety because he and Martha were lodged at the Laurens residence, in front of which, so to say, half the carriages of the town drew up, and he was scandalized by the "idleness and dissipation" he observed. Conditions in general were vastly better at the year's end than they had been twelve months previously, but Washington encountered one progressively unpleasant surprise: The quality of Delegates to Congress manifestly was declining. The strong men and the wise were fewer in number.

Washington had prepared carefully the subjects he wanted Congress to review and now, day after day, he discussed them with the committee named for that purpose. His approach was to the fundamental, "the great impediment to all vigorous measures in the state of our currency." Lack of money made defensive strategy almost the sole military policy America could pursue, except perhaps for operations to stop Indian outrages on the frontier of New York and Pennsylvania. The Army must be strengthened by vigorous recruiting and the reenlistment of men for the duration of the war, even if a substantial bounty was necessary. Officers must receive better allowances, more consideration and, on retirement, half pay for life rather than for seven years.

Washington got little of what he sought for the better defence of the country. Congress authorized the General to offer such additional bounty as he thought proper, not exceeding $200 each to qualified new soldiers and veterans who would reenter the service for the remainder of the war. Washington received orders "to superintend and direct the military operations in all the departments in these States," subject to the general orders of Congress. Nearly everything else that Washington advocated for the campaign of 1779 was deferred through indolence and suspicion or lost in the mangle of administrative detail.

Several military decisions of importance were made, some with the approval of Congress and some on Washington's own account—to abandon the joint operation against Canada, to attack Staten Island if conditions were favorable, to forego an attempt to burn British shipping at St. John on Richelieu River, and to proceed with plans against the Six Nations. More immediate was the conclusion, by January 28, that the British had landed on December 27, 1778, a considerable force in Georgia and had defeated the few troops General Howe had assembled for the defence of the southernmost State. Savannah had been occupied by the enemy; Howe had been compelled to cross the river and, in effect, abandon Georgia to the invaders; Benjamin Lincoln wrote courageously of reentering the state as soon as he had sufficient force, but he said he had been told he could expect seven thousand men, exclusive of militia, and actually had fourteen hundred. Washington did not believe the enemy would gain anything in Georgia except provisions; at the same time he could not disregard the anxiety of Delegates from the southern States. Help had to be given: whence was it to come?

That question was the companion of Washington every hour. By the end of January he had discussed all phases of it with Congress, discharged his social obligations and given hours of his time to Charles Willson Peale, whom the Executive Council of Pennsylvania had commissioned to paint his portrait. With this under the artist's finishing brush and all other duties done, Washington procured the Delegates' approval and set out for camp on February 2. He was in deep depression of spirits over the plight of the currency, the wrath of factions and the divisions in Congress. Burdened in heart, Washington reestablished himself at his former station and undertook to answer the questions which he brought back with him from Philadelphia and those he found at camp.

First, what could be done to keep the British from overrunning South Carolina? His answer was to send Pulaski's troopers there. Further aid must depend on Virginia and North Carolina.

The second question arose, in part, from the first: If the main Army could do little for itself and less for Lincoln, what assistance could be expected from allies? The term was plural, because there was a flurry of hope that Spain would enter on the side of America; to say nothing of rumors of British readiness to make peace; but Washington applied the question primarily to the French: How would they help? The American had no answer until late April when Minister Conrad Alexandre Gérard and Don Juan de Miralles, the unofficial Spanish agent, came to camp. Washington had been told he might expect from Gérard some "very important information." This proved to be a highly confidential announcement that d'Estaing was to come to the mouth of the Delaware and then might proceed to the conquest of Halifax and Newfoundland. The Admiral wished to know whether America could garrison these posts, if seized. Washington replied that he could not use militia to hold the northern posts, because these temporary troops could not be trusted. He would be compelled to employ Continentals. To detach them from the feeble main Army would be to take the risk the British would overrun the middle States. Serious as this might prove, Washington would consider the possibility of such an expedition as his French colleague had in mind, provided d'Estaing had definite naval superiority over the enemy. A better plan might be the muster of all forces, land and naval, American and French, for the defeat of the British in New York and on Rhode Island. In event d'Estaing did not have superiority of force, the Admiral should assist in the liberation of Georgia and then, perhaps, he could operate against New York. Would the French fleet be more powerful than the British? Guarantee of that had to be given before Washington could make the heavy outlay for a concentration. When Gérard could give no such assurance, the alternative of French aid in the Georgia campaign was developed.

That possibility raised the third question: If the French might come to the coast after a successful campaign in the South, was it wise to detach an expedition to the New York-Pennsylvania frontier? Congress left the question to Washington who decided to proceed. His aim was to throw a superior force into the country of the Six Nations on both sides of the boundary between New York and Pennsylvania. Over the plans for this expedition, Washington labored day after day, and when Gates declined the command he gave it to Sullivan.

During the whole time that he was working his way out of these tangles Washington had to deal with discontent among his senior officers. Schuyler resigned as Major General and felt that Washington believed him justified in doing so; Heath was anxious to be employed actively again; Greene complained that Congress was doling out money for the Quartermaster Department in an amount "no more equal to our wants than a sprat in a whale's belly"; Wayne's high spirit was rankled by slurs of Lee whom he resolved to challenge to a duel; whether Mifflin could be court-martialed after Congress at length accepted his resignation was an issue of many legal thorns; Putnam, in charge of New England winter quarters, was anxious to go home; several other Generals were in distress of one sort or another.

In dealing with most of these officers, Washington had both patience and understanding and was sufficiently experienced to administer the medicine each man needed. Many other individuals were holding reluctantly to their commissions, when every month's service cost them part of the capital they had possessed in 1775. To Washington "the discontents and distresses of the officers" were symptoms of a most dangerous disorder. Congress' refusal even to consider half-pay for life and the endless contention in the Army over rank and seniority kept scores of Washington's subordinates seething.

Washington received under date of April 6 a letter in which John Jay enclosed an extract from a communication Gates had addressed to Congress. Gates had written of the various lines of advance into Canada and had referred to an exchange in which Washington had expressed disagreement with his opinion. The commander of the Eastern Department observed: "This being the only letter I have received from his Excellency since December, Congress will immediately judge of the extent or limitation which it is proper to observe in their instructions to me." This seemed to Washington to be an effort to "prejudice" him "in the public esteem," and as such it was blasted in a long reply which was devastating in detail and accompanied by exhibits of letters that went back as far as the Conway cabal. The finished letter did not leave Gates much reputation either for strategy or for courtesy, but it might well have puzzled the man to whom it was sent. Was it necessary to employ 3500 words in order to demonstrate that Washington's dislike of Gates was justified and as deep-seated as Gates's bias against his Commander-in-Chief? In relation to the American cause, this incident made it plain that the longer the mileage between the two Generals, the better the service each of them could render.

During the winter the enemy in New York had disturbed the Americans by nothing more serious than a demonstration against Elizabeth, New Jersey, February 25 and a simultaneous futile movement by Governor Tryon to Horseneck, Connecticut. During March and April some mysterious concentration of shipping had been observed; for a few days a maritime raid on New London seemed certain; but scares and alarms died away for a time. Washington could not believe the enemy would remain inactive long after May 1 and told his subordinates again and again they must have all in order by that date.

When May came with magazines unready, ranks thin and the country as negligent and greedy as ever, Washington was depressed, wrathful and alarmed in every nerve. His observation the previous month had been: "It is a melancholy thing to see such a decay of public virtue, and the fairest prospects overcast and clouded by a host of infamous harpies who, to acquire a little pelf, would involve this great continent in inextricable ruin." Now his warning was that unless leaders in the States bestirred themselves "our affairs are irretrievably lost." He never had seen a time, he said, when, in his opinion, the issues of independence "were at so low an ebb."

Danger was created to be overcome. That was the creed of Washington. He was ready, now as always, to apply it. On May 31 he gave Sullivan final instructions, and he read with steady eye dispatches that told for the first time of a British advance to White Plains. St. Clair must proceed at once to Pompton; another division temporarily under Woodford must follow. Then, on June 2, came word that the enemy had landed at King's Ferry, which linked Stony Point on the west side of the Hudson with Verplanck's Point on the east. From Stony Point the distance by road to West Point was barely twelve miles, but King's Ferry itself was a position of prime strategic value; it was the easiest crossing of the lowest stretch of the Hudson on which it was safe for American barges to operate.

No defences of any strength had been constructed at Stony Point. At Verplanck's a small post, styled Fort Lafayette, had been erected and garrisoned with a few score men. An adversary who had warships and transports in sufficient number could reach and occupy King's Ferry by a rapid movement whenever wind and tide favored. The important duty of the American commander was, if possible, to save Fort Lafayette and, afterward, at almost any price, keep West Point from falling into hostile hands. The Virginia Division consequently was ordered to follow St. Clair immediately; the Maryland troops were put on the alert to move on June 3.

That day brought bad news: The enemy was throwing up earthworks at King's Ferry; St. Clair wrote that Fort Lafayette had surrendered and that the intelligence forecast an advance by the enemy on West Point. Kosciuszko's defences of the Hudson citadel had been declared by Duportail feeble and incomplete; the loss of the post would be a calamity that might wreck the American cause. The whole Army must march. "Appearances," said Washington, "grow more and more serious."

In the first stage of the advance from New Jersey to the Hudson, though the spirit of the Army was high, the danger of a shortage of provisions seemed so acute that Washington had to threaten seizure. Fortunately, by a reversal of usual conditions, the supply at West Point was found to be larger than had been assumed and, in general, the service of the Commissary was improved. By June 5 Washington had reached Ringwood Iron Works. The British had occupied Verplanck's Point, had closed King's Ferry to the Americans, and had begun to fortify the western bluff, Stony Point, as if they intended to remain there. Washington himself had not attempted to garrison and hold permanently the high ground on the right bank, because he had not felt he could spare troops for that purpose; Verplanck's, in turn, had been allotted little more than a nominal force. These considerations did not lessen Washington's chagrin at the loss of Stony Point and of the convenient, much-used ferry there. He moved closer to the river and opened Headquarters near the tavern in Smith's Clove. Washington perceived, of course, that Clinton had acted with wisdom in seizing the southern outpost of the highlands, even though the British commander was proceeding slowly and did not appear to contemplate an early attempt at West Point. After a few days, American officers could say with Gates: "[Clinton's] delay has ruined him; he will be beat if he attempts [to take West Point] now; if he retires he will be disgraced in the eyes of his army. . . ." Clinton seemed aware of this and appeared anxious to reach a strategical compromise. The greater part of his fleet dropped down the river ere long and left the garrisons at Stony Point and Verplanck's to fend for themselves.

Washington consequently had to wait and plan and labor at the endless task of trying to maintain a strong, well-led Army on the feeble foundation of public languor. The senior officers whom he reluctantly placed in command of the wings were Putnam and Heath. A newcomer was General Howe who had high seniority though he had not distinguished himself in the Southern Department. The troops under these men stood at ten or eleven thousand infantry. There was humiliation in a defensive when the people expected vigorous effort, and there was annoyance and waste in hauling over longer roads the supplies that previously had been moved via King's Ferry. As early as June 15 Washington, who soon established himself at New Windsor, directed Henry Lee to collect intelligence on the strength of the British at Stony Point, and after Anthony Wayne arrived at the end of the month he had that officer make a more detailed study which he supplemented by a personal reconnaissance. The conclusion was that Stony Point might be captured by a surprise night attack, but that a simultaneous effort to seize Verplanck's Point would complicate the plan excessively. Troops could be advanced on the eastern side of the river, and if all went well at Stony Point, they might be used against Verplanck's.

Washington and Wayne undertook separately to draw up detailed plans for the operation, but the Commander-in-Chief had to turn aside immediately because of reports of a British maritime raid on Connecticut towns. New Haven was damaged grievously, Fairfield destroyed, and Norwalk burned before Washington could send substantial relief.

Washington expedited as best he could the project against Stony Point. In sending Wayne his ideas of a midnight surprise, he said: "You are at liberty to depart from them in every instance where you think they may be improved for the better." The operation was set for the night of July 15/16; Wayne's moderate revision of Washington's plan was presented the Commander-in-Chief the afternoon before the attempt was to be made. That evening Washington directed McDougall to send two brigades against Verplanck's as soon as the commander at West Point heard that Stony Point had been taken.

The night of the fifteenth was dark, a condition that would favor surprise, but the hours of darkness seemed long at New Windsor, and the early morning dragged slowly until Capt. Benjamin Fishbourne, aide to General Wayne, rode up to Headquarters and handed this dispatch to Washington: "This fort & Garrison with Coln. Johnston are our's. Our Officers & Men behaved like men who are determined to be free."

Washington asked immediately whether casualties had been heavy. Fishbourne replied, to the General's vast relief, that the post had been taken with inconsiderable loss. Although Wayne himself had received a facial wound from a musket-ball, he had continued into the works with the troops. Without waiting for details, Washington had Colonel Harrison draft a brief dispatch to be sent express to Congress. Adjutant General Scammell was directed to include announcement of the victory in General Orders of the day.

Verplanck's next! If the western end of the crossing at King's Ferry had been captured, the defenders of the eastern works might be frightened or bombarded into surrender even if there could be no surprise. In addition to pursuing his original plan of sending two brigades from West Point, Washington directed Howe to hasten to the left bank and assume command. Heath was ordered to Peekskill to take general charge of the operation.

Then, late on the sixteenth or very early on the seventeenth, Washington rode down to Stony Point, but he had to delay his anticipated review of the fine achievement of Wayne's men because action was still in progress. American gunners had been firing as many as one hundred projectiles an hour against the defences of Verplanck's; the British flag still was flying, and no heavy damage was apparent. One advantage only could be observed: the wind was blowing downstream and probably would give the Americans at least the whole of the day for an attack before Clinton could reenforce the place. Washington directed that the guns at Stony Point and those of Howe's command be concentrated on the blockhouse at Verplanck's in the hope that the destruction of this might induce the garrison to surrender; but the Commander-in-Chief was mistaken in assuming that his forces on the left bank were well supplied with artillery. They had none whatsoever and in other particulars were farcically unequipped for their mission.

The next day the chance of destroying Verplanck's was gone. A small British detachment was brought up the Hudson and thrown boldly into the defences from the waterfront; overland advance of strong forces threatened to cut off Howe and Heath. Withdrawal of the American troops on the east bank had to be approved. Swiftly these men moved as far northward as Mandeville's, opposite West Point—and left Washington to decide whether it was profitable, or safe even, for Wayne's Light Infantry to remain at Stony Point. The Commander-in-Chief had not planned to garrison permanently the crossing but had reasoned that if his soldiers could capture the two posts and damage them heavily the enemy would not attempt to reoccupy them.

The requirements for holding the fort made a convincing case against the retention of Stony Point. Washington had the cannon removed, the works demolished and the houses burned, and evacuated the place. On June 19 the enemy reoccupied it. For a while Washington thought hostile tenure might be brief, but he soon concluded the British would stay there unless he drove them off again.

Wayne's losses were only fifteen killed and eighty-three wounded. The British commander reported twenty killed, seventy-four wounded, fifty-eight missing and 472 prisoners. He lost, of course, the fifteen cannon of the works at Stony Point and a considerable volume of stores, the whole of which, guns included, later was appraised at $180,655. This was a result that could not have been achieved by other than well-led, disciplined troops who acted under a good plan. Wayne in every respect earned the commendation Washington gave him: ". . . his . . . conduct, throughout the whole of this arduous enterprise, merits the warmest approbation of Congress. He improved upon the plan recommended by me and executed it in a manner that does signal honor to his judgment and to his bravery."

In contrast, no praise could be distributed, because none was deserved, for the operations against Verplanck's Point. Washington may have been correct in deciding that a simultaneous attack on both sides of the river would be too complicated, but after coming to that conclusion he failed to prepare adequately for an undertaking that inevitably would be difficult in daylight, with the British garrison alarmed and certain to receive succor in a short time. The choice of Howe as leader of the advance on Verplanck's should have been avoided because the Carolinian had served with the main Army scarcely two months and had been incapacitated approximately half that time.

Washington seldom had failed previously to shift command or assignment in such a way that he shelved his less competent lieutenants and got capable men for difficult enterprises. This time he seemed to concentrate his thought on the operation west of the river and left the other to officers readily deceived or discouraged. For mishandling this part of his enterprise, Washington was himself to blame. Whatever prospect he had of discouraging the reoccupation of King's Ferry by the British he lost through failure to design against Verplanck's an operation as adequate as the one at Stony Point. In spite of this, the operation was worth everything it cost.

That was the view of a proud Army and grateful Congress. In the rejoicing over Wayne's achievement, Howe's failure was ignored. A vote of thanks was extended to Washington and Wayne. Rightly, too, praise was given the soldiers, the men who removed the abattis and captured the sentinels, those who waded through the morass with bayonets high, and all who made a reality of the watchcry, "The fort's our own."

While the country rejoiced over the success at Stony Point, Washington had to untangle a series of administrative difficulties. Had the General listed those of the early summer of 1779 his most appreciative admirers might have asked how and why he endured such vexations. The State of Massachusetts unwisely launched an expedition against the British at Penobscot, without asking either Washington's or Gates's counsel or giving them any facts about its inception and departure. Reenforcement of South Carolina by Virginia and North Carolina was so slow that only the patience of Washington could have endured it. The General labored over his perplexities in the face of contradictory reports of enemy ship movement. Washington considered the possibility of another attack at King's Ferry, but decided, instead, to strengthen West Point. He was reluctant to maintain the defensive all summer, but the condition of the Army left no alternative. Death and desertion, sickness and the expiration of service involved a heavy subtraction. Bad as this was, Washington confessed greater fear from the condition of the country's finances than from the thinness of his ranks.

The discouraging labor was relieved somewhat, as summer came, by reports of a French victory in the West Indies and by rumors, which proved false, of American successes at Penobscot and Charleston, South Carolina. Closer at hand, Washington himself and some of his young lieutenants scrutinized the British front to see if anywhere an opportunity comparable to that of Wayne at Stony Point could be found. Washington's survey led him to believe the British were negligent at Powles Hook, the defences on the west side of the North River opposite the lower end of New York Island, and he had Maj. Henry Lee make a reconnaissance.

This showed that the approaches were difficult, across a wide salt marsh, and that the place was fortified strongly, a situation that led Washington to shake his head. The possible gains did not justify the risks, but Lee soon devised a plan to seize the post if Washington would assign him four hundred men. The Commander-in-Chief finally told Lee the attempt might be made if the Major could assure secrecy, would promise to abandon the undertaking if surprise failed, and could get the approval of Stirling, who commanded in that district.

Stirling agreed: by August 18 Lee reported everything in readiness. Detachments set out from New Bridge on the Hackensack. Difficulties were encountered quickly. The principal guide proved to be either coward or traitor and followed roundabout, narrow lanes, on which the rear was separated from the main body. This approach delayed the advance seriously but, near dawn, Lieut. Mike Rudolph, who had been sent on reconnaissance reported the fort silent. Its ditch, though nearly full of water, was passable opposite the central approach.

That decided young Major Lee. He had word passed that the way was open. Without taking time to ascertain seniors, he directed that the commanding officers of the detachments immediately at hand should lead the columns, Rudolph and Lieut. Archibald McAllister were to head the forlorn hope. Success depended upon surprise, and surprise upon silence and vigilance. Off went the men. No sound came from the fortifications; not a single shot challenged the men as the right column halted on the outer edge of the crude tidal moat.

About four o'clock Lieutenant Rudolph reached the spot below the drawbridge where he had decided he had the best chance of getting across. The men plunged in and headed for the opposite bank, but they were excited and unable to wade slowly. Their dash into the water was noisy—as if a floodgate had suddenly been opened. From the line of the abattis came the shout of a sentinel, then the ring of his musket and, in a few seconds, the sound of a general alarm. Bullets soon were screaming. The forlorn hope, with the support of Maj. Jonathan Clark's men, broke through the abattis and found in the main work an opening that had been left for easy communication with the countryside. Once in the central defence, the Americans surprised scores of men in bewildered surrender.

Now, above the rattle of British muskets, there came the b-o-o-o-m of a cannon from the left. Should the Americans load and fire? Men who put their hands on their cartridge boxes realized they could not deliver a single round; they had not been told to take off their belts and hold their cartridges above their heads. All the powder of all the men was hopelessly wet. Some cool-headed men sought out the British magazine to get powder there, but the door was too stoutly constructed to batter down. The situation was becoming more dangerous every second; Lee's men must leave as soon as they could collect their prisoners.

With little difficulty and no immediate pursuit, Lee's party withdrew and started toward Secaucus, where boats were to await them. All went well until the Hackensack was reached near the point where the banks made a small island at Secaucus: One look was enough. Not even a skiff was in sight. Something had gone awry. The crossing was impassable on foot; the men must add more miles to the thirty they had traveled since the previous afternoon. Lee immediately wrote Stirling of his plight, sent off the message, and called on the troops to make a last effort.

The torturing worst of the long ordeal came as the detachment staggered along, hungry as well as exhausted. Prisoners marched with their guards; rods stretched to miles. At Weehawken crossroads Capt. Thomas Catlett of the Second Virginia appeared with fifty men and dry ammunition. As the rear of the column dragged past the intersection of the road to Fort Lee, Lt. Col. Burgess Ball of the First Virginia arrived with fresh troops whom Stirling had dispatched. Ball immediately started for a position from which he could cover the withdrawing detachment in the last stage of its march and, as he moved out, he saw a British force emerging from woods on the right. These Redcoats opened on the American rear; but Lee also had observed these assailants and he did not wait for his rescuers to deal with them. He sent out two small parties who quickly discouraged the enemy.

Pursuit ended. Lee's haul included seven officers and 151 rank and file. Lee estimated his own losses at not more than twenty, several of whom returned later. Lee had been lucky beyond his desert. Failure to keep his column closed, issue sufficient rations, assure dry ammunition and make certain the boats were at Secaucus might readily have ruined his enterprise. Washington did not point out Lee's omissions. At the moment, inspiration was more important than admonition. The Commander-in-Chief warmly praised him in General Orders and in a dispatch to Congress, and he stood squarely by the young Major when jealous officers protested that Lee should not have been assigned to command his seniors of another arm of the service. Col. Nathaniel Gist of the Sixteenth Virginia preferred charges against Lee and demanded a court-martial. The burden of Gist's allegation was that Lee had disregarded the rules of seniority and had conducted a clumsy, unfinished enterprise—accusations that required Washington to stand aside until the wheels of military justice had ground out a verdict. Lee, in the end, had complete vindication and high praise by the court. The outcome was a relief to the Commander-in-Chief, who could cry "well done" for Powles Hook as for Stony Point, but he had to ask, Would these taunts stir the sluggard enemy to action?

Instead of swift and severe reprisal by the enemy after the attack on Powles Hook, Washington had to cope with unrest, suspense, ill-will and apprehension on the part of some of his lieutenants. Sullivan felt for a time that he had not been given adequate force for his operation against the Indians; Greene was suspicious and sensitive and wished to retain both his rank in the line of the Army and his emoluments as Quartermaster General. In dealing with these men and with others who made trouble for him, Washington held to the basic principle of his code of command—absolute candor and justice—a principle not readily accepted by some officers who were disgusted with their idleness and outraged by the progressive decline in the purchasing power of their pay. For the same all-explaining reason the men in the ranks were returning to nakedness. Clothing issued in 1778 had worn out. Continental authorities were not importing a sufficient number of uniforms, shirts, shoes, stockings and hats to supplement adequately those manufactured in America. The Board of War reported despairingly that it had to pay fifteen times as much in paper as clothing would have cost in sterling. Depreciation had risen gradually to forty to one; within three months more, the currency lost acceptance so rapidly that private individuals and some purchasing agents were paying one hundred for one. In stern words, the Board made a paralyzing prediction: "We hope we are not too much under the influence of our fears when we declare that we believe in a very short period, unless some extraordinary event takes place, the present currency will cease to be a medium of commerce."

The outlook for provisions was as gloomy. The French were buying much of the stock of flour for their fleet. Drought was making it almost impossible in several States to grind the wheat brought to mill by farmers who were loath to accept promises to pay in currency that might lose its purchasing power. Officials had on hand no more wheat and flour than would subsist the Army to November 1.

Simultaneously, the military situation became discouragingly adverse. The Penobscot expedition ended in complete defeat. The enemy appeared to be stronger, because Admiral Marriott Arbuthnot had arrived at New York on August 25, with British contingents Washington estimated as not more than four thousand. Washington thought these troops were earmarked for service in the South, but he was unable to make any move to hold the British at the mouth of the Hudson.

This was the unpromising state of affairs when, about the middle of September, Washington received a letter in which Sullivan announced that he had met and defeated a force of Indians, British and Loyalists on August 29 at Newton. As his casualties had been negligible, he soon could bring back to the Army virtually all the Continentals who had been detached for the expedition. Another item of encouraging news was a prediction that d'Estaing would return soon with a French fleet—news that prompted Washington to write out all he knew concerning British strength at New York. He explained the practicability of destroying the small British squadron in those commanding waters. "I also entreat your Excellency's sentiments on the matter of this cooperation," Washington said, "and you may depend upon every exertion in my power to promote the success of an enterprise from which such decisive advantages may be expected to the common cause." Henry Lee was hurried off to the Jersey coast to place this dispatch in the hands of d'Estaing as soon as the fleet arrived.

Rumor was the only food of curiosity until September 29. By that date, Washington knew the French had reached Georgia and had been expected to attack Savannah on the ninth. This information reduced but did not completely destroy the prospect of French cooperation in northern waters that autumn. As he saw it, the entire coast from Newport to Savannah was a chess-board on which he must move promptly and in deliberate acceptance of the fact that every man who could be spared should be sent to Lincoln. Cooperation in the South and preparation in the North became the guiding principle of the campaign. The two Carolina regiments were put on the road; Sullivan was told to rejoin as soon as he could; plans were revised to take into account the possibility that after d'Estaing had destroyed the British squadron at the mouth of the Hudson, he might wish to reduce Newport instead of undertaking the task of capturing New York.

So nearly convinced was the General of the certainty of powerful French naval aid that on October 4, he called on the nearby States for twelve thousand militia to serve three months. For a time the enemy seemed even less in doubt about the coming of a strong French fleet than Washington was. The British evacuated King's Ferry on October 22 and carried down the Hudson all their cannon, equipment and supplies. By the thirtieth, Washington learned something still more important—that the British had left Newport on the night of October 25 without committing any serious depredation. These moves were strong evidence that the British were concentrating at New York in anticipation of early attack there. This seemed ample reason for transferring Gates's troops from Rhode Island to the Hudson and moving the main Army farther down that river. Washington made these arrangements swiftly and waited, in dwindling hope and growing surprise over the paucity of news from the South. Then, on November 15, the ugly truth was disclosed in dispatches from Philadelphia:

The French and American attack on Savannah had failed; d'Estaing had been wounded; Pulaski had received mortal hurt; the siege had been abandoned; the French had sailed back to the West Indies.

Washington took care not to magnify the defeat, but he completed pending measures of defence, stopped all possible financial outlay, and took steps to put the Army in winter quarters. In keeping the Army together despite desperate hardships, Washington would require compact camps as close as possible to whatever meat and grain and forage the country could supply. This necessity was made absolute by the insistence of Commissary General Wadsworth that his resignation be accepted. Washington lost also the colorful and mercurial Sullivan, whose ill health forced resignation. Alexander McDougall was suffering from stone in the bladder and must have a quiet post; Putnam was on leave and was feeble; Gates declined the post on the Hudson and went home to Virginia for the winter. Even if Washington succeeded in getting all his troops close together and ridding himself of duties he considered those of the Clothier General, he would be taxed to the limit of his endurance.

With little loss of time, Washington marched the troops from the middle and southern States to Morristown, New Jersey, where Greene had chosen position for each brigade. When Washington himself started from West Point for that town at the end of November, he had reached the end of a campaign during which he had been wiser and more fortunate than he realized. Sir Henry Clinton had expected in the spring of 1779 that with reenforcement from England he could seize King's Ferry and lure Washington to the Valley of the Hudson where either he could defeat the Americans or drive them into the highlands and then destroy their communications. Clinton blamed the late arrival of Arbuthnot's fleet for his inability to give battle to Washington early in the spring. After that, the British Commander confessed, "nothing . . . could draw [Washington] from North Windsor." Washington's refusal to be tempted to unequal combat had been responsible for the frustration of this part of his adversary's plan.

In the next phase of the campaign, the daring that Washington had displayed in the seizure of Stony Point likewise had yielded larger returns than he had claimed. At the time Wayne took Stony Point, Clinton was expecting four regiments from the West Indies and was making ready for a move on their arrival. Later, the British Commander told an English friend he was so much retarded by having to garrison and restore Stony Point and Verplanck's that he abandoned plans for a new offensive.

Washington reached Morristown December 1, opened Headquarters at the residence of Mrs. Jacob Ford and turned to problems of a different sort. He had to keep an eye on certain indications of a British raid up Long Island Sound and he had to study the defensive security of Morristown, but his main problem was that of trying to determine in conference with Lincoln's messenger, who was John Laurens, and with a committee of two members of Congress whether substantial help could be dispatched Lincoln, or Spain be induced to organize a diversion in Florida. The decision was to send the Virginia regiments and perhaps the remnant of Baylor's Cavalry, along with the North Carolinians. Stirling declined the command because, on arrival in South Carolina, he would outrank Lincoln, whom he was unwilling to replace. As a result, the troops started their march under Brig. Gen. William Woodford.

The soldiers who took the road were less to be pitied than those who remained at Morristown in an early winter of cruel severity, where half-naked and even shoeless men had to fell stubborn trees to get timber for huts. Wretched as these men were, Washington had to devise ways of prevailing on them to reenlist, because he stood to lose by May 1, 1780, no less than eight thousand through expiration of service.

Thin ranks and filthy tatters had their usual wintry concomitant of hunger. Congress made desperate appeals for flour, but it could not overcome the loss because of the drought, nor could it prevail on farmers to accept paper money otherwise than at discounts that inflated millions of debt. When bitter December was half over, Washington had to warn the middle States that unless aid were given immediately, "there is every appearance that the Army will infallibly disband in a fortnight." The sailing of an estimated five thousand British soldiers from New York, presumably for Georgia, was reported at a time when, as he had to inform the Clothier General, a great part of the Army "could not move on the most pressing exigency" for lack of shoes.

CHAPTER / 15

Discomfort, chill and misgiving attended the birth of 1780 at Morristown. In the absence of furloughed Generals, the business of the Army took so much of Washington's time that he felt he was not devoting himself as he should to the "military parts" of his task. He was isolated as well as burdened, because Congress had ordered the dismissal of the expresses in order to save the cost of the service. Communication was rendered more nearly impossible and all the miseries of camp were made torture by extreme cold. On January 2 and 3 a storm piled up snow drifts of four to six feet, with temperature so low that prolonged venture out of doors was self-murder. For weeks before the storm, bread had been scarce. On the first of the cruel new month, some of the regiments ate the last of their meat; the second found still more of the troops with nothing except their meagre, unpalatable bread. Some increase in ration was arranged on the third. After that, the badness of the public credit, added to the severity of the weather, reduced almost to nil the provisions offered the Commissaries. Washington was not sure he could provide three days' rations even for the equivalent of one full company, assigned to special duty. Nathanael Greene broke out: "Poor fellows! They exhibit a picture truly distressing—more than half naked and two thirds starved. A country overflowing with plenty are now suffering an Army, employed for the defence of everything that is dear and valuable, to perish for want of food."

The Continentals were patient because they were powerless, so long as the storm roared over Jersey, but as soon as they could make their way, many of those who had clothing began to slip away from their quarters. Marauding parties robbed nearby farms of food and wandered about in the darkness almost as they pleased. Washington asked himself, Would it not be less of a hardship to the natives for the Commissaries to determine what the farmers could provide, and then to take this, making lawful compensation, rather than to have the householders lose even the bread of the children to desperate prowlers? Action was dictated as soon as the question was put. Provisions in surprising volume were accumulated; within a few days Washington's immediate task became one of transportation. It was not easy to get the meat, grain and flour to camp, with the few and hungry teams of the Army.

For a time, then, the troops would have full rations with which to combat the continuing cold, but this was reprieve and not release from the threat of famine. The weather grew colder and colder. Travelers soon were crossing the Hudson on the ice at King's Ferry; passage of North River to and from Powles Hook was practicable about January 19 even for heavy cannon on trucks. Once the fury of the lashing wind and the pelting snow had subsided, the worst sufferers were Lord Stirling's men, who were sent on a vain raid January 15 in the hope of catching the British garrison of Staten Island off guard. Numbers of Americans were frostbitten; a sergeant and sixteen men were captured; the failure was complete. In every respect the Army continued to decline. The roster was swollen with men listed as "absent, sick"; some companies were almost without officers, while others had more than regulations permitted. Because of lack of clothing, one Captain wrote, "many a good lad [had] nothing to cover him from his hips to his toes, save his blanket." The greatest shortage was in the most critical item—shoes.

While doing everything possible to relieve the misery of his benumbed troops, Washington had to seek recruits for 1780. He previously had outlined to Congress a plan for meeting uniformly by annual draft the deficiency in the quota of each state, but he could not prevail on the Delegates to act. Nor could he hold his half-frozen little Army to full vigilance. Although the General had given warning, the advanced parties at Elizabeth Town and Newark permitted themselves to be surprised on January 25—with the loss of more than sixty men and considerable damage to property.

About two weeks later, on the night of February 11/12, when a new snow still lay heavily on Headquarters, a hardy rider brought Washington a dispatch in which Arthur St. Clair reported that hostile parties had made an incursion into American positions—three from Staten Island and one from Powles Hook. The objective of the largest force appeared to be Elizabeth Town, but withdrawal was rapid after the American guard had been found on the alert. Little or nothing was done by detachments that went to Woodbridge and Rahway. About three hundred cavalry came from Powles Hook to Hackensack and apparently started towards Morristown but turned back because of the depth of the snow. Many officers believed this column hoped to capture Washington himself and that the weather had defeated the attempt. Next came news that an outpost near White Plains had been surprised February 2 and that the greater part of five companies of infantry had been killed or captured—an altogether discreditable affair. Then, on the nineteenth, the British attempted another raid on Newark, but they met with swift challenge and quickly retired.

One of the principal reasons for these humiliating affairs was the continuing absence of officers. The greater part of those who could find any excuse for leaving the Army during the winter procured furloughs, which Washington indulgently granted for periods unduly long. The officers who remained at their posts were overworked and, in some instances, incapacitated by sickness. In the New York regiments, no less than sixty-four ensigns, lieutenants and captains were preparing a paper to ask the privilege of leaving the service because they thought their state had failed to make decent provision for them. The General was alarmed and depressed by this disintegration of command, but he had two contrasting assurances that may have comforted him: Benedict Arnold, who had had charges brought against him in Philadelphia, soon was to return to field-duty; Charles Lee would not come back.

Arnold was convicted on two charges—that he had given permission for a ship to leave Philadelphia without the permission of the State authorities or the Commander-in-Chief, and that he had used wagons of the State of Pennsylvania to transport his personal property and that of certain disaffected residents of Philadelphia, but his punishment was to be only a reprimand in General Orders. As for Lee, he wrote Congress arrogantly in January that he had heard of a plan to strike his name from the Army list. Delegates, he said, must know him very little "if they suppose that I would accept of their money since the confirmation of the wicked and infamous sentence which was passed upon me." Congress took him at his word and terminated his service.

There was no assurance that spring would bring a sufficient number of recruits for offensive operations. Congress was hesitant and blind in assigning quotas. When Delegates finally agreed on February 9 that the call should be for a total of 35,211 men, Washington saw immediately that even if he promptly dispatched estimates to the States of the forces they were to furnish, they would not have six weeks in which to raise and equip the recruits and get these men to the assigned rendezvous by April 1, the date designated in the resolution. With the calendar confronting him, and the Treasury without funds, Washington had to face the likelier probability he had described to Steuben just before Congress acted: "I imagine we must of necessity adopt the principle of a defensive campaign and pursue a system of the most absolute economy." Even for this defensive, Washington thought a force of close to 24,000 infantry would be necessary, and he did not know where he could procure sufficient small arms if he had the men. So it was with nearly all equipment needed for 1780. Everything was scarce; prices were rising fast.

These new distresses came when the February snows were melting and the roads were bottomless in mud. Everything seemed, once more, to be collapsing simultaneously. Forage was almost exhausted with no future supply assured. The store of meat, if dealt out scantily, might suffice until almost the end of April, but disappointing deliveries and bad roads made it probable the men would have no bread after March 22.

Congress had neither specie nor credit, but when it saw its Army in danger of falling into fragments it goaded itself to a three-fold reform. The first phase of this was a determination of the quotas it would impose on the States in accordance with a plan of direct requisition. In theory, provisions were to be furnished by the States according to their special resources. Washington's somewhat embarrassed criticisms had to shape themselves to the further warning that the provisions asked of the States would not suffice for the Army. To Philip Schuyler he confided that if some parts of the plan were adhered to, "ruin must follow." Along with this desperate adventure in the supply of provisions, Congress began a painful study of the reorganization of the Quartermaster Department, though even the inquiry, without specific action, made Greene more sensitive than ever and sharpened his suspicion that Mifflin was seeking to revive the cabal against

Washington. The third phase of reform was an effort to give stability to paper money. During two months of intermittent debate, conditions went from wretched to ruinous and compelled a bewildered Congress to agree March 18 on a plan to stop the further printing of unsecured paper money and reissue a limited amount of Continental currency that could be held, it hoped, as a ratio of forty to one.

Of every phase of these ills, Washington could have written dismally and of some despairingly. The enemy raided Paramus on March 22 and might threaten even West Point. If further help was to be sent Lincoln from the main Army, it must start soon; but how could Washington spare men? Seven thousand Continentals only were left in the Jersey camps; of these, about thirteen hundred would terminate their service in May. In the foreground, hourly, remorselessly, were hunger and cold. As of March 25, Washington wrote: "The Army is now upon a most scanty allowance, and is seldom at the expiration of one day certain of a morsel of bread for the next." At the end of the month, eight inches of snow remained on the ground, and the misery of the troops seemed almost past redemption.

Slow communication with the South obscured Lincoln's defence of Charleston, but Washington feared that a concentration in that town of the small American forces might involve the loss of the whole. The first decision at Headquarters was to send the Army's Chief Engineer, Duportail, and Harry Lee's light horse to South Carolina. Next, the reported embarkation at New York of 2500 British troops led Washington to order the Delaware Regiment and the Maryland Line to start the long march southward. It was doubtful whether provisions and transportation for these troops could be found, but Washington reasoned that if they could reach South Carolina they would be valuable in any situation that might develop after the disaster that seemed almost certain at Charleston.

These days of preparation for a cruelly long journey were made hideous by the nearer approach of starvation. Greene feared the horses would perish before the forage to be supplied by the States would reach the stables. Cattle had to be killed to keep them from starving. On April 12, Washington was compelled to write: "We have not at this day one ounce of meat, fresh or salt in the magazine" and he did not know of any in transit, or procurable within reach of the Army that would suffice for more than three or four days. By the fourteenth the only issue was of bread. This was supplemented by the later arrival of some salted provisions. After this was consumed, the men at Morristown would have to keep alive, if they could, on what the Commissaries could find and deliver day by day.

With an adequate division of duty, Washington should have been able to rely on the Commissaries to do whatever was possible while he devoted himself to general command, or else, if he had to feed the Army and the horses, he should have been able to deputize other men for administration. As it was, he had now to pay the price of his generosity in granting furloughs to senior officers. The nearer the time of opening the campaign, the heavier and more cumbersome his burdens were. A pleasant, but expensive and irksome duty was the entertainment of the French Minister, the Chevalier de la Luzerne, with whom Washington had exchanged letters on the probability of early assistance from the Court of Versailles. Luzerne arrived at Morristown April 19, accompanied by his entourage and by the Spanish agent, Don Juan de Miralles. All that the poor camp could offer Washington tendered his guests—the pomp of welcome, a formal review, a visit to the outposts, and even participation in a fast day ordered by Congress. The General tried to make it plain to Luzerne that America was determined to fight until her independence was acknowledged by Great Britain but did not attempt to conceal from the Minister the condition of the Army, and he could not have done so had he tried. Luzerne left camp convinced "more than ever," as he wrote his government, "of the very great advantage which the republic derives from [Washington's] services."

Three days after Luzerne started for Philadelphia a committee of Delegates, headed by Philip Schuyler, arrived at camp to work with the Commander-in-Chief, under resolution of Congress, for the economical reorganization of the Army. Washington welcomed them gladly, and he held to his principle that the larger the information of Congressmen the better the prospect of discerning support by them. Schuyler and his colleagues observed the wretched condition and bad spirit of the soldiers. "Their patience," the committee reported to Congress, "is exhausted." More ominously, "Their starving condition, their want of pay, and the variety of hardships they have been driven to sustain, has soured their tempers and produced a spirit of discontent which begins to display itself under a complexion of the most alarming hue. . . ." A new line of communication with Congress was opened. If the committee would act for Congress and not merely report to it, Washington would have the benefit of a speed of decision he never had enjoyed previously.

This was the situation near the end of the first week of May. The troops were barely able to keep alive on the meagerest of rations; recruiting had to be pronounced as worse than slow; the enemy was close to victory in Carolina and suspiciously astir in New York; financial ruin apparently hung on the response of the States to the plan for calling in the old, discredited currency; the Army remained too weak for an offensive. In spite of all this, spring came symbolically to the wretched thousands encamped among the hills of Jersey, when on the morning of May 6, Washington received a letter from Lafayette dated at Boston Harbor, April 27, 1780, which read in its principal part:

Here I am, my dear general, and in the midst of the joy I feel in finding myself again one of your loving soldiers. I take but the time of telling you that I came from France on board of a fregatt which the king gave me for my passage. I have affairs of the utmost importance that I should at first communicate to you alone. In case my letter finds you any where this side of Philadelphia, I beg you will wait for me, and I do assure you a great public good may derive from it— tomorrow we go up to the town, and the day after I'll set off in my usual way to join my belov'd and respected friend and general.

It was natural to surmise that the "affairs" of Lafayette's letter related to the vital subject of assistance from His Most Christian Majesty—but in what manner and measure? Washington did not have long to wait. On May 10 Lafayette reached Morristown and, as soon as he could, confided the great news: Six French ships of the line and six thousand well-trained troops were to have left France for America early in April and should call at Rhode Island early in June. These allies were not to content themselves with half-measures but were to participate in joint operations for the capture of New York and its defenders, a task that Washington put above all others in desirability and possible results.

To Washington's ears this was the best news that could have come at that season of gloom, and to his mind it was reassurance of that which he never had doubted for any length of time after the receipt in 1778 of the news of the French alliance. He "considered it," Lafayette wrote later, "as deciding the successful issue of their affairs"; but it called for hard labor and a measure of cooperation on the part of Congress and the States beyond anything ever effected previously. Washington gave Lafayette the counsel the Marquis's instructions bade him seek and then, as Lafayette went on to Philadelphia to confer with the French Minister and Congress, Washington wrestled with a new aspect of his old problem of subsistence: How would it be possible to meet the needs of the French reenforcements in a country where provisions were scarce and transportation was a mockery of everything the word ought to imply: A first essential, Washington reasoned at once, was the creation of a committee with authority to speak for Congress. When he came to ask for this, Congress acted promptly but did not confer adequate powers on the committee.

Within a fortnight, the General was overwhelmed with work. Little evidence was forthcoming of any response by the States to the call for troops; Washington no longer could persuade himself, as he had for a few days, that the French would reach America in time to raise the siege of Charleston. From that city, except for the announcement of the arrival of Woodford with his Virginia troops, all the news indicated that the British noose was being pulled remorselessly tighter. It seemed incredible that hope dropped so quickly from the height of Washington's feeling when he heard that a French fleet and army were coming. After the first news and the initial rejoicing, everything went down, down, until the question, May we not end the war in this campaign? had become, Can we hold out till the French arrive? On May 25, as he reviewed the needs of the French and the effort America must sustain, he solemnly told the committee of Congress: "Drained and weakened as we already are, the exertions we shall make, though they may be too imperfect to secure success, will at any rate be such as to leave us in a state of relaxation and debility, from which it will be difficult if not impracticable to recover." Then he added, as if he were reading the counts in an indictment posterity might draw of indolent America—"the country exhausted; the people dispirited; the consequence and reputation of these States in Europe sunk; our enemies deriving new credit, new confidence, new resources."

Washington did not overwrite the tragedy of his Army. Some infantry companies had no more than four rank and file, with the average about fifteen; officers of three regiments were "so naked" they were "ashamed to come out of their huts"; the discontent of hungry men mounted daily; flour moved literally from wagon to hearth. Then, about May 21, the supply of meat failed completely. There was none in camp and no prospect of the early receipt of any.

About dusk on the twenty-fifth the drums began to roll in the camps of the Connecticut Line; in a few minutes word came to Washington that two regiments, the Fourth and the Eighth, were in armed, defiant mutiny. The Connecticut soldiers were ten days behind in their allowance of meat. They had been on the parade for hours, "growling like sore dogs," and after a sullen evening roll call, a private who was rebuked by the Adjutant suddenly called out, "Who will parade with me?" The whole Eighth Regiment fell in and formed. In a short time, the Fourth Connecticut joined the Eighth. Fortunately, the troops waited irresolutely a few minutes before they decided to go to the camp of the Third and Sixth Connecticut to arouse them. During this brief pause officers ran ahead and gave warning. The soldiers of the quiet regiments were ordered to parade immediately without their arms. After the men hurried out, a guard was thrown between them and their huts so that they could not procure their muskets. Some violence followed; Col. Return Meigs was stabbed with a bayonet; for a few seconds the issue hung on the heating or cooling of temper; presently the mutineers went angrily to their own camps. Courageously, the officers appealed to the men. One after another urged the mutineers to lay down their arms. The pleas, otherwise in vain, served one purpose: they kept the troublemakers quiet while Stewart's Brigade of the Pennsylvania Line was moved out and thrown around· the camp of the Connecticut troops. Would the Pennsylvanians act as guards or would they join the mutiny? Officers, conferring quickly, decided to take no chances. The line was withdrawn; the Connecticut regiments were left to cool down. They stirred about in darkness for a time and then returned to their quarters. Col. Walter Stewart thereupon visited them and prevailed on them to present their complaints in disciplined fashion.

The causes of discontent were indisputably the hunger of the men and the failure of Congress to put any money in their hands for five months. In deepest concern, Washington had to admit that unless food, at least, was supplied, mutiny might break out again and the Army disband. To every official who might find provisions for the Army, immediate calls were sent. The Commissary General was in Philadelphia and was doing his utmost to find meat; but he had to write on May 27: "I am loaded with debt and have not had a shilling this two months." That day, a little meat was received at camp and was issued; on the twenty-eighth the situation again seemed almost hopeless. Lafayette, who had returned from Philadelphia to Morristown, was appalled to see how low the forces had fallen. "An Army that is reduced to nothing," he wrote Joseph Reed, "that wants provisions, that has not one of the necessary means to make war, such is the situation wherein I found our troops, and however prepared I could have been to this unhappy sight, by our past distresses, I confess I had no idea of such an extremity." Washington told the same Pennsylvania leader: "Every idea you can form of our distresses will fall short of the reality. . . . If you were on the spot . . . ; if you could see what difficulties surround us on every side, how unable we are to administer to the most ordinary calls of the service, you would be convinced that . . . we have everything to dread. Indeed, I have almost ceased to hope."

The twenty-ninth and the daylight hours of the thirtieth dragged by in misery. Then, late in the night, a messenger brought from Col. Elias Dayton a copy of an extra edition of Rivington's *Gazette*: Charleston had fallen. Its garrison and all arms and equipment had been surrendered May 12. Washington forwarded the paper to the President of Congress with no comment on the effect of what he styled simply "this unfortunate event," but he looked squarely into the face of calamity: "Certain I am," he told Joseph Jones, "unless Congress speaks in a more decisive tone; unless they are vested with powers by the several States competent to the great purposes of war, or assume them as matter of right; and they, and the States respectively, act with more energy than they hitherto have done, that our cause is lost." Details of the loss of Charleston were so slow in reaching Congress and the Army through American channels that some were tempted to doubt the authenticity of the published report, though it contained documents not easily disputed. Others credited the report and wondered whether it would arouse the public. If that happened, said Reed, "heavy as it now appears," the disaster might "prove a real blessing to the country."

In order to meet the enemy's main effort, wherever directed, Washington on June 2 called for seventeen thousand militia, with instructions to rendezvous, fully armed, at designated stations by July 15. He asked a council of war on June 6 how he best could employ the twenty-four thousand he would have, presumably, by the time the state battalions were filled June 20; but the very night after the council he heard from Colonel Dayton at Elizabeth Town that the enemy had landed in force at nearby De Hart's Point and was advancing. As Washington could not afford to permit the British to march at will to the district where his heavy cannon were parked and his meager supplies stored, he decided to march his troops towards the hostile column and maneuver without engaging. By afternoon Washington was in the Short Hills that overlook Springfield. Gratifying news awaited him. Dayton's Regiment of Maxwell's Brigade had been joined promptly by the militia of the neighborhood, who had fought stubbornly and shrewdly. The advance of the enemy had been retarded with a determination that had led the foe, after reaching Springfield Bridge, to retire a short distance to high ground northwest of Connecticut Farms, a settlement about two and a half miles southeast of Springfield. There the enemy had thrown up a breastwork in front of which skirmishing continued all afternoon.

Surprise over the rally of the militiamen and the hesitation of the British was deepened the next morning, June 8, by the discovery that the invaders had withdrawn to De Hart's Point. Was the advance merely an attempt to cover an operation on the Hudson? Washington suspected this and sent cavalry to enlarge his range of vision at the same time that he organized under Brig. Gen. Edward Hand a force of five hundred to harass

the enemy from the woods. Reconnaissance showed that the British intended to hold De Hart's Point, at least temporarily, though some of the
invaders were being withdrawn to Staten Island. The British commander
at De Hart's Point, identified as Gen. Wilhelm von Knyphausen, proceeded to throw a pontoon bridge to the mainland and move baggage and
mounted troops back and forth to Staten Island—as if he intended to remain indefinitely near Elizabeth Town and threaten severance of communications between the Hudson and the South. "Our situation," said Washington on June 14, "is as embarrassing as you can imagine," and then he
had to add: "When they unite their force, it will be infinitely more so."

Knyphausen waited; the American Commander-in-Chief could not
hope to do more than maneuver slowly with broken-down teams or resist
awkwardly when assailed. Even that much seemed doubtful. The States
were indolently backward in meeting the requisitions for men and money,
meat and drink, flour and forage, without which the Army could not even
hang together. The Delegates in Philadelphia and the committee at Headquarters were pressing their pleas, but Congress, in the words of a Virginia
member, was at the time "little more than the medium through which the
wants of the Army are conveyed to the States." Washington saw the long
days of June slipping past with scarcely anything accomplished to make cooperation with the French more than mocking promise and futile hope.

Washington learned, approximately June 18, that Gates had been
directed to take charge of the Southern Department in succession to the
captured Lincoln, who was credited with a good defence of Charleston. Intelligence reports to Headquarters on and after the eighteenth indicated
that six men-of-war and at least sixty-five other sails had reached New
York—almost certainly Clinton's returning veterans of the Carolina campaign who might proceed directly against West Point. Precautionary orders
were issued for vigilance and victualling at the Hudson River posts and for
putting the main Army in condition to move, but nothing of importance
occurred until June 20. Then Washington heard that six British ships had
sailed up the Hudson as far as Verplanck's and had dropped down the
river again. This made him suspicious. If a powerful surprise attack was
about to be made on West Point, he was too far away. On the other hand,
until this hostile move was certain, he could not afford to be so far north
that troops from Staten Island could get astride his communications in
New Jersey. His solution was to leave Greene to watch and, if need be,
delay the movement of the British on the island and the shore nearby,
while the main Army proceeded cautiously to Pompton. From Pompton
three or four good marches would carry the troops to West Point.

One day was all the men spent on the road with their faces to the
North. During the night of June 22/23, Washington received two dispatches from Greene, who was puzzled by his intelligence reports. In mid-
morning there arrived from Greene, near Springfield, this alarming message: "The enemy are out on their march towards this place in full force,
having received a considerable reenforcement last night." That was
enough; soon the soldiers were marching back to support Greene. Nothing
more was heard from that officer until, in the early afternoon, he reported

the enemy driving on Springfield and moving as if to get in his rear. Then, after sunset Washington received news that the British had forced the Americans out of Springfield, burned the village and withdrawn swiftly, as if they were going all the way to Elizabeth Town.

The next morning Washington heard that the Redcoats had abandoned their position on Jersey soil. Their troops had moved across to Staten Island on the pontoon bridge and taken it up. Now none of the King's soldiers remained in the State. Washington could surmise only that West Point remained the objective of the British; and as the removal of supplies from Morristown relieved him of the necessity of guarding that base, he proceeded towards the Hudson. He advanced the main Army on July 1 to Preakness, there to rest his men, await the drafts from the States and prepare for the coming of the French.

The familiar administrative vexations of command plagued Washington from the very day the Army pitched its tents at Preakness. Expensive, devouring militia were dismissed as soon as it was apparent that West Point was not in immediate danger, but the suffering, poverty and bitterness of men in the Continental service were as bad as ever they had been, perhaps worse. Washington had an embarrassment in the fact that Robert Livingston, as well as Schuyler, now was insisting that a more vigorous man than Howe was needed at West Point, even though Washington saw to it that Steuben remained there and advised with Howe. Livingston's proposal was that the citadel be assigned Arnold. Arnold, himself, en route to Connecticut on private business, stopped at Headquarters and remarked that he wanted field command but doubted if he was physically equal to it. On returning from Connecticut, he made the same statement and intimated that he would like the assignment at West Point.

The advent of July brought no improvement. Washington had to admit that not more than thirty men had reported, of all the thousands asked of the States. Small and doubtful as was the support of the States, it had to be divided. Gates must have every man and all the supplies that Virginia and the Carolinas would furnish, but more than this Washington did not think he could spare after Clinton returned north. For his part, Gates was receiving many congratulations on his new assignment, but he confessed privately his dismay at succeeding "To the command of an army without strength, a military chest without money, a Department apparently deficient in public spirit, and a climate that increases despondency instead of animating the soldier's arm. . . ."

The whole inhuman tragedy was deepened now by uncertainty regarding the continuance of the dribble of stores Greene and his deputies had been able to divert to the Army. Congress was hammering again on the reorganization of the Quartermaster Department, and in circumstances that presaged an upheaval. Washington thought the proposed plan about as good as any that could be fitted to limitations that could not be overcome, but it was doubtful whether Greene would agree to remain as Quartermaster General or whether, in event the Rhode Islander and his deputies retired, the most essential requirements of the troops could be met. So desperate was the plight of the Army that Washington began to fear that the French might come, see the helplessness of America, and sail away. He gave warning: "If we do not avail ourselves of their succor by the most decisive and energetic steps on our part, the aid they so generously bring, may prove our ruin, and at best it will be in such case among the most unfortunate events next to that of absolute ruin, that could have befallen us."

Nearly a fortnight passed during which the enemy did nothing and the States little. As of July 13 Washington had to write: "It cannot be too much lamented that our preparations still are so greatly behindhand. Not a thousand men that I have heard of, have yet joined the Army. . . ." The pettiness of accession made a jest of the plan, nearing completion, for an attack on New York—made, indeed, an embarrassment of reports that the French fleet was off the American coast. The next day a messenger brought Washington a dispatch of July 11 from Heath: ". . . yesterday afternoon the long expected fleet of our illustrious ally appeared off [Newport]. . . , the signals were all made and the fleet standing in to the harbor. . . ."

The dispatch from Rhode Island prompted Washington to complete his outline of operations against New York and entrust Lafayette to carry it and official greetings to the commanders of the allies at Newport. For the attack on New York the General began active preparation. Then adversity trod the heels of hope: Admiral Thomas Graves was said to have arrived at Sandy Hook on the thirteenth with six ships of the line to reenforce Admiral Arbuthnot, who was credited by intelligence reports with seven large ships, three frigates and a sloop. For comparison, by July 18, a dispatch from the General in command of the French troops, Comte de Rochambeau, informed Washington that he had slightly more than five thousand men and that his naval colleague, the Chevalier de Ternay, had eight ships of the line, two frigates and two bomb-galliots. By the simplest calculation, the combined forces of Arbuthnot and Graves were far more powerful than Ternay's eight. Washington flattered America's allies when he said that the French were "rather inferior" to their adversary, but he had instant encouragement: Other French war vessels might come from the West Indies. Rochambeau assured him a second division of French ships, with more infantry, soon would arrive in America, but the prospect of early attack on New York undeniably was dimmed.

The fates seemed to be making sport of him. A new rebuff came quickly: A British force of fifteen or sixteen ships appeared off Newport, as if to establish a blockade and intercept the French second division. Within three days more, there was news that transports in large number were proceeding eastward through Long Island Sound to assail the French on Rhode Island. If the troops on these vessels were as numerous as reports indicated, a renewed opportunity presented itself of making a demonstration against New York and perhaps of attacking the city's defences; but the Quartermaster service, feeble for months, now was crippled and disorganized, because Greene had resigned as head of that department. With some difficulty Washington and John Mathews of the committee at Headquarters prevailed on Greene to continue temporarily on duty, and to their relief they found that while the machinery creaked and rumbled, the service did not collapse entirely.

The troops under the Commander-in-Chief continued their advance across the Hudson until news came at the beginning of August that Clinton's transports were returning to New York with the regiments still aboard, a movement the American commander attributed to his demonstration against the city. As soon as he was sure the British vessels were headed westward on Long Island Sound, he directed that the Army return to the Jersey side of the Hudson.

The disappointments did not exhaust Washington's patience or destroy his cheerfulness. He looked confidently for the shift in naval superiority that Admiral Ternay assured him the French King was determined to establish. The United States must do their part, conserve the little they had and organize to strike with all their might when the French squadron arrived. Greene would be available to assist him. His resignation as Quartermaster General had been accepted with no bar on service in the line. He could be assigned to command the right wing, but the man Washington desired to head the left wing, Arnold, said his wounded leg was not strong enough for so active a command. In accordance with his wishes he was assigned to the defence of West Point. None of his juniors was named to command the left wing, because the return of Clinton's fleet made an immediate order of battle unnecessary.

After New York received its full garrison again, was there any hope of striking a blow before the second division of the French fleet arrived? The British showed no initiative; the only American enterprise of any magnitude was an unsuccessful attack by Wayne July 21 on a blockhouse near Bull's Ferry. Had opportunity of achieving any larger result offered itself, Washington's acceptance would have been at the greatest risk, because all the darkest apprehensions of the failure of supply by the States were being realized. Commissary Ephraim Blaine was almost frantic; a general forage had to be authorized. Soon the only device for keeping the Army from starving was to move the camp, eat up everything in reach and then go into another district and strip it.

The misery of the men was matched by the discontent and weakened organization of the officers' corps. Maxwell resigned; Enoch Poor died; various others were cherishing grievances or debating bitterly with themselves a choice of duty. The new Quartermaster General, Timothy Pickering, failed to report promptly for field orders. By August 15 Washington had received slightly more than six thousand recruits of the 16,500 the States had been asked to supply for the main Army; a large body of Pennsylvania militia, estimated by the Commissary General at 4500, was moving forward to share in the projected attack on the British, but Washington could not feed these reenforcements. He had to order the men turned back and dismissed or encamped where provisions were abundant. He was compelled to warn the Delegates: ". . . If something satisfactory be not done, the Army . . . must either cease to exist at the end of the campaign, or it will exhibit an example of more virtue, fortitude, self denial, and perseverance than has perhaps ever yet been paralleled in the history of human enthusiasm."

Within a week, food was so scarce that Washington had to move the Army to the vicinity of Fort Lee, on the North River, in order to impress the few days' food in that area. As the march began, he had still another discouragement, so stern that it was almost a blow in the face. He learned that the useful committee at Headquarters, who had aided him in many ways, had been discharged by Congress on the ground that it had exceeded its authority. With his unflinching acceptance of civil authority, Washington made no protest, even when he attested to Congress the value of the committee's service, but he had lost advocates who had learned thoroughly the distress of the Army and could interpret it to the States.

On the evening of August 25 Washington received a dispatch of the twentieth from Rochambeau who reported the arrival at Boston of the French frigate *Alliance*. She brought much-needed arms and powder; but when she left L'Orient, the second division of the French fleet was blockaded at Brest by English squadrons. The division, with the best of fortune, could not be expected in America until October. Economy and commonsense dictated the undoing of much Washington laboriously had undertaken: he dismissed the militia, ordered the Army to return to the vicinity of Hackensack, prepared his thin battalions for a possible British advance, and warned Arnold to assemble at West Point all scattered contingents to meet a probable attack on the highlands.

While the Army was tramping to the Hackensack, rumors reached Headquarters that a disaster had befallen Gates, of whose operations in the Carolinas, Washington had heard little. On September 4 came news that Gates had suffered total defeat in a battle with Cornwallis's troops on August 16, about eight miles from Camden, South Carolina. Early accounts indicated that Gates's force had been destroyed, that he had fled 180 miles before he even could file a report, and that, because of the disaster, Virginia was exposed to invasion from the south. Washington had no comment, but he lost no time in directing a new regiment from Maryland south instead of to the main Army.

A council of war assembled on the sixth to consider plans and a new and mystifying development: the British fleet had disappeared from the vicinity of Newport August 29 and had not been heard of subsequently. The puzzled council could recommend nothing better than the suspension of the attack on New York until the arrival of the French second division. Further dispatch of reenforcements to the south likewise should await events. Washington's opinion was that the British would detach more troops to Virginia or to North Carolina. America's reliance should be on slow recovery in the South and on the creation there of a Continental force of about six thousand. If the main operations of the British should develop in the South, the whole or a part of the troops under Washington might be moved to that region.

On these and related questions Washington wished to consult the French commanders, with whom he long had desired to confer, and he now arranged a meeting at Hartford on September 20; but while he was preparing carefully for this, another calamity threatened. On the fourteenth Gen. David Forman wrote from Freehold, New Jersey: "I am this minute informed that Admiral Rodney with twelve sail of the line and four frigates are arrived off Sandy Hook from the West Indies." Instead of having the help of additional French ships to offset British strength, Washington had now to contend with a hostile superiority greater than ever, perhaps unchallengeably greater.

With regard for these developments, Washington drew up a memorandum of the subjects to be discussed, gave orders to guide the action of Greene during his absence, and on September 17, in the company of staff-officers and attendants, rode towards King's Ferry and stopped for the night at the home of Joshua Hett Smith. At Smith's Washington met Arnold. That officer had written his chief numerous letters after reaching West Point and had received hearty commendation for the spirit in which he had been discharging his duties. Now the hero of the northern campaigns wished the judgment of the Commander-in-Chief on a matter of interest. Beverley Robinson, an old-time friend of Washington's and a leading supporter of the British cause in New York, had sent Arnold a letter requesting a secret interview with him. Arnold wished to know whether he should consent to see Robinson. Washington's answer was instant and positive: By no means should Arnold do such a thing! If Robinson had any permissible private business to transact, he should address himself to the civil authorities of New York.

When Arnold transmitted a reply of this nature to Robinson, the matter ended. Perhaps this was to the satisfaction of outpost officers, because they were annoyed by frequent flags of truce. Col. Elisha Sheldon, for example, had been the go-between for reports from spies and recently had almost got himself into trouble because of a letter of one John Anderson, a New Yorker, who sought to enter the lines on a matter "of so private a nature that the public on neither side can be injured by it." Sheldon sent this paper to Arnold but he made a report of it to Washington, who inquired how the letter had come into Sheldon's hands. The Colonel explained that the communication had been brought by flag of truce. Fortunately for Sheldon, Arnold previously had mentioned the fact that he was opening a new line of intelligence from New York and now confided that Anderson was the man he wished to employ.

Washington proceeded to Hartford, where he had the pleasure of meeting Rochambeau, Ternay and other French officers. Some of these soldiers of King Louis were curious to know what manner of man the leader of the American Revolution was, and most of them were greatly pleased with him. "Enchanted" was the word Claude Blanchard used as he summarized the feelings of those fellow-countrymen who subsequently told him of Washington's "easy and noble bearing, extensive and correct views and the art of making himself beloved. . . ." Washington, in turn, found the French commanders all he could wish them to be, but he could do little more than give a pleasant personal aspect to a discussion dependent on so many contingencies that neither side could make firm promises. Everything hung on the balance between French and British naval strength, on the time and the extent of help from the Comte de Guichen, French Admiral in the West Indies.

The American leader's proposals were these: First, if de Guichen arrived by the beginning of October and won a naval victory that would give him entry into New York harbor, the capture of that city should be undertaken. In event allied naval superiority was not obtained until later in the fall, an expedition of at least twelve thousand troops, French and American, should be sent to the Southern States. A second proposal was based on a plan Greene had sketched: The French fleet might proceed to Boston, where it would be secure without the support of land forces, and Rochambeau's infantry might march towards the Hudson for cooperation with the Americans in enterprises that would keep the British from making further detachment to the South. Washington's third project was for a winter campaign in Canada. The first of these three proposals alone met with the favor of Rochambeau. Even in this particular, the French General tactfully made it plain that the King's fleet and troops were to be kept together and not to be employed contrary to his strict interpretation of his orders. Rochambeau explained that he had instructions to put his troops under Washington personally and under him only; but in the end, Washington concluded that his command of these forces was a flattering fiction.

If Washington could not hope to undertake a general offensive until French naval reenforcements arrived, he must be certain fortifications on the Hudson, and particularly at West Point, were strong enough to discourage attack. Washington wished to see them himself. So, when he left Hartford September 23, with Lafayette, Knox and the members of the staff, he took the upper road, pressed steadily on, and passed Fishkill during the next afternoon. He was continuing towards West Point when he met the Chevalier Luzerne en route to visit Rochambeau. The Minister appealed so earnestly for a conference that Washington turned back to Fishkill, where, no doubt, he traded news from Hartford for Philadelphia gossip.

The next morning, September 25, he was resolved to press straight on to the Headquarters of Arnold. Two officers were assigned to ride ahead and inform Arnold's household to prepare, if convenient, for a considerable number of hungry guests. Washington followed at a good clip and about 10:30 pulled up at Arnold's Headquarters, which were in the residence of Beverley Robinson, about two miles southeast of West Point. At the house, one of Arnold's aides, Maj. David Franks, explained that a short while previously Arnold had received a call to come at once to West Point. He sent his regrets at unavoidable absence. In approximately an hour, he would be back. Such a state of affairs was no welcome for the Commander-in-Chief, but—would the gentlemen excuse it and make themselves comfortable? Washington relieved immediately the embarrassment of Franks. If the Major would order some breakfast, all could be adjusted easily; the visitors intended to cross to the works at West Point and would see Arnold there.

After they had breakfasted the officers were rowed across the Hudson to the defences that towered on the west bank, but something evidently had gone awry. Arnold was not at the landing, nor had he been seen that morning by those who greeted the visitors. Washington concluded that the party would start its inspection and proceed from one work to another until the commander was found. As he made the rounds, Washington encountered shocking conditions of past bad planning and present neglect. Almost every part of the stronghold of the Hudson was decayed, incomplete or inflammable. Repair of the works called for the full service of Arnold's eighteen hundred militia and of all the artificers he could collect. Strangely enough, very few men were visible as garrison or masons. At each of the forts and redoubts, Washington inquired for Arnold. Nobody had seen him. Washington felt some irritation that Arnold should be negligent in attendance when word of the visit of the Commander-in-Chief had been sent; but as it was important to know the exact condition of the defences, he completed the tour of the place.

It was well past three o'clock when Washington, with vague misgiving started across the river towards Robinson's house; and it was close to four when the barge tied up at its landing. Arnold had not returned. It was very strange. Washington went to the house and into the room set aside for him. In a few minutes, Hamilton entered and handed Washington a packet that had just been received by Lt. Col. John Jameson of the First Dragoons. Washington opened the bundle and read Jameson's covering note. This explained that a man who gave the name John Anderson had been caught on the road to New York. When searched, he was found to have in his stockings papers which Jameson forwarded. The General glanced at them. One was a pass for Anderson, dated September 22. Another was a summary of the Army's strength, with a report of the troops at West Point and an estimate of the forces needed there. A return of the ordnance was in the packet, as were the arrangements for the disposition of the artillery in event of an alarm. One folio was endorsed: "Remarks on Works at Wt. Point a copy to be transmitted to his Excell'y General Washington"; still another was a copy of the minutes Washington had sent Arnold of the council of war on September 6. In short, Washington had in his hands a dossier of the most confidential papers concerning the garrison and defences of West Point and the plans of the Army. This was startling enough. The appalling fact was that two of these papers were in Arnold's handwriting. Anderson's pass was signed by the General.

Hamilton had still another document for Washington, a second letter from Jameson. The officer explained that a letter for Washington had been given him by the man who called himself Anderson and that he was forwarding this. It was an amazing communication: the arrested individual was not John Anderson but John André, a Major and Adjutant General in the British Army. He confessed that he had left the man-of-war, *Vulture*, in Hudson River, "to meet upon ground not within posts of either army, a person who was to give me intelligence." Against previous stipulations, André said, he had been conveyed "within one of your posts," whence he had been refused transit back to the vessel and forced to put on civilian dress and start to New York by land. Near Tarrytown he had been captured by some volunteers. "Thus," he continued, "as I have the honor to relate was I betrayed (being Adjutant General of the British Army) into the vile condition of an enemy in disguise within your posts."

Undoubtedly, then, this important British staff officer had held a meeting with Arnold and received from the General the papers found on him! Washington never had sustained such a shock, but he gave no indication of distress of mind. He merely made it plain that he wished to be alone with Hamilton and Harrison. When he told them what the papers disclosed, he learned for the first time of an incident that had occurred at breakfast. While Arnold was eating, he was handed a paper which he read with manifest concern. Without remark, he stuffed it in his pocket and in a few minutes got up and left the table. Whatever the origin of the sheet delivered Arnold, it must have been a warning. Arnold doubtless had fled, and if so, he probably had gone down the river to the vessel from which André had come ashore. Colonel Hamilton must take horse and, if possible, intercept the fugitive.

Then, gripping himself, Washington went to dinner at four o'clock without a word to anyone else about Arnold's disappearance. After the meal, Washington asked Lieut. Col. Richard Varick, Arnold's chief aide, to come for a walk, and, as they strolled, told him of Arnold's conduct. There was not, said Washington, the slightest ground of suspicion against Varick or Franks but, in the circumstances, they must consider themselves under arrest. Varick did not protest. Instead, he tried to explain all he knew about Arnold. As Washington listened, the Colonel told with some difficulty how he and Franks had been puzzled and troubled because they had observed an enlarging intimacy between Arnold and Joshua Hett Smith, whom they took to be a spy or a trader in illicit enemy goods, or both. Voluntarily, he and, later, Franks gave up the keys to their chests and to all those of Arnold that were under their care.

Washington took up the task of correcting mistakes deliberately made to expose an American stronghold to successful attack. Arnold had been careful to be careless. What had appeared to be the derelictions of a patriot now were disclosed as the iniquities of a traitor. It seemed that Arnold's scheme was to invite the enemy's advance. By seven o'clock Washington knew enough about the situation to begin to issue his orders: Redoubts opposite West Point were to be manned; Greene was to advance his nearest division immediately to King's Ferry, where further orders would await it; all the troops of the main Army were to be held in readiness to move; the militia and men detached as a wood-cutting party were recalled to the east bank of the Hudson; officers of known character were put on duty.

Before the last of these papers was ready Washington received this letter, which had been sent ashore by flag of truce near King's Ferry:

On board the Vulture, 25 September, 1780.

SIR: The heart which is conscious of its own rectitude, cannot attempt to palliate a step which the world may censure as wrong; I have ever acted from a principle of love to my country, since the commencement of the present unhappy contest between Great Britain and the Colonies; the same principle of love to my country actuates my present conduct, however it may appear inconsistent to the world who very seldom judge right of any man's actions.

I have no favor to ask for myself. I have too often experienced the ingratitude of my country to attempt it; but, from the known humanity of your Excellency, I am induced to ask your protection for Mrs. Arnold from every insult and injury that a mistaken vengeance of my country may expose her to. It ought to fall only on me; she is as good and as innocent as an angel, and is incapable of doing wrong. I beg she may be permitted to return to her friends in Philadelphia, or to come to me, as she may choose; from your Excellency I have no fears on her account, but she may suffer from the mistaken fury of the country. . . .

I have the honor to be with great regard and esteem, your Excellency's most obedient humble servant

BENEDICT ARNOLD

N.B. In justice to the gentlemen of my family, Colonel Varick and Major Franks, I think myself in honor bound to declare that they, as well as Joshua Smith, Esq., (who I know is suspected) are totally ignorant of any transactions of mine, that they had reason to believe were injurious to the public.

Washington did not take time to analyze this paper, with its references to the infamy Arnold knew his betrayal would bring on him. The traitor had escaped. Nothing could be done about that now. Washington then examined a communication from Beverley Robinson that accompanied the one from Arnold. It developed that Robinson, too, was aboard the *Vulture* and was immensely concerned over the apprehension of André. The former Virginian demanded the release of André on the ground that the British Adjutant General "went up with a flag at the request of General Arnold, on public business with him" and had acted as Arnold had directed, even to using a "feigned name." This argument Washington instantly rejected, but if André was so much esteemed it would be well to have the captured spy brought to West Point. The transfer consequently was ordered. Next was Smith, the man whom Arnold had described as a suspect. Find him, arrest him and bring him to Headquarters. Collect, too, all possible intelligence.

Washington's last instructions on these matters were not issued until after 10 P.M. of the twenty-fifth; movement of men to their stations at West Point went on most of the night. Before the return of daylight, there was good augury: The wind shifted and began to sweep strongly downstream, an obstacle to a British approach by water. In event the enemy planned the earliest possible attack, Washington might have the twenty-sixth in which to prepare a defence. The General put all available men to work and was standing on the piazza of the Robinson house when up clattered horsemen who had apprehended Smith. The General soon went into the house, called Lafayette, Knox and Hamilton to his room and then sent for Smith, a voluble individual who began almost immediately to protest against the arrest of so loyal an American as he. He displayed wariness, but he gave information that filled some gaps in Washington's knowledge of what had happened.

Until the examination of that loquacious individual was completed Washington had been so mired in the detail of Arnold's treason that he had not been able to stand off and look at the whole. Now he gave instruction for the drafting of a report to Congress and, in outlining what was to be said, saw that Arnold must have been fashioning for a long time a plan to get command at West Point and deliver the American citadel to the British. In the absence of suspicion, Arnold almost certainly would have succeeded but for the chance capture of André. In Washington's eyes, the circumstances attending that officer's failure to escape were beyond human fashioning. It was, said Washington, "by a most providential interposition," and he described the facts as far as he knew them. Assurance was given Congress, and Governor Clinton in a separate letter, that precautions had been taken to prevent a surprise of West Point.

The morning of the twenty-sixth brought still another development when Maj. Benjamin Tallmadge and a party of dragoons delivered to Headquarters a young man, unshorn and untidy—Maj. John André. Would Washington care to question André? No; but he was interested to hear details of the capture of the Adjutant General: On the afternoon of September 22 a number of young militiamen had procured leave of absence to waylay some of the "cowboys" engaged in stealing and driving cattle into the British lines above New York. The next morning the party divided, and three of them took station on the Old Post Road close to Tarrytown. About 9:30 they halted there a solitary rider, who was on his way to New York. In the belief that the trio were Loyalist partisans and that they had established their lookout on the British side of the "neutral ground" the horseman did not show his pass and talked so carelessly that the Americans made him dismount and strip. In the feet of his stockings they found the papers that led them to suspect he was a spy. Although he thereupon tried to bribe them into permitting him to go on his way, they took him to the nearest outpost, which was at North Castle. Jameson, temporarily in command there, read the papers and concluded they were a forgery, written to discredit the Armerican commander at West Point. He consequently wrote Arnold of the capture of André and started the captive on the way to West Point; but the vehement protests of Major Tallmadge induced the bewildered commanding officer to recall the prisoner. Jameson insisted that the letter to Arnold be forwarded but, fortunately, he dispatched to Washington, not to the commander at West Point, the documents André was carrying. Occurrences after the return of André to North Castle already were known to Washington. He did not express an opinion, so far as is known, on a question that much disturbed the more romantic of his young officers—the puzzle of Mrs. Arnold's involvement. She manifestly feared that public indignation would be visited on her for what her husband had done, and she sought permission to go to Philadelphia. As Washington saw no reason why she should be held at West Point, she left September 27, with Major Franks as her escort.

The departure of Arnold's wife was followed at once by an examination of his records, from which apparently he had not been able, in his hurry, to extract any papers. His cool request for a map of the country between West Point and New York appeared now to be a device to facilitate the march of the column that was to "surprise" the Hudson defences. Other drafts of orders and dispatches showed how carefully Arnold undertook to get a British agent into the lines without arousing suspicion. The letter of Robinson, concerning which the traitor so ostentatiously had consulted Washington, obviously was intended to make sure that Arnold had reached his station. A full set of the profiles of the West Point fortifications, each on a separate sheet, presumably had been made ready for conveyance to the enemy. The accumulating pile of papers was maddening in its disclosure of a lack of vigilance on the part of senior officers who now saw a score of acts suspicious in retrospect. One consolation only did they have: they went through all the traitor's correspondence and did not read the name of a single soldier, humble or conspicuous, who had been party to Arnold's design. Robert Howe, for example, was shown by Arnold's correspondence to have been asked, and almost ordered, to disclose the identity of his spies, a request Howe had refused politely but inflexibly. So with every other officer represented in Arnold's papers. The only American, besides the traitor himself, on whom the correspondence cast the faintest shadow of suspicion was Smith.

The Commander-in-Chief put the experienced, if half-incapacitated, Alexander McDougall in charge of West Point and its approaches, until Arthur St. Clair could arrive. It seemed wise, also, to send André and Smith to the custody of the main Army at Tappan, whither Washington himself intended to return as soon as McDougall reached West Point. Washington proceeded to Tappan September 28 and opened Headquarters at the house of John de Windt.

There he had to deal almost immediately with a sustained, desperate effort by Sir Henry Clinton to save André from execution as a spy. The British commander, writing on the twenty-sixth, stated that he had permitted André to "go to Major General Arnold at the particular request" of that general officer. An enclosed letter from Arnold, said Clinton, would show "that a flag of truce was sent to receive Major André, and passports granted for his return." Arnold's letter was a cold avowal of his treason and his delivery to the Major of "confidential papers in my own handwriting for Clinton." Arnold wrote: "I commanded, at that time, at West Point [and] had an undoubted right to send my flag of truce for Major André."

Preposterous as this contention seemed to Washington, he did not call a drumhead court-martial for the immediate sentence and execution of a spy caught in civilian dress. The American leader named, instead, a board of fourteen general officers to make a careful and speedy examination of André. Greene was designated President of the Board; the Judge Advocate General was to attend. Members assembled the day they were assigned. When André was put on the stand, he confessed readily the authorship of his letter of September 24 to Washington and then volunteered a stage-by-stage account of the manner in which he was brought ashore and subsequently told he must return by the route he was following when captured. After that statement, the Judge Advocate put to André the question his General was arguing vigorously in his behalf: Did André consider he had landed under the sanction of flag of truce? The answer recorded in the minutes of the court, was both honest and impetuous: "It was impossible for him to suppose he came on shore under that sanction, and [he] added, that if he came ashore [under flag] he certainly might have returned under it." That knocked away the last frail defence. The rest was formality. When André was asked if he acknowledged the facts in the record, he did so, with the simple remark that he "left them to operate with the board."

Insofar as all this was known in camp it created sympathy for André rather than astonishment that he seemed to be courting death. It was the duty of Washington to see that sentiment did not prompt leniency towards a man engaged in the most dangerous conspiracy the war had hatched. No comfort for the sentimentalists was presented in the report the Board of Officers filed with Washington. The Board reported " . . .That Major André, Adjutant General to the British army, ought to be considered as a Spy from the enemy, and that agreeable to the law and usage of nations, it is their opinion, he ought to suffer death."

The sentence accorded exactly with Washington's own judgment, but the report was received too late September 29 for any action on it that day. On the morning of the thirtieth, the General answered the letter in which Clinton asserted that André had immunity under Arnold's flag of truce. The American commander quoted in full the report of the Board and added simply: "From these proceedings it is evident that Major André was employed in the execution of measures very foreign to the objects of flags of truce and such as [they] were never meant to authorize or countenance in the most distant degree."

This letter was intended to be Washington's last word, though he complied readily with a request that André's servant be allowed to visit the prisoner and deliver clothing to him. Calmly, methodically, Washington proceeded as in every other death-sentence, except in one particular. In the usual formula, the findings of a court-martial were "confirmed" or "approved." This time General Orders quoted the report of the Board of Officers and then stated tersely: "The Commander in Chief directs the execution of the above sentence in the usual way this afternoon at 5 o'clock precisely."

André had spent quietly his hours of imprisonment at Tappan, and, when the General Orders were read to the young officer, he scarcely seemed to change expression; but soon the General received from him an appeal that he be sent before a firing squad rather than hanged. Washington sympathized with a soldier young and accomplished, but he could see no reason for deviating from the rule that sent spies to the gallows. All the mercy that could be shown would be to give no direct answer to André and thereby save him from certainty that he was to die on the gallows.

About 1 P.M. there arrived another letter from Clinton. The British commander still was trying to save André and insisted that the Board of

Officers who passed on the case could "not have been rightly informed of all the circumstances on which a judgment ought to be formed." Clinton continued: "I shall send his Excellency, Lieutenant General Robertson, and two other gentlemen, to give you a true state of facts, and to declare to you my sentiments and resolutions." There was no reason for listening to Robertson in any official capacity, though it would be courteous to receive an officer of his rank. Washington consequently instructed Greene to go to Dobbs Ferry and receive Robertson as an individual, not as a bargaining representative of a hostile government that had nothing to do with the enforcement of American military law. The other representatives of Clinton must not be permitted even to come ashore. Until the result of the meeting was reported, the execution of André should be postponed without any formal reprieve. Washington waited until his senior lieutenant returned with a report that Robertson merely had restated feeble arguments and, in the end, virtually had made a plea for the release of André as a personal favor to Clinton, who would reciprocate generously. Washington listened to the statement of his lieutenant but found nothing to justify any revision of the sentence imposed on André. Greene was told that he was to notify Robertson in writing the next day that the American commander had not changed his opinion. Meantime, orders must receive this addition: "Major André is to be executed tomorrow at twelve o'clock precisely a Battalion of Eighty files from each wing to attend the Execution."

On the morning of October 2 Washington took up his regular work. Before many hours passed there was much stirring in the camp, all the way from André's place of confinement to a tall gallows of two forked poles and a crosspiece on a knoll half a mile away, but there was little noise of preparation, because everything had been made ready the previous day. Presently there came the sound of marching in the vicinity of André's prison. Soon the frenzied shriek of the fife and the fast heartbeat of the drums died in the distance. Washington was left almost alone with his papers. There were vastly greater questions in his mind than that of the just fate of a spy who had come within the American lines to bargain with a traitor. After a long quiet, the sounds of the camp were renewed gradually. Officers returning from the place of execution were talking of what they had seen. It was over; André was dead; every incident of the hanging had increased the respect of witnesses for the young man in the red coat. He had faced the last ordeal as all right-minded men would pray they might if their fate had been his. Washington listened to the reports as any person of amiable nature would, but he had more of wrath towards Arnold than lament for André.

With more of sympathy for André than Washington permitted himself to feel, the country shared in other respects the emotions aroused in the Commander-in-Chief by Arnold's treason. Dismay turned quickly to wrath. Consternation sobered into amazed gratitude for providential deliverance. The response of one element of the public was less reverent. Some asked, Was there any connection between Arnold's plot and Lee's behavior during the Jersey retreat? In Philadelphia, Boston, and other towns, paraders hanged the traitor in effigy and in branding him displayed half consciously their own loyalty to the Revolution. Congress, in the words of James Lovell, was "mighty shocked," though it was admitted that those Delegates who had examined Arnold's accounts were not unprepared for disclosure of his business. Many "scandalous transactions," wrote President Samuel Huntington, were "brought to light that were before concealed." Arnold's name was erased from the roster of generals; his infamy was left to time.

Full investigation confirmed initial evidence and failed to show the involvement with Arnold of any person other than Joshua Hett Smith— who was brought to trial before a general court-martial September 30 and acquitted for lack of evidence, but he was arrested soon afterward by the New York Commissioners of Conspiracy and was imprisoned at Goshen until he escaped May 22, 1781, and went to New York City. American spies in New York and at nearby stations were alarmed and for a time afraid to employ their usual channels of communication but they escaped arrest, thanks to the earlier frustration by Howe of Arnold's efforts to ascertain their names. In the conviction that Arnold had no partner in perfidy, Washington was anxious that suspicions should not be indulged. When he heard from the Board of War that a notorious informer, whom he suspected of being a double spy, had alleged that Howe was in British pay, he protested: "It will be the policy of the enemy to distract us as much as possible by sowing jealousies, and if we swallow the bait, no character will be safe; there will be nothing but mutual distrust."

While the country still was engaged in the discussion of Arnold's crime, Washington disposed his troops to protect West Point and find subsistence in districts that had not been swept bare. So far as the northern and middle States were concerned, he felt he had written finis to an "inactive campaign," throughout which the Army had "lived upon expedients" that no longer availed. He believed a far different task faced the forces in the South. "I have little doubt," he told James Duane, "should we not gain a naval superiority, that Sir Henry Clinton will detach to the southward to extend his conquests."

Almost every development of the succeeding weeks of wretchedness bore out the warnings Washington had given. The British manifestly were reenforcing their Carolina contingents. Intelligence from New York was to the effect that Gen. Alexander Leslie was leaving that base with 2500 to 3000 men. The States below the Potomac must raise more men. If Virginia and the Carolinas were to supply recruits, they must have faith in victory. After what had happened at Camden, Gates could not hope to possess the confidence of the people. The simplest way that Congressmen could devise of getting rid of him was to order a court of inquiry into his conduct and direct Washington to put some one else at the head of the Southern Army until the court had acted. Delegates of the three southernmost States immediately asked the assignment of Greene, whom Washington undoubtedly would have selected on his own motion as the most resourceful, skilled general officer he could recommend. Greene, than at West Point, accepted the command, though with a sober understanding of the complexities of his task. Washington encouraged his lieutenant and gave him two of the best of his supporting officers, Steuben and Harry Lee. To Gates Washington sent word that the court would be held, if practicable, where and when it best suited the convenience of the defendant.

Thereafter a continuing question was whether troops could be sent from the main Army to Greene. By the end of October Washington had good news: At King's Mountain, South Carolina, on October 7 frontier militiamen overwhelmed a mixed British force, chiefly Loyalists. As this advantage might be offset by the British troops who had left New York, Washington thought it wise to consult his council of war on further detachment to Greene. A majority of the Generals replied with an unqualified "No" and urged, in answer to another question, that the Army be placed forthwith in winter quarters that would cover West Point.

The troops by that time needed shelter and everything else. Washington had all his old administrative problems. Conditions never seemed to get better; experience never was applied; each autumn found him threatened with the calamities his men barely had survived the previous winter. Scarcely a week passed that the Army did not have to do without meat one day or even two. Soon there might not be men to eat even the little that could be wrung from embittered farmers. A stripped military chest and a despised currency would not purchase the reenlistment of short-term soldiers or support the intolerable expense of militia. Many of the troops were half-naked in spite of a large accumulation of uniforms in foreign ports. The old restlessness and the ugly jealousies were reawakened angrily. Knox was outraged by the promotion of William Smallwood to Major General. Hamilton also was restive. When Colonel Scammell resigned as Adjutant General, in order to resume field command, Greene and Lafayette sent their endorsement of Hamilton for that post, but before Washington received it he chose Edward Hand. While the appointment was logical, Hamilton may not have been reconciled to it. He now had married a daughter of Philip Schuyler and was thirsting to win fame in the field.

Washington's daily service continued the same old story, in detail different but in theme so repetitious, so disheartening that it was enough to make a man wonder whether the country deserved to be free! One hope only of larger American effort was held out to Washington. On October 4 he had written John Mathews: ". . . I most firmly believe that the independence of the United States never will be established till there is an Army on foot for the war—that if we are to rely on occasional or annual levies we must sink under the expense, and ruin must follow." This appeal did not fail completely. A plan of reorganization was adopted October 3—too late to fill the ranks by January 1 but not too late to effect some improvement. The infantry regiments were to be enlisted "for and during the war" and supplemented, if necessary, by one-year drafted recruits. Several important reforms were instituted in the artillery and the mounted forces; but the most substantial gain, in Washington's judgment, was the provision that the dismissed officers of the consolidated regiments and all officers "who should continue in the service to the end of the war" were to "be entitled to half pay during life." With the beginning of November, Washington announced the new organization of the Army on a basis of long-term enlistment, adoption of which in 1776, he said privately, would have ended the war before the autumn of 1780.

Washington's immediate problems of strategy were not eased in the least by military developments. British troops established a base at Portsmouth, Virginia, and then mysteriously evacuated it. Preparations were being made at New York as if Clinton were determined to strengthen still further his southern forces. Greene received gratifying welcomes in Philadelphia and Richmond; but the farther southward he went, the more he realized the feebleness of the resources with which he hoped to conduct a partisan war until larger forces could be collected. Although it was suggested in Congress that Washington's presence in the South would do more than anything else to assure help for Greene, the Commander-in-Chief felt that in the absence of orders from Congress to this effect, he should remain where he was.

To winter quarters, then! There was no alternative. With the men apportioned in camps from West Point to Morristown, Washington fixed his own "dreary station," as he styled it, at New Windsor where Martha joined him. Whatever was procured for the Army was requisitioned or impressed. By the middle of December Washington had to confess a doubt whether there was money enough in the entire Army to pay the cost of an express to Rhode Island. At Headquarters no funds, even for table expense, had been received in nearly two months. Greene's dispatches told of like poverty. Greene was resolute but in need of encouragement as well as of money. Washington could give the one but not the other. By December 27 Washington's information was that another British fleet had left New York on the nineteenth with 2000 to 2500 troops—and that superiority at sea still hung on the second division which was to leave Brest in a short time. The year's end was gloomy; the beginning of 1781 was of the same pattern. The patience of the soldiers had worn out.

About noon on January 3 Maj. Benjamin Fishbourne drew up at Headquarters and handed Washington a letter from General Wayne that began:

The most general and unhappy mutiny took place in the Pennsylvania line about 9 o'clock last night. It yet subsists; a great proportion of the troops, with some artillery, are marching toward Philadelphia. Every exertion has been made by the officers to divide them in their determination to revolt; it has succeeded in a temporary manner with near one half; how long it will last, God knows. . . .

Wayne's dispatch described an affrighting state of affairs at Mount Kemble, near Morristown. The men had risen between 9 and 10 P.M. on the first, had seized field pieces and boldly resisted commanders who tried to restore order. One captain had been killed; several officers had been wounded. The mutineers then scoured the parade with their fire and marched away about eleven o'clock. Wayne and his subordinates retreated southward ahead of the column and kept between the troops and the British. The men said boldly they intended to proceed to Philadelphia, a threat Wayne took so seriously that he had sent warnings to Congress to leave the city.

The appalling reality was undisguised, defiant mutiny: was it to be general? Had the end come? Nothing further came that day from Wayne except confirmation of the news Fishbourne had brought; the Army around New Windsor remained quiet and apparently had not heard of the uprising. The British had not stirred, either, though, of course, the enemy would try to entice the mutineers. The night, too, was quiet. By morning of the fourth Washington concluded reluctantly that he should not attempt to go forthwith to Philadelphia or to the camp of the mutineers. By the time he could reach the scene of trouble the Pennsylvanians either would have joined the enemy or would be negotiating with a committee of Congress. To appear before the mutineers and demand that they submit to discipline without the means of compelling them to do so might impair discipline still more. Orders that could not be enforced should not be given.

In all his stern disciplinary experience as a soldier Washington had never known precisely the sort of nerve-racking suspense he now had to endure, suspense concerning both the course of the mutineers and the response of the other troops. The only sure way to prevent the spread of trouble was to relieve hunger and neglect. If there was any hope, it was in New England. He wrote the Governors of the States east of the Hudson "it is vain to think that an Army can be kept together much longer, under such a variety of sufferings as ours has experienced." Unless three months' pay were forthcoming "in money that will be of some value" to the troops and ways and means were found of clothing the men better and feeding them regularly, then, said Washington, "the worst that can befall us may be expected." This was all Washington could do—and it was ridiculously inadequate when the mutineers were said to be continuing their march towards Philadelphia.

During the evening of the sixth, Washington received a dispatch of January 4 with details of what had occurred after Wayne had sent the initial reports of the uprising. Wayne had opened negotiations with the mutinous Line, which had appointed a committee of sergeants to act for it. These NCOs asked Wayne which were the classes of men admitted to have a just title to discharge. The General's reply was that he had sent a plea that the Council of the State name representatives to confer with the soldiers and decide that subject. This arrangement was agreeable to the sergeants, who handed Wayne a list of their demands—that discharges be granted those entitled to them, arrearages of pay and of clothing be made up, and participants in the revolt be exempt from punishment.

For good or for ill, the civil authorities had intervened. They had a right to do so. When they acted, Washington ceased employing the military arm. A just settlement might reconcile the mutineers to renewed service; but the proposals of the men seemed exorbitant, and a civil settlement was almost certain to go beyond anything that military discipline could allow. These perplexities had to be faced. A day's reflection brought Washington nearer the state of mind that would interpret liberally the scope of a "fair" settlement. He so wrote Wayne on the eighth. An expression of complete confidence in the negotiators ended the letter. Nothing was firm, nothing certain—except the resolution of a few leaders.

Was resolution to be destroyed by torturing suspense? Must Washington and men of like mind remain helpless and idle at New Windsor while the mutineers made a bargain with the enemy or wrung from the Council of Pennsylvania terms that would require the discharge of hundreds from an Army already cut in half? Were the days of December 1776 back again? It must not be so! Active risk was better than passive ruin! Now, on the tenth, letters from St. Clair, Lafayette and John Laurens threw him back on his conviction that a strong hand must be employed against men who could march to the British lines if they did not receive the concessions they demanded. He would proceed to West Point, confer with his general officers, and if they thought he still could rely on the troops, he would pick one thousand men and hasten to Trenton. Then, if need be, he would move against the mutineers.

Almost at the moment Washington left his quarters for West Point he received news that Clinton had sent an emissary to the Pennsylvania troops with generous promises of welcome, pay and provisions. The committee of sergeants was said to have delivered him and his guide to General Wayne. Besides, Washington learned, a committee of Congress was in touch with the Pennsylvania troops. This put a more hopeful face on the crisis, but it did not induce Washington to abandon his plan for a council at West Point. When they assembled, the Generals expressed the belief their men could be relied upon, though there was some wavering over the proposal to detach one thousand troops in five temporary battalions. Washington ordered this and made ready to move towards the Delaware.

A new difficulty arose overnight: The report that the mutineers had delivered Clinton's agent to Wayne proved to be false. They still held the man and, as Washington saw it, "they seem to say, if you do not grant our terms we can obtain them elsewhere." Wayne, however, indicated that parleys between the mutineers and the Pennsylvania authorities were progressing, substantially on the basis of the troops' demands. If, in these circumstances, American regiments were thrown between Trenton and the British lines, this might appear to the mutineers as a show of force and might prompt them to join the enemy.

Washington remained prudently skeptical, but he did not move the detachment which might or might not be willing to fire on the mutineers. Then, one dispatch after another told of small, hopeful developments— that the British emissary and his guide had been turned over to American authorities, that the whole affair was apt to be settled, that the British "spies" had been condemned to die, and that a settlement was expected in a short time. In the evening of the fifteenth a report arrived from Sullivan, with an opening paragraph that read thus:

We are happy to inform your Excellency that the terms offered to the Pennsylvania troops are at length finally, and, as we believe, cordially and satisfactorily agreed on; and tomorrow we expect the Pennsylvania Line will be arranged in its former order. Constitutionally, no concession has been granted them that the critical situation of our affairs did not warrant and justice dictate.

Washington had expected a settlement that would thin the ranks and weaken discipline; precisely how bad was the bargain? The demand of the mutineers had been the discharge of those who had served three years, though enlistment had been for "three years *or* the war." Had the settlement been a surrender to the men on this point? It developed that if a mutineer's military papers were not available for verification, he was to be discharged by the Pennsylvania commissioners if he made oath that he had enlisted for a specific period that had expired. As the records of the regiments were fragmentary, this made the continuance of the Pennsylvania Line dependent, primarily, on the individual soldier's sense of honor. Washington believed that the Pennsylvania authorities had made the best bargain they could, but he felt that the arrangement would "not only subvent the Pennsylvania Line but have a very pernicious influence on the whole Army." It was, he thought, a result of the sort to be expected where the intervention of the civil authorities made it impossible to restore discipline by military measures.

"It is somewhat extraordinary," Washington observed to his French colleague at Newport, "that these men, however lost to a sense of duty, had so far retained that of honor, as to reject the most advantageous propositions from the enemy." Washington went on: "The rest of our Army (the Jersey troops excepted) being chiefly composed of natives, I would flatter myself, will continue to struggle under the same difficulties they have hitherto endured, which I cannot help remarking seem to reach the bounds of human patience." This was written on January 20, 1781, when Washington had no reason, so far as it is known, for regarding the parenthetical reference to "the Jersey troops" otherwise than as a casual statement of fact. The very next day, he found himself a vindicated prophet of evil: Col. Israel Shreve reported that some of those identical Jersey soldiers, then in camp at Pompton, had mutinied and were marching towards Trenton.

Were all the Jersey troops involved? Was this a movement that was to spread from one command to another until the Army was destroyed? The decision of Washington did not wait on details. This time there must be no negotiations by civil authority, no temporizing, no compromise. If the best soldiers in the Army would stand by him, he would march with them and quell the mutiny. As quickly as dispatches could be drafted and copied they were signed and sent out. Heath at West Point was to pick five or six hundred of the "most robust and best clothed" men of that garrison and place them under proper officers at once. Washington himself would be at the Point the next morning to inspect them. The next day Washington placed Robert Howe in command of the detachment. Instructions were explicit:

The object . . . is to compel the mutineers to unconditional submission, and I am to desire you will grant no terms while they are with arms in their hands in a state of resistance. The manner of executing this I leave to your discretion according to circumstances. If you succeed in compelling the revolted troops to surrender you will instantly execute a few of the most active and incendiary leaders.

The test was slower in developing than Washington had hoped. Horses were difficult to procure, and a heavy snow January 23 delayed all transportation. Washington returned to New Windsor after a single day at West Point but as late as the twenty-fifth he had received neither message nor dispatch to elaborate the first report of mutiny. Consequently, as soon as he learned that Howe's men were moving without hesitation through the snow, he determined to ride forward and ascertain the "true state of matters." When Washington reached Ringwood he learned that the number of troops who had defied their officers did not exceed two hundred. A New Jersey commission had undertaken to come to terms with the men—the very thing Washington had wished to avoid—but the commissioners had refused the mutineers' demand for the benefit the Pennsylvanians won, namely, individual discharge on oath of completed service not disproved by available records. The men had gone back to their quarters eight miles from Ringwood and had begun to riot again. Mutiny continued; military action against the offenders could be taken by Washington without violating any pledge imprudently made by civil authority.

About midnight of January 26/27 Howe marched from Ringwood with his detachment, and by dawn he had taken positions that commanded the cabins where most of the mutineers were asleep. Artillery was trained on the approaches. Howe then directed Lieut. Col. Francis Barber to order the Jersey troops to parade without arms and march to ground he would designate. Some of the men cried out, "What, no conditions?" If they were to die, others shouted, they might as well perish where they were. When Barber reported this, Howe directed Lt. Col. Ebenezer Sprout to advance his troops and cannon and sent word to the mutineers that five minutes only would be allowed for compliance with the orders by Colonel Barber.

The crisis was at hand. Tense seconds of waiting followed. Then, from their shelter, the mutineers began to appear, bundled up for the snow —but without their arms. Who, Howe asked sharply, were the chief offenders? The officers reflected and gave him names. Now, pick the three who had been most violent, one from each regiment. Send a guard directly to the parade, order the three to leave the ranks and bring them to the ground where the General had his post. Keep the mutineers standing in line, organize a field court-martial and try the principal conspirators immediately. Done . . . the three men guilty and sentenced to death . . . Verdict confirmed. Look again at the list of those most active in the meeting. Mark the twelve who had supported most loudly the three about to die. Send this dozen under guard to their huts. Have them carry their muskets to the parade. Promptly done! Let them load their pieces. Take that sergeant who had been the leader. Make him kneel—and pay no heed to his lamentation. The twelve who have loaded, divide them into parties of six each. These six are to fire first, three at the head and three at the heart of the kneeling sergeant. If he struggles after that volley, the remaining six fire. Let them protest and weep if they will. They are fortunate not to be in the sergeant's place. Fire! Still in spasm? Fire, you second party! He is dead. Now the next villain. Load for him. Proceed as before. Good! . . . dead on the first discharge. The third—are the colonels interceding for him?

Was he, as they say, endeavoring to persuade the mutineers to return to their duty? Reprieve him, then. General Washington will pass finally on his case. It is over. Now, all the troops must acknowledge their officers and pledge future good conduct.

"I then spoke to them by platoons," Howe said later, "representing to them, in the strongest terms I was capable of, the heinousness of their guilt, as well as the folly of it, in the outrage they had offered to that civil authority, to which they owed obedience, and which it was their incumbent duty to support and maintain. They showed the fullest sense of their guilt, and such strong marks of contrition, that I think I may pledge myself for their future good conduct."

Washington received the report of Howe with deep relief, and he resolved that he would prevent, if he could, any belated concession by New Jersey that would nullify the lesson taught the mutineers. Washington had anticipated, in effect, just such a report as Wayne soon was to make on the outcome of the Pennsylvania review—that more than thirteen hundred were to be discharged and part of the remaining 1150 had been furloughed to dates in March. A corresponding result in New Jersey would be an invitation to New York soldiers to mutiny for like release—and so to the death of the Army. Discipline must be maintained, relief must be afforded, the officers and the intelligent element of the men must be rallied. "The General," he said in General Orders of thanks to Howe and to that officer's detachment, "is deeply sensible of the sufferings of the Army." Then Washington wrote:

He leaves no expedient unessayed to relieve them, and he is persuaded Congress and the several States are doing everything in their power for the same purpose. But while we look to the public for the fulfilment of its engagements, we should do it with proper allowance for the embarrassments of public affairs. We began a contest for liberty and independence ill provided with the means for war, relying on our own patriotism to supply the deficiency. We expected to encounter many wants and distresses and we should neither shrink from them when they happen nor fly in the face of law and government to procure redress. There is no doubt the public will in the event do ample justice to men fighting and suffering in its defence. But it is our duty to bear present evils with fortitude, looking forward to the period when our country will have it more in its power to reward our services.

The cure of the two mutinies had been hampered at every stage by the scourging causes of the discontent—hunger, nakedness and lack of money. "There is not a single farthing in the military chest," Washington had to admit during the first week of January, and daily he had maddening evidence of the truth he put first in a statement he prepared for John Laurens' use in seeking a loan in Europe—"the absolute necessity of an immediate, ample and efficacious succor of money; large enough to be a foundation for substantial arrangements of finance, to revive public credit and give vigor to future operations."

In other respects the period of the Pennsylvanians' uprising was one of routine at Headquarters, but much of importance had beginnings during the terrible time of the disturbance among the Jersey troops. While Heath was organizing at West Point the detachment that suppressed the mutiny at the Jerseymen's barracks, Gen. Samuel Parsons on January 22/23 had executed successfully an enterprise against De Lancey's refugee corps in the vicinity of Morrisania, more than three miles within the British lines. The enemy undertook no reprisal but acted as if the hopes and the attention of all the King's men were fixed on the southern campaign, where Washington realized already that Clinton or Cornwallis or both of them had developed an admirably dangerous strategical plan. Troops that had left New York under Benedict Arnold December 22 had gone to Virginia. Arnold could render hazardous the movement of stores and provision from the middle States overland through Virginia to the Continentals in the Carolinas; and so long as the British Navy dominated Chesapeake Bay nothing could be sent Greene by water otherwise than by risky voyages to some small port on the Carolina coast that might not be blockaded by British ships. In addition, Arnold could leave the patrol of Virginia rivers to the navy and, if reenforced, could send part of his troops to harass Greene. Simultaneously, Cornwallis, based on Charleston, could close on Greene from the south. Cornwallis was strong enough to organize a vigorous offensive because Gen. Alexander Leslie's expedition, which had left New York ahead of Arnold's troops, had gone to Charleston and was moving inland to join the main British column. Greene was in danger of being caught later in the year between two hostile armies. The enemy's plan threatened complete ruin.

How could Washington frustrate the British plan? He did not dally over the answer: he must strengthen Greene, who could do no more than keep resistance alive until reenforced, and, if possible, Washington must strike a blow that would divert some of the enemy's force from Greene. The offensive manifestly could not be undertaken on any large scale otherwise than by that help for which Washington had been pleading from the hour the alliance was announced—French naval superiority on the American coast. Half-eagerly, half-wistfully, Washington wrote Laurens, "How loud are our calls from every quarter for a decisive naval superiority, and how might the enemy be crushed if we had it." Washington's observation had about it a suggestion that those answers might decide not merely the campaign but the war also. Except for keeping the main Army alive, nothing was now to bulk so large in the mind of Washington as the balance between danger and opportunity in the South.

Washington received word from Rochambeau at the end of the first week in February that a storm on January 22/23 had crippled the British squadron off Gardiner's Island at the eastern end of Long Island. The French, in the haven at Newport, sustained no damage. Superiority had shifted! The wind had done what the French King could not! Surely this was the awaited opportunity; the French naval commander, now the Chevalier Charles Destouches, might not have numerical advantage many weeks but he could proceed to Virginia waters with his entire fleet and part of Rochambeau's troops and he might destroy Arnold quickly. "If," Washington wrote Rochambeau, "Mr. Destouches should have acquired a superiority, which would make it prudent to act, Your Excellency may think this detachment an object."

Almost a week passed without word from Rochambeau or from Destouches. News from Virginia continued bad. That from the Carolinas, paradoxically, was alarming because it was good. Washington received word that on January 17, at Cowpens, South Carolina, Brig. Gen. Daniel Morgan, had defeated an attacking British force, captured more than five hundred, and pursued the enemy twenty miles. American losses were said to have been twelve killed and sixty wounded. Greene and Washington both feared the success of Morgan might lead the people to underestimate the enemy and relax their effort.

Washington received February 14 a letter Rochambeau had written him on the third: "I am going this moment aboard of the Admiral to know whether he intends going out with all his ships, or at least send a detachment of some of them to Chesapeake Bay." Was the entire force under Destouches or a part only going to Virginia? If Destouches could be prevailed upon to do so, he must use the entire French squadron and take with him approximately one thousand of Rochambeau's troops. Washington would dispatch a column of twelve hundred from his own Army to march to Virginia and share in the operations.

If the allies promptly made the utmost of their brief superiority at sea, the opportunity was immense. So great was it that Washington quickly made another resolution: Even if the French could lend no help, he would try to defeat Arnold with American troops from the Hudson and those already in Virginia, and, as a symbol of desired joint action, he would put Lafayette in command. Just as Washington completed plans to start the detachment southward, he received from Destouches on February 20 a disheartening letter that began:

I have the honor to inform your Excellency that Mr. la Luzerne has informed me of the desire of the States of Virginia and Maryland to have the fleet in shape to destroy and dissipate the pirate flotilla which is laying waste the Chesapeake Bay shores, and having the great desire to be useful to the United States of America, I sent down one ship and two frigates to accomplish that object. . . .

It seemed as if the great opportunity were being thrown away, though there was an explanation, of a sort, in other dispatches and, particularly, in one of Rochambeau's. The British fleet had not suffered as heavily as had been thought. The squadron, though small, would consist of swift, sure sailors: the ship of the line could keep up with the frigates. As Arnold was believed to have no more than a forty and some frigates, his fleet could be destroyed. Destouches' three vessels sailed February 9 under Arnaud le Gardeur de Tilly. Washington did not believe this small squadron could destroy the British vessels if Arnold gave them the protection of land batteries, and, in answering Destouches, he had to say so at the same time that he thanked the Chevalier. Whatever prospect there was of defeating Arnold by using Lafayette's detachment and forces already in Virginia would depend, Washington thought, on the ability of Destouches to "block up Arnold in the Bay" and prevent the dispatch of British help from New York. If this was expecting too much of Destouches, Rochambeau had a rumor that Admiral Comte de Grasse had met and defeated the large British fleet of Admiral Sir Samuel Hood in the West Indies. If confirmation of this could be had, Washington hastened to write Rochambeau, "I think we may regard it as an event decisive of a speedy and glorious termination of the war. . . ."

He awaited news from the Indies and from Hampton Roads and undertook to discharge an accumulation of business with a staff reduced by absence and illness and embarrassed by a most unhappy experience with Alexander Hamilton. On February 16, when the General was much perplexed over the problem of getting the French commanders to send the whole of their fleet to Virginia waters, a snapping of tensions provoked a hasty decision by Hamilton to leave the staff. Washington, in recognition of the young officer's fine qualities, decided he should make the first move to a reconciliation. He sent Tench Tilghman to Hamilton to ask that the Colonel come and talk over a difference that could have arisen only in a moment of passion. Soon Tilghman was back; the offended young gentleman would not change his mind but offered to go on with his duties as if nothing had happened until Washington could get someone in his place.

A daily ordeal was the subsistence of the Army, and more nearly torture than ordeal was doubt concerning the success Greene would have in avoiding an engagement with Cornwallis till the American forces were stronger. Washington heard nothing from de Tilly, but Rochambeau replied carefully to Washington's plea for the dispatch of the entire French fleet and one thousand French troops to Virginia waters. Destouches, said Rochambeau, had complied fully and promptly with the "requisition" of Congress and of the Virginia authorities. Had Washington's appeal for larger assistance arrived earlier, the Admiral perhaps "would have decided to go out with his whole fleet." Rochambeau himself would have been glad to send the desired infantry. As it was the damaged British ships had returned in good order to Gardiner's Bay. Destouches consequently was "less strong than the English."

Washington had to reconcile himself to the fact that the brief period of French naval superiority in American waters was at an end. He admonished Lafayette to take all precautions in moving by water south from Head of Elk. Gravely Washington analyzed the outlook: "The situation of the Southern States is alarming; the more so, as the measure of providing a regular and permanent force was by my last advices still unattempted, where the danger was most pressing and immediate. Unless all the States in good earnest enter upon this plan, we have little to expect but their successive subjugation."

February 27 brought the long-awaited news of the French in the Chesapeake. De Tilly had captured the *Romulus*, a British frigate, and had taken five hundred prisoners, two privateers and four small transports, which he had sent to Yorktown. Four other troop vessels had been burned. He had conducted a good raid, if not a successful expedition.

Then, on March 1 came the great surprise—a French visitor from Newport, Baron von Closen, placed a dispatch of Rochambeau's in Washington's hands. Its opening paragraph read thus:

The letters found on board the vessels taken by M. de Tilly have decided M. Destouches to follow in full the plan given by your Excellency, and to risk everything to hinder Arnold from establishing himself at Portsmouth in Virginia. M. Destouches is arming with the greatest diligence the forty-four-gun ship that was taken, and he hopes that this, with the frigates, will be able to go up Elizabeth River. He will protect this expedition with his whole fleet. Your Excellency has given me orders to join thereto 1000 men. I will send 1120. All my Grenadiers and Chasseurs will be there. The corps will be commanded by the Baron de Vioménil.

Fortune had shifted again! The thing most needed to be done for the American cause was to be done. Rochambeau had urged and Washington desired a conference at Newport. It must be held, if possible, before Destouches sailed. Nothing must be left to chance that could be assured by discussion and clear understanding.

All this seemed to promise fair weather, but while Washington was preparing busily, a letter arrived from Greene which confirmed previous warnings that a hazardous defensive lay ahead. The commander of the Southern Department described the hard marches that his adversary had been able to force on him because the little American army had not equipment or the support of militia in adequate number to give battle. Greene added: "Under these circumstances, I called a council, who unanimously advised to avoid an action and to retire beyond the Roanoke immediately."

Greene either was being compelled to evacuate all of North Carolina except the northeastern counties or else to seek refuge in Virginia. Cornwallis had no more than 2500 to 3000 men, but he had destroyed his wagons and was operating his entire force as light infantry with dragoon support. Greene must not be run down. North Carolina must be saved. Washington added new instructions to a letter about to be sent to Lafayette: "You are at liberty to concert a plan with the French General and naval commander for a descent into North Carolina, to cut off the detachment of the enemy which had ascended Cape Fear River, intercept if possible Cornwallis and relieve General Greene and the Southern States." This was daring strategy; could it have even a remote promise of success?

CHAPTER / 16

While Washington rode eastward on March 2, a clerk wrote carefully across the Journal in Philadelphia: "The ratification of the Articles of Confederation being yesterday compleated by the accession of the State of Maryland. . . ." Washington knew, of course, that some sort of ceremony would attend Maryland's ratification, but he had not been told when the documents were to be presented, and, had he been informed, he would not have expected an immediate change for the better. As his horse struggled with the mud of late winter, the sole question raised by the action of Maryland was whether the Articles of Confederation would help bring recruits to camp, bread and meat to the men, and full support to the French Admiral who soon was to show the fleur-de-lis again in Chesapeake Bay.

The party reached the Newport Ferry March 6 and went to the flagship, *Duc de Bourgogne,* where Rochambeau, Destouches and all the senior officers had assembled to welcome the Commander-in-Chief. After introductions, Washington went ashore, to the bark of a grand salute, and found that the French troops had been drawn up on either side of the route to Rochambeau's quarters. Splendid soldiers they were, well uniformed and finely accoutred. The interest of the General, of course, was not in the warmth of the reception accorded him but in preparations for the departure of the French fleet. Destouches must be as far south of Newport as possible before Arbuthnot had word at Gardiner's Bay that the French were weighing anchor. Everything was ready on the seventh, as Washington saw it, for Destouches to sail. Nothing happened. The next day the *Fantasque* ran aground, but Destouches sent word the vessel soon would be floated. About sunset, the French men-of-war sailed triumphantly out, the magnificence of the spectacle marred, in Washington's eyes, by the delay in staging it. Three days thereafter the worst possible result seemed probable. Lookouts reported that on March 10 the British fleet had gone to sea with as much assurance as if Arbuthnot had the reckoning of Destouches' flagship. The American commander no longer permitted himself to assume that the fleet from Rhode Island would get to Virginia before the British.

Washington's return journey was by way of Lebanon. Over an exceedingly bad road he reached Headquarters March 20, but he found there no reports that relieved his anxiety. On the twenty-first he received word of the presence of Destouches' squadron in Hampton Roads. Was it now too late? American spies and lookouts insisted a fleet of transports had left Sandy Hook March 13. These assuredly were being sent to Chesapeake

Bay and, on arrival, would make Arnold dangerous again. Recent perils were redoubled. Virginia might be subjugated and Greene destroyed. Washington reminded himself, again and again, that "we ought not to look back, unless it is to derive useful lessons from past errors, and for the purpose of profiting by dear bought experience"; but this time, when he saw America's affairs brought, as he said, "to an awful crisis," he could not deny himself the reflection that great opportunity had come when the French vessels temporarily outnumbered the British. He did not wish his friends to think he had failed to urge the utmost be made of it, and he explained the circumstances when he answered communications from Philip Schuyler, Joseph Jones, William Fitzhugh and John Armstrong, though he carefully marked the paragraph "Private." In a hasty letter to Lund Washington, he said somewhat awkwardly:

. . . this I mention in confidence, that the French Fleet and detachment did not undertake the enterprize they are now upon, when I first proposed it to them; the destruction of Arnolds Corps would then have been inevitable before the British fleet could have been in a condition to put to Sea. Instead of this the small squadron, which took the *Romulus* and other Vessels was sent, and could not, as I foretold, do anything without a Land force at Portsmouth.

For a man of cheerful self-mastery Washington's mood was of the blackest when, on March 30, doubt over the outcome of the French naval expedition was removed. He learned that Destouches and Arbuthnot had met off the Virginia Capes on the sixteenth, engaged for an hour and then broken off an action neither seemed anxious to press. Although the advantage, except in casualties, was on the side of Destouches, he had decided that the British could outsail his fleet, could get into the Chesapeake before him, and that, therefore, it seemed best to return to Newport. Details were reported within a few hours after the first news. French leaders were anxious to convince Washington that Destouches did his utmost. Next time, they said, he might have better luck.

Anxiety for Destouches' fleet had been matched by anxiety over Greene. As early as March 15 it had been known that Greene defiantly had recrossed the Roanoke River and had a somewhat less gloomy prospect, though he was weaker than some members of Congress were inclined to think. At last, on March 31, Washington received a brief dispatch from him, with a copy of a report the commander of the Southern Department had sent Congress regarding a battle with Cornwallis at Guilford Court House, North Carolina, on the fifteenth. In a hot action, British discipline and persistence had driven Greene from the position he had chosen, but he had inflicted losses that would burden British adversaries who had destroyed their wagons and had little equipment with which to care for their wounded. Some leaders, hearing this encouraging news, applied Pyrrhus's lament to Cornwallis: another such victory and he would be undone. Washington was more cautious in his judgment. He held to his belief that the troops who recently had sailed from New York had been dispatched to reenforce Cornwallis. They now were said to be fifteen to sixteen hundred in number, under Maj. Gen. William Phillips, and were free to land at Portsmouth, Wilmington, or any other harbor from which they could march expeditiously to Cornwallis. Arnold, too, might be strong enough to join Cornwallis with part of his forces or to shape his plans in cooperation with those of the General.

Whatever advantage Greene might have gained at Guilford Court House would be cancelled if Greene had to face Cornwallis, Phillips and perhaps half of Arnold's command. Could Washington give assistance? Recruiting showed no improvement; food was as scarce and transportation as feeble as ever; the prospect of the regular supply of clothing was improved by the resignation of James Wilkinson as Clothier General, but men still were being returned unfit for duty because they were almost naked. With French aid from Newport it might be possible to execute a demonstration in front of New York that would prevent further detachment of British forces to Virginia; but beyond this, what could be done to help Greene? One possibility of relief in the Southern Department was the dangerous course of sending Lafayette to Greene. Should the Marquis go to Greene despite Destouches' failure, or should he resume his place in an Army that thereby would admit its inability to reenforce Greene? Washington thought the subject of sufficient importance to justify a council of war. The unanimous decision was to reverse the march of Lafayette, who already was moving north from Annapolis, and to send him to join Greene. Orders to this effect were forwarded April 6. Approximately two weeks later Washington received from Greene a dispatch that told of Cornwallis's withdrawal from Guilford Court House to Wilmington. That town was at a greater distance than Greene could attempt to cover. "In this critical and distressing situation," said Greene, "I am determined to carry the war immediately into South Carolina." He explained: "The enemy will be obliged to follow us, or give up their posts in that State. If the former takes place, it will draw the war out of this State, and give it an opportunity to raise its proportion of men. If they leave their posts to fall, they must lose more there than they can gain here. If we continue in this State, the enemy will hold their possessions in both."

Lafayette was well advanced on his march when Washington learned of this bold plan. Would the Marquis be able to go as far as Greene might proceed? Could Lafayette afford to leave Arnold and Phillips to do their worst in Virginia while he moved to the Carolinas? Everything depended on Greene and his men, on the rally of Virginia and North Carolina, and, as always, on the hope that the French would have more ships of war on the coast than the British manned. Until that great day arrived the American cause might sink lower and lower. In a letter to Laurens, Washington reviewed some of the struggles against nakedness and hunger: ". . . why," he said, "need I run into the detail, when it may be declared in a word that we are at the end of our tether, and that now or never our deliverance must come."

To all the anguish of leadership there now was added personal humiliation of a sort Washington had not known during the entire war. In a post captured during the final days of March by Loyalist partisans near

Smith's Clove was a full and candid letter on the military situation written by Washington to Benjamin Harrison. Washington took the loss stoically and perhaps did not recall the contents of other communications that had found their way to the desk of his adversary, if indeed, he knew which had been captured and which had gone by a different post. Then, about a fortnight after this incident, the General found in Rivington's *Gazette* of April 4 a brief extract from the letter he had written Lund Washington when he had felt that the small size of de Tilly's squadron and the delay in the sailing of Destouches' ships had cost the allies an opportunity of destroying Arnold. Publication of the criticism was certain to be offensive to Rochambeau, Destouches and the other French leaders whose support was more desperately needed than ever. Washington had told Laurens it was "now or never" with French deliverance. Could it be that a careless letter had increased the chance the answer would be "never"?

Rochambeau's dispatch on the subject was so dignified and restrained that it scarcely could be called a protest. Washington left the drafting of an answer to Hamilton, who submitted a text that displayed both frankness and self-restraint. In the paper the Colonel placed before him, Washington expressed his regret "that an accident should have put it in the [enemy's] power to give the world anything from me which may contain an implication the least disagreeable to you or to the Chevalier Destouches." Washington went on: "Whatever construction it may bear, I beg your Excellency will consider the letter as to a private friend, a gentleman who has the directions of my concerns at home, totally unconnected with public affairs, and on whose discretion I could absolutely rely."

Another embarrassment came in a letter of Lund Washington's, followed by one Lafayette sent from Alexandria on April 23. These papers explained that when a British sloop came up the Potomac many Negroes left Mount Vernon and joined the enemy. Lund himself went aboard, carried food to the officers and consented to supply provisions in hope that he might procure the return of the slaves. "This," said the Marquis, "being done by the gentleman who in some measure represents you at your house will certainly have a bad effect, and contrasts with spirited answers from some neighbors that had their houses burnt accordingly." Washington's sense of justice told him that Lund had done this to save Mount Vernon from possible destruction, but he could not withhold a stiff rebuke. He told his manager: ". . . to go on board their vessels; carry them refreshments; commune with a parcel of plundering scoundrels, and request a favor by asking the surrender of my Negroes, was exceedingly ill-judged, and 'tis to be feared, will be unhappy in its consequences, as it will be a precedent for others, and may become a subject of animadversion."

Now, as usual, Washington's troops were hungry if they were not naked, without pay when not without food. Every effort to keep the Army together was hampered by the smallness of his staff. Hamilton declined to resume his regular place. The determination of the General to do absolute justice was not shaken but he could not accede immediately to Hamilton's appeal for field assignment. Washington undertook to get proper rank and seniority for the self-effacing Tench Tilghman who, with David Humphreys, temporarily constituted the official "family." Jonathan Trumbull, Jr., the choice of Washington for the post of military secretary, promised to join the staff early in June; other appointees were under consideration.

By May 13, Washington saw that large opportunity awaited his troops if they could be fed. Luzerne wrote that he was going to urge Destouches to make another effort in the Chesapeake. Washington had a thousand positive wishes for this, and forwarded Luzerne's letter to Destouches; but an express from the east brought word that command at Newport had changed: on the sixth the French frigate *Concorde* had landed at Boston the Comte de Barras, who was to relieve the temporary successor of de Ternay. The same frigate included among its passengers the Viscomte de Rochambeau, son of the General. A shower of letters from the senior, from Barras, from General the Chevalier François Jean de Chastellux, and from Destouches, conveyed intimations that the younger Rochambeau had important dispatches. An early meeting with Washington was much desired by Rochambeau and Barras. The reply of the American commander was immediate: He would be happy to meet the gentlemen on May 21, and, as the Connecticut Legislature would be in session at Hartford, he would suggest Wethersfield for the conference.

Washington set out May 18 for Wethersfield. As the second day's ride was nearing its end a group of gentlemen met the General and escorted him to Joseph Webb's house at Wethersfield. May 21 Washington and his officers rode up to Hartford to welcome Rochambeau, who arrived about noon. The French commander was accompanied by Chastellux and an official "family," but there was one disappointment: Barras had been detained in Rhode Island by the appearance of a British fleet, assumed to be that of Arbuthnot.

The next day Rochambeau confirmed the content of dispatches from France: A large fleet under the Admiral Comte de Grasse had left Brest, with infantry reenforcements on transports, and was going to the West Indies; but when this fleet had passed the Azores, vessels with six hundred troops were to be detached and, under the escort of the *Sagittaire,* were to proceed to Newport. With this accession of strength, where should the French take the field? That was what Rochambeau wished most of all to consider.

The obvious alternatives were Virginia and New York harbor. Either the French and Americans had to proceed overland to Virginia or they must conduct operations in New York. What was the judgment of Washington? The American commander did not hesitate: Could not the situation in Virginia be relieved more economically and more readily, in the controlling circumstances, by attacking New York than by attempting anything else? In event the enemy could not be challenged at sea, no better plan seemed to Washington to be within the means of the French and Americans than that of threatening vigorously the reduced garrison of New York. Clinton then would have to recall troops from Virginia or risk the loss of his most valuable base. Subtraction from the force of the enemy might serve Greene and Lafayette almost as well as additions to their own numbers. Would it not be incomparably easier to move the French from

Newport to the lower Hudson than to attempt to drag the whole Army to James River in Virginia? Nothing short of the transfer of all Clinton's troops to the South could justify that ordeal.

Rochambeau had another and exciting question: The principal French fleet was going to the West Indies—he did not say why or for how long—but if a naval reenforcement were to appear on the coast, how did Washington think it should be employed? The General replied that a choice of plan depended primarily on the size of the squadron. It might be used to help in the New York operations; it might be of largest good in circumstances not foreseen. The second of these possibilities was suggested because it was plain that a fleet of superior strength could intercept supplies for the enemy in Virginia and the Carolinas and thereby stop almost immediately the progress of Cornwallis and his columns. The nearer hope was in having de Grasse come to New York where he might cut off Arbuthnot from that base or seal the British ships in the harbor. Barras then would be free to join de Grasse. After that, any advantage that sea power could yield the allies might be within their grasp. The Frenchmen consented that Washington might bring the question to the attention of Luzerne and might say they were of one mind with the American in urging that de Grasse come to the coast of the United States. Washington forthwith addressed the French Minister, whom he urged to write the Admiral. When Washington dismounted at the New Windsor Headquarters about sunset May 25 he could tell himself that the conference had been successful, except for the absence of Barras whom it was most desirable he know personally; but, as generally happened, bad news awaited him: Martha was quite sick; the enemy's forces from Canada were said to have reached Crown Point, whence it was thought they might penetrate into the valley of the Mohawk. This danger from the direction of the New York lakes continued to hang over Washington, but it did not become acute while he was making his initial preparations for the joint attack on New York. To that operation news from Virginia and the Carolinas gave the spur of immediacy. The enemy in Virginia had advanced as far as Petersburg, and on April 25 Lord Rawdon had made a successful sally from Camden, South Carolina, which Greene had been besieging. Washington thought this investment did vast honor to Greene and forecast the loss by the British of more of their isolated posts in South Carolina, unless Cornwallis marched to relieve them; but, meanwhile, what was to be the fate of Virginia, whither the British seemed to be making ready to send still more troops from New York? There even were rumors of a transfer of the entire British army to Virginia, in which event the difficulties of land transportation could not be permitted to stand in the way of a similar movement by the Continental Army.

The very next development threatened to destroy the whole of the Wethersfield plan. As Washington had few expresses and no cipher for correspondence with Greene and Lafayette, his own seal and the vigilance of the post rider were his sole security of such military secrets as he had to transmit. In spite of previous capture of embarrassing letters, the General on May 31 wrote Lafayette via the regular public channels that the joint operation of Americans and French was to be against New York primarily because "it was thought that we had a tolerable prospect of expelling the enemy or obliging them to withdraw part of their force from the southward, which last would give the most effectual relief to those States"—the secret of all others it was important to keep from the British. This precious paper was in a mail taken from the carrier June 3 by "an artful and enterprising fellow." Sir Henry Clinton valued the seizure so highly that he gave the captor two hundred guineas, but he could not refrain from boasting of his good luck and foolishly let it be known that he was acquainted with the plans of the Americans. Washington, on his side, tried to depreciate the importance of the disclosures and sharpen the question the British soon began to ask—was the letter a ruse? The awkward reality persisted: If Washington made active preparations for an attack on New York, would not Clinton conclude that the dispatch to Lafayette was authentic and that Washington was trying to tempt the British to recall troops from Virginia?

News that came to American Headquarters in early June indicated that this plan, or a second best, had to be put into operation with the least possible delay. The situation in Virginia had become desperate. Cornwallis was known to have formed junction at Petersburg on May 20 with Phillips's troops, who now were under Arnold; additional British transports had arrived in the Chesapeake; Joseph Jones sent warning that disaster might weaken resistance. Lafayette must avoid action until he was reenforced or Greene could take some of the pressure from him.

Help must be given Lafayette. Congress immediately authorized requests for 4200 three-months' militia from Pennsylvania, Delaware and Maryland. Washington did not fail to make it plain that if Virginia was overrun, the enemy soon would be north of the Potomac. The reorganized Pennsylvania Line, which included numerous veterans, must be started from York and pushed to Lafayette by steady marches.

While these hurried measures for the relief of imperilled Virginia were still in their first stage, Washington learned that Admiral Barras disapproved the suggestion made at Wethersfield for the removal of the French fleet to Boston after Rochambeau left Rhode Island for the Hudson with the greater part of the French infantry. Besides, the French now wanted one thousand militia, not the agreed half that number, for the protection of the Newport anchorage and the stores. Washington had to ask Massachusetts and Rhode Island for five hundred each to serve with the four hundred French whom Rochambeau intended to leave there, an arrangement that was not effected otherwise than with some muttering by the state authorities. The American commander renewed his appeal to Rochambeau for the earliest possible advance of the French infantry to the vicinity of New York. He had to resist pleas that he go to Virginia and assume personal direction there. Washington needed to remain where he was and carry the heaviest of a soldier's responsibility, that of sound decision. ". . . we must not despair," he wrote John Mathews, "the game is yet in our hands; to play it well is all we have to do, and I trust the experience of error will enable us to act better in future." Washington added: "A cloud may yet pass over us; individuals may be ruined; and the country at large, or particular States, undergo temporary distress; but certain I am that it is in our power to bring the war to a happy conclusion."

Behind this now was more than hope. "Peace talk" was in the air. Washington listened but did not believe that a general treaty would be signed within a year. Then, in the last week in May, he had this intelligence from Laurens, who wrote at Passy, March 24: "The naval dispositions were made before my arrival; five ships of the line for the East Indies with troops; twenty, commanded by de Grasse, for the West Indies, twelve of which are to proceed to America. They will probably arrive on our coast in July. We have no news yet of their departure." Washington so often had been given false news by men who believed it true that his impulse was to doubt, but daily the evidence accumulated until, at length, on June 13, confirmation came. A dispatch from Rochambeau, covered one in which de Grasse stated that he was bringing the French fleet to the coast of North America for a limited time about July 15. Washington's mind ran ahead to what might be accomplished then. Rochambeau must be urged to appeal for the use of the troops that accompanied the Admiral. If they were made available, then the failure of the States to supply their quotas would not be fatal; and if the men-of-war under de Grasse were added to those of Barras and the total exceeded . . . but Rochambeau must be reminded at once: "Your Excellency will be pleased to recollect that New York was looked upon by us as the only practicable object under present circumstances; but should we be able to secure a naval superiority, we may perhaps find others more practicable and equally advisable."

What could be undertaken after de Grasse's arrival depended on the solution of a complicated equation of at least five factors—the margin of superiority the Admiral would possess, the duration of his stay in American waters, the number of troops he brought with him, the reenforcement of the British meantime, and the successful activity of the States to make the Continentals numerically effective and mobile. These were contingencies so involved and uncertain that while Washington canvassed many possible combinations, he concluded the most practicable course was to hold for the time being to the Wethersfield plan: he would bring Rochambeau's troops to New York to take the first steps in the investment of that city while he did his utmost to build up the American Army. De Grasse would decide where the French fleet should operate; the allied land forces must be ready to conform and, if need be, to shift the scene of operations.

Washington concluded that the movement of Rochambeau's troops to New York might present a chance for double surprise of the enemy at night. If Continentals could be brought down the Hudson and thrown against the outer defences of Manhattan Island at the time Rochambeau arrived from the east, advantage might be gained that could be exploited later. Washington decided to make the effort and personally supervised most of the preparations. Painstakingly he tried to make certain that he effected what he had failed at Germantown, the simultaneous convergence of columns that used different routes. When the moves were made, nothing went even decently well. Almost before a blow could be struck, the advantage of surprise was lost, and nearly all the British outposts were withdrawn over Harlem River to positions the allies could not assail. Nothing was gained beyond a good opportunity of close reconnaissance; the failure of the operation in every other particular was complete.

To Washington, as always, the lesson was, Remember the reasons for failure—and try again! He moved to a position near Dobbs Ferry, with the French infantry on his left and their cavalry still farther eastward, and he carefully took time for ceremonial visits to Rochambeau's Headquarters. The enemy remained obligingly lazy in New York and produced nothing more in the way of news than that Arbuthnot had turned over the naval command to Admiral Thomas Graves on July 4. Washington continued his struggle to procure bread and meat for his men with some prospect of finding enough to keep them alive, but recruitment by the States lagged so wretchedly that he had only 5835 Continental rank and file in mid-July. A humiliating plight this was, especially as he had told Rochambeau that he hoped to have 10,250 troops available for the operations against New York. He and the French commander continued their reconnaissances, as if preparing for action, and on July 22/23 they made a demonstration in front of King's Bridge and near Morrisania.

Startling changes were reported to Washington from Virginia. Cornwallis and his restless cavalry commanders, Banastre Tarleton and John Simcoe, had been tramping and galloping as if trying to make up for the long siesta of Clinton. Tarleton had led five hundred men half across the state to a magazine in Charlottesville. Simcoe drove Steuben and 550 recruits across James River at Point of Fork. Apparently, Cornwallis's maneuvers were designed to destroy arms and manufactories, entrap Lafayette, if possible, and, at the least, prevent the junction of the Marquis's force with Wayne's part of the reorganized Pennsylvania Line, which was moving south. Lafayette played hide-and-seek with the British in frank admission that "we cannot afford losing"; and after Cornwallis left Richmond June 20 and started toward Williamsburg, the Frenchman acted as if he were pursuing a defeated foe. On the twenty-sixth he had the temerity to assail Simcoe's Rangers. Lafayette was repulsed with the loss of at least eighteen Continentals; but when Simcoe counterattacked he had to pull back.

Cornwallis remained at Williamsburg, too strong to be attacked by Lafayette; but it was one thing to have the British commander marching unchallenged through Virginia and quite a different matter to have him halfway down the Peninsula where he was watched by the Marquis and might be assailed readily if de Grasse came to Virginia waters with the transports of a powerful fleet. Washington's prudent order to Lafayette was that he concentrate his forces and await the arrival of a confidential messenger, when one could be found to carry him information "of very great importance." The next report Washington had of the Marquis was that he had been defeated July 6 at Green Spring. Casualties of at least 139 did not spoil Lafayette's usual good luck; after the engagement Cornwallis crossed the James and marched for Portsmouth as if he were in retreat.

Greene had not called on the reenforcements Washington had di-

MAP / 14

THE MARCH TO YORKTOWN AND
THE BATTLE OF THE CHESAPEAKE CAPES

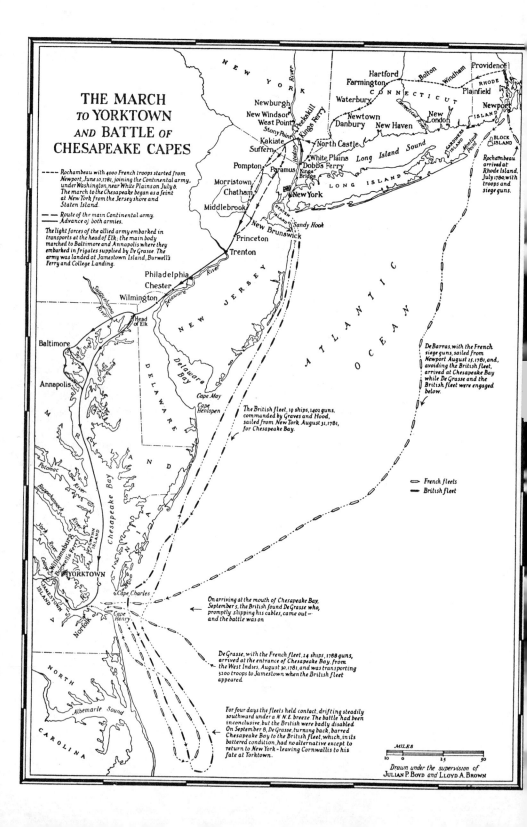

THE MARCH
TO YORKTOWN
AND BATTLE OF
CHESAPEAKE CAPES

—————— Rochambeau with 4000 French troops started from
Newport, June 10, 1781, joining the Continental army,
under Washington, near White Plains on July 6.
The march to the Chesapeake began as a feint
at New York from the Jersey shore and
Staten Island.

——————— Route of the main Continental army.
————— Advance of both armies.

The light forces of the allied army embarked in
transports at the head of Elk; the main body
marched to Baltimore and Annapolis where they
embarked in frigates supplied by De Grasse. The
army was landed at Jamestown Island, Burwell's
Ferry and College Landing.

Rochambeau
arrived at
Rhode Island,
July 1780, with
troops and
siege guns.

De Barras, with the French
siege guns, sailed from
Newport August 15, 1781, and,
avoiding the British fleet,
arrived at Chesapeake Bay
while De Grasse and the
British fleet were engaged
below.

The British fleet, 19 ships, 1402 guns,
commanded by Graves and Hood,
sailed from New York August 31, 1781,
for Chesapeake Bay.

⇒ French fleets
— British fleet

On arriving at the mouth of Chesapeake Bay,
September 5, the British found De Grasse who,
promptly slipping his cables, came out
and the battle was on.

De Grasse, with the French fleet, 24 ships, 1788 guns,
arrived at the entrance of Chesapeake Bay, from
the West Indies, August 30, 1781, and was transporting
3100 troops to Jamestown when the British fleet
appeared

For four days the fleets held contact, drifting steadily
southward under a N.N.E. breeze. The battle had been
inconclusive, but the British were badly disabled
On September 8, De Grasse, turning back, barred
Chesapeake Bay to the British fleet, which, in its
battered condition, had no alternative except to
return to New York – leaving Cornwallis to his
fate at Yorktown.

MILES

Drawn under the supervision of
JULIAN P. BOYD and LLOYD A. BROWN

rected to him because he had hoped that if Lafayette retained these men, the Marquis would be able to avoid a "capital misfortune." Greene continued to feel concern over the superiority of the enemy's mounted forces, but with his little "army" he had maneuvered the British from all their positions in Georgia, outside Savannah, and from most of South Carolina. These were strokes that Washington praised warmly and gratefully. The most likely move of the British was for Cornwallis to establish himself strongly at Portsmouth, as Washington saw it now, and then to reenforce New York with part of his troops and Charleston with the remainder. Should an operation against the lower Hudson prove impracticable, even with de Grasse's help, and the enemy still remain in Virginia, the campaign should be transferred to that state. Tactical dispositions in the Old Dominion seemed to be favorable, and Greene wrote confidently that an adequate force could dispose of Cornwallis in three weeks. The possibility of a laborious shift of scene appeared to Washington sufficiently real to prompt him to urge that Barras keep the French transports off Rhode Island in condition to sail on short notice.

Washington thought the chances of success in North River were dwindling so fast that he scarcely was justified in pursuing his plans there; but as he could not hasten by a single hour the arrival of de Grasse's fleet, he was in the difficult situation where he neither could abandon the enterprise against New York nor delay much longer the arrangements for a move south. He had simultaneously to be asking himself how he could get forage and wheat and wagonage and much besides when he had no means of paying for anything. Collapse had come in May and by the middle of July had reached the stage where hard money alone was used in the market. This perplexity was brought to Washington's own marquee by a visit from the Superintendent of Finance on August 11. By direction of Congress, Robert Morris and Richard Peters of the Board of War came to confer with Washington on the ironical question of providing an Army for 1782—though scarcely more than 50 per cent of the forces authorized for 1781 had yet been assembled. Washington undertook preparation of a paper to show why no reduction in the military establishment could safely be planned. Logically, this was not a difficult task; practically, it was hard to think clearly of what might or might not be required because every day's dispatches made plain the all-absorbing fact that bleak defeat or shining victory was close at hand.

The great, the long-awaited news arrived on August 14: Barras wrote that de Grasse was coming to the Chesapeake, not to New York, and that the Admiral had twenty-nine warships with more than three thousand troops! No such intelligence as this had been received since that glorious April 30, 1778, had brought news of the French alliance. As always, there were shadows. One of them was a warning that de Grasse could not remain later than October 15. Another was a hint by Barras that he might undertake operations with his squadron against British shipping off Newfoundland, a diversion that must be prevented if possible. The length of de Grasse's service was much too brief unless plans for the early siege of New York were abandoned and all energies devoted to transferring Rochambeau's army to Virginia, along with all American forces not imperative for the protection of West Point. New York City remained the great strategical prize, but it must be left for another campaign.

Washington started immediately his preparations. He decided that approximately 2500 men would be the maximum number he could afford to send from his own Army, along with the whole of the French, and he proceeded to select the troops who were to go. Choice of aggressive and competent command for this detachment was the next duty and a delicate one. As most of the troops named for the detachment were under Alexander McDougall, his chief thought it proper to offer him the command. When McDougall declined, Washington reverted to the rule of seniority and named Benjamin Lincoln, to the deep disappointment of Robert Howe and, in some measure, of Lafayette. In the light infantry, the command of Alexander Scammell was to be raised to its authorized strength of four hundred. A place in that expanded corps already had been found for Hamilton, whose stubborn pride Washington overlooked in careful justice to the brilliant New Yorker's shining service. Lafayette was admonished to prevent the retreat of Cornwallis into Carolina, and was authorized to retain Wayne if that officer had not marched to join Greene.

The lines of advance of the French and Americans were studied; a new appeal was to be made to the States for recruits to serve with the main Army and for militia to guard the defences of the Hudson. Rochambeau and Washington called on Barras to abandon his plan for an expedition to Newfoundland, and they succeeded in getting the Admiral's promise to join de Grasse in the Chesapeake and protect vessels that were to carry the French siege artillery and the Americans' reserve of "salted provisions." If weather favored, Barras would sail on August 21 from Newport for Virginia. This decision was of the highest importance. With Barras's squadron, de Grasse almost certainly would have a heavier broadside than the enemy could bring to bear. The guns and the rations from Rhode Island might make the difference between sure victory and possible failure on land.

Washington kept clearly before him what Lafayette stated in simplest terms, "should a French fleet now come in Hampton Roads the British army would, I think, be ours"; but Washington stressed the provisos that de Grasse should arrive opportunely and that Cornwallis should not escape meantime. Cornwallis had gone to Yorktown. At that point on the Virginia Peninsula, Washington reasoned, the British commander was in a trap that could be sprung. He and Rochambeau drafted suggestions for the guidance of de Grasse in the situations the Admiral might find on arrival. Then they faced the hard question on which nearly everything else might depend: How was the greater part of the allied Army to leave its positions north of New York and proceed southward without being attacked while in motion? General Chastellux had suggested that when de Grasse approached Boston or Newport, which then was expected to be the Admiral's port of call, the French force should advance into Jersey and remain there in a threatening position until the fleet took aboard the heavy guns and stores left in Rhode Island. Thereupon all the men-of-war should proceed to the Chesapeake and the entire Army move overland to Trenton and thence by water to Chester or New Castle. From that point the troops should tramp to Head of Elk and, reembarking, should go to Yorktown or some other landing close to the British. Washington and Rochambeau adopted this plan, or one very similar to it, and decided to develop the first phase as a ruse. Word was to be spread that de Grasse was expected hourly; the French and the American detachment intended for service in Virginia were to be moved to New Jersey, as if they were to assail Staten Island; inquiry was to be made for boats everywhere between Newark and Amboy; pontoons were to be paraded so that the dullest-witted Loyalist would guess they were intended to support a span between the mainland and the island; a bread oven built for the French at Chatham was to be mentioned as if it were the first of several to be constructed nearby. The hope was that spies would conclude that Rochambeau's troops were to remain in Jersey for weeks.

Washington surprisingly was able to begin his march by August 19. The first phase of the movement, though without material accident, was completed more slowly than Washington had hoped. He warned his officers that success might depend thereafter on speed. The British showed no curiosity as the Army crept south. Some activity was observed in Graves's fleet; otherwise the enemy kept quiet, and the march continued until the twenty-seventh when reports of an increase in British force on Staten Island led Washington to halt for a day at Springfield and close the rear. When he wrote Congress that day, reporting his advance, he made no prediction, but in less formal correspondence he expressed confidence. "The moment is critical," he said, "the opportunity precious, the prospects most happily favorable."

That evening brought news of reenforcements to the British fleet off Sandy Hook. Had not this news of British naval reenforcement created a measure of suspense, September 30 would have been rewarding to Washington. He felt that it was possible to continue the ruse of an attack on Staten Island one day longer, and to bolster this artifice he hurried his Americans forward in three columns by separate routes. Washington waited for a short time at Trenton and then set out for Philadelphia with Rochambeau, Chastellux and their entourage. The approach of the cavalcade to the Quaker City was known long enough in advance for the City Guard to serve as escort. At the city, Washington did not permit events of the day to occupy his hours so completely that he had no time for the task of procuring transportation to Head of Elk. A prudent agreement provided that the troops should march all the way. Water transportation was to be employed only for the siege guns and the heavy stores. This would delay the march of the infantry, but it was the best arrangement that could be made.

Then came news that threatened to change everything. The morning of September 1 brought a letter of August 31 which announced that the British fleet had sailed from New York. Washington's immediate conclusion was that these warships were trying to intercept the French squadron from Newport. The fleet now had reenforcements, identified as Hood's fleet and counted at thirteen. Total British strength, therefore, was twenty ships of the line, enough to overwhelm Barras. On the other hand, if Barras joined de Grasse and the two met Hood and Graves, many a British standard might fall. De Grasse alone might worst the two. If either de Grasse or Barras reached the Chesapeake and the British did not, then Cornwallis assuredly would be captured unless Lafayette most improbably let him slip past. One contingency remained, affrighting and perhaps fatal: Suppose the combined British fleets, with reenforcements for Cornwallis, should get to Virginia waters ahead of de Grasse—what would happen then?

Much business lay at hand on September 2. The American Army marched through Philadelphia in a cloud of dust that could not choke enthusiasm, but pleasures were alloyed and perplexities were aggravated by the fateful questions, Where was de Grasse; what had befallen Barras? Excellent reports from Lafayette of his measures to hamper Cornwallis were supplemented by dispatches in which Greene suggested substantially what Washington hoped to be able to do in the South. All this was gratifying and might be reassuring *if* Barras escaped and de Grasse arrived early with superior force. The contingency was similar in nature to that which Washington had faced without flinching over and over again, when the American cause had hung on some wretched uncontrollable "if." The difference was in scale. This time the "if" almost certainly would determine whether the war would be dragged on feebly or would be ended in swift victory and a peace of independence.

In half hope, half apprehension, Washington arranged in Philadelphia for the repair of roads he was to use on the southward march and, as there no longer was possibility of concealing the objective of the Army, he called on New Jersey, Delaware and Maryland for supplies. On the morning of the fifth he said farewell to Philadelphia and au revoir to Rochambeau, who elected to go by water to Chester. Three miles of sombre riding southward from Chester. Then a horseman on the road ahead, an express: Admiral de Grasse is in the Chesapeake with twenty-eight ships of the line and three thousand troops!

De Grasse had arrived with a powerful fleet and with troops more numerous than those of the American detachment under Lincoln! Joyfully Washington directed his cavalcade to turn around and trot back to Chester, in order that he might await Rochambeau's landing and announce the glorious tidings. Lafayette and the French reenforcements now could prevent the retreat of Cornwallis by land; de Grasse could cut off all relief from the sea—that was the prospect. As Washington talked of this, Rochambeau's vessel hove in sight. The waiting American General forgot his dignity the moment he recognized the figure of the Count on deck. Washington took off his hat, pulled out his handkerchief and waved both with wide sweeps of his arms. When Rochambeau stepped ashore, Washington embraced his astonished comrade. Victory was ahead, the first clear-cut major victory he ever had won in the field. He had been waiting and working six years for that!

On the morning of September 6, Washington pushed swiftly to Head of Elk. There he announced in General Orders the arrival of de

Grasse: "As no circumstance could possibly have happened more opportunely in point of time, no prospect could ever have promised more important successes, and nothing but our want of exertions can probably blast
the pleasing prospects before us." To bring more sunshine to clearing skies,
he hinted that a month's pay might be forthcoming, a half-promise that
Robert Morris contrived to redeem to the extent of twenty thousand dollars in specie, the first Continental pay ever issued the troops in "hard
money."

In projecting now the strategy of his future operations, Washington
overcame a measure of the caution that long years of defensive war had
made second nature to him. "Nothing now gives me uneasiness," Washington wrote his Chief Engineer, "but the two things you mention, not hearing from the Count de Barras . . . and the resolution for the departure of
the fleet at a certain time." Word was sent de Grasse that the utmost expedition would be employed in pushing the column forward and that, meantime, his companions in arms were confident he would do everything possible to prevent the escape of Cornwallis. Final loading and troop movement were left to Lincoln; Washington prepared to hurry forward, with
Rochambeau and Chastellux, to join Lafayette.

After an early start for Baltimore from Head of Elk on the eighth,
Washington set so rapid a pace that his French colleagues decided to spare
their horses and their thighs by letting him dash ahead while they followed
at less exhausting speed. Fast as Washington rode, the news of his coming
outstripped him. When he approached the town during the afternoon, he
found Capt. Nicholas Moore's light dragoon militia drawn up to escort
him. After darkness, every part of the town was illuminated in his honor.

With a single member of his military staff, Washington set out September 9 in an effort to have a day on his own plantation before guests arrived. At length, in deepening shadows, Washington dismounted where he
had not set foot for six years and four months. Much of interest to the
master of Mount Vernon was to be seen on the morning of the tenth, but
duties more immediate awaited a host who was to entertain under his own
roof the staffs of Rochambeau and Chastellux, as well as the two Generals
themselves and his own "family."

Dinner was made ready for a large company, made ready with ease,
because there was no shortage at Mount Vernon of any food needed to
load a table in summer. Washington's military family arrived just at meal
time and no doubt approved both the cooking and the abundance of their
General's home. That evening Rochambeau and his aides received welcome to the best quarters their host could offer. The next day, September
11, Chastellux and his staff reached Mount Vernon and had the same
handshake. Jonathan Trumbull, Jr., who was glimpsing for the first time
the life of a great plantation, wrote admiringly in his diary: "A numerous
family now present. All accommodated. An elegant seat and situation,
great appearance of opulence and real exhibitions of hospitality and
princely entertainment."

The weariness of his fellow-travelers and the delights of home kept
Washington on the Potomac September 11. He still had no report of Barras

and none of any engagement with Cornwallis; but there were ugly tidings of the old persistent foe—hunger. Little or no flour was reaching the troops between the James and the York, because drought had shut down the mills. Militia were subsisting, in part, on "roastening ears" of green corn, four for each man daily. Washington immediately wrote an appeal to the Governor of Maryland for supplies that could be sent quickly down Chesapeake Bay. Even in these matters, the commander did not eclipse the host.

On the twelfth, Washington left home once again and rode straight to bad news. Between Colchester and Dumfries he met a rider with dispatches for Congress. The man said that de Grasse, hearing the enemy was off the Virginia Capes, had carried his fleet to sea, engaged the British and then disappeared with them. The outcome had not been reported when the messenger left the Virginia Peninsula. Anxiety rose instantly. The possibilities were dark, but at the moment they dictated one order only from Washington—that the boats coming from Head of Elk should put their troops ashore or, if they were in harbor, stay there and await further instructions. The cavalcade rode on, but eager, confident hope had been chilled. The familiar and remorseless contingencies of war were nearer. Instead of certainty of success there was at least a chance of a great disaster.

The company of horsemen who reached Williamsburg on the fourteenth had been thinned to twelve by hard driving, the dispatch of aides on special errands, and the tightened rein of those who had rather miss a formal entry than endure a furious pace. Rochambeau and Adjutant General Hand had remained with Washington; a few members of the two staffs had kept their saddles, half in discomfort and half in grumbling admiration of seniors who endured so hard a journey. Washington rode through the camp of Virginia militia without ceremony, but when he approached the French camp he thought it courteous to dismount and wait. In a short while up rode Lafayette and Gov. Thomas Nelson of Virginia, who was in direct command of the state militia. Close behind them was General the Marquis Saint-Simon-Montblérn, head of the French troops that had arrived with de Grasse. Lafayette dismounted instantly and clasped Washington enthusiastically in his arms. Then he presented Saint-Simon. Saint-Simon invited the Commander-in-Chief to ride through his camp where his troops were eager to see their leader. Washington observed them with interest and satisfaction—the first reenforcement to reach Lafayette and Wayne in what was designed to be the greatest concentration Washington ever had attempted. From the French "town" Washington and his swollen entourage rode into the area where the American tents were pitched. The drums rolled; the guns barked twenty-one times.

Provisions were still scarce, though the trouble was one of organization; there was no actual shortage of grain in Virginia or Maryland; the Eastern Shore was overflowing with abundant crops. Washington noted this information which, on the morrow, he would put into urgent form for Gov. Thomas Sim Lee of the adjoining state. Governor Nelson was there to speak for himself and was able to make an encouraging report.

During the night of September 14/15 or in the early morning of the fifteenth there came news that swept away most of the doubt that had overhung the operation against Cornwallis. De Grasse was back in Chesapeake Bay, with two captured frigates, after a favorable engagement with the British fleet. What was equally, important, Barras's squadron had joined him without meeting the British or suffering any injury. Every word of this lightened Washington's load! The troops on the shores of the upper Chesapeake might now be started south again. Many felicitations doubtless were exchanged, but the Commander-in-Chief, as systematic as ever, devoted part of the day to several new aspects of old problems of supply and leadership, and particularly three special preliminaries of a siege of Cornwallis's Yorktown Lines, which were assumed to be stronger every day. The escape of the British must be prevented. Additional troops must be found to increase the odds of attack and replace men who were certain to fall. Above everything else, assurance must be sought that the French fleet would stay in Virginia waters until the campaign was closed victoriously.

On the fifteenth, Washington requested an interview with de Grasse, and, while awaiting an answer, made a reconnaissance of the British position, received additional officers, and reviewed the Virginia Line. He might have occupied himself for days with things that needed to be done, but de Grasse did not give him the time. On the seventeenth, the Admiral had in James River the fine little captured vessel, the *Queen Charlotte*. With a favoring wind she brought Washington, Rochambeau and their staffs in sight of the French fleet the next morning. Before them rode thirty-two ships of the line, the largest number Washington ever had seen together. The friendly conference that followed on the *Ville de Paris* was scarcely more than a succession of explicit answers by de Grasse to questions Washington had prepared in advance: Instructions set October 15 as the Admiral's date of departure, but he would engage to remain through October. Washington could count on Saint-Simon's troops till the warships departed.

These answers gave Washington about forty days in which to compel Cornwallis to raise the white flag. Washington turned to a somewhat less essential subject, closing of the possible British line of escape up the York. The Admiral would reserve decision until reconnaissance had been made, but he added, *"je ferai certainement tout qui sera en mon pouvoir."* De Grasse offered the use of 1800 to 2000 men from the fleet but he wished them employed only for a sudden attack, a *coup de main*. He could not detach vessels to block the port of Wilmington, North Carolina, or to take possession of Charleston harbor as his ships were not suited for these enterprises. Cannon he could supply and a small amount of powder. So the conference was satisfying.

For the moment, amity might be enjoyed on other terms than those of cannon-balls and bayonets. The Admiral gave his guests a formal dinner and afterward showed them over his flagship. Then the officers of the fleet arrived to bow to the General. Soon after the Generals reached the *Queen Charlotte* for their return trip the wind rose and shifted and the weather suddenly changed from hot to cool. The vessel could make little headway, and when the wind ceased, the calm was a veritable mooring. A breeze on the evening of the nineteenth carried her so firmly aground that Washington and his companions got into a boat the next morning and headed for the frigate *Andromaque,* whence, after a hearty welcome and a stout breakfast, they started towards the mouth of the James. They found the little *Queen* off the shoal and ready to receive them. Washington went to his cabin, wrote his note of thanks to de Grasse and prepared two brief dispatches; for other correspondence a pitching vessel did not offer a comfortable desk. Soon the *Queen* was fighting so strong a headwind that there was no alternative to getting under the shelter of the land and spending the night. On the twenty-first the storm still was rattling the shrouds, and the weather seemed to mock hope. At dawn on the twenty-second, when the wind still resisted the ascent of the *Queen,* Washington would wait no longer. Unpleasant as it might be, a boat must work its way to the left bank of the James and climb by oar to College Creek. Washington, Rochambeau and the others got into the little craft for more hours of strain before they clambered ashore. It was noon when the party reached Williamsburg.

The British had attempted nothing in Washington's absence except an abortive raid by fireships on the French vessels at the mouth of the York. The one development of possible importance occurred the day he returned to camp: An express brought news that Rear Admiral Robert Digby was off the coast of the United States with British transports and with ships of the line variously estimated from three to ten. This news was passed on to de Grasse by the Baron von Closen, but it was not alarming to Washington as there were thirty-six French ships of the line in the Bay. The French left at Newport, to guard the base after the departure of Rochambeau, had arrived under Barras's convoy and had landed. Regiments from Head of Elk were beginning to come ashore. General Lincoln had reported on the evening of the twentieth; John Laurens had hurried to the hunt, in order to be "in at the kill." Virginia authorities and those of Maryland were working vigorously to find provisions and were bringing up sufficient flour for immediate requirements. Washington did not think it prudent to open the siege of Yorktown until he had in hand a large reserve of artillery ammunition, but he found no little pride in the successful timing of the concentration already effected. He wrote Heath, who had been left in command at West Point: "By information, Lord Cornwallis is incessantly at work on his fortifications, and is probably preparing to defend himself to the last extremity; a little time will probably decide his fate; with the blessing of Heaven, I feel it will prove favorable to the interests of America."

On the twenty-fifth von Closen reported de Grasse greatly disturbed by the news of Digby's approach, and that his officers were advising him to leave. Though de Grasse held to his engagements with the combined armies, the Admiral now set forth a new plan in a paper translated immediately. After what had been said at the conference on the eighteenth, it seemed incredible that de Grasse should propose to leave a thin squadron in the Chesapeake—two ships of the line and four smaller armed vessels—and sail away with no assurance that he could or would return. Naval men might explain that de Grasse would be restricted in movement if the

British entered the Bay and attacked between the mouth of the James and the so-called Middle Ground; but in Washington's mind the Admiral's altered plan seemed to threaten complete and irretrievable ruin of the entire campaign in Virginia. Washington's anxiety rose almost to agony. As soon as he had conferred with Rochambeau, he had Laurens prepare a letter to de Grasse that did not withhold strong words in a logical plea for him to remain in the Chesapeake. This was to be delivered by Lafayette, who combined full knowledge of the situation with prestige that would assure a respectful hearing.

Until word came from de Grasse Washington must wait in suspense and must go ahead with his preparations as if he were sure de Grasse would remain in Hampton Roads. The possibility that Cornwallis might proceed suddenly up the York or across that river and northward was constantly in the mind of Washington. He decided to strengthen Weedon's Virginia militia who were facing at Gloucester Point, on the north side of the York, a veteran British contingent under Tarleton. Washington requested Rochambeau to send the Duc de Lauzun to Gloucester with infantry and cavalry. On the James, French and American forces continued to arrive from the upper Chesapeake. On the twenty-sixth there was other encouragement, a report that Greene had gained a considerable advantage in a fight of August 8 with a British force under Col. Alexander Stewart.

Then on September 27, Washington received from de Grasse a dispatch on the twenty-fifth to which the American General must have listened with fast-beating heart:

SIR: I have the honor to inform your Excellency that I this morning convened a general council of my officers and laid before them the motives I had in assembling them . . . it was decided that the major part of the fleet should proceed to anchor in York River, that four or five vessels should be stationed in the James to pass up and down the river, and that you should aid us with the means of erecting on Point Comfort a battery of thirty-six pounders and mortars . . . for the good of our operation. . . .

There was more to the dispatch, but who had an ear for that? The great fact was that the fleet would remain. De Grasse had thrown himself heartily into a campaign that must be launched immediately. Let the order of battle be announced. The whole Army would march in one column at 5 A.M. on the twenty-eighth.

When Washington issued orders for a general advance to begin on the morning of September 28, 1781, he expected to be able to open trenches in the enemy's front within four days, but he anticipated stubborn resistance by the British in the fortified posts of Yorktown and at Gloucester Point. The test of argument would be combat. About sunrise the van moved off towards the British positions, distant about twelve miles; the main American and French forces proceeded as a single supporting column for four or five miles and then Lincoln's troops held to the right and Rochambeau's men turned to the left. Marching was slow but no enemy was encountered. Towards evening the line was drawn across the fields and through the woods, part within gunshot of the British advanced works.

The only interference was offered by some British dragoons who, when challenged by a few artillery shot, withdrew. As night approached, Washington had his men camp within approximately a mile of the enemy's left.

The crossing of Great Run was effected easily on the morning of the twenty-ninth. The French heavy artillery was beginning to arrive in James River, opposite Trebell's Landing, six or seven miles from camp. Until it arrived at the front there might be continuance of the infantry skirmishing, which broke out at intervals during the day, but Washington felt that his riflemen and Rochambeau's chasseurs à pied could hold their own.

The approach was over sandy ground. Woods and open fields covered the plain. The scene of operations had military importance in three respects only: it was small, it directly commanded the deep York River, and it was confined in a most unusual way. Southwest and west of the town, ran deeply scarped Yorktown Creek. South and southeast, not so scarped, were Wormeley's Pond and Creek. Between the marsh above Moore's Mill, which was on Wormeley's Pond, and the steep ravine of Yorktown Creek the plain was not more than half a mile wide and was known in part as Pigeon Quarter. This was the line of approach, or, from the British point of view, a narrow, defensible outer line. To force it might be costly; to turn it would be almost impossible on the British right because of earthworks constructed by Cornwallis's engineers. Turning the British left in the vicinity of Moore's Mill would be less difficult but would leave the allies at a considerable distance from the town.

When Washington looked at Pigeon Quarter some of his advance guard already had crossed the marsh above Wormeley's Pond and widened the front on which his line could advance; but four British fortifications were located between the two creeks so that they could sweep all the approaches. Washington could see that these works had stout abattis and chevaux-de-frise and that from them, probably, a good view could be had both of the plain near the town and the inner fortifications. As far as he could make out, these approaches seemed easy. There appeared to be no superiority of any part of these earthworks over any other. On his left the British had two redoubts, not connected with each other or with the main lines and approximately four hundred yards in rear of them.

Washington studied as much as was visible from his points of vantage, studied it with more experienced eyes than ever had been at his command in the past. For the first time he had the two greatest luxuries of command—definite superiority of force and uniform competence of command. The result of his reconnaissance and conferences was a three-fold decision to expedite the transportation of the artillery from the James, organize large working parties for providing cover as soon as the advance could begin, and proceed on the assumption that the utmost vigor must be displayed against adversaries who would not surrender until they had lost the power to escape or fight longer.

The next morning, September 30, Washington learned that Cornwallis had saved him much labor. During the night the British had evacuated all three of their works in the plain. Abandonment of these defences led Washington to wonder if the British were preparing to retreat across

MAP / 15

YORKTOWN, 1781

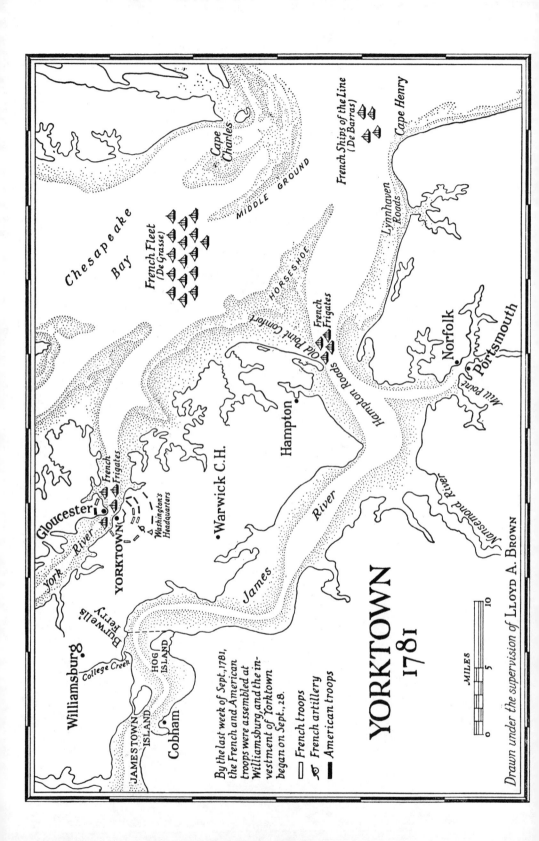

YORKTOWN
1781

Chesapeake Bay

*Cape Charles

MIDDLE GROUND

French Fleet
(De Grasse)

HORSESHOE

French Frigates

Old Point Comfort

French Ships of the Line
(De Barras)

Cape Henry

Lynnhaven Roads

Hampton Roads

Norfolk

• Portsmouth

Mill Point

Nansemond River

Hampton

Warwick C.H.

York River

French Frigates

Gloucester •

YORKTOWN •

△ Washington's Headquarters

James River

Williamsburg •

College Creek

Burwell's Ferry

JAMESTOWN ISLAND

HOG ISLAND

Cobham •

By the last week of Sept., 1781,
the French and American
troops were assembled at
Williamsburg, and the in-
vestment of Yorktown
began on Sept., 28.

— French troops
↗ French artillery
▬ American troops

MILES
0   5   10

Drawn under the supervision of LLOYD A. BROWN

the York or to the country up the river—a possibility that made him almost resentful of de Grasse's hesitancy to have ships ascend the stream and close one of these lines of withdrawal. Be that as it might, Cornwallis's withdrawal comforted Washington for a distressful incident of the day, the capture and cruel wounding of Col. Alexander Scammell, former Adjutant General and now a conspicuously able and gallant battalion commander in the light infantry.

Washington decided to tighten immediately the cord around the neck of the British: On the direct approach to Yorktown, between the two creeks, two redoubts were to be constructed in line with those the British had quit. A new effort must be made to prevail upon de Grasse to send frigates up the York. The Admiral must be requested to supply marines he had said he would lend the Army for a *coup de main*—a request granted before it was renewed. As soon as the remainder of the siege artillery was brought up, the forces would be equipped to attack; with the aid of the French, one at least of Cornwallis's avenues of escape would be closed. Next would come the swift construction of a trench opposite the enemy's main defences and then the rapid fortification of this "curtain" with redoubts and artillery.

In classical siegecraft this was the "opening of the first parallel," intended primarily to shorten the range for effective bombardment of the enemy's works. To determine the proper position of the parallel, Washington made a reconnaissance within three hundred yards of the advance posts of the British. Further study of the plain disclosed no obstacle to drawing the parallel, but Washington reasoned that nothing was to be gained by occupying the ground before all the siege guns were at hand. While gabions and fascines were being made in large number and the redoubts were being finished, the major task was to find teams to transport the last of the heavy pieces from Trebell's Landing. So long and wearing was this labor of dragging tons of iron through the sand that Washington did not celebrate and may not even have observed the completion on September 30 of what had been in many ways the great achievement of his Army after the Trenton campaign: On the final day of September, nearly all the most laggard sailing vessels from Head of Elk had cast anchor off College Creek, with the last of Rochambeau's siege artillery. That had completed on the Virginia Peninsula the concentration for which Washington had written the initial orders at Dobbs Ferry August 16.

Soon there was pleasant news from Gloucester. The Marquis de Choisy assumed command there October 1 after arriving from Newport with Barras's squadron, and he decided to draw the allied lines closer around Gloucester Point. On the morning of the third his van, passing down a lane slightly less than four miles from the Point, encountered the dragoons of Tarleton who were covering the return of a foraging party. Tarleton turned back with some of his troopers to protect the wagons—and met a prompt charge by cavalrymen as tough of fibre as his own. In a short time, the British leader pulled back. Choisy held the field and later advanced in formal siege of Gloucester Point. It was a small affair but in every way encouraging.

After the clash at Gloucester, everything indicated that the next scene was to be enacted in front of Yorktown, where the enemy kept up a steady fire October 4, 5, and the night of 5/6. Washington did not give back iron to earth in wasteful, aimless fire, but there was work enough, and rising hope besides, because reliable ox-teams now were being delivered at camp and being used to draw the guns towards the redoubts. Good augury attended good effort. On the fifth, Capt. William Pierce reached Headquarters with details of Greene's battle of September 8. The action had occurred at Eutaw Springs, South Carolina, where Greene had attacked a force of British regulars to prevent the establishment there of a permanent post. After a hard fight the American leader had been compelled to withdraw, but he did not retreat far and when he heard the British had left Eutaw Springs on the evening of the ninth, he organized pursuit of what proved to be little more than a remnant retiring towards Charleston.

Washington's engineers now were ready, they believed, "for serious operations"; the new fortifications and the strengthening of the occupied redoubts gave security to the troops who were to open the first parallel; entrenching tools and materials were adequate if used economically.

Little beyond routine occurred during the morning of the sixth except for the belated issue of lengthy General Orders that covered "Regulations for the Service of the Siege." The main task of the day was to convey fascines and gabions as far to the front as they could be carried without disclosing where the first parallel was to be. The trench was to begin directly east of the head of Yorktown Creek, cross the Hampton Road almost at right angles, and then swing on an arc to the high bank of York River, about six hundred yards from the parapet of the advanced British redoubt which also was located on the cliff. While no part of the parallel was to be nearer than this to the British defences, much of the line was to be fully eight hundred yards from them. Simultaneously with the construction of this parallel, the second part of the plan was to be executed: on the extreme allied left, next the river, some of Saint-Simon's troops were to dig a narrow support trench and a battery from which the French could challenge a star redoubt across the creek. Moreover, with the guns of the proposed battery, the artillerists hoped to reach the British shipping in the river and destroy communication during daylight hours between York and Gloucester. This digging and stir on the British right was to serve still another purpose: it was intended to fix the enemy's attention at that point and divert the British from close observation of the ground where the parallel was to be drawn.

As the afternoon of October 6 passed, Washington heard of no occurrence that would interfere with the execution of any part of the plan. At four o'clock some of the American troops paraded; at five the French were assembled and assigned their positions; as soon as night fell Rochambeau's engineers told off the fatigue-parties, which filed out two hours later and began to dig. Washington listened anxiously, but heard no sound from the enemy's front until about nine, when, on the British right, the watchdogs of the star redoubt started to bark. Soon there were growls on the centre and the right; nowhere except on the bank of the lower stretch of

Yorktown Creek, where Saint-Simon was to make his diversion, did the cannonade rise to fury. Elsewhere the hours of the night dragged past, out of step with the staccato of the picks that beat double time along the parallel. Rain hampered the British cannoneers without troubling greatly the men who were shoveling the light, sandy soil. When daylight came the allied troops had good cover in the trench and four redoubts which were sufficiently advanced in construction to protect the garrison. Losses had been few.

The opening of the first parallel and the commencement of fire were several days apart in Washington's planning. It was second nature with the thrifty American commander to conserve his ammunition. Within the time limit set by the presence of the French fleet, he would not waste a single shot until he had guns enough, close enough, to force Cornwallis's surrender or make the storming of the British defences successful at minimum sacrifice of blood. Work on redoubts and batteries was pushed without interference. The French finished their battery that afternoon. By the ninth construction was so far advanced that artillery and stores were brought up. Before noon the work on the extreme right was complete. Because the French had excelled in preparation, Washington gave them the honor of beginning the bombardment at 3 P.M. Then the American cannon joined in. Quickly the allied gunners found the range and centred their fire effectively on the embrasures of the enemy's works. To prevent repairs during the night, Washington had the two batteries continue their fire through the hours of darkness while busy hundreds of allied soldiers worked to bring more guns into position. As a reward of long toil, four additional batteries, two French and two American, were in order early on the tenth for the challenge of the enemy with approximately sixteen cannon and eight mortars, besides those that had been sounding since the previous afternoon—a total of at least forty-six.

The fire from the French left, near the river, was taken up on the Gloucester shore, when Choisy discovered a British force, crowded into six flatboats, that sought to get beyond his right flank. With help from Saint-Simon's gunners, Choisy compelled the British to creep back to Gloucester Point. Washington observed with admiration the precision of the French fire. Before long the enemy was sending over about six shots only an hour—so few that Americans and French slackened their bombardment.

A flag of truce came from the town at noon. Word soon was passed that the flag covered "Secretary" Thomas Nelson, who was uncle of Gov. Thomas Nelson and had been residing in the large residence that dominated the profile of the town as seen from the right of the American position. He was able to give the camp the first reliable news that had come from Yorktown after the siege began: The bombardment had done much damage and had forced many of the British to take shelter under the cliff, where Cornwallis had established himself in a grotto. On the Gloucester side of the river, Nelson reported, the British were contained by the forces under Choisy. To some extent, officers and men were dispirited, Nelson continued, though they professed no apprehension for the safety of the town.

The probability of attack did not increase as the sun descended. The allied guns were pugnacious; the British fire was listless; embrasures on Cornwallis's line manifestly were damaged, and even the outline of the parapets became ragged. By twilight the enemy's batteries seemed almost to be silenced. Not long after nightfall there came from within the British lines a heavy column of black smoke. A large fire it must be; the reflection, now brighter, now dimmer, was visible nearly all night. By morning, the explanation was plain: Saint-Simon's battery had turned its guns on two frigates that seemed to be maneuvering suspiciously during the afternoon. One of these, the *Guadeloupe*, got under cover of the land; the other, the *Charon*, soon was aflame from waterline to truck. This created intense alarm among the masters of other craft. Some were warped to safety; several others caught fire; Saint-Simon's guns added more redhot round shot to the confusion. The final loss, four or five vessels, was a tribute to French artillerists and a warning of things to come.

October 11 brought satisfaction in the arrival from de Grasse's fleet of two officers whom the Admiral had directed to determine whether it seemed worthwhile to run frigates past the town in order to close to Cornwallis the line of escape upstream that Washington still believed his adversary might attempt to follow. The officers said little on their return from the river, but, in Washington's opinion, they "seemed favorably disposed" to the enterprise. The American General wrote to de Grasse in some detail why he believed the operation would be as safe, with favoring wind, as it was strategically desirable.

Washington had no intention of delaying the prosecution of the siege while he awaited de Grasse's decision. Two more French batteries were going into action on the eleventh; as the British might expect further additions to the first parallel before another was opened, good strategy dictated labor on the second line at once. In undertaking this, the allies had to deal with the two advanced British redoubts on the left. So long as these redoubts were in enemy hands, they barred allied advance. Once secured, they would permit an enfilade of part of the enemy's inner line and offer shelter for the final assault. They must be taken—but how? The engineers had a simple solution: from the eastern end of the French part of the first parallel troops would move out and construct part of the second as close to the advanced British redoubts as safety permitted, and then they would erect a strong epaulement or "shoulder." If full advantage were taken of a slight rise of ground, execution of this design would reduce distance to the nearer British earthwork from 650 yards to approximately 330, perhaps even to 300 or less, without exposing the epaulement to intolerable fire. Once the advanced redoubts had been silenced or seized, the second parallel could be extended from the epaulement to the river bank.

No time was lost in carrying out the plan. Digging began at dusk. Some of the American parties escaped all cannonade; the French faced a heavy fire, which their artillery countered. Rochambeau's lieutenants moved up reenforcements in expectation of a sortie. They had to deal with one alarm during the night, but they found it merely a clash of patrols. Before morning the troops were covered. "Lord Cornwallis's conduct," Washington wrote that day, "has hitherto been passive beyond conception;

he either has not the means of defence, or he intends to reserve his strength until we approach very near him."

The only change during the day was an increase in British cannon fire, which annoyed but did not delay the allied workmen. Washington felt that several days might pass before he could get the full measure of his adversary. Meantime, in the face of an increasing, mixed fire of round shot and shell, which exacted a higher toll on the thirteenth, preparations for the next phase of the siege went steadily on. Without waiting for these to be finished, Washington ordered the guns of all the other fortifications within range to open on the advanced works opposite the American right. Saint-Simon, on the allied left, began to pound the star redoubt. The British answer was no more spirited than usual, though it included some five-inch shells which could not be seen in flight.

About 2 P.M. the Commander-in-Chief was told that the engineers considered the British positions so heavily damaged that a successful assault was practicable. Washington did not wait for details: Lafayette with four hundred light infantry must make ready to assault the advanced redoubt next the river; Rochambeau was requested to send a force of his own choice against the nearer detached work—an honor the French leader gave to General Vioménil. Simultaneously with the attacks by Vioménil and Lafayette, the French were to demonstrate against the star redoubt and British lines in Gloucester. Although several hours must pass before the new gamble with fate began, ears already were being tuned for the sound of the six guns, fired in succession, that were to give the signal for the attack.

Before the afternoon ended Washington went to the French line, met Vioménil and heard with approval the details of that officer's preparations. Then the Commander-in-Chief rode over to the ground where Lafayette's officers were waiting. Battlefield oratory was not one of Washington's acquirements, but he made a brief appeal, earnest if not eloquent: the participants in the assault, he said, must be firm, brave soldiers; the success of the attack on both redoubts depended on them. That was all. If, from the left flank, nervous fire of small arms presently was heard between the one-two of cannon shot, Washington of course knew what it meant: punctually and vigorously, Saint-Simon was launching his demonstration in the hope he might convince the British that he intended to attack. Had not distance drowned it, the sound of Choisy's feint in Gloucester might have been audible, also.

Soon the batteries ceased fire. Then, about seven o'clock, the stillness was broken by a shot from one of the French redoubts. Men started out silently from the trench. Their order was explicit: be silent, use the bayonet only. In a minute or two the vanguard disappeared in the shadows; the main body of the detachment followed. Washington and the other generals might almost have held their breath as they waited for the discovery of the attack. Then there rolled swiftly the sound of the fire of the guard. Evidently the French had been challenged and had received all the lead the men on the parapets could hurl at them. The sharp bark of small arms came from the redoubt the Americans were assaulting. Hamilton, in command of Lafayette's column of Americans, had also failed to achieve a complete surprise. Anxious minutes passed. The fire from the left became more furious; that on the right slackened. Soon the roar of voices was mingled with the crash of musketry. There were shouts, cheers. After that, fire ceased at the redoubt near the river and became intermittent from the direction of the French advance.

Both redoubts had been captured! The French had found the abattis strong and almost undamaged twenty-five yards in front of the redoubt. Time and men had been lost in breaking through. On reaching the ditch the French had thrown themselves into it, only to face a stubborn fraise and a bristling palisade. Some of the troops climbed over these obstacles and broke into the redoubt; others waited until the artificers removed the stakes. Once in the enclosure the French quickly overwhelmed the defenders, who did not make the last-ditch defence expected of them. At the other redoubt, Hamilton's main party pulled out carelessly planted palisades and swarmed over the parapet; Laurens' band swiftly closed on the rear of the redoubt.

Little time was allowed to provide for safety because the enemy soon turned on the redoubts all the guns that could be brought to bear from the inner fortifications. As this fire quickened, workers wielded their picks and within three quarters of an hour had raised earth high enough to cover the new garrison. The British shells passed over the heads of the men on the American part of the line but indicated on the French some of the heaviest losses sustained during the evening.

As the night spent its hours the enemy's cannonade took a smaller toll. By morning the workers had nearly completed the fortification of a curtain they had run all the way to the river.

The New York Brigade marched proudly into the captured work. When Washington visited the redoubt later in the day with some of the French and American officers he made his inspection under a warm fire of rifles as well as of artillery, because the lines now were close enough together for good marksmen to use small arms with some effect. He paid no heed to this and had little difficulty in deciding, with the engineers' aid, where new batteries should be placed contiguous to the captured redoubts. The troops on fatigue duty labored with zeal; the artillerists soon contrived to get two howitzers into each of the newly occupied works; by 5 P.M. they were put in action.

Before sunrise October 16 word reached Headquarters of an alarm on the lines and a sortie by the British. About four o'clock, 350 picked troops broke into the second parallel, close to the point of junction between French and Americans and near two uncompleted batteries. The British pretended to be an American relief. By this artifice they surprised a small detachment of the Agenois Regiment, most of whom had been permitted to go to sleep. When the Redcoats came to the French communication trench that led to the first parallel, they halted doubtfully. By good fortune, the Viscount de Noailles was near, guessed what the situation was and unhesitatingly attacked with the cry "Vive le Roi!" The British had been told to spike the guns with the tips of bayonets, and the men had not been deployed either for attack or defence. In a few minutes they streamed back towards their own lines. Within a few hours the spikes had been removed and every cannon had been put back in action. Washington dismissed the sortie as "small and ineffectual . . . of little consequences to either party" and devoted his energies to bringing into operation the batteries on which both French and Americans had been working diligently.

With the advanced British redoubts his own, he now had to face frontal fire only. Preparation was simplified. By 4 P.M. or a little later two of the French batteries were ready and three pieces in a large American work could be put in action. When they began a new bombardment the other batteries barked a welcome and aroused the enemy to swift, hot answer. While hundreds of Americans labored to bring up guns and strengthen the works for an even more destructive bombardment the next day, the French artillerists displayed their skill by ricocheting their shot. This did much damage to the British defences and, with good luck, sometimes placed a projectile directly over the parapet and among the men posted there. A fair day ended in a fairer prospect. The chance of naval relief of Cornwallis seemed remote; de Grasse at last was willing to send frigates up the York if the American commander provided small boats to protect against fireships, which Washington readily could do. A furious squall swept down the York after midnight, but by the morning of the seventeenth it had passed.

The camp was full of exciting news. During the night Cornwallis had made some effort to escape to the north side of the river and been frustrated by the squall. As far as the Americans could make out, none of the garrison on either side of the river had escaped. They remained where they were, exposed to the heaviest fire yet poured on them. The French had two more batteries in action; the "grand battery" of the Americans was complete. Some artillerists estimated more than one hundred guns engaged in what sounded as if it were a ceaseless bombardment. This was tearing the enemy's works apart. The only fire the allies had to face was that of small mortar shells which the enemy dropped with persistence.

If any slackening of fire was audible as Washington transacted business at Headquarters, he attached no importance to it. Pauses came often in a bombardment. The General was about to write de Grasse on the matter of pilots for the passage of the river above Yorktown when a rider pulled up his horse in front of the tents. He had a dispatch for Washington, transmitted in circumstances that had led every observer to ask the same question. Between nine and ten o'clock, a drummer had sounded a parley. A British officer thereupon had come out in front of the defences with a white handkerchief; firing had ceased, an American had run forward, bandaged the eyes of the man with "the flag," and led the emissary through the American lines. In the messenger's hand was the letter the British officer had brought:

SIR, I propose a cessation of hostilities for twenty-four hours, and that two officers may be appointed by each side, to meet at Mr. Moore's house, to settle terms for the surrender of the posts at York and Gloucester.

I have the honour to be, &c
CORNWALLIS

The proposal to surrender had come much earlier than Washington had permitted himself to hope. Now that terms were asked, they must be imposed at once, justly but rigidly. With punctuation by cannon that had renewed the bombardment when the British flag had returned, Trumbull drafted a reply which Laurens revised slightly and Washington approved. About 2 P.M. fire again halted temporarily for the paper to be passed in this form:

Camp before York, October 17, 1781

My Lord:I have had the Honor of receiving Your Lordship's Letter of this Date. An Ardent Desire to spare the further Effusion of Blood, will readily incline me to listen to such Terms for the Surrender of your Posts and Garrisons of York and Gloucester, as are admissible.

I wish previously to the Meeting of Commissioners, that your Lordship's proposals in writing may be sent to the American Lines: for which Purpose, a suspension of Hostilities during two Hours from the Delivery of this Letter will be granted. I have the Honor, etc.

In this, Washington felt he had taken decent precaution, but he had so little doubt of Cornwallis's enforced submission that he began preparations for the formal surrender. As de Grasse was the allied commander who would require the longest notice, Washington had Tilghman and Laurens draft a cordial letter in which he invited the Admiral's "participation in this treaty which will according to present appearances, shortly take place." Later in the afternoon Washington received a second letter from Cornwallis. The time allowed in a reply to Washington, said the British commander, did not permit him to enter into details of terms. Among the proposals he then sketched hastily one only was completely inadmissible—that the surrendered forces be returned on parole to Britain or to Germany. The other concessions sought by Cornwallis were not of a sort to indicate he would attempt to renew the fighting if he did not win them. Washington consequently agreed to a continued suspension of hostilities, and apparently he overlooked the possibility that the enemy might wreck or burn equipment before such acts were forbidden.

The luxury of silence and of safety now was the Army's—at least for a night. The exchanges of the day made it possible for a man to stretch out and sleep as long as he would or could in the chill October air—and have no fear of a British bayonet in his chest. At Headquarters some of the staff must have labored over the answer to be made the next day to Cornwallis, but they encountered little difficulty in giving unequivocal form to their terms. By morning Jonathan Trumbull had a draft that Washington found altogether acceptable:

Head Quarters before York, October 18, 1781

My Lord: To avoid unnecessary Discussions and Delays, I shall at Once, in Answer to your Lordships Letter of Yesterday, declare the general Basis upon which a Definitive Treaty and Capitulation must take place. The Garrisons of York and Gloucester, including the Seamen, as you propose, will be received Prisoners of

War. The Condition annexed, of sending the British and German Troops to the parts of Europe to which they respectively belong, is inadmissible. Instead of this, they will be marched to such parts of the Country as can most conveniently provide for their Subsistence; and the Benevolent Treatment of Prisoners, which is invariably observed by the Americans, will be extended to them. The same Honors will be granted to the Surrendering Army as were granted to the Garrison of Charles Town. The Shipping and Boats in the two Harbours with all their Guns, Stores, Tackling, Furniture and Apparel, shall be delivered in their present State to an Officer of the Navy, appointed to take possession of them.

The Artillery, Arms, Accoutrements, Military Chest and Public Stores of every Denomination, shall be delivered unimpaired to the Heads of Departments, to which they respectively belong.

The Officers will be indulged in retaining their Side Arms, and the Officers and Soldiers may preserve their Baggage and Effects, with this Reserve, that Property taken in the Country, will be reclaimed.

With Regard to the Individuals in civil Capacities, whose Interests Your Lordship wishes may be attended to, until they are more particularly described, nothing definitive can be settled.

I have to add, that I expect the Sick and Wounded will be supplied with their own Hospital Stores, and be attended by British Surgeons, particularly charged with the Care of them.

Your Lordship will be pleased to signify your Determination either to accept or reject the Proposals now offered, in the course of Two Hours from the Delivery of this Letter, that Commissioners may be appointed to digest the Articles of Capitulation, or a Renewal of Hostilities may take place.

I have the Honor etc.

Off went the messenger with the letter. By the time he reached the line the curiosity of thousands of adversaries was being satisfied through the bounty of the truce. On the beach of York hundreds of busy people might be seen moving to and fro. At a small distance from the shore were ships sunk down to the water's edge—farther out in the channel the masts, yards and even the top gallant masts of some might be seen without any vestige of the hulls. On the opposite side of the river was the remainder of the shipping drawn off as to a place of security. Even here the *Guadeloupe*, sunk to the water's edge, showed how vain the hope of such a place. Under the terms about to be imposed the remaining transports and other vessels must be left as they were for final disposition by the French Admiral. De Grasse, unfortunately, would not be present in person to settle the details and share the honors. Sickness had overtaken him and he designated Barras in his stead. The day brought assurance, also, that an American "fleet" as well as a French, would be in the background of the final scene. The remaining troops of St. Clair were arriving off the mouth of the York.

Cornwallis, in answering Washington, abandoned effort to have his army paroled home and contented himself with seeking three things—terms of special honor for the unassailed garrison of Gloucester Point, permission to dispatch a small vessel to New York with a cargo of private property, and immunity for Loyalists at the two posts. Washington was entirely satisfied that the British could not escape now, and he knew that at a meeting of commissioners he could impose all essential terms that honor, safety of the American cause, and decent consideration for a defeated foe demanded. More than this, Washington did not intend to exact. He named Laurens as one American commissioner and left the choice of the other to Rochambeau, who selected de Noailles, Lafayette's brother-in-law.

While Laurens and de Noailles were listening to the British commissioners, Washington made ready an American and a French detachment, each of two hundred men, to occupy British defences on the main roads and thereby prevent unauthorized entry into Yorktown or egress from it—a precaution the expectant spirit of the troops dictated. Evening came without any word on the progress of the negotiations, but Washington awaited the return of Laurens and de Noailles without concern. When they arrived they reported that British appeals and objections of one sort and another had so prolonged the meeting that the articles of capitulation were not in final form; but the American commissioners brought back a rough draft, for consideration of which they had extended the truce until nine o'clock on the morning of the nineteenth. That sufficed. The terms were those of honorable surrender, mitigated for the officers by permission to return on parole to Europe or to an American port in British hands. Cornwallis's temporary use of the sloop *Bonetta* for a voyage to New York was allowed, with the proviso that she carry dispatches and soldiers but no public property. Officers were to retain their side-arms; all baggage of individuals was to remain their own, unless it included effects taken from the inhabitants. Details of formal surrender were set forth punctiliously as to flag and music and march, and with such a "compensation" for the part of the garrison of Gloucester Point as Cornwallis had said he would expect. The sole flat denial of Cornwallis's amended proposals concerned the requested article that "natives or inhabitants of different parts of this country, at present in York or Gloucester are not to be punished on account of having joined the British army." Washington's refusal of this was brief: "This article cannot be assented to, being altogether of civil resort."

When the articles were entirely in order, Washington authorized Laurens to notify the British of certain minor changes of terms. Then the General was ready for his final move. "I had [the papers] copied," he wrote, and sent word to Lord Cornwallis "that I expected to have them signed at 11 o'clock and that the garrison would march out at 2 o'clock. . . ." The alternative was one so plain that Cornwallis could not hesitate in his choice. About eleven o'clock the text of the articles arrived from the British lines. Attached were the signatures of Cornwallis and Thomas Symonds, senior naval officer in the York River. These two names were written under a line that read: "Done at York, in Virginia, this 19th day of October 1781." Washington had this separate paragraph duly added: "Done in the trenches before Yorktown, in Virginia, October 19, 1781." Below this he quietly wrote "G. Washington." His colleague used the title, "Le Comte de Rochambeau." Barras signed: "Le Comte de Barras En mon nom & celui du Comte de Grasse." It was finished! Except for the formalities of surrender.

Time came for the great event. Washington had given his orders verbally during the forenoon—and never to subordinates more eager to obey. The people of the neighborhood were to be allowed to witness the ceremonies; the French troops were to be on one side of the road down which the British marched; the Americans were to be on the other side in two lines, the Continentals in front, the militia behind them.

When Washington rode up between the lines that had formed for a distance of about half a mile the French bandsmen were performing magnificently and the Americans were playing "moderately well"; but what was the quality of their music then to Washington? Those Continentals were symbols as surely as they were soldiers. From his left, Washington heard different music—and, doubtless, the rustle that often sweeps a silent, excited throng. The march of the British was slow and labored. Minutes passed before the head of the column approached. Washington, on his fine charger, probably looked straight ahead. Rochambeau, opposite him, was no less militarily correct in his dress uniform with the shining badges of French orders on his chest.

Louder now was the music, closer to the column. Presently came a perfectly appointed British general officer with his staff, all mounted and escorted. When the leader reached the waiting commanders he turned to his left and started to address Rochambeau, but the Count pointed to Washington. King George's officer swung around with an apology for his mistake. The American observed him instantly as a man of about forty and most courteous in his bearing—but not Lord Cornwallis. He was Brigadier Charles O'Hara of the Guards, and he came to represent his Lordship who was indisposed and unable to appear. Washington showed neither irritation nor disappointment, but, of course, if the British commander acted through a deputy, would General O'Hara be so good as to consult General Lincoln, who was directly at hand? A brief exchange sufficed: On the right of the road, a short distance beyond the position of Washington and his staff, Lincoln explained, there was an open field around which French hussars had formed a circle: The British would enter this circle, one regiment at a time, lay down their arms and await instructions to march back between the lines of allied troops.

O'Hara proceeded on his heartbreaking mission. Soon the leading platoon of the British army was in front of Washington. Many of the round-hatted English soldiers were in liquor; but most of the troops were well dressed, many of them in new uniforms, and they adhered to the letter of the articles of capitulation. The British and German flags were cased and carried ungloriously past gorgeous French standards and proudly flying American colors. All the music continued to be what Washington had prescribed, English or German, not French or American, in return for the British demand at Charleston that the drums of the despised "rebels" should "not beat a British march." Silently and slowly the troops filed to the surrender ground, and then, after a while, they began the return march, with no emblem of the soldier except uniform and knapsack.

Washington had invited General O'Hara to dinner, and O'Hara proved to be sociable and entirely at ease, with none of the air of a captive. When the meal was over and Washington could turn again to business, he

found that no news had come of any hitch in the surrender of the Gloucester post to Choisy.

At the day's end Washington undertook the most delightful of all
miltary duties. Three times previously, three times only, Washington had
addressed to Congress papers that announced major successes—the occupation of Boston, the capture of the Hessians at Trenton, and the retreat of
Clinton from Monmouth. None of these had been comparable in prisoners
and in booty to Yorktown. Washington could prepare a "victory dispatch"
in the loftiest use of the term and entrust the delivery of the paper to a
staff officer he wished particularly to honor. Trumbull must draft the paper; when it was revised and copied, it must be placed in the hands of the
faithful, selfless Tench Tilghman for delivery to Congress. No officer of the
Army had earned a better right to this conspicuous distinction.

The dispatch began: "Sir, I have the Honor to inform Congress,
that a Reduction of the British Army under the Command of Lord Cornwallis, is most happily effected. The unremitting Ardor which actuated
every Officer and Soldier in the combined Army in this Occasion, has principally led to this Important Event, at an earlier period than my most sanguine Hope had induced me to expect." The rest was praise of others.

CHAPTER / 17

Caution justified by many failures in hours of high hope made Washington dwell more on the possible ill effects than on the manifest gains of Yorktown: ". . . my only apprehension (which I wish may be groundless) is," he wrote, "lest the late important success, instead of exciting our exertions, as it ought to do, should produce such a relaxation in the prosecution of the war, as will prolong the calamities of it." His mind was shaping itself to resolution that he would make his major task for the winter that of arousing the States and assuring French naval superiority, as far as exhortation could, for the campaign of 1782.

General Orders issued the day after the surrender did not dwell upon these fears but, in congratulating the Army, put first in praise "His Most Christian Majesty" and then, rightly, the French fleet and the army of Rochambeau. Victory had been achieved by the aid of France. Feeble, inexperienced America never had a prospect of winning her independence by force of arms until her ally protected her waters and defeated or blockaded the fleet of Britain. Within less than two months after France displayed naval superiority off the coast of the United States, the only large British army not in a heavily fortified city had been compelled to surrender. Sea power made Yorktown possible.

If de Grasse's weight of metal deserved the importance that Washington attached to it, the service of Rochambeau's army most certainly came next. Particularly was the American commander indebted to Rochambeau for support, and to the French engineers and artillerists for their skill and their knowledge of siege tactics, though Washington's own engineers and artillerists were not lacking in skill. On the contrary, Washington believed that both Duportail and Knox should be promoted to Major General. It was to the credit of Knox and virtually the whole body of American officers that their emulation of the French was marred by little or no jealousy. The American Army saw a fine disciplinary example and outdid itself because it followed that example. This was undertaken, by happy chance, on ground that nowhere could have been more favorable to combined attack and blockade. Cornwallis had chosen a position convenient rather than defensible, ideally accessible to a rescuing fleet that required deep water but a trap without control of the waterways.

Washington had a final basis of victory the credit for which was primarily his own. This was the speed of his concentration. Although he had not brought everything together until the last of the heavy guns of

Rochambeau was available at Yorktown, he had established a record that must have been vastly better than his adversary expected from the previous achievements of the Continental Army in covering ground.

The next stage of the war would, it seemed to Washington, be shaped primarily by the fact that British superiority at sea would be reasserted as soon as de Grasse left American waters. That dictated utmost diligence in removing all booty from reach of a fleet that might enter the Chesapeake. De Grasse must be prevailed upon, if possible, to join in a swift attack on Charleston, South Carolina, or the destruction of the British base at Wilmington, North Carolina. De Grasse ruled out an attempt on Charleston and, after promising to convoy an expedition to Wilmington, he quickly withdrew from this commitment. Washington had to accept the decision with the appearance of cheerfulness, but he was loath to abandon plans for strengthening Greene and prepared to send infantry overland to the Southern Department in addition to the cavalry he already was assembling and equipping. Arthur St. Clair was to head this force and ascertain, as a first move, whether it was desirable and practicable to reoccupy Wilmington. In event the North Carolina port could not be captured or was not worth the effort its occupation would involve, St. Clair was to join Greene. With reenforcement and the help of the nearby States, Greene was to be left to "win those laurels," said Washington, "which from his unparalleled exertions he so richly deserves." For the winter, Rochambeau would remain in the vicinity of Yorktown. With his own troops, less St. Clair's column, Washington would return north. He then would maintain close communications with the South, resume the guard of the Hudson and prepare for the campaign of 1782. The States must be exhorted to keep their Continental regiments at full strength; Congress was reminded that "an effectual and early preparation for military operations" would give America advantage "either for war or negotiation"; a contrary course would "expose us to the most disgraceful disasters."

Hostilities had terminated only in the small area where Cornwallis had been surrounded. There was distinct possibility the sound of distant fire in Chesapeake Bay might interrupt a festive dinner in a camp near Yorktown. On October 24 Washington received an express from Gen. David Forman concerning the expected departure from Sandy Hook of a total of ninety-nine sail. This news was accepted as authentic, but Washington and de Grasse doubted whether Graves would come to the Virginia capes; both were confident he would be defeated if he did offer battle. Not until the twenty-eighth did Washington have further news. Then a message from de Grasse announced that the British fleet, or at least a part of it, had been sighted. The next morning the wind was adverse for the outward movement of the French ships. Before night the number of hostile vessels outside the capes rose to forty-four. Still Washington waited; still de Grasse let his ships swing at anchor. The British continued to maneuver until three o'clock on the afternoon of the thirtieth and then disappeared. Washington's conclusion was that Graves would not reappear while de Grasse was in the Chesapeake. In that belief Washington busied himself with preparations for his own departure and with final plans for the removal of stores from Yorktown. This would be a task that could be entrusted to subordinates, because de Grasse had promised that the French fleet would not leave until all the American troops and their supplies were at Head of Elk. Gratefully and without hitch the Commander-in-Chief discharged the final duties of courtesy.

Washington said au revoir in a round of visits November 4 and the following day rode to Williamsburg with his staff. Thence he followed the happily familiar road to Eltham—and immediately encountered tragedy. Jack Custis had ridden southward from Mount Vernon and had gone to his step-father's Headquarters, as a temporary civilian aide, but he had soon developed what was termed "camp fever." Because of this, the young man left Jones's Run and went back to his aunt's home. Martha, Jack's wife and his oldest girl, Eliza, hurried to his bedside; doctors did their feeble best. It was in vain: he was dying when Washington arrived and succumbed in a few hours. His mother was prostrated. Washington had to send his staff on to Mount Vernon while he remained at Burwell Bassett's home to arrange the funeral and comfort Martha and the young widow.

Not until the eleventh could the General set out for Mount Vernon. He stopped in Fredericksburg to see his mother, but as she was absent on a visit, the party pushed on towards Mount Vernon. It was November 13 that the soldier drew rein at his own door. He then found time for some private business and for discussion with Lund Washington of the affairs of the estate, but even to his quiet refuge came the loud echo of public applause. He received the thanks of Congress, congratulatory letters from friends, an address from his Alexandria neighbors and, doubtless, saw a few of the newspapers that were reporting celebrations, lauding him and exulting over the enemy.

Washington could not linger over the gazettes or the accounts of his steward, because he had both hopes and fears that he felt he should report to Congress. On November 20, he, Martha and a few members of his military family started for Philadelphia, via Annapolis. At the Maryland capital he had the heartiest of welcomes and the most bountiful entertainment. On the twenty-third he left on the Baltimore ferry and, to the extent that his wife's comfort permitted, hurried to his destination by the swiftest combination of road and water travel. Arrival in Philadelphia on the twenty-sixth was unannounced and unmarked by ceremony. He found a thinly attended Congress, anxious to press the war in the South and, at the same time, reduce expense and dismiss surplus officers. Washington received notice that he would "have an audience" on November 28, and when he appeared at the designated hour he had something he desired far more than compliment: With a single sentence about the glorious success of the allied arms in Virginia, the President, John Hanson, affirmed of Congress: "It is their fixed purpose to draw every advantage from [the victory] by exhorting the States in the strongest terms to the most vigorous and timely exertions." The General's reply was an expression of thanks and of pleasure that Congress would urge the States to exert themselves. "A compliance on their parts," he said with his usual conservatism of speech, "will, I persuade myself, be productive of the most happy consequences."

That "audience" by Congress fixed the pattern of Washington's labor in exact accordance with his prime concern. "My greatest fear," he already had written Greene, "is that Congress, viewing this stroke [at Yorktown] in too favorable a light, may think our work too nearly closed, and will fall into a state of languor and relaxation." Again and again, he dwelt on that fundamental: unless Congress and the States prepared adequately and soon for the campaign of 1782, the victory at Yorktown might be the preliminary of defeat. In terse words he reiterated his maxim, "without a decisive naval force we can do nothing definitive."

Thoughtful Delegates were ready to begin consideration of the future of the Army. Plans for 1782 were formulated with little delay. All the States were called upon to supply men to fill out their Continental regiments to the totals established in October 1780; the Commander-in-Chief was directed to give notice of the general officers he would need in the next campaign. The others were to be retired on half-pay with the proviso that they could be called to active duty if necessary. Surplus officers of lower rank were to be released in substantially the same manner. The unpleasant task of retiring those officers not named by Washington was delegated to the Secretary of War. That position was filled by the choice of Maj. Gen. Benjamin Lincoln, who gradually was to take from the shoulders of his senior much of the burden of staff departments. Washington had also the prospect of relief in another direction—at the hands of Robert Morris. The Superintendent of Finance made a contract with Comfort Sands & Co. to supply officers in the district of West Point with provisions—an arrangement the acceptable performance of which would save Washington many an hour of worry.

During the weeks these measures were being hammered into defensive weapons, the enemy remained quiet in New York and at adjacent posts. Washington consequently had no immediate anxiety over the secure custody of the Hudson defences. He found no added reason for alarm, even in the Southern Department. January days brought no bad news from Greene. Congress approved still another system of army inspection and put Steuben in charge of it; McDougall reported the threat of a mutiny on the Hudson but this did not appear to be serious. It was followed unpleasantly by notice from Heath that he had placed McDougall under arrest for charges tantamount to insubordination. Washington perhaps heard, also, that the contract with Comfort Sands & Co. had provoked disagreement within little more than three weeks after it had become effective.

These were vexations, but they were small in comparison with those Washington had known in every other winter of the war; nor did quiet in one month mean turmoil the next, as so often had happened. A small British raid on New Brunswick in January was followed by a long period of quiet in February. No additional British troops reached Charleston; on the contrary, when Forman announced on February 23 the departure from Sandy Hook of a transport fleet, he forwarded also a rumor that the vessels were to be used in evacuating the garrison of the South Carolina port.

Fifteen weeks now had elapsed since Washington had arrived in Philadelphia. They had been the least warlike period of the entire struggle and socially one of the most pleasant the General and his lady ever had shared. He must have been embarrassed by adulation he could not escape, but when March brought an end to weather of great severity and to his conferences with the Delegates, he felt he should return to the field. His one remaining duty in the town was drafting instructions to Henry Knox and Gouverneur Morris as commissioners for the exchange of prisoners. As Martha was going with him to camp, he had to plan a comfortable and not too hurried journey. By the eighteenth, arrangements were so near completion that he notified Congress he wished to rejoin the Army on the Hudson. In answer he was notified that Congress "would admit him to an audience of leave" at 10:30 A.M. of the twenty-first. He obediently stood with two members flanking him while the President assured him of the esteem and confidence of Congress and commended him to "the protection of Divine Providence."

When Washington reached Newburgh March 31 he found the controversy over the provision contract aflame and Heath and McDougall at war because of Heath's arrest of the New Yorker. The Commander-in-Chief deplored so unseemly a dispute between senior officers, but he always had adhered to the principle that if serious complaints were made officially, they should be submitted to a court, and he did not intervene now. The situation with respect to the provisions contract did not call for forbearance. Comfort Sands and the sub-contractors were not keeping the agreement made with the Superintendent of Finance, and the General's largest continuing labor was that of demanding in plain words that Comfort Sands or their successors fulfill their contract from stock and provisions that now were abundant.

It was a time of perplexity and of fluctuating hope that peace was near. Washington reasoned that the operations that might be undertaken in America by the allies depended on four contingencies—Britain's resolution to prosecute the war, the naval support France gave, the number of recruits the States supplied, and the money available for the Army. He did not believe it possible to make a siege of Charleston, nor could he ascertain yet whether the French fleet would be able to convoy troops to South Carolina or join in an attack on New York. As for the States, their response to the call for men was altogether unpromising and their willingness to finance the campaign was worse than doubtful. He had to await developments in the belief that reports from London of early peace were intended to deceive. Washington received on May 9 a letter from Lieut. Gen. Sir Guy Carleton, who had succeeded Sir Henry Clinton. Carleton announced his arrival and said that he was "joined with Admiral Digby in the commission of peace" and most anxious to reduce the needless severities of war. This hint of a settlement was taken up eagerly by Americans and discussed for weeks in Congress, the newspapers, and private correspondence. Washington remained skeptical.

The summer was not altogether disagreeable. Washington allowed himself a soldierly privilege previously denied him: Attended by Gov. George Clinton, he left Newburgh June 24 and proceeded to Albany, Saratoga and Schenectady, in order that he might see for himself the towns of which he had heard much. Washington reviewed troops and attended dinners; but he was concerned to find that British, Indians and refugees had made a raid down the Mohawk and that the rebuilding by them of the fortifications at Oswego was anticipated.

He was back at Headquarters July 2 in time for the celebration of the Fourth, a celebration that was doubled in its satisfaction by word from Luzerne that a great French fleet under the Marquis de Vaudreuil might arrive off the American coast in July or August. This was followed July 9 by another surprise from the Minister: Rochambeau was "moving" the French army "towards the head of the [Chesapeake] Bay where," said Luzerne, "he will be at hand to take such measures as you may judge proper as soon as we receive news from Europe." The French General suggested a conference, and Washington set out the very next day for Philadelphia. The two met in frank and cordial council on the sixteenth. Washington left Philadelphia in full accord with the French and with Congress and, by July 27, reached Newburgh again.

The weeks that followed were busy. First came the verdict in the court-martial of McDougall. A mild reprimand administered in General Orders ended the unpleasant case in a manner so satisfactory to McDougall that he declined to prosecute his countercharges against Heath. The first week of August brought word that a French fleet had reached the Chesapeake and was going to Boston with an attack on Penobscot as its principal object. At Rochambeau's instance, Washington sent the Admiral, the Marquis de Vaudreuil, a strong warning that the prize was not worth the risk.

Washington received a remarkable letter on the evening of August 4 over the signatures of Carleton and Robert Digby. It dealt with British policies of peace and exchange of prisoners and was patently an invitation to negotiate. Washington passed it on to Congress with a request that he receive "directions for my government." Washington suspected a trick to deceive America and reasoned that so long as there was doubt, the country should be vigilant and prepare more vigorously than ever for any eventuality. When Congress resolved to make public the letter the people were told that no report of any negotiations had been received from American ministers abroad; warning was given of the danger of any relaxation of effort.

Several changes in the position and organization of the Army occurred during the uncertainty that followed the receipt of the Carleton-Digby letter. Congress directed that Greene hold his troops in the Southern Department; but the northward march of Rochambeau's regiments continued, and Washington moved his Army to Verplanck's. The arrival of Rochambeau September 14 was celebrated joyfully. Horatio Gates came back to the Hudson early in October and received assignment to direct the right wing. The Army, said the Commander-in-Chief, "was better organized, disciplined and clothed" than ever it had been. Of adverse conditions, the only one that threatened trouble was a widespread discontent among officers who believed Congress was neglecting them.

The sad item in the news was that John Laurens, the brilliant, devoted young patriot, had been killed August 27 in resisting at Chehaw Neck, South Carolina, a British foraging party. Washington seldom attempted to eulogize dead comrades and the most he could say now was: "The death of Colonel Laurens I consider as a very heavy misfortune, not only as it affects the public at large, but particularly so to his family and all his private friends and connections, to whom his amiable and useful character had rendered him peculiarly dear." At approximately the same time Washington learned that Charles Lee had come to the end in Philadelphia. Washington in his correspondence noted only the fact that Lee was dead.

By the middle of October Rochambeau concluded that Charleston or New York would be evacuated and that he safely could move his troops to Santo Domingo. Lest the enemy be stirred to action, it seemed best to have it appear that Rochambeau was proceeding to New England to establish his forces around Boston or Providence for the winter. The columns moved on October 26 and 28 to the vicinity of Newburgh and Little Britain. Rochambeau, Chastellux and several of their juniors came back to Newburgh December 7 on their way south for embarkation because Vaudreuil could not transport the whole French force on his ships. The tone of exchanges with these faithful allies was that of affectionate au revoir. "I could not have bid a brother farewell," said Washington afterwards, "with more regret than I did the Chevalier Chastellux, than whom no man stands higher in my estimation."

Within ten days after Rochambeau started down the Hudson, Washington heard that the British fleet had left New York. Reports circulated once again that New York was to be evacuated. But evil auguries matched the good. Resentful officers, more outraged than ever by Congress' disdain of their applications for relief, prepared a wrathful address, which McDougall and others were to carry to Philadelphia. Signers were of a mood to demand, not to petition. Washington's word to a friendly Delegate was serious: "The temper of the Army is much soured, and has become more irritable than at any period since the commencement of the war . . . What [Congress] can or will do in the matter does not belong to me to determine; but policy, in my opinion, should dictate soothing measures. . . ."

The coming of January 1783 found Washington of opinion that Charleston had been or soon would be evacuated. When confirmation of the reported abandonment of the South Carolina city was received, the good news came at a time of some personal annoyance to Washington. Heavy use of his eyes had led him to "try" the spectacles worn by some of his companions and from these he selected lenses he asked that David Rittenhouse duplicate for him. A distress of different nature concerned a member of his family. "In God's name," he wrote, "how did my brother Samuel contrive to get himself so enormously in debt?" Besides this, Washington's mother was complaining that the overseer of the Falls Quarter was sending her nothing. Officially, there was the usual embarrassment of winter over the absence of senior officers and distress over the death of Lord Stirling.

Washington scarcely knew on what scale to project operations. Sound strategy would prompt a powerful blow against New York, in order to drive the British from their last stronghold in the United States; but he hesitated to attempt this because of Continental finance and the peace negotiations. For such a major effort he believed he could rely on the Army, nor did he question the willingness of officers to meet any challenge by the enemy. It was different with officers' attitude towards Congress and their own future. Many of Washington's subordinates displayed restlessness, discontent and ill-temper he had no means of overcoming. Some of the men close to Washington thought that Gates and his supporters were responsible for at least a part of the demoralization of the officers, but the Commander-in-Chief had no proof of this.

He did not take the full leadership in dealing with Congress that Hamilton and other Delegates urged him to display on the Army's behalf. These members were anxious for Washington to intervene persuasively after they had done the little they could in Philadelphia to remove officers' suspicion that no promise of money, or land or half pay would be remembered after the Army was discharged. The officers' address had asked money for discharging part of the accumulated pay of the troops. Congress recognized both the obligations and limitations on its ability. Argument and delay angered the officers on the Hudson, but nothing especially ominous occurred until March 10. Then Washington was handed a written copy of a call being circulated for a meeting of general and field officers the next day. He was given, also, a transcript of a fiery and rhetorical appeal to the holders of commissions to make a vigorous demand to Philadelphia. This appeal, like the call for an assembly of officers, was anonymous and violent. It meant that if the war continued, its author wished the Army to desert Congress, leave the coast defenceless, and set up a new state in the wilderness. The alternative proposed might be the maintenance, if peace came, of an Army that would refuse to lay down its weapons.

This appalled Washington. Here seemed to be defiance of civil authority, threat of mutiny of a new sort, a revolt that might have leadership sufficiently experienced and intelligent to overthrow Congress and the governments of the States. He put in General Orders of March 11 a denunciation of "such an irregular invitation" and "such disorderly proceedings." A new meeting was set by him for the fifteenth, at which representatives of all regiments would decide what further measures should be adopted "to attain the just and important object in view." Washington must go before his subordinates in person and exert all the influence he had over them to reduce the chance of a foolish step. A public appearance of this sort was worse than distasteful; but nothing less than this might suffice, and even this might not be enough.

On the fifteenth Washington went to a large wooden structure the soldiers had completed a few weeks previously. He strode to the crude lectern, visibly agitated. He had put his thoughts in writing and with the permission of his brother-officers he would read what he wished to say. The anonymous address, he said, was "calculated to impress the mind with an idea of premeditated injustice in the sovereign power of the United States, and rouse all those resentments which must inevitably flow from such a belief." He proceeded: ". . . let me entreat you, gentlemen, on your part, not to take any measures which, viewed in the calm light of reason, will lessen the dignity and sully the glory you have hitherto maintained; let me request you to rely on the plighted faith of your country, and place a full confidence in the purity of the intentions of Congress. . . ." There followed more of explanation in the same spirit that led to a fine climax: "you will, by the dignity of your conduct, afford occasion for posterity to say, when speaking of the glorious example you have exhibited to mankind, 'had this day been wanting, the world had never seen the last stage of perfection to which human nature is capable of attaining.' "

This was the finest phrase with which he ever had exhorted disgruntled, sullen or resentful men; but he was not quite sure he had convinced his comrades of the perplexities and the good faith of Congress. He had brought with him a letter he had received not long previously from Joseph Jones, a discerning member of Congress from Virginia. The reading of part of this communication, Washington told himself, perhaps might confirm whatever impression he had made. He stumbled through a few sentences, but as the manuscript was closely written, paused, took out his new spectacles, and put them on. "Gentlemen," he said, in effect, as he fumbled with the glasses, "you must pardon me. I have grown gray in your service and now find myself growing blind." That observation completed the rally to Washington. When he left the hall a few minutes later, Gates acted as presiding officer and some of the most trusted lieutenants of the Commander-in-Chief took charge of the proceedings. In the face of mild opposition by Timothy Pickering, Washington received a vote of thanks; a committee presented a report in which the officers expressed confidence in the justice of Congress, asked the General to act in their behalf, repudiated the proposals of their anonymous counsellor, and called on McDougall and his associates, who were representing their case in Philadelphia, to remain there until they accomplished their object.

Washington felt immense relief and told himself and his friends in Congress that the result was what he "had reason to expect"; but it had been an alarming experience, and most inopportune, because it had come just at the time to dampen rejoicing over the greatest news that ever had come to Headquarters, the glorious tidings of a treaty of peace that recognized the independence of the United States.

Several indirect reports of the signing of a treaty of peace between the United States and Great Britain had reached Philadelphia and had fired public rejoicing, but nothing definite came until March 12, when Capt. Joshua Barney arrived aboard a vessel most fittingly named *Washington* and brought Congress the official text. The pact had been signed in Paris November 30, 1782, and was not final. Terms were "to be inserted in, and to constitute the treaty of peace, proposed to be concluded between the Crown of Great Britain and the said United States; but which treaty is not to be concluded until terms of a peace shall be agreed upon between Great Britain and France, and his Britannick Majesty shall be ready to conclude such treaty accordingly." Acknowledgment of independence was made in the initial article of the treaty; all hostilities were to cease; prisoners were to be exchanged; the whole settlement was in accordance with American demands and was acceptable—if it actually represented a settlement. Next a messenger reached Headquarters on the night of March 26 with news of the conclusion of peace by France and Spain with Britain. Close behind came a servant whom Lafayette had sent. The papers brought by the Marquis's man left no doubt that the three belligerents had signed a treaty at Paris January 20. This, too, was preliminary, but it made operative the pact of November 30 between America and Britain.

It was true! The formal close of the war had to wait on the drafting and signing of a definitive treaty, but actual peace had come. "The news," Washington wrote Luzerne, "has filled my mind with inexpressible satisfaction"; but he turned almost immediately to the complex question of the date on which hostilities were to end, and before he could solve this, he was reminding his friends of what the States must achieve in union now they had won peace. "It remains," he told Greene, "only for the States to be wise, and to establish their independence on the basis of inviolable, efficacious union and firm confederation, which may prevent their being made the sport of European policy; may Heaven give them wisdom to adopt the measures still necessary for this important purpose."

In that spirit he completed arrangements with the British for proclaiming the termination of hostilities on an agreed date. On April 15 the treaty was ratified by Congress, and on the nineteenth, eighth anniversary of the battle of Lexington and Concord, cessation of hostilities was announced formally. After that Washington had to supervise a number of continuing tasks, among which were the exchange of prisoners and an almost futile attempt to recover slaves who had fled to the British and now were seeking to leave America. Simultaneously with these troublesome matters Washington had to labor over the preliminaries of the discharge of the Army and had to be sure he left nothing undone in redeeming his pledge to protect the officers' interests. Washington had insisted that before the men were discharged their accounts should be settled and three months' of long-overdue pay put in their hands. In painful embarrassment he undertook to get funds of some sort from the Superintendent of Finance for the use of the men on the long tramp home. All that Morris could do, with his strong box empty, was to attempt to get paper to print and deliver requisitions for three months' pay directed to the States of the individual soldiers and payable after half a year. It was a shameful and humiliating device; to see the soldiers "turned aside so disgracefully" was heartrending.

Hampering everything was uncertainty over the time that would be spent in agreeing on the definitive treaty. Washington was looking forward to the blessed hour when he could begin anew his life as a planter, but he did not think he should effect his retirement, which he hoped to be early and complete, without warning his country against the risks of broken union, lost public credit, neglected defence and uncurbed jealousies. Emergency seemed to demand strong words at that particular time because Morris almost despaired of prevailing on the States to take up the notes that were being issued. To aid imperative fiscal rescue at the same time that he gave warning on the other hazards, Washington and some of his assistants prepared during the first week of June what the General expected to be the last of his "Circulars to the States."

Washington began the "last Circular" with a reference to his prospective retirement and the hopeful future of the United States. Then he proceeded:

There are four things which I humbly conceive are essential to the well-being, I may even venture to say, to the existence of the United States as an independent power:

1st. An indissoluble Union of the States under one Federal Head.

2dly. A sacred regard to public justice.

3dly. The adoption of a proper peace establishment, and

4thly. The prevalence of that pacific and friendly disposition among the people of the United States which will induce them to forget their local prejudices and policies, to make those mutual concessions which are requisite to the general prosperity, and in some instances, to sacrifice their individual advantages to the interest of the community.

The last of these necessities of national life, he said, he would leave "to the good sense and serious consideration of those immediately concerned," and it was on the essential to which he gave first place, "an indissoluble union," that he dwelt most fervently. The circular was styled forthwith "Washington's Legacy" and was acclaimed as no paper sent out over his signature ever had been. It gave, said Elias Boudinot, the "finishing stroke to his inimitable character."

Hope was voiced that the States might respond to the call of the man their people revered; but the ironic contrast between reality and ideal, the deformity and affliction that so often had sprawled across the road when he had "come down from the mountain" awaited him now. Pennsylvania soldiers mutinied at Lancaster and marched on Philadelphia, where the men in the barracks joined them. The combined forces surrounded the State House, in which the State Executive Council as well as Congress was sitting, and threatened to storm the building unless they were permitted to name officers of their own who would present their demands. After a time they went back to their quarters, but, President Boudinot wrote, "they have secured the public magazine, and I am of opinion that the worst is not yet come." Congress desired that Washington send reliable troops towards Philadelphia.

This mutiny, in Washington's eyes, was "infamous and outrageous." He issued orders for General Howe to start fifteen hundred men for Philadelphia. Before Washington snuffed his candle that night he had another dispatch from Boudinot enclosing resolutions Congress had adopted for removal to Princeton unless the Executive Council of Pennsylvania took "effectual measures . . . for supporting the public authority." By June 30 Washington learned officially that the Delegates were establishing themselves at Princeton. The seventh anniversary of the Declaration of Independence brought word the mutiny was ended, that the men from Lancaster were back at their stations, and that Howe had reached the temporary seat of government.

Then the uprising faded into the background, with this singular effect: The departure of Howe's column of fifteen hundred to suppress the mutiny left the Commander-in-Chief so little to do that he became bored. In his dull and narrowed field Washington's correspondence underwent a change. Friends in England were free to write again. Among them was the master of Belvoir in the days before the war, George William Fairfax, who seemed unchanged in spirit. His wife, the beloved Sally Cary Fairfax, was alive and in improving health. Washington answered his letter as if there had been no break in their letter-writing and expressed the friendly hope that these long-loved neighbors would return to Virginia and reside at Mount Vernon till their own house, which had been burned, could be rebuilt. This message from the Fairfaxes was exceptional. Some from former acquaintances were anything but gratifying.

Nearly the whole of official life at Newburgh was unpalatable. Washington resolved to get away from it temporarily, and set out on the eighteenth for Albany, Saratoga, Lake George, Ticonderoga, the lower end of Lake Champlain, Crown Point and Putnam's Point. Then, starting south again, he went via Schenectady to Fort Schuyler, over the portage to Wood Creek and on to Lake Oneida. It was August 4 when Washington again reached Albany, and the sixth when he went back to his office at Newburgh.

At Newburgh Washington found a letter in which James McHenry, now a member of Congress from Maryland, intimated that the Delegates soon would summon the Commander-in-Chief to Princeton. The General would have preferred to remain at Newburgh until a single journey would carry him home. As it was, as soon as his wife recovered from a fever, he set off for Princeton. In the homage he received on the road, and through newspapers and letters, he found daily accumulating proof of a sort no man could minimize that he had become a national hero. At Princeton the Delegates had voted that an equestrian statue of him be erected at the permanent seat of government, and they received Washington cordially in a formal session August 26.

Army correspondence and meetings with committees of Congress on a peace-time Army and Indian relations were atonement to the military conscience of Washington for a variety of social affairs. In acknowledgment of hospitality shown him, Washington entertained Congress September 5 and seated his guests for dinner in a marquee captured from the British. Now that he did not have the burdens of war on his heart, the change in his expression was apparent to all. He weighed 209 when he left the Hudson, and "his front," said David Howell of Rhode Island, was "uncommonly open and pleasant, the contracted, pensive phiz, betokening deep thought and much care, which I noticed on Prospect Hill, in 1775, is done away." Washington probably enjoyed this festivity more than he thought he should while the country still had no assurance that peace actually had come; and he found pleasure in arranging for the distribution of badges of the Society of the Cincinnati, to the presidency of which the officers who organized this mild counterpart of a European order had elected him. His largest satisfaction must have been in welcoming Nathanael Greene, who reached Princeton at the end of the first week in October on his way to his home in Rhode Island. Apart from this, Washington was holding the rein less tightly on his impatience. He wanted news of the signing of the definitive treaty, wanted to discharge his last duties to the Army and the country—and wanted after that to live his old life of planter, land owner and traveler.

While he was chafing, word came about October 12 that Sir Guy Carleton intended to begin in November the evacuation of the area around New York. Congress accepted this assurance and proceeded to release the men enlisted for service "during the war." Simultaneously the Delegates accepted the resignation of Lincoln as Secretary of War and to Washington, rather than to him, was assigned the duty of announcing to the troops full release from service. Long association prompted a personal message by Washington to the soldiers who remained under his direct orders at the end, and to avoid any suggestion that he was partial to these men, he addressed himself in "Farewell Orders to the Armies of the United States," a plural he seldom had employed.

About November 1 the news that justified the orders reached Princeton: The definitive treaty had been signed in Paris on September 3. Although a peace of independence was a reality, negotiations had been spread over so long a time that delay had stripped the climax of all its trappings. Washington now lingered at Princeton only for a final decision in Congress on the inclusion of more of his officers in the promotion by brevet that previously had been approved for some. He hoped also that a conclusion could be reached on the size of the Army to be maintained; but when a vote on this issue became impossible because a sufficient number of States were not represented in Congress, the General rode back to West Point with two objects to accomplish before he started home. He would add what he could to his pleas for loyal support of the union of the States and he would see that New York and its environs were restored to American sovereignty with the least possible disorder and no reprisal. He found that the officers at West Point wished to present him an address in answer to his farewell orders. This paper, delivered to him on the fifteenth, proved to be rhetorically much better than the one to which it was a reply: "We sincerely pray God this happiness may long be yours, and that, when you quit the stage of human life, you may receive from the Unerring Judge the rewards of valor exerted to save the oppressed—of patriotism and disinterested virtue."

At the time of Washington's receipt of the officers' address, the evacuation of New York by the British and its occupation by the Americans was the theme of correspondence, polite as between Washington and Carleton but most embarrassing on the part of Washington and of Gov. George Clinton. The reason was not political. The awkwardness was in the familiar lack of money: Washington did not have funds to pay for moving the Army to New York and had to ask Clinton for an official loan of $2000. When his Excellency the Governor of New York had to admit that his treasury did not possess that much, the Quartermaster General appealed to Philadelphia for cash or bills on anyone who would accept them immediately. By the middle of November it was the understanding of Washington that the last of the enemy's troops would leave New York on the twenty-third, and, on November 20, he issued his last official paper at West Point and rode to Day's Tavern in the village of Harlem.

The first day at Harlem brought disappointment, Carleton sent notice that his troops could not complete withdrawal from New York on the twenty-third. Then came bad weather that might hold the British longer. Washington could do nothing except wait. On the twenty-fourth, Carleton gave notice that he would complete the evacuation the following day at noon. Nothing of importance occurred while the troops made ready for their last and greatest march.

The next morning, Washington, Clinton and their attendants rode southward. The enemy had disappeared now; Knox and his troops had proceeded downtown. The design was for the military to occupy the streets and assure good order. Then Clinton was to enter the city and assume its administration. Although Washington was the man of all others the people wished to see, he came, by his own desire, as a spectator and guest of Clinton. The second stage of the symbolic events of the day was to be the formal welcome and celebration.

At the Bull's Head Tavern the cavalcade waited, close to a throng of rejoicing citizens. At length all was ready. Washington touched his horse; Clinton started at the same moment. Their escort was the Westchester Light Dragoons. Past crowds that cheered and shouted and cried for joy, the column moved slowly to Tea Water Pump in Chatham Street and drew rein. When civilians assembled there joined the cavalcade, the procession started again. On Broadway Washington found the troops who had formed line to do honor to him and to Clinton. New Yorkers watched tearfully and reminiscently. "We had been accustomed for a long time," a woman spectator wrote years later, "to military display in all the finish and finery of garrison life; the troops just leaving us were as if equipped for show, and with their scarlet uniforms and burnished arms, made a brilliant display; the troops that marched in, on the contrary, were ill-clad and weather beaten, and made a forlorn appearance; but then they were *our* troops, and as I looked at them and thought upon all they had done and suffered for us, my heart and my eyes were full, and I admired and gloried in them the more, because they were weather beaten and forlorn."

There followed during the next week a succession of elaborate dinners. A higher pleasure came to Washington in other ways unnumbered. Fully did he possess abounding measure of the reward he cherished most, the good will of honest men, good will won by the devoted service he had rendered them.

Washington waited to see the back of the last Redcoat. Carleton wrote that, if wind and weather permitted, he hoped to leave December 4 with the last of his troops. Washington shaped his plans so that he could start home as soon as it was certain Sir Guy was going or had departed. Not an hour would Washington remain beyond the time all danger of a clash of arms had ended. In Philadelphia he would settle his accounts, and, as quickly as he might, go to Annapolis, where Congress was to meet, and return his commission. Then—home and a private life!

Before he started he must say farewell to the officers who remained with the troops. Gratitude, affection and courtesy alike prompted Washington to a last meeting. Twelve o'clock would be a suitable hour and Fraunces' Tavern the most convenient place for saying farewell to the officers. Notice to that effect was passed. Arrangements were made for a barge to be in waiting at nearby Whitehall to carry him to Powles Hook, where he would take horse. Steuben would go with him as far as Philadelphia, and a few dragoons would be in attendance, but the cavalcade, including the servants, would be small.

Washington entered the long room at Fraunces' soon after the clock struck the hour. He found there nearly all the officers who had entered the city on the twenty-fifth and all the others who could assemble on short notice. They were not a large company, nor were many of them exalted in rank. If all who stood when Washington entered were not renowned, they were typical of the hundreds who had remained at their posts in poverty and shabbiness while their families at home had pinched and patched though speculating neighbors had grown fat. Now, as the last representatives of a vanishing Army, they were looking at their commander and awaiting his word.

Washington did not succeed in going through even the form of refreshment, but he did achieve composure enough to fill a glass with wine, as if inviting the gentlemen to do the same. Passing this wine had the effect of permitting the officers to get a grip on themselves. By the time they had drunk it, Washington's emotions had risen so high that tears were blinding him. "I cannot come to each of you," he said in a faltering voice, "but shall feel obliged if each of you will come and take me by the hand." Chance fixed it that, in the absence of Greene, the soldier best entitled to be first among them was nearest at hand. Henry Knox stepped forward silently and held out his hand; Washington extended his own, but as he looked into those honest eyes he could not say farewell with a handshake. Impulsively he put his arms around Knox and, weeping, kissed his Chief of Artillery. Once done, this had of course to be done with all, from Steuben to the youngest officer. With streaming eyes, they came to him, received the embrace and passed on.

Washington could not endure it long. When the last weeping officer had been embraced, the General walked across the room, raised his arm in an all-inclusive, silent farewell and passed out of the tavern. The wharf was crowded with men and women of every station. Many held up children to look at the tall man who had to set his mouth and keep taut the muscles of his face lest he could not bear the parting. Without a word he climbed into the barge. At a nod from an officer the boat was shoved off. Again, Washington made that all-inclusive gesture of farewell.

The ceremonies at New York made Washington more conscious than ever that he was saying good-bye to men and places associated with the highest satisfactions and most agonizing misery of his Revolutionary career. His desire to retire was in no way diminished, but the feeling of separation took on a poignancy that showed in the papers he had David Humphreys draft as answers to addresses delivered to him as he progressed to Philadelphia. Along with this feeling, was strengthened conviction that

Providence had intervened for the achievement of American independence, which it was the duty of all honest men to preserve through justice, vigilance and right conduct. That became Washington's creed.

As he approached Philadelphia December 8, he found awaiting him at Frankfort the President of the Executive Council, now John Dickinson, together with Robert Morris, Arthur St. Clair, Edward Hand, and the notables of the town. The familiar City Troop of Light Horse was present to act as escort of honor. With Congress still absent, the citizens had opportunity of welcoming Washington when they were not eclipsed by the Delegates; and they indulged in bountiful, unrestrained celebration.

He had much to do besides shake hands with delegations, attend dinners and carry on his correspondence, mercifully lighter now. Of nothing was he more solicitous in his sojourn to Philadelphia than that all his accounts and documents should be transported with the same attention that had been given to transcribing and packing them. He purposed to store these at Mount Vernon and make them available to historians when Congress thought proper to open its archives. Washington's other concern was for settlement of the accounts from the time he had notified Congress June 16, 1775, that he would accept nothing for his services other than his expenses. He had interpreted this to mean the cost of equipment and utensils, travel, entertaining, and everything he would have purchased if he had been living away from home as a private individual on the scale he maintained at Mount Vernon. The total was accepted without question by the Comptroller of the Treasury, James Milligan, whose generous settlement undoubtedly conformed to the wishes of Congress. Washington, for his part, turned into the Treasury an unexpended balance of $27,770 from the military chest.

By the morning of the fifteenth the discharge of business had reached the stage that permitted Washington to cross the Schuylkill, homeward bound. For a short distance, the City Troop and a number of citizens attended the General, but after they turned back, Washington, Humphreys and Benjamin Walker, a recent addition to his staff, had no companions except the servants. The General, as usual, rode fast and before darkness reached the vicinity of Wilmington, Delaware. There the Governor and Council and a company of old army officers and representatives of the state and town met him, welcomed him heartily, and gave him a salute of thirteen guns. Hard riding carried the General on the seventeenth to Baltimore, where the next day he had another dinner and, in the evening, a ball that lasted till 2 A.M. He was in the saddle December 19 with the explanation that he must hurry on because he had promised Martha to dine with her on Christmas at Mount Vernon. A few miles outside Annapolis, when a number of gentlemen met Washington to escort him into the city, he found Gen. William Smallwood of the Maryland Line among them and, perhaps to his surprise, General Gates.

Congress had ajourned at Princeton on November 4 to meet in Annapolis on the twenty-sixth, but it had not been able to count a quorum until December 13. Even now, seven States only were represented. For the purposes of the General, as Congress was the body from which he had re-

ceived his commission it was also the body to which he joyfully would return it; so, on the morning of the twentieth, with his letter of resignation,
Washington waited on the President of Congress, newly elected to that
office but an old acquaintance who had been under suspicion during the
Conway cabal—no less a person than Thomas Mifflin. After Washington's
letter was read, the Delegates voted to entertain him on the twenty-second
and receive him in person December 23.

From the hour of his coming it seemed that every official, every
lawmaker and every other person of means and station in Annapolis
wished to honor Washington and be in his presence at least once before his
departure which, it was understood, would be immediately after he had returned his commission to Congress. Some of the time not consumed by entertainment had to be spent in completing a letter on the final odds and
ends of public business for the consideration of the Delegates; the responses
to the addresses had to be reviewed after Humphreys and Walker had
drafted them; hours must have been devoted to the preparation of the
brief statement Washington intended to read when he appeared before
Congress. He wrote it himself, word by word, and then reviewed it with
like care.

The morning of the twenty-third he started for the State House and,
exactly at noon, presented himself with two aides at the chamber where
Congress was sitting. The messenger bowed and asked the gentlemen to
wait. In a moment the attendant was back with Charles Thomson, who
had been Secretary of Congress when Washington himself was a member.
Escorted by this senior official, the General entered the room. Washington
took a seat pointed out to him. Doors of the chamber and the gallery then
were opened; favored ladies quickly filled the gallery; public servants,
former officers and Maryland's most eminent citizens packed along the
wall. The Secretary ordered silence; a hush of high expectancy prevailed.
Mifflin addressed Washington: "Sir, the United States in Congress assembled are prepared to receive your communications." The General arose
and bowed. Out of his pocket he drew the text of his address, and held it
in a hand that shook visibly.

He began: "Mr. President: The great events on which my resignation depended having at length taken place; I have now the honor of offering my sincere Congratulations to Congress and of presenting myself before
them to surrender into their hands the trust committed to me, and to claim
the indulgence of retiring from the service of my country." He had to grip
the paper with both hands to hold it steady enough for reading. He choked
and fought to recover his voice. If he scarcely could follow his short manuscript, there were many spectators who could not see him through their
tears. As he reached the end his voice came back strongly: "Having now
finished the work assigned me, I retire from the great theatre of action;
and bidding an Affectionate farewell to this August body under whose
orders I have so long acted, I here offer my commission, and take my leave
of all the employments of public life."

With this, he drew his commission from his uniform coat, folded the
copy of his address, went forward, handed the two papers to Mifflin,

stepped back, and remained on his feet. Mifflin then answered on behalf of Congress in a finely phrased tribute to Washington's leadership and constant respect for civil authority. Thomson handed Washington a copy of the answer. Washington took it and bowed once more to the President and Delegates. Then, George Washington, Esq., walked from the chamber. A minute later, after he had stepped into an anteroom, the spectators were dismissed, and, when they had left, Congress formally adjourned. Washington thereupon reentered the place of meeting and shook hands and said good-bye to each Delegate.

Once, by desperate riding, he had covered the distance from Annapolis to Mount Vernon in a single day. That was impossible now, because of the late start, but the General and his companions pressed on. The next morning, December 24, home was the magnet that drew him— home, Martha's embrace and the shrill, excited voices of Jack Custis' younger children—all this a richer reward than the addresses of cities, salutes of cannon, and approving words of the President of Congress.

The morrow brought the greatest of Christmas gifts, the satisfaction of knowing that when historians asked how a seemingly hopeless revolt had ended in victory and independence, the answer would include these five factors: the persistence of a few leaders, the cost of British campaigning so far from home, the blunders and sloth of most of King George's commanders, the valuable aid of France, and the service of Washington and the Army under him. The order and the relative value of four of those reasons might be disputed; the fifth certainly would not be adjudged the least weighty and, if justly considered, always would be presented in terms of the difficulties encountered as well as of the results achieved.

There was never a time during the entire period of hostilities when Washington possessed every essential of sustained operations. Something always had been lacking. The country was feeble in manufacturing and poorly organized to deliver what it could produce; the Continental government had not commanded full public support and had no central executive who could unify effort; Congress lacked effective power to collect troops, supplies and equipment. Direction of the Quartermaster Department and of the Commissary changed almost continuously. Financial support was based on paper which depreciated until it became worthless. Except for open revolt against Congress by some of the States, the American cause encountered every barrier which could have obstructed the road that led to independence. Short-term enlistment, inadequate clothing, scarcity of provisions, and feeble transportation kept the Army close to dissolution. Training was rendered doubly difficult because nearly all company officers were inexperienced and, at the outset, without any system of inspection.

The higher command throughout the war was uneven in ability and in willingness to subordinate personal interest to the common cause. Greene, Lafayette and Knox were all that a commander could ask, except for Greene's single great miscalculation at Fort Washington. Wayne probably was next to these, particularly as a combat officer, but he had an element of rashness. Heath and Sullivan showed themselves moderately good administrators. Few of the other general officers were better than average,

and some were petty or incompetent or both. Only recruitment and subsistence were more difficult tasks for Washington than the maintenance of
a qualified, contented and cooperative command.

This feeble, changing Army with mediocre leadership and crude
equipment faced troops who were admirably equipped, disciplined and
trained. Numerically, the British and German forces were adequate for
nearly all field operations and were supported by a navy which, until the
summer of 1781, usually had full command of the sea. Washington was
never able until the autumn of 1781 to assume a prolonged offensive. The
American commander had not won a single major, pitched battle, prior to
the coming of the French, and he had sustained numerous defeats.

In spite of hunger and defeat, its reeking rags and its valueless pay,
the Continental Army was kept alive, and primarily through the efforts of
its commander. When the floodwaters of calamity were at their crest,
Washington's bold action at Trenton dammed the stream of disaster. He or
Greene subsequently repaired every serious hurt the enemy inflicted. Most
of Washington's lieutenants were shaken into a cooperative mood or made
ashamed of their pettiness. Willing men were trained, the incompetent
placed where they could do the least harm. Washington overcame some of
the disadvantage of having no central executive, and he brought to troops
the little that Congress could provide. When America at last had allies, he
won and retained their goodwill and respect. Always he saw clearly the
role of seapower. The instant he had assurance of naval superiority, he
used it to effect the swift concentration that proved decisive. These were
among the reasons almost all Americans believed that the leadership of
Washington was one of the most powerful influences in winning a war
which, without him, scarcely could have ended in complete victory, even
with the aid of France.

To have described Washington's Army is to make plain the fundamental of all the cumbering factors: Washington's strategy had to be patiently defensive. He did not wish it to be so, and he used every power of
persuasion to procure strength for an offensive that would drive the enemy
from America. It was in vain he pleaded. For six years he had to adhere to
enforced defensive as the only means of avoiding the danger that his feeble
Army might suffer irretrievable defeat. While no condition tempted Washington to abandon his general defensive strategy until he felt able to do so,
he shifted to the offensive-defensive whenever he could. He was careful to
draw a line between attempting too much and doing too little. If a choice
had to be made, he preferred active risk to passive ruin; he always sought
the largest gain for the least gore.

In this investment of the lives of his men he usually was lucky and
in nothing so fortunate as in his adversary's lack of enterprise. With the
exceptions of Cornwallis and Arnold, every senior British commander opposing Washington seemed to hold blindly to the opinion that the people
of the "provinces" were erring children who could be redeemed from the
wiles of rebel leaders by a combination of severity and coaxing. To out-
guess them, Washington sought the best strategical device and had no
pride of authorship. The excellence and not the origin of a plan was de-

cisive with him. He learned by listening as well as by observing and reflecting. During the greater part of the struggle he had to be his own chief intelligence officer, and he did so with considerable success. Always he tried to learn what was not happening as well as what was, and he frequently undertook the careful analysis, in person, of conflicting intelligence reports.

In applying tactically his strategical principles and his cumulative intelligence reports, Washington overcame his initial disadvantage of having to operate on a scale much greater than that of his experience prior to the Revolution. He made surprise his chief tactical device. Frontal assault he found too costly or too hazardous; flanking operations were beyond his numerical strength and the experience of his men; until Yorktown, he never was able to employ land and naval forces together except on a small scale and with light craft, though he gave some evidence of talent for this type of warfare. Washington displayed caution in giving battle; but when necessity or opportunity led him to engage, he usually met emergency with sound decision and swift strokes. His greatest weakness tactically appears to have been his failure to apply the doctrine of concentration in superior force at the point of contact even when he was weaker than his adversary in the larger theatre of action.

Burdensome was the word to apply to Washington's administrative duties around the clock and through the year. Hundreds addressed to him their petitions, complaints and proposals for the country's good. Army business was as vexatious as it was large. Commanders of other American forces looked to him; the President and various committees and members of Congress addressed him; so did several of the state governors; visitors at Headquarters were numerous; after the arrival of the French, Washington had an extensive and delicate correspondence, half military and half diplomatic, to conduct with men who used a different language; many reports had to be compiled, sometimes at length and after much inquiry and conference. For the transaction of this business as an administrator, Washington never had an adequate staff. He consequently had to rely on his personal staff, and even this he did not enlarge adequately because he disliked to increase public expense and, in addition, could not shake off his old habit of doing too much of his own paper work. The staff officers were almost without exception able; several might be described as brilliant. The aides did their utmost for their chief, but they could not relieve him of those duties that required personal study and negotiation, as, for example, his transactions with the heads of the departments of supply. Successive Quartermasters General, Commissaries General and Clothiers General in some instances were not and had not been army officers. Their position was somewhat anomalous and consequently difficult for Washington, except insofar as the individual might be disposed to cooperate. It is not easy to say how a man with his unshakable regard for civil authority could have gone further than he did in trying to save his men from hunger and cold; but the fact remains that the Army under Washington suffered from almost every physical hardship to which men could be subjected in the temperate zone. He may have been a good administrator, but with respect to supply his Army certainly was not well administered.

If this paradox denies him first rank in that sphere of military fame where he might have been expected to shine, he had administrative distinction in his dealings with officers who commanded other geographical departments. His policy was of the simplest: all that he could do to assist Gates, Sullivan, Heath or Greene, he did promptly, and he abstained consistently from the tender of strategical advice. His inborn caution would have prompted this restraint; his poor communications with distant theatres of war made the undesirable the impossible. He did not attempt to intervene where he could not be certain either of the ground or the circumstances; and he took pains to be certain he supplied the information and the guidance properly expected of him. The great triumph of Washington as an administrator was in his relations with Congress. His practice in dealing with Delegates does not appear to have been calculated. More probably it reflected innate respect for authority, desire to avoid blame for withholding information, resolution to do his utmost for the American cause, and memory of what he personally had needed in endeavoring as a lawmaker to pass intelligently on issues of moment. Washington was not involved in any serious misunderstanding with Congress, and he never lacked the support and confidence of a majority of its members, except, perhaps, for a short time in the early winter of 1777–78, when Gates's star was at its zenith.

This, then, was the soldier, the leader, the administrator. He and his Army had lost the battles but they had won the war. His place as a captain was established in part by what he had achieved in the absolute and, still more, by what he had accomplished in terms of the forces and equipment he commanded. How had he done so much with so little?

Washington had deep and dedicated love of country, a patriotism that sprang, originally, from his belief that Americans were being denied their inherited rights, surrender of which without a struggle was unworthy of self-respecting men. As the concept of union slowly developed, he began to see that independence would establish a new empire. Combativeness and ambition hardened the steel of Washington's patriotism. The more his country was endangered, the more firmly did he resolve to defend her to the last; the more nearly hopeless his task, the greater his ambition to discharge it. His courage and will matched his patriotism; above all, he had the courage and will to go straight on where the road was blackest.

Caution was a characteristic as marked as his courage, but it never was displayed in a manner to sap his fortitude or give the least suggestion of cowardice. When he hesitated to attack, it was because he feared the defeat of his Army might be the ruin of the American cause. Personally his caution had roots that went to the very heart of the man. He did not wish to become involved in personal disputes or to make embarrassing connections. Sound judgment seemed his very nature. He would listen to half a dozen proposals, deliberate on them, and almost certainly choose the best. It was the same with the interpretation of spies' reports; so it was in his choice of men for a particular task whenever choice was open to him.

"Patience," Washington said, "is a noble virtue, and, when rightly exercised, does not fail of its reward." He exemplified his maxim and scarcely ever lost patience except in dealing with three classes—cowards, those he believed to be of habitual rascality, and, above all, those who were cheating the American people for their own profit in the life-and-death struggle for independence. He was as diligent and systematic as he was patient and, whether directing a battle or a day's affairs, usually was calm and cheerful. Another essential element of his character was inflexible justice. Infused into every other attribute and a marked virtue in itself was unfailing regard for civil authority. Nothing offended him more than the suggestion of any sort of dictatorship. Ambition had always to yield to law. The object of war was peace. Every soldier had a supreme, compelling duty to respect the government that would guard his rights and property when independence had been won.

Most of these characteristics were the flowering of qualities Washington had shown, perhaps immaturely, by the end of the French and Indian War. Besides these, Washington had numerous lesser characteristics of which his officers spoke with puzzlement, surprise, or admiration. He displayed good will to decent men, even though he might not be prepared to accept them forthwith as friends. His consideration was equally broad. Washington disliked personal clashes and sought to avoid them. If he thought he had shown temper in dealing with an individual, he went out of his way to be sure he atoned for it. The General still had no spontaneous sense of humor and when he occasionally indulged a laugh it was over a bit of horseplay or some ludicrous harmless accident. Possessed though he was of every type of courage a man might covet, public censure was his supreme fear.

The strangest mystery of Washington's life was his lack of affection for his mother. Added years and understanding brought no improvement in his relations with her. As a matter of filial duty he left instructions with Lund that his mother's calls for money were to be met, but apparently he did not write her even once during the war. He who had so much magnanimity and patience in dealing with human frailty was so much like his mother, in most money matters, that he felt she had been grasping and unreasonable. A similar contrast in his nature existed between pity and grief. He always had pity. It inspired much of his charity and no little of his effort, though his pity was mingled with wrath against those responsible for human misery. Grief was different. Doubtless it was personal to him but outwardly in his attitude to it he had not changed since his youthful days when the death of his benefactor, Col. William Fairfax, brought from his pen a tribute of one clause only.

These minor characteristics of Washington were as plain to his discerning Revolutionary associates as his major virtues were. Deeper in the soul of the man there was a frontier where he set up a barrier of defence, probably because he still was not sure of his strength and weakness there, and also because the citadel of his soul lay close beyond that line. Here was the scene of more than one spiritual dispute and here the battleground of his resentments. "Personal enmity I have none, to any man," he awkwardly wrote the Rev. Jacob Duché, when the repentant former Chaplain of Congress sought to return to the United States. Washington had wrestled with himself to achieve that goal and believed he had conquered his temper, but on occasion, he still flared up. To this same uncertain frontier of Washington's mind his personal religion had been brought after the years of peace had led him to conform without heart searching to the practices of the church. He had believed that a God directed his path, but he had not been particularly ardent in his faith. The war convinced him that a Providence intervened to save America from ruin. Now that the war had ended and the Providence that Washington would observe was that of rain and sunshine and season and storm, not that of marches and battles, it remained for the returning soldier to see whether God became personal to him.

Another uncertainty was the effect of the adulation Washington was receiving. As a young man his modesty had been listed with his amiability as one of his most attractive qualities. His distrust in 1775 of his qualifications for supreme field command may have originated in a cautious regard for the reputation he previously had acquired, rather than in modesty, but the result was the same: it led his colleagues in Congress to believe that he did not "think more highly" of himself than he should. Within less than a year after that he was subjected to the praise of the grateful city of Boston, which expressed the wish that "future generations" might "raise the richest and most lasting monuments to the name of Washington." He frankly liked this. Congress voted a medal; all America smiled in approval. Then, in the summer of 1776, began the grim succession of defeats and disappointments. These events certainly presented no temptation for Washington to exalt himself—and neither did they have contrary effect. There was nothing self-deprecatory about him, then or thereafter. Until after the French alliance, his behavior bespoke a belief that modest manners were an evidence of good taste proper for a gentleman. Later, the French soldiers, particularly some under Rochambeau, poured out a sort of praise for which Washington was not prepared. His admiring allies called it compliment; the British would have stamped it flattery; but it showed Washington that he already had in Europe a measure of the approbation he sought to win in America. When to this was added in 1783 the vote of an equestrian statue, the laudation of the continent, and receptions that had the spirit of triumphant entry, had they combined to turn Washington's head? If ultimate victory and the homage of the people failed to move him, he would have been the strangest of mortals; and if he felt no pride in the completion of his task, he would have depreciated the magnitude of what had been accomplished. He did have pride, but there was at the end of the war no evidence in him of exalted self-esteem.

Perhaps some of Washington's lieutenants knew there were at least two interpretations of some of these characteristics. Friends might have analyzed them correctly and explained his peculiarities along with his patriotism, courage, judgment, patience, systematic diligence, sense of justice and respect for civil authority. Henry Knox or Jonathan Trumbull, Jr., or David Humphreys, or almost any other of those who remained with him to the end might have taken him apart, quality by quality, but they could not easily have put him back together again. They could have said that to a certain point he was an understandable personality, of normal, integrated abilities—and, so saying, none of these men would have explained Washington or his success.

Failure to understand the inmost man was not the result of any obtuseness on the part of Washington's companions in arms. Not many of them had known him prior to 1775. He was himself responsible, in part, for the fact that he was a stranger, in his inmost self, to those around him. As man and soldier, he built up through the years of war two walls of reserve. One had a footing of personal caution. "It is easy to make acquaintances," he explained, "but very difficult to shake them off, however irksome and unprofitable they are found after we have once committed ourselves to them. . . ." The safe rule of personal relationship, as he saw it, was this: "Be courteous to all but intimate with few, and let those few be well tried before you give them your confidence; true friendship is a plant of slow growth. . . ." He loved the young Marquis as he might have loved a son, but even in this closest of friendships, Washington did not admit Lafayette all the way beyond the second wall of his reserve, the wall of military secrecy. The Commander-in-Chief knew how ears were raised in camp to catch the faintest whisper of impending movement, and he realized that gossips were almost as dangerous as spies. Even where he knew his remarks would not be passed on, reserve on military matters was a habit.

Another reason some of Washington's colleagues did not understand how he achieved what seemed impossible in the Revolution was the human disposition to assume that large results have complicated causes. These men, and many of those who came after, felt there must be some elaborate explanation of Washington's accomplishments and character. Although his words usually were the mirror of his mind and his nature was disclosed daily in the transaction of business, none of his comrades in arms could believe he actually was as simple as he had proved himself to be in the stripping ordeal of war. Washington gave an old friend, years later, the basic explanation of the success of his Revolutionary leadership when he said he "always had walked on a straight line." Early in life he acquired a positive love of the right and developed the will to do the right. There must have been derelictions, but when his fame had created curiosity concerning his youth, there did not emerge even one tale of tryst behind a haystack or of a plundering escapade with boys of the neighborhood. Item-by-item scrutiny of his cash book and ledger, which are the fullest financial record of any young American of his generation, does not disclose one entry that even hints of a liaison with a woman. He had gambled a little on horses and cards, and he had fallen harmlessly in love with his neighbor's wife, but out of this and out of all his adventures at frontier posts, there developed no scandal.

The next essential fact was his complete dedication to the duties assigned him in 1775. He had told Congress the day he accepted command: "I will enter upon the momentous duty and exert every power I possess in their service for the support of the glorious cause." In that resolution he fought "with a halter round his neck." Because Washington knew he had integrity and absolute dedication to the cause of independence, he had throughout the Revolution a positive peace of mind. This did not mean that he observed without concern the miseries of his men or the desperate fluctuation of American fortunes. Over these things he agonized endlessly; but always he could war the better against Britain because he was not at war with himself. His will and his self-discipline were his rod and his staff.

As much a part of the man as integrity, dedication and peace with himself were the two rewards Washington desired for himself. He wanted first the assurance that he had kept his promise to devote himself completely to his task. The other reward represented in developed form his youthful craving for what he had termed "honor," and if he had to be characterized in a single sentence, it would be substantially this: He was a patriot of conscious integrity and unassailable conduct who had given himself completely to the Revolutionary cause and desired for himself the satisfaction of having done his utmost and having won the approval of those whose esteem he put above every other reward.

In accepting the integrity, dedication and ambitions of Washington as realities, one does not face an insoluble problem when one asks how this life, at the end of the Revolution, had reached the goal of service, satisfaction and reward. George Washington was neither an American Parsifal nor a biological "sport." What he was, he made himself by will, effort, discipline, ambition and perseverance. For the long and dangerous journeys of his incredible life, he had the needful strength and direction because he walked that "straight line."

CHAPTER / 18

For some weeks after Washington returned to Mount Vernon as a private citizen it seemed unreal that his time was his own, to devote to private business in a world not only narrowed by retirement but dramatically imprisoned, as it chanced, by snow and ice that kept him housebound almost continuously from Christmas to the second week in February 1784. After a month and a little more Washington had convinced himself that he was a planter again. "The tranquil walks of domestic life are now beginning to unfold themselves," he cheerfully confided to Rochambeau; and to Lafayette he wrote, "I am retiring within myself, . . . envious of none . . . determined to be pleased with all."

He undertook to bring himself down to date on many subjects he had neglected. He hoped, even, for spare moments in which to enlarge his knowledge of history and, perhaps, of French, but he found quickly that legs accustomed to the saddle were not altogether at ease when stretched overlong by the fireside. His muscles made him restless; demanding duties began to devour his days, new duties as well as old, duties imposed by fame along with those exacted by ownership. Visitors arrived in large numbers, stayed at their leisure and, in some instances, returned with exacting frequency. He found that whenever he stirred from the vicinity of Mount Vernon it became a formal occasion with ceremonies, salutes and addresses. Pleasing as was the cordiality of the people to a man who found public approval the greatest of rewards, lengthy receptions and dinners were more to be avoided than enjoyed.

He did one thing that must have puzzled his friends; he wrote Capt. Daniel McCarty, vestryman of Truro Parish: "It is not convenient for me to be at Colchester tomorrow, and as I shall no longer act as vestryman, the sooner my place is filled with another, the better. This letter, or something more formal if required, may evidence my resignation, and authorize a new choice." He said no word in explanation of his withdrawal from the vestry. Subsequently, although Washington's recorded appearances at church were rare, he remained on friendly terms with his rector and probably attended Christ Church in Alexandria when weather and roads permitted.

Another experience of Washington's after he adjusted himself to renewed home-life was one for which he was in some measure prepared. Eight years of service with the troops had been eight years of neglect at home. Ante-bellum debtors who had made any payment had done so, usually, in depreciated currency. During the British raid of 1781, eighteen slaves had run away; nine had been sold in the most difficult years to provide money for taxes; plantation industries and the ferry had done well on paper for service paid in paper; Lund Washington's preoccupation on the estate and his aversion to travel and to bookkeeping had led to neglect of rent collection from western lands; current and capital accounts had been confused. The pinch of hard times had been felt everywhere except at the dining table. Yet, even when the war had been at its worst, the General had directed the continued improvement of the mansion house; and now he was ambitious to have a new room decorated in stucco. He undertook, besides, to pave the piazza with flagstones from England, built a greenhouse, made plans for a better way of keeping ice in summer, paid for and put into use French plate ordered for him by Lafayette, and replenished his stock of claret. Other drink and day-by-day food represented a continuing expense.

Within a short time the immediate household was to consist of Martha, two of her grandchildren, the General, Lund Washington for a good many of his meals, and subsequently George Augustine Washington and Fanny Bassett, a niece who served as mistress of the house. Seven or eight white persons had to be fed daily from the main kitchen, but they usually represented only a few more than half of those who sat down for dinner in mid-afternoon. On occasion as many as ten or even fifteen guests, invited or unexpected, joined the family at the meal. Several of these early guests were distinguished; most were welcome, and a few only were impostors, or persumptuous, uncouth persons who came to fill their stomachs or have an experience of which to boast; but in the aggregate they accounted for numerous young beeves, sheep and roasting pigs, to say nothing of flour and vegetables, milk and butter, fish from the river and game from the marshes. Claret, Madeira and spirits disappeared in large volume. The financial burden of this entertainment was apparent to friends and to Congress, whose members endlessly were asked by foreign travelers how arrangements might be made for interviews with the General, but a suggestion of the Pennsylvania Executive Council that Washington accept a gift from Congress was promptly and gratefully disapproved by him.

Washington had predicted that he would come home "with empty pockets" and he almost literally had done so—to find numerous, unexpected calls for money. Because of the shortage of revenue at Mount Vernon, Lund Washington had drawn no pay as steward after April 1778, but he had said nothing of this to the General. When the owner came home and found this obligation, he had no ready way of meeting it. Many unanticipated requirements for money had to be met. A hundred guineas were found somehow by the General for his nephew, George Augustine Washington, Lafayette's former aide, who needed to go to the West Indies for his health. In explaining to his nephew, Fielding Lewis, Jr., why he could not make him a loan, Washington confessed one of the main reasons for his financial distress: "My living," he said, "under the best economy I can use must unavoidably be expensive." In spite of all this, he remained optimistic that after he got his neglected affairs in order and received from London the money due on Patsy Custis's stock in the Bank of England his situation would be better.

Four months were spent in varied efforts to adjust himself to the position of a landed proprietor who had seen "the whirlwind pass." Then, in May 1784, he had to answer the first call to renewed public service in a matter that alarmed him for weeks. The Society of the Cincinnati had become unpopular with a considerable element in America, for reasons none of the founders had anticipated. Benjamin Franklin had ridiculed it; Judge Ædanus Burke of South Carolina had written a furious "address" of warning that a "race of hereditary patricians" was being created; Elbridge Gerry had become suspicious; Delegate Samuel Osgood had pictured a conspiracy against the treasury; Henry Knox had reported that antagonism was widespread and vehement in New England, where the Society was alleged to be the creation of foreign influence, the first step towards a martial oligarchy that would overthrow American democratic institutions. Washington responded as he usually had to complaints in the Army: let the justice of the protests be determined; call on the most influential of the senior officers to attend the general meeting of the Society due to be held in Philadelphia; change promptly the rules in a manner to remove all reasonable objection to it. If antagonism could not be overcome, the men who established the Cincinnati should dissolve it for the country's sake. As President-General, Washington reviewed the Society's rules (or "Institution") line by line and probably had his detailed recommendations in order on his departure for Philadelphia April 26, the first long journey he made after his home-coming.

Proceedings of the Cincinnati showed that his leadership was accepted as readily as if he still were at Field Headquarters. It was May 4 when a quorum of delegates appeared at City Tavern and the fifteenth when the debate-loving members completed their deliberations and approved a circular to be sent the State Societies. Washington's prime insistence was that the delegates "strike out every word, sentence and clause which has a political tendency." Hereditary membership was to be discontinued; no more honorary members were to be admitted; donations to the Society were not to be received except from citizens of the United States; funds were to be placed in such status that their misuse could not even be suspected. Washington urged, further, that all foreign officers meet in France as a self-governing body that would have authority to pass on applications, within the terms of the Institution. This, needless to say, was proposed to meet the charge that these officers—Frenchmen who had risked their lives in war against a common foe—were seeking to impose alien rule on America. Finally Washington advocated the abandonment of general meetings; members would assemble formally in their own States only.

The delegates adopted substantially all of Washington's proposals except the one for the abandonment of general meetings. It was their decision to recommend the whole of the revised Institution to the State Societies for acceptance, rather than to declare it the governing law of the Society. Although elections were conducted and procedure authorized by the General Society as if the revised Institution was in operation, the intent of the Delegates undoubtedly was to make the changes contingent on the approval of the State Societies. The original Institution was silent concerning amendment and revision, but congressional usage and the inclination of most men was to defer to the States. Had Washington regarded this procedure as evasive, he would not have accepted, even with the reluctance he displayed, unanimous reelection as President-General for a term of three years.

As rapidly as he could, he hurried homeward to take up the burdens of entertainment and farm management and pay another of the prices of being a national hero, the price of correspondence that became more nearly intolerable with each post. He protested that in eight years of public service, he never had been compelled to write so much in person. He daily was hampered because he had not yet been able to find a secretary or do more than make a beginning in the rearrangement of his legal papers, frightfully disordered from having been thrown into chests and hurriedly hauled away each time the British had appeared on the Potomac.

Inquiries were being made about his western lands, inquiries he usually was able to answer after much searching; but it was manifest that part of his properties in the Ohio Valley were occupied by trespassers. Some of these men boldly were offering for sale tracts Washington had patented years previously. The mill and plantation which Gilbert Simpson had mismanaged must be leased, if possible, to someone else. Washington had planned to make an early visit to these possessions beyond the mountains, and he now had an added reason for doing so. Interest was being revived in the old project of linking the upper waters of the Ohio with the Virginia rivers. Thomas Jefferson appealed to him to take the lead in this before New York State captured the western trade by opening an easy route to the Hudson. Now that he was going west on his own business he resolved to ascertain, if he could, which was the best line for a road between the navigable waters of the Potomac and some deep flowing tributary of the Ohio. If he found the route, he believed Virginia and Maryland would find the money for it.

He set out September 1 with Dr. James Craik and made his way west with few experiences he had not met before the war. By the sixth, Washington reached Berkeley Springs, now named Bath. There he met a storekeeper and builder, James Rumsey, who demonstrated an invention he claimed would enable boats to ascend easily a swiftly flowing stream. Washington grew enthusiastic and, at Rumsey's instance, wrote a testimonial in which he described what he had seen. Washington did not stop with this. He was in such good humor with Bath and so pleased with Rumsey that he authorized the inventor to build him near the springs a two-story dwelling, with a stable and a kitchen as separate buildings, the whole to be ready in July 1785.

From Bath the General and his party proceeded to the familiar settlement of Col. Thomas Cresap on the site known as Old Town. The Colonel was eighty years of age or more and of feeble eyesight, but with intellect scarcely impaired. The General then started for Simpson's in order to arrive in time for the advertised sale of the mill. Washington tried to cover the twelve miles of difficult road between Gist's and Simpson's at what he termed his "usual traveling gait of five miles an hour," but when he met travelers proceeding east with loads of ginseng, he could not resist the temptation to stop and make inquiry concerning the navigable streams. The men gave him some information on the streams up which the produce of the Ohio might be carried on batteaux, but they knew nothing about the country through which it would be necessary to open a portage. Something more personally unpleasant was told Washington by these wayfarers. Indians to the west were in ugly mood if not actually in arms. It might be dangerous for him to go down the Ohio, as he had planned, to his large holdings on the mouth of the Kanawha.

Washington reached Simpson's in the late afternoon of September 12, and not with pleasant anticipations, because nearly all his relations with Simpson had been unpleasant and expensive. Simpson had beguiled Washington time after time. Now, fresh disappointments crowded his stay at Simpson's. The mill was in disrepair; there was no reservoir; the dam had given way; it was futile to hope for any rent worth collecting from the property. Nor could a purchaser be found. The General had, in the end, to make a new and bad bargain with the wily Simpson. Ill luck continued to dog the General as he went from Simpson's to his property on Miller's Run, where numbers of families were occupying land to which he held title. After a long conference, they chose to stand suit for ejectment, alleging title of their own, rather than pay rent.

Visiting dignitaries and an officer of the Pittsburgh garrison by this time had confirmed the roadside report on Indian unrest down the Ohio. Washington's common sense told him he must turn back. Still, however, the spirit of the adventurous surveyor asserted itself. He would ride southward to Cheat River, which then seemed the most accessible tributary of the Monongahela. After examining the Cheat, he would proceed eastward to the North Branch of the Potomac. It was an arduous enterprise but inconvenience and hard riding in an unknown country did not weigh against curiosity and a belief that discovery of an easy, safe route would unify and enrich America.

Washington concluded that the best passage to the west would be from the North Branch by portage to Dunkard's Bottom and down the Cheat to the Ohio. Although he was worn by his ordeal to the extent that he had to allow himself a day's rest after he reached Fort Pleasant September 27, he counted that as nothing. The puzzle had been solved, he thought. By way of the Cheat, batteaux from the Ohio could be brought within ten miles, as he computed the distance, of water that flowed into Chesapeake Bay. The last stage of his journey was over the Alleghenies to procure from Thomas Lewis, who resided near Staunton, documents to support action for ejectment of the men occupying his land on Miller's Run.

Washington alighted at Mount Vernon October 4. If he had little to show in money for a journey of 680 miles and a month and four days of his time, he had a reward of enthusiastic interest he had not displayed in years. Peace brought a challenge to peaceful effort as absorbing as that of war. Said he: "The more the navigation of Potomac is investigated and duly considered, the greater the advantages arising from them appear." Obstacles existed, the General admitted, but they must be overcome—and could be. If there still was doubt concerning the best route, let it be resolved by careful surveys made at the instance of the government of Virginia, or on order of Congress. Meantime, companies might be organized and made ready to develop the Potomac—and the James also, if this second enterprise was necessary to remove jealousies and was believed to be profitable. To enlarge that new empire of the Ohio Valley, Congress, in Washington's opinion, should purchase from the Indians sufficient land for one or two States, "fully adequate to all our present purposes," and should sell this land at figures low enough for settlers but too high for speculators. Severest penalties should be imposed on adventurers who surveyed or attempted to settle beyond the limits of the proposed States.

To marshal arguments for presentation to Congress and the affected States was long labor for a man who composed a good letter slowly. Time was scarce, too, because of the attention the host at Mount Vernon felt he should give his guests, but Washington unflinchingly paid the price in hours for the result he hoped to achieve. Circumstance favored him. Lafayette had visited Mount Vernon in August and had left at the time Washington set out for the West. An understanding had been reached then that the Marquis would return to the estate, whence they would proceed to Richmond, Virginia, which Lafayette desired to visit again. An invitation to Richmond had come also from Gov. Benjamin Harrison, for years a friend of the retired Commander-in-Chief. Washington decided to accept and reasoned that as the General Assembly was in session, he would have an excellent opportunity of discussing with public men the improvement of the Potomac and the James.

Lafayette decided to change his route to Richmond, but Washington set out on the designated date, reached the new capital of his Commonwealth November 15 and went through ceremonials of addresses and responses. He found the General Assembly divided in support of the James and Potomac routes but willing to approve either if the other was included. Washington soon had the promise of legislators that they would take action before they adjourned. Back at home with Lafayette by the afternoon of November 24, Washington had reasons for being satisfied with the start he had made but, at the moment, the host let other matters wait while he enjoyed his guest. When Lafayette started north on the twenty-eighth, to take ship from New York, Washington went with him to Annapolis and shared festivities there. He continued with the Marquis for some distance on the road to Baltimore before turning back. "I often asked myself," he wrote later, ". . . whether that was the last sight I ever should have of you; and though I wished to say 'No,' my fears answered 'Yes.'"

Washington pressed his plea for a survey by engineers Congress employed; he renewed his suggestion for a stock company, whose capital would supplement state appropriations; and, as the legislative sessions were approaching their end in both Maryland and the Old Dominion, he urged that committees be named to confer on the drafting of identical bills. On

December 19 an express from Richmond brought him the resolutions the General Assembly had passed on the thirteenth. These set forth that acts passed by Virginia and Maryland without previous consultation might not be similar; wherefore Washington, Gen. Horatio Gates and Thomas Blackburn, or any two of them, be named to confer with Maryland authorities and report to the Assembly. Washington designated December 23 as the date of the meeting, sent the express on to Annapolis, and notified Blackburn what was contemplated. By the twenty-second he was in Annapolis with the responsibility of serving as Virginia's sole active representative. It was impossible for Blackburn to attend, and Gates had fallen sick almost immediately on arrival.

The conference progressed without hitch or halt. Unanimous recommendation was made for the survey of the various suggested routes from the Potomac to the nearest navigable streams that flowed into the Ohio. Hope was expressed that the Potomac itself could be opened as far inland as the mouth of Stony Creek. It was suggested that Maryland and Virginia each purchase fifty shares of the stock of a private company organized to develop the river and that jointly they assume the responsibility of constructing the portage roads. An initial appropriation of $3333 was advocated for each State.

The result was better than fair. The Maryland Legislature promptly passed a bill that included almost verbatim the recommendations of the commissioners. This was hurried to Washington who forwarded it to Richmond, where Virginia lawmakers adopted a similar measure January 4, 1785. Washington's popularity undoubtedly facilitated action, and his energy and his experience were almost as influential as his prestige; but the keen eye of James Madison saw something besides this in Washington's exertions: "The earnestness with which he espouses the undertaking is hardly to be described, and shows that a mind like his, capable of grand views, and which has long been occupied with them, cannot bear a vacancy."

The embarrassment of a great gift came to Washington early in January: Under an act of the General Assembly of Virginia, fifty shares of the stock of the Potomac Company and one hundred shares in the James River Company were to be purchased by the Treasurer and vested in Washington, "his heirs and assigns, forever, in as effectual a manner as if the subscriptions had been made by himself or by his attorney." A graceful preamble expressed the hope that as the public improvements sponsored by Washington would be "durable monuments of his glory," they should be made "monuments also of the gratitude of his country." He no more was disposed in 1785 than in 1775 to have it said that he served America for monetary reward. His impulse was to decline the stock. After long hesitation, he wrote Gov. Patrick Henry a careful letter in which he asked that so far as the law "has for its object my personal emolument [it] may not have its effect; but if it should please the General Assembly to permit me to turn the destination of the fund vested in me, from my private emolument, to objects of a public nature, it will be my study in selecting these to prove the sincerity of my gratitude for the honor conferred on me, by preferring such as may appear most subservient to the enlightened and patriotic views of the Legislature"—an arrangement the General Assembly at once approved.

Where an auspicious prospect of Potomac development was opening through the efforts of Washington, it was natural for stockholders to look to him for continued leadership. He was named President of the Potomac Company and was one of the active directors who undertook to find a manager. In August the retired Commander-in-Chief began periodic inspection tours of the Potomac from Harpers Ferry to the Great Falls above Georgetown. He always encountered some disappointment but usually he found encouragement. He made it plain, all the while, that development of waterways was no substitute for the maintenance and improvement of Virginia roads.

Still another enterprise that demanded a place in Washington's mind during 1785 was the Dismal Swamp Company which never had been developed with vigor. Management was feeble; records were lost, scattered or forgotten. A meeting proposed for May 1784 at Richmond had not been held until October. At a further meeting in May 1785, with Washington in attendance, a small loan for a term of seven years was authorized, but neither this nor a proposal for contructing a large canal through Dismal Swamp to Albemarle Sound yielded immediate result. Washington continued to believe that the lands of that region would "in time become the most valuable property in this country," and he declined with regret to participate in a plan Henry had in hand for extensive development of the southern end of the swamp. The reason for abstaining, the General wrote in full candor, was that "it would be most advisable for me, in my situation, not to add to my present expenditures."

Almost to be termed a calamity was hostile weather. The long, wet winter of 1784–85 was followed by what Washington described as "the most unfavorable" spring he ever knew, and an unpropitious planting season gave place to a drought that continued until August 27. The mill on Dogue Run had no water; a new insect pest sapped the corn and ruined much of the grass.

Between the backward spring and the beginning of the drought, a messenger arrived at Mount Vernon with the news that Martha's brother, Bartholomew, and their mother, Mrs. Frances Jones Dandridge, had died within a few days of each other. Mrs. Dandridge was seventy-four and had finished her active life, but Judge Dandridge was forty-eight and had in his care the tangled estate of Jack Custis. The Judge, moreover, had served as guardian of some of Jack's children and had a considerable debt to the General and Martha on his own account and because of a loan made in 1758 by Martha's estate to William Dandridge. New financial distress would be involved in any arrangement of Judge Dandridge's affairs.

The steady flow of guests to Mount Vernon was another reason for increasing financial distress. This imposition was becoming worse, not better. Some visitors came in reverence and departed in awe; an occasional guest felt disappointment because of the General's reticence or weariness or both. Washington was especially cautious and ill at ease with men whose native speech he did not understand, but where he knew his words would not be passed on, he lost some of his military reserve. Of the succession of guests, some were interesting and distinguished, all expensive and time-consuming.

Elkanah Watson, merchant adventurer and enthusiastic advocate of canals, came to Mount Vernon in January to explain what he had seen of the waterways of the Low Countries. He was then twenty-seven and already had made a fortune that had been swept away in 1783. His impression of the General was:

He soon put me at ease, by unbending, in a free and affable conversation. The cautious reserve, which wisdom and policy dictated, whilst engaged in rearing the glorious fabric of our independence, was evidently the result of consummate prudence, and not characteristic of his nature. . . . I observed a peculiarity in his smile, which seemed to illuminate his eye: his whole countenance beamed with intelligence, while it commanded confidence and respect. . . . I found him kind and benignant in the domestic circle, revered and beloved by all around him; agreeably sociable, without ostentation; delighting in anecdote and adventures without assumption; his domestic arrangements harmonious and systematic.

The next conspicuous guest was Robert Edge Pine, whose sympathy with America had cost him a profitable business as a portraitist in England. An appealing letter of introduction by George William Fairfax was followed by one from Francis Hopkinson, a favorite of Washington's. The Philadelphian wrote that he knew the General would rather fight a battle than sit for a portrait, but that Pine intended to make pictures of the Revolutionary War and could not do this without portraits of Washington. Washington replied, almost merrily:

In for a penny, in for a pound is an old adage. I am so hackneyed to the touches of the painters' pencil that I am now altogether at their beck, and sit like patience on a monument while they are delineating the lines of my face. It is a proof among many others of what habit and custom can effect. At first I was as impatient at the request, and as restive under the operation as a colt is of the saddle. The next time I submitted very reluctantly, but with less flouncing. Now, no dray moves more readily to the thill than I to the painter's chair. It may easily be conceived therefore that I yielded a ready obedience to your request and to the views of Mr. Pine.

The guest of 1785 who came on the most conspicuous mission was the French sculptor Jean Antoine Houdon. By a resolution of June 1784, the General Assembly of Virginia requested the Governor "to take measures for procuring a statue of General Washington." Under this resolution, Thomas Jefferson, then in France, had been asked to engage an artist. Jefferson's reply was: "There could be no question raised as to the sculptor who should be employed; the reputation of Monsieur Houdon of this city being unrivalled in Europe." Negotiations were concluded readily, and Houdon, after a delay occasioned by illness, left for the United States in the company of Benjamin Franklin. In a letter Washington received about

September 25, Doctor Franklin stated that Houdon was in Philadelphia. The General replied in a warm letter and sent a formal welcome to the sculptor.

On the night of October 2 Houdon arrived from Alexandria, with three assistants and with a French resident of the nearby town as interpreter. Several other guests already were occupying most of the spare beds, but room was made for the late comers. The next morning Houdon delivered letters from Lafayette, Jefferson and David Humphreys and began to prepare for modeling. The artist proceeded as if he did not intend to waste a day. Perhaps he saved time because he spoke no English and did not linger loquaciously over the Madeira or the tea. By the sixth, Houdon was ready to begin on the bust of Washington. That day and the next the General sat for him.

Houdon went with Washington and other guests to attend a funeral in the neighborhood on the ninth, and to the wedding of George Augustine Washington and Frances Bassett on the evening of October 15. The ceremony doubtless was sufficiently beautiful to have pleased an artist. Washington himself must have shared the romance of a union between Mrs. Washington's niece and his nephew. After Houdon completed his work and left on October 17 the General wrote Humphreys, "I feel great obligations [to Mr. Houdon] for quitting France and the pressing calls of the Great Ones to make a bust of me from the life." Doubtless he said as much to Houdon; doubtless the answer of the artist was urbane; but there was no au revoir, no letter of thanks from Philadelphia or from Paris, not even "I hope you like it" when the statue was finished and shipped. Houdon let the marble speak for itself. It did.

Houdon was exceptional. Other visitors were more exacting. Washington remained the generous host, and he was learning now to entrust to various persons at Mount Vernon part of the entertainment of his guests. Some relief came after July, when Washington employed William Shaw as his secretary. Even with this assistance, breakfast at seven o'clock, and the dedication of his mornings to work, Washington often left his guests for two hours between tea and supper and sometimes did not appear at the evening meal. Dinner was at 2 P.M.; nine remained his bedtime unless a visitor brought news in which he had special interest.

Washington made the best of his difficult role as national host and undoubtedly took pride in having his lands, house and table impress visitors. Improvements gave added beauty to the entire plantation. "It is impossible," wrote Joseph Hadfield, a young Manchester merchant, "to do justice to the order and management of the General's affairs." The guest continued: "His large estates, cultivated in the best manner, furnish him with all the necessaries of life, and his revenues enabled him, as well as the presents he received from all parts, to have all the luxuries of every clime. His gardens and pleasure grounds . . . were very extensive. . . . He is allowed to be one of the best informed as well as successful planters in America." More than one visitor got the same impression that Washington's style of living represented great wealth. In reality, before the end of 1785 the General confessed, "to be plain, my coffers are not overflowing with money." He never explained why it was that he scarcely ever curtailed any expenditures when income was reduced or cash depleted. His well-fed guests, drinking toasts in his champagne, would have been aghast had they known that the cash with which he was to begin 1786 was no more than £86.

Besides concern over money, Washington had in 1785 continuing and rising anxiety with respect to public affairs from which he could not divorce himself in his "retirement." The Society of the Cincinnati remained one of these cares. Washington suspected that opposition to the Society was slumbering, not dead; the State Societies should promptly approve the revised Institution and remove all reasonable objection. He confided to Hamilton that only the involvement of foreign officers and the charitable features of the organization kept him from advocating that it be abolished. He had not a single degree of enthusiasm for the Society.

Washington's deepest anxiety was for the Union of the States. The appeal of Congress in 1781 for the right to levy a 5 per cent tax on imports had been answered favorably by all the States except Rhode Island, but refusal of that State to say "Aye" and action of Virginia in repealing her statute of acquiescence had put an end to all hope of deriving from that measure money required for paying the interest on the Federal debt. In desperation, Congress in 1783 had submitted to the States the amendment of the Articles of Confederation to authorize the levy of specific taxes on certain imported luxuries and a 5 per cent ad valorem tax on all other goods brought into the United States. This was to be imposed for twenty-five years only and proceeds used exclusively for the payment on the war debt. A million and a half dollars for the support of government were to be supplied by the States annually, in specified amounts based on population. This measure was crowded with every sort of concession to pridefully asserted sovereignty, but Rhode Island, New York, Maryland and Georgia were in opposition. To persuade them to ratify the amendment was the task of those who believed the Union would perish unless it had assured revenue. Another measure presented to the States for approval authorized Congress for a period to prohibit imports from or exports to countries that had no commercial treaties with the United States—a plea for weapons with which to inflict reprisals on Britain for her discrimination against American ships and cargoes. Here again the compliance of the States was slow and hedged with so many provisos that Congress remained powerless in dealing with Britain. Other proposals were being made for amending the Articles, but the best of these, largely the work of James Monroe, were never passed and transmitted to the States.

Congress must have more power or the Union would cease to exist; ". . . it is unfortunate for us," Washington wrote, "that evils which might have been averted, must be first felt, and our national character for wisdom, justice and temperance, suffer in the eyes of the world, before we can guide the political machine as it ought to be." British commercial policy, he thought, in time would force the States to vest Congress with power necessary to protect common interests, but, at the moment, he maintained: "The Confederation appears to me to be little more than a shadow without the substance." His correspondence resounded with arguments over a stronger union and the demand, from the other camp, that the States make no additional grant of power to build up New England tyranny over the South. Washington answered with fundamentals: "We are either a united people, or we are not. If the former, let us in all matters of general concern act as a nation, which have national objects to promote, and a national character to support. If we are not, let us no longer act a farce by pretending to it." Common sense dictated union.

In that conviction, the General did not hesitate to express himself when he talked with his friends or wrote to them, though he remained the retired observer and no more than that, except as his prestige gave weight to his private remarks. While he continued to hope for the ratification of the impost and navigation acts, he saw no financial relief for Congress otherwise than through the sale of western lands ceded by the States. After tedious debate, Congress on May 20, 1785, had passed a measure that provided for surveying townships and "lots," one-seventh of which were to be assigned "for the use of the late Continental Army." Subject to various reservations, the six-sevenths were "to be drawn for, in the name of the thirteen States respectively, according to the quotas in the last preceding requisition on all the States." These lands were to be sold for not less than one dollar, specie, per acre, and the proceeds were to be made available to the Board of Treasury through the Commissioners of the Loan Office in the various States. "I confess," Washington wrote, "it does not strike me as a very eligible [mode for disposing of the western lands]," but he added with his usual caution: "however, mine is only an opinion, and I wish to be mistaken in it, as the fund would be very productive and afford great relief to the public creditors if the lands meet with a ready sale."

As for his own way of living, Washington did not permit financial distress to dampen the delights of his plantation; nor did he complain because retirement had brought him less leisure than he had expected. He decided that he would be his own manager, with his nephew, George Augustine Washington, as his assistant. In acting as steward, Lund Washington had made large sacrifice for his kinsman during the war; his long-cherished desire to resign could not in decency be disregarded further.

Christmas 1785 found numerous guests at Mount Vernon, but as soon as they left and holidays were over, the retired General became a surveyor again on his Dogue Run plantation, "with a view," as he said, "to new model the fields at that place." He was determined to reorganize his estate and make it all it could be. For this task he now had more time because his guests included fewer celebrities whose entertainment ate up his hours. Another gain of 1786 was a decrease in correspondence. He was irked by his mail but was not as heavily burdened as he sometimes thought he was. Later in the year Washington changed private secretaries and procured in Tobias Lear exactly the man he wanted. Lear was twenty-four, a well-born native of New Hampshire and a graduate of Harvard. He had resided for a time in Europe and read French well enough to translate it easily. He was good-natured, sober, industrious and companionable, and he made an excellent impression from the first.

Another change by which Washington hoped to improve his management of Mount Vernon was the employment of a type of man he had long desired, "a thorough bred *practical* English farmer." Through the efforts of George William Fairfax he made a one-year contract, at sixty guineas, with James Bloxham, "a plain, honest farmer" recently arrived in America, whose appearance and conversation were as "much in his favor" as were his recommendations. Bloxham began, unfortunately, in another adverse season. Both he and his employer had to make the best of this—the manager with lament and sighs for England, the proprietor with determination to re-divide his farms and "go into an entire new course of cropping." For this purpose, he leased new land on Dogue Run, surveyed his acquisitions and made his holdings into six distinct but cooperating plantations—Mansion House, Dogue, Ferry, River, Muddy Hole and French. Unless company or absence prevented, he visited all of these every weekday —a round of about twenty miles—and wrote in his diary what was being done at each. An overseer had general charge of each property. Under each overseer were a suitable number of the two hundred and more slaves that Washington and his wife owned.

The "new course of cropping" that Washington instituted as rapidly as he could was substantially the same on all his plantations and designed to yield food or marketable crops without exhausting the land. Prevention of this ruin depended on three essentials—the return of plowland to grass, liberal use of manure, and prompt stoppage of all flow of ground water that might create gulleys. This became the basic pattern of farming at Mount Vernon, followed in good years and in bad, when the owner had money and when he had to borrow. Progress towards a crop system that would feed his poor land was not easy, but Washington persisted in tests and finally developed a six-year rotation. Although he was not entirely satisfied with this system, it probably represented the most useful experiment Washington conducted after he returned home. Next in practical value was his determination of the wheat that gave the most satisfactory yield on his plantations.

Invaluable as horses had been to him during the war, he did not believe them the most economical beast of burden on a farm. From what he had learned of mules he concluded that they would do more and consume less, and he decided that he would import a jackass to breed them. When this plan became known, the King of Spain presented him two of these animals. One died on the voyage but the other reached Mount Vernon in December 1785 and received the name "Royal Gift." Lafayette sent from Malta a jack and two she-asses which arrived in November 1786. The master of Mount Vernon decided in February 1786 to test the qualities of South American asses and sent a consignment of flour to Surinam, Dutch Guiana, to be traded for a jenny, which in due time was delivered to him. Washington already was standing the young Arabian stallion, Magnolio, which he had taken over at £500 from the estate of Jack Custis. The General owned, also, a work-horse stallion and, with the accession of the two asses, he had a four-animal stud.

Most of his outlays had ultimate utility and in time would make

Mount Vernon more valuable as well as more attractive, but throughout 1786 they drained a strongbox into which he seldom could put cash. He did a fair business at the mill and continued his fishery, but the main sources of income were notes and bonds of kinsfolk whom it was embarrassing to press. The estate of Martha's first husband owed her—and therefore the General—£1119 balance and back payments for six years on the "rent or annuity" of £525 annually due from the yield of the properties on the Pamunkey and York; Bartholomew Dandridge on his own account and as Jack Custis's executor had died with unsettled obligations of approximately £2500 due to Gen. and Mrs. Washington; the owner of Mount Vernon still had his claim to £500 sterling of Bank of England stock from Patsy's estate, but he had not been able to compel his London agents to sell it; the General probably did not know precisely how his dead brother Samuel's account with him stood. Where kinsmen were not involved, old friends were, and if the friends were not close, then business associations had been, and the debts sometimes had been in proportion.

Washington had a surprising number of obligations, some of them pressing, some embarrassing because, though small, they had not been settled long previously. When, for example, the General came to examine his accounts with his old friend and former neighbor, George William Fairfax, he found he was in Fairfax's debt by £207, which he contrived to pay promptly. Washington still owed £800, and current interest at 7 per cent, on a tract near Fort Schuyler that he had purchased with the assistance of George Clinton. Settlement had not yet been made with Lund Washington for salary during the latter part of the war. The situation in its entirety was the worst Washington had known at any time after he became proprietor of Mount Vernon, and it was not improving. His corn crop of 1786 was 1018 barrels; his year's supply of pork, weighed fresh, was 13,867 pounds, perhaps two thousand less than he had "for family consumption" in good years. Almost the sole gain of the year with respect to his estate was the judicial establishment of his title to lands in Washington County, Pennsylvania.

Along with the embarrassment of debt, Washington had on August 31 an attack of "ague and fever." A fortnight passed before he was himself again, and then he had rheumatic pains that continued into the winter of 1786–87. He was uncomfortable, rather than alarmed, and insisted that he was reconciled to a general decline in his health, because he was "descending the hill" and, though "blessed," as he said, "with a good constitution," was "of a short-lived family." In this spirit he began to make plans for the future of George Augustine, but he was far from expectation of early death.

Washington had new reminders of the ancestral truth that war does not terminate its toll when the bullets cease to whine. During September 1785 he had heard of the death of Gov. Jonathan Trumbull, patriot, prophet and politician, who had aided Washington valiantly during the war. In May 1786 he learned that Tench Tilghman had expired April 18; June and July brought tidings that Alexander McDougall and Nathanael Greene had received their last leave. Had any of these men died in the course of hostilities, Washington would have announced it in a few words with a composure so stern that critics might have called it callous. It was different now. He wrote a careful eulogy of Trumbull, praised McDougall as a "brave soldier and disinterested patriot," and made no less than three attempts, all of them futile, to express his feeling at the death of Tilghman, the bearer of the "victory dispatch" to Congress, a man who "left as fair a reputation as ever belonged to a human character." Gloomy restraint in speaking of Greene was followed by warmer praise, and, at length, by this clumsy confession to Lafayette: "General Greene's death is an event which has given so much general concern and is so much regretted by his numerous friends that I can scarce persuade myself to touch upon it, even so far as to say that in him you lost a man who affectionately regarded and was a sincere admirer of you." He showed in another way than by words the depth of his feeling over the loss of Greene, who died with his financial affairs wretchedly entangled. Washington wrote Jeremiah Wadsworth that if Mrs. Greene and the executors thought "proper to entrust my namesake G: Washington Greene to my care, I will give him as good an education as this Country (I mean the United States) will afford and will bring him up to either of the genteel professions that his friends may choose, or his own inclination shall lead him to pursue at my own cost and expense." This offer was made in October 1786, when Washington's distress for money was acute.

Wise use of his hours had been a rule of Washington's early career; it now became so fixed a habit that interruption of his well-ordered day was painful. Duties as President of the Potomac Company during 1786 demanded attendance at six meetings of directors or committees. Because of adverse weather he had to get the consent of the legislatures of Maryland and Virginia to an extension of the authorized period during which the company was expected to improve navigation between Fort Cumberland and Great Falls; but he continued altogether optimistic that the great design could be executed.

Although narrowness of interest had been as bad after the war as during the course of hostilities and in several States perhaps had become worse, a few leaders had continued to plead for closer economic relations. There had been a promising development in the suggestion for an annual meeting of representatives of Virginia and Maryland. When this had been proposed nothing more had been contemplated than that the two States review questions of commercial relation from year to year, precisely as they had considered the joint use of the Chesapeake and the Potomac; but when the ratification of the united agreement was taken up in the Maryland Legislature, the lawmakers decided to invite Delaware and Pennsylvania to the conference. Some Virginians went further and asked, Why not invite *all* the States to be represented at such a meeting? The answer was not unanimous, but a resolution to this effect was passed January 21, 1786. Of course, this measure might mean much or little, but as Madison was quick to point out, there was a chance the conference might recommend an increase of the powers of Congress. This, said Madison, "may possibly lead to better consequences than at first occur."

Washington was not hopeful the obstacles to better relations among the States could be removed quickly. His "sentiments" with respect to the Federal Union, he wrote Henry Lee, had "been communicated without reserve," but, he went on, "I have little hope of amendment without another convulsion." His deepest dread apparently was of the slow disintegration of a union held together by waning sentiment and a Congress so pauperized and powerless that the States did not even take the trouble to see that their Delegates attended.

By May 1786 he found encouragement in the response to Virginia's invitation. He explained to Lafayette: "All the Legislatures which I have heard from have come into the proposition, and have made very judicious appointments: much good is expected from this measure, and it is regretted by many that more objects were not embraced by the meeting. A General Convention is talked of by many for the purpose of revising and correcting the defects of the federal government; but whilst this is the wish of some, it is the dread of others from an opinion that matters are not yet sufficiently ripe for such an event." He told John Jay: "I do not conceive we can exist long as a nation without having lodged somewhere a power which will pervade the whole Union in as energetic a manner as the authority of the State governments extends over the several States."

In this attitude of mind and in the face of letters predominantly pessimistic, Washington looked forward with much eagerness to the meeting which had been set for Annapolis in September. When he learned that five States only had been represented, he was disappointed and was puzzled to know why the commercial States of the East had sent no one. He soon had assurance that failure had not been complete: The fourteen Delegates unanimously had agreed to a report prepared by Hamilton which recommended that the States send Delegates to a convention in Philadelphia on the second Monday in May 1787. This proposed assembly was to:

take into consideration the situation of the United States, to devise such further provisions as shall appear to them necessary to render the constitution of the federal government adequate to the exigencies of the Union; and to report such an act for that purpose to the United States in Congress assembled, as, when agreed to by them, and afterwards confirmed by the legislatures of every State will effectually provide for the same.

Was this recommendation to be taken seriously by public men or was it to have the fate of Virginia's call for the commercial convention of all the States at Annapolis?

Before Washington could form any judgment of this, he was alarmed by news from Massachusetts. Gazettes told of discontent that had begun to take form at the end of August. On September 11, at Concord, a crowd of two or three hundred men had cowed the justices into an announcement that they would not attempt to hold court. Washington did not understand what lay behind this angry challenge of the law. Aside from the newspaper reports, all he had at first concerning events in New England, was conveyed in a letter of Humphreys that read: ". . . Our friend [David] Cobb, who is both a General of militia and a Judge of the court in the county where he resides, is much celebrated for having said 'he would die as a General or sit as a Judge.' This was indeed a patriotic sentiment. His firmness in principles and example in conduct effected a suppression of the mob—but the court was adjourned in consequence of the Governor's order." Washington wrote back: ". . . For God's sake, tell me what is the cause of all these commotions: do they proceed from licentiousness, British influence disseminated by the Tories, or real grievances which admit of redress? If the latter, why were they delayed till the popular mind had become so much agitated? If the former, why are not the powers of government tried at once?"

The General did not have to wait for Humphreys' answer. Other correspondents sent him information. Some of these reports discounted the seriousness of the outbreak, but the prevalent tone was one of alarm. The situation was going from bad to worse. There was talk of "the abolition of debts, the division of property, and reunion with Great Britain." Affairs might become so critical, Harry Lee intimated, that Congress might call on Washington to go to the eastern States, because it was taken for granted that the disorders then would subside. Other Delegates were asking whether it was not the duty of Congress to raise troops with which to support the government of Massachusetts if the authorities of that State could not put down the followers of Daniel Shays, a former Captain in the Continental Army who had emerged as the leader of the trouble-makers. "I am mortified beyond expression," Washington wrote Lee, "when I view the clouds that have spread over the brightest morn that ever dawned upon any country." As for remedy, "you talk," he continued, ". . . of employing influence to appease the present tumults in Massachusetts. I know not where that influence is to be found and, if attainable, that it would be a proper remedy for our disorders." Then he wrote solemnly: "Influence is no government." If the insurgents had grievances, correct them or acknowledge them and say that cure had to wait for better days; but if the uprising represented no real complaint, "employ the force of government against [it] at once." He insisted: "Precedents are dangerous things; let the reins of government then be braced and held with a steady hand, and every violation of the constitution be reprehended: if defective let it be amended, but not suffered to be trampled upon whilst it has an existence."

Thus was Shays's Rebellion linked in Washington's reasoning with the appeal for a stronger Federal government. From Henry Knox, Secretary of War, who had gone to Massachusetts to see the situation for himself, Washington received a long, careful letter on the uprising. The creed of the insurgents, said Knox, "is that the property of the United States has been protected from confiscation of Britain by the joint exertions of *all*, and therefore ought to be the *common property* of all. And he that attempts opposition to this creed is an enemy to equity and justice and ought to be swept from off the face of the earth." The insurrectionists reckoned twelve or fifteen thousand "desperate and unprincipled men," chiefly of "the young and active part of the community."

Manifestly, the political machinery was too frail for the duty it was called upon to perform. It must be repaired or replaced. Virginia must begin that labor. Washington had observed with admiration the diligence, patriotism and high intelligence of Madison, former representative in Congress and now member of the House of Delegates. Madison was the man to take the lead. On November 5 Washington wrote Madison. With applause for the refusal of the House to approve the emission of paper money, he joined the hope that "the great and most important of all objects, the federal government" would be considered calmly and deliberately "at this critical moment." Fervently he pleaded: "Let prejudices, unreasonable jealousies and local interest yield to reason and liberality. Let us look to our national character, and to things beyond the present period. . . . Wisdom and good examples are necessary at this time to rescue the political machine from the impending storm."

The echo of Washington's words rolled back quickly from Richmond. Dark as was the outlook described by Knox, said Madison, he himself was "leaning to the side of hope." The Assembly had voted unanimously to comply with the recommendation of the Annapolis Convention in favor of a "general revision of the federal system." A good bill was pending and soon would be passed—a bill that gave the proposal a "very solemn dress and all the weight that could be derived from a single State." Next came the return challenge of leadership: Washington's name had been placed at the head of the list of Delegates to the Convention. "How far this liberty may correspond," said Madison, "with the ideas by which you ought to be governed will be best decided when it must ultimately be decided."

That was not pleasant reading for a man whose love of retired detachment from controversies was second only to his love of country. Madison's respectful call to renewed public service was followed soon by plainspoken, New England words from Humphreys: "The troubles in Massachusetts still continue. Government is prostrated in the dust. . . .. Congress, I am told, are seriously alarmed and hardly know which way to turn, or what to expect. Indeed, my dear General, nothing but a good Providence can extricate us from our present difficulties and prevent some terrible convulsion." The personal application followed: "In case of civil discord, I have already told you it was seriously my opinion that you could not remain neuter, and that you would be obliged, in self-defence to take part on one side or the other, or withdraw from the continent. Your friends are of the same opinion. . . ."

Washington had to admit the justice of at least part of this: In such a crisis he undeniably had his share of the duty he was invoking others to discharge; but he had an embarrassment of a sort on which his mind laid particular emphasis. As President of the Society of the Cincinnati, he had notified the State Societies that private affairs, the presidency of the Potomac Company, and rheumatism made it impossible for him to attend the triennial meeting of the General Society. This meeting was to be held in Philadelphia during May 1787—the town and month set for the convention Virginia was calling. "Under these circumstances," he told Madison, "it will readily be perceived that I could not appear at the same time and place on any other occasion, without giving offence."

Soon after the beginning of December a long period of freezing covered roads and river with ice and cut Mount Vernon off completely. When the post again was operating, Washington learned that the Virginia General Assembly had passed the bill for calling a Convention of the States; that he had been elected unanimously to head a distinguished delegation of seven, and that both Madison and Gov. Edmund Randolph were urging him not to refuse, because he could not be spared from attendance.

The General read and pondered and could not bring himself to say "Yes" or to decline with a "No" so positive that someone else would of necessity be chosen in his stead. In writing Randolph, he did not quite reach the finality of refusal: Because of circumstances from which there was little prospect of disengaging himself, he said, "it would be disingenuous not to express a wish that some other character, on whom greater reliance can be had, may be substituted in my place, the probability of my nonattendance being too great to continue my appointment."

Wisely, Randolph and the Council decided not to act on Washington's declination—if declination it might be styled. Conditions might shift; another nomination could be made later, if necessary. "Perhaps, too," said the Governor, " (and indeed I fear the event), every other consideration may seem of little weight, when compared with the crisis which may then hang over the United States." With superlative tact Madison made the same appeal. Washington referred the whole correspondence to Humphreys with the query, "Should the matter be further pressed (which I hope it will not, as I have no inclination to go), what had I best do?"; but in the same letter he argued earnestly for precisely such a stronger Union as Madison and the others hoped to assure at the Convention to which they knew the presence of Washington would give prestige.

Washington had troubles enough in the early months of 1787 to have led a man of mind less resolute and ordered to put aside public affairs completely. John Augustine Washington died at the beginning of the year, a loss the General sustained with heavy heart, because Jack of all his brothers had been next only to Lawrence in his affection. Frances Bassett Washington had her first baby and lost it. These sorrows came when Washington still was suffering, sometimes acutely, from his "rheumatism" and, in a different sense, from financial "hard times." His spirits certainly were not improved by a demand from his mother for fifteen guineas. He sent the coin in February with the unabashed statement that it was literally all he had in hand. Other demands were heavy. Currently, Washington had pressing bills for more than £500. He found it exceedingly difficult to collect what was due him, even for flour, and from some of his tenants he could get nothing unless he took their horses. Lund Washington had special need of his past-due salary: the best the General could do was to tender him a bond he believed a borrower would pay on its maturity. "My estate for the last eleven years," he confessed, "has not been able to make both ends meet."

Every day public questions obtruded and overshadowed farm, family and all else. Continued alarm over the discontent and violence in Massachusetts was accompanied by a suggestion that it might be well for

Washington to pay a "private visit" to that state, but in mid-February it was hoped that a vigorous march by Benjamin Lincoln on Petersham had broken the back of the rebellion. Washington breathed less anxiously and at the appropriate time urged leniency for the insurgents, though he shared Madison's fear that discontent was spreading and the affairs of the nation approaching "some awful crisis." The threat of another flood of paper money engulfing America was, in the opinion of Washington, almost as serious as that of mobs closing Massachusetts courts. He continued to assert that America was facing a final test as to whether she could survive "without the means of coercion in the sovereign"; but insofar as this might require his participation as a Delegate to the proposed Convention, he held to his argument for declining the appointment.

On February 21 Congress voted that it was "expedient" to hold a Convention of State Delegates in Philadelphia on the second Monday in May "for the sole and express purpose of revising the Articles of Confederation." Washington still doubted whether the Convention would be well attended by men of ability and courage. On the other hand, he began to ask himself whether his refusal to participate might not be considered a lack of sympathy with republican ideals. As late as March 15 he wrote as if he would not attend, but by that date, several developments were taking form: Congress' action in endorsing the Convention was approved widely; most of the political leaders were agreed that a crisis was imminent; impressive appointments to the Convention were being made unhesitatingly by several States.

Washington reconsidered. Although he could not yet persuade himself that the Convention would be attended fully by unfettered Delegates, he found a certain sense of shame making him more and more well disposed to the Convention. His own State was holding back. Patrick Henry and Thomas Nelson, Jr., declined membership. Randolph proposed Richard Henry Lee in Nelson's place, but Lee pled ill health and said he did not think members of Congress should sit in the Convention. Was the State that initiated the gathering to have all of her best known elder sons, Washington included, absent from that body?

Pressure was becoming heavy. Anxiously and painfully Washington reviewed the arguments for and against attendance. There was danger, he felt, that his reputation might suffer if a feeble Convention ended with proposals that would not give the Union needed strength. A desperate crisis appeared to lie ahead. A supreme effort seemed necessary to prevent disintegration of the Federation into a congeries of rival States which might choke themselves with paper money. The Convention presented perhaps the only means of making this effort. If Washington did not share in it, he might be accused of lack of sympathy with it. Abstention might be greater disservice to the nation than his presence would be affront to the Cincinnati. The risk of odium from refusal might be greater than loss of popularity by taking sides in a dispute that might not, after all, be furious or defamatory.

At last, on March 28, he wrote Governor Randolph an equivocal, overcautious and self-regarding letter: If the Governor had named nobody in his place and was not considering anyone, he would undertake to go to Philadelphia, provided his health made this practicable. He took superlative pains not to commit himself beyond easy withdrawal, but in spite of ifs and provisos, the letter brought him close to a favorable decision. Randolph and Madison became so confident of Washington's participation that they began to discuss whether he should be present at the opening of the Convention or should appear later.

He had to make up his mind; this must not be a political Fort Washington, when everything might be lost by hesitation. On April 9, most unwillingly and in an egocentric strain, he wrote Randolph that he was about to act contrary to his judgment. He apprehended, moreover, that his action would be regarded as inconsistent with his statement in December 1783 that he never intended thereafter to "intermeddle in public matters." Once more he reviewed the involvement of the Society of the Cincinnati and then proceeded:

Add to these, I very much fear that all the States will not appear in Convention, and that some of them will come fettered so as to impede rather than accelerate the great object of their convening which, under the peculiar circumstances of my case, would place me in a more disagreeable situation than any other member would stand in. As I have yielded, however, to what appeared to be the earnest wishes of my friends, I will hope for the best. . . .

He scarcely could have stated it more ungraciously or with more patent regard for himself, but he said it and, after that, did not turn back.

A report of the extreme illness of his mother and of his sister sent him in great haste to Fredericksburg on April 27 and threatened to delay his departure north. Fortunately, when he reached Fredericksburg, he found Mrs. Washington better and his sister's condition the result of strain from waiting on her mother. He returned home on the thirtieth. Washington carefully gave full verbal instructions to George Augustine, whom he intended to leave in charge of Mount Vernon. Then, he set out in his carriage early May 9.

In the preliminaries of what may be regarded as a last effort to save the collapsing Union, he had been too zealously attentive to his prestige, reputation and popularity—too much the self-conscious national hero and too little the daring patriot. He had held off when he thought the Convention would be thinly attended by Delegates not of the first distinction and had accepted only when satisfied that most of the States would be represented by able men not unduly hampered by instructions. He never could have won the war in the spirit he displayed in this effort to secure the peace. But, had all the disparaging circumstances of Washington's hesitation been known, they probably would not have shaken his popularity. The people, as well as his friends, saw only that he had emerged from his cherished retirement to serve them in a time of difficulty and confusion. Knox wrote Lafayette:

General Washington's attendance at the convention adds, in my opinion, new lustre to his character. Secure as he was in his fame, he has again committed

it to the mercy of events. Nothing but the critical situation of his country would
have induced him to so hazardous a conduct. But its happiness being in danger, he
disregards all personal considerations.

He arrived on the thirteenth and was given a welcome that lacked
nothing the affection of the people could bestow. Robert Morris and Mrs.
Morris, whose invitation Washington had declined before he left Mount
Vernon, now urged him so warmly to lodge with them that he accepted.
Before he ended the day, Washington paid his first call—an official visit to
Franklin, now President of the Executive Council of Pennsylvania, whom
Washington had not seen since 1776. The meeting of course was cordial,
because each respected and admired the other, and it held out the promise
of close relations in the weeks ahead: Franklin had accepted appointment
as one of Pennsylvania's Delegates to the Convention and, feeble though
he admitted himself to be, he intended to take his seat. With this visit to
crown it, Washington's first day in Philadelphia could not be described
with a lesser adjective than triumphant. Philadelphia had not welcomed
him more eagerly when he arrived from Yorktown. The cordiality of the
reception was all the more impressive because, in a sense, it was national.
Five conventions had brought to the town representatives from nearly all
the States.

To the chagrin of the General, the most important of these conventions, the one to revise the Articles of Confederation, was the slowest in
assembling. On the fourteenth, the date set for the opening, Pennsylvania
and Virginia alone were represented. The next day individual members
from New Jersey, Delaware and North Carolina reported. While this was
deplorable, James Madison cheerfully attributed members' tardiness to a
long spell of bad weather. Washington believed that sooner or later a sufficient number of representatives would arrive to organize the Convention.
In this good hope he met daily with the other Virginians, who developed a
"plan" of government, a paper based chiefly on proposals that Madison
and Randolph had brought with them. Washington probably did not
make any specific contribution to this plan, though his common sense and
experience doubtless were employed in determining what was practicable.
In addition Washington visited friends and changed his role of host for
that of guest. His first dinner was en famille with the Morrises, his next
was with the members of the Cincinnati, a thin platoon of not more than a
score of former officers who understood readily why their President-General
had come to Philadelphia when he had said he could not do so. They gave
him their unhesitating vote of confidence by reelecting him their President,
with the understanding that the duties of the office were to be discharged
by the Vice President, Thomas Mifflin.

At last a qualified number of Delegates from seven States were
counted on May 25, and as seven were a majority of the States, men who
had been waiting almost two weeks proceeded to organize the Convention.
Morris, a member from the hostess state, arose to perform a service Franklin would have discharged if he had not been detained at home that day
by weakness and bad weather. The financier, on instructions from the

Pennsylvania delegation and on its behalf, proposed Washington as President of the Convention. John Rutledge of South Carolina seconded and expressed the hope that the choice would be unanimous. It was. Morris and Rutledge conducted the General to the chair, from which he expressed his thanks for the honor done him and asked indulgence for the unintentional mistakes into which his ignorance of the requirements of the position might lead him. Details of organization were completed quickly, a committee on rules was named, adjournment was voted to Monday the twenty-eighth. Washington did not desire this new post; but designation as President of the Convention would take him off the floor for part of his time, away from the contention of rival advocates. He was committed to the work of the Convention by accepting membership in it; he was lifted above partisanship by the duty he had to discharge. At the same time, having no speeches to prepare or committee meetings to attend, he could lend both ears to all spokesmen and thereby learn much that he had not acquired previously in camp or on his plantation. Presidency of the Convention was education and preparation.

Monday and part of Tuesday, May 28 and 29, were spent in adopting rules of procedure. Later on the twenty-ninth, speaking for the Virginia delegation, Randolph, in the stiff language of the Journal, "laid before the House, for their consideration, sundry propositions, in writing, concerning the American confederation and the establishment of a national government." These "propositions" embodied the "Virginia Plan" that had been developed in the daily meetings Washington had attended. A government of three branches, legislative, executive and judicial, was to be created. The Legislature was to consist of two chambers, one elected by the people of the several States, the other chosen by the elected branch from a list of nominees submitted by the individual state legislatures. This central bicameral body was to have all the relevant powers vested in Congress by the Articles of Confederation and, in addition, the power to pass laws where the States were unable to act or were not in harmony. All State laws that contravened the terms of union could be "negatived" by the "National Legislature" which likewise could "call forth the force of the Union against any member of the Union failing to fulfill its duty under the articles thereof." A "National Executive" would have the powers suggested by the title, insofar as the Articles of Confederation conferred authority of this type on Congress. "A general authority to execute the national laws" was added. The "National Judiciary" was to have particular regard to "questions which may involve the national peace and harmony."

These proposals and another plan of government prepared by Charles Cotesworth Pinckney of South Carolina were referred that afternoon to the Committee of the Whole. When the committee began its sittings on the thirtieth with Nathaniel Gorham of Massachusetts as its chairman, Washington could take a seat temporarily with the other members. Nine States now were represented by thirty-seven members. While a considerable part of the membership was unknown personally to Washington when the Convention assembled, he soon had ample proof that they represented high ability. It was pleasant to sit among these men during the day and in the evening meet them socially. Conversation then had to be casual because the Convention voted that "members only be permitted to inspect the journal" and that "nothing spoken in the house be printed, or otherwise published, or communicated without leave." Although this rule occasionally was violated, most members were conscientious and close-mouthed. They would not talk of the one subject every guest at tea and every frequenter of taverns wished to discuss.

Washington would take the chair each morning and, after the usual preliminaries, turn over the gavel to Judge Gorham. For nearly the entire day's sitting the members would debate the successive items of the Virginia Plan, which they approved in broad outline with alacrity. After one or another of the involved principles was discussed on a given day for three hours or more, the committee would rise, Washington would resume the chair, and Gorham would report progress, with a request for leave to sit again in committee. Adjournment usually followed at once. Among nearly all members the disposition was to find the largest basis of agreement and defer the issues on which there was wide disagreement. The spirit of accommodation seemed so pervasive that echoes of accord were audible in the newspapers, along with rumbling criticism of Rhode Island for ignoring the Convention.

Men of differing political background in dissimilar States could not hope to continue in accord. By the second week in June members were divided on the question, Should the first branch of the National Legislature be elected by the people or by the legislatures of the several States? Other issues were shaping themselves: Should the equality of State representation that had prevailed in the Continental Congress be continued? If the first branch of the lawmaking body was to be elected by the people, should slaves be counted in determining representation? To maintain the authority of the national government, must its Congress be vested with power to coerce the States or to "negative" their laws? Indeed, why should the new government be national? Could it not remain federal, with the largest freedom to the States, great and small?

After the Virginia Plan was reported, in substance, by the Committee of the Whole on June 13, these questions became spearheads of attack on the plan. Debate was as searching as if the Committee of the Whole had not discussed the "propositions" at all. Delegates from the smaller States found a rallying post in resolutions introduced by William Paterson, a New Jersey Delegate. He proposed the amendment of the Articles of Confederation in such a manner as to increase substantially the powers of Congress while preserving federal, as distinguished from national, government, except in two particulars: With the consent of an unspecified number of States a delinquent member of the Union might be forced to meet its obligations; second, acts of Congress and ratified treaties were to be "supreme law of the respective States"—a doctrine that probably made an instant appeal to some of the ablest intellects in the Convention. Powerful speeches by Randolph, James Wilson and Madison led to the rejection,

June 19, of Paterson's outline and put the Virginia Plan before the Convention again. This procedure returned Washington to duty as presiding officer.

Washington had been pleased, at the beginning of the Convention, to find members more in accord than he had expected, but the basic differences developed during the second week in June and debate became ill-tempered and tedious, particularly on the question of State representation in the legislative branch of government. By the twenty-eighth frowning factions were caparisoned for battle in a mood that made Franklin appeal unsuccessfully for prayers at the opening of each day's session. On the twenty-ninth, fighting to the last, the spokesmen of the small States were outvoted, six to four, with Maryland divided, on a resolution that established an "equitable" instead of the "equal" basis of representation they sought in the first chamber. This meant that the House of Representatives of a new Congress would be elected, by methods yet undetermined, in proportion to population.

The men who spoke for the less populous areas mustered their forces anew to win in the second chamber what they had failed to procure in the first. Washington stood with the Delegates who favored representation on the basis of population for both houses, but he did not lose his sense of reality. His counsel was simple: "To please all is impossible, and to attempt it would be vain. The only way, therefore, is . . . to form such a government as will bear the scrutinizing eye of criticism, and trust it to the good sense and patriotism of the people to carry it into effect." It looked the very next day, July 2, as if debate over representation had served only to array small States against large more stubbornly than ever. In the absence of several members, five state votes were mustered for a resolution to equalize representation in the second chamber. Defeat of the small States in the contest over the composition of the first chamber thus was offset, but at the price of a threatened impasse. When neither side would yield, Pinckney proposed and nearly all the delegations agreed that a "grand committee" of one member from each State be appointed to fashion a compromise. As the committee would require many hours for its deliberations, the Convention adjourned until July 5.

During the adjournment the General shared in patriotic services at the Reformed Calvinist Church and dined with the Pennsylvania Cincinnati at the State House, but good food and company had not relieved his apprehension when he returned to the Convention. Franklin with much difficulty had prevailed on the "grand committee" to recommend this compromise: representation in the first chamber was to be on the basis of one member for each forty thousand population of each state, with one member for any state that counted fewer than forty thousand heads; the chamber elected on this principle was to have exclusive authority to originate bills levying taxes, appropriating money and fixing salaries; the second chamber should not be empowered to amend these bills, but with respect to no other legislation was it to be subordinate; in this second branch each state was to have "an equal vote."

These proposals were regarded by the small States as a victory and they forthwith were attacked by two of the most powerful debaters in the Convention, Madison and Gouverneur Morris. Some phases of the compromise were turned over on July 6 to a special committee for review; when this group reported, its findings were referred to another "grand committee." Even the patient and innately optimistic Washington became gloomy. He wrote Hamilton: "I almost despair of seeing a favorable issue to the proceedings of our Convention, and do therefore repent having had any agency in the business."

Most of the occurrences of the next week were of a sort to deepen Washington's disgust with those he described as "narrow-minded politicians or under the influence of local views." He witnessed a seesaw of advantage between spokesmen of the large States and champions of the small until, on July 16, there was a balance of five to five that apparently could not be shifted. Some of the members were for adjournment and immediate report to the country on the differences that had arisen; others still pleaded for compromise; a few stated frankly their belief that equality of representation in the second chamber had to be conceded if the Convention was to avoid failure. Discussion was renewed at an informal conference the next morning, but so much diversity of opinion was expressed that Madison thought members from the smaller States would conclude they had no reason to fear their opponents could agree on any plan of opposition to equality in the second chamber.

From that very day, as if in acceptance of the inevitable, a spirit of reconciliation began to show itself. From July 17 through 21 more progress was made in framing a constitution than in any previous period of five days. Final decision on representation in the second branch was deferred; the motion to give the new Congress power to "negative" state laws was abandoned in favor of the clause that the acts of the Federal Legislature should be the "supreme law of the respective States." Fundamental agreement was reached on the form and function of the Judiciary, the admission of new States, the guarantee to the States of a republican form of government, a complicated scheme for the election of the Executive, and, unanimously, on the grant to the Executive of power to negative all laws of the National Legislature.

After a Sabbath in the country, Washington enjoyed on July 23 perhaps the most satisfying day he had spent, to that date, in the Convention. Members still had under consideration the powers and term of the National Executive and they wished to conclude this discussion and reach a meeting of minds. Everything else that had been decided on the floor was referred to a committee of five "for the purpose of reporting a constitution conformably to the proceedings aforesaid." A constitution was to be put on paper! Three more days sufficed to effect agreement on the Executive; the accepted resolutions on that branch were given the new committee; and the Convention adjourned to August 6 to allow the committee ample time for its difficult work.

During this intermission Washington played many parts—guest, traveler, veteran, planter, fisherman, patron of industry. Two days were given to rest and correspondence. Then on July 30, in Gouverneur Morris's phaeton, the General rode out to Mrs. Jane Moore's property, a part of which had been within the Valley Forge encampment. On Trout Creek, which Mrs. Moore's farm adjoined, Morris wished to try his hand at casting for the fish that gave their name to the creek. While his companion stumped along the bank of the stream, Washington rode over the whole of the cantonment of 1777–78, which he never had seen in summer's green. From the vicinity of Valley Forge, he returned to Philadelphia and, on August 3, went up to Trenton with a party to see whether the perch in the Delaware were interested in bait. This time the General himself used a rod with little luck one day and more success the next. He was back in Philadelphia late August 5 to be certain he did not miss the proceedings of the sixth.

Printed copies of the draft constitution were ready for members when Rutledge rose to speak on behalf of the committee. Washington and all the other members listened and some followed the type across the page, line after line, as the Secretary read the entire text. With little argument, the Convention adjourned till the next day. Rejection on August 7 of a motion to go into Committee of the Whole gave Washington the hard assignment of presiding during a floor debate that might be more tangled and retarded than ever, because of endless motions to amend.

Members now began with vigor and some impatience a detailed scrutiny of the suggested text, though some of them realized that the completion of their task still would be a work of weeks. Progress was steady, if not swift. Washington presided with what was termed "his usual dignity," and, as he had the respect and consideration of all members, he was saved from parliamentary pitfalls. From the seventh through the eleventh the Convention plodded towards agreement. The pace was slower the next week because members were of two minds over the admission of foreign-born citizens to the National Legislature and over the origin of appropriation bills.

On August 18 an armful of proposals to give specific powers to Congress was turned over to committee, and the involved question of Federal assumption of state debts was referred to a special committee. Then the Convention discussed the relation of the new government to the defence of America. On adjournment that afternoon to Monday the twentieth it was to the credit of Washington's endurance that he still had energy for an excursion on Sunday. With his friend Samuel Powel, he rode out to White Marsh, went over his old encampment there, proceeded to Germantown and probably visited the Chew House. The analogy of the struggle for a better government prompted Washington to reflect "on the dangers which threatened the American Army" at White Marsh. That camp site and Germantown exemplified the tortured hours during the dreadful months between the landing of Howe at Head of Elk in August 1777 and the debouch of the lean American forces from Valley Forge when Howe evacuated Philadelphia in May 1778. Independence had been won in woe; the dark forces that had prolonged the contest still lived. ". . . there are seeds of discontent in every part of the Union," Washington warned, "ready to produce other disorders if the wisdom of the present Convention should not be able to devise, and the good sense of the people be found ready to adopt a more vigorous and energetic government. . . ."

He returned from Germantown to Philadelphia on August 20 and began another hard week as presiding officer of the Convention. Members apparently had lost none of their positiveness and divided readily on the detail of the constitution, but few wasted the time of their colleagues in long orations. They would argue, object, defend, vote—and take up the next section of the draft constitution. On the twenty-second they paused to debate the ethics and economy of the slave trade and, in so doing, disclosed the differences between North and South, between commerical and planta-tion States, between those that found slave owning uneconomical and those that thought it profitable. The cleavage was as deep as that between large States and small and was vehemently outspoken. The Convention agreed to accept the proposal of Gouverneur Morris to refer the question of the slave trade and other disputed clauses to a committee. "These things," said Morris, "may form a bargain among the Northern and Southern States."

Then, on the twenty-third, the Convention reached the seventh arti-cle, that which made the legislative acts and existing and future treaties of the United States "the supreme law of the several States." After scrutiniz-ing and simplifying the language, the Convention adopted this article unanimously. Simultaneously the Delegates rejected the much discussed alternative, the amendment that would have empowered the National Legislature to negative any state law if two-thirds of the members of both branches so voted. An awkward obstacle was out of the way! The road was getting better. On the twenty-fifth the members accepted a compromise that forbade Congress to prohibit the importation of slaves prior to 1808. When Washington put this motion and not long afterward announced ad-journment, the week's labor had been as productive as any of the Conven-tion's life. He had much reason for satisfaction and for rekindled hope when he again rode out into the country on Sunday.

Briskly on August 27 the members began discussion of provisions re-garding the Judiciary. Despite the presentation of a theme on which every one of the twenty-nine lawyers in the Convention had opinions, debate was mild and agreement not difficult. By the last day of the month it seemed desirable to name a committee to review all postponed questions and re-port them for final action. An even better augury of the early completion of the text was the drafting of clauses on the ratification of the constitution by the States. The Articles of Confederation provided that amendment had to be by the unanimous consent of the States, but few members, if any, favored adherence to this requirement. The Convention voted to require the assent of nine States.

The last major article of the draft constitution awaiting decision was that which set forth the method by which the Executive was to be elected and vested with power. Discussion of this had become so involved that final action had been deferred. Now the Convention resumed the de-bate and in four days reached agreement. On September 8 Washington and his companions had the satisfaction of referring the draft constitution to a committee of five "to revise the style of and arrange the articles agreed to by the House." The Delegates selected for this task were admirably equipped for it—William Samuel Johnson, Hamilton, Gouverneur Morris, Madison and Rufus King, men of clear heads and precise pens. Monday September 10 was given to debate on amendment and ratification; on the eleventh the Committee on Style not being ready to report, the Convention merely assembled and adjourned. Waiting was rewarded: an admirable text was presented on the twelfth by the chairman, Judge Johnson, and, once read, was sent to the printer so that every member might familiarize himself with the precise letter of the text and with titles and terms. The "first branch of the Legislature" was, for example, to be styled the House of Representatives; the second was to be known as the Senate. "President" was the designation recommended for the Chief Executive; the court of last resort was to be called the Supreme Court of the United States. While the compositors set the type that recorded these changes the Convention debated issues concerning which there was no basic disagreement between North and South or between large States and small.

Several close votes followed on numerous sections, some of them long contested, but in no instance did the majority fall below the minimum of six. The balance had been stabilized and was not to be shaken. On his own copy of the printed text Washington inserted changes made through section 10 of Article I in the debate of September 14. The next day he noted various other verbal amendments and, as presiding officer, put no less than twenty-five motions. Before the last of these was reached, Randolph took the floor and announced he would not sign the constitution unless it included a provision, which he thereupon submitted, for another general convention to pass on amendments that might be proposed by the States. George Mason, made a similar statement; Elbridge Gerry gave a number of reasons why he would not subscribe. Nothing could be done to satisfy these men otherwise than by jeopardizing far more than was risked as a result of their opposition. All the States unflinchingly voted "No" on Randolph's motion for a second convention.

It was now almost six o'clock, nearly two hours beyond the usual time of adjournment. The last proposal from the floor for change in the text had been made. Washington waited quietly and without visible emotion for the great moment. When it came, he arose: the motion is to agree to the constitution as amended; the Secretary will call the roll of the States. From every delegation the answer of the majority was "Aye." Engrossment of the text was ordered; the gavel fell. The first stage of the battle for sound, strong American government had ended, more wisely and more easily than had seemed possible. From the Convention floor the issue must be carried to the thirteen States.

Washington was in the chair on the seventeenth for the final ceremonies of signing the engrossed Constitution. He found that a last-minute effort was to be made to persuade the three dissenters to join the majority in signing the Constitution. Franklin was present and, though too feeble to make a speech, he had written one. It was a wise and spirited appeal for the subordination of individual opinion to the nation's good, and it contained both an admission of Franklin's dislike of some articles and the cheerful declaration of his faith in the document as a whole. "It . . . astonished me, sir," he said, "to find this system approaching so near to perfection as it does; and I think it will astonish our enemies, who are waiting with confidence to hear that our councils are confounded like those of the builders of Babel; and that our States are on the point of separation, only to meet hereafter for the purpose of cutting one another's throats." The old philosopher ended with a motion which Gouverneur Morris had drafted, that the enacting clause be: "Done in Convention, by the unanimous consent of the States present the 17th of September, &c, in witness whereof we have hereunto subscribed our names."

Before this motion was put Judge Gorham proposed that the basis of representation in the House be reduced from forty to thirty thousand. King and Daniel Carroll supported Gorham and urged the members to make the concession. This was what Washington had been waiting for. When he rose to put the motion he explained that his position as President had kept him from expressing his views and that perhaps it still should impose silence, but he could not forbear voicing his wish that Gorham's motion prevail. Objections to the Constitution should be as few as possible. One was involved here. Many members believed the House so small it gave "insufficient security for the rights and interests of the people." A basis as high as forty thousand had seemed to him among the most objectionable parts of the Constitution. Late as it was in the proceedings of the Convention, he thought amendment would give much satisfaction. With that he ended the only speech he had delivered during the session, and he had immediate reward. The change was made unanimously and without further discussion—not because all members agreed but because all of them wished to do what Washington desired.

The rest was appeal, explanation, expostulation, assent, then the adoption of Franklin's motion. Although the dissenters and two of the South Carolina members were in opposition, the Constitution was accepted "by the unanimous consent of the States present." A resolution was adopted for the transmission of the finished document to Congress, with the expressed opinion that it should be submitted to popular conventions in the States. Other sections of the same resolve set forth the views of the Delegates on the manner in which the Constitution should be put into effect after nine States had ratified it. The covering letter was a persuasive appeal for a Constitution that was "liable" to as few exceptions as could reasonably have been expected. This letter was signed "Your Excellency's most obedient and humble Servants, George Washington, President. By unanimous Order of the Convention."

The rule of secrecy was repealed, and the papers of the Convention were entrusted to Washington for disposition in accordance with the order of the new Congress "if ever formed under the Constitution." Formal signing of the document followed. Continued refusal of Mason, Gerry and Randolph to attach their signatures did not dampen the satisfaction with which members completed their difficult labor, adjourned sine die, streamed to the City Tavern, had dinner together and said farewell to one another.

With Delegate John Blair as companion in his chariot, Washington set out September 18 for home. On the twenty-second he reached Mount Vernon "after an absence of four months and fourteen days," precisely reckoned and set down in his diary. They had been days during which his largest contribution was not his counsel but his presence. His votes were often on the losing side. Although he favored bringing the new government into operation when seven States ratified, the Convention decided to make nine the number. It must have been known that he thought a three-fourths vote should be required to override a Presidential veto, but the majority insisted on two-thirds. Letters from members seldom mentioned him among those at the forge where the Constitution was hammered out, blow on blow. Madison, Gouverneur Morris, Wilson, King, Randolph—these were the men, not Washington, who shaped the Constitution. Oliver Ellsworth may not have been far in error when he said, late in life, that Washington's influence in the Convention was not great.

Outside the Convention the reverse was true. In giving the body prestige and maintaining public confidence in it while deliberations dragged slowly, Washington had no peer and no second other than Franklin. Madison assured Jefferson that Washington's attendance was "proof of the light in which" the General viewed the Constitution. A writer in the *Independent Gazetteer* of Philadelphia suggested that the States which approved a new plan of government or the amendment of the old should confederate under Washington's leadership. "This," he said, "would probably stimulate the refractory states to comply also." Washington read some of this with satisfaction and some with dismay because it suggested that his retirement at Mount Vernon might again be interrupted. He did not flatter himself that he and his colleagues had devised a perfect form of government, but he knew the Convention had given the country the best Constitution on which a majority could agree.

CHAPTER / 19

A new spirit, undefined but unmistakable, was stirring the people of America. It had shown itself not only in the ready action of the States in sending Delegates to the Convention but also in the temper and standard of debates on the floor. Daily, for the greater part of the session, members had seemed to plod along and to halt often in stubborn, futile contention. Again and again even Washington had feared that differences were irreconcilable, but always the spirit of accord had triumphed over pride of opinion. The level of leaders' argument had been so high that only the most obtuse of men of small ability had taken the floor often. Nothing had been so inspiring as the rearing of a constitutional structure, stone by stone, while the eyes of the masons had been intent on the course they were laying, not on the larger design. Almost contrary to their expectations, they finished it and when they stood off and looked at it, they were surprised by the strength and the symmetry of their handiwork.

Comments on the Constitution that most disturbed Washington were predictions that he would be chosen without opposition as first President of the United States; but he told himself it was neither necessary nor modest to think of an unfilled office in a government not yet created, and he gave his thought to the reception of the document by the people rather than to its possible interruption of his way of living. The text was printed widely; Congress acted promptly and to the surprise of some in this nonpartisan language: "Resolved, unanimously that the said report with the resolutions and letter accompanying the same be transmitted to the several legislatures in order to be submitted to a convention of Delegates chosen in each State by the people thereof in conformity to the resolves of the convention made and provided in that case." Washington did not deceive himself into thinking that when the issue was presented to the States, he or any other American who had an interest in the future of the country could be neutral. He planned and hoped to do his part for ratification and did not leave his position in doubt for a moment. When he sent a report of the Constitution to Patrick Henry, the most powerful man politically in Virginia, he said in plain words that the "political concerns of the country" were "in a manner, suspended by a thread" and that if nothing had been done by the Convention, "anarchy would soon have ensued, the seeds being richly sown in every soil."

There he stood, and correspondence led him to believe a large element of the country stood with him in judgment both of the crisis and the Constitution as the weapon for combating ruin. In the taverns, shops and markets, and on the street corners, the chief reason given for support of the Constitution was this: Washington and Franklin had signed it and approved it. Praise of Washington flooded newspapers sympathetic with the Constitution, in a manifest effort to identify him with the document so that it would gain strength from his popularity. One Boston correspondent wrote of the place Washington and Franklin had won: "The military virtues of the former," he said, "and the philosophic splendour of the latter will be obscured by the new lustre they will acquire as the legislators of an immense continent." Gouverneur Morris sent the General this summary at the end of October: "I have observed that your name to the new Constitution has been of infinite service. Indeed, I am convinced that if you had not attended the convention, and the same paper had been handed out to the world, it would have met with a colder reception, with fewer and weaker advocates, and with more and more strenuous opponents." Humphreys voiced the same view with different emphasis: "What will tend, perhaps, more than anything to the adoption of the new system will be an universal opinion of your being elected President of the United States and an expectation that you will accept it for a while."

The outlook for ratification seemed most doubtful in the two States where Washington's long presence and shining service might have made his advocacy of the new government immediately influential and perhaps decisive. In New York adherents and adversaries of the Constitution were nearly balanced; in Virginia, Washington found most of the older and a few of the younger leaders in opposition at least to the extent that they demanded the earliest possible amendment of the Constitution, preferably by another general convention. Richard Henry Lee came to this view. Benjamin Harrison thought the new government vested with excessive powers to levy taxes and regulate trade. George Mason published detailed "Objections" to the Constitution, a copy of which he sent Washington.

Mason would prove a troublesome adversary, but the man who would have the largest influence in Virginia was Henry. At first there was hope he might favor the work of the Philadelphia Convention, but those who knew him best gave warning that his antagonism must be taken for granted. The great orator's objections to the Constitution were set forth with restraint in a letter to Washington, but his acts were vigorous. Washington did not underestimate the strength of his opponents, but he found encouragement in the approval shown the document by residents of northern Virginia, in support pledged by Edmund Pendleton, and in indications that Randolph was not happy in the political camp where he had pitched his tent. The greatest encouragement was that Madison, Harry Lee and other young leaders were active in behalf of stronger government for the United States. Washington made common cause with these young men, chose them as his principal correspondents, and, in particular, looked to Madison. The debates in Philadelphia had shown that Madison possessed superlatively the type of mind that could meet with calm, cold skill both the logic and the maneuver of a parliamentary opponent. Washington did not excel in compliment, but now, as he contemplated the prospect of a convention in Virginia to ratify or reject the Constitution, he wrote Madison: ". . . I hope you will make it convenient to be present. Explanations will be wanting, and none can give them with more accuracy and propriety than yourself."

The first clash in Virginia proved to be nothing more than a skirmish. Without criticism or commendation, the General Assembly referred the Constitution to a convention that was to be elected on the first day of the March court and called to order June 1, 1788. Perhaps the only sensation of the debate was the statement of Mason that he would have considered himself a traitor if he had subscribed to a Constitution he thought repugnant "to our highest interests." In spite of these angry words, the issue was not joined in the legislature. The real contest would begin when friends and hostile critics of the Constitution offered themselves as candidates for the convention.

Washington received more newspapers than he read, but he doubtless saw something of the use to which his name was being put, reasonably or otherwise. No complaint came from him. He had endorsed the Constitution and had no desire that his advocacy be kept secret. The General's arguments remained simple—the will of the majority should prevail over a selfish minority; a new general convention could accomplish nothing; the course of wisdom and safety was to ratify the document drafted at Philadelphia and, if it were found defective in operation, to amend it later. The presentation of more detailed reasons he wished to leave to those active in the debate, and, particularly, to the men writing the fine articles that were being issued over the signature *Publius,* and were soon to be styled "The Federalist."

The General did not permit the difficult situation in Virginia to blind him to encouragement coming from the States that held out hope of ratification by the required nine. On December 6 the Delaware convention ratified the Constitution unanimously; Pennsylvania followed with a vote of two-to-one, on the twelfth. Six days later, New Jersey with one voice approved the stronger Constitution. At the year's end, Connecticut seemed certain to be the fourth state; Massachusetts was expected to debate furiously and, in the end, to accept; confidence was unshaken that New Hampshire was favorable; New York remained in doubt; North Carolina was expected to follow Virginia's lead; South Carolina and Georgia were believed to favor adoption. Ratification by Rhode Island was not expected.

Before the end of January Washington received news that Connecticut had ratified the Constitution. This strengthened probability of ratification by more than nine States, but the prolongation of the campaign in Massachusetts gave concern. The decision, one way or the other, of the most powerful New England State would have great influence on New York. Washington rallied his patience and fortified his hope. By February 8 he heard that Georgia had ratified—the fifth State. One vote was as good as another in making the count of nine; but Massachusetts, New York and Virginia still were outside the ranks and, if they refused to ratify, they would leave the new Union so weak it probably would succumb. During the last week in February, the watchman at Mount Vernon had good tidings: On the evening of the sixth the Massachusetts convention had ac-

cepted the Constitution by a vote of 187 to 168. Washington felt the greatest satisfaction, only to find, as usual, a sour cup offered him after a sweet.
Maryland Anti-Federalists were urging that their state convention adjourn
until Virginia acted; conditions in North Carolina were said to be similar
to those in Virginia; the outlook in New Hampshire did not appear to be
as favorable as had been assumed.

As Virginia's action might have the largest influence on her two
nearest neighbors, the possibility of rejection by the Old Dominion must
be brought to the absolute minimum by wise leadership of the convention.
The General consequently was much pleased when he learned that Madison was willing to be a candidate for the convention. Washington, with
something of his old art in the analysis of intelligence reports, interpreted
his correspondence in terms of his own knowledge of Virginia and wrote
Rufus King: ". . . no doubt, from the first, has been entertained in my
mind of the acceptance of [the Constitution] here, notwithstanding the *in-
defatigable* pains which some very influential characters take to oppose it."

During the second week in March, Washington learned that the
convention in New Hampshire had met February 13 and, after debate, had
adjourned on the twenty-second until June 3. This reverse caused some
disappointment in Washington's mind, until it was explained to him that
the convention had risen on the motion of friends of the new government.
They knew that the majority against them included some who favored
ratification but had instructions from their constituents to oppose. If time
elapsed and other States meantime accepted, the hampering instructions
might be withdrawn.

The battle swung back to Virginia where, by the end of March, the
last of the elections to the convention had been held. Along with many
weak Delegates, some counties had chosen able spokesmen who, in Washington's words, would throw a "greater weight of abilities" against the
Constitution than opponents had mustered in any other state. Mason was
elected and was more violently hostile than ever to the document he had
helped to draw. Henry also was to be a member and was believed to be
implacable. Friends of a stronger central government began to admit that
ratification by nine States was desirable before the Virginians met. Some
were fearful the Old Dominion might reject if her Delegates were not certain the new government could become operative without Virginia. Washington believed the opposition weaker than before the polling and maintained that neither Virginia nor any other state could afford to remain
outside the Union after nine made it a certainty.

Madison went to work to form a coalition with Randolph, from
whom Washington now expected feeble opposition, if any. The General
undertook the delicate task of urging Maryland friends to prevent a move
some of the adversaries of the Constitution had in mind—to adjourn their
convention and await the action of Virginia. Postponement would be
equivalent to rejection. That was the argument Washington advanced, because indications were that if Maryland acted at all, she would ratify.
Maryland fulfilled Washington's expectations by a decisive vote for the
Constitution and thereby aided the cause in Virginia, where Henry's fol-

lowers had predicted their sister State would reject the new plan of government. Although it continued to be taken for granted that South Carolina would follow Maryland and be the eighth ratifying state, the uncertainty in Virginia alarmed northern and eastern friends of the Constitution. Washington wrote Lafayette on April 28 with something approaching awe:

A few short weeks will determine the political fate of America for the present generation and probably produce no small influence on the happiness of society through a long succession of ages to come. Should everything proceed with harmony and consent, according to our actual wishes and expectations, I must confess to you sincerely . . . it will be so much beyond anything we had a right to imagine or expect eighteen months ago that it will demonstrate as visibly the finger of Providence as any possible event in the course of human affairs can ever designate it.

Five days after Washington wrote this the Virginia convention met in Richmond. The General waited eagerly for news of its organization and initial debate, and when it came had to restrain himself lest he mistake a good beginning as assurance of a happy ending: A large number of Delegates had been present on the opening day and had voted to consider the Constitution paragraph by paragraph. On June 4, Henry began the attack with a demand for justification of the opening words, "We, the people." Why was it not "We, the States"? This challenge forecast a fight over every line of the Constitution, but there were two encouraging items in the first report Washington received: Randolph had declared himself for ratification, and South Carolina had ratified.

Some of Washington's friends in the North, though not direct parties in the struggle of the Virginia convention, were sharers with him in his hope and enthusiasm. The vote in the Old Dominion, said Tench Coxe, would have great effect on New York; Anti-Federalists in that State, Edward Carrington reported, were shocked at the prospect that Virginia would ratify; the outlook in New Hampshire was favorable, said King and Washington's young secretary, Tobias Lear; there might be a race between Virginia and New Hampshire for the honor of bringing the new government into being with the ninth state vote.

Madison wrote Washington on June 23 that the discussion of the Constitution by paragraphs had been concluded. "Tomorrow," he said, "some proposition for closing the business will be made." The conversation of Anti-Federalists "seemed to betray despair," but he concluded: "It is possible . . . that some adverse circumstance may happen." Early on the twenty-eighth amazing news was brought to Washington's door. The previous evening's mail to Alexandria had contained the glorious report that on June 25 the convention had rejected by a vote of eighty-eight to eighty a motion to propose amendments to the Constitution prior to ratification. Then the Constitution had been accepted eighty-nine to seventy-nine. On receipt of this information, the town was illuminated, cannon fired and plans made to celebrate the birth of the new government. Virginia completed the requisite nine; the State that had moved for independence had made certain the full operation of the Constitution. At least that was the joyful boast in the Potomac port until two hours before daylight on the twenty-ninth. Then an express arrived with the intelligence that New Hampshire on June 21 had accepted the Constitution by a vote of fifty-seven to forty-six. Virginia was the tenth, not the ninth.

The messenger who conveyed these happy tidings presented the General an invitation to attend the celebration in Alexandria that afternoon. With David Humphreys, who had been a guest at Mount Vernon for some months, and George Augustine he set out. A few miles outside Alexandria, Washington found a mounted group of townsmen awaiting him as an escort of honor. A salute of ten guns announced his arrival. At Wise's Tavern, thirteen toasts were drunk after an elaborate dinner, each draft with the loud "Amen" of a cannon shot. "I think," Washington wrote Pinckney, when he got home, "we may rationally indulge the pleasing hope that the Union will now be established upon a durable basis, and that Providence seems still disposed to favor the members of it, with unequalled opportunities for political happiness." That was one view. Another was expressed by James Monroe to Thomas Jefferson: "Be assured [General Washington's] influence carried this government."

Ratification by New Hampshire and Virginia relieved but did not remove the concern of Washington for successful organization of Federal government. Rhode Island, New York and North Carolina had not yet accepted the Constitution. The General thought Virginia's southern neighbor would accede, and he did not attempt to predict what might occur in Rhode Island, whose dominant faction he denounced for "infamy" that "outgoes all precedent." In spite of his own reasoning, which told him that New York must remain with her sister States, he somehow feared that powerful State might withdraw from the Union.

Another uncertainty dogged him daily as he rode over his plantations and reflected on the future of America: In the States that had ratified the Constitution, would the Anti-Federalists continue to agitate for crippling amendments and attempt to obstruct the organization of the government? For a time after Virginia accepted the Constitution he felt relief because of the apparent acquiescence of Henry in the decision of the convention. It was gratifying, also, that many of those who had voted against ratification had now rejected a plan for a protest. This satisfaction lasted a few days only. Then the report from Richmond was that Anti-Federalism was far from dead.

When James McHenry reported a whisper of a secret plan "to suspend the proper organization of the government or to defeat it altogether," Washington's counsel was realistic: In States where opposition was threatened, those "who are well-affected to the government [should] use their utmost exertions that the worthiest citizens may be appointed to the two houses of the first Congress." Then, without overturning the new system of government, proper amendments to the Constitution should be approved.

Two days after he wrote this Washington received news that was as pleasant as unexpected. On July 26 New York ratified the Constitution by a vote of thirty to twenty-seven—a victory for the Union and for Hamilton, a defeat for Governor Clinton. This action confirmed Washington in his belief that the Constitution could be put into operation without dangerous friction or strife; but he was displeased and perplexed when the New York convention sent out, over the signature of Clinton as President, a circular in which they called on the States to demand an early second convention to remove the defects of the Constitution. The North Carolina convention voted decisively against ratifying the Constitution and adjourned with a declaration that it neither ratified nor rejected the new system of government. Unaccountable as this course appeared to Washington, the refusal of Rhode Island and North Carolina to go forward with their sister States would not prevent the organization of the Union.

He and hundreds of other Americans could hope that private as well as public happiness might be enlarged, at least insofar as happiness depended on gold. In August Washington confided to Doctor Craik: "I never felt the want of money so sensibly since I was a boy of 15 years old as I have done for the last twelve months and probably shall do for twelve months more to come." To his humiliation, he had to put off the Sheriff of Fairfax County three times when that official came to collect money due on Mount Vernon and he had received warning that his lands in Greenbrier County would be sold unless taxes were paid. He could not remit the whole of what he owed Craik for medical attendance; the rector of his church was to send in November for pew rent of £5 that should have been forwarded in August. Washington had to devote many hours to finding money for day-by-day expenditures, but he maintained the confidence he always had about his own finances: his difficulties would be overcome in time, his peaceful life on the Potomac could be resumed in its quiet opulence and content. He told himself that he had performed his last public service in the Philadelphia Convention.

This was his hope, but discussion of the Presidency which he had tried to disregard in the autumn of 1787 became brisker after the New Year. The *Pennsylvania Packet* mentioned Washington frequently as President-to-be—and never once spoke of anyone else for the office. The mail brought letters from old and distinguished friends whose appeals for his acceptance of the Presidency he could not ignore. Gen. John Armstrong wrote as if the hand of the Almighty had been placed on Washington's head; a letter from Lafayette expressed some alarm over the magnitude of executive powers under the Constitution but voiced the belief that if Washington exercised the authority and found it dangerously great he would reduce it. For this and other reasons, Washington must consent to be President. A wish that he head the new government concluded a friendly letter from Rochambeau. In his answers to these letters Washington did not say he would refuse the Presidency; he affirmed only that he hoped it would not be offered him and that, if acceptance were unavoidable, it would represent the heaviest possible sacrifice.

Without any prearrangement, the people's celebration of the Fourth of July, 1788, became in large part a general call for the election of Washington as President. Public men echoed the public's demand. Appropriately, the first who spoke in words that stirred and alarmed Washington proved to be Hamilton. With persuasive logic, Hamilton reviewed the circumstances and maintained that ". . . every public and personal consideration will demand from you an acquiescence in what will *certainly* be the unanimous wish of your country." In like conviction that duty ran with public demand, Henry Lee and Benjamin Lincoln made their pleas. The newspapers, too, renewed their appeals, not so much this time in order to win Washington's consent as to assure a unanimous vote for him. Washington had to admit to himself that he almost certainly would be the choice of the electors, and he wrote in manifest distress of spirit: ". . . if I should receive the appointment and if I should be prevailed upon to accept it, the acceptance would be attended with more diffidence and reluctance than I ever experienced before in my life."

Persuasive letters of friends did not cease, but, as it chanced, Washington had a quiet period at Mount Vernon. Service to friends and neighbors was neither particularly interesting nor unusually irksome and did not take him far from home. He had time in which to fight the battle between conscience and desire—between Hamilton's "In a matter so essential . . . a citizen of so much consequence as yourself . . . has no option but to lend his services if called for" and his own "I have no wish which aspires beyond the humble and happy lot of living and dying a private citizen on my own farm."

The Congress of the Confederation by this time had carried out the recommendations made by the Convention. Presidential electors were to be chosen in the different States on the first Wednesday in January. These electors were to meet and cast their votes on the corresponding date in February. The similar Wednesday in March had been set "for commencing proceedings under the said Constitution." New York was named as the meeting place.

Washington believed in the free choice of electors but he took seriously the warning of Madison that the Anti-Federalists' plan might be to "get a Congress appointed in the first instance that [would] commit suicide on their own authority." The surest way of preventing this was to confront the Anti-Federalists boldly, resist premature amendment, and elect friends of the Constitution in sufficient number to control both Houses of Congress. In Virginia the choice of Senators by the General Assembly was completely under the control of Henry. He gave his endorsement to Richard Henry Lee and William Grayson and assured their election over Madison. Henry's antagonism did not end there. He probably was the author of an appeal by the Virginia legislature to Congress for an immediate second convention to consider amendments. Henry was charged, further, with arranging the congressional districts in such a fashion that Madison's county of Orange was put with others so strongly Anti-Federalist that Madison would have the utmost difficulty in procuring election to the House of Representatives. Virginia was divided into parties as hostile as if they had been piling up grievances for a generation. Washington did not lead the new battle, but he was heart and soul on the side of the Federalists. This was true, emphatically, of his views on the Presidency. He suspected that an effort would be made to have an advocate of destructive amendment of the Constitution placed at the head of the government. To this opinion he held, even though his informed political friends continued to assume that he would be chosen President as a matter of course.

Washington told Lincoln: ". . . nothing in this world can ever draw me from [retirement], unless it be a *conviction* that the partiality of my countrymen had made my services absolutely necessary, joined to a *fear* that my refusal might induce a belief that I preferred the conservation of my own reputation and private ease to the good of my country." In this same letter Washington expressed a decision that marked a definite change in his attitude toward the Presidency. Lincoln and others had been working with skill to have John Adams chosen as Vice President, and they sounded out Washington on his attitude towards the Massachusetts leader. The General's answer was that Massachusetts might reasonably be expected to supply the Vice President. ". . . I would most certainly treat him," said Washington of this hypothetical Vice President, "with perfect sincerity and the greatest candor in every respect. I would give him my full confidence and use my utmost endeavors to cooperate with him, in promoting and rendering permanent the national prosperity; this should be my great, my only aim, under the fixed and irrevocable resolution of leaving to other hands the helm of the State, as soon as my services could possibly with propriety be dispensed with." There he stood: If he had to accept, he would hold the office no longer than national need required. He had mentioned that possibility previously but he never had adopted it as his main line of defence. At the end of November he still permitted himself to hope that he would not be elected and that, if he were, he might contrive to decline. All the while, he showed in his letters that his reason did not sustain his hope.

The country did not share his doubt and confusion. Electors were chosen on the assumption that they would cast their votes for Washington who would not refuse the duty. Where contests were staged they were for seats in Congress. All the Senators elected in the seven States and reported by the second week in December were advocates of the Constitution or, at the least, could not be counted as Anti-Federalist, except for the two from Virginia. No less encouraging was the outlook for a sympathetic House of Representatives. Washington's chief concern was for the Representatives from his own State. Fortunately, when the contest was hottest, Madison let it be known that as the Constitution had been ratified and would be put into effect, he thought needed amendments could and should be made. This announcement destroyed the chief basis of opposition and contributed to a victory for him on February 2. Somewhat to Washington's surprise, five more Federalists, perhaps six, triumphed in the ten districts of Virginia. News of the choice of Representatives in other States came slowly, but it continued to point to the election of a Congress zealous to support the Constitution.

Anti-Federalists did not oppose Washington for President, but they appeared to be concerting for the election of a man of their own creed for second place. The individual most often mentioned as their candidate for Vice President was George Clinton to whom Washington was bound by many ties of memory and personal obligation, but he knew that Clinton or any man of like views, might seek, as Madison had put it, to have the new government commit suicide. The practical method of dealing with such a possibility was to make common cause with Adams in whose candidacy for Vice President Washington had been increasingly pleased. Adams was a safe man to whom the presidential office eventually could be entrusted; no Anti-Federalist was. Washington let it be known in Virginia and Maryland that votes for Adams would be agreeable to him and seemed "the only certain way to prevent the election of an Anti-Federalist."

It now was the end of January 1789. Soon Washington began to receive, piecemeal, news that the electors in the eastern, northern and middle States had done the expected and had cast their votes for him as President. On February 16 Knox wrote: "It appears by the returns of elections hitherto obtained, which is as far as Maryland southward, that your Excellency has every vote for President and Mr. John Adams twenty-eight for Vice-President exclusive of New Jersey and Delaware, whose votes for Vice [President] are not known." When Virginia's vote was added to those the result was beyond change by anything South Carolina and Georgia might do. Washington had been elected and, so far, unanimously! Even Henry, as a Virginia elector, had voted for him.

Most of Washington's correspondents assumed that he could not resist so overwhelming an appeal, but Washington had not yet said "Yes" and he did not intend to make any public announcement until the electors' votes had been counted officially and he had been notified of the result. All his private references to the subject still hung on an "if," but he had, of course, to make preparations, financial and other, in event he was to be absent from Mount Vernon for a long time. He would need £500 or £600 to pay pressing debts and the expenses of a journey to New York. On the very day the wheels of the new government were supposed to turn for the first time, March 4, Washington applied for a loan from a wealthy citizen of Alexandria.

Three days later Washington made what he told himself probably would be his final visit to his mother, the "last act of personal duty," as he termed it, "I may (from her age) ever have it in my power to pay [her]." She still was at Fredericksburg, about eighty years of age and in what appeared to be the fatal stage of cancer of the breast. Washington found her in the little house he had provided for her, not far from the rear of Kenmore, the home of her daughter Betty Lewis. It was part of the independent nature of Mary Washington to live in her own establishment and dress, eat, sleep and manage her servants in her own way, even though her daughter, like her son, was willing to do everything possible for her. Washington knew his mother's habits, but he did not know how fixed they were. Two years previously on one of the occasions when her demands for money had been particularly embarrassing, he had urged that she "break up housekeeping" and live with one of her children. In the same letter he had said frankly that he did not believe residence at Mount Vernon would ever "answer [her] purposes in any shape whatsoever." The house was "to be compared to a well resorted tavern, as scarcely any strangers who are going from North to South, or from South to North, do not spend a day or two at it." She had remained where she was, and there she would die. He owed her more, perhaps, than he had realized—his physical endurance, his resolution, his ambition to make his own way. Quiet words, then, at her bedside, a smile, a clasping of hands and peaceful preparation for the Great Silence that soon was to fall.

Back at Mount Vernon, Washington began to formulate the instructions he was to give George Augustine for the management of his farms. This was troublesome labor and had to be discharged when he painfully was answering the applications of those who assumed he would take office and have vast patronage to dispense at pleasure. Sadly he wrote Samuel Vaughan, to whose son he knew he could not offer a desired post:

. . . from the moment when the necessity [of accepting the Presidency] had become more apparent and, as it were, inevitable, I anticipated in a heart filled with distress, the ten thousand embarrassments, perplexities and troubles to which I must again be exposed in the evening of a life already nearly consumed in public cares. Among all these anxieties . . . I anticipated none greater than those that were likely to be produced by applications for appointments . . . my apprehensions have already been but too well justified.

Congress had been expected to assemble in New York on March 4 and, at a time of its choice, to have the certificates of the electors opened and counted by a temporary President of the Senate chosen for that purpose. Eight Senators only and no more than seventeen Representatives had made their appearance by the fifth. Frequent letters thereafter, long delayed by mud and bad weather, told of slow increase in the number of Representatives and Senators in attendance. Washington continued his efforts to put his affairs in order, and by one act, in particular, he tacitly admitted that he had despaired of finding any way of escaping the Presidency: Early in April he dispatched his secretary, Tobias Lear, and his body servant, Will, to New York. Still there was no report of a quorum for the organization of Congress.

At last, probably on April 10, an anxiously awaited regular post brought news that the House of Representatives had achieved a quorum on the first and had organized. Perhaps by the thirteenth Washington learned that the count of the electors' ballots might have been made on the sixth, but he did not know officially whether this had been done or whether the poll for him had been unanimous. On the fourteenth a clatter of hoofs and the sound of an unfamiliar voice told him a guest had arrived. When he went to the door and recognized the visitor as the old patriot Charles Thomson, Secretary of Congress, he knew what to expect: Henry Knox had written him on the second: "Mr. Thomson will set off to announce to the President the unanimous choice of the people of the United States as soon as the votes shall be opened and counted."

Thomson exchanged greetings and compliments and then addressed Washington informally, reading from a prepared statement which said in part:

. . . I was honored with the commands of the Senate to wait upon your Excellency with the information of your being elected to the office of President of the United States of America . . . I have now, sir, to inform you that the proofs you have given of your patriotism and of your readiness to sacrifice domestic separation and private enjoyments to preserve the liberty and promote the happiness of your country did not permit the two Houses to harbour a doubt of your undertaking this great, this important office to which you are called not only by the unanimous vote of the electors, but by the voice of America. . . .

Then Thomson read the formal notification:

Sir, I have the honor to transmit to your Excellency the information of your unanimous election to the Office of President of the United States of America. Suffer me, Sir, to indulge the hope, that so auspicious a mark of public confidence will meet your approbation, and be considered as a sure pledge of the affection and support you are to expect from a free and an enlightened people.

I am, Sir, with Sentiments of Respect,

Your obedient humble servant,

JOHN LANGDON

The General was prepared. From his pocket or from a table he took a paper he had made ready for the occasion:

Sir, I have been long accustomed to entertain so great a respect for the opinion of my fellow-citizens, that the knowledge of their unanimous suffrages having been given in my favor, scarcely leaves me the alternative for an option. Whatever may have been my private feelings and sentiments, I believe I cannot give a greater evidence of my sensibility for the honor they have done me, than by accepting the appointment.

I am so much affected by this fresh proof of my country's esteem and confidence, that silence can best explain my gratitude—while I realize the arduous nature of the task which is conferred on me, and feel my inability to perform it, I wish there may not be reason for regretting the choice. All I can promise is, only that which can be accomplished by an honest zeal.

Upon considering how long time some of the gentlemen of both Houses of Congress have been at New York, how anxiously desirous they must be to proceed to business, and how deeply the public mind appears to be impressed with the necessity of doing it immediately, I cannot find myself at liberty to delay my journey. I shall therefore be in readiness to set out the day after tomorrow, and shall be happy in the pleasure of your company; for you will permit me to say that it was a peculiar gratification to have received the communication from you.

That was the end of formalities. Washington prepared a brief conventional letter to President Langdon. Then he completed his arrangements for departure. On the morning of April 16 he entered his carriage with Thomson and Humphreys. His reflections were confided to his diary: "I bade adieu to Mount Vernon, to private life, and to domestic felicity, and with a mind oppressed with more anxious and painful sensations than I have words to express, set out for New York . . . With the best disposition to render service to my country in obedience to its call, but with less hope of answering its expectations." At Alexandria citizens gave him a dinner. Thirteen toasts were drunk and a most affectionate, laudatory address was delivered by Maj. Dennis Ramsay. Washington's reply was a cordial and candid statement of the struggle through which he had passed in deciding whether he would accept or decline the Presidency. ". . . words, my fellow-citizens fail me! " he said at the last: "Unutterable sensations must then be left to more expressive silence: while, from an aching heart, I bid you all, my affectionate friends and kind neighbors, farewell! "

The events that followed Washington's leave-taking at Alexandria offered the happiest possible contrast to his own gloomy foreboding. Everywhere the welcome was warm and the auguries were favorable. Always, when he was on the road, he put himself under strain to cover the greatest distance possible on a given day. Now he had a longer whip for his lead horses: Congress was waiting for him; some of its most conscientious members had been in vain attendance since the fourth of March. He resolved that he would start every morning at sunrise, if possible, and travel the entire day. Ceremonies were to be expected—and within the bounds of modesty to be enjoyed—but they must be kept as brief as possible.

On to Baltimore, then, to a welcoming salute on the afternoon of the seventeenth by its artillery and a supper at Fountain Inn. Washington was in his coach at 5:30 the next morning and, with the roaring "goodbye" of the volunteers' cannon, left Baltimore for Wilmington. On the twentieth the Burgesses and Common Council of Wilmington presented officially an address which Washington and Humphreys had seen informally long enough before the ceremonies to prepare a suitable answer. The theme was one already becoming a bit tedious—the call of the country for the General to head the new government and his acceptance of the summons in spite of a deep desire to continue in the retirement he had hoped to enjoy to the end of his days. When these felicitations had been exchanged the coach started for Philadelphia with a mounted escort of gentlemen, honorable but hampering. At the Pennsylvania line a new guard appeared. Representatives of Delaware, with the warm thanks of Washington, entrusted him and his vehicle to Philadelphians.

As he approached the city Washington found "every fence, field and avenue" lined with people. Cannon barked, church bells rang, vessels in the river ran up all their flags and joined in the salute. It was incredibly different from his march through Philadelphia that day in August 1777 when he had been pushing his ragged men southward to meet General Howe and had been able to give their tatters no other uniform than a sprig of green, the "emblem of hope." Now, twenty thousand citizens seemed to contend for a sight of him. A great dinner had been prepared at the expense of private citizens who invited "all the clergy and respectable strangers in the city." Washington remained to the end of the dinner and, "as usual, captivated every heart," though he must have been weary long before the last clinking of the glasses. From the tavern he went to the Morris home and probably to the very chamber he had occupied in the summer of 1787 when he had wondered what sort of government the members of the Convention would offer the country.

Now he had to inform President Langdon of his plans to press on to New York. He wrote: ". . . knowing how anxious both houses must be to proceed to business, I shall continue my journey with as much dispatch as possible. Tomorrow evening I purpose to be at Trenton, the night following at New Brunswick and hope to have the pleasure of meeting you at Elizabeth Town Point on Thursday at 12 o'clock." The distance to be covered in two days and a half was about seventy-five miles—not an overtaxing journey if the weather was favorable and halts were short. To get an early start was imperative, and that might be difficult. The General had to attend a display of fireworks that evening; the next morning, he was told, various addresses were to be presented. Threatening weather on Tuesday the twenty-first did not deter five committees from presenting addresses, to each of which Washington replied briefly. The hands of the clock were nearing ten when Washington could give a nod to his coachman. Off rolled the vehicle on what proved to be a damp, swift and uneventful ride up the Delaware, past villages that had witnessed many a painful march by the Continental Army.

He found a troop of horse, a company of infantry, and a large body of citizens ready to escort him into Trenton. After huzzahs and salutes, Washington took a handsome mount, thoughtfully provided for him, and rode to his assigned place in the procession. A public dinner followed at City Tavern and after that a reception. The next morning he was off at sunrise. At Princeton he received the formal address of the college, to which he spoke in brief acknowledgment. After the short ceremony he proceeded on the familiar road to New Brunswick. As he approached the town the volunteer companies of infantry and artillery, with a detachment of cavalry, formed a line past which Washington admiringly rode. A band of music played martial airs that heightened the enthusiasm of the townsfolk, nearly all of whom came out to welcome the General. Under cavalry escort, he left New Brunswick at 5 P.M. in the company of Jersey notables and with affectionate acclaim of the crowd. The night was spent at Woodbridge, and in compliment to him, light horse from New Brunswick remained nearby to share in the ceremonies of the twenty-third.

On the last stretch of his journey the procession reached Elizabeth Town before the clocks struck nine. Through a throng that overflowed the streets, Washington passed a saluting line of militia and volunteers and went to the Red Lion Inn, where he broke his fast in the company of the leading men of the community. He met there the town officials and a committee of three from the governments of New York State and City, but he punctiliously arranged that he would call on the three Senators and the five members of the House of Representatives who had come to Elizabeth Town to receive him on behalf of Congress. These gentlemen were at the home of Elias Boudinot, himself one of the committee. After pleasant conversation at Boudinot's residence, Washington proceeded to Elizabeth Town Point—the whole population, as it seemed, with him. The General walked to the craft that had been prepared for him with pride and pleasure at the expense of leading men of New York. Washington observed admiringly both craft and crew and got aboard with the joint committee of

Congress and the representatives of the civil government of New York.

By the time the barge crossed Newark Bay and reached the "Kills" opposite the southern end of Staten Island, a collection of small craft, all with flags flying and fanciful decoration, fell in behind Washington's boat, as if to form a naval parade. Soon after the barge turned into the Upper Bay, a similar handsome vessel was nearby, ready to serve as special escort. Flags and familiar faces quickly identified it as the barge of Secretary Knox, who had with him the Secretary of Foreign Affairs, John Jay, and the members of the Board of Treasury. As Washington approached the Battery on Staten Island, the familiar work on shore was wreathed with the smoke of a salute. These thirteen guns seemed to be taken as a summons by every owner of a small boat who could push it into the deep water. Minute by minute the column grew wider and longer; everywhere was color, in enthusiastic compliance with the request made by the corporation of New York City that all vessels display their flags as soon as the first salute was fired. A few minutes later, porpoises began to play around the prow of the barge as if they, too, wished to do honor to the tall man in the cocked hat.

Close now to the landing, Washington looked at thousands and thousands of New Yorkers. When the cannon of the Battery fired another salute, the spectators gave three huzzahs and then nearly all of them started to Murray's Wharf, at the bottom of Wall Street, to see the General. The flawlessly handled barge was made fast; the committees climbed out and started up carpeted steps. Then, after a fitting pause, Washington went ashore and mounted to the landing, where Governor Clinton and a coterie of officials welcomed and congratulated him. Washington thanked them with dignified regard for each individual. Thereupon an officer stepped up, saluted, and ceremoniously announced that he commanded the guard assigned the General and awaited orders. Washington's unstudied reply was almost as effective as his remarks at the Newburgh meeting or at the farewell in Fraunces' Tavern: "As to the present arrangement, I shall proceed as is directed, but after this is over, I hope you will give yourself no further trouble, as the affection of my fellow-citizens"—and he turned to the throng as he spoke—"is all the guard I want."

A formal parade had next place in the order of exercises but it was not easily started. When at last a narrow way was opened, progress was so slow and difficult that half an hour was required to move from the dock to Franklin House at No. 3 Cherry Street, previously used by the President of Congress and now assigned to Washington. A full-dress salute was rendered by the militia as the General passed their ranks; and even when finally indoors, Washington had to receive and thank the officers who had conducted the procession. Shortly Clinton's coach was at the door, and the General and the Governor proceeded without ceremony to the latter's mansion where a banquet was waiting. When, finally, Washington bade the last of his hosts goodnight and retired to the house on Cherry Street he could have told himself that in the whole of his life he never had spent a more amazing day. Emotionally, he was almost exhausted. "The display of boats . . . the decorations of the ships, the roar of cannon, and the loud acclamations of the people . . . filled my mind with sensations as painful (considering the reverse of this scene, which may be the case after all my labors to do good) as they are pleasing," he wrote.

". . . I greatly apprehend that my countrymen will expect too much from me. I fear, if the issue of public measures should not correspond with their sanguine expectations, they will turn the extravagant (and I may say undue) praises which they are heaping upon me at this moment, into equally extravagant (though I will fondly hope, unmerited) censures." That was the reflection of Washington on the events of April 23 and of the fortnight that followed. It was a shining and, at the same time, exceedingly difficult period for a man who never had served in a public executive position other than as a soldier. He completed easily the arrangements Lear had made in advance for comfortable living in the house assigned him; he carefully visited the members of Congress; he received the congratulations of the city Chamber of Commerce, and he assured a joint committee of Congress that any arrangements that body made for his induction into office would be acceptable. Congress voted to inaugurate him on April 30.

By the twenty-ninth arrangements were so nearly complete that Washington knew what to expect. If he was awake at sunrise the next day, he heard the bark of thirteen guns from the fortifications at the southern end of Manhattan Island. Not long after the guns paid homage, he had his hair powdered and dressed with proud care in a suit of brown broadcloth spun at Hartford, purchased and forwarded to Mount Vernon through Henry Knox. This apparel was to advertise American industry; it was, also, in a homely way to proclaim American liberty since the device on the buttons was that of a wing-spread eagle. The stockings were Washington's best, of white silk; his shoe-buckles were silver; he was later to fasten on a dress sword in a steel scabbard.

When Washington had eaten breakfast, the bells of city churches began to ring, some of them merrily at first and then all of them solemnly in a summons to prayer. The General and his assistants doubtless listened sympathetically, but they were busy with last-minute details. Washington's Inaugural Address was not a concern; it was ready for delivery. He had put aside completely the long statement of needed legislation he had written some weeks before at Mount Vernon and in its place, probably with help from Madison, had prepared a paper that could be read at an unhurried pace in less than twenty minutes.

Soon the General had the smallest final detail properly set in the pattern of the day's proceedings. Before his door crowds gathered and gaped. Every moment these spectators increased in number. Militia appeared in the roadway; a parade was being formed. No call came for Washington till noon was past. Then he heard the sound of horses' hoofs, the tramp of troops and the grind of carriage wheels: The joint committee of Congress was arriving to escort him to Federal Hall. Along with the eight members, whose chairman was Senator Ralph Izard, a like number of "assistants" made their bow, all except one of them veterans of the Revolution. On Izard's announcement that Congress was ready to receive him, Washington left the house and, alone, entered a grand coach that had been prepared for him. At half past twelve off rolled the General in slow stateliness, his vehicle drawn by four fine horses. Ahead were the troops and the Senate members of the joint committee; behind Washington rode his secretaries, Representatives of the committee, Chancellor Robert R. Livingston, who was to administer the oath, and, with him, the heads of the Federal Departments and a few eminent citizens.

When the procession ended its march, Washington and the others left the vehicles and walked up Broad Street towards the meeting place. Inside the remodeled Federal Hall the two Houses of Congress were sitting together in the Senate Chamber awaiting him. He mounted the stairs and came to the Chamber door, which was opened ceremoniously. As Washington walked towards the platform, the lawmakers and guests rose from the semicircle of seats; Washington bowed to both sides while he walked to the Vice President who was standing directly in front of the platform. John Adams formally welcomed Washington and escorted him to the central seat. Adams took a chair on Washington's right, and Speaker Frederick Muhlenberg one on the General's left. After a brief pause, Adams stood to address the President: "Sir, the Senate and House of Representatives are ready to attend you to take the oath required by the Constitution. It will be administered by the Chancellor of the State of New York."

"I am ready to proceed," Washington answered simply.

Adams led the way to the central door of three that led into a small portico overlooking Wall and Broad Streets. As Washington emerged, he saw crowded roof-tops and windows filled with his fellow-Americans. A second later, from the front of the portico, he beheld a multitude in the streets. Whole-hearted cheers rolled up to him and did not decrease in volume until he bowed again and again with his hand on his heart and then stepped back to the arm-chair where he took his seat. By this time the portico was jammed, but places had been left for the Chancellor, the Vice President and Governor Clinton. Immediately behind the table stood Henry Knox and Arthur St. Clair, the one still Secretary of War and the other Governor of the Northwest Territory. The historic moment was at hand. Washington arose and came forward, again in unobstructed view of the crowd. Opposite him stood Chancellor Livingston, who had been a member of Congress when the Virginian had been named as Commander-in-Chief. Samuel Otis, Secretary of the Senate, lifted the Bible and the red cushion from the table and took his station between Washington and the Chancellor. Washington saw that the Judge was ready and put his right hand on the Bible. "Do you solemnly swear," asked the Chancellor, "that you will faithfully execute the office of President of the United States and will, to the best of your ability, preserve, protect, and defend the Constitution of the United States?"

"I solemnly swear," Washington answered—and repeated the oath. Reverently he added, "So help me God." He bent forward as he spoke and, before Otis could lift the Bible to his lips, he kissed the book.

"It is done," Livingston announced, and, turning to the crowd, he made a broad gesture with his hand and shouted, "Long live George Washington, President of the United States!" The roar of the throng came back on the instant, joyful and sustained. Livingston's cry was taken up, and with it came clearly, "God bless our President." Washington bowed. The answering cheers were louder and more emotional than ever. Eyes were lifted to the cupola of the Federal Hall, where the flag was being raised. It was a signal to the Battery, which answered with the bang-bang of thirteen guns. The President bowed his acknowledgments, which evoked still more cheers, and before the ovation ended reentered the Senate Chamber, took his seat on the dais and waited for the members and guests to resume their places. All spectators rose with him and, after he had bowed again, sat down intently.

"Fellow Citizens of the Senate and House of Representatives," Washington began with embarrassment, "Among the vicissitudes incident to life, no event could have filled me with greater anxiety than that of which the notification was transmitted by your order. . . ." He repeated in well-fashioned phrases what he had said many times regarding the conflict of duty and inclination, his consciousness of his "inferior endowments," and his lack of practice "in the duties of civil administration." He followed this with "fervent supplications to that Almighty Being who rules over the Universe." In reverent tones he spoke of the "invisible hand" and the "providential agency" that had guided the people of the United States in all their struggles and had wrought the "important revolution just accomplished in the system of their United Government."

After he had dwelt on these themes for about six minutes, Washington turned to the duty imposed by the Constitution of making recommendations to Congress, but in this he deferred to Congress. The one specific suggestion he made was that Congress should decide to what extent it should advocate constitutional amendments in order to meet objections and relieve "inquietude." In this, said Washington, "I shall again give way to my entire confidence in your discernment and pursuit of the public good," but he added reflections that bespoke both his caution and his political judgment:

I assure myself that whilst you carefully avoid every alteration which might endanger the benefits of an united and effective government, or which ought to await the future lessons of experience, a reverence for the characteristic rights of freedom and a regard for the public harmony will sufficiently influence your deliberations on the question how far the former can be more impregnably fortified, or the latter be safely and advantageously promoted.

With this he turned back the pages of his public service by renewing, in effect, the statement he had made when he had been named Commander-in-Chief in 1775: he would ask that his compensation "be limited to such actual expenditures as the public good may be thought to require." A minute sufficed for his conclusion:

Having thus imparted to you my sentiments, as they have been awakened by the occasion which brings us together, I shall take my present leave; but not without resorting once more to the benign parent of the human race, in humble supplication that since He has been pleased to favor the American people, with opportunities for deliberating in perfect tranquility, and dispositions for deciding with unparalleled unanimity on a form of Government for the security of their Union and the advancement of their happiness; so his divine blessing may be equally conspicuous in the enlarged views, the temperate consultations and the wise measures on which the success of this Government must depend.

When he bowed and sat down his audience was as much moved as he had been. He had stirred deeply the feelings of most of those who had listened: the earnestness of the man, his sincerity, his simplicity and the memories that he personified set hearts to beating faster and blurred responsive eyes. The French Minister, the Comte de Moustier, reported to his government: ". . . never has sovereign reigned more completely in the hearts of his subjects than did Washington in those of his fellow-citizens. . . . He has the soul, look and figure of a hero united in him."

After his address had been delivered the President walked with Congressmen and guests, through streets lined with militia, to St. Paul's Chapel, whither Congress had voted to go in order "to hear divine service, performed by the Chaplain of Congress." Bishop Samuel Provoost did not abbreviate the petitions he made to the Almighty, and the *Te Deum* was sung, not chanted; but as Doctor Provoost did not preach a sermon, Washington was soon out doors again and in one of the carriages that awaited guests and committee. Mercifully the President was left to dine privately and reflect in his own chamber on events that would compel him at fifty-seven years of age to face the perplexities inevitably attendant on the exercise by a central government of powers eleven States jealously had guarded as the symbols and the tools of their sovereignty.

Washington's first task was not to ascertain his duties but to find time in which to discharge those awaiting him. He had to study all recent treasury reports and all foreign dispatches, and he had to confer with the heads of the departments that had existed when the Constitution became operative. In no other way than this could he so readily discover the poverty of the government and the state of negotiations with foreign powers and the Indians. Good relations with Congress had to be established and acceptable channels of communication opened, perhaps by different approaches, with House and Senate. The executive branch of government had then to be organized, revenues had to be provided, courts set up, and appointments made.

These were duties of varying complexity but the least difficult of them would demand hours on hours of work every week and some would require long attention daily; how could this be given? A rule to receive "visits of compliment" on two designated days of the week and then for an hour only was made effective forthwith. Lear, on reaching the city, had hired "Black Sam" Fraunces as steward. The former proprietor of the tavern where Washington had said farewell to his officers, "tossed off such a number of fine dishes," according to Lear, "that we are distracted in our choice when we sit down to table, and obliged to hold a long consultation on the subject before we can determine what to attack." Although it seemed bad to leave these viands untouched while members of Congress were eating poor meals at noisy taverns, the General's tentative decision to do no entertaining at dinner was approved and perhaps was prompted by old Federal lawmakers and conspicuous New Yorkers. They explained that some of the later presiding officers of Congress under the Articles of Confederation had been too lavish in the invitations extended. The General was advised that he would do well to extend no invitations and, further, to accept none.

In electing to defer entertainment under his own roof, Washington felt it prudent to continue public appearances temporarily. On May 6 he attended the commencement of Columbia College and subjected himself to ten orations by graduating students and to the final exhortation by the clear-headed President William Samuel Johnson. The next night, Washington went to a great ball at the Assembly Rooms. The evening of the eleventh was given to the theatre, with several members of Congress as guests of the President. By the fourteenth the strain of long days and late evenings may have been severe, but Washington had to go to a ball given in his honor by the French Minister. To continue this measure of social activity was out of the question. Before he had ended his experimental round of attendance on social affairs, Washington asked Adams, Hamilton, Jay and Madison for their advice: Might he safely reduce the levees? Could he with propriety set an early morning hour each day—say eight o'clock —for calls by persons who had public business to discuss? Would it be in order for him to invite men in public office and no private citizens to dine with him on the days he held levees? Were all large entertainments better barred than held? Might not a few be arranged annually at the President's house, and if so, when?

Hamilton's answer was austere: One levee a week would be sufficient and should be open only to those who were introduced properly; Washington's appearance at these affairs ought not to extend beyond half an hour; during the reception, invitations to dinner should be extended informally to six or eight guests, with whom the President would not linger overlong. No invitations were to be accepted, nor were any visits to be returned. From two to four entertainments might be held yearly. Adams's views were more liberal: Two levees a week would be necessary to accommodate the crowds; the President should not have large social gatherings but should remain free to receive unofficial guests and visit informally, because his private life should be lived at his own discretion. Public entertainment was not necessary. Tours of the country were desirable, but the expense of them ought to be separate from the compensation of the President. Washington chose, as he said, "that line of conduct which combined public advantage with private convenience and which in my judgment, was unexceptionable in itself"; he would continue two levees a week, but he would make no visits; on occasion he would indulge his fondness for the theatre; other decisions on social life could await the arrival of Martha from Virginia.

The President had in the shortest possible time to organize his personal office. He had admirable assistance in the literary veteran, Humphreys, and in Lear, whose abilities and disposition made him useful in almost every important task. Lear could effect a good bargain or have repairs executed quickly; he could write an excellent letter or manage a pleasant dinner. No young man since the days of Tench Tilghman and John Laurens had served so acceptably in Washington's household. Lear grew but so did his duties, which soon exceeded all that even his diligence could accomplish on a given day. The President had to look for another senior secretary and two juniors. It took him some months to find Maj. William Jackson, who had served in Lincoln's South Carolina campaign and in 1787 had been Secretary of the Philadelphia Convention. Washington found the Major so skillful that he well might have lamented his failure to acquire his services earlier. One junior addition to the establishment was Thomas Nelson, son of the Governor who had commanded the Virginia militia in front of Yorktown. Still another young Virginian, Washington's nephew Robert Lewis, was to come to New York with Martha. How many hours he could devote for the General and how many to the Lady of the House time alone would show. There was need also of political aides. The men to whom Washington looked for assistance were Madison and Hamilton—the Virginian for the drafting of papers too intricate for the secretaries, and the New Yorker for information on the higher political strategy of New York and the East. Both could be valuable in Washington's establishment of cordial relations with Congress.

Eight and a half years of negotiation with lawmakers while Washington was Commander-in-Chief had been added to his own training in the Virginia House of Burgesses and the Congresses of 1774 and 1775. This long instruction gave him experience for dealing with the new bicameral system of Federal legislation. The only unfamiliar phases of his duty with respect to Congress were a determination of the precise function of the Senate and the establishment of a balanced relationship of the executive departments to Congress and to him. He would use the four existing Departments—Foreign Affairs, War, Post Office and Board of Treasury—until others were created. In the absence of contrary precedents, he would have the heads of these divisions report directly to Congress on matters committed to them by resolution of the lawmakers. Washington did not feel, at the outset, that it was expedient to call for information from the Departments; but as soon as pressure on him lightened in June, he began reading the dispatches and reports on file and asked Jay, Knox and the members of the Board of Treasury to prepare a summary that would give him "a full, precise and general *idea*" of the work entrusted to them. He began to assume a positive direction of foreign affairs, control of which was vested in him by the Constitution. In careful deference to Congress, he neither made recommendations at this time nor discussed what the lawmakers debated. Scrupulously he adhered to the stand that amendment of the Constitution was proper but that in everything else he would rely on "the talents, the rectitude and the patriotism" of members. The separation of the three branches of government was to be respected. He would administer but he would not interfere—that was the basis of his executive policy.

Congress was quick to assert the prerogatives he was careful to respect. The first bill passed by Congress was one that prescribed how oaths were to be administered, an act to which Washington attached his signature June 1. An imperative measure for levying imposts had been taken up in Committee of the Whole as early as April 8 but members had much to say on this and on almost every other subject mentioned on the floor. Debate over duties on imported goods soon developed many clashes of sectional interest and numerous complicated disputes. Bills for the creation of executive Departments of Foreign Affairs, War and Treasury were soon involved in an interesting debate on the question of the right of the President to remove the heads of these Departments.

Washington believed in a strong Executive, but he did not relish constitutional analysis, and even if he had been adept in this, he would have been put temporarily out of the debate by developments of mid-June. These occurrences had a happy prelude. After much careful preparation, Martha left home during the afternoon of May 16. She rode in the family carriage with her two grandchildren and had the General's nephew, Robert Lewis of Fredericksburg, as mounted escort and majordomo. Her ride was a triumph, but not for a moment did this turn her head. She remained simple, appreciative, human and—grandmotherly. At Elizabeth Town Point Washington, Robert Morris and Humphreys had the President's new barge in waiting on May 27, and soon they conveyed the ladies and the Custis children to Peck's Slip on Manhatten Island. A salute of thirteen guns was given the First Lady as she passed the Battery; Governor Clinton stood at the dock to meet her: Martha drove at once to the President's House, which she found "a very good one and . . . handsomely furnished all new for the General." In spite of help from an excellent staff, she perceived quickly that she had heavy duties as mistress of a busy mansion and hostess at diversified affairs.

Besides her grandchildren's study, appearance and regard for the amenities of a conspicuous social position, Martha had to give her own dress and social obligations flawless and ceaseless attention. Her hair was set and dressed every day; scores of visits had to be acknowledged and were most satisfactorily disposed of, she soon found, if they were returned on the third day, without fail. It was a life far removed from the routine of Mount Vernon, where the greatest excitement of the day usually was the clatter of a strange horse's hoofs on the driveway. Martha quickly made scores of friends in her new position. "I took the earliest opportunity . . . ," wrote Abigail Adams, "to go and pay my respects to Mrs. Washington." The wife of the Vice President warmed her page as she went on: "She received me with great ease and politeness. She is plain in her dress, but that plainness is the best of every article. She is in mourning. Her hair is white, her teeth beautiful, her person rather short than otherwise. . . . Her manners are modest and unassuming, dignified and feminine, not the tincture of hauteur about her." In her next letter, Abigail confirmed her judgment: "Mrs. Washington is one of those unassuming characters which create love and esteem. A most becoming pleasantness sits upon her countenance and an unaffected deportment which renders her the object of veneration and respect. With all these feelings and sensations I found myself much more deeply impressed than I ever did before their Majesties of Britain."

Washington seldom had found himself more fortunate in her coming. He did not realize it, perhaps, but she humanized him in the eyes of his guests. What was more, she was at hand when, with little warning, he suddenly needed her in a particular manner. About the middle of June, the President developed a fever that did not yield to normal treatment. Soon there was a tenderness over the protuberance of his thigh on the left side. Medical aid was summoned by the seventeenth; Dr. Samuel Bard, a leading practitioner, and his consultants were unable to make a diagnosis. Concern was general; rumor spread that the President had a malignant tumor or else was a victim of anthrax, "wool sorters' disease." The tumor grew fast and took on a fiery hue; soreness spread to such an extent that he could not sit down except in acute pain. About the twentieth the fever disappeared and the tumor showed itself as an abscess. Dr. Bard opened it but had to make a large incision, which would heal slowly and, meanwhile, would keep the General uncomfortable, night and day. The General's steady response to this treatment has led historians of medicine to conclude that he did not have anthrax but a large carbuncle.

His progress was slow. By July 3 he could write a letter, or at least revise a draft on official business of importance; and, of course, he bestirred himself to extra effort for the observance of the Fourth of July. The New York militia were to be reviewed; the Cincinnati planned a meeting and an address to him. The day had historic beginning. To Washington's House was brought the text of "a bill for laying a duty on goods, wares and merchandizes imported into the United States"—the "impost bill." Washington signed it—without a word to indicate that he reflected on the interesting connection between political independence declared on the Fourth of July, 1776, and the fiscal independence assured by the simple bill made law thirteen years thereafter.

Washington's recovery continued but, as he was beginning to find in matters less sensitively personal, progress was slow. Had convalescence been more rapid, he could not have completed quickly the organization of the Executive, because Congress persisted in long debates on nearly all subjects. The establishment of the Departments of Foreign Affairs, War and Treasury was by separate bills, not by a single measure. All three became the object of vigorous contention, because they gave the President the power to remove the heads of Departments. The bill to set up "judical courts for the United States" passed the Senate July 17, after debate that forecast long contention in the House.

Delay in enactment of fundamental laws was embarrassing to Washington. Many men had come to New York in the hope of procuring public employment; much more numerous were the conspicuous men who sought more offices than would be available. Some of these grew impatient as weeks passed with no distribution of shining offices and exalted titles. Washington filled promptly the positions established or continued under the temporary acts for levying and collecting imposts and tonnage taxes.

Beyond this, he reminded applicants, Congress had not yet gone into the creation of offices. He let it be known that subordinate posts would not be assigned in any of the Departments till the chiefs had been appointed. In passing on official requirements and on men about whom he knew nothing, the President usually consulted the Senators from the applicant's State, though he made no pledge to do this. Applications proved a worse ordeal, if possible, than Washington had expected them to be, but towards them he displayed the caution of a man long disciplined to respect both public trust and personal reputation.

This same caution marked Washington's steps in exploring his relations with Congress. He regarded the executive branch as a "department" distinct from the Federal Legislature, but on parity with it and bound by oath and the letter of the Constitution to show proper deference towards it. If he made any suggestion for action by Congress the occasion had to be one of importance. The initiative, choice, form, scope and prompt enactment or deliberate postponement of legislation were for the determination of Congress, unhindered by the Executive. The President's power over lawmaking, as he saw it, was confined to his veto.

Washington did not understand, at the outset, exactly how he should proceed with respect to subjects that called for joint action by the President and the Senate. Would it not be well, when doubts arose, for the Senate to communicate with the President and give him opportunity of explaining why he made a nomination? Before this communication reached the Senate, a committee of that body informed him of their appointment to "confer with him on the mode of communication proper to be pursued between him and the Senate in the formation of treaties and making appointments to office." He had been considering the procedure to be followed with respect to treaties, because he planned, if Congress approved, to undertake a settlement with the southern Indians. A message on the subject was sent both Houses the day after the Senate committee was named.

Further study clarified some of his conclusions on methods of dealing with the upper house; but his survey soon involved questions of ceremonial, on which he was beginning to put undue emphasis. Two conferences with the Senate committee convinced Washington that inflexible procedure was not wise, nor was it so much a concern to the committee as was the substitution of voice votes for secret ballot in passing on nominees. Washington favored direct, open voting and said so. As between written messages and personal appearance before the Senate, he told Madison he would advocate the one that would seem "most conducive to the public good." His preference was for the black and white of a permanent record on nominations; his judgment dictated personal appearance occasionally in order to explain the provisions of treaties and ask directly for "advice and consent." In the end, he proposed that "the Senate should accommodate their rules to the uncertainty of the particular mode and place that may be preferred, providing for the reception of either oral [or] written propositions, and for giving their consent and advice in either the presence or absence of the President, leaving him free to use the mode and place that may be found eligible and accordant with other business which may be before him at the time."

The Senate acquiesced in most of this with the proviso that all questions be put by the Vice President and that Senators "signify their assent or dissent by answering, viva voce, aye or no." No sooner was this procedure tested than it was found in part unworkable. On August 7, Washington suggested that Congress approve an effort to reach an accord with the Creek Indians through "a temporary commission . . . to consist of three persons, whose authority should expire with the occasion." The two Houses agreed and appropriated $20,000 for the negotiations, whereupon Washington called on Lincoln to head the commissioners, and, with Knox as active penman, prepared to draft instructions. On the scope of these, Washington thought he should have the "advice and consent" of the Senate and, by prearrangement, he went to the Chamber on August 22, attended by Knox, and presented his questions in a paper which he passed to the Vice President. In the midst of noise from the street and confusion on the floor, Adams read this document and another that Washington had prepared, and then, after a re-reading, put the question on giving consent to the first of seven propositions submitted in the President's summary. As the subject was a complicated one, it should have been manifest that approval would be perfunctory, but William Maclay protested against immediate action and sought to have the questions sent to committee or to have action deferred. Washington disapproved. "This," he said, "defeats every purpose of my coming here," but he consented to have the whole subject deferred until the twenty-fourth. That day he received the Senate's approval of all he asked, though the debate was laboriously dull.

Washington ended the incident far less disposed than he had been to consult in person with the Senate on diplomatic affairs. Written communications would be easier and less subject to misunderstanding. If one result of the experiment with the presentation of the Indian negotiations was to establish viva voce action by the Senate, that was a desirable gain, but it concerned Congress and not the Executive. Between the two, Washington drew a clear line. Said he: ". . . as the Constitution of the United States, and the laws made under it, must mark the line of my official conduct, I could not justify my taking a single step in any matter, which appeared to me to require their agency, without its being first obtained. . . ."

Adherence to that rule was one of several factors that simplified Washington's labors. Congress gradually became more familiar with the larger issues under consideration, though it still indulged too generously its loquacious and contentious members. Washington signed on July 27 the bill for the establishment of a Department of Foreign Affairs and on August 7 a similar measure for a Department of War. Debate over the Treasury Department delayed final action until August 28; agreement on the salaries of the President and Vice President was in prospect. The bill for the compensation of the two senior executive officers fixed Washington's allotment at $25,000 and that of the Vice President at $5000. Washington continued to act on the principle that he was receiving his expenses only, but he let these mount almost precisely to the figure set by Congress as his salary. Vigorous argument over proposed constitutional amendments was under way, with Federalists determined to approve no change in the basic structure.

Washington was coming more and more to love display and he had ambition to make the Presidency "respectable." He thought it befitted the dignity of the office to drive with six cream-colored horses attached to his carriage, and apparently did not think he was making himself unduly conspicuous when he rode a white steed with leopard skin housing and saddle cloth that had a gold binding. Fourteen white servants and seven slaves were employed in his house; dinners were large, frequent and elaborate—the pomp of entry heightened by the presence of powdered lackeys; food was consumed in amazing quantities; orders for wine ran to twenty-six dozen claret and a like volume of champagne. Martha held levees Friday evening of each week, with varying attendance that her husband carefully set down in his diary. He usually came into the room to greet his wife's guests and if he found some other lady sitting on the right of Martha, where he thought Mrs. Adams should be placed, tactfully led the misplaced guest to some other part of the room. It was natural after receiving this delicate attention that Abigail should consider Washington's regard for ceremonial as proper, but she could not forget her upbringing in Massachusetts. Washington's equipage with its large team, its four servants and two gentlemen outriders, was, said Abigail, "no more state than is perfectly consistent with his station, but then I do not love to see the newswriters fib so" in asserting "he is perfectly averse to all marks of distinction. . . ."

On September 1 Washington had a dinner at which Steuben was one of the guests. "The Baron" was in a cheerful and facetious mood and made everyone merry. About the time the laughter was at its highest, Washington received a letter that put an end to jest, to dinner and to all social activities of the next few days. Late in July the General's sister, Betty Lewis, had written him that their mother's physical condition was grave. After that, it was no surprise to hear that Mrs. Washington had become speechless about August 10, had lost consciousness on the twentieth, and had died on the twenty-fifth. Washington's reflection was the natural one:

Awful and affecting as the death of a parent is, there is consolation in knowing that Heaven has spared ours to an age beyond which few attain, and favored her with the full enjoyment of her mental faculties and as much bodily strength as usually falls to the lot of fourscore. Under these considerations and a hope that she is translated to a happier place, it is the duty of her relatives to yield due submission to the decrees of the Creator. When I was last at Fredericksburg, I took a final leave of my Mother, never expecting to see her more.

He ordered black cockades, sword knots and arm-ribbons for the men of the household, but he did not "go into deep mourning." The regular levees were suspended for a week, but after that, social life flowed on as before.

From her renowned son in his manhood Mary Ball Washington never elicited the warm love a man usually has for his mother. She seemed to him grasping, unreasonable in her demands and untidy in her person.

Doubtless, too, he had been irked by her poor management and irritated by her ceaseless concern for him. She had unstinted care at the hands of her daughter, but if she was beloved in the community where she lived, no echo of affection for her survived. In old age she may have been unlovely and unlovable, yet, when she bore her son, she must have possessed qualities that reappeared in him, some softened, perhaps, and some of them disciplined. There is no reason for doubting tradition that she had fine physique and that she was a skillful horsewoman. At least a measure of her acquisitiveness was possessed by George, especially during his early manhood, and this similarity was perhaps the chief reason for misunderstanding between the two.

Her son needed in 1789 all the endurance in which he resembled her. The House of Representatives entered vehemently into a debate over the permanent seat of government which was proposed at one time or another for almost every town of any size between Trenton and Georgetown. Washington wished that the decision of Congress would be for a site on the stream that separated his own state from Maryland; but there was not a complaint from any quarter that he attempted to influence the action of the lawmakers, who, after much futile maneuver, deferred the issue to the next term. The constitutional amendments were adopted finally on September 28 in a form that met every strong demand for the guarantee of individual right and provided, in particular, that "the powers not delegated to the United States by the Constitution, nor prohibited by it to the States, are reserved to the States respectively, or to the people." No change in the division of specified powers or in the organization of the Federal government was submitted to the States. During the climactic period of this debate, the bill for the establishment of "judicial courts" was signed by Washington. The Secretary of the Treasury was directed to report to the next session of Congress a plan for the support of public credit. With these major enactments supplemented by numerous measures of less importance, Congress formally recessed September 29 to meet again on the first Monday in January 1790.

Washington regarded the session as a success. He wrote Gouverneur Morris: ". . . national government is organized, and, as far as my information goes, to the satisfaction of all parties . . . opposition to it is either no more, or hides its head." Next, perhaps, to general acceptance of the new system, the most important achievement of the session was the creation of Federal Courts. In the executive branch of government the great gain had been the acquiescence of Congress in the doctrine that the President should have the power to name and, if necessary, remove the men who would be, so to say, his divisional commanders. The desired Departments of State, Treasury, and War had been established. Provision had been made, also, for an Attorney General and for the continuance of the Post Office. Subject to Senate confirmation, the President had, likewise, the responsibility of nominating the Justices of the Supreme Court and of the lower Federal tribunals.

Appointments consequently became the most pressing task Washington faced during the last days of the session and for some weeks after adjournment. The General waited until the bill for the establishment of the Treasury Department passed and then made his principal appointments. As Secretary of War he designated the faithful man who held the corresponding office under the "old" Congress, Henry Knox. The Secretaryship of the Treasury went to Alexander Hamilton. The next appointments were those of the Judges, District Attorneys and Marshals of the eleven District Courts. Here Washington had to select the best men he could find, at the same time that he made a geographical distribution and ran the risk of offending applicants he had to pass over. He compromised in the case of James Wilson by giving the Pennsylvanian one of the seats as Associate Justice instead of the post of Chief Justice for which Wilson had applied. The other places as Associate Justice went to John Rutledge of South Carolina, William Cushing of Massachusetts, John Blair of Virginia and Robert H. Harrison of Maryland. Choice of the Chief Justice was considered carefully. No hint was dropped in the President's correspondence that he thought it desirable to shift John Jay from the office of Secretary of Foreign Affairs to the post of Chief Justice. If Washington felt that Jay's policy with respect to the navigation of the Mississippi had created antagonisms, he said nothing about it, nor did he assign any other reason for making the shift; but he sent in Jay's nomination as head of the Supreme Court September 24.

The man whom Washington selected to fill the office that corresponded to the one previously held by Jay was the United States Minister to France, Thomas Jefferson, then about to start home on leave. The President had seen comparatively little of this fellow-Virginian and had not communicated extensively with him, except during the years when Jefferson was war-time Governor of Virginia, but Washington had served with Jefferson for five years in the Virginia House of Burgesses and, as he once wrote Lafayette, he had "early imbibed the highest opinion" of the master of Monticello. The relations of Jefferson with the government of France had appeared to be cordially sympathetic. By the time he sent the nomination to the Senate, the President had learned of the incredible occurrences in Paris that had culminated in the seizure on July 14 of the Bastille. Washington knew that the information of the American representative would be of the largest value to the government in any situation that might develop in a country on whose support America in large, if lessening, measure still was dependent. Jefferson could give information and counsel on many subjects besides France. He seemed the ideal man for Secretary of State.

The last of the four executive positions of highest rank was that of Attorney General. The man appointed must be a highly competent lawyer, sympathetic with the Constitution. Such a man, in Washington's opinion, was Edmund Randolph. Although Randolph had refused to sign the Constitution, he had promoted greatly the ratification of that document in his own State. Nothing that Washington said indicated that Randolph was being rewarded for his return to the fold of Federalism. Washington's letter to Randolph urged him to make the sacrifice for the public good, though he was not sure that Randolph could afford to accept. This uneasiness was removed by Randolph's decision to serve, but he was anxious to be excused from his new duties until March 1, and certainly until January 15, 1790.

The major appointments had been made by the time Congress adjourned. Washington's duties then decreased because he left the administration of the Departments to the men temporarily or permanently in charge. Entertainment became less elaborate when members of Congress left the city. The French Minister and the Spanish agent were returning home, also. This circumstance led Washington to inquire whether the representative of Spain should depart without receiving notice that failure to press vigorously for the free navigation of the Mississippi did not mean that the United States had yielded on that score or had decided to let the issue slumber indefinitely. A diplomatic question of more immediate bearing concerned the relations of Britain and the United States. Congress had shown a disposition to levy discriminating duties on British imports because no commercial treaty between the two countries existed. The future of America's important trade with the West Indies was in doubt; slaves carried away by the British had never been restored or paid for; the western posts had not been evacuated; Americans resented the failure of Britain to send a Minister to the United States, though their country had been represented by Adams for more than three years at the Court of St. James's. Washington thought it desirable to sound out the London government and ascertain whether relations could not be improved. Jay and Hamilton were called separately into conference on this, with the result that Washington took the advice of the Secretary of the Treasury and decided to ask Gouverneur Morris, then in England, to ascertain the views of the ministry to the end that "harmony and mutual satisfaction between the two countries" might be achieved.

CHAPTER / 20

While Washington had been consulting about foreign affairs he had been also asking his advisers for their opinion on a mission that had interested him for months—a tour of the Northeastern States. They urged him to undertake such a journey. His admirers realized that he would be the symbol of government as well as of the struggle that had established American freedom. Strong as was support of the Constitution east of the Hudson, it would be stronger after a visit by him.

If he expected a tour similar to his triumphal progress to New York in April, he was not disappointed. Much that occurred from October 15 to November 13 was, in effect, a repetition of the festivity of the spring—addresses, odes, parades and dinners. Washington was pleased by what he saw of mills in New England and by the beauty and fine dress of the ladies at formal assemblies in Boston, Salem and Portsmouth. His stay in New Hampshire included a landing in Maine, an unsuccessful fishing expedition and much pleasantness in meeting old friends. He stopped on November 5 at the scene of the initial military engagement of the Revolution. As he viewed the positions the men of Massachusetts had occupied at Lexington, he told his companions that British critics had protested to Franklin that it was ill usage for the Americans to hide behind stone walls and fire at the King's soldiers; whereupon Franklin asked if there were not two sides to a wall. The good humor with which Washington repeated this story was typical of the spirit in which he finished a completely successful tour. Washington returned to New York "all fragrant," as John Trumbull remarked, "with the odor of incense."

The President promptly went to work on an accumulation of government mail. His other tasks were more troublesome than numerous. Five days before Washington reached New York, the commissioners sent to negotiate with the Creeks had returned from Georgia and reported failure. As the danger of a war with the powerful Creeks of the Southwest was only one and might not be the worst threat on the frontier, Washington began a study of relations with the unfriendly tribes beyond the American settlements. Until December this was the most complicated of Washington's puzzles. Some of his other experiences were pleasant. He proclaimed a day of Thanksgiving for November 26 and shared reverently in the services. The day of remembrance was followed by a period of work over Mount Vernon affairs. Washington had, in addition, to be counsellor on numerous financial transactions for which he had a varying measure of responsibility as his wife's agent or as a trustee. Before these were settled, the President was deep in study, with Knox and Steuben, of plans for organizing the militia.

As the time for the reassembly of Congress approached, Washington extended his activities as host, but he held rigidly to his rule to accept no invitations, not even to funerals. Martha also had placed restrictions on her daily life. Visits had to be made with discretion; she must not go to "public places." She wrote Mercy Warren:

Though the General's feelings and my own were perfectly in unison with respect for our predilection for private life, yet I cannot blame him for acting according to his ideas of duty in obeying the voice of his country. The consciousness of having attempted to do all the good in his power, and the pleasure of finding his fellow citizens so well satisfied with the disinterestedness of his conduct, will doubtless be some compensation for the great sacrifice which I know he has made. With respect to myself, I sometimes think the arrangement is not quite as it ought to have been; that I, who had much rather be at home, should occupy a place with which a great many younger and gayer women would be prodigiously pleased . . . I am still determined to be cheerful and to be happy in whatever situation I may be; for I have also learned from experience that the greater part of our happiness or misery depends upon our dispositions, and not upon our circumstances.

A New Year's reception was preliminary to a session of Congress that began four days late, January 7, 1790. North Carolina had ratified the Constitution November 21; the proposed amendments to that document had met with favor in most of the States. Washington staged with superlative care the delivery of his message on January 8, but his continuing caution deterred him from vigorous advocacy. The paper he read consisted merely of a congratulatory paragraph on "the present favorable prospects of our public affairs" and a series of unexciting proposals for common defence, protection of the frontiers, naturalization laws, uniform weights and measures, the grant of patents, the extension of the post, and the "promotion of science and literature."

When Congress had been in session a week Secretary Hamilton submitted his plan for the support of public credit, recognized immediately as a bold and strong document. Its basic argument and recommendation were: For their honor, their manifest advantage and their assurance of future credit, the United States must pay defaulted interest on their Continental debt and must fund the principal. To achieve this, the United States must treat all creditors fairly and avoid any discrimination between original purchasers and present holders of obligations. The United States must assume the war-time debts and unpaid interest of the States because these were incurred in support of the common cause and, unfunded, were a costly drain on the resources of America. The terms of such a settlement were equitable and available. A reduction in the average, long-term interest rate of the domestic debt was justified and should be effected by giving creditors a choice of alternatives that included annuities and western lands at twenty cents an acre. Refunding should begin with the foreign and domestic Continental debt; determination of the state debts in a form to make assumption practicable would take time. Interest on the foreign debt at the convenanted rate, and on the domestic Continental debt at 4 per cent would call for $2,239,000 annually. The foreign "instalments" should be met by new loans abroad; interest on the domestic debt could be provided by higher impost duties on wines, spirits, tea and coffee, together with the existing tonnage tax on foreign shipping and an increased excise on spirits distilled in the United States. Twelve million dollars should be borrowed to refund foreign obligations and begin the purchase of American notes and certificates of debt as soon as the general plan was adopted. This was to be done to discourage speculation. Finally, from the assumed profits of the Post Office, a sinking fund was to be created.

This was a dazzling plan and the most impressive possible device to demonstrate to the American people the vitality and good faith of their new government. Washington approved but he foresaw a controversy over assumption of state debts. In deference to the lawmakers who had the right to accept, reject or amend Hamilton's proposal, he wrote nothing about it and did nothing to commend it to Congress. Members did not stint other legislation while exploring the tangled problems of Federal finance. Neither House looked with favor on the measure to organize the militia, but bills to enact most of Washington's recommendations were given the consideration they required.

Within his own "department," where authority had been vested by the Constitution or voted him by Congress, Washington did not hesitate to act. The residence on Cherry Street was not as commodious as Washington desired, nor was it as handsome as he thought the President's House should be. When he learned that the Macomb House on Broadway might be vacated by the French Chargé d'Affaires, he undertook its lease. Washington convenanted to pay $1000 a year in rent and bargained for some of the fittings at £665. By frequent personal visits and through the diligence of Lear, he rearranged the contents of the rooms, ordered additional stabling and instituted a hurried search for a needed green carpet. New serving plateaux were purchased; lighting arrangements were improved; efforts were made to procure a better cook; and as a final convenience two cows were purchased. Before some of the improvements were completed, Washington moved and on February 26 had his first levee there.

Washington sent to the Senate on February 9 nominations to fill posts that original nominees had declined. Organization of the Judiciary was completed when these were confirmed. No general act was presented for Washington's signature until February 8 and, after that, none till March 1. In New York the only condition to give new concern to Washington was the vehemence of the debate over Hamilton's plan and over Quaker memorials against the slave trade. At home the situation was different. From Virginia David Stuart reported: "A spirit of jealousy which may become dangerous to the Union towards the Eastern States seems to be growing fast among us. . . . Col. Lee tells me that many who were warm supporters of the government are changing their sentiments from a conviction of the impracticability of Union with States whose interests are so dissimilar from those of Virginia." This was a serious development, one to be discussed with a gentleman who, after much delay, had accepted office and on March 21, reported in New York for duty—Thomas Jefferson, Secretary of State.

Washington found Jefferson a wise and ready counsellor on foreign affairs and the diversified questions of public policy concerning which the President asked the opinion of the heads of Departments. The Secretary had useful information also, on the possibility of procuring the release of American seamen captured and enslaved by Barbary pirates. Jefferson disclosed a strong opinion concerning the rank at which American diplomatic representatives should be accredited to European courts. It would be better, he thought, to send Chargés of prestige rather than Ministers of comparative lower standing in that category. The only exception, in his judgment, should be at Versailles. Washington was not without hopes that an American Minister would be well received at the Court of St. James's, but he had particular reason at that time for getting all the advice he could: The House had under consideration a bill for "providing the means of intercourse between the United States and foreign nations": Was it the prerogative of the President or the right of Congress to say at what rank diplomatic agents should be accredited, and if they were to have position that called for a considerable establishment, how was it to be financed? Jefferson thought the President free to decide whether he would send an Ambassador, a Minister or a Chargé to a given post, provided the expenditures did not exceed the appropriation. To have this view accepted in all its parts and get money enough for the men needed at foreign capitals Washington had "to intimate"—the verb was his—that he planned to send to Britain, as well as to France, an agent with the rank of Minister. Even after this cautious intervention, the requisite funds were not made available until months after Jefferson's arrival.

The lawmakers were in a contentious mood. The reason was the bill "to protect the public credit," the first measure to carry out the recommendations in Hamilton's report. The House was almost evenly divided—a condition that Washington thought particularly regrettable where the issue was one of high importance. Cleavage was not sectional. Massachusetts' supporters of assumption were exceeded in vehemence of argument by Representatives of South Carolina. Over and over the appeal was: These debts of the States were contracted for a common cause; the States were merely the agents of Congress; debt was the price of liberty. Madison met this with a reminder that assumption did injustice to the States which had done their duty by their creditors and now were called on to contribute to those States that had not done like duty. Almost without exception, the magnitude of the debt of a given state was the gauge of its Representatives' zeal for assumption. Men jealous of the rights of their States warned that assumption would increase the popularity of the Federal government and would weaken the States. Daily, endlessly, the debate went on.

Washington listened as the arguments were repeated in the house on Broadway, but he faced now a new and perplexing problem. The State of Georgia was alleged to have sold to private land companies large tracts that lay beyond the line of territory reserved by treaty to the Choctaw and Chickasaw and part of the Cherokee tribes. This was done after Georgia had ratified the Constitution and thereby relinquished all right to deal with the Indians. If the savages were to be restrained from violence and depredation, their rights under existing treaties must be respected, to the extent, at least, that if lands were occupied, payment should be made and new treaties negotiated. Instead of coercion there should be an opportunity for Georgia to withdraw from her position and, meantime, to preserve the status quo. It might be well to send a representative to the Indians in order "to explain to them the views of government, and to watch with their aid the territory in question."

About this time the President found himself with a bad cold. The next day he was worse. Martha took charge of the sick-room, and, as Lear was absent on his honeymoon, Major Jackson assumed direction of the office and made arrangements for medical attendance. Besides Dr. Bard, he called in Drs. John Charlton and Charles McKnight, but their combined treatment did not halt the progress of a serious form of pneumonia. Alarm seized the household. By May 12 the General's condition was so critical that the physicians asked for the counsel of Dr. John Jones of Philadelphia. Major Jackson had an express dispatched immediately and exerted every effort to have the famous surgeon make the journey with secrecy, but within a few days it was known that Washington was dangerously ill and that his death was not improbable.

On May 15 the General seemed to be close to the end. Doctor McKnight said frankly that he had every reason to expect the death of his patient. Shortly after midday, Washington seemed to be at the last of his hurried and shallow respiration. Then, about four o'clock, he broke into a copious sweat and his circulation improved. Within two hours the change was definite: he had passed the crisis. On the sixteenth he was so much improved that members of the household began to hope he was out of danger. By the twentieth this was the general opinion. After that Washington was himself again. Washington's reflections were calmly simple: He had suffered two illnesses of increasing severity within a year, he said; the next doubtless would be the last. Meantime, physicians' orders to take more exercise and do less work were hard for even so well disciplined a man as he to obey. His comfort was the prospect of going to Mount Vernon for a vacation if Congress took a recess.

Members had not advanced their legislation satisfactorily during the month Washington had been ill and convalescing. Seven acts had been passed, none of first importance, but neither the bill to provide for the public credit nor the measure to establish the seat of government had received approval. On the contrary, the two had become entangled in a manner that excited the politician and made the citizen shake a puzzled head. When division of the House of Representatives had been tested, assumption of state debts had been rejected in Committee of the Whole by a majority of two. At first, after that defeat, the resentment of New Englanders and South Carolinians ran so high that they were suspected of planning to reject all funding at that session of Congress. They were too wise and too much interested to be guilty of any such blunder. They rallied their forces while the Virginians continued in unyielding opposition to every proposal that the debts of the States be assumed. To the surprise of some members of Congress, tempers suddenly cooled. Hamilton, Jefferson, Robert Morris and others took advantage of this and made common cause. The Secretary of the Treasury had resolute ambition to see his funding plan succeed, but he lacked a vote or two and he must find them. Jefferson saw no reason why he should not use his influence with members of Congress in what he considered good causes—such, for example, as seating the government on the Potomac. Morris was desperately anxious to have the government moved temporarily to Philadelphia, doubtless in the hope the choice might be *in perpetuo*. Out of these interests came agreement whereby the advocates of assumption of state debts were to effect conversion of a few doubters, in return for which Philadelphia was to be the seat of government until 1800. After that the capital was to be near Georgetown, on the Potomac. The bill "for establishing the temporary and permanent seat of the Government of the United States" was passed and presented to the President July 12. Those who favored New York as the capital and those who opposed assumption of state debts were furious.

The President signed the bill on July 16. For this action Washington received what was almost the first direct newspaper censure that had been leveled at him since he had taken office. It was mild, guarded intimation that Washington lacked gratitude to New York. Doubtless conversation of disappointed members of Congress was sharp, but there is no record of any rebuke from the floor, nor does any letter by Senator or Representative allege that Washington was party to the bargain. Washington had hoped the valley of the Potomac would be chosen as the site of the capital, but if any member's vote was affected by the President, it was because the individual wished to do what Washington desired and not because the General asked him to do it.

The bill to move the capital was followed in little more than a fortnight by the funding measure. In final form, the bill embodied Hamilton's foundation of a new foreign loan, payment of accrued interest, and assumption of state debts; but the superstructure was simpler than in his design. If the Secretary might claim to be the architect, he still owed thanks to the draughtsmen of Congress. Washington believed in the bill and signed it with a sense of relief that the dangerous issues involved in it had been settled.

The weeks during which Congress fought over debt settlement and the seat of government witnessed several developments that encouraged or puzzled the President in his convalescence. On May 29, Rhode Island ratified the Constitution. Maj. George Beckwith, aide to Lord Dorchester (formerly Sir Guy Carleton), Governor of Canada, sought out Hamilton on July 8 and, in traditional diplomatic indirection, hinted that Britain not only might settle differences with America but also might be willing to enter into an alliance. In event of war between England and Spain, Beckwith remarked, the United States would find it to their interest to uphold Britain. There was much besides, in the Major's conversation, but these were the points of strongest emphasis.

Hamilton reported this to Jefferson and went with the Secretary of

State to inform the President what had occurred. Washington was usually cautious in his conclusions and did not clinch them until he had deliberated and heard all that the best men around him had to say. This time his judgment was clear and quickly shaped: The British had determined not to give an answer to Gouverneur Morris in London until they ascertained by Beckwith's indirect approach whether the United States were willing to make common cause with them against Spain. If America did this, then the British would negotiate a commercial treaty and would "promise perhaps to fulfil what they already stand engaged to perform" under the treaty of 1783. The result of this and another diplomatic fencing bout between Hamilton and Beckwith was a decision by Washington to let it be impressed that the United States had no understanding with Spain and had not settled with that country the question of the navigation of the Mississippi. Beyond this, civility and reticence were the course of prudence on the part of a country that desired to remain neutral and at peace with all foreign powers.

Thus the matter stood until mid-August, when there was intimation that if England and Spain opened hostilities Lord Dorchester might wish to descend the Mississippi through the territory of the United States and attack Louisiana or its outposts. If Britain made a request for her troops to have unhindered passage, what should Washington do? He thought such application would be made by Dorchester and believed that no decisive answer should be given, but he sought the advice of Hamilton, Jefferson and Knox, and of the Vice President and the Chief Justice as well. The President found these counsellors divided. Diversity of counsel underscored the warning the President's judgment gave him: he would have an unhappy decision to make—one that would outrage the West or divide the East—if the British started southward. He could not tell, as yet, whether the two powers who together hemmed in his country would go to war—with the prospect that British victory would set King George's ramparts north, west and south while the Royal fleet ruled the Atlantic.

In the exchanges between Hamilton and Beckwith there had been polite intimation and horrified denial that Britain had been exciting northwestern tribes to violence and American frontier officers had been threatening British posts verbally. The fuel for a conflagration was scattered widely north of the Ohio. Although the Six Nations no longer were a firebrand, the Miami and Wabash tribes were attacking boats on the Ohio and Wabash and were crossing into Kentucky on raids of massacre and arson. Efforts to make peace had been futile. Washington, St. Clair and Knox were of one mind in belief that nothing short of a vigorous, punitive campaign would dispose of a danger that otherwise might stop all movement on the Ohio. Washington instructed St. Clair, as Governor of the Northwest Territory, to prepare the expedition and call out militia to reenforce a small contingent of regulars, who were to have some artillery with them. On July 15 troops, presumably about fifteen hundred, were assembling at Fort Washington on the Ohio. With good fortune and good leadership, they might strike a blow in the autumn that would clear the river and make the settlements secure. The commanding officer, Brevet Brig. Gen.

Josiah Harmar, had served with Pennsylvania troops during the Revolution, but was not well known to the President.

South of the Ohio, most of the Indians were thought to be well-disposed, though a handful of Cherokee and Shawanese bandits were proving troublesome. As for the Creeks, Knox, through a shrewd and patient agent, Col. Marinus Willett, at last had accomplished what had seemed impossible: Willett had prevailed on Alexander McGillivray, the Creeks' half-breed Chief, to come to New York with twenty-nine head men. On their arrival Knox supervised negotiation of a pact by which the Creeks yielded to Georgia disputed lands on the Oconee but refused to give up their hunting-grounds southwest of the junction of that river and the Ocmulgee. Washington shared in some of the entertainment of the Indians; and gave his approval to the various measures Knox desired at the hands of Congress. He wrote Lafayette that except for the crimes of a few bandits, the treaty "will leave us in peace from one end of our borders to the other."

The adjournment of Congress on August 12 left Washington free to execute a plan he must have fashioned from the time he received news that Rhode Island had ratified the Constitution. He had not entered that State during his tour of New England. Now he would go there, meet the leaders, see the people and make it plain that he no longer kept in his heart resentments petty spokesmen of the State had aroused. The journey, begun on August 15 with Jefferson, Clinton and other notables, was the easiest Washington had made in years. The most noteworthy occurrences of the brief visit were Washington's answers to three of the addresses delivered him. Instead of perfunctory, polite avowals, he made thoughtful statements, half philosophical and admirably phrased. He told the representatives of the Jewish Congregation of Newport:

It is now no more that tolerance is spoken of, as if it was by the indulgence of one class of people, that another enjoyed the exercise of their inherent natural rights. For happily the government of the United States, which gives to bigotry no sanction, to persecution no assistance, requires only that they who live under its protection should demean themselves as good citizens, in giving it on all occasions their effectual support. . . .

Washington left Providence August 19, reached New York on the twenty-first, and took up his part of another task: the transfer of the seat of government to Philadelphia. The President took it upon himself to supervise the moving of those contents of his residence that were not too bulky or too much a part of the house to be taken down; the labor was one that Washington performed zestfully. Rehabilitation, literal or metaphorical, made a peculiar appeal to him. Details were left to Lear, who had the rare and needful combination of diligence and patience. Lear's service was more difficult and more nearly indispensable because of reorganization of the office staff. Humphreys was going to Spain and thence to Portugal on diplomatic assignment; Lewis was returning to Virginia to act as steward while George Augustine Washington went "to the mountains" in hopes of physical recovery; Nelson went, also, to Virginia on a vacation. The President consequently was left with two secretaries only, Lear and Jackson.

By August 30 all matters were arranged; amenities of departure observed, and accounts settled. On the twenty-eighth the Governor of New York, the Mayor of the city and the Aldermen had been the President's guests at dinner. In spite of his request for an unceremonious leave-taking, the Governor, the Chief Justice of the United States, the heads of Federal departments and the executive officers, state and municipal, came to his house on the thirtieth and escorted him with the utmost good will to the wharf. Although New York was losing the "seat of government" and the prestige accompanying that honor, the last minutes were impressive: "All was quietness," reported the New York *Daily Advertiser*, "save the report of the cannon that was fired on his embarkation . . . the heart was full— the tear dropped from the eye; it was not to be restrained; it was seen; and the President appeared sensibly moved by this last mark of esteem. . . ."

Lear had requested that there be "no more parade on [the President's] journey than what may be absolutely necessary to gratify the people." All went quietly until, in the afternoon of September 2, Washington reached the vicinity of Philadelphia. There he was met by a troop of light horse, militia companies and numerous citizens. Bells were rung, a *feu de joie* was tendered—everything was as if the President were visiting the city for the first time. Dinners and other ceremonies were offered, but at least some of them would have been declined with the excuse of a hurried journey had not Martha fallen sick. As it was, the President enjoyed various affairs and found time to satisfy himself concerning arrangements for a residence. The municipal corporation of Philadelphia had rented for him the home of Robert Morris, probably the handsomest dwelling in the city. Washington wrote Lear: "It is, I believe, the best *single House* in the City; yet, without additions it is inadequate to the *commodious* accommodation of my family"; and went on to describe the changes he thought necessary and the servants he would require. Then, on the sixth, Washington left for Mount Vernon. No accident worse than a harmless overturn of the chariot and the wagon delayed the remainder of the journey, and the entourage reached Mount Vernon on September 11.

Return to Mount Vernon raised the spirits of Washington and contributed to full restoration of his health. He did not have any particular problem on the plantation other than his usual need of ready cash. Correspondence did not take any large part of his time. He was able to make a leisured examination of what was being done in the improvement of the Potomac by the company he had organized and headed. Little public business was submitted for his review, though Hamilton did pass on a rumor that Spain had admitted the right of the United States to the free use of the Mississippi.

The one official concern was over absence of any report from General Harmar, who by this time was supposed to have marched against the Miami Indians. Doubt of success rose in Washington's mind when he learned St. Clair had notified the British at Detroit of Harmar's expedition and assured them the United States forces were not marching against that post. The British, in Washington's opinion, might pass this information to the Indians whom Harmar was to punish. When Washington heard later that Harmar was believed to be a heavy drinker, the President virtually abandoned hope of any substantial achievement by the American column. Knox could say nothing to reassure his Chief.

Leisure and interest prompted Washington to spend hours in planning how the Morris house in Philadelphia was to be enlarged and furnished as the official residence of the Chief Executive. No less than nine letters to Lear were devoted to the move to the Quaker City and the adornment of the dwelling. The only important point in all the long letters was insistence by the President that the house be leased by him in regular form and not accepted with the rent paid by any public body in Pennsylvania.

Washington and his party reached Philadelphia again the morning of November 27 and went at once to the Morris house. Lear had made it habitable even though the remodeling was not complete. The condition of public affairs was good and bad—good in the general prosperity and content of the people, bad in the absence of news from Harmar and in the continued hammering of Anti-Federalist newspapers, the *New-York Journal* in particular. These failed to raise a clamor or defeat any considerable number of members of Congress who stood for reelection that autumn. Washington proceeded to prepare for the coming session of Congress. On December 8 he drove to the Hall of Congress and in the Senate Chamber made his brief address, which he devoted principally to finance and Indian affairs. He had favorable credit standing to report and the recommendation that the Federal debt be reduced "as far and as fast as the growing resources of the country will permit. . . ." As for Indian depredations, it probably was fortunate that the flavor of an auspicious opening was not soured by knowledge of the failure of Harmar's expedition. At the moment, Washington could say only "the event of the measure is yet unknown to me." The President gave a paragraph to the situation in Europe and the probable curtailment of available shipping for American exports. A more cheerful statement dealt with the admission of Kentucky to the Union. The remainder of the address was devoted, briefly, to mint and militia, weights and measures, the post office and the post roads.

Knox's report on Indian affairs, submitted on the ninth, disclosed abundant reason for Harmar's expedition, but gave no account of what had befallen Harmar and his men. When the official report at length was received, it was found to be a complacent review of operations represented as successful, though actually they were a bloody failure in the defeat of two detachments and the loss of 180 men. Washington's candor in keeping Congress informed and the apparent adequacy of Knox's preparations saved the President from criticism.

Hamilton took the centre of the stage a week after the session opened and submitted two reports that forthwith made every member of Congress his advocate or his critic, to the exclusion of almost every other subject of legislative debate. Both papers were in obedience to a resolution by the House of Representatives at the previous session for a report on any further action necessary for establishing the public credit. Hamilton divided his answer into two parts, one a series of suggestions for new and higher excises, the other a plan for the establishment of a central bank. A proposal for heavier taxes on imported spirits was coupled with one for excises on liquors distilled in the United States. Estimated net revenue would be $877,500. As Hamilton designed the bank, which he frankly styled "national," it was to have a capital stock not exceeding $10,000,000, of which the President was to subscribe $2,000,000 on account of the United States. The bank was to establish branches throughout the country at its discretion and have an exclusive Federal charter; its notes and bills, if payable on demand in gold and silver coin, were to be receivable in all settlements with the United States. Details were well considered, the Bank of England serving as a model, but no provision had interest comparable to that of the exciting question: Did Congress have the power to charter any bank?

While legislators debated this issue in the taverns and in the boarding houses, before they so much as raised it on the floor, Washington labored over a small but a singularly perplexing series of tangles and wrangles. The reassurance of friendly Indians was particularly difficult when plans for new operations against the Miami scarcely were concealed. Preliminaries had to be arranged for laying off the Federal District as the permanent seat of government. Washington had to decide what further instructions should be given Gouverneur Morris, whose unofficial inquiries in England had brought to light no inclination on Britain's part to execute the provisions of the treaty of peace or open friendly commercial relations on a basis of equality. The President's conclusion was against further effort, for the time being, to press for any accord. A considerable volume of other legislation, including measures for the admission of Kentucky and Vermont to the Union, occupied Congress more than it involved the President. The sole recommendation of Washington's that met with virtual denial was for the uniform organization of the militia. This was debated in the House and killed by postponement.

Although little of this legislation aroused heat, no essential part of the bill for the excise on spirits and scarcely a clause of the measure for the establishment of the national bank failed to stir the coals of controversy. Washington felt that South and East were arrayed unpleasantly against each other—the Southern delegations in opposition and the New Englanders for the two measures—but it seemed to him that the debates were conducted with "temper and candor." The bank bill originated in the Senate; the excises, of course, were for the House to initiate. The Senate passed the bank bill January 20, 1791, and the House the excise legislation a week later. Then the two chambers exchanged bills. The Representatives made short work of the measure to establish the bank and on February 8 accepted it.

Washington had to decide for himself the constitutional question that had divided both chambers: Should he sign or disapprove the bill to charter the Bank of the United States? The Attorney General was asked for his opinion, which was adverse. Next, Jefferson's observations were sought;

they were forthcoming with convinced precision. The bill, he said, was unconstitutional, because Congress was not vested with specific authority to create such a corporation and under one of the amendments then in process of adoption, "the powers not delegated to the United States by the Constitution, nor prohibited by it to the States are reserved to the States respectively, or to the people." Jefferson's arguments were set forth succinctly and without a doubt concerning the absolute correctness of interpretation; but at the end was this candid counsel: ". . . if the pro and the con hang so even as to balance [the President's] judgment, a just respect for the wisdom of the Legislature would naturally decide the balance in favor of their opinion. It is chiefly for cases where they are clearly misled by error, ambition, or interest, that the Constitution has placed a check in the negative of the President."

Washington gave Hamilton "an opportunity of examining and answering the objections" and asked Madison to draft a proper form for returning the bill to Congress in event the decision was to refuse approval. Madison responded with a document conveniently phrased for returning the bill either on the ground of unconstitutionality or on that of a lack of merit in the measure. The argument advanced by Madison against constitutionality was condensed into a single sentence: "I object to the bill," Madison would have the President say, "because it is an essential principle of the government that powers not delegated by the Constitution cannot be rightfully exercised; because the power proposed by the bill to be exercised is not delegated; and because I cannot satisfy myself that it results from any expressed power by fair and safe rules of implication." Hamilton's answer was a complete review and attempted refutation of substantially everything Jefferson and Randolph had said. Hamilton's basic argument was:

. . . it appears to the Secretary of the Treasury that this general principle is inherent in the very definition of government, and essential to every step of the progress to be made by that of the United States, namely: That every power vested in a government is in its nature sovereign, and includes, by force of the term, a right to employ all the means requisite and fairly applicable to the attainment of the ends of such power, and which are not precluded by restrictions and exceptions specified in the Constitution, or not immoral, or not contrary to the essential ends of political society.

Thus were Washington's closest counsellors divided, to his distress and embarrassment, over the width and reach of the foundations on which the structure of government was to rise. From the beginning of the effort to give America a new Constitution, his controlling principle had been the simplest: the United States must have a strong central government if they were to keep their freedom. Because his reasoning and conviction were altogether on the side Hamilton championed, he signed the bill on February 25. The excise measure came to his desk March 1, and, as it involved no constitutional issue, it received his signature the next day.

Troubled as the government at Paris was in its desperate struggle at home, the only other large question of controversy on the floor of Congress was a French protest against the tax on tonnage of ships entering the United States. Washington asked Jefferson to report on this and the Secretary, friend though he was of France, found her contention invalid for reasons he set forth at length. He admitted that policy might dictate concession but outlined explicitly the basis of what might be said in rejecting the protest. The Senate decided to maintain the interpretation of the Secretary. When Congress at length adjourned on March 3, Washington felt that besides passing the great contested measures, the two houses "had finished much other business of less importance, conducting on all occasions with great harmony and cordiality." The majority probably agreed with Washington and shared Abigail Adams' belief: "Our public affairs never looked more prosperous." The First Congress had passed out of existence; a time of reckoning had come.

Washington was pleased not only with the achievements of the Congress but also with his success in learning his new duties. He wrote Lafayette that the American public had accepted Federal laws, which had been moderate and wise. "The administration of them," said he, "aided by the affectionate partiality of my countrymen, is attended with no unnecessary inconvenience. . . ." He owed this lack of difficulty to the same conditions that had aided him in 1789—his own cautious, sound judgment, the absence of crisis, the consideration of legislators, the undiminished esteem in which Americans held him, and the success of his dealings with Congress and with the men he had chosen as heads of the departments. Hamilton and Jefferson were Washington's closest advisers by this time and were the executive lieutenants most esteemed by Congress. Inside Congress Madison was less frequently consulted during the winter of 1790–91, not because of any cooling of affection but because he was engrossed in his labors as a legislator. Washington's unofficial communications with Congress—and some of his regular reports—were through the heads of departments. Always the approach was as deferential as when the Commander-in-Chief had been in the field during the war; in his new position he lost none of his consideration for the pride and prerogative of lawmakers. His dealings with governors, state legislatures and officials in general conformed to the same criterion, but he insisted that this golden rule of administration be followed by others as well as by himself, and he resented any encroachment by the States on the domain of the Federal government.

Within the executive precinct of the Federal government, heads of Departments exercised initiative and freedom of thought. They were at liberty to express their own views in papers they laid before Congress at his direction as well as in reports prepared on order of Congress and transmitted directly to that body. Nor was there the least complaint on the part of Washington when any document he sent to Congress was referred to one of his subordinates for study and independent report. In foreign affairs Washington had no unvarying policy of administration. He might conduct direct correspondence for a time with American representatives abroad and later might request the Secretary to act; or he might take over from Jefferson; or, still again, both he and his lieutenant might write a Minister or Chargé within the same week. On occasion, too, the President would content himself with making suggestions to the Secretary of State. Washington employed the heads of departments substantially as he had used the members of his military family during the war. Each man was consulted if and when the President desired that individual's judgment on a given issue, whether or not it was in the department for which that person was directly responsible. This had been accepted without misunderstanding and sometimes had been regarded as a convenience.

Differences over the banking bill soured amity between Jefferson and Hamilton. The opinions they had given Washington on the constitutionality of that measure had been those of men with different philosophies of government and not merely with contrary views of the implied powers of Congress. Rivalry between the two was becoming so apparent that Washington could not be unaware of it, but he chose to ignore it, and he took pains to avoid any treatment of one or the other that might seem preferential or partial.

Philadelphia most certainly was pleased with him and was able to demonstrate often during the winter its old affection for him and its pride in being the seat of his administration. He and Martha held their levees as usual. Shining affairs were the First Lady's Christmas Eve entertainment, the New Year's Day reception, and the ceremonious observance of the President's birthday February 22. Formalities were as strictly followed as ever. Washington carefully walked the line he had set for himself and respected all the amenities, but he was beginning to tire of the pomp of public appearance and was not insensitive to criticism of monarchical practices.

The President had had a series of personal and family chores to discharge during this season in Philadelphia, some so tedious and vexatious that they would have overtaxed his patience if they had not included two gratifying events. One was the birth in the President's own house of a boy to Tobias and Mary Lear, who were residing there on the hearty invitation of the General and Mrs. Washington. This young gentleman was christened Benjamin Lincoln Lear, with Washington as godfather. The other occurrence was an offer by John Joseph de Barth to purchase at a fair figure all of Washington's lands on the Ohio and the Kanawha, an offer gladly accepted.

Washington long had been making plans for a tour of the Southern States and as quickly as he could he disposed of the business that had to be transacted if the wheels of government were to revolve smoothly during an absence of three months, part of which would be in remote areas of the country. Then, on March 21, with Major Jackson, much equipment and a cumbersome entourage of five persons, he set out for the Potomac on what he regarded as the first stage of the Southern journey.

The duties Washington now had to perform were exceedingly interesting to an old surveyor. Under the law he had signed July 16, 1790, "for establishing the temporary and permanent seat of the government of the United States," he was required to appoint three commissioners and direct their survey of the district where the Federal City was to rise. The President was to decide how much land was to be acquired on the Maryland side of the river for public use. This land was then to be purchased or accepted as a gift, and on it, "according to such plans as the President shall approve," the commissioners were to provide "suitable buildings." Washington had named two citizens of Maryland—Thomas Johnson, an able former Governor, and Senator Daniel Carroll of Rock Creek. The third commissioner was David Stuart, whose wife was Jack Custis's widow. Maj. Andrew Ellicott, an experienced surveyor, had been sent to the Potomac in February to take a general view of the area and suggest "lines of experiment" for determining the exact "seat of government." Ellicott had been followed by Maj. Pierre Charles L'Enfant, who was to make detailed surveys with an eye to the location of public buildings. These appointments had been made at a time of intense excitement on the part of landowners. Almost every man who held title to an acre in the vicinity was dreaming of fortunes to be made when farms of undistinguished fertility became, overnight, priceless lots in the centre of a city.

In such a situation, George Washington, veteran in land buying, could be a wise, even shrewd, guide for the cautious President of the United States. He maintained tight-lipped secrecy concerning final bounds of the district and reserved as much latitude of purchase as possible. If one group of property owners demanded an exorbitant price, he could make a show, at least, of looking elsewhere. Washington created as much of an air of buyer's independence as he could. After he reached the area and examined the various tracts, he called the landholders together on March 29 and explained that Georgetown and Carrollsburg might defeat their own ends by rivalry or excessive prices for property desired by the Federal government. The case was not one of competition but of cooperation. Together, the towns did not cover more ground than would be required for the city. The wisdom of this counsel was for the moment irresistible. Next day Washington was informed that all the principal owners would accept the terms he proposed. A total of between three and five thousand acres was to be ceded to the United States, with these provisos: the whole was to be included in the Federal City and laid off in lots; alternate lots were to remain the property of the former proprietors, who were to donate ground for streets and alleys; for the land taken by the government, twenty-five dollars an acre was to be paid. Much pleased with this, Washington gave instructions for making the survey and for other action necessary to execute the agreement.

For his long journey through the South, a region of notoriously bad, sandy roads, Washington had prepared carefully a list of distances and contingencies; and he fixed precisely the number of days he was to spend in each of the principal towns he planned to visit. The whole arrangement he termed his "line of march," which he was to follow with no other companions than Major Jackson and the servants. Had he been superstitious he would have doubted at the very outset the wisdom of his venture, because in crossing the Occoquan, on April 7, the day of his start south, one of the animals harnessed to his new, light chariot fell into the stream, fully harnessed, and so excited the others that all went overboard. Quick work prevented loss.

At Fredericksburg, where he spent two nights and a day, he had a second disquieting experience: John Lewis, the only surviving son of Fielding Lewis by his first marriage, told of a recent interview with Patrick Henry, who made no secret of his financial interest in the so-called Yazoo Company. When Lewis had inquired how the company expected to deal with the Indians, Henry had said that an appeal would be made to Congress for protection. If this was denied, the Yazoo proprietors would organize their own force under Brig. Gen. Charles Scott. That was an ugly threat, if it was not mere gasconade. "Schemes of that sort," Washington reflected a little later, "must involve the country in trouble—perhaps in blood."

A third unpleasantness awaited Washington in Richmond, where he received ceremonious welcome April 11, and, along with salute and salutation, mail from Philadelphia. Included was a letter in which Lear remarked that Attorney General Randolph was in danger of losing slaves brought from Virginia because of a Pennsylvania law which provided that adult bondsmen would be free six months after their owner, moving into the State, became a citizen. Washington thought the difference between his situation and that of Randolph gave reasonable assurance that the law did not apply to him. In order to appear in Pennsylvania courts, Randolph had become temporarily a citizen of Pennsylvania; Washington had not. At the same time, the President felt that someone might "entice" his servants and that the Negroes might become "insolent" if they thought themselves entitled to their freedom. His old regard for his property asserted itself in the letter he wrote Lear:

As all [the slaves of the Presidential establishment] except Hercules and Paris are dower negroes, it behooves me to prevent the emancipation of them, otherwise I shall not only lose the use of them but may have them to pay for. If upon taking good advice, it is found expedient to send them back to Virginia, I wish to have it accomplished under pretext that may deceive both them and the public; and none, I think, would so effectually do this as Mrs. Washington coming to Virginia next month. . . . This would naturally bring her maid and Austin, and Hercules under the idea of coming home to cook whilst we remained there, might be sent on in the stage. Whether there is occasion for this or not, according to the result of your inquiries or issue the thing as it may, I request that these sentiments and this advice may be known to none but yourself and Mrs. Washington.

Slavery, in his eyes, was a wasteful nuisance, but so long as it existed in a country where the sentiment of honest men was divided over it, he would safeguard his rights with the least public offence.

Ceremonies in Richmond followed a familiar pattern and did not over-crowd the two days and a half that he gave to the capital of his native state. With Gov. Beverley Randolph and the directors he examined the canal the James River Navigation Company was constructing around the falls and had opportunity of talking with Col. Edward Carrington, his appointee as Marshal of the District of Virginia. The Colonel thought the people well disposed to the Federal government and ready to approve action properly explained to them. Washington heard this with much satisfaction. One of the reasons for making the tour was his wish to ascertain at first hand what the people thought of the government.

From Richmond the President drove to Petersburg on the morning of the fourteenth and there received all the honors the town could bestow. He had been warned that the next stages of his journey would be "dreary" and was not unprepared for the full, flat pinelands through which he had to pass, mile on mile. Although he soon came into a region new to him, he found little of interest except the river valleys and the possible improvement of navigation. With stops at Halifax, Virginia, and Tarboro, North Carolina, Washington proceeded to Newbern, where he had what he described as "exceedingly good lodgings." The welcome fitted the quarters, but the next stretch of the journey, the long one to Wilmington, was almost bad enough to efface the pleasant memories of the hospitable town at the confluence of the Neuse and Trent Rivers.

Wilmington was hospitable and interesting. Washington looked upstream, too, and speculated on the possibility of extending transportation as far inland as Fayetteville, which was described to him as already a "thriving place" with large markets for tobacco and flax seed. From Wilmington the road traversed more stretches of "sand and pine barrens," though he was told of better farms and a population less sparse back from the traveled route. For part of the way to Georgetown, there were no inns, but, while this compelled Washington to violate his self-imposed rule against the acceptance of private hospitality, the absence of public houses added to the comfort of his travel.

On April 29 Washington had his first contact with the rich society of South Carolina. This was at Clifton House, the seat of William Alston. Alston had the reputation of being "one of the neatest rice planters in the State of South Carolina and a proprietor of the most valuable ground for the culture of this article." Washington looked at the plantation with eyes that were keenly appreciative of trees and thriving crops. At Clifton House were Gen. William Moultrie, Col. William Washington and Edward Rutledge, who had come out to escort their State's guest to Georgetown and thence to Charleston. All three were interesting men. Besides his kinship with the President, William Washington had the fine reputation he had acquired in the main Continental Army and the fame he had won in the Southern Department. Moultrie was an officer of shining reputation, valiantly won. Edward Rutledge was the brother of the Chief Justice of the State, John Rutledge. These gentlemen brought the written greetings of Gov. Charles Cotesworth Pinckney and invitations from him.

In Georgetown, on the thirtieth, he attended a public dinner and during the afternoon bowed at a tea party to "upwards of fifty ladies." He interested himself in Georgetown and its waterways, but he felt that the town was overshadowed by Charleston, where he had decided to spend a week. May 1 was given to travel to Gabriel Manigault's plantation, where Washington spent the night. The next morning began an extraordinary week. The ceremonial crossing from Haddrel's Point to Charleston harbor was spectacular. A twelve-oared barge was rowed by American sea captains; two boats conveyed musicians; almost all light craft in the vicinity of

MAP / 16

WASHINGTON'S SOUTHERN TOUR, 1791

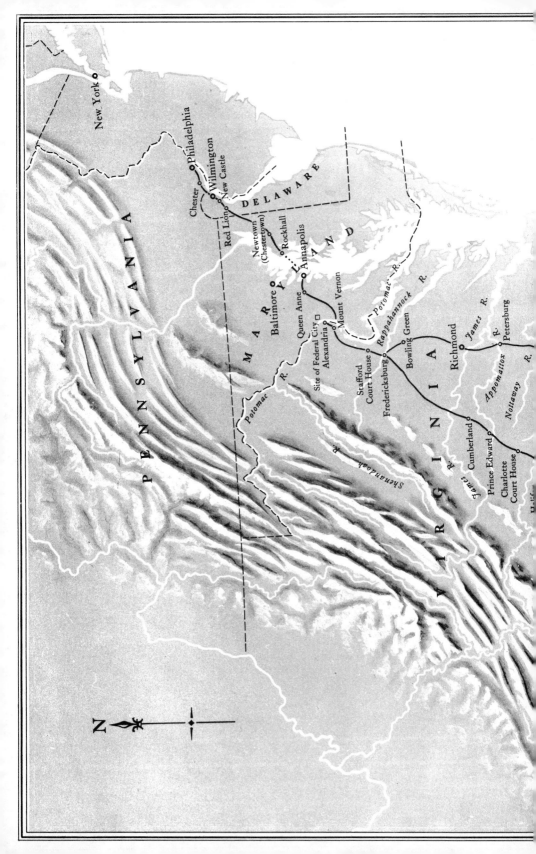

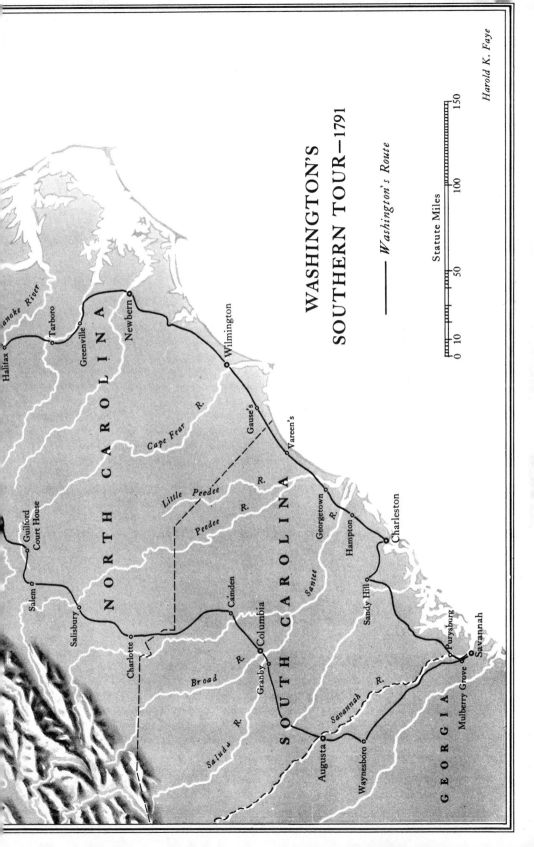

WASHINGTON'S
SOUTHERN TOUR—1791

—— *Washington's Route*

Statute Miles

0 10   50   100   150

Harold K. Faye

POLITICAL LIFE

27. Washington's Welcome at Trenton Bridge, 1789. Engraving by T. Kelley. From Washington Irving's *Life of George Washington*, vol. IV.

28. Edmund Randolph. A Copy by F. J. Fisher of the Painting by Gilbert Stuart in the State Capitol, Richmond, Virginia. *Commonwealth of Virginia. Photograph by Dementi Studio.*

29. John Jay. Portrait by Joseph Wright. *Courtesy of The New-York Historical Society.*

30. Alexander Hamilton. Painting by John Trumbull. *By Permission of the National Gallery of Art, Washington, D.C. Andrew Mellon Collection.*

31. John Adams. Painting by Charles Willson Peale. *Independence National Historical Park Collection.*

32. John Marshall. *By Permission of Mrs. Benjamin T. Woodruff of Charleston, West Virginia. Photograph by Dementi Studio.*

33. Tobias Lear. Pastel by James Sharples. *Collection of Anna Decatur Wright. Photograph Courtesy of the Frick Art Reference Library.*

34. Thomas Jefferson. Painting by Charles Willson Peale. *Independence National Historical Park Collection.*

35.   James Madison. Painting by Gilbert Stuart. *Courtesy of the Bowdoin College Museum of Art, Brunswick, Maine.*

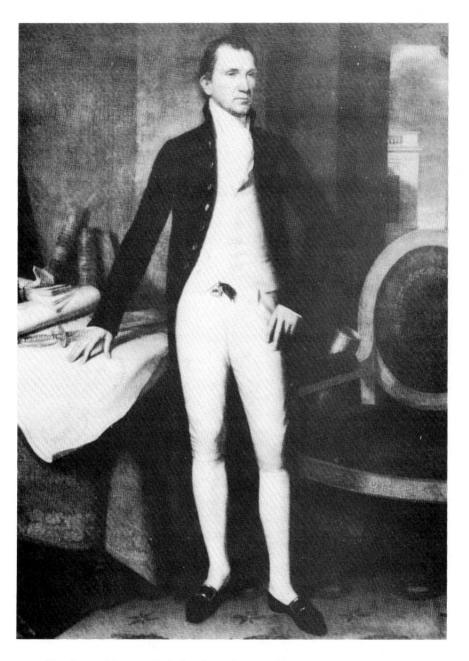

36. James Monroe. Painting by John Vanderlyn. *Courtesy of the Art
Commission of the City of New York.*

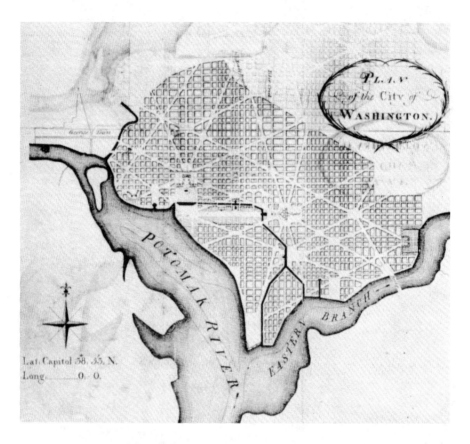

37. Major Pierre L'Enfant's Plan for a "Federal City," as Reproduced in the *Columbian Magazine* for March, 1792. *The Papers of George Washington, Library of Congress.*

Charleston attended the President; on approaching Prioleau's Wharf, Washington received a hearty artillery salute. After a formal landing and welcome, he was driven to the Exchange to see the procession pass and, when the last contingent had saluted him, he went to the residence of Judge Thomas Heyward, which had been leased and adorned for his occupancy.

Not even his "triumphant progress" from Mount Vernon to New York in 1789 equalled the entertainment that began the hour he arrived in the Carolina city. He held three receptions, attended two breakfasts, ate seven sumptuous formal dinners, listened and replied to four addresses, was the central figure at two assemblies and a concert, rode through the city, went twice to church, observed and praised a display of fireworks and drank sixty toasts. At the assembly on the evening of May 4, "the ladies," according to the *City Gazette,* "were all superbly dressed and most of them wore ribbons with different inscriptions expressive of their esteem and respect for the President such as: 'long live the President,' etc." Two evenings later, at the ball given by Governor Pinckney in Washington's honor, the homage of his feminine admirers was in their hairdress. Nearly all the coiffures included a bandeau or fillet on which was painted a sketch of Washington's head or some patriotic, sentimental reference to him.

A different attraction of the city was the line of its defence in the campaign of 1780. With deepest interest, the old Commander-in-Chief went over the ground in the company of General Moultrie and other veterans who knew every foot of it, and he concluded that the defence had been altogether honorable. Other visits of military interest were to Fort Moultrie on Sullivan's Island and Fort Johnson on James's Island. Although little remained of these earthworks, Washington had the privilege of hearing the repulse of the British fleet on June 28, 1776, described by General Moultrie, who not only was responsible for it but was able to recount it with the skill of a practiced raconteur.

En route to Savannah May 9/11 the President violated his rule against the acceptance of lodging at private homes; but he explained this carefully in his diary: He spent one night at Col. William Washington's plantation, Sandy Hill, from "motives of friendship and relationship," and he stayed at O'Brien Smith's on the tenth and Thomas Heyward's on the eleventh because there were "no public houses on the road." The next day carried him to the Savannah River at Purysburg, where notables of the fine city downstream were awaiting him with boats for the vehicles and luggage and an eight-oared barge for Washington and the committee. On the way, the President went ashore at Mulberry Grove for a brief visit to the widow of Nathanael Greene. Adversity had overtaken this brilliant woman who had enlivened many a black night in wartime winter quarters. In the brief time Washington had for this first call on her in her southern home, he could not discuss her business affairs, nor would he have talked of them, probably, had his stay been longer, because it was likely he might be called upon, as President, to sign or disapprove legislation for her relief.

With wind and tide against the bedizened sea captains at the oars, it was 6 P.M. on May 12 when the President reached Savannah, but the townsfolk still were awaiting him. The next two and a half days were crowded with ceremonial, and he visited the scene of the attempt the Comte d'Estaing and General Lincoln made in September-October 1779 to wrest Savannah from the British garrison.

From Savannah Washington returned by road to Mulberry Grove, dined with Mrs. Greene, and went on to a tavern where he lodged. Thence he rode to Augusta, which he reached May 18. Two days and a half were spent in the enjoyment of the town's hospitality. Next after Washington left Augusta May 21 was a halt of a day and a half at Columbia, South Carolina, and, unexpectedly, of a second day there because of the bad condition of a horse. Except for a welcoming escort and a public dinner at the unfinished State House, the visit to Columbia was without incident. The miles stretched out northward. An overnight halt and a public dinner at Camden on the twenty-fifth were followed by a careful examination of the ground of the action between Greene and Lord Rawdon April 25, 1781. Farther on Washington viewed the scene of the rout of Gates by Cornwallis August 16, 1780, and later wrote down his conclusion, with generosity towards the American comrade he had distrusted for years:

As this was a night meeting of both armies on their march and altogether unexpected, each formed on the ground they met without any advantage in it on either side, it being level and open. Had General Gates been half a mile farther advanced, an impenetrable swamp would have prevented the attack which was made on him by the British army, and afforded him time to have formed his own plans; but having no information of Lord Cornwallis's designs and perhaps not being apprized of this advantage it was not seized by him.

After Camden, Washington found nothing of importance on the road to Charlotte, North Carolina. Charlotte itself was disappointing but the approaches to it were through better farm lands than Washington had seen in days, and the district between Charlotte and Salisbury seemed to him "very fine."

The last day of May brought a journey to Salem, a little Moravian town that gave Washington a welcome thus charmingly described in the diary of the community:

At the end of this month the congregation of Salem had the pleasure of welcoming the President of the United States, on his return journey from the Southern States. We had already heard that he would return to Virginia by way of our town. This afternoon we heard that this morning he left Salisbury, thirty-five miles from here, so the brethren Marshall, Koehler and Benzien rode out a bit to meet him, and as he approached the town several melodies were played, partly by trumpets and French horns, partly by trombones. He was accompanied only by his Secretary, Major Jackson, and the necessary servants. On alighting from the carriage he greeted the bystanders in friendly fashion, and was particularly pleasant to the children gathered there. Then he conversed on various subjects with the brethren who conducted him to the room prepared for him. At first he said that he must go on the next morning, but when he learned that the Governor of our State would like to meet him here the following day he said he would rest here one day. He told our musicians that he would enjoy some music with his evening meal, and was served with it.

When Gov. Alexander Martin arrived, Washington talked with him about the attitude of the people to the new government. Martin confirmed for his own State all that Colonel Carrington had said of public sentiment in Virginia: opposition and discontent were subsiding fast.

In the company of the suave, conciliatory Governor, Washington rode on June 2 to Guilford, where he examined the ground of the engagement of March 15, 1781, between Greene and Cornwallis and concluded that "had the troops done their duty properly, the British must have been sorely galled in their advance, if not defeated." The day after surveying the scene of a tactical defeat that became a strategical victory, Washington bade farewell to Martin and started on the final stage of his journey, a stage broken by no ceremonial of any sort.

From Guilford the President rode to Dan River, and on to Col. Isaac Coles's plantation on Staunton River, whence in a single day he proceeded to Prince Edward Court House. By the afternoon of the tenth he was at Kenmore, his sister's home in Fredericksburg, and on June 12 he ate dinner at his own table in satisfaction over the accuracy of his timing and the sturdiness of his team. He wrote with enthusiasm of the journey:

. . . it has enabled me to see with my own eyes the situation of the country through which we traveled, and to learn more accurately the disposition of the people than I could have done by any information. The country appears to be in a very improving state, and industry and frugality are becoming much more fashionable than they have hitherto been there. Tranquility reigns among the people, with that disposition towards the general government which is likely to preserve it. They begin to feel the good effects of equal laws and equal protection. The farmer finds a ready market for his produce, and the merchant calculates with more certainty on his payments.

The journey had shown that the President was as popular in the Southern States as he was in Federalist New England. On the tour he received at least twenty-three addresses, in answering which both he and Major Jackson well might have spent their stock of friendly phrases. Particularly noticeable were the addresses from Lodges of Free Masons. This probably had no significance other than as it disclosed the strength of the Masons in the South and their pride in Washington as a brother. His answers, in turn, were in good Masonic terms, with no casualness in his references to his membership in the Order. Washington himself perhaps was unaware of it, but he was becoming increasingly fond of the homage paid him at assemblies and wherever he made his bow to ladies. Mounted escorts that deepened mud or raised dust were a nuisance, but ladies, handsome, well-dressed ladies who paid him the honor of calling on him . . . well, the Presidency was not altogether without its compensations.

Washington had transacted little public business on his tour, and he found a heavy accumulation of papers at Mount Vernon. He encountered, besides, a multitude of plantation duties, sadly increased by the progressive illness of George Augustine. Some problems of domestic management at the house in Philadelphia were posed also, in reports from that city.

A drought had ruined the hay crop and now threatened the oats;

but Washington faced his labors with his usual, well-ordered self-discipline and made the most of the fortnight at home before he started for Philadelphia on June 27 by an unfamiliar route. First he went to Georgetown and there had the pleasure of announcing where the public buildings would be located, though, by this time the President was beginning to divest himself of responsibility for the proposed seat of government and passing on the details to Jefferson. Then he proceeded, via Frederick, Maryland, to York and Lancaster, Pennsylvania, two towns he never had visited.

The week following Washington's return to Philadelphia on July 6 brought a minor illness and a move by Pennsylvania politicians to construct a new house for the President—an involvement he avoided with some difficulty. These were mere annoyances, though, compared with ominous increase of tension among European countries. The three powers that appeared to be on the verge of renewed conflict happened to be those whose holdings in the northern hemisphere were adjacent to the United States and constituted either a market or a threat or both. England still was in possession of northwestern posts and was suspected of inspiring Indian raids. Spain's hold on the Mississippi and her occupation of New Orleans and Florida gave her a position as formidable as that of the British in Canada. France was in convulsion at home and was facing a frightful slave insurrection in Santo Domingo, her richest West Indian possession.

War among these powers might be ruinous to American foreign trade. Even the possibility of a coalition between Britain and Spain, with France as their common adversary, would expose all three of the land frontiers of the United States to danger at the same time that it might involve a call by France for America to fulfill the military alliance of 1778. These were contingencies Washington faced without self-deception and with little or no prejudice. Towards them he applied certain clear principles. Efforts must be made to effect peace with the Indians by formal treaties that acknowledged the natives' territorial rights and assured American recognition of them, and Indians who chose war instead of peace were to be punished with vigor and severity; so young and weak a republic as America must keep out of foreign wars if this could be done with honor and self-respect; achievement of peace depended on drawing a distinction between conflicts with foreign interests in America and American interference in Europe; balanced policy had to be pursued separately and patiently with each of the three powers. Methods might be different; the basis of bargaining might be shifted; the goal was the same—peace, progress and the deserved larger respect of European countries.

In applying these broad rules to Britain, Washington could not disregard the feelings of his fellow countrymen who were resisting what he believed to be the general desire of peace. Something had to be conceded to the old American resentment. Said Washington:

There are . . . bounds to the spirit of forbearance which ought not to be exceeded. Events may occur which demand a departure from it. But if extremities are at any time to ensue, it is of the utmost consequence that they should be the result of a deliberate plan, not of an accidental collision; and that they should appear both at home and abroad to have flowed either from a necessity which left no alternative, or from a combination of advantageous circumstances which left no doubt of the expediency of hazarding them. Under the impression of this opinion and supposing that the event which is apprehended should be realized, it is my desire that no hostile measure be in the first instance attempted.

An understanding with Spain manifestly was difficult: Obscurity surrounded the designs of Gov. Estéban Rodriguez Miró. Dr. James O'Fallon, perhaps the most active of the frontier adventurers at this time, had been operating for the South Carolina Yazoo Company and had been loud in his professions of loyalty to the United States; but there had been suspicion that he planned to seize a region that had been acknowledged by the American government to be an Indian possession. Concern had been felt that this man might precipitate a frontier war and even might involve the country in hostilities with Spain. A proclamation against O'Fallon's activities and an order for his arrest seemed enough in the spring of 1791. Thereafter Washington gave first place in Spanish negotiations to the removal of the suspicion that the young Western Republic was eyeing covetously the Spanish West Indies.

Washington continued to follow the progress of the Revolution in France with sharpest interest, but he confessed his anxiety regarding "indiscriminate violence" from the "tumultuous populace of large cities." He wrote to the Marquis de la Luzerne:

. . . however gloomy the face of things may at this time appear in France, yet we will not despair of seeing tranquility again restored; and we cannot help looking forward with a lively wish to the period when order shall be established by a government respectfully energetic and founded on the broad basis of liberality and the rights of man, which will make millions happy and place your nation in the rank which she ought to hold.

Patience was needed if this was to be achieved, and patience America had to display in dealing with abrupt changes of policy under the revolutionary government. The new French Minister to the United States, Jean Baptiste Ternant, was received cordially and with personal consideration. The utmost was to be done in complying with a French request for money and arms to combat the slave insurrection in Santo Domingo. No advantage was to be taken of France by repaying the American debt in depreciated assignats. Friendliness was shown in the rejection of a dubious refunding plan submitted by European speculators.

Such was the simple, prudent foreign policy Washington adopted on his return to Philadelphia. It was a policy that had to be applied as opportunity offered, with respect to Britain and Spain, but it was imperative and immediate where Santo Domingo was concerned. Moreover, charges of British incitation of Indian warfare were about to be put to test. The Commander-in-Chief knew St. Clair had no experience in this type of warfare and repeated the warning he so often had given officers entrusted with troops in the wilderness: Beware of surprise. St. Clair at the proper time, presented a plan for establishing a military post at the so-called "Miami Village" as a means of over-awing nearby Indian tribes and showing the

British that the United States had no intention of abandoning that rich area to the King. The proposal was thought a good one and was taken up and entrusted to St. Clair, who was recommissioned at his wartime rank of Major General. His instructions were "to establish a strong and permanent military post" and, after garrisoning it adequately, "seek the enemy" and "endeavor by all possible means to strike them with great severity."

Determination of main lines of policy did not require many days, nor did Washington have to sit long at his desk in preparing notes for his message to Congress which, according to his calendar of events, was to assemble on October 31. Details were put aside for leisured review at Mount Vernon, whither the President turned his carriage again on September 15. This time, the reason was necessity: George Augustine Washington, in a pathetic condition—had gone to Berkeley Springs in the hope of regaining strength. The owner of Mount Vernon had to make arrangements for operating the estate during his nephew's absence. The General reached home on September 20 and commenced a survey of his affairs. His most important task after a deathly dry summer was instructing Anthony Whiting, who had succeeded Bloxham as his head farmer, in management of the property; but, as always, scores of lesser matters awaited his decision. In addition Washington had considerable correspondence with officials in Philadelphia and continued to direct the preparation of material for his address to Congress. Everything seemed to be in smooth progression, when, from a letter received October 13, Washington discovered that he had made a mistake concerning the date of the meeting of Congress: it was to assemble on the twenty-fourth, not on the thirty-first. No time was lost after that. Word was sent to Philadelphia for speed in collecting the information he would require.

Washington's address on the twenty-fifth had a cheerful opening and prime emphasis on operations against the western Indians, but it contained no important suggestion on new legislation other than that the law imposing an excise on spirits be revised where valid objection was disclosed. Most of the later paragraphs dealt with recommendations previously made and not yet enacted. Congress's response was one of unenthusiastic approval that slowly shaped itself into bills considered in leisured debate. Gradually, there developed a new vigor of dispute and a closer approach to rival philosophies, but the antagonisms of large States and small, Eastern interests and Southern, prevailed on occasion over the abstract question of the scope of Federal power.

Washington had to remain in Philadelphia throughout a session that proved inordinately long. Time-consuming was the President's continuing responsibility for the District of Columbia, though he used the services of Jefferson as far as practicable and insisted officials and employees under the District commissioners report through them. When the principal surveyor, Major L'Enfant, quarreled with the men to whom he was responsible, Washington tried several devices to retain the services of the brilliant designer but came to the conclusion that L'Enfant could not work in harness. Dismissal of the engineer was distressing, but no alternative existed.

Another continuing labor was presented by the ominous decline in the health of George Augustine. Fortunately, Whiting seemed to possess both intelligence and industry and took ever an increasing share of the work on the estate. During the autumn, because of Congress, L'Enfant and Mount Vernon, Washington had a heavy load but he carried it without getting—to use his own words—"on a stretch." October brought a development in relations with England: a British Minister, George Hammond, the first diplomatic agent to be accredited formally to America, arrived in Philadelphia to take up his residence there. As soon as practicable, Washington selected Thomas Pinckney, of South Carolina, for the corresponding post at the Court of St. James's.

No question so frequently was discussed at the President's conference with his heads of departments as that of relations with the Indians. Almost every informed public servant in the United States believed a settlement with Britain would put an end to most of the murderous raids along the Ohio and its tributaries. Peace with the Creeks would be easy when Spain no longer supplied them with powder and arms. Meantime, Washington continued to work for amity with well disposed tribes and for victory over the coalition against which St. Clair had been dispatched.

On December 8 unofficial reports were received in Philadelphia of a costly defeat sustained by St. Clair within fifteen miles of the Miami town where he was to establish a post. It was said that his casualties reached no less than six hundred and that Gen. Richard Butler and other senior officers were among the slain. The next evening, Washington received dispatches from St. Clair that included words to make the President set his jaw: "Yesterday afternoon, the remains of the army under my command got back to this place, and I now have the painful task to give you an account of as warm and as unfortunate an action as almost any that has been fought, in which every corps was engaged and worsted, except the First Regiment. That had been detached. . . ." St. Clair had been warned against surprise, yet he had permitted the Indians to gain overpowering advantage almost before the alarm could be sounded!

Washington, on reading St. Clair's report, could not have overlooked a postscript in which the ill-faring commander remarked that "some very material intelligence" had been communicated by Capt. Jacob Slough to General Butler during the night before the action but was not forwarded to St. Clair or known to him for days. A man less self-mastered than Washington might have winced at that, because he had appointed Butler to command in the face of protests. Good soldier or poor, vigilant or forgetful, Butler was dead and, with him, thirty-eight other officers. Twenty-one who held commissions were wounded. Casualties exceeded nine hundred. All the cannon with the main force had been lost. The "most disgraceful part of the business," said St. Clair, "is that the greatest part of the men threw away their arms and accoutrements, even after the pursuit . . . had ceased." Nothing so humiliating to the white man had been experienced in Indian warfare since Braddock's bewildered Redcoats had been the target of unseen marksmen on the Monongahela.

Washington, after a first wrathful outburst, took this defeat in the spirit he had shown when disasters had come to his arms in days far darker.

When members of Congress reassembled Monday the twelfth, the President sent a message in which he said: "Although the national loss is considerable, according to the scale of the event, yet it may be repaired without great difficulty, excepting as to the brave men who have fallen on the occasion, and who are a subject of public as well as private regret." Copies of St. Clair's reports were sent precisely as received, and when published, they were complete. Not even the ugliest line on the beaten troops was eliminated. Washington had learned the value of candor in dealing with the American people and he knew that one reason for their trust in him was their belief he would tell them the whole truth. Inquiry by Congress was not avoided, nor was public criticism silenced by this forthright action. Washington himself was not blamed; Knox escaped with less abuse than he might have expected; there was sympathy, rather than obloquy, for St. Clair. Chiefly, the fault was laid at the doors of army contractors. The most vigorous discussion had to do with methods of Indian warfare and with the ethics of occupying Indian territory. Feeling was moderated gradually by the successful outcome of negotiations with the Senecas and the Cherokees and by the resignation of St. Clair. Sharpened zeal was manifested for peace with the Indians. Such dealings would be enforceable by an adequate army, the command of which stirred the ambition of soldiers and the partisanship of politicians. The officers finally continued were Anthony Wayne as Major General and Rufus Putnam and Otho Williams as Brigadiers. To strengthen further the national defence, Congress passed the previously contested bill for uniform militia. All in all, St. Clair's defeat did not impair Washington's reputation and indirectly gave the Federal government the means of making its will more effective in a day of danger.

When it was intimated to Jefferson that Spain was willing to discuss free navigation of the Mississippi, Washington nominated William Carmichael, Chargé at Madrid, and William Short, who held a similar post at Paris, to undertake negotiations to extend to commercial relations with Spain and perhaps even with those of her colonial possessions. This proposal became snarled with a recommendation to send Gouverneur Morris to France with the rank of Minister, and Short to The Hague with like status, but in the end all the nominations were confirmed.

Differences of opinion concerning the policy in dealing with Spain were mild compared with the struggle in Congress over the reapportionment of representation to conform to the census of 1790. Now that reasonably accurate figures on the inhabitants of the States were available, changes from the provisional representation adopted in 1787 were required. The first Congress had sixty-five members of the House; Vermont added two more, and Kentucky, when admitted, would bring the total to sixty-nine. Those figures would be increased by any apportionment Congress was apt to endorse, because the census gave a population of 3,893,000. If the country's 697,000 slaves were reckoned at three-fifths of their actual number for purposes of representation, the net population entitled to spokesmen in Congress would be approximately 3,614,000. With one Representative for every 30,000 of these, the membership permitted in the House would be 121. Many States would gain; none would lose representation. Members of Congress went back to their school exercises in long division to determine on what basis their States would have the largest possible number of Representatives in the lower House and the lowest "remainder" of "unrepresented" population. In nearly all their calculations, these mathematicians found that gains for their own constituencies involved concessions to other States they did not wish to strengthen. Final legislation proposed a House of 120 members and seemed to some opponents a trick to enlarge the delegations from New England by bribing those from a sufficient number of other States to assure a majority for the measure.

The bill was presented to Washington on March 26, 1792. For about a week he kept his own counsel, and then, April 3, he called on Randolph for an opinion and directed the Attorney General to get the views of the heads of departments for his consideration the next day. When the opinions were summarized Washington found his counsellors equally divided: Jefferson and Randolph held the bill unconstitutional, primarily because it did not apply the same fixed ratio to each of the States separately; Hamilton and Knox did not affirm the measure constitutional beyond all dispute, but they argued that the President would do well to accept the judgment of the legislative branch.

This conflict of opinion disturbed Washington, who had until April 6 to make up his mind. If he did not return the bill by the close of proceedings that Friday, it would become law without his signature. On the morning of the fifth the President called on Jefferson before breakfast and, after a few preliminaries, described his dilemma: The principle applied in determining representation certainly was not the one the Delegates to the Philadelphia Convention had in mind, but it might be defensible. Besides, the final vote for and against the measure had been geographical: if he disapproved the bill, it might be thought that he was taking sides with a Southern party. Jefferson admitted this embarrassment but said he did not think it justified action that would be fundamentally wrong. After he left the Secretary's quarters, Washington sent a messenger for the Attorney General. Randolph was instructed to find Madison and go with the Congressman to the Secretary of State. If they united in advising that he should disapprove the bill, they were to draw up a statement for him to send to Congress. Randolph returned ere long with the draft of a brief message not favoring the bill.

The proposed message was dispatched to the House, the first "negative" of any legislation passed by Congress. The paper was received with protests by certain of Washington's Northern supporters in Congress, while most Southern members, Jefferson's followers in particular, expressed satisfaction. Resulting action of Congress vindicated Washington's veto. A motion to pass the bill in spite of him failed in the lower chamber; a revised bill that provided a House of 103 members was passed after discussion on two days only. The Senate concurred the day this bill was laid before it; Washington had the satisfaction on the fourteenth of signing a measure which increased House membership by thirty-six.

In this long contest it had seemed natural, unhappily, that South should be arrayed against East, and that Jefferson's opinion had been the reverse of Hamilton's. This was becoming the daily order of politics. In November 1791 Federalist Fisher Ames wrote that "tranquility has soothed the surface" but "faction glows within like a coalpit"; before the end of January 1792 he was saying, "I do not believe that the hatred of the Jacobites toward the House of Hanover was ever more deadly than that which is borne by many of the partisans of State power towards the government of the United States." In the larger strategy of government—funding, assumption, excise and protection of American manufactures by high duties—Hamilton still had the better of the struggle for power; but in the tactics of contest, he carelessly remained on the defensive while Jefferson enjoyed the rewards of a vigorous offensive. The fiscal policy of the government was alleged by the Republicans to be responsible for the speculative mania that ruined hundreds of men in the spring and summer of 1791. A second charge against Hamilton, and a most effective one in appealing to voters, was that he lacked sympathy with republican ideals and was at heart an enemy of the institutions established by the war for independence. Jefferson's adherents directed their third attack against the excise, which they regarded as Hamilton's creation. The Federalists had their journalistic gladiator in John Fenno, editor of the *Gazette of the United States,* and the Republicans their champion in Philip Freneau and his *National Gazette.* Although Fenno could hit hard on occasion, he did not possess the resourcefulness and skill of Freneau in finding quickly and exploiting boldly a new line of attack on the opposition.

Before the end of the session of Congress Washington had achieved the state of mind in which he paid little heed to newspaper debate that was not offensively personal to him, but he observed the widening rift between his two principal officers of administration. He listened when they talked of their differences of political opinion but, as yet, made no answer to them and contented himself with setting an example of equal regard for all honest elements in politics. There was, he believed, no personal ill will between Jefferson and Hamilton; their clashes were those of principle. He would do what he could to confine divergent opinion and would employ his most resolute endeavor to prevent a disintegration of the Union because of the antagonisms between North and South. On occasion he found himself less active and business in consequence more irksome. The prospect of retiring in March 1793 was increasingly sweet.

He passed without visible impatience through the final weeks of a session that produced better legislation than had been expected of it. Washington had made or renewed seven major recommendations. Those relating to the excise, reapportionment of representation, creation of a uniform militia, improvement of the postal service, and establishment of a mint had been enacted into law. Nothing positive had been done with respect to the introduction of a system of standard weights and measures or the disposal of vacant land. On its own initiative Congress had arranged for the succession to the Presidency, revised the system of invalid pensions and indemnified Nathanael Greene's estate for a bond he had given to supply his troops with provisions. An extension to March 1, 1793, had been granted for the tender of notes to be assumed by the Federal government; an effort to have the United States Treasury pay for a further assumption of state debts was beaten in the face of much maneuver. By the terms of a most important measure, the President was authorized to call out the militia to execute the laws of the Union, suppress insurrections and repel invasions. Not a bill was passed that seemed to Washington imprudent, nor had Congress voted adversely on any measure he was known to favor. Some actions he had recommended had been postponed but none had been denied outright.

Washington had confided to Madison and the heads of Departments his growing inclination to retire at the end of his term. Hamilton and Knox had done their utmost to dissuade him. Randolph had felt that Washington should accept reelection. Madison had said that the President's retirement would be a shock to the people. Jefferson had spoken against such a step but not as if he thought the President was to be shaken from his decision. The judgment of the Secretary of State seemed to be warranted. Washington found his duties more burdensome and the rising resentments of party more unreasonable. Newspaper criticism, he reflected, undoubtedly was aimed at him though ostensibly it was directed at subordinates. He believed "his return to private life was consistent with every public consideration," as surely as it accorded with his own inclination—and wished to settle as quickly as he could the question of how he should announce his intention in a manner to make it plain that he was not presuming he would be elected if willing to serve. On this he decided to ask the counsel of Madison, who also could be of help in preparing the text of a farewell address. Washington found Madison convinced that he should not retire. Madison's strongest argument, perhaps, was that the rise of party spirit was a reason for continuing as President rather than a reason for declining reelection. Madison had more to say that was logical but not convincing or persuasive. The two men separated with the understanding that Madison was to reflect on the question of when and how Washington's proposed retirement was to be announced, though the younger man repeated the hope that no decision would be necessary.

Washington left Philadelphia May 10 with Lear in attendance, for a hurried journey to Mount Vernon, where he found the crops flourishing. George Augustine, however, had declined sadly since the last visit of his uncle. The one available man to relieve "The Major" was Whiting, who already had taken over many of George Augustine's duties. Washington decided to give him a trial, though this would call for closer supervision from Philadelphia.

Perhaps this circumstance increased Washington's desire to return home on conclusion of his term. The more he reflected on the question of a second administration, the more firmly did he find himself disposed to decline if it were offered him. In anticipatory quiet he let his mind dwell on the valedictory statement he might make to fellow citizens about their government and themselves. On the way back to Philadelphia, he met Madison on the road and delivered a letter in which he sketched his valedictory and described his dilemma: he still could not decide in what manner he could decline reelection without posing the assumption that a second term would be his if he desired it. In his eyes, arrogance was worse than ignorance, and bad manners second only to bad morals.

Back in Philadelphia May 28, Washington found foreign relations and Indian affairs at a stage that called for much consultation with Jefferson and Knox. Minister Hammond at last was ready to discuss with the Secretary of State the execution of the peace treaty. Washington was not optimistic. The negative outcome of the first meeting consequently did not disappoint Washington greatly, but he followed subsequent cautious exchanges with care. Doubtless, too, he kept himself informed on Jefferson's instructions to Thomas Pinckney, the American Minister who was about to leave for London. The President did not look for an early settlement with Britain, but he intended to continue his efforts, especially as the activity of a Spanish agent in the Creek country was creating a suspicion that Madrid and London might be working together against America. Whether England and Spain were or were not responsible, Indian affairs had reached a distressful state. Knox was disturbed over the criticism and alarm that St. Clair's defeat had evoked. Kentucky was demanding protection against the savages; Washington unhesitatingly pledged it and, in his old fighting spirit, awaited developments. For a time, to the surprise of many, the frontier was tranquil, though military preparation continued as if an Indian war had to be faced.

Washington's prime concern remained the question of retirement. Jefferson wrote him a most earnest plea that he consent to reelection. The letter indicted the speculators and alleged monarchists and urged that Washington add "one or two more to the many years [he had] already sacrificed to the good of mankind."

"Your being at the helm," said the Secretary of State, "will be more than an answer to every argument which can be used to alarm and lead the people in any quarter into violence or secession." Then Jefferson added in a fine turn of phrase: "North and South will hang together if they have you to hang on."

When Washington left for Mount Vernon again July 11 he had a text to ponder in a carefully prepared draft by Madison of what a retiring President should say and when he should say it. As Washington approached his home he saw evidence of a drought so severe that the corn appeared to be ruined, but when he stopped at Georgetown he had the gratification of seeing much better designs for the public buildings than previously had been offered. "It was a pleasure indeed," he said, "to find, in an infant country, such a display of architectural abilities." Pleasure there was, also, in being free of the endless appointments and unrelaxed inquisition of the temporary capital, but there was no escaping the correspondence of the presidential office. It was brought in the mailbag from Alexandria as inexorably, if not as frequently, as it had been laid on his desk in Philadelphia. All this meant that Washington had much work to do with no clerical help, in a household made unhappy by the extreme illness of Major Washington, during a most unhealthy season and at a time when the General's need of money was great.

If, improbably, he had thought that private affairs could have first attention and public business be left to aestivate the summer through, developments on the frontier soon would have aroused him. It was reported that officers sent to the western Indians to negotiate peace had been murdered and that Spanish agents had been inciting the Creeks to hostility. Reports told of the arrival in New Orleans of five regiments of Spanish troops who were to be followed by a like number from Havana. Simultaneously, negotiations were under way with friendly tribes, whose failure to be satisfied with American offers might lead them to look to the British or the Spanish. War then might be inevitable. Washington gave the largest discretion to the Secretary of War. Representation should be made to the Spanish commissioners that their government was not suspected of unfriendly action in the Creek country but that the evidence against certain Spanish officers was too strong and too important to ignore. Washington declared that if the Spanish were intriguing as Americans believed this would make the President suspicious "that there is a very clear understanding in all this business between the courts of London and Madrid and that it is calculated to check, as far as they can, the rapid increase, extension and consequence of this country."

This state of affairs seemed to Washington all the more sinister because partisan division—and animosity between Hamilton and Jefferson—was deepening every hour. It was a situation that made inquiry proper. Hamilton must be given opportunity of explaining objections made by the Secretary of State. Nothing was withheld and nothing softened in a paper the President sent Hamilton with the simple statement that he sought only "to obtain light and to pursue truth." Would Hamilton write out his "ideas upon the discontents here enumerated"?

When Washington wrote this at Mount Vernon, the advantage that Freneau had won in Philadelphia over the *Gazette of the United States* was being lost. Fenno's sponsors had come to his support. While the tide of controversy was running strongly in Fenno's favor, Hamilton replied on August 18 to Washington's twenty-one inquiries. The Secretary of the Treasury said in a letter that accompanied his fourteen-thousand-word answer:

You will observe that here and there some severity appears. I have not fortitude enough always to hear with calmness calumnies which necessarily include me, as a principal agent in the measures censured, of the falsehood of which I have the most unqualified consciousness. I trust I shall always be able to bear, as I ought, imputations of error of judgment; but I acknowledge that I cannot be entirely patient under charges which impeach the integrity of my public motives or conduct. I feel that I merit them *in no degree;* and expressions of indignation sometimes escape me, in spite of every effort to suppress them. I rely on your goodness for the allowances.

The document was all denial or refutation, with the single exception that speculative dealings in government securities "had some bad effects among those engaged in it," though this doubtless was unavoidable. Much of the paper echoed the keen reasoning of the earlier reports on public credit;

allegations of stock-jobbing were met with the statement that Hamilton did not know a single member of Congress who could "properly be called a stock-jobber or a paper-dealer"; his reply to the favorite charge of Republicans that the way was being prepared for a change to a monarchy was a flat denial, with the added remark "that the project, from its absurdity, refutes itself." Towards the end of his answer, Hamilton came to the objection, "The owners of the debt are in the Southern, and the holders of it in the Northern division." Said Hamilton: "If this were literally true, it would be no argument for or against anything. It would be still politically and morally right for the debtors to pay their creditors." From that he proceeded to a discussion of economic differences between North and South and the effect of the war in determining debtors and creditors—the sort of argument most certain to impress so stoutly bottomed a nationalist as the President was.

Washington took occasion, perhaps before this letter reached Mount Vernon, in writing Jefferson concerning the danger of an Indian war, to appeal for political moderation and compromise: "How unfortunate," he exclaimed, "and how much is it to be regretted . . . that whilst we are encompassed on all sides with avowed enemies and insidious friends, that internal dissensions should be harrowing and tearing our vitals." Without more charity towards opposing opinion, he went on, "I believe it will be difficult, if not impracticable, to manage the reins of government or to keep the parts of it together. . . ." If union were thrown away before its utility were justly tried, then, he said, "in my opinion, the fairest prospect of happiness and prosperity that ever was presented to man will be lost, perhaps forever." He made his appeal simply and, as he explained, without applying the case to any individual: "My earnest wish and my fondest hope . . . is that instead of wounding suspicions and irritable charges, there may be liberal allowances, mutual forbearances and temporizing yieldings on *all sides.* Under the exercise of these, matters will go on smoothly and, if possible, more prosperously." A letter of similar import and, in part, of almost identical language was sent Hamilton.

Both men answered on September 9. Hamilton wrote regretfully of Washington's unhappiness and said plainly that if the President did not succeed in producing harmony, "the period is not remote when the public good will require substitutes for the differing members of your administration." He felt himself "the deeply injured party," said Hamilton, from the time Jefferson took office: "I have been the frequent subject of the most unkind whispers and insinuations" by the Secretary of State. "I have long seen a formed party in the Legislature under his auspices, bent upon my subversion."

Jefferson's answer set forth his chief basis of opposition to Hamilton in a broad, inclusive statement the verity of which he apparently did not think he needed to prove: "[Hamilton's] system flowed from principles adverse to liberty, and was calculated to undermine and demolish the Republic, by creating an influence of his department over the members of the Legislature." Jefferson proceeded to denounce mildly Hamilton's concept of the right of Congress to legislate for the general welfare, and then the

Secretary of State dwelt on the restrain he had shown in not opposing Hamilton's plan, though he disapproved of it. "Has abstinence from the department, committed to me, been equally observed by him?" asked Jefferson and, in answer to his own question, wrote of the manner in which Hamilton had undertaken to deal with the ministers of foreign countries. ". . . If the question be by whose fault is it that Colonel Hamilton and myself have not drawn together, the answer will depend on that to two other questions, whose principles of administration best justify, by their purity, conscientious adherence? and which of us has, notwithstanding, stepped farthest into the control of the department of the other?" The Secretary of State concluded with the statement that he intended to retire at the end of Washington's term, but he maintained: "I will not suffer my retirement to be clouded by the slanders of a man whose history, from the moment at which history can stoop to notice him, is a tissue of machinations against the liberty of the country which has not only received and given him bread, but heaped honors on his head."

These letters from his two principal officers were of doubtful comfort to Washington. They contained weak promises to seek an armistice, but they showed deep personal animosity between the two men. The prospect of party strife was increasing. That scarcely could be denied. Washington had, therefore, to wait for better opportunity of making truce and, meantime, had to consider to what extent the disputes in his official family would affect his retirement at the end of his term.

All his correspondence on the subject showed that his friends were convinced he should accept reelection, which they regarded as certainly his at the nod of his head. Lear wrote Washington that Robert Morris said he hoped the President "would not give up the government and the country to that fate which he clearly foresaw awaited them if you should determine to retire from the chair. He thought the reasons for your continuing were, if possible, more strong than those which first induced your acceptance of the office." Substantially the same argument was advanced by Randolph. Hamilton rejoiced because "there was," he thought, "some relaxation" in Washington's previously unyielding stand against reelection.

Another involvement was presented by rising opposition to the excise on whiskey, particularly in Pennsylvania. Washington said in uncompromising terms that he had the duty of enforcing the law and proceeded to draft a proclamation in which all persons were admonished and exhorted to "refrain and desist from all unlawful combinations and proceedings" that might obstruct the operation of the excise laws. Courts and officials were charged and required to exert their respective powers in seeing that the object of the proclamation was executed. Use of Federal troops was to be avoided, but if force was necessary as a last resort, the Army must be used to restore order and uphold the will of the country, expressed through an act of Congress. Washington authorized a new effort for the ransom of the American seamen held by pirates of the Barbary States; the uncertain situation in France gave him daily concern; relations with Britain were slowly approaching a settlement.

Washington completed his arrangements at Mount Vernon, as far as this was possible, and made preparations for his own leave-taking. Already he had called on several of his subordinates to give him their suggestions for his annual "speech" to Congress, and he had had opportunity of talking with Jefferson, who stopped on the Potomac en route to Philadelphia from Monticello. Before breakfast on October 1 the two had a long, frank discussion of the desire each had to retire from public service. Washington explained his state of mind and confessed that he still was in doubt about a second term, though all his inclination was to return to Mount Vernon; only there was he happy.

Jefferson affirmed that the President was "the only man in the United States who possessed the confidence of the whole; that government was founded in opinion and confidence; and that the longer [Washington] remained, the stronger would become the habits of the people in submitting to the Government, and in thinking it a thing to be maintained; that there was no other person who would be thought anything more than the head of a party." This brought the conversation to the deep division between Jefferson and Hamilton. The President had never been aware, he told Jefferson, of the magnitude of the rift. "He knew, indeed," wrote Jefferson later, "that there was a marked difference in our political sentiments, but he had never suspected it had gone so far in producing a personal difference, and he wished he could be the mediator to put an end to it." A call to breakfast ended the discussion.

The next move of Washington was to Georgetown, where on October 8 he attended a sale of lots in the new Federal City. From Georgetown, with Martha and the other members of the family, Washington went to Baltimore and Philadelphia. He arrived there on the thirteenth.

As soon as he reopened his office, Washington found that the routine of his daily life had to be changed somewhat. He had to devote much thought to Mount Vernon and write many long letters to Whiting. On them he spent a considerable part of each Sunday. His general direction of the Federal District was simplified by his insistence that a superintendent be chosen and that he deal with this official and with all others through the District commissioners only. Administrative practice in Philadelphia was modified also. Washington conferred more frequently with the heads of departments as a whole and increasingly turned over documents to these men for examination and report. He did not change his practice of seeking the advice of individuals when he needed it, even though the question at issue concerned the department of another.

Where foreign affairs were involved, relations with Spain scarcely were better, in spite of denials of any incitation of Creeks against Americans. The attitude of Spain in the probable event of war between Britain and France was the subject of earnest consideration, but, for weeks, the only result was anxiety. A new crisis was developing in France, and perhaps in that country's relations with the United States. Nothing tangible seemed likely to come of discussion until the course of the French Revolution was less obscured by doubt. The one exception was the nature and measure of assistance that could be given the French in suppressing the insurrection in Santo Domingo. With Britain, as with France, it did not appear that negotiation would progress far until the issue of war or peace was determined.

Relations with Congress, on the other hand, had now been established firmly and, in most particulars, involved little more than a continuing deference, delivery of messages, and steady compliance with the lawmakers' requests, when reasonable. The session opened November 5. Washington's annual message on November 6 was a matter-of-fact document in which Indian affairs had first place. Next came brief reference to what appeared to be diminishing resistance to the excise on whiskey, followed by recommendation that Congress revise the judiciary system and enact laws to discourage aggression against the territory of other countries. The nearest approach to a political issue was the unqualified observation that "the state of the national finances" made possible an arrangement to begin paying off the Federal debt and the loan issued for the Bank of the United States, a course of action vigorously advocated by the Republicans. The next day, word was received that on September 27 Gen. Rufus Putnam had signed with the Wabash and Illinois Indians a treaty that removed one threat to the settlers on the Ohio and some of its tributaries. By chance, Knox had submitted to Congress that same November 7 a "General View" of negotiations with the Indians. The Federal government had done all that could be expected of it in trying to maintain peace, punish murderers, and protect peaceful settlers from raids. Reports sent Congress the next week on conditions in Florida and the Creek country were equally to the credit of the government.

Important as was the President's message in what it said of Indian affairs that led to these developments, the address was most notable, to some observers, for one omission: not a word did it include concerning Washington's intentions with respect to a second term. He was silent where it might have been supposed he would speak out if he held to his purpose to retire. Truth was, he had not brought himself to announce his wish to quit public life. He had told Madison as long previously as May that he intended to make his announcement at a time most convenient to the public for choosing his successor; that he had thought of the opening of Congress as a suitable occasion but that he had laid this aside because, for one thing, the session would be late in starting. Now the States were preparing to name electors, Congress had begun its session, and he still was silent.

No rival for the office had appeared, none was so much as mentioned. Unless Washington declined almost immediately, he would be reelected. That was certain. Equally was it certain that the contest for Vice President would be hard fought. Washington took no part in the battle for the Vice Presidency, which became an ugly fight against John Adams by George Clinton and the Republicans. The President of all the people did not feel that he could be the advocate of even so admirable a public servant as he considered his second in command to be.

When questions between the followers of Jefferson and of Hamilton were brought to a test in Congress, victory was more often with the Federalists than with the Republicans. A definite victory for the Federalists, Hamilton in particular, came late in the session after the impetuous Republican representative, William B. Giles, moved and the House directed, that Washington and Hamilton respectively supply information about loans and balances with the Bank of the United States. Giles's resolutions were so worded that they might be regarded as heavy with innuendo that something was wrong. Hamilton met the demand so promptly and with such detailed and inclusive papers that even the voluble Giles was almost silenced. The other contest of importance between the parties was over a proposal to extend the assumption of state debts. After the usual debate, maneuver and minor amendment, the bill passed the House by the casting vote of the Speaker, with substantially the whole Republican contingent in opposition; but in the Senate the measure was defeated, 17 to 11, on its second reading. When defeats and victories for Hamilton and Jefferson had been set down, it might have been said that the Federalists had won the campaign but that the Republicans might win the war.

Washington observed the struggle with regret and strove both to reduce personal animosities and prevent damage to the new government. Long before the party battles ended in Congress he had evidence that the faith of Americans in him was undiminished. As the weeks had passed, he had made no statement concerning the election to the Presidency. In his own mind, he had been restrained by what he termed "strong solicitations" from saying that he would not accept reelection. Silence had been taken as consent: On February 13, 1793, when the vote was counted, John Adams was found the choice of seventy-seven electors and George Clinton of fifty for Vice President. Washington again had first place unanimously.

CHAPTER / 21

Washington was gratified at the unanimity that kept him in the presidential chair. This decision to stay on in public service had not exacted the sharp searching of the spirit as had that first decision to accept the Presidency in 1789; this time there was more of resignation than determination. There was comfort in the fact that his reputation had weathered the risk of four years' exposure in high places. Ceremony and ceremonial had consumed many hours, but at no time had all of it been unwelcome. There had been much that was pleasurable associated with the office: warm affection of the people, their demonstrations of respect and reverence, unmistakable evidence of their belief in his leadership. Perennial nostalgia for Mount Vernon, however was the more poignant because of the hopeless illness of George Augustine, word of whose death February 5 had come within the week.

It was pleasant to think upon the progress the past four years had witnessed in the nation. America's survival under the Constitution in a period mercifully unclouded by serious threat of war was satisfying and promising. The single imperative to progress, peace, now would assure extension of her enterprise and happiness to a far horizon. While the distant view was pleasing, there were, close by, objects that threatened to disturb an idyllic picture. The most intrusive was the difference between the Secretary of State and the Secretary of the Treasury. For only a few months had the President been aware of this growing disfigurement. Whether he could ignore it now seemed doubtful, though he was not without hope that Jefferson and Hamilton might be reconciled in their actions as, in his belief, they were in their principles. Their single common interest was their country's ultimate good, yet where one sought strength for the nation, the other saw only the seed of dissolution; the ideal of the one was the abomination of the other. The once disciplined differences of political opinion no longer were restrained, now that vociferous champions of each Secretary took sides in Congress. Every issue reaffirmed the diametrical opposition of Federalists and Republicans.

Another unhappy prospect was that of increasing public censure of Washington as well as of his official acts. He, personally, had been spared editorial attack until late in 1792 and had been able to ignore newspaper controversy even when the tide of invective crept close to his own door. Once it was clear that the campaign to unseat Vice President Adams had failed, editor Freneau of the *National Gazette* opened his batteries on the President himself. Freneau had one criticism only—that the President's fondness for pomp masked a tendency towards monarchism. In issue after issue the charge was reiterated. Washington said nothing, but to his sensitive spirit these remarks were agonizing. One thing the President knew for certain—he need not expect the immunity in his second term that had shielded him previously.

Alone in his carriage towards noon of March 4, Washington set out for the Senate Chamber where he would take his oath. The chair designated for him in the elegantly furnished room was the one usually occupied by the President of the Senate, Adams, who on this occasion was seated to the right. A place on the left was provided Justice William Cushing. Through the open doors of the Chamber, state and municipal personages, foreign diplomats and distinguished Philadelphians could see and be seen. Beyond them and around them every available space was filled with eager, solemn witnesses.

There was a brief pause. Then the President of the Senate arose and addressed Washington. The General stood and read his short Inaugural Address. The oath was administered and the President walked from the room as quietly as he had come. The solemnity of the occasion was the more moving because of its simplicity, but admiring restraint gave way to spontaneous cheers as the President left Congress Hall.

For weeks Washington had known that a visit to Mount Vernon would be necessary and had expressed his hope of going there by the first of April; but urgent business would have to be eased before the President could leave Philadelphia. Washington could justify no hope of immediate improvement in the troubled business of the Federal District. For months the surveyor, Andrew Ellicott, had been quarrelling with the District commissioners. The President did not know what was vexing Ellicott, but he was determined that the matter be settled and made plans to be at Georgetown about April 1. Washington was gratified that he was able to transmit to Congress Ellicott's completed plat of the District and a formal report of progress from the commissioners. He was pleased by the "grandeur, simplicity, and beauty" of a plan for the Capitol drawn by Dr. William Thornton of Philadelphia. Moreover, he concurred with the commissioners that the President's mansion should be erected only in part and built to "admit of an addition in future . . . without hurting but rather adding to the beauty and magnificence of the whole as an original plan."

Complexities of the Federal City called forth far less concern than did foreign relations, particularly with Britain. Almost a decade since ink had dried on the Definitive Treaty of Peace, and England still had not acted to evacuate the seven military and trading posts that dotted the Canadian-American frontier from Lake Champlain to Lake Superior. These posts lay well within American territory as defined by the treaty; one of them, Detroit, was more a fortified garrison than a trader's camp. All diplomatic efforts had been in vain. Another factor now complicated the situation. Throughout 1792 there had been reason to believe that the King's Canadian officials were using their possession of the posts to revive and enlarge British influence over the Indians of the Northwest. Particularly suspect was Lt. Gov. John Graves Simcoe who enjoyed transcendent prestige in the councils of the Shawnee, Miami and Kickapoo. Precisely what Simcoe's motive could be Washington did not know, but conditions north of the Ohio had become desperate in the past year. The ugly spectre of Indian war hung everywhere. The northwest frontier had been receding steadily for more than two years. In the last year, Indian depredation had caused farms to be abandoned on the Allegheny, the Muskingum and the Great Miami; families sought safety at Pittsburgh, Wheeling or Louisville; intrepid adventurers welcomed the cover of fortified posts at Marietta or Cincinnati. Military foresight was fundamental in every consideration of the problems of the West—even, in deliberations that seemed to point a way to pacification of the hostile tribes without resort to war.

Such deliberations were under way early in 1793 and the President was hopeful. During 1792 five emissaries had been sent by Knox to the Indian country, but only one, Gen. Rufus Putnam, had returned with a formal agreement, and in no way could his pact with a few unimportant headmen of the Wabash and Illinois tribes be thought prophetic. Its real significance lay in the possibility that the signers might work salutary influence on their agitated brethren, the Miami and Shawnee. This might be the outcome also of pacific exertion on the part of the Six Nations of Iroquois native councils. The Secretary of War had directed Samuel Kirkland in the spring of 1792 to solicit the help of the Six Nations and Hendrick Aupaumat was ordered abroad among the hostile tribes. The efforts of Aupaumat came to fruition early in October when a grand council of northern tribes met at Au Glaize, south of Detroit. Out of this convocation there issued a call to the United States government to treat for peace the following spring at Sandusky.

The President's first idea had been to bring Cornplanter, one of the Iroquois spokesmen, to Philadelphia for consultation; but he had to be satisfied with information culled from Wayne's dispatches, Wabash and Illinois headmen who came east with Putnam, and a commission from the Six Nations that arrived on the heels of Putnam's party and dined with Washington, Knox and others on February 11. Opportunity for negotiation must not be lost; commissioners must be selected to treat with the savages in their own camp. Appeals to Timothy Pickering, Benjamin Lincoln and Beverley Randolph were accepted and their nominations were confirmed on March 2. The hostile tribes were set on the idea that their eastern boundary should be the Ohio. In a meeting of the Cabinet on February 25 Washington propounded these essential questions: Did the Executive have the power to relinquish to the Indians any lands beyond the Ohio acquired by previous treaty? Should the commissioners be instructed to effect such recessions if necessary to the achievement of peace? Hamilton, Knox and Randolph responded to both questions in the affirmative; Jefferson dissented on both. Majority opinion prevailed—the government must be willing to make concessions "essential to peace."

The situation on the southern frontier was much the same as in the Northwest, but in this area the motive of foreign intrigue was better understood by the President. The intriguer was Spain, and for years her colonial officers in Louisiana and the Floridas had been bargaining for the friendship of the southern tribes. By the treaty of 1783 Great Britain had acknowledged the thirty-first parallel to be the southwestern boundary of the American republic; but in another article England relinquished to Spain her title to West Florida—defined at 32° 28′, that point more than a hundred miles farther north where the Yazoo River joined the Mississippi. For almost ten years the title to the Yazoo Strip, a rectangular tract extending eastward to the Chattahoochee River, had been in question. Spain preserved effective possession with a fortified post at Natchez and insisted that successful military operations had given her a rightful claim to former British territory as far north as the Tennessee and even the Ohio. Spain recognized that the most serious threat to her pretensions was the land hunger of Americans in Kentucky, the Tennessee country and Georgia. Her own twenty-five thousand subjects in Louisiana and the Floridas would not be able to check for long the pressure of aggressive American pioneers. Against this Spain must use her control of Natchez and New Orleans to close the Mississippi to American trade and maneuver for the cooperation of the four principal Indian nations of the South—their hostility to American expansion would provide a splendid barrier.

Almost continually since 1784 each development in the Southwest had been more deplorable than the one before it. Jay's negotiation in 1786 with the Spanish Minister, Don Diego de Gardoqui, failed to win for Westerners the use of the Mississippi. Now the gifted chief of the Creeks, McGillivray, was in active alliance with Gov. Estéban Miró of Louisiana and, with Choctaws and Chickasaws participating, the southern border was in a state of war. Americans were not without blame; incursions on the traditional hunting grounds of the native had been lawless, frequent and often brutal. Most despicable of all was the conspiratorial attempt of James Wilkinson and other Kentuckians, after Congress had refused their petition for statehood in 1788, to annex a part of the West to the Spanish domain in return for commercial favors from Miró. Early in the first Federal administration it appeared that the situation was to improve. Statehood was granted to Kentucky on June 1, 1792, but by that time clouds again were darkening the southern border. A new Spanish governor, Baron Hector de Carondolet, arrived at New Orleans to replace Miró. Carondolet nourished hope that he might establish the supremacy of Spain in her most extreme pretensions. What was worse, his presence revived the threat of Indian war. As reports reached Philadelphia in the fall of 1792 that Spanish agents again were in contact with McGillivray, Washington found fresh cause for concern. Jefferson instructed the American representatives at Madrid, William Short and William Carmichael, to protest to the Court of Spain, but Carondolet accelerated his activities. The most recent news was that in January 1793 he had called the principal chiefs of the Creeks, Cherokees, Chickasaws, and Choctaws to a grand council at Pensacola, that the conference was poorly attended, and that McGillivray had died suddenly in one of the sessions. What course would the unpredictable Indians take now their wily leader was gone? Neither Washington nor Secretary of War Knox ventured a guess, but this they certainly knew: Carondolet's plans were desperate and his influence was growing daily among the southern tribes. A general war might blaze on the border at any moment.

More and more the troubled affairs of France had been pressing upon the President. Each fresh report from abroad brought the thunder of the French Revolution closer to American shores. It had been known through the autumn of 1792 that the republican experiment of 1789 in France had escaped constitutional bounds and was proceeding towards a climax. Lafayette had been impeached for treasonable collusion with the King and proscribed; he fled Paris, and was captured by the Austrians and imprisoned at Olmutz. From a vantage point in the Netherlands, American Minister Short reported that "those mad and corrupt people in France . . . have destroyed their government," that total power now resided "in the hands of the most mad, wicked and atrocious assembly that was ever collected in any country."

There had come to Philadelphia in late autumn only a murmur of the Paris massacre in the first week of September. Then, on the afternoon of December 14, a cry *Ça Ira!* and a peal of bells announced the arrival of "glorious and interesting advices" from Europe. A new French army had routed the Duke of Brunswick's Austro-Prussian invaders on September 20; the National Convention had assembled in Paris, abolished the monarchy and proclaimed France a republic. These accounts satisfied the hunger of American Republicans for favorable interpretation of French affairs and provided them with an irresistible battle-cry against Federalists. Washington's first thought was for the safety of Lafayette and his family. He directed Nicholas van Staphorst of Amsterdam to place 2310 Dutch guilders at the Marquise's disposal and wrote her that this was "the least I am indebted for services rendered me by Mr. de la Fayette, of which I never yet have received the account." The President subscribed himself to her service "at all times and under all circumstances," but little could be undertaken either informally or officially to achieve the liberation of a gentleman who had given so bountifully to the cause of American freedom.

Jean Baptiste Ternant, the French Minister in Philadelphia, presented on February 8 a request that the American government make immediate advances on the debt to France of three million livres, over $500,000, to be laid out in provisions. While regular installments on the debt had been suspended in October for lack of an effective government at Paris to receive them, Washington had authorized financial aid to French colonials beset by the insurrection in San Domingo. On February 13 the President authorized an advance of $100,000 to Ternant and confided to Randolph his dread of criticism should France be disappointed in her application. The counsel of the Attorney General was compromise: assure Ternant that all arrearage to the end of 1792 would be made in good time. Washington pondered the question and a week and a day later brought it up unexpectedly in a meeting of the Cabinet. It was voted three to one that "the whole sum asked for . . . ought to be furnished." This victory of Jefferson over Hamilton was a small tactical one for American Republicans as well as a diplomatic victory for Ternant and France. The President's fear of public censure made it possible.

While the fate of his application hung suspended, Ternant sub-

mitted to Jefferson formal notice that the National Convention had constituted France a republic. The Secretary of State had been expecting such an
announcement and by February 23 had ready an exuberant reply:

The Government and the citizens of the United States . . . consider the union
of principles and pursuits between our two countries as a link which binds still
closer their interests and affections. The genuine and general effusions of joy
which . . . overspread our country on seeing the liberties of yours rise superior to
foreign invasion and domestic troubles have proved to you that our sympathies
are great and sincere. . . .

Washington approved this declaration as soon as it came to his desk.

Jefferson's extravagance may have sprung in some measure from an
interview held on February 20 with Col. William S. Smith, son-in-law of
Vice President Adams and former aide-de-camp to Washington. Smith had
just come from France as the confidential agent of the Girondist party. He
brought information that the leaders of the Gironde had shut their doors
to Gouverneur Morris and were about to send a new Minister to replace
Ternant. This diplomat, a young man named Edmond Charles Genet,
would be empowered to purchase American provisions and grant broad
commercial privileges to American shipping in the French West Indies.
France could be expected to liberate these islands within the coming year;
the adventurer Francisco de Miranda soon would strike the Spaniards at
New Orleans with forty-five ships of the line. In this event, France would
not object if the United States chose to attack the Spanish Floridas. Smith
declared to Jefferson that the Gironde had entrusted him, rather than
Ternant, to receive payments on the debt and to make extensive purchases
of American provisions until Genet's arrival.

Jefferson went to Washington with Smith's disclosures, also laying
before the President extracts of three dispatches sent to Ternant in sharp
complaint over the character and conduct of Morris. Washington was dis-
mayed. He had not expected Morris to make himself popular with the
radical rulers of France, but were not such strenuous expressions equivalent to a demand for the envoy's recall? The President felt that Morris
should be replaced at once. Jefferson suggested that Morris exchange posts
with Pinckney at London. Washington asked, instead, would not the Secretary of State himself resume for a while his old station at Paris? Jefferson
refused categorically, and added that he soon meant to retire from public
life. This irritated Washington. Jefferson had pressed him to continue in
office and now refused to do likewise himself. The Secretary of State insisted that the circumstances were not the same. Besides, Philadelphia soon
would be "the scene of action, as Genet was bringing powers to do the business here."

The President sought at once the counsel of Randolph. The Attorney General advised that no step be taken until Genet's arrival. Washington followed the course the Attorney General proposed. Smith himself
called at the President's house on February 23. Washington welcomed the

personable traveller but did not intend to acknowledge Smith as a temporary commercial agent of the French republic now that Ternant had been notified that the advance of over $500,000 would be made to him. The Colonel's application was unanimously rejected in a meeting of the Cabinet on March 2.

Smith's visit put bright focus on that factor which, Washington knew, must dictate the President's every major decision in months and years ahead: the relation of the United States to France and her Revolution. The nature of the relationship would determine every aspect of American policy towards England and Spain as well as towards France. It would cut the contour of American politics and throw long shadows into every corner of the Union. Washington's first administration had been placid; his second would be turbulent because the influence of the French Revolution now was unmistakable and inescapable. The United States must be careful to avoid any guarantee to defend the colonial empire of Spain against foreign attack. If Miranda should strike New Orleans as Smith predicted, the United States should be in a position to exact concessions from Spain—or even, if circumstances were right, to impose vengeance on Spanish authorities for their incitation of the southern Indians in the past year. Jefferson was asked to revise at once his instructions to the envoys at Madrid. On March 23 the Secretary of State set down the new rule—Carmichael and Short should make no defensive guarantee in return for any promise by Spain to open the Mississippi. Conditions had changed, Jefferson wrote; the United States must remain "free to act."

Washington continued to be distressed by the plight of Lafayette. On March 13 the President asked Jefferson to instruct Morris in Paris "to neglect no favorable opportunity of expressing *informally* the sentiments and wishes of this country respecting the M. de la Fayette." The Secretary of State wrote Morris that even a formal application for Lafayette's release might be appropriate if made with delicacy. Washington also requested Jefferson to draft a message to the Marquise which would embody "all the consolation I can with propriety give her, consistent with my public character and the national policy, circumstanced as things are."

On March 16 Philadelphia newspapers carried fragmentary accounts of the verdict of the National Convention on the fate of Louis XVI and some hint of the execution of the King by guillotine on January 21. Republicans exulted; Federalists could only endure the distressful news in silence. Washington could not bring himself to write a word on the subject. However ennobling the broad objectives of French Revolutionaries might be, the President knew better than most Americans what his country owed to the generosity of the monarch whose name had been cheered and toasted in Philadelphia only a few years before.

The spectre of general war did not diminish, but Washington hoped for America's sake that the conflagration would not spread. The welfare of his country could be served only by abstention from European difficulties and hostilities. This was the tenor of long letters of March 23 and 25 to Humphreys at Lisbon and Morris at Paris. Washington observed to Humphreys: "I trust that we shall have too just a sense of our own interest to originate any cause that may involve us in it, and I ardently wish we may not be forced into it by the conduct of other nations."

Washington readied himself for a journey to Virginia. With the turn of his carriage towards the Potomac, he could dismiss for a time the countless concerns of public office and turn his thoughts to plantation affairs. This would be his first return since George Augustine's death. Perhaps the Major's young widow and her three children soon would make Mount Vernon their home. Washington had written a tender letter to "Fanny"—an assurance of sympathy and affection, and a gracious invitation to resume residence at Mount Vernon. He thoughtfully suggested that she might bring Harriet Washington for companionship. A carriage for her use had been sent to Mount Vernon. One request the uncle made: that she entrust to him her elder son and thereby be spared concern or expense for his education.

At Baltimore on March 30 the President was handed a letter Lear had posted the day before: Philadelphia ship-owners were "under great apprehension," but there was as yet no confirmation of the rumors of war. As the distance shortened to Georgetown, Washington had to ponder what he knew of the controversy between Ellicott and the commissioners of the Federal District. The President realized that he must placate this quarrel or sacrifice the services of an experienced surveyor in much the same way that the talents of L'Enfant had been lost. Arriving at the site of the Federal City on April 2, Washington indicated in forcible terms that Ellicott, as an employee of the commissioners, was accountable to them.

Before sunset on April 2 he was home once more; his very presence on the Potomac brought him solace, but it could not bring him rest. The time was short and details of private business consumed many hours that Washington would have liked to spend in the fields. His finances demanded long, tedious correspondence. Particularly disappointing was a failure, after much expectation, to realize cash from his Kanawha lands. He had also to inquire into the standing of his account with the James River Company, and he hoped to dispose of his interests in the Great Dismal Swamp. Beyond matters of business, there remained the sad duty of arranging for the burial of George Augustine. The simple interment on April 11 was private and without a sermon.

Respite from affairs of state ended abruptly with arrival of Hamilton's letter of April 5 from Philadelphia. A ship had crossed from Lisbon with advices that Europe was in general conflagration. Pitt had ordered the French Minister to leave London; Marie Antoinette had followed her husband to the guillotine; France had declared war against England, Spain and Holland. Hamilton confirmed this in a second communication on April 8, adding his opinion that the conduct of the British navy towards American merchant vessels in the Atlantic had been "thus far . . . unexceptionable." The day before Jefferson had written that the existence of war now was "extremely probable" and that America must "take every justifiable measure for preserving our neutrality and at the same time provide for [France] those necessaries for war which must be brought across the Atlantic." Philadelphia was convulsed in speculation on what the war might mean to the United States; but, Lear was certain, "the universal hope is that [we] may not be drawn into it."

The President wrote hurriedly to Jefferson, April 12: "It behooves the Government of this country to use every means in its power to prevent the citizens . . . from embroiling us with either [England or France] by endeavoring to maintain a strict neutrality." The Secretary of State was instructed to "give the subject mature consideration" and plan steps which would guarantee a neutral role for the United States. To Hamilton, in a separate letter, Washington emphasized his desire for "immediate precautionary measures." He would set out for Philadelphia the next morning. Eruption of general European war had curtailed a vacation and ruined a rest much needed. As Lear greeted him on April 17 and he entered the office once more, Washington knew his nation was floundering in a tempest of diplomacy and domestic politics she never before had experienced. Resolution must ride out the storm.

His first day back at public business was crowded with detail that exacted minute attention and threatened to eclipse the most significant question yet to manifest itself in his Presidency: Was a plan ready or in process that would assure for the United States a strictly neutral role in the European conflict? Action was necessary and must not be postponed. For some time Hamilton had been gathering data and opinions on the status and current applicability of the Franco-American Treaties of Alliance and Commerce concluded in 1778. While Washington was not aware of the depth of Hamilton's plunges into diplomacy, he knew the Secretary of the Treasury liked to dabble in the business of the Department of State; he knew likewise that Jefferson resented these intrusions. Probably, therefore, Jefferson had not conversed a moment with Hamilton on the topic of neutrality. The widening rift in his Cabinet was to be lamented more than ever in the immediate crisis, but lamentation would never bridge it. As a last piece of business on April 18 the President sent notices to the Secretaries and the Attorney General of a meeting the next morning to deliberate on "certain matters arising from the present posture of affairs in Europe."

The Cabinet assembled in Washington's office and opened a strenuous discussion of questions the President tendered. Should a proclamation issue to prevent unneutral acts by Americans—and should it contain a "declaration of neutrality"? The necessity for a formal proclamation, Hamilton argued, was as immediate as it was obvious; Jefferson took exception on two counts. A "declaration of neutrality," he explained, was nothing less than "a declaration that there should be no war," and Congress alone had power to decide for war or peace. "It would be better," he insisted, "to hold back the declaration of neutrality as a thing worth something to the powers at war"; then each might "bid for it and we might reasonably ask [as] a price the broadest privileges" of a neutral nation. Hamilton, Knox and Randolph felt a proclamation was imperative; silence was fraught with too many perils. Finally, with an understanding that Congress would not be bound in the next session by the President's action and upon agreement that the word "neutrality" be omitted, it was decided that a statement of public policy should issue. It should forbid American citizens "to take part in any hostilities on the seas," warn them "against carrying . . . any of those articles deemed contraband by the modern usage of nations," and enjoin them "from all acts and proceedings inconsistent with the duties of a friendly nation toward those at war—" no more than an Executive warning to the citizens of the United States.

The second question was—should the Minister of the French Republic be received? Jefferson thought hesitancy to receive Genet would amount to a breach of the neutrality which was to be solemnly proclaimed. Decision to receive him was unanimous, though Hamilton expressed "great regret that any incident had happened which should oblige us to recognize the [revolutionary] government."

Should Genet be received absolutely or with some qualification? Upon this hinged all subsequent challenge to the validity of the treaties of 1778 under the stresses of 1793. The Secretary of the Treasury loosed a thunderbolt of logic. France was a monarchy in 1778, he pointed out, but now that nation styled itself a republic ". . . we have a right of election to renounce [the treaties] altogether or to declare [them] suspended till [the French] government shall be settled in the form it is ultimately to take." If the Minister of the French Republic was to be received without qualification, this would "amount to an act of election to continue the treaties"; renunciation or at least suspension of them was essential to preservation of American neutrality. Jefferson's displeasure mounted as Knox professed himself in accord with the Secretary of the Treasury. The Secretary of State's comment was terse: Hamilton's argument was ingenious but not sound—treaties bind nations rather than governments. Randolph, perhaps to the surprise of everyone, agreed with Jefferson. Then the Attorney General suggested that further time be taken to consider the status of the fifteen-year-old contracts. Randolph's conciliatory spirit eased the most distressful rupture yet to mar a meeting of the Cabinet. Prompt adjournment followed—subsequent questions postponed to another day.

It remained for Randolph to choose the words of the neutrality proclamation; the President had confidence that he could phrase a declaration moderate enough for Jefferson and forceful enough for Hamilton. When the Cabinet convened on April 22 the Attorney General displayed the draft of his handiwork. Approval was unanimous and Washington ordered a finished copy drawn up for signature and seal. Over the weekend news had reached Philadelphia that Genet had disembarked at Charleston on April 8. Very likely this intelligence was discussed in council and Hamilton may have expressed surprise that the new Minister had not come directly to the seat of government to present his credentials; but no debate followed on the questions left over from the nineteenth. The Cabinet adjourned, and Washington put his pen to the document he chose to call a "Proclamation of Neutrality," though the word "neutrality" had carefully been excluded from its text. On this warning to all citizens to abstain from unneutral acts Washington rested his hope that the nation might avoid involvement in war. Americans wanted peace; that was certain. But it was not at all certain that every American would be well pleased with the Proclamation. Ardent Federalists doubtless would consider it an ineffectual instrument. Ardent Republicans would denounce it as a royal edict, a flagrant show of hostility to the objectives of the French Revolution. Jefferson's disappointment could be expected to deepen rather than abate—in his view a great weapon had been thrown away. No longer could he hope to make Great Britain pay for American neutrality with diplomatic concessions. What might be the reaction of the British and Spanish ministers? Washington made no guess.

As if foreign affairs were not enough to harass the President, Indian problems again vied prominently for his attention. Communications from Georgia told of plundering and killing on the southern border. Early in March a party of Seminoles had pillaged a store on the St. Mary's River and killed several persons. Other outrages had followed. Alarm had spread among the settlers and Gov. Edward Telfair had called out the militia. Frontier apprehensions were by no means restricted to Georgia. Word of depredations in the Tennessee country and the Virginia borders came in letters from Govs. William Blount and Henry Lee.

Washington had no doubt that Spain was the real culprit here. Carondelet's emissaries in the Floridas were openly inviting the savages to plunder and murder. The offer of arms and ammunition removed restraint. There was some hope for peaceful settlement in the thought that not all of the Creek nation was of belligerent mind. Moreover, the Chickasaws were at war with the Creeks. This might serve to divide the combative zeal of the Redmen. On April 27 Knox submitted for approval of the President a message to the Chickasaws, whose aid would be coveted should the United States be drawn into open war with the Creeks and Cherokees.

Prospects on the Northwest frontier were momentarily brighter because the Sandusky conference was in sight. On April 18 Knox had presented a draft of instructions for the commissioners who would treat with the hostile Ohio tribes. This was to be the last proffer of the peace pipe. Pending outcome of the negotiations at Sandusky, Wayne had orders to prevent aggression by frontiersmen against all Indian towns. At the same time, Wayne held his troops in readiness for the defence of the Ohio if such action should be necessary. The forthcoming conference did not promise peace, but there was strength in the knowledge that nothing had been left undone towards that end. Justice had been and would continue to be the principle on which every exertion towards settlement revolved.

Except to pen a letter about his western lands in dismal pursuit of settling some account there, the President had no time for things at Mount Vernon until April 21. The most irksome information forwarded by his manager was that a notice of taxes due had come to the plantation—taxes its owner thought out of season. In any event, a strict economy was necessary and such an admonition went forth to Whiting that day. A letter to the overseer at Fanny Washington's was enclosed, along with a reminder to Whiting to have an eye on the place now and then.

Spectres of war which clouded the horizon of the Atlantic could not long be forgotten. Washington looked daily for the written opinions of his

Cabinet on the status of the French treaties. More and more he came of certain mind that Hamilton's argument for suspension or nullification of American pledges was unsound. The Revolutionary Commander-in-Chief could appreciate the debt of his country to the dethroned Bourbons; but vivid memories also remained of the gallant French footsoldiers at Yorktown who, still Frenchmen in every sense, now were at grips with the same foe they had helped America defeat. This human reason deterred Washington from formal abandonment of the people of France and their new republic. Jefferson furnished legal shot-and-shell with which to demolish the arguments of the Secretary of the Treasury. In the council of the nineteenth Hamilton had offered to prove from Vattel that the treaties of 1778 no longer applied. From the same authority the Secretary of State now demonstrated that precisely the opposite was true. Jefferson conceded that the guarantee in the treaties of American defence of the French West Indies against all enemies could operate to draw the United States into the war, but he felt that danger was "neither extreme, nor imminent, nor even probable." Unquestionably, Jefferson pointed out, the French Republic stood to gain more from a friendly but non-belligerent America than from an active ally whose contribution to naval hostilities in the Atlantic could be but microscopic. The sanity and sense behind this opinion must have struck the President forcibly. The matter was closed; the treaties stood. Washington was glad to have done with an unseemly squabble and told Jefferson he hoped the public would not learn of it.

Genet was expected daily at Philadelphia, but no official word had come from him. Rumor and speculation had to satisfy Washington's curiosity as to what detained this diplomat so long at Charleston, or why he had put ashore there in the first place. News arrived in the last week of April that a French ship had seized several British vessels off the capes of Delaware Bay and was proceeding towards Philadelphia with prizemasters in charge of the captures. Probably this warship was the *Embuscade,* the heavy frigate which had carried Genet to Charleston. The prizes must be admitted to the port of Philadelphia, by terms of the Treaty of Commerce, but Jefferson was uneasy. "We shall be a little embarrassed occasionally," he wrote, "till we feel ourselves firmly seated in the saddle of neutrality."

On May 2 the *Embuscade* under Captain Bompard hove in sight off the Market Street wharf with two British merchantmen in her wake. Jefferson reported that the "yeomanry" of Philadelphia flocked to the wharf by "thousands and thousands" and "rented the air with peals of exultation" as they saw the reversed position of the British colors on the halyards of the captured ships. His own delight was dampened later in the day as a sharp complaint from the British Minister crossed the Secretary's desk. Hammond claimed that Bompard had taken the British *Grange,* within Delaware Bay. Was not this belligerent act inside the territorial waters of the United States an "infringement on its neutrality"? Manifestly it was, if the charges of the British Minister proved substantial.

Jefferson submitted on May 4 dispatches from Morris, among them a report that Genet was carrying some three hundred blank commissions for privateers to be outfitted in America. This was unwelcome confirmation of

suspicions that had been general since Genet's disembarkation at Charles
ton; some step was in order to enforce the declared neutrality of the nation. Hamilton was prompt with a plan: Instruct custom-house officials to
report to the Collector of the Revenue any infringement of the President's
Proclamation, together with any evidence of intended violation—such as
construction of a vessel pierced for guns. Tench Coxe then could refer
violations to his superior, the Secretary of the Treasury, and indictment
and prosecution would follow under the Attorney General. Such a program
would impose on the Department of the Treasury almost exclusive responsibility for maintenance of neutrality. The President and the Attorney
General decided that port collectors might exercise the function Hamilton
had outlined but their information should be communicated to Federal attorneys rather than to the Department of Treasury. In Cabinet on May 7
the Secretary of the Treasury approved the sensible alteration. Jefferson,
who did not perceive the hand of the Chief Executive, was convinced Randolph had surrendered to Hamilton.

The next day Hammond delivered a second demand for release of
the *Grange,* with three new complaints of even more import. While he
could exhibit no "precise proof," the British Minister had reason to believe
that "a considerable quantity of arms and military accoutrements" soon
would be shipped to France from New York. Further, he had information
that Mangourit, the French consul at Charleston, had committed a "Judicial act" by erecting a court of admiralty and condemning for sale two
British brigantines brought into that port by the *Embuscade.* Finally, two
privateers fitted under French commissions at Charleston now were at sea
with Americans in their crews and already had captured an English ship.
Could not Great Britain expect immediate restitution? Doubtless Washington was exasperated as the implication of this last memorial became clear
to him—Genet had been busy indeed since his arrival in the United States!
On May 9 Ternant notified Jefferson that France would consider the
Grange fairly taken. The President directed that the case be submitted for
the Attorney General's prompt consideration and that Hammond's charges
be explored in Cabinet session.

Out of a meeting of the Cabinet May 15 came the draft of a letter to
Hammond which the President sanctioned the same day. The British Minister was assured that the *Grange* would be restored to her owner with
cargo intact and crew liberated. Further, while the American Government
could not restrict the freedom of her citizens to "make, vend and export
arms," the Proclamation of the Executive had stressed that exportation of
contraband to belligerents was fraught with perils of confiscation and financial loss. Assumption of admiralty powers by the French consul was entirely without basis—the United States would permit no repetition of this.
Hostile activity at sea by American citizens had been condemned "in the
highest degree"—Great Britain might be certain all means would be employed to prevent such breaches of neutrality. The outfitting of French
privateers in American ports likewise was "entirely disapproved."

One point in Hammond's memorials remained unanswered: Would
the ship seized by the Charleston privateers be restored? The ship was the

Little Sarah, taken on the open sea off the Virginia capes and now in the custody of her captor at Philadelphia. Contrary inclinations of Jefferson and Hamilton now occasioned another clash. The Secretary of State was determined to manifest no undue sympathy for England; his adversary remained equally adamant that France should gain not the smallest benefit from illegal privateering. Written opinions of Washington's advisers would have to be weighed and these were delivered to the President on the sixteenth. Opinions of the Cabinet deadlocked; the choice on restitution must be the President's alone. As he studied the statements before him, word came that Genet had arrived in Philadelphia.

The Minister's presence outside Philadelphia had been proclaimed May 16 by three salvos from the *Embuscade.* A body of citizens set forth to meet him at Gray's Ferry but somehow failed to find him, and Genet entered Philadelphia without large ovation. That evening a group of important Republicans met to prepare informal congratulations and draw up a proper address. Their report was adopted by an assemblage of enthusiastic citizens the following afternoon. A crowd gathered in City Tavern and its yard heard the congratulatory address and informal remarks by Genet and responded with "shouts and salutations."

Americans were not of one mind—and not even all Philadelphians. Considerable resentment had been displayed on the death of Louis XVI; on May 17, the day of the address to Genet, a body of merchants and traders gathered at the Coffee House to wait on the President. Their address spoke approval of the Proclamation of Neutrality and voiced firm belief that peace must prevail if prosperity and happiness were to continue.

Sometime in the course of that busy Friday Genet conversed with Jefferson and arranged for his official presentation to the President the following day. Upon introduction by the Secretary of State, the Minister stepped forward to present to Washington his credentials, his general instructions, and a memorial from the National Convention of France to the American people. The President received them and acknowledged Genet Minister Plenipotentiary from the Republic of France to the United States, but no warm word of welcome accompanied the gesture. Genet found this formal reception in sharp contrast to popular ovations that had been tendered him again and again since his arrival in Charleston. It was as though the American Executive wore the gloomy garb of the Proclamation itself for this occasion.

Just a few hours later the evening witnessed a celebration to eclipse all previous performances in honor of Genet, a feast at Oeller's Hotel that grew in gaiety with the night and with the flow of wine. After a sumptuous fare, nineteen toasts were drunk "to the glory of America and the French Republic," with the pulsing accompaniment of artillery fire out-of-doors.

If this display represented the highest pitch of partisan enthusiasm in Philadelphia since the Revolution, Washington was too busy in the next week to ponder it at length. The matter of restitution of illegal prizes remained to be settled. Of the written opinions on his desk, two were in favor of restitution and two against it. The President was most impressed by the paper of Randolph. The Attorney General sided with Jefferson against restitution of the *Little Sarah* to her British owners. Randolph reasoned that it did not matter that the French privateer which made the capture had been commissioned at Charleston. The core of Jefferson's argument was that the United States owed no special consideration to Britain and would offend France by a vindictive gesture. Randolph suggested that Americans who had enlisted in the crew of the privateer be prosecuted as violators of their nation's neutral status. This much was due the powers at war with France; even an unsuccessful prosecution would "vindicate the sincerity of our neutrality." Washington recognized at once the justice and value of this proposal. The next day he and Randolph reached what was substantially a compromise between the views of Jefferson and Hamilton on the perplexities of restitution. The *Little Sarah* would not be restored or ordered to leave Philadelphia, but the privateer which brought her there and the other French corsairs outfitted illegally at Charleston would be denied the sanctuary of American ports.

On the twenty-fourth Jefferson came to the President's house with memorials from Genet in hand. The Minister was emphasizing that his Republic had right to certain privileges under the treaties of 1778 but that power of her principles and love for the United States inclined France to overlook these stipulations. Instead, Genet had authority to negotiate a new compact with deeper, finer union of spirit and sentiments as its basis. Further, the National Convention had taken steps towards achievement of an understanding by its decree of February 19, now enclosed, which threw open French West Indian ports to American trade and suspended the regulation of 1791 against construction and sale of American vessels in France. Genet appended proposals for liquidation of the debt of the United States which bore similarity to the scheme advanced by Colonel Smith several months before. Washington would, he said, be obliged to study most carefully Genet's letter and enclosures; the Secretary of State was requested to furnish translations.

Three days later Jefferson forwarded translated copies of Genet's memorials. The President saw readily that France entertained two paramount objectives. The American Government was asked to be responsible for "the greatest part of the sustenance and stores necessary for the armies, fleets and colonies of the French Republic." If the debt were liquidated ahead of schedule and in direct payments to Genet, he could make purchases in various states and so diffuse the blessings of a large and important trade. France seemed to expect establishment of a "national pact" on a "liberal and fraternal basis." Washington pondered the two propositions. Should the United States be willing to discharge at once the entire residue of her debts, some $2,500,000, where only one-fifth of this amount was payable in 1793? Finance was the province of the Department of the Treasury; Washington gladly passed Genet's request to Hamilton for an opinion. The more general representation of the Minister had hidden implications. Clearly Genet was not going to call for defence of the French West Indies, an obligation laid down by the Treaty of Alliance—but did he intend to accept the American interpretation of Article 22 of the Treaty of Commerce and thereby repudiate his own conduct in outfitting privateers at

Charleston? The possibility here was remote. Was Genet, on the other hand, actually projecting a new commercial treaty—with Article 22 transposed and rephrased to allow himself unprecedented latitude in the commissioning of French corsairs? Such an agreement would harness the United States inevitably to the French Revolution, and war with England might be precipitated. The idea was absurdity.

Most critical among the problems of the moment was one that involved directly neither France nor England but had ultimate connection with the struggles of revolutionary armies against the monarchies of Europe. For months the Indian situation on the Georgia frontier had reflected every French military failure across the Atlantic. Now that Spain enjoyed positive alliance with Great Britain, Carondolet could be expected to incite the Indians to depredations of greater magnitude and horror. At the same time Spanish Commissioners Viar and Jaudenes at Philadelphia doubtless would assume new arrogance in their representations to the Department of State, and progress in the vexatious Mississippi navigation dispute no longer was likely. Washington continued to hope that Carmichael and Short might effect the object of their negotiations with Spain, but it seemed the day of settlement must be interminably postponed.

Knox appeared at the President's house on May 25 with correspondence which presented a distressing view of the hostile temper of the Creeks. On Monday Jefferson presented a memorial from the Spanish Commissioners which contrasted the "judicious" behavior of Carondolet with alleged inflammatory proceedings on the part of Governor Blount of the Southwest Territory. Viar and Jaudenes inferred that punitive action by the United States would be disagreeable to Spain, especially when diplomatic conversations were under way in Madrid. Did Spain propose that the American government watch a slaughter of her pioneers while negotiations at Madrid approached a standstill? If Washington felt a flush of anger on May 27, he had every justification. A meeting of the Cabinet was called for the next morning.

Hamilton's absence prevented full discussion in the session of the twenty-eighth, but the following day measures were proposed to meet the crisis in Georgia. No offensive expedition against the Indians could be authorized at present; an additional force of one hundred cavalry and a like number of infantry were to be stationed in Georgia for purely defensive purposes; Congress would be called in event of "a serious invasion . . . by large bodies of Indians." On May 30 Knox brought a letter from Governor Telfair describing recent "horrid depredations" and setting forth a peremptory view that "open war must be entered into"—zeal for vengeance by the citizens of Georgia no longer could be restrained. Washington realized the Federal Government could not engage in punitive operations on the southwestern frontier; Spanish regiments at New Orleans, Natchez and Nogales might be awaiting just such a move. The President could do no more than direct Federal agents in Georgia to renew peaceful overtures to the Creeks. If these finally availed nothing, he might encourage South Carolina militiamen to go to the defence of their beleaguered neighbors.

Washington had not been well for a week. June 1 found him so in-disposed with fever as to be unable to attend a meeting of the Cabinet called to consider the fate of another of Genet's Charleston privateers, the *Sans Culotte,* which recently had appeared at Baltimore with a British prize in tow. The President took consolation in the knowledge that Ameri-can policy had been defined—the privateer certainly would be ordered away—but the hauteur of the French Minister seemed to redouble each day. Genet now demanded immediate release of Gideon Henfield and John Singletary, two Americans who had sailed from Charleston on the corsair *Citoyen Genet* and been arrested in Philadelphia on May 30. In reply Jefferson enclosed a copy of Randolph's opinion favoring indictment for breach of the national peace and informed the Frenchman in gentle language that the accused would be fairly tried by a civil magistrate "over whose proceedings the Executive has no control."

By the end of the first week in June unseasonably cold weather, pressures of office and intensifying personal assault in the columns of the *National Gazette* combined to affect markedly the President's health and appearance. "Little lingering fevers have been hanging about him," Jeffer-son noticed, and added that Washington seemed to feel newspaper chas-tisements "more than any person I ever yet met with. I am sincerely sorry to see them." The Secretary of State knew that Washington blamed him in some measure for perpetuation of the *National Gazette,* and he had good cause now to regret the excesses of his protégé. Freneau was content no longer merely to snipe at the Proclamation; a series by "Veritas" chal-lenged the discretion and even the integrity of the man over whose signa-ture neutrality had been declared. Washington endured Freneau's contin-uing barrage of painful fire because his belief remained firm that the presi-dential office demanded granite dignity which no volley should pierce.

On June 6 Hamilton submitted in draft a negative response to Genet's request for advances on the debt, but Washington found the paper "too dry and abrupt" and sent it to Jefferson for comment. Specific reasons should support a refusal, the Secretary of State argued; so curt a denial would jeopardize Franco-American amity. Again, Hamilton's proposal for negotiation of a new Dutch loan of three million florins was met unen-thusiastically by Jefferson and Randolph, who together induced the Pres-ident to ask for explicit details. Even when they generated friction among his advisers or bore some connection to foreign affairs, questions of finance stood small at present against the enigma of neutrality. After contriving to irritate Jefferson with persistent notes, British Minister Hammond now evidenced sharp dissatisfaction over the answer sent on June 5 to his de-mand for restitution of prizes. Nor was Genet silent for long. As word came on June 8 of an "informal" application for supply of public arms to France "in such a way as to give an appearance of their being forwarded by indi-viduals," Washington must have wondered if Genet consciously sought new pinnacles of absurdity. The Cabinet agreed at once that Knox should de-cline the extraordinary requests as politely as possible. The Minister's offi-cial communication to Jefferson that day brought fresh astonishment. Was there no propriety to stay this man's impertinence? France, Genet protested, could see no justice in the American regulation against the commissioning of privateers. Out of a desire to sustain harmony between the two republics, he was willing to restrict the activities of his consuls and defer to the President's "political opinions" until Congress had assembled to confirm or reject them! The *coup de grâce* came with vehemence: Let the Federal government respond to the call of the people whose "fraternal voice has resounded from every quarter around me!" Let the United States redeem "the cowardly abandonment of their friends in the moment when danger menaces them!"

If Washington thought fleetingly that Genet's outrageous inferences were adequate reason to demand immediate recall of the diplomat, he said nothing. Despite recent evidences of popular approval of the Proclamation, the President did not fail to realize that powerful opposition existed. An accurate gauging of sentiment in Virginia would be most valuable, and Randolph set out on June 6 for an extensive tour of that state. From Annapolis the Attorney General reported that the people of Maryland seemed to appreciate the Proclamation and that Gov. Joshua Clayton of Delaware had spoken well of it. Before this heartening news arrived, Washington had to summon the Cabinet again to deal with infractions of neutrality in New York. To his credit, Governor Clinton had ordered prompt detention of the sloop *Polly*, a prize brought into the harbor and there rechristened *Republican* by her French captors and armed for privateering. Hammond complained also that the British brig *Catherine*, another prize at New York, had been captured in American territorial waters. On June 12 the President approved a unanimous verdict of the Cabinet that France was wrong in both cases and instructed the Secretary of State to take appropriate action.

It did not please Jefferson to have to respond so readily to British supplications, but on June 15 he found full reason to share Washington's mounting disapprobation of Genet. The French Minister now insisted the *Republican* was being armed merely for her own defence; and further he wished Washington to know that a United States marshal had used the President's name to interfere with sale of the prize *William* at Warder's Wharf in Philadelphia! When Hammond delivered still another appeal for guarantees, Washington ordered a Cabinet session for June 17. Was there to be no end to the stream of diplomatic depositions, protests and petitions from the emissaries of France and England? Hopeful that the Cabinet decision of June 17 and subsequent notices to Genet and Hammond would silence both men for a time, the President turned to serious consideration of Hamilton's proposal to arrange a loan in Holland. Reasons for a loan, Washington told Jefferson, were very cogent. The Secretary of State disagreed, but approval to negotiate for two million florins went forward without delay.

In the Cabinet meeting of June 20 Jefferson had in hand a communication from the Spanish Commissioners which required instant attention. Jaudenes and Viar charged that the President was countenancing incitement of the Chickasaws against the Creeks and declared that the continuance of peace was "very problematical." It was plain, in Jefferson's mind, that Carondolet meant to pick a quarrel with the United States. Washington and his counsellors expected no miracle, but a full appeal to the Court of Madrid seemed the last logical measure to avert the disaster of war with Spain and the Creeks. The President directed Jefferson to prepare comprehensive instructions for Carmichael and Short. The British Minister chose this very moment to press again for definitive assurance that French privateers would not be allowed to reenter American ports. Hammond's persistence angered the President. "I leave it to you," he instructed Jefferson, "to say what or whether any answer should be given to the British minister's letter. . . . It would seem as if neither he nor the Spanish commissioners were to be satisfied with anything this Government can do, but on the contrary are resolved to drive matters to extremity."

However manifold the President's tribulations, Genet always was enough to augment them. Washington must have been tempted to speak sharply as Jefferson presented two significant papers in a meeting of the Cabinet June 22. One was a note from Governor Mifflin of Pennsylvania; French seamen were outfitting the *Little Sarah* with cannon. The ship was in process of conversion from prize to privateer right here at Philadelphia! The President instructed Knox to determine what exactly had been done. Official patience was put to even greater test as Jefferson disclosed a communication from the French Minister which surpassed all earlier arrogance. So intense was Genet's disappointment in the American government that he threw aside "diplomatic subtleties" and challenged Jefferson to explain matters "as a republican." This was too much insolence, even for the Secretary of State; Genet's note was left unanswered. Genet had finally alienated the only man in the Cabinet on whose sympathies he might have played.

The first week of June had brought a letter from Anthony Whiting which disclosed a precarious illness. The President offered to have medical consultation on Whiting's condition and made suggestions for treatment of the malady meantime. Washington added that he would endeavor to be at Mount Vernon by July 1 for a brief stay. Not the least disturbing of Washington's domestic affairs was the decision of Lear to resign. This young man of extraordinary ability had won Washington's affection as well as his confidence and had been regarded as a member of the family. Lear was leaving to set up his own business in the Federal City. A warm letter to the commissioners of the District of Columbia in his behalf went forward from Washington's desk June 13, and the President turned over his private secretarial duties to Bartholomew Dandridge.

Although on a mission of his own, Lear responded in characteristic fashion to an emergency that developed almost immediately after his departure. Within an hour of Lear's arrival at Georgetown on June 17, he had met Doctor Craik and learned from him that Whiting's death was imminent. He would go promptly to Mount Vernon, see Whiting and ascertain conditions generally. On June 19 Lear sent a report of affairs at the plantation. Early harvest was progressing fairly well, but Whiting was "under a very great anxiety about leaving your interest without seeing some person who could inform you of the situation of it at this time." Lear's visit eased the manager's mind. Washington was acutely distressed, both because of Whiting personally and because of the probable effect on his business "present and to come." Washington's homeward journey began June 24. A letter from Lear written that day reached the President en route. It told of Whiting's death on the twenty-first, Lear's interview with the overseers from the various farms, and his intention to await Washington's arrival at Mount Vernon.

Much as he lamented the state of plantation affairs, Washington could not devote his brief visit exclusively to their betterment. One problem which accompanied the President to Mount Vernon was that of architectural design for the Capitol. At Georgetown he spent the better part of June 27 with Stephen Hallet and James Hoban and listened to their vigorous objections to Doctor Thornton's plan. Convinced that decision should wait on deliberation, Washington took to Mount Vernon papers given him by the two professional architects. After review of the problem, Washington prepared instructions for Hallet and Hoban. They were to set out for Philadelphia by the next stage with all documents necessary to effect an early decision. Jefferson was requested to call together all those concerned for a full discussion of the matter without delay. Washington admitted he had been influenced by the exterior beauty of Thornton's plan without full knowledge of the principles of architecture. He would rely on Jefferson's more experienced judgment—"A plan must be adopted and, good or bad, it must be entered upon."

It was July 11 when Washington again reached Philadelphia. The trip had been leisurely—he had no forewarning that a climax of diplomatic peril awaited him. There lay on his desk a stack of papers left by the Secretary of State and marked for "instant attention." Here were two letters from Mifflin, a statement signed by the port warden of Philadelphia, Jefferson's memorandum of a conversation with the French Minister, minutes of a meeting of the Cabinet, a note from District Attorney William Rawle, and finally Genet's letter of July 9 to the Secretary of State. All these related to the French prize *Little Sarah*. On July 5, evidently, Jefferson had been told by Hamilton that the *Little Sarah* was equipping for sea as a privateer. Immediately Knox ordered Mifflin to investigate. The warden's official report of July 6 substantiated rumors of fourteen cannon aboard the brig instead of four, six swivels and a crew of 120 men, Americans as well as Frenchmen. That Saturday night Governor Mifflin learned that the *Little Sarah* might be ready to sail immediately. He called up the state militia and rushed a message to Jefferson's country house. The Secretary of State hastened to town Sunday afternoon to find that Mifflin's assistant, Alexander J. Dallas, had gone to Genet late the previous evening for assurance that sailing orders would be withheld. No success attended this mission. The Minister refused categorically to detain the vessel, threatened to make public his diplomatic correspondence with the American government and to "appeal from the President to the people."

Jefferson went at once to Genet's quarters and was subjected to a long harangue. The Frenchman commented acidly on the American Constitution but said nothing which Jefferson could interpret as a direct insult to the President or threat of popular appeal. After Genet had spent himself in declamation, Jefferson pressed for a promise that the *Little Sarah* would be held in port until the President had returned to Philadelphia and rendered a decision. The Minister insisted that every new gun on the brig had been procured from other French vessels; he declined to give a guarantee, but declared that the ship was not yet ready to put to sea. She would merely drop down the river to another anchorage. On Monday morning, the Secretary of State met Hamilton and Knox at Mifflin's office. He rejected their proposition to establish militia and cannon on Mud Island in the Delaware as an obstacle to premature departure of the privateer. The Governor dismissed his militia, no battery was erected, and the *Little Sarah* promptly moved down the river to Chester. The next day Genet notified Jefferson that command of the vessel, rechristened the *Petite Democrate*, had been assigned to Ensign Amiot. "When ready," the Minister wrote, "I shall despatch her . . . When treaties speak, the agents of nations have but to obey."

Washington could stand no more. What superlative of insolence was this? Did Genet dare send an illegal privateer to sea from Philadelphia? Why did not the Secretary of State come in person to discuss the business? The President penned a note for instant delivery to Jefferson. Jefferson's reply, phrased formally in the third person, reached the President that evening. He had been ill for several days, and had gone home certain that Hamilton and Knox would inform the President of the facts of the case and give their views. Since neither had done so, he now enclosed a copy of their opinion favoring erection of a battery on Mud Island, together with his own argument against the proposal. He would be at his office early the next morning and available at any time the President chose.

The hours spent in Cabinet session of July 12 must have been as exasperating as any Washington yet had experienced in the Presidency. Jefferson, Hamilton and Knox met in his office to ponder a problem which emerged as the residue of months of difficult diplomacy. The *Petite Democrate's* fate was not in question. She could slip to sea on a nod from Genet. Obviously, with twenty French warships expected daily from the West Indies, the government could not so far jeopardize its neutrality as to send Federal cutters to secure the corsair by force. What really mattered was that the behavior of the French Minister had become unendurable. At his hands the sovereign dignity of the United States had suffered a gross outrage. There could be no dispute on this point; Jefferson admitted it as readily as Hamilton made the charge. Formal demand for recall was the privilege, indeed the duty, of a nation insulted by a diplomat accredited to her. The President realized America's honor was at stake—yet he hesitated when Hamilton now urged that France be asked to recall Genet and Knox proposed further that the Minister's functions meanwhile be totally suspended. All that issued from the Cabinet was a decision to apply to the Supreme Court for an opinion on general and particular aspects of neutrality. The Secretary of State was to notify the ministers of France and Great Britain that every private vessel of either nation would be expected to remain in port until the judges had forwarded recommendations to the President.

If Washington's prudence on July 12 appeared close to procrastination, the reason was plain. The *Petite Democrate* was at sea a day or two later; opportunity to obstruct her flight had been lost while he travelled from Mount Vernon. American neutrality had been breached; what damage was done could not be repaired. Peremptory suspension of Genet's ministerial status might do greater damage. The heat of faction was high. Hamilton was storming the public prints under the pseudonym "Pacificus." Popular sympathy for France stood at a new peak. Much as he wished to deal decisively with Genet, Washington would await the return of Randolph from Virginia. That trusted adviser would give valuable counsel.

For much of the next ten days the President successfully relegated the omnipresent image of Genet to a corner of his mind. It was not done easily, for the fervid Frenchman was exulting in his success, but Washington determined to ignore the Minister for the present. On July 15 the President sat down with Jefferson to discuss with Hallet and Hoban Dr. Thornton's plan for the Capitol. It was decided that Hallet, the architect in charge of construction, should proceed with his original plan but that certain of Thornton's exterior features should be incorporated. Later the same day Washington was surprised to learn from Jefferson that Secretary of War Knox had promised Governor Mifflin that army cannon would be raised on Mud Island to command the passage of the river. This should have been done before the *Petite Democrate* sailed, but the responsibility was the Governor's alone; the administration no more could be expected to supply Federal cannon for the port of Philadelphia than for a harbor in any other place. The Cabinet met and Jefferson was treated to a spectacle of Knox in discomfiture under sharp reprimand from the President. Many Republicans might believe Washington showed partiality to Hamilton and Knox as Revolutionary comrades, but impartial justice was the President's rule where duty required an official judgment.

On July 17, despite a lengthy interview with Knox on Indian affairs, Washington took time to acknowledge a letter from the Speaker of the House of Representatives, Jonathan Trumbull of Connecticut. The subject was serious and in less troubled months would have had the Executive's continuing attention. Trumbull forwarded a communication from American seamen held captive by the pirates of the Barbary States. A year earlier the President had directed Admiral John Paul Jones and Thomas Barclay, consul at Morocco, "to negotiate for the release by ransom of these unfortunate citizens." Both agents died before progress was made, and the "Algerine business" then was entrusted to Humphreys. Washington sought to quiet Trumbull's anxiety with assurance that "things are now in the best train . . . that circumstances will admit of."

His advisers had been working separately on the questions concerning neutrality to be submitted to the Supreme Court, and a Cabinet meeting on July 18 eliminated duplications and resolved the final wording of twenty-nine queries. As Washington studied the set, it gratified him to realize that here was a brilliant example of the profitable cooperation of Jefferson and Hamilton. The questions comprised a remarkable statement of the whole problem of neutrality. No one could be sure the judges would accept such an extension of their duties, but, as Jefferson remarked in transmitting the questions to them, the President would be "much relieved" to have their advice. Chief Justice John Jay and Associates James Wilson and James Iredell replied politely that they would like to delay a decision on the "propriety" of compliance until their absent colleagues reached Philadelphia. This response meant that the judges probably would decline to treat the questions, in which event Washington knew the Cabinet would have to formulate rigid rules of its own. There must be no recurrence of the affair of the *Little Sarah*.

Randolph's return from Virginia brought encouraging reports of devotion and loyalty on the part of the people of that state. With the Attorney General back, the President made ready to take action on Genet. The Minister's offensive unanswered letter of June 22 was shown to Randolph, and in Cabinet on July 23 Washington proposed that the correspondence of the envoy be sent to France with a demand for his recall. Hamilton and Knox vigorously supported this view, and the next day Randolph suggested to the President that Jefferson prepare a statement of Genet's verbal communications together with copies of the official correspondence. Washington instructed the Secretary of State accordingly on July 25.

Before the case of Genet could be reviewed in detail, the President's attention was called to other business. On July 17 Washington met Governor Blount and Gen. Andrew Pickens, both recently arrived in Philadelphia, for dinner and a discussion of Indian affairs in the South. While the delegates at Sandusky apparently were enjoying little success in negotiations with the hostile northern tribes, prospects had brightened below the Ohio, but Pickens still favored a large militia invasion of the Creek country.

By the end of the month it appeared certain that the Supreme Court would refuse to give the advisory opinions Washington sought. The President summoned his Cabinet to devise Executive Orders which would prevent further infractions of the neutral status of the nation. Out of their sessions came a set of eight "Rules Governing Belligerents." In desperation, lacking consent of Congress or judiciary counsel, the Cabinet had taken an unprecedented step. Three months of Genet's maddening conduct had forced the Executive to implement the Proclamation of April 22. A body of regulations now specifically forbade corsairs to equip in American ports or enlist American crews.

The Cabinet conference of July 29 was brief because a sad event was scheduled that afternoon—the burial of Mary Lear in Christ Church cemetery. The wife of the President's secretary, only twenty-three, had died late July 28 of a sudden illness. As readily as her able and devoted husband, "Polly" Lear had endeared herself to the Washington household. His usefulness extended to every phase of the President's activity, hers in particular to the domestic duties and social responsibilities that fell on the President's wife. Washington, who rarely attended a funeral, stood at Lear's side during the service. Three Cabinet officers and three Justices of the Supreme Court acted as pallbearers.

A meeting of the Cabinet on the first of August sealed the fate of

Genet. His entire correspondence with the Department of State was reviewed from copies Jefferson furnished. It was decided to send these documents to Morris for presentation to the Executive Council of France, together with a full statement of indiscretions of Genet and a formal demand for his recall. The Secretary of State felt that delicacy of expression was essential; Hamilton, Knox and Randolph recommended "peremptory terms." Knox found himself alone in asking the President to suspend Genet's diplomatic and consular powers at once, but Hamilton and Randolph concurred in a proposal that the Minister be duly notified of the demand for his recall. Washington seemed to favor this step in spite of Jefferson's argument that it would only stir Genet to new outrages. Washington adjourned the discussion until the next morning at nine.

August 2 was a day of disquieting and partisan discourse for Hamilton and Jefferson and one of immeasurable distress for the President. The Secretary of the Treasury opened with a long recital of reasons for public appeal and remonstrance against Genet. Jefferson replied that Hamilton "calculated to make the President assume the station of the head of a party instead of the head of a nation." Would not Genet answer such an appeal with a blatant one of his own? Washington seemed to incline towards Hamilton's proposal. Knox, instead of attempting to present a case, exhibited a broadside of "The Funeral Dirge of George Washington and James Wilson, King and Judge," one of the late pasquinades from the pen of Freneau. The President went suddenly into towering anger, spoke bitterly of the journalistic abuse to which he had been subjected in past months, and defied any critic to indicate one selfish act promulgated by him in office. He would rather be in the grave, he cried, than in his present posture! He would rather be a farmer than emperor of the world, and yet that "rascal Freneau" insinuated that his pretensions were kingly: Not for years had Washington's temper so completely possessed him. Once the fury had played out, he sank exhausted into despondency. Hamilton's effort to reintroduce the topic was fruitless. The President dismissed his advisers with a comment that no immediate decision on the proposed appeal seemed necessary. What benefit it might be to Federalists to denounce Genet officially, or what damage it might work on Republicans, the President manifestly did not care. Politics was not his province. Executive rulings would curb the menace of illegal privateering, and soon the unwelcome Minister would be replaced. At least a diplomatic nightmare was over; those decisions as yet unmade could be of secondary significance only.

The Secretary of State had indicated in a formal note of resignation on July 31 that he intended to quit office at the end of September. Hamilton, in late June had similarly expressed an intention to resign as soon as Congress assembled and completed an investigation of his public conduct. Washington was determined to prevent dissolution of the Cabinet, and on August 6 he called at Jefferson's country house in an agitated mood. The two talked at length. The President emphasized his own longing to retire and complained that Hamilton and Jefferson were about to desert him at the outset of four additional years of obligatory public service. Who could be found to replace them? Finally, the President asked Jefferson to stay until the end of the year. No promise came immediately, but on August 11 the Secretary of State consented.

Compromise was as inescapable as eventual dismemberment of the Cabinet was certain, but, "like a man going to the gallows," the President was "willing to put it off as long as he could." If this was indecision, he scarcely could be blamed. Partisan controversy grew less reasonable and more reckless every hour. At least Genet would be gone when Jefferson retired and, as long as the mercurial Frenchman remained, domestic convulsion always was possible. In fact, a convulsion seemed imminent in New York. On August 1 the inhabitants of that city were wildly excited by a sea battle off Sandy Hook. The *Embuscade* under Bompard routed the British frigate *Boston* in a dramatic action, and the next day festivities accelerated with the arrival of the entire French West Indies fleet in the roadstead. Genet hastened to New York to welcome the warships. In spite of elaborate preparations by a committee of Republicans, his reception was not extraordinary. Federalists were lively in circulating a story that Genet had maligned the President. By the middle of the month Washington learned the climax of this political drama: Rufus King and John Jay made formal charge that the French Minister had threatened an appeal to the people. Advertisement of Genet's blunders produced the effect Federalist leaders anticipated. A swell of public indignation engulfed those few Republicans who now chose to stand by Genet. In little more than a week towns and counties in half a dozen States forwarded resolution of their people: We will not suffer our Chief Magistrate to be insulted by a foreign emissary!

The President had yet to approve the letter which would request Genet's recall. In Cabinet session on August 15 Jefferson read his first draft. Five days later the paper was studied, corrected by paragraphs and approved. A meeting of August 23 determined that the letter should bear the date of the last document to accompany it. Jefferson had produced a masterpiece of eight thousand words which drew careful distinction between Genet and the French Republic. Sharp indictment was made of the errant envoy, but the "constant and unabating" good will of the United States for the people of France was guaranteed. At last Washington could feel a measure of relief, and if satisfaction accompanied it, there was reason. He had guided his nation through a storm of diplomacy, and the tempests of national politics had not turned his course.

The first six months of his second administration had taxed Washington beyond anything he had known in the Presidency. Expressions against the government more and more were directed against the man at its head. As attacks focused on him, the invectives gained in unruly strength and ugly spirit. The protests of an orderly and reasonable people fast were approaching the meaningless fury of a disorderly mob. Then quite suddenly all Philadelphians found themselves distracted by an impersonal, impartial and even more merciless foe.

On August 28 those who saw the *General Advertiser* read of the presence of yellow fever in Philadelphia, but it was not news, certainly not to Washington. By that time the disease was widespread and alarming in its manifestations. An epidemic beset the city. The newspaper article, carefully and thoughtfully prepared by a committee from the College of Physicians and printed at the instance of Mayor Matthew Clarkson, turned alarm into panic. Fear spread. Inhabitants frantically left the city. Government as well as private business was abandoned; few public offices remained open. Even the term of the Supreme Court was interrupted, and the Pennsylvania General Assembly adjourned September 5 after only eight days in session.

The President watched with concern the progress of the defiant disease, but evidently he had no personal fear of its contagion. He was disturbed over the possibility that Hamilton might be in first stages of the malady but did not withhold an invitation on September 6 to the Secretary of the Treasury and Mrs. Hamilton to dine at the President's house that afternoon. Two days later diagnosis of the Secretary's illness as yellow fever was known. Distress over Hamilton's sickness was reason for Washington's wish to delay departure for Mount Vernon, but Martha was unwilling to go without him, and there seemed no choice but to remove his family from the hazardous surroundings. The President had little hope of continuing business for the nation and made ready to leave on September 10.

If, as he rode south Washington's thoughts were of conditions he would find at Mount Vernon, this was no reason for release or relief. Plantation affairs never had obtruded more persistently than in the weeks since Whiting's death. The careful letters that went each week to Howell Lewis, his temporary manager at the Potomac estate, showed no lessening of consideration, though the boy had not taken hold readily and appeared to be disposed to procrastinate. Fanny Washington still was dependent on his counsel, and her needs seemed always to be most urgent when Washington was busy with public matters of prime importance. The overseer, James Butler, was a perennial nuisance and in Washington's opinion, scarcely could be exceeded in neglect of duty.

On the brighter side, Washington was pleased to hear that the Potomac Company prospered. Most gratifying was the prospect of obtaining a suitable plantation manager. The application of William Pearce held promise and Washington had written him on August 26. Pearce replied promptly in acceptance of the offer of one hundred guineas a year. When Pearce came to Mount Vernon September 23, Washington prepared articles of agreement between himself and the new manager which described in detail the proprietor's ideal for development of the plantation and its dependencies. A contract for one year was entered upon and Pearce was scheduled to begin his service January 1, 1794.

Wherever Washington was, there was the seat of government. A change from public to private affairs would have been welcome diversion, but more than fleeting shift from the nation's perplexities was out of the question. Scarcely had the President rested from his homeward journey than he took the road for the relatively brief ride to the Federal City. It was September 18, the date for laying the cornerstone of the Capitol. The President found the splendor of music and drums, of flying colors, of many Masons in their symbolic regalia, of happy spectators generally. It was a

memorable affair for the Masonic Order, magnified by Washington's participation as a member. When the assemblage dispersed to the echo of a final
fusillade, Washington carried with him, besides memories, more tangible
evidence of the occasion. In his pocket was a certificate of purchase for four
lots in the Federal City which he had negotiated at the sale that day.

There was a measure of reassurance in the addresses and resolves
that arrived almost daily from different parts of the Union. Washington
was grateful for this "testimony of unanimity," but it was not reassuring
that resolutions adopted in certain parts of his own Virginia were worded
with restraint—if indeed they did not imply reproof of the President by
the pallor of their praise. Seldom did the post fail to bring news of Genet's
continuing defiance, unabashed ambitions and endless activities. These
communications usually were from Jefferson, though Governor Clinton advised the President of the Frenchman's exploits in New York Harbor. If
official notification of his requested recall had dampened Genet's ardor,
there was no evidence of it. His pronouncements against the President were
more reckless and cunning than ever. Coupled with these unhappy memo-
randa was another defiance that disturbed the President profoundly—the
Democratic Societies more and more vigorously were protesting that the
cause of France should be the concern of America. In the rise of "popular"
societies Washington saw the spread of Genet's influence into the wider
rank of extreme partisanship. The aim of these clubs, he told Gov. Henry
Lee, was "nothing short of the Government of these States, even at the expense of plunging this country in the horrors of a disastrous war."

With this in mind, the President instructed the Cabinet to meet him
in Germantown on November 1. In Philadelphia fear was giving way to a
sort of mild optimism as disease lessened. By the middle of October it was
cold enough for an overcoat, and a thick frost fell on the city before the
month ended. Washington could rejoice at the recovery of his Secretary of
the Treasury, but there were many to be mourned. Perhaps his deepest
personal grief was in the loss of Samuel Powel, whose companionship and
that of his wife long had been cherished by the President and Mrs. Washington. Between the first of August and early November, death had
claimed more than four thousand Philadelphians, sometimes at the rate of
a hundred a day.

On the last stretch of the familiar journey north Washington was
glad to have the company of Jefferson, who had come as far as Baltimore
by stage. Late on November 1 they entered Germantown in a rainstorm to
find hundreds of Philadelphians plodding through deep mud, still too fearful of the plague to return to their homes in the city. So scarce were accom-
modations that Jefferson thought himself fortunate to find an empty bed in
a corner of the dining room of the King of Prussia Tavern. The President
unpacked in quarters leased for him by Randolph and, next morning,
opened his office for work. By the second week of November the fever appeared almost at an end and thousands were flocking back to their homes,
but it was decided to continue the President's office at Germantown until
December 1 as a rallying point.

Washington's thoughts went often these days to imminent crisis in the Northwest. As early as the first week of September he had definite knowledge that negotiation with the hostile Indians had broken down. After a tedious delay native chieftains had finally visited the camp of the American commissioners on July 31—but only to demand recession of the frontier to the Ohio River in accordance with the Fort Stanwix agreement of 1768. The commissioners remained two weeks more, unable to gain another direct contact with the Indians but still hopeful that some basis for peace other than the old boundary would be proposed. When no word came except a written ultimatum for the Ohio River line, the delegation left for home in disgust. Doubtless Canadian officials were plying their influence to create trouble in the borderland. Little else should have been expected, for certainly Great Britain wished to see Americans restricted as far to the south as possible. One course was left—that of open war. Major General Wayne, in cantonment near Cincinnati, had been restive all summer. On news of the collapse of the negotiation, the General put the three thousand men of his "Legion" under march on October 7. Wayne's troops within a week approached the southwest branch of the Maumee. Here he decided to pass the winter and erected a stockade which he called Fort Greeneville. Washington considered the expedition a climactic effort; the government could do no more for its pioneers north of the Ohio. Those who appreciated Wayne's talents were sure his cannon and cavalry would restore peace, and the President hoped it soon would be done.

Whatever the extent of the activities of the King's agents in Canada, his naval officers in the Atlantic had by this time given ample reason for the gravest apprehension. Late in August the President had received an alarming report from England—the British government was said to have issued an order by which naval commanders were to seize and confiscate any cargo of corn, flour or meal bound for France in a neutral vessel! Agreement had been unanimous in the Cabinet that this interpretation of contraband was preposterous. Jefferson had instructed Pinckney to demand revocation of any decree which so abridged the rights of free neutral commerce and threatened to an extreme the advancement of agriculture in the United States. Now, two months later, it was painfully evident that England did not mean to lay aside so effective a weapon in her program to reduce France to surrender by starvation. A dispatch from Pinckney verified this, and copies of his recent correspondence with Lord Grenville confirmed Washington's fear that depredations on the high seas would increase and American ships and crews often might be held indefinitely in British ports. This circumstance gave rise to dread possibility that His Majesty's navy would choose to accelerate the notorious practice of impressment of American merchant seamen. Letters in the first week of November substantiated the President's fear of impressment. It was hard to foresee any but dire consequences of Britain's new policy, and old difficulties with that nation seemed as distant from settlement as ever. Ten years after the Definitive Treaty of Peace had pledged their prompt evacuation, frontier posts remained in the occupancy of British troops. Hammond still protested that no instruction had come from London which would enable him to renew conversation on the matter.

As yet no answer had come from France to the demand for recall of Genet. While Genet's present activities were nebulous, there was reason to believe that the man's influence was spreading. The Spanish commissioners had delivered an excited complaint: four French agents were en route to Kentucky! This seemed to confirm reports that George Rogers Clark, the Revolutionary hero of the West, meant to lead an army of disgruntled frontiersmen against Spanish garrisons in Louisiana. France would welcome such a blow. Since the support Clark would have to have for even a small freebooting expedition was in Genet's power alone to supply, it appeared certain that the French envoy was involved in a scheme which, if executed, would wreck the neutrality of the United States! Any hostile gesture by Americans against Spanish Louisiana would signal disaster; it would bring immediate war with Spain, and more than likely ultimate war with England. The Secretary of State sent urgent warning to Gov. Isaac Shelby of Kentucky, and Knox wrote to authorize the use of military force if necessary.

Rumors circulated, as well, of French recruiting in South Carolina, and Genet's presumptions and utterances were more noxious than ever. Washington was angry. He was convinced, he told his Cabinet on November 8, that the troublemaker should be ordered to leave the United States at once. Hamilton and Knox agreed. Jefferson sat silent, but Randolph held that diplomatic propriety made it necessary to allow France to recall Genet. Washington restated his argument for peremptory dismissal, but in the end was sufficiently impressed with the reasoning of the Attorney General to let the matter rest.

Washington wrote late in November: "I am occupied in collecting and arranging the materials for my communications to Congress." Never before had an Annual Address been so tedious in preparation. How to explain, how to justify the Proclamation of Neutrality was the real difficulty. A session of the Cabinet on November 18 brought from Jefferson and Randolph opinion that the President must not declare anything further on the question of war or peace; Hamilton argued that the Chief Executive must compromise no part of the power to make such declarations. When, on the twenty-first, Hamilton and Randolph suggested in writing just how the Proclamation should be explained, debate flared, but the President remained uncommitted. Two days later the Attorney General was directed to prepare the address on the Proclamation and draft special messages on relations with France, Great Britain, Spain, and the Barbary Powers. When these papers were presented to the Cabinet on November 28, Hamilton insisted that England had been contrasted unfavorably with France and urged that certain documents relative to British depredations be withheld from Congress for the moment. Knox seconded this and Randolph seemed inclined to agree. The President took Jefferson's side with vehemence and declared that all pertinent papers must be laid before the legislators.

By the first of December snow was falling in Philadelphia, the last trace of the fever had vanished, and members of the Third Congress were arriving daily. Washington was at his city residence when notice came on December 2 that a quorum existed in each House. The next morning, as the President entered the Senate Chamber to deliver his fifth Annual Address, he may have taken solace in the thought that Congress now would share tribulations which had been exclusively his for so long. His explanation of the policy of neutrality was direct and unpretentious, vigorous in its simplicity. "It seemed . . . my duty to admonish our citizens of the consequences of a contraband trade and of hostile acts. Under these impressions . . . the Proclamation was issued. In this posture of affairs, both new and delicate, I resolved to adopt general rules which should conform to the treaties [of 1778] of Congress to correct, improve or enforce this plan of procedure." There followed recommendation for stronger defences, brief reference to the necessity of punitive war against Ohio tribes, and a request that newspapers be freed of transportation tax.

Two days later the President's special message on French and British relations went to Congress. Separate messages on Spain and the Barbary States were withheld until the sixteenth in order that latest dispatches from abroad might be included. Washington might have burdened each message with severe comment; instead, he let the accompanying documents speak for themselves. Only when he came to the subject of Genet did the President show asperity. The French Minister, Washington told Congress, evidenced "nothing of the friendly spirit of the nation which sent him."

As Congress began its deliberations, the business of the Executive went on. Until France recalled her unwelcome diplomat, communications from Genet must be given some formal acknowledgment. There was need now to anticipate a request by France for recall of Morris, long *persona non grata* at Paris, and, more immediate, a need to replace Jefferson. The resignation of the Secretary of State would be effective at the close of the year. To Jefferson's formal note of resignation the President replied generously. Washington invited Randolph to succeed Jefferson, and the day after Christmas an interview at the President's house confirmed the new arrangement. The Attorney General would take Jefferson's portfolio and his would go to Justice William Bradford of the Supreme Court of Pennsylvania. Randolph was the logical choice and the President's personal preference. Since the estrangement of Hamilton and Jefferson in 1792, Randolph had been his closest adviser. Time and time again Washington had sought the confidential opinion of his Attorney General; time and time again Randolph's impartial view of a question had paralleled his own. Randolph desired the appointment; the President was pleased to offer it to this old and trusted friend.

The General spent the holiday season in contemplation of the problems of a planter. Three letters went to Pearce. Washington outlined an elaborate system of crop rotation and completed a map of the five farms on the Potomac. As 1793 came to a close, one last act was characteristic. On December 31 he asked Bishop William White of Philadelphia how, "without ostentation or mention of my name," he could contribute to the relief of the widows and orphans of the city. "The pressure of public business," he wrote, "hitherto has suspended but not altered my resolution." The President's gift of $250 followed on New Year's Day.

Friends of the administration viewed the advent of 1794 with happiness and hope. To Washington clouds were visible, and they darkened with the intelligence which came in that month. General Wayne complained of poor supplies, expiring enlistments, even of sedition among officers of his Legion. Latest word from Spain told of little progress in the negotiation for commercial privileges on the Mississippi, and Pinckney wrote gloomily from London that no relaxation need be expected in the policies of the British admiralty. Worst of all, there was alarming news from South Carolina and from Kentucky which prompted the President again to consider immediate revocation of Genet's diplomatic status.

Even before the first of the year, stories were spreading to the effect that Genet had sponsored recruiting five thousand South Carolinians in the service of France. The Minister admitted that "several brave republicans" had been commissioned, but he denied any direct part in preparations against the Spanish Floridas. There followed Governor Moultrie's confirmation of recruiting activities in South Carolina and reports of the movements of Clark in Kentucky and of publication of inflammatory resolves of the Democratic Society of that State. Genet was at the bottom of an elaborate plan of war against the Spanish colonies, and discontented Americans seemed determined to carry it out. Washington's anxiety mounted. Evidences of the diplomat's intrigue were forwarded to Congress, but on the twentieth Washington was able to communicate the long awaited word that made action unnecessary: France was sending a new envoy to the United States.

The President's own relations with Congress were under strain. On January 24, with a view to embarrassing the administration, Senate Republicans asked the Chief Executive to transmit copies of the diplomatic correspondence of Gouverneur Morris, American Minister to France since June 1792. Federalists feared that Morris's dispatches would show the American envoy to have been violently at odds with both the personalities and the principles of the French Revolution. Washington watched with interest the progress of a debate which began in the House of Representatives on January 3. That day Madison, armed with Jefferson's report on foreign trade, rose to offer startling resolutions. Let Congress, the Virginian said, lay new duties against ships and goods of those nations with which the United States had no commercial treaty—let there be retaliation in kind against the maritime outrages of Britain! Federalists were aghast; these Republican resolutions seemed to invite war. By the last week of January Federalists and Republicans locked every day in verbal battle. An issue of greatest consequence had been joined. Some who wished Madison well doubted the prudence of his move at so uncertain a juncture in the foreign affairs of the nation. Federalists could interpret the resolutions only as an irresistible challenge to England, a headlong plunge to war. They tried desperately to kill the measures, but the Republican majority contrived a postponement of debate to the first Monday in March.

No sooner were Madison's resolutions put aside than the House shifted attention to the "Algerine business," business in which England again played the villain's part. Indignation against the Barbary pirates themselves was no higher than that against Great Britain, their alleged prompter. Federalists called for construction of a naval force of six frigates. The naval bill narrowly survived a test vote on February 21. Its passage seemed probable.

Washington's sixty-third birthday was notable for festive parading, pealing bells and artillery salutes. To the President, it had importance as the formal termination of Genet's nine month's residence as Minister of the French Republic. Genet's successor, Joseph Fauchet, had disembarked at Philadelphia the day before and had promptly delivered a request which both Randolph and Washington had anticipated: Robespierre's Jacobin government asked for the arrest and return of Genet to France for punishment. Washington would take no agency, even remote, in the bloody business of the French Terror; whatever Genet had done or tried to do, the President did not intend to order the young man to his doom. If Genet wished, it was agreed, he might have political asylum in America.

Randolph ushered Fauchet into the President's parlor on February 22. The new Minister spoke through an interpreter and his reception was brief, but Washington liked the grave, handsome face of this Frenchman in his mid-thirties who somehow possessed the good sense not to argue unduly for Genet's deportation. Fauchet left, and at half past twelve members of Congress came in a group to pay respects to the President. He greeted the legislators cordially, invited them to partake of cake and punch, and similarly entertained others who visited him that afternoon. In the evening Washington escorted Martha to a ball given in his honor by the City Dancing Assembly.

At last Genet was technically powerless, but movements inaugurated by him months earlier now assumed ominous proportions. Every day it became more certain that the French diplomat had planned to involve the United States in war with Spain. Evidently a two-edged attack was projected against the Spanish dependencies in North America; South Carolinians and Georgians under Samuel Hammond would strike East Florida and take St. Augustine; Kentuckians under Clark would seize St. Louis, then move down the Mississippi against Louisiana. When Clark published a call for recruits and Governor Shelby wrote defiantly from Kentucky that he possessed no authority to restrain armed men from leaving his State, Washington realized that the axe of war was poised. Hastily, he drafted a stern admonition to American citizens who might be involved and sent the paper to Randolph for suggestions. Towards the end of the month, unofficial reports of actual mobilization by Clark alarmed Federalists profoundly. Anxious to maintain the good impression he had made, Fauchet issued a proclamation on March 6 which revoked all commissions granted by Genet to Clark and his cohorts. Federalists in the Senate tried desperately to enact legislation that would define such filibustering expeditions as criminal, but only when the President submitted a documented complaint from the Spanish commissioners did Republican members yield to the bill on March 13. To Washington's chagrin, the House laid the measure aside after two readings. This left the President to take action on his own, but Randolph seemed to fear that such a gesture by the Executive would aggrieve Republicans in the West and the South. On March 24, a month after Washington had given the Secretary of State his draft, a fair copy was returned. The President signed the Proclamation the same day. Americans were warned "to refrain from enlisting, enrolling or assembling themselves for such unlawful purposes, and from being in any wise concerned . . . as all lawful means will be strictly put in execution for securing obedience to the laws and for punishing such dangerous and daring violations. . . ." General Wayne was instructed to post troops on the Ohio to intercept Clark's expedition should it attempt to pass. Clark did not move his freebooters against Louisiana. By the end of March the threat of precipitate war with Spain had passed.

Trouble with Spain would have been doubly calamitous at a time when difficulties with Great Britain were striking a new height. Multiplying reports from the Caribbean made it appear that English naval commanders were instructed to seize every neutral vessel in trade with the French West Indies. Federalists read of the depredations in stunned disbelief. Did Britain intend to force the United States out of her neutral position? It was fortunate that Congress found itself sufficiently relieved of party strife to take up problems of defence in earnest. By the beginning of March full attention focused on military preparation. Washington asked the Secretary of State to prepare an accounting of all spoliations against American vessels by the powers at war. When Randolph's report went to Congress on March 5, many were surprised at the Secretary's statement that all belligerents, France included, were in the habit of seizing neutral ships in West Indies waters. This may have given solace to Federalists who continued to hope that Britain soon would relax her maritime rigor, but many acknowledged Anglophiles wondered and doubted. Knox was heard to say that war with England had become inevitable. Radical Republicans would welcome it; some even urged immediate attack on Detroit. Before the end of the second week in March, the House had passed the naval construction bill in original form, together with a bill for harbor fortification and a large army appropriation.

While vigorous military measures were imperative, it remained the hope of Federalists to avert a rupture in England. Their faith in the President was large; their dependence on his popularity was total. They looked to the Senate for inspiration and, within that body, their spokesmen were contriving a plan to salvage the abused neutrality of the nation. The Secretary of State had suggested to Washington the idea of a special conciliatory mission to England, and on March 10 Oliver Ellsworth appeared at the President's house with definite proposals. The Connecticut Federalist asked if an envoy extraordinary might not be sent to London to negotiate a general settlement of Anglo-American quarrels. Washington was uncommunicative at first, then interested as Ellsworth enumerated the probable achievements of such an undertaking. When the Senator mentioned Hamilton as a suitable agent, Washington interrupted the discourse—Hamilton simply did not possess the confidence of the American people. Ellsworth departed without satisfaction of a commitment from the President.

Madison's "restrictive" resolutions had been all but forgotten in the excitement of preparation for war. William M. Giles made an unsuccessful effort to revive them on March 14. Two days before, Theodore Sedgwick introduced decisive resolutions of his own. The Massachusetts Federalist called for establishment of a wartime army of fifteen auxiliary regiments, each of one thousand men, and for a short-term Presidential embargo on American shipping. Madison thought he saw the hand of Hamilton behind these proposals, and he was not mistaken. Republicans showed surprise at the new belligerency of the Federalists, but certain it was that something must be done. The enforced idleness of embargo, Federalists reasoned, was at least preferable to confiscation of cargoes at sea. Perhaps an interruption of the lucrative American trade would bring England to her senses. On March 25 the House called for Executive enactment of a thirty-day embargo. The Senate concurred the next morning, and Washington received a unanimous opinion of the Cabinet that state governors be instructed to detain vessels by use of militia if necessary. On the twenty-eighth the President proclaimed the embargo in force.

Next in the business of the House were Sedgwick's proposals for invigoration of the army, and news reached Philadelphia which gave the measures fresh importance. On February 10 the Governor General of Canada, Lord Dorchester, had delivered an inflammatory address to western Indians who visited him that day at Quebec. Soon, Dorchester was alleged to have said, the United States and Great Britain would fight; soon, the King's native warriors might reoccupy much of their former territory. If war was as near as Dorchester seemed to think, it was comfort that Congress possessed the caliber to act decisively. On March 31 the House adopted resolutions for mobilization of eighty thousand effective militia. The day following, Sedgwick's proposal for an auxiliary army, now of twenty-five thousand rather than fifteen thousand troops, met approval.

In the wake of the ominous news from Canada came good news from London. On April 4 the President submitted to Congress three dispatches from Minister Pinckney. The first two told of the order of November 6, 1793, instructing British commanders to seize neutral vessels in trade with the French West Indies. The third conveyed information that, on January 8, William Pitt's government had revoked the order. Confiscations in the Caribbean would cease. George Hammond rushed to Hamilton with the glad tidings; but, to the dismay of the British envoy, he found this "most moderate of the American ministers" not at all ready to forgive and forget. Nor were other Federalists sympathetic. The fact remained that Pitt still meant to seize American cargoes of foodstuff bound for the continental ports of France. While to some members in the House the prospect of peace was bright again, unanimity did not prevail. On March 27 Jonathan Dayton of New Jersey had introduced a surprise resolution: Let the Treasury sequester all private debts due British merchants as a guarantee to American shippers for indemnification of their losses at sea! Happily for Federalists debate was postponed, but on April 7 Republican Abraham Clark rose to demand absolute suspension of commercial intercourse between Americans and Britons. Non-intercourse, Clark insisted, must be the rule until England made restitution for every illegal seizure—and until George III had withdrawn every Redcoat from posts on American soil!

Clark's proposal dramatized a situation which had become intolerable. With the King's officers in Canada poised for war, British occupation of northern posts constituted a threat of the gravest kind. In the view of Federalist leaders the frontier problem and every other Anglo-American difficulty might be resolved by fulfillment of the plan to send a special emissary to London. A month with the idea before him did not overcome Washington's reluctance to supersede Pinckney with an extraordinary mission, but Randolph's favorable argument finally convinced the President of its expediency. Who should be sent? On April 8 Robert Morris came to Washington's office as informal spokesman of Senate Federalists. Morris favored Hamilton, and once more the President had to state his firm objection. He had been thinking instead, he told Morris, of three men, the country's most experienced diplomatists—Vice President Adams, Secretary Jefferson and Chief Justice Jay. Probably Morris remarked that Adams was not suited temperamentally for the present task; Jefferson disqualified himself for the mission by his obvious adoration of France. Jay, the Senator intimated, would be acceptable. Washington wondered. To Federalists, of course, Jay would be acceptable—but to Republicans perhaps only Hamilton himself would prove more objectionable! A nomination of Jay would not be universally applauded, Washington knew, however strong national desires for peace might be, but he invited Jay to dinner that evening.

Hamilton appealed urgently and fluently in the cause of peace. A special mission to England, he argued, was imperative, and the need imminent. The President must nominate Jay, "the only man in whose qualifications for success there would be thorough confidence, and him whom alone it would be advisable to send." Hamilton, together with Senators King, George Cabot, Caleb Strong and Ellsworth, visited Jay on April 15. The Chief Justice came next morning to tell Washington that he would accept the appointment. A letter of nomination went to the Senate at once. A day in Executive session, despite objections by James Monroe, John Taylor and Aaron Burr, proved sufficient for the Senate to concur. Federalist humor, however, was spoiled by campaigning on the part of House Republicans to make a bill out of Clark's non-intercourse resolution. "As the prospects of peace brighten, the efforts of these sons of faction are redoubled," King wrote in disgust. The resolution, with minor amendments by Madison, passed on April 25. While Republicans did not expect success in the Senate, the vote on April 28 was perilously close. Vice President Adams's negative voice from the chair broke a 13–13 tie.

Two specific tasks awaited Washington's attention. Instructions must be drawn for Jay and arrangements must be made to replace Morris at Paris. Randolph thought he had a solution. Why could not Jay resign as Chief Justice and accept a permanent appointment as Minister to Great Britain? Then Pinckney might be reassigned to France. Washington made this proposal to Jay on April 29, but the Chief Justice showed no interest. In accord with Randolph's alternate suggestion the President then wrote to offer the Paris post to Robert R. Livingston, prominent New York Republican and a man of some experience in diplomacy.

Meanwhile Federalist planners were outlining a set of instructions for Jay. Immediately upon confirmation of his appointment the Chief Justice met with Hamilton, King, Cabot and Ellsworth, and in this conclave certain ideas were evolved. As was his habit, the President called for opinion from each Cabinet member, and Hamilton's letter of April 23 was the first he received. Jay should be instructed, Hamilton said, to demand compensation for all damage done to American commerce by British cruisers in the past year and press for a clarification of "contraband" to exclude foodstuffs and other non-military cargoes. Further, Jay should call for prompt evacuation of the frontier posts and indemnification for slaves carried away during the Revolution. In return he should be empowered to promise that the United States would settle the unpaid prewar debts of its citizens up to a sum, perhaps £500,000 sterling. Finally, authority should be given the plenipotentiary to negotiate a commercial treaty with Britain, provided its terms did not contradict existing American arrangements with France. On May 6 Randolph delivered a formal protest to the Federalist plan to endow Jay with treaty-making power, but by this time the President was in complete accord with the idea. Instructions which Randolph signed that day were largely a product of Hamilton's pen, though the Secretary of State was able to insert a few proposals.

When Jay left New York May 12 a thousand cheering citizens escorted him to his ship, but by this time Republican criticism of the appointment was savage. Anti-administration newspapers challenged its constitutionality and prophesied a disgraceful outcome of the venture; assaults upon his own character were the most severe Washington yet had known. He doubtless hoped Republican rancor would lessen with news of the appointment of a successor to Morris in France. By the middle of May it was clear that Livingston did not want the post. Hamilton suggested that Randolph be sent to Paris. Randolph favored James Monroe, but the Virginia Senator was hesitant so long as his friend Aaron Burr evinced a desire for the appointment. Only when Randolph declared that Burr would not be considered did Monroe finally accept on May 26. The President's message to the Senate the next day received immediate confirmation.

Federalists may not have seen it at once, but party agitation in Congress was subsiding. On the twelfth, in a landslide ballot, the House voted down a move to continue the embargo beyond May 25. No other provocative resolution made headway, but tranquillity proved brief. On May 20 Philadelphia had alarming news from the northern frontier. Lieutenant Governor Simcoe of Canada, apparently afraid that Wayne meant to attack Detroit, had ordered three companies from that garrison to Fort Miamis, the abandoned British works at the rapids of the Maumee. Randolph wrote heatedly to Hammond. What could be the explanation? On May 22 the British Minister replied indignantly that American newspapers had quoted Dorchester's February speech out of context and that there had been no authentic report of invasion of United States territory. Washington was near the end of his endurance. He sent the memorials of Randolph and Hammond to Congress as soon as copies could be made. Then he fixed attention on the crisis itself—how to prevent actual hostilities. On May 23, without the approval of the President, Governor Mifflin of Pennsylvania ordered one thousand militia to Presque Isle, on the eastern edge of Lake Erie. If Simcoe's troops were at Fort Miamis, military preparation by Americans at Presque Isle would appear a challenge to the British, and the opposite was equally true. When Mifflin learned of the President's disapproving apprehension, he promptly but reluctantly withdrew his marching orders. There would be sharp complaint from Republican pioneers in western Pennsylvania, Washington knew, but the President preferred criticism to the risk of war. Fortunately, now that Jay had embarked for England, the House was no longer disposed to punitive, precipitate measures. Congress was quiet again.

As June broke upon Philadelphia Washington could reflect with satisfaction that America still was at peace. Another period of exigency had passed. He could be sure at least of the continued service of his stalwarts, Hamilton and Knox, until, as he put it, "the clouds over our affairs, which have come on so fast of late, shall be dispersed." While both men wished to return to private life, each had consented to remain until the end of the year; and Randolph showed no inclination to resign. The President had to acknowledge that war with the Creeks seemed more likely than ever, but this intelligence delayed Congress for only a few days. The legislators adjourned June 9. Washington notified the Cabinet that he would depart for Mount Vernon no later than June 18 for a visit of two or three weeks, but small business still commanded his attention. On June 12 he examined instructions Randolph had drafted for Monroe and signed the new envoy's letter of introduction to the French government. Next, he took particular pleasure in approving the commission of John Quincy Adams, brilliant son of the Vice President, as Minister to the Netherlands. For the fourteenth, Knox had scheduled an interview with twenty Cherokee chieftains, then in the city on a mission of good will. This over, Washington left instructions with the Cabinet to effect any unanimous decision in his absence and on June 17 took the road out of Philadelphia.

While it was a flying visit to Mount Vernon, far less was accomplished by it than the returning planter had hoped. On the twenty-second, still en route, he rode from the Federal City to examine the canal and locks at the Lower Falls of the Potomac. In some manner his horse stumbled. Rider and mount seemed destined to spill onto the rocks but, by violent exertions on Washington's part, the animal recovered its footing. In the effort the President suffered a painful injury to his back that hampered him for several weeks.

As soon as he could stand the jolting carriage without excessive pain, Washington started back to the city on July 3. One of the first questions that awaited decision was whether the United States should enter a pact with Denmark and Sweden in the interest of free neutral navigation. Knox, Attorney General Bradford and Hamilton opposed the plan in the conviction that it would alarm Britain and imperil Jay's success. Randolph countered with favorable arguments and thought the matter should be left to Jay's discretion, since his instructions authorized him to sound the disposition of the ministers from Denmark and Sweden. The measure was declared inexpedient; Jay's success abroad must not be jeopardized.

Unhappy news of Kentucky called for prompt attention. Impatient Kentuckians did not appreciate the government's efforts to attain free navigation of the Mississippi by diplomatic means. In remonstrance against the administration and in hostility toward Spanish Louisiana, it seemed that Kentucky Republicans still were under the influence of Genet. For a combination of restive Americans to chance war with Spain and Great Britain was reckless beyond description, yet separation of Kentucky from the Union was unthinkable! Kentuckians must be mollified and the Spaniards placated. In Georgia also there was much to blame in the conduct of frontier inhabitants who had begun to settle on land reserved by treaty for the Creeks. Toward mid-July there was agreement in the Cabinet that a letter of admonition must go to Gov. George Matthews. Suppression of these activities was the order and, if necessary to achieve it, United States aid was the promise.

Smoldering resentment in the Allegheny region had shadowed the excise laws from their beginning. Washington had concluded that the people would comply with the law and, for the most part, in proper spirit; but he realistically observed: "It is possible . . . perhaps not improbable, that some Demagogue may start up and produce and get signed some resolutions declaratory of their disapprobation of the measure." The demagogue was Genet. The popular clubs fathered by the French Minister had, as Washington wrote Henry Lee, continued "to sow the seeds of jealousy and distrust of Government among the people by destroying all confidence in the administration of it. . . ." Armed uprising in the West, that now was real danger Washington labelled "the first *formidable* fruit of the Democratic Societies."

Many factors figured in the discontent. Distance made trade difficult, and a widening separation of other interests inevitably followed. For wholly tangible reasons, citizens of the Pennsylvania frontier were the natural enemies of an excise on liquor. Although the burden of the tax was designed to fall on the consumer, it did, in fact, work a multiple hardship on the citizens, because they were not only the largest producers of whiskey but also the largest purchasers of their product. Consequently, the measure applied as a direct tax. Whiskey to the Westerners was literally the distillation of all their efforts toward a better existence, a surer economy. More important, whiskey was legal tender, and payment of excise in cash for a commodity used also for barter was a double imposition. Grain grew abundantly in this fertile region, yet had no market value as such. Four bushels of grain, as harvested, was the load capacity of one horse, but in the form of whiskey the equivalent of twenty-four bushels could be carried in a single load—reason enough for the prevalence of stills, but no reason at all, Washington knew, for defiance of law.

United States Marshal David Lenox had served thirty-nine writs on Pennsylvania excise offenders in uneventful succession, only to meet with angry attack by armed men after the fortieth. On this last visit the marshal was accompanied by the Inspector of the Western Survey, General John Neville. The Inspector's presence aroused great indignation and led to the destruction July 17 of Neville's fine property on Chartiers Creek. The Federal officer was unpopular because he had accepted appointment as Inspector in spite of his own expressed disapproval of the excise. The fury of the mob was heightened by the fact that Maj. James McFarlane, leader of the attack on Neville's Bower Hill, was killed in the exchange of fire. The angry rabble ordered Neville and Lenox imprisoned at Pittsburgh. Thoroughly frightened and intimidated, the two men shortly made their escape and fled towards Philadelphia.

A few days later, July 23, at Mingo Creek Presbyterian Church, Hugh H. Brackenridge, prominent Pittsburgh lawyer and leader, warned those of insurgent leanings that "what had been done might be morally right, but . . . was legally wrong"—it was high treason, he said, and put it within the power of the President to call out the militia. Brackenridge ventured that the government would prefer to offer amnesty and even urged the citizens to seek it. No formal declaration of defiance was made at this meeting, but the majority showed their displeasure and thereafter excluded Brackenridge from their confidences. Washington County attorney David Bradford, on the other hand, made the most of the prevailing spirit of rebellion and emerged as undisputed leader. A circular appeared bidding militia officers to assemble their men at Braddock's Field on August 1 with arms and accoutrements and four days' rations. Bradford assumed the office of Major General. Pittsburgh residents were alarmed, but a noisy march through the streets and the burning of a single barn seemed to satisfy the rioters, at least temporarily. Meanwhile, Bradford had been persuaded, albeit reluctantly, to countermand his order for seizure of the magazine at Fort Fayette.

The Chief Executive realized the necessity for immediate, compelling measures. Congress on two occasions had modified the excise law materially, duty had been lightened and payments eased. Although Washington understood the essential causes of the Westerners' dissatisfaction, he could not understand their failure to take valid recourse by means of further appeal to Congress. He would not tolerate contempt of legislation established by that body. Every power inherent in the Executive would be used—even to the extreme of military measures.

On August 2 Washington held the first official conference in this crisis with the Cabinet. Governor Mifflin attended, accompanied by other officials of Pennsylvania. That the disturbance centered in the State wherein the seat of Government resided was itself humiliating to Washington, and he thought it proper that preliminary action come from the Governor. State officials showed unified reluctance to acknowledge the need for military measures and were disposed to minimize the gravity of the situation. Before the meeting closed, the President requested written opinions from his Cabinet members and from Mifflin.

In a last anxious effort to avoid coercive means, Washington appointed James Ross, Jasper Yeates and Attorney General Bradford as Federal commissioners to confer with representatives from western Pennsylvania. Mifflin named Pennsylvania Chief Justice Thomas McKean and William Irvine as agents of the Commonwealth on the same mission. Decisive action would wait on their word. On the President's desk by the fifth were full statements from Randolph, Hamilton, Knox, Bradford, and Mifflin. Along with these opinions, Washington could weigh the assertion of Justice James Wilson of the Supreme Court, brief but authoritative. Within a single paragraph from Wilson lay the key declaration. Authority to call out the militia was the President's—in certain circumstances—and a simple statement attested the existence of such circumstances.

The Cabinet met August 6 to debate the written opinions. Randolph's argument against immediate summons of state militia was judicious and impressive, but the case for preparedness was realistic and more impressive. Hamilton's recommendation for prompt recruitment prevailed. All concurred in the idea of a presidential proclamation to the insurgents, and it was issued the following day. Washington's charges were forthright and formidable. Clearly set down were the authority by which the President could summon the militia and his regretful determination to do so. The insurgents were commanded to disperse and all inhabitants exhorted to "prevent and suppress dangerous proceedings."

The Chief Executive found a shade of reassurance in information obtained by Randolph from Neville and Lenox, who arrived in Philadelphia August 8. Their report allayed Washington's growing alarm to the extent that it did not seem necessary further to detain Knox, who was anxious to depart for Maine on private business. The function of the Secretary of War could be transferred to Hamilton for the period of Knox's absence. Reports from the West were reviewed in a Cabinet session on the ninth, and three days later Washington ordered the garrison at Pittsburgh reinforced. By the middle of August recruitment was under way in Pennsylvania, Virginia and Maryland, and on September 1 Gov. Richard Howell issued the call in New Jersey.

While Washington anxiously "sought and weighed what might best subdue the crisis," David Bradford grasped at every means toward rebellion. He widely advertised a meeting of delegates from the various townships on August 14 at Parkinson's Ferry. In response to the circular, 226 appointees gathered in the presence of a large group of spectators. Sometime that morning word came that the government's commissioners had arrived near Pittsburgh. The Parkinson's Ferry delegates readily agreed on the necessary committee of conference—three men from each of the four counties—then proceeded to the business of shaping resolutions. One of the resolves was recognized by the more discerning as a daring endeavor to combine against state and Federal government. It anticipated "hostile attempts" by the administration against the Westerners. Albert Gallatin rose at once in admonition. His address, shrewd but mollifying, was based on the argument that "hostility" was too harsh a term and his suggestion that the matter be referred to a committee prevailed. Amended resolutions were adopted the next day, over Bradford's protest. The result of this meeting was mild compared with its original purpose of uncompromising demand for war. The hotheaded Bradford had been outmaneuvered by the cool Gallatin.

News of the President's proclamation reached Parkinson's Ferry on the second day of the meeting. It was not well received, but it was sobering. By a clever compromise move, Gallatin and Brackenridge succeeded in getting an adjournment immediately upon selection of sixty members as a standing committee of safety who would act for the people and receive the report from the committee of conference after their parley with the Federal commissioners.

On the twenty-first they met in Pittsburgh. Secret discussion lasted three days and ended with the ultimatum of the commissioners: "Perfect and entire acquiescence" in the excise law by September 1. In return the insurgents were promised pardon and amnesty. Hopes of the commissioners were high at the close of this meeting, but when the Western delegates reported to their committee of safety at Brownsville on August 28, it was apparent that few were convinced in favor of submission. The single dissenting member among the conferees at Pittsburgh had been Bradford, though he had expressed his approval of submission before the interview ended. Now he resumed his vicious opposition. The other conferees were effectively intimidated by the inflamed temper of a majority of the sixty. Bradford was eloquently refuted by Gallatin and Brackenridge, but the fever of the recalcitrants remained high. Finally, a secret ballot was taken on a resolution in favor of the proposals of the government. The result was thirty-four yeas and twenty-three nays. So far from being unanimous, such a showing certainly would not favorably impress the commissioners. With resolves from the Brownsville meeting in hand, back to Pittsburgh went nine of the conferees. They asked indemnity to persons in arrears of the excise and importuned for an extension of time to October 11. Neither request was acceptable to the commissioners, but out of this meeting came a plan to determine disposition of the inhabitants by a survey of the affected counties on September 11. Signatures of the people to a pledge of compliance would constitute proof of submission. Perhaps the spirit of moderate Westerners yet would prevail.

Moderate spirit did not prevail. Many townships declared for continued resistance and where favorable majorities did exist, the minorities were violent. By September 9 hope for amicable settlement was dwindling. Regretfully Washington approved orders for a general rendezvous of militia. On the nineteenth Philadelphians watched as infantry and horse left on the road westward. Five days later Washington received word from the commissioners that means of conciliation had been exhausted. The next day the President issued a final proclamation against the insurgents. Marching orders for the militia meant corresponding command for Washington. He would journey to Carlisle, where the militia of Pennsylvania and New Jersey were to assemble, then proceed to Bedford for the rendezvous of the army. There he would determine whether he should advance with the troops or return to Philadelphia for the opening of Congress on November 3.

Washington's carriage drove from the door of his Philadelphia residence on September 30. With the President were Hamilton, who now held the dual Department of Treasury and War, and Bartholomew Dandridge, private secretary. In the late evening a messenger met them with an official packet for Washington. In it the President found a letter from Wayne which told of brilliant successes against Indians in the Northwest Territory. Complete victory had culminated on August 20 in the Battle of Fallen Timbers against a horde of two thousand savages and their British auxiliaries. The "mortifying defeat" of Harmar and the slaughter of St. Clair's men at last were avenged. Welcome news that the far frontier was safe from hostile Indians made all the more significant the immediate problems of the nearer frontier, threatened by hostile Americans.

As the presidential coach crossed the Susquehanna October 4 the Philadelphia Light Horse were waiting to escort the General and his party over the seventeen remaining miles to Carlisle. Some distance outside the town they were met by Governors Mifflin and Howell. Troops at the camp formed a long line of passage for the President, who advanced on horse-back. Citizens, as well as soldiers, showed their joy at sight of him. Washington began on the sixth a week the like of which he had not experienced since the Revolution.

Washington had reason to hope that present trials would emerge in early triumph. As soon as proper alinement and provisioning of the troops at Carlisle were assured, he would proceed to Williamsport, Fort Cumberland and Bedford. By the first of November, if possible, he would return to Philadelphia. Meanwhile, his Annual Address must be prepared, whether or not he would present it in person. Washington requested Randolph to arrange the subject matter topically and forward it at once. The Secretary of War now had returned from Maine and his suggestions also were sought. Randolph remained alert to Washington's requests and kept his chief informed of affairs in other quarters—encouraging evidence of improved conditions in Kentucky and reassurances that fear of another epidemic in Philadelphia had dissipated.

Militia were continually pouring into Carlisle, many of them well uniformed and equipped; but their arrival was unsystematic. The sooner Mifflin and Howell could start their men to Bedford the better. Washington himself mapped the course and planned the timing of the march. He directed Mifflin in coordinating the various units and secured Gen. Edward Hand as Adjutant. Assignments for the principal officers posed no problems. Governor Lee would rank them all, and in the event that Washington need not accompany the troops beyond Bedford, would be their Commander-in-Chief. Mifflin was second in authority and Howell, third. The dates of commission would determine which of the two Major Generals, Daniel Morgan and William Irvine, would serve in fourth place. By October 9 militia were welding into an impressive Army, and Washington was pleased with their appearance and with the spirit they exemplified. Now that General Orders were ready, he could divert his attention from military matters to the "Whiskey Boys" themselves.

About seven o'clock on the morning of October 9, William Findley and David Redick, emissaries from the insurgents, appeared at the President's quarters. Washington received them politely, and explained that other duties must postpone examination of the paper they put into his hands—resolutions unanimously passed at a second meeting of the committee at Parkinson's Ferry on October 2—but that he would confer with them the following morning. Before the deputies returned, Washington studied the three resolves. The first was an attempt at explanation for failure to obtain universal signatures of compliance—not so much owing to opposition to law as to lack of time or information to achieve the proper sentiment; the second was an assurance of submission on the part of the committee and of a "general disposition" to submit; the third commissioned Findley and Redick to wait on the President and Mifflin with these resolutions in order that Washington might judge whether armed force was necessary. When the two Western delegates appeared at the appointed hour, Washington addressed the deputies a forceful indictment against the grave evil and immeasurable injury caused by the insurrection. Findley and Redick then zealously presented the case of the malcontents.

Washington acknowledged hopeful evidences disclosed in the reports but pronounced them not convincing enough to justify a countermand to the troops. Offices of inspection could not yet be safely established except in the shadow of the Pittsburgh garrison. The President reminded Findley and Redick that in the face of approaching winter he could not vacillate in the matter of a military expedition. What earlier might have sufficed to stay a marching order now must be strengthened by "unequivocal proofs of absolute submission." Such proofs still were lacking; the Army would proceed over the mountains. Reluctant to close the conference on this unhappy note, the deputies sought a second interview. Washington, in the company of Hamilton, saw them again that afternoon, only to reiterate his resolve. The General assured them that revengeful behavior of the troops would not be tolerated; that their duty lay in support of civil authority, not in execution of the laws themselves. Every precaution would be taken to keep them subordinate, but there must be no armed resistance; he could not answer for the consequences if a single gun was fired by the insurgents.

Even before Findley and Redick had their last interview with the President the march of men from Carlisle to Bedford had begun. On October 12 Washington, Hamilton and their entourage started the journey to Fort Cumberland. Two days at Fort Cumberland sufficed for a survey of the troops and gave opportunity for a review of plans with General Lee. Washington was pleased with what he found, and his spirits rose accordingly. The 3200 well provisioned men soon would be augmented by seventeen hundred additional soldiers from Virginia. A variety of reports and rumors caught up with the President at Fort Cumberland. Intelligence from the western counties was consistent; the people were alarmed but not yet completely chastened; submission was in proportion to the fear of nearby forces; let the Army withdraw and the rebellion again would rise. The Army would not withdraw.

The General was met outside Bedford by officers of distinction and was lodged in the town "very comfortably." Homage to the President bore the exquisite compliment of dignity. Admiration of the crowds gathered in Bedford streets was the more impressive because it was silent. The same scarcely could be said of public response at the seat of government, for criticism of the President had not been lacking in the East. Republicans found pleasure in the charges of Westerners that the administration had sought an excuse to raise arms against them. Washington continued to denounce the Democratic Societies as fomenters of this antagonism; he was of a mind to reproach them in his forthcoming address to Congress. Nor was silence an attribute of Benjamin Franklin Bache, grandson of Franklin and editor of the Philadelphia avidly Republican *Aurora,* and when Washington made known his plan to return by the end of October, he wished it understood that Bache's impertinence in challenging his right to command the Army during a session of Congress had no influence on that decision.

On the twentieth staff officers met for a final conference with Washington and Lee. It was decided to put the Army in motion by October 23 and converge the two wings on Parkinson's Ferry. Full instructions for Lee were finished, but the departing Commander-in-Chief wished still to write a farewell message to the militia. It was addressed to Lee to be published with General Orders. Once again Washington emphasized the priority of civil over military discipline—his unvarying political principle. As he climbed into his carriage October 21, his most particular good-bye was said to Hamilton, who would proceed with Lee at the head of the left wing. By noon October 28 the Chief Executive was again in Philadelphia.

Since the session of Congress was to open November 3, Washington turned immediately to the preparation of his annual message. Randolph had promised to have a draft "in sufficient forwardness" on the President's return, but so much diverse communication had gathered in the past month that Washington would be compelled to read for hours to acquaint himself with the closer points of each piece of national business.

Washington did not have to hurry a final draft of his address to Congress. Neither the Senate nor the House was ready for business on November 3, and a week and a day passed before the House alone could count a quorum. This gave the President time to make thoughtful choice of matters to be emphasized and words with which to portray them. A month earlier Randolph had suggested that the moment was at hand to deliver a fatal blow to the widespread Democratic Societies. Washington needed little support for his conviction that the clubs must be chastised. He would discuss the insurrection roundly in his message to Congress, and he would censure the Democratic Societies in an explicit way.

By November 6 the language of the address had been chosen, but thoughts of the insurrection disturbed the Chief Executive for at least two weeks more, though letters from Hamilton came in almost every post and were reassuring. By the second week of November he was detailing a plan for seizure of stills and mass arrests to begin on November 12 in Washington County. On the fifteenth he wrote that, though twenty leaders already were confined, "the bad spirit is evidently not subdued" and it appeared "indispensable" that a military force be left to police western Pennsylvania that winter. Two days later some 150 insurgents were under guard and awaiting civil trial at Pittsburgh, and Lee's Army stood ready for the homeward march. Maj. Gen. Daniel Morgan was assigned to camp for the winter on the Monongahela with a small body of troops, and Hamilton notified the President November 19 that the Army was in motion and that he was setting out for Philadelphia. Only when Washington received this word did his last apprehension disappear.

CHAPTER / 22

Mention of Wayne's dramatic victory over the Indians would lend cheer to the Annual Address, but Washington might have wished that later news from the Northwest had been as auspicious as the account of the battle of August 20. Wayne was again complaining of poor recruitment and urging a large army to insure the peace of the pioneer country. Nor was there promising word from Timothy Pickering, who had been sent to Canandaigua to reaffirm the friendship of Joseph Brant and the Six Nations. More disquieting would be the omission from Washington's text of any news of improvement in relations with Great Britain. Jay's communications could be considered encouraging to a limited degree only. As yet there had been no dispatch from Monroe, though it was said unofficially that the Jacobins had fallen from power in July and that he had been received at Paris. The European war could be expected to proceed on a large scale, for, despite domestic upheaval, France had enjoyed spectacular success in the summer campaign. Reflective of this was Fauchet's attitude, which had become abrasive in recent months, but Randolph maintained that it was more important than ever to keep France in "good humor" because the outcome of Jay's negotiation with the British was so uncertain. Finally, on November 18, the Senate formed its quorum and to a joint committee of legislators who visited him that afternoon Washington announced his intention to address Congress the next day.

Almost his first words gave the clue that Washington meant to describe at some length the background, incipiency and suppression of the Whiskey Rebellion, and he was fully twenty minutes on this topic. He had, he declared, done all in his power to preserve and defend the Constitution as the oath of office required. Then came the President's plea: "On you, gentlemen, and the people by whom you are deputed, I rely for support." The rest of his text Washington finished in five or six minutes. Wayne's victory, he said, was decisive, but always the object of Indian policy would be peace rather than punishment. To the House he directed a request for some plan to redeem the public indebtedness. On external affairs he could declare only that the Executive continued to strive for amity with every power. He made pointed reference to recent domestic dissensions caused by the spread of the so-called Democratic Societies. In closing he urged all Americans to "implore the Supreme Ruler of nations to spread His holy protection over these United States, to turn the machinations of the wicked to the confirming of our Constitution, to enable us at all times to root out internal sedition, and to put invasion to flight. . . ." Washington then handed copies of the address to the Vice President and the Speaker. The audience stood at silent attention as he left the chamber.

On November 20 the President's office transmitted to Congress all documents on the Pennsylvania insurrection, as well as reports from Wayne and the Georgia frontier. The next day Washington advised the Senate of his plan to send Thomas Pinckney from London to Spain as envoy extraordinary. Although he continued to have full confidence in William Short, now the sole Minister at Madrid, it was his hope that a special mission would bring to "a happy and speedy issue" the protracted negotiation for commercial rights on the Mississippi. So aware was the President of growing unrest in Kentucky that already he had dispatched Col. James Innes to Lexington to assure disgruntled Westerners that their needs had not been forgotten.

It did not take the Senate long to make formal acknowledgment of the President's annual message. On the twenty-third Adams brought the Senate in a group to Washington's house and read the statement which had been adopted the day before. The Senate approved unequivocally the use of militia by the President and shared his condemnation of "the proceedings of certain self-created societies." Washington replied gratefully, but he was to be disappointed if he expected the House to render promptly like acknowledgment. That body found itself so divided by the tenor of the address that a debate of five days' duration followed the introduction of a draft reply on November 24. Madison, its principal author, had phrased a paragraph so as to withhold any specific endorsement of the measures of the Executive in the realm of foreign relations; but after sustained argument the Virginian and his Republican cohorts retreated somewhat on this point. They retreated not at all in the face of a Federalist resolution to include an expression approving the President's denunciation of the Democratic Societies. Madison's draft with a minor amendment was adopted November 28, and the next day Washington met the legislators who came to deliver the formal statement of the House. The address was polished, but there was nowhere the hint of a reference to the clubs. The President noted this and replied politely but briefly. Later the same day he signed an act by which Congress authorized the Executive to station a corps of militia in western Pennsylvania for a limited time.

A resolution of thanks to General Wayne was approved on December 4, and Congress fell quiet for many days thereafter. Together with weekly letters to Pearce, Washington found time for correspondence on a matter that had been in the back of his mind since he returned to Philadelphia. As he had expressed to Adams in November, it was an old opinion of his that "a national university in this country is a thing to be desired," and he looked forward to "a full and free conversation" with the Vice President on that subject. His hope was that a university would be built in the Federal City and, thinking of his fifty shares in the Potomac Company as an endowment for this purpose, he asked Randolph to consult with Madison "to mature the measures which will be proper for me to pursue in order to bring my designs into view."

Since both Hamilton and Knox were about to leave the Cabinet,

Washington's great concern at the moment was the choice of their successors. Hamilton had notified the President that he wished to be relieved on the last day of January; Knox mentioned early in the month that December 31 would be his last day, and a formal note to that effect came to Washington's desk on the twenty-eighth. In acknowledgment, the President assured Knox of "my most perfect persuasion that you have deserved well of our country," and two days later sent to Congress the long summation by the Secretary of War on the condition of the frontier. Knox was sharply critical of the encroachments of pioneers upon Indian land guaranteed by treaty; he suggested that punishment for violations be meted out to white man and red man alike. Washington added his own comment that "the disorders and the great expenses which incessantly arise upon the frontiers are of a nature and magnitude to excite the most serious considerations." As yet there was no hint of Hamilton's successor; but the new Secretary of War would be an experienced Indian negotiator, Postmaster General Timothy Pickering.

On New Year's Day 1795 President Washington entertained members of Congress at his house with a repast of cake and wine. The next morning Pickering's nomination went to the Senate, together with the fine treaties he had obtained from the Six Nations and the Oneidas. While the month was as quiet in Philadelphia as the weather was mild, the President longed more and more to return to the life of a planter. "I can religiously aver," he wrote Edmund Pendleton, "that no man was ever more tired of public life, or more devoutly wished for retirement than I do."

On January 28 the President showed manifest satisfaction in a letter to the commissioners of the Federal City:

It has always been a source of serious reflection and sincere regret with me that the youth of the United States should be sent to foreign countries for the purpose of education. . . . We ought to deprecate the hazard attending ardent and susceptible minds from being too strongly and too early prepossessed in favor of other political systems before they are capable of appreciating their own. For this reason, I have greatly wished to see a plan adopted by which the arts, sciences, and belles lettres could be taught in their *fullest extent.* . . .

If, therefore, he declared, a plan for a national university in the Federal City could be devised and set in motion, he would endow the project with his fifty shares of Potomac Company stock.

Hamilton's departure from office was imminent and, he was retiring just as the House of Representatives entertained proposals for the gradual extinction of the public debt, some $78,000,000 which the government had assumed under Hamilton's stewardship of national finance. On January 16, the day debate on redemption of the debt reached momentary climax in the House, Hamilton announced his wish to submit sweeping recommendations on the subject. Caught unaware, Republicans acceded to his request, but further debate was postponed. Three final communications from Hamilton came to the President's desk on Saturday the thirty-first; Washington notified the Secretary formally on Monday that his resignation was accepted. "In every relation which you have borne to me," the President testified, "I have found that my confidence in your talents, exertions and integrity has been well placed." This same day Oliver Wolcott, Comptroller of the Treasury since 1789, was named as Hamilton's successor. By the middle of February, as a plan for debt reduction took shape in the House, the retired Secretary was en route with his family to their home in Albany.

Washington submitted to Congress on February 4 a report Randolph had drafted on the Dutch loan, a subject the President thought "extremely interesting and urgent." More interesting yet would be the next official mail from England, for the last day of January had at last brought unofficial news that Jay had concluded a treaty with the British late in November. The text of the treaty should come in time to be delivered to the Senate before adjournment of Congress on March 3. Meanwhile the President had private correspondence to answer and routine duties to perform. On February 17 he conferred with the Secretary of War on a matter which alarmed both men; that morning he sent to Congress copies of two recent acts of the legislature of Georgia which had thrown open some fifty million acres of Indian land to purchase by speculators. Georgia was giving legal countenance to a dangerous practice which Washington thought might "deeply affect the peace and welfare of the United States." Congress, he hoped, would take appropriate action.

Sudden severe weather and an incidence of pleurisy in Philadelphia made Congress anxious to adjourn, but still the European mail yielded no communication from Jay. The President was obliged to announce in a confidential message February 28 that nothing had come. There was fresh news from Wayne to offset this disappointment: preliminary articles of a treaty of peace had been approved by chiefs of the four principal tribes of the Northwest. Fourteen bills, most of them of minor importance, came for Washington's signature on March 2 and 3. Late on the third, just before adjournment, the President notified Adams and each Senator individually that their presence in a special session would be required on June 8, 1795, to deliberate upon "certain matters touching the public good." If Washington's language was guarded, it was because he was increasingly unsure that a treaty with Great Britain actually had been concluded. If indeed Jay had signed a treaty in November, where was it?

On March 7 the long wait ended. David Blaney, a homeward-bound Virginian whom Jay had entrusted to deliver a set of the important papers, reached Randolph's office that morning after a hard ride from Norfolk, his port of debarkation. Evidently Jay's originals had gone astray, for these letters and documents were third copies, but the papers were complete and their seal unbroken. Here, at last, was the text of the "Treaty of Amity, Commerce and Navigation" signed by Jay and Lord Grenville on November 19, together with dispatches to the Secretary of State and a letter to the President. Jay's words to Randolph were those of a man who had done his best: "I have no reason to believe or conjecture that [a treaty] more favorable to us is attainable." To Washington he wrote simply, "It must speak for itself. . . . To do more was not possible."

Jay's meaning came clear as soon as the twenty-eight articles had been examined closely. Certainly their terms appeared to be much more advantageous to Great Britain than to the United States. Only Article Two, England's pledge to evacuate the western posts, seemed a real achievement for Jay—and this was marred by a condition that complete withdrawal need not be effected until June 1, 1796. The third article gave Canadian trappers, traders and Indians free access to the Northwest Territory and use of its rivers, the Mississippi included; Americans were granted the same privileges, however valueless, in Canada. Under the fifth and sixth articles, provision was made for eventual establishment of commissions to study the question of boundaries and the intricate problem of pre-Revolution debts owed to British merchants. Article Seven provided joint arbitration on recent American losses at sea as a result of illegal captures by English commanders. The remainder of the treaty dealt with conditions on which trade between the two nations was to be regulated in the future. Rules for commercial reciprocity between the United States and the British homeland were the usual ones in this kind of agreement, but Washington scarcely could have been satisfied with Article Twelve. Here the important intercourse between the United States and the British West Indies was tilted heavily in favor of English carriers. Only American ships of seventy tons or less could engage in this traffic; British merchant vessels of any capacity were allowed to compete. Worse was the stipulation that no American ship could clear a West Indies port, or any British port, with certain cargoes bound for France or a neutral station. These cargoes were largely the products for which France was willing to pay a premium. A final blow came as Washington read the eighteenth article: England reserved the right to declare and seize, whenever she chose, all foodstuffs and provisions as contraband of war.

Jay's pact had fallen woefully short of the objectives of his assignment. Nowhere was there reference to compensation for slaves carried off during the Revolution. Nor was there acknowledgment of the claim for losses arising out of England's retention of the western posts. The treaty failed to restrict the flagrant practices of the British admiralty—search and impressment; it did nothing to credit the cherished American principle that free ships made their cargoes free. Yet the final product of Jay's extended negotiation did dispel for the United States the imminence of war against the most formidable naval power in the world. With all its limitations, Jay's treaty did seem to guarantee peace; this was its basic accomplishment, a great one. As the Constitution required the consent of the Senate to ratification, the treaty would have to remain for three months in the custody of the Executive. The President and the Secretary of State agreed that its text must be kept exclusively in their confidence until the instrument could be delivered to the Senate for verdict. Perhaps by that time Jay would be home from England and able to defend his handiwork against attacks which seemed inevitable.

Washington had not seen Mount Vernon for eight months. With spring before him, the President's weekly letters to Pearce grew more detailed in instruction and deeper in concern. As soon as the condition of the roads permitted, he would make a brief visit to Virginia. Before he took leave of Philadelphia, he meant to clear his mind of the persistent vexation of Indian affairs. Now that Congress had risen without adopting a measure to avert possible hostilities between the Creeks and the State of Georgia, Washington thought it necessary "to take up the subject upon a full and comprehensive scale, that some systematic plan may be resolved on and steadily pursued during the recess." He asked Pickering to study the question and devise a program. Towards the end of March the Secretary of War had ready careful instructions for Governor Blount of the Southwest Territory and for James Seagrove, Indian agent in Georgia. The President wished to consider also the situation of the northwest frontier. Accordingly, he requested Pickering to develop a plan for establishment of the Presque Isle garrison on Lake Erie and prepare orders for Wayne's peace negotiation with the hostile tribes.

On April 2 the President and Martha gave a formal dinner to which the English, Spanish, Portuguese and Dutch ministers brought their wives. Two days later Washington signed credentials for David Humphreys, returning to the Barbary States as Commissioner Plenipotentiary after a short visit to America. His own departure for Mount Vernon could not be too soon, but a rainstorm on April 13 delayed it one day more.

In his passage south the President's attention necessarily was fixed on a complexity of problems that awaited him in the Federal City. Thomas Johnson, former Federal commissioner, had written graphically: "The success of the City has now become important to your reputation. It is a favorite object with you and not less so with me, though the reward will be as unequal as our powers and merits. For you will stand as the first figure . . . whilst I shall be junk in the undistinguished group in the background." Johnson's carping tone was the result of a dispute between him and the incumbent commissioners. Washington regretted this altercation between the present commissioners and "one of the old set" and in March had asked Lear to investigate discreetly. In Georgetown on April 19 the President was disappointed to find that Lear was in Portsmouth, New Hampshire. He did see Johnson and talked briefly with Commissioners Carroll and Stuart. Then Washington encountered William Thornton and quickly perceived that this commissioner was inimicable towards Johnson. When Thornton declared he would forward all evidence in the dispute to Mount Vernon at once, Washington saw a way to say good-bye and hurried across the Potomac in time to reach his door before nightfall.

It had been the President's hope "to take a transient view of the situation of my private concerns," but there was little time for this in the single week he planned to remain at Mount Vernon. A letter arriving on April 25 recalled the President's thoughts disagreeably to Philadelphia. Randolph had written to say that the Dutch Minister Resident, Van Berckel, had dismissed his counsul, Heinaken, and desired the United States to take formal notice of the action. Compliance in this would be tantamount to a renewal of American recognition of the United Netherlands. This would be awkward, for it was known unofficially that unrest prevailed in Holland—that the government was tottering as French agitators attempted to erect a "Batavian Republic" on the Jacobin model.

Would the Secretary of State please conduct a Cabinet study of Heinaken's case and have written opinions assembled when the President returned?

Late on Sunday April 26 Washington began his return ride to Philadelphia. In Georgetown on the twenty-eighth he chose Alexander White, a lawyer of Frederick County, to fill the vacancy among the commissioners of the Federal District which had been created by the resignation of Carroll. The President was back at the seat of government by noon on May 2, his desk clear of urgent business. He was aware of a deepened estrangement between Secretary of State Randolph and Minister Fauchet and received the warning of Gouverneur Morris that the new rulers in Paris meant to annul the Franco-American treaties of 1778. But in the month that followed the President's most significant occupation was with the projects of Secretary of War Pickering towards a fresh negotiation with the Creeks.

Towards the end of May the President and the Secretary of State were in daily expectation of the arrival of Jay from England. In the partisan opinion of Republican John Beckley their eagerness for Jay's return betrayed a deep fear that the treaty would fail in the Senate if its architect did not appear beforehand to explain and support his work. Beckley proceeded to hint that Randolph was weary of the Secretaryship and longed to replace Jay in the chair of Chief Justice. Jay's resignation from the Court had become imminent by reason of his election as Governor of New York. Confirmation of Jay's victory preceded by just two days his debarkation at New York on May 28. The envoy notified Randolph that evening that his unsettled state of health would not permit a journey to Philadelphia at the moment. On June 1 he wrote to ask Randolph to visit him in New York. The Secretary of State ruled out this possibility and set forth instead seven questions on Jay's negotiation with Grenville, "thrown together from memory only," but admittedly in search of "views more striking than those which have originated with myself." Jay had written philosophically in February "that no attainable settlement or treaty would give universal satisfaction." To this belief he held. His reply to Randolph was so matter-of-fact as to be of no use in the formulation of a presidential message to accompany the treaty in its hour of trial.

Speculation was frenzied over the probable fate of the treaty at the hands of the Senate, over the consequences at home and abroad if ratified and if not. On June 8, the day designated for the special session, twenty-four members of the Senate had taken their seats. Caleb Strong and John Langdon came that morning to inform the President that a quorum existed; Washington replied he would deliver the treaty and pertinent documents immediately, and did so with only the barest message of transmission.

Washington received regular news of the debate that now engaged the Senate in closed chambers. Federalist Senators moved in phalanx to strike down two motions which proposed an immediate publication of the treaty and pertinent papers. Republican Senators muttered and tightened their line of battle. By the fifteenth both sides were poised for a war of dialectics—and Article XII provided the material for contention. This was the "West India article," which allowed small American ships to trade with the British islands but forbade reexportation of their produce to Europe. Federalists saw real inequity in the clause and recognized it as a large obstacle to ratification. Better to remove the barrier themselves, they thought, than to permit it to become a rallying point for hostile opinion. On the sixteenth, Federalist tacticians shifted attention to other sections of the treaty and the next day made a motion to approve the remaining twenty-seven articles and "recommend . . . further friendly negotiations" on Article XII. Deliberation of the proposal occupied the Senate the rest of the week.

The debate was of such significance that the President found it difficult to turn his mind to routine matters, but he was diverted briefly by the arrival of a new envoy from France. He was Pierre Adet, sent by the Directory to replace the representative of the fallen Jacobins, Fauchet. Adet was the third young man in two years to come from France with full ministerial powers; Washington hoped he would prove more a diplomat than Fauchet or Genet.

On June 22 deliberations in the Senate took an alarming turn. Aaron Burr, the able New York Republican, moved that further consideration of the treaty be postponed and that the Executive be asked to reopen negotiation on seven points. Burr's motion was killed on the twenty-third, but it stimulated a defection in Federalist solidarity which made the next day one of crisis and climax. When John Adams's gavel summoned the Senate to order on June 24, Jacob Read of South Carolina, a newly seated Federalist whose regularity was taken for granted, asked that an addition be made to the motion of June 17: England should be required to make compensation for Negroes carried away during the Revolution. Federalist managers persuaded Read to withdraw his unexpected proposal, but the Federalist column appeared to be weakening. Republicans took the offensive with a sweeping suggestion to reject the treaty forthwith and recommend that the President "continue his endeavors . . . to adjust the real causes of complaint" between the United States and Great Britain. The initiative then passed to the Federalists, who urged an immediate roll call on their motion to consent to all of the treaty except Article XII. The motion carried 20 to 10. By exactly the Constitutional requirement of a two-thirds vote, the Senate had agreed to a conditional ratification of Jay's treaty.

Washington could not know what was expected of him at this juncture. The language of the Senate was inconclusive. It might imply that the President should draft and submit immediately a substitute for Article XII; then, on approval of the new clause, he would be free to ratify the treaty provisionally and send it to England for change. This, thought Randolph, was what the Federalist majority wished Washington to do. The question of procedure, he felt, would involve "some critical, delicate and hazardous points." Apparently without formal request the Secretary offered his observations: "If [the President] sends an article already drawn, it will be asked: Why did he do so? . . . Does he mean to exhibit his approbation of the treaty so *strikingly*? . . . Does he mean to ratify it *now*, so as to render it unnecessary for the treaty to come back to *himself* after the new suspending article is inserted?" Randolph's remarks were enough to convince Washington that a revised article should not be submitted at this time. But ought he acknowledge the action of the Senate in some other way? In the view of the Secretary, Washington's possible choices were three. He could be silent; or make a "positive declaration" of his understanding of the intention of the Senate; or offer a "qualified declaration," together with a casual sketch of Article XII as the Executive planned to recast it. Randolph advocated no particular course. Washington made his choice without looking elsewhere for counsel. He would remain silent; the Senate would adjourn without word from him.

News of the action of the Senate went out in every direction, and with as much praise, criticism or innuendo as excited pens could call forth. Washington was occupied on June 25 with two unrelated messages for the Senate, the more important of which concerned impending negotiation with the Creeks in Georgia and embodied his nomination of Benjamin Hawkins, Andrew Pickens and George Clymer as commissioners of peace. Both communications went forward that day and were confirmed the next. In the afternoon George Cabot and John Brown called to say that the Senate was about to adjourn sine die. Perhaps in private conversation with Cabot, Washington learned of the passage of a significant motion, the only one of the session: strict secrecy was rescinded, but Senators were enjoined not to disclose any part of the treaty until it had been ratified by presidential signature. One Federalist, Oliver Wolcott, felt the secret was out. "The right of conversing generally about it," he said, "will be found equivalent to a publication." Washington still had no comment, but he and Randolph were ready to accept the advice of Senator King and release an official copy for publication in Andrew Brown's *Philadelphia Gazette*. Before this could be done, Bache's *Aurora* on June 29 offered an abstract over the pseudonym "A Citizen." Then, two days later, Bache advertised a pamphlet edition of the full text for twenty-five cents, and gave an explanation by Senator Stevens T. Mason, a Virginia Republican, that he had surrendered his copy in order to correct the "false impressions" of the abstract. As Madison later described it, the treaty now "flew with an electric velocity to every part of the union."

The Chief Executive now faced a mighty problem of procedure. As Randolph intimated, it had become the desperate design of the opposition "to embarrass the treaty by objecting to the course which is at hand." Washington put the problem before his Cabinet on June 29. Opinions of Wolcott and Pickering came the next morning. They were unequivocal: the President need not deliver the revised clause to the Senate. Randolph reiterated this counsel in terms slightly less positive. For two full days Washington turned the problem of the treaty in his mind and reached no decision. Then he posted a letter to Hamilton. "My desire," Washington wrote, "is to learn from dispassionate men, who have knowledge of the subject and abilities to judge of it, the genuine opinion they entertain of *each* article of the instrument, and the result of it in the aggregate. . . . My wishes are to have the favorable and unfavorable side of *each* article stated and compared together, that I may see the bearing and tendency of them and, ultimately, on which side the balance is to be found." The President's request ended on a hopeful note that Hamilton would find time to comply.

Perhaps he sought only the views of "dispassionate men," but Washington scarcely could fail to observe the reaction of citizens who hated the treaty with passion. Eleazer Oswald's *Independent Gazetteer* opened the Fourth of July with a notice that henceforth the national anniversary would be an occasion of national mourning. Oswald's harangue produced no immediate result; Philadelphians paid the President visits of congratulation in the usual manner. Then, towards midnight, a boisterous crowd appeared in the streets. A parade began, and overhead the rioters carried an illuminated effigy of Jay. The excited demonstrators marched on to Kensington, a suburb of the city, where the effigy was burned with shouts and huzzas. When Captain Morrell's Light Horse appeared to disperse the mob, his men were stoned and a placard erected to mark the spot: "Morrell's Defeat—Jay Burned—July 4, 1795."

These proceedings drew comment neither from the President nor from Jay, and the latter's retirement from the Supreme Court caused Washington to write warmly to him in appreciation of six years of sterling service. The day he received Jay's resignation, the President offered the Chief Justiceship to John Rutledge, who had been a member of the Court before his return to South Carolina in 1791 to become the leading jurist of that State. The Charlestonian, Washington knew, coveted the appointment; he knew also that Rutledge, an old and ardent Republican, was no admirer of Jay or of the present Court, but Rutledge was a seasoned jurist and a brilliant one. Washington made his choice "without hesitating a moment."

He must decide whether to ratify now, or whether to follow the counsel of his Cabinet and do so before Article XII had been adjusted. While he awaited the advice of Hamilton, routine duties occupied him. Then, on July 7 and 8, the mail from New York brought confirmations from Hamilton and Jay of a shocking report in the public prints: British cruisers again were seizing as contraband cargoes of American grain ships bound for France! Were not these confiscations proof that a new instruction had been issued which restated the obnoxious provision order of June 8, 1793? Washington was exasperated. England gave him cause to believe that the United States was the victim of a diplomatic deception, that no true basis of accommodation underlay the treaty. The President conferred at once with the Secretary of State. Randolph submitted a conclusive opinion on July 12: "The order for capturing provisions is too irreconcilable with a state of harmony for the treaty to be put in motion during its existence." Here was Randolph's idea of a way to remove every difficulty: He could be sent to the British Minister to declare unreservedly that the President had determined to sign the treaty without submitting a revision of Article XII to the Senate. Once this was understood, Randolph would attach a proviso: "The President cannot persuade himself that he ought to ratify during the existence of the order. . . . That order being removed, he will ratify without delay or further scruple." If Hammond was agreeable, he would receive a memorial in this sense, to be delivered to his government with a revised draft of Article XII. The British Foreign Office could make reply to William A. Deas, chargé ad interim at London, and final ratifications could be exchanged at Philadelphia. This procedure, Randolph thought, would be attractive to Hammond because it gave him a role in the exchange of ratifications; it would be attractive to Grenville, who was eager for final action, because it overcame all delays foreseen in the assignment of a new American representative to perform the function of the absent Pinckney.

Randolph's plan seemed a sensible one. Washington gave the Secretary permission to carry it out. Soon Randolph was back to report an unsatisfactory conversation with Hammond. The British Minister actually had asked if it might be sufficient to lift the order temporarily, then renew it after the ratification! Further, he wished to know if the President was "irrevocably determined" not to ratify while the order remained in effect. When Randolph told Washington he had given no positive answer to this second question, the President's comment was sharp. Hammond might have been informed, he said, that he would never sign a pact with Great Britain while her warships seized American cargoes and insulted the American flag in the Atlantic! If Pitt and Grenville came to their senses, he would ratify; if they failed to do so, he would not. Randolph was instructed to draft a memorial for Hammond and prepare a revision of Article XII so that the American government would be ready for the eventuality of a ratification.

While England's caprice had resolved the mind of the President, he was glad to receive in the post of the thirteenth a paper Hamilton called "Remarks on the Treaty" though it bore signs of necessary haste. The New Yorker's comment was extensive on several articles but fragmentary on others. Article XII he dismissed as "an exceptionable one" without analysis of the reasons which made it so. On the whole, he concluded, the treaty was in "the true interest of the United States" and ought to be accepted. A second mail from Hamilton came, and a third. In the last he gave his opinion that the revision of Article XII must be approved by the Senate before ratification. This view surprised Washington; would Hamilton please amplify in further correspondence? "Notwithstanding one great object of my visit to Mount Vernon is relaxation," the President wrote on July 14, "yet to hear from you in the sentiments entertained of the treaty . . . would be considerable gratification."

Washington started for Mount Vernon July 15. It was good to leave the city; and perhaps more so this time than previously. In Washington's word, Philadelphia had been "suffocating" for the past week. Although he did not say it, the problems of the presidential office were more oppressive at this moment than the heat. His responsibilities never were larger, his role never more difficult. "A hot and disagreeable ride," Washington said of the six days of travel that took him down the familiar road to Virginia. He made Wilmington the first night and Susquehanna Ferry the next, but not until the eighteenth did the President's entourage reach Baltimore, and there came another unexpected delay. An express from Boston was put into his hands: the people of Boston had voiced disapproval of the treaty and, by way of the enclosed address of their Selectmen, implored the President not to sign it. Washington wrote hastily to Randolph: "The application is of an unusual and disagreeable nature and . . . is intended, I have no doubt, to place me in an embarrassed situation from whence an advantage may be taken." Would the Secretary of State consult with his colleagues and decide whether a reply was proper? If so, one should be drafted in "accord with *all* your ideas," and sent quickly to Mount Vernon for signature.

The President the next night lodged at Georgetown and was ready on July 20 for a conference with thé commissioners of the Federal District. To his dismay, the commissioners presented a complaint that went much beyond the usual personal bickering. Payments were not arriving on schedule from Robert Morris and John Nicholson, whose extensive holdings now included seven thousand lots originally purchased by James Greenleaf. Further deficiencies in the stipulated monthly payment of $12,000 would necessitate discharge of irreplaceable workmen. Such a circumstance could result in suspension of work on the public buildings. The President saw yet another danger: Morris's failure to make good his obligations "would throw such a cloud over the public and private concerns of the City, and would be susceptible of such magnified and unfavorable interpretation, as to give it a vital wound." When Washington took leave of the commissioners after a full day of discussion, he promised to urge Morris and Nicholson to deliver funds at once.

The President reached Mount Vernon by the dinner hour. He planned to extend this vacation to the end of September if possible, but it was only too obvious that public affairs could not be forgotten even for a day. Two communications from Randolph awaited him, one enclosing a recent issue of the *Pittsburgh Gazette* which featured an inflammatory speech against the treaty by H. H. Brackenridge, the Western agitator. "A Solomon is not necessary to interpret the design of the oration of Mr. Brackenridge," Washington noted cryptically in reply to the Secretary of State on the twenty-second. This same letter set forth the President's decision on the treaty; Randolph was instructed to make sure the other Cabinet officers understood the decision. Should it prove that no British maritime order was in effect, "a conditional ratification . . . may on all fit occasions be spoken of as my determination. . . . My opinion respecting the treaty is the same now that it was: namely, not favorable to it—but that it is better to ratify it than to suffer matters to remain as they are, unsettled." In the next post came Randolph's excited report that other towns appeared to be following the example of Boston; the commotion over the treaty, he thought, was "the greatest in its consequences which had occurred under this Government." Should he hasten to Mount Vernon to consult with the President?

The spread of popular protest might have been expected. Republican newspapers were lending much space to criticisms of the treaty, and the *Aurora* urged all American towns to emulate the proceedings of the

Boston Selectmen. While he could not yet have known details, Washington must have heard of the mass meetings a week earlier in Portsmouth and in Charleston. "The same leaven that fermented a part of the town of Boston," he answered Randolph on July 24, "is at work, I am informed, in other places. But whether it will produce the same fruit remains to be decided." If circumstances became such that he must consult with the Secretary of State, Washington would prefer to return to Philadelphia rather than summon Randolph to Virginia: "If matters are peculiarly embarrassed, I should be on the theatre of information with documents and other aids about me that could not be had here."

Three days later news from New York crystallized every dread expectation. A recent commotion in that metropolis dwarfed the tumult of lesser towns. By wide newspaper advertisement and circulation of handbills, New York Republicans had been able to arouse great enthusiasm for a town meeting scheduled July 18, in front of City Hall. Federalist merchants hastily declared their approbation of the treaty in the press, but the crowd which gathered in Wall Street at the appointed hour was large and rowdy. Hamilton appeared to defend the treaty, but shouts for "A Chairman! A Chairman!" subdued him and allowed Col. William S. Smith to be elevated to that role. When Hamilton and Peter Livingston appealed to Smith for a chance to present their opposite views, Smith appealed to the crowd and Hamilton was overruled. The chairman then asked the multitude to divide left and right, for and against the treaty, and confusion was compounded. Hamilton called for full and free discussion, but Brockholst Livingston deprecated this as a waste of precious time. Thereupon, those who had gone to the right marched off to the Battery and burned copies of the treaty before the residence of Governor Jay. Soon they returned, carrying French flags and accompanied by seamen from French ships in the harbor, and Hamilton became the target of a barrage of stones. When one struck him in the head and drew blood, he left the scene and every supporter of the treaty departed with him. Brockholst Livingston then moved that an address be prepared and sent to the President; a list of fifteen committeemen for this work was read rapidly by another Republican. As soon as these names were affirmed by acclamation, the crowd dispersed and the chosen ones retired to draft a set of resolutions.

Their twenty-eight resolves Washington now read with care. They repeated and enlarged the charges of the Boston Selectmen. The treaty was damned for the permission it gave British troops to remain eighteen months more in the northwest posts and its failure to obtain compensation for twelve years' illegal occupancy; its failure to secure payment for slave property carried away during the Revolution; its failure to stipulate restitution for recent maritime outrages; its indulgence of the old claims of English creditors; the heavy advantage given to Britain in every commercial clause; and, above all, the patent hostility of the whole instrument to France. "Not willing to lose a post day," the President wrote instantly to Randolph, "I hasten to send these resolutions. . . ." Would the Cabinet please consider the advisability of a reply?

The next post brought an address favorable to the treaty, adopted in counter action by the New York Chamber of Commerce July 21, but vastly more significant was news from Wolcott of demonstrations in Philadelphia on July 23 and 25. As announced by an inflammatory handbill, a town meeting was held on the twenty-third in the yard of the State House. The turnout was poor—no more than 1500—and adjournment followed the selection of a committee of fifteen, under Dr. William Shippen, to frame resolutions for the President. A second meeting on the twenty-fifth also proved thin in numbers; but those who came included such conspicuous Philadelphians as Alexander J. Dallas and Thomas McKean, respectively the Commonwealth Secretary and Chief Justice, the merchant prince Stephen Girard, and the popular Irish orator Blair McClenachan. An address, primarily the work of Dallas, was read aloud; a show of hands gave almost unanimous approval to each paragraph. Then McClenachan, in a high state of excitement, waved a printed sheet above his head and shouted: "What a damned treaty! I make a motion that every good citizen in this assembly kick this damned treaty to hell!" His followers immediately impaled the treaty on a pole and carried it to the house of Pierre Adet, but the French Minister did not respond to their calls to join the riot. The mob then paraded to George Hammond's residence, stoned his windows and burned the treaty on his doorstep. Another copy was destroyed in front of the house of the British consul, Phineas Bond, and Senator William Bingham was insulted similarly.

Four enclosures from the Secretary of State came in the same mail that brought Wolcott's account of the agitation in Philadelphia. Here were the Cabinet consensus of an appropriate reply to the Boston Selectmen, Randolph's draft of the memorial to be presented to the British Minister, a proposed revision of Article XII, and an outline of instructions for the American agent who would handle the exchange of ratifications in London should the treaty be signed. Washington examined each, then made up his mind to return to Philadelphia. A meeting of the Potomac Company in Alexandria on August 3 would prevent his departure until that date; but he might be expected at the seat of government a few days thereafter.

The President meant to attend the meeting in Alexandria and then start for Philadelphia on the same evening, but torrential rain made travel impossible. Water was high and rising in every stream; most of the bridges were gone. Not until August 5 was there a regular delivery of mail to Mount Vernon. That post brought word from Lear that the Potomac Company would convene in Georgetown the next day. He would try to be there, Washington replied; but "such an accumulation" of official mail was expected momentarily that probably it would be the eighth before he had answered it and could start for Philadelphia. Would Lear please represent him if he did not appear?

The Philadelphia mail arrived and was found to contain three overdue letters. One from the Secretary of State dated July 29 gave the unanimous opinion of the Cabinet that the President ought not to return hurriedly to the seat of government; obvious haste, it was thought, would show the Chief Executive to be excited by the recent town meetings and would endow these demonstrations with a new importance. Randolph reversed this advice in a communication of July 31; late developments, he wrote, made it necessary for the President to be at Philadelphia. A letter from Pickering was more specific and more alarming: The British Minister had been recalled and would be leaving in three weeks; "some useful and perhaps very important arrangements" might be made before Hammond's departure. Then the Secretary of War added this passage:

On the subject of the treaty I confess that I feel extreme solicitude, and for a *special reason* which can be communicated to you only in person. I entreat, therefore, that you will return with all convenient speed to the seat of government. In the meanwhile, for the reason above referred to, I pray you to decide on no important political measure in whatever form it may be presented to you. Mr. Wolcott and I, Mr. Bradford concurring, waited on Mr. Randolph and urged his writing to request your return. He wrote in our presence, but we concluded a letter from one of us also expedient.

Washington made up his mind to start to Philadelphia without further delay. Early on August 6 he said good-bye to his family and ordered the coach away. At Georgetown he attended the meeting of the Potomac Company and conferred briefly with the commissioners of the Federal City. The condition of the roads worsened as he proceeded, and it was noon on August 11 before the President finally alighted in Philadelphia.

Anxious to know what had prompted Pickering's letter, Washington sent to ask the Secretary of War to call at his earliest convenience. Pickering came during the dinner hour and found Washington and Randolph at table and in cheerful conversation. The President rose and, taking a glass of wine, indicated to Pickering alone to step into the next room. As soon as the door closed behind them, Washington asked, "What is the cause of your writing me such a letter?" Pickering pointed at the door and replied, "That man is a traitor!"

Pickering explained his charge. Shortly after the President had gone to Mount Vernon, he said, the British Minister received from London intercepted despatches which had been sent the previous year by Fauchet to his superiors at Paris. Hammond invited Wolcott to his house on July 26 and read to him, in English, several passages from one of these, Despatch No. 10 of October 31, 1794. It appeared from this, said Pickering, that Randolph had asked Fauchet for money and had intimated that American policy could be influenced by it! Information of "such magnitude," Wolcott told Hammond, ought not to remain exclusively with one Cabinet officer; but allegations could not be communicated further unless the original of Fauchet's letter was in hand to substantiate them. Hammond agreed to deliver the document. Accordingly, on July 28, he gave Wolcott the original and a certified copy of Despatch No. 10. Wolcott then presented Fauchet's letter to Pickering, who made a rough translation with the aid of a French grammar, and together they visited Attorney General Bradford on the twenty-ninth. These three vowed the strictest secrecy until the President returned to Philadelphia and decided he should be called back immediately. On July 31 Pickering and Wolcott, giving a fictitious reason, asked Randolph to write the necessary letter. The Secretary of State complied unwittingly, and Pickering also wrote. When the President had studied Fauchet's despatch, Pickering said, he could judge for himself how far Randolph was implicated in treason. Wolcott would bring him the document that evening. The President accepted Pickering's terrible report in silence. "Let us return to the other room," he said at last, "to prevent any suspicion of the cause of our withdrawing."

Alone in his study that evening Washington read Fauchet's incrimination of the Secretary of State. Midway in the opening paragraph of the long despatch Randolph's name appeared. Fauchet had written: "Besides, the precious confessions of Mr. Randolph alone throw a satisfactory light upon everything that comes to pass." The implication was unmistakable—Randolph had given away state secrets! The President read on rapidly. One passage after another yielded nothing but Fauchet's denunciation of the excise tax and observations on the insurrection in western Pennsylvania. Then, in the fourteenth paragraph, Randolph was said to have declared "that under pretext of giving energy to the government, it was intended to introduce absolute power and to mislead the President in paths which would conduct him to unpopularity." Fauchet commented in the next paragraph that "the influence of Mr. Randolph over the mind of the President" was paramount, and that this had determined the Executive to send commissioners to placate the insurgent counties. The sixteenth paragraph named Mifflin and Dallas as ardent Pennsylvania Republicans, then gave the confirmation of Pickering's spoken words that Washington dreaded but could not discount:

. . . these men, with others unknown to me, all having without doubt Randolph at their head, were balancing to decide on their party. Two or three days before the proclamation [of August 7, 1794] was published, and of course before the Cabinet had resolved on its measures, Mr. Randolph came to see me with a countenance expressive of much anxiety, and made to me the overtures of which I have given you an account in my No. 6. Thus with some thousands of dollars the [French] Republic would have decided on civil war or on peace! Thus the consciences of the pretended patriots of America have already their scale of prices! . . . What will be the old age of this government, if it is thus early decrepit! Such, Citizen, is the evident consequence of the system of finances conceived by Mr. Hamilton. He has made of a whole nation a stock-jobbing, speculating, selfish people. Riches alone here fix consideration. . . . they are universally sought after.

What could all this mean except that the Secretary of State had asked Fauchet for money? The French Minister said no more of "overtures" than that they were described in an earlier dispatch, No. 6, the content of which Washington did not know. But here before his eye in No. 10 a damning inference glared. "Overtures" and "some thousands of dollars," used as they were in this sequence, conveyed a single idea and stamped an awful impression: Randolph was corrupt! Remaining passages in Fauchet's letter carried smaller connotations of guilt, but added little to the ugly image of "precious confessions" and "overtures." The President could not question the genuineness of this intercepted dispatch; nor could he simply dismiss Fauchet's words as contrived or exaggerated. However much Washington may have wished to avoid them, conclusions were inescapable. He had to acknowledge that his most intimate associate might be faithless and venal, might be even what Pickering called him—a traitor.

Not since an autumn day in 1780, when the first fragmentary hints of Benedict Arnold's defection came to him, had Washington faced this kind of thing. He was loath then to believe the worst of Arnold, but that subordinate soon evidenced his treason. Would Randolph's conduct likewise indicate a real guilt? If the Secretary's financial harassments were severe enough a year ago to lead him into collusion with the French Minister, he might be in the pay of France at this very moment! If so, would he not make efforts at this time to delay ratification of the treaty with England in the hope of finally preventing it altogether? For a month the President's intention had been firm: Great Britain should be notified, by way of a memorial to Hammond, that the treaty would be signed as soon as the offensive "provision order" was rescinded. This resolve he had reached in sole collaboration with the Secretary of State. If Randolph's tactic was to postpone ratification indefinitely, the President was playing into his hands!

Washington summoned the Cabinet to his office the next morning. His colleagues greeted Randolph civilly if coolly, and nothing in the President's demeanor betrayed his state of mind. The draft of the memorial to Hammond, which had been approved tentatively at Mount Vernon and returned to Randolph, was in the Secretary's pocket; he expected now to submit it for minor revision. The President called instead for comments on the advisability of immediate ratification. Wolcott and Pickering argued in favor of such action. Randolph gave a statement of his view that Britain must be made to abandon the "provision order" before the President assented to the treaty. This order, he said, was totally incompatible with a spirit of diplomatic accord and with the principle of freedom of the seas; the government would emasculate its protests against British naval arrogance by acquiescing in the order; and surely the United States risked the justifiable wrath of France by combining with England to starve her. To the consternation of the Secretary of State, Washington seemed suddenly oblivious to this reasoning. Wolcott and Pickering renewed their polemics, and Bradford inclined to their side. Finally the President arose and declared, "I will ratify the treaty." Hammond should be so notified and a memorial delivered to him in course, without the stipulation Randolph desired. Instructions must be hurried to the American agent who now was to proceed with the formal exchange of ratifications in London.

If Washington later chose to explain his decision, he may have advanced the multiplying arguments of other Federalists that only an immediate ratification could counter the dangerous tide of opposition to both the treaty and the Government—and indeed this seemed the case. Addresses and resolutions were arriving from every corner of the land; a swell of diatribe threatened to obliterate public appreciation of every good feature of the treaty and erode the cement of the Union. Certain addresses were, in Washington's opinion, so unreasonable, so abusive as to merit no acknowledgment at all. "Tenor indecent—no answer returned," he wrote across the paper from Petersburg, Virginia. Others would have to be noticed. Accordingly, the President directed Randolph to release the reply to the Boston Selectmen and prepare similar answers for Portsmouth, Charleston, New York, Philadelphia, Richmond, Trenton, Baltimore and Wilmington, Delaware. All these were posted in the next two days.

The week which followed the Cabinet meeting of August 12 must have been a torturing time for Washington. He met often with Randolph. Yet, because the Secretary's part was essential in the ratification, the President thought it necessary to keep from his friend all knowledge of Fauchet's incriminating despatch. If he exhibited the letter to Randolph or hinted its content, a storm would break over the Cabinet and its thunder would echo through the remotest town in the nation. The treaty would be irretrievably lost; the government would be shaken to its roots. Washington was convinced that the interest of the United States required an immediate ratification of the treaty. The guilt or innocence of the Secretary of State must not be brought to question until the treaty was safe.

A private interview with Randolph on the thirteenth must have tapped the deepest resources of Washington's control. Randolph submitted for his inspection three diplomatic letters which had gone abroad in the last month and each of which announced unequivocally that there would be no ratification while the "provision order" remained operative. One, a circular to American envoys, was dated July 21; the others were to Monroe in Paris and bore dates of July 14 and 29. The last of these arrested Washington's attention—here was a critique, a sharp one, of the Secretary's most recent impressions of the departed Fauchet. Randolph had written:

Most thoroughly I am now persuaded that Mr. Fauchet has wrapped himself round with intrigue from the first moment of his career in the United States. He found me in no manner turned towards Britain, but warm towards France. He affected a confidence in me . . . He has more than once asserted his conviction that Mr. [Laforest, the French consul-general]—was perfidious and confederated with the enemies of France. He expressed his disgust and suspicions against Genet, endeavoring to inculcate an opinion that they were irreconcilable. He pretended great attachment to the President. The reverse of all this is now fixed upon my mind. His chief associates have been enemies of the Government and of the administration. His conversation has been steadily hostile to the Executive. I believe he has been instrumental in many of the printed attacks upon its reputation; that he has been in close league with Genet; that he has been plotting how to embroil this country with France; and that he has insidiously covered, with charges against the fidelity of [Laforest],—a bait to procure information from members of the Executive to whom he resorted. I was not one of them. . . .

There was more, much more. When the Secretary had gone, Washington read the letter again and made a précis. It could have been at this moment that the last vestige of his faith in Edmund Randolph was destroyed. Why, he may have asked himself, did Randolph attempt to connect other "members of the Executive" with Fauchet, and who could these have been? Of the officers of the Cabinet during Fauchet's sixteen months at Philadelphia, Randolph alone was sympathetic in some degree to France. Was the Secretary afraid now that Fauchet would speak to Monroe in Paris and disclose a confidence he had obtained in America? Was Randolph trying to obscure the fact that *he* had conversed too freely with the French Minister? Did Randolph's own letter bear out the allegation of "precious confessions" in Fauchet's intercepted despatch? If questions like these arose in Washington's mind, his sole conclusion could have been that Edmund Randolph had done something very wrong.

On August 14 the President visited Randolph at the Secretary's house. They discussed the memorial for Hammond which had been reworded to exclude Randolph's declaration that the treaty would go unsigned until the "provision order" was rescinded. The paper now stated that the President would ratify subject to the excision of Article XII as stipulated by the Senate and asserted a mild formal objection to the interpretation of contraband upon which the British admiralty based its orders-in-council. Since Hammond was leaving for New York the next morning, the Secretary was instructed to deliver the memorial that day. Before he left, the President had Randolph's countersignature on the form of the ratification.

Every mail to Philadelphia brought new resolutions against the treaty. This popular movement, Pickering wrote Jay, could be halted only by a proclamation of the President's intention to accept the treaty. He hoped Washington would issue "a solemn declaration . . . of the principles of his administration," which might explain "the purity and patriotism of his conduct on the present occasion" by "his appealing to the train of actions which have marked his whole life." Jay did not agree; nor did Washington, if the idea was presented to him. The treaty would be signed in two or three days; that action would speak for itself. On Saturday August 15 the President entertained a group of friends at dinner, among them Randolph. A note from Pickering awaited Washington Monday morning: the Secretary of War had completed his own draft of the ratification form, "somewhat different" from Randolph's, and immediately would consult Wolcott and Bradford on this paper and the instructions to be sent to the American agent in London. All seemed in readiness. On August 18 the President signed the treaty.

Washington conversed that evening with Randolph, who was again his guest at table, but still he said nothing of Fauchet's despatch and gave not the smallest clue that the Secretary was suspect. Now that the treaty was beyond danger the President could have taken this occasion to exhibit the letter to Randolph and interrogate him privately. He might have done so, except that his faith in his friend was failing by the hour. Sometime in the last six days, probably before the eighteenth, Washington had delivered a confidential memorandum to Pickering and Wolcott. The questions in it and the language of those questions were indicative. They showed the President was sure Randolph could not exculpate himself and that his removal was contemplated and its justification before the public planned. Washington retained no copy of this paper or of the replies of Pickering and Wolcott, if indeed these were in writing. Whether written or oral, their advice set a stage for the scene which followed on August 19.

Randolph was expected at the President's office at nine o'clock for routine business, but word was sent that he should delay his call until half past ten. Meanwhile Washington met with Pickering and Wolcott to determine the manner in which the intercepted letter should be presented to the Secretary of State. Apparently on the ground that a request might be considered improper and be refused—the President and his counsellors decided not to apply to Fauchet's successor for extracts of Despatches No. 3 and No. 6. Instead, they thought, a close observation of Randolph's reactions would furnish "the best means of discovering his true situation and of duly estimating the defence he might make." Accordingly the President decided that Pickering and Wolcott should be present when Despatch No. 10 was shown to Randolph and asked them to study Randolph's countenance as he read the letter.

When he arrived at 10:30 the Secretary of State learned from the doorkeeper that Pickering and Wolcott were already in the President's office and had been there for some time. He went up immediately, thinking that perhaps Washington's messenger had misinformed him and he was late for a meeting of the Cabinet. The President greeted Randolph with unusual formality, and Pickering and Wolcott followed his example. After a few words Washington drew a paper from his pocket. It was the original of Fauchet's Despatch No. 10. "Mr. Randolph," he said, "here is a letter which I desire you to read, and make such explanations as you choose." Randolph took the document and read it through in silence; his composure was perfect, except for a slight flush at the very beginning. When he had finished, Randolph remarked that the letter must be an intercepted one; Washington nodded his head. "I will explain what I know," the Secretary said; but, he added, his recollection might not be accurate on so spontaneous a call. He began his explanation, paragraph by paragraph, and was not interrupted; but the comments impressed Wolcott as profuse, "desultory" and contrived to produce time in which to concoct some justification for the incriminating passages. Of "precious confessions" Randolph said only that he could remember no improper communication to the French Minister—and that the words might be elucidated by that section of Despatch No. 3 to which Fauchet referred. When he came to "overtures" and "prices" in the sixteenth paragraph, he declared simply that he could not be sure, without access to Despatch No. 6, what was connoted by this language. Never, he declared positively, had he asked or received money from Fauchet; but he did recall that the French Minister once complained that Hammond was conspiring with certain New Yorkers to destroy him, Governor Clinton and other acknowledged Republicans, Randolph among them. He had answered this by suggesting that such machinations might be countered effectively by several able Americans whom Fauchet knew well, men with whom he had contracted for the purchase of flour. By way of conclusion, Randolph said he would be glad to throw all his ideas on paper if he were permitted to retain the letter. "Very well," replied the President, "retain it." Washington then asked Pickering and Wolcott if they cared to interrogate their colleague. This "style of proceeding" nettled Randolph. Pickering had no query, but Wolcott wished to know exactly what was meant by the observation that Hammond sought to "destroy"

Fauchet, Clinton, Randolph and others. Obviously, Randolph replied, this meant that Hammond was attempting to destroy the influence and popularity of the men named. He turned to the President and asked if indeed there had not been a rumor in 1794 that Hammond was so engaged. Randolph then received a retort that shocked and chagrined him. He for one, Washington announced, certainly was not trying to conceal anything!

At this point the President was called from the room. While he was out Randolph inquired of Pickering and Wolcott how the intercepted despatch had come to the Executive's attention. "The President will, I presume, explain that to you," Wolcott replied coldly. Immediately upon returning, Washington directed Randolph to step into the adjoining room while he, Pickering and Wolcott conferred; and the Secretary did so. For the next forty-five minutes Randolph's reactions and explanations were discussed. All agreed that he had betrayed no emotion during the interview, but when Randolph returned his control had broken. The President asked him if he still wished to commit his representations to writing. It would be done, Randolph replied abruptly—but without access to Despatches No. 3 and No. 6 he scarcely could be expected to dispel the false impression that he had encouraged the Pennsylvania insurrection! Washington chose to ignore the remark. How soon could the Secretary produce a paper? "As soon as possible," Randolph flared, and declared he never could remain in office after such treatment as he had just received at the President's hands. With this said, he turned and departed.

Randolph's letter of resignation, dated the nineteenth, was delivered to the President the next day. Randolph had written:

> Immediately upon leaving your house this morning, I went to [my] office . . . where I directed the room, in which I usually sat, to be locked up, and the key to remain with the messenger. My object in this was to let all the papers rest as they stood. Upon my return home, I reflected calmly and maturely upon the proceedings of this morning. Two facts immediately presented themselves. One . . . was that my usual hour of calling upon the President had not only been postponed for the opportunity of consulting *others* upon a letter of a foreign minister highly interesting to my honor, before the smallest intimation to me, but they seemed also to be perfectly acquainted with its contents and were requested to ask questions for their satisfaction. The other was that I was desired to retire into another room until you should converse with them upon what I had said. Your confidence in me, Sir, has been unlimited and, I can truly affirm, unabused. My sensations, then, cannot be concealed when I find that confidence so immediately withdrawn without a word or distant hint being previously dropped to me! This, Sir, as I mentioned in your room, is a situation in which I cannot hold my present office, and therefore I hereby resign it. It will not, however, be concluded from hence that I mean to relinquish the inquiry. No, Sir, far from it. I will also meet any inquiry. And to prepare for it, if I learn this morning that there is a chance of overtaking Mr. Fauchet before he sails, I will go to him immediately. . . . I am satisfied, Sir, that you will acknowledge one piece of justice due on this occasion, which is that until an inquiry can be made, the affair shall continue in secrecy under your injunction. For, after pledging myself for a more specific investigation of all these suggestions, I here most solemnly deny that any overture ever came from me which was to produce money to me, or any others for me; and

that in any manner, directly or indirectly, was a shilling ever received by me. Nor was it ever contemplated by me that one shilling should be applied by Mr. Fauchet to any purpose relative to the insurrection.

Randolph closed with a request that the President furnish him a copy of the intercepted letter and with Fauchet's Despatch No. 6 if that document was also in his possession.

Washington replied at once, but he neither acknowledged the grievance nor expressed regret at the resignation. "Candor induces me," he wrote,

to give to you, in a few words, the following narrative of facts. The letter from Mr. Fauchet . . . was, as you supposed, an intercepted one. It was sent by Lord Grenville to Mr. Hammond; by him put into the hands of the Secretary of the Treasury; by him shown to the Secretary of War and the Attorney General; and a translation thereof was made by the former for me. . . . Whether it is known to others, I am unable to decide. While you are in pursuit of means to remove the strong suspicions arising from this letter, no disclosure of its contents will be made by me. And I will enjoin the same on the public officers who are acquainted with the purport of it, unless something shall appear to render an explanation necessary on the part of the Government—of which I will be the judge. A copy of Mr. Fauchet's letter shall be sent to you. No. 6, referred to therein, I have never seen.

The President wrote Randolph on August 22, "Agreeably to your request and my promise, and as soon as it has been in my power, I send you a copy of Mr. Fauchet's Letter No. 10." Although Randolph had left Philadelphia and was hurrying to Rhode Island to overtake Fauchet before the diplomat sailed for France, the President made no mention of this in his note of one sentence only. If this reticence was callous, the press of other matters explained it in part. Before he could resume his interrupted vacation at Mount Vernon, Washington must take steps to fill the office of Secretary of State; he must induce some able man to succeed Attorney General Bradford, whose lingering illness ended in death on August 23; he must approve instructions for the American agent who was to carry out the formal exchange of treaty ratifications in London; and he must look into a complaint from Gov. Arthur Fenner of Rhode Island that the British cruiser *Africa* was hovering off Newport.

Washington considered John Marshall of Richmond particularly fitted for the Attorney Generalship and wrote accordingly to the Virginian. His choice for the Department of State was William Paterson of New Jersey, but the Supreme Court Justice declined an oral invitation, and the offer went next to Thomas Johnson of Maryland. Johnson pleaded failing health, and a similar invitation then was forwarded to Charles Cotesworth Pinckney. It would take some time for Pinckney's answer to return from Charleston; until an appointment could be made, Pickering had agreed to handle the business of the Department of State as well as that of his own office. Pickering's first task in the new capacity gave him a challenge—he had to prepare definitive instructions for the American diplomat who was to execute the exchange of treaty ratifications with Great Britain. The only United States official at the London legation was William A. Deas, secretary to Thomas Pinckney and now chargé ad interim. The President knew nothing of Deas's character or qualifications and much preferred to assign the exchange to a diplomat of rank, the most available of whom was the American minister resident at The Hague, John Quincy Adams. It was decided that Adams should be ordered to London; but as delay must be avoided, Deas should have authority to proceed if Adams had not arrived by October 20. Pickering had a set of instructions ready August 25, and the President approved it that day. The American agent, Adams or Deas, was to carry out the exchange, qualifying the treaty by excision of Article XII, and then protest orally against the recent "provision order." Finally, he was to urge immediate evacuation of British troops from the western posts. As soon as Pinckney was back in London, further negotiation should be left to him.

On August 31 Washington wrote Hamilton of the activities of Capt. Rodman Home of His Majesty's cruiser *Africa* off Newport. While hovering there in the hope of intercepting the French frigate *Medusa* when that vessel put to sea, Home had impressed several seamen from American merchant ships. Then, on July 31, Home and British Vice Consul Thomas W. Moore demanded that Governor Fenner assist them in reclaiming British sailors on shore leave in Newport. The next day Home entered American territorial waters to stop and search the coastal packet *Peggy,* on which Fauchet had embarked at New York on his journey to Newport where the *Medusa* awaited him. Forewarned, Fauchet left the *Peggy* at Stonington, but his baggage was ransacked by Home's searchers. In spite of a formal protest by Pickering to Consul Phineas Bond, senior British diplomat in the United States now that Hammond was gone, no explanation of Home's and Moore's conduct had been given. The President complained to Hamilton, ". . . it would seem next to impossible . . . to keep peace between the United States and Great Britain." Washington waited two days more for some apology from Bond, but patience proved fruitless. On September 2, determined that the sovereignty of the United States should not be affronted without redress, he approved a detailed indictment of Home and Moore which had been drafted by Pickering for transmission to Bond. Three days later the British diplomat was notified that the exequatur of Moore had been revoked by the President and that henceforth all intercourse was prohibited between the people of Newport and the *Africa.*

Popular response to his acceptance of the treaty was exactly what Washington had anticipated; Federalists lauded the action and Republicans denounced it. Washington ignored the whispers that came to his ears, as likewise he ignored the abusive memorials now arriving in every mail. His state of mind at the close of August was much the same as it had been the day he signed the treaty. On the thirty-first he sent this reply to an address from the Republicans of Savannah:

Next to the consciousness of having discharged my duty according to my best judgment, nothing could have afforded me a greater pleasure than to have found my decision consistent with the wishes of all my fellow citizens. On this occasion I have, however, been directed by the great principle which has governed all my public conduct: a sincere desire to promote and secure the true interest of my country.

A note from Pickering on September 7 informed the President that no public business remained to prevent his departure for Mount Vernon the next morning. This word was gratifying, but that night Washington received a private communication which disturbed him and which called for an immediate decision. A letter from Knox in Boston enclosed a message from George Washington Lafayette, son of the Revolutionary hero, who recently had disembarked in that town after a voyage from France. Young Lafayette's letter expressed a desire to hurry to Philadelphia and place himself in the care of the President. Such action, Washington feared, could have embarrassing repercussions; yet Washington felt deeply responsible for the welfare of his namesake. With emotions as strong as they were mixed at the moment, the President penned a hasty letter to Senator George Cabot of Massachusetts. He asked Cabot to act temporarily as the lad's sponsor, enroll him at Harvard College that fall, and impress upon the boy the great necessity for moderate behavior and prudence. National interest made it impossible for him to disclose his sentiments at present, Washington told Cabot, but he added emphatically, "Let me in a few words declare that I *will be his friend . . . a father, friend, protector and supporter . . .* My friendship for his father, so far from being diminished, has increased in the ratio of his misfortune."

On September 8 the President left Philadelphia in the expectation of being absent five or six weeks. At Elkton, Maryland, he interrupted his journey to write an urgent letter to Pickering. Late news from Rhode Island had reached him: the *Medusa,* with Fauchet aboard, had slipped to sea from anchorage in Newport the night of August 31, but had been pursued at once by Captain Home in the *Africa.* Washington was distressed; the flight of the *Medusa* had occurred before he took action against the offensive British commander. "This circumstance . . . I regret exceedingly," he told Pickering, "because the effect of [my] order for the departure of the [*Africa*] will be the same to the British as if she had been in the harbour of Newport, and we shall obtain no credit for it from the French and their partisans." He directed Pickering to inform Monroe of the facts of the case and stress to the Minister at Paris the necessity of presenting the American position accurately and well.

The President was at Georgetown the twelfth and spent most of the next day in conference with the commissioners of the Federal City. No money at all had been paid as yet by Morris and Nicholson on their contract for lots. Work on the public buildings was almost at a standstill. Washington still refused to believe that Morris and Nicholson were engaged in speculation and had no real interest in the progress of the city, but rumors of such duplicity were gaining every day.

His first full day at home, the fourteenth, brought the President news most welcome. Wayne had concluded a treaty with the northwest tribes, though no text of the pact had yet come to Philadelphia. Washington instructed the Secretary of War to send Indian Agent James Seagrove to the southwest border to arrange a cessation of hostilities between Creeks and Chickasaws. It would be "a pleasing circumstance," the President thought, to report to Congress in November that the United States enjoyed peace with every Indian nation and, as well, had been instrumental in negotiating a truce between two warring tribes. Towards the end of the month, Pickering was able to forward a certified text of the accord Wayne had signed with the Ohio tribes at Greeneville on August 9.

Washington had not been long on the Potomac shore when he was visited by Henry Lee on a matter of personal business. Lee wished to know if the President would sell or trade his plantation in the Dismal Swamp. Lee held stock in the Bank of Columbia in the Federal City and was willing to exchange it; but Washington could not set a price on his share in the Dismal Swamp Company, because he had no idea of the current value of the land. The President would attempt to ascertain its worth. On the twenty-fifth Washington rode to Alexandria to spend the night at the home of Lear and his bride of one month, Frances Bassett Washington. Doubtless the President took this occasion to ask Lear's opinion of the prospects of the Bank of Columbia and of the real value of Lee's stock.

On September 27 the President went to his desk for a task he did not relish; he must write Randolph. Recent mails had brought three communications from him, two dated September 15 and the third September 21. Randolph had pursued Fauchet to Newport and overtaken him there August 31. He had described to Fauchet the circumstances of his resignation and asked for a statement that no secrets had been divulged to him and that no money ever was received, requested or suggested by the Secretary of State. Fauchet promised to furnish such a certificate, then embarked suddenly when the captain of the *Medusa* saw an opportunity to slip out of Newport. Randolph's distress at this was relieved when the pilot returned with the certificate Fauchet had written as the vessel put to sea. He returned immediately to Philadelphia and secured extracts of Fauchet's Despatches No. 3 and No. 6 from Adet. Then, on September 15, he wrote Washington: ". . . I trust that I am in possession of such materials . . . as will convince every unprejudiced mind that my resignation was dictated by considerations which ought not to have been resisted for a moment, and that everything connected with it stands upon a footing perfectly honorable to myself." His letter of the twenty-first asked Washington for information and employed a tone more aggressive than aggrieved, language tart and altogether unpleasant. Washington replied September 27 in a note conspicuously unspecific. "It is not in my power to inform you," he told Randolph, "at what time Mr. Hammond put the intercepted letter of Mr. Fauchet into the hands of Mr. Wolcott. I had no intimation of the existence of such a letter until after my arrival in Philadelphia the 11th of August." Then the President added: "No man would rejoice more than I should to find that the suspicions, which have resulted from the intercepted letter, were unequivocally and honorably removed." Some days later Washington received from Wolcott a report that Randolph had released the letter of September 15 to Republican newspapers. In answer on October 2, Washington enclosed for Wolcott's and Pickering's inspection the letters from Randolph and the reply to the last of them. Annoyance, distrust and a hardening of attitude were manifest in the President's words. If, as Washington supposed, Randolph had made similar inquiries of Wolcott and Pickering, his aim was only "to see if he could involve inconsistencies in the answers . . . and to know what kind of superstructure he might build on the information he has obtained (if any) from Mr. Fauchet. . . ." Whatever defence Randolph might produce, Washington expected the worst of him now.

In spite of vexations, the President's month at Mount Vernon might have provided a fine rest from the cares of office had it not been for the pressing need to fill vacancies in the Executive. Appointment of Elias Boudinot as Director of the Mint established an able man in that minor position, but the posts of Secretary of State and Attorney General still were unoccupied. Washington had been at home only a few days when he received Marshall's declination of the Attorney Generalship. A satisfactory Attorney General, the President thought, might be James Innes of Virginia, and the opinion of Edward Carrington would be valuable here. Before he had Carrington's reply, Washington was visited again by Lee on October 4. As Charles Cotesworth Pinckney had by now declined the office of Secretary of State, conversation turned to this vacancy and Lee repeated an intimation that Patrick Henry no longer was antagonistic to the Federal government. Lee thought that Henry would accept the Secretaryship and could be expected to serve with credit in that post. Not at all sure that Lee was correct in either assumption, the President weighed his estimate for several days and finally composed a careful offer to Henry. The President signed this letter but did not send it immediately. Instead, he enclosed it in a message to Carrington on October 9. If Carrington felt that Innes would not do or would not accept the offer, the letter to Henry should be forwarded from Richmond. Nomination of two Virginians to high office at the same time would violate his rule of geographical distribution, Washington explained to Carrington; and, very likely, Henry would not accept a portfolio in any case. A last alternative, then, would be the formal transfer of Pickering to the Department of State. If this were done, would Carrington himself accept the Secretaryship of War?

It was the President's intention to depart for Philadelphia early October 12 and confer that day with the commissioners at Georgetown, but Washington and his family did not arrive at Georgetown until the afternoon of the twelfth. Most of the following day was given to consultation with the commissioners. After that, wet weather so hampered the progress of his carriage that not until October 18, did it reach Elkton. Then a touch of sickness overtook young Washington Custis and one of the coachmen, and that night was spent in Wilmington. Late on the twentieth, eight days after he had taken leave of Mount Vernon, the President alighted at his house in Philadelphia.

"Pressing and important business . . . has accumulated in my absence," Washington wrote soon after his return. A part of that business had to do with Randolph. Randolph released a paragraph of his letter to Washington of October 8 to the *Philadelphia Gazette*. The extract announced in belligerent tone that Randolph was preparing a public statement of his innocence, a "vindication" to be corroborated by his official correspondence while Secretary of State. In the full letter Randolph charged that Pickering had refused to surrender from the files of the Department of State the letter Washington had written Randolph on July 22. "I hold that letter," Randolph asserted to Washington,

to be important to one of the views which the question will bear . . . and therefore request the inspection of it. . . . You must be sensible, Sir, that I am inevitably driven into discussion of many confidential and delicate points. I could with safety immediately appeal to the people of the United States, who can be of no party. But I shall wait for your answer . . . [and] shall also rely . . . that you will consent to the whole of this affair, howsoever confidential and delicate, being exhibited to the world.

Washington and Pickering composed an answer to Randolph which the President signed October 21:

It is not difficult from the tenor of [your] letter to perceive what your objects are. But that you may have no cause to complain of the withdrawing of any paper . . . I have directed that you should have the inspection of my letter of the 22nd of July, agreeably to your request; and that you are at full liberty to publish, without reserve, *any* and *every* word I have ever uttered, to or in your presence, from whence you can derive any advantage in your vindication. I grant this permission inasmuch as the extract manifestly tends to impress on the public mind that something has passed between us which you should disclose with reluctance from motives of delicacy which respect me. . . . I request that this letter may be inserted in the compilation you are now making, as well to show my disposition to furnish you with every means I possess toward your vindication, as that I have no wish to conceal any part of my conduct from the public. That public will judge, when it comes to see your vindication, how far and how proper it has been for you to publish private and confidential communications which oftentimes have been written in a hurry, and sometimes without even copies being taken. And it will, I hope, appreciate my motives, even if it should condemn my prudence in allowing you the unlimited license herein contained.

If Washington expected that his reply would quiet Randolph, he was mistaken. Within three days the President received another letter, this one bright with anger and bristling with sarcasm and implication. "Whatsoever my objects may be supposed to be," Randolph flared, "I have but one, which is *to defend myself*. Your unlimited permission of publication is therefore, as you must be persuaded, given without hazard. For you never could believe that I intended to exhibit to public view *all* and *every* thing which was known to me. I have indeed the sensibility of an injured one; but I shall disclose even what I am compelled to disclose, under the necessity which you yourself have created. I have been the meditated victim of party spirit. . . ." Washington proceeded to compose a rejoinder. Then on considering his draft, he decided not to answer Randolph's last letter at all. On October 25 he laid the entire correspondence aside and turned his thoughts elsewhere.

CHAPTER / 23

Wherever Washington fixed his concentration at the moment, there could be no shelter from the deluge of abuse which now poured upon him from Republican editors and contributors to their gazettes. Attacks immediately after his decision to ratify the treaty had been only the first drops in a great storm. Now, the tempest was here. A writer in the *Independent Chronicle* of Boston laughed at Federalists who attempted to defend the British treaty with the bland assertion that the wisdom of the President was behind it. How absurd it was, cried this correspondent, to think that Washington's mind was superior to that of Jefferson, Madison, Clinton or other patriots who disapproved the treaty! "Pittachus" in the *Aurora* called the President "Saint Washington," a man distinguished only by "the seclusion of a monk and the supercillious [*sic*] distance of a tyrant"; another mocked him with the offer of a crown.

Washington felt the cruelest blow on October 23 at the hands of "A Calm Observer" in Bache's *Aurora*. This writer declared that the President was overdrawing his appropriation of $25,000 per annum! With or without Washington's expressed sanction, Wolcott wrote at once to Bache. It was the common practice of his Department, the Secretary of the Treasury admitted, to advance monies to the President's secretary for household expenses, and at times these disbursements may have exceeded the regular quarterly division of $6250; but, if this procedure was to be censured, the Department of the Treasury and Congress must be considered responsible for it—not the President. "Calm Observer" labelled the Secretary's explanation "a complete acknowledgement of guilt" and demanded to know if Washington ever had received more than $25,000 in a year or $100,000 in four years. "One of the People" supplied specific answers: the President had overdrawn $5150 by April 30, 1791; he was still $4150 in arrears a year later and $1037 short on March 4, 1793, the day of his second inauguration; he received $11,200 instead of the authorized disbursement of $6250 in the first three months of the new term; and he remained heavily overdrawn at this moment.

This information was correct. The facts were indisputable, and Wolcott could make no refutation; but the President never received a dollar for which there was not explicit appropriation by Congress and at no time had he drawn in advance as much as a full quarter's allotments. Wolcott insisted that John Beckley was the contriver of the articles and that the pertinent data had been furnished by Edmund Randolph! In the *New-York Daily Advertiser* of November 11 Hamilton published a defence of the disbursement policy of the Treasury and gave proof that the President had not requested the advances. Republican editors scoffed at this logic and baldly repeated the charge: President Washington was overdrawing his salary. Even the warmest admirers of the President were powerless to combat the evidence of advance payments which now made Washington's reputation an easy and attractive target. The only rejoinder left to Federalists was the simple truth, typically voiced by a Connecticut newspaper, that the charges were "prompted more by ill nature than by any love for the good of the people."

Welcome as was any diversion from politics at this moment, Washington found little comfort in the necessity of dealing again with the affairs of the Federal City. In the first week of November the President was visited by George Hadfield, an Englishman who had succeeded James Hoban as architect of the Capitol. Hadfield journeyed to Philadelphia to get Washington's consent to proposed structural changes which the Federal commissioners would not approve. His professional reputation, he insisted, would suffer if a dome was not erected over the circular lobby. Washington secured the architect's promise to "stick by the building until it was finished," but he extended no pledge to support Hadfield's ideas. While the President thought well of the plan for a dome, he considered himself too deficient in a knowledge of the related problems of the City to judge in this matter.

On another matter concerning the Federal City, Washington was quite ready to give counsel. The mansion which Robert Morris was building in Philadelphia proclaimed that the famous financier enjoyed greater wealth than ever; yet Morris and Nicholson still had not rendered a single payment on their contract for lots in the Federal City. In desperate need of money to support construction schedules, the commissioners decided to apply for a loan either to Congress or the State of Maryland. They wished the President's advice before proceeding. "If . . . upon more mature consideration and inquiry you concur in the opinion that it can be done," he wrote on October 30, "I think you ought not hesitate to make the attempt." Then, five days later, he sharply qualified this approval. If Maryland lawmakers rejected the application, Washington warned, Congress might follow this negative example.

Not many days of November had passed when Washington determined to wait no longer in the appointment of a Secretary of State. Since Randolph's resignation, offers had gone to five men—William Paterson, Thomas Johnson, Charles Cotesworth Pinckney, Patrick Henry and Rufus King—and each had declined the position. Pickering exhibited little interest in permanent assignment to the vacancy. Washington was resolved to end the search and urged Pickering to transfer. He refused at first, then promised to consider. Wolcott's prompting and a desire to save the Executive from the embarrassment of a conspicuous vacancy in the Cabinet when Congress convened in December at last brought Pickering to accept. This left the administration without a Secretary of War, but Pickering could continue to manage the business of this Department until a replacement was found. An invitation went to John Eager Howard, but the Marylander declined. An offer of the Attorney Generalship to Charles Lee was accepted, much to the President's relief. By the end of the month only the portfolio of War remained unassigned.

On December 7 both the Senate and the House of Representatives easily assembled a quorum. When Washington came to the chamber of the House on December 8, the Chief Executive's seventh Annual Address was markedly moderate in everything except his own exuberant ambitions for the future of the American Republic. Three days after his address to Congress, Washington was disturbed to learn that a rumor was circulating among legislators that the administration had no definite program for further conciliation of the Indians. He instructed Pickering to send without delay detailed recommendations of the War Department. On December 12 Adams and the members of the Senate called to present their formal reply to the annual message. Drafted by a committee of three Federalists, the declaration reflected the sympathies of the majority of the Senate, and Washington responded gratefully. The reply of the House five days later was scarcely less cordial. The spirit of the House augured well; Washington expressed warm thanks in answer.

The President had never found it more difficult to sustain enthusiasm for his own role than now. He experienced one of the unhappiest hours of his life as he sat down to read the pamphlet Randolph published December 18 and styled *A Vindication*. Randolph began with a recital of the circumstances of his resignation, wove into this extracts of his correspondence, then offered the English text of Fauchet's Despatches No. 3 and No. 6 as well as that of the intercepted No. 10, and finally rested his case on the certificate he had obtained from Fauchet. All of this consumed not so much as half of the 103-page pamphlet; the balance was taken up by an open letter to the President, an analytical statement incisive and insulting.

Randolph offered no new argument, but his words pierced the President's composure and hung like barbs in his mind. Many times in recent months Washington had seen his name grossly slandered and his character blasted in print, but this publication might go further than all others in damage to his reputation. Randolph's pamphlet was self-suffering rather than scurrilous, plaintive rather than punitive, the more potent for its less aggressive tone. Washington took time to study it with the closest attention. On December 22 he wrote Hamilton: "Ere this, I presume you have seen the long promised vindication, or rather accusation. What do you think of it and what notice should be taken of it? . . . I shall leave you to judge of it, without any comments of mine." Hamilton's reply was as concise as the President's question. The *Vindication,* he thought, was "a confession of guilt"; the author's "attempts" against the Executive were "base" and "will certainly fail of their aim. . . ." The New Yorker did not equivocate: "By you, no notice can be or ought to be taken of the publication. It contains its own antidote."

Randolph had established a case for himself with documents which could not be denied; Fauchet, his accuser, had disavowed the accusation. No publication by the President could alter the facts; the *Vindication* omitted no evidence, misquoted no document, and committed no error of narrative which could be exposed. Randolph had all the evidence on his side; his paper was irrefutable. Washington realized this; there was nothing for the President to say. Any effort to answer the *Vindication* would be received as an acknowledgment that the President's reputation was in jeopardy and as a desperate defence of his conduct. Worse yet, it would open floodgates of controversy and engulf the administration in a new deluge of protest against the British treaty. Randolph's pamphlet tied the circumstances of his resignation to the President's decision to ratify the treaty; any debate over the justice of the *Vindication* would threaten the pact anew. At a moment when the treaty seemed safe and popular agitation was subsiding, no greater disaster than this could visit the nation.

Washington could hardly expect that his silence might silence others. Federalists were certain to castigate Randolph for what he had done to Washington's name. "The feelings of good men," wrote Fisher Ames, "are wrought up to *revolutionary* pitch by the abuse on the President." William Plumer, a New Hampshire Federalist, expressed a reaction that was typical: "I do not believe President Washington . . . was ever influenced by any other motive than love of country and of fame." Republicans were delighted with the *Vindication*, but more because the President's reputation had been damaged than because Randolph had established his innocence. Jefferson wrote Monroe: "[Randolph's] *Vindication* bears hard on the Executive . . . and though it clears him . . . of the charge of bribery, it does not give . . . high ideas of his wisdom or steadiness." In the view of Madison, Randolph's "greatest enemies will not easily persuade themselves that he was under a corrupt influence of France, and his best friends can't save him for the self condemnation of his political career as explained by himself." Influential Republicans did not, however, fly to Randolph's side as he may have expected. What solace Randolph derived from the publication, he was destined to enjoy alone. Newspapers of neither party gave large notice to his pamphlet. Randolph's career in politics manifestly was at an end. The President recognized no other course than to put the man altogether out of his thoughts. The asperities of the *Vindication* had destroyed the last cord of a relationship which once was Washington's closest bond in public life.

Never, it seemed, would there be an end to the plague of vacancies in high station. Pickering's transfer to the Department of State solved one difficulty, but the President continued in anxiety over empty offices elsewhere. Not until the middle of January was he sure that the new Attorney General would assume his duties. As yet he had no Secretary of War and now, unexpectedly, there were two vacant seats on the Supreme Court. Justice John Blair resigned and then, on December 15, the Senate refused to confirm Washington's nomination of John Rutledge as Chief Justice. The President attempted unsuccessfully to secure Patrick Henry for the War Department and finally decided in favor of his Revolutionary aide, Dr. James McHenry of Baltimore. His invitation carried the request that McHenry ask another Maryland Federalist, Samuel Chase, to take Blair's seat on the Court. McHenry wished time to consider, but on January 24 he replied affirmatively and added that Chase also would accept. Two days later the President appointed McHenry and Chase and nominated William Cushing, on the Court since 1789, for Chief Justice. The Senate concurred on January 27, but Cushing now upset the arrangement by declining promotion. After more exasperating delays, Senator Oliver Ellsworth of Connecticut was nominated and confirmed as Chief Justice.

In accord with Pickering's suggestion that he advise Congress of the urgent need for Federal action against ruthless men in the Southwest Territory who continued to persecute the Cherokee natives, Washington delivered a short, meaningful message on February 2. Both Houses were too engrossed in trifling argument to pay heed. Indeed, it seemed that Congress would be content merely to quibble until Jay's treaty or Thomas Pinckney's pact with Spain was presented for debate. Already it was known in Philadelphia that Pinckney's special mission to Madrid had resulted in a sweeping agreement, but neither the compact made with the Spaniards nor the ratified British treaty had yet reached the United States.

Unaccustomed leisure early in February gave the President time to put on paper a plan which had been in his thoughts for two years. His holdings in land, Washington came to realize, were too extensive, the problems of proprietorship too worrisome for a man who had reached a period of life which, as he said, "requires tranquility and ease." Determined to relieve himself of the greater burdens of land ownership, he now drafted an advertisement which set forth parallel objectives. He would accept offers on all of his western properties—thirteen tracts, some forty-one thousand acres—and would sell to the bidders who were high on September 1, 1796; and he would lease three of the farms at Mount Vernon to substantial tenants at a yearly rental of one and one-half bushels of wheat, or its market value in cash, for each acre of arable soil.

Two days before the sixty-fourth anniversary of Washington's birth, editor Bache of the *Aurora* reminded his readers that previous celebrations of this occasion had been so extravagant that it was little wonder the President behaved "with all the insolence of an Emperor of Rome." Bache's pronouncement had no effect. February 22, 1796, was hailed in Philadelphia with what Wolcott called "unusual joy and festivity." At one minute past midnight bells announced the day; another peal and a cannon salute welcomed the dawn. The President greeted crowds of well-wishers at his house with cake and punch. The evening included a supper at Oeller's Hotel and a grand ball at Ricketts' "amphitheatre" on Chestnut Street. Commemoration of the President's birthday was so universal and enthusiastic as to elicit from one Republican newspaper a mocking reference to America's "Political Christmas."

Washington's birthday was as auspicious as festive, and for a particular reason. Pinckney's treaty with Spain reached Philadelphia sometime on February 22. Probably Washington found no chance to read it that day, but he was highly gratified when he studied its terms. The agreement of October 27, 1795, signed at San Lorenzo by Pinckney and Foreign Minister Manuel de Godoy, gave American citizens unrestricted use of the Mississippi waterway, granted the right of tax-free deposit of goods brought to

New Orleans for export, acknowledged the thirty-first parallel as the south-west boundary, and pledged to restrain Indian violations of the frontier. Whatever Godoy's reason for these sweeping concessions, Spain now relin-quished a position which her agents had sought desperately for more than a decade to maintain. Pinckney's mission had produced a diplomatic achievement of first importance to the United States, one in which men of both parties could rejoice equally. Washington delivered the treaty to the Senate February 26. Unanimous approval on March 3 presaged an enthusi-astic reception in all quarters.

Another occasion for rejoicing, though qualified by certain condi-tions, was the President's promulgation of a treaty with the Dey of Algiers. This agreement, concluded the previous September, committed the Bar-bary tyrant to release Americans held in captivity and in future to spare American vessels in the Mediterranean. These concessions would prove "enormously expensive" said Wolcott, because the Dey was to receive a ransom of $800,000 and a yearly tribute of $24,000. The achievement was worth the price and the humiliation, everyone agreed, but Secretary of War McHenry wondered if this treaty did not abrogate a Naval Construc-tion Act of 1794. Despite a recommendation of the House that work be sus-pended on four of six heavy frigates that had been ordered, the keel of each ship already was laid and the framework going up. Washington now asked Congress to consider the inexpediency of "derangement in the whole system" on which the nation's maritime security was predicated. If an Amer-ican fleet once could be put to sea, the degrading practice of diplomatic bribery could be forsaken.

When no official mail from England arrived in the last week of Feb-ruary, the felicity of Federalists changed to chagrin. Deas was under in-structions to send attested copies of Jay's treaty to Philadelphia as soon as ratifications were exchanged, but evidently he had failed to do so. To his mortification, Washington learned that a ratified copy had been received at Charleston and published there. The President could maintain official si-lence no longer. Sympathy for the treaty had gained remarkably since De-cember. Even so ardent a Republican as Dr. Benjamin Rush was ready by mid-January to admit: "General Washington is still much esteemed . . . and his treaty with Great Britain becomes less unpopular in proportion as it is understood." Six weeks later he earnestly lamented that Jay's treaty "once reprobated by 19/20 of our citizens" now was "approved of, or peaceably acquiesced in, by the same proportion of the people." The Charleston publication might create a belief that the administration pos-sessed a ratified copy which was being withheld; such speculation would harm the popularity of the treaty. Washington felt free to do what was imperative at the moment. On February 29 he proclaimed the treaty in effect, and on March 1 the document was transmitted to Congress.

Now that the British treaty was in their hands, Republican mem-bers of the House might be expected to dissect it in debate. On March 2 Edward Livingston of New York arose to declare that "some important constitutional questions" surely would develop in discussion of the treaty, and that "every document which might throw light on the subject should be before the House." He moved that the President be requested to submit copies of Jay's instructions and all connected correspondence. Washington was shocked by the implications of the motion. The position of Republicans was marked unmistakably by Jefferson: "On the precedent now to be set will depend the future construction of our Constitution, and whether the powers of legislation shall be transferred from the President, Senate and House of Representatives to the President, Senate, Piarningo or any other Indian, Algerine or other chief." If Livingston's motion should succeed, what could the President do? Must he deliver the papers and thereby acknowledge the right of the House to request them, or could he refuse? Chief Justice Ellsworth advised him privately that Livingston's presumption "to participate in or control the treaty-making power" was "as unwarranted as it is dangerous."

On March 7, and for two weeks and four days thereafter, Livingston's resolution held the stage in a verbal spectacle that called forth the talents and pretensions of dozens of Congressmen. Excitement deepened and tempers shortened. In expectation of a vote after the weekend recess, Livingston held the floor most of Friday March 18 with remarks he hoped would counter every Federalist objection. Republicans who expected a roll call on Monday were unduly optimistic. Not until the House had heard the last determined or loquacious Federalist could there be a count. When Speaker Jonathan Dayton put Livingston's proposal to test late on March 24, Republican control of the House assured its passage by vote of 62 to 37.

In anticipation of the success of Livingston's motion, Washington wrote to Hamilton for advice on March 22. He scheduled a meeting of the Cabinet on the twenty-sixth and posed three questions: Did the House have a constitutional right to call for documents of a diplomatic negotiation? If not, would it be "expedient under the circumstances of this particular case to furnish them?" What tone and language might be most appropriate in a compliance or a refusal? Pickering, Wolcott, McHenry and Attorney General Lee answered unanimously that the Constitution did not authorize the House to demand such documents, but Lee counseled the President to submit the papers for the sake of accommodation. Wolcott and McHenry vigorously opposed this as a sacrifice of important principles. On March 29 Washington made his decision and the draft of a message was supplied by Pickering: The President would refuse to deliver all or any part of the material the House had requested. A letter from Hamilton, received that day or the next, reinforced Washington's determination.

An atmosphere of expectancy gripped Philadelphia, and tensions were building in Congress. "Anxiety is on the tiptoe . . . our galleries have been crowded," wrote Representative Francis Preston of Virginia, who felt with many Republicans that the documents would be surrendered gracefully. When the President's message was delivered March 30, it turned expectancy to angry disappointment. These were Washington's words:

I trust that no part of my conduct has ever indicated a disposition to withhold any information which the Constitution has enjoined upon the President as a duty to give . . . The nature of foreign negotiations requires caution and their success must often depend on secrecy . . . a full disclosure of all the measures, demands or eventual concessions, which may have been proposed or contemplated, would be extremely impolitic . . . To admit, then, a right in the House of Representatives to demand, and to have as a matter of course, all the papers respecting a negotiation with a foreign power, would be to establish a dangerous precedent . . . it is perfectly clear to my understanding that the assent of the House of Representatives is not necessary to the validity of a treaty . . . A just regard to the Constitution and to the duty of my Office . . . forbids a compliance with your request.

Republicans professed amazement at the President's positive declination. The message, said Senator Henry Tazewell, was "couched in terms to bring on a contest between the Executive and the House of Representatives of a more serious nature than has ever yet taken place in the political affairs of the Union." Federalists were ecstatic in their praise of Washington's stand. According to William Plumer, enthusiasm in New Hampshire was boundless: "The incomparable answer of our great Chieftain . . . is very popular with the sovereign people. More than nineteen-twentieths approve it."

Explicit as Washington's declaration had been—no assent of the House was required by the Constitution to validate a treaty—the Constitution left a powerful tool in the hands of the Representatives. The majority could invalidate the treaty simply by refusing to vote money for its implementation. Washington had experienced enough of politics to foresee a desperate effort by Republicans and a furious debate in the days ahead. It was in this expectation that he made two significant gestures in the last week of March. On the day before his reply to Livingston's resolution the President forwarded Pinckney's popular Spanish Treaty to the House with a suggestion that necessary funds be legislated at once. Endorsement of Pinckney's treaty might stimulate new sympathies for Jay's. Then, on March 31, he evinced a firm intention of carrying out the articles of that agreement which specified Anglo-American arbitration of boundaries and claims by announcing the nomination of commissioners. As debate resumed in the House Washington's expectations were substantiated, his fears justified. Republicans launched their attack with a demand by Thomas Blount that the President's message be referred to a Committee of the Whole. This, said the North Carolinian, would enable the House to enter in the *Journal* its various reasons for endorsement of Livingston's resolution. Blount's motion carried 55 to 37, but the business was postponed until April 6.

To Washington, nothing could have been more welcome at the moment than this pause. Unanswered personal correspondence was accumulating and now two visitors, Lear and young Lafayette, were expected daily. Before either appeared the President received sad news that was not altogether a surprise: Lear's wife, Fanny, had succumbed to a lingering illness. "To say how much we loved and esteemed our departed friend is unnecessary. . . . but she must be happy because her virtue has a claim to it," he wrote Lear in a note of condolence that Martha also signed. Another letter congratulated Elizabeth Parke Custis on her recent marriage to

Thomas Law of Georgetown. Once Lear arrived he doubtless gave some secretarial assistance, but the bereaved man's motherless children were with him and the President had to arrange for their care. By April 11 the household was crowded; George Washington Lafayette and his tutor, who had been waiting eight months to visit, were at last in Philadelphia, and entertainment had to be provided.

The next day the President sat for his portrait by the celebrated artist, Gilbert Stuart; but whatever his preoccupations, Washington could not remain oblivious to the renewal of activity in the House on the sixth. Federalist Nathaniel Smith of Connecticut opened the day with a plea to set aside Blount's motion, but it was reaffirmed by the consistent party vote of 57 to 36. As soon as the House had resolved into a Committee of the Whole, Blount was on his feet to deliver the preconceived reply of Republicans to the declination of their call for the treaty papers. Blount's rebuttal took the form of two motions, the more significant of which declared the House to have "the Constitutional right and duty . . . to deliberate on the expediency" of execution of any treaty. Madison's dispassionate and well ordered speech in support of this was so long as to prevent any rejoinder that day, and without difficulty on April 7 the majority recorded their viewpoint in the *Journal* of the House. Federalists regarded their position with diminishing cheer. Republicans had it in their power to wreck Jay's treaty if they really wished to do so. So long as their majority was firm, they could reject the necessary appropriation.

A Federalist campaign to rally public opinion was in motion everywhere. The prospect of failure of the treaty so frightened merchants in New York that business came to a standstill; underwriters refused to issue maritime insurance; Federalists were certain their petition would be signed "by almost every decent man in the city." Even in Virginia, Marshall observed, clamor for the treaty all but equalled the noise against it. But nowhere were Federalist efforts more successful than in the Northeast; Bostonians endorsed the treaty by mock vote of 2400 to 100 in a public meeting.

In Philadelphia apprehensions grew as each day's discussion in the House seemed to place the treaty in greater hazard. Theodore Sedgwick moved to vote common funds for all four treaties under consideration. By amendment to Sedgwick's motion, Albert Gallatin led his Republican colleagues into a successful vote for consideration of the Spanish, Indian, and Algerine treaties in that order, and three separate appropriations were passed on April 14.

April 18 opened a week of pyrotechnics that brought men to their feet in every corner of the House. Then on Friday April 22 Republican Samuel Smith of Maryland stood to say that he would accept the treaty, much as he despised it, because the people of his state had petitioned in its favor—and because acquiescence might "restore harmony and unanimity to our public measures." Here was the crack in the dike for which Federalists had worked assiduously. Isaac Smith of New Jersey seized the opportunity for conciliation and possible conversion of other Republicans. In like theme, and saying scarcely a word for the merits of the treaty, Thomas

Henderson of New Jersey finished the day with an earnest reminder that the Constitution would suffer if the House refused this appropriation. Washington must have been encouraged by this time. The majority was breaking down.

Then, on the twenty-sixth, the leader of the irreconcilables, Gallatin, asked for the floor. Silent for two weeks while he listened to lesser colleagues argue with the Federalists, Gallatin had saved himself for this crisis. Now he brought forth the heaviest artillery in the arsenal of the opposition. He cut sure and deep into the sinews of Federalist logic. He displayed the commercial articles of the treaty in full and merciless light, mocked as ridiculous the probability of war with England, and then slashed with sarcasm the contention of many Federalists that the national government would collapse if the appropriation was refused in this session.

If Gallatin's powerful speech accomplished its purpose, it would draw wavering Republicans back into opposition. Its effect must be counteracted. On April 27 two Federalists held the floor, morning and afternoon, and both used to a limit that technique of last resort, personal abuse. Ezekiel Gilbert contrasted Gallatin's Swiss nativity against his own American background. After the New Yorker had emphasized that real American patriots were demanding "redress for all the injuries, outrages, insults and depredations received from the British nation" and that, short of a war for national honor, the treaty alone could offer satisfactory balm, Uriah Tracy of Connecticut repeated this theme in language still more disparaging to Gallatin. He for one, Tracy declared, "[could not] feel thankful" to Gallatin "for coming all the way from Geneva to give Americans a character of pusillanimity!" This attack upon their leader and Tracy's insulting reference to their Western constituents were too much for certain Republicans—on their feet with calls to order. When Chairman Frederick Muhlenberg declined to repress Tracy, the Connecticut Federalist apologized briefly for his warmth and continued in the same strain. He wished it to be remembered, he said, that Gallatin had placed the stamp and stigma of fear upon the President's negotiation with Britain. He would say, again and again, "it [is] madness or worse to suppose we [can] defeat this treaty and avoid a war!"

Whatever the effect of ridicule of Gallatin, the debate was drawing to a close. Now that the most talented spokesmen of the House, and some not so gifted, had been heard, for or against the treaty, a decisive vote seemed imminent. Indeed, both sides were all but exhausted. Republican opposition had reached its crescendo in Gallatin's delivery; Federalist defenders were at the bottom of their store of logic and words. On April 28 a Republican hitherto silent, Francis Preston, asked the indulgence of weary colleagues while he recited the weaknesses of certain articles. As Preston went on, expectancy was in the air. The galleries suddenly filled. The whisper was that Fisher Ames would arise next. Until now, the most eloquent of Federalists, the greatest speaker in Congress, had been perfectly still—either because his talent was saved, strategically, for this climax, or because poor health would not permit the effort of oration. When Preston ended his remarks, Ames stood. "Mr. Chairman," he said, "I entertain the hope, perhaps a rash one, that my strength will hold me out to speak a few minutes."

Ames spoke for an hour and a half. Without notes he proceeded in brilliant style from the broad to the particular, from a rational consideration of the Constitutional role of the House to a stirring portrayal of the consequences of rejection of the treaty. First, he insisted, his colleagues must cast aside the hypocritical concept that they could weigh any great issue objectively and without heat. Even the bitterest enemies of the treaty, said Ames, admitted that this pact was lawfully negotiated, ratified and proclaimed—and all of this without the participation of the House. A treaty, "the promise of a nation," had been made. There remained, then, only one point of real dispute—"the naked question," he called it: "Shall we break the treaty? . . . Shall we break our faith?" Conceivably it could be wise and right to do so, if indeed the agreement with Britain was "really so very fatal" to the welfare of the United States, "bad not merely in the petty details, but in its character, principle and mass . . . evil to a fatal extreme . . . intolerably and fatally pernicious" to American interests. But who among the critics had lodged so sweeping an indictment? Not even "loose and ignorant declaimers" had taken this ground; no, every criticism of the treaty had been in small points, not in total. Would public opinion, Ames asked, allow the nation to break its faith on a tiny wheel? He thought not. Republican objections to certain articles served only to mask a fundamental objection, a deep horror—this was a treaty with the enemy of France. No treaty with England, neither Jay's nor another more favorable in parts, would suit Anglophobes. It might be well, Ames conceded, if "Britain was sunk in the sea," but Americans need never fear the return of English influence to their councils. Finally a masterful summation: "Let us not hesitate . . . to agree to the appropriation to carry it into faithful execution. Thus we shall save the faith of our nation, secure its peace, and diffuse the spirit of confidence and enterprise . . . The vast crop of our neutrality is all seed wheat, and is sown again to swell . . . the future harvest of prosperity."

As Ames finished Justice James Iredell turned to John Adams, who sat beside him in the gallery, and exclaimed in tears, "My God! How great he is!" From Federalists on the floor there came a cry, "The Question!" —but Republicans were shouting, "Committee, Rise!" When Abraham Venable of Virginia urged one more day's discussion for so important a vote, seventy members agreed and the committee adjourned. The next morning Federalists brought in more petitions; Nathaniel Smith held the floor for half an hour, obviously to use time; and Speaker Jonathan Dayton followed with remarks that upheld Ames's logic and complemented his effort. Finally a Republican who had criticized the treaty, Gabriel Christie of Maryland, announced he would vote for it. The question was put to the Committee of the Whole. A tie—49 in favor, 49 against—left the decision to Chairman Frederick Muhlenberg, whose vote would carry the treaty to the House in open session or kill it in committee. Muhlenberg, a Pennsylvania Republican, was a Federalist this day. He voted in the affirmative.

The grand debate was over, the crisis surmounted, the treaty safe. Those ten Republicans who endorsed the appropriation one day would do so the next; their opposition had been dissipated by petitions and demolished by the dialectics of Ames. In open session on April 30, by 51 to 48, the House formally approved funds for the treaty in the sum of $80,808. Federalists scarcely could contain their joy.

Washington had followed with deepest concern the debate in each day's newspaper, but while it raged he kept his own counsel. Throughout April he wrote not a word to any correspondent on the subject of the treaty. Finally on May 1 he was free to express himself. "Few," he wrote Charles Carroll at Annapolis, ". . . conceive that the *real* question was not whether the Treaty with Great Britain was a *good* or *bad* one; but whether there should be a *treaty at all* without the concurrence of [the] House . . . No occasion more suitable might ever occur to establish the principle and enlarge the power they aimed at . . . [They] resolved to attempt at *every* hazard to render the treaty-making power a nullity without their consent; nay worse, to make it an absolute absurdity . . . These measures . . . have not only brought the Constitution to the brink of a precipice, but the peace, happiness and prosperity of the Country into imminent danger." A week later he wrote meaningfully to Jay: "These things do . . . fill my mind with much concern and with serious anxiety. Indeed, the troubles and perplexities which they occasion, added to the weight of years which have passed over me, have worn away my mind more than my body." Then Washington made reference to "ease and retirement" which he thought "indispensably necessary" to his health "during the short time I have to stay here." He hoped circumstances would not "prevent the public annunciation of [his retirement] in time to obviate a waste or misapplication of votes at the election . . . in December next, upon myself." It was clear that the President meant to retire at the expiration of his term.

On the day that Washington wrote Jay, a letter to Hamilton dealt with one of those "troubles and perplexities" from which there seemed no escape. Hamilton had forwarded a communication from Gouverneur Morris which warned that the French Directory was about to send a special envoy to the United States. The diplomat would be escorted by a war fleet, and the French would demand "in the space of fifteen days a categorical answer to certain questions." The President was shocked by this intimation. He wrote Hamilton:

. . . I cannot bring my mind to believe that they seriously mean, or that they could accompany this envoy with a fleet, to *demand* the annihilation of the Treaty with Britain in fifteen days; or that war, in case of refusal, must follow as a consequence. Were it not for the unhappy differences among ourselves, *my* answer would be short and decisive, to this effect: "We are an independent nation and act for ourselves . . . We will not be dictated to by the politics of any nation under Heaven, farther than treaties require of us." Whether the *present* or any circumstances should do more than *soften* this language, may merit consideration. But if we are to be told by a foreign power . . . what we *shall* do and what we shall *not* do, we have independence yet to seek, and have contended hitherto for very little.

To the delight of many Federalists, who already thought of him as an excellent presidential candidate, Thomas Pinckney was returning home after five years in the diplomatic service. His successor at the Court of St. James's, Hamilton advised, should be Rufus King, who was "tired of the Senate and . . . will resign at all events." The President decided to appoint King. His nomination went to the Senate May 19 and was confirmed the next day. Then, on the twenty-eighth, Washington named John Quincy Adams as Minister Plenipotentiary to Portugal. Adams' appointment to Lisbon and Humphreys' transfer to Spain with equivalent rank necessitated a new appropriation of $23,500. Republicans in the House objected, but the funds were approved by vote of 39 to 25.

If he needed the reminder, a note from Hamilton turned the President's thoughts in May to the "public annunciation" of his retirement. Hamilton, who was to "re-dress . . . the body" of such an announcement, felt it "important that a thing of this kind should be done with great care and much at leisure, touched and retouched." Washington agreed. His draft of a valedictory address, which incorporated ten paragraphs written by Madison in 1792, now was ready for Hamilton's inspection. The President sent the manuscript to New York remarking: "My wish is that the whole may appear in a plain style and be handed to the public in an honest, unaffected, simple garb."

His expectation that Congress would rise before the end of May was unfulfilled, but the President enjoyed relief from public pressures in the closing weeks of the session. Aside from a request to Congress for funds to establish civil authority in the posts of the Northwest, no national business required his attention save the routine signing of bills. One was a measure to admit the Southwest Territory into the Union as a sixteenth State, Tennessee. A meeting with the newly arrived British Minister, Robert Liston, may have borne out Pinckney's estimate of the diplomat as "a sensible, well informed man of pleasing manners and dispassionate temper." The unofficial call of another Englishman, Thomas Twining, must have afforded diversion, for this traveler had just come from India and the service of the Governor-General, Lord Cornwallis. The visitor later recorded:

So completely did [the President] look the great and good man he really was, that I felt rather respect than awe in his presence . . . Although his deportment was that of a general, the expression of his features had rather the calm dignity of a legislator than the severity of a soldier.

Congress adjourned June 1 and Ames, who thought it remarkable "we should finish and leave the world right side up," came to dinner the next afternoon. Then, on the fifth, Washington sent word to Pearce at Mount Vernon: ". . . there is yet a good deal for me to do before I can leave the Seat of Government. My present expectation, however, is that I shall be able to do this tomorrow week." On June 12, the evening before his departure, in his first letter in months to Humphreys, he opened a troubled heart as he wrote:

I am attacked for a steady opposition to every measure which has a tendency to disturb the peace and tranquility . . . But these attacks, unjust and unpleasant as they are, will occasion no change in my conduct; nor will they work any other effect in my mind than to increase the anxious desire . . . to enjoy in the shades of retirement the consolation of having rendered my Country every service my abilities were competent to . . . Malignity, therefore, may dart her shafts, but no earthly power can deprive me of the consolation of knowing that I have not . . . been guilty of a wilful error, however numerous they may have been from other causes.

The pressure of recent weeks made the prospect of a Mount Vernon visit more than ever welcome. Even now, there would be one delay to hold him from his cherished destination for a matter of two days; he must allow ample time for matters in the Federal City. There and at Georgetown on June 18 and 19 Washington did what he could to facilitate a much needed loan from Holland. He also emphasized the need for constant supervision of the buildings by those in authority and pointed out irregularities and delays that had occurred because the commissioners had been inaccessible.

On the twentieth, as his carriage moved along the last miles towards Mount Vernon, Chief Executive deferred to plantation proprietor. Scarcely had he shaken the dust of the road when on June 25 information came from Hamilton which, Washington feared, might require his early return to Philadelphia. An American merchant ship, the *Mount Vernon,* had been seized by the French privateer *Flying Fish* off the Delaware coast. Regardless of the specific circumstances, the President saw that France was determined to continue such captures in its resentment against Anglo-American commerce. He wrote at once to Wolcott and the Secretary of State. Pickering was requested to call a meeting of the Cabinet and report its consensus to him. He wished particularly to know their views on two points: whether Adet should be asked to explain the incident, and whether the President had power during recess of the Senate to send a special envoy to Paris for the purpose of giving and requesting explanations in the present strained relationship between the two countries.

By July 8 the President's mind was made up—he would recall the American Minister at Paris. Once he had read Pickering's letter of July 4 and the enclosed opinions of the department heads, his decision was firm. The Cabinet criticized Monroe's failure to present his government's views faithfully. Whether this was because of an undue attachment for France or mistaken judgment on Monroe's part, the unfortunate result was the same and something must be done. As soon as he had examined the papers bearing on Monroe, Washington sent them to Attorney General Lee, then in Alexandria, and requested his prompt opinion. Lee's view was that Monroe's recall was "indispensably necessary." With removal of the Minister one problem would be resolved, but another would be created by the necessity of finding someone to replace him. The new envoy must be inclined to promote the neutral policy of the administration and, "as far as the nature of the case will admit, be acceptable to all parties." Consequently the post was offered to John Marshall, in whose letter Washington enclosed another to be forwarded to Charles Cotesworth Pinckney, in event Marshall refused.

It appeared to Washington that French discontent with the American government had its origin in Monroe's neglect of diplomatic duty. But his own course was clear. "The Executive have a plain road to pursue, namely: to fulfill all the engagements which his duty requires; be influenced beyond this by none of the contending parties; maintain a strict neutrality, unless obliged by imperious circumstances to depart from it; do justice to all, and never forget that we are Americans; the remembrance of which will convince us that we ought not to be French or English." Good news came at last with Pinckney's acceptance of the post at Paris.

But "envenomed pens" would not run dry for lack of subject. Even while Washington and Hamilton were busy shaping paragraphs for the President's message of farewell, Republicans were exerting themselves to make certain Washington would have need of a valedictory. The edge of invective was sharpened every morning by new or renewed charges in their gazettes. Many Federalists still were uncertain of Washington's intentions; some hoped and believed he would not decline the office, others feared and believed he would retire. There was speculation as well as accusation. Jefferson predicted that the Federalist party "will run Mr. [Thomas] Pinckney, in which they regard his southern position rather than his principles." The question in Washington's mind was not whether he would say farewell, but when and how it best could be done. A cursory reading of Hamilton's "Original Major Draft" for the Address, based on the paper the President had sent him, was pleasing as to content, but Washington was doubtful about the great length the paper was taking.

On August 17 Washington set out for Philadelphia on a journey that promised to be arduous. By the time of his departure he knew, unhappily, that Pearce's rheumatic pains would compel the plantation manager to resign. Washington had been well pleased with Pearce, but search for a suitable replacement began at once. Business in the Federal City consumed most of the seventeenth, but on the eighteenth the master of Mount Vernon wrote to James Anderson, a likely applicant referred to him by Col. John Fitzgerald.

Not until he reached Philadelphia on the evening of August 21 could Washington know the contents of a letter received at Mount Vernon on the tenth. This was a communication from Monroe, dated March 24, 1796, and written in cipher. It disclosed that the French Directory was offended by Washington's letter of December 22, 1795, to Gouverneur Morris, which had fallen into their hands. Whether Monroe's cipher communication further tried the President's patience, it scarcely had been decoded when he authorized Pickering to send the American Minister's official notice of recall without delay.

At this pause in a possible crisis, Washington again could turn attention to his valedictory. He had gone carefully over the most recent draft by Hamilton and found it superior to all the others. Further revision seemed unnecessary but since Hamilton had suggested it, Washington would forward the piece once more for the New Yorker's scrutiny, with the request that it be returned shortly. It was vital that it appear well ahead of the time for choosing Presidential electors.

Only publication of his valedictory and the necessity of a talk with Charles Cotesworth Pinckney now held him at the seat of government. When Pinckney arrived he was furnished with copies of Morris' letter of July 3, 1795, and of Washington's reply, to which, according to Monroe, the Directory had taken exception. Certain of the President's correspondence with Monroe also was enclosed in a letter Washington wrote Pinckney on September 12. These documents might prove useful in appraising the situation in Paris, he thought.

On the fifteenth the President submitted a copy of his valedictory to the Cabinet for review. Then on the sixteenth he received David C. Claypoole of the *American Daily Advertiser*. Washington explained that he had some thoughts and reflections on the occasion of his retirement in the form of a Farewell Address and desired Claypoole's paper "to usher it to the world." Monday September 19 was agreeable to both as the date for publication.

"I have the consolation to believe," Washington had written in his Farewell, "that while choice and prudence invite me to quit the political scene, patriotism does not forbid it." At the moment that he looked forward to the joys of private life, he looked backward in acknowledgment —of opportunity for service, honors bestowed on him by the people, their confidence and constancy "in situations in which not unfrequently want of success had countenanced the spirit of criticism." His invocation forever would be: "That your Union and brotherly affection may be perpetual; that the free Constitution, which is the work of your hands, may be sacredly maintained; that its administration in every department may be stamped with wisdom and virtue; that, in fine, the happiness of the people of these States, under the auspices of liberty, may be made complete. . . ." After greetings, acknowledgments, and good wishes, might have come the final farewell. Actually, these remarks became merely the introduction to more compelling passages. Washington's first theme was that of inseparable union. Only through "a government for the whole" could there be "efficacy and permanency" in a union. Religion and morality, two "great pillars of human happiness," the President continued, were indispensable to "private and public felicity." Nor, he counselled, can it be expected "that national morality can prevail in exclusion of religious principle." Here he inserted a paragraph on education: "Promote, then, as an object of primary importance, institutions for the general diffusion of knowledge. In proportion as the structure of a government gives force to public opinion, it is essential that public opinion should be enlightened." As an important source of security, "cherish public credit," he specified. In nothing was Washington more earnest or eloquent than in his plea for a true neutrality. "Observe good faith and justice towards all nations. Cultivate peace and harmony with all," he exhorted, but—his warning rang out—"Against the insidious wiles of foreign influence (I conjure you to believe me, fellow citizens), the jealousy of a free people ought to be *constantly* awake." He proceeded to further advice: ". . . Even our commercial policy should hold an equal and impartial hand. . . . 'Tis folly in one nation to look for disinterested favors from another. . . . There can be no greater error than to expect or calculate upon real favors from nation to nation." These, he said, were the "counsels of an old and affectionate friend" who dared not hope they would make "the strong and last impression I could wish."

A few more remarks, personal and poignant, and Washington was done. "How far in the discharge of my official duties," he said, "I have been guided by the principles which have been delineated, the public records and other evidences of my conduct must witness to you and to the world. . . . I have at least believed myself to be guided by them." The closing paragraphs declared him to be "unconscious of intentional error" but "nevertheless too sensible of my defects not to think it probable that I may have committed many errors." And then the last words of the Farewell: ". . . I anticipate with pleasing expectations that retreat, in which I promise myself to realize without alloy the sweet enjoyment of partaking, in the midst of my fellow citizens, the benign influence of good laws under a free Government, the ever favorite object of my heart and the happy reward . . . of our mutual cares, labors and dangers."

With the appearance of the Farewell Address, the last of Washington's immediate plans was completed. That same September 19 his coach began its Potomac journey. By the hour when Philadelphians had refolded their newspapers, the Chief Executive could reflect that President Washington had left the seat of government for the last time, that when his carriage moved southward again, its same passenger would be simply George Washington, Esq.

If his hours were crowded during a month at Mount Vernon, they were filled primarily with plantation affairs. On October 5 the contract with James Anderson for a year was signed. The new manager was expected to take over on or before January 1. Correspondence was light and little that was burdensome came from Philadelphia. While relations with France still were critical, the President expected no encouraging word until Pinckney reached Paris. "A few months more will put an end to my political existence," Washington observed to Landon Carter, "and place me in the shades of Mount Vernon under my vine and fig tree. . . ." On October 25 all was in readiness for Washington's last presidential journey. The family set out that afternoon for the Federal City where, as usual, Washington would tarry for a conference with the Commissioners. The most persistent problem with respect to the future Capital City was that of obtaining money for continuance of building; but in spite of tedious business and discouraging difficulties with plans and with personalities, the Federal City was shaping steadily, if slowly, towards Washington's ideal.

It was October 31 when Washington reached the President's house. The Chief Executive had expected to be "immersed in papers and preparing for the approaching session and busy scenes with Congress," but the first major item that confronted him was a development in French affairs of such serious import that it had no rival in the rank of problems on his desk. Under date of October 27 Minister Adet had delivered a disturbing letter to the Secretary of State—and the Frenchman already had published the note in the *Aurora,* an act of indignity towards the United States. The purpose of the letter ostensibly was to transmit to the American government an extract from the *arrêt* declared by the French Directory on July 2, 1796, relative to its conduct towards neutral ships. "The flag of the Republic," Adet declared, "will treat the flag of neutrals in the same manner as they shall suffer it to be treated by the English." This measure, he added, was "dictated by imperious circumstance, and approved by justice," for, in the face of British disregard for treaties, France suffered "real disadvantage" in holding its compact of 1778 with the United States. While the English continued to take American ships into port and "dragged from them Frenchmen and French property," the Republic could not continue to abide by its promise to regard as American any English cargo found aboard American ships. Instead of employing every effort to enforce protection of their trade, Adet charged, the United States had negotiated a "treaty of friendship, navigation and commerce" with Great Britain—and the English went on with their seizures, and with impressment. Remonstrances had followed, but the French Minister's dispatches went unanswered, Adet complained. If the United States desired respect for her neutrality, she should not suffer the English to sport with it; nor could Americans complain if France, "to restore the balance of neutrality to its equilibrium, shall act in the same manner as the English."

Pickering prepared his answer at once. In keeping with the manner of Adet's communication, the letter was delivered to the Minister and the press simultaneously on the morning of November 5. Washington had approved the draft and acquiesced in the printing of it after consultation with the Secretary and others whose opinions he trusted. Pickering argued that the people expected an open reply to Adet, and the consensus was in favor of a prompt one. In the Secretary's answer there was nothing new. Pickering stated the distinction between uncommitted powers whose conduct was governed only by the law of nations and those between whom some explicit agreement had imposed "special obligations." In the twenty-third article of the Franco-American compact of 1778 it was plainly set forth that "free ships make free goods"; that the principle of reciprocity "was to operate at different periods. . . that is, at one time in favor of one of the contracting parties, and of the other at another time." Now, the Secretary protested, France desired the United States "to gratuitously renounce this right." In response to Adet's complaint that certain remonstrances had gone unanswered, the Secretary asserted that they required no answer, the topic having been "officially and publicly discussed" already. Furthermore, the insinuations and "indecent charges" embodied in the notes were too offensive to deserve acknowledgment. In closing he called on Adet for an explanation of the inconsistent behavior of France and the real intentions of the Directory towards the United States.

Washington faced long hours of work on his annual speech to Congress. As usual, he had requested his department heads to submit items for inclusion in the message, but he desired also Hamilton's views on their views. All doubts as to the propriety of giving to Congress a full statement of French affairs were removed when, on November 21, there appeared in

Claypoole's paper an extravagant manifesto from Adet to the Secretary of State. Washington wrote Hamilton that day: "The necessity of bringing the matter before Congress is now rendered indispensable, and through that medium it is presumed it will make its way to the public with proper explanations." The French Minister's temerity and insolence more and more were reminiscent of Edmond Genet, whose rascality Washington had thought could not be exceeded.

Representative Ames, now less active but not less astute, had predicted from his home in Dedham that Washington's Farewell would "serve as a signal, like dropping a hat, for party racers to start. . . ." Both Republicans and Federalists had been conjecturing quietly—the one party fearful, the other hopeful that the present system in government might be preserved. The contest of principles was emblazoned in the gazettes as that of "monarchy versus Republicanism"; that of personalities fell to John Adams and Thomas Jefferson as the foremost contenders.

The campaign in progress bore no resemblance to that of 1792. Republicans agreed that Aaron Burr should place with Jefferson; but intra-party differences among Federalists caused increasing mention of Thomas Pinckney over Adams. Hamilton and his friends were determined to sponsor Pinckney; New England Federalists remained just as determined to elevate Adams from his eight-year apprenticeship. While Adams and Pinckney appeared to have equal strength north of the Potomac, Pinckney was the more popular in the South and West. The clash of men, principles and parties promised to grow loud and spirited. States had varying days for their balloting and the final result ostensibly would not be known until electors voiced their preferences late in January. Prophets abounded, and Federalists were increasingly worried over Jefferson's apparent strength and what should be done at this late hour to assure victory.

Nothing claimed more of Washington's thoughts than his annual message to Congress, and when the usual preliminaries of the open session were over he was ready. He arrived at the House of Representatives on December 7 to find the room and gallery filled "with the largest assemblage of citizens, ladies and gentlemen ever collected on a similar occasion." This last of his Annual Addresses touched on a dozen subjects; its delivery took some thirty minutes. He began with a reassuring report on Indian affairs and the good prospect of continuing friendship. At last he could say that the posts in the Northwest were evacuated and that a final decision on the boundary of the St. Croix River, mentioned in the 1783 treaty, was in the making; other provisions both in Jay's treaty and the pact with Spain were proceeding favorably. Liberation of Americans imprisoned in Algiers was the bright fact in an otherwise halting business with that country. Towards future protection of commerce and a secure neutrality, Washington proposed that the United States "look to the means, and . . . set about the gradual creation of a navy." He advocated support and encouragement in the field of manufactures. In nothing was the President more earnest than in his perennial plea for a national university, and he recommended a military academy. Moreover, if good men were to be had for the administration of good government, then important public positions must offer better pay so that choice of able officers need not be confined to the wealthy. Brief reference to the harassment of American commerce in the West Indies brought the President to the last topic, a statement that a full review of French relations would be reserved for a special communication to Congress. Three days later the Senate waited on the President and responded in gracious form through its spokesman, Adams. The address of the House, delivered on the sixteenth, also was cordial and admiring, in spite of all the articulate William B. Giles of Virginia could do to make it otherwise.

It was late December before a definite trend in the national election could be narrowed. Early in January, weeks before the electoral votes were counted officially, the results were known. John Adams had won the Presidency by a margin of three votes over Jefferson. Republicans found adjustment to the prospective executive order easy, in fact pleasant, and none seemed more elated than Jefferson. For Federalists, the victory was bittersweet. Jefferson's Vice Presidency was the "formidable evil" Ames had feared. "Two Presidents, like two suns in the meridian," he augured, "would meet and jostle for four years, and then Vice would be first." Washington believed that Adams would pursue his own never-ending and most cherished policy to preserve the United States "in peace and friendship with all the world." It was to be expected that the enemies of government would harass the administration in the future as in the past, but he was confident that the public weal would be well guarded; that even though "we may be a little wrong, now and then, we shall return to the right path with more avidity."

No diversion as 1797 opened could erase entirely the stings of personal abuse that seemed to increase towards the finish of the President's official career. The apparent purpose was to effect an early end to present government through degradation of its first Chief Executive. Every other French inspired scheme having failed of its ultimate purpose, batteries had been levelled at the President. The epitome of the abuse was a composition by Thomas Paine—an open letter to Washington dated July 30, 1796. It had been brought from Paris to the eager presses of Bache. This industrious editor saw to it that Paine's pamphlet had wide distribution. Whereas the letter was addressed to Washington, it was about him rather than to him and was meant for all eyes everywhere. Paine's charges against Washington ranged from fraud to murder. So violent was his climax that, inadvertently, the words may have served Washington well:

As to you, sir, treacherous in private friendship (for so you have been to me, and that in the day of danger) and a hypocrite in public life, the world will be puzzled to decide, whether you are an apostate or an impostor; whether you have abandoned good principles, or whether you ever had any.

Washington probably would not have gone so far as to say with William Plumer that "censure from the depraved Payne [sic] is a better reward than his eulogium," but he believed his best rejoinder to all Americans under the spell of France lay in his promised communication on French affairs. On January 19 the President sent to Congress documents relating to transactions between the United States and France since the early period of the current European war. His covering message was brief, but the documents were so voluminous that they were ordered to be printed without first being read in session. The presentation was the work of Pickering, but Washington had kept in close touch with his Secretary of State and cautioned him to be careful of his facts, his candor and expression, as every sentence would be scrutinized to find a basis for further charges. Washington had furnished Pickering with some excellent ideas for summary remarks in his September letter to Charles Cotesworth Pinckney, among them this:

That this government . . . [being] conscious of its fair dealing towards all the Belligerent Powers; and wrapt up in its own integrity; it little expected . . . upbraidings it has met with. Notwithstanding, it now is, as it always has been, the earnest wish of the government . . . to be on the best and most friendly footing with the Republic of France; and we have no doubt, after giving this candid exposition of facts, that the Directory will revoke the orders under which our Trade is suffering, and will pay the damages it has sustained thereby.

Business could not relieve the Chief Executive of excessive entertainment during the last weeks in office. Guest lists were longer, drawing rooms more crowded and dinners more frequent. To Washington, official hospitality was an important part of his presidential duty and he was careful not to neglect it. A variety of personal matters claimed attention also. In particular, he would need considerable cash to negotiate the final move from Philadelphia. Mount Vernon was often on his mind. He was pleased with his new manager's ideas and encouraged his views; Anderson, he realized, had both ability and promise. Washington sought help from his dentist, Dr. John Greenwood, for the relief of discomfort and disfigurement caused by his artificial teeth. In anticipation of his homeward journey, he bought two draft horses to pull a light wagon loaded with trunks.

Other preparations that centered on the President were in the making too, but for these he had no responsibility beyond the arduous role of honored guest for the whole of a day and evening. The occasion was the twenty-second of February—a great and yet a sad time for those who participated, because they knew it was the last birthday Washington would celebrate in Philadelphia. The city awoke to a general holiday, "ushered in by the ringing of bells and firing of cannon." Schools were out, servants had liberty, uniformed militia strutted along the streets, artillery paraded and fired a midday salute. Washington received Congressmen, the Governor, the Pennsylvania Legislature in a body, and the Society of the Cincinnati. In the evening the President and Martha went to the "elegant entertainment" at Ricketts' where there was a supper and dancing for some twelve hundred persons. These marks of affection and respect moved him more deeply than the sharpest strokes from Republican pens could cut.

Had it been written in the statutes that the District of Columbia was to be Washington's sole responsibility through all the years of his Presidency, he scarcely could have found the future seat of government more time consuming, but his faith in the final achievement of a worthy Capital endured every test. On March 3, the last day of his presidential authority, the "City of Washington" was an important item on his agenda. In the letter he wrote the Commissioners that day, every reference to the city bore his name, as if now to admit that he cherished the honor and wished to sanction his namesake for the acceptance of posterity.

Mindful of the caution that had been his unfailing rule in official appointments, Washington took pains to advise his successor against undue sensibility with respect to John Quincy Adams. Washington wrote John Adams "in a *strong hope* that you will not withhold merited promotion . . . because he is your son. For . . . I give it as my decided opinion that Mr. Adams is the most valuable public character we have abroad, and that he will prove himself to be the ablest of all our diplomatic corps." Then there were farewells to be written, good-byes to be said. The last strictly personal letters from President Washington went to Henry Knox and Jonathan Trumbull. His only regret on retiring, he wrote, was "at parting with (perhaps never more to meet) the few intimates whom I love. . . ."

On the afternoon of March 3 Washington entertained at dinner "to take my leave of the President elect, of the foreign characters, the heads of departments, &ca." The company was large; host and guests were gay. When the tablecloth had been removed, Washington filled his wine glass and, smiling at his guests, said: "Ladies and gentlemen, this is the last time I shall drink your health as a public man. I do it with sincerity, and wishing you all possible happiness!" Suddenly the gaiety was gone and Bishop William White, who glanced at the wife of British Minister Robert Liston, saw that "tears were running down her cheeks."

Near noon on Saturday March 4 Washington walked alone to Congress Hall. As readily as he had assumed the bearing of Commander-in-Chief or the stately posture of President, he put on this morning the modest appearance of private citizen. Solemnity and dignity were the order of the day; firing of cannon marked the important hour. As the General came in sight at the door of the House, he was greeted with a burst of tremendous applause. Washington quickened his step as if to shorten the ovation and took his proper place. In a moment the hand-clapping swelled again as the straight figure of Jefferson entered the room. In his long blue frock coat, the Vice President seemed even taller than usual as he made his way down the aisle. Renewed and warm acclaim rose as the President of the United States approached. John Adams had just stepped from his new carriage wearing, quite in contrast to his customary simple mode, a pearl-colored broadcloth suit, a sword and cockade. He proceeded to the Speaker's chair on the elevated dais. Every space in the room was filled, but the multitude was quiet as the ritual began. When his Address was finished, Adams stepped forward and Chief Justice Ellsworth administered the oath of office. The occasion is best described by the new President himself:

A solemn scene it was indeed, and it was made affecting to me by the presence of the General, whose countenance was as serene and unclouded as the day. He seemed to me to enjoy a triumph over me. Methought I heard him say, "Ay! I am fairly out and you fairly in! See which of us will be happiest!"

The first act of George Washington as once more a private citizen, was to call on the President of the United States. When the inaugural ceremony was over, he made his way to the Francis Hotel where Adams was lodging. A throng followed at respectful distance and watched as the General was lost to view within the building. Then suddenly, as if in answer to their unvoiced bidding, the door reopened and Washington turned to acknowledge the homage of the crowd. His eyes were wet with tears as he then slowly closed the door. Private citizen he might be, but the public still had a claim on its first President. The pageantry of the day was not yet over. In the evening Philadelphians honored him with a farewell dinner at Ricketts' Amphitheatre. Although surrounded with homage, Washington knew that not all expressions on his retirement were those of appreciation. The *Aurora* published its pleasure at Washington's exit and proposed the exit of Jay's treaty also—the instrument by which, it asserted, Washington had provoked probable war with France. But positive evidences of approbation, both planned and impromptu, by their very intensity and earnestness more truly represented the measure of the man in the eyes of the people.

Expectations of most Federalists had been realized and suspicions of most Republicans quieted by Adams' Inaugural Address. It appeared that Adams was indeed a man of no party—or so Republicans thought for a brief time. Even Jefferson was convinced for a day. Soon after his inauguration the Chief Executive sought an interview with his Vice President to discuss the pressing need of a new mission to France and ascertain whether Jefferson himself would serve as the all-important emissary. No one else, Adams believed, was so uniquely qualified. But Jefferson's inclination was against it, and Adams dismissed the idea. Thereupon the two began to consider other eligible characters. They were clearly in agreement that Madison would make an ideal member, but Jefferson predicted that the retiring Congressman would decline. On the evening of the sixth Adams and Jefferson dined with Washington as his guests. When they were out of the house, Jefferson resumed the discussion of the previous day by informing the new President that Madison positively refused to consider an assignment to France. Adams quickly indicated a change of mind in the matter, due, he added, to certain unexpected objections raised in a consultation. Jefferson saw embarrassment in Adams' effort at excuses and sensed a reason: That morning Adams had met with his Cabinet and, Jefferson concluded, had been led back into the partiality of the Federalist fold. Collaboration ceased as suddenly as it had begun. Unlike President Washington, President Adams was not to enjoy the full favor of his Vice President. Nor was there to be the same happy circumstance of continuing harmony between President and Cabinet. Adams chose to retain the department heads and Attorney General Lee, but full allegiance to the Chief Executive did not necessarily follow. The men he inherited in turn chose to inherit and seek the constant counsel and approval of that high Federalist leader in New York, Hamilton.

Washington turned from Executive matters to different duties and spent many hours in preparation for the move to Mount Vernon. The sorting and transfer of furniture and furnishings, the disposition of countless belongings, presidential and personal, were exacting for him and his staff. The General himself made detailed lists of government property in the residence, with accounts of articles long ago worn out and replaced through his private funds and of certain objects to be offered for public sale. On March 8 Washington appeared at the President's quarters to pay farewell respects to his successor, and by the morning of the ninth everything was in readiness for the departure of the former President and his entourage. Besides Martha, himself and Nelly Custis, George Washington Lafayette and his tutor, Felix Frestel, made up the family party. Tobias Lear and Bartholomew Dandridge remained in Philadelphia to supervise final packing, shipping and the thorough cleaning that must be done before the Adamses took up residence in the President's House. After everything was in order, Lear would bring the final accounts to Mount Vernon, but the parting with Dandridge was a definite farewell. The young man soon would leave to become secretary to William Vans Murray, American Minister at The Hague.

CHAPTER / 24

Wherever he tactfully could do so on his journey home, Washington avoided escort and parade. As always, he was mindful of the honor and pleased with the intent, but he was eager to be at Mount Vernon and ceremonies took time. It was desirable for Martha's sake, too, that they not tarry, for she was suffering from a severe cold. The few first days were without ceremonial, but on March 12, 1797, Baltimore was eagerly waiting to bestow all its honors. Salutations were spectacular and prolonged from a crowd said to be the largest ever assembled in the city. On the fourteenth the City of Washington brought out its artillery escort and as the General reached the Capitol he heard the sound of cannon. Later, as the returning planter rode by the President's House of future years, now under construction, the salute of sixteen guns found its echo in the hearty huzzas of spectators. Georgetown citizens presented their own complimentary address the following day. It was for Alexandria to extend the final tribute of the journey; townspeople gathered at the ferry landing and accompanied their illustrious neighbor to the door of Mount Vernon.

The master of Mount Vernon soon discovered that fields and buildings were in serious need of repair. Within ten days after his return, painters had begun their work in preparation for the expected furnishings from Philadelphia. Soon joiners and masons were busy in all parts of the mansion and many of the outbuildings. James McHenry's concern lest retirement bring to Washington restlessness was groundless. He had no time and no need for a period of readjustment. He explained,

I find myself in the situation of a young beginner; for although I have not houses to build (except one, which I must erect for the accommodation and security of my military, civil and private papers which are voluminous, and may be interesting) yet I have . . . scarcely anything else about me that does not require considerable repairs.

By March 25 the plantation proprietor had word that the sloop *Salem* was on its way with the furniture and other articles from Philadelphia. The invoice, enclosed in a letter from Lear, listed ninety-seven boxes, fourteen trunks, forty-three casks, thirteen packages, three hampers and various other items. The postscript of the General's acknowledgment to Lear—"it would be very pleasing to me to have you here"—was understatement. He had need of every competent, helpful hand. Along with the confusion of these days, Washington had also the anxiety of Martha's health. Her cold persisted, though at last he could say she was better. Sometime before March 31 favorable winds brought the *Salem* and the much beloved Lear. Many duties could be shifted onto his younger shoulders and those not shifted could be shared with this tried and understanding friend. Moreover, Lear would have fresh observations and information from the seat of government on which the former Chief Executive could rely.

In April only Washington's pen was less busy than usual. The few letters he wrote were concerned for the most part with irksome matters of personal business—to some extent due to the way his old friend Henry Lee had sought to discharge his indebtedness for purchase of the Dismal Swamp land. The stock Lee proposed to transfer in part payment was reputed to be worthless—a fact that did not please the seller and one not altogether disguised in the General's communications concerning it. All this must have been the more annoying because of the indifference of George Ball, who had contracted for Washington's Gloucester lands. Ball not only had neglected to comply with the terms, but also was an elusive correspondent. The General was further vexed by "dribbling payments" from Israel Shreve, purchaser of his lands in western Pennsylvania, which made it necessary for Washington to employ a business agent in Philadelphia. Word from George Lewis on the fifth brought news of the death of the General's sister, Betty Washington Lewis. The melancholy of his nephew's letter, Washington replied, filled him with "inexpressible concern."

Washington soon discovered that in addition to tedious proprietary responsibility, he faced exacting parental responsibility also. George Washington Parke Custis was more nearly son than grandson and, had he lived up to the flavor of his letters, a more exemplary youth would have been hard to find; but his pen portrayed more promise than performance. His behavior was reminiscent of that of his father, John Parke Custis. Young Custis, sixteen, was now enrolled in the College of New Jersey at Princeton. From his sister Nelly he had learned details of the family's homeward journey. In proper spirit he addressed a letter of congratulation to his grandfather on the "marks of approbation and esteem" along the way and added that he would be hurrying home for a visit of perhaps twenty days. No doubt the General and Martha looked forward to his return, and if there was cause for displeasure during this visit, there was no mention of it; but after his departure, information about him, rather than from him, brought distress to Washington. On April 24, in manifest disappointment, the General acknowledged a letter from the Rev. Samuel Stanhope Smith, president of the College, that had contained disquieting reports of the boy. Then there began an exchange between the General and Custis that indicated full forgiveness for some unnamed offense in return for remorse and firm resolution. The boy wrote disarmingly and convincingly that he had "shockingly abused" Washington's goodness, though now he was the "sincere penitent"; he promised that "your grandson shall once more deserve your favor." Except for Custis' reference to "the late contest with the passions," there was no hint as to the nature of his misconduct. At a season when Washington's every exertion was needed in home affairs, when his every thought not of home was disturbed by the condition of national affairs, indiscretions of an adolescent grandson scarcely could be regarded as diversion.

Washington had asked Secretary of War McHenry to communicate to him important developments in state affairs, within, of course, the bounds of official propriety. McHenry had written on March 24 of the French Directory's refusal to receive Pinckney and the insulting form of the rejection—an indirect message to the new Minister by way of the re-called Monroe. "The conduct of the French government is so much beyond calculation," Washington replied, "and so unaccountable upon any princi-ple of justice or even of plain understanding, that I shall not *now* puzzle my brains in attempting to develop their motives to it."

Now letters from Secretary of State Pickering disclosed ominous de-velopments. Turbulence and tension seemed to mount, and party spirit more than ever was pervading the United States. It was a stormy season, and most of the thunderheads on both sides of the Atlantic had risen from France. The Directory was not alone in labelling resentment towards the United States the "fruit of the British Treaty." Jefferson so named it, and like-minded Republicans everywhere evinced similar scorn. The two politi-cal factions referred to one another as the "British Party" or the "French Party" with increasing frequency and venom. The friends of government in America feared the force of their enemies at home far more than the threats of their enemies abroad. It was estimated that thirty thousand Frenchmen resided in the United States, reputedly allied in devotion to France. The American Society of United Irishmen numbered fifty thou-sand, and their animosity towards Great Britain made fears more formida-ble. Feelings of Federalist merchants intensified with growing French dep-redations on American shipping.

The burden of French remonstrance against the United States was based on Jay's treaty which, the Directory continued to insist, was a viola-tion of the Franco-American alliance of 1778. The maritime policy against American commerce was provoked and justified, it was declared, by this outrageous infraction. Yet the French ministry could not explain on these grounds its demands of Hamburg, Bremen and Denmark to sever com-merce with England. The objective was to choke off British commerce everywhere; Jay's treaty interfered with French strategy. The Directory had taken umbrage in the frustrating fact that the negotiation of 1795 had eased friction between America and England. Such accord jeopardized the license France had enjoyed. Her desire and designs grew with the extraor-dinary success of her campaigns, and she became more menacing with each new conquest.

Washington was glad to observe that Adams did not equivocate. The new President courageously proceeded with his first step towards negotiation—approval of a special mission to France. He then issued a proclamation on March 25 for Congress to assemble in extra session May 15. Republicans now turned against Adams as vigorously as ever they had opposed Washington. They had some justification for their retort that the very men who, not many months ago, were so aghast at the idea of war with England now seemed to invite conflict with France. Government officials theoretically closest to Adams—his department heads themselves—favored a war declaration, but Pickering, Wolcott and McHenry reckoned without their oracle, Hamilton, who was of the same opinion as Adams. Realistically, the two recognized that no provocation short of the most humiliating would justify open war. Consequently, towards the middle of May the Chief Executive found his policy strengthened by the approval of his Cabinet, though their deference was to Hamilton rather than to Adams.

By the last week in May the General had read a copy of Adams' speech to Congress May 16 and studied the documents to which it referred. Adams had spoken well. His speech reviewed the events leading to crisis—the abuses, demands and rebuffs of the French Directory; in particular, the indignity of Pinckney's treatment. Yet, Adams continued to explain, the conduct of the Directory towards the recalled Monroe was more significant even than its refusal of Pinckney and "evinces a disposition to separate the people of the United States from the Government . . . and thus to produce division fatal to our peace." France must be persuaded by whatever instrument necessary that "national honor, character, and interest" still prevailed in the United States. Humiliation and indignity America would not tolerate, but national pride did not preclude certain concessions. On this premise, then, he would proceed, and no reasonable effort towards amicable settlement would be left untried. Republicans denounced the speech as a war cry. Washington, hopeful that the address would unify national sentiment, was disappointed that so great a minority continued in opposition. This was the more lamented by those friends of government who believed the principles of Washington's administration were on trial.

When Washington began a letter to Thomas Pinckney on May 28 consuming anxiety encouraged his pen to record his thoughts on national affairs. Every principle on which the Constitution was based, it seemed, now was being challenged. "Things cannot, ought not to remain any longer in their present disagreeable state. Nor should the idea that the government and the people have different views be suffered any longer to prevail, at home or abroad." Whether the United States would "stand upon independent ground, or be directed in its political concerns by any other nation," Washington knew, would not remain long in doubt. "A little time will show who are its true friends or, what is synonymous, who are true Americans."

The last week in June brought to Mount Vernon one of its master's most welcome guests. On his way from Richmond to Philadelphia, whence he would sail to join Charles Cotesworth Pinckney, John Marshall "spent an evening" with Washington. There was much to be said on the crisis and of the task on which Marshall was embarked. On May 31 President Adams had named him and Francis Dana to join Pinckney for the special envoy to France. Senate approval was forthcoming on June 5, but Judge Dana declined to serve. Then, solidly against Cabinet advice, Republican Elbridge Gerry was nominated as the third member of the mission. Washington's confidence in Marshall's excellent mind and discriminating judgment had been attested a year earlier by his own first choice of his fellow-Virginian as replacement for Monroe. As Marshall left the Potomac haven, he was given three letters from Washington for delivery in Europe—to the Comte Guillaume Dumas, former aide to Rochambeau; the Comte de Ségur, friend of Lafayette, and Pinckney. The closing paragraph of each of the communications introduced the bearer and his mission. Washington said of this emissary: "You will find him well worthy of your friendship and confidence. He is a firm friend, upon true principles to his country, sensible and discreet."

If visitors to Mount Vernon had any notion of its existing turmoil, few of them were influenced by it. The busy proprietor never knew when he came in from his afternoon inspection of the farms what company would share his table. Instead of the relaxation of friendly faces across the board and the ease of familiar, favorite topics of conversation—sometimes quiet, sometimes stimulating, as the need might be—there often were strangers, "come as they say, out of respect to me." But Washington was prompted to ask: "Pray, would not the word curiosity answer as well?" With its owner's retreat to private life, the "well-resorted tavern" of earlier years, as the General had once described Mount Vernon, lost none of its fascination for the stranger. Friends and distant family came often on invitation and Washington delighted in their presence, but his rigid daily routine did not allow him to tarry long of an evening to talk or listen, however interesting or dear the company might be. On July 31 Washington penned this note to Lear: "I am alone at *present*, and shall be glad to see you this evening. Unless someone pops in, unexpectedly—Mrs. Washington and myself will do what I believe has not been done within the last twenty years by us—that is to set down to dinner by ourselves." Even with his rule for retiring early, the burden of entertainment made it desirable that a proper person be brought to Mount Vernon to bestow its hospitality. Hopefully, he wrote to his nephew, Lawrence Lewis: "Whenever it is convenient to you to make this place your home, I shall be glad to see you at it . . . As both your aunt and I are in the decline of life, and regular in our habits, especially in our hours of rising and going to bed, I require some person . . . to ease me of the trouble of entertaining company, particularly of nights . . . In taking these duties, which hospitality obliges one to bestow on company, it would render me a very acceptable service. . . ."

Correspondence of a far different nature engaged Washington on July 3, when he read a paper of startling implications enclosed in a letter posted at Knoxville on June 11. The enclosure was a confidential letter from Senator William Blount of Tennessee, former Governor of the Southwest Territory, to James Carey, Indian interpreter, dated April 21, 1797. This communication had been intercepted and sent to Philadelphia by David Henley, who simultaneously directed a copy to Mount Vernon. The former President saw in it the basest designs and intrigue. A scheme to involve the Creeks and Cherokees in conspiracy with the British against Spain was there in unmistakable words. The paragraphs penned by the Tennessean were puzzling but were explicit in their implication of British Minister Liston and of Capt. John Chisholm, United States agent to the Indians.

Blount exhorted Carey to raise native suspicion and hostility against Benjamin Hawkins, present Governor of the Southwest Territory, and against "any other person in the interest of the United States or Spain." Then, with bold effrontery, Blount directed Carey to spread abroad among the southern Indians an explanation that Washington was responsible for any dissatisfaction they might feel as to their boundary line—that he, Blount, simply had been strapped by instructions.

Washington observed:

The intercepted letter, *if genuine,* is really an abomination, disgraceful to the author; and to be regretted, that among us, a man in high trust and a responsible station, should be found so debased in his principles as to write it. With respect to the sentiment which relates to me, as late President of the United States, I hold it, as I shall do the author, if he uttered it, in the most sovereign contempt; but such an attempt as is therein exhibited to poison the minds of the Indians, and destroy the utility and influence of the agents employed by the government for the express purpose of preserving peace and harmony with the Indians, and this too for the avowed design of facilitating a plan which he is unwilling, or ashamed to express; and more than probable from the complexion of the letter, is of an injurious nature to the country, deserves an epithet which he can be at no loss to apply.

Within a few days Washington knew that the disgraceful affair had been laid before Congress on July 3. Full reports submitted to Congress by Pickering and McHenry, based on correspondence with the British and Spanish ministers and latest advices from the southern border, sustained the accusations against the Senator. When Blount was confronted with the letter on the floor of the Senate, the case against him was irrefutable. On July 8 he was expelled from the Senate.

As the summer progressed Martha began to show the fatiguing effects of the hospitality extended at Mount Vernon. Her weariness was the greater because her health was not consistently good. It distressed Washington to see her going about supervisory tasks and entertaining guests even when one side of her face was badly swollen. There were always sufficient servants, but they did not function automatically. "These require instructions in some cases," Martha confided, "and looking after in all." Someone, if possible, must be obtained to relieve the mistress of Mount Vernon. The General advertised for a competent housekeeper at a wage of $150 a year. Disappearance of the cook added a further complication and it seemed Washington would have to resort to purchase rather than hire for a replacement. "I had resolved never to become the master of another slave by *purchase,*" he wrote George Lewis, "but the resolution I fear I must break." On this business of slavery he had previously written Lawrence Lewis on August 4: "I wish from my soul that the Legislature of this State could see the policy of a gradual abolition of slavery; it would prevent much future mischief."

There soon were two less in the Mount Vernon family. George Washington Lafayette and Felix Frestel left October 12 for Georgetown where they would take a stage for New York, there to embark for France.

The General accompanied them to the Federal City, gave young Lafayette $300 for the voyage and sent in his care a warm, devoted letter to the boy's father. Reunion of the Marquis and his family had been rumored for weeks, and when report of his liberation came to Mount Vernon the over-joyed son determined to depart as quickly as possible. Washington thought it would be wiser to await authenticated information, but he had not the heart to oppose the boy in his eagerness "to fly to the arms of those whom he holds most dear." Young Lafayette had won the admiration and affec-tion of the entire Mount Vernon family and said he had been as happy as possible in their tender care. Frestel also expressed appreciation for Wash-ington's "kind, tender and truly paternal affection." He had come away, he added, with the lasting impression "that all who are truly great are consequently—and necessarily good."

By the first of November circumstances on the plantation had bet-tered with the arrival of the new gardener and prospect of a new house-keeper, but no personal business of his could shut out the General's con-cern in public matters. European developments were discouraging and in-ternal discord undiminished. While the Republican press was prophesying that the three envoys would be received, Washington believed it unlikely that pride would allow the Directory of France to "acknowledge its errors and tread back its steps immediately." Any change for the better on the part of France would occur by slow degrees, and, the French would insist, entirely to the credit of their own magnanimity. Unofficial word had come that preliminary articles of peace between that country and Great Britain had been signed at Lisle. The tendency among many Americans to mini-mize defensive measures in the face of this news was deplored as "a false and fatal security." In his Annual Address on November 22 President Adams warned Congress: "I hold it most certain that permanent tranquil-ity and order will not soon be obtained."

Direct word came at last to Washington in letters from Marshall and Pinckney of their meeting at The Hague. The General had only news-paper reports of their subsequent arrival in Paris. As he wrote each of them on December 4, his thoughts were of the negotiation which, he presumed, already had begun. "What has been the reception of the embassy by the French Directory is to me unknown; and what will be the result of it, is not for me to predict." Uncertainty became anxiety as week after week went by without further communication from the envoys. It was an unwel-come, ominous silence.

Washington found an unexpected diversion and encouragement in his private affairs when, on November 24, a stranger presented himself with a letter of introduction from Gen. Daniel Morgan. Although Morgan said little more than that he knew the bearer to be one James Welch, Washington invited the visitor to dine. The Greenbrier County resident came with an offer for the lease of lands on the Great Kanawha. This roughshod caller with his smooth-spoken propositions must have given Washington pause, for he asked the opinion of Dr. James Craik, who began an investigation of the man. Craik reported he was not favorably impressed and would be hesitant to bargain, especially when he learned the eagerness with which Welch hoped to acquire the acreage belonging to Craik as well as that of Washington. The master of Mount Vernon was not sufficiently wary to dismiss the backwoods trader, in spite of Craik's caution. After several interviews and a considerable exchange of letters, Washington instructed his attorney, James Keith, to draw up a contract for long lease of the property—more than 23,000 acres—with an option for purchase. The price was computed at 6 per cent interest on $200,000, payable annually, beginning January 1, 1799. As security Washington accepted promise of a trust deed from Welch for some one hundred thousand acres which the buyer certified he owned in Randolph County. In any event, a substantial cash income would furnish a commodity rare at Mount Vernon. What Washington's Potomac plantation could not produce, western lands might yield.

The New Year began auspiciously. The Maryland Legislature approved a loan towards continuance of public buildings in the Federal City, and Washington had reason to hope that similar consideration would be given another "favorite object of his heart"—full navigation of the Potomac. Best of all, welcome word of the safe arrival of Lafayette and his family at Hamburg came directly from the consul there—authentic news for which Washington long had waited. The reunion of George Lafayette with his parents and sisters still was unverified, but Washington hoped the meeting had been accomplished. The General was not too busy with his correspondence and with plantation matters to put in writing the system and daily conduct expected of his grandson, who was at Mount Vernon for an indefinite stay. Young Custis may have been unimpressed by his elder's instructions and unmindful of their valuable application in the General's own self-discipline, but he was now exposed to example as well as precept.

Newspaper accounts from France were not, for Washington, adequate proof of diplomatic progress, or indeed of the well being of the three envoys. Only direct word from them would satisfy him. He was puzzled by their silence. At the same time, he was made curious by the lack of silence of the recalled Monroe, and requested Pickering to send him the pamphlets now in circulation from the pens of Monroe and his counterpart, Fauchet. The master of Mount Vernon wished to be told "with the most unreserved frankness," the public sentiment respecting them, especially Monroe's *View of the Conduct of the Executive of the United States.* Pickering reported that Monroe's *View,* like Randolph's *Vindication,* "is considered his own condemnation or death warrant" when he sent the pamphlets. As for Fauchet's bold assertions, the Secretary added, they had little regard for truth or reason of decency and were of so little merit as to be below animadversion.

Sometime during March the General took up his copy of the *View* and simultaneously took up his pen. When he had finished, the margins were heavy with comments. The pungency of his sentences disclosed satisfaction in the mere process of pulling apart these morsels Monroe had offered for general consumption. In the first place, Washington questioned the propriety of employing private instructions and official correspondence as a means of personal vindication. Then, topic by topic, in unequivocal phrases, he inscribed his own review and refutation. With that, he closed the subject because, he explained, "I shall leave it to the tribunal to which he himself has appealed. . . ."

On February 12 the General and his family rode into Alexandria to a ball in honor of his birthday. At Philadelphia ten days later the former President's birthday was celebrated with a banquet in Concert Hall. Governors and Judges there were, and others of high station, but the one who ranked them all, the President of the United States, did not attend. When the card of invitation from a committee of Philadelphians arrived, Adams "took the earliest opportunity to inform them that he declined accepting it." The President's absence provoked hearty criticism from many Federalists and friends of Washington, but the Vice President's failure to participate apparently disturbed no one and called forth comment only from the President's Lady, who assumed Jefferson's absence to be out of deference to her husband.

Whether the plantation proprietor had expected it, his first post-presidential birthday evoked comparisons between himself and his successor. Most incisive was Madison's observation:

There never was perhaps a greater contrast between two characters than between those of the present President and his predecessor. . . . The one cool, considerate and cautious, the other headlong and kindled into flame by every spark that lights on his passions; the one ever scrutinizing into the public opinion, and ready to follow where he could not lead it; the other insulting it by the most adverse sentiments and pursuits. Washington a hero in the field, yet overweighing every danger in the Cabinet—Adams with a single pretension to the character of a soldier, a perfect Quixotte as a statesman; the former Chief Magistrate pursuing peace everywhere with sincerity, though mistaking the means; the latter taking as much pains to get into war, as the former took to keep out of it. . . .

Washington, in the single brief letter he wrote on his sixty-sixth birthday, lamented to Senator Alexander Martin of North Carolina that "when all hearts should be united . . . ready to rejoice at the good, or repel the evil which awaits us . . . nothing but internal dissensions and political hostilities are to be found in the councils of our common country."

Plantation problems seemed never to diminish. Restoration of his estate would consume many months yet; Martha's frequent indispositions troubled him; and something must be decided about the future of Washington Custis. Mount Vernon would not afford the necessary discipline or direction. In consultation with the youth's stepfather, David Stuart, arrangements were made for Custis to enter St. John's College at Annapolis. On March 5 Doctor Stuart and his stepson set out for the college. In the weeks that followed the pattern of correspondence between Mount Vernon and Annapolis became unhappily familiar—exhortations, promises, disappointments, more exhortations, more promises. Washington at length displayed undisguised pique when Custis inquired whether he should withdraw from St. John's on his forthcoming visit to Mount Vernon. "The question . . . really astonishes me!" replied the General, "for it would seem as if *nothing* I could say to you made more than a *momentary* impression." But somehow this grandson usually had his way, though Washington did not tolerate the idea, much less foresee the fact, of the boy's failure to resume his studies in the fall.

Almost constant concern for public affairs made correspondence burdensome and, as the work at Mount Vernon necessitated much extra bookkeeping, the General resolved to employ a clerk, if one could be found at a moderate wage. Consequently, the arrival of clerical assistance in the person of Albin Rawlins, who "wrote a good hand and had a knowledge of accounts," was most welcome.

Anxiety approached anguish as weeks grew into months without word from Pinckney, Marshall and Gerry. On March 4 Washington's apprehension was betrayed in his query to McHenry: "Are our commissioners guillotined, or what else is the occasion of their silence?" As it happened, the first dispatches from the envoys after their arrival in Paris were received at Pickering's office that very evening, and the next day President Adams notified Congress. The dispatches were in cipher, except the last—a letter of January 8, 1798. This paper with its enclosure—a translation of the astounding decree of the French Directory declaring all neutral ships with any British-made cargo to be lawful prizes and all French ports closed to any vessel that had touched an English port in the course of its voyage—accompanied Adams' brief message. It had seemed to Washington that continuance of French depredations on American commerce "would have united all parties and all descriptions of men . . . in a firm and temperate demand of justice, or in preparations for the worst. . . ." but the natural expectation had not followed. The unnatural response of many Americans—censure of their own government and leniency towards France —was a disturbing fact. Early in April brought the further information that the envoys had not been received. Moreover, Washington saw no encouragement in the President's message to Congress on March 19. In the light of communications from the envoys, Adams declared that the mission evidently could not be accomplished "on terms compatible with safety, honor and essential interests of the nation." He recommended that merchant vessels be permitted to arm and exhorted Congress to proceed with "zeal, vigor and concert, in defence of the national rights, proportioned to the danger with which they are threatened."

Reassurance did not issue from Congress. Albert Gallatin had predicted that little business would be done there before the fate of the French mission became known; but the President's intimation of its failure and appeal for prompt defensive measures disturbed few members of the House of Representatives. When at last the House resolved itself into a Committee of the Whole to consider the state of the Union, discussions still were trifling. Then on April 2, when a resolution to demand the official communications was proposed, it passed readily. On the third the desired documents were presented in full, with a short message from Adams.

By mid-April Washington also had received the revelatory dispatches. Now the conjecture of recent months was ended, the long silence explained. Washington saw revealed the wisdom and the wiles of men and nations. From the moment of their arrival in Paris October 4, 1797, the envoys had met only delay and indirection. Their dispatches told an astonishing story: On the afternoon of the eighth, Monsieur Talleyrand admitted them to his house as unofficial callers but insisted he was "too busy" to promise a further interview. Official reception of the Envoy Extraordinary then was postponed on the ground of the Directory's wounded feelings due to certain phrases in President Adams' address to Congress on May 16, 1797. But, the envoys soon were informed, if the speech were abrogated and a *douceur* of $250,000 placed at Talleyrand's disposal, the Minister's hurt would be healed. Moreover, a loan to the French Republic would mollify the Directory and set the stage for negotiation. Suddenly it was obvious to the three Americans what the real grievance was: they had not come bearing money or offers of money. This was made abundantly clear, though not by Talleyrand himself. Instead, one by one there appeared spokesmen in his behalf. Whereas these agents claimed they were not sent by the French Minister, they professed to know his mind and each in turn stated Talleyrand's propositions with supreme assurance, always with a single object—money to bribe the privilege of a stay in Paris and more money to buy an authoritative audience. When on April 3 President Adams disclosed the documents to Congress, he omitted the names of Talleyrand's unofficial deputies and denoted them simply as W, X, Y and Z. The first to call had been Monsieur W, whose part was only that of introducing Monsieur X. At the envoys' request, Monsieur X put in writing the monetary demands already stated on behalf of the French Minister. This done, he ushered in a confidant of Talleyrand—Monsieur Y— who came forward with suggestions to ensure a successful mission. Monsieur Y described a subtle arrangement for the requisite loan to France: The United States could purchase certificates of a mandatory Dutch loan to the French Republic, valued at $12,800,000—but worth about half that amount on the current market—with the apparent expectation of a return to par when peace came again to Europe. In that way a gift of some $6,000,000 could be made to France without arousing English fury. But, Monsieur Y was careful to insist, the loan and the private gift of *douceurs* must be considered separate matters and must be kept so. In any event, these pecuniary procedures and a revocation of the offending speech were imperatives to further transaction.

The plenipotentiaries were commissioned with ample authority to make treaties, but they were not empowered to make a loan. The envoys countered that one of the three would return to the United States to consult on that point *if* the French would discontinue depredations on American commerce in the interim. As for the President's speech, that could not be recanted. Monsieur X then made a more impassioned plea for money. Over and over again payment was importuned. Until that was accomplished all words would be useless and other efforts futile. At this point Gerry was approached by yet another caller in the person of Monsieur Z, who came to reaffirm Talleyrand's good disposition towards the United States. As proof, he would arrange a private though unofficial interview between the French Minister and one of the envoys, preferably Gerry, since both Talleyrand and Monsieur Z had known him in Boston. The meeting finally was effected, but nothing was accomplished beyond a certain satisfaction on the part of Gerry that he was singled out for conference.

Marshall and Pinckney saw only frustration in the attempt to cope with Talleyrand's preposterous proposals; they discerned also efforts to divide the envoys and evidences of Gerry's growing susceptibility to French flattery. They wished to end the useless bickering, but at Gerry's insistence the absurd arguments with one or another of the agents were continued day after day. Anything suggested met only the refrain—"it is money; it is expected that you will offer money." Finally, the thoroughly exasperated Pinckney shouted: "It is no, no; not a sixpence!"

The determined French finally brought feminine influence to bear. A lady, "well acquainted with Talleyrand," explained to Pinckney that the Directory had not *demanded* the loan but left it to the more delicate device of an offer from the envoys. She did not fail to reiterate the menacing strength of the French party in America and the disastrous results the uncompliant commissioners might bring upon their country. Yet another means of effecting the bribe—this one at no actual cost to the United States—was devised by Talleyrand, only to be deprecated by Marshall to whom the subject was presented. Pinckney and Marshall were consistently in accord, but Talleyrand's artfulness was not lost on Gerry. Flattered by attentions turned to him, Gerry fancied that much might be accomplished in the climate of the dinner table, and he did not confide all that passed privately between himself and Talleyrand or with Monsieur Y. On December 17 Talleyrand consented to dine as guest of the New Englander ten days later. However sanguine Gerry's expectations, Marshall and Pinckney did not share them, and on Christmas Eve the envoys prepared a realistic report to the Secretary of State. Their covering note on January 8, 1798, concluded: "Nothing new has occurred since our last, in date of the 24th ultimo. We can only repeat that there exists no hope of our being officially received by this Government, or that the objects of our mission will be in any way accomplished." This was the final word in the dispatches that had reached Pickering March 4.

As Washington had hoped, publication of the dispatches brought patriotic outbursts from many quarters. Growing dismay beset Republicans and increasing delight stirred Federalists. Whatever might eventuate in Paris between the envoys and the French Foreign Minister, failure of the mission soon was acknowledged throughout the United States. Accusations of the "peace party" against the "war party" were shouted in vain. Popular protests against the administration in many instances gave way to praise for Adams. Hamilton noted that a good spirit was gaining ground in Congress, though "measures march slowly." Washington continued to express regret at the lack of national unity, but said resignedly: "To expect that all men should think alike upon political, more than on religious or other subjects, would be to look for a change in the order of nature."

In a letter to the Secretary of War the first week in May, Washington urged that steps be taken to complete and utilize the arsenal and foundry at the mouth of the Shenandoah—in his opinion one of the most important and strategic of measures. Between this and the end of the month there was but a single reference to national affairs from his pen. On

May 16 he addressed a long letter to Sally Cary Fairfax in Bath, England—the first since she and her late husband, Col. George William Fairfax, had left twenty-five years ago to make their home abroad. Washington mentioned briefly the threatening behavior of the French, stated his wish "to spend the remainder of my days (which cannot be many) in rural amusements," and remarked on the additions and alterations at Mount Vernon. Then, almost wistfully: ". . . it is a matter of sore regret, when I cast my eyes towards Belvoir, which I often do, to reflect that the former inhabitants of it, with whom we lived in such harmony and friendship, no longer reside there; and that the ruins can only be viewed as a memento of former pleasures." There followed a description of the progress of the two enterprises most dear to his heart: the Federal City and the opening of inland navigation. "In a word," he declared, "if this Country can steer clear of European politics . . . and be wise and temperate in its government, it bids fair to be one of the greatest and happiest nations in the world."

Eight days' absence in visits with relatives and friends did not altogether relieve Mount Vernon's proprietor of plantation problems. One that followed him to the Federal City was of the utmost importance—farm manager Anderson's resignation. Washington had no wish to part with this competent man, yet he had no wish to retain a discontented person, or one who might better himself elsewhere. At the end of a year of service Washington had written his observations on Anderson's work, in praise of those things that had pleased him and in criticism of those that had not. The manager had been offended by candid comments. In reply to Anderson's resignation, Washington spoke plainly:

If I cannot remark upon my own business, passing every day under my eyes, without hurting your feelings, I must discontinue my rides, or become a cypher on my own Estate. You will, I am persuaded, do me the justice to say that I have never undertaken any new thing, or made any material change, or indeed any change at all in the old without consulting with you thereupon; and you must further acknowledge, that I have never been tenacious of any matters I have suggested, when you have offered reasons against the adoption of them. If your feelings have been hurt by my remarks on the bad clover seed that was purchased, I cannot help that; my view and plan have been much more hurt by it.

Washington then proposed an arrangement whereby Anderson's efforts would be confined to the mill, distillery and fishery. Washington hoped these three industries would pay him better if managed better. On the twenty-ninth he learned from Lear that Anderson had tendered his services to William Fitzhugh. He wrote Fitzhugh a frank appraisal of Anderson, in which the Scotsman's faults were far outweighed by his abilities, and stated that it had been his hope to retain Anderson. The matter was settled happily; Anderson elected to stay on at Mount Vernon after certain adjustments were made: Overseer William Stuart was assigned full management of River Farm; Albin Rawlins in future would do all necessary writing for Anderson and some of the inspection of the plantation.

A sobering letter from Hamilton awaited Washington on his return home. Hamilton was aware of a continuing opposition and feared it could not easily be overcome. Mindful of its power and alarmed that French sympathizers still were numerous in Virginia and North Carolina, Hamilton sought the best means of combating them. No influence with the people could equal that of Washington. Would it not be expedient for the General to make a tour of those States, he wrote, ostensibly for reasons of health, and in response to inevitable addresses, public dinners and toasts, impart to the people the truths they should know and the sentiments they should accept? He could win approval for present administrative policies because they were also his own. Although "deeply impressed with the present situation of public affairs, and not a little agitated by the outrageous conduct of France," Washington declined the idea. The object of the tour could not be attributed to his health which, he explained, "never was better."

So far as Washington personally was concerned, the last paragraph of Hamilton's letter augured something far beyond his expectation:

You ought to be aware, my dear sir, that in the event of an open rupture with France, the public voice will again call you to command the armies of your country; and, though all who are attached to you will, from attachment, as well as from public considerations, deplore an occasion which should once more tear you from that repose to which you have so good a right, yet it is the opinion of all those with whom I converse, that you will be compelled to make the sacrifice.

Washington still believed invasion of American soil was unlikely and so assured Hamilton. There was encouragement in recent evidences of stronger adherence to government in the States south of Virginia, he observed. Then Washington made a simple declaration: In event of open war, he was not convinced that he could serve more ably than many other men; but should he be called, it must not be out of respect to him but from an unequivocal preference for him; before he should accept, he would wish to know who would be his general officers and, lastly, whether Hamilton himself would take an active part. Precisely what Washington's innermost thoughts were at the moment he did not disclose, but one thing was certain: he might protest, but full-time planter would give over to full-time patriot if he must. Whatever was required of him in a national crisis he would do.

Among the invited visitors at Mount Vernon in early June was Julian Ursin Niemcewicz, a Polish officer who had recently come to America with Kosciuszko. During the twelve days of his visit, Washington talked with Niemcewicz on many subjects, but only once did the conversation turn to the topic which probably occupied the General's thoughts more than any other—the crisis between the United States and France. The subject was prompted by receipt of a letter from Paris June 13. Discussion turned immediately to the threatened war with France, and Washington's indignation was aroused. "I never heard him before speak with so much fire and candor," Niemcewicz recalled, and quoted the General's words as he remembered them:

Whether we consider the wrongs and the plunder which our trade is suffering . . . or the outrage to the independence [and] to the dignity of the nation
in ejecting our ministers, or whether we think at last of the oppression, ruin,
and destruction of free nations produced by this military government, we always
see the necessity of arming ourselves with a power and cunningness equaling the
danger which threatens us. Patience and submission will not avail us any more
than it did Venice. Submission is cowardice. Rather than that, America will
arouse; everyone of us, myself in spite of my age, will give all the blood that
remains in my veins. Mr. Adams is censured for too much passion in deeds
and too much boldness in speech. From the moment I left the administration,
I have not written a single word to Mr. Adams; neither have I received from
him anything except the dispatches which we have seen in public papers. I
do not know where his other sources of information are from. But I am persuaded
that, as a reasonable and honest man and as a good American, he cannot act
otherwise. I myself should be perhaps not less emphatic in his place in words, but
certainly I would prepare not any less steadily and energetically.

Nothing in later dispatches from Paris improved the gloomy picture.
Washington observed to James Lloyd late in June: "When the *whole* correspondence between our Envoys and the French Minister . . . is brought
into one view and laid before the public, it will be extremely interesting;
and must, I conceive, carry conviction to every mind that is open to it, of
what the French now are, and have been aiming at, from the beginning of
their Revolution; or from an early period of it, at least." With Marshall's
arrival in Philadelphia on June 18, had come latest intelligence of the ill-
fated mission. The General rejoiced at Marshall's safe return, and regretted only that his colleagues had not accompanied him. He understood
the necessity of Pinckney's lingering in the south of France because of his
daughter's illness, but of Gerry he wrote: "The stay of one of them has a
mysterious appearance." The French Minister's "invidious distinction"
should have filled Gerry "with resentment instead of complaisance," he
thought. Talleyrand had waited six weeks after he received the American
memorial of January 17 before he deigned to reply. Then the audacity of
his answer was matched only by Gerry's servile willingness to be the bearer
of it. Talleyrand named Gerry the single member with whom the Directory
could and would negotiate. Pinckney described the memorial as "weak in
argument, but irritating and insulting in style." Marshall prepared the
refutation which, after much quibbling and many self-righteous remarks,
Gerry agreed to sign. To the abusive behavior of the French Minister now
was added the humiliation of Gerry's performance. Flattered into conviction that by remaining to negotiate singly he could prevent a French declaration of war, Gerry could not be moved from his decision. His companions consequently took leave of him and Paris as soon as their passports
were issued. Among the papers submitted to Congress on June 21 was a
copy of Pickering's renewed instructions of March 23—that the envoys consent to no loans in any circumstances. Adams announced the negotiation at
an end and concluded with the statement: "I will never send another
minister to France without assurances that he will be received, respected,
and honored as the representative of a great, free, powerful and independent nation."

Marshall, Washington learned, was escorted into Philadelphia with parade and song. At a dinner given in his honor June 18 toasts were many and registered the happy temper of the Federalist party. First, to the United States, the people, the President. The 120 glasses then were raised to General Washington—"His name a rampart and the knowledge that he lives a bulwark against mean and secret enemies of his Country's Peace." But the toast that expressed the real spirit of the occasion was the inspired phrase of Robert Goodloe Harper: "Millions for Defence, but not a cent for Tribute." The voice of the banqueters resounded in the Philadelphia streets and echoed throughout the country as the voice of all patriotic Americans.

Hamilton's intimation that Washington would be called again to public service now seemed prophetic. Two letters that claimed his attention the Fourth of July brought evidence of coming events. The Secretary of War had asked plainly on June 26: "May we flatter ourselves, that, in a crisis so awful and important, you will accept the command of all our armies?" Adams' letter of June 22 had implied the wish that Washington become military chief; in the organization of an Army, Washington's counsel would be imperative. In the very name of Washington, Adams concluded, "there will be more efficacy . . . than in many an army." Washington's answer to McHenry admitted, "I see, as you do, that clouds are gathering and that a storm may ensue." However painful it would be "to quit the tranquil walks of retirement and enter the boundless field of responsibility and trouble," he would find it difficult "to remain an idle spectator under the plea of age or retirement." Personal desires would be no obstacle, but the General laid down unequivocal conditions that must be met before he would assume command. In his mind these provisions were not personal, yet they indicated a continuing concern for his place with posterity. "That reputation the partiality of the world has been pleased to confer for past services," cherished as it was, must be protected by every possible means.

The burden of his reply to the President was the same as that to McHenry. In the matter of choosing general officers and the general staff, Washington spoke plainly. Adams had given the cue when he confessed the perplexity he might face in the selection of officers—"whether to call out all the old generals, or to appoint a young set." In event of French invasion men must march with quick step, the President said. On this Washington wrote: ". . . it will not be an easy matter, I conceive, to find among the *old set* of Generals, men of sufficient activity, energy and health, and of sound politics, to train troops to the *quick step,* long marches, and severe conflicts they may have to encounter . . . recourse must be had (for the greater part at least) to the well known, most experienced, best proved, and intelligent officers of the late Army, without respect to grade." Then came his *sine qua non:* "As it is of the utmost importance to the public, to the Army, and to the officer commanding it, be he whom he will, I will take the liberty of suggesting it *now:* It is, that the greatest circumspection be used in appointing the General Staff." As he saw it, these officers were as "so many limbs or parts of the Commander-in-Chief." Whatever Adams' ideas, he should have no doubt of Washington's sentiments in the present situation or of his expectations if called to command the Army.

The first authentic report of his appointment came to Washington in a newspaper account accompanied by a note from McHenry, both dated July 4. Pickering's letter of the sixth reached Mount Vernon July 10, but the official notification was not a surprise, except in the manner of it. On July 11 Washington's carriage set out for Alexandria to meet the Philadelphia mail stage and bring back an official guest in the person of McHenry. It was evening when the Secretary of War alighted at Mount Vernon and handed Washington a communication from the President: "Mr. McHenry, the Secretary of War, will have the honor to wait on you in my behalf, to impart to you a step I have ventured to take, and which I should have been happy to have communicated in person if such a journey had been, at this time, in my power . . . if it had been in my power to nominate you to be President of the United States, I should have done it with less hesitation and more pleasure." Next, the enclosure ". . . I have nominated and by and with the Advice and Consent of the Senate, do appoint him Lieutenant General and Commander in Chief of all the Armies raised or to be raised for the service of the United States. . . ." The Commission was dated July 4, 1798.

Should he acquiesce in the appointment, Washington observed to McHenry, it would be with the clear reservation that he would not be called to active duty until the Army required his presence in the field. He would expect to take part in the arrangement and organization of the Army, of course, with the understanding that "principal officers in the line and of the staff shall be such as I can place confidence in." Washington took pains to establish his stand as he and the Secretary conversed.

The General furnished McHenry with names of officers for the General Staff and of "prominent characters" from which to select field officers. The three at the head of the list, Washington knew, would present the larger difficulty. At the top was Hamilton, Inspector General with the rank of Major General. Next came Charles Cotesworth Pinckney and Henry Knox, Major Generals also. The order was all-important. However firmly Washington might favor the position next his own for Hamilton, the question of relative rank had to be weighed carefully. Knox had seniority. He had also Washington's "love and esteem." Nor could the first President forget that Knox had been the first Secretary of War. Personal affection, however, did not alter the conviction that Knox was not the proper choice for second in command of the Army of 1798. Actually, Washington concluded, Knox should rank after Pinckney. Whether the "spirited, active and judicious" Pinckney would accept position below that of Hamilton was a definite doubt in Washington's mind. The South Carolinian's reputation, already high militarily, had been exalted by his conduct in France. He had the further advantage of seniority over Hamilton. Pinckney's connections were numerous and his influence powerful; to invite discontent among his large following might be to invite danger. In any event, Washington recommended Hamilton, Pinckney, Knox, in that order—unless among themselves these officers agreed to an altered arrangement. The decision had not been easy, but now it was determined, Washington assumed it would stand, certainly so far as the President was concerned.

Should a replacement be required for Hamilton, Knox or Pinckney, Washington suggested Henry Lee be designated Major General, otherwise that he rank as Brigadier. John Brooks of Massachusetts, William S. Smith of New York, or John E. Howard of Maryland, also were proposed as Brigadiers. Jonathan Dayton, Jr., from New Jersey, was Washington's choice for Adjutant General, and Edward Carrington, Virginian, for Quartermaster General. As Director of the Hospital, he put down James Craik, for whom, in Washington's opinion, there was no substitute.

Most of the two and a half days of McHenry's stay at Mount Vernon were spent in seclusion as he and Washington weighed military positions and personalities. When McHenry departed on July 14 he carried a letter to the President. In it Washington repeated his reluctance to reenter public life, reviewed the deplorable conduct of France, and commended the "wise and prudent measures of the administration." Most important were these words: "I have determined to accept the Commission. . . ." On July 18 a copy of Washington's letter of acceptance was transmitted to the Senate by President Adams. The official communication, immediately and widely published, was received with high satisfaction.

By the end of July the patriot-planter found his correspondence increasingly crowded with applications, introductions and recommendations. The first of at least a dozen to seek membership in Washington's military family was John Marshall's brother, James. Other would-be aides-de-camp, whose names might have stirred Washington's memories of Revolutionary years were Charles Carroll, Jr., Thomas Cadwalader and Thomas Nelson, Jr. The General explained to one and all his resolve to postpone selection until he was called into the field.

If the pay of a secretary was allowable, Washington had need of someone promptly. That someone he wished to be Lear, whose "abilities, prudence and integrity" had been proved by fourteen years of close association. As soon as presidential authority was received, Washington urged Lear to take up the station at once. The invaluable secretary resumed his Mount Vernon residence none too soon. On August 18 Washington was seized with an ague. He ignored it at first and pursued his usual rides and occupations, but after two days he yielded to a fever that did not break for a week. For a time the illness alarmed his family and friends. The General was greatly debilitated and convalescence seemed slow; a loss of twenty pounds made the ravages of his illness marked.

Washington was buoyed in spirit by the prospect of a visit from John Marshall and Bushrod Washington, whom he had invited to Mount Vernon. The General had written his nephew: "The crisis is important. The temper of the people of this State in many (at least in some) places, are so violent and outrageous, that I wish to converse with General Marshall and yourself on the elections which must soon come." The travelers arrived in time for breakfast September 3. During the three days that followed, the General pressed Marshall to run for Congress as a Federalist candidate. At length the Virginian consented.

On September 3, probably before Marshall and Bushrod arrived, the General had written at length to the Secretary of War on various matters of military importance. At the close of the letter he said: "If any change should take place in settling the relative rank of the Major Generals, I shall hope and expect to be informed of it." From McHenry's "confidential and private" letter of August 25 Washington had observed that the President's idea of relative rank was not in accord with his, though Adams had presented the names to the Senate in the order submitted. Almost immediately afterward Adams had left Philadelphia and wrote later from Quincy his altered opinion: the only satisfactory arrangement would be Knox, Pinckney, Hamilton. Knox deserved it, was legally entitled to it. "You may depend upon it," the President cautioned McHenry, "the five New England States will not patiently submit to the humiliation that has been meditated for them."

These words were those of Knox also, one of the arguments he had set forth in a bitter communication of July 29 directed to Mount Vernon. Knox questioned the high estimation of Hamilton and hinted that Washington had been misled on behalf of the New Yorker. Finally he had said that "unless the relative rank of the late war should govern according to the established and invariable usage of the former war," which he believed to be in line with past principles and military law, he must decline appointment. Washington was disquieted by Knox's observations. On August 9 the Commander-in-Chief endeavored to explain and defend what had been done, though nothing he could say to Knox, he feared, would compensate for lack of precedence over Hamilton and Pinckney. As for a reference by Knox to the inconstancy of his friendship, Washington said: "I will pronounce with decision that it ever has been, still is, and notwithstanding the unkindness of the charge, ever will be . . . warm and sincere." The unexpected nature of his own appointment and the impropriety of any action on his part before the general officers were nominated, he added, had made consultation with Knox out of the question. In justification of Hamilton's precedence, Washington went on to say: ". . . from information I had no cause to distrust, no doubt remained on my mind that Colonel Hamilton was designated second in command—and first if I should decline acceptance—by the Federal characters of Congress, whence alone anything like a public sentiment relative thereto, could be deduced." Besides this evidence, Washington listed five other factors that contributed to the decision. Nor did Washington believe any of the efforts in Hamilton's behalf were intrigue. Whether these explanations would mollify Knox, the General could not guess, but his own satisfaction lay in the "utmost sincerity and frankness of heart" with which he had disclosed his thoughts.

If he was not reconciled militarily, Knox was softened in his personal attitude towards Washington. In his answering letter of August 26 he said that he had ascertained to his satisfaction how Washington had determined upon "the transcendent military talents of General Hamilton," and admitted "the opinions formed on that head may be entirely accurate." His most pleasing gesture was the expressed wish to serve as Washington's aide-de-camp in event of invasion. None would be more welcome in his military family, the Commander-in-Chief replied, provided he could come without rancor, but Washington continued to hope that Knox might yet accept his commission as Major General.

President Adams, meanwhile, had warmed increasingly to Knox's cause. With Adams at Quincy and Washington at Mount Vernon, understanding was not easily reached. The President had Constitutional authority in this question, Adams reminded McHenry, and in his letter of August 29 reiterated that the order would stand—Knox, Pinckney, Hamilton. Thoroughly apprehensive of the situation, McHenry confided to Washington that he had laid the whole of his correspondence with the President before Wolcott, Pickering and Secretary of the Navy Benjamin Stoddert. A respectful protest to the President was considered imperative. Wolcott was designated to write the letter. This he did on September 17, and two days later McHenry reviewed the entire affair in a communication to Mount Vernon.

Now that the President knew the Commander-in-Chief had been apprised of developments, Washington could set forth his own views to Adams without betraying McHenry's confidences. Such a letter as the General prepared on September 25 never would have come from the pen of planter and proprietor. Whereas deference still was due the President, the Commander-in-Chief had certain perquisites also. He had no wish to increase his own powers or diminish those of the President, Washington carefully explained, but the terms of his acceptance—declared *after* his appointment because he had no opportunity of declaring them *before*—were explicit. He had retained the commission in the belief that his conditions would be met. Yet, changes in the general staff had been determined upon and others contemplated without intimation to the Commander-in-Chief. "In the arrangement made by me with the Secretary of War," Washington wrote, "the three Major Generals stood, Hamilton, Pinckney, Knox; and in this order I expected their commissions would have been dated. But you have been pleased to order the last to be first, and the first to be last. . . ." Washington asked, "if no regard was intended to be had to the *order* of my arrangement, why was it not altered before it was submitted to the Senate?" In nothing did Washington equivocate, least of all concerning the two most conspicuous personalities. Of Hamilton he said: "That he is ambitious I shall readily grant, but it is of that laudable kind which prompts a man to excel in whatever he takes in hand. He is enterprising, quick in his perceptions, and his judgment is intuitively great; qualities essential to a military character and therefore I repeat that his loss will be irreparable." Then his comment on Knox: ". . . I can say with truth, there is no man with whom I have been in habits of greater intimacy; no one whom I loved more sincerely, nor any for whom I have had a greater friendship. But esteem, love and friendship can have no influence in my mind when . . . possibly, our all is at stake." Lengthy though the letter was, Washington had one more compelling point to make: In over two months there had been no recruiting and now the spirit of the people noticeably was lagging.

There could have been no doubt in Adams' mind that he must say at once how matters stood. On October 9 he answered the letter that had come from Mount Vernon the day before. Wolcott's forceful communication of September 17 had probably conditioned him for the concession he was called upon to make. Already, the President wrote Washington, he had signed and dated commissions for the three Major Generals on the same day. Should controversies as to rank arise, they would be submitted to the Commander-in-Chief, Adams added, whose judgment he was resolved to confirm.

On October 15 the General had the satisfaction of reading in the gazettes that Pinckney, his wife and daughter had arrived at New York. Washington promptly wrote the returned envoy a warm invitation for the family to visit at Mount Vernon whenever they passed through Virginia on the way to Charleston. Relieved of his apprehension for Pinckney's safety, there came immediately to Washington's mind apprehension of another sort. "I hope," Washington wrote Pickering, "he will not play the second part of the difficulty created by General Knox."

Pickering had recalled Gerry in unequivocal terms under date of June 25, but by the time the lagging envoy left Paris he had been buffeted about by Talleyrand for three months and more. Although the New Englander believed himself favored of the French Minister, Talleyrand displayed no more respect or consideration for him than he had for his colleagues. By mid-July the dispatches of the American envoys had been published and widely distributed in England and on the continent. The prevailing reaction was sympathy with the United States. Talleyrand demanded that Gerry deny these disclosures and brazenly declared that demands for redress for Adams' speech or for money never had been made. Then Talleyrand called on Gerry to communicate to him the names of those persons designated in the dispatches as W, X, Y, and Z. In absurd acquiescence, Gerry complied, as if he had not known that they were the chosen tools of Talleyrand.

The effect of the X Y Z dispatches on the majority of Americans had eased the way for Federalists in Congress. Proper measures for defence—a new army, a first navy, and taxes for their establishment and support—had been legislated with little difficulty. Only a declaration of war was lacking as a guarantee of unanimity. It was the opinion of the more ardent administration enthusiasts that since France had not proclaimed it, Congress should have done so. George Cabot proclaimed that "war, open and declared would not only deprive our external enemy of his best hopes, but would also extinguish the hopes of our internal foes." Towards this end, therefore, measures were sought with a zeal that rivalled that for soldiers and ships.

Federalists, pleased and overconfident in their new popularity, took the offensive and chose as their weapons a Naturalization Bill and Alien and Sedition Laws. The Naturalization Bill prescribed a residence of fourteen years instead of five before application for citizenship. The second measure invested the President with authority to remove enemy aliens in event of war or threatened invasion and with arbitrary powers to deport aliens suspected of "treasonable or secret machination against the government." The Sedition Act was designed to suppress written, printed, published or spoken expressions of a "false, scandalous and malicious" nature against government or anyone associated with government.

Immediately and most conveniently, these measures became, in Washington's words, "the desiderata in the opposition"—the ideal Republican restorative. Doubtless the General was correct in his assertion that the "Jacobins" would have clamored on some other account had this one not been offered, but they scarcely could have contrived to do better for themselves than the Federalists had done for them. When the Alien bill was scarcely more than an idea, Hamilton deprecated it as a dangerous move, but the admonition went unheeded.

Washington believed the measures justifiable. The knowledge that objectors to the government were persistent and numerous in his own State of Virginia was exceedingly painful to him. Protection must be provided against aliens who acknowledged no allegiance to the United States and "in many instances are sent among us . . . for the express purpose of poisoning the minds of our people and to sow dissensions among them . . thereby endeavoring to dissolve the Union." No true American need fear the laws; only Jacobins and disloyal persons would be affected. Where Jefferson saw monarchical intent, Washington saw simply an effort towards stronger national unity.

It remained for Virginia to display the most serious disaffection and administer the most severe rebuke to the national government. Although the Assembly of Kentucky was the first to act officially, Washington knew beyond doubt that the motivating influence was that of Virginians; that the Vice President was subtly at work in close collaboration with the brilliant Madison. Kentucky, in a legislative action of November 16, anticipated by more than a month adoption of similar measures by its sister State. The Kentucky Resolutions and those of Virginia denounced the Alien and Sedition Acts as the exercise of unconstitutional powers. What could there be but potential dissolution of national government, thought Washington, in the declaration that the compact among the States had been violated, that the States "have the *right* . . . to interpose for arresting the progress of the evil, and for maintaining, within their respective limits, the authorities, rights and liberties appertaining to them"? Furthermore, the Virginia Assembly appealed to other States to take "necessary and proper measures" to protect their rights and liberties. The General wrote Henry that Kentucky alone had countenanced Virginia's action. Where right-minded men would not exert themselves singly against the "torrent that carries away others" they would embark against it with "an able pilot to conduct them." Henry would be just such a pilot. Although the week before Washington wrote his letter, Henry had declared himself "too old and infirm ever again to undertake public concerns" he answered that he would consent to be a candidate for the Virginia Assembly. In so doing, Henry, now in his sixty-third year, allied himself unequivocally and finally with Washington and the Federalist cause.

In early August another foe than France had threatened Americans—Federalists and Republicans alike. Yellow fever made its third invasion in five years, and its worst. Newspapers and letters brought to Mount Vernon the "extremely painful" accounts of its spread in the North. Philadelphians lost no time in capitulation to the mysterious enemy, and within the month business there virtually ended. Taverns and markets closed; government offices moved to Trenton, and other public offices joined them there or went to Germantown. Federalists believed the ill wind had brought at least one blessing in the death of Benjamin F. Bache. An arch enemy and an able one was silenced. Republicans had similar satisfaction in the death of John Fenno. By the end of October, when the malady retreated before the frosts, death had taken almost 3700 of those who stayed in the stricken city, but most of the 40,000 who had fled were flocking back into Philadelphia.

Neither the pathological fever that had racked him nor the more persistent "French fever" could diminish for long Washington's activity on behalf of the Federal City. The city a century hence, he predicted, would become a capital "though not as large as London, yet of a magnitude inferior to few others in Europe." Continuance of public building was assured, at least for a time, by a loan voted by Congress. Although Washington urged that private building parallel public construction, his own enterprise there had been delayed because of demands at Mount Vernon. By September 20 he felt well enough to spend two days in the Federal City for the purpose of settling upon a location for two houses. Washington had calculated that $8000—at the most, $10,000—would cover the aggregate cost, but the appraisal was higher and Washington thought it excessive. He was back in the city for three days in October. After considerable consultation and correspondence, the price was fixed at $11,250, exclusive of painting, glazing and ironwork. The General was pleased that this enterprise, undertaken "more with a view to promote the necessary improvements in the City, than for any expectation of private emolument," was under way. In further accord with his enthusiasm, on October 24 Washington bought five shares "toward building a hotel in the City of Washington."

Washington had been uneasy about McHenry's ability to discharge the mounting duties of the War Department. These apprehensions were sharpened by Hamilton's opinion of McHenry's utter inadequacy. Washington wrote plainly to the Secretary of War. Although "called to the Army in a moment of danger," the General remonstrated, he was now "as ignorant of its foundation, its munitions and everything else relating thereto, as if I had just dropped from the clouds." Call out the Inspector without delay, he entreated. Hamilton went to Philadelphia on November 1, but soon confessed to Washington his conviction that "the administration of the War Department cannot prosper in the present very well disposed but very unqualified hands."

At the end of October McHenry made firm an earlier intimation that the Commander-in-Chief and the Major Generals should gather in Philadelphia by November 10. Knox had declined and the President could not attend, the Secretary wrote October 30, but General Pinckney would remain in the North until after the conference and Hamilton would be there. Washington agreed to be in Philadelphia but advised McHenry that he might not reach there until the eleventh.

On the morning of November 5 General Washington and Colonel Lear drove away from the Potomac. Cavalry escort met the Commander-in-Chief outside Alexandria and military honors awaited him within the city. As it began, so it continued. Alexandria escort gave over to Georgetown soldiery. Nor was Baltimore to be outdone. Washington found the Baltimore Horse ready to join him on a twelve-mile ride into the city. At the Susquehanna he was met by the Harford Horse and escorted to Elkton. On the tenth the General entered Philadelphia. Cavalry and infantry were drawn up along the streets, and on the commons waiting to receive him was the colorful corps of the MacPherson Blues.

Washington had need of both the good health and good spirits that accompanied him. Hours not taken by conferences with McHenry, Hamilton and Pinckney were given to reports of other Department heads or to consultation with them. Besides the difficult business of army organization, there were countless visits and almost daily state entertainment. A few days after Adams returned from Quincy, Commander-in-Chief and President dined together at the residence Washington had occupied as Chief Executive. To this same house, now rebuilt into one of Philadelphia's finest, the General had come during the Constitutional Convention as the guest of Robert Morris. As it chanced, the very day after he dined with the President, Morris was again his host, but at the humblest of tables—for that friend now resided in Debtor's Prison.

With December, members began to arrive for the second session of the Fifth Congress. On the eighth Lieutenant General Washington entered the Hall of the House where the two bodies of Congress were assembled. With him were Major Generals Pinckney and Hamilton and Colonel Lear. They took their seats at the right of Speaker John Laurance's chair. After a bit, President Adams rose to make his Annual Address. The major portion of the speech was devoted to French affairs. In his summary of the crisis Adams mentioned an apparent aversion of the French government to war with the United States, but he declared: "Nothing is discoverable in the conduct of France which ought to change or relax our measures of defence." While he exhorted to defensive arms, he was careful to reassert that the objective was peace, that there would be "no obstacle to the restoration of a friendly intercourse," and that the option for peace rested with the French Directory.

Political reconciliation continued to be Washington's concern, but it was not now his particular responsibility. The Provisional Army was. The work proved tedious; there was much to be done. Sunday the ninth Hamilton and Pinckney worked the whole day with him in an effort to finish by the end of the week. Many hours of the thirteenth, his last full day in Philadelphia, Washington spent in preparation of a report on the business accomplished during his stay. Three letters to the Secretary of War, all in Hamilton's autograph, went forward in first draft, with various inserts and corrections. There was not time, the General explained, to have fair copies made. Questions McHenry had posed were treated in detail. Other matters of military importance were presented in a long communication whose principal subject was that of a proper plan for organization of military forces throughout the country.

The General and Lear set out after dinner on December 14. They stayed the night at Chester and before he retired Washington wrote to McHenry. Again it was a military matter, but a decidedly personal one. Young Custis had been nominated to serve as Cornet in the Troop of Light Dragoons, but to prevent probable disappointment and the natural resentment of youth, the General cautioned McHenry against any mention of his grandson's name until the way was cleared for his acceptance through consultation with his mother and grandmother. The boy would covet such a colorful assignment as that suggested for him under Capt. Lawrence Lewis, Washington knew, but, remembering Martha's anxiety and uneasiness over her own son, consent was by no means to be taken for granted.

On November 19 Washington sat down to dinner at his own table. For six weeks and three days he had given himself to the duties of Commander-in-Chief. If he could not now put aside public business completely, he could enjoy again in part his role as plantation proprietor. About two weeks later Richard Parkinson, an Englishman with whom Washington had corresponded concerning possible tenancy of River Farm and who had recently arrived at Alexandria, braved the December weather and drove out to spend the day. Parkinson spoke often of the beautiful river, but "did not like the land at all." His lack of interest in the tenancy by no means diminished Washington's consideration and courtesy towards him. Impressed with the earnestness of the newcomer, he gave a careful description of the countryside and the important cities in order to help Parkinson choose a location for the small acreage he wished to acquire. The Englishman learned that "Baltimore was and would be the risingest town in America, except the Federal City . . . that Philadelphia would decline, but New York would always maintain an eminent commercial rank. . . ." At length, the visitor declining to stay the night, Washington tactfully sent Lear to inquire whether his departing guest needed money. He did. Such was the friendliness of the busy man, of whom Parkinson later said: "His behavior to me was such that I shall ever revere his name."

Christmas was perhaps less gay at Mount Vernon since Nelly Custis had gone to Hope Park to be with her parents. Washington Custis and Lawrence Lewis also were away. The General spent the early morning at his desk, his thoughts and pen dedicated to Lafayette in a long letter, the first in over a year. Washington explained he had not written sooner because for months he thought Lafayette and George had embarked for America. In relief that such a voyage had not begun, Washington urged Lafayette to postpone it until differences between France and America were settled. Even without actual war, Washington feared Lafayette's return at this time would be misinterpreted by both sides. When "harmony between the nations is again restored," the General wrote, "no one in the United States would receive you . . . with more ardent affection than I should." Within the limitations of a letter, Washington sketched his view of the crisis. If, as Lafayette had stated, the Directory were disposed to peaceful accommodation, "let them accompany it by action for words unaccompanied therewith will not be much regarded now." From distant friends he turned to those close by. The master of Mount Vernon and Martha had gathered with their guests, Judge and Mrs. William Cushing, at the Christmas table when the sound of carriage wheels announced the expected arrival of General Pinckney, his wife and daughter. The holiday dinner was heightened in enjoyment by the addition of this charming company.

As 1799 commenced news from the War Department was disquieting. McHenry, it appeared, was inept when he was not inactive. Washington regretted that the Secretary of War had not reported to Congress the proceedings with Hamilton and Pinckney in full rather than in part. Furthermore, where Executive action was required, could not McHenry obtain it promptly? Many valuable officers and recruits already had been lost by dilatoriness, and others soon would become impatient. Besides these complaints, there was one on a private account the General did not fail to mention, though he was careful to call it "incidental" : When costs of his Philadelphia trip were reckoned, expenditures were found to be in excess of the two months' pay he had drawn. Exclusive of $300 paid for a horse, he had spent $1115.55. But he urged that McHenry not consider this a plea for further pay—he had no wish to incur public criticism and preferred to sustain loss rather than be suspected of mercenary motives. Even the pinch of unpaid bills would be more endurable than wounded pride. Besides, there were other means by which he might obtain money to finance his houses in the Federal City and for other needs. The General hoped to realize £800 from three jacks, descendants of Royal Gift. If John Tayloe declined to purchase these fine animals, then Washington might have to borrow from the bank, "at its ruinous interest."

The General was intensely interested in Pickering's report on French relations, made to Congress on January 21, and even more in the passages concerning Gerry that the President had deleted over the Secretary's protest—Pickering's observations on the "improper" and "inexcusable" conduct of the envoy. Washington lamented that the missing portions had not been retained. He applauded Pickering's realistic view of the crisis and did not wonder that Republican hearers "disrelished" it.

The General might have spared himself worry where his grandson's military appointment was concerned. Martha had no objection, and the permission of his mother, Mrs. David Stuart, soon followed. Possibly they had less fear for him on a field of battle than in the sea of matrimony on which he seemed determined to embark. No doubt it was a happy young gentleman who set out for a visit at Doctor Stuart's January 22. It was an even happier young lady who returned to Mount Vernon just at this time. Eleanor Parke Custis, the adored "Nelly" of the household, was to be married soon to Lawrence Lewis. Even if Washington had discerned a growing attraction between Nelly and his nephew, the culmination of the romance came as a complete surprise, "they having, while I was at Philadelphia, without my having the smallest suspicion that such an affair was in agitation, formed their contract. . . ." Washington drove to Alexandria January 23 to become Nelly's legal guardian, that he might authorize a license for her marriage.

February 11 found the General back in Alexandria for celebration of his sixty-seventh birthday. At eleven o'clock, when the General appeared on the streets, he was escorted by three companies of dragoons. The ceremonial was carefully planned and colorfully executed. Military maneuvers showed marching men at their best. There was a sham battle between defensive land forces and three companies of "enemy" infantry on ships. The General watched intently and approvingly until the "invaders" were forced to surrender. The climax of the occasion came with an elegant ball and supper, and before the revelry was ended toasts had vied with artillery salutations in number and grandeur.

Back at the Potomac plantation on the twelfth, all eyes were centered on the twenty-second, the "new calendar" date usually observed as the General's birthday—this year of special significance because Nelly and Lawrence had chosen it for their wedding. By dinner time that day the Rev. Thomas Davis had arrived in the company of Nelly's kinsman, George Calvert. Then, as the General recorded, "Miss Custis was married abt. Candle light to Mr. Lawe. Lewis."

During the week beginning February 18 Washington had penned scarcely a dozen lines, but communications from Hamilton and McHenry soon called him back to his desk. Many were the reports, but few the explanations, of the unaccountable delay in recruiting. Although he hesitated to ascribe causes, the General did not hesitate to predict that "unless a material change takes place, our military theatre affords but a gloomy prospect to those who are to perform the principal parts in the drama."

This state of affairs was alarming, but news that soon followed was nothing short of astounding: On February 18, when the Senate turned to Executive business, President Adams, without previous hint, nominated William Vans Murray, American Minister resident at The Hague, to be minister plenipotentiary to the French Republic. With this pronouncement Adams transmitted a copy of a communication from Talleyrand to Citizen Louis André Pichon, chargé d'affaires at The Hague, dated September 28, 1798. Pichon had shown the paper to Murray, and Murray had forwarded it to Adams. On its content the President apparently rested his determination to send another mission to France. Washington was surprised, but if France had made plea for peaceful negotiation, he was thankful that the nation's tranquility soon might be restored. When he learned that no overtures had come direct from the French Republic, he was amazed and perplexed at Adams' apparent indiscretion. In Washington's view, it was not enough that the French Minister had communicated his altered sentiments circuitously through Murray. If there was no intrigue, why should there be the methods of intrigue? Washington wondered what influence, if any, a communication he had just sent the President might have had on his sudden decision. He had the answer almost at once in a letter from Adams written the day after his startling statements in the Senate Chamber.

The communication Washington had forwarded was a long letter received on January 31 from Joel Barlow in Paris. Barlow had written urging Washington to use his influence towards a new attempt at negotiation with France. The dispute was simply a misunderstanding, he said; he enumerated reasons for belief in the Directory's peaceful and tractable intent and listed concessions that France was willing to make. If the United States refused these generous overtures, Barlow admonished, "war of the most terrible and vindictive kind will follow." Washington transmitted the letter "without delay and without comment, except to say that it must have been written with a very good or a very bad design. . . ." Adams explained in his reply to Washington that, as he saw it, Talleyrand had met the conditions prescribed in the message to Congress on June 21, 1798. Hence Murray's appointment—though Adams said he would instruct the envoy not to make a move until formal assurances pledged his proper reception and treatment.

The proposed new mission was at once the topic of tongues and pens and presses throughout the country. Stunned Federalists soon became articulate and active against this "degrading and mischievous measure." This appointment—"dishonorable to the United States, and disastrous to prospects of other foreign negotiations"—was altogether Adams' own, Pickering hastened to inform Washington. Then, in an effort to ameliorate both the wound and its after effects, the nomination was referred to a committee of the Senate. When the committee found that the President was fixed in his intention to send an envoy, Adams perceived that they too were fixed in their intention to defeat the proposal. Thereupon, he nominated two additional envoys to serve with Murray—Chief Justice Oliver Ellsworth and Patrick Henry. Senators saw that they must approve the mission; the alteration from a single to a three-member envoy appeased Federalists in the only possible way. At least Adams had named safe men for his unsafe mission. Republicans, meanwhile, kept a cautious quiet. There was satisfaction enough in watching the schism within the Federal party.

From Pickering's letters and the newspapers, Washington was kept well informed politically; but militarily, the bulk of his communications was cause for justifiable complaint. He now had questions and comments he no longer could forbear stating, and on March 25 he set them down in an unflinching manner to McHenry. What, the General wished to know, kept back commissions of officers already appointed; and what continued to arrest recruiting? "Blame is in every mind," he said, "attached by some to the President, by some to the Secretary of War." Still others, "fertile in invention," might censure the Commander-in-Chief. Washington was exasperated that he had been left "in the field of conjecture." Every accusation, every argument against conditions in the War Department, the General repeated and reemphasized. "These, my dear McHenry, are serious considerations to a man who has nothing to gain, and is putting everything to hazard." The most delicate of his criticisms, Washington left for the last. He had come to the unhappy conclusion, he wrote, that predictions of McHenry's complete inability to conduct his Department in event of war were well founded.

Washington feared he might lose a friend, but this was not the first time he had put principle above personality. He need not have worried. McHenry did not take offense at the candor of Washington, but asked, that the General "continue to give me such proofs of your friendship." In return, McHenry had the satisfaction of some reassurance from Washington: He often had stated his belief, the General replied, that circumstances beyond the Secretary's control accounted largely for his conduct, and that all the blame should not be attached to him personally.

Whatever his potential worth in lands, Washington faced this spring the most awkward financial situation of his life. Within the last four years he had sold lands to the amount of $50,000, but all the money received from this source, from crops and rents, Washington admitted, had "scarcely been able to keep me afloat." Out of $15,000 due him a year ago and a like amount payable this June, he had received only $1700. To the embarrassment of insufficient funds, long familiar, was added the painful necessity of borrowing money. For the first time Washington had to negotiate a bank loan. He wrote early in March that his real want of cash had driven him to "a ruinous mode of obtaining money." Reproachfully he explained to George Ball, whose payment of £303 due in April 1798 had not yet come, that he had sold those most valuable Gloucester lands only because he lacked funds and exhorted Ball to forward his overdue instalment; and he warned James Welch that he no longer was to be "trifled with." That deception was a part of Welch's dealings Washington now had no doubt. Earlier Washington had warned Israel Shreve that his judgment bond would be enforced. The knowledge that Shreve had sold part of the property bought from Washington for more than he owed the General was particularly annoying. The best Washington could expect from Henry Lee's obligation was a shipment of corn, for which he would allow a credit of fifteen shillings per barrel.

Non-payment for lands and poor collections on rentals did not completely account for the General's financial embarrassments. Taxes were heavy. Mount Vernon hospitality, still extensive and expensive, continued and the number of mouths to be fed on the plantation grew by natural increase. Furthermore, others close to him had need of money also, and they were not refused. On May 1 Washington made a loan of $1500 to Lear. In answer to his nephew, Samuel Washington, threatened with attachment of his Negroes, he wrote that he would lend $1000, "but not one cent beyond; as that sum will take nearly every farthing I have in the bank and is insufficient to meet demands which, every moment, I expect will be made upon myself." The imminent call was for his houses in the Federal City, on which advances were to be paid the builder at the beginning of the work.

On the morning of April 24 Washington rode to Alexandria. It was election day in Virginia. As he cast his vote for Henry Lee, Congressional candidate from Fairfax, Washington wished success also for John Marshall, Congressional candidate from the Richmond district. A few days later, he learned with "infinite pleasure" of Marshall's victory, though the margin of votes was less than Washington had hoped. Lee also had been elected, by an even smaller majority.

The end of May found the General in the Federal City for two days. His houses were under construction at last, and he wished to make inspection. Soon after his return to Mount Vernon, rumors of Patrick Henry's death that had persisted for several weeks were displaced by the fact that he had passed away June 6. "I sincerely lament his death as a friend," Washington wrote Marshall, "and the loss of his eminent talents as a patriot I consider as peculiarly unfortunate at this critical juncture of our affairs."

The General was puzzled at the delay in his old friend Jonathan Trumbull's letter, dated June 22 but received at Mount Vernon July 20. He was not aware that it had been sent to Oliver Wolcott first, with a suggestion that the Secretary of the Treasury pass it to Pickering and any others to whom the subject properly might be disclosed. Evidently, the communication was pondered leisurely before Wolcott sent it on to Mount Vernon. Washington had not come forward in a statement to George Cabot, if indeed he knew the Senator had expressed the belief that he "would doubtless yield to the necessity" of a third term rather than submit to election of a "French President," but now to like proposals by Governor Trumbull and his brother John he answered: "Prudence on my part must arrest any attempt at the well meant, but mistaken views of my friends, to introduce me again to the chair of government." He would serve in defence of his country, "which every citizen is bound to do," but nothing, Washington knew, ever could persuade him to reenter civil service.

"It would be a matter of sore regret to me," Washington said, "if I could believe that a serious thought was turned towards me as [Adams'] successor." In realistic fashion he explained: "For although I have abundant cause to be thankful for the good health with which I am blessed, yet I am not insensible to my declination in other respects. It would be criminal therefore in me, although it should be the wish of my countrymen, and I could be elected, to accept an office under this conviction. . . ." He urged, let there be "no eye, no tongue, no thought" turned towards him for this purpose. "A mind that has been constantly on the stretch since the year 1753, with but short intervals and little relaxation," he concluded, "requires rest and composure. . . ."

For a time the General feared an indisposition might prevent a ride to Georgetown on August 5 for an important meeting of the Potomac Company stockholders, but recovery was quick and he rode over from Mount Vernon. Washington did not feel altogether secure about the Company's future because of half-hearted support, but he hoped the business could be "rescued from its present sloth." So convinced was he that to complete the navigational project would be to establish "one of, if not the most productive funds . . ." of any business in the country, that he told Charles Carroll: "If I had the means and was anxious to provide for those who may step into my shoes when I go hence, I would not hesitate a moment to complete the work at my own expence, receiving proportionate tolls." There was time also for a view of his Federal City houses, and he went prepared to pay the builder another $1000. The sooner the houses were ready, the sooner Washington could enjoy return on his investment.

Information that France finally had met with effective resistance in Europe and that her internal situation was not easy augured well for America—at least the Commander-in-Chief had thought so for a while. Now he feared that the Directory's knowledge of the new mission might cost the United States the advantage. "I wish this nomination and appointment may not be productive of embarrassment in the measures of this Government," he said. He knew the choice was one between difficulties. To pursue the plan for negotiation was to invite unpredictable consequences; to withdraw from it would be to "arm the opposition with fresh weapons" for renewed attack on the administration.

Civil government long had been the object of Republican attack, and now it appeared that the military was to share the invectives of the press. Washington certainly had no wish for active campaigning at the head of the Army, but most certainly he wished there might be an effective force and one worthy of the name. The staffing and recruiting had shown little perceptible progress, though Hamilton continued his exertions to establish a fine provisional force. He wrote often to Mount Vernon and, Washington knew, his letters of instruction and inquiry to McHenry were almost continuous.

While Washington read with regret of yellow fever again in Philadelphia, he watched a severe drought parch the Potomac cornfields and ruin the oats. More direct distress came to the Mansion House towards the end of August. Martha was taken with an ague and fever, though she kept on her feet for a time. At midnight on September 5 she became very ill, and Washington summoned Doctor Craik, who arrived with the early morning. After a second visit from the Doctor, the patient showed slight improvement. To add to his harassment, Washington's farm manager also was indisposed and it looked as if he could not perform his duties properly without jeopardy to his health. Washington must devise a way by which he could simplify his manager's business without complicating his own. When his anxiety for Martha was lessened somewhat, he wrote Anderson the result of his deliberations: Perhaps the manager would like to confine his efforts to the mill and distillery which Washington would rent him on such terms as Anderson thought fair and operate them for his own benefit, while Washington would plan to take over the management of the plantation as soon as it could be reduced in scale. There should be no difficulty in leasing the fishery at the ferry. Then, if a further idea for the disposal of one of his farms matured, the compass of Mount Vernon affairs would be narrowed sufficiently "to make the superintendence of them a mere matter of amusement."

In references that were casual and quite matter-of-fact, Washington had by 1799 come to speak frequently of the limited days that remained to him. This was not due to apprehension of imminent death, but simply to his awareness that he was not far from the Biblical "three score and ten." His "greatest anxiety" was to leave all his own affairs and those of others for which he was responsible "in such a clear and distinct form . . . that no reproach may attach itself to me when I have taken my departure for the land of spirits."

Washington had thought seriously about his will during the months after Nelly's wedding. Before the document could be written many decisions had to be made. What he wished to administer and perpetuate was more than mere investment in lands and houses, servants and time, crops and horses and equipment; it was investment in a way of living. Much of the owner and his forebears was represented in the worldly wealth Washington now contemplated as a whole. His deepest interest and his untiring energy had gone into its acquisition; his best efforts had been devoted to its care. He must use his wisest judgment in its disposition; something of himself would be a part of each bequest. What he had acquired with ambition and protected with zeal, he would distribute with infinite care.

Ready at last, he wrote on July 9: "In the name of God amen, I George Washington of Mount Vernon—a citizen of the United States,—and lately President of the same, do make, ordain and declare this Instrument . . . to be my last Will & Testament, revoking all others."

A brief paragraph directed that all his debts be "punctually and speedily paid" and then—the first Item: "To my dearly beloved wife Martha Washington I give and Bequeath the use, profit, and benefit of my whole Estate, real and personal, for the term of her natural life, except such parts thereof as are specifically disposed of hereafter. . . ." His improved lot in Alexandria, the household furnishings and supplies of every sort he would leave to her in fee simple. For the rest of his possessions, when their usefulness for her would have ended in her death, he must make specific bequests.

Before further treatment of material things, his desire concerning the Negroes must be made clear. Had there been a practicable way by which he could dispossess himself of slaves, he would have done so long ago, but he was "principled against selling Negroes, as you would cattle in the market." It would give him the greatest satisfaction now if he could with a sweep of his pen order their freedom at the time of his death, but this he could not do. Dower Negroes had married with other dower slaves in some instances, more often with other Negroes on the estate or in the neighborhood. Unless all were freed together, an insuperable problem would result. But if he offered them freedom upon Martha's demise, then all could be manumitted at the same time. This he would do. His body servant, William, was the single exception; Washington would grant him immediate freedom if he wished it. The choice would be Billy's but in either event, he should receive an annuity of thirty dollars, "as a testimony of my sense of his attachment to me and for his faithful services during the Revolution."

His thoughts next turned to education. He assigned twenty shares of his stock in the Bank of Alexandria, in trust, to the free school for poor and orphan children attached to the Alexandria Academy. Still intent upon a national university, the General designated his shares of Potomac Company stock for that purpose. With confirmation of his earlier gift of shares in the James River Company to Liberty Hall Academy, he turned from public to personal bequests.

At last, Washington must have thought, he could clear up the estate of his brother Samuel which had given him so much concern. He would release it of all money owing him and at the same time acquit the heirs of Samuel's deceased son, Thornton, and two other sons, George Steptoe and Lawrence Augustine, from repayment of funds advanced for their schooling. Likewise, he would erase the balance due from the estate of Martha's brother, Bartholomew Dandridge. Charles Carter, husband of Washington's niece, Betty Lewis, had purchased Fredericksburg lots from him; if the titles were not secured at the time of his death, the General wished them to be made so without further payment. A nephew, William Augustine Washington, should have the claim to certain property in and near Richmond, as well as a parcel of land in Prince George County, Virginia. All the papers in his possession relating to his civil and military administrations, as well as those of a private nature, the General would leave to Bushrod Washington. His library should be given this nephew on Martha's demise.

Any money collected from the lands he had sold, leased, or conditionally sold was to be invested in bank stock; the dividends from this and other stock to be paid Martha during her lifetime. The gold-headed crabtree cane left him by Benjamin Franklin—what better hands could hold it than those of his one surviving brother, Charles? Lawrence and Robert Washington, of Chotank, Washington wished to be remembered with his two other gold-headed canes, and each of them should have one of the spyglasses he had used in the Revolution. "To my compatriot in arms, and old and intimate friend"—the devoted Doctor Craik—should go his bureau or tambour secretary and the circular chair now in his study. For Doctor Stuart, warm friend and member of the family by marriage, there should be the large shaving and dressing table and his fine telescope. His Bible in three large folio volumes, with notes—who but the Reverend Fairfax, more recently Bryan, Lord Fairfax, should receive it? That pair of "finely wrought steel pistols" taken from the British in the Revolutionary War— they should be fitting and pleasing to General Lafayette. There should be mourning rings, valued at one hundred dollars each, for two sisters-in-law, Hannah Washington and Mildred Washington; for Eleanor Stuart, Hannah Washington of Fairfield, and Elisabeth Washington. "These bequests," wrote the General, "are not made for the intrinsic value of them, but as mementos of my esteem & regard."

Next on the list was Lear. There had been no one who enjoyed a comparable position both in Washington's business life and his affection. From the hour he took up his duties, Lear had discharged them with taste, discernment and precision, after the very heart of his employer. Lear had shared the confidences and concerns of the General. How best reward this friend? When all the possibilities were weighed, Washington wrote: "To Tobias Lear, I give the use of the Farm which he now holds, in virtue of a Lease from me to him and his deceased wife (for and during their natural lives) free from Rent, during his life. . . ."

Five of his nephews should choose five of his swords, with the injunction "not to unsheath them for the purpose of shedding blood except it be for self-defence, or in defence of their country and its rights, and in the latter case to keep them unsheathed, and prefer falling with them in their hands, to the relinquishment thereof."

Washington now came face-to-face with distribution of the "more important parts" of his estate. The greatest gift he could bestow was Mount Vernon. More than a gift, it was a trust—one that should be committed to a Washington. The General had watched with uncommon interest and mounting approval the development of his nephew, Bushrod. In him Washington had an apt pupil. So it was that the future of Mount Vernon was decided, and as he copied from his notes, these words in Washington's bold script fell across the page: "To my Nephew Bushrod Washington and his heirs (partly in consideration of an intimation to his deceased father while we were Bachelors, & he had kindly undertaken to superintend my Estate during my Military Services in the former War between Great Britain & France, that if I should fall therein, Mount Vernon (then less extensive in domain than at present) should become his property) I give and bequeath all that part thereof which is comprehended within the following limits. . . ."

What of his grand-nephews, George Fayette and Charles Augustine Washington? These sons of Martha's niece Fanny Bassett Washington and his nephew George Augustine, both deceased, were doubly close by their double kinship. Should not these kinsmen inherit the land on Dogue Neck he had planned in earlier years to give their father? The two thousand acres and more which would be theirs in time should embrace also the farm now occupied by their stepfather, Tobias Lear.

Next, his children—his and Martha's—for her grandchildren had been for years in every sense like their very own, "more especially . . . the two whom we have reared from their earliest infancy." The tie with Nelly had been strengthened still more by her marriage to his sister's son:— "Wherefore," wrote the General, "I give and bequeath to the said Lawrence Lewis and Eleanor Parke Lewis, his wife, and their heirs, the residue of my Mount Vernon Estate, not already devised . . . together with the Mill, Distillery, and other houses and improvements on the premises, making together about two thousand Acres. . . ." As for his grandson, a large tract overlooking Alexandria already belonged to him through his father's inheritance. Through his mother's dower right, George Washington Parke Custis would also come into full possession of adjoining property, where she and his stepfather now lived. In view of this, Washington set aside his contiguous estate on Four Mile Run—approximately twelve hundred acres—for this only male heir in the family. Custis would receive also Square 21 in the Federal City.

Washington then instructed his executors to sell "all the rest and residue of the Estate," the money thus realized to be divided into twenty-three equal parts. The four children of his half-brother Augustine each should receive one share, as should the five children of his sister, Betty Lewis; three parts should go to the surviving children of his brother Samuel—one share for each—and a fourth share should be divided among the heirs of a deceased son. One part was assigned to Bushrod's brother Corbin and one to the heirs of their sister Jane. Similarly, he remembered the three children of his brother Charles. He designated that one share should be divided among George Augustine's three children. A full part each should go to Eliza Law, Martha Peter and Nelly Lewis. Finally, one part should be divided among his nephews, Bushrod Washington and Lawrence Lewis, and Martha's grandson, Washington Custis.

A word of advice and a caution not to act hastily in disposition of the landed property now seemed in order—and a request about the family vault. Then he wrote: "Lastly, I constitute and appoint my dearly beloved wife Martha Washington, My Nephews William Augustine Washington, Bushrod Washington, George Steptoe Washington, Samuel Washington, & Lawrence Lewis, & my ward George Washington Parke Custis (when he shall have arrived at the age of twenty years) Executrix & Executors of this Will & testament,—"

CHAPTER / 25

As the summer of 1799 ended and Washington pondered the realities of a complex plantation and the changes he should make towards its simplification, he was much alone at his work and in his thoughts. Martha's illness denied him her cheerful company; the reliable Lear had gone "to try the air of the mountains"; the light-hearted, lovable Nelly and her Lawrence had not yet returned from a trip to the mineral springs; and manager Anderson still was ailing. Although his need for cash continued, no spark of response from his debtors was visible. Both time and forage were exacted of him by military "applicants, recommenders of applicants and seekers of information," who, with their servants and horses, made pilgrimages to Mount Vernon. But even in these circumstances, Washington declined McHenry's offer of two months' military pay. Sorrow was added to Washington's anxiety and irksome duties when, on September 20, he received news of the death of Charles Washington, his younger brother. "I was the *first*, and am now the *last*, of my father's children by the second marriage who remain," the General observed, and added, "when I shall be called upon to follow them, is known only to the giver of life."

About this time Washington wrote Lawrence Lewis a letter he had been contemplating for some weeks. If the General's proposal was well received, a step towards reduction of the lands immediately under his care would be accomplished to his own satisfaction and, he hoped, to his nephew's delight. Washington explained and described to Lawrence the lands he had bequeathed jointly to him and Nelly in his will, with the suggestion that they might choose a site for their house and commence building at pleasure. Until it was ready Mount Vernon would continue to be their home. Washington then offered the mill and distillery, which James Anderson apparently had declined, in addition to the farm on Dogue Run, at "a just and equitable rent," and the hire of the hands there also; "it being necessary," the General observed, "that a young man should have objects of employment." He sealed and sent the letter to Alexandria, but somehow it missed the mail and was returned to Mount Vernon. Anderson, meanwhile, had advised the General of his decision to rent the distillery and mill after all and to relinquish his position as manager at the end of the year. Washington explained this to Lawrence in a letter of September 28, which he attached to the earlier communication. He did not wish to hurt the feelings of the "obliging and zealous" manager by dismissing him, but if Anderson engaged in the business of milling and distilling, his withdrawal as manager would be his own act and Washington's wishes thus would be served without embarrassment.

Washington did not wait for Lawrence's answer. In expectation of the young couple's early return to Mount Vernon, and in belief that the plan would be agreeable to Lawrence, the General made firm his earlier offer to Anderson for rental of the mill and distillery, but he made clear that when Lewis returned he wished to work the mill and the distillery. With Anderson's acquiescence, that became the accepted arrangement.

There were fewer visitors at Mount Vernon for a while. Late in September Gov. William R. Davie, who had replaced Henry for the mission to France, called on Washington. Towards the end of October British Minister Liston and his lady came for three days. By this time Martha was regaining her strength, Lawrence and Nelly were settled again in the mansion, and Lear had returned. The complexion of plantation life took on a brighter hue.

The same could not be said for the aspect of national affairs. When Washington heard of the President's order for the immediate embarkation of Judge Ellsworth and Governor Davie, he hoped the measure had been "considered in all its relations," but Hamilton had little reassurance and Pickering none. Without prior word to anyone Adams on October 10 ordered the mission to proceed. Although his department heads were available, he neither asked their counsel nor heeded the advice they volunteered. Washington, in a private letter of October 27, expressed misgivings at the President's "late decision" and commented to Hamilton: "I was surprised at the *measure,* how much more so at the manner of it? This business seems to have commenced in an evil hour, and under unfavorable auspices; and I wish mischief may not tread in all its steps, and be the final result of the measure." But Washington was not without that faith he had voiced in other and darker days. His closing words to Hamilton were: ". . . I have the same reliance on Providence which you express, and trust that matters will end well, however unfavorable they may appear at present."

Correspondence in recent months made it desirable for Washington to resurvey his property on Difficult Run and check a small tract close by. A visit to the Federal City was made on November 9, and there he inspected his buildings. He was pleased that the houses were ready for occupancy and hoped to find reliable tenants. The General figured that an income of $7\frac{1}{2}$ per cent on his investment would be a fair return and on this basis computed the rent at $1200 annually.

For a time after his return on November 10 master of Mount Vernon had preponderance over General of the Army. Although the question of winter quarters for the troops required his attention, much of the correspondence could be handled by Lear, who was thoroughly familiar with the problem and with the possibilities of hutting at and in the vicinity of Harpers Ferry. Moreover, Lear could answer appeals for the Commander-in-Chief in matters of minor military rank by referring them to General Pinckney for decision. When he learned of Bryan Fairfax's return from England, Washington went promptly to Mount Eagle with warm greetings for his old friend. Sunday the seventeenth he was in his pew at Christ Church and afterward dined at the Alexandria residence of William Fitzhugh. By the time he was well on his way homeward, evening had over-taken him and his companions, Lawrence Lewis, young Custis and a neighbor. The General was astride a new Narragansett horse and the riders were proceeding at a pleasant gait when Washington drew rein and dismounted to look more closely at fields or fences. As he stepped into the stirrup again the horse lurched forward and the General fell heavily to the ground. Almost before his startled companions could alight, he was on his feet with assurances that he was unhurt, but in the confusion the frightened horses sped away. The deserted riders continued their journey on foot. They had gone only a short distance when the horses came in sight, subdued by some neighborhood servants, and the travelers soon were remounted for the few miles that would bring them to Mount Vernon.

If he followed his usual pattern, the General had attended to his correspondence early on that Sunday morning. It consisted of a single letter to James McHenry, but by no means was it comparable in length to the one he had just received from the Secretary of War—"with the contents of which I have been stricken dumb," the General confessed. McHenry's communication was so laden with disturbing confidences that all the anxious and painful fears of recent months seemed close to realization. He had begun by transferring the rumor of a serious rift between President and Cabinet from the realm of the conjectural to that of the positive. The rupture had become irreparable with the recent mission to France, when, in deciding the measure, Adams had ignored his Secretaries. "The President believes, and with reason," McHenry wrote, "that three of the heads of departments have viewed the mission as impolitic and unwise . . . I find that he is particularly displeased with Mr. Pickering and Mr. Wolcott, thinking they have encouraged opposition to it to the eastward; seemingly a little less so with me. . . ." Whether the President would find it expedient to dismiss any of the Cabinet, McHenry could not predict, but he observed: "The evil does not lie in a change of secretaries . . . but in the mission which . . . is become an apple of discord to the Federalists, that may so operate upon the ensuing election of President, as to put in jeopardy the fruits of all their past labors, by consigning to men devoted to French innovations and demoralizing principles, the reins of government. It is this dreaded consequence which afflicts and calls for all the wisdom of the Federalists."

There was much more that augured ill for the United States and for Federalism: Pennsylvania's election of a Republican governor; attack by enemies of the administration on the renewal of trade with San Domingo; the continued charge of British influence; the unfortunate effects on the public mind produced by the schisms between President and Cabinet and among Federalists generally. All in all, it could not have been a gloomier presentation. "I see rocks and quicksands on all sides," the Secretary concluded, "and the administration in the attitude of a sinking ship. It will . . . depend very much upon the President, whether she is to weather the storm or go down." To McHenry's appeal for counsel, Washington answered resolutely: ". . . I believe it is better that I should remain mute than express any sentiment on the important matters which are related.

. . ." Then, with a rally of his philosophic resources, he added: "The vessel is afloat, or very nearly so, and considering myself as a passenger only, I shall trust to the mariners whose duty it is to watch, to steer it into a safe port."

On the afternoon of November 22 the sound of carriage wheels called Washington to welcome Col. and Mrs. Edward Carrington, who had come from Richmond. Presently, they were joined in the parlor by Martha and five "pleasant and agreeable" younger women. Nelly was among them, though she was expecting a child soon, and a midwife had been established in the household for the event. Perceiving this, the thoughtful Colonel and his lady, over Washington's protest, departed the next morning to spend several days with friends in and near the Federal City. Doctor Craik, who now paid his visits with more than usual frequency, was summoned early on the morning of the twenty-seventh, and before noon Nelly was delivered of a daughter. The following day the Carringtons returned to finish out their visit. Washington's attachment for the Colonel was more than ever manifest during the few days they were together. The two had shared many memorable experiences and with Carrington Washington felt free in conversation. Eliza Carrington was impressed with those hours of the day enjoyed under Martha's sole hospitality. After breakfast on the thirtieth, good-byes were said and the Carrington carriage headed for Richmond. The last days of November had been just such ones as Washington might wish to be the pattern for his years of retirement.

After breakfast on December 9 the General stood at the front steps to wish Lawrence Lewis and Washington Custis a pleasant journey as they set out for New Kent. That same morning he said good-bye also to Lawrence's brother Howell and his wife, who had been at Mount Vernon for ten days. "It was a bright frosty morning," one of the nephews later recounted; "he had taken his usual ride and the clear healthy flush on his cheek and his sprightly manner, brought the remark from both of us that we had never seen the General look so well. I have sometimes thought him decidedly the handsomest man I ever saw; and when in lively mood, so full of pleasantry, so agreeable to all with whom he associated, that I could hardly realize that he was the same Washington whose dignity awed all who approached him."

The master of Mount Vernon did not find it convenient to attend the meeting of the Potomac Company in Alexandria on the tenth. That day he put into final form a plan for cropping and managing the Mount Vernon estate, to be followed for the year 1800 and several years thereafter. By a fixed procedure he hoped to maintain the optimum in quality of land and quantity of production and through an established system to achieve in time the best possible economy of labor. Specific directions for operating the plan, field by field, were set down for each of the farms remaining in his own hands—River, Union and Muddy Hole.

Early in the morning of December 12 the General wrote Hamilton on the subject of a military academy. Hamilton had proposed a plan for establishment of such an institution in a letter to McHenry and had forwarded a copy to Washington for his criticism, but the Commander-in-

Chief declined to counsel. Whereas he always had been impressed with the importance of a training school for soldiers, Washington explained, and during his Presidency repeatedly had called it to the attention of the legislators and recommended it to the people in his public speeches, he never had gone into the details of organization. Rather he chose to leave this task to others, "whose pursuits in the paths of science . . . better qualified them for the execution of it." With the interest and help of the Secretary of War, he hoped the measure soon would be approved. By ten o'clock, the master of Mount Vernon was in the saddle and off for his ride around the plantation.

The General had not long been out when a change in the weather brought snow, then sleet, then settled for a while into cold, steady rain that turned again to snow before the ride was ended. By the time he reached the Mansion House at the end of his circuit he had been in the open for more than five hours. As soon as he came in Lear brought some letters to be franked. Washington took them, but remarked that the weather was too severe to send a servant to the Post Office that evening. Lear saw that snow still clung to the General's hair and that his neck was wet, but Washington assured the secretary his greatcoat had kept him dry. He then went directly in to dinner, which had been kept waiting for him and, contrary to his usual custom, did not change his clothes beforehand. "In the evening," Lear later recorded, "he appeared as well as usual."

The cold northeast wind persisted, but during the night it began to bring only snow and on the thirteenth Washington looked out onto white-covered fields. He went to his desk, wrote a brief note to Anderson to accompany his copy for the over-all farm plan and to admonish his manager about the condition of the cattle pens. Had his throat not been sore, he probably would have defied the weather in favor of his usual ride, but the combination of circumstances induced him to stay indoors for the better part of the day. In the early afternoon the snow ceased and by four o'clock "it became perfectly clear." There remained almost an hour before sunset, and Washington saw no reason why he should not go out on the front lawn and mark certain trees he wished removed.

After the evening meal, Martha sat in the parlor with the General and Lear. In spite of a hoarseness that had developed with his cold and noticeably worsened, Washington read aloud from recently arrived gazettes various items of interest or amusement, as often he did. Presently Martha withdrew from the cheerful conversation to visit with Nelly. After she went upstairs Washington asked his secretary to read to him the debates in the Virginia General Assembly on the selection of a governor and a Senator. When the two said good night, Lear suggested that his chief take something for his cold, but Washington reminded his companion that he never took anything for a cold but preferred to "let it go as it came." The General, as did Lear, probably attributed the disorder to his exposure the day before. Certainly his health and spirits seemed at their best otherwise.

At that darkest of hours, long before the dawn of a mid-December day, Washington suffered a severe ague. Sometime between two and three o'clock he woke Martha and told her he was ill. He breathed with difficulty and scarcely could speak. Her impulse was to go at once for a servant, but fearful lest she contract another of her dangerous colds, the General would not allow her to get up in the chilled room. With the sunrise, which was after seven o'clock, the housemaid Caroline came to make the morning fire. Martha directed her at once to call Lear and, at Washington's request, a summons also was sent to overseer Rawlins at Union Farm to come and bleed him, since it would be some time before the doctor could arrive.

Lear dressed quickly and hurried to the bedchamber. Martha was up and told him of the General's seizure. His breathing still was labored and his words almost unintelligible. Lear dispatched his own servant in all haste with a note for Doctor Craik. This done, he returned to the bedside and saw there was no change. Washington tried to take some of a mixture of molasses, vinegar and butter that was offered him in the hope it might relieve his throat, but he could not swallow it. Each effort to do so brought on a spasm and it seemed almost as if he would suffocate.

Soon after daybreak Rawlins arrived, and as the overseer tremulously began his unhappy task, Washington said, "Don't be afraid." When the incision was made, the General observed, "The orifice is not large enough," though the blood flowed rather freely. Martha feared the procedure might be harmful rather than helpful, and at her earnest request Lear moved to stop the bleeding, but Washington gestured otherwise and as soon as he could speak said "More." Shortly, out of respect to Martha's continuing concern, the measure was stopped after about half a pint was taken. Still there was no change. Lear then, gently as he could, applied sal volatile externally to the throat. As his fingers touched the affected area, Washington remarked, " 'Tis very sore." A soft cloth soaked in the solution then was wrapped around his neck, and his feet were bathed in warm water. It was past eight o'clock and still there was no change.

About this time Washington said he would like to get up. His clothes were brought and he was dressed, probably by his body servant Christopher, who had come in the early morning to wait on his master and remained to attend him throughout the day and evening. Washington was helped to a chair by the fire, where he sat for almost two hours, without relief. Martha, meanwhile, remembering Doctor Craik's suggestion that in event of serious illness at Mount Vernon, Dr. Gustavus Richard Brown of Port Tobacco should be called, asked Lear to send for him. The groom Cyrus was dispatched at once on the urgent mission. It was about nine o'clock. Shortly afterward, Doctor Craik alighted at the door and hurried to his friend's bedside. As soon as he ascertained the nature of the affliction, which he diagnosed as "inflammatory quinsy," the Doctor put a blister of cantharides on the throat in the hope of drawing the inflammation to the surface. A second bleeding then was done. Washington was able to inhale from a steaming kettle of vinegar and water, but could not gargle. When he leaned back to let a mixture of sage tea and vinegar run down his throat, he again almost suffocated. There was an involuntary effort to cough, in which Doctor Craik encouraged him, but Washington could do no more than make the attempt. Still there was no change.

Doctor Craik became increasingly anxious for a consultant. Doctor

Brown, he feared, might not arrive in time, and he requested that Dr. Elisha Cullen Dick be summoned. It was close to eleven o'clock when a messenger mounted and made off towards Alexandria. The lone physician turned again to the patient. A third bleeding was done. Still Doctor Craik saw sorrowfully there was no change. Near three o'clock Doctor Dick arrived. After he examined Washington and conferred briefly with Doctor Craik, the General again was bled. The blood came reluctantly, but the patient did not grow faint. About this time, Doctor Brown was shown into the sickroom. He stood at the bedside and felt the feeble pulse, then he and his colleagues withdrew. In a little while Doctor Craik returned and upon observing that Washington could swallow a little, prescribed a dose of calomel and tartar emetic. Still there was no change for the better.

In great distress from embarrassed respiration, Washington was exceedingly restless and repeatedly sought to change his position in bed during the long afternoon. Each time the watchful Lear would lie beside him, raise the weakened body and turn it with all the quiet strength he could muster. The General occasionally asked what time it was, and when he realized that Christopher had been standing all the while, Washington motioned him to sit down. About four-thirty he asked that Martha be called to his bedside. She came and at his request went downstairs and brought from his desk the two wills he said she would find there and handed them to him. Washington gave her one and asked her to burn it; this done, she went out with the other and placed it in her closet.

Lear then came back to the General's side and took his hand. Washington said: "I find I am going, my breath cannot continue long; I believed from the first attack it would be fatal; do you arrange and record all my late military letters and papers—arrange my accounts and settle my books, as you know more about them than anyone else, and let Mr. Rawlins finish recording my other letters which he has begun." He again was helped to his chair in the late afternoon, but in half an hour asked to be put back to bed. Doctors Dick and Brown then joined Doctor Craik for another look at their patient. Doctor Craik asked if he could sit up in bed, and Washington held out his hand to Lear. When he was raised from the pillows he addressed the doctors in a low, strained voice: "I feel myself going. I thank you for your attention. You had better not take any more trouble about me; but let me go off quietly; I cannot last long."

Lear laid him gently down and the consultants left the room. Craik could not speak. He pressed Washington's hand. Then, helpless in the shadow of approaching death, heartsick that there was no measure known to medical skill that now could stay the life that was ebbing, the physician friend sat by the fire "absorbed in grief." Yet unreconciled to final retreat, the doctors rallied once more and about eight o'clock blisters were produced on the legs and feet, and soft poultices of wheat bran applied to the throat. Nothing changed, except that the breathing seemed less difficult. Washington still was restless and, with Lear's help, moved his position constantly in an effort to get relief, though neither sigh nor word of complaint came from his lips. About the time the clock struck ten, Lear saw that the General wished to speak and leaned close in an effort to catch what the broken voice was trying to say. At length the words came: "I am just going. Have me decently buried, and do not let my body be put into a vault in less than two days after I am dead." Lear nodded, unable to speak, but Washington looked at him directly and said, "Do you understand me?" Lear answered, "Yes, sir." Washington spoke once more: " 'Tis well."

Martha kept vigil near the foot of the bed. Doctor Craik had returned to his chair by the fire. Christopher stood nearby and several other servants were gathered at the door. A little after ten, the General's breathing became much easier and he lay quietly. Lear still held his hand. Then unexpectedly Washington withdrew it to feel his own pulse. There was a change in his countenance. On the instant, Lear spoke to Doctor Craik, who stepped to the bedside. In a moment Washington's fingers slipped away from his wrist, Lear took the hand and again clasped it to his breast. Doctor Craik laid his hand gently over Washington's eyes. There was not "a struggle or a sigh." Almost as if he realized that everything now was in readiness for his last command, George Washington withdrew in the presence of Death.

Not a word was spoken until out of the stillness came Martha's voice, firm and calm. "Is he gone?" she asked. Lear choked and silent, gestured that it was so. " 'Tis well," she said simply, echoing Washington's last words, perhaps unconsciously. "All is now over," she added. "I have no more trials to pass through. I shall soon follow him." Martha's fortitude reflected that of the General. The quietness with which he had borne his pain through the long day and she her sorrow made them the more poignant for those who merely watched and worked.

Lear kissed the cold hand he still held and laid it down. He walked over to the fire and stood there "lost in grief." For him had come that moment when a dreadful reality is not yet real—acknowledged by the mind, but not yet accepted by the senses. Presently Christopher brought him the keys and other articles that were in Washington's pockets, as Martha directed him to do. Lear, thus gratefully recalled to duty, wrapped them in the General's handkerchief and went downstairs. Near midnight the General's body was brought down to the drawing room and placed in front of the chimney-piece.

Early on the fifteenth Martha asked Lear to have a coffin made in Alexandria. Accordingly, Doctor Dick took the necessary body measurements. Lear noted them as follows: "In length 6 ft. 3½ inches exact. Across the shoulders 1— 9—. Across the elbows 2— 1—." Lear conferred with Doctor Craik as to the proper fee for his consultants, and before their departure gave them each forty dollars. The faithful secretary then took up the sad and difficult task of preparing and dispatching letters about the General's death. That evening Lear discussed the date for the burial with Doctor Craik, Thomas Peter, Thomas Law and Doctor Thornton. The physicians advised against waiting until the end of the week, as Lear suggested, so that distant relatives might gather. The time was set for Wednesday the eighteenth, with the understanding that in event of extreme weather that day the service would be held on Thursday. Lear sent notice of the plans to various friends and neighbors whom Martha wished advised and wrote to ask the Rev. Thomas Davis to read the service. Washington had made the "express desire" in his will that his interment be "in a private manner, without parade or funeral oration," but it soon became clear that his wishes in this respect could not be carried out precisely.

On Monday the family vault was opened and cleaned. It was not to be sealed with brick after the funeral as formerly. Instead, Martha requested that a door be made, convinced "that it will soon be necessary to open it again." Washington had specified in his will that the old vault, "requiring repairs, and being improperly situated besides," be replaced by a larger one of brick, to be "built at the foot of what is commonly called the Vineyard Inclosure." Just five days before his death, the General had pointed out the spot for the new vault to one of his nephews as they walked about the grounds and talked of various improvements the proprietor had planned. "First of all, I shall make this change," Washington had remarked, and added, "for after all, I may require it before the rest."

Mourning clothes must be made for the family, the overseers and the house servants. When word came that the Freemasons and the military would attend the funeral in a body, Lear began to arrange for the hospitality that would be expected. Forty pounds of cake, which would be served with a simple punch or a beverage from the Mount Vernon wine cellar, were ordered. Anderson went to Alexandria to procure a number of items, and the many preparations occupied many hands, all under Lear's direction.

On the morning of December 17 the Adjutant from the Alexandria Regiment arrived to look at the ground over which the procession would pass. Early that afternoon a stagecoach drew rein at the door of the Mansion House. The mahogany coffin and the bier were carried from the coach to the room where the body lay. The head of the casket was adorned with the inscription, *Surge Ad Judicium;* about halfway down were the words *Gloria Deo,* and on a silver plate was inscribed: "General/ George Washington/ Departed this life on the 14th of December/ 1799, Aet. 68." The case provided for the coffin was lined and covered with black cloth. Before the shrouded figure was placed against the folds of lace in the dark casket, Lear cut a lock of the General's hair as a keepsake for Martha.

December 18 dawned fair, but when it became known that many of the military who were proceeding from Alexandria on foot could not arrive by twelve o'clock, the ceremony was postponed until afternoon. Persons from many miles around had begun to assemble by eleven that morning, and there on the lofty portico where the casket had been placed early that day, the General's last visitors filed by for a last look at the familiar face.

About three o'clock, from Robert Hamilton's schooner anchored close by in the Potomac, minute guns began their firing. At the same time the solemn procession began to move to the music of a dirge and muffled drums. At the head was the cavalry. The infantry followed, and the guard, all with arms reversed. Next came the band and after them the clergy. The General's horse, accoutered with his saddle, holsters and pistols, was led by the two postilions, Cyrus and Wilson. Col. Thomas Blackburn walked alone just ahead of the bier, which was borne by four lieutenants of the Virginia militia. The six honorary pallbearers marched alongside, three to the left, three to the right. They were Cols. Charles Little, Charles Sims, William Payne, George Gilpin, Dennis Ramsay and Philip Marsteller. Close behind came the principal mourners: Eliza Law and her mother, Mrs. David Stuart; Nancy and Sally Stuart; Miss Fairfax and Miss Dennison; Thomas Law and Thomas Peter; James Craik and Tobias Lear; Bryan, Lord Fairfax, and his son Ferdinando. A large representation from the Masonic Order followed; next came the Mayor and Corporation of Alexandria; Washington's farm manager James Anderson, and his clerk Albin Rawlins, walked just ahead of the overseers. All the other persons fell in to complete the long procession.

The cavalry took their places near the tomb and foot soldiers formed a line through which the rest of the procession passed. The bier was placed at the opening of the sepulchre. The Reverend Mr. Davis and Doctor Dick took their places at the head of the casket, and the family gathered at the foot. The voice of the minister was heard against the silence: "I am the resurrection and the life, saith the Lord. . . ." When he had read the Order of Burial from the Episcopal Prayer Book, Washington's rector spoke a brief eulogy. Doctor Dick, Grand Master of the Alexandria Lodge, then stepped forward and with the assistance of the Reverend Mr. Muir, Chaplain, conducted full Masonic rites. As the ceremony ended, the minute guns repeated from the Potomac and echoed in the hills. From behind the vault came the answering boom of eleven artillery cannon. Then the company moved away.

INDEX

Index

(Prepared by William C. Kiessel)